AF765942

HOUSE PRACTICE

A Guide to the Rules, Precedents, and Procedures of the House

Wm. Holmes Brown
Parliamentarian of the House
1974–1994

Charles W. Johnson
Parliamentarian of the House
1994–2004

John V. Sullivan
Parliamentarian of the House
2004–

Preface

The Parliamentarian of the House of Representatives is appointed by the Speaker without regard to political affiliation. The Office of the Parliamentarian and its subsidiary Office of Compilation of Precedents comprise lawyers and clerks who render nonpartisan assistance to the Speaker, to the other presiding officers, and to the House on legislative and parliamentary procedure and, in addition, compile the parliamentary precedents of the House.

The parliamentary law of the House of Representatives emanates from the Constitution and from rules adopted pursuant to section 5 in article I of the Constitution. These rules include not only the standing rules adopted from Congress to Congress but also *Jefferson's Manual*, as customarily incorporated by reference in the standing rules. They also include rules enacted as law and special rules adopted from time to time. On this foundation rests a body of precedent established by decisions of presiding officers on actual parliamentary questions or by long custom and tradition.

The overarching role of the Office of the Parliamentarian is to strive for consistency in parliamentary analysis by attempting to apply pertinent precedent to each procedural question. In resolving questions of order, the Speaker and other presiding officers of the House adhere to the jurisprudential principle of *stare decisis* – a commitment to stand by earlier decisions. This fidelity to precedent promotes analytic consistency and procedural predictability and thereby fosters legitimacy in parliamentary practice. The commitment of the House to stand by its procedural decisions requires rigor concerning what constitutes precedent. In the parliamentary context, the term does not refer to a mere instance in which something occurred or was suffered; rather, it refers to a decision or order actually disposing of a question of order.

The compilation of the parliamentary precedents of the House is as important as any other function of the Office of the Parliamentarian. For each procedural decision made on the floor of the House, the Parliamentarian extracts the proceedings from the daily *Congressional Record* and writes a parliamentary syllabus. These ''headnotes'' must be precise, stating the real substance of the decision and its legal rationale in suitably narrow terms. To ensure a current digest of these matters, the Parliamentarian biennially publishes a *House Rules and Manual*. For the longer term, the Parliamentarian compiles the most salient precedents for formal, scholarly publication. These precedents presently fill 28 volumes comprising thousands of decisions over the 224 years of parliamentary practice in the House. They are published as *Hinds' Precedents* (1907); *Cannon's Precedents* (1936); and *Deschler's*, *Deschler-Brown*, and *Deschler-Brown-Johnson Precedents* (ongoing).

To bridge the span between a digest of decisions and formally published precedents, the Parliamentarian also publishes this work as a condensed compilation of procedures of current application as of the first session of the 112th Congress. The scope of this volume is thus limited. It is a summary review of selected precedents and not an exhaustive survey of all applicable rulings. The *House Rules and Manual* and the published volumes of precedents remain the primary sources for more comprehensive analysis and authoritative citation.

An earlier, condensed work of this kind is *Cannon's Procedure in the House of Representatives*. That summary by Clarence Cannon was first published in 1949 and last published in 1959. A later summary, entitled *Deschler's Procedure in the U.S. House of Representatives*, was prepared by Lewis Deschler in 1974 and was revised and updated in 1978, 1979, 1982, 1985, and 1987.

This third edition of *House Practice* reflects the efforts of all of the members of the Office of the Parliamentarian – Tom Wickham, Ethan Lauer, Carrie Wolf, Jay Smith, Anne Gooch, Brian Cooper, Lloyd Jenkins, Monica Rodriguez – and of its Office of Compilation of Precedents – Andrew Neal, Max Spitzer, Deborah Khalili, and Bryan Feldblum – as well as former Parliamentarian Charles W. Johnson, III. Their diligence in annotating the decisions of the Chair and other parliamentary precedents reflected in this volume and their devotion to the pursuit of excellence in the procedural practices of the House are gratefully acknowledged. Particular appreciation goes to Max Spitzer for his skilled management of the project.

References to frequently cited works are to the *House Rules and Manual* for the 112th Congress, by section (*e.g.*, *Manual* § 364); to the volume and section of *Hinds'* or *Cannon's Precedents* (*e.g.*, 6 Cannon § 570); to the chapter and section of *Deschler's*, *Deschler-Brown*, or *Deschler-Brown-Johnson* (*e.g.*, Deschler Ch 5 § 2); to the *Congressional Record*, by Congress, session, date and page (*e.g.*, 108-2, May 20, 2004, pp 10618-29); and to the United States Code, by title and section (*e.g.*, 2 USC § 287).

John V. Sullivan
Parliamentarian
2004–

Chapter Outline

Chapter 1
Adjournment

Research References

U.S. Const. art. I, § 5

5 Hinds §§ 5359-5388

8 Cannon §§ 2641-2648

Deschler-Brown-Johnson Ch 40

Manual §§ 82-84, 911-913

A. Generally; Adjournments of Three Days or Less

§ 1. In General

Types of Adjournments

Adjournment procedures in the House are governed by the House rules and by the Constitution. There are: (1) adjournments of three days or less, which are taken pursuant to motion (or by unanimous consent when only the Chair is present in the chamber) (§ 5, infra); (2) adjournments of more than three days, which require the consent of the Senate (§ 10, infra); and (3) adjournments *sine die*, which end each session of a Congress and which require the consent of both Houses. Adjournments of more than three days or *sine die* are taken pursuant to concurrent resolutions. §§ 10, 13, infra.

Adjournment Versus Recess

Adjournment is to be distinguished from recess. The House may authorize a recess under a motion provided in clause 4 of rule XVI. The Speaker also may declare a recess when no other business is pending (clause 12(a) of rule I) or when notified of an imminent threat to the safety of the House (clause 12(b) of rule I). During a period of recess, the House remains in session. The mace remains in place on its pedestal, reports may be filed with the Clerk, and bills may be placed in the hopper. See RECESS.

Emergency Convening Authority

During any recess or adjournment of not more than three days, if the Speaker is notified by the Sergeant-at-Arms of an imminent impairment of the place of reconvening, then the Speaker may, in consultation with the Minority Leader, postpone the time for reconvening within the three-day limit prescribed by the Constitution. In the alternative, the Speaker, under the same conditions, may reconvene the House before the time previously appointed solely to declare the House in recess within that three-day limit. Clause 12(c) of rule I; § 10, infra.

§ 2. Adjournment Motions and Requests; Forms

Motions

The motion to adjourn authorized by clause 4(a) of rule XVI is in order in simple form only. 5 Hinds §§ 5371, 5372. The form is as follows:

MEMBER: M__. Speaker, I move that the House do now adjourn.
Note: The motion must be in writing if demanded.

The proponent of the motion may not include argument in favor of the adjournment or impose conditions under which it is to be taken. 5 Hinds §5371; 8 Cannon §2647. The motion may not be amended to set forth the day on which the House is to reconvene. §6, infra. However, the simple motion to adjourn may be preceded at the Speaker's discretion by a non-debatable and unamendable motion provided by clause 4(c) of rule XVI that, when the House adjourns, it stand adjourned to a day and time certain. *Manual* §911. This motion is used when the House wishes to make some change in the day or hour of its next regularly scheduled meeting. *Manual* §621.

MEMBER: M__. Speaker, I move that when the House adjourns today it stand adjourned to meet at __________(time) on __________(date).

This motion cannot be used to circumvent the constitutional restriction against adjournments for more than three days without the consent of the Senate.

Unanimous-Consent Requests

Adjournments of three days or less may be taken pursuant to a unanimous-consent request:

MEMBER: M__. Speaker, I ask unanimous consent that when the House adjourns today, it adjourn to meet at ____ on ____, ____ (any time on a day within three calendar days not including Sundays).

For adjournments of more than three days, see §§10-12, infra.

Legislative Days and Calendar Days Distinguished

The duration of a legislative day does not conform to the 24 hours of a calendar day, nor does a legislative day automatically terminate by reason of the arrival of the time for a regularly scheduled meeting of the House. The legislative day continues until terminated by an adjournment, irrespective of the passage of calendar days. 5 Hinds §§6738, 6739. The House has convened and adjourned twice on the same calendar day pursuant to a motion to fix the day to which the House shall adjourn, thereby meeting for two legislative days on the same calendar day. *Manual* §913. However, a legislative day cannot extend into a new Congress or a new session. 96-1, Jan. 3, 1980, p 37774.

§3. When in Order; Precedence and Privilege of Motion

The motion to adjourn is a motion of highest privilege and is in order whenever the floor can be secured. See *Manual* §912; 5 Hinds §§5359, 5360. Other motions may not intervene between the motion to adjourn and the vote thereon. 5 Hinds §5361. The motion to adjourn is specifically given precedence over all other secondary motions permitted by clause 4 of rule XVI, including the motions to lay on the table, for the previous question, to amend, to refer, or to postpone. *Manual* § 911. The motion to adjourn takes precedence over all other motions because, as Jefferson noted, the House might otherwise be kept sitting against its will and indefinitely. *Manual* § 439.

The motion to fix the day and time to which the House shall adjourn is of equal privilege to the simple motion to adjourn but is entertained only at the Speaker's discretion. *Manual* §§ 911, 912. The motion to fix the day, if made first, need not give way to the simple motion. 5 Hinds § 5381.

The motion to adjourn may not interrupt a vote being taken in the House. 5 Hinds § 5360. However, the motion to adjourn is in order:

- Between the putting of the question on a proposition and the ensuing vote. *Manual* § 439.
- Between the different methods of voting, as between a vote by division and a vote by yeas and nays. *Manual* § 439.
- After a recorded vote is ordered and before the vote begins. 5 Hinds § 5366.
- After a vote has been objected to for lack of a quorum. *Manual* § 913.

The motion to adjourn permitted by clause 4 of rule XVI applies both when a question is "under debate," and when other business is before the House as well. *Manual* §§ 911, 912. The motion is in order and takes precedence over the motions delineated in clause 4(a) of rule XVI and:

- The reading of the Journal. 4 Hinds § 2757.
- The Speaker's approval of the Journal. *Manual* § 621.
- A motion for a call of the House. 8 Cannon § 2642.
- A resolution offered as a question of the privileges of the House. *Manual* § 699.
- The consideration of an impeachment proceeding. 91-2, Apr. 15, 1970, p 11940.
- A motion to reconsider. 5 Hinds § 5605.
- A motion to instruct conferees. *Manual* § 912.
- The filing of a privileged report from a committee. *Manual* § 912.
- The consideration of conference reports. 5 Hinds §§ 6451, 6453.
- A report from the Committee of the Whole. 8 Cannon § 2645.
- The consideration of a veto message from the President. 4 Hinds § 3523.

When Not in Order

The motion to adjourn does not take precedence and may not be entertained:

- When another Member holds the floor in debate. *Manual* § 912; 5 Hinds § 5360.
- During time yielded for a parliamentary inquiry. Deschler-Brown-Johnson Ch 40 § 3.18.
- When the House is voting, such as by the yeas and nays or other recorded vote. 5 Hinds § 6053.
- Pending a vote pursuant to a special order of business providing for such vote "without intervening motion." 4 Hinds §§ 3211, 3212.
- During the presentation of a conference report. 5 Hinds § 6452.
- Pending or during the administration of the oath to a Member. 1 Hinds § 622.

In certain situations, the motion cannot be repeated after one such motion has been defeated. See § 9, infra. Repetition is not permitted:

- Pending consideration of a report from the Committee on Rules. Clause 6(b) of rule XIII; 8 Cannon § 2260.
- Pending consideration of a motion to suspend the rules. Clause 1(b) of rule XV.

§ 4. In Committee of the Whole

The motion to adjourn is not in order after the House has voted to resolve into the Committee of the Whole. 4 Hinds § 4728; 5 Hinds § 5367. The motion is not in order in the Committee of the Whole. 4 Hinds § 4716. It also is not entertained when the Committee of the Whole rises to report proceedings incident to securing a quorum (8 Cannon § 2436) or when it rises "informally" to receive a message. However, the motion to adjourn is permitted when the House is meeting as in the Committee of the Whole. 4 Hinds § 4923.

§ 5. Who May Offer Motion; Recognition

The motion to adjourn may be made by any Member (91-1, Oct. 14, 1969, pp 30054-56). The Chair may declare the House adjourned by unanimous consent when no Member is available. Deschler-Brown-Johnson Ch 40 § 3.28.

§ 6. Debate on Motion; Amendments

Debate on the simple motion to adjourn is precluded by clause 4(b) of rule XVI. *Manual* § 911; 5 Hinds § 5359. Clause 4(c) precludes debate on the motion to fix the day to which the House shall adjourn. *Manual* § 911; 5 Hinds §§ 5379, 5380. The stricture against debate on a motion to adjourn includes a prefatory statement leading up to the motion. Such statement, if made, is not carried in the *Congressional Record.* 107-2, Feb. 13, 2002, p 1419.

Unless the House has yet to adopt its customary standing order that fixes the daily hour of meeting for each day of the week, the simple motion to adjourn is not subject to amendment. *Manual* § 585. Thus, the motion may not be amended by language alluding to the purpose of the adjournment. *Manual* § 912. The motion also may not be amended by language specifying the day (5 Hinds § 5360) or hour (5 Hinds § 5364) to which adjournment is to be taken. *Manual* § 912. Similarly, the separate motion under clause 4(c) of rule XVI that when the House adjourns it stand adjourned to a day and time certain also is not subject to amendment. An older precedent (5 Hinds § 5754) indicating otherwise predates the 1973 change in clause 4(c) of rule XVI, which enabled the motion at the Speaker's discretion. See *Manual* § 911.

§ 7. Voting

The vote on a motion to adjourn may be taken by any of the voting methods authorized by the House rules, including a division vote or a vote by the yeas and nays. 99-1, Dec. 20, 1985, p 38733; 88-2, Feb. 8, 1964, pp 2616, 2639. The adoption of a resolution providing for adjournment *sine die* on a day certain does not preclude a demand for the yeas and nays on the motion to adjourn on that day. 87-1, Sept. 27, 1961, p 21528. A negative vote on a motion to adjourn is not subject to the motion to reconsider. 5 Hinds §§ 5620, 5622; see also RECONSIDERATION.

§ 8. Quorum Requirements

A quorum is required for a motion to fix the time of adjournment to a day and time certain. *Manual* § 913.

The simple motion to adjourn may be agreed to notwithstanding the absence of a quorum. See *Manual* §§ 52, 1025. Indeed, no motion is in order in the absence of a quorum except to adjourn or for a call of the House. 4 Hinds §§ 2950, 2951, 2988; 6 Cannon §§ 680, 682. The motion to adjourn is in order on failure of a quorum, even where the House is operating under a special order of business requiring the consideration of the pending business. 5 Hinds § 5365.

The motion to adjourn takes precedence over a motion for a call of the House. § 3, supra. In one instance, following a point of order that a quorum was not present, and before the Chair so ascertained, a Member moved a call of the House while another Member immediately moved to adjourn. The Chair recognized for the more privileged motion. 88-1, June 12, 1963, p 10739.

It is not in order to demand an ''automatic'' roll call under clause 6 of rule XX on an affirmative vote on a simple motion to adjourn because that motion may be agreed to by less than a quorum. *Manual* § 1025. However, a vote by the yeas and nays in such a case would be in order, if demanded by one-fifth of those present, no quorum being required. *Manual* §§ 75, 76. Where the vote on an adjournment is decided in the negative, and a point of order that a quorum is not present is sustained, an ''automatic'' roll call on the motion then occurs under clause 6 of rule XX. 100-1, Nov. 2, 1987, pp 30386-90; Deschler-Brown-Johnson Ch 40 § 3.8.

> MEMBER: I move that the House do now adjourn.
>
> SPEAKER: On this vote (by division, or by voice) the noes have it.
>
> MEMBER: I make a point of order that a quorum is not present and (pursuant to clause 6 of rule XX) I object to the vote on the ground that a quorum is not present.
>
> SPEAKER: A quorum is not present, and the yeas and nays are ordered. Members will record their votes by electronic device.

Although a motion to adjourn is in order pending a point of order that a quorum is not present, it is not entertained after the Clerk has begun to call the roll. 5 Hinds § 5366; 86-2, June 3, 1960, p 11828. After the call has been completed, the motion to adjourn is again in order; and it is not necessary that the Chair announce that a quorum has failed to respond before entertaining the motion. 91-1, Oct. 14, 1969, pp 30054-56.

§ 9. Dilatory Motions; Repetition of Motion

Clause 1 of rule XVI, which precludes the Speaker from entertaining dilatory motions, is applicable to motions to adjourn. *Manual* § 903. Although of the highest privilege, the motion to adjourn is not in order when offered for purposes of delay or obstruction. 5 Hinds §§ 5721, 5731; 8 Cannon §§ 2796, 2813. On one occasion, a point of order was sustained against the motion where a House rule gave the Speaker the discretion to recognize for a motion to adjourn. 8 Cannon § 2822.

The motion to adjourn, once disposed of, may ordinarily be repeated, but not until after intervening business, such as debate, a decision of the Chair on a question of order, or the ordering of the yeas and nays. *Manual* § 912; 5 Hinds §§ 5373, 5374, 5376-5378; 8 Cannon § 2814.

In some cases the rules specifically provide that only one motion to adjourn is to be permitted. This restriction applies during the consideration of certain reports from the Committee on Rules and during the consideration of motions to suspend the rules. *Manual* §§ 858, 890; § 3, supra. In such cases the motion to adjourn—once having been rejected—may not again be entertained until the pending matter has been disposed of. 5 Hinds §§ 5740, 5741. However, if a motion to adjourn is made and rejected, and a quorum then fails, a second motion to adjourn is admitted. 5 Hinds §§ 5744-5746.

B. Adjournments for More Than Three Days

§ 10. In General; Resolutions

House-Senate Action

Under article I, section 5, clause 4 of the Constitution, neither House can adjourn (or recess) for more than three days without the consent of the other. The consent of both Houses is required even when the adjournment is sought by only one House. *Manual* § 84. In calculating the three days, either the day of adjourning or the day of meeting (excluding Sundays) must be taken into the count. *Manual* § 83; 5 Hinds § 6673. Thus, the House can adjourn by motion from Thursday to Monday, or from Friday to Tuesday, because Sunday is a *dies non*. However, it cannot, for example, adjourn from Monday to Friday without the Senate's assent. Consistent with this requirement, the House has authorized the Speaker to declare the House in recesses subject to calls of the Chair during discrete periods, each not more than three days. *Manual* § 83.

Adjournments for more than three days are provided for by concurrent resolution. The resolution may provide for the adjournment of one House or of both Houses. *Manual* § 84. Senate concurrent resolutions for adjournment are laid before the House by the Speaker as privileged. 101-1, Mar. 16, 1989, p 4480. Whether originating in the House or Senate, such concurrent resolutions are not debatable and require a quorum for adoption. *Manual* § 84.

The concurrent resolution is generally offered by the Majority Leader or a designee:

> MEMBER: M__. Speaker, I send to the desk a privileged concurrent resolution and ask for its immediate consideration.

The resolution may set forth the times at which the adjournment is to begin and end, but frequently the resolution will provide optional dates so as to give each House some discretion in determining the exact period of adjournment. *Manual* § 84. Recent resolutions have provided for one period of adjournment of the House and a different period for the Senate. Thus, the resolution may provide for an adjournment of the House for more than three days to a day certain, and a recess of the Senate for more than three days to a day certain as subsequently determined by the Senate before recessing. *Manual* § 84. For a discussion of the authority of the President to determine the period of adjournment when the two Houses are unable to agree with respect thereto, see *Manual* § 171; for convening, see ASSEMBLY OF CONGRESS.

Conditional Adjournments; Recall Provisos

An adjournment resolution may include various conditions or provisos, such as that the Senate shall adjourn pursuant to the resolution after it has disposed of a certain bill. *Manual* § 84; 95-2, June 29, 1978, p 19466.

A concurrent resolution adjourning both Houses for more than three days, or *sine die*, normally includes authority for the Speaker and the Majority Leader of the Senate, acting jointly, to reassemble the Members whenever the public interest shall warrant it. *Manual* § 84. Recently, such recall authority has allowed the respective designees of the Majority Leader and the Speaker to so reassemble. It has also allowed reassembly at such place as may be designated. Deschler-Brown-Johnson Ch 40 § 2.2. In the 108th Congress, the two Houses granted anticipatory consent to assemble the 108th Congress at a place outside the District of Columbia whenever the public interest shall warrant it. 108-1, H. Con. Res. 1, Jan. 7, 2003, p 21; see also *Manual* § 82a. A concurrent resolution also may provide for the *sine die* adjournment of one House following a single House recall. *Manual* § 84.

The House has entered an order authorizing the Speaker or a designee, during any recess or adjournment of not more than three days, to reconvene the House at a time other than that previously appointed, within the limits of clause 4, section 5, article I of the Constitution, based on a determination that the public interest so warrants and after consultation with the Minority Leader. 112-1, H. Res. 479, Dec. 6, 2011, p ____.

Amendments; Voting

Adjournment resolutions originating in one House are subject to amendment by the other. 95-2, June 29, 1978, p 19466; 95-2, Aug. 17, 1978, p 26794. Such an amendment is not in order after the previous question is ordered (except pursuant to a motion to commit with proper instructions). 96-2, Oct. 1, 1980, p 28576. Voting on the motion may be by voice, division, or any of the methods of voting established by rule XX or by article I, section 5 of the Constitution.

§ 11. Privilege of Resolution

A concurrent resolution providing for an adjournment of the House or of the Senate (or of both Houses) is privileged. *Manual* § 84; 5 Hinds § 6701. The resolution is privileged even though it provides for an adjournment of the two Houses to different days certain. 93-2, Apr. 11, 1974, p 10775. An adjournment resolution remains privileged, despite its inclusion of additional matter, so long as such additional matter would be privileged in its own right. For example, an adjournment resolution including a declaration asserted as a question of the privileges of the House relating to the ability of the House to receive veto messages during the adjournment retains its privilege. 101-1, Nov. 21, 1989, p 31156. An adjournment resolution including a provision establishing an order of business for the following session of the Congress was not considered privileged. 102-1, Nov. 26, 1991, p 35840.

Amendments of the Senate to adjournment resolutions are privileged in the House. 97-2, Feb. 10, 1982, p 1471.

A House concurrent resolution providing for an adjournment may be subject to a point of order if the House is not in compliance with sections 309 or 310(f) of the Congressional Budget Act, which preclude such resolutions until the House has approved its regular appropriation bills and completed action on any required reconciliation legislation. *Manual* § 1127; 108-2, June 25, 2004, p 14153. However, these provisions of the Act may be waived by unanimous consent or by adoption of a resolution reported by the Committee on Rules. See, *e.g.*, 101-1, June 23, 1989, p 13271.

§ 12. August Recess

The Legislative Reorganization Act of 1946 provides that unless otherwise provided by Congress, the two Houses shall either (a) adjourn *sine die* by July 31 of each year, or (b) in odd-numbered years, adjourn in August (for a specified period) pursuant to a concurrent resolution adopted by roll call vote in each House. 2 USC § 198. The House has not adjourned *sine die* by July 31 under this Act for many years, and the provisions in the Act to that effect have been routinely waived by concurrent resolution, thereby permitting the two Houses to continue in session. *Manual* §§ 1106, 1106a. In the absence of such a resolution, a simple motion to adjourn, made at the conclusion of business on July 31, is in order and would permit the House to meet on the following day. *Manual* § 1106a.

The House and Senate may adopt a concurrent resolution adjourning in August in an odd-numbered year as specified by the Act. Such a resolution is called up as privileged, requires a yea and nay vote for adoption, and is not debatable. *Manual* § 1106a. Concurrent resolutions waiving the provisions of the Act are not privileged and have been called up by unanimous consent (Deschler-Brown-Johnson Ch 40 § 12.4) or by resolution reported by the Committee on Rules (105-1, July 31, 1997, p 17018).

C. Adjournment Sine Die

§ 13. In General; Resolutions

Adjournments *sine die* (literally, without day) are used to terminate the sessions of a Congress, and are provided for by concurrent resolution. A session terminates automatically at the end of the constitutional term. See 96-1, Jan. 3, 1980, p 37774; 104-1, Jan. 3, 1996, p 38609. Adjournment resolutions may be offered from the floor as privileged. 5 Hinds § 6698.

The resolution is not debatable. 8 Cannon §§ 3371-3374. However, a Member may be recognized during its consideration under a reservation of objection to a unanimous-consent request. *Manual* § 84. It requires a quorum for adoption. 92-2, Oct. 18, 1972, p 37061.

A *sine die* resolution may specify the particular legislative or calendar day of adjournment or may specify alternate dates. *Sine die* adjournment in the latter case is effected by a motion offered pursuant to the resolution. *Manual* § 84. *Sine die* resolutions may be amended to provide for an adjournment on a date other than that specified. 98-2, Oct. 11, 1984, p 32314. The resolution need not specify the date of convening because, under section 2 of the 20th amendment to the Constitution, a regular session of a Congress automatically begins at noon on January 3 of every year unless Congress sets a different date by law. *Manual* § 242; 96-2, Jan. 3, 1980, p 3.

Under clause 1(o) of rule X, the Committee on Rules has jurisdiction of matters relative to final adjournment of Congress. *Manual* § 733.

The time of adjournment *sine die* having been fixed by concurrent resolution, the House may not finally adjourn before that time. 5 Hinds § 6714. However, a *sine die* resolution may be recalled prior to action thereon by the other House. 5 Hinds § 6699. Also, it is subject to rescission by a subsequent concurrent resolution. 5 Hinds § 6700. A resolution rescinding an order for adjournment *sine die* is open to amendment, and an amendment assigning a new date is germane. 5 Hinds § 5920. For waivers of statutory provision as to adjournment *sine die* on July 31, see § 12, supra.

Under the current practice, *sine die* adjournment resolutions normally contain House-Senate leadership recall authority. For a discussion of recall authority generally, see § 10, supra.

The House customarily authorizes the Speaker to appoint a committee to notify the President of the completion of business and the intention of the two Houses to adjourn *sine die* unless the President has some further communication to make. 100-1, Dec. 21, 1987, p 37618. This committee is usually composed of the Majority and Minority Leaders of the House, and joins a similar committee appointed by the Senate. 106-1, Nov. 18, 1999, p 30735.

§ 14. Procedure at Adjournment; Motions

The House may adjourn at the time specified in the adjournment resolution even though other business, such as a roll call, may be pending. 5 Hinds §§ 6325, 6719, 6720. Adjournment *sine die* can occur notwithstanding the absence of a quorum if both Houses have adopted a concurrent resolution providing for *sine die* adjournment on that day. *Manual* § 55; 5 Hinds § 6721.

A motion to adjourn may invoke a concurrent resolution that gives it particular meaning on the instant day. The motion is offered pursuant to the concurrent resolution:

> M__. Speaker, pursuant to House Concurrent Resolution ____, ____th Congress, I move that the House do now adjourn.

The yeas and nays may be ordered on this motion. The adoption of a concurrent resolution providing for adjournment *sine die* on a day certain does not preclude a demand for the yeas and nays on the motion to adjourn on that day. 87-1, Sept. 27, 1961, p 21528.

Chapter 2
Amendments

Research References
5 Hinds §§ 5753-5800

8 Cannon §§2824-2907a
Deschler Ch 27
Manual §§413, 456, 469, 902, 905, 911, 919-927, 978-981, 986-989, 991

A. Amendments Defined and Distinguished; Forms

§1. In General; Formal Requisites

Generally

The four forms of amendment are specified by clause 6 of rule XVI. They are:

- The amendment to the pending proposition
- Amendments to the amendment
- Substitute amendments
- Amendments to the substitute

An amendment to a pending amendment is in order as an amendment in the second degree, as is an amendment to a pending substitute. Amendments in the third degree are not in order. § 14, infra.

The amendment to the original text must, of course, be offered first, and generally only one amendment to the text may be pending at any one time. 5 Hinds §5755; Deschler Ch 27 §1. Once that amendment is offered, however, the other three forms of amendment may be offered and all four amendments may be pending at one time. 5 Hinds §§5753, 5785; 8 Cannon §§2883, 2887; Deschler Ch 27 §1; see also §13, infra.

Recognition for the purpose of offering amendments is within the discretion of the Chair. See §20, infra. Members may offer amendments in their own names at the request, or as the designee, of other Members. But Members may not offer them in other Members' names or jointly. Deschler Ch 27 §1.11. Furthermore, Members may not offer amendments to their own amendments; an amendment once offered may not be directly modified by its proponent except by unanimous consent. §37, infra.

Formal Requirements; Written or Oral Motions

Pursuant to clause 1 of rule XVI, the Chair or any Member may require that an amendment be reduced to writing before being offered. Deschler Ch 27 §1.1. In the Committee of the Whole, the Clerk transmits copies of offered amendments to the majority and the minority tables in accordance with clause 5(b) of rule XVIII, although the failure of the Clerk to promptly transmit such copies is not the basis for a point of order against the amendment. Deschler Ch 27 §22.11.

An amendment must contain instructions to the Clerk as to the portion of the text it seeks to amend. Deschler Ch 27 § 1.28. Similarly, an amendment to an amendment should specify and identify the text to be amended. Amendments to a substitute should be drafted to the proper page and line number of the substitute rather than to comparable provisions of the original text. Deschler Ch 27 §§ 1.9, 1.10. A Member who intends to propose such an amendment may ascertain the appropriate page and line number by inspecting the pending amendment at the Clerk's desk or obtaining a copy thereof at the committee tables. Deschler Ch 27 § 22.10.

The Chair may examine the form of an offered amendment to determine its propriety and may rule it out of order where improper in form and therefore not in order at that time, even where no point of order is raised from the floor and debate has begun. Deschler Ch 27 § 1.39. However, an ambiguity in the wording of an amendment, or a question as to the propriety of draftsmanship of an amendment to accomplish a particular legislative purpose, should not be questioned on a point of order; that is an issue to be disposed of by a vote on the merits of the amendment. Deschler Ch 27 § 1.31.

Order or Sequence

A distinction should be made between the order or sequence of voting on amendments and the sequence in which they may be offered. Amendments must be voted on in a definite sequence. The first-degree amendment to the text is voted on last, thereby giving the Members the fullest opportunity to perfect it before addressing its adoption. (For the order of voting on amendments, see § 28, infra.) However, this sequence is reversed with respect to the *offering* of amendments, because amendments to the text are proposed before the offering of amendments to the amendment, and substitute amendments must precede the offering of amendments to the substitute. § 21, infra. Nevertheless, considerable latitude is permitted in the order of offering amending propositions. For example, in one instance five amendments were offered in the following order: (1) an amendment in the nature of a substitute for the pending measure, (2) a substitute therefor, (3) a perfecting amendment to the original text, (4) a perfecting amendment to the substitute, and (5) a perfecting amendment to the amendment in the nature of a substitute. Deschler Ch 27 § 5.28. Indeed, under this scenario, three further amendments would have been in order: (1) a substitute to the perfecting amendment to the original text; (2) a perfecting amendment to the substitute; and (3) a perfecting amendment to the amendment to the original text.

Effect of Special Orders of Business

Bills are frequently considered pursuant to the terms of a resolution reported by the Committee on Rules. The resolution may specify whether amendments may be offered to the bill, the kind and number of amendments that may be offered, whether they can be amended, and the order of consideration and voting thereon. The resolution may also ''self-execute'' an amendment by considering that amendment as adopted. § 11, infra. Such special orders of business are themselves subject to germane amendment while the rule is pending if the Member in control yields for such amendment or offers such amendment, or if the motion for the previous question is defeated. Deschler Ch 27 § 3.1.

§ 2. Perfecting Amendments

Generally

Generally, the House follows the Jeffersonian principle that an amendment should be perfected before agreeing to it. *Manual* § 456. The term ''perfecting amendment'' includes amendments to insert as well as amendments to strike and insert. Deschler Ch 27 § 15. Furthermore, a perfecting amendment may take the form of a motion to strike a lesser portion of the words encompassed in a pending motion to strike. Deschler Ch 27 § 15.17. There are no degrees of preference as between perfecting amendments. Deschler Ch 27 § 5.9.

A perfecting amendment may be offered to the text of a bill or to an amendment to a bill. Once a perfecting amendment to an amendment is disposed of, the original amendment, as amended or not, remains open to further perfecting amendment, and all such amendments are disposed of before voting on substitutes. Deschler Ch 27 § 23.9.

Perfecting Amendments and the Motion to Strike

Perfecting amendments to a section or paragraph may be offered—one at a time—while a motion to strike the section or paragraph is pending, and are disposed of first. Deschler Ch 27 § 15.15. Indeed, all perfecting amendments to a section of a bill must be disposed of before the vote on a pending motion to strike the section. Deschler Ch 27 § 24.3. If the perfecting amendment changes all the words proposed to be stricken, the motion to strike necessarily falls and is not voted on because the entirety of the amendment has been changed. Deschler Ch 27 § 24.15.

§ 3. Motions to Insert

A motion to insert may be pending at the same time as a motion to strike, with the vote taken first on the motion to insert, then on the motion to strike, which is consistent with the principle that text should be perfected before stricken or retained. See § 21, infra. They need not be offered in the order in which they are voted on. Deschler Ch 27 § 15.1.

It is not in order to reinsert the precise language stricken by amendment. Deschler Ch 27 § 31.4. However, an amendment similar to the stricken language may be offered if germane to the pending portion of the bill. Deschler Ch 27 § 31.6.

After an amendment to insert has been agreed to, the matter inserted ordinarily may not then be amended insularly. 5 Hinds § 5761; 8 Cannon § 2852; see § 38, infra. However, an amendment may be added at the end of the inserted material. 5 Hinds § 5759; *Manual* § 469.

§ 4. Motions to Strike and Insert

A motion to strike and insert is usually a perfecting amendment (Deschler Ch 27 § 16), and is not divisible under clause 5 of rule XVI. A motion to strike and insert may be offered as a perfecting amendment to a pending section of a bill, and is voted on before a pending motion to strike that section. However, even if agreed to, the perfected language is subject to being eliminated by subsequent adoption of the motion to strike in cases where the perfecting amendment has not so changed the text as to render the original motion to strike an improper change of language already adopted. Deschler Ch 27 § 17.12 (note). See also § 23, infra.

§ 5. Motions to Strike

A motion proposing to strike a section of a bill is in order after perfecting amendments to the section are disposed of. If offered first, the motion to strike is held in abeyance until perfecting amendments have been disposed of. § 21, infra. A motion proposing to strike a section that has been perfected, but not changed in its entirety, is in order. Deschler Ch 27 § 17.29. The motion to strike, if adopted, strikes the entire section, including provisions added as perfecting amendments to that section. Deschler Ch 27 § 31.1.

A motion to strike the enacting clause of a bill is a parliamentary motion used for rejecting the bill. Deschler Ch 27 § 15. It takes precedence over a motion to amend the bill under clause 9 of rule XVIII. *Manual* § 988.

§ 6. Substitute Amendments

A substitute always proposes to replace all the words of a pending amendment. The amendatory instructions contained in a substitute direct changes to be made in the original language rather than to the pending amendment. Although a substitute may change parts of a bill not changed by the pending amendment, the substitute must be germane to the pending amendment. 8 Cannon §§ 2879, 2883; Deschler Ch 27 § 18.6. A substitute may result in similar language to the original text proposed to be changed by the pending amendment but may not result in identical language. Deschler Ch 27 § 18.15.

A substitute for a motion to strike is not in order. Deschler Ch 27 § 18.8. A motion to strike is not in order as a substitute for a pending motion to strike and insert (Deschler Ch 27 § 17.18) or for a perfecting amendment to text generally (Deschler Ch 27 § 17.17).

A proposition contained in a substitute may sometimes be reoffered in a different form after it has failed of approval. 8 Cannon § 2843.

Members may not offer substitutes for their own amendments. Deschler Ch 27 § 18.22.

§ 7. Amendments in Nature of a Substitute

An amendment in the nature of a substitute is an amendment that is offered to the text of a bill; it generally replaces the entire bill. It should be distinguished from a substitute amendment, which is merely a substitute for another amendment that has been offered. Deschler Ch 27 § 12.

An amendment in the nature of a substitute takes the form of a motion to strike and insert. However, the term ''amendment in the nature of a substitute'' properly applies only to those motions that propose to strike an entire pending bill, though it is sometimes used, less precisely, to describe motions proposing to strike an entire pending section or title of text and to insert new matter. It should not be used to describe those motions to strike and insert, which are properly characterized as ''perfecting amendments'' and which go only to a portion of the pending text. Deschler Ch 27 § 25. An amendment in the nature of a substitute for a pending bill may be offered after the first section is read and is then open to amendment in its entirety. Deschler Ch 27 § 12.

An amendment in the nature of a substitute for a bill may be proposed before perfecting amendments to the pending portion of the original text have been offered, but may not be voted on until after such perfecting amendments have been disposed of. 8 Cannon § 2896; Deschler Ch 27 § 25.

Where an amendment in the nature of a substitute for a bill has been adopted in the Committee of the Whole, the measure is no longer open to amendment and further amendments, including pro forma amendments for debate, are not in order except by unanimous consent. Deschler Ch 27 § 32.6; see also *Manual* § 923.

§ 8. Pro Forma Amendments

Pro forma amendments have been in use during debate in the Committee of the Whole under the five-minute rule as early as 1868. 5 Hinds § 5778. A pro forma amendment is a procedural formality—a parliamentary device used to obtain recognition during consideration of a bill being read for amendment. Such an amendment does not contemplate any actual change in the bill. Although pro forma amendments are phrased to make some superficial change in the language under consideration, such as "to strike the last word," the underlying purpose is merely to obtain time for debate that might otherwise be prohibited because of the time limitations of the five-minute rule. Clause 5 of rule XVIII; Deschler Ch 27 § 2. A special order of business may limit the offering of substantive amendments but enable pro forma amendments for the purpose of debate. A pro forma amendment may be offered after a substitute has been adopted and before the vote on the amendment, as amended, by unanimous consent only because the amendment has been amended in its entirety and no further amendments, including pro forma amendments, are in order. *Manual* § 981.

A Member who has occupied five minutes on a pro forma amendment:

- May not lengthen this time by making a second pro forma amendment or by offering a pro forma amendment to the original amendment. *Manual* § 981; 5 Hinds § 5222; 8 Cannon § 2560.
- May not extend this time by offering a substantive amendment while other Members are seeking recognition. *Manual* § 981.
- May offer a second-degree amendment and then offer a pro forma amendment to debate the underlying first-degree amendment. *Manual* § 981.

Debate on a pro forma amendment must be confined to the portion of the bill to which the pro forma amendment has been offered. Deschler Ch 27 §§ 2.5, 28.38. If the point of order is raised, a Member may not under a pro forma amendment discuss a section of the bill not immediately pending. Deschler Ch 27 § 2.4. A Member recognized to debate a pro forma amendment may not allocate or reserve time. *Manual* § 981.

§ 9. Precedence of Motion Generally

In General

Clause 4 of rule XVI specifies the motions that are in order when a question is under debate in the House and assigns precedence to those motions in the order named in the rule. The motion to amend is listed in the sixth position, taking precedence over the motion to postpone indefinitely. Under that rule, the motion to amend yields to the motion to adjourn, to lay on the table, for the previous question, to postpone to a day certain, and to refer. *Manual* § 911. Because the motion to refer takes precedence over the motion to amend (5 Hinds § 5555), the motion to amend is not entertained while the motion to refer is pending (6 Cannon § 373).

Explaining or Opposing an Amendment

In the Committee of the Whole, under the five-minute rule where an amendment is offered, the initial 10 minutes of debate—five for the proponent to explain the amendment, five for a speech in opposition—takes precedence over a motion to amend it. 4 Hinds § 4751.

The Previous Question

In the House, a motion for the previous question takes precedence over a motion to amend. *Manual* § 926; 8 Cannon § 2660. Thus, the previous question may be moved pending the offering of an amendment by a Member to whom the floor was yielded for that purpose; and the previous question must be voted down before that Member is recognized to offer the amendment. Deschler Ch 23 § 18.3. The previous question having been defeated, an amendment may be offered. However, if the amendment is ruled out on a point of order, the previous question may again be moved and takes precedence over the offering of another amendment. Deschler Ch 23 § 20.3. Once the proponent of an amendment has been recognized for debate, such Member may not be taken from the floor by another Member seeking to move the previous question. Deschler Ch 23 § 20.7.

In the House as in the Committee of the Whole, a Member recognized to debate a pro forma amendment may not be taken from the floor by the motion for the previous question. 92-2, May 8, 1972, pp 16154, 16157.

The Motion to Strike the Enacting Clause

Under clause 9 of rule XVIII, the motion to strike the enacting clause takes precedence over a motion to amend. *Manual* § 989. The motion may be offered while an amendment is pending. 5 Hinds § 5328; 8 Cannon § 2624.

In the Committee of the Whole, where the motion is utilized under the modern practice, the motion must be phrased as a recommendation, because only the House can directly reach the enacting clause. Where the House rejects a recommendation to strike the enacting clause, the House resolves itself without motion into the Committee of the Whole for further consideration of the bill. Deschler Ch 19 § 10.9.

> The gentle______ from __________ moves that the Committee do now rise and report the bill back to the House with the recommendation that the enacting clause be stricken.

In the Committee of the Whole, the motion is subject to debate under the five-minute rule. Only two five-minute speeches are in order, one in favor of, one in opposition to, the motion. Although the motion to strike the enacting clause is pending, not even a pro forma amendment to strike the last word is entertained. 8 Cannon § 2627.

For general discussion of the motion to strike the enacting clause, see COMMITTEE OF THE WHOLE.

The Motion to Rise

With one exception in the Committee of the Whole, a motion to amend a bill has precedence over a motion to rise and report it to the House. 4 Hinds §§ 4752-4758. However, the motion to amend yields to the simple motion that the Committee rise. 4 Hinds § 4770. Under clause 2(d) of rule XXI, the motion to rise and report, if offered by the Majority Leader (or designee), takes precedence over an amendment proposing a limitation after a general appropriation bill has been completely read for amendment. *Manual* § 1040. In the 109th Congress, the House adopted a resolution creating a point of order against a motion to rise and report an appropriation bill that exceeded an applicable allocation of new budget authority under section 302(b) of the Congressional Budget Act of 1974. Such a point of order has been carried forward in subsequent Congresses by separate order contained in the opening-day rules package. *Manual* § 1044b.

For precedence as between particular forms of amendment, see § 21, infra.

§ 10. Amending Other Motions

Generally

The motion to amend may be applied, with certain exceptions, to other motions that are in order in the House or the Committee of the Whole. 5

Hinds §5754; *Manual* §927. Unless precluded by the operation of the previous question, the motion to amend may be applied to a motion:

- To postpone. 5 Hinds §5754; 8 Cannon §2824.
- To amend. 5 Hinds §5754.
- To refer. 5 Hinds §5754.
- To recommit. 5 Hinds §5521; 8 Cannon §§2695, 2738, 2762.
- To recommit with instructions. 8 Cannon §§2698, 2699, 2712, 2759.
- To declare a recess. 5 Hinds §5754.
- To instruct conferees. 8 Cannon §§3231, 3240.
- To change the reference of a public bill if the amendment is authorized by the appropriate committee. *Manual* §825; 7 Cannon §2127. But see 4 Hinds §4378.

When Not Permitted

A motion to amend may not be applied to a motion:

- To order the previous question. *Manual* §452.
- To table. 5 Hinds §5754.
- To suspend the rules, although a motion to suspend the rules and pass a measure may include a proposed amendment to the measure. 5 Hinds §§5405, 6858, 6859.
- To adjourn, as by specifying a particular day. 5 Hinds §§5360, 5754.
- To go into the Committee of the Whole to consider a privileged bill. *Manual* §927; 6 Cannon §§52, 724.
- To take up a designated bill in the Committee of the Whole. 8 Cannon §2865.
- To strike the enacting clause. 8 Cannon §2626.

An amendment may not be offered to a motion against which a point of order is pending. See POINTS OF ORDER; PARLIAMENTARY INQUIRIES. For discussion of the general rule that the motion to amend is not in order on questions on which the previous question is operating, see PREVIOUS QUESTION. Amendments to conference reports, see CONFERENCES BETWEEN THE HOUSES.

§11. Effect of Special Orders of Business

Bills are frequently considered pursuant to the terms of a special order of business resolution reported by the Committee on Rules. Such special orders may specify the amendments that may be offered to the bill, the kind and number of amendments that may be offered, and the order of consideration and voting thereon. Deschler Ch 27 §3. The Committee on Rules may report a resolution providing procedures to govern the consideration of a measure even where the measure is already pending in the Committee of the Whole. Deschler Ch 27 §3.77; see also SPECIAL ORDERS OF BUSINESS.

Legislation may be considered:

- Under an "open" rule, which places no restrictions on amendment.
- Under a rule that is "closed" or "modified-closed" that strictly restricts the universe of amendments to, for example, amendments specified in the report of the Committee on Rules accompanying the rule.
- Under a rule that is "open in part," "closed in part," or "open for a time, closed thereafter."
- Under a rule that is "modified open," which places minor restrictions on amendments, for example, requiring preprinting in the *Congressional Record.*

Where a bill is being considered in the Committee of the Whole under an "open" rule, germane amendments to the bill are in order under the standing rules of the House. Deschler Ch 27 § 3.7. Where a bill is being considered under a "closed" rule, even pro forma amendments are not in order. Deschler Ch 27 § 3.34. A "modified-closed rule" permits only designated amendments or a designated class of amendments. Deschler Ch 21 § 22.8.

The Committee of the Whole may not substantively restrict the offering of amendments in contravention of a special order of business adopted by the House. *Manual* § 993; Deschler Ch 27 § 3. However, a unanimous-consent request may be entertained in the Committee of the Whole if its effect is to allow procedures that differ only in minor or incidental respects from the procedure required by a special order of business adopted by the House. By unanimous consent, the House may delegate to the Committee of the Whole authority to entertain unanimous-consent requests to change procedures contained in such a rule. Deschler Ch 27 § 3.29 (note). For a list of unanimous-consent requests that have been permitted in the Committee of the Whole, see *Manual* § 993.

A special order of business may waive points of order against a bill or against specified amendments thereto. Deschler Ch 27 § 3. Such a waiver will not be implied. A special order of business merely "making in order" an amendment offered by a designated Member but not specifically waiving points of order does not permit consideration of the amendment unless in conformity with the rules of the House. Deschler Ch 27 § 3.72 (note). A waiver of points of order against a bill does not apply to amendments offered from the floor. Deschler Ch 27 § 3.

The so-called "self-executing" special order of business has been applied in recent years to expedite the amendment process. Such a rule may provide that a specified amendment "shall be considered to have been adopted." The committee has also reported rules that have "self-executed" the adoption of an amendment that became original text for the purpose of further amendment. *Manual* § 855; Deschler-Brown Ch 31 § 10.14.

§ 12. — Amendments Printed in the Congressional Record

The Committee on Rules may report a rule that precludes amendments that have not been printed in the *Congressional Record.* An amendment similar but not identical to the text of an amendment printed in the *Record* has been held out of order under such a rule. Only the House, by unanimous consent, may permit the offering of an amendment that differs in any way from an amendment permitted under the rule. However, an offeror may modify an amendment by unanimous consent in the Committee of the Whole once pending. *Manual* § 993; Deschler Ch 27 §§ 3.25-3.27.

Where a special order of business restricts the offering of amendments to those printed in the *Congressional Record* but does not specify the Members who must offer them, the right to propose amendments properly inserted in the *Record* inures to all Members. 105-2, Sept. 17, 1998, pp 20838, 20839.

A special order of business prohibiting amendments to a bill except those printed in the *Congressional Record* does not apply to amendments in the second degree unless so specified. Deschler Ch 27 § 3.13.

B. Permissible Pending Amendments

§ 13. In General; The Stages of Amendment

The checklist below and the above chart show the four common motions that may be pending simultaneously under clause 6 of rule XVI (5 Hinds § 5753) and the order in which they are voted on (see also § 28, infra):

- To amend the text (4)
- To amend the proposed amendment (1)
- To amend by a substitute (3)
- To amend the substitute (2)

Generally, only one amendment to the text may be pending at any one time. 5 Hinds § 5755; Deschler Ch 27 § 1. Once that amendment is offered, however, the other three forms of amendment shown above may be offered and all four amendments may be pending at one time. 5 Hinds § 5753; 8 Cannon § 2883; Deschler Ch 27 § 1.

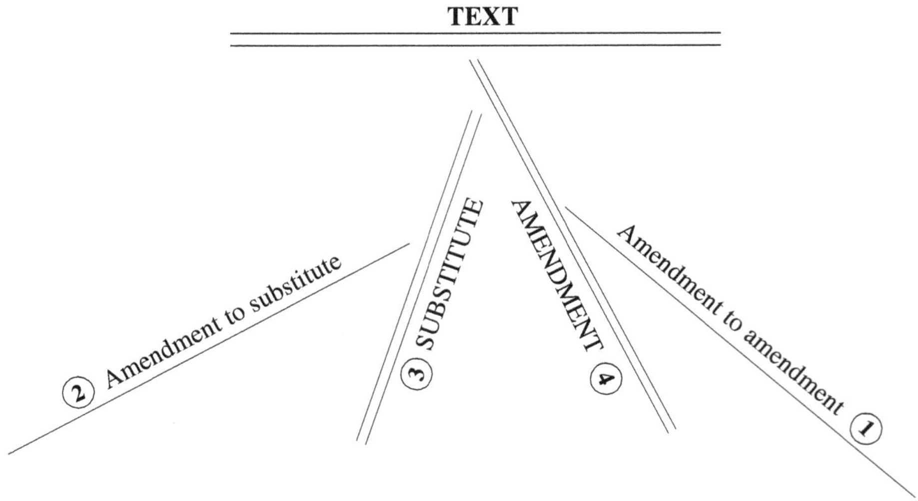

The amendments shown in the chart are amendments in the first or second degree. Amendments beyond the second degree, such as an amendment to the amendment to the amendment to the pending text, are not in order. See § 1, supra; § 14, infra. Frequently, however, as by a special order of business, an amendment in the nature of a substitute may be considered as an original text for purposes of amendment, thereby extending the permissible degrees of amendment. Deschler Ch 27 § 1. Indeed, a special order of business reported by the Committee on Rules may specifically permit the offering of amendments beyond the second degree. 94-1, Feb. 27, 1975, p 4593. In one instance, pursuant to a special order of business, up to eight amendments to the pending text were pending simultaneously. 96-1, May 15, 1979, p 1050.

There is no limit to the number of amendments that may be offered either to an amendment or to a substitute so long as not changing a previously adopted amendment. When one second-degree amendment has been disposed of, another can be offered. Deschler Ch 27 § 5.16. Where both an amendment and a substitute have been offered, each may have one amendment pending to it at one time. Deschler Ch 26 §§ 5.14, 5.15.

Perfecting the Original Text

It is in order to offer a perfecting amendment to the pending portion of original text, even though there is pending an amendment in the nature of a substitute for the pending measure. Deschler Ch 27 § 5.34. Likewise, where there is pending a motion to strike a title of a bill, perfecting amendments to that title may nevertheless be offered and voted on before voting on the motion to strike. Deschler Ch 27 § 5.11.

Amending Pending Amendments

Only one amendment to a pending amendment may be pending at one time. Deschler Ch 27 §§ 5.7, 5.17, 5.24. However, as soon as an amendment to an amendment is adopted or rejected another is in order seriatim until the amendment is perfected; and only after disposition of the amendment will further amendment of the bill be allowed. Deschler Ch 27 § 5.5.

Amending Substitute Amendments

A substitute for an amendment is subject to amendment. Deschler Ch 27 §§ 5.3, 5.4. Thus, where an amendment, an amendment thereto, and a substitute for the original amendment are pending, it is in order to offer an amendment to the substitute. Deschler Ch 27 § 5.13. Other amendments to the substitute are in order following disposition of the pending amendment to the substitute. Deschler Ch 27 § 5.25.

Amending Amendments in the Nature of a Substitute

When specifically made in order, an amendment in the nature of a substitute may be considered as original text for purposes of amendment. Accordingly, where pursuant to a special order of business a committee amendment in the nature of a substitute is being read as original text for purpose of amendment, there may be pending to that text (1) an amendment, (2) a substitute therefor, and (3) amendments to both the amendment and the substitute. Deschler Ch 27 § 5.32. As often as amendments to the amendment are disposed of, further amendments may be offered and voted upon before voting on the amendment to the substitute. Deschler Ch 27 § 5.21.

§ 14. Amendments in the Third Degree

The following chart shows the four common forms of amendments in the first or second degree and distinguishes them from amendments in the third degree.

Amendments in the third degree are not in order. 5 Hinds § 5754; 8 Cannon § 2580; Deschler Ch 27 § 6.1. ''The line must be drawn somewhere,'' wrote Thomas Jefferson, ''and usage has drawn it after the amendment to the amendment.'' *Manual* § 454. This principle is reflected in clause 6 of rule XVI and is considered fundamental in the House of Representatives. *Manual* § 922; Deschler Ch 27 § 6. Thus, as shown by the chart, an amendment to an amendment to an amendment is in the third degree and

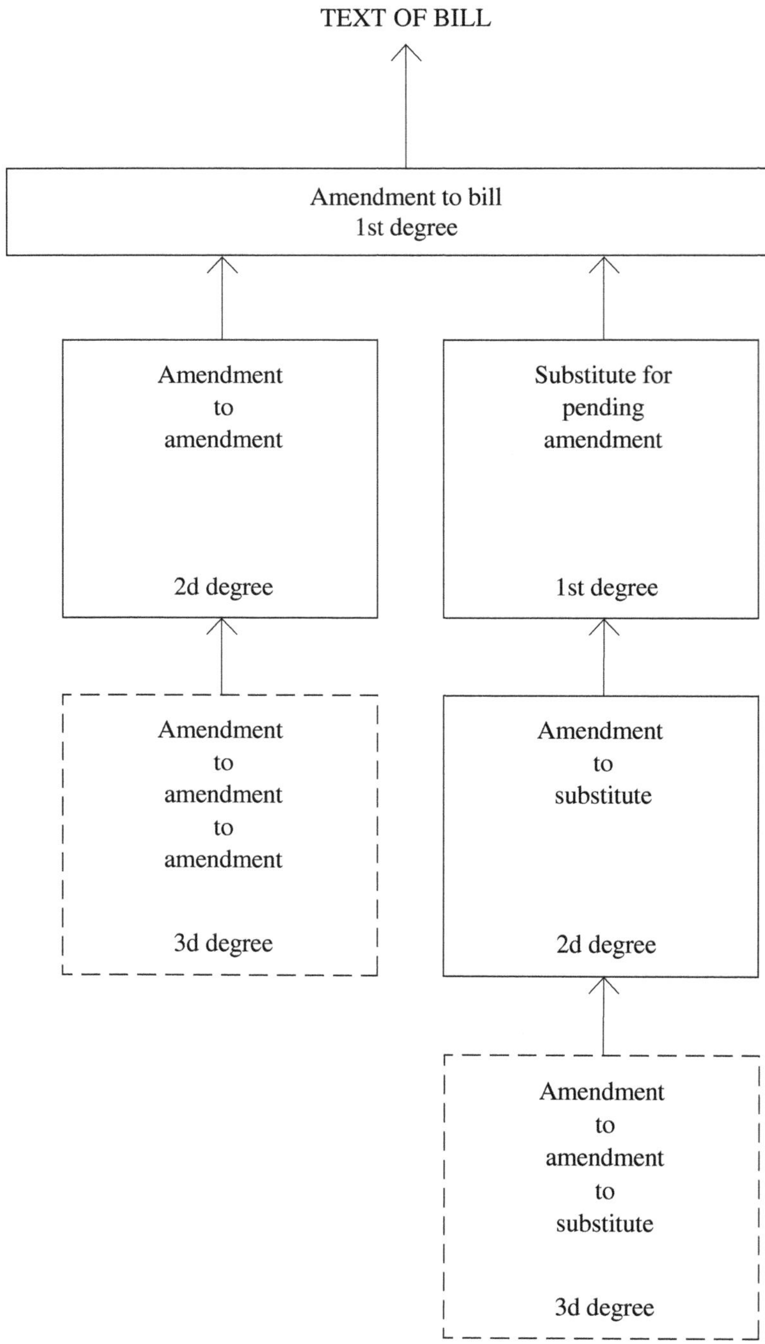
TEXT OF BILL
Amendment to bill
1st degree
Amendment
to
amendment
2d degree
Substitute for
pending
amendment
1st degree
Amendment
to
amendment
to
amendment
3d degree
Amendment
to
substitute
2d degree
Amendment
to
amendment
to
substitute
3d degree

not in order. Deschler Ch 27 § 6.2. Until the amendment to the amendment is disposed of, no further amendment to the amendment may be offered. Deschler Ch 27 § 6.12.

The prohibition against amendments in the third degree also applies to amendments between the House and Senate. If a bill originating in one House is amended by the other, the originating House may amend the amendment; and the second House may again amend. Any further amendment between the Houses would be in the third degree. *Manual* § 529. However, the House has on occasion adopted a special order of business (waiving applicable points of order) that provided for consideration of a motion to concur in a Senate amendment with a further House amendment that broached the third degree. 110-2, June 19, 2008, p 13052; 110-2, July 23, 2008, p ____; 110-2, Sept. 28, 2008, p ____; 111-2, Mar. 4, 2010, p ____.

Substitutes for Pending Amendments Distinguished

As shown by the following chart, a substitute for a pending first-degree amendment is subject to amendment, whereas a perfecting amendment to an amendment is not, as that would be in the third degree. *Manual* § 923; Deschler Ch 27 § 6. The substitute permitted by clause 6 of rule XVI is an alternative to the original first-degree amendment and not for the amendment to that amendment. Indeed, when an amendment and a perfecting amendment thereto are pending, neither an amendment to, or substitute for, the perfecting amendment is in order, both such amendments being in the third degree. Deschler Ch 27 § 6.2.

Although a perfecting amendment to a pending substitute should retain some portion of the substitute so as not to be in effect a substitute in the third degree, the Chair does not look behind the form of the amendment in the absence of a timely point of order from the floor. Deschler Ch 27 § 6.21.

Amendments in the Nature of a Substitute

Normally, an amendment to or a substitute for an amendment to an amendment in the nature of a substitute would be in the third degree and not in order. This principle, however, would not apply if the amendment in the nature of a substitute were being considered as original text for purposes of amendment. Deschler Ch 27 § 6.15 (note). Where an amendment in the nature of a substitute is considered as original text for the purpose of amendment, pursuant to a special order of business, an amendment to an amendment thereto is not in the third degree and is in order. Deschler Ch 27 § 6.18.

Amendments While Motion to Strike Pending

While a motion to strike is pending, it is in order to offer an amendment to perfect the language proposed to be stricken; such a perfecting amendment (which is in the first degree) may be amended by a substitute (also in the first degree), and amendments to the substitute are thus in the second degree and therefore in order. Deschler Ch 27 § 6.20.

Pro Forma Amendments

In the Committee of the Whole, pro forma amendments are technically not in order where the four permitted amendments are pending if the point of order is raised, as they would constitute amendments in the third degree. However, the Chair has hesitated to rule out of order pro forma amendments as being in the third degree, because the Committee has the power to close debate when it chooses and has permitted such amendments to be offered by unanimous consent. Deschler Ch 27 § 6.22.

C. When to Offer Amendment; Reading for Amendment

§ 15. In General; Reading by the Clerk

A second reading occurs in the Committee of the Whole after general debate when a measure is read for amendment under clause 5 of rule XVIII. Under clause 5(a) of rule XVIII, amendments are not in order in the Committee of the Whole until general debate has been closed. 4 Hinds § 4744. Amendments are then debated under the five-minute rule. *Manual* § 978. The bill is read for amendment, and amendments are offered and debated at the appropriate point in the reading. Thus, when a bill is being read for amendment in the Committee of the Whole by section, it is not in order to offer amendments except to the one section under consideration. Deschler Ch 27 § 7. After a section or paragraph has been passed, it is no longer subject to amendment. *Manual* §§ 413, 980.

Bills are ordinarily read for amendment by section or paragraph in sequence. However, the House, by unanimous consent or special order of business, may vary the reading of a bill for amendment under the five-minute rule in the Committee of the Whole, which may include dispensing with the reading entirely. Deschler Ch 27 §§ 7.1, 7.18.

House Practice Distinguished

In the House, amendments to measures on the House Calendar are made where the Member calling up the measure yields for an amendment, or if the previous question is not moved or ordered, pending the engrossment and third reading. 5 Hinds § 5781; 7 Cannon § 1051; Deschler Ch 27 § 13.3. Amendments may be offered to any part of the bill without proceeding by section or paragraph. 4 Hinds § 3392.

Practice in House as in the Committee of the Whole

Where a bill is by unanimous consent considered in the House as in the Committee of the Whole, the bill is considered as read and open to amendment at any point under the five-minute rule. Deschler Ch 27 § 11.22. This is so despite the fact that the House has previously adopted a special order of business providing that the bill be read by title in the Committee of the Whole because that order of the House had been superseded by a subsequent order of the House. Deschler Ch 27 § 7.2.

§ 16. Amendments to Text Passed in the Reading

In the Committee of the Whole, amendments to a section are in order after the section has been read or the reading dispensed with and remain in order until the reading of the next portion to be considered. Deschler Ch 27 § 7. Generally, an amendment comes too late when the Clerk has read beyond the section to which the amendment applies. 8 Cannon § 2930; Deschler Ch 27 § 8.1.

An amendment offered as a new section is in order to a bill being read by section after the Clerk has read up to, but not beyond, the point at which the amendment would be inserted. The amendment must be offered after the consideration of the section of the bill that it would follow, and comes too late after the next section of the bill has been read for amendment. Deschler Ch 27 § 8.17. A section is considered passed for the purpose of amendment after an amendment inserting a new section has been adopted following that section. Deschler Ch 27 § 8.12. An amendment adding a new section at the end of a bill is in order after the last section of the bill has been read, even though other amendments adding new sections have been adopted. Deschler Ch 27 § 7.35.

To be timely, an amendment must be offered at the appropriate place in the reading. A point of order that an amendment to a section or a paragraph of a bill comes too late does not lie where the Member offering the amendment was standing and seeking recognition before the section or paragraph was passed in the reading. Deschler Ch 27 § 8.22. The Chair has on occasion directed the Clerk to reread a paragraph of a bill where there was doubt as to how far the Clerk had read. Deschler Ch 27 § 8.4.

§ 17. Amendments to Text Not Yet Read; Amendments En Bloc

It is not in order to strike or otherwise amend portions of a bill not yet read for amendment. Deschler Ch 27 § 9. Even committee amendments printed in a bill are not considered until the section where they appear is read for amendment. Deschler Ch 27 § 9.4. Unless permitted by a special order of business, amendments to a pending title of a bill and to a subsequent title may be offered en bloc only by unanimous consent. Deschler Ch 27 § 9.13. Similarly, to a bill being read for amendment by section, amendments to more than one section may be considered en bloc by unanimous consent only. Deschler Ch 27 § 9.14.

During the reading of an appropriation bill, clause 2(f) of rule XXI permits the offering of certain budget-neutral amendments to text not yet read. Such amendments may propose only to transfer appropriations among objects in the bill and are not subject to division. *Manual* § 1042.

§ 18. Amendments to Bills Considered as Read and Open to Amendment

Unless permitted by a special order of business, a bill may be considered as read and open to amendment at any point only by unanimous consent. A motion to that effect is not in order. Deschler Ch 27 § 11.2. Similarly, during the reading of a section for amendment, that section can be considered as read and open to amendment at any point only by unanimous consent. Deschler Ch 27 § 11.4. Where consent is granted that the remainder of the bill be open to amendment at any point, amendments may then be offered to any portion of the bill not yet read for amendment at the time the permission is granted and amendments remain in order to that portion of the bill pending when the request was granted. Deschler Ch 27 § 11.9; 94-1, June 4, 1975, p 16899. However, an agreement that the remainder of the bill be considered read and open for amendment at any point does not admit an amendment to a portion of the bill already passed in the reading. Deschler Ch 27 § 11.8. Points of order against the text open to amendment are disposed of before the offering of amendments. See POINTS OF ORDER; PARLIAMENTARY INQUIRIES.

§ 19. Amendments in the Nature of a Substitute

Unless the bill is considered as having been read for amendment, an amendment in the nature of a substitute for a bill is in order only after the first section (or paragraph) of the bill has been read for amendment or following the reading of the final section (or paragraph) of the bill. Deschler

Ch 27 §§ 12.1, 12.2, 12.4. To a bill being read for amendment by title, an amendment in the nature of a substitute for the entire bill may be offered either after the reading of the ''short title'' of the bill (which is normally a separate section of the bill preceding title I) or at the conclusion of the reading of the whole bill. Deschler Ch 27 § 12.

An amendment in the nature of a substitute for a bill is not in order at an intermediate stage of the reading unless the bill is considered as having been read for amendment, in which case an amendment in the nature of a substitute may be offered at any time during consideration of the bill. Deschler Ch 27 §§ 12.3, 12.10.

Although an amendment in the nature of a substitute may ordinarily be offered after the reading of the first section of a bill being read by section and before committee amendments adding new sections, where a bill consists of one section and is therefore open to amendment at any point when read, committee amendments adding new sections are considered perfecting amendments and are disposed of before the offering of amendments in the nature of a substitute. Deschler Ch 27 § 12.13.

An amendment in the nature of a substitute is in order after an entire bill has been read and perfecting amendments have been adopted thereto, as long as such perfecting amendments have not changed the bill in its entirety. Deschler Ch 27 § 12.16. Similarly, an amendment in the nature of a substitute may be offered for a bill (or for an amendment being considered as original text) after the reading thereof has been completed, if another amendment in the nature of a substitute has not been previously adopted. Deschler Ch 27 § 12.6. For substitutes for amendments in the nature of a substitute, see § 24, infra.

§ 20. Recognition to Offer Amendments; Priority

Necessity of Recognition

Under clause 2 of rule XVII, decisions on recognition rest with the Chair. Therefore, a Member wishing to offer an amendment must first be recognized by the Chair for that purpose; and a Member holding the floor under the five-minute rule may not yield to another Member to offer an amendment. 2 Hinds § 1422; Deschler Ch 27 §§ 4.1, 4.6.

Discretion of Chair

Except where governed by a special order of business, recognition for the purpose of offering amendments is within the discretion of the Chair. Deschler Ch 27 §§ 4.2, 4.3. No point of order lies against the Chair's recognition of one Member over another. Deschler Ch 27 § 4.4. Nevertheless, in the absence of a controlling special order of business, the Chair ordinarily follows the many precedents and practices that serve as guidelines to the Chair in according recognition to Members to offer amendments. Deschler Ch 27 § 4.35. For example, the Chair may accord recognition pursuant to the principle of alternation between majority and minority parties or on the priority of perfecting amendments over motions to strike. Deschler Ch 27 § 4.19. Decisions on questions of recognition are not subject to appeal. *Manual* § 949.

Priority of Committee Amendments

Amendments recommended by a committee reporting a bill are normally considered before amendments offered from the floor, including instances where a bill is considered read and open to amendment. Deschler Ch 27 § 4.34. Thus, perfecting committee amendments to a paragraph under consideration are disposed of before amendments from the floor are considered. Deschler Ch 27 § 4.33. A special order of business will often make in order a committee amendment in the nature of a substitute as the base text for purposes of further amendment.

Committee Membership as Basis for Recognition

The Chair ordinarily accords priority in recognition to members of the committee reporting the bill, if on their feet seeking recognition. Deschler Ch 27 § 4.8. This is so despite the party affiliation of such Members. Deschler Ch 27 § 4.10.

Members of the reporting committee or committees are normally accorded prior recognition in order of full-committee seniority and not by the sequence of lines in the pending paragraph to which those amendments may relate. Deschler Ch 27 §§ 4.11, 4.13, 4.30. It is within the discretion of the Chair as to whether a majority or minority member of the committee will be recognized first. Deschler Ch 27 § 4.18.

Effect of Parliamentary Inquiries

The fact that the Chair has recognized a Member to raise a parliamentary inquiry does not prohibit the Chair from then recognizing the same Member to offer an amendment. The principle of alternation of recognition does not require the Chair to recognize a Member from the minority to offer an amendment after recognizing a Member from the majority to raise a parliamentary inquiry. Deschler Ch 27 § 4.13 (note).

D. Offering Particular Kinds of Amendments; Precedence and Priorities

§ 21. Introductory; Perfecting Amendments

Generally, the House follows the Jeffersonian principle that language should be perfected before taking other action on it. Deschler Ch 27 § 15. ''[T]he friends of the paragraph,'' Jefferson wrote, ''may make it as perfect as they can by amendments before the question is put for inserting it. . . . In like manner, if it is proposed to amend by striking a paragraph, the friends of the paragraph are first to make it as perfect as they can by amendments, before the question is put for striking it out.'' *Manual* § 469. An important exception to this rule is that a motion to strike the enacting words of a bill, being a device used for purposes of rejecting the bill, has precedence over a motion to amend the bill. Clause 9 of rule XVIII; *Manual* § 988.

A motion to strike and a perfecting amendment may be pending simultaneously. They must be voted on separately and in a specified order. § 28, infra. When a motion to strike is pending, an amendment to perfect the text proposed to be stricken may be offered as preferential. When an amendment to perfect is pending, a motion to strike must wait. Deschler Ch 27 § 15.1. They may not be offered as amendments to or substitutes for one another. When a motion to strike a pending portion of a bill is pending, perfecting amendments are in order to the *text* proposed to be stricken—not to the motion to strike. Deschler Ch 27 § 15.13.

Precedence Over the Motion to Strike

A perfecting amendment to the text of a bill is in order and takes precedence over a pending motion to strike the text and is first to be voted on. Deschler Ch 27 §§ 15.3, 15.4. Thus, an amendment inserting new words is in order and takes precedence over a pending motion to strike that portion of the text. Deschler Ch 27 § 15.7.

Perfecting amendments to a paragraph may be offered (one at a time) while a motion to strike the paragraph is pending, and such perfecting amendments are first disposed of. Deschler Ch 27 §§ 15.5, 15.15. Under this rule, where a perfecting amendment is offered and rejected, a second perfecting amendment may be offered and disposed of before the vote on a motion to strike. If the motion to strike is ultimately defeated, further perfecting amendments to the pending text are yet in order. Deschler Ch 27 §§ 15.8, 15.26.

A motion to strike a pending portion of a bill will be held in abeyance until perfecting amendments to that portion are disposed of. *Manual* § 469. However, a Member who has been recognized to debate the motion to strike may not be deprived of the floor by another Member who seeks to offer a perfecting amendment. After the Member so recognized has completed five minutes in support of the motion to strike, but before the question is put on the motion to strike, the perfecting amendment may be offered and voted upon. Deschler Ch 27 § 15.11.

In the case of preferential perfecting amendments to the text offered pending a motion to strike that text, such a motion to strike must still be voted upon regardless of whether or not such perfecting amendments are adopted (assuming that the perfecting amendments do not change the entire pending text). Deschler Ch 27 § 15.24. However, if perfecting amendments are agreed to, and are coextensive with the material proposed to be stricken, the motion to strike the amended text falls and is not acted on. Deschler Ch 27 § 15.25.

Precedence Over Amendment in the Nature of a Substitute

Where a bill consists of several sections, an amendment in the nature of a substitute should be offered after the reading of the first section and following disposition of perfecting amendments to the first section. Deschler Ch 27 § 15.40 (note). Indeed, a perfecting amendment to the first section of a bill may be offered while an amendment in the nature of a substitute for the entire bill is pending. Deschler Ch 27 § 15.32. A perfecting amendment to a pending paragraph of a bill is in order and is not precluded by the intervention of a single substitute for the paragraph and several of those following. Deschler Ch 27 § 15.33.

§ 22. Motions to Strike

Amendments proposing to strike a section of a bill are in order after perfecting amendments to the section are disposed of. Deschler Ch 23 § 17.3. A motion to strike a section or paragraph is not in order while a perfecting amendment is pending. Deschler Ch 27 §§ 16.6, 17.1. The motion to strike, if already pending, must remain in abeyance until the amendment to perfect has been disposed of. *Manual* § 469; 5 Hinds § 5758; 8 Cannon § 2860. Because a provision must be perfected before the question is put on striking it out, a motion to strike a paragraph or section may not be offered as a substitute for a pending motion to perfect the paragraph or section, including where the pending perfecting amendment is a motion to strike and insert new text. Deschler Ch 27 §§ 17.15-17.18. Although the motion to strike is not in order in this situation as a substitute, it may be offered after disposition of the perfecting amendment to strike and insert if more comprehensive in scope. Deschler Ch 27 §§17.30-17.32.

Although an amendment that has been agreed to may not be modified, a proposition to strike it from the bill with other language of the original text is in order. 8 Cannon §2855. Thus, if the pending title of a bill is perfected by an amendment adding a new section thereto, and the Committee of the Whole thereafter agrees to a motion to strike the entire title, the words added by the perfecting amendment are eliminated along with the rest of the title. 91-1, Oct. 3, 1969, p 28454.

To a motion to strike certain text and insert new language, a simple motion to strike all that text may not be offered as an amendment, as it would have the effect of dividing the motion to strike and insert, which is prohibited by clause 5 of rule XVI. Deschler Ch 27 §17.23.

§23. Motions to Strike and Insert

As a perfecting amendment, a motion to strike and insert takes precedence over a pending motion to strike. 8 Cannon §2849. It may be offered while the motion to strike is pending and is first acted upon. Deschler Ch 27 §16.3. If the perfecting amendment is agreed to, and is coextensive with the motion to strike, the motion to strike the amended text falls and is not acted on. Deschler Ch 27 §16.4.

Under clause 5 of rule XVI, a motion to strike and insert is indivisible. *Manual* §920. For this and other reasons, a motion to strike is not in order as a substitute for a pending motion to strike and insert. Deschler Ch 27 §17.18. Conversely, a motion to strike and insert a portion of a pending section is not in order as a substitute for a motion to strike the section, but may be offered as a perfecting amendment to the section and is first voted upon, subject to being eliminated by subsequent adoption of the motion to strike. Deschler Ch 27 §17.7. See also §4, supra.

§24. Substitute Amendments

Generally

A ''substitute'' is a substitute for an amendment, and not a substitute for the original text. §6, supra. A substitute can be entertained only after an amendment is pending. 8 Cannon §2883. In the Committee of the Whole, the proper time to offer a substitute for an amendment is after the amendment has been read and the Member offering it has been permitted to debate it under the five-minute rule. Deschler Ch 27 §18.2. The substitute is then in order until the Chair puts the question on the amendment. Deschler Ch 27 § 18.3.

Substitutes for Amendments in the Nature of a Substitute

An amendment in the nature of a substitute is subject to amendment by a substitute therefor, and the substitute is in order even after perfecting amendments have been adopted to the amendment in the nature of a substitute. Deschler Ch 27 §§ 18.18, 18.19.

Reoffering Substitute Propositions

Whether a proposition contained in a substitute may be reoffered in a different form after it has failed of approval depends on the circumstances. If the language of the substitute is reoffered in such a way as to present precisely the same question that has already been voted on, it would not be in order. Where an amendment is altered by adoption of a substitute, and then is rejected as so amended, the language of the substitute cannot be reoffered at that point as a first-degree amendment. See Deschler Ch 27 § 18.25 and note. Clearly, however, where the actual proposition was never voted on because of changes made through the amendment process, the proposition may be offered again as, for example, an amendment to text. Where an amendment is offered, and then a substitute for that amendment, the consideration of that substitute necessarily proceeds with reference only to the particular amendment to which offered. This may present a different question from that which would arise if the language of the substitute were considered with reference to the text of the bill. *Manual* § 923; see also 5 Hinds § 5797, 8 Cannon § 2843, and Deschler Ch 27 § 18.25 (note).

§ 25. Offering Amendments During Yielded Time

In the House

A measure being considered in the House is not subject to amendment unless the Member in control yields for that purpose or the previous question is either not moved or is rejected. Deschler Ch 27 § 13.6; see § 26, infra. Ordinarily, an amendment to the measure may be offered only by the Member having the floor unless such Member yields to another for that purpose; and it is within the discretion of the Member in charge whether, and to whom, to yield. Deschler Ch 27 § 13.3. An amendment may not be offered in time yielded for debate only. 8 Cannon § 2474; Deschler Ch 27 § 13.1.

A Member controlling debate in the House on a measure may yield to another to offer an amendment, despite a prior announced intention not to yield for such purpose. 8 Cannon § 2470. The Member so yielded to may then offer an amendment, be recognized for an hour, and may yield time to others. Deschler-Brown Ch 29 § 30.7.

A Member who has the floor in debate in the House may not yield to another Member to offer an amendment without losing control of the time. 5 Hinds § 5021. By yielding to another to offer an amendment a Member loses the right to resume. 5 Hinds § 5031. However, a Member may yield to permit an amendment to be read for information without losing control of the time. 8 Cannon § 2477.

In the Committee of the Whole

A Member recognized under the five-minute rule may not yield to another Member to offer an amendment. A Member wishing to offer an amendment under the five-minute rule must seek recognition from the Chair and may not be yielded the floor for that purpose by another Member. Deschler Ch 27 § 13.7.

§ 26. Effect of Previous Question; Expiration of Time for Debate

Generally; House Practice

The adoption of the previous question precludes further debate or amendment on the pending measure and brings the House to an immediate vote thereon. Clause 1 of rule XIX; 5 Hinds §§ 5486, 5487; Deschler Ch 27 § 14.1. The previous question may be moved (1) on a pending amendment; (2) on the underlying measure; or (3) on both propositions. See PREVIOUS QUESTION. Thus, where the previous question is ordered in the House on a pending resolution *and* the amendment thereto, the vote immediately recurs on the adoption of the resolution after the disposition of the amendment, and no intervening amendment is in order. Deschler Ch 27 § 14.3. However, a motion to commit may be in order under clause 2 of rule XIX. *Manual* §§ 1001, 1002; see REFER AND RECOMMIT.

The previous question is sometimes ordered on nondebatable motions for the specific purpose of preventing amendments thereto. 5 Hinds § 5490.

Expiration of Debate Time in the Committee of the Whole

An amendment to a pending section of a bill being considered in the Committee of the Whole may be offered notwithstanding the expiration of all time for debate on the section and any amendments thereto. Deschler Ch 27 § 14.9. Under clause 8 of rule XVIII, the expiration of a limitation on debate under the five-minute rule does not prohibit the offering of further amendments, but such amendments are not subject to debate if not printed in the *Congressional Record*. *Manual* § 987; Deschler Ch 27 § 14.10. However, where a special order of business limits the time for consideration of amendments, an amendment may not be offered upon the expiration of that time limitation. *Manual* § 993; see also CONSIDERATION AND DEBATE.

E. Consideration and Voting

§ 27. In General; Reading of Amendment

Generally

Amendments to a bill must be read in full or their reading dispensed with in accordance with the rules. 8 Cannon § 2339. This is so even where the bill itself is considered as having been read for amendment pursuant to a special order of business. Deschler Ch 27 § 22. The reading of an amendment must be completed before an amendment thereto is in order. Deschler Ch 27 § 22.5.

Amendments at the Clerk's desk must be offered by a Member before they will be read by the Clerk. Deschler Ch 27 § 7.27. They need not be reoffered after they have been reported by the Clerk notwithstanding suspension of consideration of the bill. Where the Committee of the Whole resumes its consideration of a bill after an interval of time, the Chair sometimes (without objection) directs the Clerk to re-report the amendments that were pending at the time the Committee rose. Deschler Ch 27 § 22.3.

Numbering Amendments

Amendments printed in the *Congressional Record* are numbered in the order submitted for printing. Clause 8 of rule XVIII.

Dispensing with Reading

The reading of an amendment may be dispensed with by unanimous consent or waived pursuant to the provisions of a special order of business. Deschler Ch 27 § 22. The reading of an amendment in the Committee of the Whole may also be dispensed with by motion if the amendment has been printed in the bill as reported or if printed in the *Congressional Record* by the offeror of the amendment. Clause 7 of rule XVIII; *Manual* § 986.

Re-reading Amendments

An amendment that has been once read may not be read again except by unanimous consent. Deschler Ch 27 § 22.2. It is not within the province of the Chair to analyze the effect of amendments, and the Chair has declined to recognize for unanimous consent that the Clerk read the ''differences'' between two pending amendments. Deschler Ch 27 § 1.33.

Amendment in the Nature of Substitute

The reading of an amendment in the nature of a substitute must be completed before an amendment thereto is in order. Deschler Ch 27 § 22.5. An amendment in the nature of a substitute is not read by section in the absence of a special order of business that specifies to the contrary, and it is open to amendment at any point when read in its entirety. Deschler Ch 27 § 22.6. Where, pursuant to a special order of business, an amendment in the nature of a substitute is being read as an original bill for the purpose of amendment, the amendment is read section by section, and substantive as well as pro forma amendments are in order following the reading of each section. Deschler Ch 27 § 22.7.

§ 28. Order of Consideration Generally; Postponed and Clustered Votes on Amendments

Voting Sequence

The four forms of amendment permitted by clause 6 of rule XVI may be pending simultaneously. § 13, supra. However, as shown by the following chart, they must be voted on in the sequence shown, as follows: (1) amendments to the amendment, if any, are disposed of first, seriatim, until the amendment is perfected; (2) amendments to the substitute are next voted on, seriatim, until the substitute is perfected; (3) the substitute is next voted on; and (4) the amendment is voted on last, so that if the substitute has been agreed to, the vote is on the amendment as amended by the substitute. *Manual* § 922; Deschler Ch 27 § 23.

An amendment to an amendment must be offered before the question is put on the underlying amendment. Deschler Ch 27 §§ 18.3, 18.4. Once a perfecting amendment to an amendment is disposed of, the original amendment, as amended or not, remains open to further perfecting amendment, and all such amendments are disposed of before voting on substitutes for the original amendment and amendments thereto. Deschler Ch 27 § 23.9.

Disposition of a perfecting amendment to a substitute amendment does not preclude the offering of further perfecting amendments to the substitute or the underlying amendment. However, once the substitute is adopted, the Chair immediately puts the question on the original amendment as amended by the substitute and further perfecting amendments (including pro forma amendments) are not in order. Deschler Ch 27 §§ 23.8, 23.9.

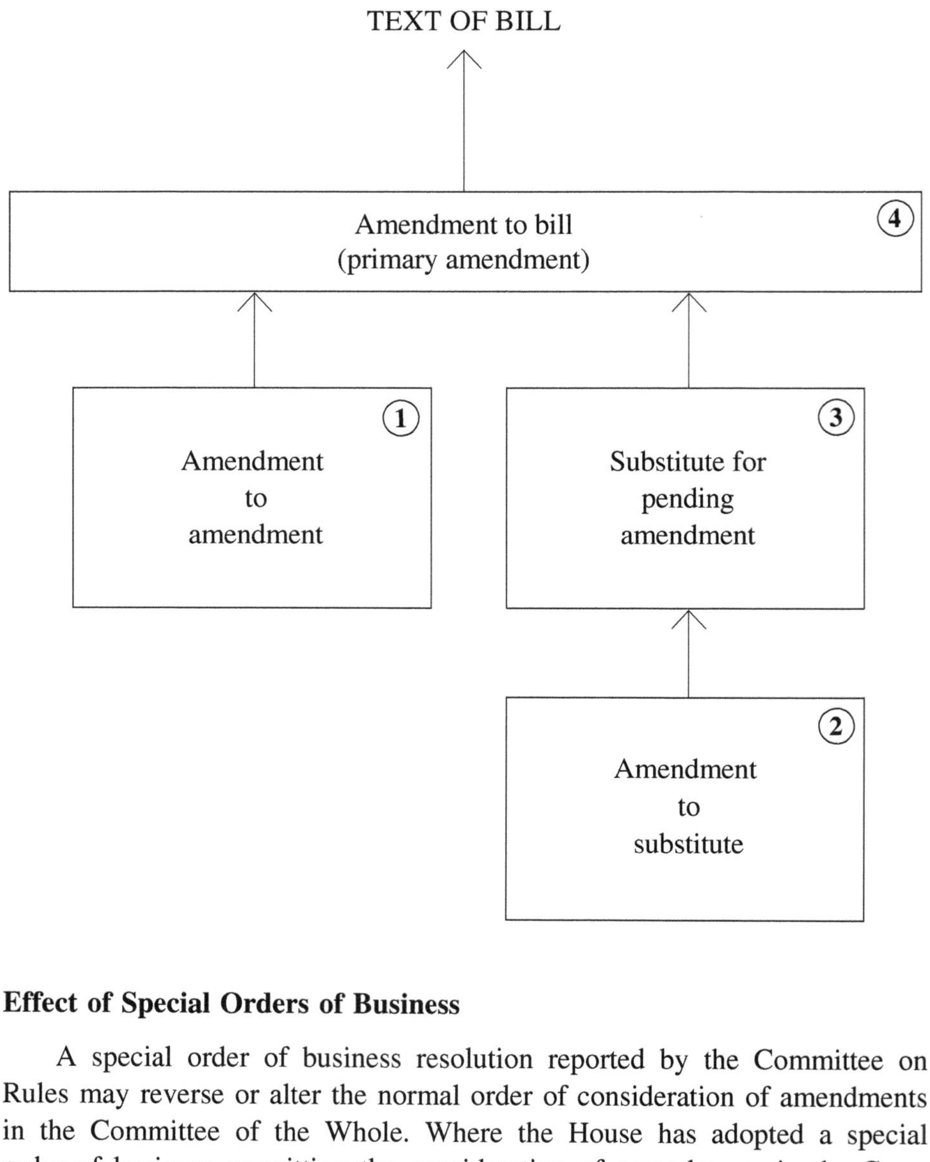

Effect of Special Orders of Business

A special order of business resolution reported by the Committee on Rules may reverse or alter the normal order of consideration of amendments in the Committee of the Whole. Where the House has adopted a special order of business permitting the consideration of amendments in the Committee of the Whole only in a prescribed order, the Committee of the Whole must rise to permit the House, by unanimous consent, to change that order of consideration. *Manual* § 993; Deschler Ch 27 § 23.

Postponed and Clustered Votes on Amendments

Under clause 6(g) of rule XVIII, the chair of the Committee of the Whole may postpone and cluster requests for recorded votes on amendments to a subsequent place and time during the amendment process as determined by the Chair. Special orders of business from the Committee on Rules, before adoption of clause 6(g), routinely provided the chair of the Committee of the Whole such authority. *Manual* § 984.

Where a special order of business provided such authority, the Chair has held:

- Use of that authority, and the order of clustering, was entirely within the discretion of the Chair.
- An amendment pending as unfinished business where proceedings on a request for a recorded vote had been postponed could be modified by unanimous consent on the initiative of its proponent.
- A request for a recorded vote on an amendment on which proceedings had been postponed could be withdrawn by unanimous consent before proceedings resumed on the request as unfinished business, in which case the amendment stood disposed of by the voice vote thereon.
- Unanimous consent is not required to withdraw a request for a recorded vote on an amendment on which proceedings had been postponed when the question recurs as unfinished business.
- Such authority did not permit the Chair to postpone a vote on an appeal of a ruling of the Chair (even by unanimous consent).
- The Committee of the Whole by unanimous consent could vacate postponed proceedings, thereby permitting the Chair to put the question *de novo*.
- The Committee of the Whole could resume proceedings on unfinished business consisting of a ''stack'' of amendments even while another amendment was pending.

Manual § 984.

Clause 6(g) also provides the Chair the ability to reduce to five minutes the time for electronic voting on any such postponed question that follows another electronic vote without intervening business. The offering of a pro forma amendment to discuss the legislative program, or an extended one-minute speech by a Member to express gratitude to the Members on a personal matter, may be considered intervening business such as to preclude a five-minute vote under this authority except by unanimous consent. *Manual* § 984.

§ 29. Committee Amendments

Pending amendments, whether favorably or adversely recommended by the committee reporting the bill, must be voted on. 8 Cannon § 2865. The

Committee of the Whole must vote on a pending amendment even though it has been "accepted" by members of the committee reporting the bill. Deschler Ch 27 § 26.10.

Absent a special order of business that provides otherwise, committee amendments to a bill are ordinarily taken up before amendments from the floor, although they are not voted on until after they have been perfected. 5 Hinds § 5773. Floor amendments to the bill are normally in order following the disposition of pending committee amendments perfecting that bill, even though the bill is open to amendment at any point. Deschler Ch 27 §§ 26.3, 26.5.

Absent a special order of business that provides otherwise, where a committee amendment proposes to strike a portion of the text, a perfecting amendment from the floor may intervene before the vote is taken on the committee amendment. See § 21, supra.

A committee amendment to the first paragraph or section of a bill is voted on before a vote is taken on an amendment in the nature of a substitute to strike all after the enacting clause and insert new matter. Deschler Ch 27 § 26.1.

§ 30. Amendments En Bloc; Use of Special Orders of Business

Generally

Amendments may be considered en bloc only by unanimous consent or pursuant to a special order of business. Deschler Ch 27 §§ 27.2, 27.3, 27.14-27.16. Amendments considered en bloc by unanimous consent are subject to germane amendment after they have been read. Once pending they are open to perfecting amendment at any point. Deschler Ch 27 § 27.7.

En bloc amendments may be offered to a pending amendment, but it is not in order to consider en bloc amendments to committee amendments that have not yet been reported. Deschler Ch 27 § 27.10. For en bloc amendments to appropriation bills, see APPROPRIATIONS.

The en bloc consideration of amendments in the Committee of the Whole pursuant to a unanimous-consent request therein does not necessarily result in an en bloc vote in the House, because that is merely an order of the Committee and not binding on the House. Moreover, even amendments considered en bloc pursuant to a special order of business are subject to a demand for a division of the question in the House if divisible, unless prohibited by the rule. Deschler Ch 27 § 27.15 (note).

Points of Order

Where unanimous consent is requested that two or more amendments be considered en bloc, points of order against any or all of them may be made or reserved pending agreement to the request. Deschler Ch 27 §27.5. Amendments offered en bloc by unanimous consent are considered as one amendment, and a single point of order against any portion thereof renders the entire amendment subject to a point of order. Deschler Ch 27 §27.5.

Consideration Pursuant to Special Order of Business

To expedite consideration of perfecting committee amendments to a bill, the House may adopt a special order of business permitting their consideration en bloc in lieu of separate consideration in the order printed in the bill. Under such a special order of business, the manager of the bill may request en bloc consideration after the pending text is read and unanimous consent is not required. Deschler Ch 27 §§27.13, 27.14.

"King of the Hill" Rule

The Committee on Rules has provided for the consideration of two or more amendments under what is sometimes termed a "king of the hill" procedure. The special order of business may provide that such amendments be considered in a specified order and that if more than one such amendment is adopted, only the last amendment so adopted shall be considered as finally adopted and reported to the House. 102-2, June 3, 1992, p 13239.

"Top Vote Getter" or "Queen of the Hill" Rule

On occasion, the Committee on Rules has reported a rule that permitted several alternative amendments to be considered in a specified order with the one receiving the largest majority being reported back to the House. See, *e.g.*, 104-1, Jan. 25, 1995, p 2360.

"First Amendment Adopted" Rule

On rules providing for the consideration of the concurrent resolution on the budget, or on other rare occasions, the Committee on Rules has waived all points of order against the amendments in the nature of a substitute printed in the report accompanying the rule, except that the adoption of an amendment in the nature of a substitute constituted the conclusion of consideration of the concurrent resolution for amendment. See, *e.g.*, 106-2, Mar. 23, 2000, p 3342.

§ 31. Perfecting Amendments; Motions to Strike

Preference as Between Perfecting Amendments

There are no degrees of preference as between perfecting amendments. Deschler Ch 27 § 24.1. However, perfecting amendments to a section are considered before amendments proposing to insert new sections. 8 Cannon § 2356; Deschler Ch 27 § 24.2.

Preference as Between Perfecting Amendment and Motion to Strike

All perfecting amendments to a section of a bill must be disposed of before the vote on a pending motion to strike the section. Deschler Ch 27 § 24.3. After the first perfecting amendment has been disposed of, another may be offered and the vote on the motion to strike is again deferred until the amendment is disposed of. Deschler Ch 27 § 24.5. If the perfecting amendment as adopted changes all the text proposed to be stricken, the motion to strike necessarily falls and is not voted on. Deschler Ch 27 § 24.15. The principle of perfecting text before considering an amendment striking it from the bill is followed even where the motion to strike is improperly drafted as a second-degree amendment. Deschler Ch 27 § 24.12.

§ 32. Substituting Amendments

Substitute Amendments

A substitute for an amendment is not voted on until after amendments to the amendment have been disposed of. 8 Cannon § 2895. If the substitute is rejected, the amendment is open to further amendment; if the substitute is adopted, the question recurs on the amendment as amended by the substitute. Deschler Ch 27 § 25.1. Thus, where an amendment in the nature of a substitute to a bill is amended by the adoption of a substitute therefor, the question recurs on the amendment in the nature of a substitute, as amended. Deschler Ch 27 § 25.2. The defeat of the amendment as amended by the substitute results in the rejection of the language included in the substitute as amended. Deschler Ch 27 § 23.

Amendments in the Nature of a Substitute

An amendment in the nature of a substitute for a bill may be proposed before perfecting amendments to the pending portion of the original text have been offered or acted on, but may not be voted on until after such perfecting amendments have been disposed of. 5 Hinds § 5787; 8 Cannon § 2896; Deschler Ch 27 § 25. Thus, an amendment in the nature of a substitute having been proposed, amendments to the portion of the original text that have been read are in order and are voted on before the question is taken on the substitute. 8 Cannon § 2861.

Where a substitute—striking all of the text and inserting new matter—for an amendment in the nature of a substitute is adopted, the vote occurs immediately on the amendment, as amended, and no further amendments to either proposition are in order, because the original amendment has been changed in its entirety by the substitute. Deschler Ch 27 § 25.

§ 33. Points of Order

Generally

Points of order may lie against amendments that do not conform to established rules and practices. For example, an amendment may be barred because it violates the rule against amendments in the third degree, the ''germaneness'' rule, the prohibition against inclusion of legislation in an appropriation bill, or the prohibition against inclusion of an appropriation in a legislative bill. See § 14, supra; APPROPRIATIONS; and GERMANENESS OF AMENDMENTS. For points of order against amendments en bloc, see § 30, supra.

Reserving Points of Order

It is within the discretion of the Chair whether to permit a reservation of a point of order against an amendment, how long such a reservation can be maintained, and whether to dispose of the point of order before debate on the amendment. If a point of order is reserved, the Chair, with the sufferance of the Committee of the Whole, may permit debate by the proponent on the merits of the amendment before hearing argument on the point of order. The Chair then has the discretion to insist that the point of order be made following debate by the proponent of the amendment and before recognition of other Members. If the point of order is made rather than reserved, the Member making the point of order is immediately recognized for argument thereon. See POINTS OF ORDER; PARLIAMENTARY INQUIRIES.

Reservation as Inuring to Other Members

One Member's reservation of a point of order against an amendment protects the rights of all Members to insist on a point of order. The reserving Member need not specify the basis of the reservation. The reservation of the point of order inures to all Members, who may raise other points of order before the intervention of further debate if the original point of order is overruled or withdrawn. See POINTS OF ORDER; PARLIAMENTARY INQUIRIES.

§ 34. — Timeliness

Generally

Except as provided in the last paragraph of this section, a point of order against an amendment is properly made (or reserved) immediately after the reading thereof, following agreement to a unanimous-consent request that the amendment be considered as read, or at any time before debate has begun on the amendment. It should be disposed of before amendments to that amendment are offered. Similarly, a point of order against certain language should be decided before recognition of another Member to offer an amendment to the challenged language. See POINTS OF ORDER; PARLIAMENTARY INQUIRIES.

Effect of Intervening Amendment or Debate

A Member must exercise due diligence in raising a point of order. A point of order against an amendment should be made or reserved before the proponent of the amendment has been recognized to debate the amendment. It cannot be raised after the proponent of the amendment has been recognized and has begun debate. A point of order against an amendment is not entertained where business has intervened between the reading of the amendment and the making of the point of order unless the intervening business is vacated. A unanimous-consent request to modify the amendment does not constitute intervening business. 106-1, Mar. 11, 1999, pp 4335-37. The re-reading of the amendment by unanimous consent after there has been debate does not permit the intervention of a point of order against the amendment. See POINTS OF ORDER; PARLIAMENTARY INQUIRIES.

Although a point of order against an amendment ordinarily comes too late if debate has begun thereon, the Chair has recognized a Member to make or reserve a point of order against an amendment where the Member raising the point was standing, seeking recognition, at the time the amendment was read. See POINTS OF ORDER; PARLIAMENTARY INQUIRIES; Deschler Ch 27 § 1.

Points of Order That May Be Made ''At Any Time''

Clause 4 and clause 5(a) of rule XXI refer to points of order that may be ''raised at any time.'' Clause 4 deals with appropriations in a bill reported by committees not having jurisdiction to report appropriations and prohibits amendments carrying appropriations during consideration of a bill reported by a committee not having that jurisdiction. Clause 5(a) is aimed at tax or tariff measures contained in a bill reported by a committee not having that jurisdiction, or amendments of the Senate or amendments in the

House that are offered to a bill not reported therefrom. Points of order under these rules must still be raised when the offending bill or amendment is before the House for consideration. However, intervening debate or amendments will not preclude a proper point of order from being cognizable by the Chair when raised during the pendency of the amendment under the five-minute rule. See POINTS OF ORDER; PARLIAMENTARY INQUIRIES.

§ 35. Debate on Amendments

When general debate is closed in the Committee of the Whole, under the five-minute rule the proponent of an amendment is allowed five minutes in which to explain it, after which the Member who first obtains the floor has five minutes in opposition. Clause 5 of rule XVIII; *Manual* § 978. These time limitations do not apply, of course, where the measure is called up pursuant to a special order of business that specifies other terms of debate. Under clause 3(c) of rule XVII, a manager of a measure who opposes an amendment thereto is entitled to close controlled debate thereon. See CONSIDERATION AND DEBATE.

Where all time for debate on a section of a bill and amendments thereto has expired, amendments may still be offered to the section, but are voted on without debate, except in certain cases where a Member has caused an amendment to be printed in the *Congressional Record* pursuant to clause 8 of rule XVIII. Deschler Ch 27 § 14.9. For a discussion of limiting debate on amendments, see CONSIDERATION AND DEBATE.

§ 36. Withdrawal of Amendment

In the Committee of the Whole

Under clause 5(a) of rule XVIII, an amendment may not be withdrawn in the Committee of the Whole except by unanimous consent, unless withdrawal authority is conferred by the House. *Manual* §§ 905, 978; 5 Hinds §§ 5221, 5753; 8 Cannon §§ 2465, 2859; Deschler Ch 27 § 20.1. Thus, where a Member has been recognized by the Chair to offer an amendment and the amendment has been reported by the Clerk, unanimous consent is required to withdraw the amendment. Deschler Ch 27 § 20.4. However, unanimous consent is not required to withdraw an amendment that is merely at the Clerk's desk and has yet to be offered. Deschler Ch 27 § 20.5.

Where a point of order is made or reserved against an amendment and a unanimous-consent request is then made for the withdrawal of the amendment, the Chair will first dispose of the unanimous-consent request. Deschler Ch 27 § 20.6.

The withdrawal of an amendment by unanimous consent does not preclude its being subsequently reoffered, and unanimous consent is not required to reoffer the amendment if otherwise in order. Deschler Ch 27 § 20.10.

In the House

Although unanimous consent to withdraw an amendment is required in the Committee of the Whole, an amendment in the House may be withdrawn by the proponent at any time before a decision or amendment is rendered thereon. Clause 6 of rule XVI. The same right to withdraw an amendment exists in the House as in the Committee of the Whole and in standing committees where general procedures in the House as in the Committee of the Whole apply. *Manual* § 905.

§ 37. Modification of Amendment

The proponent of an amendment may modify such amendment only by unanimous consent. Deschler Ch 27 §§ 21.1-21.3. However, where there is pending an amendment and a substitute therefor, the Member who offered the original amendment may also offer an amendment to the substitute, such action not constituting an amendment to one's own amendment. Deschler Ch 27 § 21.4. A unanimous-consent request may be entertained in the Committee of the Whole to permit the modification of a designated amendment made in order by a ''modified-closed'' special order of business, once pending. *Manual* § 993.

The modification of a pending amendment by its proponent should be offered before the amendment is voted on. 106-2, Mar. 29, 2000, p 4017. However, in one instance, pending a request for a recorded vote following a voice vote on an amendment, the Committee of the Whole, by unanimous consent, vacated the Chair's putting of the question on the amendment so as to permit its modification. Deschler Ch 27 § 21.7.

The fact that a decision of the Chair is pending on a point of order against an amendment does not necessarily preclude a request by its proponent that it be modified. Deschler Ch 27 § 21.6. However, the Chair or any Member may insist that a proposed modification be submitted in writing and read by the Clerk. Deschler Ch 27 § 21.8.

In the event of objection to a unanimous-consent request to modify a pending amendment, any Member—other than the proponent of the amendment—may offer a proper amendment thereto. Deschler Ch 27 § 21.10. Indeed, a request to modify an amendment, when made by a Member who is not the proponent thereof, is sometimes treated as a motion to amend rather than as a unanimous-consent request. 99-1, Dec. 5, 1985, pp 34730, 34731.

F. Effect of Adoption or Rejection; Changes After Adoption

§ 38. In General; Effect of Adoption of Perfecting Amendment

Generally

It is fundamental that it is not in order to amend an amendment previously agreed to. *Manual* §§ 468-474; 8 Cannon § 2856; Deschler Ch 27 § 29.2. Once the text of a bill has been perfected by amendment, the perfected text cannot thereafter be amended. Deschler Ch 27 § 29.8. Similarly, the adoption of an amendment to a substitute precludes further amendment to those portions of the substitute so amended. *Manual* § 469; see § 41, infra.

However, in order for an amendment to be ruled out of order on the ground that its substance has already been passed on by the House, the language thereof must be practically identical to that of the proposition already acted on. 5 Hinds § 5760; 8 Cannon § 2839; Deschler Ch 27 § 29.1. The precedents do not preclude the offering of an amendment merely because it is similar to, or achieves the same effect as, an amendment previously agreed to. *Manual* § 466. Although it is not in order to reinsert precise language stricken by amendment, an amendment similar but not identical to the stricken language may be offered if germane to the pending portion of the bill. A simple change in substance in the words sought to be inserted, such as changing the word ''shall'' to ''may,'' allows the amendment to be offered. Deschler Ch 27 § 31.8.

Effect of Inconsistency

The Chair will not rule out an amendment as being inconsistent with an amendment previously adopted, as the consistency of amendments is a question for the House to determine by its vote on the amendment. *Manual* § 466; Deschler Ch 27 § 29.23. It follows that an amendment is not subject to a point of order that its provisions are inconsistent with a section of the bill already considered under the five-minute rule. Deschler Ch 27 § 29.25.

Amendments Negating Proposition Previously Adopted

The Committee of the Whole may not amend a section of a bill already passed during the reading. However, it may adopt an amendment to a later section that has the effect of negating the provisions of the earlier section because the Committee of the Whole may consider a subsequent amendment which contradicts a proposition previously agreed to. Deschler Ch 27 §§ 29.20, 29.26.

Changes Following Amended Text

The adoption of a perfecting amendment only precludes further amendments changing the perfected text; amendments are in order that add language to an unamended portion at the end of the amended text. *Manual* § 469. Likewise, the adoption of an amendment inserting a new subsection in a bill does not preclude consideration of another amendment inserting another new subsection immediately thereafter which does not textually change the amendment already agreed to. Deschler Ch 27 § 29.21.

The "Bigger Bite" Rule

Although an amendment may not be offered to change only that portion of the pending text which has been altered by amendment, a further amendment changing a more comprehensive portion of the pending text is in order. Deschler Ch 27 § 31.18. In other words, an amendment taking a "bigger bite" of the pending text than that altered may be permitted. Thus, although it is not in order to further amend an amendment previously agreed to, an amendment encompassing a more comprehensive portion of the bill, including original text not yet amended, is in order. Deschler Ch 27 § 29.9. Similarly, it is in order to offer an amendment which strikes language changed by amendment as well as other matter and inserts language which proposes substantive changes going beyond the original amendment or strikes out matter not only in the amendment previously agreed to but also in additional portions of the pending bill. *Manual* § 474; Deschler Ch 27 § 29.

Effect of Special Orders of Business

The general principle that an amendment may not be offered which directly changes an amendment already agreed to does not apply where the House has adopted a special order of business permitting amendments to be offered even if changing portions of amendments already agreed to. Deschler Ch 27 § 29.48. In addition, where a special order of business permits a motion to recommit "with or without" instructions, a motion to recommit may include an amendment that changes an amendment already adopted by the House. See § 47, infra.

§ 39. Adoption of Amendment as Precluding Motions to Strike

It is not in order to offer an amendment merely striking an amendment previously agreed to. 94-1, Aug. 1, 1975, pp 26946, 26947. For example, where by amendment a new paragraph or section has been added to the text, it is not in order to offer an amendment that merely strikes that new paragraph or section. *Manual* § 474; Deschler Ch 27 § 30.10.

On the other hand, the adoption of a perfecting amendment to a *portion* of the text of a bill does not preclude a vote on a pending motion to strike the entire text as amended. Deschler Ch 27 § 30.4. Similarly, although a provision inserted by amendment may not thereafter be stricken, a motion to strike more than the provision previously inserted is in order. Deschler Ch 27 § 30.7.

Although the adoption of an amendment changing all the text of a section precludes a vote on a pending motion to strike that section, the motion to strike will still be voted on where the perfecting amendment to the section changes some but not all of that text. Deschler Ch 27 § 30.3. However, in this situation another perfecting amendment to strike the remainder of the section not yet perfected may be offered and voted on before the motion to strike the entire section and, if adopted, the motion to strike the section falls and is not voted on, the whole text having been changed. Deschler Ch 27 § 30.14.

The adoption of a perfecting amendment to part of a section does not preclude a motion to strike the section and insert new text. Deschler Ch 27 § 30.12. Similarly, the adoption of a perfecting amendment inserting language at the end of a paragraph does not preclude an amendment striking the entire perfected paragraph and inserting new language. Deschler Ch 27 § 30.15. However, where a bill is being read by section, and committee amendments adding new sections at the end of a bill have been adopted, an amendment proposing to strike a section of the original bill and the new sections is not in order. Deschler Ch 27 § 30.9.

§ 40. Effect of Adoption of Motions to Strike

Adoption of Motion to Strike

A motion to strike a section of a bill, if adopted by the Committee of the Whole, strikes the entire section including a provision that was added as a perfecting amendment to that section. Adoption by the Committee of the amendment striking the section vitiates the Committee's prior adoption of perfecting amendments to that section, and only the motion to strike is reported to the House. Deschler Ch 27 §§ 31.1, 31.2. The bill returns to the form as originally introduced upon rejection by the House of the amendment reported by Committee. Deschler Ch 27 § 31.3. Where an amendment has been adopted striking language in a bill, a perfecting amendment to the stricken language comes too late and is not in order. Deschler Ch 27 § 31.9.

Although it is not in order to reinsert precise language stricken by amendment, an amendment similar but not identical to the stricken language may be offered if germane to the pending portion of the bill. Deschler Ch 27 § 31.6. See also *Manual* § 468; 5 Hinds 5760.

Adoption of Motion to Strike and Insert

If an amendment to strike a portion of a bill and insert new language is agreed to, a pending amendment proposing to strike the same portion falls and is not voted on. *Manual* § 469; Deschler Ch 27 §§ 31.11, 31.12. When an amendment striking certain language and inserting other provisions has been adopted, it is not in order to further amend the provisions so inserted. *Manual* § 469; Deschler Ch 27 § 31.14.

The adoption of a perfecting amendment to strike and insert does not preclude the offering of another amendment to strike and insert which goes beyond the changes made by the first amendment. Deschler Ch 27 § 31.18. Similarly, although it is not in order to perfect or reinsert language which has been stricken, an amendment may be offered to insert new language if it is germane to the bill and not identical to the language stricken. Deschler Ch 27 § 31.7. However, if a motion to strike all after the first word of text and insert a new provision is agreed to, the language thus inserted cannot thereafter be amended. Deschler Ch 27 § 31.14.

§ 41. Adoption of Amendment in the Nature of a Substitute

The adoption of an amendment in the nature of a substitute ends the amendment stage; and further amendment is not in order, including pro forma amendments for debate. Deschler Ch 27 §§ 32.1, 32.2, 32.22. Thus, absent a special order of business to the contrary, the adoption of an amendment in the nature of a substitute precludes the offering of another. Deschler Ch 27 § 32.4. Debate having been closed, adoption of the amendment causes the stage of amendment to be passed and amendments—though printed in the *Congressional Record*—cannot thereafter be offered. Deschler Ch 27 § 32.3.

The adoption of an amendment in the nature of a substitute, as amended by a substitute, precludes further amendment to the amendment and to the bill. Deschler Ch 27 § 32.8. When the substitute is agreed to, the question recurs immediately on the amendment as amended by the substitute, and further perfecting amendments to the amendment (including pro forma amendments) are not then in order. Deschler Ch 27 § 32.22.

§42. Amendments Pertaining to Monetary Figures

When a specific amendment to a monetary figure in a bill has been agreed to, further amendment of that specific sum is not in order. Deschler Ch 27 §§33.1-33.3; *Manual* §455. However, an amendment inserted following the figure agreed upon and providing funds ''in addition thereto'' is in order. Deschler Ch 27 §33.13. An amendment adding a new section having the indirect effect of changing amended amounts in the bill may also be in order. Deschler Ch 27 §33.10. In recent practice an amount in an appropriation bill has been changed by inserting a parenthetical ''increased by'' or ''decreased by'' after the amount rather than by directly changing the figure in order to avoid such a point of order. *Manual* §455.

Where the Committee of the Whole has adopted an amendment changing the total figure in a paragraph of an appropriation bill, it is not in order to further amend such figure. Deschler Ch 27 §33.9.

Although it is not in order to offer an amendment merely changing an amendment already adopted, it is in order to offer a subsequent amendment more comprehensive than the amendment adopted, changing unamended portions of the bill as well. Deschler Ch 27 §33.7 (note); §38, supra. Thus, after adoption of amendments changing monetary figures in a bill, an amendment making a general percentage reduction in all figures contained in the bill and indirectly affecting those figures, is still in order. Deschler Ch 27 §33.10. Likewise, the adoption of a perfecting amendment to a concurrent resolution on the budget changing several figures would preclude further amendment merely changing those amended figures but would not preclude more comprehensive amendments changing other portions of the resolution which had not been amended. Deschler Ch 27 §29.47.

Although it may be in order to offer an amendment to the pending portion of the bill that changes not only a provision already amended but also an unamended pending portion of the bill, it is not in order merely to amend a figure already amended. Even if the amendment also changes other matter not already amended (including where it is drafted to address figures as though the earlier amendment had not been adopted), it is still out of order. *Manual* §469.

Members have offered ''fetch-back'' amendments to appropriation bills, which are new paragraphs inserted to change amounts contained in previous paragraphs. ''Fetch-back'' amendments may be in order as long as the amendment is germane to the portion of the bill to which offered and amounts only to a reduction of funds contained in previous paragraphs. See, *e.g.*, 106-1, Aug. 5, 1999, pp 20143, 20144. However, a ''fetch-back'' amendment increasing an amount contained in a prior paragraph must be supported by an authorization. Such support is necessary because the precedents that admit a germane perfecting amendment to an unauthorized item permitted to remain deal with actual changes in the figure permitted to remain and not with the insertion of new matter beyond that permitted to remain. *Manual* § 1058; see APPROPRIATIONS.

§ 43. Effecting Changes by Unanimous Consent

By unanimous consent, it is in order to amend an amendment which has already been agreed to. Deschler Ch 27 § 34.1. For example, unless otherwise restricted by a special order of business governing consideration of a measure (*Manual* § 993), the Committee of the Whole may by unanimous consent:

- Permit Members to offer amendments to change an amended figure in an appropriation bill. Deschler Ch 27 § 34.7.
- Permit a previously adopted amendment to an amendment to be considered as adopted instead to a pending substitute for the underlying amendment. 99-2, Aug. 5, 1986, pp 19107, 19108.
- Permit a modification of an amendment by its proponent. *Manual* § 993.
- Permit a page reference to be included in a designated printed amendment made in order under a special order of business where the printed amendment did not include that reference. *Manual* § 993.

In one instance, the Committee of the Whole by unanimous consent vacated the proceedings whereby it had agreed to an amendment, agreed to an amendment to that amendment, and then adopted the original amendment as amended. Deschler Ch 27 § 34.2.

§ 44. Amendments Previously Considered and Rejected

Generally

It is not in order to offer an amendment identical to one previously rejected. Deschler Ch 27 §§ 35.1, 35.2. However, an amendment that raises the same question by the use of different language may be admissible. Deschler Ch 27 § 35. An amendment similar but not identical to one previously rejected may be considered if a substantive change has been made. Deschler Ch 27 §§ 35.3, 35.4. Rejection of an amendment changing a figure in a bill does not preclude the offering of a different amendment to that provision. Deschler Ch 27 § 35.21.

An amendment in different form may be entertained even though its effect may be similar to that of a rejected amendment. Deschler Ch 27 §§ 35.11, 35.13. Thus, in one instance, after an amendment containing a limitation on the use of funds in an appropriation bill had been rejected, the

Chair held that another amendment—containing a similar limitation and also stating an exception from that limitation—was not an identical amendment and therefore could be offered. Deschler Ch 27 § 35.18. Presiding officers have been reluctant to rule out an amendment as dilatory merely because of its similarity to one previously rejected. Deschler Ch 27 § 35.7.

A motion offered as a substitute for an amendment and rejected may be offered again as a separate amendment. Deschler Ch 27 § 35.8. Similarly, a proposition offered as an amendment to an amendment and rejected may be offered again, in identical form, as an amendment to the bill. Deschler Ch 27 § 35.9.

A portion of a rejected amendment may be subsequently offered as a separate amendment if presenting a different proposition. Thus, rejection of an amendment consisting of two sections does not preclude one of those sections being subsequently offered as a separate amendment. Deschler Ch 27 § 35.17.

Rejection of Motion to Strike

A motion to strike certain language having been previously rejected, it may not be offered a second time. Deschler Ch 27 § 35.22. However, a motion to strike that language and insert a new provision is in order. Deschler Ch 27 § 35.23. Conversely, if the motion to strike and insert is rejected, the simple motion to strike is in order. Deschler Ch 27 § 35.11.

Rejection of En Bloc Amendments

Rejection of several amendments considered en bloc by unanimous consent does not preclude their being offered separately at a subsequent time. Deschler Ch 27 § 35.15. It follows that where an amendment to a figure in a bill considered en bloc with other amendments has been rejected, no point of order lies against a subsequent amendment to that figure which specifies a different amount and which is offered as a separate amendment. Deschler Ch 27 § 33.16.

G. House Consideration of Amendments Reported From the Committee of the Whole

§ 45. In General; Voting

Generally

Only amendments adopted in the Committee of the Whole are reported to the House. All amendments so reported stand on an equal footing and must be voted on by the House, notwithstanding inconsistencies among them, and are subject to amendment in the House unless the previous question is ordered. 4 Hinds §§ 4871, 4881; 8 Cannon § 2419. However, under modern practice, the previous question is ordered by special order of business upon the rising and reporting of the Committee of the Whole. Where in the unusual case it is in order to submit additional amendments to the pending bill, the first question is on the amendments reported from the Committee of the Whole. 4 Hinds § 4872.

Kinds of Amendments Reported to the House

Some amendments adopted in the Committee are not reported to the House. Pursuant to a practice originating in the 19th Congress (1825), the Committee reports amendments only in their perfected form. 4 Hinds § 4904; Deschler Ch 27 § 36.1. Thus, if the Committee of the Whole perfects a bill by adopting certain amendments and then adopts an amendment striking those provisions and inserting a new text, only the adopted motion to strike and insert is reported to the House. Deschler Ch 27 §§ 36.5, 36.13. Similarly, the adoption by the Committee of an amendment striking a section of a bill vitiates the Committee's prior adoption of perfecting amendments to that section, so that only the motion to strike is reported to the House. Deschler Ch 27 § 31.2. However, when the bill is being considered under a special order of business permitting separate consideration in the House of *any* amendments adopted in the Committee, all amendments adopted in the Committee are reported to the House, regardless of their inconsistency. Deschler Ch 27 § 36.13.

Demanding a Separate Vote

Although the House may act at once on all the amendments to a bill reported from the Committee of the Whole *en gros*, it is the right of any Member to demand a separate vote on any reported first-degree amendment. 4 Hinds §§ 4893, 4894; 8 Cannon § 2419. However, a special order of business may prohibit a demand for separate votes on sundry amendments, requiring all amendments to be acted upon *en gros*. In the absence of a special order of business providing therefor, a separate vote may not be had in the House on an amendment to an amendment which has been adopted by the Committee of the Whole. Deschler Ch 27 § 36.6. This principle precludes a separate vote in the House on an amendment to an amendment in the nature of a substitute adopted in the Committee. Deschler Ch 27 § 36.8. Because the Committee in reporting a bill with an amendment to the House reports such amendment in its perfected form, it is not in order in the House to have a separate vote upon each perfecting amendment to the amendment that has been agreed to in the Committee absent a special order of business providing to the contrary. Deschler Ch 27 § 36.

A special order of business may, of course, provide for separate votes on second-degree amendments. Deschler Ch 27 § 36. However, where separate votes are permitted, only those amendments reported to the House from the Committee of the Whole are voted on; it is not in order to demand a separate vote in the House on amendments rejected in the Committee. Deschler Ch 27 § 36.12. The House theoretically has no information as to actions of the Committee of the Whole on amendments not reported therefrom. Deschler Ch 27 § 36.

Where a special order of business permits a demand in the House for a separate vote on an amendment adopted to an amendment in the nature of a substitute for a bill reported from the Committee of the Whole, the Speaker inquires whether a separate vote is demanded before putting the question on the amendment in the nature of a substitute. Deschler Ch 27 § 36.14. A Member must demand the separate vote before the question is taken on the substitute. Deschler Ch 27 § 36.18. A demand in the House for a separate vote on an amendment to the amendment comes too late after the amendment, as amended, has been agreed to. Deschler Ch 27 § 36.19.

En Bloc Amendments

Where the Committee of the Whole reports a bill back to the House with amendments, some of which were considered en bloc pursuant to a special order of business, the en bloc amendments may be voted on again en bloc on a demand for a separate vote. Deschler Ch 27 § 36.27. A separate vote being demanded, the Chair puts the question separately on the amendments en bloc in the House, where no Member demands a division of the question. Deschler Ch 27 § 36.28. However, another amendment separately considered in Committee may not be voted on with the en bloc amendments in the House (absent unanimous consent). Deschler Ch 27 § 36.27.

For division of an amendment for voting, see VOTING.

Order of Consideration

When demand is made for separate votes in the House on several amendments adopted in the Committee of the Whole, such amendments are read and voted on in the House in the order in which they appear in the bill as reported from the Committee of the Whole—not in the order in which agreed to in Committee or in which demanded in the House. *Manual* § 337; Deschler Ch 27 §§ 36.16, 37.1. However, where a special order of business prescribes the order for consideration of amendments (with the bill being considered as read) in the Committee of the Whole, then separate votes demanded in the House on adopted amendments are taken in that same order, regardless of the order in which the amendments may appear in the bill. *Manual* § 337.

Where a special order of business provides for a separate vote on an amendment to an amendment in the nature of a substitute reported from the Committee of the Whole, the Speaker puts the question first on the amendment on which a separate vote is demanded, then on the amendment in the nature of a substitute, as amended. Deschler Ch 27 § 37.6.

§ 46. Effect of Rejection of Amendment

Generally

When the House rejects an amendment adopted in the Committee of the Whole, the original text of the bill is before the House. Deschler Ch 27 § 38.1. Thus, if an amendment in the nature of a substitute is reported from the Committee of the Whole and rejected by the House, the original bill is before the House. Deschler Ch 27 § 38.5. Similarly, if an amendment striking and inserting is reported from the Committee of the Whole and rejected by the House, the language of the original bill is before the House. Deschler Ch 27 § 38.12.

Rejection of Motion to Strike

Where the Committee of the Whole adopts perfecting amendments to the language of a bill and then agrees to an amendment striking that language, only the latter amendment is reported to the House. In the event of its rejection by the House, the original language, and not the perfected text, is before the House. Deschler Ch 27 §§ 38.3, 38.8. However, the practice may be otherwise where the House is operating under a special order of business allowing separate votes in the House on *any* amendment adopted in the Committee of the Whole. As indicated elsewhere (§ 45, supra), under such a rule all amendments adopted in Committee to the amendment are reported to the House regardless of their inconsistency. The House may retain a section as perfected in the Committee of the Whole by first adopting on separate votes the perfecting amendments to the section and then rejecting on a separate vote the motion to strike that section. Deschler Ch 27 § 38.11 (note).

§ 47. Motions to Recommit with Instructions Pertaining to Amendments

The House may recommit a bill to committee with instructions to report it back ''forthwith'' with an amendment. 5 Hinds § 5545. In such cases the chair of the committee reports the amendment at once without awaiting committee action. 5 Hinds §§5545-5547. Instructions to report "forthwith" accompanying a motion to recommit must be complied with immediately. *Manual* §1002b. However, it is not in order to propose as instructions anything that might not be proposed directly as an amendment, such as to propose an amendment that is not germane to the bill, or to propose an amendment containing legislation or a limitation on a general appropriation bill not in order in the Committee of the Whole. *Manual* §1002b; 5 Hinds §§5529-5541; 8 Cannon §§2705, 2712.

A motion to recommit may not include instructions to modify any part of an amendment previously agreed to by the House. 8 Cannon §§2720, 2721, 2740; Deschler Ch 27 §32.5. However, where a bill is being considered under a special order of business permitting a motion to recommit "with or without instructions," a motion to recommit may include an amendment which changes an amendment already adopted by the House, even where the House has adopted an amendment in the nature of a substitute. Clause 6(c) of rule XIII precludes the Committee on Rules from reporting a rule that would prevent a motion to recommit a bill or joint resolution with or without instructions if offered by the Minority Leader or a designee. See generally REFER AND RECOMMIT.

The rejection of an amendment in the Committee of the Whole does not preclude the offering of the same amendment in the House in a motion to recommit with instructions. Deschler Ch 27 §35.27.

H. Amendments to Titles and Preambles

§48. In General

Amending Titles

Amendments to the title of a bill are not in order until after passage of the bill, and are then voted upon without debate. Deschler Ch 24 §9.4; Deschler Ch 27 §19.1; clause 6 of rule XVI. An amendment in the Committee of the Whole proposing an amendment to the title is not in order. *Manual* §922; Deschler Ch 27 §19.4. Committee amendments to the title of a bill are automatically reported by the Clerk after passage of the bill, although an amendment to a committee amendment to the title may be offered from the floor. Deschler Ch 27 §19.6.

Amending Preambles of Joint Resolutions

In the Committee of the Whole, amendments to the preamble of a joint resolution are considered following disposition of any amendments to the body of the resolution. Deschler Ch 27 §§ 19.7, 19.8; *Manual* § 414. In the House an amendment to the preamble of a joint resolution reported from Committee of the Whole is considered following engrossment and before the third reading of the resolution. 4 Hinds § 3414; Deschler Ch 27 § 19.9.

An amendment to the preamble of a Senate joint resolution is considered after disposition of amendments to the text of the joint resolution and pending the third reading. 97-1, Nov. 19, 1981, pp 28208, 28209.

Amending Preambles of Simple or Concurrent Resolutions

Amendments to the preamble of a simple or concurrent resolution are considered and voted on in the Committee of the Whole after amendments to the body of the resolution. Amendments to the preamble of such a resolution are voted on in the House after the resolution has been adopted. 7 Cannon § 1064; Deschler Ch 27 §§ 19.11-19.13. In the House the previous question is ordered separately on the preamble after adoption of the resolution if amendments to the preamble are offered. Deschler Ch 24 § 9.9. The motion for the previous question may be applied at once to both a resolution and its preamble. 105-2, Feb. 12, 1998, pp 1333, 1334.

Chapter 3
Appeals

Research References
5 Hinds §§ 6877, 6938-6952
8 Cannon §§ 3435, 3452-3458
Deschler-Brown Ch 31 § 13
Manual §§ 379, 627-629, 641, 884, 902, 903

§ 1. In General; Forms

The right to appeal from a decision of the Chair on a question of order is derived from the English Parliament and is recognized under clause 5 of rule I, which dates from 1789. *Manual* §§ 379, 627, 629. This right of appeal, which may be invoked by any Member, protects the House against arbitrary control by the Speaker. 5 Hinds § 6002.

MEMBER: I (respectfully) appeal the ruling of the Chair.
CHAIR: The question is, shall the decision of the Chair stand as the judgment of the House [or the Committee]?

An appeal is debatable but is subject to the motions for the previous question and to table in the House. §§ 4, 5, infra. In the Committee of the Whole, an appeal is subject to the motion to limit debate and to rise and close debate in the House. *Manual* § 629.

The vote on an appeal may be taken by record vote. 98-2, June 26, 1984, p 18861. A majority vote sustains the ruling. *Manual* § 971. The weight of precedent indicates that a tie vote (especially where the Chair has not voted to make the tie) sustains the ruling as well. 4 Hinds § 4569; 5 Hinds § 6957. The Chair may vote to make or break a tie and may cast a vote in favor of the decision. 4 Hinds § 4569; 5 Hinds §§ 5686, 6956. An appeal from a ruling of the Chair goes only to the propriety of the ruling; the vote thereon should not be interpreted as a vote on the merits of the issue at hand. Deschler-Brown Ch 31 § 13.2.

§ 2. When in Order

Clause 5 of rule I provides the right of appeal from decisions of the Speaker on questions of order. Examples of appeals from decisions of the Chair include the following:

- The priority of business. 5 Hinds § 6952.
- Whether a certain resolution gives rise to a question of privilege. *Manual* § 713.
- The propriety of an exhibit. *Manual* § 622.
- Whether a Member has engaged in personalities in debate. *Manual* § 622.

An appeal may also be taken from the ruling of the chair of the Committee of the Whole on a question of order. *Manual* § 971. For example, an appeal may be taken from a ruling of the Chair on the germaneness of an amendment or that an amendment proposes to change a portion of the bill already passed in the reading. Deschler-Brown Ch 31 § 13.7; 105-1, Sept. 25, 1997, 20181.

An appeal is in order during a call of the House. 6 Cannon § 681.

§ 3. When Not in Order

The Speaker's decision on a question of order is not subject to appeal if the decision is one that falls within the discretionary authority of the Chair. For example, an appeal may not be taken from the following:

- Chair's decision on recognition. 2 Hinds §§ 1425-1428; 8 Cannon §§ 2429, 2646, 2762.
- Chair's decision on dilatoriness of motions. 5 Hinds § 5731.
- Chair's count of the number rising to demand tellers, a recorded vote, or the yeas and nays. *Manual* § 629; 8 Cannon § 3105.
- Chair's call of a voice vote. *Manual* § 629.
- Chair's refusal to recapitulate a vote. 8 Cannon § 3128.
- Chair's count of a quorum. *Manual* § 629.
- Chair's determination that a Member's time in debate has expired. *Manual* § 629.
- Chair's response to a parliamentary inquiry. 5 Hinds § 6955; 8 Cannon § 3457.
- Chair's announcement of an adjustment to the whole number of the House. Clause 5(d) of rule XX.

- Chair's announcement of the content of a catastrophic quorum failure report by the Sergeant-at-Arms (or a designee). Clause 5(c)(5) of rule XX.

An appeal from a ruling of the Chair declining to consider the question of the constitutionality of a provision is not in order. The question of the constitutionality of a provision in a pending measure is a matter for the House to determine by its vote on the merits, rather than by voting on a possible appeal from the Chair's decision declining to rule on that constitutional issue. Deschler-Brown Ch 31 § 13.1.

An appeal from a ruling of the Chair is not in order if the effect of the appeal, if sustained, would be to change a rule of the House, such as where the underlying rule does not involve discretion on the part of the Chair. Thus, the Speaker's refusal under clause 7(a) of rule XX to entertain a point of order of no quorum when a pending question has not been put to a vote is not subject to an appeal, because that rule contains an absolute and unambiguous prohibition against such a point of order. To allow an appeal in such a case would permit a direct change in the rule itself. Deschler-Brown Ch 31 § 13.5.

Untimely or Dilatory Appeals

An appeal is not in order if it is dilatory. 5 Hinds §§ 5715-5722; 8 Cannon § 2822. An appeal also is not in order if it is untimely. An appeal is not in order:

- While another appeal is pending. 5 Hinds §§ 6939-6941.
- On a question on which an appeal has just been decided. 4 Hinds § 3036; 5 Hinds § 6877.
- During a call of the yeas and nays. 5 Hinds § 6051.
- Between the motion to adjourn and vote thereon. 5 Hinds § 5361.

§ 4. Debate on Appeal

Appeals are customarily subject to debate, both in the House and the Committee of the Whole (8 Cannon §§ 3453-3455). However, debate is not in order on an appeal from a ruling of the Chair on the priority of business (Clause 6 of rule XIV; 5 Hinds § 6952) or on a ruling as to the relevancy of debate (5 Hinds §§ 5056-5063).

Debate in the House on an appeal is under the hour rule but may be closed at any time by the adoption of a motion for the previous question or to lay on the table. *Manual* § 629. Debate on an appeal in the Committee of the Whole is under the five-minute rule and may be closed by motion to close debate or to rise and report. 5 Hinds §§ 6947, 6950; 8 Cannon §§ 2347, 3453-3455.

Members may speak but once on appeal, unless by permission of the House, the Chair alternating between those favoring and those opposing. *Manual* § 627; 8 Cannon § 3455.

It is not in order in debating an appeal to discuss the merits of the proposition under consideration at the time the decision was made. 5 Hinds § 5055.

§ 5. Motions

Although an appeal is debatable, it is normally disposed of in the House without debate by a motion to lay the appeal on the table. If the motion to table is adopted, the appeal is disposed of adversely and the ruling of the Speaker is sustained. See *Manual* § 706. The House has tabled a motion to reconsider the vote whereby an appeal from a decision of the Chair was laid on the table. Deschler-Brown Ch 31 § 13.16. An appeal in Committee of the Whole may not be laid on the table, because that motion does not lie in the Committee. 4 Hinds § 4719.

Other motions that may be offered pending an appeal include:

- A motion to postpone the appeal to a day certain (where underlying matter was postponed). 8 Cannon § 2613.
- A motion for the previous question (in the House). 5 Hinds § 6947.
- A motion to close or limit debate (in the Committee of the Whole). 5 Hinds §§ 6947, 6950.
- A motion that the Committee rise and report to the House. 8 Cannon § 3453.

§ 6. Withdrawal

An appeal may be withdrawn at any time before action thereon by the House. 5 Hinds § 5354. An appeal can be withdrawn before the question is put on a motion to lay the appeal on the table. Deschler-Brown Ch 31 § 13.10. Ordering the yeas and nays on a motion to lay an appeal on the table has been held sufficient House action as to preclude withdrawal. 5 Hinds § 5354.

§ 7. Effect of Adjournment

An appeal pending at adjournment ordinarily comes up for consideration on the next legislative day. 5 Hinds § 6945. However, an appeal pending at adjournment on a day set apart for Private Calendar business and related to private business goes over to the next day provided for consideration of business on the Private Calendar. Where the House has adjourned and reconvened to meet again on the same calendar day and the call of the

Private Calendar is still in order, the appeal comes up as unfinished business. 97-1, Nov. 17, 1981, pp 27772, 27773.

Chapter 4
Appropriations

I. Introductory

II. General Appropriation Bills

A. Introductory

B. Authorization of Appropriation

C. Authorization for Particular Purposes or Programs

III. Legislation in General Appropriation Bills; Provisions Changing Existing Law

IV. Limitations on General Appropriation Bills

V. Reappropriations

VI. Reporting; Consideration and Debate

A. GENERALLY

B. SENATE AMENDMENTS

VII. Other Appropriation Measures

VIII. Appropriations in Legislative Bills

Research References
U.S. Const. art. I, §§ 7, 9
4 Hinds §§ 3553-4018
7 Cannon §§ 1116-1720
Deschler Chs 25, 26
Manual §§ 143, 716, 717, 747, 853, 1035-1065, 1127, 1130(6A)

I. Introductory

§ 1. In General; Constitutional Background

Article I, section 9, clause 7 of the Constitution provides that no money "shall be drawn from the Treasury" but in consequence of appropriations made by law. Appropriation bills are the device through which money is permitted to be "drawn from the Treasury" for expenditure. Deschler Ch 25 § 2.

This constitutional provision is construed as giving Congress broad powers to appropriate money in the Treasury and as a strict limitation on the authority of the executive branch to exercise that function. The Supreme Court has recognized that Congress has wide discretion with regard to the details of expenditures for which it appropriates funds and has approved the frequent practice of making general appropriations of large amounts to be allotted and expended as directed by designated government agencies. *Cincinnati Soap Co.* v. *United States*, 301 U.S. 308, 322 (1937).

§ 2. Power to Originate Appropriation Bills; House and Senate Roles

Under article I, section 7, clause 1 of the Constitution, it is exclusively the prerogative of the House to originate "revenue" bills. That clause provides:

> All Bills for raising Revenue shall originate in the House of Representatives; but the Senate may propose or concur with Amendments as on other Bills.

The House has traditionally taken the view that this prerogative encompasses the sole power to originate all general appropriation bills. Deschler Ch 25 § 13. On more than one occasion, the House has returned to the Senate a Senate bill or joint resolution appropriating money on the ground that it invaded the prerogatives of the House. Deschler Ch 13 §§ 20.2, 20.3. In 1962, when the Senate passed a joint resolution continuing funds for the Department of Agriculture, the House passed a resolution declaring that the Senate's action violated article I, section 7 of the Constitution and was an infringement of the privileges of the House. Deschler Ch 13 § 20.2. In support of the view that the House has the sole power to originate appropriation bills, it has been noted that at the time of the adoption of the Constitution the phrase ''raising revenue'' was equivalent to ''raising money and appropriating the same.'' S. Doc. 62-872.

§ 3. Definitions; Kinds of Appropriation Measures

Generally

An appropriation is a provision of law that provides budget authority for Federal agencies to incur obligations. ''Budget authority'' means the authority provided by law to incur financial obligations as defined by section 3(2)(A) of the Congressional Budget Act of 1974.

An appropriation Act is the most common means of providing budget authority. Deschler Ch 25 § 2. It has been held that language authorizing the Secretary of the Treasury to use the proceeds of public-debt issues for the purposes of making loans is not an appropriation. Deschler Ch 25 § 4.43.

Types of Appropriation Acts

The principal types of appropriation Acts are general, supplemental, special, and continuing.

- General appropriation bills provide budget authority to departments and agencies, usually for a specified fiscal year. Today, there are 12 regular appropriation Acts for each fiscal year. See § 6, infra.
- A supplemental appropriation is an Act appropriating funds in addition to those in the 12 regular annual appropriation Acts. Supplemental appropriations provide additional budget authority beyond the original estimates for an agency or program. Such a bill may be used after the fiscal year has begun to provide additional funding. Supplemental bills also may be general bills within the meaning of rules XIII and XXI if covering more than one agency. See § 73, infra.

- A special appropriation provides funds for one government agency, program, or project. See § 74, infra.
- Continuing appropriations—also known as continuing resolutions—provide temporary funding for agencies or programs that have not received a regular appropriation by the start of the fiscal year. They are used to permit agencies to continue to function and to operate their programs until their regular appropriations become law. Continuing resolutions are usually of short duration, but they have been used to fund agencies or departments for an entire fiscal year. See § 72, infra.

Privileged and Nonprivileged Appropriations Distinguished

The term ''general appropriation bill'' is used to refer to those bills that may be reported at any time and are privileged for consideration. See § 6, infra. A joint resolution continuing appropriations also may be reported and called up as privileged under the general rules of the House if reported after September 15 preceding the beginning of the fiscal year for which it is applicable. See § 72, infra. Other continuing appropriation measures, and special appropriation bills, are not privileged and are therefore considered under other procedures that give them privilege—such as a unanimous-consent agreement, a special order of business reported from the Committee on Rules, or a motion to suspend the rules. Deschler Ch 25 §§ 6, 7.

To file a report on a general appropriation bill, a member of the Committee on Appropriations seeks recognition and presents the report as follows:

MEMBER: M__. Speaker, by direction of the Committee on Appropriations, I submit a privileged report for printing under the rule.

SPEAKER: The Clerk will report the title. [*After Clerk reports title.*] Referred to the Union Calendar and ordered printed. Pursuant to clause 1 of rule XXI, all points of order are reserved.

Note: For a discussion of reserving points of order on appropriation bills, see § 65, infra.

§ 4. Committee and Administrative Expenses

Generally

Funding for House committees is provided by resolutions that allocate resources made available to the House in certain accounts in annual Legislative Branch Appropriation Acts. Authorization for payment may be obtained pursuant to clause 6 of rule X, which provides detailed provisions for the consideration of a primary expense resolution and for subsequent supplemental expense resolutions. With the exception of the Committee on Appropriations, the rule applies to ''any committee, commission, or other entity.'' *Manual* § 763; see generally COMMITTEES.

Under clause 1(b) of rule XI, the authority of all committees, and other entities, to incur expenses, including travel expenses, is made contingent upon adoption by the House of expense resolutions as required under clause 6 of rule X.

Appropriations from accounts for committee salaries and other administrative expenses of the House are under the jurisdiction of the Committee on House Administration. Clause 1(k) of rule X; *Manual* § 724. A resolution reported by that committee providing for such an expenditure is called up as privileged under clause 5(a) of rule XIII. Such a resolution, if not reported by the committee, may be called up and agreed to by unanimous consent. Deschler Ch 17 § 4. In recent years the resolution, although reported as privileged, has been considered under a special order of business (105-1, Mar. 21, 1997, p 4672), under suspension of the rules (109-1, Apr. 27, 2005, p 7990) and by unanimous consent (112-1, Mar. 17, 2011, p ____).

§ 5. Authorization, Appropriation, and Budget Processes Distinguished

There are three processes by which Congress allocates the fiscal resources of the Federal government. There is an authorization process under which Federal programs are created, modified, and extended in response to national needs. There is an appropriations process that provides funding for these programs. The congressional budget process, which may place spending ceilings on budget authority and outlays for a fiscal year and otherwise provides a mechanism for allocating Federal resources among competing government programs, interacts with and shapes the other phases. The budget process is treated separately in this work. See BUDGET PROCESS.

In the authorization process, the legislative committees establish program objectives and may set dollar ceilings on the amounts that may be appropriated. Once this authorization process is complete for a particular program or department, the Committee on Appropriations recommends the actual level of "budget authority," which allows Federal agencies to enter into obligations. The House may decline to appropriate funds for particular purposes, even though authorization has been enacted. Deschler Ch 25 § 2.1.

As a general rule, these two stages should be kept separate. With certain exceptions, authorization bills should not contain appropriations (§ 76, infra), and, again with certain exceptions, appropriation bills should not contain authorizations (§ 27, infra). This general rule is complicated by the fact that some budget authority becomes available as the result of previously enacted legislation and does not require current action by Congress. Examples include the various trust funds for which the obligational authority is already provided in basic law. See § 9, infra. This general rule is further complicated by the fact that Congress may combine authorizations and appropriations into ''omnibus'' or ''consolidated'' bills at the end of a fiscal year. In addition, some spending, sometimes referred to as direct spending, is controlled outside of the annual appropriations process. It is composed of entitlement and other mandatory spending programs. Such programs are either funded by provisions of the permanent laws that created them or by annual appropriation Acts providing liquidating cash or other funds mandated by law. See BUDGET PROCESS. Moreover, the authorization for a program may be derived not from a specific law providing authority for that particular program but from more general existing law—''organic'' law—mandating or permitting such programs. Thus, a paragraph in a general appropriation bill purportedly containing funds not yet specifically authorized by separate legislation was upheld where it was shown that all of the funds in the paragraph were authorized by more general provisions of law currently applicable to the programs in question. *Manual* § 1045.

II. General Appropriation Bills

A. Introductory

§ 6. Background; What Constitutes a General Appropriation Bill

Today, much of the Federal government is funded through the annual enactment of 12 regular appropriation bills. The subjects of these bills are determined by and coincide with the subcommittee jurisdictional structure of the Committee on Appropriations. Typically the 12 regular appropriation bills are identified as:

- Agriculture, Rural Development, Food and Drug Administration, and related agencies.
- Commerce, Justice, Science, and related agencies.
- Defense.
- Energy and Water Development.
- Financial Services and General Government.
- Homeland Security.
- Interior, Environment, and related agencies.
- Labor-Health and Human Services-Education, and related agencies.
- Legislative Branch.
- Military Construction, Veterans Affairs, and related agencies.
- State, Foreign Operations, and related agencies.
- Transportation, Housing and Urban Development, and related agencies.

The question as to what constitutes a general appropriation bill is important because clause 2 of rule XXI, which precludes unauthorized appropriations and legislation in appropriation bills applies only to general appropriation bills. *Manual* § 1044; Deschler Ch 26 § 1.1; § 27, infra. In the House the 12 regular appropriation bills and measures providing supplemental appropriations to two or more agencies are general appropriation bills. Deschler Ch 25 § 6; Deschler Ch 26 § 1.3.

Measures that have been held *not* to constitute a general appropriation bill include:

- A joint resolution continuing appropriations for government agencies pending enactment of the regular appropriation bills. Deschler Ch 26 § 1.2.
- A joint resolution making supplemental appropriations for one agency. Deschler Ch 25 § 7.4.
- A joint resolution making an appropriation to a department for a specific purpose. Deschler Ch 25 § 7.3.
- A bill providing appropriations for specific purposes. 8 Cannon § 2285.
- A joint resolution providing an appropriation for a single government agency even where permitting transfer of a portion of those funds to another agency. *Manual* § 1044.
- A joint resolution reported from the Committee on Appropriations transferring appropriated funds from one agency to another. *Manual* § 1044.
- A joint resolution transferring unobligated balances to the President to be available for specified purposes but containing no new budget authority. *Manual* § 1044.
- A bill making supplemental appropriation for emergency construction of public works. 7 Cannon § 1122.

§ 7. The Restrictions of Clause 2 of Rule XXI

Generally

Clause 2 of rule XXI contains two restrictions relative to appropriation bills: it (1) prohibits the inclusion in general appropriation bills of "unauthorized" appropriations, except for works in progress, and (2) prohibits provisions "changing existing law"—usually referred to as "legislation on an appropriation bill"—except for provisions that retrench expenditures under certain conditions, and except for rescissions of amounts provided in appropriation Acts reported by the Committee on Appropriations. *Manual* §§ 1036, 1038. The "retrenchment" provision is known as the Holman rule and is discussed in section 46, infra.

In practice, the concepts "unauthorized appropriations" and "legislation on general appropriation bills" sometimes have been applied almost interchangeably as grounds for making points of order pursuant to clause 2 of rule XXI. This occurs because an appropriation made without prior authorization has, in a sense, the effect of legislation, particularly in view of rulings of long standing that a ‘‘proposition changing existing law’’ may be construed to include the enactment of a law where none exists. Deschler Ch 26 § 1; see also § 28, infra. The two concepts are treated separately in this chapter, however, because they derive from different paragraphs of clause 2 of rule XXI and constitute distinct restrictions on the authority of the Committee on Appropriations. *Manual* §§ 1036, 1038.

Enforcement of Rule

As all bills making or authorizing appropriations require consideration in the Committee of the Whole, it follows that the enforcement of the rule would ordinarily occur during consideration in the Committee of the Whole, where the Chair, on the raising of a point of order, may rule out any portion of the bill in conflict with the rule. *Manual* § 1044; 4 Hinds § 3811. Because portions of the bill thus stricken are not reported back to the House, clause 1 of rule XXI reserves points of order to empower the Committee of the Whole to strike offending provisions without adopting an amendment to that effect. The enforcement of the rule also can occur in the House. For example, a motion to recommit a general appropriation bill may not propose an amendment in violation of the rule. Deschler Ch 26 § 1.4. It should be stressed, however, that the House may, through various procedural devices, waive one or both requirements of the rule, and thereby preclude the raising of such points of order against provisions in the bill. See § 68, infra.

§ 8. Committee Jurisdiction and Functions

Generally

Today, under clause 1(b) of rule X the Committee on Appropriations has jurisdiction over all appropriations, including general appropriation bills. *Manual* § 716. Special Presidential messages on rescissions and deferrals of budget authority submitted pursuant to sections 1012 and 1013 of the Impoundment Control Act of 1974, as well as rescission bills as defined in section 1011, are referred to the Committee on Appropriations if the proposed rescissions or deferrals involve funds already appropriated or obligated. *Manual* § 717. For a discussion of impoundments generally, see BUDGET PROCESS.

Under the Congressional Budget Act of 1974, the committee was given jurisdiction over rescissions of appropriations, transfers of unexpended balances, and the amount of new spending authority to be effective for a fiscal year. Clause 1(b) of rule X; *Manual* § 716.

Committee Reports

Under clause 3(f) of rule XIII, a report from the Committee on Appropriations accompanying any general appropriation bill must contain a concise statement describing the effect of any provision of the accompanying bill that directly or indirectly changes the application of existing law. *Manual* § 847. Provisions in the bill that are described in the report as changing existing law are presumed to be legislation in violation of clause 2(b) of rule XXI, absent rebuttal by the committee. *Manual* § 1044. Clause 2(f) of rule XIII further requires that such reports contain a list of appropriations in the bill for expenditures not previously authorized by law.

§ 9. Duration of Appropriation

Annual Appropriations

The most common form of appropriation provides budget authority for a single fiscal year. All of the 12 regular appropriation bills, for example, are annual, although certain accounts may "remain available until expended." Where a bill provides budget authority for a single fiscal year, the funds have to be obligated during the fiscal year for which they are provided. The funds lapse if not obligated by the end of that year. Indeed, unless an Act provides that a particular fund shall be available beyond the fiscal year, appropriations are made for one year only and any unused funds automatically go back into the Treasury at the end of the current fiscal year. *Norcross* v. *United States*, 142 Ct.Cl. 763 (1958).

An appropriation in a regular appropriation Act may be construed to be permanent or available continuously only if the appropriation expressly provides that it is available after the fiscal year covered by the law in which it appears, or unless the appropriation is for certain purposes such as public buildings. 31 USC § 1301.

The fiscal year for the Federal government begins on October 1 and ends on September 30. The fiscal year is designated by the calendar year in which it ends.

Multi-year Appropriations

A multi-year appropriation is made when budget authority is provided in an appropriations Act that is available for a specified period of time in excess of one fiscal year.

Permanent Appropriations

A permanent appropriation is budget authority that becomes available as the result of previously enacted legislation and that does not require current action by Congress. Examples include the appropriations for compensation of Members of Congress and the various trust funds for which the obligational authority is already provided in basic law. Pub. L. 97-51, § 130(c); S. Doc. 105-18.

B. Authorization of Appropriation

§ 10. In General; Necessity of Authorization

Generally

Clause 2(a) of rule XXI prohibits the inclusion in general appropriation bills of ''unauthorized'' appropriations, except for ''public works and objects that are already in progress.'' *Manual* § 1036. The House may, however, waive this rule. See §§ 67, 68, infra.

Authorization to Precede Appropriation

The enactment of authorizing legislation must occur before, and not following, the consideration of an appropriation for the proposed purpose. Thus, delaying the availability of an appropriation pending enactment of an authorization will not protect that appropriation against a point of order. Deschler Ch 26 § 7.3. A bill may not permit a portion of a lump sum—unauthorized at the time the bill is being considered—to subsequently become available; a further appropriation upon the enactment of authorizing legislation would be needed. Deschler Ch 25 § 2. Likewise an appropriation will not be permitted that is conditioned on a future authorization. Deschler Ch 26 §§ 7.2, 47.4. However, where lump sums are involved, language that limits use of an appropriation to programs ''authorized by law'' or that permits expenditures ''within the limits of the amount now or hereafter authorized to be appropriated,'' has been held to insulate the provision against the point of order. Deschler Ch 26 § 7.10 (note).

The requirement that the authorization precede the appropriation is satisfied if the authorizing legislation has been enacted into law between the time the appropriation bill is reported and the time it is considered in the Committee of the Whole. Deschler Ch 25 § 2.21.

It should be emphasized that the rule applies to general appropriation bills. A joint resolution containing continuing appropriations is not considered a general appropriation bill within the purview of the rule, despite inclusion of diverse appropriations that are not continuing in nature. Deschler Ch 25 § 2.

§ 11. Duration of Authorization

Generally; Renewals

Until recent years, many authorizations were permanent, being provided for by the organic statute that created the agency or program. Such statutes often include provisions to the effect that there are hereby authorized to be appropriated "hereafter" such sums "as may be necessary" or "as approved by Congress," to implement the law, thereby requiring the appropriate budget authority to be enacted each year in accordance with this permanent authorization. See, *e.g.*, Deschler Ch 26 § 11.1.

The Congress often authorizes appropriations for only a certain number of years at a time. For example, authorizations may extend for two, five, or 10 years and may be renewed periodically. The trend toward periodic authorizations is reflected in the rule adopted in 1970 that requires each standing committee to ensure that appropriations for continuing programs and activities will be made annually "to the maximum extent feasible," consistent with the nature of the programs involved. Programs for which appropriations are not made annually may have "sunset" provisions that require their review periodically to determine whether they can be modified to permit annual appropriations. Clause 4 of rule X; *Manual* § 755.

§ 12. Sufficiency of Authorization

Generally

The term "authorized by law" in clause 2 of rule XXI is ordinarily construed as a "law enacted by the Congress." *Manual* § 1036. Statutory authority for the appropriation must exist. Deschler Ch 25 § 2.3. It has been held, for example, that a bill passed by both Houses but not signed by the President or returned to the originating House is insufficient authorization to support an appropriation. 92-1, May 11, 1971, p 14471. Similarly, an executive order does not constitute sufficient authorization in the absence of proof of its derivation from a statute enacted by Congress. Deschler Ch 26 § 7.7. On the other hand, sufficient authorization for an appropriation may be found to exist in a treaty that has been ratified. 4 Hinds § 3587; Deschler Ch 26 § 17.9. Sufficient authorization also may be found in legislation contained in a previous appropriation Act that has become permanent law. Deschler Ch 25 § 2.5.

Authorization From Specific Statutes or General Existing Law

Authorization for a program may be derived from a specific law providing authority for that particular program or from a more general existing law—''organic law''—authorizing appropriations for such programs. Thus, a paragraph in a general appropriation bill purportedly containing funds not yet specifically authorized by separate legislation was held not to violate clause 2 of rule XXI, where it was shown that all of the funds in the paragraph were authorized by more general provisions of law currently applicable to the programs in question. Deschler Ch 26 § 10.8. Organic statutes or general grants of authority in law constitute sufficient authorization to support appropriations only where the general laws applicable to the function or department in question do not require specific or annual authorizations or a periodic authorization scheme has not subsequently occupied the field. *Manual* § 1045.

Similarly, a permanent law authorizing the President to appoint certain staff, together with legislative provisions authorizing additional employment contained in an appropriation bill enacted for that fiscal year, constituted sufficient authorization for a lump-sum supplemental appropriation for the White House for the same fiscal year. Deschler Ch 25 § 2.6. The legislative history of the law in question may be considered to determine whether sufficient authorization for the project exists. Deschler Ch 25 § 2.7. The lack of appropriations during a series of years for a program previously authorized by law does not repeal the law, and it may be cited as providing authorization for a subsequent appropriation. 4 Hinds § 3595.

Some statutes expressly provide, however, that there may be appropriated to carry out the functions of certain agencies only such sums as Congress may thereafter authorize by law, thus requiring specific subsequently enacted authorizations for the operations of such agencies and not permitting appropriations to be authorized by the ''organic statute'' creating the agency. Deschler Ch 26 § 49.2 (note).

Effect of Prior Unauthorized Appropriations

An appropriation for an object unauthorized by law, however frequently made in former years, does not warrant similar appropriations in succeeding years, unless the program in question is such as to fall into the category of a continuation of work in progress, or unless authorizing legislation in a previous appropriation Act has become permanent law. *Manual* §§ 1036, 1045; 7 Cannon § 1150; § 25, infra.

Incidental Expenses; Implied Authorizations

A general grant of authority to an agency or program may be found sufficiently broad to authorize items or projects that are incidental to carrying out the purposes of the basic law. Deschler Ch 25 § 2.10. An amendment proposing appropriations for incidental expenses that contribute to the main purpose of carrying out the functions of the department for which funds are being provided in the bill is generally held to be authorized by law. Deschler Ch 26 § 7.15. For example, appropriations for certain travel expenses for the Secretary of the Department of Agriculture were held authorized by law as necessary to carry out the basic law setting up that department. Deschler Ch 25 § 2.10.

On the other hand, where the authorizing law authorizes a lump-sum appropriation and confers broad discretion on an executive in allotting funds, an appropriation for a specific purpose may be ruled out as inconsistent therewith. Deschler Ch 26 § 15.5 (note); see also 105-1, Sept. 8, 1997, p 18042. The appropriation of a lump sum for a general purpose having been authorized, a specific appropriation for a particular item included in such general purpose may be a limitation on the discretion of the executive charged with allotment of the lump sum and not in order on the appropriation bill. 7 Cannon § 1452. Such a limitation also may be ruled out on the ground that it is "legislation" on an appropriation bill. See § 43, infra. An appropriation to pay a judgment awarded by a court is in order if such judgment has been properly certified to Congress. Deschler Ch 25 § 2.2.

§ 13. Proof of Authorization; Burden of Proof

Burden of Proof Generally

Under House practice, those upholding an item of appropriation have the burden of showing the law authorizing it. 4 Hinds § 3597; 7 Cannon §§ 1179, 1276. Thus, a point of order having been raised, the burden of proving the authorization for language carried in an appropriation bill falls on the proponents and managers of the bill, who must shoulder this burden of proof by citing statutory authority for the appropriation. Deschler Ch 25 § 9.5; Deschler Ch 26 § 9.4. The Chair may overrule a point of order upon citation to an organic statute creating an agency, absent any showing that such law has been repealed or amended to require specific annual authorizations. Deschler Ch 26 § 9.6; see also § 27, infra.

Burden of Proof as to Amendment

The burden of proof to show that an appropriation contained in an amendment is authorized by law is on the proponent of the amendment, a point of order having been raised against the appropriation. *Manual* § 1044; Deschler Ch 26 §§ 9.1, 9.2. If the amendment is susceptible to more than one interpretation, it is incumbent upon the proponent to show that it is not in violation of the rule. *Manual* § 1044a.

Evidence of Compliance with Condition

An authorizing statute may provide that the authorization for a program is to be effective only upon compliance by executive officials with certain conditions or requirements. In such a case, a letter written by an executive officer charged with the duty of furthering a certain program may be sufficient documentary evidence of authorization in the manner prescribed. Deschler Ch 26 §§ 10.2, 10.3.

§ 14. Increasing Budget Authority

Increases within Authorized Limits

Authorizing legislation may place a ceiling on the amount of budget authority that can be appropriated for a program or may authorize the appropriation of ''such sums as are necessary.'' Absent restrictions imposed by the budget process, it is in order to increase the appropriation in an appropriation bill for a purpose authorized by law if such increase does not exceed the amount authorized for that purpose. Deschler Ch 25 §§ 2.13, 2.15. An amendment proposing simply to increase an appropriation for a specific purpose over the amount carried in the appropriation bill does not constitute a change in law unless such increase is in excess of that authorized. Deschler Ch 25 § 2.14. An amendment changing the figure in the bill to the full amount authorized does not violate clause 2 of rule XXI. Deschler Ch 25 § 2.16. Likewise, if the authorization does not place a cap on the amount to be appropriated, an amendment increasing the amount of the appropriation for items included in the bill is in order. Deschler Ch 25 § 11.16.

Increases in Excess of Amount Authorized

An appropriation in excess of the specific amount authorized by law may be in violation of clause 2 of rule XXI, the rule prohibiting unauthorized appropriations. Deschler Ch 26 § 21. Thus, where existing law limited annual authorizations of appropriations for incidental expenses of a program to $7,500, an appropriation for $10,000 was held to be unauthorized and was ruled out on a point of order. 94-1, Sept. 30, 1974, p 30981.

The rule that an appropriation bill may not provide budget authority in excess of the amount specified in the authorizing legislation has also been applied to:

- An amendment proposing an increase in the amount of an appropriation authorized by law for compensation of Members of the House. Deschler Ch 26 § 21.2.
- A provision increasing the loan authorization for the rural telephone program above the amount authorized for that purpose. Deschler Ch 26 § 33.3.

- A provision providing funds for the Joint Committee on Defense Production in excess of the amount authorized by law. Deschler Ch 26 § 21.5.
- A provision containing funds in excess of amounts permitted to be committed by a Federal agency for mortgage purchases. 97-2, July 29, 1982, p 18636.
- An amendment en bloc transferring appropriations among objects in the bill, offered under clause 2(f) of rule XXI, increasing an appropriation above the authorized amount. *Manual* § 1063a.

Waiver of Ceiling

Where a limitation on the amount of an appropriation to be annually available for expenditure by an agency has become law, language in an appropriation bill seeking to waive or change this limitation gives rise to a point of order that the language is legislation on an appropriation bill. Deschler Ch 26 § 33.2.

C. Authorization for Particular Purposes or Programs

§ 15. In General

Absent an appropriate waiver, language in a general appropriation bill providing funding for a program that is not authorized by law is in violation of clause 2(a) of rule XXI and also may ''change existing law'' in violation of clauses 2(b) or 2(c). Provisions that have been ruled out as unauthorized under clause 2 of rule XXI include:

- Appropriations for fiscal year 1979 for the Department of Justice and its related agencies. Deschler Ch 26 § 18.3.
- An appropriation for expenses incident to the special instruction and training of United States attorneys and United States marshals, their assistants and deputies, and United States commissioners. Deschler Ch 26 § 18.1.
- An appropriation for Coast Guard acquisitions, construction, research, development, and evaluation. 95-1, June 8, 1977, pp 17945, 17946.
- An appropriation for the U.S. Customs Service air interdiction program. 98-2, June 21, 1984, pp 17693, 17694.
- An appropriation for liquidation of contract authority to pay costs of certain subsidies granted by the Maritime Administration. 92-1, June 24, 1971, p 21901.
- A provision permitting the Secretary of Labor and the Secretary of Health, Education, and Welfare to use funds for official reception and representation expenses. Deschler Ch 26 § 20.19.
- A provision making funds available for distribution of radiological instruments and detection devices to States by loan or grant for civil defense purposes. Deschler Ch 26 § 20.1.

- A provision making funds available for reimbursements of government employees for use by them of their privately owned automobiles on official business. Deschler Ch 26 § 20.6.
- An appropriation for the American Revolution Bicentennial Commission. 91-2, May 19, 1970, p 16165.
- An appropriation for the National Cancer Institute where a lapsed periodic authorization scheme had preempted reliance on an organic statute as the source of authorization. 105-1, Sept. 9, 1997, p 18197.
- An appropriation for the President to meet "unanticipated needs." *Manual* § 1045.

The rulings cited in this division illustrate the application of the rule requiring appropriations to be based on prior authorization and are thus dependent on the state of current law at the time the appropriation is considered.

§ 16. Agricultural Programs

Held Authorized by Existing Law

- An appropriation to be used to increase domestic consumption of farm commodities. Deschler Ch 26 § 11.1.
- Appropriations for cooperative range improvements (including construction, maintenance, control of rodents, and eradication of noxious plants in national forests). Deschler Ch 26 § 11.3.
- An appropriation to enable the Secretary of Agriculture to carry out the provisions of the National School Lunch Act of 1946. Deschler Ch 26 § 11.5.
- Appropriations for the acquisition and diffusion of information by the Department of Agriculture. 4 Hinds § 3649; Deschler Ch 26 § 11.10.
- Appropriations for agricultural engineering research and for programs relating to the prevention and control of dust explosions and fires during the harvesting and storing of agricultural products. Deschler Ch 26 § 11.11.
- An appropriation for the purchase and installation of weather instruments and the construction or repair of buildings of the Weather Bureau. Deschler Ch 26 § 11.16.

Ruled Out as Unauthorized

- An appropriation for a celebration of the centennial of the establishment of the Department of Agriculture. Deschler Ch 26 § 11.2.
- A provision providing for the organization of a new bureau to conduct investigations relating to agriculture. 4 Hinds § 3651.
- A provision providing for cooperation by and with State agriculture investigators. 4 Hinds § 3650; 7 Cannon §§ 1301, 1302.
- An appropriation to collect, compile, and analyze data relating to consumer expenditures and savings. Deschler Ch 26 § 11.7.

- An appropriation to permit the Department of Agriculture to investigate and develop methods for the manufacture and utilization of starches from cull potatoes and surplus crops. Deschler Ch 26 § 11.9.
- A provision for the refund of certain penalties to wheat producers. Deschler Ch 26 § 11.6.
- An amendment appropriating funds for the immediate acquisition of domestic meat and poultry to be distributed consistently with provisions of law relating to distribution of other foods. 93-2, June 21, 1974, p 20620.
- An appropriation for the control of certain crop diseases or infestations. Deschler Ch 26 §§ 11.12, 11.13.

§ 17. Programs Relating to Business or Commerce

Held Authorized by Existing Law

- An appropriation for the Director of the Bureau of the Census to publish monthly reports on coffee stocks on hand in the United States. Deschler Ch 26 § 12.1.
- An appropriation for the Office of the Secretary of Commerce for expenses of attendance at meetings of organizations concerned with the work of his office. Deschler Ch 26 § 12.6.

Ruled Out as Unauthorized

- An appropriation for sample surveys by the Census Bureau to estimate the size and characteristics of the nation's labor force and population. Deschler Ch 26 § 12.2.
- An appropriation for necessary expenses in the performance of activities and services relating to technological development as an aid to business in the development of foreign and domestic commerce. Deschler Ch 26 § 12.4.
- An appropriation for travel in privately owned automobiles by employees engaged in the maintenance and operation of remotely controlled air-navigation facilities. Deschler Ch 26 § 12.5.
- An appropriation for necessary expenses of the National Bureau of Standards (including amounts for the standard reference data program) for fiscal year 1979. Deschler Ch 26 § 12.9.

§ 18. Defense Programs

Held Authorized by Existing Law

- An appropriation for paving of streets and erection of warehouses incident to the establishment of a naval station. 7 Cannon § 1232.
- An appropriation to enable the President, through such departments or agencies of the government as he might designate, to carry out the provisions of the Act of March 11, 1941, to promote the defense of the United States. Deschler Ch 26 § 13.3.

Ruled Out as Unauthorized

- An appropriation for transportation of successful candidates to the Naval Academy. 7 Cannon § 1234.
- An appropriation for establishment of shooting ranges and purchase of prizes and trophies. 7 Cannon § 1242.
- An appropriation for the construction and improvement of barracks for enlisted men and quarters for noncommissioned officers of the Army. Deschler Ch 26 § 13.5.
- An amendment striking funds for a nuclear aircraft carrier program and inserting funds for a conventional-powered aircraft carrier program. Deschler Ch 26 § 13.6.
- A provision increasing the funds appropriated for a fiscal year for military assistance to South Vietnam and Laos. 93-2, Apr. 10, 1974, p 10594.
- An appropriation for Veterans' Administration expenses for the issuance of memorial certificates to families of deceased veterans. Deschler Ch 26 § 13.1.

§ 19. Funding for the District of Columbia

Held Authorized Under Existing Law

- An appropriation for opening, widening, or extending streets and highways in the District of Columbia. 7 Cannon § 1189.
- An appropriation for streetlights or for improving streets out of a special fund created by the District of Columbia Gasoline Tax Act. Deschler Ch 26 §§ 11.15, 14.7.
- An appropriation for expenses of keeping school playgrounds open during the summer months. Deschler Ch 26 § 14.5.
- An appropriation for the preparation of plans and specifications for a branch library building in the District of Columbia. Deschler Ch 26 § 14.13.

Ruled Out as Unauthorized

- Appropriations for certain Federal office buildings in the District of Columbia that were not approved by the Public Works Committees of the House and Senate as required by the Public Buildings Act of 1959. Deschler Ch 26 § 19.2.
- A provision permitting the use of funds by the Office of the Corporation Counsel to retain professional experts at rates fixed by the commissioner. Deschler Ch 26 § 14.1.
- An appropriation for the preparation of plans and specifications for a new main library building in the District of Columbia. Deschler Ch 26 § 14.12.
- An appropriation for the salary and expenses of the Office of Director of Vehicles and Traffic out of the District Gasoline Tax Fund. Deschler Ch 26 § 14.14.

- A provision permitting the Commissioners of the District of Columbia to purchase a municipal asphalt plant. Deschler Ch 26 § 14.19.
- An amendment making funds available for expenditure by the American Legion in connection with its national convention. Deschler Ch 26 § 14.3.
- An appropriation to reimburse certain District of Columbia officials for services and expenses. 7 Cannon § 1184.

§ 20. Interior or Environmental Programs

Held Authorized Under Existing Law

- An appropriation for suppression of liquor or peyote traffic among Indians. 7 Cannon §§ 1210, 1212.
- An appropriation for the examination of mineral resources of the national domain. 7 Cannon § 1222.
- An appropriation for the development of an educational program of the National Park Service. Deschler Ch 26 § 15.17.
- An appropriation for the purpose of encouraging industry and self-support among Indians and outlining areas of discretionary authority to be exercised by the Secretary of the Interior. Deschler Ch 26 § 15.26.
- Appropriations for irrigation projects that had been recommended by the Secretary of the Interior and approved by the President. Deschler Ch 26 § 15.30.

Ruled Out as Unauthorized

- An appropriation to enable the EPA to obtain reports as to the probable adverse effect on the economy of certain Federal environmental actions. Deschler Ch 26 § 15.1.
- An appropriation to the EPA to establish an independent review board to review the priorities of the agency. Deschler Ch 26 § 15.2.
- A provision authorizing the Secretary of the Interior, in administering the Bureau of Reclamation, to contract for medical services for employees and to make certain payroll deductions. Deschler Ch 26 § 15.9.
- An appropriation for the Division of Investigations in the Department of the Interior, to be expended under the direction of the Secretary, to meet unforeseen emergencies of a confidential character. Deschler Ch 26 § 15.12.
- An appropriation ''out of the general funds of the Treasury'' (and not the reclamation fund) for investigations of proposed Federal reclamation projects. Deschler Ch 26 § 15.28.
- A provision requiring that part of an appropriation for general wildlife conservation be earmarked expressly for the leasing and management of land for the protection of the Florida Key deer. Deschler Ch 26 § 15.5.
- An appropriation for the National Power Policy Committee to be used by the committee in the performance of functions prescribed by the President. Deschler Ch 26 § 15.7.

§ 21. Programs Relating to Foreign Affairs

Held Authorized by Existing Law

- An appropriation for transportation and subsistence of diplomatic and consular officers en route to and from their posts. 7 Cannon § 1251.
- A provision earmarking an amount for a contribution to the International Secretariat on Middle Level Manpower. Deschler Ch 26 § 17.2.
- An appropriation for the obligation assumed by the United States in accepting membership in the International Labor Organization. Deschler Ch 26 § 17.3.
- An amendment providing funds for a health exhibit at the Universal and International Exhibition of Brussels. Deschler Ch 26 § 17.6.
- An appropriation for commercial attachés to be appointed by the Secretary of Commerce. 7 Cannon § 1257.
- An appropriation to compensate the owners of certain vessels seized by Ecuador. Deschler Ch 26 § 17.1.

Ruled Out as Unauthorized

- An amendment to earmark part of the appropriation for the United States Information Agency to provide facilities for the translation and publication of books and other printed matter in various foreign languages. Deschler Ch 26 § 17.7.
- Appropriations for incidental and contingent expenses in the consular and diplomatic service. 4 Hinds § 3609.
- An appropriation for the Foreign Service Auxiliary. Deschler Ch 26 § 17.14.
- An appropriation for the salary of a particular U.S. minister to a foreign country where the Senate had not confirmed the appointee. Deschler Ch 26 § 17.17.
- An amendment providing funds for acquisition of sites and buildings for embassies in foreign countries. 4 Hinds § 3606.

§ 22. Legislative Branch Funding

It is not in order to provide for payments to employees of the House in an appropriation bill unless the House by prior action has authorized such payments. 4 Hinds § 3654. Such authorization is generally provided for by resolution from the Committee on House Administration. The House in appropriating funds for an employee may not go beyond the terms of the resolution creating the office. 4 Hinds § 3659.

A resolution of the House has been held sufficient authorization for an appropriation for the salary of an employee of the House. 4 Hinds §§ 3656-3658, 3660. A resolution intended to justify appropriations beyond the term of a Congress may be ''made permanent law'' by a legislative provision in a Legislative Branch Appropriation Act.

Held Authorized

- Funds for employment of counsel to represent Members and to appear in court officially. 7 Cannon § 1311.
- Funds for expenses incurred in contested election cases when properly certified. 7 Cannon § 1231.
- Salaries for certain House employees. 91-1, Aug. 5, 1969, p 22197.
- An increase in the salary of an officer of the House. 89-2, Sept. 8, 1966, p 22020.
- The salary of the Chief of Staff of the Joint Committee on Internal Revenue Taxation. 92-2, Oct. 4, 1972, p 33744.
- Salary adjustments for certain House employees. 92-2, Jan. 27, 1972, p 1531.
- Overtime compensation for employees of the Publications Distribution Service (Folding Room). 92-2, Mar. 2, 1972, p 6627.
- Costs of stenographic services and transcripts in connection with a meeting or hearing of a committee. *Manual* § 789.
- Certain costs associated with the organizational meeting of the Democratic Caucus or Republican Conference. *Manual* § 1126.
- The transfer of surplus prior-year funds to liquidate certain current obligations of the House. Deschler Ch 25 § 5.3.

Ruled Out as Unauthorized

- An increase in the total amount for salaries of Members beyond that authorized. Deschler Ch 26 § 21.2.
- An allowance payable to the attending physician of the Capitol. 86-2, May 17, 1960, p 10447.
- Funds for a parking lot for the use of Members and employees of Congress. Deschler Ch 26 § 20.3.
- Funds for employment by the Committee on Appropriations of 50 qualified persons to investigate and report on the progress of certain contracts entered into by the United States. Deschler Ch 26 § 20.2.

§ 23. Salaries and Related Benefits

Language in a general appropriation bill providing funding for salaries that are not authorized by law is in violation of clause 2(a) of rule XXI. Such propositions, whether to appropriate for salaries not established by law or to increase salaries fixed by law, are out of order either as unauthorized or as changing existing law. 4 Hinds §§ 3664-3667, 3676-3679; Deschler Ch 26 § 43. The mere appropriation for a salary for one year does not create an office so as to justify appropriations in succeeding years. 4 Hinds §§ 3590, 3697. However, it has been held that a point of order does not lie against a lump-sum appropriation for increased pay costs as being unauthorized where language in the bill limits use of the appropriation to pay costs "authorized by or pursuant to law." Deschler Ch 25 § 2.20.

Ruled Out as Unauthorized

- Funds for necessary expenses for a designated number of officers on the active list of an agency. 98-2, May 31, 1984, p 14590.
- Funds for salaries and expenses of the Commission on Civil Rights above the amount authorized by existing law for that purpose. 92-1, June 24, 1971, p 21902.
- Funds for salaries and expenses of additional inspectors in the U.S. Customs Service. 98-2, Aug. 1, 1984, pp 21904, 21905.
- A salary of $10,000 per year for the wife of the President for maintaining the White House. Deschler Ch 26 § 20.13.

D. Authorization for Public Works

§ 24. In General

Language in a general appropriation bill providing funding for a public work that is not authorized by law is in violation of clause 2(a) of rule XXI, unless the project can be deemed a work in progress within the meaning of that rule. Deschler Ch 26 § 19.13; see § 25, infra. An appropriation for a public work in excess of the amount fixed by law, or for extending a public service beyond the limits assigned by an executive officer exercising a lawful discretion, is out of order. 4 Hinds §§ 3583, 3584, 3598; 7 Cannon § 1133.

Held Authorized by Existing Law

- An appropriation for necessary advisory services to public and private agencies with regard to construction and operation of airports and landing areas. Deschler Ch 26 § 19.4.
- An amendment proposing to increase a lump-sum appropriation for river and harbor projects. Deschler Ch 26 § 19.6.
- An appropriation for the Tennessee-Tombigbee inland waterway. Deschler Ch 26 § 19.9.
- An appropriation for construction of transmission lines from Grand Coulee Dam to Spokane. Deschler Ch 25 § 19.11.

Ruled Out as Unauthorized

- Language providing an additional amount for construction of certain public buildings. Deschler Ch 26 § 19.1.
- Appropriations for certain Federal office buildings in the District of Columbia where not approved by the Public Works Committees of the House and Senate as required by the Public Buildings Act of 1959. Deschler Ch 26 § 19.2.
- An appropriation for construction of a connecting highway between the United States and Alaska. Deschler Ch 26 § 19.5.

- An amendment making part of an appropriation to the Army Corps of Engineers for flood control available for studying specified work of the Bureau of Reclamation. Deschler Ch 26 § 19.8.
- A provision appropriating certain trust funds for expenses relating to forest roads and trails. Deschler Ch 26 § 28.2.

§ 25. Works in Progress

Clause 2(a) of rule XXI, the rule that bars appropriations not previously authorized by law, provides for an exception for appropriations for ''public works and objects that are already in progress.'' *Manual* § 1036. Thus, when the construction of a public building has commenced and there is no limit of cost, further appropriations may be made under the exception for works in progress. Deschler Ch 26 § 8.1. The exception for works in progress under rule XXI may apply even though the original appropriation for the project was unauthorized. 7 Cannon § 1340; Deschler Ch 26 § 8.2.

Historically, the works-in-progress exception has been applied only to projects funded from the general fund of the Treasury for which no authorization has been enacted. It does not apply to language changing existing law by extending the authorized availability of funds or in contravention of law restricting use of a special fund. An appropriation for construction that is in violation of existing law, which exceeds the limit fixed by law, or is governed by a lapsed authorization is not permitted under the works-in-progress exception of rule XXI. *Manual* § 1048; 4 Hinds §§ 3587, 3702; 7 Cannon § 1332.

The tendency of later decisions is to narrow the application of the exception under clause 2(a) of rule XXI making in order appropriations for works in progress. 7 Cannon § 1333. The work in question, to qualify under the rule, must have moved beyond the planning stage. 7 Cannon § 1336. To come within the terms of the rule, it must be actually ''in progress,'' according to the usual significance of those words, with actual work having been initiated. 4 Hinds § 3706; Deschler Ch 26 § 8.5. Merely selecting or purchasing a site for the construction of a building is not sufficient. 4 Hinds §§ 3762, 3785. However, the fact that the work has been interrupted—even for several years—does not prevent it from qualifying under the works-in-progress exception of clause 2(a). 4 Hinds §§ 3707, 3708.

To establish that actual work has begun on the project, the Chair may require some documentary evidence that work has been initiated. Deschler Ch 26 § 8.5. To this end, the Chair may consider a letter from an executive officer charged with the duty of constructing the project. Deschler Ch 26 § 8.2. News articles merely suggesting that work may have begun have been regarded as insufficient evidence that work is in progress within the meaning of the rule. Deschler Ch 26 § 8.7.

§ 26. —What Constitutes a Work in Progress

The term ''works and objects'' in the exception to the rule prohibiting unauthorized appropriations is construed as something tangible, such as a building or road. 4 Hinds §§ 3714, 3715; see also Deschler Ch 26 § 8. The term does not extend to projects that are indefinite as to completion and intangible in nature, such as the gauging of streams or an investigation. 4 Hinds §§ 3714, 3715, 3719. The term does not extend to the ordinary duties of an executive or administrative office. 4 Hinds §§ 3709, 3713.

Appropriations for extension or repair of an existing road (4 Hinds §§ 3793, 3798), bridge (4 Hinds § 3803), or public building have been admitted as in continuation of a work (4 Hinds §§ 3777, 3778), although it is not in order as such to provide for a new building in place of one destroyed (4 Hinds § 3606). The purchase of adjoining land for a work already established has been admitted under this principle (4 Hinds §§ 3766-3773), as well as additions to or extensions of existing public buildings (4 Hinds §§ 3774, 3775). However, the purchase of a separate and detached lot of land is not admitted. 4 Hinds § 3776.

Appropriations for new buildings as additional structures at government institutions have sometimes been admitted (4 Hinds §§ 3741-3750), but propositions to appropriate for new buildings that were not necessary adjuncts to the institution have been ruled out (4 Hinds §§ 3755-3759).

Projects that have qualified as a work in progress under clause 2(a) of rule XXI include:

- A topographical survey. 7 Cannon § 1382.
- The continuation of construction at the Kennedy Library, a project owned by the United States and funded by a prior year's appropriation. *Manual* § 1049.
- A continuation of aircraft experimentation and development. 69-1, Jan. 22, 1926, p 2623.

Projects that have been ruled out because they did not qualify as a work in progress under clause 2(a) of rule XXI include:

- New Army hospitals. 4 Hinds § 3740.
- A new lighthouse. 4 Hinds § 3728.
- An extension of an existing road. *Manual* § 1049.

III. Legislation in General Appropriation Bills; Provisions Changing Existing Law

A. Generally

§ 27. The Restrictions of Clause 2 of Rule XXI

In General; Historical Background

Almost continuously since the 44th Congress, the rules have contained language forbidding the inclusion in general appropriation bills of language ''changing existing law.'' In 1835, when it became apparent that appropriation bills were being delayed because of the intrusion of legislative matters, John Quincy Adams suggested the desirability of a plan that such bills ''be stripped of everything but the appropriations.'' 4 Hinds § 3578.

Today, clause 2 of rule XXI provides that, with two exceptions, ''A provision changing existing law may not be reported in a general appropriation bill . . .'' and that ''An amendment to a general appropriation bill shall not be in order if changing existing law.'' The exceptions set forth in clause 2(b) are for germane provisions that change existing law in a way that would ''retrench'' expenditures, and for rescissions of previously enacted appropriations. *Manual* § 1038; see § 46, infra.

Language changing existing law in violation of rule XXI often is referred to as ''legislation on an appropriation bill.'' Deschler Ch 26 § 1. What ''legislation'' means in this context is a change in an existing law that governs how appropriations may be used.

Like the rule generally prohibiting unauthorized appropriations, the restriction against legislating on general appropriation bills is only enforced if a Member takes the initiative to enforce it by raising a point of order. See § 67, infra. Such a point of order may be waived pursuant to various procedural devices. See § 68, infra.

The rule against legislation in appropriation bills is limited to general appropriation bills. Thus, a joint resolution merely continuing appropriations for government agencies pending enactment of the regular appropriation bills is not subject to the prohibitions in clause 2 of rule XXI against legislative language. A point of order under this rule does not apply to a special order of business reported from the Committee on Rules ''self-executing'' the adoption in the House of an amendment changing existing law. *Manual* § 1044.

Construction of Rule

The rule that forbids language in a general appropriation bill that changes existing law is broadly construed. Deschler Ch 26 § 64.23. The restriction is construed to apply not only to changes in an existing statute but also to the enactment of law where none exists, to language repealing existing law (§ 28, infra), to a provision making changes in court interpretations of statutory law (96-2, Aug. 19, 1980, p 21978), and to a proposition to change a rule of the House (4 Hinds § 3819). The fact that legislative language may have been included in appropriation Acts in prior years and made applicable to funds in those laws does not permit the inclusion in a general appropriation bill of similar language. *Manual* § 1054.

Under clause 2(c) of rule XXI, the restriction against changing existing law applies specifically to amendments to general appropriation bills. *Manual* § 1039. It follows that if a motion to recommit with instructions constitutes legislation on an appropriation bill, the motion is subject to a point of order. Deschler Ch 26 § 1.4.

Burden of Proof

Where a point of order is raised against a provision in a general appropriation bill as constituting legislation in violation of clause 2 of rule XXI, the burden of proof is on the Committee on Appropriations to show that the language is valid under the precedents and does not change existing law. Deschler Ch 26 § 22.30. Provisions in the bill, described in the accompanying report as directly or indirectly changing the application of existing law, are presumably legislation in violation of clause 2 of rule XXI, in the absence of rebuttal by the committee. Deschler Ch 26 § 22.27. Similarly, the proponent of an amendment against which a point of order has been raised as constituting legislation on an appropriation bill has the burden of proving that the amendment does not change existing law. *Manual* § 1044a; Deschler Ch 26 § 22.29; see also § 13, supra.

§ 28. Changing Existing Law by Amendment, Enactment, or Repeal; Waivers

The prohibition of clause 2 of rule XXI against inclusion of a "provision changing existing law" has been construed as follows:

- A change in the text of existing law. Deschler Ch 26 §§ 23.11, 24.6.

  Note: Existing law may be repeated verbatim in an appropriation bill, but the slightest change of the text causes it to be ruled out. 4 Hinds §§ 3414, 3817; 7 Cannon §§ 1391, 1394.
- The enactment of law where none exists.

Note: The provision of the rule forbidding legislation in a general appropriation bill is construed as the enactment of law where none exists, such as permitting funds to remain available until expended or beyond the fiscal year covered by the bill, or immediately upon enactment, where existing law permits no such availability. *Manual* § 1052; 4 Hinds §§ 3812, 3813.

- The repeal of existing law. 7 Cannon § 1403; Deschler Ch 26 §§ 24.1, 24.7.
- A waiver of a provision of existing law. *Manual* § 1056; Deschler Ch 26 §§ 24.5, 34.14, 34.15.

Note: A waiver may be regarded as legislation on an appropriation bill where it uses such language as "notwithstanding the provisions of any other law" or "without regard to [sections of] the Revised Statutes." Deschler Ch 26 §§ 24.8, 26.6.

§ 29. Imposing Contingencies and Conditions

Generally; Conditions Precedent

Provisions making an appropriation contingent on a future event are often presented in appropriation bills. *Manual* § 1055. Such contingencies may be phrased as conditions to be complied with, as in "funds shall be available when the Secretary has reported," or as restrictions on funding, as in "No funds until the Secretary has reported." Similar tests are applied in both formulations in determining whether the language constitutes legislation on an appropriation bill: Is the contingency germane or does it change existing law? Deschler Ch 26 § 49.2. Does it impose new duties (for example, to report) where none exist under law? See § 31, infra.

Precedents discussed in sections 29-31, relating to "conditions," could in many instances be cited under the discussion in sections 50-59a, relating to "limitations." Language imposing a "negative restriction" on funds in the bill is not a proper limitation if it creates new law or requires positive determinations and actions where none exist in law. See §§ 56, 59, infra.

The proscription against changing existing law is applicable to those instances in which the whole appropriation is made contingent upon an event or circumstance as well as those in which the disbursement to a particular participant is conditioned on the occurrence of an event. Deschler Ch 26 §§ 47, 48. The terms "unless," "until," or "provided," in an amendment or proviso are clues that the language may contain a condition that is subject to a point of order under clause 2(b) or (c) of rule XXI. Language that has been ruled out pursuant to this rule include:

- An amendment providing that funds shall not be available for any broadcast of information about the U.S. until the radio script for such broadcast has been approved by the Daughters of the American Revolution. Deschler Ch 26 § 47.1.
- An amendment to require, as a condition on the availability of funds, the imposition of standards of quality or performance. Deschler Ch 26 § 59.1.
- A provision providing that none of the funds should be used unless certain procurement contracts were awarded on a formally advertised basis to the lowest responsible bidder. Deschler Ch 26 § 23.14.
- An amendment making the money available on certain contingencies that would change the lawful mode of payment. Deschler Ch 26 § 48.1.
- An amendment denying the obligation or expenditure of certain funds unless such funds were subject to audit by the Comptroller General. Deschler Ch 26 § 47.8. (A subsequent amendment that denied the use of funds not subject to audit "as provided by law" was offered and adopted.)
- A provision making certain funds for an airport available for an access road (a Federal project) provided Virginia makes available the balance of funds necessary for the construction of the road. Deschler Ch 26 § 48.7.
- A provision providing that no part of the appropriation for certain range improvements shall be expended in any national forest until contributions at least equal to such expenditures are made available by local public or private sources. Deschler Ch 26 § 48.6.
- A provision stating that no part of the funds shall be used "unless and until" approved by the Director of the Bureau of the Budget. Deschler Ch 26 § 48.3.
- A proviso that no funds shall be available for certain expenditures unless made in accordance with a budget approved by the Public Housing Commissioner. Deschler Ch 26 § 48.4.
- An amendment specifying that no funds made available may be expended until total governmental tax receipts exceed total expenditures. Deschler Ch 26 § 48.11.
- An amendment containing certification requirements and mandating certain contractual provisions as a condition on the receipt of funds. *Manual* § 1054.

§ 30. —Conditions Requiring Reports to, or Action by, Congress

Reporting to Congress as a Condition

It is legislation on a general appropriation bill in violation of clause 2 of rule XXI to require the submission of reports to a committee of Congress where existing law does not require that submission. *Manual* § 1054. Thus, an amendment to a general appropriation bill precluding the availability of funds therein unless agencies submit reports to the Committee on Appropriations—reports not required by existing law—constitutes legislation in violation of that rule. 98-1, Nov. 2, 1983, p 30496; 99-1, July 25, 1985, pp 20806, 20807.

Congressional Action as Condition

Under the more recent precedents, it is not in order by way of amendment to make the availability of funds in a general appropriation bill contingent upon subsequent congressional action. *Manual* § 1055; 90-2, June 11, 1968, p 16692; 96-1, Sept. 6, 1979, pp 23360, 23361. Such a condition changes existing law if its effect is to require a subsequent authorization which, when enacted, will automatically make funds available for expenditure without further appropriations. Such a result is contrary to the process contemplated in rule XXI whereby appropriations are dependent on prior authorization. Deschler Ch 26 § 49.2 (note). Language making the availability of funds contingent upon the enactment of authorizing legislation raises a presumption that the appropriation is then unauthorized. 98-1, Sept. 19, 1983, pp 24640, 24641. Indeed, a conditional appropriation based on enactment of authorization is a concession on the face of the language that no prior authorization exists. Deschler Ch 26 § 47.3 (note); 109-1, May 19, 2005, p 10377.

It is not in order on a general appropriation bill to direct the activities of a committee, such as to require it to promulgate regulations to limit the use of an appropriation. *Manual* § 1055. As such, an amendment to a general appropriation bill including language to direct the budget scorekeeping for amounts appropriated was held to constitute legislation and was ruled out of order under clause 2 of rule XXI. 103-1, May 26, 1993, p 11317-19.

Other conditions relative to congressional action that have been ruled out as legislation include:

- An amendment providing that no part of the funds in the bill shall be used for the enforcement of any order restricting sale of any article or commodity unless such order shall have been approved by a concurrent resolution of the Congress. Deschler Ch 26 § 49.2.
- A provision requiring that certain contracts be authorized by the appropriate legislative committees and in amounts specified by the Committees on Appropriations of the Senate and House. Deschler Ch 26 § 49.5.
- An amendment making the availability of funds in the bill contingent upon subsequent enactment of legislation containing specified findings. *Manual* § 1055.

- An amendment changing a permanent appropriation in existing law to restrict its availability until all general appropriation bills are presented to the President. *Manual* § 1055.
- An amendment limiting funds in the bill for certain peacekeeping operations unless authorized by Congress. 103-2, June 27, 1994, p 14613.
- A provision restricting certain District of Columbia funds unless appropriated by Congress where existing law allowed use without congressional approval. *Manual* § 1055.

§ 31. — Conditions Imposing Additional Duties

Where a condition in an appropriation bill or amendment thereto seeks to impose on a Federal official non-incidental duties that are different from or in addition to those already contemplated in law, the provision may be ruled out as legislative in nature. *Manual* § 1054. Thus, although it is in order on a general appropriation bill to prohibit the availability of funds therein for a certain activity, that prohibition may not be made contingent upon the performance of a new affirmative duty on the part of a Federal official. Deschler Ch 26 § 50. Other provisions that have been ruled out under this rule include:

- An amendment providing that no part of the money appropriated shall be paid to any State unless and until the Secretary of Agriculture is satisfied that such State has complied with certain conditions. Deschler Ch 26 § 50.2.
- A provision providing that no part of a certain appropriation shall be available until it is determined by the Secretary of the Interior that authorization therefor has been approved by the Congress. Deschler Ch 26 § 50.3.
- An amendment providing that none of the money appropriated shall be paid to persons in a certain category unless hereafter appointed or reappointed by the President and confirmed by the Senate. Deschler Ch 26 § 50.4.
- A provision prohibiting the use of funds to pay for services performed abroad under contract "unless the President shall have promulgated" certain security regulations. Deschler Ch 26 § 50.5.
- An amendment providing that no part of the appropriation shall be used for land acquisition for airport access roads until the Federal Aviation Administration shall have held public hearings. Deschler Ch 26 § 50.6.
- An amendment rendering an appropriation for energy conservation services contingent upon recommendations by Federal officials. Deschler Ch 26 § 50.7.
- A provision making the availability of certain funds contingent on legal determinations to be made by a Federal court and an executive department. 100-2, June 28, 1988, p 16261.
- An amendment requiring a determination of "successor agency" status. *Manual* § 1054.
- An exception to a limitation on funds requiring determinations of "equivalence" of health benefits plans. *Manual* § 1054.

§32. Language Describing, Construing, or Referring to Existing Law

Generally

It is in order in a general appropriation bill to include language descriptive of authority provided in law as long as the description is precise and does not change that authority in any respect. Deschler Ch 26 §23.1. However, language in an appropriation bill construing or interpreting existing law, although cast in the form of a limitation, is legislation and not in order. Deschler Ch 26 §24. Likewise, an amendment that does not limit or restrict the use or expenditure of funds in the bill, but that directs the way in which provisions in the bill must be interpreted or construed, is legislation. Deschler Ch 26 §25.15. The rationale underlying this rule is that a provision proposing to construe existing law is in itself a proposition of legislation and therefore not in order. *Manual* §1056; 4 Hinds §§3936-3938. Provisions that have been ruled out pursuant to this rule include:

- A provision broadening beyond existing law the definition of services to be funded by an appropriation. Deschler Ch 26 §25.8.
- A provision defining certain expenses as "nonadministrative," for purposes of making a computation. Deschler Ch 26 §§22.13, 25.4.
- A provision making appropriations available for the purchase of station wagons "without such vehicles being considered as passenger motor vehicles." Deschler Ch 26 §22.12.
- An amendment construing certain language so as to permit the withholding of funds for specific military construction projects upon a determination that elimination of such projects would not adversely affect national defense. Deschler Ch 26 §25.9.
- An amendment providing that nothing in the Act shall restrict the authority of the Secretary of Education to carry out the provisions of title VI of the Civil Rights Act of 1964. 96-2, Aug. 27, 1980, p 23535.
- A provision stating that a limitation on funds in the pending appropriation bill is to be considered a prohibition against payments to certain parties in administrative proceedings. 100-2, May 17, 1988, p 11305.
- A provision directing the Selective Service Administration to issue regulations to bring its classifications into conformance with a Supreme Court decision. *Manual* §1055.
- An amendment that expresses the sense of Congress that reductions in appropriations in other bills should reflect the proportionate reductions made in the pending bill. 101-2, Oct. 21, 1990, p 31709.

Incorporation by Reference to Existing Law

An amendment to a general appropriation bill that incorporates by reference the provisions of an existing law not otherwise applicable may be subject to a point of order. 88-1, Oct. 10, 1963, pp 19258-60. Thus a paragraph in a bill containing funds for the Corporation for Public Broadcasting to be available "in accordance with the provisions of titles VI and VII of the Civil Rights Act of 1964" was ruled out as legislation in violation of clause 2 of rule XXI, where it could not be shown that the corporation was already subject to the provisions of that law. 94-2, June 24, 1976, pp 20414, 20415. Other provisions ruled out for the same reason include:

- A provision referring to conditions imposed on certain programs in other appropriation Acts and making those conditions applicable to the funds being appropriated in the bill under consideration. Deschler Ch 26 § 22.6.
- A provision in a general appropriation bill prescribing that the provisions of a House-passed resolution "shall be the permanent law with respect thereto." Deschler Ch 26 § 22.7.

§ 33. Particular Propositions as Legislation

The prohibition of clause 2 of rule XXI against a provision changing existing law has been applied to a wide variety of proposals. A sampling of these provisions, classified by subject matter, is set out below.

Provisions Relating to Agriculture

- An amendment curtailing the use of funds for price support payments to certain persons and defining the term "person" to mean an individual, partnership, firm, joint stock company, or the like. Deschler Ch 26 § 39.10.
- An amendment providing that certain loans be exclusively for the construction and operation of generating facilities for furnishing electric energy to persons in certain rural areas. Deschler Ch 26 § 39.5.

Provisions Relating to Commerce

- A provision carrying an appropriation for all expenses of the Bureau of the Census necessary to collect, compile, analyze, and publish a sample census of business. Deschler Ch 26 § 40.5.
- A provision providing that functions necessary to the compilation of foreign trade statistics be performed in New York instead of Washington, DC. Deschler Ch 26 § 40.4.

Provisions Relating to Foreign Affairs

- A provision expressing the sense of Congress concerning the representation of the Chinese government in the United Nations. Deschler Ch 26 § 41.4.
- An amendment providing that "a reasonable amount" of the funds provided to the Organization of American States may be available for distribution in certain underdeveloped areas in the United States. Deschler Ch 26 § 41.9.

Provisions Relating to Federal Employment

- A provision permitting an executive official to delegate to an administrative officer the authority to make appointments of certain personnel. Deschler Ch 26 §45.5.
- A provision providing that the Secretary of State may, in his discretion, terminate the employment of an employee whenever he shall deem such termination necessary or advisable in the interests of the United States. Deschler Ch 26 §43.4.

Provisions Relating to Congressional Employment and Compensation

- A provision increasing or providing additional salary to Members of Congress. Deschler Ch 26 §§44.1, 44.2.
- An amendment requiring a committee to promulgate rules to limit the amount of official mail sent by Members. Deschler Ch 26 §44.10.
- A provision mandating that House offices institute a waste recycling program. 106-1, June 10, 1999, p 12513.

Provisions Relating to Housing and Public Works Programs

- A provision restricting the contract authority of the Housing and Home Finance Administrator to an amount "within the limits of appropriations made available therefor." Deschler Ch 26 §45.3.
- An appropriation for the construction of buildings for storage of certain equipment and including a stated limit of cost for construction of any such building. Deschler Ch 26 §45.7.

B. Changing Prescribed Funding

§34. In General

Generally; Mandating Expenditures

Language in a general appropriation bill is permitted where it is drafted simply as a negative restriction or limitation on the use of funds. §50, infra. Such limitations may negatively affect the allocation of funds as contemplated in existing law, but may not explicitly change statutory directions for distribution. *Manual* §1056; Deschler Ch 26 §77.2. It is in violation of clause 2 of rule XXI to include language in a general appropriation bill directing that funds therein be obligated or distributed in a manner that is contrary to existing law. *Manual* §1057. Language directing that funds in the bill shall be distributed "without regard to the provisions" of the authorizing legislation is subject to a point of order. Deschler Ch 26 §36.1.

The Committee on Appropriations may report a limitation on the availability of funds within the reported bill. However, a limitation on the obligation of funds, or a removal of an existing statutory limitation on the obligation of funds contained in existing law, is legislation and in violation of clause 2 of rule XXI. 103-1, Sept. 23, 1993, p 22203.

If existing law places a limit or cap on the total amount that may be spent on a program, language in a general appropriation bill may not direct an increase in that amount. 4 Hinds §§3865-3867. Similarly, a provision making available indefinite sums for a particular program may be ruled out as legislation in violation of clause 2 of rule XXI where existing law provides that a definite amount must be specified for that purpose in annual appropriation bills. Deschler Ch 26 §33.1. Where mandatory funding levels have been earmarked for certain programs by existing law, a provision in a general appropriation bill rendering them ineffective may be ruled out as in violation of clause 2 of rule XXI. Deschler Ch 26 §36.5. A paragraph in a general appropriation bill directing that "not less" than a specified sum be available for a certain purpose was ruled out as legislation constituting a direction to spend a minimum amount and not a negative limitation. *Manual* §1057. An amendment to a general appropriation bill denying funds therein for a program at *less* than a certain amount constitutes legislation where existing law confers upon a Federal official discretionary authority to determine minimum levels of expenditures. 95-2, July 20, 1978, p 21856. Language mandating a certain allotment of funds at "the maximum amounts authorized" has also been ruled out as legislation on an appropriation bill. Deschler Ch 26 §36.2.

Language in a general appropriation bill may not authorize the adjustment of wages of government employees or permit an increase in Members' office allowances only "if requested in writing." Also, it may not mandate reductions in various appropriations by a variable percentage calculated in relation to "overhead." *Manual* §1054. A proposal to designate an appropriation as having a special status (such as "emergency spending") within the meaning of the budget-enforcement laws is fundamentally legislative in character. *Manual* §1052.

Change in Source or Method of Funding

Where existing law authorizes appropriations out of a special fund for a particular purpose, it is not in order in an appropriation bill to direct that the money be taken from the general funds of the Treasury for that purpose. Deschler Ch 26 §§35.1, 35.2. Thus, language in a bill providing funds for an agricultural project, for which funding had been authorized from the receipts of timber sales and not from appropriated funds, was ruled out as legislation in violation of clause 2 of rule XXI. Deschler Ch 26 §35.3. The language in an appropriation bill appropriating funds in the Federal Aid

Highway Trust Fund for expenses of forest roads and trails was held to be legislation and not in order where no authorization existed for the expenditure from that trust fund for those proposed purposes. Deschler Ch 26 § 28.2. A provision providing that airport funding be derived from a certain source, thereby changing the source and method of funding under existing law, was held to constitute legislation. 106-1, June 23, 1999, p 14002.

Language in a general appropriation bill that substitutes borrowing authority in lieu of a direct appropriation is subject to a point of order if contrary to existing law. Deschler Ch 26 § 35.4.

Changing Allotment Formulas; Setting Priorities

A provision in a general appropriation bill that changes the legislative formula governing the allotment of funds to recipients is legislation on an appropriation bill in violation of clause 2 of rule XXI. *Manual* § 1056; Deschler Ch 26 § 36.10. It is not in order in a general appropriation bill to establish priorities to be followed in the obligation or expenditure of the funds where such priorities are not found in existing law. Thus, a proviso specifying that an appropriation for veterans' job training be obligated on the basis of those veterans unemployed the longest was conceded to be legislation where existing law did not require that allocation of funds, and was ruled out as in violation of clause 2 of rule XXI. Deschler Ch 26 § 36.17. Similarly, where existing law establishes priorities to be followed by an executive official in the distribution of funds, an amendment to an appropriation bill requiring that those funds be distributed in accordance with such priorities may under some circumstances be regarded as constituting a stronger mandate as to the use of those funds and ruled out as a modification of the authorizing law, and therefore out of order. Deschler Ch 26 § 23.8.

However, where existing law prescribes a formula for the allocation of funds among several categories, an amendment merely reducing the amount earmarked for one of the categories is not legislation, as long as it does not textually change the statutory formula. *Manual* § 1057.

§ 35. Affecting Funds in Other Acts

Generally

Language in a general appropriation bill that is applicable to funds appropriated in another Act may constitute legislation under clause 2 of rule XXI. Deschler Ch 26 § 30.10. Thus, an amendment to an appropriation bill seeking to change a limitation on a previous appropriation bill may be held to be legislation and not in order. Deschler Ch 26 § 27.26.

Rescissions

Under clause 2(b) of rule XXI, the Committee on Appropriations may report in a general appropriation bill ''rescissions of appropriations contained in appropriation Acts.'' However, under clause 2(c) of rule XXI, an amendment to a general appropriation bill may not change existing law, as by rescinding an appropriation contained in another Act or by rescinding contract authority. *Manual* § 1052; 103-1, May 26, 1993, p 11310.

§ 36. Transfer of Funds— Within Same Bill

A provision in a general appropriation bill that authorizes an official to transfer funds among appropriation accounts in the bill changes existing law in violation of clause 2 of rule XXI by including language conferring new authority. However, direct transfers of appropriations within the confines of the same bill are normally considered in order. 7 Cannon § 1468; Deschler Ch 26 § 29. Such a direct transfer may not include legislative language, such as requiring the approval of an official. In addition, the transfer of an appropriation for a purpose authorized to be carried out by a specified agency may not be transferred to another agency, even within the same bill. The following illustrations may clarify these distinctions:

In Order

- $500,000 is hereby transferred from the Capital Improvement and Maintenance appropriation to the State and Private Forestry appropriation.

Not in Order

- Funds appropriated in title III of this Act for the Department of Defense Pilot Mentor-Protege Program may be transferred to any other appropriation contained in this Act.
- Not to exceed 1 percent of any discretionary funds (pursuant to the Balanced Budget and Emergency Deficit Control Act of 1985, as amended) that are appropriated for the Department of Education in this Act may be transferred between appropriations.
- $500,000 shall be transferred from the Capital Improvement and Maintenance appropriation to the State and Private Forestry appropriation upon approval of the Director of the Office of Management and Budget.
- $500,000 for repair of the official residence of the Vice President shall be transferred from the General Services Administration [only agency authorized by law to carry out such repair] to any department or agency for expenses of carrying out such activity.

A provision in an appropriation bill may permit certain funds to be available ''interchangeably'' for expenditure for various authorized purposes. Deschler Ch 26 § 29.8. Similarly, an amendment providing that a particular authorized project should be financed out of ''any available unallocated funds contained in this act'' was held to be in order. Deschler Ch 26 § 29.10.

See also § 63, infra, for a discussion of amendments permitted to be offered en bloc under clause 2(f) of rule XXI that only transfer appropriations among objects in the bill.

§ 37. —Transfer of Previously Appropriated Funds

Language in an appropriation bill that is applicable to funds appropriated in another Act constitutes legislation in violation of clause 2(b) of rule XXI (Deschler Ch 26 § 30.10) and also may constitute a reappropriation of unexpended balances in violation of clause 2(a) (Deschler Ch 26 § 30.20). For a discussion of reappropriations generally, see § 60, infra. Thus, an amendment to an appropriation bill proposing the transfer of funds previously appropriated in another appropriation bill is legislation. Deschler Ch 26 § 30.1. A point of order will lie against language that attempts to transfer such funds from one department to another. Deschler Ch 26 §§ 30.16, 30.25.

§ 38. Making Funds Available Before, or Beyond, Authorized Period

Generally; Availability of Balances

It is provided by statute that the balance of an appropriation limited for obligation to a definite period is available only for payment of expenses properly incurred during the period of availability or to complete contracts properly made within that period of availability. 31 USC § 1502. As such, it is not in order in a general appropriation bill to provide that funds therein are to be available beyond the fiscal year covered by the bill unless the authorizing law permits that availability. Deschler Ch 26 §§ 32.1, 32.10. Such language is held to ''change existing law'' in violation of clause 2 of rule XXI because it extends the use of the funds beyond the period permitted by law. Deschler Ch 26 § 32.11.

By statute, an appropriation in a regular, annual appropriation Act may be construed to be permanent or available continuously only if the appropriation expressly provides that it is available after the fiscal year covered by the law, or unless the appropriation is for certain purposes, such as public buildings. 31 USC § 1301. Amounts appropriated to construct public buildings remain available until completion of the work. When a building is completed and outstanding liabilities for the construction are paid, balances remaining revert immediately to the Treasury. 31 USC § 1307.

Provisions in appropriation bills that have been ruled out under clause 2 of rule XXI on a point of order include:

- A provision appropriating funds to collect and publish certain statistics on voting, to be available until the end of the next fiscal year. Deschler Ch 26 § 32.6.
- A provision making fees and royalties collected pursuant to law available beyond the current fiscal year. Deschler Ch 26 § 32.9.
- A provision appropriating funds for a census available beyond the time for which it was originally authorized. Deschler Ch 26 § 22.2.
- A provision appropriating funds for the Migratory Bird Conservation Fund for the current year ''and each fiscal year thereafter'' from the sale of stamps. Deschler Ch 26 § 32.8.
- A provision appropriating funds for the Tennessee Valley Authority to be available for the payment of obligations chargeable against prior appropriations. Deschler Ch 26 § 32.16.

Funds ''To Be Immediately Available''

Language in an appropriation bill stating that the funds shall be immediately available—that is, before the start of the fiscal year covered by the bill—is subject to a point of order. A prior ruling permitting immediate availability has been superseded by more recent rulings proscribing such immediate availability. *Manual* § 1052; 7 Cannon §§ 1119, 1120. Making funds available in an earlier fiscal period also may have implications under the Congressional Budget Act of 1974.

§ 39. Funds ''To Remain Available Until Expended''

Generally

Authorization laws or statutes sometimes provide that appropriated funds are ''to remain available until expended.'' Such language is permitted where existing law authorizes the inclusion of language extending the availability of funds for the purpose stated in that law. *Manual* § 1052. Conversely, where the authorizing statute does not permit funds to remain available until expended or without regard to fiscal year limitation, the inclusion of such availability in a general appropriation bill has been held to constitute legislation in violation of clause 2 of rule XXI. Deschler Ch 26 §§ 32.1, 32.2, 32.10. However, language that certain funds be ''available until expended'' may be included where other existing law can be interpreted to permit that availability. Thus, a provision in a general appropriation bill that funds therein for the construction of the west front of the U.S. Capitol shall ''remain available until expended'' was held not to constitute legislation in violation of clause 2 of rule XXI, where an existing law provided that funds for public building construction shall remain available until the completion of the work. Deschler Ch 26 § 32.1.

Authority of Committee on Appropriations to Confine Expenditure to Current Fiscal Year

Although authorizing legislation sometimes provides that funds authorized therein shall "remain available until expended," the Committee on Appropriations has never been required, when appropriating funds for those purposes, to specify that such funds *must* remain available until expended. Indeed, the Committee on Appropriations often confines the availability of funds to the current fiscal year, regardless of the limit of availability contained in the authorization, and it may do so absent a clear showing that the language in question was intended to require appropriations to be made available until expended. Deschler Ch 26 § 32.21.

§ 40. Reimbursements of Appropriated Funds

If not authorized by existing law, language in a general appropriation bill providing for the use of funds generated from reimbursement, repayment, or refund, rather than from a direct appropriation, may be ruled out as legislation under clause 2 of rule XXI. Deschler Ch 26 § 38.1. Provisions in appropriation bills that have been ruled out under this rule include requirements:

- That "all refunds, repayments, or other credits on account of funds disbursed under this head shall be credited to the appropriation." Deschler Ch 26 § 38.1.
- That appropriations contained in the Act may be reimbursed from the proceeds of sales of certain material and supplies. Deschler Ch 26 § 38.2.
- That any part of the appropriation for salaries and expenses be reimbursed from commissary earnings. Deschler Ch 26 § 38.4.
- That repayment of Federal appropriations for a certain airport be made from income derived from operations. Deschler Ch 26 § 38.10.
- That money received by the United States in connection with any irrigation project constructed by the Federal government shall be covered into the general fund until such fund has been reimbursed. Deschler Ch 26 § 38.11.
- That receipts from non-Federal agencies representing reimbursement for travel expenses of certain employees performing advisory functions to such agencies be deposited in the Treasury to the credit of the appropriation. Deschler Ch 26 § 38.13.
- That certain advances be reimbursable during a fixed period under rules and regulations prescribed by an executive officer. Deschler Ch 26 § 38.14.

C. Changing Executive Duties or Authority

§ 41. In General; Requiring Duties or Determinations

Generally

Where an amendment to or language in a general appropriation bill explicitly places new duties on officers of the government or implicitly requires them to make investigations, compile evidence, or make judgments and determinations not otherwise required of them by law, then it assumes the character of legislation under clause 2 of rule XXI and is subject to a point of order. *Manual* § 1054; 4 Hinds §§ 3854-3859; Deschler Ch 26 § 52. The extra duties that may invalidate an amendment as being ''legislation'' are duties not now required by law. The fact that they may be presently in effect, as required for present and prior years in annual appropriation Acts, does not protect an amendment from a point of order under clause 2 of rule XXI. Deschler Ch 26 § 63.7 (note). The point of order will lie against language requiring new determinations by Federal officials whether or not State officials administering the Federal funds in question routinely make such determinations. Deschler Ch 26 § 52.33. Thus, in a general appropriation bill, if not already mandated by existing law, an executive official may not be required:

- To make substantial findings in determining the extent of availability of funds. Deschler Ch 26 § 59.19.
- To make evaluations of propriety and effectiveness. *Manual* § 1054.
- To include information in the annual budget on transfers of appropriations. Deschler Ch 26 § 52.10.
- To make determinations, in implementing a personnel reduction program, as to which individual employees shall be retained. Deschler Ch 26 § 22.17.
- To implement certain conditions and formulas in determining amounts to be charged as rent for public housing units. Deschler Ch 26 § 52.20.

Approval or Certification Duties

Where existing law authorizes the availability of funds for certain expenses when certified by an executive official, language in a general appropriation bill containing funds for that purpose to be accounted for solely upon certification may be held in order as not constituting a change in existing law. 93-2, June 18, 1974, pp 19715, 19716. For example, appropriations for traveling expenses at meetings ''considered necessary'' in the exercise of the agency's discretion for the efficient discharge of its responsibilities were held authorized by a law permitting inclusion of such language in the bill. Deschler Ch 26 § 52.28. However, language in a general appropriation bill authorizing the expenditure of funds on the approval of an executive official and on a ''certificate of necessity for confidential military purposes'' was held to change existing law and was ruled out in violation of clause 2 of rule XXI when the Committee on Appropriations failed to cite statutory authority for that method of payment. Deschler Ch 26 § 22.19. Even a proviso that certain vouchers ''shall be sufficient'' for expenditure from the appropriation has been ruled out as legislation in violation of clause 2 of rule XXI. Deschler Ch 26 § 22.20.

Duty to Submit Reports

It is not in order on a general appropriation bill to require an executive official to submit reports not required by existing law. 7 Cannon § 1442. For example, a provision requiring the Commissioner of Indian Affairs to report to Congress all interchanges of appropriations was ruled out as legislation. Deschler Ch 26 § 52.9.

§ 42. Burden of Proof

Generally

The burden of proof is on the proponent of an amendment to a general appropriation bill to show that a proposed executive duty or determination is required by existing law, and the mere recitation that it is imposed pursuant to existing law and regulations, absent a citation to the law imposing that responsibility, is not sufficient to overcome a point of order that the amendment constitutes legislation. *Manual* § 1044a; Deschler Ch 26 § 22.25.

Determinations Incidental to Other Executive Duties

If a proposed executive determination is not specifically required by existing law, but is related to other executive duties, then the proponent has the burden of proving that it is merely incidental thereto. Thus, language in a general appropriation bill in the form of a conditional limitation requiring determinations by Federal officials may be held to change existing law in violation of clause 2 of rule XXI, unless the Committee on Appropriations can show that the new duties are merely incidental to functions already required by law and do not involve substantive new determinations. Deschler Ch 26 § 52.

§ 43. Altering Executive Authority or Discretion

Generally

A proposition in a general appropriation bill that interferes with authority that has been conferred by law on an executive official ''changes existing law'' under clause 2 of rule XXI. 4 Hinds § 3846; Deschler Ch 26 § 51.3. A proposition that significantly alters the discretion conferred on the official also ''changes existing law'' within the meaning of that rule. *Manual* § 1054; 4 Hinds §§ 3848-3852; 7 Cannon § 1437. Thus, where existing law authorized the expenditure of funds for a program under broad supervisory powers given to an executive official, provisions in an appropriation bill that impose conditions affecting both the exercise of those powers and the use of funds may be ruled out as legislation. Deschler Ch 26 § 51.4.

Language in a general appropriation bill conferring discretionary authority on an executive official where none exists under existing law is subject to a point of order under clause 2 of rule XXI. Deschler Ch 26 § 55.1. A proposition having the purpose of enlarging, rather than restricting, an official's discretion also may be viewed as changing existing law. Deschler Ch 26 § 51. Language granting discretionary authority to the Secretary of the Army to use funds for purposes ''desirable'' in expediting military production was held to be legislation and not in order. Deschler Ch 26 § 59.7.

A provision in a general appropriation bill requiring the performance of a duty by a Federal official which, under existing law is entirely discretionary, constitutes legislation in violation of clause 2 of rule XXI. Deschler Ch 26 § 59.20. Although it is in order on a general appropriation bill to limit the availability of funds therein for part of an authorized purpose (§ 52, infra), language that restricts not the funds but the discretionary authority of a Federal official administering those funds may be ruled out as legislation. *Manual* § 1054; Deschler Ch 26 § 51.14.

Earmarking Funds as Affecting Executive Discretion

The earmarking of funds for a particular item from a lump-sum appropriation may constitute a limitation on the discretion of the executive charged with allotment of the lump sum and thus be subject to a point of order under clause 2 of rule XXI. 7 Cannon § 1452; Deschler Ch 26 § 51.5. Language earmarking some of the appropriations for the Veterans' Administration for a special study of its compensation and pension programs was conceded to be legislation and held not in order. Deschler Ch 26 § 55.12.

§ 44. Mandating Studies or Investigations

Language in a general appropriation bill describing an investigation that may be undertaken with funds in the bill at the discretion of an official upon whom existing law imposes a general investigative responsibility does not constitute legislation and is not in violation of clause 2 of rule XXI. 93-2, Apr. 9, 1974, pp 10208, 10209. However, where existing law gives an agency discretion to undertake an investigation, language in a general appropriation bill that requires the agency to make the investigation is legislation. Deschler Ch 26 §51.7. Although an executive official may have broad investigative responsibilities under existing law, it may not be in order in a general appropriation bill to impose a duty to undertake a specific additional study. 93-2, Apr. 9, 1974, pp 10205, 10206.

The mere requirement in a general appropriation bill that an executive officer be the recipient of information at one time was not considered as imposing any additional burdens. 90-2, June 11, 1968, p 16712. In the 105th Congress, clauses 2(b) and 2(c) of rule XXI were amended to treat as legislation a provision that conditions the availability of funds on whether certain information not required by existing law has been "made known" to an executive official, thus superseding 7 Cannon §1695. *Manual* §1054. In addition, language imposing new responsibilities on Federal officials beyond merely being the recipients of information may constitute legislation in violation of clause 2 of rule XXI. 95-1, June 17, 1977, p 19699. Thus, in 1974, language in a general appropriation bill was ruled out as legislation when the Committee on Appropriations conceded that agencies funded by the bill would be required to examine extraneous documentary evidence—including hearing transcripts—in addition to the language of the law itself, to determine the purposes for which the funds had been appropriated. 93-2, June 21, 1974, pp 20612, 20613.

§45. Granting or Changing Contract Authority

Granting Authority

Language in a general appropriation bill authorizing a governmental agency to enter into contracts is legislation in violation of clause 2 of rule XXI if such authority is not provided for in existing law. 4 Hinds §§3868-3870; Deschler Ch 26 §37.4. Although under existing law it may be in order to appropriate money for a certain purpose, it may not be in order in a general appropriation bill to grant authority to incur obligations and enter into contracts in furtherance of that purpose. Deschler Ch 26 §§37.3, 37.4. Thus, language authorizing the Secretary of the Interior to enter into contracts for the acquisition of land and making future appropriations available to liquidate those obligations was held to be legislation on an appropriation bill and not in order. Deschler Ch 26 §37.8.

Waiving Contract Law

Language in a general appropriation bill that waives the requirements of existing law as to when certain contracts may be entered into may be ruled out as legislation in violation of clause 2 of rule XXI. Deschler Ch

26 § 37.14. Thus, language providing that contracts for supplies or services may be made by an agency without regard to laws relating to advertising or competitive bidding was conceded to be legislation on an appropriation bill and held not in order. Deschler Ch 26 § 34.1.

Restricting Contract Authority

A provision in a general appropriation bill changing existing law by restricting the contract authority of an executive official may be ruled out on a point of order as legislation under clause 2 of rule XXI. Deschler Ch 26 § 45.3. This is so notwithstanding clause 1(b) of rule X, which gives the Committee on Appropriations jurisdiction over rescissions of appropriations (as distinguished from rescission of contract authority) (Deschler Ch 26 § 24.4 (note)) and clause 2(b) of rule XXI, which permits rescissions of appropriations contained in appropriation Acts. In one instance, an amendment requiring the Civil Aeronautics Authority to award contracts to the highest bidder only after previously advertising for sealed bids was ruled out as legislation. Deschler Ch 26 § 46.3. Language authorizing an agency to enter into contracts for certain purposes in an amount not to exceed $7 million was conceded to be legislation on an appropriation bill and was ruled out absent citation to an existing law authorizing inclusion of such limitation. Deschler Ch 26 § 37.12. Language in an appropriation bill seeking to reduce or rescind contract authority contained in a previous appropriation bill has also been ruled out as legislation changing existing law. Deschler Ch 26 §§ 22.14, 24.4.

The rulings in this section should be considered in the light of section 401(a) of the Congressional Budget Act, which precludes consideration of measures reported by legislative committees providing new contract authority, new authority to incur certain indebtedness, or new credit authority, unless the measure also provides that such authority is to be effective "only to such extent or in the amounts provided in advance in appropriation Acts." Since the adoption of this law, language properly limiting the contractual authority of an agency, if specifically permitted by law, would not render that language subject to a point of order under clause 2 of rule XXI. Deschler Ch 26 § 37.

D. The Holman Rule; Retrenchments

§46. In General; Retrenchment of Expenditures

Generally

Clause 2(b) of rule XXI, which precludes the use of language changing existing law in a general appropriation bill, makes an exception for ''germane provisions that retrench expenditures by the reduction of amounts of money covered by the bill'' as reported. This exception is referred to as the Holman rule, having been named for the Member who first suggested it in 1876, William Holman of Indiana. *Manual* §1038.

Decisions under the Holman rule have been rare in the modern practice of the House. *Manual* §1062. The rule applies to general appropriation bills only and is not applicable to funds other than those appropriated in the pending bill. 7 Cannon §§1482, 1525. In 1983, the House narrowed the Holman rule exception to apply only to retrenchments reducing the dollar amounts of money covered by the bill. *Manual* §1062.

Retrenchments and Limitations Distinguished

A distinction should be noted between retrenchments offered under the criteria of the Holman rule and ''limitations'' on appropriation bills, discussed in §§50-59a, infra. Under the Holman rule, a provision that is admittedly ''legislative'' in nature is nevertheless held to fall outside the general prohibition against such provisions, because it reduces the funds in the bill. The limitations discussed in later sections are not ''legislation'' and are permitted on the theory that Congress is not bound to appropriate funds for every authorized purpose. Deschler Ch 26 §4.

Under the modern practice, the Holman rule does not apply to limiting language that does not involve a reduction of dollar amounts in the bill. An amendment that does not show a reduction on its face and that is merely speculative is not in order under the rule. *Manual* §1062.

The words ''amounts of money covered by the bill'' in the rule refer to the amounts specifically appropriated by the bill, but as long as a provision calls for an obvious reduction at some point during the fiscal year, it is in order under the Holman rule even if the reduction takes place in the future in an amount actually determined when the reduction takes place (for example, by formula). *Manual* §1062. Language held in order as effectuating a retrenchment has included a proposition—legislative in form—providing that total appropriations in the bill be reduced by a specified amount. Deschler Ch 26 §4.5.

It has been said that the Holman rule should be strictly construed in order to avoid the admission of ineligible legislative riders under the guise of a retrenchment. 7 Cannon § 1510.

§ 47. Germaneness Requirements; Application to Funds in Other Bills

The Holman rule, although permitting certain retrenchment provisions as an exception to the prohibition against legislation in appropriation bills, requires that such provisions be germane. *Manual* § 1038. An amendment providing that appropriations "herein and heretofore made" be reduced by a reduction of certain employees was held to be legislative and not germane to the bill, because it went to funds other than those carried therein, and was therefore not within the Holman rule exception. *Manual* § 1062. An amendment proposing to change existing law by repealing part of a retirement Act was held not germane and not in order under the Holman rule. Deschler Ch 26 § 5.15.

§ 48. Reporting Retrenchment Provisions

At one time, retrenching provisions in general appropriation bills were reported by the legislative committees of the House. 7 Cannon § 1561. In 1983, the Holman rule was amended to eliminate the separate authority of legislative committees to report amendments retrenching expenditures. The new rule permits legislative committees to merely recommend such retrenchments to the Committee on Appropriations for discretionary inclusion in the reported bill. *Manual* §§ 1038, 1062.

§ 49. Floor Consideration; Who May Offer

Under the earlier practice, retrenching amendments to general appropriation bills could be offered during the reading of the bill for amendment in the Committee of the Whole. In 1983, rule XXI was narrowed to permit the consideration of retrenchment amendments only when reading of the bill has been completed and only if the Committee of the Whole does not adopt a motion to rise and report the bill back to the House. *Manual* § 1040; see generally § 64, infra.

IV. Limitations on General Appropriation Bills

§50. In General; When in Order

Generally

Although general appropriation bills may not contain legislation, limitations may validly be imposed under certain circumstances, where the effect is not to change existing law. Deschler Ch 26 §1. The doctrine of limitations on a general appropriation bill has emerged over the years primarily from rulings in the Committee of the Whole. Deschler Ch 26 §22.26. The basic theory of limitations is that, just as the House may decline to appropriate for a purpose authorized by law, it may by limitation prohibit the use of the money for part of the purpose while appropriating the remainder of it. The limitation cannot change existing law but may negatively restrict the use of funds for an authorized purpose or project. Deschler Ch 26 §64.

The following tests are applied to determine whether language in an appropriation bill or amendment thereto constitutes a permissible limitation:

- Does the limitation apply solely to the appropriation under consideration?

  Note: A limitation may be attached only to the appropriation under consideration and may not be made applicable to moneys appropriated in other Acts. See §59, infra.

- Does it operate beyond the fiscal year for which the appropriation is made?

  Note: A limitation must apply solely to the fiscal year(s) covered by the bill and may not be made a permanent provision of law. 4 Hinds §3929.

- Is the limitation coupled with a phrase applying to official functions; and, if so, does the phrase give affirmative directions in fact or in effect, even if not in form?

  Note: A proposition to establish affirmative directions for an executive officer constitutes legislation and is not in order on a general appropriation bill. 4 Hinds §3854.

- Is it accompanied by a phrase which might be construed to impose additional duties? Does it curtail or extend, modify, or alter existing powers or duties or terminate old or confer new ones?

  Note: A limitation that changes the duties imposed by law on an executive officer in the expenditure of appropriated funds is not in order. See §54, infra.

- Is the limitation authorized in existing law for the period of the limitation?

  Note: Under clause 2(c) of rule XXI, an amendment proposing a limitation not authorized in existing law for the period of the limitation is not in order during the reading of the bill by paragraph. *Manual* §1039.

7 Cannon §1706; Deschler Ch 26 §64.

A restriction on authority to incur obligations contained in a general appropriation bill is legislative in nature and is not a limitation on use of funds in the bill. *Manual* § 1053.

Certain amendments proposing limitations are in order only after the reading of the bill for amendment has been completed and a privileged motion to rise and report by the Majority Leader or a designee is either not offered or is rejected. Clause 2(d) of rule XXI permits consideration at this time of amendments proposing limitations not contained or authorized in existing law or proposing germane amendments that retrench expenditures. For a discussion of retrenchment of expenditures, see § 46, supra.

Construction of Rule; Burden of Proof

The doctrine permitting limitations on a general appropriation bill is strictly construed. Deschler Ch 26 § 80.5. The language of the limitation must not be such as, when fairly construed, would change existing law (4 Hinds §§ 3976-3983) or justify an executive officer in assuming an intent to change existing law (4 Hinds § 3984; 7 Cannon § 1707). The language of clause 2(c) of rule XXI, which permits limitation amendments during the reading of a bill by paragraphs only if authorized by existing law, is likewise strictly construed. It applies only where existing law requires or permits the inclusion of limiting language in an appropriation Act, and not merely where the limitation is alleged to be "consistent with existing law." *Manual* § 1043.

The limitation must apply to a specific purpose, or object, or amount of appropriation. If a proposed limitation goes beyond the traditionally permissible objectives of a limitation, as for example by restricting discretion in the timing of the expenditure of funds rather than restricting their use for a specific object or purpose, the Chair may rule that the amendment constitutes legislation in the absence of a convincing argument by the proponent that the amendment does not change existing law. Deschler Ch 26 § 80.5.

As a general proposition, whenever a limitation is accompanied by the words "unless," "except," "until," "if," or the like, there is ground to view the provision with the suspicion that it may be legislation. In case of doubt as to its ultimate effect, the doubt should be resolved on the conservative side. Deschler Ch 26 § 52.2. The limitation may not be accompanied by language stating a motive or purpose in carrying it out. Deschler Ch 26 § 66.4. Where terms used in a purported limitation are challenged because of their ambiguity or indefiniteness, the burden is on the proponent to show that no new duties would arise in the course of applying its terms. Deschler Ch 26 § 57.17 (note).

Effecting Policy Changes

Although a limitation on a general appropriation bill may not involve changes to existing law or affirmatively restrict executive discretion, its simple denial of the use of funds may have the effect of changing administrative policy and still be in order. Deschler Ch 26 § 51.15. For example, during consideration of an army appropriation bill, an amendment was allowed that provided that the funds appropriated could not be used for compulsory military training in certain schools. The Chair noted that the amendment "simply refuses to appropriate for purposes that are authorized by law and for which Congress may or may not appropriate as it sees fit," and that while the amendment did have the effect of changing a policy of the War Department, "a change of policy can be made by the failure of Congress to appropriate for an authorized object." 7 Cannon § 1694.

Limitations Relating to Tax and Tariff Measures

Tax and tariff measures fall within the jurisdiction of the Committee on Ways and Means under clause 1(t) of rule X. *Manual* § 741. Under clause 5(a) of rule XXI, such measures may not be reported by any committee not having jurisdiction thereof. In the 108th Congress, clause 5(a) was amended to include in the definition of a tax or tariff measure an amendment proposing a limitation on funds in a general appropriation bill for the administration of a tax or tariff. This change established a different standard for determining a violation of this rule by an amendment to a reported general appropriation bill than for a provision in the bill itself. For an amendment, the Chair needs to find merely a textual relationship between the amendment and the administration of a tax or tariff. 108-1, Jan. 7, 2003, p 12. For a provision reported in the bill, the Chair must find that the provision impacts revenue collections or tax statuses or liabilities inevitably and with certainty. *Manual* § 1066. For example, a limitation on the use of funds reported in such a bill may be held to violate this clause where the limitation has the effect of requiring the collection of revenues not otherwise provided for by law. *Manual* § 1066.

§ 51. Limitations on Amount Appropriated

Generally

A negative restriction on the use of funds above a certain amount in an appropriation bill is in order as a limitation. 91-1, July 30, 1969, p 21471. As long as a limitation on the use of funds restricts the expenditure of Federal funds carried in the bill without changing existing law, the limitation is in order, even if the Federal funds in question are commingled with non-Federal funds that would have to be accounted for separately in carrying out the limitation. *Manual* § 1053.

"Not To Exceed" Limitations

Language that an expenditure "is not to exceed" a certain amount is permissible. Deschler Ch 26 § 67.36. However, the fact that funds in a general appropriation bill are included in the form of a "not to exceed" limitation does not necessarily preclude a point of order under clause 2(a) of rule XXI that the funds are not authorized by law. *Manual* § 1045.

Ceilings on Total Expenditures

Many limitations on funding that are offered to general appropriation bills apply to only one of the agencies covered by the bill. However, a limitation may be drafted in such a way as to place a ceiling on the total amount to be expended by all agencies covered by the bill. Deschler Ch 26 §§ 80.1, 80.2.

Spending "Floors"

Precedents holding in order negative restrictions on the use of funds must be distinguished from cases where an amendment, though cast in the form of a limitation, can be interpreted to require the spending of *more* money. For example, an amendment prohibiting the use of funds to keep fewer than a certain number of people employed is not in order. A "floor" on employment levels is tantamount to an affirmative direction to hire no fewer than a specified number of employees and would be subject to a point of order as legislation. Deschler Ch 26 § 51.15 (note). That point of order will also lie against an amendment requiring not less than a certain sum to be used for a particular purpose where existing law does not mandate such expenditure. *Manual* § 1057.

§ 52. Limitations on Particular Uses

Generally

An amendment prohibiting the use of funds in a general appropriation bill for a certain purpose is in order, although the availability of funds for that purpose is authorized by law. Deschler Ch 26 § 64.1. Such limitations are in order even though contracts may be left unsatisfied thereby. Deschler Ch 26 § 64.25. An amendment to a general appropriation bill that is strictly limited to funds appropriated in the bill, and that is negative and restrictive in character and prohibits certain uses of the funds, is in order as a limitation even though its imposition will change the present distribution of funds and require incidental duties on the part of those administering the funds.

Deschler Ch 26 §67.19. Thus, it has been held in order in a general appropriation bill to deny the use of funds:

- To formulate or carry out tobacco programs. 95-1, June 20, 1977, p 19882.
- To pay certain rewards. 96-1, July 13, 1979, p 18451.
- To implement any plan to invade North Vietnam. Deschler Ch 26 §70.1.
- To operate and maintain facilities where intoxicating beverages are sold or dispensed. Deschler Ch 26 §70.4.
- To pay government employees a larger wage than that paid for the same work in private industry. 7 Cannon §1591.
- To pay for work on which naval prisoners were employed in preference to registered laborers and mechanics. 7 Cannon §1646.
- To pay for salaries or compensation for legal services in connection with any suit to enjoin labor unions from striking. 7 Cannon §1638.
- To pay for agriculture commodity programs under which payments to any single farmer would exceed a certain dollar amount. Deschler Ch 26 §67.33.
- To expand court facilities at Flint, Michigan. Deschler Ch 26 §69.6.
- To disseminate market information over government-owned or government-leased wires serving privately owned newspapers, radio, or television. Deschler Ch 26 §67.9.

Partial Restrictions

An amendment to a general appropriation bill that restricts the use of money in the bill to a part of an authorized project is in order though the bill would otherwise permit full funding of the authorization. 91-1, July 22, 1969, p 20329. Although it is not in order as an amendment to a general appropriation bill to directly restrict the discretionary authority of a Federal agency (§53, infra), it is permissible to limit the availability of funds in the bill for part of an authorized purpose while appropriating the remainder. *Manual* §1053. In the 95th Congress, the Chair indicated that an amendment to a general appropriation bill negatively restricting funding therein for part of a discretionary activity authorized by law would be in order if no new affirmative duties or determinations were thereby required. 95-2, June 9, 1978, p 16996.

Restrictions Relating to Agency Regulations

It is in order on a general appropriation bill to deny the use of funds to carry out an existing agency regulation. Deschler Ch 26 §64.28. Thus, an amendment providing that no part of a lump sum shall be used to promulgate or enforce certain rules or regulations precisely described in the amendment was held to be a proper limitation restricting the availability of funds and in order. Deschler Ch 26 §79.7. The fact that the regulation for which funds are denied may have been promulgated pursuant to court order and pursuant to constitutional provisions is an argument on the merits of the amendment and does not render it legislative in nature. Deschler Ch 26 § 64.28.

§ 53. Interference with Executive Discretion

Assuming that it does not change existing law, a negative restriction on the availability of funds for a specified purpose in a general appropriation bill may be a proper limitation even though it indirectly interferes with an executive official's discretionary authority by denying the use of funds. Deschler Ch 26 § 64.26. The limitation may in fact amount to a change in policy, but if the limitation is merely a negative restriction on use of funds, it will normally be allowed. 7 Cannon § 1694; Deschler Ch 26 § 51. Thus, it is in order on a general appropriation bill to provide that no part, or not more than a specified amount, of an appropriation shall be used in a certain way, even though executive discretion be thereby negatively restricted. 4 Hinds § 3968; Deschler Ch 26 § 51.9.

On the other hand, it is not in order, under the guise of a limitation, to affirmatively interfere with executive discretion by coupling a restriction on the payment of funds with a positive direction to perform certain duties contrary to existing law. Deschler Ch 26 § 51.12. For example, an amendment prohibiting funds from being used to handle parcel post at less than attributable cost was ruled out on the point of order that its effect would directly interfere with the Postal Rate Commission's quasi-discretionary authority to establish postal rates under guidelines in law. Deschler Ch 26 § 51.22.

The point of order lies against language enlarging or granting new discretionary authority as well as against language curtailing executive discretion. An amendment in the form of a limitation providing that no part of the appropriated funds shall be paid to any State unless the Secretary of Agriculture is satisfied that the State has complied with certain conditions was held to be legislation imposing new discretionary authority on a Federal official. Deschler Ch 26 § 52.25.

§ 54. Imposing Duties or Requiring Determinations

Generally; Imposing Executive Duties

Although it is in order in a general appropriation bill to limit the use of funds for an activity authorized by law, the House may not, under the guise of a limitation in the bill, impose additional burdens and duties on an executive officer. Such a provision may be ruled out as legislation on a general appropriation bill in violation of clause 2 of rule XXI. *Manual*

§ 1054. Of course, the application of any limitation on an appropriation bill places some minimal extra duties on Federal officials, who, if nothing else, must determine whether a particular use of funds is prohibited by the limitation; but when an amendment, while curtailing certain uses of funds carried in the bill, explicitly places new duties on officers of the government or inevitably requires them to make investigations, compile evidence, discern the motives or intent of individuals, or make judgments not otherwise required of them by law, then it assumes the character of legislation and is subject to a point of order. Deschler Ch 26 § 52.4.

Requiring Executive Determinations

A restriction on the use of funds in a general appropriation bill which requires a Federal official to make a substantive determination not required by any law applicable to such official's authority, thereby requiring new investigations not required by law, is legislation in violation of clause 2 of rule XXI. Deschler Ch 26 § 52.38. Thus, it is not in order to require Federal officials, in determining the extent of availability of funds, to make substantial findings not required by existing law, or to make evaluations of propriety and effectiveness not required to be made by existing law. *Manual* § 1054. Language requiring new determinations by Federal officials is subject to a point of order regardless of whether or not State officials administering the Federal funds in question routinely make such determinations. Deschler Ch 26 § 61.12.

On the other hand, if the determinations required by the language are already required by law, no point of order lies. For example, an amendment denying funds to rehire certain Federal employees engaged in a strike in violation of Federal law was held in order as a limitation not requiring new determinations on the part of Federal officials administering those funds, because existing law and a court order enjoining the strike already imposed an obligation on the administering officials to enforce the law. Deschler Ch 26 § 74.6.

Impermissible Duties or Determinations

Set out below are provisions that have been ruled out under clause 2 of rule XXI as imposing new duties or requiring new determinations not found in existing law:

- An amendment proposing a reduction of expenditures through an apportionment procedure authorized by law, but requiring such reduction to be made ''without impairing national defense.'' Deschler Ch 26 § 52.6.
- A provision prohibiting use of funds for the furnishing of sophisticated weapons systems to certain countries ''unless the President determines'' it to be important to national security, such determination to be reported within 30 days to the Congress. Deschler Ch 26 § 56.1.
- An amendment providing that no part of the appropriation could be used to make grants or loans to any country that the Secretary of State believed to be dominated by the foreign government controlling the world Communist movement. Deschler Ch 26 § 59.17.
- An amendment prohibiting payment of funds in the bill for the support of any action resulting in the destruction of a structure of historic or cultural significance. Deschler Ch 26 § 52.17.
- A provision providing funds for grants to States for unemployment compensation ''only to the extent that the Secretary finds necessary.'' Deschler Ch 26 § 52.14.
- A paragraph requiring that appropriations in the bill be available for expenses of attendance of officers and employees at meetings or conventions ''under regulations prescribed by the Secretary.'' Deschler Ch 26 § 52.13.
- An amendment restricting the availability of funds for certain countries until the President reports to Congress his determination that such country does not deny or impose more than nominal restrictions on the right of its citizens to emigrate. Deschler Ch 26 § 55.5.
- An amendment denying the use of funds for foreign firms that receive certain government subsidies but permitting the President to waive such restriction in the national interest with prior notice to Congress. Deschler Ch 26 § 56.7.
- An amendment denying the use of funds for a certain publication until there had been a review of all conclusions reached therein and a determination that they were factual. 96-2, July 30, 1980, pp 20504-506.
- A provision limiting the availability of funds for grants-in-aid to any airport that failed to provide designated and enforced smoking and nonsmoking areas for passengers in airport terminal areas. 99-2, July 30, 1986, p 18188.
- A section restricting funds for special pay of physicians or dentists whose ''primary'' duties were administrative. 98-1, Nov. 2, 1983, p 30494.
- A provision restricting funds to carry out any requirement that small businesses meet certain prequalifications of ''acceptable'' product marketability to be eligible to bid on certain defense contracts. 98-1, Nov. 2, 1983, p 30495.

Determinations as to Intent or Motive

An amendment curtailing the use of the funds for certain purposes if the funds are used with a certain intent or motive requires new determinations by the officials administering the funds and is subject to a point of order as legislation. 91-1, July 31, 1969, pp 21653, 21675. Thus, an amendment prohibiting the use of funds in the bill to pay rewards for information leading to the detection of any person violating certain laws, or "conniving" to do so, was ruled out as legislation because the amendment required the executive branch to determine what constitutes "conniving" in violating the law. 96-1, July 13, 1979, p 18451. Similarly, an amendment denying use of funds in the bill to grant business licenses to persons selling drug paraphernalia "intended for use" in drug preparation or use was ruled out as legislation requiring new duties and judgments of government officials. Deschler Ch 26 § 23.18.

An amendment prohibiting the use of funds in the bill for abortions or abortion-related services, and defining abortion as the "intentional" destruction of unborn human life, was conceded to impose new affirmative duties on officials administering the funds and was ruled out as legislation. Deschler Ch 26 § 25.14. Similarly, a paragraph prohibiting the use of funds to perform abortions except where the mother's life would be endangered if the fetus were carried to term (or where the pregnancy was a result of rape or incest) was held to impose new affirmative duties. *Manual* § 1054.

A paragraph denying use of funds in the bill to sell certain loans except with the consent of the borrower was conceded to be legislation requiring new determinations of "consent" and was ruled out in violation of clause 2(c) of rule XXI. 98-2, May 31, 1984, p 14590.

Negative Prohibition and Affirmative Direction Distinguished

To be permitted in a general appropriation bill, a limitation must be in effect a negative prohibition on the use of the money, not an affirmative direction to an executive officer. 4 Hinds § 3975. When it assumes affirmative form by direction to an executive in the discharge of duties under existing law, it ceases to be a limitation and becomes legislation. 7 Cannon § 1606. The limitation must be in effect a negative prohibition that proposes an easily discernible standard for determining the application of the use of funds. Deschler Ch 26 § 52.23.

Imposing "Incidental" Duties

The fact that a limitation on the use of funds may impose certain incidental burdens on executive officials does not destroy the character of the limitation as long as it does not directly amend existing law and is descriptive of functions and findings already required to be undertaken by existing law. *Manual* § 1053; Deschler Ch 26 § 71.2. Thus, an amendment reducing the availability of funds for trade adjustment assistance by amounts of unemployment insurance entitlements was held in order where the law establishing trade adjustment assistance already required the disbursing agency to take into consideration levels of unemployment insurance in determining payment levels. Deschler Ch 26 § 61.21.

The proponent must be prepared to show that the new duties are merely incidental to functions already required by law and do not involve substantive new determinations. 99-1, July 26, 1985, p 20808.

Effect of Information "Made Known"

As noted above (§ 44, supra) and in the *Manual* § 1054, clauses 2(b) and 2(c) of rule XXI were amended in the 105th Congress to render legislation a provision that conditions the availability of funds on certain information not required by existing law on being "made known" to an executive official, superseding 7 Cannon § 1695.

Imposing Duties on Non-Federal Official

Under the modern practice, it is not in order to make the availability of funds in a general appropriation bill contingent upon a substantive determination by a State or local government official or agency that is not otherwise required by existing law. 81-1, Mar. 30, 1949, p 3531; 99-1, July 25, 1985, p 20569; Deschler Ch 26 § 53 (note).

§ 55. —Duties Relating to Construction or Implementation of Law

Duty of Statutory Construction

Although all limitations on funds on appropriation Acts require Federal officials to construe the language of that law in administering those funds, that duty of statutory construction, absent a further imposition of an affirmative direction not required by law, does not destroy the validity of the limitation. Deschler Ch 26 § 64.30. Thus, an amendment restricting the use of funds for abortion or abortion-related services and activities was upheld as a negative limitation imposing no new duties on Federal officials other than to construe the language of the limitation in administering the funds. Deschler Ch 26 § 73.8. Similarly, it is in order on a general appropriation bill to deny funds for the payment of salary to a Federal employee who is not in compliance with a Federal law, if the limitation places no new duties on the Federal official who is already charged with enforcing that law. Deschler Ch 26 § 52.34.

On the other hand, it is not in order in a general appropriation bill to limit the use of an appropriation or to provide how existing laws, rules, and regulations should be construed in carrying out the limitation. Also, it is not in order to condition the availability of funds or contract authority upon an interpretation of local law where that determination is not required by existing law. *Manual* §§ 1054, 1056.

Implementation of Existing Rules or Policies

It is in order on a general appropriation bill to make the availability of funds therein contingent upon the implementation of a policy already enacted into law, providing the description of that policy is precise and does not impose additional duties on the officials responsible for its implementation. 92-1, Nov. 17, 1971, p 41838. Similarly, an amendment prohibiting the use of funds in the bill to an agency to implement a ruling of the agency may be held in order as a limitation, where the amendment is merely descriptive of an existing ruling already promulgated by that agency and does not require new executive determinations. Deschler Ch 26 § 64.27.

§ 56. Conditional Limitations

Generally

The House may by limitation on a general appropriation bill provide that an appropriation shall be available contingent on a future event, such as a date certain. 7 Cannon § 1579. However, it is not in order:

- To make the availability of funds in the bill contingent upon a substantive determination by an executive official which is not otherwise required by law. *Manual* § 1054.
- To impose additional duties on an executive officer and to make the appropriation contingent upon the performance of such duties. *Manual* § 1054.
- To condition the use of such funds on the performance of a new duty not expressly required by law. *Manual* § 1054.

To a bill making appropriations for the U.S. contribution to various international organizations, an amendment providing that none of the funds might be expended until all other members had met their financial obligations was ruled out as legislation that imposed a duty on a Federal official to determine the extent of such obligations. Deschler Ch 26 § 59.16.

In one instance, an amendment limiting funds for foreign aid until the President submitted a report analyzing the effectiveness of U.S. economic assistance for each recipient country was held to change existing law and was ruled out of order as a violation of clause 2 of rule XXI. 100-2, May 25, 1988, p 12270. However, the imposition of certain incidental burdens on executive officials will not destroy the character of the limitation as long as those duties—such as statistical comparisons and findings of residence and employment status—are already mandated by law. *Manual* § 1053.

Language in a general appropriation bill in the form of a conditional limitation requiring determinations by Federal officials will be held to change existing law in violation of clause 2 of rule XXI unless the Committee on Appropriations can show that the new duties are merely incidental to functions already required by law and do not involve substantive new determinations. *Manual* § 1053.

A conditional limitation in a general appropriation bill may also be subject to a point of order where the condition is not related to the expenditures specified in the bill. Where a bill contained funds not only for certain allowances for former President Nixon but also for other departments and agencies, an amendment delaying the availability of all funds in the bill until Nixon had made restitution of a designated amount to the U.S. government was ruled out as not germane and as legislation, where that contingency was not related to the availability of other funds in the bill. 93-2, Oct. 2, 1974, pp 33620, 33621. For a discussion of conditions as legislation on appropriation bills generally, see § 29, supra.

Condition Subsequent

Where the expenditure of funds made available in an appropriation bill is subject to a condition subsequent—so that spending is to cease upon the occurrence of a specified condition—the language may be upheld as a proper limitation on an appropriation bill, provided that it does not change existing law. This is so even though the contingency specified may never occur. Deschler Ch 26 § 67.2. Thus, a provision that an appropriation for the pay of volunteer soldiers should not be available longer than a certain period after the ratification of a treaty of peace was upheld as a limitation. 4 Hinds § 4004. Other conditions subsequent that have been upheld as limitations include:

- An amendment stating that if the appropriations Act were to be declared unconstitutional by the Supreme Court, none of the money provided could thereafter be spent. Deschler Ch 26 § 76.6.
- An amendment terminating the use of the appropriated funds after the enactment of certain legislation pending before the Congress. Deschler Ch 26 § 64.10.

On the other hand, it is not in order in a general appropriation bill to restrict the discretionary authority of an executive official by a condition subsequent that changes existing law. *Manual* § 1054. For example, where existing law confers discretionary authority on an executive agency as to the submission of health and safety information by applicants for licenses, an amendment to a general appropriation bill restricting that discretion by requiring the submission of such information as a condition of receiving funds constitutes legislation. 96-1, June 18, 1979, pp 15286, 15287.

Conditions Relating to the Application or Interpretation of State Law

A limitation in a general appropriation bill may be upheld where it denies funds for a certain activity where that activity would be in violation of State law. However, such a limitation may be subject to a point of order if it imposes on Federal officials a duty to become conversant with a variety of State laws and regulations. Whether such duty would constitute a new or additional duty not contemplated in existing law would then be at issue. Deschler Ch 26 § 67.8.

Language in an appropriation bill that specifies that funds therein shall not be used for any project which ''does not have local official approval'' has been upheld as not imposing additional duties, and in order. 89-1, Oct. 14, 1965, p 26994.

§ 57. Exceptions to Limitations

An exception to a valid limitation in a general appropriation bill is in order, providing the exception does not add legislative language in violation of clause 2 of rule XXI. Deschler Ch 26 §§ 64.14, 64.15, 66.7. An exception from a limitation on the use of funds stating that the limitation does not prohibit their use for certain designated Federal activities may be held in order as not containing new legislation if those activities are already mandated by law. Deschler Ch 26 § 66.6. Other exceptions to limitations in general appropriation bills that have been held in order include:

- An amendment inserting ''Except as required by the Constitution'' in provisions prohibiting the use of funds to force a school district to take action involving the busing of students. Deschler Ch 26 § 64.14.
- A paragraph denying use of funds for antitrust actions against units of local government, but providing that the limitation did not apply to private antitrust actions. Deschler Ch 26 § 66.10.
- A provision excepting a limitation on funds for food stamp assistance for certain households eligible for general assistance from a local government. Deschler Ch 26 § 64.15.
- A provision excepting a limitation on funds for the Office of Personnel Management to enter contracts for health benefit plans that excepted certain specified coverage and plans. *Manual* § 1054.

Exceptions to limitation amendments that fail to comply with the principle that limiting language must not contain legislation are subject to a point of order under clause 2 of rule XXI. Deschler Ch 26 § 63.7. That point of order will lie, for example, against an exception from a limitation if it contains legislation requiring new executive determinations. *Manual* § 1054.

However, an exception from a limitation may include language precisely descriptive of authority provided in law as long as the exception only requires determinations already required by law and does not impose new duties on Federal officials. Deschler Ch 26 § 66.3.

§ 58. Limitations as to Recipients of Funds

Although it is not in order in a general appropriation bill to legislate as to qualifications of the recipients of an appropriation, the House may specify that no part of the appropriation shall go to recipients lacking certain qualifications. *Manual* § 1053; 7 Cannon § 1655; Deschler Ch 26 § 53. It is in order to describe the qualifications of the recipients of the funds and to deny the availability of those funds to recipients not meeting those criteria, the restriction being confined to the fiscal year covered by the bill. Deschler Ch 26 § 64.15. It is likewise in order to deny the availability of funds in the bill to an office that fails to satisfy certain factual criteria, as long as no new substantive determinations are required. 95-2, June 14, 1978, p 17668.

Amendments requiring the recipients of funds carried in the bill to be in compliance with an existing law have been permitted where the Federal officials concerned are already under an obligation to oversee the enforcement of existing law and are thus burdened by no additional duties by the amendment. 91-1, July 31, 1969, p 21633.

Limitations relating to the qualifications of recipients that have been held in order include:

- A provision limiting payments from appropriated funds to persons receiving pay from another source in excess of a certain amount. 7 Cannon § 1669.
- An amendment providing that none of the funds for a program shall be paid to any person having a certain net income in the previous calendar year. Deschler Ch 26 § 67.3.
- An amendment proposing that no part of an appropriation for an agency shall be used for salaries of persons in certain positions who are not qualified engineers with at least 10 years' experience. Deschler Ch 26 § 76.2.
- An amendment denying funds to pay the compensation of persons who allocate positions in the classified civil service subject to a maximum age requirement. Deschler Ch 26 § 74.1.

An amendment to a general appropriation bill that denies the availability of funds in the bill for the benefit of a certain category of recipients but which requires Federal officials to make additional determinations not required by law as to the qualifications of those recipients is legislation. Deschler Ch 26 § 53.4. Such an amendment is legislation if it requires a Federal official to subjectively evaluate the propriety or nature of individual conduct. 96-2, Sept. 16, 1980, p 25604. Provisions ruled out of order as requiring additional determinations include:

- An amendment denying funds for financial assistance to college students who had engaged in certain types of disruptive conduct, and requiring that the college initiate certain hearing procedures. Deschler Ch 26 § 61.4.
- An amendment prohibiting the use of ''impacted school assistance'' funds for children whose parents were employed on Federal property outside the school district. Deschler Ch 26 § 52.18.
- An amendment prohibiting the expenditure of funds in any workplace that was not free of illegal substances by requiring contract recipients to so certify and requiring contracts to contain provisions withholding payment upon violation. *Manual* § 1054.
- An amendment requiring an agency to investigate and determine whether a person or entity entering into a contract with funds under the pending bill is subject to a legal proceeding commenced by the Federal government and alleging fraud. *Manual* § 1054.

§ 59. Limitations on Funds in Other Acts

A limitation must apply solely to the money of the appropriation under consideration and may not be applied to money appropriated in other Acts. A limitation that is not confined to funds in the pending bill is legislation on an appropriation bill under clause 2 of rule XXI and not in order. 4 Hinds § 3927; 7 Cannon § 1495; Deschler Ch 26 §§ 27.2, 27.7, 27.8, 27.12, 27.16. An amendment to an appropriation bill seeking to change a limitation on expenditures carried in a previous appropriation bill has been held to be legislation and not in order. Deschler Ch 26 §§ 22.9, 22.10. Language requiring future fiscal year funding to be subject to limitations to be subsequently specified is legislation and not in order. *Manual* § 1053.

Provisions in general appropriation bills that have been held out of order because they imposed a limitation that was not confined to the funds in the bill include:

- An amendment providing that funds appropriated ''or otherwise made available'' for a public works project be limited to a certain use. 95-2, June 15, 1978, p 12831.
- A provision limiting the appropriation contained ''in this or any other act'' to a certain purpose. Deschler Ch 26 § 27.20.
- A provision providing that no part of ''any appropriation'' shall be used for a specified purpose. Deschler Ch 26 § 27.18.
- An amendment providing that ''no appropriation heretofore made'' be used for a certain purpose. Deschler Ch 26 § 27.21.
- An amendment declaring that ''hereafter no part of any appropriation'' shall be available for certain purposes. Deschler Ch 26 §§ 27.16, 27.25.

- An amendment providing that none of the funds in the bill "or elsewhere made available" be used for a certain purpose. Deschler Ch 26 § 27.12.
- An amendment providing that "total payments to any person" under a soil conservation program shall not exceed a certain amount. Deschler Ch 26 § 27.5.

§ 59a. Funding Floors

Highway Trust Fund

Clause 3 of rule XXI, as amended in the 112th Congress, prohibits consideration of a general appropriation bill proposing certain expenditures from the Highway Trust Fund. As originally added by the Transportation Equity Act for the 21st Century (Pub. L. 105-178), that clause required a minimum level of obligation limitations for certain categories of surface transportation funding. For additional background on the prior iteration of that clause, see APPROPRIATIONS, § 59a of House Practice (2003) and *Manual* § 1064 for the 111th Congress (H. Doc. 110-162).

Funding for Aviation Programs

Section 106 of the Wendell H. Ford Aviation Investment and Reform Act for the 21st Century (Pub. L. 106-181) added a provision establishing points of order to guarantee a certain level of budget resources available from the Airport and Airway Trust Fund each fiscal year through fiscal year 2003 (subsequently extended to 2007), to restrict the uses of those resources, and to guarantee a certain level of appropriations. The chairs of the Committee on Rules and the Committee on Transportation and Infrastructure inserted in the *Congressional Record* correspondence concerning points of order established in this section. *Manual* § 1064a; 106-2, Mar. 15, 2000, p 2805.

V. Reappropriations

§ 60. In General

Generally; Transfers Distinguished

A restriction against the inclusion of reappropriations in general appropriation bills is set forth in clause 2(a) of rule XXI. *Manual* § 1037. Reappropriations are to be distinguished from transfers of funds, which are permitted under some circumstances. See §§ 36, 37, supra.

Before enactment of the Legislative Reorganization Act of 1946, provisions that reappropriated in a direct manner unexpended balances and continued their availability for the same purpose for an extended period of time were not prohibited by rule XXI, because they were not deemed to change existing law by conferring new authority. 4 Hinds § 3592; 7 Cannon § 1152; Deschler Ch 26 § 30. Today, however, with two exceptions, clause 2(a) of rule XXI precludes the reappropriation of unexpended balances in a general appropriation bill or amendment thereto. *Manual* § 1037. The rule specifically excludes (1) appropriations in continuation of appropriations for public works on which work has commenced, and (2) transfers of unexpended balances within the department or agency for which they were originally appropriated. *Manual* § 1037. As to what constitutes a public work in progress under clause 2 of rule XXI, see § 26, supra.

Clause 2(a) of rule XXI is limited by its terms to general appropriation bills and amendments thereto, and the exceptions specified by it apply only to propositions reported by the Committee on Appropriations. *Manual* § 1037. An unreported joint resolution carrying a transfer of unobligated balances of previously appropriated funds—and not containing an appropriation of any new budget authority—is not a general appropriation bill within the meaning of that rule. *Manual* § 1044.

Provisions Subject to a Point of Order

Language in a general appropriation bill making available unobligated balances of funds appropriated in prior appropriation Acts may constitute a reappropriation in violation of clause 2(a) of rule XXI. Deschler Ch 25 § 3.2. A provision transferring previously appropriated funds to extend their availability and to merge them with current-year funds is likewise in violation of clause 2(a). 98-1, Oct. 26, 1983, pp 29416, 29417. Unless permitted under one of the exceptions specified in clause 2, the reappropriation is subject to a point of order, even though the funds are sought for the same purpose as the original appropriation and the original appropriation was authorized in law. *Manual* § 1063; Deschler Ch 25 § 3.3.

Authorization Bills and Reappropriations

Language in an appropriation bill continuing the availability of unobligated balances of prior appropriations is in order where provisions of the original authorizing legislation permit such a reappropriation and are still in effect. Deschler Ch 25 § 3.8. Clause 2(a) of rule XXI is not applicable to appropriation bills when the reappropriation language is identical to legislative authorization language enacted subsequent to the adoption of the rule, because the authorizing law is a more recent expression of the will of the House. Deschler Ch 25 § 3.7.

VI. Reporting; Consideration and Debate

A. Generally

§ 61. Privileged Status; Voting

Generally

General appropriation bills have long enjoyed privileged status under the rules of the House. Such bills may be reported ''at any time'' under clause 5 of rule XIII. *Manual* § 853; see also COMMITTEES. In 1981, this privilege was extended to joint resolutions continuing appropriations for a fiscal year if reported after September 15 preceding the beginning of such fiscal year. *Manual* § 853. The privilege does not extend to special appropriations to address a specific purpose. 8 Cannon § 2285. Similarly, a joint resolution providing an appropriation for a single government agency is not a general appropriation bill and is not reported as privileged. Deschler Ch 25 § 7.4. Consideration of a privileged appropriation bill is subject to layover requirements. § 62, infra.

Nonprivileged appropriation bills may be made in order by unanimous consent or pursuant to a special order of business reported by the Committee on Rules. Deschler Ch 25 § 6; see also § 75, infra.

Prior Consideration in the Committee of the Whole

All bills or joint resolutions ''directly or indirectly making appropriations'' require initial consideration in the Committee of the Whole, and a point of order may be made under clause 3 of rule XVIII at any time before the consideration of a bill or joint resolution has commenced. *Manual* § 973. Motions to resolve into the Committee of the Whole for the purpose of considering general appropriation bills have precedence under clause 4(b) of rule XVIII. *Manual* § 977.

Consideration in the House as in the Committee of the Whole

Pursuant to an order of the House, an appropriation bill may be called up as if privileged and considered in the House as in the Committee of the Whole (meaning that the bill is considered as read and open to amendment at any point under the five-minute rule, without general debate). 89-1, July 28, 1965, p 18578; 89-1, Oct. 13, 1965, p 26881; 91-2, June 24, 1970, p 21239.

§62. When Bills May Be Considered

The privilege given to general appropriation bills is subject to the requirement of clause 4 of rule XIII that such bills may not be considered in the House until printed committee hearings and a committee report thereon have been available for at least three calendar days (excluding Saturdays, Sundays, and legal holidays if not in session). *Manual* §§850, 852. Availability may be measured by electronic availability under clause 3 of rule XXIX or by access to printed copies. *Manual* §1105b.

The three-day layover requirement may be waived by unanimous consent or pursuant to the adoption of a special order of business from the Committee on Rules.

§63. Debate; Consideration of Amendments; Perfecting Amendments; En Bloc Amendments

Generally; Perfecting Amendments

Under clause 5(a) of rule XVIII, amendments perfecting a general appropriation bill are considered in the Committee of the Whole during the reading of the bill for amendment under the five-minute rule. *Manual* §§978, 980. General appropriation bills are read for amendment by paragraph—unless a special order of business provides otherwise—whereas bills appropriating funds for a specific purpose are read by sections. 4 Hinds §§4739, 4740; Deschler Ch 25 §11.8.

However the bill is read—either by paragraph, section, or other subdivision—an amendment to a given portion must be made after that portion has been read or is considered as read by the Clerk. An amendment to a paragraph that has been passed in the reading of the bill may be offered only by unanimous consent. Deschler Ch 25 §11.13. For more on the proper time to offer amendments, see AMENDMENTS.

Where the reading proceeds by paragraph, a paragraph that is composed of discrete sub-units of indented text is nonetheless treated as a single paragraph for purposes of offering amendments. 102-2, July 1, 1992, pp 17272, 17273, 17277 (reversing a ruling at 98-2, Nov. 30, 1982, p 28066).

En Bloc Amendments

Under clause 2(f) of rule XXI, en bloc amendments proposing only to transfer appropriations among objects in the bill, without increasing the levels of budget authority or outlays in the bill, are in order during the reading of the bill for amendment in the Committee of the Whole. Such amendments may amend portions of the bill not yet read for amendment and are not subject to a demand for division of the question. The burden of proof is on the proponent with regard to the levels of budget authority or outlays. *Manual* § 1063a.

Consideration in the House

Amendments adopted in the Committee of the Whole are reported to the House for action. During consideration of the bill in the House, it is in order to demand that those amendments be voted on separately. Deschler Ch 25 § 11.21.

Under clause 10 of rule XX, the yeas and nays are automatically ordered when the Speaker puts the question on final passage or adoption of any bill, joint resolution, or conference report making general appropriations. *Manual* § 1033.

§ 64. —Limitation Amendments; Retrenchments

Amendments Authorized in Existing Law

Limitation amendments ''specifically contained or authorized in existing law for the period of the limitation'' may, pursuant to clause 2(c) of rule XXI, be offered in the Committee of the Whole during the reading of a general appropriation bill for amendment. *Manual* §§ 1039, 1053. However, that rule is strictly construed to apply only where existing law requires or permits the inclusion of limiting language in an appropriation Act, and not merely where the limitation is alleged to be ''consistent with existing law.'' *Manual* § 1053.

Limitation Amendments Not Authorized in Existing Law; Retrenchment Amendments

In 1983 and in 1995, the House adopted and then modified procedures for the consideration of retrenchment and limitation amendments: such amendments are in order only (1) when reading of the bill has been completed and (2) if the Committee of the Whole does not adopt a motion, if offered by the Majority Leader or a designee, to rise and report the bill back to the House. *Manual* §§ 1040, 1043. Pursuant to clause 2(d) of rule XXI, a general appropriation bill must be read for amendment *in its entirety* (including the short title of the bill if part of the text) before retrenchments or amendments proposing limitations are in order. In practice, however, the Committee of the Whole may choose to entertain such amendments before the short title is read. After the bill has been read, the motion that the Committee of the Whole rise and report the bill to the House with the amendments adopted takes precedence over any other amendment. *Manual* § 1043. Under clause 2(d), an amendment proposing a limitation not specifically contained or authorized in existing law for the period of the limitation is not in order during the reading of the bill, and if offered at the completion of the reading, can be entertained only if a preferential motion to rise and report, if offered, is rejected. *Manual* § 1043. However, the amendment with the limitation if offered first may be considered as pending upon rejection by the Committee of the preferential motion to rise and report. 99-1, July 30, 1985, pp 21534-36.

Unlike an amendment proposing a limitation or a retrenchment, an amendment simply reducing an amount provided in a general appropriation bill is not subject to the requirements of clause 2(d) of rule XXI. Such amendment need not await the completion of the reading and the disposition of other amendments or yield to a preferential motion to rise and report. 102-2, June 30, 1992, pp 17139-41.

§ 65. Points of Order—Reserving Points of Order

Generally

Under the former practice, points of order ordinarily had to be reserved against a general appropriation bill at the time the bill was reported to the House and referred to the Union Calendar and could be reserved after the bill had been referred to the Committee of the Whole only by unanimous consent. Deschler Ch 25 § 12.1. Under clause 1 of rule XXI, however, it is not necessary to reserve points of order at the time the bill is referred to the Union Calendar; the right of a Member to raise them at a later time is automatically protected. *Manual* § 1035.

Against Amendments

In the Committee of the Whole, the reservation of a point of order against an amendment to an appropriation bill is within the discretion of the Chair. If the reservation is permitted, the point of order must be reserved before debate begins on the amendment. Deschler Ch 26 § 2.2; see also POINTS OF ORDER; PARLIAMENTARY INQUIRIES.

§ 66. — Timeliness

Generally; Points of Order Against Paragraphs

A point of order against a provision in a general appropriation bill may not be entertained during general debate but must await the reading of that portion of the bill for amendment. 103-1, June 18, 1993, pp 13359, 13360. Such a point of order cannot be reserved. 108-1, July 22, 2003, p 18984. The time for making points of order against items in an appropriation bill is after the House has resolved itself into the Committee of the Whole and after the paragraph containing such items has been read for amendment.

Deschler Ch 25 § 12.8. A point of order against the paragraph on the ground that it is legislation will not lie before the paragraph is read. Deschler Ch 26 § 2.10. A point of order against two consecutive paragraphs comprising a section in the bill can be made only by unanimous consent. Deschler Ch 25 § 12.5.

Points of order against a paragraph must be made before an amendment is offered thereto or before the Clerk reads the next paragraph heading and amount. *Manual* § 1044; Deschler Ch 26 § 2. A point of order against a paragraph that has been passed in the reading for amendment may be made only by unanimous consent. See POINTS OF ORDER; PARLIAMENTARY INQUIRIES.

A point of order must be made against a paragraph after it is read and before an amendment is offered thereto, including a pro forma amendment offered for the purpose of debate only and an amendment that is ruled out of order. Deschler Ch 26 § 2.21. However, the point of order is not precluded by the fact that, by unanimous consent, an amendment had been offered to the paragraph before it was read. Deschler Ch 26 § 2.10. As required by clause 2(f), the Chair will query for points of order against the provisions of an appropriation bill unprotected by waiver and not yet reached in the reading but addressed by an amendment offered en bloc under that clause. *Manual* § 1058.

Timeliness Where Bill is Considered as Read

Where a general appropriation bill or a portion thereof (a title, for example) is considered as read and open to amendment by unanimous consent, points of order against provisions therein must be made before amendments are offered and cannot be reserved pending subsequent action on amendments. *Manual* § 1044; Deschler Ch 26 § 2. In this situation, the Chair first inquires whether any Member desires to raise a point of order against any portion of the pending text. The Chair then recognizes Members to offer amendments to that text. Deschler Ch 26 § 2.15. A point of order comes too late if it is made after the Chair has asked for amendments after having asked for points of order. Deschler Ch 26 § 2.16.

Where an appropriation bill partially read for amendment is then opened for amendment "at any point" (rather than for "the remainder of the bill"), points of order to paragraphs already read may yet be entertained. Deschler Ch 26 § 2.14.

Points of Order Against Amendments

Points of order against proposed amendments to a general appropriation bill must be made or reserved immediately after the amendment is read.

After a Member has been granted time to address the Committee of the Whole on an amendment, it is too late to make a point of order against it. Deschler Ch 26 § 12.13.

§ 67. —Points of Order Against Particular Provisions

Generally; Against Paragraphs of Bill

Points of order against unauthorized appropriations or legislation on general appropriation bills may be raised against an entire paragraph or a portion of a paragraph. 4 Hinds § 3652; 5 Cannon § 6881. If raised against only a portion of a paragraph, any Member may extend the point of order to the entire paragraph. *Manual* § 1044.

Where a point of order is made against an entire paragraph in an appropriation bill on the ground that a portion thereof is in conflict with the rules of the House and the point of order is sustained, the entire paragraph is eliminated. *Manual* § 1044; Deschler Ch 26 § 2.4. Similarly, where a point of order is made against an entire proviso on the ground that a portion of it is subject to the point of order, and the point of order is sustained, the entire proviso is eliminated. Deschler Ch 26 § 2.6.

Against Amendments

If any portion of an amendment to an appropriation bill constitutes legislation, the entire amendment is subject to a point of order. *Manual* § 1044.

A point of order against an amendment as legislation on a general appropriation bill must be determined in relation to the bill in its modified form (as affected by disposition of prior points of order). Deschler Ch 26 § 2.24.

§ 68. —Waiving Points of Order

Generally; Alternative Procedures

Points of order against a general appropriation bill may be waived in various ways:

- By unanimous consent. Deschler Ch 26 § 31.
- By special order of business from the Committee on Rules. *Manual* § 1058; 4 Hinds §§ 3260-3263; Deschler Ch 26 § 3.
- By motion to suspend the rules. 4 Hinds § 3845.
- By failure to make a timely point of order. Deschler Ch 26 § 3.17.

> *Note:* Although legislation in an appropriation bill may be subject to a point of order under clause 2 of rule XXI, such language ultimately included in an appropriation Act becomes permanent law where it is permanent in its language and nature. Deschler Ch 26 § 3.17.

Waiver of Points of Order by Special Order of Business

A waiver of points of order pursuant to a special order of business from the Committee on Rules may be couched in broad terms, as where it seeks to protect the entire bill against points of order. Deschler Ch 26 § 3.14. The waiver also may be confined to points of order directed at a particular title or a specified chapter of the bill. Deschler Ch 26 §§ 3.7, 3.8. A waiver may be very limited in scope, as where it permits points of order against portions of certain paragraphs but not against entire paragraphs. See Deschler Ch 26 § 3.5.

Waiver of Particular Points of Order

The House, by adoption of a special order of business from the Committee on Rules, may waive any point of order, including:

- Against certain paragraphs in an appropriation bill not authorized by law or containing legislative language. Deschler Ch 26 §§ 3.2, 3.6.
- Against reappropriations in violation of clause 2(a) of rule XXI. 97-1, July 30, 1981, p 18803.
- Against consideration of a bill containing new budget authority in excess of allocations to subcommittees and for failure of the committee report to contain a comparison of spending in the bill with subcommittee allocations. 99-2, Apr. 22, 1986, pp 8343, 8344, 8348.
- Against consideration of the bill until printed committee hearings and the committee report have been available for three days as is required by clause 4 of rule XIII. Deschler Ch 25 § 10.3.

Application of Waiver to Points of Order Against Amendments

Although points of order against the particular provisions of a bill may be waived by unanimous consent or special order of business, such waiver will not preclude points of order against amendments offered from the floor unless the waiver is made specifically applicable to such amendments. Deschler Ch 26 § 3. Thus, where a general appropriation bill is considered under terms of a special order of business waiving points of order "against said bill," the waiver applies only to the provisions of the bill and not to amendments thereto. Deschler Ch 26 § 3.14. However, a special order of business waiving points of order may be drafted in such a way as to protect a specific amendment or to protect "any amendment offered by direction of the Committee on Appropriations." Deschler Ch 26 §§ 3.10, 3.11.

§69. Amending Language Permitted to Remain

When in Order

Language that has been permitted to remain in a general appropriation bill or amendment by virtue of a waiver may be modified by a further amendment if it is germane and does not contain additional legislation or additional unauthorized items. *Manual* §1058; 4 Hinds §3862; 7 Cannon §1420; Deschler Ch 26 §3. The Chair will examine an entire legislative provision permitted to remain when ruling that an amendment to a portion of the provision was merely perfecting. *Manual* §1058.

Where an unauthorized appropriation is permitted to remain in the bill by failure to raise, or by waiver of, a point of order, an amendment merely changing the amount and not adding legislative language or earmarking separate funds for another unauthorized purpose is in order. *Manual* §1058; Deschler Ch 26 §3.38. However, an increase in the amount may violate certain budget-related rules. An amendment adding a new paragraph indirectly increasing an unauthorized amount contained in a prior paragraph passed in the reading is subject to a point of order because the new paragraph is adding a further unauthorized amount not textually protected by the waiver. However, a new paragraph indirectly reducing an unauthorized amount permitted to remain in a prior paragraph passed in the reading is not subject to a point of order, because it is not adding a further unauthorized amount. *Manual* §1058. Merely narrowing the application of an unauthorized appropriation permitted to remain by way of germane exception is not subject to a point of order. Deschler Ch 26 §§3.23, 3.24.

To a legislative provision permitted to remain conferring assistance on a certain class of recipients, an amendment adding another class is further legislation and is not merely perfecting in nature. On the other hand, to a legislative provision permitted to remain, an amendment particularizing a definition in the language was held not to constitute additional legislation where it was shown that the definition being amended already contemplated inclusion of the covered class. *Manual* §1058.

When Not in Order

Although legislative language in a general appropriation bill that is permitted to remain therein because of a waiver of points of order may be perfected by germane amendment, such an amendment may not add additional legislation. *Manual* §1058; 4 Hinds §§3836, 3837; 7 Cannon §§1425-1434; 101-1, Aug. 2, 1989, p 18166. Such an amendment may not earmark funds for an unauthorized purpose or direct a new use of funds not required by law. *Manual* §1058; Deschler Ch 26 §3.30. The figures in an unauthorized item permitted to remain may be perfected. However, the provision may not be changed by an amendment substituting funds for a different unauthorized purpose. Deschler Ch 26 § 3.45. An increase in such figure may not be accompanied by legislative language directing certain expenditures. Deschler Ch 26 § 3.42. Amendments to language permitted to remain in an appropriation bill that have been ruled out under clause 2 of rule XXI include:

- An amendment adding additional legislation prohibiting the availability of funds in other Acts for certain other purposes. Deschler Ch 26 § 3.18.
- An amendment adding an additional class of recipients to those covered by a legislative provision permitted to remain. Deschler Ch 26 § 3.34.
- An amendment adding further unauthorized items of appropriation or adding legislation in the form of new duties. 99-2, July 23, 1986, pp 16850, 16851.
- An amendment broadening the application of a legislative provision permitted to remain so as to apply to other funds. *Manual* § 1058.
- An amendment adding a new paragraph in another part of the bill that indirectly increases an unauthorized amount passed in the reading, because not textually protected by the waiver. *Manual* § 1058; 104-1, July 12, 1995, pp 18627-29.
- An amendment increasing an authorized amount above the authorized ceiling. *Manual* § 1058.
- An amendment in the form of a motion to strike, extending the legislative reach of the pending text. *Manual* § 1058.
- An amendment extending restrictions on recipients of a defined set of Federal payments and benefits to persons benefiting from a certain tax status determined on the basis of wholly unrelated criteria. *Manual* § 1058.
- An amendment explicitly waiving a different provision of law than that addressed in language permitted to remain. *Manual* § 1058.

B. Senate Amendments

§ 70. In General

Senate Amendments Before Stage of Disagreement

Clause 3 of rule XXII requires any Senate amendment involving a new and distinct appropriation to be first considered in the Committee of the Whole. However, the modern practice bypasses this requirement by sending appropriation bills with Senate amendments directly to conference, either by unanimous consent or a motion under clause 1 of rule XXII, notwithstanding the fact that the stage of disagreement has not been reached. *Manual* §§ 1070, 1073, 1074. Thus, earlier precedents (4 Hinds §§ 4797-4806; 8 Cannon §§ 2382-2385) governing initial consideration of Senate amendments to appropriation bills in the Committee of the Whole are largely anachronistic, and the practices discussed below regarding disposition of Senate amendments normally involve the post-conference stage of consideration where the stage of disagreement has been reached and motions in the House to dispose of Senate amendments are privileged (*Manual* §§ 528a-d, 1075).

Amending Senate Amendments

A point of order under clause 2 of rule XXI does not lie against a Senate amendment to a House general appropriation bill. *Manual* §§ 1059, 1076; 7 Cannon § 1572. Where a Senate amendment on a general appropriation bill proposes an expenditure not authorized by law, it is in order in the House to perfect such Senate amendment by germane amendments. Deschler Ch 25 § 13.13; Deschler Ch 26 § 6.1. Similarly, where the Senate attaches a ''legislative'' amendment to the bill, it is in order in the House to concur with a perfecting amendment provided such amendment is germane to the Senate amendment. Deschler Ch 25 § 13.14. In amending a Senate amendment, the House is not confined to the limits of the amount set by the original bill and the Senate amendment. Deschler Ch 25 § 13.15.

Amendments Reported in Disagreement

A Senate amendment containing legislation reported from conference in disagreement (see § 71, infra) may be amended by a germane amendment even though the proposed amendment also is legislative. *Manual* § 1059; Deschler Ch 26 § 6.9. Although clause 5 of rule XXII prohibits House conferees from agreeing to a Senate amendment that proposes legislation on an appropriation bill without specific authority from the House, that rule is a restriction upon the managers only. It does not provide for a point of order against such amendment when it is reported in disagreement and comes up for separate action by the House. 7 Cannon § 1572. It is customary for the managers to report such amendments in technical disagreement. After disposing of the conference report, which includes those Senate amendments not in violation of clause 2 of rule XXI, amendments reported in technical or true disagreement are taken up in order and disposed of directly in the House by separate motion. *Manual* § 1076; 7 Cannon § 1572. Accordingly, where a Senate amendment proposing legislation on a general appropriation bill is reported back from conference in disagreement, a motion to concur in the Senate amendment with a further amendment is in order, even if the proposed amendment adds legislation to that contained in the Senate amendment, and the only test is whether the proposed amendment is germane to the Senate amendment reported in disagreement. *Manual* §§ 1059, 1076; Deschler Ch 26 § 6.5.

§71. Authority of Conference Managers

Generally

Under clause 5 of rule XXII, the managers on the part of the House may not agree to any Senate amendment to a general appropriation bill if that amendment, had it originated in the House, would have been in violation of clause 2 of rule XXI, unless such agreement is specifically authorized by separate vote prior thereto. That restriction has been interpreted to extend to Senate amendments in the form of limitations because limitation amendments are in violation of clause 2(c) unless offered at the end of reading for amendment in the Committee of the Whole. It has therefore been the practice of the managers at a conference on a general appropriation bill to bring Senate amendments containing limitations back to the House in technical disagreement. The House may then dispose of them by proper motion, the stage of disagreement having been reached.

Clause 5 of rule XXII also precludes House managers from agreeing in conference to Senate appropriation amendments on any bill other than a general appropriation bill unless authorized by separate vote. *Manual* § 1076. Under this rule, a conference report may be ruled out when conferees present to the House a conference report on a legislative measure on which the conferees agreed to a Senate amendment appropriating funds. Deschler Ch 25 §§ 13.8, 13.9. However, a point of order against an appropriation in a conference report on a legislative bill will lie under the rule only if that provision was originally contained in a Senate amendment and will not lie against a provision permitted by the House to remain in its bill. Deschler Ch 25 § 13.12. Moreover, because the rule applies only to Senate amendments that are sent to conference, it does not apply to appropriations contained in Senate legislative bills. Deschler Ch 25 § 13.11; see generally CONFERENCES BETWEEN THE HOUSES; § 76, infra.

Authorization by Special Order of Business

The managers on the part of the House may be authorized by a special order of business reported by the Committee on Rules to agree to Senate amendments carrying appropriations in violation of clause 2 of rule XXI. 7 Cannon § 1577. Where the special order of business waives points of order against portions of an appropriation bill that are unauthorized by law, and the bill passes the House with those provisions included and goes to conference, the conferees may report back their agreement to those provisions even though they remain unauthorized, because the waiver carries over to the consideration of the same provisions when the conference report is before the House. *Manual* § 1076.

Authorization by Unanimous Consent

A Member may seek unanimous consent to send an appropriation bill to conference and authorize the House conferees to agree to Senate legislative amendments notwithstanding the restrictions contained in clause 5 of rule XXII. Deschler Ch 26 § 6.3. However, unanimous consent merely to take from the Speaker's table and send to conference a bill with Senate amendments does not waive the provisions of the rule restricting the House conferees' authority. 7 Cannon § 1574.

VII. Other Appropriation Measures

§ 72. In General; Continuing Appropriations

A continuing appropriations measure is legislation enacted by the Congress to provide budget authority for specific ongoing Federal programs when a regular appropriation for those programs has not been enacted. Deschler Ch 25 § 7.1.

Joint resolutions continuing appropriations pending enactment of general appropriation bills for the ensuing fiscal year are not general appropriation bills and therefore are not reported or called up as privileged unless reported after September 15 preceding the beginning of such fiscal year. Clause 5(a) of rule XIII; *Manual* § 853; 8 Cannon § 2282; Deschler Ch 25 § 7. A continuing resolution may be called up by unanimous consent, by a motion to suspend the rules, or under a special order of business. See § 75, infra.

A continuing resolution is not a general appropriation bill within the meaning of clause 2 of rule XXI and is therefore not subject to its provisions. The restrictions against unauthorized items or legislation in a general appropriation bill or amendment thereto are not applicable to a continuing resolution despite inclusion of diverse appropriations that are not continuing in nature. 94-1, June 17, 1975, p 19176; Deschler Ch 26 § 1.2.

§ 73. Supplemental Appropriations

A supplemental appropriation provides budget authority in addition to regular or continuing appropriations already made. Bills making supplemental appropriations for diverse agencies are considered general appropriation bills and are reported as such. Deschler Ch 25 § 7.

A waiver of points of order against a supplemental appropriation bill may be provided for by a special order of business from the Committee on Rules. The rule may waive points of order against the entire bill or against a specific paragraph in the bill. Deschler Ch 25 §§ 9.6, 9.7. Such a rule has been considered and agreed to by the House even after general debate on the bill has been concluded and reading for amendment has begun in the Committee of the Whole. Deschler Ch 25 § 9.1.

§ 74. Appropriations for a Single Agency

A measure making an appropriation for a single department or agency might not be a general appropriation bill within the meaning of clause 5(a) of rule XIII. Such a measure is not privileged for consideration when reported by the Committee on Appropriations and is not subject to points of order under clause 2 of rule XXI. Deschler Ch 25 §§ 7.3, 7.4; 95-1, Feb. 3, 1977, p 3473.

§ 75. Consideration of Other Appropriation Measures

By Special Order of Business, Unanimous Consent, or Suspension

The consideration of nonprivileged appropriation measures may be made in order by a special order of business from the Committee on Rules (Deschler Ch 25 § 7.3), may be made in order by unanimous consent (98-2, Oct. 1, 1984, p 27961), or may be considered pursuant to a motion to suspend the rules (Deschler Ch 25 § 13.18). A joint resolution continuing appropriations for a fiscal year is reported under clause 2 of rule XIII, relating to the filing of nonprivileged reports. *Manual* § 831; Deschler Ch 25 § 8.8.

Consideration in House as in the Committee of the Whole

Formerly, joint resolutions continuing appropriations pending enactment of regular annual appropriation measures were often considered in the House as in the Committee of the Whole. More rarely they were considered in Committee of the Whole to permit more extensive general debate. Deschler Ch 25 § 6 (note). Joint resolutions providing supplemental appropriations also may be considered in the House as in the Committee of the Whole. Deschler Ch 25 §§ 11.5, 11.6. Such consideration may be provided for by unanimous consent or pursuant to a special order of business from the Committee on Rules. Deschler Ch 25 §§ 8.4, 8.7.

Consideration in House

Under modern practice, continuing appropriation joint resolutions are often considered by unanimous consent or by special order of business in the House, and often with the previous question considered as ordered to prevent amendment. Deschler Ch 25 §§ 8.9-8.12; 102-1, Sept. 24, 1991, p 23725.

VIII. Appropriations in Legislative Bills

§76. In General

Generally

Restrictions against the inclusion of appropriations in legislative bills are provided for by clause 4 of rule XXI. A bill or joint resolution carrying appropriations may not be reported by a committee not having jurisdiction to report appropriations. The rule also prohibits amendments proposing appropriations on a reported legislative bill. *Manual* §1065. Under this rule, a provision appropriating funds that is included in a bill reported by a legislative committee is subject to a point of order. 7 Cannon §2133; Deschler Ch 25 §4.24. However, because the rule by its terms applies to appropriations ''reported'' by legislative committees, the point of order does not apply to an appropriation in a bill that has been taken away from a nonappropriating committee by a motion to discharge. 7 Cannon §1019a. It also does not apply to a special order of business reported from the Committee on Rules ''self-executing'' the adoption to a bill of an amendment containing an appropriation, because the amendment is not separately before the House during consideration of the special order of business. *Manual* §1065.

Application to Senate Bills or Amendments Between the Houses

The rule forbidding consideration of items carrying appropriations in bills reported by nonappropriating committees applies to Senate bills as well as to House bills. 7 Cannon §§2136, 2147. The point of order may be made against an appropriation in a Senate bill under consideration (in lieu of a reported House bill) even though the bill has not been reported by a committee of the House. 7 Cannon §2137. This rule also applies to an amendment proposed to a Senate amendment to a House bill not reported from the Committee on Appropriations. *Manual* §1065.

Application to Private Bills

Clause 4 of rule XXI does not apply to private bills, because the committees having jurisdiction of bills for the payment of private claims may report bills making appropriations within the limits of their jurisdiction. 7 Cannon §2135.

§77. What Constitutes an Appropriation in a Legislative Bill

Generally

As used in clause 4 of rule XXI, an appropriation means taking money out of the Treasury by appropriate legislative language for the support of the general functions of government. Deschler Ch 25 § 4.43. Language that restricts or negates funding does not ''carry'' an appropriation within the meaning of clause 4. Rulings on points of order under clause 4 have frequently depended on whether language allegedly making an appropriation was in fact merely language authorizing an appropriation. Deschler Ch 25 § 4. Thus, a provision that disbursements ''shall be paid from the appropriation made to the department for that purpose'' was construed merely as an authorization and not an appropriation and was, therefore, not subject to a point of order under clause 4. 7 Cannon § 2156.

Provisions Held in Order

Provisions in a legislative bill that have been held not to violate clause 4 include:

- A provision authorizing an appropriation of not less than a certain amount for a specified purpose. Deschler Ch 25 § 4.34.
- A provision providing that an appropriation come out of any unexpended balances heretofore appropriated or made available for emergency purposes. Deschler Ch 25 § 4.35.
- A provision providing that all funds ''available'' for carrying out the Act ''shall be available'' for allotment to certain bureaus and offices, no use of existing funds being permitted. Deschler Ch 25 § 4.36.
- A provision authorizing and directing an executive officer to advance, when appropriated, sums of money out of the Treasury. Deschler Ch 25 § 4.38.
- A provision authorizing the withdrawal of money from the Treasury belonging to a governmental agency, even though it would otherwise eventually revert to the government. 7 Cannon § 2158.
- A provision authorizing the Secretary of the Treasury to use proceeds of public-debt issues for the purpose of making loans. Deschler Ch 25 § 4.43.

Provisions Held out of Order

Provisions in a legislative bill, or amendments thereto, that have been held to violate clause 4 include:

- A provision directing that funds previously appropriated be used for a purpose not specified in the original appropriation. 7 Cannon § 2147.
- A provision reappropriating or diverting an appropriation for a new purpose. 7 Cannon § 2146; Deschler Ch 25 §§ 4.1, 4.4.
- An amendment requiring the diversion of previously appropriated funds in lieu of the enactment of new budget authority. *Manual* § 1065.
- A provision providing for the transfer of unexpended balances of appropriations and making such funds available for expenditure. Deschler Ch 25 § 4.5.
- A provision making available an appropriation or a portion of an appropriation already made for one purpose to another or for one fiscal year to another. *Manual* § 1065.

- A provision providing for the collection of certain fees and authorizing the use of the fees so collected for the purchase of certain installations. Deschler Ch 25 §4.16.
- An amendment establishing a user charge and making the revenues collected therefrom available without further appropriation. Deschler Ch 25 §4.19.
- A provision making available for administrative purposes money repaid from advances and loans. Deschler Ch 25 §4.21.
- A provision directing disbursements from Indian trust funds. 7 Cannon §2149.
- An amendment permitting the acquisition of buses with funds from the highway trust fund. 92-2, Oct. 5, 1972, p 34115.
- A provision establishing a special fund, to be available with other funds appropriated, for the purpose of paying refunds. 7 Cannon §2152.
- A provision making excess foreign currencies available to stimulate private enterprise abroad. Deschler Ch 25 §4.22.
- A provision providing that the cost of certain surveys would be paid from the appropriation theretofore or thereafter made for such purposes. Deschler Ch 25 §4.10.
- A provision making available unobligated balances of appropriations ''heretofore'' made to carry out the provisions of the bill. Deschler Ch 25 §4.11.
- An amendment waiving provisions in an appropriation Act that limited the availability of funds appropriated therein for a specified purpose, thereby increasing the availability of appropriated funds. 93-2, Apr. 4, 1974, pp 9846, 9847.
- An amendment providing for the transfer of existing Federal funds into a new Treasury trust fund and for their immediate availability for a new purpose. 93-2, June 20, 1974, pp 20273-75.
- A provision authorizing the Treasurer to honor requisitions of the Archivist in such manner and in accordance with such regulations as the Treasurer might prescribe. Deschler Ch 25 §4.15.
- A provision in an omnibus reconciliation bill reported by the Committee on the Budget making a direct appropriation to carry out a part of the Energy Security Act. 99-1, Oct. 24, 1985, p 28812.

§78. Points of Order; Timeliness

Generally

A point of order under clause 4 of rule XXI against an appropriation in a bill reported by a non-appropriating committee should be raised at the appropriate time in the Committee of the Whole and does not lie in the House before consideration of the bill. 94-1, Sept. 10, 1975, pp 28270, 28271. The provision in clause 4, that a point of order against the appropriation can be made ''at any time'' has been interpreted to require the point of order to be raised during the pendency of the amendment under the five-minute rule. Deschler Ch 25 § 12.14. Such a point of order comes too late after the amendment has been agreed to and has become part of the text of the bill, and cannot then be raised against further consideration of the bill as amended. *Manual* § 1065.

Although a point of order under clause 4 against an amendment carrying an appropriation operates as one against consideration of the amendment, when applied to a provision in a bill it applies to the appropriation against which it is directed and not against consideration of the bill. A point of order under clause 4 does not lie in the standing committees of the House. A point of order in the House that the bill is improperly on the Union Calendar does not lie. 7 Cannon § 2140. The point of order should be directed to the item of appropriation in the bill at the proper time and not, in the House, to the act of reporting the bill. 7 Cannon § 2142. It follows that motions to discharge nonappropriating committees from consideration of bills carrying appropriations are not subject to points of order under the rule. 7 Cannon § 2144.

The intervention of debate or the consideration of amendments following the reading do not preclude points of order under clause 4. Points of order against appropriations in legislative bills may be raised even after the merits of the proposition have been debated. Deschler Ch 25 § 12.15. A point of order against an amendment to a legislative bill containing an appropriation can be raised "at any time" during its pendency, even in its amended form, though the point of order is against the amendment as amended by a substitute and though no point of order was directed against the substitute before its adoption. *Manual* § 1065.

Waiving Points of Order

Points of order based on clause 4 may be waived by order of the House. Deschler Ch 25 § 4.3. Where the House has adopted a resolution waiving points of order against certain appropriations in a legislative bill, a point of order may nevertheless be raised against an amendment to the bill containing an identical provision. 94-1, Apr. 23, 1975, p 11512.

§ 79. —Directing Points of Order Against Objectionable Language

A point of order under clause 4 of rule XXI against an appropriation in a legislative bill should be directed against that portion of the bill (or against the amendment thereto) in which the appropriation is contained and cannot be directed against the consideration of the entire bill. 7 Cannon

§ 2142; Deschler Ch 25 § 4.2. If such a point of order is sustained with respect to a portion of a section of a legislative bill containing an appropriation, only that portion is stricken. However, if the point of order is directed against the entire section for inclusion of that language, the entire section will be ruled out. 93-2, Apr. 4, 1974, pp 9845, 9846.

Chapter 5
Assembly of Congress

Research References
1 Hinds §§ 1-10; 5 Hinds §§ 6758-6762
6 Cannon §§ 1-5
Deschler Ch 1
Manual §§ 60, 242, 243

§ 1. In General; Day of Convening

Generally

The Constitution provides that each regular session of Congress shall begin on January 3 unless Congress by law appoints a different day. U.S. Const. amend. XX, § 2. A joint resolution, which is not privileged, is used for such appointment. For laws appointing a different day for assembling, see *Manual* § 243. The joint resolution may originate in either House. 93-1, Dec. 17, 1973, p 42059; 95-1, Dec. 15, 1977, p 38948.

The President has the constitutional authority to convene the Congress earlier than on the day it has fixed for its reconvening. The President may exercise this authority on ''extraordinary occasions'' by convening either or both Houses. U.S. Const. art. II, § 3. A number of early Congresses were convened by Presidential proclamation. 1 Hinds §§ 10, 12. The last session so convened was in the 76th Congress. Deschler Ch 1 § 2.1.

For examples of provisions in concurrent resolutions authorizing the recall of the House or of both Houses, see *Manual* § 84 and ADJOURNMENT.

Pro Forma Meetings

Upon completion of the legislative business for a session, the House may schedule pro forma meetings for the remainder of the constitutional term. 96-1, Dec. 14, 1979, p 36200. For example, as the first session of the 96th Congress drew to a close, the House, by unanimous consent, agreed to convene every third day for the remainder of the session, including a final pro forma meeting immediately before the constitutional expiration of the session at noon on January 3, 1980. 96-1, Dec. 20, 1979, p 37317. Similarly, in the 102d Congress, pursuant to the concurrent resolution that placed the two Houses in an intrasession adjournment from November 27, 1991, until January 3, 1992, the House convened at 11:55 a.m. on that day for its final meeting of the first session. A similar situation prevailed at the end of the 110th Congress, where the House was adjourned from December 10, 2008, until January 3, 2009, and the House convened at 11:00 a.m. on that day for the final meeting of the Congress. Alternatively, the House may recess or adjourn pursuant to a rule reported from the Committee on Rules at the end of a session for periods not in excess of three days. *Manual* § 83.

On January 3 of an even-numbered year, in the absence of a law appointing a different convening date, the Speaker may either (1) announce the adoption of a simple motion to adjourn the last day of the first session just before noon to declare the House adjourned *sine die* so that the second session may convene at noon (102-2, Jan. 3, 1992, p 36367) or (2) unilaterally declare the House adjourned *sine die* just before noon (without a simple motion) so that the second session may convene at noon (105-2, Jan. 3, 1996, p 35).

§ 2. Hour of Meeting

Generally; Hourly Schedules

Each House has plenary power over the time of its meetings during the session. If the time of meeting has not been set previously by resolution, the House, by long-standing practice having the force of a standing order, meets each day at noon. Deschler Ch 1 § 3. However, it is the customary practice of the House to adopt a resolution establishing times for its daily meetings. *Manual* § 621.

Times of meeting originally were selected to provide sufficient committee time for hearings and markups early in the session, and sufficient floor time later for authorization and appropriation bills. Resolutions setting daily meeting times are privileged, even though they are not reported from the Committee on Rules, because they are incidental to the organization of the House. 97-2, Jan. 25, 1982, p 62. However, subsequent resolutions changing the hour of meeting, unless reported as privileged from the Committee on Rules, require unanimous consent for consideration (although ad hoc arrangements from day to day may be effected by privileged motion under clause 4 of rule XVI). 95-2, June 29, 1978, p 19507.

Adjournments to a Different Hour

The meeting hour may be subsequently changed on certain days of the week pursuant to the adoption of a resolution setting forth the new convening time. 95-1, June 30, 1977, p 21685. The House may by unanimous consent vacate a previous order providing for the House to meet at a certain time and agree to meet at a different time. Deschler Ch 1 §§ 3.12, 3.13. The motion that when the House adjourns it adjourn to a day and time certain also may be used to enable the House to meet at an hour different from that provided by the standing order. For a general discussion of this motion (which is a privileged motion entertained at the Speaker's discretion), see ADJOURNMENT.

Emergency Convening Authority

During any recess or adjournment of not more than three days, if the Speaker is notified by the Sergeant-at-Arms of an imminent impairment of the place of reconvening, then the Speaker may, in consultation with the Minority Leader, postpone the time for reconvening within the three-day limit prescribed by the Constitution. In the alternative, the Speaker in such case may reconvene the House before the time previously appointed solely to declare the House in recess within that three-day limit. Clause 12(c) of rule I; 111-1, Dec. 19, 2009, p ____.

The House has entered an order authorizing the Speaker or a designee, during any recess or adjournment of not more than three days, to reconvene the House at a time other than that previously appointed, within the three-day limit prescribed by the Constitution, based on a determination that the public interest so warrants and after consultation with the Minority Leader. 112-1, H. Res. 479, Dec. 6, 2011, p ____.

§ 3. Place of Meeting

Under article I, section 5, clause 4 of the Constitution, neither House may, without consent of the other, adjourn "to any other Place than that in which the two Houses shall be sitting." The requirement for consent has been interpreted to apply to the seat of government, which has been, since 1800, the District of Columbia. Therefore, the House may convene in another place within the District of Columbia without the consent of the Senate. Deschler Ch 1 § 4.1. Under clause 12(d) of rule I, the Speaker may convene the House in a place at the seat of government other than the Hall of the House whenever, in the Speaker's opinion, the public interest shall warrant it.

In the 107th Congress, the two Houses authorized joint leadership recall from an adjournment ''at such place and time as they may designate if, in their opinion, the public interest shall warrant it'' (permitting recall from an adjournment to a place outside the District of Columbia). 107-1, H. Con. Res. 251, Oct. 17, 2001, pp 20210, 20211; 107-1, S. Con. Res. 85, Nov. 16, 2001, p 22922. In the 108th Congress, the two Houses granted blanket joint leadership authority to assemble at a place outside the District of Columbia whenever the public interest shall warrant it. 108-1, H. Con. Res. 1, Jan. 7, 2003, p 21.

The President may convene Congress at places outside the seat of government during hazardous circumstances. 2 USC § 27; Deschler Ch 1 § 4.

§ 4. Organizational Business—First Session

Functions of the Clerk

Under clause 2(a) of rule II, the Clerk from the prior Congress (including one appointed pursuant to section 75a-1 of title 2, United States Code), creates a roll of the Representatives-elect and calls the House to order at the beginning of a new Congress. 2 USC § 26; *Manual* § 643. In the event of the Clerk's absence or incapacity, the Sergeant-at-Arms from the prior Congress creates the roll and calls the House to order. 2 USC § 26; *Manual* § 656. After the opening prayer and Pledge of Allegiance, the Clerk:

- Announces the receipt of credentials of Members-elect.
- Causes a quorum to be established, by roll call by State, by electronic device.
- Announces the filing of credentials of Delegates-elect and of the Resident Commissioner.
- Recognizes for nominations for Speaker.
- Appoints tellers for the roll call vote (alphabetical by surname) for Speaker.
- Announces the vote.
- Appoints a committee to escort the Speaker to the Chair.

Election of Speaker

The first order of business after the ascertainment of a quorum at the opening of a new Congress is ordinarily the election of the Speaker. *Manual* § 27. Pursuant to statute and precedent, nominations for election of the Speaker are of the highest privilege and take precedence over a question of the privileges of the House relating to the interim election of a Speaker pro tempore pending an ethics investigation of a nominee for Speaker. 2 USC § 25; *Manual* § 27; 1 Hinds § 212.

Candidates for the office are nominated by the respective chairs of the Democratic Caucus and the Republican Conference. Deschler Ch 1 § 6.1. The Speaker is elected by a majority of Members-elect present and voting by surname. *Manual* § 27. The Speaker was at first elected by ballot but, since 1839, has been chosen by *viva voce* vote by surname in response to a call of the roll. 1 Hinds § 187; Deschler Ch 1 § 6. Although the Clerk appoints tellers for the election, the House, and not the Clerk, determines what method of voting to use. *Manual* § 27; Deschler Ch 1 § 6. On two occasions, by special rules, Speakers were chosen by a plurality of votes; but in each case the House by majority vote adopted a resolution declaring the result. 1 Hinds §§ 221, 222. The House has declined to choose a Speaker by lot. 1 Hinds § 221.

Status and Rights of Members-elect

Where the certificate of election of a Member-elect, in due form, is on file with the Clerk, such Member-elect is entitled as of right to be included on the Clerk's roll. *Page v. United States*, 127 U.S. 67 (1888). Those Members whose names appear on the Clerk's roll are entitled to vote for a new Speaker at the beginning of a Congress and to participate in other organizational business before the administration of the oath. They may debate propositions, propose motions, offer resolutions, and make points of order. Deschler Ch 2 § 2. Once sworn, Members may be named to serve on House committees and may introduce bills. *Manual* § 300; 4 Hinds §§ 4477, 4483, 4484.

All Members-elect whose credentials have been received by the Clerk are included on the first roll call on opening day to establish a quorum. Members-elect not responding to that call and not appearing to take the oath when it is administered *en masse* on opening day are not included on further roll calls until they have taken the oath. See generally OATHS. Pursuant to article I, section 2 of the Constitution, because the House is composed of Members elected by the people of the several States and because the House elects its Speaker, the Delegates-elect and the Resident Commissioner from Puerto Rico are not constitutionally qualified to vote in the House for Speaker. Therefore, the Clerk does not include them on the roll. *Manual* § 675.

Notices and Messages

At the beginning of a new Congress, the House by various resolutions: (1) directs that a message be sent to inform the Senate that a quorum of the House has been established and that the Speaker and Clerk have been elected, (2) establishes a select committee to notify the President that a quorum of the House has assembled and is ready to receive any communication desired to be made, and (3) directs the Clerk to inform the President of the selection of the Speaker. Deschler Ch 1 § 7.

§ 5. Organizational Business—Second Session

At the beginning of a second session of a Congress, the House is ordinarily called to order by the Speaker, although, where the Office is vacant, the House may be called to order by the Clerk. Deschler Ch 1 § 5. Alternatively, the House may be called to order by a previously designated Speaker pro tempore. Deschler Ch 1 § 7.4. Under clause 8(b)(3) of rule I, the Speaker is required to deliver to the Clerk a list of Members in the order in which each shall act as Speaker pro tempore in the case of a vacancy in the Office of Speaker. A Speaker pro tempore designated under this rule also may convene the second session of a Congress. Following the opening prayer, the Speaker orders, without motion, a call of the House to establish a quorum. Deschler Ch 1 § 7.5. The call of the House is normally taken by electronic device, but the Speaker may elect not to use the electronic system. Deschler Ch 20 § 4.

Members-elect, elected to fill vacancies occurring in the first session, are not included on the roll call to ascertain the presence of a quorum when the second session convenes. Their names are included on the roll only after their certificates of election have been laid before the House and their oaths have been administered. Similarly, the names of those Members who resigned or died during adjournment are stricken from the roll and are not called to establish a quorum. Deschler Ch 2 § 4.10.

§ 6. Adoption of Rules and Separate Orders

The Constitution gives each House the power to determine the rules of its proceedings. U.S. Const. art. I, § 5, cl. 2. The Supreme Court has interpreted this clause to mean that the House possesses broad power to adopt its own procedural rules. *United States* v. *Ballin*, 144 U.S. 5 (1892). This power cannot be restricted by the rules or statutory enactments of a preceding House. For example, the adoption of a layover requirement by the 91st Congress did not bind the 92d Congress. Deschler Ch 1 § 10.1.

The rules of the House for each Congress are adopted by resolution. See, *e.g.*, 112-1, H. Res. 5, Jan. 5, 2011, p ____. Ordinarily, the House adopts the rules of the prior Congress but with various amendments. 5 Hinds § 6742. Separate orders also may be adopted in the same resolution. Separate orders are not amendments to the standing rules but have the same force and effect for a Congress or portion thereof. See, *e.g.*, 108-1, H. Res.

5, Jan. 7, 2003, pp 10, 11. The House in the 106th Congress adopted a recodified version of the rules of the House in existence at the close of the 105th Congress, which rewrote and renumbered the rules, many without substantive change. 106-1, Jan. 6, 1999, pp 47-223.

A resolution adopting rules is subject to the motion for the previous question and subject to amendment if the previous question is voted down. Deschler Ch 1 § 9.6. The resolution is not subject to a demand for a division of the question absent prior adoption of a special order of business permitting a division of the resolution. *Manual* § 60; Deschler Ch 1 § 10.8.

The motion to commit is permitted after the previous question has been ordered on the resolution adopting the rules but is not debatable. It is the prerogative of the minority to offer a motion to commit even before the adoption of the rules. However, at that point the proponent need not qualify as opposed to the resolution. *Manual* § 60; Deschler Ch 1 § 9. Such a motion to commit is not divisible. However, if it is agreed to and more than one amendment is reported back pursuant thereto, then separate votes may be had on the reported amendments. The motion to refer also has been permitted upon the offering of a resolution adopting the rules, and before debate thereon, subject to the motion to lay on the table. *Manual* § 60; 5 Hinds § 5604.

As with other House-passed measures, the House may by unanimous consent direct the Clerk, in the engrossment of a House resolution providing for the adoption of rules, to make certain technical corrections in the text of the resolution. Deschler Ch 1 § 10.12.

§ 7. Procedure Before Adopting Rules

Before the adoption of formal rules, the House operates under general parliamentary law, as modified by certain customary House rules and practices and by portions of *Jefferson's Manual. Manual* § 60; 5 Hinds §§ 6761-6763; 8 Cannon § 3386. Statutes incorporated into the rules of the prior Congress do not control the proceedings of the new House. Deschler Ch 1 § 10.1. They must be re-adopted as part of the rules of the new House.

Before the adoption of rules by the House, rules that embody practices of long-established custom will be enforced as if already in effect. 6 Cannon § 191. Thus, before adoption of the rules, the Speaker may maintain decorum by directing a Member who has not been recognized in debate beyond an allotted time to be removed from the well or by directing the Sergeant-at-Arms to present the mace as the traditional symbol of order. *Manual* § 60.

Procedures common to general parliamentary law applicable in the House before the adoption of its formal rules include:

- The motion for a call of the House. 4 Hinds §2981; Deschler Ch 1 §9.
- Points of order of no quorum. *Manual* §60.
- The motion to refer, subject to the motion to table. *Manual* §60.
- Demands for the yeas and nays. 5 Hinds §§6012, 6013; Deschler Ch 1 §9.
- The motion for the previous question, which takes precedence over a motion to amend. 5 Hinds §§5451-5455.
- The motion to amend after rejection of the previous question (Deschler Ch 3 §10.10), with any amendment being subject to the point of order that it must be germane (Deschler Ch 1 §12.7).
- The practice that Members may engage in debate only when recognized, such recognition being at the discretion of the Speaker. *Manual* §60.
- The hour rule for debate on a question. Deschler Ch 1 §12.3.
- Losing the right to resume after yielding the floor. 5 Hinds §§5038-5040.
- Recognition for an amendment after the defeat of the previous question, under the hour rule, with the proponent of the amendment controlling the time. Deschler Ch 23 §22.4.
- The nondebatable motion to commit after ordering of the previous question. *Manual* §60; 5 Hinds §6758. Proponent of the motion to commit need not qualify as opposed to the resolution. *Manual* §60.
- Withdrawal of a resolution before action is taken thereon. Deschler Ch 1 §10.6.
- The motion to lay on the table. 5 Hinds §5390; Deschler Ch 1 §9.
- The motion to postpone to a day certain. Deschler Ch 1 §10.7.
- The motion to adjourn. 1 Hinds §89; Deschler Ch 1 §9.

Specific standing rules of the House held *not* applicable before adoption of its formal rules include:

- The rule permitting 40 minutes of debate after the moving of the previous question on a matter on which there has been no debate. 5 Hinds §5509.
- The three-day availability rule for the consideration of committee reports. Deschler Ch 1 §12.9.

§8. Taking Up Legislative Business

Generally

Congress is not assembled until both the House and Senate are in session with a quorum present. 6 Cannon §5. Once the two Houses have assembled, elected officers, sworn Members, and adopted rules, the resumption of legislative business is in order. 1 Hinds §§130, 140, 237; Deschler Ch 1 §11. In rare instances a major bill has been considered and passed even before the completion of organization by the adoption of rules. Deschler Ch 1 §12.8. However, a bill will not be considered in the House before the administration of the oath to Members-elect because of the statutory requirement that the oath precede the consideration of general business. 2 USC § 25. On occasion the House has convened for its second session, but then conducted no legislative business (including approval of its Journal or referral of bills) for several days. *Manual* § 84.

Old Business

Upon convening for a second or subsequent session during the term of a Congress, the House resumes all business that was pending before the House or its committees at the adjournment *sine die* of the preceding session. Clause 6 of rule XI; *Manual* § 814; 5 Hinds § 6727. Similarly, conference business between the two Houses continues over an adjournment between the first and second sessions of a Congress. 5 Hinds §§ 6760-6762. However, because past proceedings of one Congress do not bind its successor, business remaining at the end of one Congress does not carry over to the beginning of a new Congress. Deschler Ch 1 § 11.

Chapter 6
Bills and Resolutions

Research References
4 Hinds §§ 3266-3297, 3364-3390
7 Cannon §§ 846-871, 1027-1053
Deschler Ch 16; Deschler Ch 24 §§ 1-4, 9, 10

A. Generally

§ 1. In General; Resolutions Distinguished

Bills are used for purposes of general legislation. Joint resolutions are used to propose constitutional amendments and for special or subordinate legislative purposes. Simple or concurrent resolutions are used primarily to regulate the administrative or internal business of the House (or Houses), to express facts or opinions, or to dispose of some other nonlegislative matter. Deschler Ch 24 § 1. However, unlike simple or concurrent resolutions, a joint resolution is a bill so far as the rules of the House are concerned. 4 Hinds § 3375.

The introduction of certain types of private bills is prohibited by clause 4 of rule XII. See § 17, infra.

The various stages in the passage and enactment of a bill (reading, engrossment, enrollment, etc.) are treated elsewhere. See READING, PASSAGE, AND ENACTMENT; see also CONSIDERATION AND DEBATE; VOTING; and VETO OF BILLS.

§ 2. Public and Private Bills Distinguished

Bills and resolutions may be either public or private. A private bill is a bill for the benefit of one or several specified persons or entities, and a public bill relates to public matters and deals with individuals by classes only. 3 Hinds § 2614; 4 Hinds § 3285; 7 Cannon § 856; Deschler Ch 24 § 1. Whether a law is to be regarded as public or private depends on the attendant circumstances, having regard to the effect rather than the form of the legislation. *Bollinger* v. *Watson*, 63 S.W. 2d 642 (Ark. 1933). The distinction is important because the procedures followed in the enactment of private bills are significantly different from those applicable to public bills. § 15, infra.

A bill may be regarded as a public bill, and thus referred to the House or Union Calendar when reported, where it:

- Contains provisions applicable to the general public, although benefiting a named individual. 4 Hinds § 3286.
- Relates to a classes or groups of persons and not to persons as individuals. 7 Cannon § 870; Deschler Ch 24 § 3.3.

- Indemnifies a foreign government for injury to one of its nationals. 7 Cannon § 865; Deschler Ch 24 § 3.2.
- Includes among provisions for the relief of private persons one item to pay a claim of a foreign nation. 4 Hinds § 3287.
- Grants an easement over public lands to a private company. 7 Cannon § 864.
- Authorizes an exchange of government-owned land for privately owned land. 7 Cannon § 862.
- Provides for the reimbursement of "all the depositors" of a certain bank, the depositors not being identified by name. 8 Cannon § 2373.

§ 3. Form; Component Parts

Generally

The form of bills in the House is governed by statute and by the practices and customs of the House. Any deviation from the form so prescribed may be authorized by joint resolution or be waived by passage under suspension of the rules. 7 Cannon § 1035. Alleged errors in the drafting of a bill are to be resolved by the House during its consideration of the measure and not by the Speaker on a point of order. Deschler Ch 24 § 2.2.

Although there is no mandatory uniform style that is to be followed in the drafting of legislative measures, general guidelines are available through the Office of the Legislative Counsel.

The component parts of a bill introduced in the House include:

- A bill title (an identifying bill number is subsequently added thereto).
- A preamble—used often in simple and concurrent resolutions, less often in joint resolutions, and, in modern practice, never in bills. § 5, infra.
- An enacting or resolving clause, which must appear in the first section of the Act. 1 USC § 103.
- The text of the bill.

On rare occasions, a bill may contain an illustration, as where it shows a required warning label. 99-2, Feb. 3, 1986, p 1326. Also rare, one House may pass a bill with blanks to be filled in by the other House. 5 Hinds § 5781. Members distributing copies of bills on the floor containing personal interpretations or notations must abide by the Speaker's announced policies regarding handouts. *Manual* § 622; see also Deschler Ch 24 § 2.1.

Enacting Clauses

The form prescribed by section 101 of title 1, United States Code for the enacting clause of a bill is as follows:

> *Be it enacted by the Senate and House of Representatives of the United States of America in Congress assembled.*

Resolving Clauses

The form prescribed by section 102 of title 1, United States Code for the resolving clause of a joint resolution is:

> *Resolved by the Senate and House of Representatives of the United States of America in Congress assembled.*

If the joint resolution proposes to amend the Constitution, it is customary to add to the resolving clause the words ''two-thirds of both Houses concurring.'' 4 Hinds § 3367.

Sections; Headings and Subheadings

The United States Code requires that each section of a bill be numbered and that it ''contain, as nearly as may be, a single proposition of enactment.'' 1 USC § 104. Section headings and subheadings may be used, and in cases of ambiguity it is proper to consult both a section heading and the section's content in order to ascertain the clear meaning of the legislation. *House* v. *Commissioner*, 453 F.2d 982 (5th Cir. 1972).

Page and Line Numbers

When a bill is introduced or reported, each page of the text is numbered and each line in the text is given a separate number in the margin so that reference may quickly be made to specific provisions of the bill. However, the pagination and marginal numerals are not part of the text of the bill, and after amendment they may be altered, changed, or transposed by the Clerk to conform to the amended text without the necessity of a House order. 5 Hinds § 5781; 8 Cannon § 2876.

§ 4. Titles

All bills are given a title that indicates the subject matter of the bill. A title is used strictly for purposes of identification and is not considered in passing on points of order relating to the provisions of the bill. 7 Cannon § 1489; Deschler Ch 24 § 9.1. The title, also known as the ''long title,'' should be distinguished from the ''short title'' of a bill, which is typically contained in a separate section of the bill, and indicates a proposed legal citation for the bill.

Under the guidelines suggested by the Office of the Legislative Counsel, a title should accurately and briefly describe what a bill does. For bills amending primarily a particular law, the form ''To amend [citation of law] to . . .'' is ordinarily used. For constitutional amendments, the form ''Proposing an amendment to the Constitution of the United States concerning

. . .'' is used. If the bill covers multiple items, the phrase ''and for other purposes'' may be used at the end of the title.

The title is retained on the bill during the various stages of enactment, including engrossment and is entered on the Journal and printed in the *Congressional Record. Manual* §§431, 831. However, it is not considered to be part of the enacted statute and is generally published only in the *Statutes at Large*. Indeed, when an enacted statute is codified and included in the United States Code, its title may be excluded or greatly abbreviated.

A title cannot be used to negate the obvious meaning of the statute. However, a title may, as part of the legislative history, assist in resolving ambiguities. 4 Hinds §3381. In such cases the title of an Act may be resorted to by courts as an aid in determining legislative intent. *Brotherhood of R.R. Trainmen* v. *Baltimore and Ohio Railroad Co.,* 331 U.S. 519 (1947). In this context, the title of a bill at the time of its enactment is said to be indicative of the true intention of Congress in enacting it. Corpus Juris Secundum, *Statutes* §351.

§5. Preambles

Preambles are sometimes used to indicate the underlying reason for a measure. 4 Hinds §3413. Preambles (''whereas'' clauses) often appear in concurrent or simple resolutions. Such clauses appear less often in joint resolutions (and, in modern practice, never in bills) because sections containing separate statements of findings serve the same purpose. 4 Hinds §3412.

The House may amend or delete the preamble from a joint resolution before its passage or the preamble from a concurrent or simple resolution following its adoption. *Manual* §414. This is done either by unanimous consent or pursuant to a motion to strike the preamble. This cannot be done simply by moving to strike all after the enacting or resolving clause because the preamble always precedes that clause. Deschler Ch 24 §9.5. Preambles to simple resolutions may also be disposed of pursuant to a motion to lay on the table, and the adoption of such motion does not affect the status of the resolution. 5 Hinds §5430. The motion for the previous question may be applied at once to the resolution and the preamble. *Manual* §996. Of course, where no action is taken to strike the preamble, and the joint resolution is passed, the preamble remains part of the joint resolution. Deschler Ch 24 §9.5.

B. Introduction and Reference

§ 6. Introduction of Measures in the House; Sponsorship

Bills and Resolutions

Bills and resolutions are introduced by being deposited in the hopper at the Clerk's desk anytime the House is in session. Deschler Ch 16 § 1. A Member may introduce a bill during a pro forma meeting even though no legislative business is being conducted. *Manual* § 816.

At its organization for the 106th Congress, the House adopted an order reserving the first ten bill numbers for assignment by the Speaker during a specified period. For the 107th and 108th Congresses, the House adopted the same order and extended the applicable time period to the entire first session. For subsequent Congresses, the time period has been extended to the entire Congress. In the 112th Congress, the second ten bill numbers were reserved for the Minority Leader. *Manual* § 825.

A bill or resolution may be introduced by any Member who has taken the oath, and one need not seek recognition for that purpose. Deschler Ch 16 § 1. A Member may introduce a bill even though personally opposed to its passage. Deschler Ch 16 § 1.6. The rules do not limit the number of bills a Member may introduce.

Once introduced, the bill becomes the property of the House. As such, the House may consider it notwithstanding the death, resignation, or replacement of its sponsor. Deschler Ch 16 § 1.9.

Bills Introduced ''By Request''

Only a Member, Delegate, or the Resident Commissioner may introduce a bill. The House does not permit the names of citizens requesting the introduction of a bill to be printed in the *Congressional Record*, but the rules do permit the words ''by request'' to be entered on the Journal, printed on the bill, and printed in the *Record. Manual* § 826. These words appear following the name of the primary sponsor or the names of some or all of the initial cosponsors. Deschler Ch 16 § 1.2.

Petitions and Memorials

Petitions and memorials addressed to the House are delivered to the Clerk and may be presented by the Speaker as well as by any Member. *Manual* § 818; 4 Hinds § 3312. Members may present petitions from the citizens of States other than their own. 4 Hinds §§ 3315, 3316.

Sponsorship; Endorsements and Signatures

By House rule, all bills, resolutions, and memorials must be endorsed with the name of the Member or Members introducing or presenting them. *Manual* §§ 818, 825. By directive of the Speaker, all such measures must bear the original signature of the chief sponsor or first-named Member. *Manual* § 821. A bill falsely introduced in a Member's name involves a question of privilege, and the House may agree to an order providing for its cancellation. 4 Hinds § 3388.

Cosponsorship

Unlimited cosponsorship of a public bill is permitted until such time as all committees authorized to report the bill have filed their reports with the House or have been discharged from consideration thereof. Before the bill is reported, Members may remove their names as cosponsors by unanimous consent. *Manual* § 825. Alternatively, a cosponsor may announce withdrawal of support for a bill, or a statement indicating that an error was made in the listing of a cosponsor's name may be made on the floor for publication in the *Congressional Record*. Deschler Ch 16 §§ 2.5, 2.6. At its organization for the 104th Congress, the House resolved that each of the first 20 bills and each of the first two joint resolutions introduced in that Congress could have more than one Member reflected as a first sponsor.

By unanimous consent, Members may add their own names as cosponsors of an unreported bill where the primary sponsor is no longer a Member of the House. Similarly, a designated Member may be authorized to sign and submit lists of additional cosponsors where the primary sponsor is no longer a Member. However, the Chair will not otherwise entertain a unanimous-consent request to add cosponsors by a Member other than the primary sponsor, whether such request includes only the Member making the request, all Members, or a specified additional sponsor. Such requests must be made by a primary sponsor through the hopper not later than the last day on which all committees authorized to report the bill have filed their reports with the House. *Manual* § 825. In the case of an unreported bill considered pursuant to a special order of business, cosponsors may be added or removed prior to the calling up of such bill pursuant to the special order of business. For other unreported bills (such as those considered by suspension), cosponsors may be added prior to the vote on final passage.

§ 7. Reference

Generally

When a bill is introduced, it is referred by the Speaker to committee in accordance with clause 1 of rule X, the rule fixing the jurisdiction of committees over particular subjects, and in accordance with the referral procedures contained in clause 2 of rule XII. Deschler Ch 16 § 3. However, a bill referred by the House itself may be sent to any committee without regard to the rules of jurisdiction. 4 Hinds § 4375; 7 Cannon § 2131. Jurisdiction in such a case is deemed conferred by the action of the House. 4 Hinds §§ 4362-4364; 7 Cannon § 2105.

Absent specific authority or the authority to originate, a committee may not report a measure that has not been properly referred to it by the Speaker or by the House. 4 Hinds §§ 4355-4360; 7 Cannon §§ 1029, 2101. The following committees are authorized to originate and file from the floor as privileged, pursuant to clause 5 of rule XIII, certain bills and resolutions: Appropriations, Budget, House Administration, Rules, and Ethics. *Manual* §§ 412, 853.

Erroneously Referred Bills

Clause 7 of rule XII provides for procedures to be followed in case of an error in the reference of a public bill. For a discussion of erroneous referral of a private bill, see § 14, infra. The House rerefers public bills without debate, usually pursuant to a unanimous-consent request. Deschler Ch 16 §§ 3.13-3.15. A motion to rerefer also is available. However, that motion has not been offered since the 82d Congress. *Manual* § 825; Deschler Ch 16 §§ 3.10-3.13. The motion to rerefer:

- Must apply to a bill erroneously referred. 7 Cannon § 2125.
- Must be made immediately following the Pledge of Allegiance. Clause 7 of rule XII; 7 Cannon §§ 1809, 2119, 2120.
- Must apply to a single bill and not to a class of bills. 7 Cannon § 2125.
- May be amended. 7 Cannon § 2127.
- May not be divided. 7 Cannon § 2125.
- May not be debated. 7 Cannon §§ 2126-2128.

Bills Reported From Committee; Referrals to Calendars

Bills reported from committees are ordinarily referred to the proper calendar under the direction of the Speaker. *Manual* §§ 828, 831. Once a bill has been reported by committee, points of order against its reference and motions for its rereferral are not entertained. 7 Cannon § 2110; Deschler Ch 16 § 3.6. Under clause 2 of rule XII, a bill reported from committee (even a bill previously referred to a calendar) may be sequentially referred by the

Speaker to other committees. § 8, infra. Moreover, once consideration of the reported measure has begun in the House, a motion to refer or recommit is in order in differing situations under the rules of the House. *Manual* §§ 916, 917, 1001; see REFER AND RECOMMIT.

§ 8. Multiple Referrals; Sequential or Split Referrals

Before the 94th Congress, a bill could not be referred to two or more committees, even though it contained matters properly within the jurisdiction of several committees. 4 Hinds § 4372. However, in 1975 the House adopted clause 2(b) of rule XII, stating that every referral must be made so as to ensure "to the maximum extent feasible" that each committee having jurisdiction over the subject matter of a provision will have responsibility for considering it and reporting thereon to the House. Since 1995, clause 2(c)(1) of rule XII has required the Speaker to designate a committee of primary jurisdiction upon the initial referral of a measure to a committee (except where it is determined that extraordinary circumstances justify review by more than one committee as though primary). The Speaker has discretion to:

- Refer the measure to other committees either initially (at the time of introduction) or sequentially (following the primary committee's report); in either case, subject to time limits imposed after the primary committee has reported.
- Refer designated portions of the same measure to other committees (split referral).
- Refer a measure to a special ad hoc committee, established by the House, consisting of members of committees with shared jurisdiction over the measure.

The Speaker's referrals are always for consideration of such provisions as fall within a committee's jurisdiction, and bills referred to more than one committee are endorsed with an explicit statement to that effect.

§ 9. Bills Reported with Amendments

A bill reported from a committee with an amendment may be sequentially referred to another committee where the amendment falls within the jurisdiction of the second committee. *Manual* § 816. In determining whether the matter falls within the jurisdiction of the second committee, the Speaker may base the referral on either (1) the text of an amendment as well as the text of the original bill; or (2) solely on the text of a reported substitute amendment in lieu of the original bill. *Manual* § 816. The second committee may report an amendment to the amendment adopted by the first committee if the amendment to the amendment is within the jurisdiction of the second committee.

The Speaker has exercised the authority to base referrals on committee amendments to reported bills by sequentially referring:

- A reported bill to another committee solely for consideration of provisions of the first committee's amendment within its jurisdiction, and not for consideration of the entire bill.
- A reported bill to two other committees for different periods of time, solely for consideration of designated sections of the first committee's recommended amendment.
- A reported bill solely for consideration of designated portions of the first committee's amendment.
- Only a portion of the original text where the primary committee's amendment would delete portions of the bill within the sequential committee's jurisdiction.

Manual § 816.

§ 10. Matters Subject to Referral

Generally

Clause 2 of rule XII, the rule establishing the referral procedures to be followed by the Speaker, applies to ''each bill, resolution, or other matter'' relating to a subject falling within the jurisdiction of a standing committee under clause 1 of rule X. Thus, the Speaker may, pursuant to the rule, refer bills and resolutions, a portion of a bill, a Presidential message, an executive communication, or a select committee report. *Manual* § 816.

Senate Amendments to House Bills

Pursuant to clause 2 of rule XIV, the Speaker may refer to a standing committee a Senate amendment to a House-passed bill. Formerly, where a House bill was returned from the Senate with an amendment relating to a new and different subject, the Speaker referred it to the committee having jurisdiction of the original bill. 4 Hinds §§ 4373, 4374. Under the modern practice, the Speaker rarely exercises the authority to refer Senate amendments at all. When so doing, the Speaker may impose a time limitation for consideration of a certain portion of the amendment. *Manual* § 816. On being reported from a standing committee, the House bill with the Senate amendment is referred to the Committee of the Whole. 4 Hinds § 3108; 8 Cannon § 3187. Under clause 2 of rule XXII, House bills with Senate amendments that do not require consideration in Committee of the Whole may be disposed of by privileged motion.

Senate Bills and Messages

Pursuant to clause 2 of rule XIV, the Speaker may refer bills and joint and concurrent resolutions messaged from the Senate to committees in the same manner as public bills originating in the House. Senate amendments requiring consideration in Committee of the Whole and Senate bills (with certain exceptions, as where a similar House measure has been reported or ordered reported) are referred to the appropriate standing committees under the direction of the Speaker without action by the House. 4 Hinds §3101; 6 Cannon §727. Simple resolutions of the Senate that do not require any action by the House are not referred. 7 Cannon §1048.

§11. Time Limitations on Referred Bills; Extensions

Generally

Pursuant to clause 2 of rule XII, the Speaker may impose a time limit for the consideration by any committee of a bill that is initially or sequentially referred, but normally does so only for a sequential referral. The Speaker may sequentially refer a bill without setting such limit or may set a limit as short as one day. *Manual* §816.

On the last day of an expiring sequential referral, a committee has until midnight to file its report with the Clerk. *Manual* §816.

Clause 2 of rule XII is not construed to prevent another committee from reporting before the primary committee. It is the intent of the rule to allow the primary committee to report before a measure is scheduled for floor consideration. However, the measure may be considered without a report by the primary committee pursuant to a special order of business. The measure also may be considered when the Speaker exercises discretion to impose a time limit on the primary committee for reporting (although such discretion is rarely exercised) and such committee fails to meet the deadline. In that case, the primary committee will be considered to have been discharged from further consideration of the measure. *Manual* §816.

Extensions of Time

The Speaker may extend the time limit set for the consideration of a referred bill, and has exercised such authority with respect to bills that have been sequentially referred, or divided for reference. Where the Speaker extends the time limit on a sequentially referred bill, the bill may also be referred to another committee for the same period. More than one extension of time may be given. *Manual* §816.

Discharge of Committee

Where a committee does not report a measure to the House on or before the date specified by the Speaker pursuant to the authority under clause 2 of rule XII, the Speaker may discharge the committee from further consideration of the measure and refer it to the appropriate calendar or to another committee. Also, the House may adopt a special order of business accomplishing the discharge. *Manual* § 816.

§ 12. Referrals to Select and Ad Hoc Committees

The Speaker may refer bills, resolutions, and other matters (including messages and communications) to select or ad hoc committees established with the approval of the House. The House order authorizing the select or ad hoc committee may require that referrals to the committee be by initial or sequential reference or by some other method provided by clause 2 of rule XII. *Manual* § 816. For more information on select and ad hoc committees, see COMMITTEES.

C. Private Bills

§ 13. In General

Background

The practice of Congress in passing private bills for the benefit of specific persons or entities was taken from the English Parliament and began with the First Congress. The use of private bills steadily increased thereafter, so much so that in some years the Congress enacted more private bills than it did public bills. The 59th Congress, for example, enacted more than 6,000 private bills, while it enacted fewer than 700 public bills. 7 Cannon § 1028. In recent years, and especially since the adoption of the Legislative Reorganization Act of 1946, the number of private bills enacted into law has been steadily declining. In the 110th and 111th Congresses, only two private bills were enacted.

Because it lacks the generality of application that is normally found in public laws, a private law is considered a legislative anomaly. Congressional action in passing such laws has been based on the rationale that because public laws cannot cover every situation or extraordinary circumstance that might arise, Congress may, as part of its general law-making function, create ''equitable law'' to cover such circumstance. *Note, Private Bills in Congress*, 79 Harv. L. Rev. 1684 (1966).

Constitutionality

Although the constitutionality of private laws has not been subjected to extensive critical analysis by the courts, their use is regarded as a proper legislative function. The Supreme Court in 1940 held that the passage of a private law does not constitute a congressional intrusion into the judicial function. *Paramino Lumber Company* v. *Marshall*, 309 U.S. 370 (1940).

Omnibus Bills

Clause 5 of rule XV permits the use of ''omnibus'' private legislation—that is, a measure containing two or more private bills that are considered as a single package. *Manual* §§ 895, 897.

§ 14. What Constitutes a Private Bill

A private bill may be generally defined as a bill for the benefit or relief of one or several specified persons or entities. 4 Hinds § 3285; 7 Cannon § 856. It is generally enacted only for those who have no other remedy available to them. Deschler Ch 24 § 3. A bill for the benefit of a named individual is classed as a private bill, even though it deals with government property. 7 Cannon § 859. An ''omnibus claim bill,'' which contains provisions for payments to many different claimants, also is treated as a private bill rather than a public bill, where all claimants are of the same class and each claimant is specified by name. 4 Hinds § 3293.

§ 15. Introduction, Reference, and Consideration

Private bills may be presented to the House only through a sponsoring Member and may not be cosponsored. They are otherwise introduced in the same manner as public bills. A Member with a private bill to present (1) endorses the bill by signature and (2) delivers the bill to the Clerk. Clause 3 of rule XII; *Manual* § 818.

Under clause 6 of rule XII, errors in the referral of private bills may be corrected without action by the House at the suggestion of the committee in possession of the bill. Because an erroneous reference of a private bill does not confer jurisdiction on the committee to report it, a point of order will lie against the bill when it comes up for consideration in the House or in the Committee of the Whole. *Manual* § 824. A subcommittee may have specific rules governing the consideration of private bills. Committee approval of the bill is generally contingent upon a showing that the applicant has no other remedy. A private bill reported out of committee is referred to the Private Calendar.

Private bills called on the Private Calendar are reviewed by a committee of ''official objectors'' consisting of six Members—three from each party. As a matter of policy, the official objectors have traditionally required that bills must be on the Private Calendar for seven days before being called up. See PRIVATE CALENDAR. A Member serving as an official objector has periodically included in the *Congressional Record* an explanation of how bills on the Private Calendar are considered. *Manual* § 896. If two or more Members of the House object to a bill, it is recommitted to the committee that reported it. *Manual* § 895. However, such a bill may be ''passed over without prejudice'' by unanimous consent for subsequent consideration. Also, the provisions of a private bill may be reported back in an omnibus bill. See PRIVATE CALENDAR. In modern practice, private bills have not been scheduled by the Speaker for consideration under suspension of the rules. This procedure has been reserved for public bills.

If the bill is unopposed, it is taken up in the House as in the Committee of the Whole. The procedure is as follows:

> SPEAKER: This is the day for the call of the Private Calendar. The Clerk will call the first omnibus bill on the calendar. . . . The Clerk will read the bill by title for amendment. [*The Clerk reads the bill, and any committee amendments are reported and disposed of; thereafter, motions to amend are in order.* See § 16, infra.]
>
> MEMBER: M__. Speaker, I offer a motion [*to strike all or part of the pending paragraph.*]
>
> > *Note:* Amendments are in order only if they strike or reduce amounts of money or provide limitations. *Manual* § 895. Motions to strike the last word are not permitted, nor are reservations of objection. See PRIVATE CALENDAR.
>
> SPEAKER [*after disposition of amendments*]: The question is on the engrossment and third reading of the bill.
>
> MEMBER: M__. Speaker, I offer a motion to recommit.
>
> SPEAKER [*after disposition of the motion to recommit*]: The question is on the passage of the omnibus bill.

After being passed by the House, an omnibus private bill is resolved into the various private bills of which it is composed, and each is sent to the Senate as if individually passed. *Manual* § 897. A private bill that has passed both Houses must be approved by the President or enacted over a veto to become law.

§ 16. — Amendments

A private bill is subject to amendment under the five-minute rule, pursuant to clause 5 of rule XV. *Manual* §§ 895, 897. However, a private bill for the benefit of one individual may not be amended so as to extend its provisions to another individual, even indirectly through a motion to recommit with instructions. 4 Hinds § 3296. Under the germaneness rule, it is not in order to amend a private bill by extending its provisions to a general class of individuals, which would be public in character. 4 Hinds § 3292; 7 Cannon § 860; see GERMANENESS OF AMENDMENTS. Motions to strike the last word—pro forma amendments—are not entertained. Deschler-Brown Ch 29 § 70.7.

When an amendment is offered, members of the reporting committee have priority in recognition to oppose the amendment. Deschler-Brown Ch 29 § 13.23.

§ 17. Uses of Private Bills

Generally

Under the modern practice, most private bills granting relief to individuals fall into one of four major categories: (1) bills involving claims *against* the United States or waiving claims *by* the Federal Government against specific individuals; (2) bills excepting named individuals from certain requirements of the immigration or naturalization laws; (3) conveyances of real property rights; and (4) tariff treatment for private entries. See §§ 18, 19, infra.

Some private bills granting relief to identified individuals merely permit the taking of some action that would otherwise be prohibited by general law. For example, one favorably reported private bill authorized Federal employees of the Social Security Administration in Syracuse, New York, to transfer annual leave to a fellow employee who had exhausted her sick leave during her treatment for cancer. 100-2, H.R. 3625, H. Rept. 100-554. Another private bill authorized the Secretary of Defense to allow the children of a secret service agent killed while on duty to attend school at a United States military facility in Puerto Rico (the family had been notified that his children were no longer eligible to attend the school because the children were no longer dependents of a Federal employee in Puerto Rico). 100-2, H.R. 3439, H. Rept. 100-552.

Measures Barred From Consideration

Under clause 4 of rule XII, a private bill may not be introduced or considered if it authorizes or directs the payment of money for property damages or for personal injuries or death for which suit may be instituted under the Federal Tort Claims Act (FTCA). Private pension bills (other than those to carry out a provision of law or treaty stipulation) are also barred, as are bills providing for the construction of a bridge across a navigable stream.

Private bills providing for the correction of a military record are likewise proscribed. However, a private bill that merely changes the computation of retired pay for a former member of the armed services has been held permissible. *Manual* § 822. The barring of private bills in such cases is based on the availability to claimants of other judicial or administrative remedies. Deschler Ch 24 § 3. The FTCA, for example, provides both administrative and judicial remedies in certain personal injury cases involving the negligence of Federal employees. 28 USC § 2671.

§ 18. — Claims By or Against the Government

Generally; Constitutionality

Many private bills grant relief to an individual who has a meritorious claim against the Federal government that cannot otherwise be remedied. Deschler Ch 24 § 3. The constitutional basis for such bills is found in the first amendment, which sets forth the right to petition the government for the redress of grievances, and in article I, which allocates to Congress the power to pay the debts of the United States. U.S. Const. art. I, § 8, cl. 1; *Pope* v. *United States*, 323 U.S. 1 (1944).

Procedure

Under clause 2(d) of rule XII, unanimous consent is required for the reference of a private claim bill to a committee other than the Committee on the Judiciary or the Committee on Foreign Affairs. *Manual* § 817. Most private bills involving claims against the government are referred to the Committee on the Judiciary, which has jurisdiction over such claims under clause 1(l) of rule X. For example, a private bill providing to a named individual an entitlement to social security benefits was referred as a private claim only to the Committee on the Judiciary (in accord with clause 2(d) of rule XII) and, when reported by that committee, was referred to the Private Calendar and not sequentially to the Committee on Ways and Means. 106-2, Feb. 14, 2000, p 1170.

The Committee on the Judiciary refers a private claim bill to its Subcommittee on Immigration Policy and Enforcement. The subcommittee may hold a hearing on the matter. The full committee files its report with the House, and the Speaker refers it to the Private Calendar. See also § 15, supra.

> *Note:* An alternative to this procedure is provided for in law. It authorizes either House of Congress, by adopting a resolution, to refer bills (except pension bills) to the Chief Judge of the U.S. Court of Federal Claims, and

stipulates that the Chief Judge is to report the findings of fact and conclusions in each case to the House that made the reference. 28 USC §§ 1492, 2509. These reports are provided to Congress for use in deciding whether certain private claims warrant legislative relief. *Zadeh* v. *United States*, 111 F. Supp. 248 (Ct. Cl. 1953).

Granting Relief; Consideration of Particular Claims

In exercising its jurisdiction over claims against the government, and in determining whether relief should be granted to persons seeking redress of grievances under its rules, the subcommittee with jurisdiction over private claims has been guided by "principles of equity and justice." The task of the subcommittee has been to determine whether the equities and circumstances of a case create a "moral obligation" on the part of the government to extend relief to an individual who has no other existing remedy. For example, relief has been granted in private legislation:

- To provide for the payment to settle certain property damage claims of residents arising out of the 1973 occupation of Wounded Knee, South Dakota. 100-2, H.R. 2711, H. Rept. 100-559.
- To provide for a payment to a child who had been sexually assaulted by an employee of the Postal Service, who was delivering mail at the time. A civil action against the United States on behalf of the six-year-old claimant was filed under the FTCA on the basis of negligent supervision of the employee by the Postal Service, but this suit was unsuccessful, intentional torts such as assault being excluded under the provisions of the Act. 100-2, H.R. 4099, H. Rept. 100-556.
- To authorize certain firefighters to sue the United States for injuries or death under the FTCA because the Secretary of Labor had determined that the firefighters were Federal employees covered by another statute—the Federal Employee Compensation Act—which precluded claims under the FTCA. 100-2, H.R. 2682, H. Rept. 100-547.
- To waive the discretionary-function and foreign-country exceptions to the FTCA, thereby granting jurisdiction for a claimant to sue the government for claims arising at a U.S. Army health facility in Germany for improperly administered smallpox vaccination. 100-2, H.R. 2684, H. Rept. 100-442.
- To provide compensatory relief in a contract case based on a moral obligation of the government, such as when money was promised and not paid. 87-1, Priv. L. 87-195, H. Rept. 87-232; 100-2, H.R. 3185, H. Rept. 100-549.
- To adjust or credit the account of a Federal official or to reimburse a government employee for expenditures made by him at the direction of his employer. 7 Cannon § 863; 100-2, H.R. 3388, H. Rept. 100-551.

- To permit claimants to receive an annuity under the Civil Service Retirement System. 100-2, H.R. 2889, H. Rept. 100-548; 100-2, H.R. 1864, H. Rept. 100-546.
- To relieve a Federal employee of liability for repayment of travel expenses erroneously paid to him by his employer. 100-2, H.R. 3941, H. Rept. 100-555; 100-2, H.R. 3347, H. Rept. 100-550.
- To suspend or waive a statute of limitations where the government has been unjustly enriched at the expense of the claimant (87-1, Priv. L. 87-23, H. Rept. 87-176), or where to do so would be in the interests of "justice and equity" (100-1, H.R. 1491, H. Rept. 100-439).
- To provide payment to an individual injured by a government-prescribed fire. 104-2, S. 966, H. Rept. 104-638.
- To provide reimbursement to an entity for emergency work under the Robert T. Stafford Disaster and Emergency Assistance Act. 104-1, H.R. 419, H. Rept. 104-359.

§ 19. —Immigration and Naturalization Cases

Private bills are sometimes used to exempt individuals from the application of the immigration and naturalization laws in hardship cases where the law would otherwise prohibit entry into or require deportation from the United States. Deschler Ch 24 § 3.

Private bills have been used in specific cases to:

- Restore a prospective immigrant to his place on a quota waiting list when that place was lost through no fault of the immigrant. 83-2, Priv. L. 601, H. Rept. 83-2078.
- Grant asylum to a Communist aviator who flew his plane to the West. 83-2, Priv. L. 380, H. Rept. 83-650.
- Grant permanent-residency status to a Philippino woman who became pregnant while visiting the United States under a temporary visa, where the father had acquired permanent-residency status, and where the alternative would have been to separate the family, with the mother and infant returning to the Philippines and the father remaining in the United States. 100-1, S. 393, H. Rept. 100-354.
- Reinstate U.S. citizenship to a man who had renounced citizenship in 1950 due to family obligations when he was married to a Mexican national. 100-1, H.R. 2358, H. Rept. 100-381.
- Enable a record-holding swimmer from East Germany who had defected to the United States to file a petition for naturalization, without regard to residence or Communist Party membership. 100-2, H.R. 446, H. Rept. 100-598.
- Grant the status of permanent residence to a sports and media figure retroactively to 1950 and provide that he be considered to have complied with residential and physical presence requirements of the Immigration and Naturalization Act. 86-2, Priv. L. 86-486, H. Rept. 1506.

- To permit certain individuals who were evacuated from Kuwait during the Persian Gulf War to file for permanent-residency status. 106-2, H.R. 3646, H. Rept. 106-580.

D. Restrictions on Certain Public Bills

§ 20. Appropriations

Appropriations on Legislative Bills

Restrictions against the inclusion of appropriations in legislative bills are provided for by clause 4 of rule XXI. A bill or joint resolution carrying appropriations may not be reported by a committee not having jurisdiction to report appropriations; and points of order lie against those provisions when the bill is read for amendment. The rule also prohibits amendments proposing appropriations on a reported legislative bill. *Manual* § 1065; see also APPROPRIATIONS, § 76.

Transportation Obligation Limitations

Clause 3 of rule XXI provides a restriction against general appropriation bills that provide spending authority from balances in the Highway Trust Fund (other than transfers from the general fund of the Treasury) or reduces or limits the accruing balances of that trust fund for anything other than activities authorized for highway or mass transit programs. A former version of this rule enforced specified minimum levels of surface transportation obligation limitations. *Manual* § 1064; see also APPROPRIATIONS, § 59a.

Funding for Aviation Programs

Section 206 of the Wendell H. Ford Aviation Investment and Reform Act for the 21st Century (Pub. L. 106-181) added a provision establishing points of order to guarantee a certain level of budget resources available from the Airport and Airway Trust Fund each fiscal year through fiscal year 2003 (updated to 2007 by Pub. L. 108-176), to restrict the uses of those resources, and to guarantee a certain level of appropriations. *Manual* § 1064d; see also APPROPRIATIONS, § 59a.

§ 21. Tax and Tariff Measures

Under clause 5(a) of rule XXI, a bill or joint resolution carrying a tax or tariff measure may not be reported by a committee other than the Committee on Ways and Means; and points of order lie against those provisions when the reported bill is read for amendment. The prohibition extends to consideration of an amendment in the House or proposed by the Senate that carries a tax or tariff measure offered during the consideration of such bill or joint resolution. For a discussion of the restrictions against bills and amendments carrying a tax or tariff, see *Manual* § 1066.

Clause 5(c) of rule XXI precludes consideration of a bill, joint resolution, amendment, or conference report that carries a retroactive Federal income tax rate increase. The rule defines a ''Federal income tax rate increase'' as any amendment to subsection (a), (b), (c), (d), or (e) of section 1, or to section 11(b) or 55(b), of the Internal Revenue Code of 1986, that imposes a new percentage as a rate of tax and thereby increases the amount of tax imposed by any such section. The rule further specifies that a Federal income tax rate increase is retroactive if it applies to a period beginning before the enactment of the provision. *Manual* § 1068.

§ 22. Designation of Public Works

Clause 6 of rule XXI precludes consideration of a bill, joint resolution, amendment, or conference report that provides for the designation or redesignation of a public work in honor of an individual then serving as a Member, Delegate, Resident Commissioner, or Senator. *Manual* § 1068a.

§ 23. Prohibition on Commemorations

Clause 5 of rule XII precludes introduction and consideration of a bill or resolution, or an amendment thereto, if it establishes or expresses a commemoration. The term ''commemoration'' is defined by the rule as a remembrance, celebration, or recognition for any purpose through the designation of a specified period of time. *Manual* § 823.

§ 24. Earmarks

Clause 9 of rule XXI precludes the consideration of bills and joint resolutions unless a list of congressional earmarks, limited tax benefits, and limited tariff benefits, are included in the committee report. For unreported bills and certain amendments, this list must be printed in the *Congressional Record.* In lieu of such a list, a statement that the legislation contains no such earmarks, tax or tariff benefits may also be submitted. Clause 9 of rule XXI also precludes the consideration of conference reports whose joint explanatory statement fails to include the requisite earmark statement.

The point of order raised against consideration of a measure under this rule must be based solely on the failure to include the requisite earmark statement. The Chair does not rule on the sufficiency or accuracy of such statements, but merely takes cognizance of their presence or absence in the report, the joint explanatory statement, or the *Congressional Record*, as applicable. See 110-1, May 10, 2007, pp 12190, 12191.

Pursuant to clause 9(c) of rule XXI, it is not in order to consider a special order of business or other order of the House that waives the earmark statement requirements in clause 9(a) or (b) of rule XXI. A point of order under that paragraph is decided by the question of consideration. See QUESTION OF CONSIDERATION.

§ 25. Budget-related Restrictions

Certain budgetary schemes contained in House rules or enacted into law place restrictions on the consideration of measures that violate those budgetary rules. For a detailed discussion of these restrictions, see BUDGET PROCESS.

Chapter 7
Budget Process

Research References

Deschler Ch 13 § 21
Manual §§ 169, 719, 748, 853, 990, 1068c, 1068f, 1129-1130
Budget and Accounting Act of 1921
Congressional Budget and Impoundment Control Act of 1974
Balanced Budget and Emergency Deficit Control Act of 1985 (Gramm-Rudman)
Balanced Budget and Emergency Deficit Control Reaffirmation Act of 1987

Budget Enforcement Act of 1990
Omnibus Budget Reconciliation Act of 1993
Unfunded Mandates Reform Act of 1995
Budget Enforcement Act of 1997
Statutory Pay-As-You-Go Act of 2010
Budget Control Act of 2011
Introduction to the Federal Budget Process, CRS, Dec. 2, 2010
Budget Enforcement Act of 1997: Summary and Legislative History, CRS, Oct. 8, 1997

§ 1. In General

There are three stages in the complex process by which the Congress allocates the fiscal resources of the Federal government. First, there is an *authorization* process, under which Federal programs are created in response to national needs. Second, there is an *appropriations* process under which funding is provided for those programs. See APPROPRIATIONS. Finally, there is a congressional *budget* process that annually establishes an overall fiscal policy of spending and revenues and that institutes a complex web of procedures to enforce those budgetary decisions. The overall fiscal policy is established by the annual adoption of a concurrent resolution on the budget. The congressional budget process includes the development and consideration of reconciliation legislation to implement its most significant budget policies. These three stages are not necessarily considered or completed in chronological order.

The enforcement of budgetary decisions encompasses both congressional and executive actions. Such enforcement is rooted principally in three statutes—the Congressional Budget Act of 1974 (the Budget Act), the Balanced Budget and Emergency Deficit Control Act of 1985 (Gramm-Rudman), and the Statutory Pay-As-You-Go Act of 2010 (Stat-Paygo). A recent law, the Budget Control Act of 2011, also provides new enforcement mechanisms for budgetary decisions. See § 24, infra. The Budget Act permits enforcement through parliamentary points of order against legislation violating its requirements and procedures. However, the enforcement mechanisms are not automatically applied and timely points of order from the floor are required to bring them into play. Gramm-Rudman made significant revisions to the Budget Act and its budgetary control mechanisms. See § 2, infra. Stat-Paygo provides for a scorecard and a procedure that will result in sequestration (automatic spending cuts) if the scorecard shows a debit. The Budget Control Act of 2011 establishes a point of order if discretionary spending caps are violated and provides for sequestration if the product of a joint select committee on deficit reduction is not enacted into law by December 2011.

§ 2. —Earlier Statutes

The Budget and Accounting Act of 1921

Budget reform began with the passage of the Budget and Accounting Act of 1921. That Act established a new budget system that permitted all items relating to a department to be brought together in the same bill; required the President to submit an annual national budget to Congress in place of the previous uncoordinated agency submissions; created the Office of Management and Budget (OMB) to assist in this respect; and established the General Accounting Office and made it the principal auditing arm of the Federal government. 31 USC § 1101.

The Congressional Budget Act of 1974

Until 1974 Congress lacked a comprehensive uniform mechanism for establishing priorities among its budgetary goals and for determining national economic policy regarding the Federal budget. Responsibility for the budget remained fragmented throughout the Congress. The size of the budget, and the size of the surplus or deficit, were not subject to effective controls. To address these problems, both Houses enacted over President Nixon's veto the Congressional Budget and Impoundment Control Act of 1974. Deschler Ch 13 § 21. The Act (2 USC § 601) consisted of 10 titles that established:

- New committees on the budget in both the House and the Senate, and a Congressional Budget Office (CBO) designed to improve Congress' informational and analytical resources with respect to the budgetary process.
- A timetable and controls for various phases of the congressional budget process centered on a concurrent resolution on the budget to be adopted before legislative consideration of revenue or spending bills.
- Various enforcement procedures and provided for program review and evaluation.
- Standardized budget terminology.
- Procedures for congressional review of Presidential impoundment actions.

Titles I through IX constitute the Congressional Budget Act of 1974 and title X constitutes the Impoundment Control Act. The Unfunded Mandates Reform Act of 1995 added a new part B to title IV of the Budget Act.

The central purpose of the process established by the Budget Act is to coordinate the various revenue and spending decisions that are made in separate tax, appropriations, and legislative measures.

The Balanced Budget and Emergency Deficit Control Act of 1985

The Balanced Budget and Emergency Deficit Control Act of 1985 (Gramm-Rudman) made further significant changes in the budget process, and in the Budget Act procedures. 2 USC § 900. Conceived as a statutory response to the burgeoning Federal deficit, Gramm-Rudman instituted a single binding budget resolution, binding committee allocations, reconciliation, and enforcement of spending through sequestration. Gramm-Rudman included provisions amending the Budget Act to permit a new point of order against legislation exceeding the appropriate committee allocation (§ 302(f) of the Budget Act), exempting the title II Social Security program from reconciliation (§ 310(g) of the Budget Act), and precluding the breaching of budget authority or outlay ceilings or revenue floors, with certain exceptions (§ 311 of the Budget Act). Pursuant to section 275 of Gramm-Rudman, several provisions of Gramm-Rudman expired on September 30, 2002, including two provisions providing for sequestration to enforce discretionary spending (§ 251) and deficit targets (§ 253).

Budget Enforcement Act of 1990; Revisions and Extensions

The Budget Enforcement Act of 1990 (BEA of 1990) revised the Gramm-Rudman deficit targets, made deficit targets adjustable, and extended the sequestration process. It set limitations on distinct categories of discretionary spending and created a PAYGO process that would trigger a sequestration of funds should increases in direct spending or decreases in revenues cause a net increase in the deficit for a given year. §§ 13-16, infra.

Budget Enforcement Act of 1997

The Budget Enforcement Act of 1997 (BEA of 1997) extended the discretionary spending limits and PAYGO process through fiscal year 2002 and further changed the congressional budget process. For a more detailed discussion of its revisions, see *Budget Enforcement Act of 1997: Summary and Legislative History*, CRS, Oct. 8, 1997.

§ 3. —The Paygo/Cutgo Rule (Clause 10 of rule XXI)

Generally

At different times over the past three decades, different procedures in the House have fallen under the label "Pay-As-You-Go" or PAYGO. The term PAYGO was first used in law in section 252 of Gramm-Rudman as part of a process that required that direct spending and revenue legislation enacted into law be deficit neutral. The original statutory PAYGO process, as noted above, was first instituted in 1990 and, while textually still in law, only applies to legislation enacted prior to the end of the fiscal year 2002. Today the House operates under another statutory PAYGO process (Stat-Paygo), enacted on February 12, 2010 (Pub. L. 111-139). See §4, infra.

The House first adopted a separate PAYGO rule providing a point of order against measures in the 110th Congress (clause 10 of rule XXI). That rule was converted to a procedure known as CUTGO in the 112th Congress. ''Cut-As-You-Go'' changed the focus of the rule to increases in mandatory spending. As so amended, the rule operates independently of revenue changes and the status of the deficit or surplus. This section will address primarily the parliamentary procedures found in the House rules. For a more detailed description of Stat-Paygo, see *The Statutory Pay-As-You-Go Act of 2010: Summary and Legislative History*, CRS, Sept. 13, 2010. For more on the former House PAYGO rule, see *Manual* §1068e for the 111th Congress (H. Doc. 110-162).

The Cutgo Rule (clause 10 of rule XXI)

The House CUTGO rule establishes a point of order against measures that cause an increase in mandatory spending over a six- or eleven-year time period. The effect of the measure is determined on the basis of estimates made by the Committee on the Budget. 112-1, Jan. 26, 2011, p ____. The rule also provides special procedures when evaluating measures that (1) are considered under a rule that directs the Clerk to add the text of one measure to another after passage, or (2) contain provisions designated as an emergency.

Definitions and Time Periods

The CUTGO rule only addresses measures that affect mandatory spending. The rule equates ''mandatory spending'' with ''direct spending'' and uses the definition of direct spending found in section 250 of Gramm-Rudman with an exception for certain provisions in appropriation Acts. The rule also uses the definitions of ''budget year'' and ''current year'' found in section 250 of Gramm-Rudman.

The rule provides both a six- and eleven-year time period in which a measure may not increase mandatory spending. Specifically, the measure may not increase mandatory spending for the period comprising either: (1) the current year, the budget year, and the four years following that budget year; or (2) the current year, the budget year, and the nine years following that budget year.

Estimates

The effect of the measure on mandatory spending is based on estimates provided by the Committee on the Budget. This is similar to the authority vested in the Committee on the Budget by section 312 of the Budget Act over estimates of levels of new budget authority, outlays, direct spending, new entitlement authority, and revenues for purposes of titles III and IV of the Budget Act. The Chair is authoritatively guided by estimates from the Committee on the Budget as to the net effect of a measure as compared to the proposition to which it was offered. 112-1, Jan. 26, 2011, p ____.

Linking Measures

The rule provides for a special evaluation when a measure is being considered under a special order of business that directs the Clerk to add the text of one measure to another measure following passage. Specifically, the rule provides that if a bill, joint resolution, or amendment is considered pursuant to a special order of the House directing the Clerk to add as new matter at the end of such measure the entire text of a separate measure or measures as passed by the House, the new matter shall be included in the evaluation of the bill, joint resolution, or amendment. Clause 10(b) of rule XXI. See SPECIAL ORDERS OF BUSINESS.

Emergency Designations

The rule excludes provisions designated as emergencies in certain measures from the CUTGO evaluation. The rule specifically excludes a provision designated as an emergency under Stat-Paygo in the case of a point of order against: (1) a bill or joint resolution; (2) an amendment made in order as original text by a special order of business; (3) a conference report; or (4) an amendment between the Houses. Clause 10(c)(1) of rule XXI. The rule also provides that in the case of an amendment (other than an amendment in the nature of a substitute made in order as original text or an amendment between the Houses) the evaluation of the Committee on the Budget shall give no cognizance to any designation of emergency. Clause 10(c)(2) of rule XXI. This provision creates a level playing field for amendments by requiring the Committee on the Budget to evaluate amendments offered from the floor (including those proposed in a motion to recommit) to the underlying text as if both the amendment and the underlying text did not include such emergency designations. For a discussion of the treatment of emergency designations under the Budget Control Act of 2011, see § 24, infra.

Reconciliation Directives

Clause 7 of rule XXI also provides a point of order against concurrent resolutions on the budget that contain reconciliation directives that are not CUTGO-compliant. Specifically, it is not in order to consider a concurrent resolution on the budget, or an amendment thereto, or a conference report thereon, that contains reconciliation directives under section 310 of the Congressional Budget Act of 1974 that specify changes in law that would cause an increase in net direct spending for the period of the concurrent resolution on the budget.

§4. —The Statutory Pay-As-You-Go Act of 2010 (Stat-Paygo)

Generally

The Statutory Pay-As-You-Go Act of 2010 (Pub. L. 111-139) was enacted on February 12, 2010. That Act established a new budget enforcement mechanism to require that new direct spending and revenue legislation enacted into law not increase the deficit. Under this procedure, the budgetary effects of direct spending and revenue legislation are carried on PAYGO scorecards covering five- and ten-year periods. If at the end of a congressional session a scorecard shows a net debit, the President issues an order known as a ''sequestration order'' that results in a largely across-the-board cut in certain programs equal to the amount of the debit.

Section 4 of the Act establishes a procedure whereby budgetary effects of certain measures for purposes of maintaining a PAYGO scorecard are determined by Congress. This procedure permits the House and Senate to include language in bill text to direct that the scoring of a measure be determined by reference to an estimate submitted in the *Record* by the chair of either the House or Senate Budget Committee or both acting together in the case of a conference report. If such language is not included, the budgetary effects are determined by the Office of Management and Budget.

Section 4 of the Act provides that the provisions that are designated as emergency requirements under the Act are not counted as budgetary effects. The Act further provides that the Chair must put the question of consideration with regard to each measure carrying an emergency designation. See QUESTION OF CONSIDERATION.

Budgetary Effects Procedure

Stat-Paygo establishes a procedure where the budgetary effects of legislation are determined by either the Congress or by the Office of Management and Budget. The Act provides for congressional scoring to be used if (1) specified legislative language is contained in the measure and (2) a statement issued by the relevant chair of the Committee on the Budget (or jointly by both chairs in the case of amendments between the Houses and conference reports) has been printed in the *Record* prior to the final vote on the measure. The language required to be included in the measure is as follows:

> The budgetary effects of this Act, for the purpose of complying with the Statutory Pay-As-You-Go Act of 2010, shall be determined by reference to the latest statement titled 'Budgetary Effects of PAYGO Legislation' for this Act, submitted for printing in the *Congressional Record* by the chair of the (House and/or Senate) Budget Committee, provided that such statement has been submitted prior to the vote on passage (or in the House acting first on this conference report or amendments between the Houses).

For examples of *Congressional Record* submissions to accompany the textual reference, see 111-2, Feb. 25, 2010, p ____ (submission with respect to a bill); 111-2, May 28, 2010, p ____ (submission with respect to a House amendment to a Senate amendment), and 111-2, Nov. 15, 2010, p ____ (joint submission with respect to a conference report). Any deviation from the statutory formula in terms of content or timing could result in the budgetary effects being measured by the Office of Management and Budget rather than Congress.

Emergency Designations

Section 4 of the Act provides that a provision of direct spending or revenue legislation may be designated as an emergency for purposes of the Act. The budgetary effects of such a provision are not included in the estimate provided under the Act by CBO or OMB, as applicable. § 4(g). The Act also provides that if an emergency designation under the Act is included in a measure in the House, the Chair must put the question of consideration on such measure. § 4(g)(2). The Budget Control Act of 2011 provides a separate treatment for emergency designations and motions to strike such designations. See § 24, infra.

§ 5. Committee Jurisdiction; Reports and Estimates

Committee on the Budget Jurisdiction

To implement the congressional budget process, the Budget Act created the Senate and House Budget Committees and CBO. 2 USC § 601. The Budget Committees were authorized to draft the concurrent resolution on the budget. Unlike the authorizing and appropriating committees, which focus on individual Federal programs, the Budget Committees focus on the Federal budget as a whole and on how it affects the national economy.

Clause 1(d) of rule X gives the Committee on the Budget jurisdiction over matters relating to the congressional budget, including concurrent resolutions on the budget and measures on budget process and on the enforcement of budget controls. *Manual* § 719. Section 310 of the Budget Act provides conditions for the reporting by the Budget Committees of reconciliation measures.

Section 306 of the Budget Act prohibits the consideration in either House of a bill or resolution dealing with a matter within the jurisdiction of its Committee on the Budget if not reported from that committee or discharged therefrom. The following were held to violate this section:

- An amendment directing that certain lease-purchase agreements be scored on an annual basis for budget purposes. 106-1, July 19, 1999, pp 16615, 16616.
- An amendment designating an appropriation as ''emergency spending'' within the meaning of the budget-enforcement laws. 106-1, Sept. 8, 1999, pp 20928-30.

Separate orders contained in opening-day rules packages have confined the point of order under section 306 to bills and joint resolutions only. See, *e.g.*, 107-1, H. Res. 5, Jan. 3, 2001, p 26; 108-1, H. Res. 5, Jan. 7, 2003, p 10; 109-1, H. Res. 5, Jan. 4, 2005, p 44; 110-1, H. Res. 6, Jan. 4, 2007, p 23; 111-1, H. Res. 5, Jan. 6, 2009, p ____; 112-1, H. Res. 5, Jan. 5, 2011, p ____.

Committee on Rules Jurisdiction

The Committee on Rules has the special oversight function of review of the budget process. Clause 3(j) of rule X. Under section 301(c) of the Budget Act, the Speaker must refer a concurrent resolution on the budget reported from the Committee on the Budget sequentially to the Committee on Rules for not more than five legislative days if it includes any procedure or matter having the effect of changing a rule of the House. After such a referral, an additional one-day layover follows the report of the Committee on Rules. § 305(a)(1) of the Budget Act. In modern practice, this sequential referral is obviated in favor of the review by the Committee on Rules when reporting a special order of business governing consideration of the budget resolution. This process allows the Committee on Rules to review suggested rules changes. In the 108th Congress, composition of the Committee on the Budget was changed to include one member of the Committee on Rules. Clause 5(a)(2) of rule X.

Committee Reports; Cost Estimates and Scorekeeping

CBO provides economic and programmatic analyses and cost information on most reported public bills and resolutions. Under the Budget Act, five-year cost estimates are prepared and published in the reports accompanying these bills. §§ 308(a)(1)(B), 402 of the Budget Act. A committee cost estimate identifying certain spending authority as recurring annually and indefinitely was held necessarily to address the five-year period required by this section. *Manual* § 844.

Committee reports on legislation providing new budget authority or a change in revenues or tax expenditures are required to contain the estimates and other detailed information mandated by section 308(a) of the Budget Act. The information mandated by section 308(a) also is required under clause 3(c) of rule XIII, except that the estimates with respect to new budget authority must include, when practicable, a comparison of the total estimated funding level for the relevant program (or programs) to the appropriate levels under current law. *Manual* § 840.

If a bill providing new budget authority is reported without an estimate of its cost, a point of order under clauses 3(c)(2) and 3(c)(3) of rule XIII (requiring that an estimate under sections 308 and 402 of the Budget Act be included in the report) may be made against consideration of the bill. However, a special order of business for the consideration of a bill that "self-executes" the adoption of an amendment providing new budget authority into a bill to be subsequently considered does not, itself, provide new budget authority within the meaning of section 308 of the Budget Act (so as to require a report by the Committee on Rules to include such a cost estimate). *Manual* § 1127. The Committee on the Budget has certain scorekeeping responsibilities under section 312 of the Budget Act, the House CUTGO rule, and Stat-Paygo.

The Director of CBO is required to issue to the committees of the House and the Senate monthly reports detailing and tabulating the progress of congressional action on specified bills and resolutions. § 308(b)(1) of the Budget Act. The Budget Committees of each House are required to prepare budget "scorekeeping" reports and to make them available frequently enough to provide Members of each House with an accurate representation of the current status of congressional consideration of the budget. § 308(b)(2) of the Budget Act.

For a discussion of committee allocations, see § 12, infra.

§ 6. The Budget Timetable

Section 300 of the Budget Act includes a nonmandatory timetable for various stages of the congressional budget process:

- On or before first Monday in February—President submits a budget to Congress

  Note: Additional time for submission of the President's budget can be provided by law. Shortly after its submission, the two Budget Committees begin hearings on the budget, the economic assumptions upon which it is based, the economy in general, and national budget priorities.

- On or before February 15—CBO submits annual report to the Budget Committees

  Note: This report deals primarily with overall economic and fiscal policy and alternative budget levels and national budget priorities.

- Not later than six weeks after President submits a budget—committees submit views and estimates to Budget Committees

  Note: These reports provide the Budget Committees with an early and comprehensive indication of committee legislative planning. These reports include estimates of new budget authority and outlays.

- On or before April 1—Senate Budget Committee reports concurrent resolution

- On or before April 15—Congress completes action on concurrent resolution on the budget

  Note: Congress may revise its budget resolution before the end of the appropriate fiscal year (§ 304 of the Budget Act); although this may be done at any point, the Congress in some years has followed the practice of revising the budget plan for the current fiscal year as part of the budget resolution for the ensuing fiscal year.

- May 15—Annual appropriation bills may be considered in the House

  Note: General appropriation bills, and amendments thereto, may be considered in the House after May 15 even if a budget resolution for the ensuing fiscal year has yet to be agreed to. § 303(b)(2) of the Budget Act.

- On or before June 10—House Committee on Appropriations reports last annual appropriation bill

- June 15—Congress completes action on reconciliation legislation

  Note: The mandatory June 15 deadline was repealed by the BEA of 1990. However, the Congress may not adjourn for more than three calendar days during the month of July until the House has completed action on the reconciliation legislation (§ 310(f) of the Budget Act) and the annual appropriation bills (§ 309 of the Budget Act).

- On or before June 30—House completes action on annual appropriation bills
- October 1—Fiscal year begins

  Note: The fiscal year begins on October 1 and ends on September 30. If action on appropriation bills has not been completed by October 1, Congress may pass a "continuing resolution" to provide appropriations on a temporary basis until the regular appropriation bills are enacted.

Deadlines for other stages in the budget process, such as notification of adjustment in maximum deficit amounts, the President's mid-session budget review, and various CBO and OMB sequestration reports, were provided for in section 254(a) of Gramm-Rudman. Other than October 1 (beginning of new fiscal year), the dates established in section 300 are targets to be met each year. Failure to meet the targets does not inhibit consideration of measures beyond those dates.

Under clause 2(d) of rule X, each standing committee must submit its oversight plan for the Congress to the Committees on Oversight and Government Reform and House Administration by February 15 of the first session. These plans must be reported to the House by the Committee on Oversight and Government Reform by March 31 of the session. Clause 2(d) of rule X.

§ 7. Budget Resolutions; Consideration and Debate

Generally

The budget resolution is a concurrent resolution; as such it is not a law. It serves as an internal framework for Congress in its action on separate revenue, spending, and other budget-related measures. The content of budget resolutions and accompanying reports is governed by section 301 of the Budget Act. Budget resolutions set forth budgetary levels for the upcoming fiscal year and for at least the four succeeding fiscal years, including amounts for total spending and total revenues. The budget resolution gives the Congress a mechanism for establishing Federal spending priorities. The budget resolution accomplishes this by dividing up Federal spending among various "major functional categories," such as national defense, agriculture, and health. *Manual* § 1127.

Section 301(b)(4) of the Budget Act permits a concurrent resolution on the budget to "set forth such other matters, and require such other procedures, relating to the budget, as may be appropriate to carry out the purposes of [the] Act.'' This provision is sometimes referred to as the ''elastic clause.'' Textually, the ''other matters'' and ''procedures'' admitted by this section must: (1) relate to the budget; and (2) be appropriate to carry out the purposes of the Budget Act.

Note: Matter included under the ''elastic clause'' must not include matter that would destroy the privilege of the concurrent resolution on the budget, such as by effecting a special order of business. The only matter in the nature of a special order of business that may be included in a privileged concurrent resolution on the budget is a reconciliation directive. See § 11, infra.

Consideration of Budget Resolutions

A concurrent resolution on the budget that has been reported as privileged pursuant to clause 5(a) of rule XIII is privileged for consideration under procedures set forth in section 305 of the Budget Act, but those procedures do not apply to unreported budget resolutions. 98-2, Apr. 5, 1984, pp 7992, 7993. The House may vary the parameters of consideration by unanimous consent, by suspension of the rules, or by adoption of a special order of business, because the statutory provisions concerned were enacted as exercises of the rulemaking powers of the House under the Constitution. § 904(a) of the Budget Act. It is customary for the House to vary the parameters for consideration of a budget resolution by adopting a special order of business recommended by the Committee on Rules. In recent Congresses such rules have permitted only designated amendments in the nature of substitutes, and perfecting amendments have been precluded. See, *e.g.*, 103-2, H. Res. 384, Mar. 10, 1994, p 4346; 107-1, H. Res. 100, Mar. 28, 2001, p 4758; 111-1, H. Res. 305, Apr. 1, 2009, p ____.

Section 305(a)(1) of the Budget Act requires a three-day layover period that starts when the report on the resolution first becomes available. Clause 4(a) of rule XIII. Section 305(a) of the Budget Act also provides for consideration in the Committee of the Whole; limits general debate to not more than ten hours, with up to an additional four hours permitted on economic goals and policies; and provides for consideration of amendments under the five-minute rule. § 8, infra. After the Committee of the Whole rises and reports the resolution back to the House, the previous question is considered as ordered on the resolution and any amendments thereto to final passage without intervening motion. Neither a motion to recommit the resolution nor a motion to reconsider is in order. § 305(a)(2)-(5) of the Budget Act. The yeas and nays are required to be put on the question of final adoption of a concurrent resolution on the budget. Clause 10 of rule XX.

A budget resolution being considered in Committee of the Whole has been held subject to a motion to rise and report the resolution back to the House with the recommendation that the resolving clause be stricken. 103-1, Mar. 18, 1993, p 5658. However, a motion to recommit pending House adoption of the concurrent resolution is not in order under section 305(a) of the Budget Act.

A budget resolution may under some circumstances be divided so as to permit a separate vote on particular sections therein. *Manual* § 921. The question of adoption of a budget resolution containing one section revising the congressional budget for the fiscal year, preceded by sections setting forth budget targets for ensuing fiscal years as well as reconciliation instructions, and followed by a final section on reporting of certain fiscal information, was divided on the demand of a Member for two separate votes (1) on the first and final portions of the resolution and then (2) on the separable section in between. 96-2, May 7, 1980, pp 10185-87. The rule providing for the consideration of a budget resolution normally precludes a demand for a division on the question of its adoption. See, *e.g.*, 107-1, H. Res. 100, Mar. 28, 2001, p 4758.

§ 8. — Amendments to Resolutions

Generally

Under section 305(a)(5) of the Budget Act, amendments to budget resolutions are considered in the Committee of the Whole under the five-minute rule in accordance with rule XVIII. Under clause 10 of rule XVIII, the resolution is open to amendment at any point, so that the Committee of the Whole may amend the functional categories section before consideration of the total budget allocations. *Manual* § 1127. As stated above, a special order of business resolution from the Committee on Rules typically structures the amendment process.

Amendments to Achieve Mathematical Consistency

Clause 10 of rule XVIII requires, with certain exceptions, that amendments to concurrent resolutions on the budget be mathematically consistent. Under this rule, amendments making changes in budget authority and outlay aggregate totals must be accompanied by comparable changes in functional categories. A point of order will lie against an amendment to the resolution increasing the aggregates and a functional category for budget authority and outlays but not changing the amount of the deficit. However, an amendment that only transfers an amount of budget authority from one functional category to another—that is, reduces one category by a certain amount and adds the same amount to another category—need make no changes in the aggregates to achieve mathematical consistency. 96-1, May 8, 1979, p 10271.

An amendment to achieve mathematical consistency throughout the resolution may either change the functional categories to conform with the aggregates, or vice versa, and if such an amendment is offered and rejected, another amendment in different form to achieve mathematical consistency may be offered. 96-1, May 14, 1979, pp 10967-75. Under section 305(a)(5) of the Budget Act, an amendment or amendments to achieve mathematical consistency can be offered at any time up to adoption.

A change in the public debt limit from that figure reported by the Committee on the Budget is not in order, except as part of an amendment offered at the direction of the Committee on the Budget to achieve mathematical consistency. Clause 10 of rule XVIII. For more on the public debt limit, see § 18, infra.

Germaneness

Unless protected by a special order of business, an amendment to a concurrent resolution on the budget must be germane to the text of the resolution. An amendment expressing the sense of Congress that the Impoundment Control Act be repealed for a fiscal year and calling for a review of the Budget Act and the budget process has been conceded to be not germane. 96-2, Nov. 18, 1980, p 30026.

§ 9. —Debate on Conference Reports

Unless limited by a special order of business, there can be up to five hours of debate in the House on a conference report on a concurrent resolution on the budget under section 305(a)(6) of the Budget Act, to be equally divided between the majority and minority parties. Where the conferees report in total disagreement, debate on the motion to dispose of the amendment in disagreement is not governed by the statute and is instead considered under the general ''hour'' rule in the House. See, *e.g.*, 95-2, May 17, 1978, p 14117. Under section 305(a)(6) of the Budget Act, neither a motion to recommit nor a motion to reconsider is available on a conference report.

§ 10. —Budget Resolution to Precede Consideration of Related Legislation

Section 303 of the Budget Act precludes consideration of certain budget-related legislation for a fiscal year until the budget resolution for that year has been adopted by both Houses. The essence of this section is timing. It reflects a judgment that legislative decisions on expenditures and revenues for the coming fiscal year should await the adoption of the budget resolution for that year. 101-2, July 25, 1990, p 19161. Legislation ruled out under section 303 has included:

- A conference report containing new spending authority in the form of entitlements to become effective in fiscal years 1978 through 1980, where the concurrent resolution on the budget for those fiscal years had not yet been adopted. *Manual* § 1127.
- An amendment providing new entitlement authority to become effective in a fiscal year before adoption of the budget resolution for that year. *Manual* § 1127.
- An amendment providing new budget authority for a fiscal year, before adoption of a budget resolution for that year. *Manual* § 1127.
- A motion to recommit proposing an amendment providing an increase in revenues for a fiscal year before adoption of a budget resolution for that year. 105-2, July 24, 1998, pp 17198, 17276.

While section 303 provides that a point of order lies only against a bill or joint resolution that has been reported (§ 303(b)(3) of the Budget Act), clause 8 of rule XXI provides that title III of the Budget Act operates without regard to whether the measure concerned has been reported.

Waivers of section 303 of the Budget Act have been provided pursuant to a special order of business from the Committee on Rules. See § 4, supra. Section 303 does not apply after April 15 if the measure would not increase the deficit or lower revenues below the aggregate level of Federal revenues set forth in the concurrent resolution on the budget. § 302(g) of the Budget Act.

§ 11. Reconciliation Procedures

Section 301(b)(2) of the Budget Act provides for the inclusion of reconciliation instructions in a budget resolution and for the reporting and consideration of reconciliation legislation. Reconciliation instructions direct committees to recommend changes in existing law to achieve the goals in spending or revenues contemplated by the budget resolution. If reconciliation instructs more than one committee in each House, then all committees instructed are to submit their recommendations to their respective Budget Committees. The Budget Committees then assemble, without substantive revision, all the recommendations into one bill for action by the House or Senate. § 310 of the Budget Act. Reconciliation instructions may contemplate several reconciliation bills, including a bill that reduces revenues. See, *e.g.*, 104-2, May 21, 1996, p 11939-41 (decision of Chair sustained on appeal in the Senate); 106-1, H. Con. Res. 68, Mar. 25, 1999, pp 5754, 5755

(House adoption of budget resolution). Section 310 provides expedited consideration in both Houses of reconciliation legislation, provided the reconciliation bill has been reported as privileged pursuant to clause 5(a) of rule XIII. However, it is customary for the House to vary the parameters for consideration of a reconciliation bill by adopting a special order of business resolution recommended by the Committee on Rules. See, *e.g.*, 107-1, H. Res. 142, May 16, 2001, p 8191. Clause 7 of rule XXI provides a point of order against reconciliation instructions that are not CUTGO-compliant.

Section 310(c)(1)(A) of the Budget Act permits committees, in meeting their reconciliation targets, to alternatively substitute revenue and spending changes by up to 20 percent of the sum of the absolute value of reconciled changes as long as the result does not increase the deficit relative to the reconciliation instructions. Section 310(d) of the Budget Act requires that amendments offered to reconciliation legislation in either the House or the Senate must not increase the level of deficit (if any) in the resolution. Section 313 of the Budget Act addresses the subject of ''extraneous'' material in a reconciliation bill—the so-called ''Byrd Rule.'' The enforcement of this section applies only in the Senate but can be directed against matter originating in the House.

§ 12. Adherence to Budget Resolution Spending and Revenue Levels

The various parliamentary enforcement mechanisms established in the Budget Act—those sections establishing points of order against consideration of certain propositions—constitute rules of the House and, as such, are liable to waiver by unanimous consent, by suspension of the rules, or by adoption of a special order of business. It is not unusual for the House to waive such a point of order by adopting a special order of business resolution recommended by the Committee on Rules.

Adherence to Total Spending and Revenue Levels (§ 311(a) of the Budget Act)

With certain exceptions, section 311(a) of the Budget Act precludes specified measures—including amendments and conference reports—that would cause total budget authority or total outlays to exceed, or total revenues to be below, the level set forth in the budget resolution. The provision is enforced by points of order against the consideration of reported measures that would breach the ''appropriate levels'' of total new budget authority or total outlays or total revenues in the budget resolution.

The Chair has sustained points of order under section 311(a) of the Budget Act in the following instances:

- An amendment striking a rescission of existing budget authority where its effect would be to increase the net new budget authority in the bill in breach of the applicable total. 97-1, May 12, 1981, p 9314.
- An amendment reducing revenues for the fiscal year below the total level of revenues contained in the concurrent resolution on the budget for that year. See 94-2, Oct. 1, 1976, pp 34554-57.
- A motion to amend a Senate amendment providing new budget authority for official mail costs to be available immediately where the applicable total of new budget authority contained in the budget resolution had already been exceeded and where the Committee on Appropriations had exceeded its section 302(a) allocation (thereby rendering the section 311(b) exception inapplicable). 101-1, Sept. 28, 1989, p 22267.

''Deemers''

The House has adopted resolutions to ''deem'' budget parameters to be in place for temporary enforcement. These ''deemers'' have typically been carried in either a special order of business reported from the Committee on Rules or as a separate order in an opening-day resolution adopting the standing rules for a Congress. See, *e.g.*, 105-2, H. Res. 477, June 19, 1998, pp 12991, 12998; 106-1, H. Res. 5, Jan. 6, 1999, p 76; 107-2, H. Res. 428, May 22, 2002, p 8675; 108-1, H. Res. 5, Jan. 7, 2003, p 13. These resolutions often empower the chair of the Committee on the Budget to place allocations in the *Record* that are ''deemed'' in place for purposes of enforcing the Budget Act.

Committee Allocations (§ 302 of the Budget Act)

Section 302(a) of the Budget Act provides for an allocation to each committee of ''appropriate levels'' of new budget authority and outlays, which are published in the joint statement of managers accompanying a conference report on the budget resolution.

Each committee is allocated an overall level for discretionary spending that is consistent with the congressional budget plan. Under section 302(b) of the Budget Act, the Committee on Appropriations of each House then subdivides its allocations among its subcommittees. Section 302(c) of the Budget Act precludes consideration of an appropriation measure until that committee has made its suballocation under section 302(b). Points of order under section 302(c) apply separately to the consideration of bills and amendments. Thus, a waiver of points of order against consideration of an appropriation bill before filing of a report from the Committee on Appropriations allocating new budget authority among its subcommittees does not extend to an amendment providing new budget authority in addition to the amounts contained in the bill. 100-1, July 13, 1987, p 19514; 108-1, Jan. 8, 2003, p 194.

Any Member may raise a point of order under section 302(f) of the Budget Act against a bill, amendment, or conference report that would exceed the relevant committee allocation. An amendment that provides no new budget authority or outlays but instead results in outlay savings is not subject to a point of order under these provisions. 100-1, June 30, 1987, p 18308. The Chair has sustained points of order under section 302(f) of the Budget Act in the following instances:

- An amendment to a general appropriation bill increasing the level of new discretionary budget authority in excess of the relevant allocation under 302(b) of the Budget Act. 108-1, July 25, 2003, p 19722-24; 109-2, June 27, 2006, p 12802.
- An amendment to a general appropriation bill proposing to strike a provision scored as negative budget authority and thus providing new budget authority in excess of the relevant allocation under section 302(b) of the Budget Act. 106-2, June 13, 2000, p 10505.
- An amendment to a general appropriation bill offsetting an increase in the level of discretionary budget authority with a decrease in an account designated as "emergency spending," such designation rendering that account invisible under the Budget Act and thus unavailable for an offsetting transfer. 109-1, Mar. 15, 2005, p 4696.
- An amendment to a general appropriation bill proposing to strike a provision stating that a specified increment of new discretionary budget authority provided by the bill would "become available for obligation only upon the enactment of future appropriations legislation," thus causing the bill to provide additional new discretionary budget authority in that incremental amount in excess of the relevant 302(b) allocation. 104-2, June 26, 1996, p 15563.
- A motion to commit a bill with instructions proposing to provide new budget authority in excess of the relevant 302(a) allocation. 108-1, Jan. 8, 2003, p 193, 194.
- A motion to recommit a bill with instructions proposing to provide new budget authority in excess of the relevant 302(a) allocation. 106-2, June 28, 2000, p 12750; 108-2, Apr. 2, 2004, p 6374; 108-2, July 22, 2004, p 17321.

The Section 311(c) Exception

As noted above, section 311(a) of the Budget Act precludes Congress from considering legislation that would cause total revenues to fall below, or total new budget authority or total outlays to exceed, the appropriate level set forth in the budget resolution. However, section 311(a) does not apply in the House to spending legislation if the committee reporting the measure has stayed within its section 302(a) allocation of new budget authority. See § 311(c) of the Budget Act. Accordingly, for the purposes of section 311, the House may take up any spending measure that is within the appropriate committee allocations, even if (solely due to excessive spending within another committee's jurisdiction) it would cause total spending to be exceeded.

Emergency Spending

In prior years, Congress used a variety of mechanisms to exempt spending designated as emergency spending from constraints imposed by the Budget Act. For example, an amount designated as an emergency might be rendered ''invisible'' and not taken into account for certain Budget Act purposes, as under section 606(d) (now repealed). Under other procedures, automatic adjustments in budget levels and committee allocations would be triggered to account for amounts designated as emergencies, as under section 314 (now revised).

The Budget Control Act of 2011 provided for new treatment in the House for provisions containing amounts designated as an emergency and made substantial changes to the operation of section 314 of the Budget Act. See § 24, infra. In addition, emergency spending is sometimes governed by provisions in the concurrent resolution on the budget. Finally, emergency designations are also accorded special treatment under clause 10 of rule XXI and Stat-Paygo. See §§ 3, 4, supra.

Chair Guided by Committee on the Budget Estimates

When the Chair decides questions of order under titles III and IV of the Budget Act, section 312(a) of the Budget Act requires the reliance on estimates provided by the Committee on the Budget in determining levels of new budget authority, outlays, direct spending, new entitlement authority, and revenues for a fiscal year. See, *e.g.*, 106-2, June 8, 2000, pp 9940-3. A similar authority is provided in the House CUTGO rule and Stat-Paygo.

§ 13. Other Spending Controls

Generally

For a detailed explanation of deficit targets, discretionary spending limits, and PAYGO processes, see *Introduction to the Federal Budget Process*, CRS, Dec. 2, 2010.

§ 14. —Sequestration

Sequestration (an automatic spending reduction process) involves the issuance of a Presidential order that permanently cancels budgetary authority (except for special funds and trust funds) for the purpose of achieving a required amount of outlay savings. Currently, sequestration authority is provided by Stat-Paygo and the Budget Control Act of 2011. Pursuant to Stat-Paygo, the budgetary effects of direct spending and revenue legislation are carried on scorecards covering five and ten year periods. The President is required to issue a sequestration order (prepared by OMB) if, at the end of a congressional session, either scorecard shows a net debit. The sequestration order results in a largely across-the-board cut equal to the amount of the debit, the specifics of which can be found in section 6 of Stat-Paygo.

The Budget Control Act of 2011 established annual discretionary spending limits for security and non-security spending for a ten-year period. The Act also mandated sequestration procedures to eliminate a breach in either category. The Act also established a point of order in section 314 of the Congressional Budget Act against any bill, joint resolution, amendment, motion, or conference report that would cause the discretionary spending caps to be exceeded.

Direct Spending

A conventional authorization establishes or continues a government agency or program. Although it may limit the amount of budget authority that may be appropriated for that purpose, the authorized funds are available only to the extent provided for in appropriation Acts originated by the Committee on Appropriations. Deschler Ch 25 §2.13; see APPROPRIATIONS. Spending legislation that circumvents the appropriations process is called ''direct spending'' (sometimes referred to as ''mandatory spending''). Under clause 10 of rule XXI, direct spending includes spending described in section 250(c)(8) of Gramm-Rudman (budget authority provided by law other than appropriation Acts, entitlement authority, and the Supplemental Nutrition Assistance Program) and, additionally, provisions in appropriation Acts that make outyear modifications to substantive law as described in section 3(4)(C) of Stat-Paygo.

§15. —New Contract Authority; New Borrowing Authority

New budget authority provided by law other than appropriation Acts may take the form of new contract authority or new authority to incur indebtedness (often referred to as ''borrowing authority'').

With certain exceptions, section 401(a) of the Budget Act requires new contract authority and new authority to incur indebtedness to be effective only as provided in appropriation Acts. The various authorities referred to in section 401(a) of the Budget Act do not apply to bills that provide legislative authorizations that are subject to the appropriations process. A conference report authorizing the Secretary of Health, Education, and Welfare to borrow funds by issuing government notes as a public debt transaction, not subject to amounts specified in advance in appropriation Acts, was conceded to violate section 401(a) of the Budget Act and was ruled out on a point of order. 94-2, Sept. 27, 1976, p 32655. Whether or not an amendment to a pending measure violates section 401(a) of the Budget Act is determined by its marginal effect on the pending measure (rather than current law). See 102-2, Mar. 26, 1992, p 7183.

§ 16. —Entitlement Authority

Section 401(b) of the Budget Act precludes ''new entitlement authority'' that becomes effective during the current fiscal year. Entitlement authority is the authority to make payments to a person or government under a provision of law that obligates the United States to make such payments to those who meet the requirements established by that law, including the food stamp program. § 3(9) of the Budget Act; *Manual* § 1127. The Chair contemplates immediate enactment to determine when an entitlement takes effect. *Manual* § 1127.

The following examples have been held to provide new entitlement authority within the meaning of the Budget Act:

- A conference report requiring the Secretary of Agriculture to pay a cost of transporting agricultural commodities to major disaster areas.
- A Senate amendment requiring the Secretary of Labor to certify a new group of workers as eligible for adjustment assistance under the Trade Act of 1974.
- An amendment enlarging the class of persons eligible for a government subsidy.

Manual § 1127.

The following examples have been held not to provide new entitlement authority within the meaning of the Budget Act:

- A provision requiring payments to individuals meeting certain qualifications but also requiring such payments to be ratably reduced to the amounts of appropriations actually made if sums appropriated pursuant thereto are insufficient.
- An amendment establishing a new executive position at a specified compensation level but subjecting its salary to the appropriation process.

Manual § 1127.

In recent Congresses, the House has adopted an order of the House excluding Federal compensation from the definition of entitlement authority. See, *e.g.*, 112-1, H. Res. 5, Jan. 5, 2011, p ____.

Points of Order under Section 401 of the Budget Act

A point of order under section 401 lies against a reported bill or joint resolution and not against an unreported measure. *Manual* § 1127. The spending authorities subject to constraints under section 401, as forms of direct spending, are also subject to the spending constraints on new budget authority under sections 302(f), 303, and 311(a) of the Budget Act.

§ 17. Social Security Funds

Receipts and disbursements of the Social Security trust funds are not to be counted as new budget authority, outlays, receipts, or as deficit or surplus. Under section 13301 of the BEA of 1990, the off-budget status of these programs applies for purposes of the President's budget, the congressional budget, and under Gramm-Rudman. *Manual* § 1129. Section 13302 of the BEA of 1990 creates a ''fire wall'' point of order in the House to prohibit the consideration of legislation that would change certain balances of the Social Security trust funds over specified periods. *Manual* § 1129.

Section 310(g) of the Budget Act prohibits the consideration of reconciliation legislation that contains recommendations with respect to the title II program under the Social Security Act (OASDI).

§ 18. The Budget Process and the Public Debt Limit

A limit on the public debt is fixed by law. 31 USC § 3101. The public debt limit may be changed by enactment of a bill or joint resolution. See, *e.g.*, 101-2, H.R. 5350, Aug. 4, 1990; the Omnibus Budget Reconciliation Act of 1993. A former rule of the House generated and deemed passed a joint resolution automatically upon adoption by Congress of a concurrent resolution on the budget that sets forth a level of the public debt that is different from the statutory limit. Rule XXVIII was first adopted in the 96th Congress. It was rendered inoperative on occasion. See, *e.g.*, 104-1, H. Res. 149, May 17, 1995, pp 13275, 13276; 105-1, H. Res. 152, May 20, 1997, p 8904. It was repealed in the 107th Congress, reinstated in the 108th Congress, and repealed again in the 112th Congress. *Manual* § 1104.

The Budget Control Act of 2011 provided for incremental increases in the debt limit by the President and expedited procedures for the Congress to disapprove of those increases. For a description of the procedures for increasing the debt limit under the Budget Control Act of 2011, see § 24, infra.

Section 301(a)(5) of the Budget Act requires the budget resolution to set forth the appropriate level for the public debt. Under clause 10(c)(1) of rule XVIII, it is not in order to consider an amendment to the budget resolution that proposes to change the appropriate level for the public debt. Reconciliation directives relative to changes in the public debt may be included in the concurrent resolution on the budget under section 310(a)(3) of the Budget Act.

§ 19. Impoundments Generally

Executive Branch Authority; Types of Impoundments

The executive branch has no inherent power to impound appropriated funds. In the absence of express congressional authorization to withhold funds appropriated for implementation of a legislative program, the executive branch must spend all the funds. *Kennedy* v. *Mathews*, 413 F. Supp. 1240 (D.D.C. 1976); see also *Train* v. *City of New York*, 420 U.S. 35 (1975). Accordingly, if the controlling statute gives the officials in question no discretion to withhold the funds, a court may grant injunctive relief directing that they be made available. *Kennedy*, 413 F. Supp. 1245.

The impoundment of appropriated funds may be proposed by the President pursuant to the Impoundment Control Act of 1974. *Manual* § 1130(6A). Two types of impoundments are referred to by this statute: (1) rescissions, which are the permanent cancellation of spending, and (2) deferrals, which impose a temporary delay in spending. §§ 1012, 1013 of the Impoundment Control Act; 2 USC § 681.

The Impoundment Control Act was enacted by Congress in an effort to control the budgetary impoundment powers asserted by the President. As the court noted in *City of New Haven, Conn.* v. *United States*, 634 F. Supp. 1449 (D.D.C. 1986), in the early 1970's the President began to use impoundments as a means of shaping domestic policy, withholding funds from various programs he did not favor. The legality of these impoundments was repeatedly litigated, and by 1974, impoundments had been vitiated in many cases. See, *e.g.*, *National Council of Community Mental Health Centers, Inc.* v. *Weinberger*, 361 F. Supp. 897 (D.D.C. 1973) (public health funds).

§ 20. — Rescissions

Under the Impoundment Control Act, the President may propose to rescind all or part of the budget authority Congress has appropriated for a particular program. To propose a rescission, the President must send a special message to Congress detailing the amount of the proposed rescission, the reasons for it, and a summary of the effects the rescission would have on the programs involved. § 1012(a) of the Impoundment Control Act. Under the Act, Congress then has 45 days within which to approve the proposed rescission by a "rescission bill" that must be passed by both Houses.

§1012(b) of the Impoundment Control Act. If the rescission bill is not approved, the President must allow the full amount appropriated to be spent. *City of New Haven, Conn.* v. *United States*, 634 F. Supp. 1449, 1452 (D.D.C. 1986).

The 45-day period prescribed by the Act applies only to the initial consideration of the bill; the consideration of a conference report on such a bill is subject only to the general rules of the House relating to conference reports and is not prevented by the expiration of the 45-day period following the initial consideration of the bill. *Manual* §1130(6A).

The Impoundment Control Act sets forth detailed procedures expediting and governing the consideration of a rescission bill introduced under its provisions. §1017(a)-(c) of the Impoundment Control Act. These procedures are rarely invoked in the modern practice, and the ''rescission bill'' referred to in the Act is not the only means by which the House may take action on such a matter. The House may address the question through other legislation without following the procedures set forth in section 1017 of the Impoundment Control Act. 94-1, Mar. 25, 1975, p 8484.

Rescissions of prior appropriations are more often reported in general appropriation bills, and the inclusion of rescission language by the Committee on Appropriations is excepted from the prohibition against provisions ''changing existing law'' under clause 2(b) of rule XXI. See *Manual* §§1038, 1043, 1052. However, this exception does not extend to amendments or to the rescission of contract authority provided by a law other than an appropriations Act. *Manual* §1052.

§21. —Deferrals

Under section 1013(a) of the Impoundment Control Act of 1974, the President must notify Congress of the proposed deferral of any budget authority, the reasons for the deferral, the impact the deferral will have on the programs involved, and ''any legal authority invoked to justify the proposed deferral.'' 2 USC §684(a).

Until 1986 the Act was used frequently as the basis for Presidential deferral proposals and for their consideration by the Congress. Section 1013 of the Impoundment Control Act allows a deferral to be overridden by a resolution of disapproval passed by either House. Congress could reject the proposal by one-House veto or in subsequent legislation. Today, the Congress may disapprove a deferral only through the enactment of a law (often an appropriation Act). It may not do so through a resolution of disapproval only by one House under court rulings. *Manual* §1130.

In 1986 a suit was brought to contest the validity of certain deferrals proposed by the President under section 1013 of the Impoundment Control Act. In November 1985, the President had signed the fiscal year 1986 appropriations bill for the Department of Housing and Urban Development, which appropriated funds for certain community development programs. In February 1986, the President sent impoundment notices to Congress pursuant to the Act announcing his deferrals of the expenditure of funds for the programs at issue. The plaintiffs in the suit included various cities, community groups, and Members of Congress. The plaintiffs challenged as unconstitutional the provision allowing a so-called one-House legislative veto of impoundments proposed by the President, such vetoes having been declared unconstitutional under the Supreme Court decision in *Immigration and Naturalization Service* v. *Chadha*, 462 U.S. 919, 103 (1983). The plaintiffs argued that the unconstitutional legislative veto provision contained in section 1013 rendered the *entire* section invalid, leaving the President without statutory authority on which to base the deferrals in question. After analyzing the intent of Congress in enacting section 1013, the District Court for the District of Columbia held that the section's unconstitutional legislative veto provision was inseverable from the remainder of the section. *City of New Haven, Conn.* v. *United States*, 634 F. Supp. 1449 (D.D.C. 1986). Accordingly, the court declared section 1013 void in its entirety and ordered the defendants to make the deferred funds available for obligation. *City of New Haven*, 634 F. Supp. 1460. The judgment of the District Court in striking down section 1013 in its entirety was affirmed by the U.S. Court of Appeals. *City of New Haven, Conn.* v. *United States*, 809 F.2d 900 (D.C. Cir. 1987).

In 1987, after section 1013 of the Impoundment Control Act was declared unconstitutional, the Act was amended to exclude the one-House legislative veto procedure, and limitations were placed on the purposes for which deferrals could be made. Section 1013 of the Impoundment Control Act now permits deferrals only in three specified situations: "to provide for contingencies," "to achieve savings made possible by or through changes in requirements or greater efficiency of operations," or "as specifically provided by law." The same language is used in the Anti-Deficiency Act. 31 USC § 1512(c)(1). The purpose of such language was to preclude the President from invoking section 1013 as authority for implementing "policy" impoundments, while preserving the President's authority to implement routine "programmatic" impoundments. *City of New Haven, Conn.* v. *United States*, 809 F.2d 906 (note).

Unreported Deferrals

Section 1015(a) of the Impoundment Control Act (2 USC §686(a)) requires the Comptroller General to report to the Congress whenever it is found that any officer or employee of the United States has ordered, permitted, or approved a reserve or deferral of budget authority, and the President has not transmitted a special impoundment message with respect to such reserve or deferral.

§22. Unfunded Mandates

The Unfunded Mandates Reform Act of 1995 added a new part B to title IV of the Budget Act that imposes several requirements on committees with respect to ''Federal mandates,'' establishes points of order to enforce those requirements, and precludes the consideration of a rule or order waiving such points of order in the House. 2 USC §§658-658g. Section 425 of the Budget Act establishes a point of order against consideration of a bill, joint resolution, amendment, motion, or conference report containing unfunded intergovernmental mandates. Section 426(a) of the Budget Act establishes a point of order against consideration of any rule or order that waives the application of section 425. Points of order under sections 425 and 426(a) of the Budget Act are disposed of by the House voting on the question of consideration. *Manual* §1127.

Section 426(b) of the Budget Act requires a Member raising a point of order under section 425 to specify the precise language upon which the point of order is based. 104-2, May 23, 1996, p 12283. Debate on the point of order is on the question of consideration of the underlying text that is the subject of the point of order. The Members controlling debate on the point of order may reserve their time, and a manager of a measure who controls time for debate against the point of order has the right to close debate. A point of order under section 426 against consideration of a resolution providing a special order of business that waives section 425 or self-executes the adoption of an amendment must be made when the special order of business is called up and comes too late after the resolution has been adopted. 104-2, July 18, 1996, p 17668. A point of order under section 425 against consideration of a bill is properly raised pending the Speaker's declaration that the House resolve into the Committee of the Whole for such consideration. 105-1, Oct. 29, 1997, p 23712.

§23. Earmarks

While only indirectly related to the congressional budget process, the subject of earmarks has engendered special scrutiny in the House in recent years. The House rules define a congressional earmark as "a provision or report language included primarily at the request of a Member, Delegate, Resident Commissioner, or Senator providing, authorizing, or recommending a specific amount of discretionary budget authority, credit authority, or other spending authority for a contract, loan, loan guarantee, grant, loan authority, or other expenditure with or to an entity, or targeted to a specific State, locality or Congressional district, other than through a statutory or administrative formula-driven or competitive award process." Clause 9(e) of rule XXI. This clause also defines "limited tax benefit" and "limited tariff benefit" which are treated in the same fashion as earmarks.

The House attempts to limit or restrict the use of earmarks through the mechanism of a disclosure requirement. Clause 9(a) of rule XXI provides for a point of order against consideration of bills and joint resolutions (whether or not reported from committee), "manager's" amendments to bills or joint resolutions (offered at the outset of consideration), or conference reports that do not comply with the disclosure requirement. Clause 9(b) provides a similar point of order for conference reports accompanying general appropriation bills.

In each case, the disclosure required to be made is a list of all congressional earmarks, limited tax benefits, and limited tariff benefits contained in the measure, or, alternatively, a statement that the measure contains no such earmarks, or tax or tariff benefits. Depending on the measure at issue, such disclosure is required to be made in the committee report (for reported bills or resolutions), printed in the *Congressional Record* prior to consideration (for unreported bills or joint resolutions), or contained in the joint explanatory statement of managers (for conference reports).

Clause 9(c) of rule XXI provides a point of order against a special order of business reported from the Committee on Rules that waives the application of either clause 9(a) or 9(b) of rule XXI. Disposition of this point of order is decided by the question of consideration, which the Chair puts to the House when the point of order is made. Such question of consideration is debatable for 20 minutes, with 10 minutes controlled by the Member raising the point of order and 10 minutes controlled by a Member opposed. The question of consideration is decided without intervening motion, except for one motion that the House adjourn. This same procedure is followed with respect to points of order made under clause 9(b) regarding conference reports accompanying regular general appropriation bills. For a further discussion of questions of consideration, see QUESTION OF CONSIDERATION.

It is important to note that the disclosure requirement is fulfilled by the mere presence of the disclosure statement in the required document, whether that be a committee report, the *Congressional Record*, or a joint statement accompanying a conference report. When ascertaining the validity of a point of order under clause 9(a), the Chair consults the pertinent document and notes the presence or absence of the required statement. The Chair does not assess the accuracy or sufficiency of the required earmark statement. See 110-1, May 10, 2007, pp 12190, 12191.

For additional precedents regarding the timing and application of this rule, see *Manual* § 1068d.

§ 24. Recent Developments: The Budget Control Act of 2011

Generally

The Budget Control Act of 2011 was enacted on August 2, 2011. The Act combined a series of budget control mechanisms with a proposal to increase the limit of the public debt. The procedural aspects of the Act included (1) the establishment of annual discretionary spending caps over a ten-year period enforceable by a point of order and sequestration; (2) altering the treatment for funding designated as emergencies including protections for a motion to strike such a designation; (3) requiring a vote in each body on a joint resolution proposing a balanced budget amendment to the Constitution by a time certain and providing expedited treatment of such a joint resolution in the other body; (4) allowing for staged increases in the limit of the public debt by the President with expedited procedures for joint resolutions disapproving each increase; and (5) creation of a joint select committee required to produce a measure by a date certain that would achieve a specified amount of deficit reduction and which would then be considered by each House on an expedited basis (with failure to enact such legislation by such date resulting in automatic sequestration).

Discretionary Spending Caps

The Budget Control Act of 2011 established annual discretionary spending limits for security and non-security spending for a ten-year period. The Act also mandated sequestration procedures to eliminate a breach in either category. The Act also established a point of order in section 314 of the Budget Act against any bill, joint resolution, amendment, motion, or conference report that would cause the discretionary spending caps to be exceeded.

Emergencies

The Budget Control Act of 2011 provided for new treatment in the House for provisions containing amounts designated as an emergency. Under the law, a provision contained in a reported bill or joint resolution, or amendment thereto, or conference report thereon providing new budget authority or outlays or reducing revenue and designated as an emergency under Gramm-Rudman would be entitled to special scoring by the chair of the House Committee on the Budget. Specifically, the chair of the Committee on the Budget does not count the budgetary effects of the provision under titles III and IV of the Congressional Budget Act and the rules of the House. The Act also removes procedural hurdles for a motion to strike an emergency designation under Gramm-Rudman and attach thereto an accompanying across-the-board cut to achieve budget neutrality. Specifically, a motion to strike an emergency designation under Gramm-Rudman is not counted by the chair of the Committee of the Budget for purposes of titles III and IV of the Congressional Budget Act and the rules of the House. Such a proposal to strike an emergency designation may also contain an across-the-board cut that may be offered at any point in the reading of a measure. These two steps obviate a point of order that striking an emergency designation would increase the budget authority or reduce revenues above or below enforceable levels and allow for an across-the-board cut to address each account in the pending measure regardless of how far the reading has progressed.

Balanced Budget Amendment

The Budget Control Act of 2011 provided for a vote in each body on a joint resolution proposing a balanced budget amendment to the Constitution by a date certain. The law required that each body vote after September 30, 2011 and before December 31, 2011, on final passage of a joint resolution with the title: ''Joint resolution proposing a balanced budget amendment to the Constitution of the United States.'' The Act also prescribed expedited procedures for consideration of a qualifying joint resolution passed by the other body.

Debt Limit Increases

The Budget Control Act of 2011 provided for incremental increases in the debt limit by the President and expedited procedures for the Congress to disapprove of those increases. The congressional disapproval procedures for the debt limit increases were modeled on those found in the Emergency Economic Stabilization Act of 2008 (Pub. L. 110-343). Those procedures included an overall calendar day cap on congressional consideration (including tolling in the event of a veto), referral to the Committee on Ways and Means, a privileged motion to discharge the committee after six calendar days, unamendability in the committee and the full House, and a vote on passage following two hours of debate.

Joint Select Committee on Deficit Reduction

The Budget Control Act of 2011 provided for a Joint Select Committee on Deficit Reduction composed of six Senators and six Members of the House equally divided by party. The goal of the joint committee was "to reduce the deficit by at least $1.5 trillion over the period of fiscal years 2012 to 2021." The joint committee was required to report recommendations back to Congress and such product of the committee would then be subject to expedited procedures in both Houses. The Act provided that the joint committee terminate on January 31, 2012.

Chapter 8
Calendar Wednesday

Research References
7 Cannon §§ 881-971
Deschler Ch 21 § 4
Manual §§ 900, 901

§ 1. In General; Forms

Under clause 6 of rule XV, the Calendar Wednesday rule, Wednesdays are set apart for the consideration, pursuant to a call of committees, of unprivileged bills on the House and Union Calendars. The Calendar Wednesday procedure is utilized infrequently due to its cumbersome operation and to the fact that unprivileged bills may be considered more effectively pursuant to other procedures, such as a special order of business from the Committee on Rules, suspension of the rules, or unanimous consent. Deschler Ch 21 § 4.

At the beginning of the 111th Congress, the Calendar Wednesday rule was changed to require the committee chair, or other member authorized by the committee, to announce an intention to request a call of the committees. Absent such a request, the call of the committee does not occur. This change obviated the need for weekly unanimous-consent requests to waive the Calendar Wednesday rule, which had become more frequent in modern practice. The Calendar Wednesday rule does not apply during the last two weeks of a session. *Manual* § 900; § 10, infra.

Form

SPEAKER: Today is Calendar Wednesday, and the Clerk will call the roll of those committees whose chair or other member authorized by the committee has so requested.

MEMBER (when the appropriate committee is called): M__. Speaker, by direction of the Committee on __________, I call up H.R. ______.

> *Note:* Calendar Wednesday business may be called up only on formal authorization by the committee. A Member without such authorization may not call up the bill if objection is made. § 6, infra.

SPEAKER: This bill is on the House Calendar. The Clerk will report the bill.

[or, if the bill is on the Union Calendar . . .]

SPEAKER: This bill is on the Union Calendar, and under the rule the House automatically resolves itself into the Committee of the Whole House on the state of the Union, with the gentle______ from ______ in the Chair.

CHAIR: The House is in the Committee of the Whole House on the state of the Union for the [further] consideration of the bill H.R. ______, which the Clerk will report [by title].

> *Note:* When first called up, the bill is read in full unless reading is dispensed with by unanimous consent. If consideration is extended beyond the day, it is read by title when called up on subsequent days.

CHAIR: Under the rule, general debate is limited to two hours, and the Chair will recognize the gentle______ from ______ [usually the chair of the committee], for the hour in favor of the bill and later the gentle______ from ______ [usually the ranking minority member of the committee], for the hour in opposition. The gentle______ from ______ is recognized.

§ 2. Business Considered on Calendar Wednesday

Committees called under the Calendar Wednesday rule may call up for consideration any unprivileged bill on either the House or the Union Calendar but not on the Private Calendar. *Manual* § 900; Deschler Ch 21 § 4. No priority is given to bills on the House or the Union Calendar. 7 Cannon §§ 938, 963.

The Calendar Wednesday procedure applies only to bills reported from committee and not to amendments between the Houses or to unreported bills. 98-2, June 28, 1984, p 19770. Another limitation of clause 6 of rule XV is that it applies only to unprivileged public bills. *Manual* § 900. A privileged bill is ineligible for consideration under the Calendar Wednesday rule, whether it is reported from the floor or delivered to the Clerk. 7 Cannon § 936. Unprivileged bills given privileged status by unanimous-consent agreement or special order of business are ineligible for consideration under the Calendar Wednesday procedure. 7 Cannon §§ 932-935.

The purpose of the Calendar Wednesday rule is to preserve that day for the class of legislation specified by the rule—namely, unprivileged bills. *Manual* § 900. Committee *reports* on bills may be filed on Calendar Wednesday, but they may not be called up for consideration or other action on such days. 7 Cannon § 907.

When Calendar Wednesday business is being considered under the rule, it is not in order to:

- Move a change of reference. 7 Cannon §§ 884, 2117.
- Call up a conference report. 7 Cannon §§ 899-901.
- Offer a motion for recess. *Manual* § 900.
- Call up a privileged bill, pursuant to a special order of business. 7 Cannon §§ 932, 934, 935.
- Call up a private bill. Deschler Ch 21 § 4.10.
- Consider business coming over from a prior legislative day with the previous question ordered. 7 Cannon § 890.
- Call up a resolution of inquiry or move to discharge a committee from the consideration of such a resolution. 7 Cannon §§ 896-898.

On Calendar Wednesdays, the Speaker ordinarily declines to entertain unanimous-consent requests not connected with Calendar Wednesday business. 7 Cannon §§ 882-888. However, the House may by unanimous consent, prior to the call of committees on Calendar Wednesday, permit a one-minute speech (Deschler-Brown Ch 29 § 10.62), allow a bill to be sent to a conference (*Manual* § 901), or permit consideration of a resolution electing a committee chair (98-2, Jan. 25, 1984, p 357).

§ 3. —In Committee of the Whole

When a bill on the Union Calendar is called up on Calendar Wednesday, the House automatically resolves into the Committee of the Whole without motion from the floor. *Manual* § 901. When such a bill comes up as the unfinished business on the next Calendar Wednesday when the same committee can be recognized, the House automatically resolves into the Committee of the Whole immediately without waiting for the call; and debate is resumed from the point at which it was discontinued on the previous Wednesday. 7 Cannon §§ 940, 942, 966; Deschler Ch 21 § 4.26.

On rejection by the House of a recommendation by the Committee of the Whole for peremptory disposition of a bill under consideration on Calendar Wednesday, the House automatically resolves into the Committee of the Whole for its further consideration. 7 Cannon § 943.

For a discussion of resolving into the Committee generally, see COMMITTEES OF THE WHOLE.

§4. Privilege and Precedence of Calendar Wednesday Business

No business in order on Calendar Wednesday may precede a properly requested call of committees. *Manual* §900; 7 Cannon §881. However, a motion to adjourn may interrupt the call of committees. 110-2, May 7, 2008, p 7996. Calendar Wednesday business is privileged matter which may interrupt the daily order of business as specified in rule XIV clause 1. *Manual* §871. It takes precedence over other business privileged under the rules, but not over a veto message privileged under the Constitution (Deschler Ch 21 §4.6), a question of privilege (7 Cannon §§908-911; Deschler Ch 21 §4.5), or the administration of the oath to Members (6 Cannon §22). When the call of committees is completed on Calendar Wednesday, business otherwise in order may be called up on that day. 7 Cannon §921.

The call of committees on Calendar Wednesday has precedence over:

- The consideration of conference reports. 7 Cannon §§899-901.
- The motion to go into Committee of the Whole to consider revenue and appropriation bills. 7 Cannon §904.
- Business on which the previous question is operating and undisposed of at adjournment on the preceding day. 7 Cannon §890.
- The motion for change of reference to committees. 7 Cannon §§883, 884.
- Privileged resolutions of inquiry. 7 Cannon §896.
- Contested election cases. 7 Cannon §903.
- Motions to reconsider. 7 Cannon §905.
- Certain procedural propositions relating to impeachment. 7 Cannon §902.
- Budget messages from the President. 7 Cannon §914.
- Senate bills privileged because of similarity to a bill on the House Calendar. 7 Cannon §906.
- Unanimous-consent requests generally. 7 Cannon §§882-888.

Motions to reconsider may be entered but not considered. 7 Cannon §905. Privileged reports may be presented for printing but without the right to call up for immediate consideration. 7 Cannon §907.

§5. The Call of Committees

Committees are called seriatim in the order in which they appear in rule X, the call being limited to those duly-noticed committees which have been elected. 7 Cannon §§922, 923, 925. Select committees with legislative jurisdiction are called after standing committees. Deschler Ch 21 §4. When a committee is reached during a Calendar Wednesday call of committees, it is ordinarily not in order to ask recognition for any purpose other than to call up a bill for consideration. 6 Cannon § 754.

During a call of committees under the rule, a committee may not yield or exchange its order of rotation. 7 Cannon § 927. Any committee declining to proceed with consideration of a bill when called on Wednesday loses that opportunity until again called in regular order. 7 Cannon § 926.

§ 6. Calling Up Calendar Wednesday Business; Authorization

Generally

The Calendar Wednesday rule permits committees to call up unprivileged bills from either the House Calendar or the Union Calendar, provided that there has been compliance with other rules of the House requiring that the measure and the report thereon be available for three days prior to consideration. *Manual* §§ 850, 900.

In addition to the notice requirement established in the 111th Congress, Calendar Wednesday business may be called up only on formal authorization by the reporting committee. 7 Cannon § 929. Clause 2(b) of rule XIII, requiring the chair of each committee to take necessary steps to bring reported measures to a vote, is sufficient authority for the chair to call up a bill on Calendar Wednesday. Deschler Ch 21 § 4.16. However, any other committee member must obtain specific authorization from the committee to call up a reported bill on Calendar Wednesday. *Manual* § 901; 4 Hinds § 3128; 7 Cannon §§ 928, 929. Committee authorization to a committee member to "use all parliamentary means to bring the bill before the House" is sufficient authorization to the member to call up the bill on Calendar Wednesday. 8 Cannon § 2217. Authority having been given to one Member to call up a bill, another may not be recognized for that purpose if objection is made. 7 Cannon §§ 928, 929. Only the Member authorized by the committee reporting the bill may call up that bill on Calendar Wednesday. Deschler Ch 21 § 4.12. It is within the discretion of the committee to determine which member to authorize to call up the bill. Deschler Ch 21 § 4.15.

Withdrawal

After a bill has been called up on Calendar Wednesday, it may be withdrawn at any time before amendment. 7 Cannon § 930.

§ 7. The Question of Consideration

The question of consideration may be demanded on a bill called up under the Calendar Wednesday rule. Deschler Ch 21 § 4.18. The question is properly raised after the Clerk has read the title of the bill. Deschler Ch

21 § 4.20. The question of consideration is properly raised on a Union Calendar bill in the House before going into Committee of the Whole. 7 Cannon § 952. If the question is decided in the affirmative, the House automatically resolves itself into the Committee of the Whole for the consideration of the bill. Deschler Ch 21 § 4.20.

The refusal of the House to consider a bill called up under the Calendar Wednesday rule does not preclude the bill from being brought up under another procedure, such as pursuant to a special order of business from the Committee on Rules. Deschler Ch 21 § 4.19.

It is not in order to reconsider the vote whereby the House has declined to consider a proposition under the Calendar Wednesday rule. Deschler Ch 21 § 4.25.

§ 8. Consideration and Debate

In the House

The hour rule for debate applies to House Calendar bills called up in the House on Calendar Wednesday as on other days, and the Member in charge of the bill may move the previous question at any time after debate begins. 7 Cannon §§ 955-957.

In Committee of the Whole

The Calendar Wednesday rule allows not more than two hours of general debate on any measure called up on Calendar Wednesday, to be confined to the subject and to be equally divided between those favoring and those opposing. *Manual* § 900. This provision has been construed as applying only in the Committee of the Whole. 7 Cannon § 955. The two hours permitted by the rule may be reduced by the House by unanimous consent to one hour. 98-2, Jan. 25, 1984, pp 357, 358. However, time allotted for debate under the rule may not be extended in the Committee of the Whole even by unanimous consent. 7 Cannon § 959. When a bill previously debated by another means is called up for the first time on Calendar Wednesday, consideration may proceed in the Committee of the Whole as if there had been no previous debate. 7 Cannon § 954.

In recognizing Members to control the time in opposition to the bill, the Chair recognizes minority members of the committee reporting the bill in the order of their seniority on the committee. Deschler Ch 21 § 4.24. They are entitled to prior recognition to oppose it, but if no member of the committee rises to oppose it, any Member may be recognized in opposition. 7 Cannon §§ 958, 959. The bill is read for amendment at the conclusion of an hour in favor of the bill if no one rises in opposition. 7 Cannon §§960, 961.

Amendments

In the Committee of the Whole, amendments may not be offered until the close of the two hours of debate, and the bill is taken up under the five-minute rule and read by section for amendment. 7 Cannon §960. Committee amendments are considered first as each section is reached. When the reading of the bill under the five-minute rule has been completed, the Committee rises and reports to the House. See COMMITTEES OF THE WHOLE.

§9. Unfinished Business; Effect of Previous Question

Where the previous question has been ordered on a bill on Calendar Wednesday, and the House adjourns, the bill becomes the unfinished business on the next legislative day. 8 Cannon §§895, 967; Deschler Ch 21 §§4.17, 4.28. Where a quorum fails on ordering the previous question on a bill under consideration on a Calendar Wednesday, and the House adjourns, the vote goes over until the next Calendar Wednesday available to the committee reporting the bill. Deschler Ch 21 §4.29.

When the House adjourns on Tuesday without voting on a proposition on which the previous question was ordered, the question occurs not on Wednesday but on Thursday. 7 Cannon §§890-894. In one instance, a Calendar Wednesday bill on which the previous question had been ordered at adjournment on Wednesday was taken up as the unfinished business on Thursday and took precedence over a motion to go into the Committee of the Whole for the consideration of a bill privileged by a special order of business. 8 Cannon §2674. A bill postponed from a Wednesday to a subsequent Wednesday becomes unfinished business to be considered when the committee calling it up is again called. 7 Cannon §970.

§10. Dispensing with Calendar Wednesday

Previously, it was possible by motion or unanimous consent to dispense with Calendar Wednesday business. Before the 111th Congress, Calendar Wednesday business was dispensed with routinely pursuant to a request made by the Majority Leader the previous week. Beginning in the 111th Congress, however, the call of the committees only occurs if specifically requested by the chair or other authorized member of a committee, obviating the need to dispense with such call.

Chapter 9
Calendars

Research References
4 Hinds §§ 3115-3118
7 Cannon §§ 881-1023
Deschler Ch 22 §§ 1, 2
Manual §§ 828-830, 892, 898, 899

§ 1. In General; Kinds of Calendars

Under clause 1 and rule XIII, the House maintains various calendars to facilitate the scheduling and consideration of its legislative business. These include:

- The House Calendar. This calendar receives referrals of public bills that do not raise revenue or directly or indirectly make or require an appropriation of money or property. *Manual* § 828.
- The Union Calendar. Measures belonging on the Union Calendar are those on subjects that fall within the jurisdiction of the Committee of the Whole. Deschler Ch 22 § 2. Subjects that must be considered in the Committee of the Whole are specified in clause 3 of rule XVIII. Bills appropriating money or property are referred to the Union Calendar. *Manual* §§ 828, 973. The same is true of bills authorizing an undertaking by a governmental agency that will incur an expense to the government, however small. 8 Cannon § 2401.
- The Private Calendar (to which are referred bills of a private character). See PRIVATE CALENDAR.
- The Discharge Calendar (to which are referred motions to discharge committees). *Manual* §§ 830, 892; see DISCHARGING MEASURES FROM COMMITTEES.

These calendars—the Discharge Calendar excepted—consist primarily of lists of measures on which committee action has been completed and which are ready for floor action. They are printed daily and appear in *Calendars of the United States House of Representatives.*

Calendar Wednesday and the ''suspension calendar'' are not legislative calendars. Calendar Wednesday refers to the procedure for the call of committees on Wednesday for the consideration of unprivileged bills on the House and Union Calendars. See CALENDAR WEDNESDAY. Bills listed on the leadership's ''suspension calendar'' are those intended to be taken up by motions to suspend the rules on Mondays, Tuesdays, and Wednesdays. See SUSPENSION OF RULES.

§ 2. Referrals to Calendars

Measures Reported Favorably

Bills that are favorably reported from a committee are referred to the appropriate calendar under the direction of the Speaker unless referred to other committees under clause 2 of rule XII. *Manual* § 816. Public bills favorably reported are referred either to the Union Calendar or to the House Calendar. Deschler Ch 22 § 2. Bills reported without recommendation are also referred to the appropriate calendar.

The reference of a bill to a particular calendar is governed by the text of the bill as referred to committee, and amendments reported by a committee are not considered in making this determination. 8 Cannon § 2392.

Measures Reported Unfavorably

Bills and resolutions that are adversely reported from committee are not referred to a calendar unless a request to that effect is made by the committee or a Member. Deschler Ch 22 § 1.1. Under clause 2(a)(2) of rule XIII, Members have three days in which to request such a referral. *Manual* § 832. Such request is normally communicated by the committee to the Clerk at the time of reporting, although it also may be made by a Member from the floor. Absent such a request, an adversely reported measure is laid on the table. *Manual* § 832. Thereafter, it may be taken from the table and placed on the calendar only by unanimous consent. 6 Cannon § 750.

Privileged measures are excepted from the general rule that only favorably reported bills are referred to a calendar. Adverse reports on privileged resolutions (including resolutions of inquiry) are referred to the proper calendar by the Speaker. 6 Cannon § 411.

Measures Reported Improperly

A bill that has been improperly reported from a committee is not entitled to a place on a calendar, and should be recommitted. 4 Hinds § 3117.

§3. —Erroneous Referrals

A bill that is on the wrong calendar is subject to a point of order when it is called up for consideration. *Manual* §828; 6 Cannon §§746, 747. Such a point of order is untimely if made after consideration of the measure has begun. 7 Cannon §856.

The Speaker has general authority to correct an erroneous reference of a reported bill to a calendar, and to transfer the bill to the proper calendar. *Manual* §828; 7 Cannon §859. Thus, a private bill erroneously referred to the Union Calendar may be transferred to the Private Calendar by direction of the Speaker. *Manual* §828. The transfer of the bill to the proper calendar may be made effective as of the date of the original reference. Deschler Ch 22 §1.2. The Speaker may correct such a reference at any time before consideration of the bill begins and while the question of consideration is pending. 6 Cannon §748. The authority of the Speaker to correct a calendar reference does not apply where the reference was made by the House itself. 6 Cannon §749.

An error in the referral of a bill to a calendar may also be corrected pursuant to motion. Such a motion presents a privileged question. 3 Hinds §§2614, 2615. However, a mere clerical error in the calendar, such as an incorrect date, does not give rise to such a question. 3 Hinds §2616.

§4. Discharge From Calendars

Although the Speaker has no specific authority under the House rules to remove a reported bill from the Union Calendar, such a bill may be discharged for reference to another committee pursuant to the Speaker's general responsibility under clause 2 of rule XII to fashion sequential referrals where appropriate. *Manual* §816. Section 401(b) of the Congressional Budget Act of 1974 and clause 4(a)(2) of rule X give the Speaker discretionary authority to discharge a bill from the Union Calendar and refer for 15 days to the Committee on Appropriations bills reported by another committee providing certain new entitlement authority. *Manual* §§747, 1127.

§5. The Corrections Calendar

The former Corrections Calendar (established in the 104th Congress as a replacement for the Consent Calendar) was abolished in the 109th Congress. *Manual* §898.

Chapter 10
Chamber, Rooms, and Galleries

Research References
5 Hinds §§ 7270-7311
8 Cannon §§ 3632, 3636-3643
Deschler Ch 4; Deschler-Brown Ch 29 § 85
Manual §§ 677-684

§ 1. In General; Use of the Hall

The Hall of the House and unappropriated rooms in the House (rooms not specifically assigned by action of the House) are under the general control of the Speaker. Clause 3 of rule I; *Manual* § 623. Control of the appropriated rooms in the House wing is exercised by the House itself. 5 Hinds §§ 7273-7279. Resolutions assigning a room to a committee have been considered as privileged. 5 Hinds § 7273.

Under clause 1 of rule IV, the Hall may be used only for (1) the legislative business of the House; (2) caucus meetings of its Members, including joint party caucuses; (3) ceremonies in which the House votes to participate; and (4) classified briefings of Members, if authorized by the Speaker, during recesses declared under clause 12 of rule I. *Manual* §§ 623, 677. In rare instances the House has permitted the Hall to be used for ceremonial or special occasions. 8 Cannon § 3632; Deschler Ch 4 §§ 3.1, 3.4. However, a House and Senate ceremony of religious reconciliation to be conducted in the Hall of the House during a recess requires adoption of a concurrent resolution by both Houses. See, *e.g.*, 107-1, H. Con. Res. 184, Oct. 23, 2001, pp 20388-90 (never adopted by the Senate). Beginning in the 111th Congress, the Speaker has announced a policy that when the House stands adjourned, its chamber remains on static display and shall not be used for any proceedings that might be taken to carry the imprimatur of the House. 111-1, Jan. 6, 2009, p ____; 112-1, Jan. 5, 2011, p ____.

Disorderly or disruptive acts in the Capitol are unlawful, and unauthorized demonstrations are prohibited by law. 40 USC § 5104(e)(2)(D). The unauthorized presence of persons on the floor of either House or in the gallery of either House is prohibited. 40 USC § 5104(e)(2)(B). Disorder in the House, see CONSIDERATION AND DEBATE.

§ 2. Admission to the Floor

Generally

Clause 2 of rule IV enumerates those persons entitled to be admitted to the floor or rooms leading thereto. *Manual* § 678. Among those who may be admitted to the Hall are Members and Members-elect of Congress, the President and Vice President, Judges of the Supreme Court, governors of States, heads of departments, foreign ministers, contestants in election cases during the pendency of their cases on the floor, one attorney for a Member-respondent during consideration of a disciplinary resolution reported from the Committee on Ethics, and other named officials. *Manual* § 678. The term "heads of departments" has been construed to mean members of the President's Cabinet, and the term "foreign ministers" has been construed to mean the representatives of foreign governments duly accredited to the United States, and not necessarily those with the title of "minister" in their own parliaments. 5 Hinds § 7283. The term "contestants in election cases" has been construed to include challengers in an election contest, even though the challenger was not a candidate in the election in which the sitting Member was reelected. Deschler Ch 4 § 4.5.

It is not in order to refer to persons temporarily on the floor of the House as guests of the House, such as Members' children, other children, or Senators exercising floor privileges. *Manual* § 678. Although Senators have floor privileges, they are not entitled to address the House. Deschler Ch 4 § 4.8.

The rule is strictly enforced during regular meetings. However, the rule is less strictly enforced on ceremonial occasions (5 Hinds § 7290) or when the House is in recess during a joint meeting with the Senate (Deschler Ch 4 § 4). The rule is not applicable to joint sessions of the two Houses. 5 Hinds § 7292. The Speaker sometimes announces guidelines for use of the chamber during a recess. During a regular meeting, a point of order will lie to object to the presence of any unauthorized persons. 92-2, June 21, 1972, p 21704. Under clause 2(b) of rule IV, motions or unanimous-consent requests to suspend the rule may not be entertained by the Speaker or by the chair of the Committee of the Whole. 5 Hinds § 7285.

The Speaker has the authority to exclude an individual who abuses the privileges of the floor. 5 Hinds § 7288. An alleged abuse of the privilege of the floor may be made the subject of an inquiry by a special committee. 5 Hinds § 7287.

Former Members

A former Member must observe the rules of proper decorum while on the floor, and the Chair may direct the Sergeant-at-Arms to assist the Chair in maintaining such decorum. *Manual* § 622. The question of banning a former Member engaged in indecorous behavior on the floor gives rise to a question of the privileges of the House. *Manual* § 680. A former Member may not manifest approval or disapproval of the proceedings. 8 Cannon § 3635. For more information on floor privileges of former Members, see *Manual* § 680.

Although former Members, officers, and certain former employees have access to the floor under clause 2 of rule IV, such individuals are not entitled to the privileges of the floor, or rooms leading thereto, if they (1) are a registered lobbyist or agent of a foreign principal; (2) have a direct personal or pecuniary interest in legislation under consideration in the House or reported by any committee; or (3) represent any party or organization for the purpose of influencing the disposition of legislation pending before the House or reported by a committee or under consideration in a committee. *Manual* § 680. For a list of regulations issued by the Speaker under this rule, see *Manual* § 680.

Staff; Committee Clerks

Clause 2(a)(7) of rule IV permits on the floor staff of a committee when business from their committee is under consideration and no more than one person from the staff of a Member when that Member has an amendment under consideration. This rule has been interpreted by the Speaker to allow the presence on the floor of four professional staff members and one clerk from a committee during consideration of that committee's business and to require that such individuals remain unobtrusively by the committee tables. *Manual* § 678. Clause 2(a)(7) of rule IV also permits on the floor staff of the respective party leaderships when so assigned with the approval of the Speaker. The privileges of the floor do not extend to departmental employees assisting committees in the preparation of bills. 6 Cannon § 579. Where several committees are involved with a pending measure, the rule permits authorized majority and minority staff (up to five persons) from each committee. 97-1, June 26, 1981, p 14574. Clerks other than those employed by a committee involved in the bill under consideration are not entitled to the floor. Deschler Ch 4 § 4. The Speaker has announced an intention to strictly enforce the rule to prevent a proliferation of staff on the floor and has required committee staff to display staff badges when on the floor. *Manual* § 678. Under clause 5 of rule IV, and regulations promulgated by the Speaker thereunder, staff on the floor are not permitted to pass out literature or otherwise attempt to influence Members in their votes or to applaud during debate. *Manual* § 681.

Secret Sessions

Before a secret session of the House commences, the Speaker may direct that the Chamber be cleared of all persons except Members and those officers and employees, specified by the Speaker, whose attendance on the floor is essential to the functioning of the session. Clause 9 of rule XVII; *Manual* § 969; Deschler-Brown Ch 29 § 85. A point of order will not lie against the presence in the Chamber of those persons whose attendance on the floor is permitted by the Speaker's directive. Deschler-Brown Ch 29 § 85.15; see CONSIDERATION AND DEBATE. Secret classified briefings of Members may be permitted during recesses of the House declared by the Speaker under clause 12 of rule I. Under clause 13 of rule XXIII, a Member, officer, or employee must execute an oath of secrecy before having access to classified material. *Manual* § 1095.

§ 3. Electronic Devices; Signals, Bells, and Clocks

Various electronic devices and computer services are used by the House to expedite quorum calls and votes and for other purposes. *Manual* §§ 1012-1016. For example, a legislative bell and light system alerts Members to quorum calls, the taking of certain votes, and other occurrences on the floor. *Manual* §§ 1014, 1016. Changes in the system are announced by the Speaker from time to time. The failure of the signal bells to announce a vote does not warrant repetition of the record vote, nor does such a failure permit a Member to be recorded following the conclusion of the call. *Manual* § 1016; 8 Cannon §§ 3153, 3155, 3157; see also VOTING.

The use of a mobile electronic device on the floor of the House that impairs decorum is prohibited under clause 5 of rule XVII, and the Chair has admonished Members to disable wireless telephones on entering the Chamber. The Chair has also announced that the use of wireless telephones is not permitted in the gallery. *Manual* § 962.

Microphones have been placed on the floor of the House for the use of Members. A Member making an appropriate request should use one of the floor microphones so that all Members may hear the request. 94-1, Oct. 28, 1975, p 34027. A Member may speak at any microphone on the floor.

Manual § 364. Clause 2 of rule I directs the Speaker to preserve order and decorum in the House, and authorizes the Speaker to order the microphones turned off if they are being utilized by a disorderly Member who has not been properly recognized. Deschler-Brown Ch 29 § 11.19.

§ 4. Galleries and Corridors

Under clause 3 of rule I, control over the corridors leading to the House Chamber is vested in the Speaker. *Manual* §§ 622, 623. The Speaker may order the corridors cleared during quorum calls and the taking of votes to ensure unimpeded access to the Chamber. *Manual* § 623. Under clause 2 of rule I, the Speaker preserves order and decorum in the galleries, and in the event of a disturbance, may order the galleries cleared. *Manual* § 622. The chair of the Committee of the Whole may exercise similar power in preserving order in the galleries. *Manual* § 970.

Guests in the House gallery must maintain order and refrain from manifestations of approval or disapproval of proceedings on the floor, and admonitions may be expressed either by the Speaker or by the chair of the Committee of the Whole. Deschler Ch 4 § 5.6. Under clause 7 of rule XVII, it also is out of order to refer to visitors in the galleries, even with permission to proceed out of order; and the Speaker, *sua sponte*, may declare such remarks to be out of order. Deschler Ch 4 §§ 5.3, 5.4.

§ 5. Photographs; Radio and Television Coverage

Photographs

Under the practice of the House, permission must be obtained before photographs may be taken inside the House Chamber. Rules regarding the taking of such pictures may be enforced by the Speaker. Deschler Ch 4 § 3.5 (note). Official photographs of the House while in session may be permitted by resolution. See, *e.g.*, 107-2, H. Res. 378, June 5, 2002, p 9285; 111-1, H. Res. 658, July 17, 2009, p ____.

Media Coverage of Floor Proceedings

Prior to the 95th Congress, the rules and precedents of the House did not permit public radio and television broadcasts of House proceedings. In 1977, the House adopted a privileged resolution reported from the Committee on Rules to provide a system of closed-circuit viewing of House proceedings and for the orderly development of a broadcasting system. Under rule V, the Speaker directs the audio and visual broadcasting and recording of the proceedings of the House, including periods of voting. Under this rule, broadcasts are made over closed-circuit television in House offices and have been made available to the news media and to cable television systems. Broadcasts made available under the rule may not be used for political or commercial purposes. *Manual* § 684.

In 1984, a question arose as to the authority of the Speaker to require wide-angle television coverage of the House Chamber during special-order speeches. In that instance, the Speaker's directive that television cameras covering special-order speeches of the House at the completion of legislative business include periodic wide-angle coverage of the entire House Chamber was held to be consistent with the authority conferred upon the Speaker under rule V. *Manual* § 684. Beginning in the 103d Congress, the Speaker has followed a policy under which television cameras would not ''pan'' the Chamber during morning-hour or special-order speeches. However, the Speaker directed that a caption run at the bottom of the screen indicating the conduct of morning-hour debate or to show that legislative business has been completed for the day. *Manual* § 684.

Although clause 2 of rule V requires complete and unedited broadcast coverage of the proceedings of the House, it does not require in-House microphone amplification of disorderly conduct by a Member no longer under recognition. Deschler-Brown Ch 29 § 11.19.

Chapter 11
Committees

Research References

4 Hinds §§4019-4703
7 Cannon §§1721-2170; 8 Cannon §§2171-2317
Deschler Ch 17
Manual §§714-814, 816, 831-863

A. Generally; Establishing Committees

§1. The Committee System; Standing, Select, and Joint Committees

The Role of Committees

The committee system is as old as the House itself, having been patterned after the English House of Commons, the colonial assemblies, and the Continental Congress. Although during its first quarter century the House relied primarily upon select committees and the Committee of the Whole, the first standing committee dates from 1789.

The committees of the House play a prominent role at every stage of the legislative process. As a general rule, proposed legislative measures are referred to committees before receiving consideration in the House itself. *Manual* §446. A committee may report a measure with or without amendments (which may rewrite the measure entirely), report adversely, or fail to report the measure at all. For a discussion of discharge procedures, see DISCHARGING MEASURES FROM COMMITTEES.

The role of the committee does not terminate with the reporting of the bill to the House. When a bill reaches the floor, members of the committee reporting it are entitled to priority in recognition for the purpose of offering amendments, and general debate is generally under the control of the chair and ranking minority member. See CONSIDERATION AND DEBATE and AMENDMENTS. Finally, members of the reporting committees are often appointed by the Speaker to serve on the conference committee to resolve differences between competing forms of the bill. See CONFERENCES BETWEEN THE HOUSES.

Standing, Select, and Joint Committees Distinguished

House committees are of three distinct types: (1) standing committees, whose members are *elected* by the House, (2) select committees (also called special committees), whose members are *appointed* by the Speaker, and (3) joint committees, whose members are chosen according to the provisions of the statute or concurrent resolution creating them. Variations of these three categories are discussed in later sections.

Standing committees (created in the standing rules) receive bills and other measures within their jurisdiction upon referral from the Speaker. See INTRODUCTION AND REFERENCE OF BILLS. Select committees are established (usually outside the standing rules) to consider a particular matter or subject and may or may not have legislative jurisdiction. A select committee often expires when it issues its final report on the matter for which it was created. 4 Hinds §§ 4403-4405; see § 12, infra. Joint committees take up matters of concern to both Houses. See § 14, infra.

Committee of the Whole Distinguished

The Committee of the Whole has been described as a committee of the House, although it is not a committee in the customary sense. 4 Hinds § 4706. The Committee of the Whole, unlike regular committees, does not have a fixed membership. All Members of the House may attend and participate in its deliberations under special rules designed to encourage wide-ranging debate and to expedite legislation. The Committee of the Whole itself has no power to authorize or appoint a committee. 4 Hinds § 4710. Because of its unique role in the procedures of the House, the Committee of the Whole is addressed in a separate chapter of this work. See COMMITTEES OF THE WHOLE.

Conference Committees Distinguished

Conference committees are used primarily to resolve differences between the House and Senate on measures that have passed the two Houses and also are addressed in a separate chapter. See CONFERENCES BETWEEN THE HOUSES.

Subcommittees

Standing committees may establish subcommittees to study legislation, hold hearings, and make reports to the full committee. With certain exceptions, clause 5(d) of rule X precludes a committee from establishing more than five subcommittees. In addition to the exceptions found in the rule itself, the House has occasionally made further exceptions to that stricture. See, *e.g.*, 107-1, H. Res. 5, Jan. 3, 2001, p 26; 108-1, H. Res. 5, Jan. 7, 2003, p 11. Clause 5(d) was adopted in the 104th Congress to replace a requirement that all standing committees having more than 20 members establish at least four subcommittees. *Manual* § 762; see § 11, infra.

Subcommittees have no power to report directly to the House, absent specific authority to do so and are subject to the control of the full committee. *Manual* § 787. Other subunits of committees, such as "task forces," have no formal recognition or authority under the standing rules of the House unless formally established by the House. See, *e.g.*, 102-2, H. Res. 258, Feb. 5, 1992, p 1621.

Commissions

Commissions are analogous to select committees in that they are established to study a particular problem; but a commission is distinguishable from a select committee in that its membership may include private citizens, Members of the House and Senate, and representatives from other branches of government. See, *e.g.*, 94-2, H. Res. 1368, July 1, 1976, p 21795 (creating the Commission on Administrative Review); 6 USC § 101 note (creating the National Commission on Terrorist Attacks Upon the United States).

Duration of Committees

The committees of the House remain in existence only during the two-year term of a Congress which created them. The standing committees of the House are usually reconstituted by a new Congress after the standing rules or resolutions specifically creating new committees are adopted. Deschler Ch 17 § 1.2 (note).

Select committees expire with the term of the Congress in which they were created or at such earlier date as may be specified in the resolution creating them. Deschler Ch 17 §§ 1, 5.5. Unless permanently established, a select committee ceases to exist when it finally reports in full on the subject committed to it but may be revived by action of the House in referring a new matter to it. 4 Hinds §§ 4403-4405. A select committee that expires in one Congress may be reconstituted in the next. Deschler Ch 17 § 5.5. In one instance, a select committee was reconstituted (and its existence extended through subsequent resolution) solely for the purpose of completing activities directly associated with the declassification and public release of its report. *Manual* § 1112a.

Joint committees established by statute remain in existence beyond the Congress in which they were created unless otherwise provided, although the members thereof must be chosen anew in each Congress. Deschler Ch 17 § 1.

§ 2. Establishing Committees

Standing Committees

Standing committees are ordinarily established with the adoption of the standing rules on opening day for a Congress. They also may be subsequently established by a simple resolution reported from the Committee on Rules, usually by way of amendment to the House rules. Deschler Ch 17 §§ 2.1, 2.3. For a discussion of adoption of rules of a new Congress, see ASSEMBLY OF CONGRESS.

A resolution reported by the Committee on Rules during a Congress establishing a new committee, changing the name or authority of a committee, or abolishing a committee and transferring its jurisdiction and records to another committee is called up as privileged and is debatable under the hour rule in the House. Deschler Ch 17 §§ 2.1, 2.4, 2.6.

Select Committees

Select committees are normally established by a resolution reported from the Committee on Rules. Deschler Ch 17 §§ 5.3, 5.5. However, in one instance, a select committee was created pursuant to a floor amendment (offered to the Committee Reform Amendments of 1974). 93-2, H. Res. 988, Oct. 8, 1974, p 34470. In another instance, a select committee was created as a separate order included in a resolution adopting the standing rules of the House. 108-1, H. Res. 5, Jan. 7, 2003, p 11. The House also has adopted a privileged resolution reported from the Committee on Rules establishing a new select subcommittee of a standing committee. 104-2, H. Res. 416, May 8, 1996, p 10484. A select subcommittee of a standing committee has also been created by an unreported resolution considered under a separate order included in a resolution adopting the standing rules of the House. 110-1, H. Res. 35, Jan. 9, 2007, p 567. For a list of current select committees, see *Manual* §§1112a, 1112b.

A resolution creating a select committee may specify the jurisdiction and powers of the select committee and may place it under the authority of a standing committee. Deschler Ch 17 §§5.2, 5.3; §12, infra.

A resolution creating a select committee is reported and called up as privileged, because the Committee on Rules may report at any time on rules, and the creation of such a committee is the equivalent of a new rule. *Manual* §853; Deschler Ch 17 §5.1. If such a resolution is not reported by the Committee on Rules, it is not privileged, and unanimous consent or a special order of business reported by the Committee on Rules is necessary to permit its consideration. 95-1, Jan. 4, 1977, p 72. The Committee on Rules itself may not report such a resolution as privileged if it contains provisions outside the jurisdiction of the committee. Deschler Ch 17 §1.1 (note). However, if such a resolution is referred to another committee for consideration of a provision that also is privileged, both committees may report the resolution as privileged. See, *e.g.*, 102-1, H. Res. 258, Nov. 19, 1991, p 32903 (resolution contained a provision funding the select committee from the "applicable accounts of the House").

Special Ad Hoc Committees

Under the earlier practice of the House, special committees to consider a particular matter could be established by way of a motion or other proposition to refer. 4 Hinds §§4401, 4402; 5 Hinds §§6633, 6634. Thus, the House could refer a message of the President to a special committee to be appointed by the Speaker. At the same time the House could instruct the committee and specify the number of members to be appointed. 5 Hinds §6633. It was held in this regard that the House need not refer to a special committee already in existence but could refer to one to be subsequently appointed. 5 Hinds §6634. An ad hoc select committee may be established by a resolution called up as a question of the privileges of the House. 102-2, H. Res. 431, Apr. 9, 1992, p 9029 (resolution laid on the table); 110-1, H. Res. 611, Aug. 3, 2007, p 22769.

Special ad hoc committees may be established pursuant to clause 2(c) of rule XII. Under this rule, the Speaker has authority to refer a matter to a special ad hoc committee appointed by the Speaker to consider that matter and report thereon to the House. The appointment must be made with the approval of the House and include members of the committees having legislative jurisdiction. Pursuant to this authority, the Speaker may, with the approval of the House, appoint a special ad hoc committee to consider a particular measure, or a particular bill and similar subsequent bills. A resolution authorizing the Speaker to take such action is privileged when offered from the floor at the Speaker's request. *Manual* § 816b.

Joint Committees

Joint committees are created by law or by concurrent resolution. *Manual* §§ 1108-1112; Deschler Ch 17 § 7; see § 14, infra. A joint committee may be created and vested with jurisdiction as one part of a comprehensive bill or as the sole purpose of a joint resolution. 6 Cannon § 371; Deschler Ch 17 §§ 7.4, 7.5. A joint committee created by concurrent resolution must expire (unless reconstituted) with the Congress in which it was created. 4 Hinds § 4409.

A concurrent resolution establishing a joint committee, if reported by the Committee on Rules, is called up as privileged by that committee. Deschler Ch 17 § 7.1. However, such a resolution may not be reported as privileged if it contains an authorization for appropriations. Deschler Ch 17 § 7.5. Debate on the resolution is under the hour rule. Deschler Ch 17 § 7.1.

Commissions

Commissions are ordinarily created by statute. See, *e.g.*, the Abraham Lincoln Bicentennial Commission (36 USC § 101 (note)). They may also be created by House resolution. See, *e.g.*, the Commission on Administrative Review, 94-2, H. Res. 1368, July 1, 1976, p 21795; the House Democracy Partnership, 109-1, H. Res. 135, Mar. 14, 2005, p 4527 (re-established in succeeding Congresses); and the Tom Lantos Human Rights Commission, 110-2, H. Res. 1451, Sept. 24, 2008, p ____ (re-established in succeeding Congresses).

§ 3. Committee Expenses; Funding

Authorization for the payment of committee expenses for a particular Congress is obtained pursuant to "one primary expense resolution" for each committee (the Committee on Appropriations excepted). Clause 6 of rule X. The request for such authorization is made to the Committee on House Administration, which has jurisdiction over such expenditures. Clause 1(k) of rule X. In recent years, the Committee on House Administration has combined the individual committee funding resolutions into a single resolution to expedite consideration in the House. See, *e.g.*, 112-1, H. Res. 147, Mar. 17, 2011, p ____.

Authorization for the payment of additional committee expenses not covered by the primary expense resolution may be obtained pursuant to one or more "supplemental expense resolutions." Clause 6(b) of rule X.

The primary and supplemental expense resolutions, are subject to a one-calendar-day layover requirement. A supplemental expense resolution that is not reported by the Committee on House Administration may be considered by unanimous consent (subject to the Speaker's guidelines for recognition of unanimous-consent requests). 107-2, H. Res. 359, Mar. 7, 2002, p 2738.

Funds for the Committee on Appropriations are appropriated by the annual appropriation bill for the legislative branch.

B. Chairs, Members, and Staff; Elections and Appointments

§ 4. In General; Membership and Seniority

Standing and Select Committees Distinguished

Until 1911, the members and the chairs of the standing and select committees of the House were generally appointed by the Speaker, although in rare instances a committee chose its own chair. See 4 Hinds § 4524. Since 1911, standing committee chairs and members have been elected by the House as part of a three-step procedure. First, with certain exceptions, a selection committee—sometimes called a committee on committees or a steering committee—of each party caucus recommends candidates for committee assignments. Second, the party caucus approves the recommendations of the selection committee. Third, the House approves the recommendations of the caucuses, which are brought before the House as privileged resolutions. Clause 5(a)(1) of rule X; *Manual* §§ 317, 757; 4 Hinds § 4513; 8 Cannon § 2201. The rules of the Democratic Caucus and the Republican Conference may prescribe different nomination procedures for certain committees. Furthermore, the Speaker has retained the authority, under clause 11 of rule I, to appoint Members to select committees. *Manual* § 637.

Electing Chair

Pursuant to nominations submitted by the majority party caucus, one member of each standing committee is elected as its chair at the commencement of each Congress. *Manual* § 761. A Member's service as chair of the same committee (with the exception of the Committee on Rules) is limited to three consecutive Congresses. Clause 5(c)(2) of rule X. Nominations for chairs are submitted to the House for its approval in the election resolution. Deschler Ch 17 § 8.1. Such a resolution is normally called up as privileged by the chair of the majority party caucus, often as part of a resolution electing all majority members to those committees. Deschler Ch 17 § 8.7 (note). For an example of a resolution electing only committee chairs, and one electing only ranking minority members, see 111-1, H. Res. 8 and H. Res. 12, Jan. 6, 2009, p ____, p ____.

In the event of a permanent vacancy in the elected chair, the House elects a successor pursuant to a privileged resolution. *Manual* § 761. This procedure is followed when a vacancy is created on a standing committee by the death of its chair or after a chair has resigned. Deschler Ch 17 §§ 8.3, 8.5, 8.6. In the absence of the chair, the member next in rank as named in the resolution electing the committee acts as chair. *Manual* § 761.

Where the chair is unable to carry out the responsibilities of the position, the House may, in the election resolution, provide for a delegation of powers and duties to an acting chair until further ordered by the House. *Manual* § 761. Similarly, the resolution electing minority members to a committee may devolve the role of ranking minority member to the next-senior minority member of a standing committee (where the ranking minority member remained absent due to physical infirmity). 105-2, H. Res. 369, Feb. 25, 1998, p 1967.

Election of Members

Resolutions electing Members to standing committees have traditionally been offered from the floor and called up as privileged at the direction of the party organization. 8 Cannon §§ 2171, 2179, 2182. Each party's resolution, if adopted, elects en bloc those Members from that particular party to the various standing committees. Deschler Ch 17 § 9.1. Such a resolution is not divisible under clause 5(b)(1) of rule XVI. *Manual* § 919. However, it is debatable and subject to amendment until such time as the previous question is ordered. 8 Cannon §§ 2172, 2174.

Under clause 5(b)(1) of rule X, service on a standing committee is contingent upon continuing membership in the nominating party caucus. Such service automatically ceases upon termination of caucus membership. *Manual* § 760.

No Member may serve simultaneously as a member of more than two standing committees or four subcommittees unless approved by the House on recommendation of the caucus. Clause 5(b)(2) of rule X. A Member may be removed from a committee by privileged resolution. See, *e.g.*, 109-2, H. Res. 872, June 16, 2006, p 11618.

Seniority

Committee seniority is shown by the order in which the Members' names are listed in the election resolution. Deschler Ch 17 § 11.1. A resolution electing a Member to a committee may include the designation of rank on the committee (Deschler Ch 17 § 9.6) and may be made effective retroactively (Deschler Ch 17 §9.16). A resolution may also alter the rank among sitting committee members. See, *e.g.*, 107-1, H. Res. 85, Mar. 8, 2001, p 3295.

§5. Numerical Composition of Committees; Party Ratios

Committee Size

Clause 5(a)(3) of rule X limits the size of only one standing committee of the House, the Committee on Ethics, which is set at five majority and five minority members. *Manual* §759. The sizes of other committees of the House are negotiated by the Majority and Minority Leaders at the direction of their respective party organizations. Deschler Ch 17 §9. The size of each committee is ultimately determined by the number of Members elected to each committee pursuant to clause 5(a) of rule X. *Manual* §757.

Party Ratios

The allocation of majority party and minority party representation on committees is normally determined through negotiations between the majority and minority leadership. Historically, the party ratios on most standing committees have tended to reflect the relative membership of the two parties in the House as a whole. Deschler Ch 17 §9.4. Sometimes, however, the membership of a committee is equally divided between the majority and minority parties where bipartisan deliberations are considered essential. See, *e.g.*, clause 5(a)(3) of rule X, requiring the members of the Committee on Ethics to be five from the majority party and five from the minority party.

Disproportionate party ratios on committees may also be traced to the rules of the party caucus. Deschler Ch 3 §9. Moreover, some House committees, such as the Committee on Rules and the Committee on House Administration, have traditionally reflected disproportionate ratios in favor of the majority party. See, *e.g.*, 8 Cannon §2184.

§6. The Chair's Role

The powers and duties of the full committee chairs are derived from custom and from the rules of the House. The chair of a committee:

- Presides over committee meetings. *Manual* §317.
- Schedules meetings and hearings subject to rule XI.
- Administers oaths to witnesses in hearings in the committee or delegates that authority. *Manual* §805; 2 USC §191. In one instance, the chair of an investigating committee administered the oath to himself and testified. 3 Hinds §1821.
- May punish breaches of order and decorum by censure and exclusion from hearings. *Manual* §803.

- Authorizes and issues subpoenas when the power to do so has been delegated by the committee. *Manual* § 805.
- Fixes, within certain guidelines, the salaries of staff. *Manual* § 777.
- Submits committee reports to the House, even if not concurring therein. Clause 2(b)(1) of rule XIII; 4 Hinds §§ 4670, 4671. However, a committee may order its report to be made by some other member or even by a member of the minority party. 4 Hinds §§ 4669, 4672, 4673.
- Submits privileged reports to the House from the floor. *Manual* § 418.
- Manages bills of the committee in the House under the responsibility to take steps necessary to bring the measure or matter to a vote. Such managerial status entitles the chair at all stages to prior recognition for allowable motions intended to expedite it. *Manual* § 834; 2 Hinds §§ 1452, 1457; 6 Cannon §§ 296, 300.
- Receives priority in recognition when Senate amendments to the bill are debated. 2 Hinds § 1452.

§ 7. Committee Employees and Staff

The employment of committee staff is governed by clause 9 of rule X (*Manual* §§ 771-781) and by statute (see, *e.g.*, 5 USC §§ 5315, 5316, setting permissible rates of staff pay).

The House rules place a limit on the number of professional staff members which may be appointed to a standing committee (the Committee on Appropriations excepted) and on the number of professional staff members which may be selected by the minority. *Manual* §§ 771-774. The Committee on Appropriations is subject to a separate rule permitting the appointment, in addition to a clerk and assistants for the minority, of such staff as are determined by majority vote to be necessary. Clause 9(d) of rule X.

C. Committee Functions; Jurisdiction and Authority

§ 8. Legislative Jurisdiction

Generally; Referrals and Rereferrals

The legislative jurisdiction of each standing committee is specified and defined by rule X. *Manual* §§ 714-41. Areas of legislative interest have been divided under rule X into distinct subject matter classifications, with jurisdiction over each being allocated to a standing or select committee. The Speaker refers bills and other matters to committees pursuant to the jurisdiction of each committee as defined by rule X, taking into account any relevant precedents. Under clause 2 of rule XII, the Speaker is required to refer a measure to more than one committee where it involves subject matter assigned to different committees. *Manual* § 816. Under clause 2(c)(1) of rule

XII, the Speaker is required to indicate a primary committee of jurisdiction (except where it is determined that extraordinary circumstances justify review by more than one committee as though primary). Additional committees of initial referral are listed after the primary committee. The Speaker imposes time limits on the additional committees once the primary committee reports. Clause 2(c) of rule XII; *Manual* § 816. Under clause 2 of rule XII, the Speaker also may refer a measure sequentially to a committee upon reporting by the committees of initial referral. The Speaker imposes time limits on sequential referrals. For a discussion of referrals generally, see BILLS AND RESOLUTIONS.

Rule X requires the Speaker to refer public measures in accordance with its terms and gives some discretion to Members in referring private bills. *Manual* §§ 714, 818. However, the House itself may refer bills to any committee without regard to the rules of jurisdiction, and jurisdiction is thereby conferred. 4 Hinds §§ 4362-4364, 4375; 5 Hinds § 5527; 7 Cannon §§ 2105, 2131.

The committees, because they are created by the House, exercise no authority or jurisdiction beyond that specifically conferred by the rules or by special authorization of the House itself. 7 Cannon § 780. However, the House may confer jurisdiction on a committee by the adoption of a special order of business from the Committee on Rules. 7 Cannon § 780. A bill may be originated by a committee which has been given jurisdiction to do so by order or rule of the House. 4 Hinds § 3365. Jurisdictional authority, in addition to that specified in rule X, may be vested in a committee pursuant to:

- A resolution enlarging the jurisdiction of a committee or authorizing it to study and report on a particular matter. 3 Hinds § 1753.
- A change in the rules of the House by adoption of a resolution from the Committee on Rules. 91-2, July 8, 1970, p 32136.
- A motion to rerefer or recommit.

The erroneous reference of a public bill, if it remains uncorrected, gives the committee authority to report that measure. 4 Hinds §§ 4365-4371; 7 Cannon § 2108. However, such is not the case with respect to a private bill unless the reference is made by action of the House itself. 4 Hinds §§ 3364, 4382-4391; 7 Cannon § 2131.

Informal Agreements

Questions relating to the jurisdiction over a subject by two or more committees are sometimes resolved pursuant to an informal agreement or memorandum of understanding between the committees involved. See, *e.g.*, 96-2, Mar. 25, 1980, pp 6405, 6406, 6408-10 (memorandum of understanding among six different committees on energy measures); 104-1, Jan. 4, 1995 (memorandum of understanding between two committees concerning the budget process); 104-1, Jan. 30, 1995, p 2888 (memorandum of understanding between two committees concerning jurisdiction over the merchant marine resulting from the dissolution of the Committee on Merchant Marine and Fisheries); 110-1, Jan. 4, 2007, p 16 (memorandum of understanding between two committees concerning jurisdiction over departments, agencies, and programs relating to homeland security). Although these memoranda may explain understandings, they may not alter explicit jurisdictional statements in the rules. Committee reports often contain an exchange of letters between committee chairs waiving a committee's claim to review a particular bill, with the understanding that this surrender of jurisdiction over the matter is not permanent. See, *e.g.*, 106-2, H. Rept. 106-616.

Points of Order; Erroneous Referrals

The Speaker's referral of a bill is not subject to a point of order. *Manual* § 825; 4 Hinds § 4372; Deschler Ch 17 §§ 26, 27.9. Under clause 7(a) of rule XII, a motion to correct an erroneous reference is privileged if authorized either by the committee to which the bill had been erroneously referred or by the committee claiming jurisdiction. The motion is not debatable. Under the modern practice, however, erroneous referrals are corrected by unanimous consent. The Speaker may also sequentially refer a measure (upon reporting by the committee of initial referral) to a committee that was erroneously excluded from the initial referral.

The Speaker's standard phrasing for multiple referral of measures is as follows: "in each case for consideration of such provisions as fall within the jurisdiction of the committee concerned." As a result, a committee may not mark up portions of a bill that fall entirely outside the jurisdiction of the committee (though they may mark up portions with shared jurisdiction). In a committee of referral, a point of order lies against an amendment that falls entirely outside the jurisdiction of the committee.

§ 9. Oversight Jurisdiction

Generally

The oversight function of the House arises from its duty to exercise continuous vigilance over the administration and execution of the laws by the departments and agencies of the Federal government. Legislative oversight as a continuing function was given to all standing committees by the Legislative Reorganization Act of 1946, which provided that each standing committee "shall exercise continuous watchfulness" over administrative agencies, and by the Legislative Reorganization Act of 1970, which required periodic reports by committees on their oversight activities. Clause 2 of rule X requires the standing committees to exercise general oversight. *Manual* §§ 742, 743. In the 111th Congress, clauses 2(n), (o), and (p) were added to rule XI, requiring committees to hold hearings on ''waste, fraud, abuse, or mismanagement in Government programs,''and related financial statement disclaimers by agency auditors or Comptroller General reports.

General and Special Oversight Distinguished

The House rules impose both general and special oversight responsibilities on standing committees. General legislative oversight is performed by all standing committees, although special oversight functions, under clause 3 of rule X, are given to certain standing committees. *Manual* §§ 742, 744. Additional budget and other oversight-related functions are delineated in clause 4 of rule X. *Manual* §§ 745-756.

§ 10. Investigative Jurisdiction and Authority

Standing Committees

Under clause 1(b) of rule XI, each standing committee is authorized to conduct such investigations as it considers necessary or appropriate in carrying out the jurisdictional responsibilities given to it under rule X. *Manual* § 788. To carry out its duties, each committee and each subcommittee is authorized by clause 2(m) of rule XI to hold hearings and to subpoena witnesses or compel the production of documents. *Manual* § 805. As to the issuance and enforcement of subpoenas, see § 24, infra.

Select or Joint Committees

Lacking general investigative authority, a select or joint committee must be given specific authority to undertake an investigation. Such authority may be given pursuant to:

- A statute conferring investigative powers. See, *e.g.*, 26 USC § 8022 (conferring investigative duties on the Joint Committee on Internal Revenue Taxation).
- A concurrent resolution. See, *e.g.*, 102-2, H. Con. Res. 192, Aug. 6, 1992, p 21961 (establishing the Joint Committee on the Organization of Congress).
- A standing rule of the House. See, *e.g.*, clause 11 of rule X (establishing the Permanent Select Committee on Intelligence).

- A simple resolution. See, *e.g.*, 105-2, H. Res. 463, June 18, 1998, pp 12876-80, (establishing the Select Committee on U.S. National Security and Military/Commercial Concerns with China); 110-1, H. Res. 202, Mar. 8, 2007, p 5797 (establishing the Select Committee on Energy Independence and Global Warming).

Scope; Limitations

The investigative power that is exercised by the House through its committees is inherent in the power to make laws. *Watkins* v. *United States*, 354 U.S. 178 (1957). In so ruling, courts have reasoned, "A legislative body cannot legislate wisely or effectively in the absence of information respecting the conditions which the legislation is intended to affect or change." *McGrain* v. *Daugherty*, 273 U.S. 135 (1927); *Eastland* v. *United States Servicemen's Fund*, 421 U.S. 491 (1975).

This investigative power encompasses inquiries concerning the administration of existing laws and the need for proposed legislation. It extends to studies of social, economic, or political problems, and probes departmental corruption, inefficiency, or waste at the Federal level. *Watkins*, 354 U.S. 178. Although broad, this power of investigation is not unlimited. It may be exercised only in aid of the "legislative function." *Kilbourn* v. *Thompson*, 103 U.S. 168 (1881). It is said that Congress has no general power to inquire into private affairs and that the subject of inquiry must be one "on which legislation could be had." *McGrain*, 273 U.S. 135.

Since 1952, the courts have declined to presume the existence of a legislative purpose and have narrowly construed resolutions granting authority to committees to conduct investigations. *United States* v. *Rumely*, 345 U.S. 41 (1952). The investigative power cannot be used to expose merely for the sake of exposure or to inquire into matters which are within the exclusive province of one of the other branches of government or which are reserved to the States. Deschler Ch 15 § 1.

A further requirement for the validity of a committee investigation is that it must have been expressly or implicitly authorized in accordance with congressional procedures. Deschler Ch 15 § 1. Thus, the courts have refused to convict a witness for contempt arising out of a subcommittee investigation where that investigation had not been approved by a majority of the parent committee, as was required by the committee rule. *Gojack* v. *United States*, 384 U.S. 702 (1966).

The courts will not look to the motives which may have prompted a congressional investigation. *Watkins*, 354 U.S. 178. The courts also will not question the wisdom of the investigation or its methodology. *Doe* v. *McMillan*, 412 U.S. 306 (1973). The very nature of the investigative function is such that it may take the searchers up some ''blind alleys'' and into nonproductive enterprises. The validity of a legislative inquiry is not contingent on a predictable end result. *Eastland*, 421 U.S. 491.

Obstructing Committee Investigation

A Federal statute provides criminal penalties for those who corruptly influence, obstruct, or impede ''due and proper'' congressional inquiry. 18 USC § 1505. Indictments under § 1505 have been upheld despite contentions that the committee violated its own rules and those of the House. *United States* v. *Poindexter*, 725 F. Supp. 13 (D.D.C. 1989); *United States* v. *Mitchell*, 877 F.2d 204 (4th Cir. 1989).

§ 11. Standing Committees

Standing committees were not used extensively during the earliest Congresses. It was the general practice of the House to refer matters to a Committee of the Whole to develop the primary objectives of a proposal, and then to commit such matters to select committees to draft specific bills.

At the start of the 19th century, standing committees began to proliferate. By mid-century the House had 34 standing committees, and by 1900 it had 58. Subsequent additions raised the number of standing committees to 61 by 1905. However, in the 1920's the House consolidated numerous committees and again vested in the Committee on Appropriations jurisdiction over all general appropriation bills. 7 Cannon § 1741. Further reductions in the number of committees in the House were made by the Legislative Reorganization Act of 1946 (60 Stat. 812). By dropping relatively inactive committees and by merging those with similar functions and jurisdiction, the Act reduced the total number of standing committees in the House from 44 to 19. Between 1946 and 1995, this number fluctuated only slightly with minor additions and consolidation.

In 1995 the House again reorganized its committee system, reestablishing the number at 19 by abolishing three committees and altering the jurisdiction of several others. 104-1, H. Res. 6, Jan. 4, 1995, p 462. Under clause 5(d) of rule X, a standing committee may have no more than five subcommittees. However, clause 5(d) excepts from that stricture (1) a committee that maintains a subcommittee on oversight, which may have six subcommittees; (2) the Committee on Appropriations, which may have 13 subcommittees; and (3) the Committee on Oversight and Government Reform, which may have seven subcommittees. *Manual* § 762. The House has occasionally excepted other committees from that stricture. See, *e.g.*, 107-1, H. Res. 5, Jan. 3, 2001, p 26; 108-1, H. Res. 5, Jan. 7, 2003, p 11.

In the 109th Congress, the House established a Committee on Homeland Security as a standing committee, replacing a prior select committee. Corresponding changes were made to the jurisdictions of the Committees on the Judiciary, Transportation and Infrastructure, and Ways and Means. The Speaker announced that referrals to the prior select committee would not constitute precedent for referrals to the standing committee. 109-1, Jan. 4, 2005, p 71.

The standing committees of the House, with their antecedent committees, are shown in the following table. This table provides citations to relevant statutes or precedents and to the authority for legislative jurisdiction and/or oversight functions, where applicable.

Standing Committees (112th Cong.)

JURISDICTION, OVERSIGHT FUNCTION, AND ANTECEDENTS

STANDING COMMITTEES (112TH CONG.)	ANTECEDENT COMMITTEES
Agriculture	
Established 1820; 4 Hinds §4149	
Legislative jurisdiction, *Manual* §715	
Oversight functions, *Manual* §§742, 755, 756	
Appropriations	
Established 1865; 4 Hinds §4032	Ways and Means (in part), 1802
Legislative jurisdiction, *Manual* §716	
Oversight and additional functions, *Manual* §§744-747, 755, 756	
Armed Services	
Established 1947; 60 Stat. 812	Military Affairs, 1822
Legislative jurisdiction, *Manual* §718	Naval Affairs, 1822
Oversight and additional functions, *Manual* §§742-744, 755, 756	Militia, 1835
Formerly known as ''National Security'' 1995, *Manual* §718	Atomic Energy (Joint Committee), 1946
Budget	
Established 1974; 88 Stat. 299	
Legislative jurisdiction, *Manual* §719	
Oversight functions, *Manual* §§742-744, 748, 756	

Standing Committees (112th Cong.)—Continued

JURISDICTION, OVERSIGHT FUNCTION, AND ANTECEDENTS

STANDING COMMITTEES (112TH CONG.)	ANTECEDENT COMMITTEES
Education and the Workforce	
Established 1947; 60 Stat. 812	Education, 1867
Legislative jurisdiction, *Manual* § 720	Labor, 1883
Oversight functions, *Manual* §§ 742-744, 755, 756	
Formerly known as ''Education and Labor'' 1947, ''Economic and Educational Opportunities'' 1995, ''Education and the Workforce'' 1997, ''Education and Labor'' 2007, *Manual* § 720	
Energy and Commerce	
Established 1795; 4 Hinds § 4096	Commerce and Manufacturers, 1795
Legislative jurisdiction, *Manual* § 721	Coinage, Weights and Measures, 1867
Oversight functions, *Manual* §§ 742-744, 755, 756	Atomic Energy (Joint Committee), 1946
Formerly known as ''Interstate and Foreign Commerce'' 1892, ''Commerce and Health'' 1975, ''Interstate and Foreign Commerce'' 1975, ''Energy and Commerce'' 1980, ''Commerce'' 1995, *Manual* § 721	
Ethics	
Established 1967; 90-2, H. Res. 418	Standards and Conduct (Select Committee), 1966
Legislative jurisdiction, *Manual* §§ 721b, 721c	Ethics (Select Committee), 1977
Oversight functions, *Manual* § 742	
Formerly known as ''Standards of Official Conduct'' 1967, *Manual* § 721b	
Financial Services	
Established 1865; 4 Hinds § 4082	
Legislative jurisdiction, *Manual* § 722	
Oversight and additional functions, *Manual* §§ 742, 743, 755, 756	

Standing Committees (112th Cong.)—Continued

JURISDICTION, OVERSIGHT FUNCTION, AND ANTECEDENTS

STANDING COMMITTEES (112TH CONG.)	ANTECEDENT COMMITTEES
Formerly known as ''Banking and Currency'' 1865, ''Coinage, Weights and Measures'' 1867, ''Banking, Currency and Housing'' 1974, ''Banking, Finance and Urban Affairs'' 1977, ''Banking and Financial Services'' 1995, *Manual* § 722	
Foreign Affairs	
Established 1822; 4 Hinds § 4162	Atomic Energy (Joint Committee), 1946
Legislative jurisdiction, *Manual* § 723	
Oversight functions, *Manual* §§ 742-744, 755, 756	
Formerly known as ''Foreign Affairs'' 1822, ''International Relations'' 1975, ''Foreign Affairs'' 1979, ''International Relations'' 1995, *Manual* § 723	
Homeland Security	
Established 2005	Homeland Security (Select Committee), 2002
Legislative jurisdiction, *Manual* §§ 723a, 723b	Homeland Security (Select Committee), 2003
Oversight and additional functions, *Manual* §§ 742-744, 755, 756	
House Administration	
Established 1947; 60 Stat. 812	Enrolled Bills, 1789
Legislative jurisdiction, *Manual* §§ 724-728	Elections, 1794, 1895
	Accounts, 1805
Oversight and additional functions, *Manual* §§ 742, 743, 750-756	Mileage, 1837
	Printing, 1846
Formerly known as ''House Oversight'' 1995, *Manual* § 724	Disposition of Executive Papers, 1889
	Ventilation and Acoustics, 1893
	Memorials, 1929
Judiciary	
Established 1813; 4 Hinds § 4054	Claims, 1794
Continued, 1947, 60 Stat. 812	Patents, 1837

Standing Committees (112th Cong.)—Continued

JURISDICTION, OVERSIGHT FUNCTION, AND ANTECEDENTS

STANDING COMMITTEES (112TH CONG.)	ANTECEDENT COMMITTEES
Legislative jurisdiction, *Manual* §§ 729, 730 Oversight functions, *Manual* §§ 742, 743, 755, 756	Revision of the Laws, 1868 War Claims, 1883 Immigration and Naturalization, 1893 Internal Security, 1969
Natural Resources	
Established 1805; 4 Hinds § 4194 Legislative jurisdiction, *Manual* § 731 Oversight functions, *Manual* §§ 742-744, 755, 756 Formerly known as "Public Lands" 1805, "Insular Affairs" 1899, "Interior and Insular Affairs" 1951, "Natural Resources" 1993, "Resources" 1995, *Manual* § 731	Private Land Claims, 1816 Indian Affairs, 1821 Territories, 1825 Mines and Mining, 1865 Merchant Marine and Fisheries (in part), 1887 Irrigation of Arid Lands, 1893 Atomic Energy (Joint Committee), 1946
Oversight and Government Reform	
Established 1927; 7 Cannon § 2041 Legislative jurisdiction, *Manual* § 732 Oversight and additional functions, *Manual* §§ 742-744, 749, 755, 756 Formerly known as "Expenditures in the Executive Departments" 1927, "Government Operations" 1952, "Government Reform and Oversight" 1995, "Government Reform" 1999, *Manual* § 732	District of Columbia, 1808 Public Expenditures, 1814 State, Treasury, War, Navy, and Post Office, 1816 Justice, 1874 Agriculture, 1889 Commerce and Labor, 1905 Post Office and Civil Service, 1947
Rules	
Established 1880; 4 Hinds § 4321 Mandated by law, 1947, 60 Stat. 812 Legislative jurisdiction, *Manual* §§ 733, 734 Oversight functions, *Manual* §§ 742-744, 756	Rules (Select Committee), 1789

Standing Committees (112th Cong.)—Continued

JURISDICTION, OVERSIGHT FUNCTION, AND ANTECEDENTS

STANDING COMMITTEES (112TH CONG.)	ANTECEDENT COMMITTEES
Science, Space, and Technology	
Established 1958; 85-2, H. Res. 496 Legislative jurisdiction, *Manual* §735 Oversight functions, *Manual* §§742-744, 755, 756 Formerly known as "Science and Astronautics" 1958, "Science and Technology" 1975, "Science, Space, and Technology" 1987, "Science" 1995, "Science and Technology" 2007, *Manual* §735	Merchant Marine and Fisheries (in part), 1887 Atomic Energy (Joint Committee), 1946 Astronautics and Space Exploration (Select Committee), 1958
Small Business	
Established 1975; 93-2, H. Res. 988 Legislative jurisdiction, *Manual* §736 Oversight functions, *Manual* §§742-744, 755, 756	Small Business (Select Committee), 1941 Small Business (Permanent Select Committee), 1971
Transportation and Infrastructure	
Established 1947; 60 Stat. 812 Legislative jurisdiction, *Manual* §739 Oversight functions, *Manual* §§742, 743, 755, 756 Formerly known as "Public Works and Transportation" 1975, *Manual* §739	Public Buildings and Grounds, 1837 Mississippi Levies, 1875 Rivers and Harbors, 1883 Merchant Marine and Fisheries (in part), 1887 Roads, 1913 Flood Control, 1916
Veterans' Affairs	
Established 1947; 60 Stat. 812 Legislative jurisdiction, *Manual* §740 Oversight functions, *Manual* §§742, 743, 755, 756	Pensions and Revolutionary Claims, 1813 Revolutionary Pensions, 1825 Invalid Pensions, 1831 World War Veterans' Legislation, 1924
Ways and Means	
Established 1802; 4 Hinds §4020 Legislative jurisdiction, *Manual* §741 Oversight functions, *Manual* §§742, 743, 755, 756	Ways and Means (Select Committee), 1789

§ 12. Select Committees

Select (or special) committees were used extensively by the House during the early Congresses. In the Jeffersonian era, it was common practice to refer each proposal to a select committee created to draft the appropriate legislative language for the measure. *Manual* § 401. By the Third Congress, 350 select committees had been named. However, as standing committees came to be recognized as the most appropriate forum for the development of legislation, the use of select committees declined steadily. By the 23d Congress, the number of select committees had been reduced to 35. By the 106th Congress, only the Permanent Select Committee on Intelligence remained. Clause 11 of rule X; *Manual* § 1112a. A select committee identified as permanent is reconstituted in each Congress upon adoption of the rules of the House. Select committees have been established with oversight jurisdiction only (for example, the Select Committee on Energy Independence and Global Warming. *Manual* § 1112c).

In the modern era, select committees are created primarily to investigate conditions or events. As pointed out elsewhere, all committee investigations must be undertaken in furtherance of a constitutionally assigned function of Congress. Deschler Ch 15 § 1; see § 10, supra.

Select committees have also been created to study and report on matters with a view toward legislative action. Most select committees of this type lacked authority to report legislation. Instead, they were directed to assess the adequacy of existing laws and, if necessary, to make legislative recommendations. However, several select committees have been empowered to report legislation directly to the House. Deschler Ch 17 § 6. For example, the Select Committee on Homeland Security was required to report to the House its recommendations on a bill establishing a Department of Homeland Security. In making its recommendation, the select committee was required to take into consideration recommendations by each committee to which such bill was initially referred. 107-2, H. Res. 449, June 19, 2002, p 10722. In the 108th Congress, the House established a successor to the Select Committee on Homeland Security, granting it jurisdiction over matters relating to the Homeland Security Act of 2002 (the law enacted on the recommendation of the predecessor select committee). In the 109th Congress, the Committee on Homeland Security became a standing committee of the House. For further discussion on the establishment of select committees, see Guidelines for the Establishment of Select Committees, Committee on Rules, 98-1, February, 1983.

Finally, select committees have been created to supervise certain routine housekeeping functions; for example, the Select Committee on the House

Beauty Shop (95-1, H. Res. 1000), the Select Committee on the House Recording Studio (Pub. L. 84-624), the Select Committee on the House Restaurant (95-1, H. Res. 472), and the Select Committee to Regulate Parking on the House Side of the Capitol (95-1, H. Res. 282).

§ 13. — Particular Uses of Select Committees

The House has established more than 20 select committees since passage of the Legislative Reorganization Act of 1946. The table below identifies some of these committees for purposes of illustration. The table shows these committees by name (or paraphrase thereof), dates of creation and termination, and authority, including legislative authority. With the two exceptions noted—Campaign Expenditures and Small Business—the table excludes those committees existing before 1947 which were subsequently reconstituted.

Select Committees

Committee	Jurisdiction—Investigative Authority	Reporting Authority
Aging Established Jan. 3, 1975; 93-2, H. Res. 988 Terminated Jan. 5, 1993, *Manual* § 784	Problems of the older American; income maintenance, housing, and health; welfare programs	To report annually to the House; no legislative authority
Astronautics and Space Exploration Established Mar. 25, 1958; 85-2, H. Res. 496 Terminated July 21, 1958; became standing Committee on Science and Astronautics	All aspects and problems relating to the exploration of outer space; resources, personnel, equipment, and facilities; legislation	To report to the House, by bill or otherwise
Assassinations Established Sept. 17, 1976; 94-2, H. Res. 1540 Terminated Jan. 3, 1979	Circumstances surrounding the death of John F. Kennedy and the death of Martin Luther King, Jr.	To report to the House on the result of its investigation (see H. Rept. 95-1828); no legislative authority

Select Committees—Continued

Committee	Jurisdiction—Investigative Authority	Reporting Authority
Campaign Expenditures		
Established May 29, 1928; 70-1, H. Res. 232 Reestablished by each Congress through 92-2	Election disputes; electoral fraud; excessive campaign expenditures of Presidential or congressional candidates	Reporting authority varied from Congress to Congress
Chemicals, Pesticides, and Insecticides Affecting Foods		
Established June 20, 1950; 81-2, H. Res. 323 Terminated Jan. 3, 1953	Chemicals, compounds, and synthetics in the production of food products; health factors; the agricultural economy; toxic residues; effect on soil and vegetation	To report to the House on its investigation with recommendations for legislation (see H. Rept. 82-2182); no legislative authority
Children, Youth and Families		
Established Sept. 29, 1982, 97-2, H. Res. 421 Reestablished by each Congress through 102-2.	Income maintenance; health; nutrition; education; welfare; employment	To report to the House on the results of its investigations; no legislative authority
Committees		
Established Jan. 31, 1973; 93-1, H. Res. 132 Terminated Dec. 20, 1974; reestablished 1979; 96-1, H. Res. 118; records transferred to Committee on Rules, Apr. 1, 1980	Rules X and XI of the rules of the House; committee structure; number and size of committees; jurisdiction; committee procedure; meetings, staffing, and facilities	To report to the House by bill, resolution, or otherwise (see H. Rept. 96-866)

Select Committees—Continued

COMMITTEE	JURISDICTION—INVESTIGATIVE AUTHORITY	REPORTING AUTHORITY
Communist Aggression		
Established July 27, 1953; 83-1, H. Res. 346 Terminated Dec. 31, 1954	Seizure of Latvia and Estonia by the U.S.S.R.; treatment of the Baltic peoples during this period	To report to the House on its study together with recommendations (see H. Rept. 83-2650); no legislative authority
Congressional Operations		
Established Mar. 28, 1977; 95-1, H. Res. 420 Terminated Jan. 3, 1979	Organization and operation of the U.S. Congress; cooperation between the Houses; relationship with other branches of government	To report recommendations on subjects specified (see H. Rept. 95-1843); no legislative authority
Congressional Pages		
Established Sept. 30, 1964; 88-2, H. Res. 847 Terminated Jan. 4, 1965	General welfare and education of congressional pages	To report on the results of its investigations (see H. Rept. 88-1945); to make recommendations
Covert Arms Transactions with Iran		
Established Jan. 7, 1984; 100-1, H. Res. 12 Terminated Nov. 13, 1987	Investigation of the ''Iran-Contra affair''; met jointly with Senate Select Committee	To report on the results of its investigations (see H. Rept. 100-433)
Crime		
Established May 1, 1969; 91-1, H. Res. 17 Terminated June 30, 1973	All aspects of crime in the United States; its elements, causes, and extent; reciprocity of information; urban crime	To report on its investigation with recommendations (see H. Rept. 93-358); no legislative authority

Select Committees—Continued

COMMITTEE	JURISDICTION—INVESTIGATIVE AUTHORITY	REPORTING AUTHORITY
Energy Established Apr. 21, 1977; 95-1, H. Res. 508 Terminated Jan. 3, 1979; jurisdiction transferred to Energy and Commerce, 97th Cong.	Message of the President dated Apr. 20, 1977, and other communications relating thereto; bills or resolutions sequentially referred thereto	To report to the House by bill or otherwise (see H. Rept. 95-543)
Energy Independence and Global Warming Established Mar. 8, 2007; 110-1, H. Res. 202 Terminated Jan. 3, 2011	To investigate reducing U.S. dependence on foreign sources of energy and reducing activities that contribute to climate change and global warming.	To report on policies, strategies, and new technologies related to its investigations
Ethics - Standards and Conduct of Members Established Oct. 19, 1966; 89-2, H. Res. 1013 Terminated Dec. 27, 1966; standing Committee on Standards of Official Conduct (now Ethics) created Apr. 13, 1967	Rules or regulations necessary or desirable to ensure proper standards of conduct by Members and by officers or employees of the House; reporting of statutory violations	To make recommendations to the House by report or resolution
Ethics Established Mar. 9, 1977; 95-1, H. Res. 383 Terminated Jan. 3, 1979	Certain bills and resolutions relating to ethical standards of Members contained in standing rules; regulations relating thereto; advisory opinions	To report to the House on the measure specified (see H. Rept. 95-1837); to report regulations; to recommend legislation

Select Committees—Continued

COMMITTEE	JURISDICTION—INVESTIGATIVE AUTHORITY	REPORTING AUTHORITY
Ethics		
Established Jan. 7, 1997; 105-1, H. Res. 5 Terminated Jan. 21, 1997	Continue investigation of a Member by the Committee on Standards of Official Conduct (now Ethics), begun in the prior Congress	To resolve the inquiry and report to the House (see H. Rept. 105-1; H. Res. 31)
Export Controls		
Established Sept. 7, 1961; 87-1, H. Res. 403 Terminated May 31, 1962	The Export Control Act of 1949; assessment of accomplishments under that Act; improvements in administration and enforcement; congressional oversight	To report on its investigation together with any recommendations (see H. Rept. 87-1753); no legislative authority
Foreign Aid		
Established July 22, 1947; 80-1, H. Res. 296 Terminated May 3, 1948	Basic needs of foreign nations and peoples; relief in terms of food and clothing; resources and facilities; agencies	To report to the House as deemed appropriate; no legislative authority
Government Research		
Established Sept. 11, 1963; 88-1, H. Res. 504 Terminated Jan. 3, 1965	Research programs of Federal agencies; expenditures for research programs; costs of government research	To report its findings to the House with recommended legislation (see H. Rept. 88-1143)
Homeland Security		
Established June 19, 2002; 107-2, H. Res. 449 Terminated after final disposition of specified bill (Nov. 25, 2002)	Develop recommendations on such matters that relate to the establishment of a department of homeland security as may be referred to it by the Speaker and on recommendations submitted to it by standing committees to which the Speaker referred a bill establishing such department	To report its recommendation to the House on a bill establishing a department of homeland security (see H. Rept. 107-609)

Select Committees—Continued

Committee	Jurisdiction—Investigative Authority	Reporting Authority
Homeland Security		
Established Jan. 7, 2003; 108-1, H. Res. 5 Terminated Jan. 3, 2005	Develop recommendations on such matters that relate to the Homeland Security Act of 2002 as may be referred to it by the Speaker; to conduct oversight of laws, programs, and Government activities relating to homeland security; to conduct a study of the operation and implementation of the rules of the House, including rule X, with respect to homeland security	To report its recommendations to the House by bill or otherwise on matters referred to it by the Speaker; to report its recommendations on changes to House rules to the Committee on Rules
Hunger		
Established Feb. 22, 1984; 98-2, H. Res. 15 Reestablished each Congress through 102-2; Reestablishment rejected Feb. 4, 1993; 103-1, H. Res. 18	International programs; world food security; malnutrition; food production and distribution; agribusiness role	To conduct studies and make recommendations about possible legislation
Hurricane Katrina		
Established Sept. 15, 2005; 109-1, H. Res. 437 Terminated Mar. 16, 2006	The local, State, and Federal preparation for, and response to, Hurricane Katrina	To conduct an investigation and report its findings to the House by Feb. 15, 2006
Intelligence		
Established Feb. 19, 1975; 94-1, H. Res. 138 Terminated Feb. 11, 1976; became permanent select committee, July 14, 1977, H. Res. 658 (clause 11 of rule X; *Manual* § 785)	Proposals concerning the intelligence and intelligence-related programs and activities of the U.S. Government; oversight; proposed legislation and other matters relating to the CIA	To report to the House on the nature and extent of intelligence activities of U.S. departments and agencies by legislation or otherwise (see H. Rept. 94-833)

Select Committees—Continued

Committee	Jurisdiction—Investigative Authority	Reporting Authority
Katyn Forest Massacre Established Sept. 18, 1951; 82-1, H. Res. 390 Terminated Dec. 22, 1952	The massacre of thousands of Polish officers in the Katyn Forest in territory then under the control of the U.S.S.R.	To report to the House on completion of its hearings (see H. Rept. 82-2505); no legislative authority
Lobbying Activities Established Aug. 12, 1949; 81-1, H. Res. 298 Terminated end of the 81st Cong.	Lobbying activities intended to influence legislation; activities of Federal agencies intended to influence legislation	To submit reports on the results of its study (see H. Rept. 81-3239); no legislative authority
Narcotics Abuse and Control Established July 29, 1976; 94-2, H. Res. 1350 Reestablished each Congress through 102-2	International traffic in narcotics; prevention; enforcement; organized crime; drug abuse; treatment; rehabilitation	To report to the House on its investigations; no legislative authority
Newsprint Established Feb. 26, 1947; 80-1, H. Res. 58 Terminated Dec. 31, 1948	Need for adequate supplies of newsprint and related products; production possibilities and prospects	To submit reports with recommendations (see H. Rept. 80-2471); no legislative authority
Offensive and Undesirable Literature Established May 12, 1952; 82-2, H. Res. 596 Terminated Dec. 31, 1952	The extent to which books, magazines, and comic books contain immoral, obscene, or otherwise offensive matter; availability through the U.S. mails; adequacy of existing laws	To report to the House with recommendations, including recommendations for legislation (see H. Rept. 82-2510); no legislative authority

Select Committees—Continued

Committee	Jurisdiction—Investigative Authority	Reporting Authority
Outer Continental Shelf		
Established Apr. 12, 1975; 94-1, H. Res. 412 Terminated Jan. 3, 1979; succeeded by another select committee on the same subject (96-1, H. Res. 53), which terminated July 31, 1980	A bill relating to the management of oil and natural gas in the Outer Continental Shelf; marine and coastal environments; certain related matters on this subject on referral to it by the Speaker	To report the bill and other legislation referred to it; transmit its findings and make a full report to the House (see H. Rept. 96-1214)
Population		
Established Sept. 28, 1977; 95-1, H. Res. 70 Terminated end of the 95th Cong.	Causes of changing population conditions; population characteristics relative to limited resources; population planning; global population-related issues	To report on the results of its investigation (see H. Rept. 95-1842); no legislative authority
Professional Sports		
Established May 18, 1976; 94-2, H. Res. 1186 Terminated Jan. 3, 1977	Need for legislation with respect to professional sports	To report to the House on the results of its inquiry (see H. Rept. 94-1786); no legislative authority
Right of Member To Be Sworn In		
Established Jan. 10, 1967; 90-1, H. Res. 1 Terminated Feb. 23, 1967	The right of Adam Clayton Powell (N.Y.) to be sworn in in the 90th Congress and to a seat therein	To report to the House within five weeks (see H. Rept. 90-27); no legislative authority

Select Committees—Continued

Committee	Jurisdiction—Investigative Authority	Reporting Authority
Small Business Established Dec. 4, 1941; 77-1, H. Res. 294 Reestablished each Congress until 1970; became a standing committee 1975; 94-1, H. Res. 988; clause 1 of rule X; *Manual* §736	Assistance to small business; small business protection; financial aid; small business participation in Federal procurement	Reported to the House on results of its investigations; no legislative authority before becoming a standing committee
Survivors' Benefits Established Aug. 4, 1954; 83-2, H. Res. 549 Terminated Jan. 15, 1956	Benefits provided under Federal law for dependents of deceased members and former members of the armed forces	To prepare such legislation; to report on the results of its investigation (see H. Rept. 83-9282)
Tax-exempt Foundations and Organizations Established Apr. 4, 1952; 82-2, H. Res. 561 Terminated Dec. 16, 1954	Educational and philanthropic foundations and related organizations exempt from Federal income taxation; use of foundations	To report to the House on the results of its investigation (see H. Rept. 82-2681); no legislative authority
Transactions on Commodity Exchanges Established Dec. 18, 1947; 80-1, H. Res. 404 Terminated Dec. 31, 1948	Purchases and sales of commodities; commodities for future delivery; activities of Federal agencies and individuals therein as affecting the price of commodities	To report to the House on completion of its investigation (see H. Rept. 80-2472); no legislative authority
U.S. Military Involvement in Southeast Asia Established June 8, 1970; 91-2, H. Res. 976 Terminated July 6, 1970	All aspects of U.S. military involvement in Southeast Asia	To report on its investigation (see H. Rept. 91-1276); no legislative authority

Select Committees—Continued

Committee	Jurisdiction—Investigative Authority	Reporting Authority
U.S. National Security and Military/Commercial Concerns with China		
Established June 18, 1998; 105-2, H. Res. 463; reestablished Jan. 6, 1999, 106-1, H. Res. 5; extended Mar. 24, Apr. 29, May 13, 1999, 106-1, H. Res. 129, H. Res. 153, H. Res. 170 (respectively) Terminated May 31, 1999	Investigate technology transfers to China; successor select committee assigned to produce unclassified version of report filed by predecessor committee	To report on its investigation (see H. Rept. 105-851) (declassified, in part, pursuant to H. Res. 5 (106-1)); no legislative authority
U.S. Servicemen Missing in Action in Southeast Asia		
Established Sept. 11, 1975; 94-1, H. Res. 335 Terminated Mar. 13, 1977	U.S. servicemen identified as missing in action; recovery of bodies of known dead; international inspection teams	To report to the House on its investigation (see H. Rept. 94-1764); no legislative authority
Voting Irregularities of Aug. 2, 2007		
Established Aug. 3, 2007; 110-1, H. Res. 611 Terminated Jan. 3, 2009	The circumstances surrounding a vote on Aug. 2, 2007	To conduct an investigation and produce an interim report by Sept. 30, 2007, and a final report by Sept. 15, 2008
White County Bridge Commission		
Established May 25, 1955; 84-1, H. Res. 244 Terminated Apr. 25, 1956	Financial position of the White County Bridge Commission; monies received and expenditures made; anticipated toll-free use	To report to the House with recommendations (see H. Rept. 84-2052); no legislative authority

Select Committees—Continued

COMMITTEE	JURISDICTION—INVESTIGATIVE AUTHORITY	REPORTING AUTHORITY
World War II Veterans		
Established Aug. 28, 1950; 81-2, H. Res. 474 Terminated Feb. 2, 1951	Abuses in education, training and loan guarantee programs of World War II veterans	To report on the results of its investigation (see H. Rept. 2501); no legislative authority

§ 14. Joint Committees

Generally

Joint committees are composed of Members from both Houses. Jefferson noted that joint committees were used by the two Houses of the English Parliament. *Manual* § 325. Since the First Congress, a joint committee has been used to make arrangements for the inauguration of the President and Vice President. *Manual* § 1112; 3 Hinds § 1986. The early congresses formed joint standing committees on the Library and Printing, which exist to this day. *Manual* §§ 1110, 1111; 4 Hinds §§ 4337, 4347. For a current list of joint committees, see *Manual* §§ 1108-1112.

Joint committees, or committees of the House and Senate acting jointly, have been used to investigate problems relating to immigration (4 Hinds § 4415), to resolve a dispute relating to the electoral count (3 Hinds § 1953), and to investigate the revision and codification of the laws (4 Hinds § 4410).

Jurisdiction, Functions, and Duties

Joint committees are used for study and investigation, supervision and oversight, and sometimes for purely ceremonial activities. Joint committees generally function in areas beyond the jurisdiction of any particular committee of either House. Deschler Ch 17 § 7. Joint committees may report to both Houses if so directed (4 Hinds §§ 4421, 4422), or to either House (4 Hinds § 4432; 7 Cannon § 2167).

A joint committee created by concurrent resolution may be instructed by the two Houses acting concurrently or, if so authorized, by either House acting independently. 4 Hinds § 4421. However, a joint committee created by statute is not susceptible to control by one House; and its duties may not be enlarged or diminished by either House acting independently. 7 Cannon § 2164. A joint committee created by concurrent resolution must be re-established by a subsequent Congress.

Composition; Voting

Recent joint committees have featured an equal number of Members from both Houses, with the chair alternating between the House and Senate, and with each member having one vote. Deschler Ch 17 § 7.

The table below shows the major joint committees that were established during the post-1946 era, their composition, and their jurisdiction and functions:

Joint Committees

Committees	Jurisdiction and Functions
Atomic Energy Established 1946; 42 USC § 2251 House members: 9 Senate members: 9 Terminated Jan. 4, 1977	Development, use, and control of atomic energy; to report legislation and make recommendations within its jurisdiction; legislative jurisdiction abolished 1977; 95-1, H. Res. 5
Congressional Operations Established 1970; 2 USC §§ 411-417 House members: 5 Senate members: 5 Inactive since 94th Cong.; Select Committee on Congressional Operations created, 95-1, H. Res. 420	Identification of court proceedings affecting Congress; organization and operation of the Congress; supervision of the Office of Placement and Management; no legislative jurisdiction
Defense Production Established 1950; 50 USC App § 2161 House members: 5 Senate members: 5 Terminated Mar. 1, 1992; no appointments after Sept. 30, 1978	Review of programs established by the Defense Production Act of 1950; Federal emergency preparedness and mobilization policy; integrity of defense contracts and the procurement process; to report to the House and Senate on its studies, with recommendations
Deficit Reduction Established 2011; Pub. L. 112-25 House members: 6 Senate members: 6 Terminated Jan. 31, 2012	Report recommendations to Congress to reduce the deficit by at least $1.5 trillion over the period of fiscal years 2012 to 2021

Joint Committees—Continued

Committees	Jurisdiction and Functions
Economic Established 1946; 15 USC § 1021 House members: 10 Senate members: 10 (*Manual* § 1108)	Economic Report by the President; means of promoting national policy on employment; short-term and medium-term economic goals; to report to the House and Senate (by March 1) and to each Budget Committee (by March 15)
Housing Established 1947; H. Con. Res. 104 House members: 7 Senate members: 7 Terminated 80th Cong.	Housing needs in U.S.; building material shortages; building costs; building codes and zoning laws; housing loans and insurance; veterans' preferences; findings to be reported to the House and Senate
Inaugural Ceremonies Established 1789; reestablished every other Congress by concurrent resolution House members: 3 Senate members: 3	The necessary arrangements for the inauguration of the President-elect and the Vice President-elect
Internal Revenue Taxation Established 1926; 26 USC § 8002 House members: 5 Senate members: 5 (*Manual* § 1109)	Operation and effects of Federal system of internal revenue taxation; to report to the Committee on Ways and Means, and, in its discretion, directly to the House
Library Established 1806; 2 USC § 132b House members: 5 Senate members: 5 (*Manual* § 1110)	Management and expansion of the Library of Congress; rules and regulations for the government of the Library; development of Botanic Garden; gifts for the benefit of the Library; statues and other works of art in the Capitol
Organization of Congress Two separate joint committees Established 1965; S. Con. Res. 2 Established 1992; H. Con. Res. 192; (Reestablished Pub. L. 102-392) House members: 12 Senate members: 12 Terminated Dec. 31, 1967 Terminated Dec. 31, 1993	Organization and operation of Congress; relationship between the two Houses and between the Congress and other branches of government; committees; to report to the House and Senate

Joint Committees—Continued

Committees	Jurisdiction and Functions
Printing Established 1846; 44 USC § 901 House members: 5 Senate members: 5 (*Manual* § 1111)	Inefficiencies or waste in the printing, binding, and distribution of government publications; arrangement and style of the *Congressional Record*; printing of the legislative program for each day; listing of committee meetings and hearings
Washington Metropolitan Problems Established 1957; H. Con. Res. 172 House members: 3 Senate members: 3 Terminated 86th Cong.	Growth and expansion of the District of Columbia and its metropolitan area; effectiveness of agencies and instrumentalities concerned therewith; to report to the House and Senate

D. Procedure in Committees

§ 15. Committee Rules; Applicable House Rules

Generally

House committees are required to follow the procedures prescribed by the rules of the House ''so far as applicable.'' Clause 1(a) of rule XI; *Manual* § 787. They are also bound by those provisions of *Jefferson's Manual* that are consistent with the rules of the House. *Manual* §§ 792, 1105. Finally, they are bound by their written rules which are adopted by each standing committee under clause 2(a) of rule XI. *Manual* § 791. Committee rules must be published in the *Congressional Record* and made publicly available in electronic form within 30 days after the chair of the committee is elected and are compiled by the Committee on Rules each Congress as a committee print. *Manual* § 791. If a committee meets pursuant to a rule which has not been published, the proceedings may be held insufficient to support a perjury conviction for alleged false testimony given to that committee. *United States* v. *Reinecke*, 524 F.2d 435 (D.C. Cir. 1975).

Clause 1(a)(2) of rule XI states that each subcommittee of a committee is a part of that committee and subject to its authority, direction, and rules. However, clause 2 of rule XI grants certain authorities specifically to subcommittees, such as authorizing and issuing subpoenas. See, *e.g.*, clause 2(m) of rule XI.

Points of Order

A point of order does not ordinarily lie in the House against consideration of a bill by reason of defective committee procedures occurring before the time the bill is ordered reported to the House. *Manual* § 792. Thus, a point of order that a measure was ordered reported in violation of a committee rule requiring advance notice of the committee meeting will not lie in the House—the interpretation of committee rules being within the cognizance of the committee and not the House. *Manual* § 791.

On the other hand, if a committee procedure directly violates a rule of the House, or if a rule specifically permits, a point of order may be raised in the House, which may result in the recommittal of the bill. *Manual* §§ 792, 799. For example, a point of order against a measure on the ground that the hearings on such measure were not properly conducted as required by the rules may be raised in the House by a committee member if the point of order was timely made and improperly overruled or not properly considered in committee. Clause 2(g)(6) of rule XI.

A deficiency in a committee report may be the subject of a point of order in the House. *Manual* §§ 837-849. A committee report that erroneously reflects the information required under clause 3 of rule XIII—for example, that committee reports reflect the total number of votes cast for and against any public measure or matter and any amendment thereto and the names of those voting for and against—may be subject to a point of order. *Manual* § 839. This error may be corrected by a supplemental report that need not be separately available for three days. *Manual* § 838.

§ 16. Records, Files, and Transcripts; Disclosure and Disposition; Member Access

Generally; Voting Records

Each committee must keep a complete record of all committee action. *Manual* § 794. A meeting or hearing transcript (if made) must include, under clause 2(e)(1) of rule XI, a substantially verbatim account of remarks actually made. All committee records and files must be kept separate from the office records of the member serving as chair. *Manual* § 796. The text of any amendment adopted in committee must be made publicly available in electronic form no later than 24 hours after adoption. *Manual* § 796.

The record of committee action must include the votes on any question on which a roll call vote is demanded, and the result of each such vote must be made available by the committee for inspection by the public and made publicly available in electronic form. *Manual* § 795. In addition, committee reports must include all record votes on motions to report and on any amendments. *Manual* § 839.

Members' Right of Access; Disclosure

Under clause 2(e) of rule XI, the records and files of a committee are considered the property of the House and accessible to all Members of the House. However, clause 2(e) of rule XI includes an exception to that rule for certain records of the Committee on Ethics and clauses 11(c) and 11(g) of rule X include exceptions for the Permanent Select Committee on Intelligence. On one occasion the House restricted access to executive session material of a committee, notwithstanding clause 2(e) of rule XI, to members of the committee and to such employees of the committee as were designated by the chair after consultation with the ranking minority member. 105-2, H. Res. 525, Sept. 11, 1998, pp 20020, 20021.

Clause 2(e) does not entitle a Member to bring committee materials into the well of the House and does not necessarily apply to records within the possession of the executive branch that members of the committee have been allowed to examine under limited conditions at the discretion of the agency. 96-2, July 31, 1980, p 20765. Furthermore, committees may prescribe regulations to govern the manner of access, such as limiting examination of files to committee rooms or prohibiting the making of photocopies. *Manual* § 796; 85-1, Aug. 14, 1957, p 14737.

Use of Information Obtained in Executive Session

Testimony or evidence taken in an executive session of a committee is under the control of and subject to the regulation of the committee and, under clause 2(k) of rule XI, cannot be released or made public without the consent of the committee. Thus, although a Member's right of access under clause 2(e) of rule XI may allow examination of executive session materials in committee rooms, it does not permit copying or taking of personal notes from such materials, keeping such notes in personal office files, or releasing such materials to the public without the consent of the committee or subcommittee. *Manual* § 796. Evidence or testimony taken in executive session of a committee may later be made public by vote of the committee. Deschler Ch 17 § 22.2. A committee may take such action even with respect to evidence or testimony taken in executive session under clause 2(k)(5) of rule XI that tends to degrade, defame, or incriminate. Deschler Ch 17 § 22.3. A committee may also take such action with respect to threshold discussions held in executive session under clause 2(g)(2)(B) of rule XI to explore whether evidence or testimony should be received in executive session.

Clause 2(k)(7) of rule XI, which requires a majority of the committee to constitute a quorum for closing a meeting or hearing, also requires a full quorum to release or make public evidence or testimony received in executive session. The chair has no unilateral authority to release such material. Under clause 2(k)(7), executive session material may be released only when authorized by the committee, a majority being present. *Manual* § 803.

Clauses 11(c) and 11(g) of rule XI provide that classified material transmitted by the Permanent Select Committee on Intelligence to another committee of the House becomes the executive session material of the recipient committee by virtue of the nature of the material and the injunction of clause 11(g) of rule X, which prohibits disclosure of such information to Members of the House except in a secret session. Clause 3(b)(6) of rule XI prohibits the public disclosure of complaints or information received by the Committee on Ethics except as specifically authorized by that committee in each instance.

Under clause 6(b) of rule VIII, minutes or transcripts of executive sessions, or evidence received during such sessions, may not be disclosed or copied in response to a subpoena. A subpoena duces tecum requesting production of executive session records of a committee from a prior Congress may be laid before the House pending a determination as to its propriety. 97-1, Apr. 28, 1981, p 7603.

Disposition of Committee Records

The House may adopt a resolution providing for the disposition of the records and files of a select or other committee. On one occasion, the House required that the files of a select committee be held intact and turned over to a newly created committee with similar jurisdiction. Deschler Ch 17 § 19.3. On another occasion, the House gave a select committee the authority to dispose of its records consistent with the rules and laws concerning classified information. 106-1, sec. 2(f)(3), H. Res. 5, Jan. 6, 1999, p 76. Pursuant to that authority the select committee transferred its records to the Clerk and instructed the Clerk to grant access to those records only with the approval of the chair and ranking minority member of the former select committee (so long as each remains a Member) and, thereafter, with the approval of the Permanent Select Committee on Intelligence. *Manual* § 1112a. In the absence of specific disposition by the House, clause 1 of rule VII requires the chair of each committee to deliver to the Clerk all noncurrent records of the committee. *Manual* § 695. Clause 3 of rule VII outlines the procedures for the public release of noncurrent records.

Reference in Debate to Transcripts or Minutes

Under early decisions of the House, it was not in order in debate to refer to the proceedings of a committee except as had been formally reported to the House. 5 Hinds §§ 5080-5083; 8 Cannon §§ 2485-2493; Deschler Ch 17 §§ 20.1, 20.2. The rationale for the early decisions was to protect the confidentiality and independence of committee proceedings and to permit flexibility and compromise in committee deliberations. 8 Cannon § 2491. Today, however, the rules require that committee meetings be open to the public unless properly closed by vote of the committee. Committee proceedings are widely available on television and by other means. These considerations mitigate against the application of the rule of nondisclosure to meetings and hearings which are open to the public. *Manual* § 360; Deschler Ch 17 § 20.1. On the other hand, it is clear that the rule protecting committee proceedings from disclosure in House debate is applicable to executive session proceedings. 8 Cannon § 2493; Deschler Ch 17 § 20. Thus, it has been held not in order in debate in the House to refer to or quote from the minutes of an executive session of a committee, unless the committee has voted to make such proceedings public. *Manual* § 319. The precedents clearly prevent reference in debate to committee actions which impugn the motives of committee members, whether or not by name. Deschler-Brown Ch 29 § 54.3.

§ 17. Meetings

Regular Meetings; Calling Additional Meetings

Standing committees must fix regular meeting days. *Manual* § 793. These meeting days may be on a weekly, biweekly, or monthly basis but must be at least once a month. Clause 2(b) of rule XI; *Manual* § 407. Additional meetings may be called by the chair as deemed necessary, and a mechanism exists that allows a majority of the committee to require that a special meeting be held to consider a particular measure or matter. *Manual* § 793. Pursuant to clause 3(g) of rule XI, a committee meeting may not commence until the third day on which members have notice thereof, and text of the legislation to be marked up must be available to members in electronic form 24 hours prior to the commencement of the meeting. Where a committee has a fixed date to meet, a quorum of the committee may convene on that date without call of the chair and transact business regardless of the chair's absence. Clause 2(d) of rule XI; 8 Cannon § 2214. In the absence of the chair or vice chair designated by the chair, the ranking majority member who is present presides at the meeting. Clause 2(d) of rule XI.

§ 18. —Consideration and Debate; Voting

Generally; Motion Practice

Committees generally conduct their business under the five-minute rule and may employ the ordinary motions and procedures which are in order in the House under clause 4 of rule XVI, as well as those procedures which are in order in the House as in the Committee of the Whole. *Manual* §§ 424, 427, 792, 911. These include:

- The reading for amendment by section as in the Committee of the Whole and the reading of the measure and amendments thereto in full. *Manual* § 792.
- Dispensing with the first reading (in full) of a bill or resolution if printed copies are available. Clause 1(a)(2)(A)(ii) of rule XI.
- Limiting the time for debate and the motion to limit debate under the five-minute rule. *Manual* § 792; 4 Hinds § 4573.
- The motion for the previous question. *Manual* § 994.
- Voting by the yeas and nays. 4 Hinds § 4572.
- The motion to refer. *Manual* § 916.
- The motion to lay on the table, but tabling an amendment also carries the bill to the table. 3 Hinds § 1737; 4 Hinds § 4568.
- The motion to reconsider. 4 Hinds §§ 4570, 4571.
- The taking of an appeal from a decision of the Chair. 4 Hinds § 4569.
- The motion to recess from day to day or subject to the call of the Chair (within 24 hours). *Manual* § 787.

A proposed investigative or oversight report shall be considered as read in committee if it has been available to the members for at least 24 hours (excluding Saturdays, Sundays, or legal holidays except when the House is in session on such a day). Clause 1(b)(2) of rule XI.

Proxy Voting

Proxy voting in committees, once permitted under certain conditions, was banned beginning in the 104th Congress under clause 2(f) of rule XI. *Manual* § 797.

Postponed Votes

In the 108th Congress, clause 2(h) of rule XI was amended to permit each committee to adopt a rule authorizing the chair of a committee or subcommittee to postpone a record vote on the question of approving a measure or matter or on adopting an amendment. Proceedings may be resumed on a postponed question at any time after reasonable notice. A committee rule permitting such postponed votes must provide that when proceedings resume on a postponed question, notwithstanding any intervening order for the previous question, the underlying proposition must remain subject to further debate or amendment to the same extent as when the question was postponed.

§ 19. Hearings

Generally; Uses of Hearings

The three most common uses of hearings held by the committees of the House are: (1) to consider the enactment of a measure into law and to provide a forum where information and opinions on the measure can be presented; (2) to inform the House as to activities that may call for legislation; and (3) to invoke the investigative powers of the House as overseer of Federal programs and operations.

Hearings have included such publicized investigations as the Credit Mobilier Corporation bribery charge investigation of 1872 (2 Hinds § 1286), the Un-American activities investigations beginning in the 1930's (Deschler Ch 15 § 1.32), the investigation of covert arms transactions with Iran in 1988 (100-1, H. Res. 12, Jan. 7, 1987, p 821), the investigation of political fundraising improprieties (105-1, H. Res. 167, June 20, 1997, p 11677), and the investigation of whether the impeachment of President Clinton was warranted (105-2, H. Res. 581, Oct. 8, 1998, p 24679).

Announcement of Hearings

A chair must announce a hearing at least one week in advance, although the chair and ranking minority member acting jointly, or the committee by majority vote with a business quorum present, may determine that there is good cause to begin the hearing sooner. In such a case the chair must make the announcement at the earliest possible date. The announcement must be published in the *Daily Digest* and made publicly available in electronic form. *Manual* § 798. The Committee on Rules is exempted from this requirement.

§ 20. Hearings and Meetings as Open or Closed

Generally

All committee or subcommittee meetings and hearings must be open to the public, including the media, unless the committee, in open session with a majority present, votes to close all or part of the remainder of the meeting or hearing on that day for one of the permissible reasons stated in the rule. Clause 2(g) of rule XI; see also clause 2(k)(5) of rule XI. Permissible reasons include national security, the compromise of sensitive law enforcement information, violation of a law or rule of the House, or a situation where testimony might incriminate, defame, or degrade a person.

Only members of the committee and such noncommittee Members, staff, and departmental representatives as the committee may authorize may be present at a meeting held in executive session. Clause 2(g)(1) of rule XI. A committee or subcommittee may not exclude noncommittee Members from nonparticipatory attendance at a hearing unless so authorized by the House. Clause 2(g)(2) of rule XI.

A motion to close a committee meeting or hearing, like the motion for a secret session in the House, is not debatable. *Manual* § 969. Under rule XI clause 2(g)(2)(D), all committees may vote to close a hearing for one additional day. The Committees on Appropriations and Armed Services and the Permanent Select Committee on Intelligence may close a hearing for up to five additional, consecutive days. *Manual* § 798.

Evidence or Testimony Tending to Defame, Degrade, or Incriminate

Clause 2(k)(5) of rule XI requires certain procedural steps whenever a member of the committee asserts that evidence or testimony before a committee hearing may tend to defame, degrade, or incriminate any person. Witnesses also may make such assertions with respect to themselves. *Manual* §§ 798, 803. A majority of those present may vote to (1) receive the evidence or testimony in executive session under clause 2(k)(5) or (2) go into executive session under clause 2(g)(2)(B) of rule XI to hold threshold discussions to explore whether the evidence or testimony may tend to defame, degrade, or incriminate. To continue the hearing in open session, a majority quorum of the committee or subcommittee must be present to entertain a motion that the evidence or testimony is in fact not defamatory, incriminating, or degrading and the committee should proceed in open session. Such a motion requires a majority for adoption. An opportunity to appear voluntarily must be afforded to the witness in either case. *Manual* § 803.

A point of order may be raised against a privileged report of a committee relating to the contemptuous refusal of a witness to testify on the ground that the committee had violated clause 2(k)(5) of rule XI. Deschler Ch 15 § 15. If a witness appears in response to a subpoena and, when called, properly asserts grounds for an executive session, the committee must determine whether the testimony will tend to defame, degrade, or incriminate, even though the witness may have ignored a previous opportunity to appear voluntarily to testify. However, the proper assertion must be made by the witness to the committee. If the witness leaves the hearing room without making any statement other than a refusal to testify, the committee is not obligated to go into executive session, because the proceedings have not reached the point where the witness has demanded that the committee determine whether the testimony would tend to degrade, defame, or incriminate.

The determination that evidence or testimony may tend to degrade, defame, or incriminate lies with the committee and not with the witness. Deschler Ch 15 § 15.

§ 21. Quorum Requirements

Generally

Historically, a majority of a committee constituted a quorum for the transaction of business. *Manual* § 409; 4 Hinds §§ 4540, 4552. Under current clause 2(h) of rule XI, committees may fix the quorum required for the taking of testimony at a hearing to not less than two and (except for Appropriations, Budget, and Ways and Means) may fix the quorum for the conduct of business, other than actions for which a majority of the committee is required, at not less than one-third.

Minimum quorum requirements for committees and subcommittees of the House are as follows:

Action	Minimum Quorum	Clause 2 of Rule XI
To report a measure or recommendation	A majority of the committee, ''actually present''	(h)(1) *Manual* § 799
To report contempt	A majority of the committee	(h)(1) *Manual* § 799
To authorize and issue a subpoena	A majority of the committee	(m)(2) *Manual* § 805
To close a meeting or hearing	A majority of the committee	(g)(1), (2) *Manual* § 798
To make public evidence taken in executive session	A majority of the committee	(k)(7) *Manual* § 803
To immunize a witness	A majority of the committee	18 USC § 6005
To take evidence or testimony in open session after assertion that it defames, degrades or incriminates	A majority of the committee	(k)(5) *Manual* § 803

ACTION	MINIMUM QUORUM	CLAUSE 2 OF RULE XI
To take testimony or receive evidence at hearing	Two members	(h)(2) *Manual* § 800
To close a hearing where assertion of defamatory testimony or evidence is made	Two members	(k)(5) *Manual* § 803
To take any other action	One-third of membership	(h)(3) *Manual* § 800

§ 22. —In Ordering a Report to the House

Generally

A standing committee cannot validly report a measure unless the report has been authorized at a formal meeting of the committee with a quorum present. Clause 2(h) of rule XI; *Manual* § 799; 8 Cannon §§ 2220-2222; Deschler Ch 17 § 23.2.

A point of order of no quorum may provoke a quorum call to obtain the presence of a majority of the committee in the committee room. *Manual* § 799.

Contemporaneous Meeting

The report is not valid unless authorized with a quorum of the committee *actually* present at the time the vote is taken. *Manual* § 799. This rule is derived from *Jefferson's Manual*, which states that a committee may act only when together—"nothing being the report of the committee but what has been agreed to in committee actually assembled." *Manual* § 407. This requirement means that a majority must be contemporaneously assembled when the question is put or at some point while the vote is taken.

Although Speakers have indicated that committee members may come and go during the course of the vote if the roll call indicates that a quorum was present, where it is admitted that a quorum was not in the room at any time during the vote and the committee transcript does not show a quorum acting as a quorum, the Chair will sustain the point of order against the measure when called up in the House. 8 Cannon §§ 2212, 2222. A poll of committee members by telephone will not suffice. Deschler Ch 17 § 23.2.

Obsolete "Rolling Quorum"

In the 103d Congress the rules were amended to permit a "rolling quorum" by allowing a majority to be deemed present if the committee records showed that a majority responded on a roll call vote on the motion to report in question. 103-1, H. Res. 5, Jan. 5, 1993, p 49. This language was deleted in the 104th Congress, thus restoring the previous requirement that a "majority of the committee be actually present" at the time a measure is ordered reported. Unlike a House floor vote, during which Members may come and go during the course of a vote, the committee quorum rule, absent the old "rolling quorum" latitude, means a committee cannot simply leave a vote open until a sufficient number of Members have responded to their names.

§ 23. —Points of Order Based on Reporting Requirements

Generally

Unless a point of order is raised, the House assumes that reports from committees are authorized with a quorum present. Deschler Ch 17 § 23. Quorum issues raised by a point of order are often determined on the basis of information in the report or supplied by the chair of the committee in question, and the Speaker may question the chair as to the circumstances of the meeting and the number of committee members present at that meeting. *Manual* § 799; Deschler Ch 17 § 23.5. Where the chair admits that the bill was reported when a quorum was not present, the point of order against the bill on that ground will be sustained. Deschler Ch 17 § 25.2. If the point of order is sustained, the bill is automatically recommitted. Deschler Ch 17 §§ 23.2, 25.2.

Where a bill is being considered under suspension of the rules, a point of order will not lie against the bill on the ground that a quorum was not present when the bill was reported from committee. Deschler Ch 17 § 24.8.

The absence of a quorum at the time a "clean" bill is ordered reported gives rise to a point of order on the House floor, even though the chair had been previously instructed by the committee to report the bill. *Cf.* Deschler Ch 17 § 23.6.

Timeliness

A point of order that a bill was reported from a committee in the absence of a quorum is properly raised in the House when the bill is called up for consideration or pending the Speaker's declaration, or a vote on a motion, that the House resolve itself into the Committee of the Whole for the consideration of the bill. Deschler Ch 17 §§ 24.2, 24.4; 101-1, May 16,

1989, p 9356. It has been ruled that such a point of order comes too late if raised:

- After consideration of the bill has begun in the House. 8 Cannon § 2223.
- After the House has resolved into the Committee of the Whole for the consideration of the measure. Deschler Ch 17 § 24.5.
- After debate on the measure has started in the House. Deschler Ch 17 § 24.6.
- After adoption of the measure. Deschler Ch 17 § 24.7.

The point of order is premature and will not be entertained:

- Where a resolution providing for the consideration of the bill is before the House. Deschler Ch 17 § 24.2.
- Pending a unanimous-consent request to consider the measure otherwise not privileged for consideration. 90-2, Oct. 11, 1968, p 30751.

Clause 2(g)(6)(B) of rule XI precludes a point of order against consideration of a reported measure, on the ground that hearings on such measure were conducted without a proper quorum, unless that point was timely made and improperly disposed of in committee.

§ 24. Witnesses

Summoning Witnesses; Subpoenas

Witnesses are summoned before a committee pursuant to authority conferred on it by the House to send for persons or papers. 3 Hinds § 1750. Clause 2(m) of rule XI permits committees and subcommittees to issue a subpoena when authorized by a majority of the members voting, a majority being present. This authority does not extend to other subunits of a committee such as "task forces." Full-committee chairs may authorize and issue subpoenas when that authority is delegated by the full committee, either on an ad hoc basis or by committee rule. Such subpoenas must be signed by the chair of the committee or by a member designated by the committee. Subpoenas issued to persons are returnable at the committee or subcommittee. A subpoena duces tecum, one that commands the production of documents, may specify terms of return other than at a meeting or a hearing. Clause 2(m)(3)(C) of rule XI.

Clause 2(k)(5) of rule XI requires committees and subcommittees to afford any person who may be defamed, degraded, or incriminated by testimony or evidence the opportunity to voluntarily appear as a witness. That clause and clause 2(k)(6) also require committees and subcommittees to dispose of requests from such person, or requests made by committee members during hearings, to subpoena additional witnesses. Such interlocutory requests can cover the full range of persons and papers for which subpoenas may be authorized under clause 2(m).

Under clause 2(m) of rule XI, compliance with a committee subpoena may be enforced only as authorized by the House. This clause has been interpreted to require authorization by the full House before a subcommittee chair may intervene in a lawsuit in order to gain access to documents subpoenaed by the subcommittee. *In re Beef Industry Antitrust Litigation*, 589 F.2d 786 (5th Cir. 1979); see also CONTEMPT. Clause 2(m) does not authorize a committee to conduct a deposition or interrogatory before one member or before staff of the committee. Except in the case of the Committee on Oversight and Government Reform under clause 4(c) of rule X, such authority must be conferred by separate action of the House. *Manual* §§ 800, 805.

Interrogation of Witnesses

Under clause 2(j)(2)(A) of rule XI, questioning of a witness appearing before a committee proceeds under the five-minute rule. Each member must be given an opportunity to question a witness for five minutes. Where more than one witness testifies in a ''panel,'' each member is permitted to question each witness in the panel for five minutes. Clauses 2(j)(2)(B) and 2(j)(2)(C) enable committees to permit extended examinations of witnesses for 30 additional minutes by designated members, or by staff, of each party.

Witnesses Called by the Minority

Under clause 2(j)(1) of rule XI, whenever a hearing is conducted by a committee on a measure or matter, the minority members on the committee have the right to call witnesses of their own choosing to testify on that measure or matter of a hearing for one day. Such a request must be supported by a majority of the minority members and submitted to the chair before completion of the hearing. The chair may set the day under a reasonable schedule. *Manual* § 802.

Perjury

It is a felony to give perjurious testimony before a congressional committee. 18 USC § 1621. It is a felony to make false, fictitious, or fraudulent statements before any department or agency of the United States, including congressional committees. 18 USC § 1001. However, the courts have ruled that the facts sought must be in aid of the committee's legislative purpose. The committee may recall a witness for additional testimony on a point already testified to, or question such witness about a prior denial, or address questions which are not clearly in aid of legislation, but a perjury indictment may not be found on false testimony in response to questions which are not asked for the purpose of eliciting facts material to the committee's investigation. *United States* v. *Cross*, 170 F. Supp. 303 (D.D.C. 1959).

A quorum of a committee must be present when testimony is given to support a charge of perjury. *Manual* §§343, 409, 803; *Christoffel* v. *United States*, 338 U.S. 84 (1949). The absence of a quorum of a committee at the time a witness willfully fails to produce subpoenaed documents is not a valid defense in a prosecution for contempt where the witness failed to raise that objection before the committee. *United States* v. *Bryan*, 339 U.S. 323 (1950); *United States* v. *Fleischman*, 339 U.S. 349 (1950).

Use of Written Statements

Under clause 2(g)(5) of rule XI, committees are encouraged to require each prospective witness to file a written statement of proposed testimony in advance and limit oral presentation to a summary thereof. The committees also must require, to the greatest extent practicable, nongovernmental witnesses who submit written statements to submit with such statement curriculum vitae and disclosures of Federal grants or contracts received over the previous three years. Under clause 2(k)(8) of rule XI witnesses are permitted, at the discretion of the committee, to submit brief, sworn statements in writing for inclusion in the committee record.

Subpoena Duces Tecum

Under clause 2(m)(3)(B) of rule XI, a subpoena for documents may specify terms of return other than at a meeting or hearing of the committee or subcommittee authorizing the subpoena, such as at committee offices.

Witness Fees

Clause 5 of rule XI authorizes the Committee on House Administration to establish the per diem and travel rates of reimbursement of witnesses. Some committees, in their rules, prescribe procedures for disbursing such fees, such as the signing of appropriate vouchers.

§25. —Rights or Privileges of Witnesses

Generally; Under the Constitution

Committee investigations must be conducted in accordance with the Constitution, particularly the first, fourth, and fifth amendments. Witnesses appearing at hearings cannot be compelled to give evidence or testimony against themselves, cannot be subjected to unreasonable search and seizure, and cannot have their first amendment freedoms of speech, press, religion, or political belief and association abridged. *Watkins* v. *United States*, 354 U.S. 178 (1957).

The Privilege Against Self-incrimination

The privilege against self-incrimination may be invoked by a person subpoenaed to testify or produce materials before a House committee notwithstanding the fact that a congressional investigation is not a ''criminal case'' in the conventional sense. 3 Hinds §§ 1699, 2514. The assertion of the privilege against self-incrimination need take no particular form, provided the committee can reasonably be expected to understand it as an attempt to invoke the privilege. *Quinn* v. *United States*, 349 U.S. 155 (1955). At the same time, a witness may waive the privilege by failing to assert it, expressly disclaiming it, or testifying on the same matters concerning which the privilege is later claimed. Deschler Ch 15 § 9. Thus, after testifying to an incriminating fact, a witness may not refuse to answer more questions on the same subject on the ground that such answers would further incriminate. *Rogers* v. *United States*, 340 U.S. 367 (1951).

Immunity Procedures

A witness who refuses to testify before a congressional committee on the basis of the privilege against self-incrimination may be granted immunity by court order and, under certain conditions, compelled to testify or provide information to the committee. 18 USC §§ 6002, 6005. Under the statute, the request for the court order must have been approved by two-thirds of the entire membership of the committee. The statute has been upheld as constitutional. *Application of U.S. Senate Select Committee on Presidential Campaign Activities*, 361 F. Supp. 1270 (D.D.C. 1973); see also 6 Cannon § 354.

Under the Rules of the House

A witness appearing at a hearing before a committee of the House is entitled to certain rights or privileges under the rules of the House. Clause 2(k) of rule XI; *Manual* § 803. Under these rules, a witness is entitled:

- To a copy of the committee rules (upon request).
- To be accompanied by counsel to advise on constitutional rights.
- To seek a closed hearing if the evidence or testimony tends to defame, degrade, or incriminate.
- To submit requests for committees to subpoena additional witnesses.
- To submit brief and pertinent sworn statements in writing for inclusion in the committee record (at discretion of committee).
- To a transcript of such witness's testimony if given in an open hearing.

Although the applicable rule permits witnesses to have counsel at hearings to advise on constitutional rights, it is the witness, not counsel, who has ultimate responsibility for protecting the witness's rights and invoking the procedural safeguards guaranteed under the rules of the House. The attorney for the witness may not, as a matter of right, present argument or make demands on the committee. Deschler Ch 15 § 14.3.

§ 26. —Proceedings Against Recalcitrant Witnesses

An individual who fails or refuses to comply with a House subpoena may be cited for contempt of Congress. The Supreme Court has found the subpoena power to be an ''indispensable ingredient'' of the legislative powers granted to Congress by the Constitution. *Eastland* v. *United States Servicemen's Fund*, 421 U.S. 491 (1975). Although the Constitution does not expressly grant Congress the power to punish witnesses for contempt, that power has been deemed an inherent attribute of the legislative authority of Congress. See *Anderson* v. *Dunn*, 19 U.S. 204 (1821). To supplement this inherent power, the Congress in 1857 adopted an alternative statutory contempt procedure. Under this statute, the House may certify to the appropriate U.S. Attorney the witness's refusal to comply with a congressional subpoena. House certification is effected by its adoption of a report from the committee where the refusal took place. The contempt is punishable by fine and imprisonment. 2 USC §§ 192, 194. For comprehensive discussion, see CONTEMPT; *Manual* §§ 293-299.

§ 27. Media Coverage of Hearings and Meetings

Clause 4 of rule XI requires that open committee hearings and meetings be open to audio, video, and photographic coverage by accredited press representatives. *Manual* §§ 807-812. The rule also requires committees to adopt written rules to govern such coverage within certain parameters set forth in the rule. Clause 2(e)(5) of rule XI provides that, to the maximum extent practicable, committees shall provide audio and video coverage of each meeting or hearing and make such coverage (and recordings thereof) easily accessible to the public.

E. Committee Reports

§ 28. In General

Necessity of Report; Chair's Duty to Report

Under clause 2 of rule XIII (first adopted in 1880), a bill reported from a committee must be accompanied by a written report. *Manual* § 833. Reported bills that are not accompanied by a written report are not placed on a calendar. 8 Cannon § 2783.

The report of a committee is in the nature of argument or explanation. The report on a legislative measure does not itself come before the House for amendment or other specific action. 4 Hinds § 4674; Deschler Ch 17 § 58. The Speaker makes no determinations as to the sufficiency of a report beyond specific requirements of House rules. 2 Hinds § 1339.

It is the duty of each committee chair to ''promptly'' report measures approved by the committee to the House. Clause 2(b)(1) of rule XIII; *Manual* § 834. Under this rule, if the report on such a measure is not filed by the chair of the committee, a majority of its members may file a written request for the filing of the report. Within seven calendar days (exclusive of the days on which the House is not in session) after the filing of the request, the committee report is to be filed. Excepted from this rule are certain reports of the Committee on Rules and reports on resolutions of inquiry. *Manual* § 835.

Committee Authorization or Approval

When a committee concludes consideration of a bill, a motion to order the measure reported is in order. 4 Hinds § 4667. In this respect, the House has adhered to the principle that the reporting of a measure must be authorized by the committee acting together at a formal meeting of the committee with a quorum present. Clause 2(h)(1) of rule XI; *Manual* § 407; 4 Hinds § 4585; 8 Cannon §§ 2221, 2222, 2249.

Objection being made that the text of a report does not reflect the actions of a committee, the question as to the reception of the report may be submitted to the House. 4 Hinds § 4591. If a bill is held to be improperly reported, the bill is not entitled to a place on the calendar. 4 Hinds § 3117. After the House has voted to consider a bill or after consideration has begun in the House, it is too late to raise the question of authorization or to question the validity of the committee's action in reporting the bill. 4 Hinds §§ 4598, 4599; 8 Cannon §§ 2223, 2225.

The rules of the House do not require that committees separately approve legislative reports. A point of order that a committee did not vote to approve a report as required by the rules of the committee is properly made in committee and not in the House. Deschler Ch 17 § 58.5.

Recommittal

The failure of a committee report to comply with the rules of the House, such as the reporting requirements contained in rule XIII, may result in automatic recommittal of the bill if a point of order is sustained. See, *e.g.*, 8 Cannon § 2237. Under clause 3(a)(2) of rule XIII, a committee may file a supplemental report to correct technical errors in its initial report. Such supplemental report is subject to a new three-day availability under clause 4(a) of rule XIII, except that a supplemental report only correcting errors in the depiction of record votes under clause 3(b) of rule XIII is not subject to such availability requirement. If the bill is recommitted because of a defective report, further proceedings are *de novo* and all committee formalities necessary to the first report are likewise necessary to authorize a second report. 8 Cannon §2221.

Adverse or Unfavorable Reports

A committee may report a bill adversely, even though the committee originated the bill. *Manual* §832; 4 Hinds §4659. A committee may also report a bill to the House with no recommendation for action. 4 Hinds §§4661, 4662. If the committee is unable to agree on a recommendation for action, it may submit a statement of this fact in the report (4 Hinds §4665), in which case the report may include minority views alone (2 Hinds §945) or simply set forth the propositions representing the opposing contentions (3 Hinds §2497; 4 Hinds §4664). Motions to report favorably, unfavorably, or with no recommendation have no priority over each other in committee and are not in order as amendments to each other.

Multiple Reports; Supplemental Reports

The report of a committee must be confined to a single volume, and ordinarily only one report is filed on each bill. §29, infra. Indeed, it has been held that two reports may not be filed from the Committee on Rules to accompany the same rule or order of business. Deschler Ch 17 §58.2.

However, clause 3(a)(2) of rule XIII permits the filing of a supplemental report to correct a technical error in a previous report, and unanimous consent is not required. Deschler Ch 17 §64.1. The authority to file a supplemental report to correct a technical error in a previous report does not include the authority to file a supplemental report (1) to correct the failure of a committee to comply at all with the reporting requirements set forth in rule XIII (such as the requirement to include a committee cost estimate); (2) to change a statement of legislative intent contained in the initial report (Deschler Ch 17 §64.1 (note)); (3) to include additional views not timely submitted for inclusion with the report; or (4) to outline substantive interpretations of a previously reported bill. In those cases, unanimous consent is required for a committee to file a supplemental report. In any case, a supplemental report is subject to the three-day layover requirement under clause 4(a) of rule XIII unless it only corrects errors in the depiction of record votes. Clause 3(a)(2) of rule XIII.

Reporting Bills with Amendments; "Clean" Bills

A committee may report a bill with sundry amendments for the consideration of the House. Where a bill has been extensively amended in the committee, its members may instruct the chair to incorporate the changes into an amendment in the nature of a substitute or to introduce a "clean" bill, which reflects the committee's action. If the latter course is chosen, the new bill must be introduced through the hopper. In either case, the committee cannot vote to report until it has the perfected text before it. Deschler Ch 17 § 23.6.

§ 29. Form and Contents of Report

Rule XIII governs the form and content of committee reports. Clauses 2(a) and 3(a) of rule XIII, respectively, require that committee reports be printed and confined to a single volume. Verbal statements will not be received in the House as the report of a committee. 4 Hinds §§ 4654, 4655.

Under rule XIII, a report on any measure or matter shall include:

- Minority, supplemental, or additional views if properly submitted. Clause 3(a).
- The total number of record votes cast in committee for or against the reporting of the measure or matter and on any amendment thereto, and the names of those voting for or against. Clause 3(b).
- Oversight findings and recommendations required pursuant to clause 2(b)(1) of rule X. Clause 3(c)(1).
- A statement of performance goals and objectives. Clause 3(c)(4).

Under rule XIII, a report on any public bill or joint resolution shall include:

- A statement describing fiscal ramifications of the measure as required by section 308 of the Congressional Budget Act of 1974, if the measure provides new budget authority or new or increased tax expenditures. Clause 3(c)(2).
- An estimate and comparison required under section 402 of the Congressional Budget Act as to the costs anticipated in carrying out the bill or joint resolution over specified periods of time, if timely submitted. Clause 3(c)(3).
- An estimate by the committee of the costs incurred in carrying out the bill or joint resolution in the fiscal year it is reported and in each of five following fiscal years (which may be satisfied by including a section 402 estimate). Clause 3(d)(1).
- A comparative print indicating changes in existing law (the Ramseyer Rule). Clause 3(e); § 30, infra.

Clause 3(f) of rule XIII requires a report of the Committee on Appropriations on a general appropriation bill to include:

- A description of the effect of any provision of the accompanying bill that changes the existing law.
- A list of unauthorized appropriations contained in the bill.
- A list of rescissions and transfers.

In addition, clause 3(f)(2)(A) requires an appropriation bill or joint resolution to include separate headings for ''Rescissions'' and ''Transfers of Unexpended Balances'' contained in the bill or joint resolution.

Clause 3(g) of rule XIII requires a report of the Committee on Rules on a resolution proposing to repeal or amend a standing rule of the House to include a ''Ramseyer'' comparison of the proposed text with the existing rule. §30, infra.

Clause 3(h) of rule XIII requires a report of the Committee on Ways and Means on a measure proposing to amend the Internal Revenue Code of 1986 to include (or to be printed in the *Congressional Record* by the chair of the Committee on Ways and Means before consideration) a ''tax complexity analysis'' and a ''macroeconomic impact analysis'' prepared by the Joint Committee on Internal Revenue Taxation.

Reports are also required to contain identification and cost-estimates of Federal mandates under the Unfunded Mandates Reform Act of 1995 (*Manual* §§843, 1127) and a description of the applicability of the measure to the Legislative Branch under the Congressional Accountability Act of 1995 (*Manual* §842). Under clause 9 of rule XXI, a point of order lies against consideration of a bill or joint resolution reported by a committee where the committee report fails to include a list of congressional earmarks, limited tax benefits, and limited tariff benefits contained in the measure (or a statement that the measure contains no such provisions). For a more detailed discussion of earmarks, see BUDGET PROCESS.

§30. Comparative Prints; The Ramseyer Rule

Generally

Clause 3(e) of rule XIII, the Ramseyer rule, was first incorporated into the House rules in 1929. It was named for its author, C. William Ramseyer. 8 Cannon §2234. This rule provides that whenever a committee reports a measure repealing or amending a statute, the committee report must include the text of the statute and a comparative print showing the proposed omissions and insertions by stricken-through type and italics, parallel columns, or other appropriate typographical devices. The purpose of the rule is to inform Members of any changes in existing law by the proposed legislation. Deschler Ch 17 § 60.

The Ramseyer rule requires that the statute proposed to be amended be quoted in the report; it is not sufficient that it is incorporated in the bill. 8 Cannon § 2238. However, a comparative print need only be prepared for the affected part of the law. Deschler Ch 17 § 60.6. If the bill amends existing law by the addition of a proviso, the report should quote in full the section immediately preceding the proposed amendment. 8 Cannon § 2237.

Where a committee reports a bill with amendments, the comparative print required by the rule must show the changes in existing law proposed by the bill as amended, rather than by the bill as introduced. Deschler Ch 17 § 60.4. Where there has been a multiple referral of a measure to two or more committees, each committee need only depict the changes it recommends and not the changes recommended by the other committees. *Manual* § 816.

Application of Rule

To fall within the purview of the Ramseyer rule, a bill must repeal or amend a statute directly, and a general reference to the subject treated in a statute without the proposition of a specific amendment is not sufficient. 8 Cannon § 2235. Provisions in a bill which merely waive certain statutory requirements or grant an exemption therefrom are not specifically amendatory of existing law and therefore are not subject to the Ramseyer rule requirements. Deschler Ch 17 § 60.7. Thus, the Ramseyer rule has been held inapplicable to a joint resolution extending the period for State ratification of a constitutional amendment submitted to the States, where the resolution did not specifically change the deadline for ratification, but merely extended the period "notwithstanding" any provision in the prior law. 95-2, Aug. 15, 1978, p 26204. A point of order will not lie against a committee report merely because the comparative print required by the Ramseyer rule includes laws which are not affected by the reported bill but which are included to give full information to the Members. Deschler Ch 17 § 60.3.

The Ramseyer rule is applicable whenever a committee reports a bill repealing or amending "a statute or part thereof." *Manual* § 846. Thus, the rule is not applicable to:

- A bill changing the rules of evidence for the District of Columbia courts. Deschler Ch 17 § 6.8.
- Bills discharged from a committee (as distinguished from bills reported by a committee). Deschler Ch 17 § 60.10.
- Bills amending simple resolutions. 8 Cannon § 2239.

The Ramseyer rule is not applicable to reports accompanying simple resolutions. 93-2, Sept. 30, 1974, p 32956. However, a Ramseyer-type comparative print is required under clause 3(g) of rule XIII whenever the Committee on Rules reports a resolution proposing to repeal or amend a standing rule of the House or part thereof. This clause does not apply to resolutions that merely provide temporary waivers of rules during the consideration of particular legislative business and does not apply to a resolution providing for the consideration of a bill with textual modifications that would effect certain changes in House rules on enactment of the bill into law but not itself repealing or amending any rule. *Manual* § 848.

The Ramseyer rule applies to general appropriation bills where such bills include legislative provisions. 8 Cannon § 2241. General appropriation bills are also subject to a separate rule requiring that the report contain a statement of the effect of any changes in existing law. Clause 3(f) of rule XIII.

Substantial Compliance

A Ramseyer rule violation may occur even though the bill in question proposes but one minor and obvious change in existing law. 8 Cannon § 2236. Under the doctrine of substantial compliance, however, the Speaker has overruled Ramseyer points of order on the rationale that the committee had substantially complied with the requirements of the rule and that deviations were minor and inconsequential. Deschler Ch 17 §§ 60.11-60.14. Thus, the Speaker has upheld a report, even though it contained errors in typography and punctuation and failed to indicate a relatively insignificant date change. Deschler Ch 17 § 60.14.

Points of Order

The point of order that a report fails to comply with the Ramseyer rule is properly made when the bill is called up in the House and before the House has resolved into the Committee of the Whole for its consideration. 8 Cannon §§ 2243, 2245; Deschler Ch 17 §§ 60.15-60.18. The point of order does not lie in the Committee of the Whole. Deschler Ch 17 § 60.16. Thus, the proper time to raise the point of order is when the motion is made to go into, or the Speaker declares the House resolved into, the Committee of the Whole to consider the bill. If that motion is withdrawn, the Chair is not obliged to rule on the point of order. *Manual* § 905. When a point of order is raised that a report is in violation of the Ramseyer rule, it is incumbent on the proponent of the point of order to cite the specific statute which will be amended by the pending bill. 8 Cannon § 2246.

Compliance with the Ramseyer rule may be waived by unanimous consent or by a special order of business. Deschler Ch 17 §§ 60.19, 60.20. However, a special order of business providing for the consideration of a bill, unless specifically waiving points of order, does not preclude the point of order that the report on such a bill fails to comply with the Ramseyer rule. 8 Cannon § 2245.

Recommittal; Supplemental Report

Technical defects in a Ramseyer may be remedied by a supplemental report, which may be filed with the Clerk under clause 3(a)(2) of rule XIII without unanimous consent. 8 Cannon § 2247. Two remedies are available to the Chair when a point of order for failure to comply with the Ramseyer rule is sustained. The Chair may recommit the bill to the respective committees reporting it. 8 Cannon § 2237; Deschler Ch 17 § 60.2. This was the automatic remedy before the adoption of clause 3(a)(2) of rule XIII. When a bill was recommitted for failure to conform to the rule, further proceedings were *de novo* and the bill was considered again and reported by the committee as if no previous report had been made. 8 Cannon § 2249. In the alternative, the Chair may announce that consideration of the bill must await the filing of a supplemental report under clause 3(a)(2) to cure the defect. The latter remedy is most suitable where the violation is merely technical.

§ 31. Printing; Referral to Calendars

Generally

Unless a report is privileged for immediate consideration, it is delivered to the Clerk for printing and reference to the proper calendar under the direction of the Speaker. *Manual* § 831; § 33, infra. Privileged reports are filed from the floor while the House is in session and referred to the appropriate calendar and ordered printed by the Speaker. Deschler Ch 17 § 58.

For more discussion of referrals, including sequential referrals, see BILLS AND RESOLUTIONS.

Adverse Reports

Under clause 2(a)(2) of rule XIII, a bill reported adversely is laid on the table unless the reporting committee or a Member requests the Clerk to refer the bill to a calendar. Nonprivileged reports on resolutions adversely reported are not printed unless a request is made that they be referred to a calendar. Deschler Ch 17 § 59.1. However, reports on resolutions of inquiry are privileged, are reported as such (whether favorable or adverse) and are printed and referred. *Manual* § 864; see also CALENDARS.

Correcting an Error

A ''star print'' is a reprint of a committee report or reported bill to correct errors in the first printing of the report. A ''star print'' may be authorized by the Speaker to correct an error made by the Government Printing Office. 95-2, June 23, 1978, p 18806. A committee may correct a technical error in its report by filing a supplemental report under clause 3(a)(2) of rule XIII. § 28, supra.

§ 32. Supplemental, Minority, and Additional Views

The members of a committee who are in the minority may not present a proposition of legislation but have the right to file views to accompany the report. 4 Hinds §§ 4601-4605. Unless filed with the report, minority views may be presented only by consent of the House. 4 Hinds § 4600; 8 Cannon § 2231.

Clause 2(l) of rule XI entitles a member of the committee who gives notice to two additional calendar days to file with the clerk of the committee supplemental, additional, or minority views. The member must give notice at the time of the approval of the report. The right to submit additional views inures to all members of the committee and not simply the member who gives notice. The two calendar days begin the day after the measure is ordered reported and do not count Saturdays, Sundays, and legal holidays except when the House is in session. Such views must be in writing and signed by the submitting member. *Manual* § 804. If one member makes a timely request for filing views, all other members of the committee may submit views for inclusion in the report within the two-day window. Deschler Ch 17 § 64. Views may also be called ''separate,'' ''concurrent,'' or ''dissenting.''

Under clause 2(c) of rule XIII, views submitted under clause 2(l) of rule XI must be included in, and must be part of, the report. Under clause 3(a) of rule XIII, the cover of the report must recite the inclusion of such views. When the two additional days guaranteed by clause 2(l) of rule XI expire, the committee may arrange to file its report with the Clerk not later than one hour after the expiration of such time, even if the House is not in session. Clause 2(c) of rule XIII.

§ 33. Filing Reports

Nonprivileged reports are filed by delivering them to the Clerk for reference to the calendars under the direction of the Speaker. *Manual* § 831. Privileged reports are filed from the floor and referred to the appropriate calendar by the Speaker. *Manual* § 853; Deschler Ch 17 § 58.

Ordinarily, a committee report on a bill or other measure reported to the House must accompany the reported measure. *Manual* §§ 831, 853. Except as provided in clause 2(c) of rule XIII, or in the case of an expiring referral, unanimous consent is required to file a committee report when the House is not in session, and such permission may not be obtained by motion. *Manual* § 418; Deschler Ch 17 § 62; § 32, supra. A special order of business may provide committees with authority to file supplemental reports. 110-2, Apr. 23, 2008, p 6706.

The House may extend the time for a select committee to file a report pursuant to a simple resolution (105-1, H. Res. 170, May 13, 1999, p 9499) or by agreement to a unanimous-consent request (94-2, Aug. 2, 1976, p 25086). An extension of time to file has been given to a joint committee pursuant to a joint resolution and to a unanimous-consent request agreed to in each House. Deschler Ch 17 §§ 62.10, 62.11.

§ 34. Calling Up; Time to Report

Privileged and Nonprivileged Reports Distinguished

Certain committee reports may be called up as privileged under the rules and precedents of the House. If privileged, a report may be filed from the floor at any time; its consideration is preferential and does not require a special order of business from the Committee on Rules. Deschler Ch 17 § 63. The report may be privileged even though the measure in question is reported adversely. 6 Hinds § 413; 8 Cannon § 2310; Deschler Ch 17 § 63.3.

Privileged status is accorded to:

- Reports on Presidential vetoes. Deschler Ch 17 §§ 63.1, 63.2.
- Reports on impeachments and matter incidental thereto. Deschler Ch 17 § 63.3.
- Reports on questions involving the privileges of the House, such as reports relating to the refusal of a witness to testify or produce documents. Deschler Ch 17 §§ 63.4-63.7.
- Reports on resolutions of inquiry. 6 Cannon § 404.
- Reports by those committees specified by clause 5 of rule XIII to report at any time on particular matters, subject to applicable layover requirements. *Manual* § 855.
- Reports which may be reported at any time by specific authorization of a House resolution. Deschler Ch 17 § 63.10.
- Reports on measures which may be reported at any time pursuant to statute, as in the case of certain resolutions of disapproval. *Manual* § 1130; Deschler Ch 17 § 63.11 (note).

As noted above, certain committees are, under clause 5 of rule XIII, given leave to report at any time on matters particularized in the rule. *Man-*

ual §§853, 855. This privilege to report at any time does not extend to matters not specified by the rule. 4 Hinds §4622; 8 Cannon §2286. The committees with leave to report at any time on specified matters under this rule are shown in the table below:

Committee	**Eligible Matters and Measures**
Rules	Rules, joint rules, and the order of business.
Appropriations	General appropriation bills, certain joint resolutions continuing appropriations, but not appropriations for specific purposes (8 Cannon §2285)
Budget	Matters under titles III and IV of the Congressional Budget Act of 1974
House Administration	Enrolled bills; election contests; printing; noncurrent House records; expenditures of applicable accounts of the House
Ethics	Certain resolutions recommending action with respect to a Member, officer, or employee

The right to report at any time is said to carry with it the right to consideration at any time (4 Hinds §3131), subject to applicable layover requirements (see §35, infra). However, such right does not exist when in conflict with other rules of the House. 8 Cannon §2291. Measures reported under a leave to report at any time yield to matter enjoying a higher privilege in the order of business, to questions of privilege (*Manual* §854; 6 Cannon §557), and to measures already given a priority by a special order of business (4 Hinds §§3175, 3176).

Where a committee has been given the privilege of reporting at any time with respect to a certain matter, it may report Senate bills as well as House bills under the privileged status given. Deschler Ch 17 §63.10.

Generally, nonprivileged reports are made by delivering them to the Clerk. *Manual* §831. Reports privileged under the rules must be made from the floor. *Manual* §853; 4 Hinds §3146; 8 Cannon §§2230, 2233.

Who May Call Up; Reading

A committee ordinarily authorizes its chair to submit and call up its report. *Manual* § 834; 4 Hinds § 4669. The chair may do so even though not concurring therein. 4 Hinds § 4670. However, the committee may authorize other members of the committee to present reports, and under some circumstances minority members of the committee have been ordered to present the report of the committee. 4 Hinds §§ 4669, 4672, 4673; 8 Cannon §§ 2314, 2315.

Reports are not normally read by the Clerk. However, in a few cases, where a report does not accompany a bill or other proposition of action, but presents facts and conclusions under consideration by the House, it is read by the Clerk (such as the predicate for a contempt resolution). *Manual* § 422.

Withdrawal

The chair of a committee, having made a report to the House in accordance with instructions from the committee, may not withdraw it except by consent of the House. 4 Hinds § 4690; 8 Cannon § 2312. When placed on the calendar, a bill is not subject to further consideration by the committee reporting it. 8 Cannon §§ 2218, 2307.

§ 35. Availability (''Layover'') Requirements

With certain exceptions, clause 4(a) of rule XIII requires that a committee report on a measure or matter be available to Members for three calendar days (excluding Saturdays, Sundays, and legal holidays, unless in session) before the measure may be considered in the House. The rule permits consideration of a measure on the third day a report is available rather than on the fourth day following its availability. *Manual* § 850. The three-day rule runs anew from the time of availability of a supplemental report to correct a technical error in a previous report, except to correct errors in the depiction of record votes. Clause 3(a) of rule XIII; Deschler Ch 17 § 64.1. A measure or matter made publicly available in electronic form at a location designated by the Committee on House Administration is considered as having been made available to Members. Clause 3 of rule XXIX.

Clause 4 of rule XIII exempts the following from the three-day layover requirement:

- A resolution from the Committee on Rules providing a rule, joint rule, or order of business (clause 4(a)(2)(A)), such reports being subject to a separate one-day layover requirement unless the House determines by a vote of two-thirds to consider the resolution on the same day (clause 6(a)(1)).
- A resolution from the Committee on House Administration providing committee expenses (clause 4(a)(2)(B)), such reports being subject to a separate one-day layover requirement (clause 6(a) of rule X).
- A resolution presenting a question of the privileges of the House. Clause 4(a)(2)(C).
- A measure for the declaration of war or national emergency. Clause 4(a)(2)(D).
- A measure providing approval or disapproval of impending actions or determinations by a government agency. Clause 4(a)(2)(E).

Points of order against consideration of a bill for failure of the report thereon to be available for three days may be waived pursuant to a resolution from the Committee on Rules (see, *e.g.*, 106-1, H. Res. 136, Apr. 13, 1999, p 6284), which waiver may be called up the same day reported from Committee on Rules without a two-thirds vote (clause 6(a)(2) of rule XIII).

§ 36. Points of Order Relating to Reports

Generally

A point of order will lie in the House against consideration of a measure for failure of the committee report on the measure to include any of the reporting requirements outlined in § 29, supra.

A point of order will also lie in the House against consideration of a measure for failure of the committee report to meet the availability requirements (§ 35, supra) and to report a measure without a sufficient quorum (§ 21, supra).

Points of order against consideration for noncompliance with the rules in the preparation of the report should be made in the House. A point of order that a committee report is not in proper form does not lie in the Committee of the Whole. Deschler-Brown Ch 29 § 20.28.

The Chair does not rule on points of order relating to the sufficiency, insufficiency, or legal effect of committee reports, those being matters for the House to decide. 4 Hinds § 1339; Deschler Ch 17 §§ 58.3, 58.4. Similarly, a point of order will not lie against a committee report that included an executive communication on the ground that the communication failed to comply with the statute that required the communication. Deschler Ch 17 § 58.1.

Points of order as to reports on appropriation bills, see APPROPRIATIONS.

Waiving Points of Order

Points of order against a measure for defects in a committee report may be waived by adoption of a special order of business from the Committee on Rules, an order of the House granted by unanimous consent, and by consideration of the bill under suspension of the rules. Deschler Ch 17 § 58.

Chapter 12
Committees of the Whole

Research References

4 Hinds §§ 4704-4922
8 Cannon §§ 2318-2430
Deschler Ch 19
Manual §§ 326-340; 970-993

A. Generally

§ 1. In General

Role and Functions; Historical Background

The Committee of the Whole has been described as an ancient parliamentary institution, having been derived from the practice of the English House of Commons. 4 Hinds § 4705; Deschler Ch 19 § 5. The Continental Congress frequently used the Committee of the Whole for important business. The concept that the Committee of the Whole should receive what were called ''the greater matters of legislation'' has gradually resulted in the usage now crystallized in clause 3 of rule XVIII, which requires the reference to its calendar of all bills directly or indirectly raising revenue, general appropriation bills, and public bills appropriating money or property. See 4 Hinds § 4705.

The Committee of the Whole meets to consider matters referred to it under rules designed to expedite consideration and to allow greater participation by Members. The Committee of the Whole is in this respect comparable to a standing committee. 4 Hinds § 4706. The Committee of the Whole is never completely dissolved. The House merely resolves into and out of Committee of the Whole, and bills remain on its calendar until reported therefrom. 4 Hinds § 4705.

Every Member of the House is a member of the Committee of the Whole. However, the Committee may sit with a smaller number (100 Members) than is required to transact business in the House (218 Members). Clause 6(a) of rule XVIII. For a discussion of quorums generally, see QUORUMS.

Distinguishing the Committee of the Whole

The term ''Committee of the Whole'' refers to the ''Committee of the Whole House on the state of the Union,'' which considers public bills. Deschler Ch 19 § 1. Prior to 1935, the term was also used to refer to the ''Committee of the Whole House,'' which formerly considered business on the Private Calendar. Since 1935, however, bills on the Private Calendar have been considered in the ''House as in the Committee of the Whole.'' Thus, the term ''Committee of the Whole House'' has no application in the modern practice of the House (Deschler Ch 19 § 1) and was deleted from the rules when they were recodified in 1999.

House as in the Committee of the Whole

When the House sits as in the Committee of the Whole, it does not actually resolve into the committee; it sits ''as in'' Committee of the Whole to allow consideration of bills under the five-minute rule without general debate and with the bill considered as read and open to amendment at any point. *Manual* §§ 424, 427; 4 Hinds § 4924. This practice is permitted in the consideration of public bills only by unanimous consent or pursuant to a special order of business from the Committee on Rules. *Manual* § 424. A motion that a proposition be considered under that procedure is not in order. *Manual* § 424; 4 Hinds § 4923.

The Speaker remains in the Chair, and a quorum of the House (and not of the Committee of the Whole) is required. 6 Cannon § 639. The measure is considered to have been read for amendment, and is open to amendment at any point. *Manual* § 427. A motion to close debate on the pending measure (or an amendment) is in order. *Manual* § 427.

When the House is sitting as in the Committee of the Whole, it may invoke many procedures that are not available to it when it is meeting in the Committee of the Whole. *Manual* § 427. For example, it may:

- Order the yeas and nays by one-fifth of those present or upon objection for lack of a quorum. 4 Hinds § 4923.
- Receive messages from the President or the Senate. 4 Hinds § 4923.
- Permit withdrawal of amendments before action thereon. 4 Hinds § 4935.
- Refer to a committee. 4 Hinds §§ 4931, 4932.
- Entertain the previous question. 4 Hinds §§ 4926-4929; 6 Cannon § 639.
- Entertain the motion to reconsider. 8 Cannon § 2793.
- Entertain the motion to adjourn. 4 Hinds § 4923.

The procedures applicable in the House as in the Committee of the Whole apply generally to proceedings in standing committees of the House. *Manual* § 427; see also COMMITTEES.

Significance of the Mace

The position of the mace in the Chamber signifies to the Members whether the House has resolved itself into the Committee of the Whole. When the mace is in position on the higher pedestal at the Speaker's right, the House is in regular session. When the Members begin deliberations in the Committee of the Whole, the mace is placed on the lower pedestal next to the desk of the Sergeant-at-Arms. Deschler Ch 19 § 1.1.

§ 2. Jurisdiction and Authority; Reference

Generally; Public Bills

Under clause 1(a)(1) of rule XIII, bills raising revenue, general appropriation bills, and bills of a public character directly or indirectly appropriating money or property are referred to the Union Calendar and considered in the Committee of the Whole. See also clause 3 of rule XVIII. Where the purpose of a bill is to raise revenue, even though that purpose is affected indirectly, the bill is within the jurisdiction of the Committee of the Whole. 8 Cannon § 2399.

Whether a bill should be referred to the Union Calendar is governed by the text of the bill as introduced, and amendments recommended by the committee reporting it are not considered. Thus, a bill that includes a charge on the Treasury is referred to the Union Calendar notwithstanding a committee amendment striking that charge. 8 Cannon § 2392.

Measures Other Than Public Bills

Although the jurisdiction of the Committee of the Whole is devoted primarily to the consideration of public bills, other matters are sometimes referred to the Committee pursuant to House order. For example, the annual message of the President is customarily referred to the Committee of the Whole by motion. Propositions to change the rules of the House have been considered in Committee of the Whole pursuant to a special order of business. 4 Hinds § 4822; Deschler Ch 21 § 21.15.

Referrals; Effect of Special Orders of Business

Measures referred by the Speaker to the Union Calendar for consideration in the Committee of the Whole are considered therein under special orders of business reported by the Committee on Rules or by the standing rules applicable to the Committee of the Whole. See rule XVIII.

The Committee has no authority to change an order of the House governing the consideration of a particular measure in the Committee of the Whole, although minor modifications may be accomplished by unanimous consent. *Manual* § 993; see also SPECIAL ORDERS OF BUSINESS. Thus, where the Committee of the Whole is considering a bill under a special order of business that fixes the time for debate and the amendments that may be offered, a Member may not be recognized to seek unanimous consent to offer a measure that is beyond the scope of the special order of business (4 Hinds §§ 4712, 4713) or to extend the time for general debate as fixed thereby (5 Hinds §§ 5212-5216).

Bills are sometimes referred to the Committee of the Whole as a result of action in the House resulting in its recommittal thereto (*Manual* § 988; 4 Hinds § 4784) or in unusual situations pursuant to a motion to recommit in the House either with or without instructions (5 Hinds §§ 5552, 5553).

Presidential Messages

The President's state of the Union message is referred by motion to the Committee of the Whole. See, *e.g.*, 106-2, Jan. 27, 2000, p 162; 112-1, Jan. 25, 2011, p ____. Other Presidential messages are normally referred to the committee having jurisdiction by order of the Speaker. *Manual* § 873. At one time, annual messages of the President were referred to and reported by the Committee of the Whole with recommendations for reference to the proper standing or select committee, but this practice was discontinued in the 64th Congress. 8 Cannon § 3350.

Limitations on Authority

Many procedures and motions traditionally available in the House may not be invoked in the Committee of the Whole. See § 8, infra. For example, the Committee of the Whole may not:

- Appoint, authorize, or discharge committees. 4 Hinds §§ 4697, 4710.
- Entertain the question of consideration (7 Cannon § 952) except pursuant to those provisions of the Congressional Budget Act and the Statutory Pay-As-You-Go Act of 2010 that permit the question of consideration in the disposition of certain points of order (*Manual* §§ 910, 991).
- Transact proceedings regarding words demanded to be taken down in debate. 2 Hinds §§ 1257-1259; 8 Cannon § 2539.
- Recess without permission of the House (5 Hinds §§ 6669-6671), except in case of emergency (clause 12(b)(2) of rule I).
- Instruct conferees. 8 Cannon § 2320.
- Consider questions of privilege under rule IX. *Manual* § 711; 2 Hinds § 1657; Deschler Ch 11 § 4.3.
- Authorize extraneous matter to be included in the *Congressional Record*. *Manual* § 688.

Similarly, unanimous-consent requests may not be entertained in the Committee of the Whole if they materially alter procedures required by a special order of business or other order adopted by the House. For example, the Committee of the Whole may not:

- Permit a perfecting amendment to be offered to the underlying bill where a special order of business permitted its consideration only as a perfecting amendment to a committee amendment.
- Permit a substitute to be read by section for amendment where the special order of business did not so provide.
- Extend the time limitation for consideration of amendments beyond that set by a special order of business requiring the Chair to put the question on the pending amendments at the expiration of certain hours of consideration.
- Restrict authority granted in a special order of business to offer amendments "en bloc."
- Change the scheme for control (other than among committees controlling time) or duration of general debate specified by the House.
- Reduce below 15 minutes the minimum time for the first recorded vote in a series.
- Preempt the Chair's discretion to postpone and cluster votes.
- Permit an amendment to an amendment rendered unamendable by a special order of business or permit a subsequent amendment changing an unamendable amendment already adopted.
- Permit consideration of an amendment out of the order specified in a special order of business.
- Permit consideration of an additional amendment or authorize a supplemental report from the Committee on Rules in lieu of the original report referred to in the special order of business.
- Permit a different Member to offer an amendment vested in a specified Member.
- Permit a division of the question on an amendment rendered indivisible by a special order of business.

Manual § 993.

Where the Committee of the Whole reports a recommendation that is ruled out as in excess of its powers, the accompanying bill stands recommitted to the Committee of the Whole. *Manual* § 335; 4 Hinds § 4908.

On the other hand, unanimous-consent requests may be entertained in the Committee of the Whole if they do not materially alter procedures required by special order of business or other order adopted by the House.

For example, unanimous-consent requests have been entertained in the Committee of the Whole to:

- Permit one of two committees controlling time for general debate pursuant to a special order of business to yield control of its time to the other.
- Permit the modification of a designated amendment made in order by a special order of business, once offered, if the request is propounded by the proponent of the amendment, including as unfinished business where proceedings on a request for a recorded vote have been postponed.
- Permit a page reference to be included in a designated amendment made in order as printed where the printed amendment did not include that reference.
- Permit a supporter of an amendment to claim debate time allocated by a special order of business to an opponent, where no opponent seeks recognition.
- Shorten the time set by a special order of business for debate on a particular amendment.
- Lengthen the time set by a special order of business for debate on a particular amendment under terms of control congruent with those set by the order of the House.
- Permit en bloc consideration of several amendments under a ''modified-closed'' special order of business providing for the sequential consideration of designated separate amendments.
- Reach ahead in the reading of a general appropriation bill to consider one amendment without prejudice to others earlier in the bill under a special order of the House contemplating that each remaining amendment be offered only at the ''appropriate point in the reading of the bill.''
- Permit the reading of an amendment that was considered as read under a special order of business.

Manual § 993.

Authority to Originate Measures

In the early practice, the Committee of the Whole could consider a matter even though the matter had not been referred to it by the House. 4 Hinds § 4705. Today, the Committee of the Whole no longer originates measures, but receives only such measures as have been referred to it, usually by way of a special order of business. *Manual* § 326; 4 Hinds § 4707. Under this practice, the House may not resolve into the Committee of the Whole for the purpose of originating a measure except by unanimous consent. *Manual* § 412. Absent an appropriate referral, the Committee of the Whole may not report a recommendation, that, if carried into effect, would change a rule of the House. 4 Hinds §§ 4907, 4908.

Conference Reports

Conference reports are considered in the House rather than in the Committee of the Whole, and this is so notwithstanding a point of order that the report contains matter ordinarily requiring consideration in the Committee. 5 Hinds §§ 6559, 6561.

§ 3. Matters Requiring Consideration in the Committee of the Whole

Generally

Clause 3 of rule XVIII specifies the matters that must be considered in the Committee of the Whole before consideration in the House. The matters so specified include all motions or propositions involving a tax or charge upon the people, all proceedings involving appropriations of money or property, requiring such appropriation to be made, or authorizing payments out of appropriations already made. Also included within the rule are bills releasing any liability to the United States for money or property, or referring any claim to the Court of Claims. A point of order under this rule may be raised at any time before the consideration of a bill has commenced.

The consideration of a measure by unanimous consent waives any requirement as to consideration in Committee of the Whole. 4 Hinds § 4823; 8 Cannon § 2393. Similarly, the effect of a special order of business may be to discharge the Committee of the Whole and bring the bill directly before the House. *Manual* § 973. In the modern practice, special orders of business reported from the Committee on Rules often provide for consideration of a measure on the Union Calendar in the House where no amendments, or only one amendment, are made in order. See, *e.g.*, 107-1, H. Res. 199, Apr. 26, 2001, p 6299.

The requirement of clause 3 of rule XVIII is that the class of business specified by the rule must be ''first'' considered in the Committee of the Whole. *Manual* § 973. It follows that a bill considered in the Committee of the Whole, reported to the House, and then recommitted by the House to a standing committee, is not, when again reported to the House, necessarily subject to the point of order that it must be considered in Committee of the Whole. *Manual* § 973; 4 Hinds § 4828; 5 Hinds §§ 5545, 5546.

Measures Requiring Consideration in the Committee of the Whole

The following measures require consideration in the Committee of the Whole:

- Increasing the rate of postage. 4 Hinds § 4861.
- Creating a new Federal office. 4 Hinds § 4846.

- Authorizing an undertaking by a government agency that will incur an expense, however small, to the government. 8 Cannon § 2401.
- Requiring an expenditure with some probability. Deschler Ch 19 § 1.
- Setting in motion a chain of circumstances destined ultimately to involve certain expenditures. 4 Hinds § 4827; 8 Cannon § 2399.

Measures Not Requiring Consideration in the Committee of the Whole

The following measures do not require consideration in the Committee of the Whole:

- Not directly making an appropriation of money or requiring one to be made. 4 Hinds § 4856.
- Making an expenditure that is to be borne otherwise than by the Federal Government. 4 Hinds § 4831.
- Proposing an amendment to the Constitution to extend the term of office of certain officials. 8 Cannon § 2395.

§ 4. —Amendments Between the Houses

Clause 3 of rule XVIII, requiring that any proposition involving a tax or an appropriation of money or property must be considered in the Committee of the Whole, is applicable to Senate amendments to House measures. § 3, supra. Accordingly, where a House bill returned with Senate amendments involving a new matter of appropriation has been referred by the Speaker to a standing committee, it is, upon being reported therefrom, referred to the Committee of the Whole. *Manual* § 874; 4 Hinds §§ 3094, 3108-3110. Similarly, a House amendment to a Senate amendment is subject to clause 3. 4 Hinds § 4795. Normally, such Senate and House amendments are not referred to committee, but are held at the Speaker's desk (pursuant to the Speaker's discretionary authority under clause 2(b) of rule XIV) for disposition by the House. *Manual* §§ 874, 1073.

The question as to whether a Senate amendment involves a tax or an appropriation so as to require consideration in Committee of the Whole is applied to each amendment received from the Senate. The fact that the original House bill was considered in Committee of the Whole is not taken into consideration in determining this question. 8 Cannon § 2381.

A Senate amendment to a House bill is subject to the point of order that it must first be considered in the Committee of the Whole if, had it originated in the House, the amendment would be subject to that point of order. Clause 3 of rule XXII; *Manual* § 1072. Hence, a Senate amendment that on its face places a charge on the Treasury must be considered in Committee of the Whole absent proof to the contrary. 8 Cannon § 2387. However, a Senate amendment that merely modifies a House proposition, such as an increase or decrease in the amount of an appropriation and that does not involve a new and distinct expenditure, is not required to be considered in the Committee of the Whole. *Manual* § 1073; 4 Hinds §§ 4797, 4800; 8 Cannon §§ 2382, 2385. Moreover, the requirement that certain Senate amendments be considered in the Committee of the Whole applies only before the stage of disagreement has been reached on the Senate amendment (and not thereafter), and it is too late to raise a point of order that Senate amendments should have been considered in the Committee after the House has disagreed thereto and the amendments are reported from conference in disagreement. *Manual* §§ 1073, 1074. The fact that one of several Senate amendments must be considered in Committee does not prevent the House from proceeding with the disposition of those not subject to the point of order. 4 Hinds § 4807.

The requirement of clause 3 of rule XXII that the amendment be ''first considered'' in the Committee of the Whole does not apply if the House has agreed to a special order of business providing that the amendment is ''hereby'' considered as adopted. *Manual* § 1073; see, *e.g.*, 103-1, H. Res. 71, Feb. 4, 1993, p 2500.

§ 5. Resolving Into the Committee of the Whole

Generally; Declaration by Speaker

The House may resolve into the Committee of the Whole pursuant to motion or by declaration of the Speaker pursuant to clause 2 of rule XVIII after the House has adopted a special order of business from the Committee on Rules providing for consideration of a measure in the Committee of the Whole and permitting such declaration. 4 Hinds § 3214; 7 Cannon §§ 783, 794; Deschler Ch 19 § 4; § 6, infra. When employing the latter method, the Speaker may at any time after adoption of the resolution, when no other question is pending, declare the House resolved into the Committee of the Whole for consideration of a measure. Under the modern practice, this is the generally used mechanism for resolving into the Committee for the consideration of both nonprivileged bills and privileged general appropriation bills.

Resolving Automatically Into the Committee of the Whole

The House automatically and without motion resolves itself into the Committee of the Whole to consider a measure:

- When a special order of business from the Committee on Rules provides for the immediate consideration of the measure in the Committee of the Whole. 7 Cannon §§ 783, 794; Deschler Ch 19 § 4.1.
- After the Speaker has ruled on words taken down in the Committee of the Whole. Deschler Ch 19 § 4.8.
- After a recommendation of the Committee of the Whole that the enacting clause of the measure be stricken is rejected by the House. Deschler Ch 19 § 10.9.
- When a bill on the Union Calendar is timely called up (or is the unfinished business) on Calendar Wednesday. *Manual* § 901; 7 Cannon §§ 939, 940, 942.

§ 6. —By Motion

Although rarely used in recent years, the House may resolve into Committee of the Whole pursuant to motion (Deschler Ch 19 § 4), as follows:

> MEMBER: M__. Speaker, I move that the House resolve itself into the Committee of the Whole House on the state of the Union for the [further] consideration of __________.

This motion is listed eighth in the daily order of business. *Manual* § 869. However, the motion is usually given more preferential status by the adoption of a special order of business reported from the Committee on Rules. Deschler Ch 19 § 4. Where a motion that the House resolve itself into the Committee of the Whole is pending, the motion that the Committee be discharged and that the bill be laid on the table is not preferential and not in order. Deschler Ch 19 § 4.13. The question of consideration may not be raised against the motion to resolve into the Committee, for the motion to resolve is itself a test of the will of the House on consideration. Deschler Ch 19 § 4.10.

A Member may withdraw a motion that the House resolve itself into the Committee of the Whole at any time before the motion is acted upon. Deschler Ch 19 § 4.11.

A motion to resolve into the Committee of the Whole to consider general appropriation bills and continuing appropriations after September 15 is privileged under clause 5 of rule XIII, if called up by direction of the Committee on Appropriations. *Manual* §§ 853, 856. The motion is neither debatable nor amendable (4 Hinds § 3078), is not subject to a demand for the previous question (4 Hinds § 3077), and may not be laid on the table or indefinitely postponed (6 Cannon § 726). Although highly privileged, the motion does not take precedence over a motion to reconsider or a motion to change the reference of a bill. 4 Hinds § 3087; 7 Cannon § 2124.

Former Practices

Prior to 1975 the use of the motion to consider revenue bills in the Committee of the Whole was of equal privilege, but there no longer is a privileged status for that motion. *Manual* § 856; Deschler Ch 19 § 4 (note 17).

Some procedures regarding consideration of business in the Committee of the Whole are seldom used in modern practice. After refusing to go into Committee of the Whole to consider a particular bill, the House may then consider business prescribed by the regular order. 4 Hinds § 3088. Thus, the House may reach legislation of lesser privilege by rejecting the motion to resolve into the Committee of the Whole to consider an appropriation bill. Deschler Ch 19 § 4.4. Nonprivileged matters are considered in the Committee of the Whole pursuant to a special order of business from the Committee on Rules or pursuant to a unanimous-consent request.

Under an earlier practice found in clause 4 of rule XVIII, the Committee of the Whole can determine its own order of business unless the House so determines, with general appropriation bills taking precedence.

§ 7. The Chair

The chair of the Committee of the Whole is appointed by the Speaker. *Manual* § 970. Following a custom of the British Parliament, the House requires the Speaker ''in all cases'' to leave the chair after appointing the chair of the Committee of the Whole. *Manual* § 970; Deschler Ch 19 § 5. Where the Member named by the Speaker to act as Chair is unavailable, the Speaker may ask another Member to assume the chair as acting Chair. Where the Member appointed to preside over the Committee of the Whole is female, the proper form of address is ''Madam Chair.'' Deschler Ch 19 § 5.3.

In general, the Chair recognizes for debate and decides questions of order arising in the Committee of the Whole independently of the Speaker. Deschler Ch 19 § 5.1. Where words are ''taken down'' in debate, the Chair reports them to the Speaker, who rules on their admissibility. Otherwise, points of order relating to procedure in the Committee of the Whole are decided by the Chair (*Manual* § 961; 5 Hinds § 6927; § 16, infra) and are subject to appeal (5 Hinds § 6928; Deschler Ch 19 § 9.1). In exceptional cases, the Committee of the Whole may rise and report the question to the House. 4 Hinds § 4783.

The Chair has a duty to enforce the rules of decorum in debate. 8 Cannon §§2515, 2520. Under clause 1 of rule XVIII, the Chair may cause the galleries or lobbies to be cleared in case of disturbance or disorderly conduct. *Manual* §971.

The Chair directs the Committee of the Whole to rise when the hour previously fixed for adjournment arrives, when the hour fixed by the House for termination of the consideration of the bill in Committee arrives, or when a rule provides for automatic rising after general debate. *Manual* §971.

§8. —Limitations on Jurisdiction and Authority of Chair

The functions of the chair of the Committee of the Whole are not unlimited; certain determinations are reserved to the Speaker, the House, or the Committee itself. *Manual* §971. Thus, the Chair does *not*:

- Decide whether the Committee may sit in executive session (reserved to the House). Deschler Ch 19 §7.18.
- Entertain unanimous-consent requests to materially alter an order of the House governing the consideration of a measure in the Committee of the Whole. *Manual* §993.
- Respond to inquiries concerning the legislative schedule outside the Committee of the Whole (97-2, July 29, 1982, p 18605); including whether or when a pending bill will be taken up again after the Committee rises (Deschler Ch 19 §§7.14, 7.15).
- Rule on procedural questions that may arise when a bill is reported back to the House (Deschler Ch 19 §7.10) or predict what action may take place in the House after the Committee of the Whole rises (Deschler Ch 19 §7.9).
- Consider a question that had arisen in the House just before the Committee began to sit. *Manual* §971.
- Interpret the application of a rule of the House that sets forth the vote required to adopt a resolution in the House. Deschler Ch 19 §7.13.
- Determine whether the House can rescind a time limitation imposed by the Committee. Deschler Ch 19 §7.12.
- Determine the privileges of a Member under general ''leave to print.'' 5 Hinds §6988.

For examples of limitations on the authority of the Committee of the Whole, see *Manual* §993; §2, supra. For the practice governing the Chair in deciding points of order and responding to parliamentary inquiries (both Speaker and chair of the Committee of the Whole), see POINTS OF ORDER; PARLIAMENTARY INQUIRIES; *Manual* §§628, 628a.

B. Consideration and Debate in Committee

§ 9. In General; Quorums

Generally

The conditions under which a particular measure is to be considered and debated are ordinarily determined pursuant to a special order of business from the Committee on Rules or other House order. The Committee of the Whole may not set aside or materially modify such an order, even by unanimous consent. *Manual* § 993.

Quorum Requirements

Until 1890 a quorum of the Committee of the Whole was the same as a quorum of the House. *Manual* § 329. In that year a rule was adopted fixing a quorum of the Committee of the Whole at 100 Members. *Manual* § 982. Where the Chair has announced the absence of a quorum in the Committee of the Whole, no further business may be conducted until a quorum is established. *Manual* § 982. When a vote is taken in Committee of the Whole notwithstanding the absence of a quorum, a timely point of order having been made, the vote is invalid. 6 Cannon §§ 676, 677. However, a quorum is inferred (or presumed) if no question is raised with respect thereto; that is, a quorum is presumed to be present unless otherwise determined. See 4 Hinds § 2895; 6 Cannon §§ 565, 624.

Under the modern practice, when a Committee of the Whole finds itself without a quorum and a timely point of order is made, the Chair directs that the Members record their presence by electronic device. *Manual* § 982. It is a quorum of the Committee of the Whole—100 Members—and not a quorum of the House that must appear. Deschler Ch 20 § 7.1. In ascertaining the presence of a quorum, the Chair includes those Members present but not voting as well as those voting. 6 Cannon §§ 641, 671; Deschler Ch 20 § 7.7.

Where, following a timely point of order, the Chair announces that a quorum is not present, a motion that the Committee of the Whole rise is in order and does not require a quorum for adoption. 8 Cannon § 2369; Deschler Ch 20 § 7.13. If a quorum develops on a negative vote on the motion to rise, the Committee of the Whole proceeds with its business. 6 Cannon §§ 670, 671; 8 Cannon § 2369. For a discussion of motions to rise generally, see §§ 26-28, infra.

Clause 6 of rule XVIII sharply limits the circumstances under which a point of order of no quorum may be raised once the House has resolved into Committee. After a quorum has been established in the Committee of the Whole on any given day (by quorum call or recorded vote), the Chair may not thereafter entertain a point of order that a quorum is not present unless (1) the Committee of the Whole is operating under the five-minute rule (which has been interpreted to include any ''modified-closed'' amendment process under the terms of a special order of business) and (2) the Chair has put the pending motion or proposition to a vote. *Manual* § 982. During general debate, there is no requirement of a quorum; but the Chair is given the discretion to recognize for a point of order of no quorum. Clause 6(b)(1) of rule XVIII.

The Chair must entertain a point of order of no quorum during the five-minute rule if a quorum has not yet been established in the Committee of the Whole on the bill then pending; the fact that a quorum of the Committee has previously been established on another bill on that day is irrelevant. *Manual* § 982. This precedent applies even when a measure is considered in the Committee of the Whole under a modified-closed rule that specifies the amendments that may be offered and establishes the time for their debate, such rule declaring the measure read for amendment under the five-minute rule. Where a recorded vote on a prior amendment or motion during the five-minute rule on that bill on that day has established a quorum, a subsequent point of order of no quorum during debate is precluded except by unanimous consent. *Manual* § 982.

§ 10. First Reading

When a bill is taken up in the Committee of the Whole, clause 5(a) of rule XVIII requires its reading in full before general debate begins, unless such reading has been properly dispensed with by unanimous consent or by a special order of business from the Committee on Rules. The first reading is normally dispensed with in this manner. *Manual* § 942. A motion to dispense with the first reading of the bill is not in order. 8 Cannon §§ 2335, 2436.

§ 11. General Debate

Control by the House

The duration and allocation of time for general debate in Committee of the Whole is controlled by the House, not the Committee. 91-2, Dec. 17, 1970, p 42222. The Committee may not, even by unanimous consent, extend the general debate time as fixed by the House. *Manual* §§ 979, 993.

The control of the House over general debate time in the Committee of the Whole may be exercised through a unanimous-consent request or through the adoption of a special order of business from the Committee on Rules. See, *e.g.*, Deschler-Brown Ch 29 §§ 76.1, 76.7. Where the House has divided general debate time among certain Members, it is not in order for a Member to whom time has been yielded to ask unanimous consent for additional time because time is controlled by those to whom it is allotted by the House and is not subject to extension by the Committee of the Whole. *Manual* § 979. However, time may be reallocated by unanimous consent among committees controlling debate time pursuant to an order of the House.

When the House has vested control of general debate in the Committee of the Whole in certain Members, their control may not be abrogated during that debate by another Member moving to rise, unless one of them yields for that purpose, nor may Members yielded time in general debate yield to another for such motion. *Manual* § 334.

The Hour Rule

In the absence of a House order limiting general debate in Committee of the Whole, debate in the Committee of the Whole is under the hour rule. A Member having control of such time may not consume more than one hour. *Manual* § 978.

Prior to 1841 there was no limit on the time that a Member might occupy when in possession of the floor in the Committee of the Whole. This practice hindered the ability of the Committee of the Whole to complete action on bills. 5 Hinds § 5221. In that year the rule of the House that no Member could speak for more than one hour was applied to the Committee of the Whole. *Manual* §§ 957, 978. This one-hour limitation applies to each Member recognized to speak in the Committee of the Whole. Deschler Ch 19 § 15. However, a Member recognized for one hour of debate may yield time to a Member who has just occupied an hour. 8 Cannon § 2470.

Yielding Time

Members managing general debate under the hour rule in Committee of the Whole may yield any portion of their time to another Member, who may in turn yield to a third Member while remaining standing. 8 Cannon § 2553. Of course, if the first Member retains control of the floor, yielding to a second Member only for a question, it is the first Member who would subsequently yield to a third. Deschler Ch 19 § 15. Conversely, where a matter is being debated pursuant to a special order of business vesting control of the time for debate in certain Members, one of those Members may yield a specific block of time to a second Member, in which case the second Member may yield to a third (although not a block of time) while remaining standing, and permission of the first Member is not necessary. Deschler Ch 19 § 15.

Members may speak in general debate on a bill as many times as they are yielded to by those in control of the debate. *Manual* § 959; Deschler Ch 19 § 15.8. Those in control of such debate time may yield as many times as they desire to whom they desire. Deschler Ch 19 § 15.4.

§ 12. — Closing General Debate

The right to close general debate inures to the majority manager of the primary committee who has opened. *Manual* § 979. General debate in Committee of the Whole is closed or terminated pursuant to an order of the House or sooner if no Member desires to participate further. *Manual* § 978; 4 Hinds § 4745; 5 Hinds § 5221. Amendments may not be offered in the Committee of the Whole until general debate has been closed or yielded back, and motions for the disposition of the pending bill are not in order before that time. 4 Hinds §§ 4744, 4778; 5 Hinds § 5221. However, those Members in control of the time for general debate need not use all of the time for the purpose prescribed by House order. Rather, they may agree among themselves to close further general debate, yield their remaining time, and allow consideration of the bill under the five-minute rule to begin. Deschler-Brown Ch 29 § 76.1.

For general discussion of the practice of limiting or closing general debate, see CONSIDERATION AND DEBATE.

§ 13. Debate Under the Five-minute Rule; Amendments

Generally

Amendments to measures pending in Committee of the Whole are in order following the close of general debate. Deschler Ch 19 § 15. Amendments are offered under the so-called five-minute rule. This rule provides that any Member "shall be allowed" five minutes to explain any amendment such Member may offer, after which the Member who first obtains the floor is allowed five minutes to oppose it. *Manual* §§ 978, 980. Thereafter, a Member may obtain five minutes for debate by offering a pro forma amendment "to strike the last word." No actual change in text is contemplated by the offering of such amendment. *Manual* § 981. For a discussion of pro forma amendments generally, see § 14, infra.

The Committee of the Whole may not, even by unanimous consent, prohibit the offering of an amendment otherwise in order under the five-minute rule. 98-2, July 31, 1984, p 21701. To guard against abuse of the rule by Members offering an amendment for the sole purpose of gaining debate time (5 Hinds § 5221), the rule also provides that amendments may be withdrawn only by unanimous consent. *Manual* § 978.

The five-minute rule is applicable to amendments that are offered to amendments. *Manual* § 978. However, where an amendment to a bill has been offered, the right to explain or oppose that amendment has precedence over a motion to amend it. 4 Hinds § 4751.

Under the modern practice of the House, bills increasingly are considered in the Committee of the Whole under a "modified-closed" amendment process. Such process vitiates, in part, the five-minute rule by considering the bill as having been read for amendment, restricting amendments that may be offered, and by limiting and controlling debate time on amendments made in order.

Limiting or closing five-minute debate, see CONSIDERATION AND DEBATE.

Yielding Time During Five-minute Debate

Members who have been recognized for debate under the five-minute rule may not yield time to another Member and then be seated. 100-1, Dec. 10, 1987, p 34686. Although Members recognized in debate under the rule may yield to other Members while remaining on their feet, they may not yield designated amounts of time. 5 Hinds §§ 5036, 5037; Deschler Ch 19 § 15. They may not yield to another Member to offer an amendment. 93-1, Dec. 14, 1973, p 41716; 94-2, Sept. 8, 1976, p 29243.

Where debate on an amendment is limited or allocated by a special order of business, or by the Chair, to a proponent and an opponent, the Members controlling the debate may yield and reserve time; but debate time on an amendment under the five-minute rule cannot be reserved. *Manual* § 980.

Reading for Amendment

In Committee of the Whole, bills are read for amendment by section pursuant to a practice dating from 1789, because each section normally contains a substantive legislative provision. *Manual* § 980. General appropriation bills, on the other hand, are ordinarily read by paragraphs, because such bills are normally drafted so that each paragraph contains an appropriation. However, whether a bill shall be read by paragraphs, sections, or titles is determined by unanimous consent or special order of business reported by the Committee on Rules, which may provide that the bill is to be "considered as read" and open to amendment at any point. Changing the reading cannot be accomplished by motion. *Manual* § 980; Deschler Ch 21 § 25.

When a paragraph or section has been passed in the reading, it is not in order to return thereto except by unanimous consent. *Manual* § 980. However, the Chair may direct a return to a section where, through inadvertence, no action was taken on a pending amendment. 4 Hinds §4750.

§14. —Pro Forma Amendments

Generally

Pro forma amendments have been permitted in the Committee of the Whole since at least as early as 1868, when they were used during the consideration of articles of impeachment against President Andrew Johnson. 5 Hinds §5778. Pro forma amendments are those offered during debate under the five-minute rule to make some ostensible change in a measure—by tradition "to strike the last word"—where the underlying purpose is to obtain time for debate or to offer an explanation, no actual change in the measure being contemplated. *Manual* §981; Deschler Ch 19 §15.

When in Order

Like substantive amendments, pro forma amendments are in order following the reading of a section or paragraph of the pending measure and are liberally permitted during debate under the five-minute rule. See AMENDMENTS. A Member who has expended five minutes on a pro forma amendment may not lengthen this time by making another pro forma amendment at that point in the reading. 5 Hinds §5222; 8 Cannon §2560; Deschler Ch 19 §15. A Member who has offered a substantive amendment and then debated it for five minutes may not extend the time by offering a pro forma amendment, as it is not in order to amend one's own amendment except by unanimous consent. *Manual* §981. Conversely, a Member recognized on a pro forma amendment may not automatically extend the time by offering a substantive amendment, not having been recognized for that purpose. Deschler Ch 19 §15.11.

Pro forma amendments are not in order when a bill is being considered under a "closed" or "modified-closed" rule prohibiting all amendments or permitting only certain amendments, unless the rule specifies to the contrary. Deschler-Brown Ch 29 §77.20. Similarly, the offering of a pro forma amendment requires unanimous consent after a substitute has been adopted and before the vote on the amendment, as amended, because the amendment has been amended in its entirety; and no further amendments, including pro forma amendments, are in order. *Manual* §981.

§15. Relevancy in Debate

Latitude in general debate is normally limited by a special order of business from the Committee on Rules or other order of the House, which routinely confines general debate to the subject of the measure. *Manual* § 948. Latitude in debate under the five-minute rule is limited by clause 5(a) of rule XVIII, which permits five minutes to ''explain'' an amendment and five minutes to speak ''in opposition'' to the amendment. *Manual* § 978. For a more thorough discussion of relevancy of debate in the Committee of the Whole, see CONSIDERATION AND DEBATE.

§ 16. Calling Members to Order

Jefferson suggested that, as a matter of parliamentary law, to avert the ''danger of a decision by the sword'' in the Committee of the Whole, the Speaker could take the Chair to restore order. *Manual* § 331. In several early instances, the Speaker did in fact exercise this authority. 2 Hinds §§ 1648-1652. Under the modern practice, the Chair directs the Committee of the Whole to rise and report to the House when objections have been made to words spoken in debate. *Manual* § 971; Cannon §§ 2533, 2538; Deschler Ch 19 § 17.

Under this procedure, a Member must be seated when called to order by the Chair. Deschler Ch 19 § 17.1. The Chair or any Member may cause the words to be taken down at the Clerk's desk and read in the Committee of the Whole, which then rises automatically without debate. 8 Cannon §§ 2533, 2538, 2539. The words are then reported to the House and are again read. 2 Hinds §§ 1257-1259. The words reported are then taken up in the House, with consideration being limited to the words reported. 8 Cannon § 2528. The Member uttering the words may withdraw them in the Committee of the Whole or in the House only by unanimous consent. 8 Cannon §§ 2528, 2538, 2540; Deschler Ch 19 § 17.7. If the words are not withdrawn, the Speaker rules on whether the words are unparliamentary (Deschler Ch 19 § 17.5), and such ruling is subject to appeal (*Manual* §§ 629, 961; 5 Hinds §§ 5157, 5178, 5194; Deschler-Brown Ch 29 § 50.8). Withdrawal of a demand that words be taken down is a matter of right and does not require unanimous consent.

If a Member's words are ruled out of order, motions in the House to strike unparliamentary words from the *Record* and to permit the offending Member to proceed in order are available before the Committee of the Whole resumes its sitting. Instances of disorder during debate in the Committee of the Whole may be disposed of in the House pursuant to a motion to expunge the offending language from the *Record* (8 Cannon §§ 2538, 2539) or, in especially flagrant instances, pursuant to a resolution of censure (2 Hinds §§ 1257, 1259). However, censure is not a remedy available for words spoken if debate or business has intervened. Clause 4(b) of rule XVII.

After disposition of the matter in the House, the Committee of the Whole automatically resumes its sitting. *Manual* § 961; 8 Cannon § 2541; Deschler Ch 19 § 17.5.

For general discussion of disorder in debate, see CONSIDERATION AND DEBATE.

§ 17. Voting

The methods and procedures by which Members vote in Committee of the Whole are prescribed by the rules of the House, particularly rule XX and clause 6 of rule XVIII. They include:

- *Voice vote*—Based on volume of sound of Members responding aye or no. Clause 6 of rule I; *Manual* § 630.
- *Division (or standing) vote*—May be invoked by the Chair or any Member, and is in order following a voice vote. Under this procedure, Members stand to be counted, first those voting in the affirmative, then those voting in the negative. Clause 1 of rule XX; *Manual* § 1012.
- *Recorded vote*—The Members insert a personalized electronic voting card to be recorded as "yea," "nay," or "present." The request for such a vote must be supported by at least 25 Members. A recorded vote may be preceded by a point of order of no quorum, which requires the Chair to first count for 100 Members. Clause 6 of rule XVIII; *Manual* §§ 982, 983. The Chair's count is not subject to challenge. *Manual* § 629.
- *Record vote by tellers or a "roll call"*—During a record vote by tellers, the Members cast their votes by depositing a signed green (yea) or red (no) card in a ballot box. Clause 4 of rule XX; *Manual* § 1019. During a "roll call" the Chair directs the Clerk to call the roll alphabetically. Clause 3 of rule XX; *Manual* § 1015. These procedures have been supplanted by the use of the electronic voting equipment and are used primarily as a backup voting system when that equipment becomes inoperative.

A vote by the yeas and nays, which may be demanded in the House under the Constitution or obtained automatically under clause 6 of rule XX, is not in order in Committee of the Whole. *Manual* §§ 76, 1026.

Under clause 6(g) of rule XVIII, the Chair may postpone a request for a recorded vote on any amendment; and may resume proceedings on that request at any time. An electronic vote ordered on the postponed request may be reduced to not less than two minutes, provided the first vote in a series is 15 minutes. *Manual* § 984.

For a discussion of voting procedures generally, see VOTING.

§ 18. Points of Order

Generally

In Committee of the Whole, questions of order relating to procedure (except for words taken down) are decided by the Chair, not the Speaker. *Manual* § 971; 5 Hinds §§ 6927, 6928; Deschler Ch 19 § 19. The Speaker cannot rule on a point of order arising in the Committee of the Whole unless the point of order is reported to the House for a decision. 5 Hinds § 6987. Appeals from a decision of the Chair on a point of order are ordinarily resolved in the Committee of the Whole, but in rare cases an appeal from a decision on a point of order may be reported to the House for its determination. 4 Hinds § 4783.

Debate on a point of order raised in the Committee of the Whole is within the discretion of the Chair and must be confined to the point of order. Deschler Ch 19 § 19.2.

When in Order

Generally, points of order in the Committee of the Whole against a provision in a bill or amendment are properly made when that provision or amendment is reached in the reading. For a discussion of points of order in the Committee of the Whole against provisions in general appropriation bills and amendments thereto, see *Manual* § 1044. A point of order against an amendment comes too late after there has been debate on the amendment (*Manual* § 924) or when the amendment has been reported to the House (92-2, June 1, 1972, pp 19479, 19483). However, clauses 4 and 5(a) of rule XXI permit the raising ''at any time'' of a point of order against a legislative bill carrying an appropriation or a tax or tariff if the bill was reported by a committee not having jurisdiction to report such matters. *Manual* §§ 1065, 1066; see also APPROPRIATIONS.

Points of order against consideration of bills are properly raised in the House pending resolution into the Committee and may not subsequently be raised in Committee of the Whole. Deschler Ch 19 § 20. This rule has been applied to points of order against consideration of the measure for:

- Violations of committee reporting requirements, such as the Ramseyer rule (that proposed changes in law be indicated typographically). *Manual* § 846; Deschler Ch 19 §§ 20.1-20.3.
- Availability requirements prior to floor consideration of measures. *Manual* § 850.

For points of order generally, see POINTS OF ORDER; PARLIAMENTARY INQUIRIES; for points of order relating to particular measures or matters, see

APPROPRIATIONS, BUDGET PROCESS, and CONFERENCES BETWEEN THE HOUSES.

§ 19. Unfinished Business

Business unfinished when the Committee of the Whole rises remains unfinished, to be considered first in order when the House next goes into the Committee to consider that business. 4 Hinds §§ 4735, 4736; see also UNFINISHED BUSINESS. Thus, when the Committee of the Whole rises before the time fixed for debate expires, debate continues when the Committee resumes its deliberations. Deschler Ch 19 § 26.1. When a recommendation of the Committee of the Whole that the enacting clause of a bill be stricken is rejected by the House, the House, without motion, resolves itself into the Committee for the further consideration of the bill. Deschler Ch 19 § 26.2.

Absent a special order of business to the contrary, when the Committee of the Whole rises on the adoption of a simple motion to rise, a bill pending at that time remains the unfinished business for subsequent consideration in the Committee. *Manual* § 977. Similarly, if such a motion intervenes pending a request for a recorded vote, that request remains the pending business upon resumption of consideration of the bill in Committee. Deschler-Brown Ch 30 § 33.15.

C. Motions in Committee

§ 20. In General

Motions Permitted

The principal motions used in Committee of the Whole are as follows:

- Motions to amend under the five-minute rule. *Manual* § 978; see also § 13, supra.
- Motions to close five-minute debate. *Manual* § 987; see also CONSIDERATION AND DEBATE.
- Motions relating to the enacting clause. *Manual* § 988; for a comprehensive discussion, see § 22, infra.
- Motions to rise. Deschler Ch 19 § 22; see also § 26, infra.

Motions Not Entertained

The Committee of the Whole may not entertain motions involving functions properly performed by the House. Of the motions specified by clause 4 of rule XVI—to adjourn, to lay on the table, for the previous question, to postpone, to refer, or to amend—only the motion to amend is authorized in the Committee of the Whole. *Manual* § 911. The Committee may not entertain a motion to:

- Limit general debate (as distinguished from five-minute debate). Deschler Ch 19 § 2; for a general discussion, see CONSIDERATION AND DEBATE.
- Close general debate. *Manual* § 979; 5 Hinds § 5217.
- Dispense with the reading of a bill unless authorized pursuant to a special order of business from the Committee on Rules. Deschler Ch 19 § 2.11.
- Return to a section of the bill passed in the reading. Deschler Ch 19 § 2.10.
- Effect a conference or instruct conferees. 8 Cannon §§ 2319, 2320; Deschler Ch 19 § 2.
- Order a call of the House. 8 Cannon § 2369.
- Expunge remarks from the *Record*. Deschler Ch 19 § 3.2.
- Order the previous question. 4 Hinds § 4716; Deschler Ch 19 § 2.6.
- Reconsider. 4 Hinds §§ 4716-4718; 8 Cannon §§ 2324, 2325; Deschler Ch 19 § 2.5.
- Recommit. 4 Hinds § 4721; 8 Cannon § 2326.
- Postpone or rise and resume sitting on a day certain. *Manual* § 915; Deschler Ch 19 § 22.2.
- Lay on the table. 4 Hinds §§ 4719, 4720; 8 Cannon § 2330; Deschler Ch 19 § 2.7.
- Recess (absent permission of the House). 5 Hinds §§ 6669-6671; 8 Cannon § 3357; Deschler Ch 19 § 2.
- Adjourn. Deschler Ch 19 § 2.4.

Motions Recommending House Action

As noted above, the motions to postpone, recommit, or lay on the table are not in order in the Committee of the Whole. However, under certain circumstances, the Committee of the Whole may entertain a motion to rise and report with the *recommendation* that the House entertain such an action. Whether such a motion will or will not lie in the Committee of the Whole is ordinarily determined by the terms of the special order of business under which the measure is being considered. Under the modern practice, a special order of business normally provides that after consideration the Committee of the Whole shall rise and report the measure to the House, with the previous question to be considered as ordered on the bill and amendments thereto to final passage. In that case, the Committee of the Whole may not report to the House a recommendation that the bill be recommitted. Deschler Ch 19 § 23.12. In the exceptional circumstance where this language is not included in the special order of business, the Committee of the Whole may entertain a motion to rise and report with:

- A recommendation that the consideration of the bill be postponed. 4 Hinds §§ 4765, 4774; 8 Cannon § 2372; Deschler Ch 19 § 22.
- A recommendation that the bill be referred or recommitted. 4 Hinds § 4774; Deschler Ch 19 § 23.12.
- A recommendation that the bill lie on the table. 4 Hinds § 4777.

Requirement That Motions Be Written

Although motions made in the Committee of the Whole are often put forward orally, any Member may demand that a motion be made in writing. See, *e.g.*, Deschler Ch 19 § 2.1.

Withdrawal

A motion may be withdrawn in the Committee of the Whole only by unanimous consent. Deschler Ch 23 § 2.10. Clause 5(a) of rule XVIII specifically prohibits the withdrawal of an amendment except by unanimous consent, whether or not debate has proceeded. 5 Hinds § 5221; 8 Cannon § 2859. This principle has also been applied to the motion to close debate under the five-minute rule (8 Cannon § 2564) and to the motion to recommend the striking of the enacting clause (98-1, July 29, 1983, p 21675).

§ 21. Precedence of Motions

Motions to Rise

The simple motion to rise is of highest privilege. *Manual* §§ 334, 983; Deschler Ch 19 §§ 23.1, 23.2. It takes precedence over motions to amend (*Manual* § 983; Hinds § 4770) and over amendments pending under the five-minute rule (Deschler Ch 19 § 23.3), though it may not interrupt other Members in debate (Deschler Ch 19 § 23.6; § 26, infra). The motion takes precedence over a demand for a recorded vote on a pending amendment (97-1, July 15, 1981, p 15921), and over a point of order of no quorum pending such a demand (see 95-1, Sept. 21, 1977, p 30126). The motion is in order pending the Chair's count of a quorum (Deschler Ch 19 § 23.5) and pending a decision of the Chair on a point of order (Deschler Ch 19 § 23.7). The simple motion to rise also takes precedence over a pending motion to rise and report with the recommendation that the enacting clause be stricken. Deschler Ch 19 § 23.13.

Motion Relating to the Enacting Clause

The motion that the Committee of the Whole rise and report to the House with the recommendation that the enacting clause be stricken is of high privilege. Deschler Ch 19 § 10.4. The motion is preferential because, if adopted, it constitutes a final disposition of the bill in the Committee of the Whole. Deschler Ch 19 § 11.11 (note). The motion may be offered where another Member seeks recognition to offer an amendment (Deschler-Brown Ch 29 § 12.13) or when an amendment is pending. However, the motion may not interrupt debate. *Manual* § 989. The motion also takes precedence over a motion to limit debate (*Manual* § 989) and over a motion to rise and report with a favorable recommendation (8 Cannon § 2620). See also § 22, infra.

Motions to Amend

With one exception, a motion to amend a bill takes precedence over a motion to rise and report the bill. 4 Hinds §§ 4752-4758; 8 Cannon § 2364; Deschler Ch 19 § 23.14. The exception is in clause 2(d) of rule XXI, which specifies that when a general appropriation bill has been read for amendment, a motion to rise and report, if offered by the Majority Leader or a designee, takes precedence over an amendment.

The initial right of the proponent to explain an amendment offered under the five-minute rule, or of a Member to rise in opposition thereto, takes precedence over a motion to amend that amendment. 4 Hinds § 4751.

§ 22. Motion Relating to Enacting Clauses

Generally; Effect of Rejection or Adoption

Every bill that becomes law contains the phrase: "Be it enacted by the Senate and House . . . in Congress assembled. . . ." It is in order to move that the Committee of the Whole rise and report a bill back to the House with the recommendation that this clause, known as the enacting clause, be stricken. 5 Hinds §§ 5326-5346; 8 Cannon §§ 2618-2638; Deschler Ch 19 § 10. Such a motion is not, strictly speaking, an amendment, because it can be dispositive of the entire bill. See Deschler Ch 19 § 10 (note 13). If the House agrees to the recommendation, its action is equivalent to a rejection of the bill. *Manual* § 988; 5 Hinds § 5326; Deschler Ch 19 § 10.6. If the House rejects the recommendation, it automatically resolves itself back into the Committee of the Whole for the further consideration of the bill. Deschler Ch 19 § 10.9.

The motion must be in writing and in the proper form. *Manual* § 988.

> MEMBER: I move that the Committee of the Whole do now rise and report the bill to the House with the recommendation that the enacting clause (or the resolving clause) be stricken. Deschler Ch 19 § 10.2.

Motions that deviate from this form are subject to a point of order. Deschler Ch 19 § 10.3. Thus, a simple motion to strike the enacting clause, although at one time permitted in the Committee of the Whole, is, under the modern practice, not in proper form and not in order. 5 Hinds § 5332; Deschler Ch 19 § 10.1. A motion to strike ''all after the enacting clause'' is likewise out of order. Deschler Ch 19 § 10.3. The recommendation that the enacting clause be stricken may not be combined with a provision that the bill be recommitted to a committee. Deschler Ch 19 § 10.10.

Application to Particular Measures

The motion that the Committee of the Whole rise and report to the House the recommendation that the enacting clause be stricken is also applicable to the enacting clause of a Senate-passed bill. Deschler Ch 19 § 10.14. The motion has also been used to recommend the striking of the resolving clause of a simple resolution (Deschler Ch 19 § 11.10), the resolving clause of a concurrent resolution on the budget (96-1, May 9, 1979, p 10490), and the resolving clause of a joint resolution (Deschler Ch 19 § 11.4).

Who May Offer or Oppose

A Member offering the motion to rise and report with the recommendation that the enacting clause be stricken must qualify as being opposed to the bill when challenged. A Member in favor of the bill may not offer the motion. *Manual* § 989; Deschler Ch 19 § 12.2. A challenge being made by another Member, the Member offering the motion must declare opposition to the bill. Deschler Ch 19 § 12.1. Generally, in recognizing a Member for the motion, the Chair will accept the statement that such Member is opposed to the bill. Deschler Ch 19 § 12.5. Similar rules are applied with respect to the qualification of a Member to oppose the motion. To obtain recognition to oppose the motion, a Member must qualify by stating opposition thereto. Deschler Ch 19 § 12.11.

The practice of offering the motion merely to obtain time for debate, though subject to criticism, has been permitted. Deschler Ch 19 §§ 12.8-12.10. In fact, under the modern practice, extending debate is usually the intent of the offeror, who then withdraws the motion by unanimous consent.

Repetition of Motion

A second motion on the same day to recommend the striking of the enacting clause is not entertained in the absence of any material modification of the bill. 8 Cannon § 2636; Deschler Ch 19 §§ 14.1, 14.2. Thus, a second motion is in order if the bill has been amended since disposition of the first motion (Deschler Ch 19 § 14.4) but is not in order if the only action of the

Committee of the Whole in the interim has been the rejection of a proposed amendment to the bill (Deschler Ch 19 § 14.5). If the first such motion is withdrawn by unanimous consent, a second motion relating to the enacting clause is in order. *Manual* § 989; Deschler Ch 19 § 14.7. The motion may be renewed on a subsequent day regardless of any modification of the bill. Deschler Ch 19 § 14.8.

§ 23. — When in Order

The motion that the Committee of the Whole rise and report with the recommendation that the enacting clause be stricken is not in order during general debate on the measure. Deschler Ch 19 § 10. The motion is in order only after the Clerk has begun reading the bill for amendment under the five-minute rule (Deschler Ch 19 § 11.2), assuming that another Member has not obtained the floor for purposes of debate (96-1, June 13, 1979, p 14710). The motion is no longer in order when the stage of amendment is passed. The stage of amendment is passed in Committee where a bill is being considered under a rule permitting only committee amendments, and where no committee amendments are offered at the conclusion of general debate. *Manual* § 989. The adoption of an amendment in the nature of a substitute also may foreclose the opportunity to offer the motion. Deschler Ch 19 § 11.6.

§ 24. — Debate

Generally; Time Limitations

The debate on a motion that the Committee of the Whole rise and report with the recommendation that the enacting clause be stricken is governed by the five-minute rule. 5 Hinds §§ 5333-5335; 8 Cannon §§ 2628-2631; Deschler Ch 19 § 13. Debate on the motion is thus limited to 10 minutes, five minutes in favor and five minutes in opposition. Deschler Ch 19 § 13.1. The Chair has declined to recognize for requests to extend the five minutes (Deschler Ch 19 § 13.2), and a Member may not merge the time with time made available to debate the remainder of the bill and amendments thereto (Deschler-Brown Ch 29 § 31.33). Debate is limited to two five-minute speeches even though the proponent and the Member in opposition both speak in favor of the motion. Deschler Ch 19 § 13.3. The Chair will not announce in advance who will be recognized in opposition to the motion. *Manual* § 989.

Time may not be reserved. Where a Member recognized for five minutes in opposition to the motion yields back the time, another Member may not claim the unused portion thereof. *Manual* § 989.

Members of the committee managing the bill have priority in recognition for debate in opposition to the motion. *Manual* § 989.

Effect of Limitation of Time for Debate

A limitation of all debate time on a bill and amendments thereto to a time certain does not preclude debate on a motion to recommend the striking of the enacting clause during the time remaining under the limitation. 97-1, Oct. 5, 1981, p 23154. However, the motion is not debatable after all time for debate on the bill and all amendments thereto has expired. Deschler Ch 19 § 13.7. On the other hand, where debate has been closed only as to amendments to a bill, and not on the bill itself, a Member offering the motion to strike the enacting clause is entitled to five minutes to debate that motion. Deschler-Brown Ch 29 § 6.28. A similar practice is followed where the limitation is only on an amendment in the nature of a substitute being read as an original bill for the purpose of amendment under a special order of business. *Manual* § 989.

Scope of Debate

Since the motion to rise and report with the recommendation that the enacting clause be stricken applies to the entire bill, debate may be directed to any part of the bill—or to a pending amendment—and need not be confined to the merits of the preferential motion. Deschler-Brown Ch 29 § 37.11. Thus, the motion may be used by a Member to secure five minutes to debate a pending amendment notwithstanding a limitation of time for debate on the pending amendment and all amendments thereto. Deschler-Brown Ch 29 § 37.8. However, debate on the motion may not include matters beyond the provisions of the bill. 5 Hinds § 5336.

D. Rising; Reporting to the House

§ 25. Generally

Formal and Informal Rising Distinguished

When the Committee of the Whole terminates or suspends its proceedings, it ''rises,'' either formally or informally. Deschler Ch 19 § 21.1. When the Committee of the Whole rises formally, it normally does so by motion or by operation of a special order of business. § 26, infra. When the Committee of the Whole rises informally, it does so by unanimous consent (4 Hinds § 4788) or simply at the direction of the Chair without a formal motion from the floor (Deschler Ch 19 § 21.1).

The Committee of the Whole may rise informally to permit the House to transact administrative business, such as to swear in a Member, to receive a message, or to lay down a signed enrolled bill. *Manual* § 330; Deschler Ch 19 § 21.1. Having no power to receive a message, the Committee of the Whole rises informally to permit the House to do so. *Manual* § 330; 4 Hinds § 4786. At this rising, the House may not have the message read or transact other business except by unanimous consent. 4 Hinds §§ 4787-4791.

Effect of Special Orders of Business

The Committee of the Whole rises automatically and without motion when it rises pursuant to a special order of business providing that at the conclusion of consideration of the bill for amendment the Committee of the Whole ''shall'' rise and report back to the House (94-1, July 30, 1975, p 25881) or pursuant to a House order limiting general debate to a time certain and providing that the Committee rise at the conclusion of that time (Deschler Ch 19 § 21.3). However, a motion to rise is required to enable the Committee of the Whole to rise prior to the time fixed by the applicable special order of business. 7 Cannon § 793.

Beginning in the 110th Congress, opening-day rules packages have included separate orders establishing a point of order against the motion to rise and report if the bill under consideration exceeds certain budgetary allocations. 112-1, H. Res. 5, Jan. 5, 2011, p ____.

§ 26. Motions to Rise

Generally; Forms

In the Committee of the Whole, the motion takes two forms: (1) the simple motion to rise and (2) the motion to rise and report. 4 Hinds §§ 4766, 4767; Deschler Ch 19 §§ 22.1, 23.13. The motions are expressed as follows:

M__. Chair, I move that the Committee do now rise.

M__. Chair, I move that the Committee do now rise and report the bill back to the House with the recommendation that __________.

The motion to rise and report may recommend to the House either a favorable or adverse disposition of the bill. It may recommend that the consideration of the reported measure be postponed, or that it be recommitted or tabled. However, under the modern practice, such motion is normally precluded by the applicable special order of business. § 20, supra. For the motion to rise and report with the recommendation that the enacting clause be stricken, see § 22, supra. For reporting amendments, see § 30, supra.

The simple motion to rise in the Committee of the Whole is analogous to the motion to adjourn in the House. The motion to rise (or to rise and report) must be in writing if the demand is made. Deschler Ch 19 §22.3. The simple motion to rise does not require a quorum for adoption, although a negative voice vote is subject to a point of order of no quorum pending a request for a recorded vote. *Manual* §983; 4 Hinds §§2975, 2976; Deschler Ch 19 §22.7. However, a quorum is required on an affirmative vote on a motion to rise and report. See 4 Hinds §2973. Neither motion is debatable. 4 Hinds §§4766-4768; Deschler Ch 19 §22.4. Either may be withdrawn by unanimous consent. Deschler Ch 19 §22.9. They may not include restrictions on the amendment process or limitations on future debate on amendments. *Manual* §334.

§27. —When in Order

The motion that the Committee of the Whole rise is privileged during debate under the five-minute rule. *Manual* §334. The motion is in order notwithstanding an informal agreement among the floor managers of a bill to conclude consideration at a different time. Deschler Ch 19 §23.4. The motion is in order:

- While an amendment is pending, except where another Member has the floor. *Manual* §334.
- Pending a decision on a point of order. Deschler Ch 19 §§23.7, 23.8.
- After agreement to a motion to limit debate on an amendment. Deschler Ch 19 §23.10.
- Pending a count of a quorum. Deschler Ch 19 §23.5.
- After the absence of a quorum has been ascertained and pending a vote on an amendment (*Manual* §982) but comes too late when the Chair has announced the absence of a quorum and the roll call has begun (91-2, Sept. 16, 1970, p 32229).
- Pending a demand for a record vote but prior to the time the Chair begins the count to determine whether a sufficient number support the demand. 94-1, Aug. 1, 1975, p 26947.
- During general debate if offered by a manager or by a Member to whom a manager has yielded for that purpose. *Manual* §334.

A motion that the Committee of the Whole rise may be made between the time an amendment is offered and read and before recognition of its proponent for debate thereon. 97-1, May 12, 1981, pp 9320, 9323. Where a special order of business provides that the Committee rise and report at the conclusion of the consideration of a bill for amendment, a motion that the Committee of the Whole rise and report the bill with certain amendments, before the bill has been completely read for amendment, is not in order. However, a simple motion that the Committee of the Whole rise is in order at that time. 96-1, Dec. 5, 1979, p 34755.

§ 28. — Who May Offer

In the Committee of the Whole, any Member may move to rise and the Chair is constrained to recognize for that purpose, unless another Member controls the floor. Deschler Ch 19 § 24.2; 8 Cannon § 2369. Although the motion may be offered by any Member entitled to the floor, the motion is commonly made by the Member managing the bill before the Committee. Deschler Ch 19 §§ 22.5, 22.8, 23.1. The motion also may be made by a Member who holds the floor by virtue of having offered an amendment, but such Member must yield back before offering the motion. Deschler Ch 19 § 24.1.

A Member recognized by the Chair may not be interrupted by a motion to rise even though such Member has not yet begun to speak. 8 Cannon § 2370. Members may not, in time yielded to them for debate, move that the Committee of the Whole rise (Deschler Ch 19 § 10) or yield to another Member for such a motion (Deschler Ch 29 § 23). However, a Member controlling the time for general debate may yield for a motion that the Committee of the Whole rise, and may do so without losing the right to continue at the next sitting of the Committee on the same matter. 5 Hinds §§ 5012, 5013.

For precedence of a motion to rise and report a general appropriation bill, if offered by the Majority Leader, over an amendment, see § 21, supra.

§ 29. Reporting to the House

Generally

When a matter is concluded in the Committee of the Whole, it is reported to the House. The permission of the House is neither required nor sought when the Chair reports on a measure. The report is made and received and is then before the House for action. *Manual* § 334. When the Committee of the Whole rises without concluding the matter, the Chair reports that it "has come to no resolution thereon." Under this procedure the Chair does not report the measure back to the House. Deschler Ch 19 § 21.4. The measure remains as unfinished business for subsequent consideration in the Committee of the Whole. § 19, supra.

The Speaker recognizes only reports from the Committee of the Whole made by the Chair thereof. 5 Hinds § 6987. The Speaker has no official knowledge of proceedings in the Committee of the Whole beyond those reported by its Chair. A matter alleged to have arisen therein but not reported may not be brought to the attention of the House. 8 Cannon §§ 2429, 2430.

§30. House Action on Committee Reports

Generally

When the Committee of the Whole reports to the House, the House usually acts at once on the report without reference to select or other committees. *Manual* §326. The recommendation of the Committee being before the House, the motion to carry out the recommendation is usually considered as pending without being offered from the floor. 4 Hinds §4896.

The recommendation of the Committee of the Whole may be favorable or adverse, and the bill may be reported with or without amendments:

> CHAIR: M__. Speaker, the Committee of the Whole House on the state of the Union, having had under consideration the bill H.R. ______, directs me to report it back to the House with sundry amendments and with the recommendation that the amendments be agreed to and the bill as amended do pass.
>
> SPEAKER: The chair of the Committee of the Whole reports that the Committee of the Whole House on the state of the Union, having had under consideration the bill H.R. ______, directs him/her to report . . . .

For House action on amendments reported from the Committee of the Whole, including the demand for separate votes, see AMENDMENTS. For steps to be taken in the passage of a bill in the House, see PREVIOUS QUESTION and READING, PASSAGE, AND ENACTMENT.

Recommittal to the Committee of the Whole

Bills are sometimes recommitted to the Committee of the Whole as the result of the action of the House (4 Hinds §4784) or on motion either with or without instructions (5 Hinds §§5552, 5553). If the bill is reported from the Committee of the Whole with an adverse recommendation, and such recommendation is disagreed to by the House, the bill stands recommitted to the Committee without further action by the House, unless the bill is disposed of pursuant to a motion to refer. *Manual* §988. When a recommendation of the Committee of the Whole that the enacting clause of a bill be stricken is rejected by the House, the House, without motion, resolves itself into the Committee of the Whole for the further consideration of the bill. *Manual* §989; 7 Cannon §943.

Chapter 13
Conferences Between the Houses

Research References
5 Hinds §§ 6254-6589
8 Cannon §§ 3209-3332
Deschler-Brown Ch 33
Manual §§ 530-559, 637, 1069-1094

I. Generally

§ 1. In General; Purpose

Before a measure can become law, both Houses must agree to the same bill—either a House bill or a Senate bill—and they must agree on each provision of the bill. 5 Hinds §§ 6233-6240. Although the two Houses may pass similar measures on the same subject, neither can become law unless both Houses pass the same numbered bill with identical text. 4 Hinds § 3386.

In many cases disagreements between the House and Senate over the provisions in a bill can be resolved through amendments that are messaged between the Houses. Such action is taken in the expectation that one House will eventually concur (or recede and concur) with the amendments of the other House and thereby finally pass the bill. See SENATE BILLS; AMENDMENTS BETWEEN THE HOUSES. Another approach aimed at reconciling differences is a conference committee, consisting of managers from each Chamber, with authority to report on negotiated agreements. Sometimes these procedures are pursued simultaneously: one House will (1) concur as to certain amendments and (2) insist on disagreement as to other amendments and request a conference thereon. 5 Hinds §§ 6287, 6401. If a conference fails to reconcile the differences, and reports this fact back to the two Houses, motions to dispose of any amendments remaining in disagreement are permitted. §§ 36-38, infra.

The request for a conference is made by the House in possession of the papers. § 4, infra. The House receiving the request may agree to the conference or it may disregard the request and act on the pending unresolved amendments. 5 Hinds §§ 6313-6315. In the latter case it may simply concur in the amendments or recede from disagreement, thereby rendering a conference unnecessary if no further issues remain to be disposed of between the Houses. 5 Hinds §§ 6316-6318. It also has the option of postponing action on the request to a time certain or indefinitely. 5 Hinds § 6199.

§ 2. Questions Sent to Conference

It was Jefferson's view that a House-Senate conference may be sought "in all cases of difference of opinion between the two Houses on matters depending between them." *Manual* § 530. Conferences between the two Houses are usually held over differences as to amendments to a particular bill. 5 Hinds § 6254. On occasion, several bills have been sent to conference by a single House action. Deschler Ch 21 § 27.6. Differences over a joint or concurrent resolution also may be sent to conference. 5 Hinds §§ 6258, 7063.

House-Senate conferences have sometimes been sought to resolve questions unrelated to any pending bill or other legislative proposition. Conference committees have on rare occasions been used to resolve differences as to:

- The prerogatives of the two Houses in the origination of revenue measures. 2 Hinds § 1487.
- The instructions given by one House to its managers. 5 Hinds § 6401.
- The procedures to be followed in an impeachment proceeding. 3 Hinds § 2304.
- The time for the convening of the next session of Congress. 5 Hinds § 6255.
- Papers in the nature of petitions. 5 Hinds § 6263.

§ 3. Sending to Conference

Generally; By Unanimous Consent

Amendments in disagreement between the Houses may be sent to conference by unanimous consent. The disagreement may relate to a Senate amendment or to an insistence by the House on its own amendment. *Manual* § 533; 6 Cannon § 732.

> MEMBER: M__. Speaker, I ask unanimous consent to take from the Speaker's table the bill H.R. ______, with the Senate amendment[s] thereto, disagree to the Senate amendment[s], and [ask for a conference with the Senate] [agree to a conference asked by the Senate] on the disagreeing votes of the two Houses.

By Motion

A matter may be sent to conference pursuant to a motion offered under clause 1 of rule XXII. The motion is privileged in the discretion of the Speaker if the motion is offered by direction of the primary committee and of all reporting committees that had initial referral of the measure. *Manual* §§ 1069, 1070. This restraint is intended to prevent the use of that motion as a dilatory tactic. *Manual* § 535. The motion may be offered only while the House is in possession of the papers.

Initial Senate amendments may be taken from the Speaker's table and sent to conference by motion under this rule. *Manual* §§ 533, 1069, 1070. The motion permitted by the rule also may be raised at subsequent stages of the amendment process between the Houses and may include a motion to disagree to a Senate amendment to a House amendment to a Senate bill and request a conference (92-2, Mar. 8, 1972, p 7540) or a motion to insist on a House amendment to a Senate amendment to a House bill and request a conference (*Manual* § 1070).

A Member offering a motion to send a bill to conference under this rule is recognized for one hour and is in control of the debate on the motion. Deschler-Brown Ch 33 § 2.14. When the previous question is ordered on the motion, further debate may occur only by unanimous consent. Deschler-Brown Ch 33 § 2.15.

Clause 1 of rule XXII requires a separate committee authorization with respect to each particular bill to be sent to conference. Clause 2(a)(3) of rule XI allows committees to adopt a committee rule authorizing the chair of the committee to offer a motion under clause 1 of rule XXII whenever the chair considers is appropriate. Where a measure has been reported by two or more committees of initial referral, each reporting committee must authorize the motion sending it to conference. A committee receiving sequential referral of a bill or not reporting thereon need not authorize the motion. On a Senate bill with a House amendment consisting of the text of two corresponding House bills that were previously reported to the House, the motion must be authorized by the committees reporting those corresponding bills. *Manual* § 1070. The primary committee of jurisdiction may authorize the motion on an unreported measure. 106-2, Oct. 11, 2000, p 22250.

Motions to send a measure to conference pursuant to clause 1 of rule XXII are generally made by the chair of the legislative committee with primary jurisdiction over the measure, acting by direction of that committee as follows:

> MEMBER: M__. Speaker, pursuant to clause 1 of rule XXII and by direction of the Committee on __________, I move to take from the Speaker's table the bill (H.R.______) with the Senate amendment[s] thereto, disagree with the Senate amendment[s] and agree to the conference requested by the Senate [or request a conference with the Senate thereon].
>
> MEMBER: M__. Speaker, pursuant to clause 1 of rule XXII and by direction of the Committee on __________, I move to take from the Speaker's table the bill (S.______) with the House amendment[s] thereto, insist on the House amendment[s] and agree to the conference requested by the Senate [or request a conference with the Senate thereon].

A motion to send a bill to conference may not be amended to include instructions to House managers; instructions are properly offered by separate motion following the adoption of the motion to go to conference and before managers are appointed. Deschler-Brown Ch 33 § 2.18. For a discussion of motions to instruct, see § 11, infra.

§ 4. — When in Order; Stage of Disagreement

Generally

Under the former practice, it was customary to allow the House insisting on its amendment (the other House having disagreed thereto) to request a conference. 5 Hinds §§ 6278-6280. Under the modern practice, a conference may be requested as soon as one House has either disagreed to an amendment of the other or has insisted on its own amendment. 5 Hinds §§ 6273-6277. In any event, the request for a conference must always be by the House that is in possession of the papers. *Manual* § 530. For a discussion on when the stage of disagreement is reached, see SENATE BILLS; AMENDMENTS BETWEEN THE HOUSES, § 16.

Motions

A motion to disagree or insist and request a conference is in order before, or after (subject to preferential motions), the Houses have reached the stage of disagreement if made pursuant to clause 1 of rule XXII. *Manual* §§ 528, 535, 1070; see also SENATE BILLS; AMENDMENTS BETWEEN THE HOUSES.

Once a motion to request a conference has been rejected, its repetition at the same stage of the proceedings has not been permitted where no other motion to dispose of the matter in disagreement has been considered. 5 Hinds § 6325. However, a motion under clause 1 of rule XXII may be repeated, if authorized by the committee concerned, and if the Speaker again agrees to recognize for that purpose, even though the House has once rejected a motion to send the same matter to conference. *Manual* §§ 535, 1070.

Unanimous-consent Requests

A unanimous-consent request to seek a conference is in order even though the House and Senate have not yet reached the stage of disagreement. Indeed, there have been rare instances where the House by unanimous consent has ''deemed'' a House bill with *possible* Senate amendments sent to conference before Senate passage of the bill with amendment, effective when subsequently in possession of the papers, in order to permit managers to be appointed and to formally meet if the House is not in session. See, *e.g.*, 105-2, Apr. 1, 1998, p 5735.

§ 5. Effect of Special Orders of Business

Amendments may be sent to conference pursuant to a special order of business from the Committee on Rules. 4 Hinds §§ 3242-3249. The special order of business may or may not preclude intervening motions, and may direct the Speaker to appoint the managers. 4 Hinds § 3242. The special order of business may:

- Take a House bill with Senate amendments from the Speaker's table and send it directly to conference. 7 Cannon § 826.
- Make in order a motion to take a bill with Senate amendments from the Speaker's table, disagree to the amendments, and request a conference. 7 Cannon § 822.
- Deem a Senate bill amended with House text and a conference requested thereon, upon passage of House text and receipt of Senate bill, and authorizing the appointment of conferees before the motion to instruct. 108-2, Oct. 7, 2004, 21723.
- Provide for consideration of Senate amendments and for a motion to agree to a conference, and for appointment without instructions to the managers. 4 Hinds §§ 3243, 3244.

- Discharge a committee from consideration of a bill with Senate amendments and ask for, or agree to, a conference thereon. 7 Cannon §§820, 821.

II. Conference Managers

§6. In General; Appointment of Managers

Generally

Appointments of Members to serve as managers on the part of the House at a conference are made by the Speaker pursuant to clause 11 of rule I. *Manual* §637. The terms ''manager'' and ''conferee'' are used synonymously in the modern precedents and are so used in this chapter. Clause 11 of rule I contains guidelines for the Speaker to observe when appointing conferees. Conferees should include:

- A majority of Members who generally supported the House position, as determined by the Speaker.
- Members who are primarily responsible for the legislation.
- To the fullest extent feasible, Members who were the principal proponents of the major provisions of the bill as it passed the House.

These guidelines permit the exercise of broad discretion by the Speaker in making appointments. *Manual* §637. The Speaker may specify the legislative issues on which individual managers are to confer. *Manual* §536.

Number of Managers

In the early practice of the House, three Members were usually appointed to a conference by the Speaker. 5 Hinds §6336. Today, the number of Members to be designated is at the discretion of the Speaker, and the complexity of the bill and the number of committees with jurisdiction may be considered. 8 Cannon §3221. A motion to instruct the Speaker as to the number of managers to be appointed is not in order. *Manual* §637; 8 Cannon §3221.

Conference agreements are reached when a majority of House managers agree with a majority of Senate managers, which is indicated by their signing of the conference report. The number of managers appointed by the Senate does not affect the Speaker's determination as to the number of House managers because the managers of one House vote separately from those of the other. 5 Hinds §6334. For a discussion of conference meetings, see §10, infra.

Time of Appointment

Conferees are usually appointed by the Speaker immediately after the request for a conference is granted, but they may be appointed at a subsequent time. In one instance, the Speaker did not announce his appointment of conferees until the second session on a bill on which the House had requested a conference in the first session. Deschler-Brown Ch 33 § 6.17.

§ 7. Committee Representation

The Speaker in making appointments to a conference normally consults with the chair of the committee having jurisdiction over the bill. Members of that committee are ordinarily designated as managers. Deschler-Brown Ch 33 § 6.1. The Speaker may make such appointments without regard to committee seniority. 99-2, July 16, 1986, p 16705. On a comprehensive matter, the Speaker may appoint separate groups of conferees from several committees for consideration of provisions within their respective jurisdictions. *Manual* § 637.

The Speaker may appoint members from a nonreporting committee as conferees on a provision in a Senate measure within that committee's jurisdiction. *Manual* § 637. The Speaker may, after appointing general conferees from a reporting committee on all Senate provisions, appoint additional conferees from an additional reporting or nonreporting committee on a specified section. 107-2, Mar. 7, 2002, p 2747.

In the current practice, the Speaker has announced a policy of simplifying conference appointments by noting on the occasion of a relatively complex appointment that, inasmuch as conference committees are select committees that dissolve when their report is acted upon, conference appointments should not be construed as jurisdictional precedent. *Manual* § 637.

§ 8. Changing or Adding Managers; Removal or Resignation

At any time after the appointment of a conference committee, the Speaker may remove a conferee or appoint additional conferees. Clause 11 of rule I; 5 Hinds §§ 6341-6368. In making additional appointments, the Speaker may specify that a conferee be authorized to act only with respect to a certain provision (96-1, Aug. 2, 1979, p 22101), or that additional conferees from certain committees act solely on matters within those committees' jurisdictions (99-1, Oct. 24, 1985, p 28743). Under clause 11, the Speaker may supplement an appointment of conferees by modifying the array of separate panels and by further specifying the subject matter to be considered by such panels. Deschler-Brown Ch 33 § 8.7.

Vacancies on a conference committee are filled through appointment by the Speaker. 5 Hinds § 6372; 8 Cannon § 3228. The Speaker may appoint a conferee to fill a vacancy caused by death or ill health, resignation, or removal. Deschler-Brown Ch 33 §§ 8.3, 8.8. The Speaker may appoint the successor conferee with all or part of the authority of the original conferee. 98-2, Mar. 21, 1984, p 6249.

Usually a conferee resigns by sending a letter of resignation to the Speaker. The letter is laid before the House. A conferee may be excused by unanimous consent at the request of another Member, particularly where time is of the essence. Deschler-Brown Ch 33 § 8.2.

Managers have resigned from conference committees because of policy differences with other managers. In one instance, a Member declared that his resignation was based on the fact that other House conferees had agreed to a motion in conference limiting their participation to specified portions of the matters committed to conference, though originally all Members had been appointed without restriction. The Member's resignation was accepted by unanimous consent. Deschler-Brown Ch 33 § 8.10.

Under clause 11 of rule I, conferees may be removed from a conference committee by the Speaker. Before the adoption of that rule, conferees were removed only by action of the House by unanimous consent. Deschler-Brown Ch 33 § 8.1.

In the modern practice of the House, a bill is normally sent only to a single conference. However, in earlier years, several conferences were sometimes held on the same bill, and it was common to change managers at each conference. 5 Hinds §§ 6288-6291, 6324. So fixed was this practice that their reappointment had a special significance, indicating an unyielding temper. 5 Hinds §§ 6352-6368. However, later practice was to reappoint the same managers (5 Hinds §§ 6341-6344) unless a change was necessary to enable the sentiment of the House to be represented (5 Hinds § 6369). For motions to discharge and appoint new conferees, see § 14, infra.

§ 9. Power and Discretion of Managers

Generally

There are limitations on the authority of the managers with respect to the legislative matters they may address. The managers:

- May not change text that has already been agreed to by both Houses. 5 Hinds §§ 6417, 6418, 6420.
- May not address new items or a new subject not committed to the conference. 5 Hinds §§ 6407, 6408; 8 Cannon §§ 3254, 3255; 107-2, Nov. 14, 2002, p 22408.

- Must confine themselves to matters that are within the scope of the difference between the House position and the Senate position. *Manual* § 1088.

These limitations stem from the fundamental principle that when a bill is sent to conference, matters in disagreement between the Houses—and only matters in disagreement between the Houses—are before the conferees. *Manual* § 1088. A matter not within the scope of the differences committed to the conference lies beyond the authority of the managers even though germane to the question at issue. 5 Hinds § 6419.

Clause 9 of rule XXII permits managers to propose a substitute that is a "germane modification" of the matter in disagreement but proscribes the presentation of "specific additional" matter not committed to conference. Clause 9 further prohibits the report of the managers from including matter not committed to the conference by either House or a modification of any specific matter committed to the conference if that modification is beyond the scope thereof. *Manual* § 1088. For a discussion of points of order against the report, see § 22, infra; for the use of special orders of business to waive the point of order for exceeding "scope," see § 28, infra.

Differences as to Time Periods

When the two Houses fix different periods of time for certain legislative action, the conferees have latitude to compromise only between the two time frames, and may not exceed the longer or go below the shorter. 8 Cannon § 3264. Likewise, where the Senate has amended a House-passed bill to change the effective date therein, the authority of the conferees on the bill is limited to the time frame between the dates in each version. Where the dates contained in both versions have since passed, the conferees may report the Senate amendment back in technical disagreement so that the effective date can be reconsidered. Deschler-Brown Ch 33 § 7.12.

Differences as to Numbers or Amounts

Where the legislative differences between the two Houses on a measure involve numerical figures, managers at conference are limited to the range between the highest figure proposed by one House and the lowest proposed by the other. If, for example, the House proposes a tariff rate of 30% for a certain product and the Senate proposes a 35% tariff, the managers may agree on 30% or 35% or any tariff falling within that range; but they may not agree on a tariff that is less than 30% or more than 35%. 8 Cannon § 3263. Similarly, where sections of a conference report contain higher entitlements for certain veterans' benefits than those contained in either the House bill or in the Senate amendment, the conferees may be held to have exceeded their authority. Deschler-Brown Ch 33 § 7.7. By the same token, conferees may report back in total disagreement where the informal decisions reached by the conferees would have exceeded the scope of the differences committed to conference by reducing certain aggregate totals below those in either the House or the Senate version. 95-1, Sept. 13, 1977, p 29021.

Amendments to Existing Law

Where one House has amended an existing law and the other House has implicitly taken the position of existing law by remaining silent on the subject, the scope of differences committed to conference lies between those issues presented in the amending language on the one hand and the comparable provisions of existing law on the other. 95-2, Feb. 28, 1978, p 5010. In such cases, the Speaker may examine existing law to determine whether House conferees have remained within the scope of the differences committed to conference. *Manual* § 1088.

Extending Authority of Managers by Resolution

On rare occasions, the managers of a conference have been permitted to take up a matter not in issue between the Houses pursuant to a concurrent resolution. 5 Hinds §§ 6437-6439. Concurrent resolutions permitting managers to consider matters not technically committed to conference are considered by unanimous consent. *Manual* § 527.

§ 10. Meetings

Generally; Voting

The managers of the two Houses while in conference vote separately, the majority in each body determining the attitude to be taken toward the proposition(s) at issue. 5 Hinds § 6336. When the report is made, the unqualified signatures of a majority of the managers from each House are sufficient. For a more thorough discussion of signatures on a conference report, see § 18, infra.

Meetings as Open or Closed

Clause 12 of rule XXII requires a meeting of each conference committee to be open to the public except where the House by record vote determines otherwise. *Manual* § 1093. The rule permits a point of order in the House against the report if the House managers fail to meet at least once in open session as required. See *Manual* § 548. If the point of order is sustained, it results in rejection of the report (signatures notwithstanding) and in an automatic request for a new conference, and it permits the appointment of new conferees without intervening motion to instruct. Deschler-Brown Ch 33 § 5.13.

Motions to Close a Conference Meeting

Under clause 12 of rule XXII, a motion to authorize conferees to close a conference meeting is privileged for consideration in the House after the House has agreed to go to conference. The motion is not debatable and must be decided by the yeas and nays. The motion may be amended only if the Member offering the motion yields for that purpose (or the previous question is rejected). *Manual* § 1093. The motion may provide for exceptions or limitations, such as a stipulation that the meeting may be closed only when certain matters are under discussion or that any sitting Member of Congress shall have the right to attend such meeting. 95-2, July 14, 1978, p 20960.

Points of Order as to Meeting Irregularities

There are few formal House rules that govern procedures to be followed in conducting a meeting of the conferees. Pursuant to clause 12 of rule XXII, managers on the part of the House should abide by certain guidelines with respect to notice of meetings, topics open to discussion, and security of papers, and shall be provided with a ''unitary time and place'' to examine the final conference report. Clause 12(b) provides for a point of order against a conference report where the conference committee did not comply with these strictures. Clause 13 of rule XXII also prohibits the consideration of any conference report that differs in any way from the text that reflects the action of the conferees on all differences between the two Houses.

Beyond these minimal requirements, the conferees may offer motions or consider and debate propositions according to their own informal guidelines or ad hoc rules, with each House having one vote. The Speaker will not normally sustain a point of order against consideration of a conference report signed by a majority of House and Senate conferees based upon irregularities at the conference meeting, other than the requirement for one open meeting and the other guidelines of clause 12. 96-2, Mar. 25, 1980, p 6430. This position reflects the policy that unqualified signatures of a majority of House and Senate conferees constitute a ratification of any procedural irregularity alleged to have occurred in a conference committee. The Speaker will not look behind the signatures to determine whether the report has incorporated all the agreements informally made in conference, except as otherwise provided in clauses 12 and 13 of rule XXII. Deschler-Brown Ch 33 § 18.2. In one instance the Speaker overruled a point of order against a conference report signed by a majority of the conferees, although the Member raising the point of order alleged that the form of the report was inconsistent with a motion agreed to in the conference meeting. Deschler-Brown Ch 33 §7.13.

III. Instructions to Managers; Motions

§11. In General

Instructions In Order

Instructions are used primarily to indicate priorities considered important to the House or to identify positions or amendments it would support or oppose. The House may instruct its conferees to:

- Insist on a portion of a House amendment to a Senate bill. 93-1, July 24, 1973, pp 25539-41.
- Agree to a numbered Senate amendment with an amendment that is within scope. *Manual* §541.
- Insist on certain provisions in a House-passed bill. 96-1, Dec. 19, 1979, p 36895.
- Disagree to one of several Senate amendments (notwithstanding that the House has just disagreed to all Senate amendments in toto). 91-1, Oct. 9, 1969, p 29315.
- Insist on a meeting with Senate conferees. *Manual* §1079.

Limitations on Instructions

Instructions may not direct conference managers to do that which they might not otherwise do (5 Hinds §§6386, 6387; 8 Cannon §§3235, 3244), such as to change a part of a bill not in disagreement (5 Hinds §§6391-6394). In addition, instructions may not:

- Change the text to which both Houses have agreed. 5 Hinds §6388.
- Direct the conferees to agree to something not committed to conference. *Manual* §1088.
- Agree to the deletion of certain language committed to conference if the effect of such deletion results in broadening the scope of the matter in disagreement. *Manual* §1088.
- Direct conferees to concur in a Senate amendment with an amendment not germane thereto. 8 Cannon §3235.
- Include argument. Clause 7(d) of rule XXII.

One House has no jurisdiction over conferees appointed by the other. Instructions apply only to managers on the part of the House giving the instructions. 8 Cannon §§3241, 3242.

Conferring Authority to Agree to Certain Senate Amendments

A motion to instruct also may be used to authorize House conferees, pursuant to clause 5 of rule XXII, to agree to certain Senate amendments. Clause 5 requires such authorization for Senate amendments that, if originating in the House, would violate clause 2 of rule XXI (legislation on an appropriation bill or an unauthorized appropriation) or propose an appropriation on a bill other than a general appropriation bill. *Manual* § 1076. However, clause 5 does not permit a motion to instruct conferees on a general appropriation bill to include additional legislation to that contained in the Senate amendment. *Manual* § 1076.

§ 12. Consideration of Motions to Instruct

Generally

The opportunity for the House to instruct conferees arises at three distinct stages of the legislative process: (1) at the time the House votes to go to conference, (2) 20 calendar days and, concurrently, 10 legislative days after the second House has appointed conferees, the conferees having failed to report (§ 14, infra), and (3) immediately before adoption of a conference report by the first House, in a motion to recommit the conference report to conference (§ 15, infra). For a discussion of recognition and debate of such motions, see § 13, infra.

On Going to Conference

After the House has voted to go to conference with the Senate, the House may consider a timely motion to instruct its managers. A motion to instruct the House managers at a conference is in order after the House has agreed to a conference and before the appointment of the conferees, although the motion may be postponed by unanimous consent until a time after the appointment. 5 Hinds §§ 6379-6382. The motion is not in order until the House has voted to ask for or agree to a conference. Deschler-Brown Ch 33 § 10.5. Only one motion to instruct conferees is in order at this stage. *Manual* § 541; 8 Cannon § 3236.

Tabling of Motion

A motion to instruct House managers at a conference is subject to the motion to lay on the table; and, if adopted, does not carry the bill to the table. *Manual* § 541. The motion to lay the motion to instruct on the table is in order after the motion to instruct has been read or after debate thereon before ordering the previous question. If the motion to table is voted down, the previous question may be moved on the motion to instruct. Deschler-Brown Ch 33 § 9.13.

Withdrawal or Postponement of Motion

A motion to instruct the House managers at a conference has been withdrawn after debate thereon. Deschler-Brown Ch 33 § 9.14. The postponement of consideration of such a motion is permitted by unanimous consent. Deschler-Brown Ch 33 § 10.4. Under clause 8 of rule XX, the Speaker may postpone the vote on a motion to instruct. However, proceedings may not resume on a postponed question of agreeing to a motion to instruct under clause 7 of rule XXII after the managers have filed a conference report in the House. *Manual* § 1079.

§ 13. —Debate on Motion; Recognition and Amendments

Recognition and Debate

Recognition to offer the initial motion to instruct House conferees, and recognition to offer the motion to recommit a conference report with instructions, are the prerogative of the minority. The Speaker recognizes the ranking minority member of the committee reporting the bill when that member seeks recognition to offer the motion. *Manual* § 541.

A motion to instruct conferees is debatable under the hour rule. Under clause 7(b) of rule XXII, the hour is equally divided between the majority and minority parties unless both support the motion. *Manual* § 1078. In that case a Member in opposition to the motion may demand one-third of the time for debate. No additional debate thereon is in order unless the previous question is rejected or unless the Member having the floor yields for amendment. See, *e.g.*, Deschler-Brown Ch 33 § 9.7. The hour of debate time on a motion to instruct may be terminated by laying the motion to instruct on the table before debate. Deschler-Brown Ch 29 § 68.29.

Amendments to Motion

No amendment to a motion to instruct is in order unless the previous question is rejected or unless the Member having the floor yields for amendment. *Manual* § 541.

Divisibility

Neither the initial motion to instruct, nor instructions in a motion to recommit a conference report, are subject to a division of the question for voting. Deschler-Brown Ch 30 § 45.2. However, the 20-day motion to instruct (see § 14, infra) is divisible, provided separate substantive propositions are presented. *Manual* § 921. For more on the divisibility of motions, see DIVISION OF THE QUESTION FOR VOTING.

§ 14. Motions After Failure of Managers to Report

Where conferees have been appointed for 20 calendar days and, concurrently, 10 legislative days (or for 36 hours during the last six days of a session) and have failed to file a report, motions to instruct the House managers—or discharge and appoint new ones—are in order. Clause 7(c) of rule XXII. This period runs from the time that the conference committee has been formed by appointment in both Houses. Deschler-Brown Ch 33 § 14.3. The Member offering such motion must give notice of one legislative day under the rule, and recognition does not depend on party affiliation. *Manual* § 1079. When the House adjourns while such motion is pending, the motion becomes unfinished business on the next day and does not need to be re-noticed. *Manual* § 877.

The practice that precludes more than one motion in the House to instruct conferees before their appointment (§ 12, supra) is not applicable to motions to instruct (or discharge and appoint new) conferees who have failed to report to the House within the requisite period. *Manual* § 541. Indeed, a motion to instruct House conferees who have failed to report for 20 calendar days and, concurrently, 10 legislative days is in order even though its instructions are the same as those given to the conferees at the time the bill was sent to conference. 92-2, May 11, 1972, pp 16838-42. The motion remains available when a conference report is recommitted by the first House to act thereon, because the conferees are not discharged and the original conference remains in existence. *Manual* § 1079.

§ 15. Instructions in Motions to Recommit

A motion to recommit a conference report may include instructions to the House conferees. 8 Cannon § 3241; § 35, infra. A report may be recommitted with instructions to insist on disagreement or take other action on an amendment contained in the report. Deschler-Brown Ch 33 § 32.38; 94-2, Sept. 28, 1976, p 33034.

However, the motion may not instruct House conferees to include matter that is beyond the scope of differences committed to conference. For example, a motion to instruct conferees on a general appropriation bill may not instruct the conferees to include a funding limitation not contained in the House bill or Senate amendment or to add legislation to that contained in a Senate amendment. *Manual* § 1076. Similarly, a motion to recommit a conference report may not instruct conferees to expand definitions to include classes not covered under the House bill or Senate amendment or to include provisions not contained in the House bill or Senate amendment. A waiver of all points of order against a conference report and against its consideration does not inure to instructions contained in a motion to recommit such measure to conference. *Manual* § 1088.

Under clause 7(d) of rule XXII, instructions to conferees in a motion to recommit to conference may not include argument.

§ 16. Instructions as Binding on the Managers

Instructions by the House to its conferees are advisory in nature and are not binding as a limitation on their authority. *Manual* § 550. A failure of conferees to adhere to such instructions does not render their report subject to a point of order. *Manual* § 541; 5 Hinds § 6395; 8 Cannon §§ 3246-3248. Conferees are not required to seek further guidance if they are unable to comply with instructions suggested to them. Deschler-Brown Ch 33 § 12.4. For these reasons, a point of order will not lie against a conference report because it is in contravention of instructions imposed on House conferees. It is for the House to determine by its vote on the report whether to accept or reject it or to recommit it. *Manual* § 541. For a discussion of voting on the report, see § 36, infra.

IV. Conference Reports

A. Generally; Form

§ 17. In General; Preparation and Filing

Generally; Partial Reports

A conference report contains the recommendations of the conference committee to the two Houses as to the disposition of the matter in disagreement. The report may recommend, for example, that the House (or Senate) recede from disagreement to a certain numbered amendment, or that it agree to a certain amendment with an amendment. A conference report may contain an entirely new amendment in the nature of a substitute. *Manual* § 543; 5 Hinds §§ 6465-6467.

The report will normally identify those amendments on which the committee has been unable to agree. Managers may report an agreement as to a portion of the numbered amendments in disagreement, leaving the remainder to be disposed of by subsequent House action. 5 Hinds §§ 6460-6464. For a discussion of disposition of amendments remaining in disagreement between the Houses, see SENATE BILLS; AMENDMENTS BETWEEN THE HOUSES.

A conference report is jointly prepared by the managers from the House and the Senate. The report must be signed by a majority of the managers of the House and a majority of the managers on the part of the Senate. Under House precedents, the signatures must be without qualification, exception, or argument. § 18, infra. Minority views are not in order. *Manual* § 543. The managers in the minority have no authority to make a formal report concerning the conference. 5 Hinds § 6406.

Filing a conference report and subsequent printing in the *Congressional Record* are necessary to initiate the three-day waiting period that must precede the consideration of the report on the floor of the House. *Manual* § 1082; § 30, infra. Under clause 7 of rule XXII the filing of a conference report is privileged. Permission to file and print a report when the House is not in session may be given by unanimous consent.

In the case of recommittal of a conference report to a committee of conference, the subsequent conference report is filed as privileged, assigned a new number, and otherwise treated as a new and separate report. Deschler-Brown Ch 33 § 16.2.

Explanatory Statements

Under clause 7(e) of rule XXII, conference reports are to be accompanied by an explanatory statement prepared jointly by the conferees on the part of the House and the conferees on the part of the Senate. This statement must inform the House as to the effect that the matter contained in the report will have upon the pending measure. *Manual* § 1080. This statement is signed by a majority of the managers of each House, which, under House precedents, must be without qualification, exception, or argument. *Manual* § 543.

A report may not be received without the accompanying statement. *Manual* § 1080. The Speaker may require the statement to be in proper form, but it is for the House, and not the Speaker, to determine its sufficiency. 5 Hinds §§ 6511-6513.

Pursuant to clause 9 of rule XXI, the joint explanatory statement must contain a listing of congressional earmarks and tax and tariff benefits, or a statement that the proposition contains no such provisions.

Although minority views are not in order on a conference report, the majority of the managers may, in the statement accompanying the report, indicate exceptions taken or objections raised by certain conferees who signed with the majority. Deschler-Brown Ch 33 § 20.4. A conferee may not revise or supplement a joint statement of managers by inserting in the *Con-*

gressional Record by unanimous consent extraneous material. *Manual* § 1080.

§ 18. Signing and Signatures

To be valid in the House, a conference report must be signed by a majority of the managers of the House and by a majority of the managers of the Senate without qualification, exception, or argument. *Manual* § 543; 5 Hinds §§ 6497-6502 (even though under Senate practice signatures with conditions or exceptions are counted toward a majority). In the House each provision must be signed by a majority of the Members appointed for that provision only (including general and additional conferees). However, under Senate practice, signatures are counted strictly per capita. Reports bearing insufficient signatures are subject to a point of order and will not be received. 5 Hinds § 6497; 8 Cannon § 3295.

Reports are made in duplicate for the two Houses, the House managers signing first the report for their House and the Senate managers signing the other report first. 5 Hinds § 6500. The name of an absent manager may not be affixed to a conference report. A quorum among the managers on the part of the House at a committee of conference is established by their signatures on the conference report and joint explanatory statement. *Manual* § 1080. Pursuant to clause 12 of rule XXII, managers on the part of the House must be provided a unitary time and place to sign (or not) the conference report and joint explanatory statement. *Manual* § 1093.

Signatures with Qualifications

Under prior practice, conferees were permitted to sign a conference report with qualification or exception. 5 Hinds §§ 6489-6496, 6538. However, recent precedents in the House weigh against allowing such signatures to be counted with the majority in support of the report. Signatures bearing exception, qualification, or argument are redacted. This is consistent with the general rule that conferees may not file separate or minority views. Managers on the part of the House must act on a conference report as a whole, either by signing it to indicate their support for all that is included in the report or by declining to sign it to indicate their opposition to any part thereof. *Manual* § 543; 8 Cannon § 3302. However, under Senate practice, House and Senate signatures with conditions or exceptions are counted toward a majority.

§ 19. Correction of Errors

A correction to language appearing in a conference report may be made by the Clerk or the Secretary of the Senate in the enrollment of the bill if authorized by concurrent resolution. Such a concurrent resolution may be considered by unanimous consent, under suspension of the rules, or by report from the Committee on Rules. *Manual* § 527. In one instance, a conference report and concurrent resolution making changes therein (by correcting the enrollment) were simultaneously adopted under a motion to suspend the rules. Deschler-Brown Ch 33 § 30.28.

The inadvertence of the conferees in failing to dispose of an amendment to a title does not prevent the amendment from coming back to the House for disposition by motion or unanimous consent following adoption of the conference report. 94-2, Apr. 28, 1976, p 11598; 94-2, Sept. 10, 1976, p 29759; 107-2, Oct. 10, 2002, p 20333.

B. Limitations on Reports; Points of Order

§ 20. In General

A conference report is subject to a point of order for failure to comply with a rule of the House when the report is called up for consideration in the House and before debate on it begins. Deschler-Brown Ch 33 § 25.9. For a discussion of raising points of order, see § 27, infra.

§ 21. Reports Exceeding Authority of Managers

A point of order will lie against a conference report on the ground that the conferees have agreed to a provision that was beyond the limits of their authority. *Manual* § 1088; § 9, supra. If the point of order is sustained, the conference report is vitiated; and the bill and amendments are again before the House for consideration. *Manual* § 547; 8 Cannon § 3256; 107-2, Nov. 14, 2002, p 22408.

Sustaining a point of order on a conference report on the ground that it contains a provision beyond scope does not preclude subsequent consideration of the same provision in the House by motion. The bill and amendments are again before the House and, the stage of disagreement having been reached, motions relating to amendments and a further conference are in order. Deschler-Brown Ch 33 § 25. A matter ruled out as beyond scope may constitute a germane amendment to a Senate amendment remaining in disagreement.

For a discussion of the Senate scope rule, clause 2 of Senate Rule XXVIII, see Deschler-Brown Ch 33 § 19.4.

§ 22. — Conference Substitutes or Modifications

Under clause 9 of rule XXII, a conference report containing a substitute agreed to by the managers may not include matter not committed to the conference by either House. *Manual* § 1088. Points of order under the rule are confined to language in the conference report and do not extend to expressions of intent in the joint statement. Deschler-Brown Ch 33 § 7.4. Even a modification of a proposition will give rise to a point of order if it is beyond the scope of either the bill or the amendment as committed to conference. Deschler-Brown Ch 33 § 7.11. The deletion of provisions ''not committed to conference'' because the text has been agreed to by both Houses or is identical in the bill and the amendment also may give rise to a point of order. *Manual* § 527. The managers may eliminate specific words or phrases contained in either version and add words or phrases not included in either version only if they remain within the scope of their differences and do not incorporate additional topics, issues or propositions. Deschler-Brown Ch 33 § 7.4.

§ 23. Nongermane Senate Matter

A Member may raise a point of order against certain language in a conference report if such matter originated in the Senate but would have been considered as not germane if offered to the text when under consideration in the House. The point of order may be raised with respect to a Senate amendment, a conference substitute, or a provision in a Senate bill (if not included in the House-passed version). The point of order must be raised before the report itself is debated. Clause 10(a) of rule XXII.

If the Chair sustains a point of order that conferees have agreed to a nongermane Senate provision, a motion to reject that provision is in order, which is debatable for 40 minutes, equally divided between the Member offering the motion and a Member opposed. Clause 10(b) of rule XXII. Recognition is not based on party affiliation. Deschler-Brown Ch 29 § 17.10. No other point of order under clause 10(a) may be made until disposition of the motion to reject. *Manual* § 1090.

Under clause 10(d) of rule XXII, if the House votes in favor of any motion to reject the nongermane matter, the report itself is considered as rejected. The House then automatically proceeds to consider a motion to recede and concur with an amendment (consisting of that portion of the report not rejected) or to insist on its own amendment. *Manual* § 1089. The adoption of clause 10(d) was based on the principle that a conference report must be acted on as a whole. It must be either agreed to or disagreed to in its entirety. *Manual* § 549.

If, after disposition of all motions to reject, the conference report is not rejected, the nongermane Senate matter is retained, and debate commences on the conference report itself. Deschler-Brown Ch 33 § 30.24.

Points of order arising under clause 10(a) of rule XXII are normally waived by a special order of business from the Committee on Rules or by unanimous consent. § 28, infra.

§ 24. Senate Appropriations on House Legislative Bill

Under clause 5 of rule XXII, the House managers may not agree to a Senate amendment providing for an appropriation on any bill other than a general appropriation bill unless specific authority to agree to such amendment is first given by the House. *Manual* § 1076. Therefore, where a House legislative measure has been committed to conference and the conferees agree to a Senate amendment appropriating funds, the conference report thereon is subject to a point of order and may be ruled out. *Manual* § 1076. This point of order:

- Applies only to Senate amendments that are reported from conference and not to appropriations reported in Senate legislative bills. *Manual* § 1076.
- Does not apply if House conferees were authorized to agree to the amendment by separate House vote, such as a motion to instruct or a motion to recommit with instructions. *Manual* § 1076.
- Does not apply to a provision permitted by the House to remain in its own bill. *Manual* § 1076.
- May be waived by a special order of business or by unanimous consent. § 28, infra.

§ 25. Senate Legislation on House Appropriation Bill

Language changing existing law in violation of clause 2(c) of rule XXI—often referred to as ''legislation on an appropriation bill''—may give rise to a point of order if it appears in a Senate amendment agreed to by the conference managers. The House managers may not agree to such an amendment unless specific authority to agree to the amendment is first given by the House by a separate vote, such as a vote on a motion to instruct or a motion to recommit with instructions. *Manual* §§ 1039, 1076. The purpose of this restriction is to prevent conference committees from using appropriation bills to legislate or to agree to unauthorized appropriations without the permission of the House. 7 Cannon § 1574.

Because of the point of order that will lie against the conferees' agreement to a Senate legislative amendment to an appropriation bill under the rules, it was at one time a customary practice to report such amendments in technical disagreement, where such Senate amendments were separately numbered. The House would first consider a partial report consisting of the matter agreed to in conference and not in conflict with rule XXI, and then consider separately those amendments reported in real or technical disagreement. Such Senate amendments are not subject to a point of order when reported from conference in disagreement, and may be called up for disposition by separate motion. *Manual* § 1076. Under clause 8(b)(3) of rule XXII, a preferential motion to insist on disagreement to the Senate amendment is in order if offered by the House committee having jurisdiction thereof and if the original motion to dispose of the Senate legislative amendment offered by the House manager proposes to amend existing law. *Manual* § 1084; see SENATE BILLS; AMENDMENTS BETWEEN THE HOUSES. However, under modern practice, the Senate ordinarily amends a House-passed general appropriation bill with one amendment in the nature of a substitute, which precludes reporting in partial disagreement of portions thereof and necessitates waivers of points of order in the House.

§ 26. Congressional Budget Act Violations

Congressional action on legislation reported from a conference committee is subject to the Congressional Budget Act of 1974. *Manual* § 1127. The following Congressional Budget Act points of order lie against a conference report:

- Containing spending, revenue, or debt-limit legislation for a fiscal year before a budget resolution for that year has been adopted. § 303(a).
- Containing matter within the jurisdiction of the House and Senate Budget Committees but not reported by those committees. § 306.
- On reconciliation legislation if containing a recommendation that changes Social Security. § 310(g).
- Breaching the allocation—to each committee with jurisdiction—of appropriate levels of budgetary spending authority. § 302(f).
- Breaching certain budgetary levels as set forth in the applicable concurrent resolution on the budget. § 311(a).
- Providing certain budget authority beyond that provided for in advance in appropriation acts. § 401.
- Increasing the costs of Federal intergovernmental mandates by amounts that exceed specified thresholds (to be determined by a vote on the question of consideration). § 425.
- On reconciliation legislation (in the Senate only) that includes extraneous provisions (the "Byrd Rule"). § 313.

§ 27. Raising Points of Order

Generally

A point of order against a conference report comes too late after debate has been had on the report. The point of order should be made when the report is called up for consideration and before debate thereon. Deschler-Brown Ch 33 § 25.9. Where a reading is required, a point of order against the report is not entertained until after the report has been read and cannot be reserved during a reading of the report. Deschler-Brown Ch 33 § 25.12; 94-1, Dec. 15, 1975, p 40671. Under clause 8(c) of rule XXII, a conference report is considered as read if it has been available for three days (having been printed in the *Congressional Record* on the day filed). The report also may be considered as read by a special order of business or by unanimous consent.

Multiple Points of Order

The Chair may rule on all points of order raised against a conference report, whether they are made separately or at one time. Deschler-Brown Ch 33 § 25.18. However, the Chair entertains and rules on points of order that, if sustained, will vitiate the entire conference report before entertaining points of order against certain portions of the report under clause 10 of rule XXII. *Manual* § 1090.

Where a point of order against a conference report is overruled, a second point of order may be pressed against the report, providing that debate on the report has not intervened. Deschler-Brown Ch 33 § 25.17.

Points of Order and the Question of Consideration

The question of consideration may be raised against a conference report before the Chair entertains points of order against the report on the ground that it is useless to entertain points of order if the House is not going to consider the report. However, a point of order should be decided first if it concerns whether the matter is privileged to come up for consideration in the first instance. *Manual* § 909.

Under section 426 of the Congressional Budget Act of 1974, which provides for disposition of points of order that preclude unfunded Federal intergovernmental mandates, a question of consideration can be raised against a conference report that contains a provision increasing the costs of such mandates above levels specified in section 424 of that Act. If the provision is precisely identified in the point of order, the House can then, by voting on the question of consideration, determine whether or not to allow the entire conference report to be considered.

Earmarks

Clause 9(a) of rule XXI provides that a conference report must be accompanied by a disclosure statement for it to be considered in the House. Such a statement lists the congressional earmarks, limited tax benefits, and limited tariff benefits contained in the conference report or joint explanatory statement, or states that the conference report or joint statement contains no such provisions. Such statements must also include the names of Members requesting such items. *Manual* § 1068d. A point of order will be sustained against a conference report that is not accompanied by a disclosure statement. The Chair will assess merely its inclusion in the joint explanatory statement and not its accuracy or sufficiency. 110-1, May 10, 2007, pp 12190, 12191.

Clause 9(b) of rule XXI provides for similar treatment of conference reports accompanying general appropriation bills. The joint explanatory statement must include an earmark disclosure statement listing all congressional earmarks, limited tax and tariff benefits that were neither committed to the conference by either House nor contained in a report of a committee of either House on such bill or companion measure (or a statement that the conference report contains no such provisions).

Clause 9(c) of rule XXI provides for a point of order against a special order of business that waives either clause 9(a) or 9(b). See § 28, infra.

§ 28. Waiving Points of Order

By Special Order of Business

Points of order against a conference report—or against the consideration of a conference report—may be waived pursuant to a resolution reported by the Committee on Rules and adopted by the House, and this has become the normal practice. See, *e.g.*, 107-1, H. Res. 312, Dec. 12, 2001, p 25089. The resolution normally waives all points of order but may waive one or more specific points of order. Such a resolution may also waive all points of order against a conference report *except* against certain provisions, for example, sections therein that contain matter beyond the House conferees' scope of authority in violation of clause 9 of rule XXII. Deschler-Brown Ch 33 § 26.8.

While a resolution may waive the earmark point of order (clauses 9(a) and 9(b) of rule XXI), such a resolution would then itself be subject to a point of order under clause 9(c) of rule XXI. The point of order is disposed of by the question of consideration, with 20 minutes of debate permitted by the rule. Similarly, a resolution that waives the unfunded mandates point of order under the Congressional Budget Act is likewise subject to a point of order disposed of by the question of consideration. See QUESTION OF CONSIDERATION and UNFUNDED MANDATES.

By Unanimous Consent

By unanimous consent the House may waive some or all of the points of order that would otherwise lie against a conference report and may take such action before the report has been filed or even before the conferees have reached agreement. 98-2, June 18, 1984, p 16841; 99-1, Dec. 16, 1985, p 26559. By unanimous consent, the House has provided for the following:

- The consideration of a report (on a bill on which conferees had just been appointed) on that same day or any day thereafter (if filed). 99-1, Aug. 1, 1985, p 22640.
- The consideration of a report not yet filed and amendments reported in disagreement, subject to one-hour availability to Members. Deschler-Brown Ch 33 § 2.24.
- The consideration of a report containing no joint statement of the managers. 98-2, June 29, 1984, p 20206.
- The midnight filing of a new report on a bill recommitted to conference, and the consideration of the report on the following day. 97-2, Aug. 17, 1982, pp 21397, 21398.

By Motion to Suspend the Rules

A conference report may be adopted pursuant to a motion to suspend the rules. Deschler-Brown Ch 33 § 30.26. The Speaker may recognize a Member to move to suspend the rules and agree to a conference report that has been ruled out of order because the conferees exceeded their authority in violation of clause 9 of rule XXII or because the conference report has not met its availability requirement under clause 8 of rule XXII. Deschler-Brown Ch 33 § 26.28; Deschler-Brown Ch 33 § 27.9.

C. Consideration and Disposition of Reports

§ 29. In General; Custody of Official Papers

Both Houses of Congress must agree to a conference report, and they do so seriatim. Either House must be in possession of the official papers before it can act. *Manual* § 549. Under a practice suggested by Jefferson, at the close of an effective conference, the official papers change hands from the House asking the conference to the House agreeing to the conference. The managers on the part of the House agreeing to the conference take possession of the papers and submit them and the report to their House, which acts first on the report. However, the managers for the agreeing

House may nevertheless surrender the papers to the asking House so that it may act first on the report. *Manual* § 555; 8 Cannon 3330.

In the event that the matter in disagreement is an amendment of the House that requested the conference, the papers may be surrendered to the other House to permit it to act first on, and respond to, that amendment. Deschler-Brown Ch 33 § 24.13.

§ 30. Layover and Availability Requirements

Generally

The floor consideration of conference reports is subject to layover and availability requirements under clause 8(a) of rule XXII. *Manual* § 1082. They require that conference reports:

- Be printed in the *Congressional Record* on the day filed and be available for three calendar days (excluding Saturdays, Sundays, and legal holidays unless the House is in session).
- Be available to Members on the floor for at least two hours before consideration thereof.

The three-day layover requirement does not apply during the last six days of a session. *Manual* § 1082. This is construed to mean that, during the last six calendar days before the constitutional end of a session on January 3, a conference report may be called up on the same day it is filed. Deschler-Brown Ch 33 § 22.5.

Waivers

The three-day layover rule may be waived by unanimous consent, by suspension of the rules, or, more commonly, by adoption of a special order of business. § 28, supra. A resolution only waiving the availability requirement may be considered on the same day the resolution is reported under clause 8(e) of rule XXII and clause 6(a)(2) of rule XIII. Such a resolution may permit a waiver of the three-day layover requirement for the remainder of a session. 93-2, Dec. 18, 1974, pp 40846, 40847.

Even if the three-day layover requirement is waived, the conference report is still to be available at least two hours before the matter is taken up for consideration, although the two-hour requirement may likewise be waived pursuant to a special order of business. Deschler-Brown Ch 33 § 27.10. The two-hour requirement also may be waived pursuant to a unanimous-consent agreement providing for consideration ''immediately'' after filing. Deschler-Brown Ch 33 § 27.9.

§ 31. Filing and Calling Up Report; Reading

Generally; Precedence

A conference report may be called up in the House as privileged business after the report has been filed and is in compliance with the three-day layover and two-hour availability requirements of rule XXII. § 30, supra.

Because of its potential value in settling House-Senate differences, the filing of a conference report is considered as a matter of high privilege. Clause 7 of rule XXII; *Manual* § 1077; 5 Hinds § 6443. A conference report must be filed by a conferee. Its presentation or filing takes precedence over:

- Unfinished business. *Manual* § 1077.
- The reading of a bill. 5 Hinds § 6448.
- A Member occupying the floor in debate. 5 Hinds § 6451.
- The ordering of (or demand for) the previous question. 5 Hinds §§ 6449, 6450.
- The question of ordering a recorded vote. 5 Hinds § 6447.
- A motion to refer a Senate bill. 5 Hinds § 6457.
- A motion to reconsider. 5 Hinds § 5605.
- A motion to adjourn (although as soon as the report is presented the motion to adjourn may be put). *Manual* § 1077.

Who May Call Up

A conference report may be called up for consideration in the House by the senior manager on the part of the House at the conference. Such report may be called up by a manager who is in fact opposed to the report and who did not sign it. Deschler-Brown Ch 33 § 23.3. If the senior House manager is unable to be present on the floor to call up the report, the Speaker will recognize another majority member of the conference committee. Deschler-Brown Ch 33 § 23.1.

Reading

Under clause 8(c) of rule XXII, a conference report that meets the availability requirements need not be read when called up for consideration in the House. If it has not been available for the three-day period, it must be read in full when called up for consideration, unless dispensed with by a special order of business or by unanimous consent. The statement of the managers accompanying a conference report may by unanimous consent be read in lieu of the report. Deschler-Brown Ch 33 § 20.9.

Withdrawal; Postponement

A conference report may be withdrawn from consideration in the House by the Member calling it up at any time before action thereon. Deschler-

Brown Ch 33 § 20.9. Similar practice in the Senate has been criticized. 5 Hinds § 6549.

A motion to postpone the consideration of a conference report to a day certain is permitted until the previous question is ordered on the report. Thereafter, postponement is permitted only by unanimous consent (except for the Speaker's authority to postpone the vote on adoption of a conference report under clause 8 of rule XX). Deschler-Brown Ch 33 § 30.9. Under clause 1(c) of rule XIX, adopted in the 111th Congress, where the previous question is operating to adoption of a conference report pursuant to a special order of business, the Speaker has authority to postpone further consideration of the conference report until a later time. *Manual* § 1000a.

§ 32. En Bloc Consideration

Reports

Ordinarily, it is not permissible to consider several conference reports en bloc. Each conference report should be considered and voted upon separately. Deschler-Brown Ch 33 § 30.2. However, pursuant to a resolution from the Committee on Rules, the House may consider and vote on two or more conference reports en bloc. Deschler-Brown Ch 33 § 22.10.

Amendments in Disagreement

Where two or more amendments have emerged from conference in disagreement, they may by unanimous consent be considered en bloc where the same motion is to be applied to each amendment. Deschler-Brown Ch 33 § 29.42. Proposed motions to dispose of the amendments that were not all the same (as where they proposed to recede and concur with different amendments) also may be considered by unanimous consent. Deschler-Brown Ch 32 § 11.10. For disposition of Senate amendments generally, see SENATE BILLS; AMENDMENTS BETWEEN THE HOUSES.

§ 33. Debate

Generally; Extending Time

Debate on a conference report is under the hour rule. Clause 2 of rule XVII; clause 8(d) of rule XXII; *Manual* §§ 957, 1086. Such debate may be extended by unanimous consent or by special order of business reported by the Committee on Rules but not by motion. Deschler-Brown Ch 33 §§ 28.2, 28.3. The one hour of debate could also be continued if the motion for the previous question were rejected. 93-2, Feb. 27, 1974, p 4397.

Division of Time

Under clause 8(d) of rule XXII, the time for debate on a conference report or an amendment emerging from conference in disagreement is equally divided between the majority and minority parties. The rule has been interpreted to require an equal allocation of time on a motion to dispose of an amendment in disagreement following rejection of a conference report by the House or following the sustaining of a point of order against a conference report. Indeed, it has become the practice of the House to equally divide the time on all motions to dispose of amendments emerging from conference in disagreement, whether the amendment has been reported in disagreement or has come before the House at some other stage for disposition. *Manual* § 1086.

Three-way Division of Debate

Clause 8(d) of rule XXII provides that, if both the floor manager for the majority and the floor manager for the minority support a conference report, the hour of debate thereon may be divided three ways—among the two managers and a Member who is opposed. *Manual* § 1086. This allocation may not be claimed if the minority manager indicates opposition to the report. 99-2, Oct. 15, 1986, p 31515. Recognition of a Member to control the 20 minutes of debate in opposition does not depend upon party affiliation. Priority in such recognition is accorded to a member of the conference committee. *Manual* § 1086.

To open debate, the Chair recognizes first the majority manager calling up the conference report, then the minority manager, then the Member in opposition. The right to close the debate where the time is divided three ways falls to the manager calling up the conference report. A similar three-way division of time applies to the motion offered by the floor manager to dispose of an amendment remaining in disagreement if the floor managers for the majority and minority favor the motion. *Manual* § 1086.

§ 34. —Recognition; Control of Debate Time

Generally

When a conference report is called up or a Senate amendment in disagreement is pending, the hour of debate time is equally controlled by the majority and minority parties. *Manual* § 1086. Where the Member calling up the report does not seek recognition as a majority member to offer a motion to dispose of the matter reported in disagreement, another majority member may be recognized to offer such a motion and to control one-half of the time thereon. Deschler-Brown Ch 32 § 8.11. Where conferees have been appointed from two committees of the House, the Speaker may recognize the chair of one committee to control 30 minutes and a minority member of another committee to control 30 minutes. Deschler-Brown Ch 33 § 28.6. By unanimous consent, the time allocated to the majority and minority may be reallocated to other Members, with the right of those Members to yield time to other Members. 99-2, Oct. 8, 1986, p 29714.

Debate in the House on a Senate amendment reported from conference in disagreement having been divided, the minority member in charge controls 30 minutes for debate only and may yield to other Members for debate only. Another minority member, merely by offering a preferential motion, does not thereby control one-half of the time under the original motion. *Manual* § 1086.

However, if the original motion is defeated, recognition may shift and a second motion to dispose of the amendment may be offered; and if the second motion is offered by a minority member, the Chair may allocate the hour of debate between such minority member and a majority member, although neither controlled time on the initial motion. *Manual* § 1086.

Debate Following Division of the Question

Where a preferential motion to recede and concur in an amendment reported from conference in disagreement has been divided, one hour of debate, equally divided between the majority and minority, is permitted on the motion to recede. If the previous question is ordered only on the motion to recede and if the House then recedes and a preferential motion to concur with an amendment is offered, another hour of debate equally divided is permitted. 95-1, Aug. 2, 1977, p 26206; 95-2, Oct. 5, 1978, p 33698. The Chair may put the question on receding without debate if the majority and minority floor managers do not seek recognition to debate that portion of the original motion, because the subsequent question of concurring, or concurring with an amendment, is debatable for one hour, equally divided between the managers. 98-2, Oct. 10, 1984, p 31694.

§ 35. Recommittal of Report

Generally; By Motion

A motion to recommit a conference report to the existing conference committee is in order if the other House has not acted on the report and thereby discharged its managers. Manual § 550. After one House has acted on a report, the other House has only the option of accepting or rejecting it. Deschler-Brown Ch 33 § 32.6. After both Houses have acted on the report, it may be recommitted to conference only by concurrent resolution. *Manual* § 550; 8 Cannon § 3316.

The motion to recommit is initially the prerogative of the minority. See REFER AND RECOMMIT. However, the Speaker has recognized a majority member to offer a motion to recommit a conference report in the absence of a minority member seeking recognition to offer the motion. Deschler-Brown Ch 33 § 32.20.

A motion to recommit a conference report is not in order until the previous question has been ordered on the report. Deschler-Brown Ch 33 § 32.10. Only one valid motion is permitted, so if the motion is voted down, the question before the House is on the adoption of the report. Deschler-Brown Ch 33 § 32.52. However, if a recommittal motion with instructions is ruled out on a point of order, a valid motion may still be offered. A motion to recommit comes too late after the report has been agreed to. Deschler-Brown Ch 33 § 32.13.

Under section 305(a)(6) of the Congressional Budget Act of 1974, a motion to recommit a conference report on a concurrent resolution on the budget is not in order.

Where a conference report is recommitted to conference, the House managers carry the original papers back to conference. Deschler-Brown Ch 33 § 32.51. The same conferees remain appointed. Deschler-Brown Ch 33 § 32.2. To produce a new conference report, the conference must meet again and obtain new signatures for the second report. If a second report is then filed by the conferees, it is numbered and otherwise treated as a new and separate report. Deschler-Brown Ch 33 § 32.48. Because the same conference remains in being after recommittal, the time period regarding the availability of a subsequent motion to instruct resumes from where it was tolled when the conference report was filed. 101-2, June 28, 1990, p 16157. See § 14, supra.

For a discussion of instructions in a motion to recommit, see § 15, supra.

Recommittal by Unanimous Consent or Special Order of Business

Conference reports are sometimes recommitted by unanimous consent in the House acting first. Deschler-Brown Ch 33 § 32.40. This procedure may be used:

- To recommit a report in which an error has been discovered. Deschler-Brown Ch 33 § 32.40.
- To permit the conferees to make certain changes and to file a new report. Deschler-Brown Ch 33 § 32.41.

- Where the conferees have exceeded their authority in reporting a matter not in disagreement. 90-1, June 28, 1967, p 17738.

A conference report also may be recommitted by a special order of business reported by the Committee on Rules. See, *e.g.*, 107-1, May 8, 2001, pp 7358-62; 108-1, Oct. 28, 2003, p 25990.

§36. Final Disposition of Report; Voting

Generally

As a general rule, when a conference report has been debated and its final disposition is pending, only three courses of action are available to the Members: (1) agree, (2) disagree, or (3) recommit to conference. 5 Hinds §§6546, 6558. For recommittal, see §35, supra. Conference reports may not be:

- Disposed of by the motion to table after the previous question is ordered. 5 Hinds §§6538-6544.
- Referred to a standing committee. 5 Hinds §6558.
- Amended (5 Hinds §§6534, 6535), except by concurrent resolution (5 Hinds §6536).
- Sent to Committee of the Whole. 5 Hinds §§6559-6561.

A report having been called up, the motion to agree to the report is regarded as pending. The Speaker may put the question on the report without motion from the floor. 5 Hinds §6517; 8 Cannon §3300. Although most reports are agreed to by majority vote, a two-thirds vote is required on a report relating to a constitutional amendment (5 Hinds §7036) and under clause 5(b) of rule XXI, a three-fifths vote is required on a conference report carrying a Federal income tax rate increase. For Speaker's discretion to postpone a vote on a conference report, see clause 8 of rule XX; *Manual* §1030. For postponement of conference reports, see §31, supra.

Under clause 10 of rule XX, the yeas and nays are considered ordered on the adoption of a conference report on a general appropriation bill, on a concurrent resolution on the budget, or on a bill increasing Federal income tax rates.

Partial Reports

A conference report must generally be acted on as a whole and either agreed to or disagreed to in its entirety. Rejection of a portion of a conference report under a special order of business permitting such a separate vote results in the rejection of the entire report. Deschler-Brown Ch 33 §30.5. Until the report has been acted on, no motion to deal with individual amendments reported in disagreement is in order. 5 Hinds §§6323, 6389,

6390. In some cases, however, the managers return to the House with a partial conference report dealing with the amendments on which they have reached agreement but specifying one or more amendments that remain in disagreement. 5 Hinds §§ 5460-5464. In such cases, the vote first occurs on agreeing to the conference report on those matters on which agreement has been reached. The amendments reported therein in disagreement are reported and acted on seriatim thereafter. Deschler-Brown Ch 33 § 29.3. For a discussion of amendments reported in total disagreement, see § 38, infra.

Motions to Reconsider the Vote

After disposition of the report and any or all amendments reported from conference in disagreement, it is in order to move to reconsider the vote on a motion disposing of one of the amendments. Deschler-Brown Ch 33 §§ 30.35, 30.36. The Speaker may put as one question reconsideration of multiple votes (subject to demand for a separate vote on reconsideration of any question) and a Member may then move to lay all motions to reconsider on the table. 95-2, Oct. 4, 1978, p 33480. Under section 305(a)(6) of the Congressional Budget Act of 1974, a motion to reconsider the vote on a conference report on a concurrent resolution on the budget is not in order.

§ 37. Effect of Rejection of Report; Further Conferences

When either House disagrees to a conference report, the matter is left in the position it was in before the conference was asked. 5 Hinds § 6525. Motions for the disposition of amendments in disagreement or to send the matter to further conference are again in order. Clause 4 of rule XXII; *Manual* §§ 551, 1075; 8 Cannon § 3303. Thus, the House may reject a conference report, insist on disagreement to a Senate amendment, and ask for a further conference. *Manual* § 528d. However, a motion to instruct House managers at a new conference is not in order until the motion to go to further conference has been agreed to. Deschler-Brown Ch 33 § 31.8.

D. Disposition Where Managers Report in Total Disagreement

§ 38. In General

Where the managers at a conference are unable to come to any agreement on the matters committed to them, they prepare and sign a written report to that effect. 5 Hinds §§ 6565-6570. The report is filed and ordered printed. *Manual* § 545. Under the former practice, amendments reported in total disagreement could be taken up for immediate consideration in the

House. 8 Cannon §§ 3299, 3332. Today the matter in disagreement is subject to the three-day layover requirement of clause 8(b) of rule XXII.

House action on amendments reported in total disagreement differs from that of the Senate. In the Senate a conference report in total disagreement is considered before disposition of the reported amendments. Deschler-Brown Ch 33 § 29.13. In the House, after the report is called up, action is taken on the amendment in disagreement but not on the report. Deschler-Brown Ch 33 § 29.3. Thus, where conferees report in disagreement absent a special order of business, and the Senate then recedes and concurs in the House amendments with an amendment, the conference report is not acted on in the House; the Speaker merely directs the Clerk to report the Senate amendments to the House amendments for disposition by motion. Deschler-Brown Ch 33 § 29.28. Debate (including possible three-way debate) and voting proceeds in the same manner as on amendments reported from conference in partial disagreement. See § 33, supra. Motions to dispose of amendments in disagreement, see SENATE BILLS; AMENDMENTS BETWEEN THE HOUSES.

Chapter 14
Congressional Procedures Enacted in Law

Research References
U.S. Const. art. I, § 7
Manual § 1130

§ 1. In General

Congress has enacted numerous laws reserving for itself the right of review by approval or disapproval of certain actions of the executive branch or of independent agencies. These laws take various forms, often including expedited procedures. For example, the Alaska Natural Gas Transportation Act of 1976 permits the privileged consideration of joint resolutions approving Presidential decisions on the Alaska natural gas transportation system when those resolutions are reported from committee or are discharged after 30 days. 15 USC §§ 719f, 719g; *Manual* § 1130(18); 95-1, Nov. 1, 1977, p 36347. Another statute sets forth a similar procedure for congressional approval or disapproval of certain actions by the District of Columbia Council. District of Columbia Home Rule Act, §§ 602(c), 604; *Manual* § 1130(5). The *House Rules and Manual* carries a compilation of current texts of congressional disapproval provisions that include expedited procedures. *Manual* § 1130.

§ 2. Constitutionality

Federal court decisions indicate that congressional action to approve or disapprove an executive branch determination should be undertaken by way of a bill or joint resolution and not by way of a simple or concurrent resolution or through committee action. In 1983, the Supreme Court declared in *Immigration and Naturalization Service* v. *Chadha* (462 U.S. 919 (1983)) that a statute permitting the disapproval of a decision of the Attorney General by simple resolution of one House was unconstitutional. The Court said the device violated the doctrine of separation of powers, the principle of bicameralism, and the clause of the Constitution requiring that legislation passed by both Chambers must be presented to the President for signature or veto. In an earlier decision, the Court of Appeals specifically held a one-House legislative veto provision in the Natural Gas Policy Act of 1978 (15 USC § 3341(b)) unconstitutional. In its decision, the circuit court for the District of Columbia said that the primary basis for its holding was that the one-House veto violates article I, section 7, of the Constitution both by preventing the President from exercising the veto power and by permitting legislative action by only one House of Congress. The circuit court also found the one-House veto to contravene the separation of powers principle implicit in articles I, II, and III because it authorizes the legislature to share powers properly exercised by the other two branches of government. The court declared that article I, section 7, sets forth the fundamental prerequisites to the enactment of Federal laws—bicameral passage of legislation and presentation for approval or disapproval by the President— and held that congressional disapproval of final agency rules must comply with these requirements. The court added that Congress may choose to use a resolution of disapproval as a means of expediting action, but only if it acts by both Houses and presents the resolution to the President. *Consumer Energy Council of America, et al.* v. *FERC*, 673 F.2d 425 (D.C. Cir. 1982), *aff'd* 463 U.S. 1216 (1983).

In the light of these decisions, Congress has amended several statutes to convert procedures involving simple or concurrent resolutions of approval or disapproval to procedures requiring joint resolutions to be presented to the President for signature or veto. *Manual* § 1130.

§ 3. Consideration in the House

Many ''legislative procedure'' statutes prescribe special procedures for the House to follow when reviewing executive branch actions. For a compilation of the relevant provisions of such statutes, see *Manual* § 1130. These procedures technically are rules of the House, enacted expressly or implicitly as an exercise of the House's rule-making authority. At the beginning of each Congress, it is customary for the House to reincorporate by reference in the resolution adopting its rules such legislative procedures as may exist in current law. Nevertheless, because the House retains the constitutional right to change its rules at any time, the Committee on Rules may report a resolution varying such procedures. *Manual* § 1130.

Where a law enacted as a rule of both Houses provides special procedures during consideration of a joint resolution approving a Presidential determination, and the House adopts a special order of business providing for consideration of such a joint resolution in the House, the Speaker will nevertheless interpret the special statutory provisions to apply if consistent with the special order of business. 97-1, Dec. 10, 1981, p 30486.

Chapter 15
Congressional Record

Research References
5 Hinds §§ 6958-7024
8 Cannon §§ 3459-3502
Deschler Ch 5 §§ 15-20
Manual §§ 685-692, 967, 968

§ 1. In General; Control Over the Congressional Record

The present system of reporting the proceedings of the House for the *Congressional Record* is the result of gradual evolution. The first debates, beginning in 1789, were published in condensed form in the *Annals of Congress*. The *Congressional Globe* began in 1833 and continued until 1873, when the *Record* began. 5 Hinds § 6959.

The *Congressional Record* is governed by statutory provisions and rules as to its format and content. 44 USC §§ 901-910. Control over the arrangement and style of the *Record*, including maps, diagrams, and illustrations, is vested in the Joint Committee on Printing. 44 USC §§ 901, 904. Neither the Speaker nor the House may order changes in the type size or printing style without the approval of the Joint Committee on Printing. Deschler Ch 5 §§ 15.1, 15.2.

The proceedings of the House and the proceedings of the Senate are published in separate portions of the *Congressional Record*, and each House separately controls the content of its portion of the *Record*. 8 Cannon § 2503. The statement of a Senator that would normally appear in the Senate portion of the *Record* may not be inserted in that portion of the *Record* dealing with the proceedings of the House. 87-2, Jan. 16, 1962, p 291.

Both the Joint Committee on Printing and the House have adopted supplemental rules governing publication in the *Congressional Record*. For the text of these rules, see *Manual* § 686. Under clause 1(k) of rule X, the Committee on House Administration has jurisdiction of matters relating to printing and correction of the *Record*.

A Member is not entitled to inspect the reporter's notes of remarks of others not reflecting on that Member nor may such Member demand that they be read. 5 Hinds §§ 6964, 6967; 8 Cannon § 3460.

§ 2. Matters Printed in the Congressional Record

Generally

The content of the House portion of the *Congressional Record* is governed by statute, the House rules, and the customs and practices of the House. In addition, the House often agrees by unanimous consent to permit certain matter to be inserted in the *Record* which would not ordinarily be included. Deschler Ch 5 § 16.

Clause 8 of rule XVII and section 901 of title 44 of the United States Code require the *Congressional Record* to be a substantially verbatim account of the proceedings of the House. *Manual* § 967. Clause 8 applies to statements and rulings of the Chair as well as to debate. *Manual* § 968. Because of this requirement, the Speaker will not entertain a unanimous-consent request to give a special-order speech ''off the Record.'' *Manual* § 687.

Additional matters required by statute or House rules to be printed in the *Congressional Record* include:

- The oath of office subscribed to by a Member. 2 USC § 25.
- Referrals to committee under clause 7 of rule XII. *Manual* § 825.
- The filing of committee reports. *Manual* § 831.
- Reports submitted to Congress pursuant to a statute requiring publication in the *Record.* See, *e.g.*, 2 USC § 1383.
- Amendments to be protected for debate time under clause 8 of rule XVIII. *Manual* § 987.
- Conference reports and accompanying statements. *Manual* § 1082.
- Messages received from the Senate and President giving notice of bills passed or approved under clause 1 of rule XII. *Manual* §§ 815, 875.
- Motions to discharge. *Manual* § 892.
- Certain changes in votes. Deschler Ch 5 § 16.14.
- The addition or deletion of the name of a cosponsor. *Manual* § 825.
- Measures introduced ''by request.'' *Manual* § 826.

The *Congressional Record* is for the proceedings of the House and Senate only, and unrelated matters are rigidly excluded. 5 Hinds § 6962. It is not, however, the official record of business, that function being fulfilled by the Journal. See JOURNAL.

As a general principle, the Speaker has no control over the *Congressional Record.* 5 Hinds §§ 6983, 7017. The House, and not the Speaker, determines the extent to which a Member may be allowed to extend remarks (5 Hinds §§ 6997-7000; 8 Cannon § 3475), whether or not a copyrighted article shall be printed therein (5 Hinds § 6985), or whether there has been an abuse of the leave to print (5 Hinds § 7012; 8 Cannon § 3474).

The House frequently agrees by unanimous consent to permit insertions of matters of general interest in the *Congressional Record* at the request of Members. Matters that have been inserted in the *Record* under this procedure include:

- Information relative to the installation of voting equipment in the Chamber. 91-2, Nov. 25, 1970, p 39085.
- Records from litigation involving the House. 90-1, Apr. 10, 1967, pp 8729-62.
- Summaries of the work of Congress or its committees at adjournment. Deschler Ch 5 § 16.
- Extraneous and tabular matter to establish legislative history concerning the codification of the standing rules. 106-1, Jan. 6, 1999, p 78.

Printing Bills in the Congressional Record

Measures considered in the House are printed in the *Congressional Record* at the beginning of consideration. If an amended version of the measure is made in order under the special order of business providing for its consideration, that amended version is printed at the beginning of consideration, unless further amendments are made in order. In that case, the amended version is printed after debate.

Measures considered in the Committee of the Whole are printed in the *Congressional Record* following general debate. The only version of the measure printed is the one made in order as original text for the purpose of amendment by the special order of business providing for its consideration. The measure is printed as read by the Clerk. For example, if under a special order of business the measure is considered as read, it is printed in its entirety after general debate. If the measure is read by title, each title is printed at the point the Clerk either reads or designates it. No other version of the measure is printed in the *Record.*

§ 3. Corrections; Deletions

Under clause 8 of rule XVII, the substantially verbatim account of remarks made during debate and published in the *Congressional Record* is subject only to technical, grammatical, and typographical corrections authorized by the Member making the remarks involved. Unparliamentary remarks may be deleted only by permission or order of the House. Under clause 8(c) of rule XVII, this requirement may be investigated by the Committee on Ethics. *Manual* § 967.

The remarks of a Member, if in order, cannot be stricken from the *Congressional Record* by the House. 5 Hinds § 6974; 8 Cannon § 3498. However, remarks that are out of order may be excluded from the *Record* by House order. Deschler Ch 5 § 19.8. Remarks by a Member not under recognition do not appear in the *Record*. *Manual* §§ 687, 946.

The Committee of the Whole has no authority over the *Congressional Record*. 5 Hinds § 6986; Deschler Ch 5 § 17.22.

Substantive insertions submitted under leave to ''revise and extend'' are printed in distinctive type. A speech that has been substantively revised is printed as delivered and then separately printed as revised in distinctive type. *Manual* § 686.

§ 4. Printing Errors

Generally

The House may correct errors in the printing of the *Congressional Record* in order to ensure that the proceedings of the House are accurately recorded. 5 Hinds § 6972. The authority to correct such errors is vested in the House, not the Speaker. 5 Hinds § 7019; Deschler Ch 5 § 18.

The correction of an error in the *Congressional Record* may present a question of the privileges of the House where the integrity of House proceedings is in question. *Manual* §§ 690, 704; Deschler Ch 5 §§ 18.1, 18.2. However, this question may not be raised until the daily edition of the *Record* has appeared (Deschler Ch 5 § 18), and no corrections may be submitted after the permanent edition of the particular volume is published (Deschler Ch 5 § 18.12).

Errors that may be corrected under this procedure are errors in the transcript or printing of the proceedings, not errors of fact made by a Member during debate. The House may not change the *Congressional Record* merely to show what should have been said on the floor. 5 Hinds § 6974; 8 Cannon § 3498; Deschler Ch 5 § 18. A mere typographical error or proper revision of a Member's remarks does not give rise to a question of privilege. *Manual* § 690.

By Motion or Resolution

A motion or resolution to correct the *Congressional Record*, if constituting a question of privilege, is in order after the approval of the Journal. *Manual* § 690; Deschler Ch 5 § 18.6. A motion or resolution to correct the *Record* also may be offered after a unanimous-consent request to that effect has been objected to. Deschler Ch 5 § 18.9. Such motion or resolution is debatable under the hour rule and is subject to motions under clause 4 of rule XVI. Deschler Ch 5 §§18.7-18.10.

A resolution alleging inaccuracies in the President's state of the Union message and authorizing corrections to the *Congressional Record* does not give rise to a question of the privileges of the House. 108-1, Oct. 20, 2003, p 25256.

§5. Extensions of Remarks; Insertions

Generally

In 1968 the Appendix of the *Congressional Record* was replaced by a new heading, "Extensions of Remarks," for the inclusion of material in the *Record* that is extraneous to the proceedings on the floor. Members, with permission of the House, may be permitted to extend their remarks in this part of the *Record* so as to insert (1) speeches that were not actually delivered on the floor and (2) extraneous materials related to the subject under discussion. 5 Hinds §§6990-6993; Deschler Ch 5 §20. This has been a long-standing practice, dating from as early as 1852, when it was the custom to print undelivered speeches in the Appendix to the *Record*. 5 Hinds §6993. Under the modern practice, such insertions are normally permitted by unanimous consent, a motion to do so not being privileged. Deschler Ch 5 §20.11. Beginning in the 106th Congress, the House has, by unanimous consent, authorized all Members to revise and extend their remarks and include extraneous material (within two *Record* pages) during either one session or an entire Congress. See, *e.g.*, 106-1, Jan. 6, 1999, p 247; 112-1, Jan. 5, 2011, p ____.

Permission to include extraneous materials may be granted only by the House. To eliminate the need for daily requests, the House has recently adopted the practice of granting all Members permission to revise and extend their remarks in the "Extensions of Remarks" portion of the *Congressional Record* and include extraneous material (within two *Record* pages) at the beginning of each Congress. See, *e.g.*, 106-1, Jan. 6, 1999, p 247. The chair of the Committee of the Whole may recognize Members to extend their own remarks, but the Committee of the Whole lacks the power to permit the inclusion of extraneous materials. Deschler Ch 5 §20.12.

Permission to extend in the body of the *Congressional Record* must be sought by the Member whose remarks are to be inserted, although general permission to extend is sometimes given to all Members. Deschler Ch 5 §20. Typically, the manager of a bill will propound a unanimous-consent request to authorize such extensions, to be submitted within five legislative days. If submitted on the day the bill was considered, such extensions will appear in the daily *Record* immediately after general debate on the bill, in a different typeface. If submitted at a later time, such extensions appear in the ''Extensions of Remarks'' portion of the daily *Record.* When the permanent *Record* is published, all such extensions are printed immediately following general debate.

The revised material inserted under permission to extend remarks must be clearly distinguishable, by different typeface, from the substantially verbatim account of proceedings. The Speaker has instructed the Official Reporters of Debates to adhere strictly to this requirement. *Manual* § 687.

Timeliness

Permission to extend must be sought at the proper time. Requests to insert made prior to the reading and approval of the Journal will not be entertained. Deschler Ch 5 § 20.4.

Strict Construction

Authorizations to extend remarks in the *Congressional Record* are strictly construed. Deschler Ch 5 § 20. A Member who has received permission only to extend remarks may not also include in such remarks extraneous matter, such as an article or speech by another person. 8 Cannon § 3479; Deschler Ch 5 § 20.23. Similarly, a Member who has obtained the consent of the House only to extend remarks on a specific bill must confine the insertions to the subject matter of the bill and may not include extraneous materials such as letters, editorials, or articles. Deschler Ch 5 § 20.24.

The Chair will decline to entertain a request that a Member be permitted to revise and extend remarks on a point of order or to insert, immediately following a record vote on an amendment, the results of a previous record vote on the same subject. *Manual* § 628; 96-2, Jan. 30, 1980, p 1319.

Limitations on Insertions

Under leave to extend, a Member may not insert matter that:

- Would be out of order if stated on the House floor. 5 Hinds § 7003; Deschler Ch 5 § 20.
- Fails to comply with statute or the rules of the Joint Committee on Printing as to format (44 USC § 904) or cost-estimate requirements for extraneous matter exceeding two *Congressional Record* pages (*Manual* § 692).
- Fails to conform to the descriptions implicit in the request to which the House consented. 5 Hinds § 7001; 8 Cannon § 3479; Deschler Ch 5 §§ 20.25, 20.26.
- Fails to include the Member's signature. *Manual* § 686.
- Alters the nature of colloquies as delivered on the floor or changes the meaning of what another Member said. Deschler Ch 5 §§ 19.3, 19.17, 20.3.

- Inserts an entire colloquy between two or more Members that was not actually delivered. *Manual* § 692.
- Includes newspaper articles or other extraneous matter without having obtained authority to do so. *Manual* § 692; 8 Cannon §§ 3480-3483.

Abuse of Leave to Print

Abuse of the leave to print may give rise to a question of privilege. 5 Hinds §§ 7008, 7011; 8 Cannon §§ 3491, 3495. A resolution to investigate the propriety of remarks as constituting such abuse, or for the appointment of a committee to consider the propriety of remarks inserted under leave to print, is privileged but is not in order until the daily edition of the *Congressional Record* appears. 5 Hinds §§ 7020, 7021; 8 Cannon §§ 3493, 3495. An inquiry by the House as to alleged abuse of leave to print does not necessarily entitle the Member implicated to recognition on a question of personal privilege. 5 Hinds § 7012. A committee having been appointed to investigate the propriety of a Member's remarks in the *Record*, the Member was afforded an opportunity to be heard. 8 Cannon § 3491.

Expungement

The extension of remarks in the *Congressional Record* by a Member without the permission of the House constitutes grounds for a question of the privilege of the House, and the House may expunge such remarks from the *Record*. Deschler Ch 5 § 20.2. A resolution to expunge remarks alleged to be an abuse of leave to print is privileged and is debatable. 8 Cannon §§ 3475, 3479, 3491.

The House may exclude in whole or in part an insertion by a Member under leave to print in the *Congressional Record* that would not have been in order if uttered on the floor. *Manual* § 692.

Form

MEMBER: M__. Speaker, I ask unanimous consent to extend my remarks and to include extraneous material on H.R. __________.

MANAGER: M__. Speaker, I ask unanimous consent that all Members may have five legislative days in which to revise and extend their remarks and include extraneous material on H.R. __________.

MAJORITY LEADER: M__. Speaker, I ask unanimous consent that for the __________ Congress all Members be permitted to extend their remarks and to include extraneous material within the permitted limit in that section of the *Congressional Record* entitled "Extensions of Remarks."

Chapter 16
Consideration and Debate

Research References

5 Hinds §§4978-5299
8 Cannon §§2448-2608
Deschler-Brown Ch 29
Manual §§359, 364, 369-371, 465, 622, 891, 945-969, 978-981, 987, 994-999

A. Introductory; Initiating Consideration and Debate

§1. In General; In the House

Generally; Initiating Consideration

Whether and how a matter is to be considered depends on many factors—the way it is brought to the floor, the nature and precedence of the proposal, and agreements reached by the leadership and membership on the method of consideration. The House may reject a proposal to consider a matter by voting on the question of consideration. See QUESTION OF CONSIDERATION.

There are four common procedures under which measures may be called up for consideration: (1) special orders of business reported from the Committee on Rules; (2) motions to suspend the rules; (3) unanimous-consent agreements; and (4) standing rules for certain measures reported as privileged under clause 5 of rule XIII. *Manual* §§853-868. However, non-privileged matter contained in a measure reported under clause 5 of rule

XIII destroys the privilege of the measure; and consideration must depend on one of the three remaining procedures. *Manual* §§ 854, 855.

House rules expressly preclude introduction or consideration of certain commemorative measures (clause 5 of rule XII), as well as consideration of certain private bills (clause 4 of rule XII) and measures carrying a retroactive Federal income tax rate increase (clause 5(c) of rule XXI).

Generally, questions are not considered on the floor unless reported or discharged from House committees, although rule IX and practices of the House permit the immediate consideration of introduced bills under certain circumstances. §§ 3, 4, 6 infra. Certain time periods or ''layover'' requirements may be a condition precedent to consideration in the House after a committee has reported. See COMMITTEES. If a bill or joint resolution is unreported, clause 11 of rule XXI prevents consideration until the third calendar day on which such measure has been available to Members. For recognition by the Chair to call up measures under the various procedures, see RECOGNITION.

Other factors bearing on consideration include whether the proposal has been referred to the House or Union Calendar or whether the proposal is called up from a particular special calendar, such as the Private Calendar. See § 5, infra.

Initiating Debate

As a general rule, debate is not in order until a debatable motion has been offered and stated by the Chair or read by the Clerk. 5 Hinds §§ 4982-4985, 5304. However, debate may be initiated without motion:

- Under a reservation of the right to object to a unanimous-consent request. 4 Hinds § 3058.
- When questions of personal privilege are raised. 3 Hinds § 2546.
- When conference reports are considered, the question on agreeing being regarded as pending. *Manual* § 550; 5 Hinds § 6517.
- When the Committee of the Whole reports its recommendation to the House, unless the previous question is ordered. 4 Hinds § 4896.
- When personal explanations are made by unanimous consent. 5 Hinds § 5064.
- When special orders of business providing for consideration of a measure have been adopted. *Manual* §§ 734, 972.
- When a measure on a special calendar or on a special day has been called up. Rule XV.

§2. Order of Consideration

The "daily order of business" is set forth in rule XIV, which specifies the sequence in which certain matters are to be taken up. *Manual* §869. The order of consideration may be varied by unanimous-consent agreements or by special orders of business reported from the Committee on Rules and adopted by the House. See §§3, 6; see also ORDER OF BUSINESS; PRIVILEGED BUSINESS; and SPECIAL ORDERS OF BUSINESS. Indeed, the preface to clause 1 of rule XIV establishes a daily order of business "unless varied by the application of other rules and except for the disposition of matters of higher precedence."

Among the privileged matters that may affect the order of consideration are: (1) general appropriation bills under clause 5 of rule XIII; (2) conference reports under clause 7(a) of rule XXII; (3) special orders of business reported by the Committee on Rules under clause 5 of rule XIII; and (4) questions of privilege under rule IX. *Manual* §§698, 871; see also QUESTIONS OF PRIVILEGE.

Some propositions are privileged for consideration on certain days of the week or month. On any Monday, Tuesday, or Wednesday, for example, the Speaker may recognize Members to move to suspend the rules. *Manual* §885; see also §§4, 5, infra.

§3. Use of Special Orders of Business

A major portion of the legislation taken up in the House is considered pursuant to resolutions, also called "special rules" or "special orders of business," reported by the Committee on Rules and adopted by the House. Although the general effect of the adoption of a resolution making in order the consideration of a bill is to give the bill a privileged status, the adoption of the resolution does not make the consideration mandatory unless so stated in the resolution. Deschler Ch 21 §16. For example, the resolution may: (1) provide that "the House shall immediately consider" the bill; (2) permit the Speaker to declare the House resolved into the Committee of the Whole for the consideration of the bill (see clause 2 of rule XVIII); or (3) provide for consideration at some specified time in the order of business. If the special order of business authorizes a specified Member to call up a bill (either directly or indirectly, such as "it shall be in order to consider"), the consideration of the bill must await the initiative of that Member. See Deschler Ch 21 §20.17.

Special orders of business may provide for the consideration of a bill or resolution in the Committee of the Whole, in the House, or in the House as in the Committee of the Whole. Deschler Ch 21 §§20.16, 20.17.

A special order of business may be limited in scope, as where it provides only for initial consideration of a measure, provides for general debate, and precludes further consideration absent a further order of the House. See, *e.g.*, 105-2, H. Res. 435, May 19, 1998, pp 9742, 9743.

The resolution may waive one or more House rules that impede the consideration of the bill or amendment thereto. Points of order do not lie against the consideration of such a resolution, as it is for the House to determine, by a majority vote on the adoption of the resolution, whether certain rules should be waived. Deschler Ch 21 §§ 16.9-16.14. See generally SPECIAL ORDERS OF BUSINESS. However, section 426 of the Unfunded Mandates Reform Act of 1995 permits a point of order against consideration of a rule or order that waives points of order against a measure for violating that Act (subject to a separate vote on the question of consideration). *Manual* § 1127. In similar fashion, clause 9 of rule XXI establishes a point of order against consideration of certain measures for failure to disclose (or disclaim the presence of) certain earmarks, tax benefits, and tariff benefits, and permits a vote on the question of consideration of a rule or order waiving such a point of order. See BUDGET PROCESS.

§ 4. Consideration Under Suspension of the Rules

A privileged motion to suspend the rules may be used to bring a matter before the House under clause 1 of rule XV. *Manual* §§ 885, 887; 5 Hinds §§ 6846, 6847. Additionally, the motion to suspend may provide for a series of procedural steps, including the reconsideration of a bill already passed, agreement to an amendment, and repassage as amended. 5 Hinds § 6849. For examples of proposals for which the motion may be used, see SUSPENSION OF RULES. However, the motion is in order only on Mondays, Tuesdays, and Wednesdays of each week and on the last six days of a session or when the House by unanimous consent or rule gives the Speaker authority to recognize for such motions on other days of the week. In any case, recognition for the motion is within the discretion of the Speaker. The motion is debatable for 40 minutes, is not amendable, and requires a two-thirds vote for adoption. See SUSPENSION OF RULES.

§ 5. Role of Calendars

The House maintains various calendars to facilitate the consideration of different classes of legislative business. The primary calendars are (1) the Union Calendar, for business to be taken up in the Committee of the Whole, (2) the House Calendar, for matters to be considered in the House, and (3) the Private Calendar, to which all reported private bills are referred. Most legislative business reported from committee is referred to one of these calendars. *Manual* § 828. In addition, the House maintains a Calendar of Motions to Discharge Committees. *Manual* §§ 830, 892. The former Consent Calendar and Corrections Calendar have been abolished. *Manual* §§ 898, 899. For a discussion of the various calendars, see CALENDARS.

§ 6. Consideration by Unanimous Consent

The House, pursuant to a unanimous-consent agreement, sometimes permits the consideration of a measure that is not otherwise in order under the rules, for example, one not yet introduced. *Manual* §§ 381, 872, 956; 4 Hinds § 3058. For a discussion of consideration by unanimous consent (including the Speaker's guidelines requiring approval by floor and committee leaderships before recognition), see UNANIMOUS-CONSENT AGREEMENTS.

§ 7. In Committee of the Whole

Certain legislative measures are referred to the Union Calendar by the Speaker for subsequent consideration in the Committee of the Whole. Their consideration therein is governed by special orders of business, orders of the House, or the standing rules applicable to the Committee. See rule XVIII; 4 Hinds §§ 3214, 4705, 4822; Deschler Ch 19 §§ 1, 4.

For comprehensive discussion of consideration of measures in Committee of the Whole, see COMMITTEES OF THE WHOLE.

§ 8. In the House as in the Committee of the Whole

Bills and other measures sometimes are taken up by the House when it sits ''as in'' the Committee of the Whole. *Manual* § 427. This practice permits consideration of a measure under the five-minute rule rather than the hour rule, but without general debate. 4 Hinds § 4924; *Manual* § 424. For a discussion of consideration of measures in the House as in the Committee of the Whole, see COMMITTEES OF THE WHOLE.

§ 9. Limitations on Debate; Nondebatable Matters

Generally; Time Limitations

Debate is subject to many limitations under the rules and precedents of the House. Most of the limitations imposed by House rule concern the duration of time allowed for the debate of a particular proposition. These include, for example, the hour rule (*Manual* § 957), the 40-minute rule (*Manual* §§ 891, 999), the 20-minute rule (*Manual* § 892), the ten-minute rule (*Manual* § 987), the five-minute rule (*Manual* § 978), and the time limits that are imposed on the one-minute speeches or special-order speeches that are often permitted when no legislative business is pending (*Manual* § 950). For a more detailed discussion of these time limitations, see §§ 44-50, infra.

Most of these are rules of general applicability. In addition, the House may adopt a special order of business from the Committee on Rules that places a different limit on the duration of debate on a particular legislative proposal. This practice enables the House, by majority vote, to specify time for, and control of, debate depending on the complexity of the proposed measure.

Unless otherwise provided by House rule or by a special order of business from the Committee on Rules, a proposition considered in the House is debated under the hour rule. §§ 44, 45, infra. However, the various motions that may apply to a proposition often carry their own time limitations for debate and, in some instances, preclude debate entirely.

Matters Not Subject to Debate

The relevant standing rule and the precedents must be consulted in order to determine whether debate on a motion or question is precluded. The following are examples of questions that are not subject to debate:

- A motion that the Journal be read in full. *Manual* § 621.
- A motion for the previous question. Deschler Ch 23 § 21.
- A motion to go into the Committee of the Whole. 4 Hinds §§ 3062, 3078; 6 Cannon § 716.
- A motion that the Committee of the Whole rise and report. 4 Hinds §§ 4766, 4782; Deschler Ch 19 § 22.4.
- A motion for a call of the House or incidental to a call of the House. *Manual* § 1024; 6 Cannon §§ 683, 688.
- A resolution authorizing the Sergeant-at-Arms to arrest absentees. 6 Cannon § 686.
- A motion that the Speaker be authorized to declare a recess or that when the House adjourns it stand adjourned to a day and time certain. Rule XVI; *Manual* § 913.
- A concurrent resolution providing for a *sine die* adjournment or for adjournment to a day certain. *Manual* § 84.
- A motion to adjourn. *Manual* § 911; Deschler-Brown-Johnson Ch 40 § 5.
- A motion to lay on the table. 6 Cannon § 415; 8 Cannon § 2465.
- A motion to reconsider an undebatable proposition. 5 Hinds §§ 5694-5699.
- A motion to close general debate or to limit five-minute debate. *Manual* § 979; 5 Hinds § 5203.
- A motion to strike unparliamentary language from the *Congressional Record*. 6 Cannon § 617.
- An incidental question of order after a demand for the previous question. *Manual* § 1000.

- An incidental question of order arising during a division. 5 Hinds §5926.
- A motion that the Committee of the Whole take up a bill out of calendar order. 8 Cannon §§2331, 2333.
- A motion for a change of reference of a bill. *Manual* §825.
- A question of consideration (with limited exceptions). *Manual* §906.
- A question relating to the priority of business. *Manual* §884.
- An appeal from a decision of the Chair on the priority of business. 5 Hinds §6952; *Manual* §884.
- An appeal from a decision of the Chair on relevancy of debate. 5 Hinds §§5056-5063.
- An amendment to the title of a bill. Clause 6 of rule XVI; 8 Cannon §2907.

B. Control and Distribution of Time for Debate

§10. In General; Role of Manager

Under long-standing practice, and as usually provided by special orders of business, one or more designated Members manage a bill during its consideration. Such managers are normally the chair and ranking minority member of a committee reporting the measure. §14, infra.

The majority manager of a measure has procedural advantages enabling its expeditious consideration and passage. The majority manager is entitled to the prior right to recognition unless the control of time is surrendered or otherwise lost or unless a preferential motion to recommit is offered by an opponent of the bill. See RECOGNITION. If the bill is to be taken up in the House under the standing rules, the manager calling it up is entitled to one hour of debate, which may be yielded to other Members. See §15, infra. The manager may at any time during such hour move the previous question, thereby bringing the matter to a vote and terminating further debate, unless control of time has been yielded to another. See §45, infra; see also PREVIOUS QUESTION.

The manager of a bill enjoys a similar advantage in the Committee of the Whole where the bill is being considered under a special order of business or unanimous-consent agreement. General debate therein typically is controlled and divided by the majority and minority managers. The majority manager has the right to close general debate. *Manual* §959. When the bill is read for amendment in the Committee, the managers have the prior right to recognition, whether to offer an amendment or oppose an amendment or to move to close or to limit debate or to move that the Committee rise. Similarly, if the bill is taken up in the House as in the Committee of the

Whole, priority in recognition is extended during debate to members in charge of the bill from the reporting committee. See RECOGNITION.

Once a measure has been approved by a standing committee of the House, its chair has a duty under the rules to report it promptly and to take steps to have the matter considered and voted upon. Clause 2(b) of rule XIII. When the measure is called up, the reporting committee manages the bill during the various stages of its consideration. The designated managers from the committee, and then other members of the committee in order of seniority, have priority in recognition at all stages of consideration. See RECOGNITION. When a chair is opposed to a bill (although rare), the responsibility for managing the bill may be delegated to the ranking majority member of the committee. Deschler-Brown Ch 29 § 26.7. Such delegation of control is ineffective where challenged unless communicated to the Chair. Deschler-Brown Ch 29 § 26.30. The chair also may relinquish control where the Committee of the Whole has adopted amendments to the bill to which the chair is opposed. Deschler-Brown Ch 29 § 26.8.

Where the measure falls within the jurisdiction of two standing committees, the chair of one of them may yield to the chair of the other to control part of the available time and to move the previous question. Deschler-Brown Ch 29 § 26.10.

For further discussion on control of debate by managers, see also § 12, infra.

§ 11. Distribution and Alternation; Closing General Debate

The distribution of available time for debate, and the alternation of time between majority and minority Members, is governed by principles of comity and by House tradition, as well as by standing rules of the House and by special orders of business. *Manual* § 955. A division of time for debate on certain motions may be required, and a Member opposed may claim a priority to control a portion of the time. For example, clause 1(c) of rule XV requires a division of time for debate on a motion to suspend the rules between those in favor and those opposed. *Manual* § 891. Under rule XXII, one-third of the time may be claimed by a Member opposed to conference reports, motions to instruct conferees, and amendments reported from conference in disagreement, where both the majority and minority managers support the proposition.

The Chair alternates recognition between those favoring and those opposing the pending proposition where a rule or precedent gives some control to an opponent or, traditionally, between the parties where time is limited. Special orders of business commonly divide control of time for general debate equally between the chair and ranking minority member of the committees reporting the measure. When a special order of business itself is being considered, the majority floor manager customarily yields half of the time to the minority. For a discussion of alternation generally, see RECOGNITION.

A majority manager of the bill who represents the primary committee of jurisdiction is entitled to close general debate, as against another manager representing an additional committee of jurisdiction. Where an order of the House divides debate on an unreported measure among four Members, the Chair will recognize for closing speeches in the reverse order of the original allocation. Similarly, where general debate on an adversely reported measure is controlled by two Members allocated time under a previous order of the House and by two other Members deriving subdivisions of that time under a later order by unanimous consent, the Chair may recognize for closing speeches in the reverse order of the original allocation, concluding with the Member who opened the debate. Where a Member derives time for debate from the manager of a measure by unanimous consent, that Member also derives the right to close debate thereon. Where a member of the minority is recognized under a special order of business to call up a Senate concurrent resolution from the Speaker's desk, such Member is recognized to open and close debate thereon. *Manual* §959.

§12. Management by Committee; Closing Controlled Debate on an Amendment

Special orders of business providing ''modified rules'' governing the amendment process commonly limit and divide control of debate between a proponent and an opponent of the amendment. Deschler-Brown Ch 29 §28. Similarly, the Committee of the Whole may by unanimous consent limit and divide control of debate between a proponent and a Member in opposition. Deschler-Brown Ch 29 §27.3. Under clause 3(c) of rule XVII, the manager of a bill or other representative of the committee in opposition—and not the proponent of an amendment—has the right to close debate on an amendment where debate has been so limited and allocated without regard to the party affiliation of the proponent. *Manual* §959. Clause 3(c) is an exception to the rule set forth in clause 3(a) of rule XVII, which otherwise provides that the mover, proposer, or introducer of the pending matter has the right to open and close debate. The exceptional treatment of the right to close debate on an amendment elevates the manager's prerogative over the proponent's burden of persuasion. This is so even when the majority manager offers an amendment that has not been recommended by the committee. In that case, a member of the committee in opposition to such amendment has the right to close. 107-2, July 25, 2002, p 14723.

Clause 3(c) applies to the manager of an unreported measure, even where the rule providing for the consideration of the unreported measure designates managers who do not serve on a committee of jurisdiction. It also applies to a measure reported by the committee without recommendation. The minority manager may claim the right to close debate under clause 3(c), as may a member of a committee of sequential referral to close debate against an amendment to a provision recommended by that committee. *Manual* § 959. However, the proponent of an amendment has the right to close where a manager does not oppose the amendment but nevertheless, by unanimous consent, claims the time reserved for opposition. *Manual* § 959.

For further discussion on control of debate by managers, see § 10, supra.

§ 13. Designation of Member Who May Call Up a Measure

The committee reporting a measure occasionally designates the Member who may call up a measure for consideration, in which case the Chair may recognize only that Member. Deschler-Brown Ch 29 §§ 27.1, 27.2. A special order of business also may designate the Member. § 14, infra. If a Member has not been specifically designated, the Chair has the discretion to recognize a committee member to call up a measure. 91-1, Dec. 23, 1969, p 40982.

§ 14. Effect of Special Orders of Business

Generally

The designation of certain Members to control debate on a measure is frequently provided by special order of business from the Committee on Rules. Typically the Committee on Rules will draft a special order of business providing that debate be equally divided and controlled by the chair and ranking minority member of the reporting committee or committees. Deschler-Brown Ch 29 § 28. That control can be delegated to a designee on the committee.

Dividing Debate Between Multiple Committees

A special order of business from the Committee on Rules may specify that debate be divided between and controlled by two or more standing committees. Deschler-Brown Ch 29 § 28.13. The special order of business may provide that debate be controlled by the chairs and ranking minority members of the several committees reporting a bill, sometimes with the secondary committees controlling a lesser amount of time. Deschler-Brown Ch 29 § 28.16. Debate also may be divided between the standing committee reporting a bill and a permanent select committee. 95-1, Sept. 9, 1977, p 28367.

Where a special order of business divides the control of general debate on a bill among the chairs and ranking members of two standing committees, but does not specify the order of recognition, recognition is within the Chair's discretion. The Chair may allow one committee to use its time before recognizing the other, or may rotate among the four managers. Deschler-Brown Ch 29 § 28.18.

If the rule divides control of debate among a primary reporting committee and several sequentially reporting committees in a designated order, the Chair may allocate time between the chair and ranking minority member of each committee in the order listed, if and when present on the floor, and permit only the primary committee to reserve a portion of its time to close general debate. Deschler-Brown Ch 29 § 28.16. When the Chair has announced the intention to permit the primary committee to so reserve a portion of its time, the sequential committees are required to use all of their time before the closing debate by the primary committee. 99-1, Dec. 5, 1985, pp 34638, 34644. A majority manager of the bill who represents the primary committee of jurisdiction is entitled to close general debate (as against another manager representing an additional committee of jurisdiction). *Manual* § 959.

Division of Time Between a Member in Favor and a Member Opposed

In the event that a specified amount of time for debate is equally divided and controlled between the proponent of the amendment and a Member opposed thereto, only one Member may be recognized to control the time in favor of the amendment and only one Member may be recognized to control the time in opposition, though each may in turn yield blocks of time to other Members. 99-2, Aug. 11, 1986, pp 20678, 20679. Pro forma amendments are not permitted where second degree amendments are prohibited unless so specified. 99-2, Aug. 14, 1986, p 21655. Time for debate on the amendment having been divided between the proponent and an opponent, the Chair has the discretion to recognize the manager of the bill in opposition, there being no requirement for recognition of the minority party. Indeed, the Chair ordinarily recognizes the chair of the committee managing the bill if such individual qualifies as opposed to the amendment. *Manual* § 959; § 10, supra.

A special order of business may provide that, after general debate divided between the chair and ranking minority member of the reporting committee, a certain amount of time for general debate be divided and controlled by a Member in favor of and a Member opposed to a certain section of the bill. 96-1, Sept. 13, 1979, pp 24168, 24192. In one instance, the House adopted a special order of business providing for one hour of general debate to be equally divided and controlled by the chair and ranking minority member of the reporting committee, and two hours to be divided and controlled by Members to be designated by the chair. 95-2, July 31, 1978, p 23451.

§ 15. Yielding Time—For Debate

In General; Who May Yield

In an earlier era, a Member could not yield time for debate without losing the right to reoccupy the floor. A Member could not yield the floor unless it was yielded unconditionally. 5 Hinds §§ 5023, 5026. That practice began to change with the adoption of the hour rule for debate in 1841. 5 Hinds § 5021.

Under current practice, a Member controlling the time during debate may yield blocks of time for debate to others, be seated, and still retain the right to resume debate or move the previous question. 8 Cannon § 3383. The yielding of time for debate is discretionary with the Members who have control thereof. Deschler-Brown Ch 29 §§ 31.1, 31.2. A Member may not yield for purposes of debate when rising merely to make or reserve a point of order. Deschler-Brown Ch 31 § 7.5. A Member may not yield to another for debate while under recognition merely for a parliamentary inquiry. Deschler-Brown Ch 29 § 20.7.

A Member who seeks yielded time should address the Chair and request the permission of the Member speaking. Deschler-Brown Ch 29 § 42. Where a Member interrupts another Member during debate without being yielded to, the time consumed by such remarks are not charged against the time for debate of the Member controlling the floor and the remarks are not carried in the *Congressional Record*. *Manual* § 946.

The time used by yielding is ordinarily charged against the yielding Member. Deschler-Brown Ch 29 § 29.5. Unused time reverts to the yielding Member. Deschler-Brown Ch 29 § 31.36. A Member may yield to another for a parliamentary inquiry, but the time consumed by the inquiry and the response of the Chair comes out of the time of the Member yielding. Deschler-Brown Ch 29 § 29.5.

Clause 3(b) of rule XVII, which prohibits a Member who is not a manager from speaking more than once on a question, often is superseded in modern practice by special orders of business that vest control of debate in designated Members and permit them to yield more than once to other Members. *Manual* § 959.

In the House

The Member in control of debate in the House under the hour rule has the discretion to yield for debate. Deschler-Brown Ch 29 § 29. Indeed, although not required to do so by standing rule, majority members in control under the hour rule frequently yield one-half the time to the minority. Deschler-Brown Ch 29 § 29.15. Of course, the yielding of time must be consistent with any division of time that is required by House rule or a special order of business from the Committee on Rules.

In the Committee of the Whole

In the Committee of the Whole, a Member in control of time for general debate may yield a block of time (up to one hour) to another Member. Deschler-Brown Ch 29 § 31.24.

During five-minute debate Members may yield, as for a question or comment, but may not yield blocks of time. 5 Hinds §§ 5035-5037. A Member yielding to a colleague during debate under the five-minute rule should remain standing to protect such Member's right to the floor. Deschler-Brown Ch 29 § 29.8. If a Member uses only part of the time, such five-minute period is treated as exhausted, as it cannot be reserved, and another Member cannot claim recognition for the unused time. 8 Cannon § 2571. However, where debate on an amendment is limited or allocated by a unanimous-consent agreement or motion, or by a special order of business, to a proponent and an opponent, the five-minute rule is abrogated and the Members controlling the debate may yield blocks of time or reserve time. *Manual* § 980.

Yielding During Debate on Special Orders of Business

The traditional practice with regard to resolutions from the Committee on Rules providing special orders of business for the consideration of measures is for the Member in charge of the resolution to yield one-half of the time to the minority, who then may yield specified portions thereof. Although the minority member of the Committee on Rules to whom one-half of the time for debate is yielded customarily yields portions of that time to other Members, another Member to whom a portion of time is yielded may in turn yield blocks of that time only by unanimous consent. Deschler-Brown Ch 29 § 31.23. However, where a Member has been recognized under the hour rule following refusal of the previous question on such a resolution, such Member has control of the time and is under no obligation to yield half of that time as is the customary practice of the Committee on Rules. Deschler-Brown Ch 29 § 15.20.

Yielding Time During Yielded Time

A Member to whom time has been yielded during debate under the hour rule in the House may, while remaining standing, yield to a third Member for comments or questions but may not in turn yield blocks of time, except by unanimous consent. Deschler-Brown Ch 29 § 31.21. A similar rule is followed in the Committee of the Whole. Deschler-Brown Ch 29 § 31.24.

Where a Member is yielded time in the House for debate only, time may not be yielded to a third Member for purposes other than debate. Deschler-Brown Ch 29 § 31.19.

§ 16. — Yielding for Amendment

In General

A measure being considered in the House is not subject to amendment by a Member not in control of the time unless the Member in control yields for that purpose. Deschler-Brown Ch 29 §§ 30.1, 30.4. A Member may not offer an amendment in time secured for debate only or request unanimous consent to offer an amendment unless yielded to for that purpose by the Member controlling the floor. *Manual* § 946; 8 Cannon § 2474; Deschler-Brown Ch 29 § 30.6.

Members to whom time is yielded for the purpose of offering an amendment in the House are recognized in their own right to discuss the amendment for one hour and may themselves yield time. 8 Cannon §§ 2471, 2478; Deschler-Brown Ch 29 § 30.11.

Loss of Control by Yielding Member

A Member may not yield to another Member to offer an amendment without losing the floor. 5 Hinds §§ 5021, 5030, 5031; 8 Cannon § 2476; *Manual* § 946. Where a Member controlling the time on a measure in the House yields for the purpose of amendment, another Member may move the previous question on the measure before the Member yielded to is recognized to debate the amendment. *Manual* § 997. The previous question takes precedence over an amendment. Clause 4 of rule XVI; *Manual* § 911. If the Member calling up a measure offers an amendment and then yields to another Member to offer an amendment to that amendment, the first Member loses the floor and the Member yielded to is recognized for one hour and may move the previous question on the amendments and on the measure itself. Deschler-Brown Ch 29 § 33.9.

Under the Five-Minute Rule

A Member recognized under the five-minute rule may not yield to another Member to offer an amendment. It is the prerogative of the Chair to recognize Members offering amendments under the five-minute rule. *Manual* §946. However, a Member recognized under the five-minute rule may by unanimous consent yield the balance of the time to another Member, who may thereafter offer an amendment when separately recognized by the Chair for that purpose. Deschler-Brown Ch 29 §19.25.

A Member offering a pro forma amendment under the five-minute rule may not yield to another Member during that time to offer an amendment. *Manual* §981.

§17. Interruptions; Losing or Surrendering Control

In General

With few exceptions, a Member may interrupt another Member in debate only if yielded to. A Member desiring to interrupt another in debate should address the Chair to obtain the permission of the Member speaking. The Member speaking may then decide whether or not to yield. The Chair will take the initiative in preserving order when a Member declining to yield in debate continues to be interrupted by another Member. Deschler-Brown Ch 29 §42.14; *Manual* §946.

A Member in control of time for debate in the House may voluntarily surrender the floor by simply so stating or by withdrawing the measure. A Member recognized under the hour rule may yield the floor upon expiration of that hour without moving the previous question, thereby permitting another Member to be recognized for a successive hour. *Manual* §957. A Member also may lose the floor if ruled out of order for disorderly language. Deschler-Brown Ch 29 §33. Finally, a Member loses the floor if yielding for other legislative business (8 Cannon §2468) or for an amendment (§16, supra).

A Member may be interrupted by a point of order or by the presentation of certain privileged matter, such as a conference report. 5 Hinds §6451; 8 Cannon §3294. In addition, it is customary for the Speaker to request a Member to yield for the reception of a message. *Manual* §946. However, a parliamentary inquiry may not be used to interrupt a Member. *Manual* §628a.

Although a motion proposed by the Member in charge may be displaced by a preferential motion, a Member may not by offering such motion deprive the Member in charge of the floor. 8 Cannon § 3259. A Member having the floor may not be deprived of the floor:

- By a motion to adjourn. 5 Hinds §§ 5369, 5370; 8 Cannon § 2646.
- By a demand for the previous question. 8 Cannon § 2609.
- By a question of personal privilege. 5 Hinds § 5002; 8 Cannon § 2459; 98-1, Sept. 29, 1983, pp 26508, 26509.

Interruptions for Parliamentary Inquiries

An interruption for a parliamentary inquiry is not in order unless the Member having the floor yields for that purpose. *Manual* § 628a; 8 Cannon §§ 2455-2458. If a Member does yield for that purpose, control of the floor is not lost because the right to resume is retained. Thus, a Member who has been yielded time for a parliamentary inquiry may not during such inquiry move that the House adjourn, for that would deprive the Member holding the floor of the right to resume. 88-2, June 3, 1964, p 12522.

Where the Member controlling the time yields to another for debate, the latter may, during the time so yielded, propound a parliamentary inquiry. 90-1, July 17, 1967, p 19033. The time consumed to state and answer the inquiry is deducted from the time for debate. 94-1, Sept. 25, 1975, p 30196. When the Member holding the floor during general debate yields solely for a parliamentary inquiry, such Member's time continues to run. Deschler-Brown Ch 31 § 15.6. However, when the Chair entertains a parliamentary inquiry before the Member managing the pending measure in the House has been recognized for debate, or between recognitions, the time consumed by the inquiry does not come out of the manager's time. Deschler-Brown Ch 31 § 15.8.

C. Relevancy in Debate

§ 18. In General; In the House

Members addressing the House must confine themselves ''to the question under debate. . . .'' Clause 1 of rule XVII; *Manual* § 945. The rule, which was adopted in 1811, enables the House to expedite proceedings when a specific proposition is before it for action. *Manual* § 945; 5 Hinds §§ 4979, 5043-5048; 8 Cannon § 2481. The rule is directed against irrelevant discussion, not mere redundancy. Although *Jefferson's Manual* enjoins superfluous or tedious remarks, in practice the House has never suppressed debate of this character, the hour rule being regarded as sufficiently restrictive in that regard. *Manual* § 359.

Debate on a reported resolution pending before the House should be confined thereto and should not be extended to an unreported bill even though on the same subject. 5 Hinds § 5053. The rule is also applicable to debate on private bills. 8 Cannon § 2590. On a motion to suspend the rules, debate is confined to the object of the motion and may not range to the merits of a bill not scheduled for such consideration. *Manual* § 948.

It was the custom of earlier Speakers to hold the Member speaking strictly to the question before the House, without waiting for the point to be made on the floor. See 5 Hinds § 5043 (note). Under modern practice, however, the Chair waits for a point of order to be made and rarely calls a Member to order *sua sponte* for speaking on an unrelated question. *Manual* § 948.

Under modern practice Speakers have applied the rule of relevancy with more tolerance and latitude than under the earlier practice. Deschler-Brown Ch 29 § 35. A Member is sometimes permitted to discuss matters other than the pending measure by unanimous consent. Deschler-Brown Ch 29 § 35. Absent unanimous consent, if a point of order is made and sustained, the Speaker must direct the Member speaking to confine remarks to the question (5 Hinds §§ 5044-5048) and to maintain an ongoing ''nexus'' between the pending bill and any broader policy issues (*Manual* § 948).

The relevancy requirement of rule XVII is applicable to floor debate on pending propositions. It is not normally applicable to a Member making a one-minute or special-order speech. See § 50, infra. However, if a unanimous-consent request for a Member to address the House for one hour specifies the subject of the address, the Chair may enforce the rule of relevancy in debate by requiring that the remarks be confined to the subject so specified. *Manual* § 948.

When a resolution reported from the Committee on Rules is pending, debate must be confined to that special order of business and to the merits of the bill made in order thereby. Debate should not extend to the merits of a bill that is not to be considered under the special order of business. *Manual* § 948. However, debate may extend to the merits of a germane amendment to the special order of business, which a proponent is prepared to offer in the case that the previous question is not ordered on the special order of business.

Debate on a question of personal privilege must be confined to the statements or issue that gave rise to the question of privilege. 5 Hinds §§ 5075-5077; 6 Cannon §§ 576, 608; 8 Cannon §§ 2448, 2481; Deschler-Brown Ch 29 § 36. Debate on a privileged resolution recommending disciplinary action against a Member may include comparisons with other such actions taken by or reported to the House for purposes of measuring the severity of punishment but should not extend to the conduct of another Member who is not the subject of a committee report. Debate on a resolution electing a Member to committee should not extend to that committee's agenda. *Manual* § 948.

§ 19. In the Committee of the Whole—General Debate

In the Committee of the Whole, during the general debate that precedes the reading of the bill for amendment under the five-minute rule, a Member is allowed great freedom and latitude in debate. 5 Hinds §§ 5234-5238. "Anything may be discussed which may by the liveliest imagination be supposed to relate to the state of the Union in any particular or in any degree, however remote." 8 Cannon § 2590. However, such license is normally suppressed by the special order of business or other House order setting the duration and scope of the debate. 5 Hinds §§ 5233-5238; 8 Cannon § 2590; Deschler-Brown Ch 29 § 37. If the bill is being considered under the terms of a special order of business that requires that debate be confined to the bill, a Member may exceed those bounds only by unanimous consent. Deschler-Brown Ch 29 § 37.3.

§ 20. —Under the Five-Minute Rule

The scope of debate under the five-minute rule is more narrowly confined than is the scope of general debate. *Manual* § 948; 5 Hinds §§ 5240-5256; 8 Cannon § 2591. Debate on a pending amendment must be confined to the subject of the amendment and its relation to the bill. Deschler-Brown Ch 29 §§ 38.5, 38.11. This is due in part to the language of clause 5 of rule XVIII, which states that a Member is to be allowed five minutes "to explain" an offered amendment. *Manual* § 978. It has been held that remarks on the general merits of the bill are not in order as "explaining" an amendment, and remarks touching on the demerits of the bill are not in order as opposing an amendment. 5 Hinds § 5242. Nevertheless, the Chair may accord Members latitude to put their amendment in context, such as permitting debate on a series of amendments in the nature of a substitute to a concurrent resolution on the budget to include amendments not yet offered. 106-1, Mar. 25, 1999, pp 5725-27, 5733-44.

Relevancy in debate may be enforced even if a Member is attempting to respond to previous extraneous remarks in debate against which no point of order was raised. Deschler-Brown Ch 29 § 38.13; 110-1, July 31, 2007, p 21963. However, a Member may speak to another subject by unanimous consent. This is permitted even where the Committee of the Whole is proceeding pursuant to the provisions of a special order of business permitting only designated amendments to be offered. Deschler-Brown Ch 29 § 38.17. Where a general provisions title is pending, debate may relate to any subject covered by the bill. *Manual* § 948.

D. Disorder in Debate

§ 21. In General

Generally

Among the oldest rules of the House are those that authorize the Speaker to maintain order and decorum in the House (clause 2 of rule I) and to call a Member who had transgressed the rules of the House ''in speaking or otherwise'' to order (clause 4 of rule XVII). This language makes it clear that Members must not only follow all the rules and requirements for the conduct of business in the House, but must also observe the principles of decorum and courtesy in debate, as set forth in rule XVII and by related provisions in *Jefferson's Manual*. *Manual* §§ 353-379, 945-962.

Time consumed by proceedings incident to a call to order is not charged against the time of the Member under recognition. 102-2, Oct. 3, 1992, p 31009.

A Member may be called to order by another Member's timely demand that the words used be taken down and read aloud at the Clerk's desk. The Speaker then rules whether the words or actions of the Member are disorderly. Whether an offending Member is to be allowed to proceed in order or is to be disciplined is determined by the House. § 26, infra.

Disorderly Acts

Decorum or comportment in the conduct and behavior of Members on the floor of the House is governed in part by clause 5 of rule XVII. *Manual* § 962. Prohibited conduct under the rule includes:

- Walking out of or across the hall while the Speaker is addressing the House.
- Passing between the Chair and a Member under recognition.
- Wearing a hat.
- Using a mobile electronic device that impairs decorum.
- Remaining by the Clerk's desk during roll calls.
- Smoking.
- Wearing a communicative badge while under recognition.

A Member's comportment may constitute a breach of decorum even though the content of that Member's speech is not, itself, unparliamentary. Deschler-Brown Ch 29 § 41.2; 103-2, July 29, 1994, p 18609.

Demonstrations of approval or disapproval, such as applause, are not a part of the formal proceedings of the House and are not carried in the *Congressional Record.* Deschler-Brown Ch 29 § 41.8. A Member having the floor may not request Members to conduct a straw vote, such as showing hands or rising in support of a certain measure. Deschler-Brown Ch 29 § 41.10.

The Chair may entertain a demand to clear the well in the event of disorder therein. 88-1, Dec. 9, 1963, p 23831. Under clause 3 of rule II, the Sergeant-at-Arms attends the sittings of the House and the Committee of the Whole and maintains order under the direction of the Speaker or Chair. *Manual* § 656; 1 Hinds § 257. On one occasion the Speaker requested the Sergeant-at-Arms to assist him in maintaining decorum disrupted by a former Member. *Manual* § 622. Former Members may be banned from the floor for indecorous behavior as a matter of privilege. *Manual* § 680.

Acts of physical violence by one Member or between two Members during or after heated debate have occurred. 2 Hinds §§ 1642-1644, 1655, 1656. Assaults or affrays in the Committee of the Whole are dealt with by the House. 2 Hinds §§ 1648-1651.

Attire

The Speaker has announced as proper the customary traditional attire for Members while in attendance in the House Chamber, including a coat and tie for male Members and appropriate attire for female Members. In one instance, the Speaker refused to recognize for debate a Member in violation of the practice that Members were expected to follow traditional standards of dress, and requested the Member in question to remove himself from the floor and don proper attire. The House subsequently agreed to a resolution, offered as a question of privilege, requiring Members to wear proper attire as determined by the Speaker, and denying noncomplying Members the privilege of the floor. *Manual* § 622.

Exhibits and Charts; Badges

Under clause 6 of rule XVII, the Chair has the discretion to submit to the House the question of the use of an exhibit, such as a chart, during debate. In addition, the Speaker's responsibility to preserve decorum requires that an exhibit in debate that would be demeaning to the House or that would be disruptive of its proceedings be disallowed. *Manual* §§ 622, 963; see § 61, infra.

In recent years, Members occasionally have worn badges on the floor to convey political messages to their colleagues and to the television audience. The Speaker has advised Members that the wearing of badges on the floor while engaging in debate is inappropriate and in contravention of clause 1 of rule XVII. *Manual* § 945.

Speaker's Announcements

On the opening day of recent Congresses, the Speaker has stressed the importance of various rules of decorum in the House. The Speaker has prefaced this customary announcement with a general statement concerning decorum in the House, including adjurations against engaging in personalities, addressing remarks to spectators, and passing in front of the Member addressing the Chair. "It is essential," the Speaker said, "that the dignity of the proceedings of the House be preserved, not only to assure that the House conducts its business in an orderly fashion but to permit Members to properly comprehend and participate in the business of the House." 107-1, Jan. 3, 2001, p 40. See also §§ 60-62, infra.

At the beginning of the 112th Congress, the Speaker's announcement regarding recognition for special-order speeches affirmed that the Speaker retains the ability to withdraw such recognition should circumstances (such as disorderly conduct) so warrant. 112-1, Jan. 5, 2011, p ____.

§ 22. Disorderly Language

Members have been censured or otherwise disciplined for the use of disorderly words in debate, whether the words were uttered in the House or the Committee of the Whole. *Manual* § 960; 2 Hinds §§ 1254, 1259, 1305; 6 Cannon § 236. A Member may likewise be disciplined for the insertion of disorderly words in the *Congressional Record*. 6 Cannon § 236. Members have been cautioned against the use of vulgarity or profanity in debate. *Manual* § 945. The Chair may call to order a Member engaging in or tending toward personalities in debate or for a verbal outburst following the expiration of time for debate. *Manual* §§ 361, 622. For a discussion of critical references to Members, see § 37, infra.

Remarks in debate have been the subject of a resolution collaterally raising a question of the privileges of the House, such resolution alleging that the remarks brought discredit upon the House and proposing that the Member in question be censured. 110-1, Oct. 23, 2007, p 27966; see also QUESTIONS OF PRIVILEGE.

The context of the debate itself must be considered in determining whether the words objected to constitute disorderly criticism or do in fact fall within the boundaries of appropriate parliamentary discourse. The present-day meaning of language, the tone and intent of the Member speaking, and the subject of the remarks, must all be taken into account by the Speaker. There have been instances in which the same or similar word has on one occasion been ruled permissible and on another ruled unparliamentary. Thus the word ''damn'' has been ruled out of order, whereas ''damnable'' has been permitted. Deschler-Brown Ch 29 § 43.

§ 23. — Critical References to the Senate and to Senators

A rule of comity prohibiting most references in debate to the Senate was first enunciated in *Jefferson's Manual* and was strictly enforced in the House through the 108th Congress (albeit with certain exceptions adopted in the 100th and 101st Congresses). *Manual* § 945. The former rule prohibited most references to the Senate except in a general or neutral way and prohibited any references to individual Senators (beyond their status as sponsors of legislation).

In the 109th Congress, the rule was changed to permit references to the Senate generally and to subject individual Senators to the same standards of debate used for Members of the House. Thus, Members may not engage in ''personalities'' with regard to individual Senators. For example, it is not in order to refer to a Senator in a derogatory fashion, to question a Senator's personal motives, or to accuse a Senator of falsehood or deception. For further information on the kinds of personal remarks prohibited as to both House Members and Senators, see §§ 37-43, infra. The Chair will take the initiative to call Members to order for unparliamentary references with regard to the Senate. *Manual* § 371.

§ 24. — References to the Press, Media, or Gallery

References to the Media

A Member should address all remarks to the Chair, and only the Chair; it is not in order for a Member to address remarks to ''the press'' or to the ''television audience,'' including Members watching in their offices. The rule is enforced on the Chair's own initiative. *Manual* § 945.

References to the Gallery

By rule of the House adopted in 1933, no Member may introduce or refer to any occupant of the galleries of the House. Clause 7 of rule XVII; *Manual* § 966. The rule is strictly enforced, and the Speaker ordinarily intervenes *sua sponte* to prevent infraction thereof. Deschler-Brown Ch 29 §§ 45.4, 45.7. The rule may not be suspended by permission to proceed out of order, even by unanimous consent. *Manual* § 966. The rule has been invoked to prevent a Member from making references to:

- An honored guest in the gallery who had exhibited ''great heroism.'' Deschler-Brown Ch 29 § 45.1.
- A Member's constituents sitting in the gallery. Deschler-Brown Ch 29 § 45.2.
- A Federal official present in the gallery who had an interest in the pending bill. Deschler-Brown Ch 29 § 45.3.
- A ''disinterested, objective observer'' sitting in the gallery. Deschler-Brown Ch 29 § 45.5.
- Family members present in the gallery. 99-2, July 29, 1986, p 17956.

§ 25. — References to Executive Officials

Jefferson wrote that in Parliament it was out of order to speak ''irreverently or seditiously'' against the King. *Manual* § 370. No analogous constraint exists in the rules of the House. Members in debate are permitted wide latitude in the use of language that is critical of the President, other officials of the executive branch, and the government itself. 5 Hinds §§ 5087-5091; 8 Cannon §§ 2499, 2500; Deschler-Brown Ch 29 § 47. Such criticism is considered as inherent in the exercise of legislative authority. As a report adopted by the House in 1909 read, ''The right to legislate involves the right to consider conditions as they are and to contrast present conditions with those of the past or those desired in the future. The right to correct abuses by legislation carries the right to consider and discuss [them].'' 8 Cannon § 2497. Members may employ strong language in criticizing the government, government agencies, and governmental policies. For example, it has been held in order for a Member to:

- Refer to the government as ''something hated, something oppressive.'' Deschler-Brown Ch 29 § 47.6.
- Refer to the President as ''using legislative and judicial pork.'' 8 Cannon § 2499.
- Refer to certain unnamed officials as ''our half-baked nitwits who are handling the foreign affairs. . . .'' Deschler-Brown Ch 29 § 47.3.
- Refer to a Federal agency as a ''Socialist, Communist'' experiment. Deschler-Brown Ch 29 § 47.4.
- Refer to the government as a ''labor dictatorship.'' Deschler-Brown Ch 29 § 47.5.

On the other hand, the rules do not permit the use of language that is personally offensive toward the President. *Manual* § 370; 5 Hinds § 5094. For example, it is out of order to call the President a ''liar'' or a ''hypocrite'' or to refer to accusations of sexual misconduct. *Manual* § 370; 8 Cannon § 2498; Deschler-Brown Ch 29 § 47.16. A Member may refer to political motives of the President in debate. However, personal criticism, innuendo, ridicule, or terms of opprobrium are not in order. 8 Cannon § 2497. For example, a Member may not in debate describe the President's veto of a bill as ''cowardly'' (*Manual* § 370), charge that the President has been ''intellectually dishonest'' (Deschler-Brown Ch 29 § 47.15), refer to the President as ''giving aid and comfort'' to the enemy (Deschler-Brown Ch 29 § 47.17), or describe the President's actions as ''arrogant'' (110-1, Jan. 11, 2007, p 998) or ''mean-spirited'' (110-2, July 15, 2008, p ____).

Members must abstain from personally offensive language even during impeachment proceedings. It is not in order to refer to evidence of alleged impeachable offenses by the President contained in a communication from an Independent Counsel pending before a House committee but not before the House itself. *Manual* § 370.

The Speaker has advised that the traditional protections against unparliamentary references to the President do not necessarily extend to the President's family. Deschler-Brown Ch 29 § 47.18. The Speaker enunciated a minimal standard of propriety for all debate concerning nominated candidates for the Presidency, based on the traditional proscription against personally offensive references to the President even in the capacity of candidate. *Manual* § 370.

References in debate to the Vice President are governed by the standards of reference permitted toward the President or Senators. Therefore, a Member may criticize in debate the policies or candidacy of the Vice President but may not engage in personality. *Manual* § 371.

Under rule XVII a Member may be called to order for alleged unparliamentary references to the President by a demand that the words be taken down. Deschler-Brown Ch 29 § 49.32.

§ 26. Procedure; Calls to Order

In the House

Procedures are available under rule XVII that enable the House to deal with disorderly words or actions by Members. A Member transgressing the rules may be called to order by the Speaker or by another Member. *Manual* § 960. The Member calling the offending Member to order may demand that the words objected to be ''taken down'' and read to the House by the Clerk. *Manual* § 960.

Briefly summarized, procedures available to deal with disorder include:

- Point of order raised against alleged unparliamentary language.
- Demand that words be ''taken down.''

- The Chair gavels the proceedings to a halt and directs the offending Member to be seated.
- Words taken down reported to the House by the Clerk.
- Unanimous-consent request to withdraw words taken down.
- Motion to allow Member to explain words taken down.
- Speaker rules whether words are out of order.
- Member ruled out of order must be seated and discontinue debate.
- Motion to strike (or expunge) words.
- Censure or other disciplinary action by the House if (with certain exceptions) there has been no intervening debate or business.
- Motion that the Member be allowed to proceed in order.

Not all cases involving disorderly words require the taking down of words and other formal action by the House. In many instances, the Chair will observe that debate is becoming personal and approaching a violation of the rules, in which case the Chair may simply request that Members proceed in order. See, *e.g.*, Deschler-Brown Ch 29 § 48.1. The Chair also may caution all Members, on the Chair's own initiative or in response to a parliamentary inquiry, not to question the integrity or motivation of other Members in debate. Deschler-Brown Ch 29 § 49.36. Likewise, where a Member objects to unparliamentary remarks delivered in debate, but does not demand that the words be taken down, it is appropriate for the Chair to sustain the point of order and then direct the Member to proceed in order. Deschler-Brown Ch 29 § 49.34.

Ordinarily, a question of personal privilege may not be based upon language uttered in debate, the proper course being the timely demand that words be taken down under rule XVII. *Manual* § 708. However, remarks in debate have been the subject of a resolution collaterally raising a question of the privileges of the House, such resolution alleging that the remarks brought discredit upon the House and proposing that the Member in question be censured. 110-1, Oct. 23, 2007, p 27966; see also QUESTIONS OF PRIVILEGE.

§ 27. —Procedure in the Committee of the Whole

A point of order may be raised against the use of disorderly language during debate in the Committee of the Whole. The chair of the Committee may respond by sustaining the point of order and admonishing the offending Member to proceed in order. Deschler-Brown Ch 29 § 49.34.

The use of disorderly language in the Committee of the Whole also is subject to a demand that the words be taken down and reported to the House for a ruling by the Speaker. 8 Cannon § 2539. The Chair does not rule on whether the words taken down are out of order. 8 Cannon §§ 2533,

2540. There is no debate in the Committee on the propriety of the words used. 8 Cannon § 2538. The Committee rises automatically to report the words to the House after the words are reported by the Clerk. 2 Hinds §§ 1257-1259, 1348; 8 Cannon §§ 2533, 2538, 2539. The business of the Committee is suspended until the words objected to are reported to the House. Deschler-Brown Ch 29 § 49.42.

Form

> CHAIR: M__. Speaker, the Committee of the Whole House on the state of the Union having under consideration the bill H.R.____, certain words used in debate were objected to and on request were taken down and read at the Clerk's desk, and I herewith report the same to the House.
>
> SPEAKER (after announcing report of Chair): The Clerk will read the words reported from the committee.

All of the words objected to in the Committee of the Whole should be reported to the House. The Speaker can pass only on the words as reported; a demand that additional words uttered in Committee be reported is not in order in the House. Deschler-Brown Ch 29 § 50.10.

After the Speaker rules on the words objected to and the House has disposed of any disciplinary proceedings, the Committee of the Whole resumes its sitting without motion. 8 Cannon §§ 2539, 2541; *Manual* § 961.

§ 28. — Taking Down Words

The taking down of words objected to in debate was a practice of the House even before the procedure became part of its formal rules in 1837. Clause 4 of rule XVII; *Manual* § 960. The words taken down may consist of a single phrase (Deschler-Brown Ch 29 § 61.3) or an entire colloquy between two Members (Deschler-Brown Ch 29 § 49.13). The demand should indicate the words excepted to and the identity of the Member who uttered them. *Manual* § 960. The objecting Member may indicate briefly the basis for the demand, such as impugning the motives of a colleague; but the objecting Member may not at that time debate the grounds for a finding that the words are disorderly. Deschler-Brown Ch 29 § 49.18.

Ordinarily, debate on or interpretation of the words objected to is not in order pending a ruling by the Speaker. Although words objected to in debate may be withdrawn pursuant to a unanimous-consent request, no debate is in order pending such a request. Deschler-Brown Ch 29 § 49.20. However, the offending Member may by unanimous consent (or on motion by another Member) be permitted to explain the words. Deschler-Brown Ch 29 § 52.16; § 30, infra.

While a demand that a Member's words be taken down is pending, that Member should be seated immediately. *Manual* § 961. It is a breach of decorum for a Member to ignore the Chair's gavel and the instruction to be seated. Deschler-Brown Ch 29 § 41.2.

The business of the House is suspended until the words are reported to the House. Deschler-Brown Ch 29 § 49.32. During that time the Speaker may refuse to entertain a parliamentary inquiry or a unanimous-consent request that a Member be allowed to proceed for one minute. Deschler-Brown Ch 29 §§ 49.14, 49.15.

Form

MEMBER: M__. Speaker (or M__. Chair), I ask that the gentle______'s words be taken down.

CHAIR: The gentle______ will be seated. The Clerk will report the words.

Timeliness of Demand

A demand that words be taken down is in order only if made in a timely manner under rule XVII. *Manual* § 960; 110-1, Jan. 22, 2007, p 1899. The demand should be made immediately after the words are uttered. Where debate has intervened, the demand comes too late unless the objecting Member was standing and seeking recognition at the proper time. The Chair's determination whether a Member's point of order constitutes a demand that those words be "taken down," is not such intervening debate or business as to render the demand untimely. *Manual* § 961; 8 Cannon § 2528. The Chair may not respond to a parliamentary inquiry regarding the propriety of words pending a demand that words be taken down or after the words have been uttered and no such demand has been made. *Manual* § 628.

Taking Down Words Read From Papers

Papers read during debate are subject to a timely demand that words be "taken down" as an unparliamentary reference to other sitting Members, but the demand must be made before subsequent reading intervenes. That certain words may already have been published elsewhere does not make them admissible in debate, and words not admissible in debate may not be inserted in the *Congressional Record*. Deschler-Brown Ch 29 § 83.6.

Withdrawal of Demand

Before a ruling by the Speaker, a demand in the House or in the Committee of the Whole that words be taken down may be withdrawn by the Member making the demand, and unanimous consent is not required. *Manual* § 961.

§ 29. — Withdrawal or Modification of Words

Generally; In the House

Words objected to in debate in the House may be withdrawn or modified by unanimous consent, even after the words have been taken down on demand and read by the Clerk. 8 Cannon §§ 2543, 2544; Deschler-Brown Ch 29 §§ 51.1, 51.2.

Pending a demand that words spoken in debate be taken down and ruled unparliamentary, the Chair may inquire whether the Member whose remarks are challenged wishes to request unanimous consent to modify the remarks before directing the Clerk to read them. Deschler-Brown Ch 29 § 51.11. However, the withdrawal of unparliamentary language may be made even after the Speaker has ruled the language out of order or even recognized another Member on a motion to strike the words from the *Congressional Record.* 8 Cannon § 2539.

The Speaker does not rule retrospectively on the propriety of words withdrawn by unanimous consent. *Manual* § 628.

In the Committee of the Whole

A Member may withdraw or modify words objected to in the Committee of the Whole by unanimous consent. 8 Cannon §§ 2528, 2538. In one instance, two Members demanded that each other's words be taken down and then, by unanimous consent, withdrew their remarks in the Committee before they were reported to the House. Deschler-Brown Ch 29 § 51.5.

Deletions From the Record

Clause 8 of rule XVII mandates that the *Congressional Record* be a ''substantially verbatim'' account of debate and permits the deletion of unparliamentary remarks only by order of the House. This clause establishes a standard of conduct within the meaning of that provision of the rules giving rise to the investigative jurisdiction of the Committee on Ethics.

§ 30. — Permission to Explain

Ordinarily, a Member whose words are taken down must sit down and may not explain the remarks pending a ruling by the Speaker. *Manual* § 961. However, the rules specifically provide for a motion to allow the Member to explain, which motion may be made only by another Member. Clause 4 of rule XVII; *Manual* § 960. Moreover, the Speaker has the discretion, before ruling on the words, to request the Member called to order to make a brief explanation of the remarks. Deschler-Brown Ch 29 § 52.16.

§ 31. —Speaker's Ruling

The Speaker (or Speaker pro tempore) has the sole power to rule whether words objected to constitute a breach of order in debate. *Manual* §§ 960, 961; 2 Hinds § 1249; 5 Hinds §§ 5163-5169. This determination is made by the Speaker after the words have been taken down (whether in the House or in the Committee of the Whole) and have been reported by the Clerk. The question of whether words taken down violate the rules is for the Speaker to decide and is not debatable. Deschler-Brown Ch 29 § 50.7. The Chair judges the words as read by the Clerk and not as alleged to have been uttered. *Manual* § 961. No Member may engage the Chair until the demand has been disposed of. *Manual* § 961.

The Speaker's ruling on a question of order has been appealed in the House in numerous instances, the Speaker generally being sustained. See, *e.g.*, 5 Hinds §§ 5157, 5173, 5178, 5194, 5196, 5198, 5199. Such an appeal is subject to the motion to table. *Manual* § 629. Also, the House may, by voting on a proper motion, dictate the consequences of that ruling by imposing disciplinary action or by allowing the Member to proceed in order.

The Speaker, in ruling on the words objected to, weighs the importance of freedom in debate against the need to maintain the order and dignity of the House. 5 Hinds § 5163. The Speaker considers the meaning of the words as well as the context in which they were used. Deschler-Brown Ch 29 § 50.6. Pending the ruling, the Speaker may recognize the Member who made the statement to ask unanimous consent to withdraw or modify the words. Deschler-Brown Ch 29 §§ 51.1, 51.2. The Speaker also may put questions to the offending Member about the words and may consult dictionaries to determine the meaning of certain words or terms. Deschler-Brown Ch 29 §§ 50.3, 50.4.

§ 32. —Discipline; Post-Ruling Motions

Generally

Censure or other disciplinary action is a matter for the House and not the Chair to decide. *Manual* § 961. However, no House action is in order until the Chair has ruled on the words objected to. Deschler-Brown Ch 29 § 51.21. If the words used are ruled to be unparliamentary, and if such words have not been withdrawn, the House may entertain certain motions enabling it to dispose of the breach of order.

Striking Words From the Record

Under modern practice, words ruled out of order are normally stricken from the *Congressional Record* by unanimous consent initiated by the Chair.

Manual § 961. If there is an objection, a motion to strike or expunge the words from the *Record* is in order. 8 Cannon §§ 2538, 2539; *Manual* § 960. A motion to expunge is in order even though the House by vote has authorized the Member to proceed. Deschler-Brown Ch 29 § 51.23. The motion, which is debatable within narrow limits under the hour rule, is not in order until the Chair has decided that the words are out of order. *Manual* § 961; Deschler-Brown Ch 29 § 51.21. The motion is not in order in the Committee of the Whole. *Manual* § 961.

Proceeding In Order

After a Member's words have been ruled out of order, the Member may be permitted to proceed in order on that same day either by unanimous consent or by motion. *Manual* § 961. It is the practice to test the opinion of the House by a motion "that the gentle______ be allowed to proceed in order." 5 Hinds §§ 5188, 5189; 8 Cannon § 2534. This motion may be stated on the initiative of the Chair. It is debatable within narrow limits of relevance under the hour rule, and is subject to the motion to lay on the table. *Manual* § 961. The motion is privileged for consideration in the House. Deschler-Brown Ch 29 § 51.22. A motion to strike the objectionable words also generally precedes a proposition to permit a Member to proceed in order. See, *e.g.,* Deschler-Brown Ch 29 § 52.7.

If a Member is not granted permission to proceed on that same day, the Member cannot speak even on yielded time and may not insert unspoken remarks in the *Congressional Record*. *Manual* § 961; 5 Hinds §§ 5147, 5196-5199. However, the Member may exercise the right to vote or to demand the yeas and nays. 8 Cannon § 2546. Whether the Member is to be allowed to proceed in order or is to be subjected to censure or other disciplinary measure is for the House to determine. *Manual* § 960.

E. Critical References to the House, Committees, or Members

§ 33. In General; Criticism of the House

Generally

In early Congresses it was held not in order to "cast reflections" on the House or its membership, present or past. 5 Hinds §§ 5132-5138. Today, in the interests of free and full debate in conducting legislative deliberations, Members are permitted to voice critical opinions of Congress, of the House, and of the political parties. Deschler-Brown Ch 29 § 53. Statements that are critical of Congress or a portion of its membership will not be ruled out of order for that reason alone. Thus, a statement in debate claiming that the campaign expenses of Members were paid by certain interest groups has been held to be in order. Deschler-Brown Ch 29 §53.1.

However, such criticism is subject to the rules and settled practices of the House that require courtesy and decorum in debate. *Jefferson's Manual* states that no one is permitted to use ''indecent language'' in referring to the proceedings of the House. *Manual* §360. The language used must not be offensive in itself. 5 Hinds §5135. The words must be stated in such a way as to avoid personal criticism of individual Members. §37, infra.

Ruled In Order

Following are precedents in which criticism in debate was held parliamentary or in order as not referring to any particular Member:

- A question whether it was a parliamentary inquiry to ask that a bill be printed in ''words of one syllable so that [Members of the opposing party] can understand it.'' Deschler-Brown Ch 29 §53.4.
- A statement that a Member was leading his party in a policy of opportunism. Deschler-Brown Ch 29 §53.5.
- A statement referring to ''irresponsible actions by members of the President's own party.'' Deschler-Brown Ch 29 §53.2.
- ''[Y]ou have your definition of consistency. My definition is that consistency is a virtue of small minds.'' Deschler-Brown Ch 29 §62.2.
- A reference to Members as having praised a foreign dictator in prior debate. Deschler-Brown Ch 29 §60.10.
- Words characterizing unnamed Members as taking ''potshots'' and as lacking judgment. Deschler-Brown Ch 29 §51.16.
- A reference to the consideration of a bill under procedures representing ''a classic example of duplicity.'' 100-2, Apr. 19, 1988, pp 7330, 7335-39.

Ruled Out of Order

Following are examples in which remarks in debate were held unparliamentary:

- ''Talk not to me of vindicating your insulted dignity. . . . You have no dignity to vindicate.'' 5 Hinds §5132.
- ''[T]he proceedings of the House had been such as not only to degrade it as a body, but also to degrade the country.'' 5 Hinds §5133.
- A statement declaring the opinions and decisions of the House ''damnable heresies.'' 5 Hinds §5135.
- A reference to ''[T]he right of the minority to stay indefinitely the right of the majority to legislate is as disgraceful, as dishonorable. . . .'' 5 Hinds §5136.
- ''Drunken Members have reeled about the aisles—a disgrace to the Republic. Drunken speakers have debated grave issues on the floor. . . .'' 5 Hinds §5186.

- A statement alleging that the Republican Conference believed that lynching was a ''proper means of justice.'' Deschler-Brown Ch 29 § 53.3.
- A statement alleging that a Member lacks ''decency.'' 110-1, Mar. 21, 2007, p 7074.

To show the distinction between words that are permissible and language that may be ruled out, illustrations in this chapter are drawn from debates from earlier as well as recent Congresses. However, precedents from earlier eras must be evaluated in their historical and cultural context; whether a word or expression is to be ruled out of order depends on its current meaning and usage. See § 38, infra.

§ 34. Criticism of Committees

A Member in debate may express general criticism of the actions of a committee, as by alleging an abuse of its powers. Deschler-Brown Ch 29 § 54.1. Criticisms of committee procedure are also permitted. Deschler-Brown Ch 29 § 54.6. However, a Member may not in debate impugn the personal motives of a committee or its members or make unparliamentary claims of unlawful activity. Deschler-Brown Ch 29 §§ 54.2, 54.3. Debate may not include critical characterizations of members of the Committee on Ethics who have investigated a Member's conduct. *Manual* § 361.

Ruled In Order

Following are examples in which remarks in debate were held parliamentary:

- A reference to the action of a committee as ''more or less pusillanimous.'' Deschler-Brown Ch 29 § 54.7.
- An editorial read by a Member charging a committee with ''pigeon-holing'' certain legislation. Deschler-Brown Ch 29 § 54.6.
- ''Did the gentleman's committee also find paid agents of Hitler on the congressional payroll?'' Deschler-Brown Ch 29 § 54.12.
- A reference to a committee investigation of ''the recent wave of policy lynch murder in Mississippi.'' Deschler-Brown Ch 29 § 54.9.
- A statement that a Member ''has been the victim of the abusive, vicious, and irresponsible use of the power of a congressional committee.'' Deschler-Brown Ch 29 § 54.1.

Ruled Out of Order

Following are examples in which remarks in debate were held unparliamentary:

- A statement that certain fascist organizations exercised extensive influence on a special House committee. Deschler-Brown Ch 29 § 54.3.
- Language referring to "lies and half-truths" of a House committee report. Deschler-Brown Ch 29 § 54.4.
- "I cannot respect the actions or even the sincerity of some of the committee members." Deschler-Brown Ch 29 § 54.5.
- A reference to the Committee on Un-American Activities as "the Un-American Committee." Deschler-Brown Ch 29 § 54.11.

§ 35. Criticism of Speaker

The prescription of clause 1 of rule XVII that Members confine themselves to the question under debate, "avoiding personality," has been applied to critical references to the Speaker's personal conduct. *Manual* § 362. It is not in order in debate to refer invidiously to the Speaker. 8 Cannon § 2531. It also is not in order to speak disrespectfully of the Speaker. 2 Hinds § 1248. For example, it has been held out of order to assert that the Speaker was "kowtowing" to persons who would desecrate the U.S. flag or to refer to the Speaker as a "crybaby." *Manual* § 362. It is not in order in debate to refer in a personally critical manner to the Speaker's political tactics or to arraign the Speaker's personal conduct. Deschler-Brown Ch 29 § 57. Any complaint as to the conduct of the Speaker should be presented directly for the action of the House and not by way of debate on other matters, such as the approval of the Journal. *Manual* § 362; 5 Hinds § 5188. Personal criticisms of the Speaker can be challenged even after debate has intervened. 2 Hinds § 1248; Deschler-Brown Ch 29 § 57.7.

It is not in order in debate for a Member to charge that the Speaker, while presiding, committed a dishonest act or that the Speaker repudiated and ignored the rules of the House. Deschler-Brown Ch 29 § 57.2. In one instance, however, an assertion of a personal belief that a sufficient number had been standing to demand a recorded vote was held parliamentary as not necessarily charging the Chair with disregard of the rules, in the context of those words alone. Deschler-Brown Ch 29 § 57.4. It is not in order to refer to official conduct of the Speaker that is either under investigation or has been resolved by the Committee on Ethics or by the House. *Manual* § 362.

If words impugning the Speaker are uttered, the Speaker may choose not to rule on the words personally but to appoint a Member to occupy the Chair and deliver a decision. Deschler-Brown Ch 29 § 57.1.

§ 36. Criticism of Legislative Actions or Proposals

Generally

Although remarks in debate may not include personal attacks against a Member or an identifiable group of Members, they may address political motivations for legislative positions. *Manual* § 363. Statements in debate, although critical of House action or of the legislation at issue, may be ruled in order if they do not improperly reflect on the House or a particular Member. Deschler-Brown Ch 29 § 58.4. Harsh words may be used to criticize a bill unless they fail to "avoid personality" as mandated by rule XVII. Deschler-Brown Ch 29 § 58.1. For example, although it may be appropriate in debate to characterize the effect of an amendment as deceptive or hypocritical, to characterize the motivation of a Member in offering an amendment with those terms is not in order. Deschler-Brown Ch 29 § 58.12. A statement in debate that "it is only demagoguery or racism which impel such an amendment" was held by the Speaker to be unparliamentary as impugning the motives of the Member offering the amendment. Deschler-Brown Ch 29 § 58.6.

Ruled In Order

Criticisms of legislative actions or proposals or political motivations that have been held in order in debate include:

- A statement that "sinister influences" were working in the interest of certain unnamed Members opposing a bill. Deschler-Brown Ch 29 § 58.9.
- A statement accusing unnamed colleagues who opposed a measure of talking "loosely and recklessly with the truth." Deschler-Brown Ch 29 § 58.8.
- A statement accusing unnamed Members of attempting to "cut off debate" on important legislation in order to attend an engagement at a hotel. 78-2, Feb. 3, 1944, p 1216.
- A statement that all lawyers know "that the adoption of this language neither adds to nor takes from a single item of the substance of this bill." Deschler-Brown Ch 29 § 58.3.
- A reference accusing unnamed opponents of a proposal of "blind," "slavish," and "shameful" opposition. Deschler-Brown Ch 29 § 58.7.
- In reference to an amendment: ". . . where I come from . . . the people . . . do not like slippery, snide, and sharp practices." Deschler-Brown Ch 29 § 58.5.
- A statement referring to a tactic of "withholding" votes until it could be determined whether they would be necessary on the pending question. Deschler-Brown Ch 29 § 58.10.
- A statement that a Member "has already admitted his amendment does not make sense, and he will take any alternative that is offered." Deschler-Brown Ch 29 § 58.4.

§37. Critical References to Members

Jefferson stressed the importance of preserving ''order, decency and regularity . . . in a dignified public body.'' *Manual* §285. The House rules provide that Members must confine themselves to the question under debate, ''avoiding personality.'' Rule XVII. The Chair may interrupt a Member engaging in ''personalities'' with respect to a fellow Member as is the case with respect to improper references to Senators or the President. However, under modern practice the Chair normally awaits a point of order from the floor with respect to references to other Members. *Manual* §961. The Chair may announce an intention to take the initiative in calling Members to order during debate on disciplinary resolutions. *Manual* §361.

The Speaker will hold language unparliamentary where it improperly reflects on another Member under rule XVII. *Manual* §361. A Member may not in debate impugn the personal motives of another Member (§39, infra), charge another Member with falsehood or deception (§40, infra), or denigrate a Member's intelligence (§41, infra). It also is not in order in debate to refer in a personally critical manner to the political tactics of a Member. *Manual* §361. The truth of allegations involving unethical behavior of a Member is not a defense to a point of order that the remarks are unparliamentary as engaging in personalities explicitly or by innuendo. 104-1, Jan. 18, 1995, p 1444. On the other hand, it is recognized that free and full debate is necessary in conducting legislative business, and a Member is allowed considerable latitude in criticizing the position, arguments, or contentions of another Member. Deschler-Brown Ch 29 §59.2; §36, supra.

It is not in order during debate to refer to a particular Member of the House in a derogatory fashion, even though that Member is not named, and the Chair may intervene to prevent improper reference where it is evident that a particular Member is being described. *Manual* §361. In one instance, after a Member had expressed an absence of ''good faith on the other side,'' he was granted unanimous consent to withdraw any reference to any individual Member. 100-1, June 18, 1987, pp 16761-63.

Members should refrain from references in debate to the official conduct of other Members where such conduct is not under consideration in the House by way of a report of the Committee on Ethics or as a question of the privileges of the House. *Manual* §361.

The rule requiring Members to avoid ''personality'' during debate prohibits reference to outside accounts whose criticism of a sitting Member would be unparliamentary if uttered on the floor as the Member's own words. *Manual* §361.

It is not unparliamentary to describe in debate the effect that a Member's remarks may have, especially where that description includes a disclaimer disavowing any intention to impugn a Member's motives. Deschler-Brown Ch 29 § 59.8.

Ruled In Order

Following are examples in which remarks in debate were held parliamentary:

- A statement that if a certain Member were to sponsor a measure it would receive only one or two votes. Deschler-Brown Ch 29 § 58.2.
- A reference to another Member's remarks as ''yapping.'' Deschler-Brown Ch 29 § 61.13.
- A statement accusing a Member of trying ''to becloud'' an issue. Deschler-Brown Ch 29 § 59.1.
- A reference in debate to another Member as not representing a certain class of people in his State. Deschler-Brown Ch 29 § 60.7.
- A reference to another Member's statement as ''intemperate.'' Deschler-Brown Ch 29 § 59.5.
- A description of a Member's statement that ''this is an example of the spurious reasoning that [an interest group] has with regard to their opposition to this bill.'' Deschler-Brown Ch 29 § 43.2.
- A Member's statement that another Member's demand that words be taken down during a special-order speech was ''an unfair stealing of time.'' Deschler-Brown Ch 29 § 59.10.
- A Member's assertion that ''even though that may not be the intention, I think [certain statements] have the tendency to try to assassinate the character of the person making the statement rather than to effectively assassinate the argument.'' Deschler-Brown Ch 29 § 59.8.
- A Member's general reference that ''big donors'' receive ''access to leadership power and decisions'' because it does not identify a specific Member as receiving a contribution specifically in exchange for votes or other legislative action. *Manual* § 361.

Ruled Out of Order

Following are examples in which remarks in debate were held unparliamentary:

- A reference to the remarks of another Member as ''malignant shafts'' or as a ''base insinuation.'' 5 Hinds § 5162.
- A reference to another Member as a ''snooper.'' Deschler-Brown Ch 29 § 61.11.
- ''The gentleman took the floor in his self-appointed role as spokesman for the committee [and] referred to me in my absence in a disgraceful and unparliamentary manner.'' Deschler-Brown Ch 29 § 59.3.
- Referring to another Member as a demagogue or as a ''president of the Demagogue Club.'' Deschler-Brown Ch 29 §§ 60.3, 60.4.

- ''[D]on't you start comparing anybody's record, because I have got yours . . . with . . . the FBI.'' Deschler-Brown Ch 29 § 60.24.
- A reference to another Member as a ''pinko.'' Deschler-Brown Ch 29 § 61.9.
- A reference to an identifiable group of sitting Members as the perpetrators of a crime, such as ''stealing an election.'' Deschler-Brown Ch 29 § 60.22.
- A reference suggesting that another Member ''did not have the nerve'' to make a statement on the floor. 104-2, July 25, 1996, p 19170.
- A statement alleging that a Member lacks ''decency.'' 110-1, Mar. 21, 2007, p 7074.

§ 38. —Use of Colloquialisms; Sarcasm

The Members are allowed considerable latitude in the use of colloquialisms, euphemisms, figures of speech, and even sarcastic comments in debate. A statement in debate that ''you are going to skin us'' was held merely a colloquialism that did not reflect on any Member and was held in order. Deschler-Brown Ch 29 § 61.10. In another instance, a Member used the word ''crime'' in referring to another Member, but the Chair ruled the term in order, finding that in the context of the debate, the term was being used as a synonym for, or figure of, speech meaning ''wrong.'' Deschler-Brown Ch 29 § 59.2.

The use in debate of colloquial expressions, figures of speech, or sarcasm is governed by their current meaning and by the context in which they are uttered. 5 Hinds §§ 5165, 5167. Unparliamentary references in debate, even when phrased as satiric compliments, are not in order. 112-1, July 22, 2011, p ____. The tone and mannerisms of a Member may be taken into account by the Chair in determining whether the criticism voiced is personally offensive to another Member. Deschler-Brown Ch 29 § 60.21.

Ruled Out of Order

Following are examples in which remarks in debate were held unparliamentary:

- A reference to another Member ''whose name is synonomous [*sic*] with falsehood . . . who is the apologist of thieves; who is such a prodigy of vice and meannesses that to describe him would sicken imagination and exhaust invective.'' 2 Hinds § 1251.
- ''[N]obody but a gambler or cutthroat would have thought of tacking such a thing as that to such a bill as this.'' 2 Hinds § 1258.
- ''The devotion of the gentleman . . . to the truth is so notorious that I shall not reply.'' 8 Cannon § 2545.
- A reference to another Member as a ''stool pigeon.'' Deschler-Brown Ch 29 § 61.12.

- References to a Member as having a ''hand like a ham,'' grasping a microphone until it ''groaned from mad torture,'' and striding the House floor ''like a wild man.'' Deschler-Brown Ch 29 § 61.1.
- A reference to another Member's proceeding in a ''cheap, sneaky, sly way.'' Deschler-Brown Ch 29 § 61.2.

§ 39. — Impugning Motives

In the early practice of the House, the Speaker intervened in debate to prevent even the mildest imputation on the motives of a Member. 5 Hinds § 5161. It is still the rule that Members may not in debate impugn the personal motives of other named Members in the performance of their legislative duties. *Manual* § 363. An opinion on the general motives of the House or a political party in adopting or rejecting a proposition may be expressed. § 36, supra. References to political motivation for legislative actions may be in order. *Manual* § 363. However, an assertion that a Member's use of the legislative process is motivated by personal gain (5 Hinds § 5149) or by ''the prospect of a junketing trip'' (8 Cannon § 2546) is not in order. Merely to question the sincerity of a Member has been held to impugn the motives of such Member. 5 Hinds § 5148.

Members should refrain from references in debate to the motivations of Members who file complaints before the Committee on Ethics. *Manual* § 361.

Ruled Out of Order

- Charging another Member, in his capacity as custodian of certain public money, with ''[m]aking a parade of his charity, he has been gorging himself and speculating with this money.'' 5 Hinds § 5152.
- Characterizing the motivation of a Member in offering an amendment as deceptive and hypocritical. *Manual* § 363.
- An observation that a Member stood in the well before an empty House and challenged the Americanism of other Members, ''and it is the lowest thing that I have ever seen in my 32 years in Congress.'' Deschler-Brown Ch 29 § 59.9.
- An observation that a Member was ''one of the most impolite I have ever seen.'' *Manual* § 361.
- Characterizing another Member as ''speaking out of both sides of his mouth.'' Deschler-Brown Ch 29 § 51.36.
- A reference to an identifiable group of sitting Members as the perpetrators of a crime, such as ''stealing an election.'' Deschler-Brown Ch 29 § 60.22.

§40. —Charging Falsehood or Deception

During debate on the floor, an assertion by one Member may be declared untrue by another. However, in so doing, an accusation of intentional misrepresentation must not be implied. *Manual* §363; 5 Hinds §§5157, 5159, 5189; 8 Cannon §2542. Any term or language implying a deliberate misstatement of the truth, for whatever motive, is unparliamentary, including allegations of lying, slander, or hypocrisy. A Member's expression of disbelief may be construed as meaning that the Member referred to was merely mistaken. Deschler-Brown Ch 29 §63.3. In one instance, a Member's statement in referring to another Member that ''That is not true, and he knows it,'' was held in order, the Speaker observing that the words were not uttered in an offensive tone. 5 Hinds §5158.

A Member may refer to falsehoods in the media without violating the rules of the House, even if such remarks are made during debate with another Member. Deschler-Brown Ch 29 §63.2.

Ruled In Order

Following are examples in which remarks in debate were held parliamentary:

- A Member's statement that he did ''not believe a word that [another Member] said.'' Deschler-Brown Ch 29 §63.3.
- A statement referring to another Member ''when he comes here to defend some slime-monger who goes on the radio and lies about me. . . .'' Deschler-Brown Ch 29 §63.2.
- ''Let us be sincere and honest about this thing.'' 78-2, Jan. 21, 1944, p 560.

Ruled Out of Order

Following are examples in which remarks in debate were held unparliamentary:

- A Member's declaration that the words of another Member were ''a base lie.'' 2 Hinds §1249.
- The use of the words ''grossly false,'' as applied to statements made by another Member in a pamphlet published by him during a recess of Congress. 5 Hinds §5157.
- ''I cannot believe that the gentleman . . . is sincere in what he has just said.'' Deschler-Brown Ch 29 §63.7.
- A statement that the remarks of a Member were ''false and slanderous.'' Deschler-Brown Ch 29 §63.4.
- A statement in referring to another Member that ''pretexts are never wanting when hypocrisy wishes to add malice to falsehood or cowardice. . . .'' Deschler-Brown Ch 29 §63.6.

- "I cannot respect the actions or even the sincerity of some of the committee members." Deschler-Brown Ch 29 § 54.5.
- Language read in the House that repudiated "lies and half-truths" in a House committee report. Deschler-Brown Ch 29 § 63.5.
- Use of the word "canard"—meaning falsehood—in referring to the statement of another Member. Deschler-Brown Ch 29 § 63.1.
- Words accusing another Member of hypocrisy. *Manual* § 363.

§ 41. —Lack of Intelligence or Knowledge

A Member in debate may be critical of the understanding or knowledge of other Members or groups of Members in relation to pending bills or amendments. However, such remarks should not denigrate the intelligence of another Member because this would be personally critical and offensive. Deschler-Brown Ch 29 § 64.

§ 42. —References to Race, Creed, or Racial Prejudice

Gratuitous references in debate to the race or religion of another Member are not in order. A reference to "the Jewish gentleman from New York," for example, has been ruled out by the Speaker. Deschler-Brown Ch 29 § 65.4.

It is not in order in debate to accuse a Member of bigotry or racism. Remarks characterizing the motives behind certain legislation as "demagogic and racist" have been ruled out of order, as has a reference to another Member as having reached "bigoted" conclusions. Deschler-Brown Ch 29 §§ 65.5, 65.6.

§ 43. —Charges Relating to Loyalty or Patriotism

Unless the subject is relevant to disciplinary proceedings then pending as the question before the House against a Member, remarks in debate impugning the patriotism or loyalty of a Member are not in order. Deschler-Brown Ch 29 § 66. Words impeaching the loyalty of a portion of the membership also have been ruled out. 5 Hinds § 5139. However, if such language is directed at the House or at its membership in general, the remarks may not be improper. See § 33, supra.

Ruled In Order

Following are examples in which remarks in debate were held parliamentary:

- A statement referring to all opponents of the Committee on Un-American Activities as communist enemies. Deschler-Brown Ch 29 § 66.2.
- A statement that another Member had been published in a newspaper ''dedicated to the destruction of this Government.'' Deschler-Brown Ch 29 § 66.10.
- A statement referring to (unnamed) Members who give ''aid and comfort'' to enemies and traitors. Deschler-Brown Ch 29 § 66.3.
- A statement referring to ''people'' who would rip down the American flag and replace it with the Soviet flag. Deschler-Brown Ch 29 § 66.5.
- A statement characterizing the Committee of the Whole as an agency of the Soviet Union. Deschler-Brown Ch 29 § 66.11.
- A statement accusing another Member of past opposition to ''every bill necessary for the defense of our country.'' Deschler-Brown Ch 29 § 62.5.

Ruled Out of Order

Following are examples in which remarks in debate were held unparliamentary:

- A statement that insertions in the *Congressional Record* by another Member were taken from ''Nazi elements.'' Deschler-Brown Ch 29 § 66.6.
- A statement by a Member that internal fascist organizations exercised extensive influence over a special House committee. Deschler-Brown Ch 29 § 66.7.
- A statement, in response to critical comments by another Member, that ''I am not going to sit here and listen to these communistic attacks made on me.'' Deschler-Brown Ch 29 § 66.1.
- ''There is nothing more subversive than the kind of red baiting tactics [of] the gentleman from ________.'' Deschler-Brown Ch 29 § 66.8.
- A statement referring to another Member as attempting to undermine the government. Deschler-Brown Ch 29 § 66.9.
- A reference to the Committee on Un-American Activities as ''the Un-American Committee.'' Deschler-Brown Ch 29 § 66.12.
- A reference to certain Members as ''apostles of doom'' whose utterances would give ''great aid and comfort'' to the Soviet Union. Deschler-Brown Ch 29 § 66.4.
- A reference to another Member as ''kowtowing'' to persons who would desecrate the flag. *Manual* § 362.

F. Duration of Debate in House

§ 44. In General

Limitations on Time for Debate

Before 1841, there was no limit on the time that a Member might occupy once in possession of the floor. 5 Hinds § 5221. Under the modern practice, the duration of debate in the House is invariably limited. Such limitations are imposed pursuant to the standing rules of the House, special orders of business from the Committee on Rules, and unanimous-consent agreements adopted by the House. Certain types of legislative propositions, such as concurrent resolutions on the budget, are subject to statutory time limitations. § 48, infra.

On major bills, a special order of business typically specifies the length of time for general debate—usually a number of hours—and identifies the Members who are to control that time. § 48, infra. Such time limits also may be imposed pursuant to a unanimous-consent agreement. Deschler-Brown Ch 29 § 67. If a bill or resolution comes to the House floor without such a time limit, clause 2 of rule XVII applies to limit the time for debate to one hour. *Manual* § 957. A Member calling up a measure in the House pursuant to a unanimous-consent request or special order of business that does not specify time for debate controls one hour of debate thereon. Deschler-Brown Ch 29 § 68.

Other limitations on the duration of debate are found in those standing rules of the House that authorize specific motions, such as the motion to suspend the rules for which debate is limited to 40 minutes under clause 1(c) of rule XV. *Manual* § 891. For a discussion of 40-minute debate, see § 46, infra.

Discretion of Chair as Affecting Time for Debate

On certain incidental questions of order, the duration of debate is within the discretion of the Chair. This practice is followed with respect to:

- Debate on points of order. 5 Hinds §§ 6919, 6920; 8 Cannon §§ 3446-3448; Deschler-Brown Ch 29 § 67.3.
- Debate under the five-minute rule on an appeal in the Committee of the Whole. 8 Cannon § 2347.

Timekeeping

The Chair monitors the time of Members who take the floor in debate. The Chair announces when their time has expired under the rules, and that announcement is not subject to challenge. See, *e.g.*, Deschler-Brown Ch 29

§67.1. For a discussion of extensions of time, see §48, infra. Traditionally, the time of the Speaker, the Majority Leader, and the Minority Leader is not monitored if they have been yielded a nominal amount of time (typically one minute) to allow such individuals the courtesy of extended and unfettered debate. *Manual* §953.

§45. The Hour Rule

Clause 2 of rule XVII limits to one hour the amount of time that a Member may occupy in debate on a pending question, and no Member may address the House for more than one hour, even by unanimous consent. *Manual* §957; Deschler-Brown Ch 29 §§68, 68.3; §48, infra.

The practice under the hour rule often serves to limit the total time for debate on the measure itself to one hour. This is because, at the conclusion of the controlling Member's hour, ordering the previous question cuts off further debate. *Manual* §994. If the Member controlling the hour successfully moves the previous question, all debate is terminated and the measure is voted on by the House.

If the House rejects the previous question, the measure is then open to further debate. Recognition passes to an opponent of the measure, who may offer an amendment and be recognized for one hour. See PREVIOUS QUESTION. A Member recognized under the hour rule may yield the floor upon expiration of that hour without moving the previous question, thereby permitting another Member to be recognized for a successive hour. *Manual* §957.

The hour rule is one of general applicability; it is often overtaken by an order of the House or a special order of business from the Committee on Rules, and it is not applicable where another rule of the House specifies otherwise. The hour rule applies to the following:

- A resolution presenting a question of the privileges of the House, subject to the division of time specified in rule IX. *Manual* §698.
- A resolution reported as a question of the privileges of the House, such as a resolution presenting impeachment charges. *Manual* §699.
- A question of personal privilege. *Manual* §713.
- A privileged resolution reported from committee, such as a rule, joint rule, or order of business reported from the Committee on Rules or a committee funding resolution reported from the Committee on House Administration. Deschler-Brown Ch 29 §§68.32, 68.37.
- A resolution of inquiry. Deschler-Brown Ch 29 §68.33.
- A District of Columbia bill on the House Calendar called up on District Day under clause 4 of rule XV. Deschler-Brown Ch 29 §68.5.
- A private bill called up in the House by unanimous consent. Deschler-Brown Ch 29 §68.9.

- A measure not requiring consideration in the Committee of the Whole before the House pursuant to a motion to discharge. Deschler-Brown Ch 29 § 68.34.
- A motion to refer, or the direct consideration of, a vetoed bill. Deschler-Brown Ch 29 §§ 68.55, 68.56.
- A motion to reconsider (if debatable). *Manual* § 1010.
- A motion to discharge a committee from further consideration of a resolution disapproving a reorganization plan. Deschler-Brown Ch 29 § 68.64.
- A motion to expunge from the *Congressional Record* certain remarks used in debate and ruled out of order. Deschler-Brown Ch 29 § 68.61.
- A motion to send a bill to conference under clause 1 of rule XXII. Deschler-Brown Ch 29 § 68.26.
- A motion to instruct House managers at a conference, subject to the division of time specified in clause 7(b) of rule XXII. *Manual* § 1078.
- A conference report or a motion to dispose of a Senate amendment reported in disagreement by a conference committee, subject to the division of time specified in clause 8(d) of rule XXII. *Manual* § 1086.
- A preferential motion to insist on disagreement to a Senate amendment reported in disagreement by a conference committee, subject to the division of time specified in clause 8(b)(3) of rule XXII. Deschler-Brown Ch 29 § 68.12.
- A Senate amendment considered in the House. Deschler-Brown Ch 29 § 68.12.

The hour rule applies even before the adoption of the rules at the inception of a Congress. *Manual* § 60. Thus, a Member offering a resolution on the seating of a Member-elect is entitled to one hour of debate. Deschler-Brown Ch 29 § 68.1

§ 46. Ten-minute, 20-minute, and 40-minute Debate

The House rules specify fixed periods of time for debate, equally divided between the proponents and opponents, on certain motions and questions.

Ten-minute Debate

The House rules permit the proponent and an opponent each five minutes of time for debate on an amendment offered after closing of general debate in the Committee of the Whole, subject to additional pro forma or second-degree amendments. Similarly, 10 minutes for debate is permitted on an amendment offered after the closing of five-minute debate by the Committee under clause 8 of rule XVIII if printed as required in the *Congressional Record* and if not dilatory. *Manual* §§ 978, 981, 987.

In addition, the House rules permit five minutes in support and five minutes in opposition to the following motions:

- A motion to recommit with instructions a bill or joint resolution under clause 2 of rule XIX, with the time subject to extension under some circumstances. *Manual* § 1001.
- A motion to dispense with the call of the Private Calendar under clause 5(c) of rule XV. *Manual* § 895.

Twenty-minute Debate

The House rules permit 20 minutes of time for debate on motions to discharge a committee, the time to be equally divided under clause 2 of rule XV. *Manual* § 892. The right to close such debate is reserved to the proponents of the motion. 7 Cannon § 1010a. The chair of the committee being discharged, if opposed to the motion, is recognized to control the 10 minutes in opposition. Deschler-Brown Ch 29 § 69.3. If the motion to discharge is successful, and the measure is properly before the House rather than the Committee of the Whole, the Member moving its consideration is recognized in the House under the hour rule. *Manual* § 892.

Twenty minutes of debate also is permitted where a point of order is raised against an unfunded Federal intergovernmental mandate under section 425 of the Congressional Budget Act. *Manual* § 1127. Points of order under the Act are disposed of by putting the question of consideration, debatable for 20 minutes—10 by the Member making the point of order, 10 by a Member in opposition. § 426(b)(4) of the Congressional Budget Act. Similarly, clause 9 of rule XXI establishes a point of order against consideration of certain measures for failure to disclose (or disclaim the presence of) certain earmarks, tax benefits, and tariff benefits, and permits a vote on the question of consideration of a rule waiving such a point of order. Such question of consideration is debatable for 20 minutes—10 by the Member making the point of order, 10 by a Member in opposition. See BUDGET PROCESS.

Forty-minute Debate

The House rules permit 40 minutes of time for debate, to be divided between proponents and opponents, on the following:

- A motion to suspend the rules under clause 1 of rule XV. *Manual* § 891.
- A debatable proposition on which there has been no debate before the ordering of the previous question under clause 1 of rule XIX. *Manual* § 994; 5 Hinds § 6821.
- A motion to reject certain portions of a conference report or Senate amendment objected to as nongermane under clause 10 of rule XXII. *Manual* § 1089.

Other chapters in this work dealing with specific motions and questions should be consulted. See, *e.g.*, PREVIOUS QUESTION; CONFERENCES BETWEEN THE HOUSES; and SUSPENSION OF RULES.

§ 47. Debate in the House as in the Committee of the Whole

Debate on a bill being considered in the House as in the Committee of the Whole is under the five-minute rule, with no general debate. *Manual* §§ 424-427. Five minutes in favor of and five in opposition to an amendment are permitted. Deschler-Brown Ch 29 § 70.7. Members also may gain five minutes of debate by offering pro forma amendments and motions to strike the enacting clause. Deschler-Brown Ch 29 §§ 70.11, 70.12.

Normally, five-minute debate on a bill considered in the House as in the Committee of the Whole may be extended by unanimous consent. Deschler-Brown Ch 29 § 70.6. However, the Chair does not recognize for such extensions of time during consideration of a private bill in the House as in the Committee of the Whole. Deschler-Brown Ch 29 § 70.10.

§ 48. Limiting or Extending Time for Debate

Generally

The House may by unanimous consent or by special order of business limit or extend the time for debate on propositions considered in the House. Deschler-Brown Ch 29 § 71. However, a motion to extend the time for debate in the House is not in order. Deschler-Brown Ch 29 § 73.17.

By Special Order of Business

A special order of business from the Committee on Rules may extend the time for debate that may be devoted to a proposition to be considered in the House. Deschler-Brown Ch 29 § 71.1. It may specify, for example, that debate shall not exceed a certain number of hours. Deschler-Brown Ch 29 § 25.17. Similarly, though conference reports are ordinarily considered under the hour rule, a special order of business may provide for more extended debate. Deschler-Brown Ch 29 § 71.18.

By Unanimous Consent

Time for debate in the House under the hour rule may be modified by unanimous consent. Deschler-Brown Ch 29 § 71. For example, by unanimous consent, debate has been extended on a resolution presenting articles of impeachment (Deschler-Brown Ch 29 § 71.13) and on a disciplinary resolution (Deschler-Brown Ch 29 § 71.6; 107-2, July 24, 2002, p 14310).

Debate on a privileged resolution in the House is ordinarily under the hour rule, but such debate may be extended beyond one hour by unanimous consent or by rejecting the motion for the previous question. Deschler-Brown Ch 29 §§68.41, 68.42; §49, infra. Thus, the House may agree to a unanimous-consent request to extend the time for debate in the House on a special order of business reported from the Committee on Rules. Deschler-Brown Ch 29 §71.4.

Unanimous-consent agreements extending time may further provide for a division of time between various Members. However, a Member may not extend a special-order speech (or debate on a question of personal privilege) for more than one hour, even by unanimous consent. *Manual* §957; Deschler Ch 11 §22.1; Deschler-Brown Ch 29 §71.20.

Effect of Statutory Time Limitations

Time for debate on certain kinds of legislative propositions is limited by statute. *Manual* §1130. Examples include:

- Congressional Budget Act of 1974 (limits debate on concurrent resolutions on the budget to 10 hours; specifies up to four hours for debate on economic goals and policies; amendments considered under five-minute rule). §305(a); 2 USC §636.
- Impoundment Control Act of 1974 (limits debate on rescission bill or impoundment resolution to not more than two hours). §1017(c); 2 USC §688.
- Trade Act of 1974 (limits debate on implementing bills and certain resolutions to 20 hours). 19 USC §2191.
- Pension Reform Act (limits debate on joint resolutions approving certain schedules to not more than 10 hours). §4006(b)(6); 29 USC §1306(b).
- Marine Fisheries Conservation Act (limits debate on fishery agreement resolutions to not more than 10 hours). §203(d)(4); 16 USC §1823(d).
- Nuclear Waste Policy Act of 1982 (limits debate on certain resolutions of approval to not more than two hours). §115(e)(4); 42 USC §10135(e).

Such statutory provisions (compiled in *Manual* §1130) are enacted as an exercise of the rulemaking power of both Houses, with full recognition of the ability of either House to change them at any time. In one instance, the Committee of the Whole was considering a resolution disapproving a reorganization plan pursuant to the Reorganization Act of 1949, which limited time for debate to 10 hours. The House agreed by unanimous consent to limit debate in the Committee to five hours and subsequently consented to limit further debate to 30 minutes. Deschler-Brown Ch 29 §71.7.

§ 49. Terminating Debate

The usual motion for closing debate in the House (as distinguished from the Committee of the Whole) is the motion for the previous question under rule XIX. *Manual* § 994; 5 Hinds § 5456; 8 Cannon § 2662. This motion also is used to close debate in the House as in the Committee of the Whole. Deschler-Brown Ch 29 § 72.7. The Member controlling debate on a proposition in the House may move the previous question and (if ordered by the House) thereby terminate further debate. Deschler-Brown Ch 29 § 72.2. However, the House may by unanimous consent vacate the ordering of the previous question in order to extend debate. Deschler-Brown Ch 29 § 72.4. If the previous question is ordered on a debatable proposition, and that proposition has not in fact been debated, then, under clause 1 of rule XIX, 40 minutes of debate is permitted. *Manual* § 994; 5 Hinds § 6821; 8 Cannon § 2689.

Other methods of terminating or precluding debate in the House include the use of the motion to lay on the table and the raising of the question of consideration. For a discussion of such methods, see PREVIOUS QUESTION, LAY ON THE TABLE, and QUESTION OF CONSIDERATION.

§ 50. One-minute and Special-order Speeches; Morning-hour Debates

Generally

The ability of Members to address matters not on the daily legislative agenda is facilitated by allowing "one-minute speeches" and "special-order speeches." Neither procedure is specifically provided for in the standing rules. Their use is permitted by a long-standing custom and is based on the Speaker's discretionary power of recognition under clause 2 of rule XVII. *Manual* § 950.

One-minute Speeches

The practice of limiting recognition before legislative business to one minute began on August 2, 1937, and was reiterated by Speaker Rayburn on March 6, 1945. 75-1, Aug. 2, 1937, p 8004; Deschler Ch 21 § 6.1. One-minute speeches are normally entertained at the beginning of the legislative day, although the Speaker has discretion to recognize Members to proceed for one minute after legislative business has been completed or at some other time or place in the legislative day (for example, to follow a scheduled recess). Deschler-Brown Ch 29 § 73.6. Indeed, when the House has a heavy legislative schedule, the Speaker may refuse all requests to recognize Members for one-minute speeches. Deschler-Brown Ch 29 § 73.5. More commonly, the Speaker limits one-minute speeches to a certain number for each side of the aisle, entertaining any remaining requests at the end of legislative business before special-order speeches.

Where a guest chaplain leads the House in prayer at the beginning of the legislative day, it is typical for the Member representing the guest chaplain's district to give the first one-minute speech of the day in order to introduce the guest chaplain to the House. See, *e.g.*, 110-2, July 24, 2008, p 16367.

The evaluation of the time consumed on a one-minute speech is a matter for the Chair and is not subject to challenge on a point of order. Deschler-Brown Ch 29 § 73.3. The Chair has refused to put to the House unanimous-consent requests for extensions of that time. Deschler-Brown Ch 29 § 73.10. Moreover, under the Speaker's power of recognition as traditionally exercised before legislative business, a Member can be recognized for a one-minute speech only once, and a second unanimous-consent request on that day will not be entertained. *Manual* § 950.

The order of recognition for one-minute speeches before legislative business is within the discretion of the Chair and is not subject to challenge on a point of order. Deschler-Brown Ch 29 § 10.55. However, the Chair endeavors to recognize majority and then minority Members by allocating time in a nonpartisan manner. Deschler-Brown Ch 29 § 10.50. In 1984, the Speaker instituted the policy of requiring alternate recognition of majority and minority Members in the order in which they seek recognition. *Manual* § 950.

Morning-hour Debate

Morning-hour debate was first initiated in the second session of the 103d Congress. The House by unanimous consent agreed that on Mondays and Tuesdays the House would convene 90 minutes earlier than the time otherwise established by order of the House, solely for the purpose of conducting morning-hour debate, to be followed by a recess declared by the Speaker. In the 104th Congress, the House extended and modified that order to accommodate earlier convening times after May 14 of each year. In the 112th Congress, the House expanded that order to include morning-hour debate on Wednesdays and Thursdays as well. Debate is limited and allocated to each party, with initial and subsequent recognition alternating daily between parties pursuant to lists submitted by the leadership. Under the customary order of the House establishing morning-hour debate, a Member may not be recognized for more than five minutes (with certain leadership exceptions). The Chair does not entertain a unanimous-consent request to extend this five-minute period. *Manual* § 951. When the House convenes solely for morning-hour debate, the Chair does not entertain unanimous-consent requests to remove cosponsors from bills. 103-2, Apr. 26, 1994, p 8544. The Chair may receive messages during morning-hour debate (103-2, May 10, 1994, p 9697) and, beginning in the 112th Congress, privileged reports may also be filed (112-1, Jan. 5, 2011, p ____).

Special-order Speeches

The Chair normally recognizes Members for special orders to address the House at the conclusion of business of the day. The Speaker may reserve the right to return to business. Deschler-Brown Ch 29 § 10.69. Under clause 2 of rule XVII, no Member may be recognized beyond one hour, even by unanimous consent. *Manual* § 957. Furthermore, a Member may not be recognized for two special-order speeches on the same legislative day, even though special orders have been interrupted by legislative business. Deschler-Brown Ch 29 §73.15.

The Speaker has announced the following policies for recognition of special-order speeches:

- Recognition alternates between majority and minority Members.
- Recognition shall be only pursuant to lists submitted by the leadership.
- Recognition does not extend beyond ten o'clock in the evening.
- Recognition for special-order speeches is limited to four hours equally divided between the majority and minority.
- The first hour for each party is reserved to its respective Leader or designees. The second hour is divided into 30-minute periods.
- The first recognition within a category alternates between the parties from day to day.
- The respective Leaders may establish additional guidelines for entering requests.

Manual § 950.

The Chair will recognize for subdivisions of the first hour reserved for special orders only on designations (and reallocations) by the leadership concerned. A Member who is recognized to control time during special orders may yield to colleagues for such amounts of time as the Member may deem appropriate but may not yield blocks of time to be enforced by the Chair. Members regulate the duration of their yielding by reclaiming the time when appropriate. *Manual* § 950.

At the beginning of the 112th Congress, the Speaker's announcement regarding recognition for special-order speeches affirmed that the Speaker retains the ability to withdraw such recognition should circumstances (such as disorderly conduct) so warrant. 112-1, Jan. 5, 2011, p ____.

G. Duration of Debate in the Committee of the Whole

§51. In General; Effect of Special Orders of Business

At one time, there was no limit on the time that a Member might occupy in debate in the Committee of the Whole when once in possession of the floor. A Member might speak an unlimited time, whether in general debate or on an amendment. 5 Hinds §5221. Today time limitations on general debate are imposed on measures by unanimous consent or special order of business. Deschler-Brown Ch 29 §74. In the unlikely event a measure is considered in the Committee of the Whole without fixing the time for general debate, each Member may be recognized for one hour. §52, infra.

The chair of the Committee of the Whole monitors the time used by each Member for debate and announces the expiration thereof.

§52. General Debate

The duration and allocation of time for general debate in the Committee of the Whole is controlled by the House; and the Committee may not, even by unanimous consent, extend the time for general debate fixed by the House. *Manual* §993; Deschler-Brown Ch 29 §75.7. The House establishes such time for general debate through a unanimous-consent agreement or the adoption of a special order of business from the Committee on Rules. Deschler-Brown Ch 29 §74.

If the House does not limit the time for general debate in the Committee of the Whole, such debate is under the hour rule. Deschler-Brown Ch 29 §75.1. A Member having control of such time may not consume more than one hour. Deschler-Brown Ch 29 §75.5.

Normally, the House order limiting time for general debate in the Committee of the Whole also will divide the control of the time between certain Members, such as the chair of the reporting committee and its ranking minority member. Although under the special order of business a Member may have control of more than one hour of general debate on a bill in the Committee, Members may not, under the general rules of the House, yield themselves more than one hour for debate. Deschler-Brown Ch 29 §74.4. It also is not in order for a Member to whom time has been yielded to ask unanimous consent for additional time, for time is controlled by those to whom it is allotted by the House and is not subject to extension by the Committee. Deschler-Brown Ch 29 §75.8.

The Committee of the Whole may not, even by unanimous consent, change the control of general debate to Members other than those specified by the House. However, unanimous consent has been permitted in the Committee to permit one of two committees controlling time under a special order of business to yield control of its time to the other. *Manual* § 993.

Effect of Absence of Members in Control

Where no member of the reporting committee is present at the appropriate time during general debate in the Committee of the Whole, the Chair may presume the time to have been yielded back. *Manual* § 978.

§ 53. Limiting General Debate

By Unanimous Consent in the House

Pending a motion to resolve into the Committee of the Whole, the House may by unanimous consent limit general debate to a time certain. Deschler-Brown Ch 29 § 76.8. If objection is raised to such unanimous-consent request, the Speaker puts the question on the initial motion to go into the Committee. Deschler-Brown Ch 29 § 3.5.

By Motion in the House

After unlimited general debate has begun in the Committee of the Whole and the Committee rises, a motion in the House to close or limit further general debate is in order. *Manual* § 979; 5 Hinds §§ 5204-5206. The motion is not in order until after debate in the Committee has begun and is made in the House pending the motion that the House resolve itself into Committee for further consideration of the bill, and not after the House has voted to go into Committee. 5 Hinds §§ 5204, 5208. The motion may not apply to a series of bills, and the motion must apply to the whole and not to a part of a bill. 5 Hinds §§ 5207, 5209. The motion may not be made in the Committee. 5 Hinds § 5217; 8 Cannon § 2548.

By Unanimous Consent in the Committee

Although the motion to close general debate is not in order in the Committee of the Whole, the Committee may, in the absence of an order of the House, close debate by unanimous consent. 8 Cannon §§ 2553, 2554.

Although a bill is being considered in the Committee of the Whole under a special order of business specifying the time for general debate, the managers of the bill need not use all of the prescribed time. The Members in control of the time are permitted to yield it back and thereby shorten general debate. Deschler-Brown Ch 29 § 76.1.

§54. Five-minute Debate

Generally

When general debate is closed in the Committee of the Whole, debate on amendments proceeds under the five-minute rule. Clause 5 of rule XVIII, which provides:

> When general debate is concluded or closed by order of the House, the measure under consideration shall be read for amendment. A Member, Delegate, or Resident Commissioner who offers an amendment shall be allowed five minutes to explain it, after which the Member, Delegate, or Resident Commissioner who shall first obtain the floor shall be allowed five minutes to speak in opposition to it. There shall be no further debate thereon, but the same privilege of debate shall be allowed in favor of and against any amendment that may be offered to an amendment.

Under this rule the proponent of an amendment is entitled to five minutes of debate in favor of the amendment before a perfecting amendment may be offered thereto. Deschler-Brown Ch 29 §30.20. If, after a speech in favor of an amendment, no one claims the floor in opposition, the Chair may recognize another Member favoring the amendment. 8 Cannon §2557.

Speaking More Than Once

Generally, a Member may speak only once for five minutes on a pending amendment, although a point of order under this rule comes too late after that Member has been recognized and has begun to speak. 92-1, June 9, 1971, p 18988. Even when the Committee of the Whole resumes consideration of an amendment that has been debated by its proponent on a prior day, the proponent may speak again for five minutes on such amendment only by unanimous consent. *Manual* §981. A Member recognized for five minutes on an amendment may not extend the time by offering another amendment. 8 Cannon §§2560, 2562. However, a Member who has offered an amendment and spoken thereon is not precluded from seeking recognition to speak to a proposed amendment to that amendment. Deschler-Brown Ch 29 §21.16. Where there is pending an amendment and a substitute therefor, the Member offering the substitute may debate it for five minutes and subsequently be recognized to speak for or against the original amendment. Moreover, if debate on the pending amendment is limited, the five-minute rule is abrogated and Members who have already spoken on an amendment may be recognized again under the limitation. Deschler-Brown Ch 29 §22.9.

Precluding Amendments; Effect of Special Orders of Business

The House, and not the Committee of the Whole, controls the extent to which the offering of amendments may be precluded under the five-minute rule. The Committee cannot, even by unanimous consent, prohibit the offering of amendments otherwise in order under the rule. *Manual* § 993.

A special order of business or other order of the House providing for the consideration of a bill may preclude the offering of amendments under the five-minute rule. For example, if a special order of business permits only designated amendments and prohibits amendments to amendments, then only two five-minute speeches are in order on each designated amendment, one speech in support and one in opposition. Deschler-Brown Ch 29 § 77.19. A Member may obtain additional time for debate only by unanimous consent. Because only the two five-minute speeches are in order, pro forma amendments are not permitted, and a third Member may be recognized only by unanimous consent. *Manual* § 993. A third Member is not entitled to recognition, notwithstanding the fact that the second Member, recognized in opposition, actually spoke in favor of the amendment. Deschler-Brown Ch 29 § 21.23.

Yielding Time

A Member recognized under the five-minute rule may not reserve time or yield a specific amount of time to another Member. *Manual* § 980; 5 Hinds §§ 5035-5037. Members so recognized may yield a portion of their time while remaining on their feet, but may not yield to another to offer an amendment. Deschler-Brown Ch 29 § 21.5. If a Member yields back or sits down before expiration of the five minutes, another may not be recognized for the remainder of that time. 8 Cannon § 2571.

A Member may yield during debate under the five-minute rule while remaining standing to permit another Member to pose questions, to make a comment, or to make a unanimous-consent request. However, the time consumed thereby comes out of that of the Member holding the floor. Deschler-Brown Ch 29 § 29.6. Time consumed in yielding for a parliamentary inquiry also is charged against the five minutes. Deschler-Brown Ch 31 § 15.6.

Extending Time

A motion to require a certain amount of debate under the five-minute rule is not in order in the Committee of the Whole. Deschler-Brown Ch 29 § 78.101. A Member recognized under the five-minute rule may extend the time for debate (by not more than five minutes) only by unanimous consent, and a motion to that effect is not in order. Deschler-Brown Ch 29 § 21.13; § 57, infra.

Where debate on an amendment is limited and allocated to a proponent and an opponent, the Members controlling the debate may yield and reserve time, whereas time for debate on amendments cannot be reserved under the five-minute rule. *Manual* §980.

Pro Forma Amendments

The pro forma amendment—to ''strike the last word''—is used under the five-minute rule only for purposes of debate or explanation, the proponent having no intent to offer a substantive amendment. A Member who has been recognized for five minutes on a pro forma amendment cannot thereafter extend the time by offering a second pro forma amendment. Deschler-Brown Ch 29 §77.8. Members who have consumed five minutes in support of an amendment that they have offered cannot obtain additional time by offering a pro forma amendment to their own amendment. However, they may extend their time or speak again on the amendment by unanimous consent. Deschler-Brown Ch 29 §77.9. A Member who has occupied the five minutes in opposition to an amendment may subsequently offer a pro forma amendment to the amendment. 84-1, June 30, 1955, p 9614. A pro forma amendment may be offered after a substitute has been adopted and before the vote on the amendment, as amended, by unanimous consent only, because the amendment has been amended in its entirety and no further amendments, including pro forma amendments, are in order. A Member recognized on a pro forma amendment may not allocate or reserve time, but may, in yielding, indicate to the Chair an intention to reclaim time after a certain point. The Chair endeavors to alternate recognition to offer pro forma amendments between majority and minority Members (giving priority to committee members) rather than between sides of the question. *Manual* §981.

Motions to Strike the Enacting Clause

The preferential motion to rise and report back to the House with the recommendation that the enacting clause be stricken is sometimes used to gain an additional five minutes for debate in the Committee of the Whole. Clause 9 of rule XVIII; *Manual* §§988, 989. Debate on the preferential motion is limited to two five-minute speeches, and the Chair declines to recognize for requests for extensions of that time. Deschler Ch 19 §13.2. Only two five-minute speeches are permitted, notwithstanding the fact that the second Member, recognized in opposition to the motion, spoke in favor thereof. Deschler Ch 19 §13.3. Time for debate may not be reserved. *Manual* §989. Debate may go to the merits of the underlying bill. 5 Hinds §5336.

Members of the committee managing the bill have priority in recognition for debate in opposition to the motion. Deschler-Brown Ch 29 §23.43.

However, the Chair will not announce in advance who will be recognized in opposition. *Manual* § 989.

If the House acts to strike the enacting clause as recommended by the Committee of the Whole, the bill is considered rejected. *Manual* § 989; 5 Hinds § 5326. For a general discussion of this motion, see COMMITTEES OF THE WHOLE.

§ 55. —Limiting or Extending Five-minute Debate—By House Action

By Unanimous Consent

The House, by unanimous consent, may agree to limit or extend debate under the five-minute rule in the Committee of the Whole, whether or not that debate has commenced. The House may by unanimous consent agree to an extension of time for such debate even after the Committee has previously agreed to terminate debate at an earlier time. Deschler-Brown Ch 29 § 78.41.

By Motion

A timely motion to limit debate on a matter pending in the Committee of the Whole under the five-minute rule has been held to lie in the House as well as in the Committee once that debate has begun. In an early decision Speaker Crisp held that the Committee did not have the exclusive right to limit debate on matters pending before it, and that a motion to limit debate on a section of a bill pending in Committee would lie in the House. 5 Hinds § 5229. However, in modern practice the motion is made in the Committee under clause 8 of rule XVIII. § 56, infra.

§ 56. —By Motion in the Committee of the Whole

Generally; When in Order

A motion in the Committee of the Whole to limit or close five-minute debate is permitted by clause 8 of rule XVIII. *Manual* § 987. The motion may propose to close debate at once or at the expiration of a designated time. 8 Cannon § 2572. As noted above, a motion to extend debate is not in order in the Committee. § 54, supra.

Until a bill has been read for amendment in full or its reading dispensed with by unanimous consent or special order of business, a motion to close or limit debate on the entire bill is not in order. Deschler-Brown Ch 29 § 78.27. Likewise, a motion to close debate on a portion of a bill not yet reached in the reading of the bill for amendment is not in order. Deschler-Brown Ch 29 § 78.29. A motion to close debate on a portion of a bill that has been read and on which there has been debate is in order. Deschler-Brown Ch 29 § 78.34. For a discussion of unanimous-consent requests to close or limit debate, see § 57, infra.

A motion to limit or close debate under the five-minute rule is not in order until debate has begun. 5 Hinds § 5225. Thus, a motion to close debate on a section of a bill or on an amendment is not in order until there has been some debate thereon. Deschler-Brown Ch 29 § 78.22. However, the motion to close debate has been held in order after only one speech, even though brief (5 Hinds § 5226), and although the Member making the speech, after gaining recognition to strike the last word, obtained consent to speak out of order (Deschler-Brown Ch 29 § 78.25).

Under clause 8 of rule XVIII, a motion in the Committee of the Whole to close debate under the five-minute rule is privileged. However, the motion cannot deprive another Member of the floor. Deschler-Brown Ch 29 § 78.14. Once pending, the motion must be disposed of before further recognition by the Chair. Deschler-Brown Ch 29 § 22.1.

Although it is customary for the Chair to recognize the manager of the pending bill to offer motions to limit debate, any Member may, pursuant to clause 8 of rule XVIII, move to limit debate at an appropriate time in the Committee of the Whole. Deschler-Brown Ch 29 § 23.28. However, the Member managing the bill is entitled to prior recognition to move to close debate on a pending amendment (after the proponent has yielded back) over other Members seeking to debate or amend the amendment. Deschler-Brown Ch 29 § 24.16.

It is in order in the Committee of the Whole to move to limit or close debate under the five-minute rule with respect to:

- The portion of the text that is pending and all amendments thereto. Deschler-Brown Ch 29 § 78.7.
- An amendment and all amendments thereto. Deschler-Brown Ch 29 § 78.65.
- All amendments to the bill (after the bill has been read) and all amendments thereto. Deschler-Brown Ch 29 § 78.30.

A proposition to control or divide the time is not in order as a part of a motion to limit debate under the five-minute rule. 8 Cannon § 2570.

Where there is a time limitation on debate on a pending amendment in the nature of a substitute and all amendments thereto, but not on the underlying original text, debate on perfecting amendments to the original text proceeds under the five-minute rule, absent another time limitation. Where the time for debate on a pending amendment in the form of a motion to strike (and all amendments thereto) has been limited, a subsequently offered perfecting amendment considered as preferential to (rather than as an amendment to) the motion to strike remains separately debatable outside the limitation. *Manual* § 987.

A limitation on debate on a section of a bill and amendments thereto does not affect debate on an amendment adding a new section to the bill. Deschler-Brown Ch 29 § 79.31. The Chair may decline to recognize a Member to offer such an amendment until perfecting amendments to the pending section have been disposed of under the limitation. Deschler-Brown Ch 29 § 79.137.

Consideration of Motion; Debate and Amendments

A motion to limit debate under the five-minute rule must be reduced to writing if demanded by any Member. Deschler-Brown Ch 29 § 78.52. The motion is not debatable (*Manual* § 987), although it is subject to amendment (5 Hinds § 5227; 8 Cannon § 2578).

The motion in the Committee of the Whole to limit debate is not subject to a motion to reconsider because the motion to reconsider does not lie in the Committee. Deschler-Brown Ch 29 § 78.79. However, the Committee may by unanimous consent rescind or modify such an agreement. Deschler-Brown Ch 29 § 78.84.

§ 57. —By Unanimous Consent in the Committee of the Whole

Generally

Debate under the five-minute rule in the Committee of the Whole may be closed or limited by the Committee by unanimous consent, even on portions of the bill not yet read. Deschler-Brown Ch 29 § 78.29. However, such request should include the condition that the portion of the bill sought to be limited be considered as read and open to amendment at any point. Deschler-Brown Ch 29 § 78.93. Similarly, the Committee may limit and allocate control of time for debate on amendments not yet offered by unanimous consent. *Manual* § 987.

In limiting debate by unanimous consent under the five-minute rule, the Committee of the Whole may include provisions to control and allocate the time. Deschler-Brown Ch 29 § 78.37. For example, the Committee may, by unanimous consent, limit debate to a certain number of hours, or to a time certain, to be equally divided and controlled by the managers of the bill. Deschler-Brown Ch 29 § 78.62.

Rescission or Modification of Limitation

A time limitation on debate imposed by the Committee of the Whole may be rescinded or modified by the Committee by unanimous consent (but not by motion). Deschler-Brown Ch 29 §§ 78.42, 78.43. The Committee may by unanimous consent permit additional debate on an amendment before it is offered, notwithstanding a previous limitation imposed by the Committee on all amendments to the bill. Deschler-Brown Ch 29 § 79.63. The Committee can effect minor changes in procedures set by a special order of the House only by unanimous consent and only where congruent with the terms of the special order of business. *Manual* § 993.

§ 58. Motions Allocating or Reserving Time

A motion to limit debate under the five-minute rule in the Committee of the Whole is not in order if it includes a reservation of time for any special purpose, including a reservation of time for a particular Member. Deschler-Brown Ch 29 §§ 78.37, 78.61, 78.67, 78.72. However, the Committee may limit debate and include a reservation of time by unanimous consent. For example, part of the time under a limitation may be reserved for the reporting committee by unanimous consent. Deschler-Brown Ch 29 § 78.69.

§ 59. Timekeeping; Charging Time

Generally

A limitation on debate under the five-minute rule may take the form of a restriction on time for debate (for example, "for 60 minutes") or as a limitation on debate to a time certain (for example, "until 5 p.m."). The form of the limitation is particularly significant in determining how the time is to be accounted for under the limitation.

When time for debate on a proposition is limited to a fixed period, such as 60 minutes, the time consumed for purposes other than debate is not counted or charged against the allowable time for debate (such as votes, quorum calls, maintaining order, points of order, reading amendments, or offering and debating preferential motions to strike the enacting clause). *Manual* § 987; Deschler-Brown Ch 29 §§ 79.10, 79.13. However, if time is limited to a fixed period on the entire bill and all amendments thereto, the time for the preferential motion does consume time under the limitation. Deschler-Brown Ch 29 § 79.17.

On the other hand, where the time for debate has been fixed to a time certain, such as 5 p.m., the time consumed by matters other than debate (such as parliamentary inquiries, points of order, rereading of amendments, maintaining order, votes, quorum calls, or offering and debating preferential motions to strike the enacting clause) is charged against the time remaining. Deschler-Brown Ch 29 §§ 79.5, 79.9. Such a limitation terminates all debate at the time specified, notwithstanding any allotted time remaining. Deschler-

Brown Ch 29 § 79.8. In such cases, no point of order lies against the inability of the Chair to recognize each Member desiring recognition. Deschler-Brown Ch 29 § 22.31. The time specified can be rescinded or modified only by unanimous consent. *Manual* § 987. A unanimous consent-request or motion to close debate at a time certain should specify that the debate cease at a certain time, and not that the Committee of the Whole vote at a certain time, because the Chair cannot control time consumed by quorum calls or votes on other intervening motions. Deschler-Brown Ch 29 § 78.75. If the Committee rises before the expiration of such a limitation, and does not resume consideration before the time certain arrives, no further time for debate remains. Deschler-Brown Ch 29 § 79.128.

If debate is closed instantly on the entire bill and all amendments thereto, no further debate is in order for any purpose (including the preferential motion that the enacting clause be stricken); and further amendments may be offered but not debated unless they have been printed in the *Congressional Record.* Deschler-Brown Ch 29 §§ 79.1, 79.23.

Role of the Chair in Allocating Time

Where debate on an amendment has been limited, the Chair has several options in allocating the remaining time. The Chair may (1) continue to recognize under the five-minute rule; (2) divide the time between Members indicating a desire to speak; or (3) as is increasingly the case under the modern practice, divide time between the proponent of the amendment and an opponent (giving priority in recognition among opponents to committee members) and allow them in turn to yield time to other Members. *Manual* § 987.

The Chair also has the discretion to give priority in recognition under a limitation to those Members seeking to offer amendments, over other Members standing at the time the limitation was agreed to. Where time for debate on a bill and all amendments thereto has been limited to a time certain several hours away, the Chair has the discretion to continue to proceed under the five-minute rule until deciding to allocate remaining time on possible amendments. The Chair may then divide that time among proponents of anticipated amendments and committee members opposing those amendments. The Chair also has discretion to reallocate time to conform to the limit set by unanimous consent of the Committee of the Whole. *Manual* § 987.

Time Remaining After Committee Rises

The adoption of a motion to rise during debate on an amendment in the Committee of the Whole does not affect the time remaining on the amendment when the bill is resumed as unfinished business in the Committee of the Whole, where debate is limited to a number of minutes and not to a time certain. Deschler-Brown Ch 29 § 79.131. However, where a measure has been limited to a time certain, and the Committee rises before that time without having completed action on the pending measure, no time is considered to be remaining when the Committee, on a later day, resumes consideration of the measure. Deschler-Brown Ch 29 § 79.127. The Committee may extend debate on the subsequent day only by unanimous consent. Deschler-Brown Ch 29 § 78.84.

Where after limiting debate under the five-minute rule the Committee of the Whole is about to rise on motion, the Chair has the discretion to defer the allocation of that time until the Committee resumes consideration of the bill on a subsequent day. Deschler-Brown Ch 29 § 79.52.

H. Reading Papers; Displays and Exhibits

§ 60. Reading Papers

In the early practice of the House, the reading of papers, including a Member's own written speech, was usually permitted without question; and Members usually read such papers as they pleased. *Manual* § 964; 5 Hinds § 5258. However, that privilege was subject to the authority of the House if another Member objected under a former version of clause 6 of rule XVII. *Manual* § 964. If objection was made to such a reading under the former rule, the question was determined by the House without debate. The rule was amended in 1993 to apply only to exhibits and not to readings and the question no longer must be submitted to the House. *Manual* § 963.

§ 61. Use of Exhibits

Generally

Members often use relevant exhibits in debate for the information of other Members. The display of exhibits in debate was at one time automatically subject to House consent under clause 6 of rule XVII if objection was made. However, the clause was amended in the 107th Congress to give the Chair the discretion to submit the question of its use to the House. *Manual* § 963.

For procedures under the former rule, see *Manual* § 963.

It is not a proper parliamentary inquiry to ask the Chair to judge the accuracy of the content of an exhibit. It is not in order to request that the electronic voting display be turned on during debate as an exhibit to accompany a Member's debate. *Manual* § 963.

Exhibits that have been permitted by the House or the Committee of the Whole, either by vote or because no objection was raised, include:

- A pair of oversized dice. Deschler-Brown Ch 29 § 84.2.
- Models prepared by the Committee on Science and Astronautics. Deschler-Brown Ch 29 § 84.4.
- Electronic voting equipment to be installed in the House Chamber. Deschler-Brown Ch 29 § 84.
- A bottle of liquor alleged to be ''government rum.'' Deschler-Brown Ch 29 § 84.1.
- A chart showing complex funding formulas. Deschler-Brown Ch 29 § 84.5.
- Photographs of missing children. Deschler-Brown Ch 29 § 84.14.
- A display of dismantled weapons. Deschler-Brown Ch 29 § 84.17.
- A chart showing stockpiled weaponry. 99-1, June 19, 1985, p 16359.

The Speaker or chair of the Committee of the Whole may under rule I direct the removal of an exhibit from the well if the exhibit is not being used in debate. Deschler-Brown Ch 29 §§ 84.9, 84.10.

The Speaker has denied a request that a Member be permitted to use a video recorder on the floor of the House during a special-order speech, as an audio-visual display of comments by non-Members would be contrary to precedents limiting the privilege of debate to Members. Deschler-Brown Ch 29 § 80.8. The Speaker has disallowed the use of a person on the floor as a guest of the House as an ''exhibit.'' *Manual* § 622; § 21, supra.

Beginning in the 111th Congress, the Speaker has announced guidelines for appropriate comportment in the chamber when the House is not in session. Such guidelines re-affirm the Speaker's responsibility for control of the Hall of the House under clause 3 of rule I, indicate that the chamber remains on static display during periods of adjournment, and prohibit any activity (including audio or video recording) that might be taken to carry the imprimatur of the House. 111-1, Jan. 6, 2009, p ____.

§ 62. — Decorum Requirements

The Speaker's responsibility under clause 2 of rule I to preserve decorum requires that the use of exhibits in debate that would be demeaning to the House or that would be disruptive of the decorum thereof be disallowed. Deschler-Brown Ch 29 § 84.16. Thus the Speaker may inquire of a Member's intentions as to the use of exhibits before conferring recognition to address the House. Deschler-Brown Ch 29 § 84.11. In one instance, the Chair declined to permit a bumper sticker to be attached to the lectern in the House Chamber. 101-1, Sept. 13, 1989, p 20362. In 1995, a caricature of the Speaker presented during debate was ruled out of order. 104-1, Nov. 16, 1995, p 33393-95. In another instance, where a Member during debate on a bill funding the arts indicated his intention to show as exhibits certain photographs—some innocuous and some alleged to be pornographic—the Chair announced that he would prevent the display of *all* such exhibits on the pending bill. The Chair observed that although the first amendment to the Constitution provides that Congress shall make no law abridging the freedom of speech, the Constitution also provides in article I that the House may determine the rules of its proceedings, and in clause 2 of rule I the House has assigned to the Chair the responsibility of preserving order and decorum. *Manual* § 622.

At the request of the Committee on Ethics, the Speaker announced that (1) all handouts distributed on or adjacent to the floor must bear the name of a Member authorizing the distribution; (2) the content of such handouts must comport with the standards applicable to words used in debate; (3) failure to comply with these standards may constitute a breach of decorum and thus give rise to a question of privilege; (4) staff are prohibited in the Chamber or rooms leading thereto from distributing handouts and from attempting to influence Members with regard to legislation; and (5) Members should minimize the use of handouts to enhance the quality of debate. *Manual* § 622.

I. Secret Sessions

§ 63. In General

Generally; Historical Background

In the early days of the Congress, secret sessions of the House were frequent. The sessions of the Continental Congress were secret. Up to and during the War of 1812, secret sessions of the House were held often. Normally, the House sat with galleries open. When the occasion required, as on receipt of a confidential communication from the President, the galleries were cleared by House order. 5 Hinds §§ 7247, 7251 (note). Following that period, the practice fell into disuse, remaining dormant for almost a century, and there have been but few secret sessions in the modern era. 6 Cannon § 434.

It has been held that each House has a right to hold secret sessions whenever in its judgment the proceedings should require secrecy. In 1848, the Circuit Court of the District of Columbia upheld a Senate contempt proceeding conducted in a secret session arising out of the publication of a treaty pending before the Senate in executive session. *Nugent v. Beale*, 18 F. Cas. 141 (C.C.D.C. 1848) (No. 10375); 2 Hinds § 1640.

Procedure

The oath of office taken by elected House officers obligates them to ''keep the secrets of the House'' under clause 1 of rule II. *Manual* § 640. Clause 9 of rule XVII, dating from 1792, authorizes the holding of a secret session (1) whenever confidential communications are received from the President, or (2) whenever the Speaker or any Member informs the House that such individual has communications that such individual believes ought to be kept secret. *Manual* § 969.

The House, and not the Committee of the Whole, determines whether to conduct a secret session under clause 9 of rule XVII. *Manual* § 969; Deschler-Brown Ch 29 § 85.6. Provision for the session is generally made pursuant to a motion considered in the House. See § 64, infra. The material to be presented in the secret session is not required to be relevant to any particular legislation. Deschler-Brown Ch 29 § 85.9. No point of order lies in the secret session that the material in question must be produced for the Members in advance to determine whether secret or confidential communications are involved. Deschler-Brown Ch 29 § 85.14.

For procedures governing a secret session of the House called to resolve a conflict between the Permanent Select Committee on Intelligence and the President with respect to disclosure of classified information, see clause 11(g) of rule X. *Manual* § 785.

Use of Special Orders of Business

In 1983, for the first time, a secret session was held pursuant to a special order of business reported from the Committee on Rules and adopted by the House. The special order of business provided for preliminary general debate on a bill in secret session of the Committee of the Whole and for further consideration of the bill in open session of the Committee of the Whole. 98-1, H. Res. 261, July 14, 1983, p 19133. Following the secret session, the Speaker stated that Members were bound not to release or revise or make public any of the transcript thereof until further order of the House, and that pursuant to the special order of business the transcript would be referred to the two committees reporting the bill. 98-1, July 19, 1983, pp 19776, 19777. Six months later, the Speaker laid before the House communications transmitting the recommendations of those committees that the transcript of the secret session not be publicly released. 98-2, Jan. 23, 1984, p 84.

In 2008, for the first time, a secret session was held pursuant to a unanimous-consent request that, similar to a special order of business, provided the terms for debate. *Manual* § 969.

§ 64. Motions; Debate

A motion to go into a secret session is in order when any Member informs the House that such Member has communications that should be considered in confidence. The motion takes precedence over a motion to resolve into the Committee of the Whole for the consideration of privileged legislative business such as an appropriation bill. 8 Cannon § 3630.

The motion to resolve into secret session may be made only in the House and not in the Committee of the Whole. *Manual* § 969; Deschler-Brown Ch 29 § 85.6. The Member offering the motion must qualify by asserting that such Member has a secret communication to make to the House. Deschler-Brown Ch 29 § 85.5. The motion may be repeated on the same legislative day if the proponent asserts additional qualifying communications. *Manual* § 969. The motion is not debatable, although the Chair may explain the operation of the rule and respond to parliamentary inquiries after the motion has been agreed to and before the secret session commences. *Manual* § 969; Deschler-Brown Ch 29 §§ 85.7, 85.9. The motion to resolve into secret session is subject to the motion to lay on the table. *Manual* § 969.

After a motion to resolve into a secret session has been adopted, the Member who offered the motion may be recognized for one hour of debate. The normal rules of debate, including the principle that motions are in order only when the Member in control yields for that purpose, apply. Deschler-Brown Ch 29 § 85.13.

A motion in secret session to make the proceedings public is debatable for one hour, within narrow limits of relevancy. At the conclusion of debate in secret session, a Member may be recognized to offer a motion that the session be dissolved. Deschler-Brown Ch 29 § 85.18. In 2008, the unanimous-consent agreement pursuant to which the House resolved into secret session provided for adjournment of the House immediately following the secret session. *Manual* § 969.

§ 65. Secrecy Restrictions and Guidelines

The Speaker may announce before a secret session commences that the galleries will be cleared. The Speaker also may announce that the Chamber will be cleared of all persons except Members and those officers and employees whose attendance is essential to the functioning of the secret session and so specified by the Speaker, and that all proceedings in the secret session must be kept secret until otherwise ordered by the House. Deschler-Brown Ch 29 §§ 85.8, 85.9. In one instance, the Speaker directed all officers and employees designated by him as essential to the proceedings to come to the desk and sign an oath of secrecy. The Speaker announced that violation of the oath was punishable by the House and that Members and employees were subject to standards of conduct and disciplinary proceedings under House rules. Deschler-Brown Ch 29 § 85.9. Where the House has concluded a secret session and has not voted to release the transcripts of that session to the public, the injunction of secrecy remains and the Speaker may informally refer the transcripts to appropriate committees for their evaluation and report to the House as to their ultimate disposition. Deschler-Brown Ch 29 § 85.10. Under clause 13 of rule XXIII (which was added to the Code of Official Conduct in the 104th Congress), all Members, officers, and employees are required to execute an oath before they are given access to classified information. The list of Members signing this oath is published weekly in the *Congressional Record*. For a discussion of committee meetings in executive session, see COMMITTEES.

Chapter 17
Contempt

Research References
2 Hinds §§ 1597-1640; 3 Hinds §§ 1666-1724
6 Cannon §§ 332-334
Deschler Ch 15 §§ 17-22
Manual §§ 293-299
2 USC §§ 192, 194

§ 1. In General

An individual who fails or refuses to comply with a House subpoena may be cited for contempt of Congress. *Eastland* v. *United States Servicemen's Fund*, 421 U.S. 491 (1975). Although the Constitution does not expressly grant Congress the power to punish witnesses for contempt, that power has been deemed an inherent attribute of the legislative authority of Congress (*Anderson* v. *Dunn*, 19 U.S. 204 (1821)) so far as necessary to preserve and exercise the legislative authority expressly granted (*Marshall* v. *Gordon*, 243 U.S. 521 (1917)). However, as a power of self-preservation, a means and not an end, the power does not extend to infliction of punishment. *Manual* §§ 294-296.

To supplement this inherent power, Congress in 1857 adopted an alternative statutory contempt procedure. § 2, infra. Thus, the House may either (1) certify a recalcitrant witness to the appropriate United States Attorney for possible indictment under this statute or (2) exercise its inherent power to commit for contempt by detaining the witness in the custody of the Sergeant-at-Arms. *Manual* § 296. The statutory procedure is the one used in modern practice, but the ''inherent power'' remains available. In one instance, the House invoked both procedures against a witness. 3 Hinds § 1672.

In contrast, the Senate may invoke its civil contempt statute (2 USC § 288d) to direct the Senate legal counsel to bring an action in Federal court to compel a witness to comply with the subpoena of a committee of the Senate.

Under the inherent contempt power of the House, the recalcitrant witness may be arrested and brought to trial before the bar of the House, with the offender facing possible incarceration. 3 Hinds § 1685. At the trial of the witness in the House, questions may be put to the witness by the Speaker (2 Hinds § 1602) or by a committee (2 Hinds § 1617; 3 Hinds § 1668). In one instance, the matter was investigated by a committee, the respondent was then brought to the bar of the House, and a resolution was reported to the House for its vote. 2 Hinds § 1628.

The inherent power of Congress to find a recalcitrant witness in contempt has not been invoked by the House in recent years because of the time-consuming nature of the trial and because the jurisdiction of the House cannot extend beyond the end of a Congress. See *Anderson* v. *Dunn*, 19 U.S. 204 (1821). The first exercise of this power in the House occurred in 1812, when the House proceeded against a newspaper editor who declined to identify his source of information that had been disclosed from executive session. 3 Hinds § 1666. Such powers had been exercised before the adoption of the Constitution by the Continental Congress as well as by England's House of Lords and House of Commons. *Jurney* v. *MacCracken*, 294 U.S. 125 (1935). Although the use of such powers was supported by the Supreme Court in *Jurney*, neither House has used them since 1935.

§ 2. Statutory Contempt Procedure

Generally

An alternative statutory contempt procedure was enacted in 1857. Under this statute the wrongful refusal to comply with a congressional subpoena is made punishable by a fine of up to $1,000 and imprisonment for up to one year. A committee may vote to seek a contempt citation against a recalcitrant witness. This action is then reported to the House. 2 USC § 192. If a resolution to that end is adopted by the House, the matter is referred to a U.S. Attorney, who is to seek an indictment. See 2 USC § 194; *Manual* § 299.

In the 97th Congress the House adopted such a resolution following the failure of an official of the executive branch (EPA Administrator Anne M. Gorsuch) to submit executive branch documents to a House subcommittee pursuant to a subpoena. This was the first occasion on which the House cited a cabinet-level executive branch official for contempt of Congress. *Manual* § 299; H. Rept. 97-968. In the same Congress, Secretary of the Interior James G. Watt was cited for contempt for withholding from a committee subpoenaed documents and for failure to answer its questions. The contempt citation was reported to the House by the oversight and investigations subcommittee through the full Committee on Energy and Commerce. H. Rept. 97-898. An accommodation was reached on the documents, and the House took no action on the report. Similarly, in 1998, a committee report recommended the adoption of a resolution finding Attorney General Janet Reno in contempt of Congress for failing to produce documents subpoenaed by the Committee. H. Rept. 105-728. The House took no action on the report.

In 1983, a committee report recommended the adoption of a resolution finding Rita M. Lavelle (former EPA Assistant Administrator) in contempt of Congress for failing to appear in response to a subpoena. H. Rept. 98-190. The House then adopted a resolution certifying such refusal to the U.S. Attorney. *Manual* § 299.

In 2008, the House adopted (by special order of business) a resolution, reported by the Committee on the Judiciary, directing the Speaker to certify to the United States Attorney the refusal of the White House Chief of Staff to produce documents to a committee, and the refusal of former White House Counsel to appear and testify and produce documents to a subcommittee, each as directed by subpoena. 110-2, H. Res. 979, Feb. 14, 2008, p 2190; *Manual* § 299.

Floor Consideration

A contempt citation must be reported to the House pursuant to formal action by the committee. *Ex parte Frankfield*, 32 F. Supp. 915 (D.D.C. 1940). A committee report relating to the refusal of a witness to testify is privileged for consideration in the House if called up by the chair or other authorized member of the reporting committee. *Manual* § 299. A report relating to the refusal of a witness to produce certain documents as ordered is also privileged. Deschler Ch 15 § 20.9. The report is presented and read. A resolution may then be offered directing the Speaker to certify the refusal to a U.S. Attorney. *Id.* Such a resolution may be offered from the floor as privileged, because the privileges of the House are involved, and a committee report to accompany the resolution may be presented to the House without regard to the three-day availability requirement for other reports. Clause 4(a)(2)(C) of rule XIII; *Manual* §§ 299, 850.

A resolution with two "resolved" clauses separately directing the certification of the contemptuous conduct of two individuals is subject to a demand for a division of the question as to each individual (contempt proceedings against Ralph and Joseph Bernstein, *Manual* § 299); as is a resolution with one "resolved" clause certifying contemptuous conduct of several individuals. *Manual* § 299; *cf.* Deschler-Brown Ch 30 § 49.1. A contempt resolution may be withdrawn as a matter of right before action thereon. *Manual* § 299.

§ 3. — Duties of the Speaker and U.S. Attorney

The controlling statute provides that when a witness fails or refuses to answer or produce the required documents, and such failure is reported to the House—or to the Speaker when the House is not in session—it ''shall be the duty'' of the Speaker to certify the facts to the United States Attorney for presentation to a grand jury. 2 USC § 194. Notwithstanding the language in the statute referring to the ''duty'' of the Speaker, the court in *Wilson* v. *United States*, 369 F.2d 198 (D.C. Cir. 1966) held that the Speaker erred in construing the statute to prohibit any inquiry into the matter by him, and that his automatic certification of a case to the U.S. Attorney during a period of *sine die* adjournment was invalid. Since the incident that gave rise to this decision, no contempt reports have been produced following a *sine die* adjournment, so the authority of the Speaker has not been used.

§ 4. — Defenses; Pertinence Requirement

The statute that penalizes the refusal to respond to a congressional subpoena provides that the question must be ''pertinent to the question under inquiry.'' 2 USC § 192. That is, the answers requested must (1) relate to a legislative purpose that Congress may constitutionally entertain, and (2) fall within the grant of authority actually made by Congress to the committee. Deschler Ch 15 § 6. In a prosecution for contempt of Congress, it must be established that the committee or subcommittee was duly authorized and that its investigation was within the scope of delegated authority. *United States* v. *Seeger*, 303 F.2d 478 (2nd Cir. 1962). A clear chain of authority from the House to its committee is an essential element. *Gojack* v. *United States*, 384 U.S. 702 (1966).

The statutory requirement that a question be pertinent is an essential factor in prosecuting the witness for contempt. Pertinence will not be presumed. *Bowers* v. *United States*, 202 F.2d 447 (D.C. Cir. 1953). The right of a witness to refuse to answer a nonpertinent question is not waived by mere lack of assertion. The committee has a burden to explain to the witness that a question is pertinent and that despite the witness's objection, the committee demands an answer. *Barenblatt* v. *United States*, 252 F.2d 129 (D.C. Cir. 1958), *aff'd*, 360 U.S. 109 (1959); *Davis* v. *United States*, 269 F.2d 357 (6th Cir. 1959), *cert. denied*, 361 U.S. 919 (1959).

In judicial contempt proceedings brought under the statute, constitutional claims and other objections to House investigatory procedures may be raised by way of defense. *United States* v. *House of Representatives*, 556 F. Supp. 150 (D.D.C. 1983). The courts must accord a defendant every right "guaranteed to defendants in all other criminal cases." *Watkins* v. *United States*, 354 U.S. 178 (1957). All elements of the offense, including willfulness, must be proven beyond a reasonable doubt. *Flaxer* v. *United States*, 358 U.S. 147 (1958). However, the courts have been extremely reluctant to interfere with the statutory scheme by considering cases brought by recalcitrant witnesses seeking declaratory or injunctive relief. See, *e.g.*, *Eastland* v. *United States Servicemen's Fund*, 421 U.S. 491 (1975); *United States* v. *House of Representatives*, 556 F. Supp. 150 (D.D.C. 1983).

During committee proceedings, where a report to the House is contemplated, a witness's defense (including objections based on relevance, attorney-client privilege, or executive privilege) may be considered separately by the committee or may merge with a vote on reporting to the House.

To justify withholding subpoenaed information, a witness sometimes contends that the President has claimed executive privilege with respect thereto or has directed the witness not to disclose the information. However, the Supreme Court has rejected the claim that the President has an absolute, unreviewable executive privilege. See *United States* v. *Nixon*, 418 U.S. 683 (1974). Moreover, noncompliance with a congressional subpoena by government officials may not be justified on the ground that they were acting under the orders of a superior. See *United States* v. *Tobin*, 195 F. Supp. 588 (D.D.C. 1961).

§ 5. Purging Contempt

A witness in violation of a House subpoena has been permitted to comply with its terms before the issuance of an indictment. 3 Hinds §§ 1666, 1686. However, once judicial proceedings to enforce the subpoena have been initiated, the defendant cannot be purged of contempt merely by producing the documents or testimony sought. See *United States* v. *Brewster*, 154 F. Supp. 126 (D.D.C. 1957), *cert. denied*, 358 U.S. 842 (1958). At this stage, the House itself must consider and vote on whether to permit a discontinuance. The committee that sought the contempt citation submits a report to the House indicating that substantial compliance on the part of the witness has been accomplished; the House then adopts a resolution certifying the facts to the U.S. Attorney to the end that contempt proceedings be discontinued. *Manual* § 299; Deschler Ch 15 § 21. For example, in the 98th Congress, after EPA Administrator Anne M. Gorsuch had been cited by a prior Congress for contempt for failure to produce certain documents to a House subcommittee, the House adopted a resolution certifying to the U.S. Attorney that an agreement giving the committee access to those documents had been reached. *Manual* § 299.

Although witnesses cannot purge contempt after judicial proceedings have begun, a court may suspend the sentence of witnesses convicted of contempt and give them an opportunity to avoid punishment by providing the testimony sought. Deschler Ch 15 § 21.

Chapter 18
Delegates and Resident Commissioner

Research References
1 Hinds §§ 400-410
6 Cannon §§ 240-246
Deschler Ch 7 § 3
Manual §§ 675, 676

§ 1. In General

Generally

The Delegates and Resident Commissioner are those statutory officials who represent in the House the territories and properties owned or administered by the United States but not admitted to statehood. Deschler Ch 7 § 3. The Virgin Islands, Guam, American Samoa, the Northern Mariana Islands, and the District of Columbia are each represented in the House by a Delegate. Puerto Rico is represented by a Resident Commissioner. *Manual* § 675.

§ 2. In the House

The floor privileges of a Delegate or a Resident Commissioner in the House include the right to debate (2 Hinds § 1290), offer motions (2 Hinds § 1291), and raise points of order (6 Cannon § 240). However, such individual cannot vote in the House (*Manual* § 675) or serve as its presiding officer (*Manual* § 970). A Delegate or a Resident Commissioner may offer any motion a Member may offer, including the motion to adjourn, but not the motion to reconsider, which is itself dependent on the right to vote. 2 Hinds § 1292; Deschler-Brown Ch 29 § 23.65. Such individual may file reports for committees (*Manual* § 675) and may object to the consideration of a bill (6 Cannon § 241; Deschler Ch 7 § 3.7). Impeachment proceedings have been moved by a Delegate. 2 Hinds § 1303.

§ 3. In Committees

Under clause 3 of rule III, Delegates and the Resident Commissioner are elected to serve on standing committees in the same manner as Members, and possess in such committees the same powers and privileges as the other members. *Manual* § 675. They have the right to vote in committees on which they serve. Seniority accrual rights on committees have also been extended to the Delegates and Resident Commissioner. Deschler Ch 7 § 3.11. They may be appointed by the Speaker to any conference committee. The Speaker also has the authority to appoint them to any select committee, an appointment that previously required the permission of the House. *Manual* § 676.

§ 4. In Committee of the Whole

Under a rule first adopted in 1993 (but since stricken), when the House was sitting in Committee of the Whole, the Delegates and Resident Commissioner had the same right to vote as Members, subject to immediate reconsideration in the House where their votes were collectively decisive in the Committee. The Speaker also had authority to appoint a Delegate or Resident Commissioner to serve as chair of the Committee of the Whole. The constitutionality of that rule was upheld based on the feature of the rule providing for immediate reconsideration. *Michel* v. *Anderson*, 14 F.3d 6723 (D.C.Cir. 1994). These provisions were stricken in 1995, reinstated in 2007, and stricken again in 2011. *Manual* § 985.

Chapter 19

Discharging Measures From Committees

Research References

7 Cannon §§ 1007-1023
Deschler Ch 18
Manual §§ 892, 1130

§ 1. In General; Alternative Methods

There are certain procedures that effectively discharge a committee or that may be invoked whenever a committee fails or refuses to report a measure. These methods include:

- The motion to discharge a public bill or resolution available under clause 2 of rule XV after the measure has been pending in committee for more than 30 days. *Manual* § 892; see § 2, infra.
- A motion to discharge the Committee on Rules from a resolution proposing a special order of business for consideration of certain public bills or resolutions under clause 2 of rule XV after the special order of business has been pending before it for seven days. *Manual* § 892; see § 3, infra.
- The motion to suspend the rules available under clause 1 of rule XV pursuant to a vote of two-thirds of the Members. *Manual* § 885.

Note: The motion to suspend the rules may be applied to unreported measures. 8 Cannon § 3421; see generally SUSPENSION OF RULES.

- The Speaker's referral under clause 2 of rule XII of a measure pursuant to time limits that result in the discharge of the measure from committee at the end of the designated time. *Manual* § 816.
- A resolution reported by the Committee on Rules providing for the consideration of an unreported measure; the effect of the resolution, if adopted, is to discharge the committee before which the measure is pending. 5 Hinds § 6771.
- A unanimous-consent request agreed to by the House (the procedure does not apply in the Committee of the Whole). 4 Hinds § 4697.

  Note: Although a unanimous-consent request is within the discretion of the Chair, the Speaker will not entertain such a request without the consent of the chair and ranking minority member of the committee considering the measure and the majority and minority floor leadership. See *Manual* § 956.
- A statutory procedure for discharging certain measures of congressional disapproval or approval. *Manual* § 1130; 4 Hinds § 4697.

As to the procedures for discharging a committee from a resolution of inquiry, see RESOLUTIONS OF INQUIRY. Discharge of vetoed bills, see § 8, infra; discharge pursuant to statute, see § 9, infra.

§ 2. The Discharge Rule; Motions to Discharge

Generally

Under clause 2 of rule XV, a Member may file with the Clerk a motion (normally called a discharge petition) to discharge a committee from the consideration of a public bill or resolution that was referred to the committee 30 days prior thereto. *Manual* § 892. The word ''days'' has been construed to mean legislative days and has been so recodified in clause 2 of rule XV. Deschler Ch 18 § 3.1 The period of time specified by the rule does not begin to run until the committee is appointed or elected. 7 Cannon § 1019.

The Clerk makes the petition available at the rostrum for Members to sign while the House is in session. Under clause 2 of rule XV, when the requisite number of signatures are obtained (a majority of the total membership), the motion is entered on the Journal, printed in the *Congressional Record*, and referred to the Discharge Calendar. Deschler Ch 18 § 1.3. When the motion has been on the calendar for seven legislative days, it may be called up in the House under the discharge rule on the second or fourth Monday of a month. The motion is then debated for 20 minutes and voted on. If the motion prevails on a public bill or joint resolution, it is in order to proceed to consider the discharged measure pursuant to a motion to that effect. See §6, infra. If the motion prevails on a special order of business, the House proceeds to immediate consideration of the rule. See §7, infra.

Petitions to discharge committees are filed with the Clerk and are not presented from the floor, but Members may give notice of the filing of such petitions, either from the floor or by letter. 7 Cannon §1008. Once the motion has been filed, the Clerk makes the signatories a matter of public record on the last day of each week, and they are available for public inspection in the Clerk's office on any day of the business week. *Manual* §892.

Reoffering of Motion

Under clause 2 of rule XV, when a perfected motion to discharge a committee from the consideration of a measure has once been acted on by the House, it is not in order to entertain during the same session another motion for the discharge of that measure or any other bill or resolution substantially the same as such measure.

§3. —Application and Use; What Measures May Be Discharged

Public Bills and Resolutions

A motion to discharge a committee from the consideration of a bill applies to the bill as referred to the committee and not as it may have been proposed to be amended in the committee. 7 Cannon §1015.

The motion to discharge a bill may not be entertained if the bill against which it is directed has been reported from committee before the motion is called up in the House. The filing of the motion to discharge does not preclude the committee from reporting the measure in question at any time before the motion is called up. *Manual* §892; Deschler Ch 18 §1.13.

Application to Special Orders of Business From the Committee on Rules

Under the modern practice, the rule is often invoked to discharge the Committee on Rules from the consideration of a resolution specified in clause 2(b)(1)(B) of rule XV. Such a resolution would enable consideration of a reported public bill or public resolution that has been reported by a standing committee or has been referred to a standing committee for 30 legislative days under terms therein specified by the sponsor of the resolution rather than under the general rules of the House. A petition to discharge the Committee on Rules from consideration of a special order of business making in order a balanced budget constitutional amendment received the requisite number of signatures on two occasions. *Manual* §892.

The motion applies only to special orders of business that have been pending before the Committee on Rules for at least seven legislative days. *Manual* § 892. Moreover, it is not in order to move to discharge the Committee on Rules from the consideration of a resolution not specified in the discharge rule. For example, the Committee on Rules may not be discharged from the further consideration of a resolution providing merely for the appointment of a committee to investigate. Deschler Ch 18 § 2.6.

Since the 105th Congress, clause 2(b)(2) of rule XV has required that a special order of business subject to a discharge motion address the consideration of only one measure and must not propose to admit or effect a nongermane amendment.

Timetable

The discharge of a measure pursuant to clause 2 of rule XV is subject to the following timetable:

- Expiration of 30 legislative days after the measure is referred to committee and the concurrent expiration of seven legislative days after a petition is filed against a special order of business referred to the Committee on Rules. § 2, supra.
- Requisite number of signatures. § 4, infra.
- Expiration of seven legislative days, which begins the day the motion is referred to the discharge calendar. § 6, infra.
- Privilege of motion only on second or fourth Monday of month following expiration of seven-day period. § 6, infra.

§ 4. — Signatures Required

The requirement that a discharge motion be signed by a majority of the Members has been interpreted to mean that the motion requires the signatures of a majority of the entire membership, or 218 Members. Deschler Ch 18 § 1.2. Non-voting Delegates may not sign a discharge petition, even by unanimous consent. 108-1, Oct. 1, 2003, p 23853. This numerical requirement is in contrast to the vote needed for actual passage of legislation under ordinary conditions, which requires only a majority of those present and voting, a quorum being present. See VOTING. However, a hard majority is necessary for a discharge motion because the death or resignation of a signatory of the motion does not invalidate such individual's signature. Deschler Ch 18 § 1.5. To enable a Member elected in a special election to sign a petition, the signature of the predecessor must be removed by the successor. *Manual* § 892; Deschler Ch 18 § 1.4.

Clause 2 of rule XV requires the preparation of daily cumulative lists of the names of those signing the petition. Such lists must be made available for public inspection.

Additional signatures are not admitted after the requisite number have been affixed. Deschler Ch 18 § 1.4. Under clause 2 of rule XV, a signature may be withdrawn by a Member in writing at any time before the petition is signed by the requisite number and entered on the Journal. The signing of discharge motions by proxy is not permitted. 7 Cannon § 1014.

§ 5. —Privilege and Precedence of Motions

A motion to discharge a committee, when called up pursuant to the provisions of the discharge rule, is privileged; and the Speaker may decline to recognize for a matter not related to the proceedings. 7 Cannon § 1010. Such motions take precedence over business merely privileged under the general rules of the House. 7 Cannon § 1011. The motion takes precedence over motions to resolve into Committee of the Whole (7 Cannon §§ 1016, 1017), over unfinished business (Deschler Ch 18 § 3.4), and over motions to suspend the rules (7 Cannon § 1018). However, prior to the consideration of a motion to discharge, the Speaker has the discretion to recognize Members for one-minute speeches by unanimous consent. Deschler Ch 18 § 3.8.

§ 6. —Calling Up and Debating the Motion

Generally

Under clause 2 of rule XV, a motion to discharge that has been on the Discharge Calendar at least seven days may be called up for consideration on the second and fourth Mondays of each month except during the last six days of a session. The consideration of such a motion may be made in order on a day other than the specified Mondays by unanimous consent. Deschler Ch 18 § 3.5. The House may dispense with a motion to discharge by unanimous consent and agree to consider the underlying matter on a date certain under the same terms as if discharged by motion. *Manual* § 892.

To call up the motion, a Member must qualify as having signed the discharge petition. Deschler Ch 18 § 3.6.

Intervening Motions

Clause 2 of rule XV does not permit intervening motions except for one motion to adjourn. Accordingly, it has been held that when a motion to discharge a committee is called up, it is not in order to move to table the motion or to move to postpone consideration thereof to a day certain. Deschler

Ch 18 §§ 3.14, 3.15; see also 96-1, July 24, 1979, p 20358; 103-2, Mar. 11, 1994, p 4772.

Debate on Motion

Debate on the motion to discharge is limited to 20 minutes—10 minutes under the control of the proponent and 10 minutes under the control of a Member recognized in opposition. *Manual* § 892. The Speaker has denied recognition for requests to extend the time. 7 Cannon § 1010.

The 20-minute period for debate is divided according to position on the pending matter and not according to membership in a particular political party. 7 Cannon § 1010. The proponents of a motion to discharge are entitled to open and close debate on the motion. 7 Cannon § 1010a; Deschler Ch 18 § 3.13. The chair of the committee being discharged, if opposed, is ordinarily recognized to control the 10 minutes in opposition. Deschler Ch 18 § 3.10.

A Member recognized to control half of the debate on the motion may yield part of that time to another Member, but that Member may not yield part of that time to a third Member. Deschler Ch 18 §§ 3.11, 3.12.

§ 7. —Consideration of Discharged Measure; Forms

Motion to Consider the Discharged Measure

Under clause 2 of rule XV, following agreement to a motion to discharge a measure pending before a committee, it is in order for any Member who signed the motion to move to proceed to the immediate consideration of that measure. Deschler Ch 18 § 4.3. The motion to consider the measure is privileged and is decided without debate. Deschler Ch 18 § 4.3. If the motion for immediate consideration is adopted, the legislation is taken up under the general rules of the House. Deschler Ch 18 §§ 4.4, 4.6. Otherwise, the discharged measure is referred to its proper calendar. Deschler Ch 18 § 4.7.

Under the modern practice of the House, many discharge motions propose to discharge the Committee on Rules from further consideration of a resolution pending before that committee. Under clause 2 of rule XV, if that motion is adopted, the House immediately considers the resolution. During such consideration, the Speaker may not entertain any dilatory or other intervening motion except one motion to adjourn. Deschler Ch 18 § 4. Amendments to the resolution are not in order, unless the previous question is not ordered. *Manual* § 892. If the discharged resolution is adopted, the House then considers the discharged measure under the terms of the resolution.

Motions to Expedite Consideration; Debate

A bill having been discharged pursuant to the rule, its proponents are entitled to recognition for allowable motions to expedite consideration of the discharged measure. 7 Cannon § 1012. Measures requiring consideration in Committee of the Whole are taken up therein. 7 Cannon § 1021; Deschler Ch 18 § 4.4. Where the discharged measure does not require consideration in Committee of the Whole, the Member who offered the motion for its immediate consideration is recognized in the House under the hour rule. *Manual* § 892. For example, when a joint resolution proposing an amendment to the Constitution was considered in the House pursuant to a motion to discharge, the proponent of the joint resolution was recognized to control one hour of debate. Deschler Ch 18 § 4.6. However, a special order of business discharged from the Committee on Rules under this procedure normally specifies the procedures under which the underlying bill is to be considered.

Under clause 2 of rule XV, the bill to which the discharge motion applies is read by title only and may not be read in its entirety. 7 Cannon § 1019a.

The point of order provided by clause 4 of rule XXI—interdicting provisions containing appropriations not reported by the Committee on Appropriations—does not apply to an appropriation in a bill that has been the object of a successful motion to discharge. *Manual* § 892; 7 Cannon § 1019a.

Form

MEMBER: M__. Speaker, pursuant to clause 2 of rule XV, I call up the petition to discharge the Committee on __________ from the further consideration of the bill, H.R. __________.

Or

M__. Speaker, pursuant to clause 2 of rule XV, I call up the petition to discharge the Committee on Rules from the further consideration of the resolution, H. Res. __________, providing for consideration of the bill, H.R. __________.

SPEAKER: Did the gentle______ sign the petition?

MEMBER: I did, M__. Speaker.

SPEAKER: The gentle______ from __________ calls up a motion to discharge the Committee on __________ from the further consideration of the bill [resolution], which the Clerk will report by title.

SPEAKER: The gentle______ from __________ will control ten minutes in favor of the motion, and the gentle______ from __________ will control ten minutes in opposition. The gentle______ from __________ [proponent of the motion] is recognized.

SPEAKER: The time of the gentle______ has expired. All time has expired. The question is on the motion to discharge the Committee on __________ from further consideration of the bill (or resolution). As many as favor the motion will say "Aye." As many as are opposed say "No."

SPEAKER: The ayes have it and the motion is agreed to. The committee is discharged.

§ 8. Discharge of Matters Privileged Under the Constitution

Certain matters arising under the Constitution are privileged for consideration at any time and may therefore be discharged at any time irrespective of the requirements for petitions under the discharge rule, subject to a two-day notice and scheduling requirement under rule IX. Examples include propositions to discipline a Member and impeachment resolutions. Deschler Ch 18 § 5. Similarly, a motion to discharge a committee from the further consideration of a vetoed bill that has been returned to the House and referred back to committee by the House presents a privileged question and is in order at any time. Deschler Ch 18 § 5.1. It is likewise in order to move to discharge a proposition involving a contested election. See discussion in 8 Cannon § 2316; see generally QUESTIONS OF PRIVILEGE.

Although a motion to discharge a committee from the consideration of a vetoed bill is privileged and debatable, that motion is subject to the motion to lay on the table but remains renewable on a subsequent day. *Manual* § 108; 4 Hinds § 3532; Deschler Ch 18 § 5.1.

§ 9. Discharge of Resolutions of Disapproval; Statutory Motions

Congressional actions approving or disapproving certain executive branch decisions are sometimes made subject, by statute, to automatic discharge or to a motion to discharge after the lapse of a certain period of time. For various examples, see *Manual* § 1130.

Chapter 20
District of Columbia Business

Research References
U.S. Const. art. I, § 8
4 Hinds §§ 3304-3311
7 Cannon §§ 872-880
Deschler Ch 21 § 5
Manual §§ 135, 894, 1130(5)

§ 1. In General; Constitutional Background

Generally

Under the Constitution, the Congress is empowered to "exercise exclusive Legislation in all Cases whatsoever, over [the District of Columbia]." U.S. Const. art. I, § 8. Although the Constitution gives "exclusive" jurisdiction to the Congress over such legislation, the Congress is not precluded from delegating its powers over the District to a local government. The Supreme Court has indicated that the "exclusive" jurisdiction granted was meant to exclude any question of power by adjoining States over the area and was not intended to prevent an appropriate delegation of legislative authority to the District. *District of Columbia* v. *John R. Thompson Company*, 346 U.S. 100 (1946); see also *Stoutengurgh* v. *Hennick*, 129 U.S. 141 (1889).

Home Rule

Pursuant to its authority under this constitutional provision, Congress provided in 1970 for the people of the District to be represented in the House by a Delegate and for a commission to report to the Congress on the organization of the government of the District. 2 USC § 25a. In 1973, the District of Columbia Self-Government and Governmental Reorganization

Act, also known as the District of Columbia Home Rule Act, was enacted. Pub. L. 93-198, 87 Stat. 774 (1973). It reorganized the governmental structure of the District, provided for a charter for local government, delegated certain legislative powers to the District, and implemented certain recommendations of the commission. That Act sets forth a procedure for congressional approval or disapproval of certain actions by the District of Columbia Council. *Manual* § 1130(5).

District of Columbia Appropriations

Section 446 of the District of Columbia Home Rule Act reserved to Congress the authority to appropriate all Federal and local funds for the District. As a result, general matters relating to the District of Columbia are most frequently considered in the context of the annual general appropriation bill that provides funding for the District, albeit often in the form of legislation in violation of clause 2 of rule XXI.

§ 2. Jurisdiction; When District Business is in Order

All measures relating to the municipal affairs of the District, with the exception of appropriation bills, fall within the jurisdiction of the Committee on Oversight and Government Reform. Clause 1(n) of rule X.

Clause 4 of rule XV sets apart the second and fourth Mondays in each month for the consideration of District business, if claimed by the committee, to be considered after the disposition of motions to discharge and referral business on the Speaker's table. District of Columbia business is in order on one of the designated Mondays after other more privileged business, such as a motion to suspend the rules, and the fact that the House has considered some District business before such a motion does not affect the eligibility of further such business after suspensions have been completed. *Manual* § 894.

District Day may be transferred to another day not specified in the controlling rule either by unanimous consent or by adoption of a special order of business from the Committee on Rules. Deschler Ch 21 § 5.12.

§ 3. Privilege; Precedence

The consideration of District business on the specified days is of qualified privilege only. Deschler Ch 21 § 5. District business yields to:

- Questions of the privileges of the House. Deschler Ch 21 § 5.3.
- Referral business on the Speaker's table. *Manual* § 894; Deschler Ch 21 § 5.
- Conference reports. 8 Cannon § 3292; Deschler Ch 21 § 5.

- A privileged resolution on the order of business from the Committee on Rules. Deschler Ch 21 § 5.4.
- Motions to suspend the rules (within the discretion of the Speaker). Deschler Ch 21 § 5.1.
- Motions to discharge. *Manual* § 894; 7 Cannon § 872.
- Motions to resolve into the Committee of the Whole for the consideration of appropriation bills. 6 Cannon §§ 716-718; 7 Cannon § 876; Deschler Ch 21 § 5.

On a District Day a motion to go into the Committee of the Whole to consider District business and a motion to go into the Committee to consider business generally privileged under a special order of business are of equal privilege, and recognition to move either is within the discretion of the Chair. 7 Cannon § 877.

§ 4. Consideration; Forms

Procedure

Business reported by committee relating to the District of Columbia is normally taken up for consideration in the House as in the Committee of the Whole. Deschler Ch 21 § 5.7. If such business is on the Union Calendar, it also may be considered in Committee of the Whole by motion (Deschler Ch 21 § 5.9), by unanimous consent (Deschler Ch 21 § 5.7), or by a special order of business (Deschler Ch 21 § 5.15).

The question of consideration may not be raised against District business generally, but may be raised against a particular bill when presented. 4 Hinds §§ 3308, 3309.

When reported, private bills relating to the District of Columbia may be called up for consideration on a District Monday. 4 Hinds § 3310; 7 Cannon § 873; Deschler Ch 21 § 5.10.

Form

Union Calendar Bills

MEMBER IN CHARGE: M__. Speaker, I move that the House resolve itself into the Committee of the Whole House on the state of the Union for the [further] consideration of District of Columbia business on the Calendar.

> *Note:* The motion to go into the Committee of the Whole is not debatable, is not subject to amendment, and may not be laid on the table or indefinitely postponed. See COMMITTEES OF THE WHOLE.

Pending that, I ask unanimous consent that general debate be limited to __________ hours, equally divided and controlled by myself and the gentle______ from __________.

Note: General debate in the Committee of the Whole may be limited and divided in the House by unanimous consent, but a motion to limit such debate is not in order until after general debate has begun and the Committee rises. See CONSIDERATION AND DEBATE.

In the House as in the Committee of the Whole

SPEAKER: This is District of Columbia day. The Chair recognizes the gentle______ from __________, chair of the Committee on Oversight and Government Reform.

MEMBER: M__. Speaker, by direction of the Committee on Oversight and Government Reform, I call up the bill (H.R.__________) to ________________________.

SPEAKER: The Clerk will report the title of the bill.

MEMBER (*after the reading*): I ask unanimous consent that the bill be considered in the House as in the Committee of the Whole.

§ 5. — Debate

Members of the committee with jurisdiction over District of Columbia business have precedence in recognition for debate during consideration of District business. 7 Cannon § 875. General debate in the Committee of the Whole is under the hour rule unless otherwise provided by the House or the Committee. 7 Cannon § 874; Deschler Ch 21 § 5.7 (note). Such debate properly alternates between those favoring and those opposing the pending proposition. Debate is general debate and is not confined to the bill under consideration. 7 Cannon § 875. Where the bill is considered in the House as in the Committee of the Whole, as is usually the case by unanimous consent, there is no general debate. The bill is considered as read, and debate and amendments proceed immediately under the five-minute rule. See COMMITTEES OF THE WHOLE.

§ 6. Disposition of Unfinished Business

District business that is unfinished on a day assigned to the committee with jurisdiction normally goes over to the next eligible day for that committee. 4 Hinds § 3306. Accordingly, unless the previous question has been ordered, unfinished business on District Day does not come again before the House until the next District Day (Deschler Ch 21 § 5.13), at which time it must be affirmatively called up by the Member in charge (Deschler Ch 21 § 5.14). Unfinished business on one District Day does not come up on the next District Day unless called up by the committee. *Manual* § 894; 4 Hinds § 3307; 7 Cannon §§ 879, 880.

§ 7. Procedure Under Home Rule Act

Under the District of Columbia Home Rule Act, the Congress retains control over amendments to the District of Columbia Charter. An amendment to the District of Columbia Charter is deemed repealed if within 35 days a joint resolution disapproving such amendment is enacted. Likewise, the enactments of the District of Columbia Council, with certain exceptions, are deemed repealed if the Congress within a specified period enacts a joint resolution of disapproval thereof. In the House, such resolutions are referred to the Committee on Oversight and Government Reform. A privileged motion to discharge that committee is authorized under certain circumstances where matters affecting the District of Columbia Criminal Code are involved. The motion is debatable under the hour rule. The motion is privileged if made after the 20-day period specified by the Home Rule Act. District of Columbia Home Rule Act, §§ 303, 602, 604; *Manual* § 1130(5).

The present Home Rule Act requires that congressional disapproval be expressed in a joint resolution (a concurrent resolution was formerly permitted). *Manual* § 1130(5). For a discussion of the validity and constitutionality of resolutions of disapproval, see CONGRESSIONAL PROCEDURES ENACTED IN LAW.

Disapproval resolutions are considered in the House unless the enactment in question affects the U.S. Treasury, in which case they are considered in the Committee of the Whole. *Manual* § 1130(5).

When the committee has reported the resolution, or has been discharged from its consideration, it is in order to move to consider the resolution. This motion is highly privileged and is not debatable or amendable. Debate on the resolution is limited to not more than 10 hours, to be equally divided. Motions to further limit debate are permitted but are themselves not debatable. The resolution is not subject to amendment or recommittal. Motions to postpone or to proceed to the consideration of other business are not debatable. *Manual* § 1130(5).

Chapter 21

Division of the Question for Voting

Research References

5 Hinds §§ 6106-6162

8 Cannon §§ 3163-3176

Deschler-Brown Ch 30 §§ 42-52

Manual §§ 480-482, 919-921

A. Generally

§ 1. In General; Form

Under clause 5 of rule XVI, a question that consists of two or more separable substantive propositions is subject to a division of the question, if demanded, so as to obtain a separate vote on each proposition. Deschler-Brown Ch 30 § 42. The procedure is applicable in the Committee of the Whole as well as in the House. See, *e.g.*, Deschler-Brown Ch 29 § 42.12.

The rule prohibits its application to special orders of business from the Committee on Rules, to propositions electing Members to standing or joint committees, and to a motion to strike and insert. *Manual* § 919. The entire rule may be suspended by the adoption of a resolution from the Committee on Rules. 7 Cannon § 775.

§ 2. Tests of Divisibility

To be divided for a vote, a question must consist of at least two separate and distinct propositions both grammatically and substantively, so that if one proposition is rejected, a separate proposition logically will remain. *Manual* § 921; 8 Cannon § 3165; Deschler-Brown Ch 30 §§ 42.1, 42.3. In passing on a demand for division, the Chair considers only the severability of the propositions and not the merits of the question presented. 5 Hinds § 6122.

The requirement that there must be at least two substantive propositions in order to justify division is strictly enforced. 5 Hinds §§ 6108-6113. If either proposition, standing alone, is not a distinct substantive proposition, the question is not divisible, even though each portion is grammatically complete. 7 Cannon §§ 3165, 3167. However, in dividing a question into separate propositions, some restructuring of the language used is permissible. *Manual* § 921; 5 Hinds §§ 6114-6118.

§ 3. Demanding a Division

A request for a division of the question does not require unanimous consent, and no motion is made. Deschler-Brown Ch 30 § 42.4. The Member seeking a division rises and addresses the Chair:

MEMBER: M__. Speaker, I demand a division of the question.

SPEAKER: The gentle______ will indicate the proposition(s) on which a separate vote is desired. . . .

SPEAKER: The gentle______ requests a division, and that portion of the proposition will be divided for a separate vote.

[*Or*]

OPPONENT: M__. Speaker, I make the point of order that the question is not susceptible of division, and that the portions indicated by the gentle______ do not constitute separate substantive propositions.

A demand for a division of a question is in order even after the previous question has been ordered. 5 Hinds §§ 5468, 6149; 8 Cannon § 3173. Under clause 5 of rule XVI, the demand for a division is in order before the question is put to the House for a vote. Deschler-Brown Ch 30 § 42.4. The question may not be divided after it has been put or after the yeas and nays have been ordered. 5 Hinds §§ 6160-6162. The demand is likewise untimely if the question is one against which a point of order has been raised and is pending. 8 Cannon § 3432.

A demand for a division of the question may be withdrawn. However, withdrawal is permitted only by unanimous consent once the Chair has put the question on the first portion to be voted on. *Manual* § 921; Deschler-Brown Ch 30 § 42.11. A demand having been made by one Member, another Member may demand a further division, if the proposition is susceptible to such further division. 111-2, May 28, 2010, p ____.

B. Division of Particular Propositions

§ 4. In General

Generally; Distinction Between Bills and Resolutions

Whether a division of the question may be demanded depends on the nature of the pending matter and on whether it meets the tests of divisibility imposed by rule XVI. § 2, supra. Certain House resolutions—whether simple or concurrent—are subject to the demand. § 5, infra. However, bills and joint resolutions are not divisible. A separate vote may not be demanded on various provisions set forth in such a measure or on its preamble. 5 Hinds §§ 6144-6147; 8 Cannon § 3172. When the previous question has been ordered on adoption of a measure containing a series of simple resolutions, they may be divided. 5 Hinds § 6149.

The question of engrossment and third reading of a bill under clause 8 of rule XVI is not subject to a demand for a division of the question. *Manual* § 943. Certain amendments, such as a compound motion to strike (§ 10, infra), may be divided. However, most other motions are not divisible. A motion for the previous question on a proposition and an amendment thereto is not divisible. *Manual* § 996; Deschler-Brown Ch 30 § 46.1. Division of the question is possible on a motion that a Member-elect's credentials be referred to committee and that such individual be sworn. 5 Hinds § 6117.

Appeals

There may be a division of the question on an appeal from a decision of the Speaker if the decision involves two or more separate and distinct questions. 5 Hinds § 6157.

§ 5. Simple or Concurrent Resolutions

A simple or concurrent resolution may be subject to a demand for a division of the question if it satisfies the test of divisibility imposed by rule XVI. § 2, supra. Thus, a concurrent resolution on the budget is subject to a demand for a division of the question if the resolution grammatically and substantively relates to different fiscal years or includes a separate, hortatory section having its own grammatical and substantive meaning. *Manual* § 921; Deschler-Brown Ch 30 § 42.5. An impeachment resolution has been divided for a separate vote on each article. *Manual* § 921; 6 Cannon § 545.

To be subject to a demand for a division of the question, a resolution must present two or more separate and distinct substantive propositions. It has been held that a resolution (1) censuring a Member and (2) adopting the committee report recommending such censure on the basis of the committee's findings is not divisible because these questions are substantively equivalent. Deschler-Brown Ch 30 § 42.2. An adjournment resolution that also authorizes the receipt of veto messages from the President during the adjournment is not subject to a division of the question, as the receipt authority would be nonsensical standing alone. *Manual* § 921.

It is not in order to demand a division of the question on matters that are merely incorporated by reference in the pending resolution. For example, when a resolution to adopt a series of rules, referred to but not made a part of the resolution, is before the House, it is not in order to demand a separate vote on each rule. 5 Hinds § 6159.

§ 6. —Resolutions Naming Two or More Individuals

Under clause 5 of rule XVI, a resolution electing Members to standing or joint committees is not divisible. However, other types of resolutions relating to two or more named individuals may be divided for the purpose of voting. Deschler-Brown Ch 30 § 49. For example, a resolution confirming the nomination of certain individuals to executive branch offices is subject to a division of the question so as to obtain a separate vote on each nominee. Deschler-Brown Ch 30 § 49.2. A resolution with two resolve clauses separately certifying the contemptuous conduct of two individuals is divisible. *Manual* § 921. Similarly, a resolution with one resolve clause certifying contemptuous conduct of several individuals may be divisible. *Manual* § 299; but see Deschler-Brown Ch 30 § 49.1.

A resolution relating to two or more named individuals may be divided even though that may require a grammatical reconstruction of the text. 5 Hinds § 6121. A word that is a mere formality, such as "resolved," is sometimes supplied by interpretation of the Chair. 5 Hinds §§ 6114-6118.

§ 7. —Special Orders of Business

Under clause 5 of rule XVI, resolutions reported from the Committee on Rules providing a special order of business are not divisible. However, other types of special orders of business from that committee are subject to a demand for a division where the resolution contains separate and distinct substantive propositions. For example, a resolution reported from that committee establishing two or more select committees is subject to a demand for a division of the question. *Manual* § 921.

§ 8. Amendments

Generally

Clause 5 of rule XVI permits a division of the question on an amendment on the demand of any Member where the amendment is properly divisible into two or more substantive propositions. A division is in order on an amendment if the amendment contains propositions so distinct in substance that, one being taken away, a substantive proposition remains. *Manual* § 921; Deschler-Brown Ch 30 § 42.13. Thus, an amendment offered to an appropriation bill providing that no part of the appropriation may be paid to named individuals may be divided for a separate vote on each name. Deschler-Brown Ch 30 § 49.4. An amendment in the form of a motion to strike and insert is not divisible. See § 11, infra.

Amendments in Committee of the Whole

The rule permitting a division of the question is applicable to an amendment (other than a motion to strike and insert) consisting of two or more substantive propositions under consideration in the Committee of the Whole. Deschler-Brown Ch 30 § 43. A request for a division of the question on such an amendment may be made at any time before the Chair puts the question thereon. 5 Hinds § 6162. An amendment reported to the House from the Committee of the Whole as a discrete amendment is not subject to a division of the question in the House. 4 Hinds §§ 4883-4892; see generally COMMITTEES OF THE WHOLE.

Perfecting Amendments; Substitute Amendments

An amendment adding language to the pending text is divisible if the language to be added contains two or more distinct propositions. 5 Hinds §§ 6129, 6133. However, an amendment in the nature of a substitute is not subject to a demand for a division of the question. 5 Hinds § 6127; 8 Cannon § 3168. The division of a motion to strike and insert is precluded by House rule. § 11, infra.

A division of the question may be demanded on an amendment either before amendments are adopted thereto, or on the amendment as amended (assuming that perfecting amendments or an adopted substitute do not destroy the divisibility of the amendment as amended). *Manual* § 921.

A negative vote on a motion to strike a portion of a pending amendment does not prevent a demand for a division of that portion of the amendment if it is a separate proposition and therefore properly severable. Deschler-Brown Ch 30 § 43.1.

§ 9. —En Bloc Amendments

Consideration of several amendments en bloc by unanimous consent or otherwise does not prevent a division of the question from being demanded so as to obtain a separate vote on one of the amendments. Deschler-Brown Ch 30 §§ 43.4-43.6. In fact, a Member may be permitted to offer several amendments en bloc and then demand a division of the question for a separate vote on each one. Deschler-Brown Ch 30 § 43.4. However, amendments en bloc proposing only to transfer appropriations among objects in a general appropriation bill (without increasing the levels of budget authority or outlays in the bill), when considered en bloc pursuant to clause 2(f) of rule XXI, are not subject to a demand for division of the question in the House or in the Committee of the Whole.

§ 10. Motions to Strike

A motion to strike various separate provisions of a pending proposition may be divided for purposes of voting. 8 Cannon § 3166. Thus, an amendment proposing to strike two or more sections of a pending amendment may be divided in order to obtain separate votes on the proposal to strike each section. *Manual* § 921. However, an amendment proposing to strike a provision in a bill—and to redesignate subsequent paragraphs accordingly—is not subject to a demand for a division because it contains only one substantive proposition. 93-2, Dec. 10, 1974, p 38746. A motion to strike is not grammatically divisible. However, where there is pending a motion to strike a pending provision, a perfecting amendment to the underlying text may be offered to strike a lesser portion of the provision; and the perfecting amendment is voted on first. Deschler Ch 27 §§17.26, 24.13.

§11. Motions to Strike and Insert

Although a motion to insert may be divisible (§8, supra), the division of a motion to strike and insert is precluded by clause 5(c) of rule XVI. *Manual* §920. The indivisibility of a motion to strike and insert under clause 5(c) operates not only between each branch of the motion (*i.e.* the striking branch and the inserting branch) but also within each branch. 8 Cannon §3169; see also 5 Hinds §6124. An amendment comprising two discrete instructions to strike and insert may be divided. *Manual* §921. 105-2, June 4, 1998, pp 11063, 11064, 11071-75.

A simple motion to strike may not be offered as a substitute for a motion to strike certain words and insert others, as that would have the effect of dividing the motion to strike and insert. *Manual* §920.

§12. Motions to Suspend the Rules

A question being considered pursuant to a motion to suspend the rules may not be divided for a vote. 5 Hinds §§6141-6143; 8 Cannon §3171. Although a proposition may be subject to a division of the question under rule XVI, it cannot be divided if rule XVI is suspended. 5 Hinds §6143; see generally SUSPENSION OF RULES.

§13. Motions to Recommit; Motions to Instruct Conferees

A motion to recommit with instructions is not subject to a demand for a division of the question. It is not in order to demand a separate vote even where the motion includes separate branches of instructions to the reporting committee. *Manual* §921; 5 Hinds §§6134-6137; 8 Cannon §3170. However, an amendment reported forthwith pursuant to instructions contained in a successful motion to recommit may be divided on the question of its adoption if composed of substantively and grammatically distinct propositions. *Manual* §921.

Instructions in a motion to recommit a conference report may not be divided. Deschler-Brown Ch 30 §45.2. Likewise, an initial motion to instruct conferees may not be divided, as only one such motion is permitted. 8 Cannon §3236. However, a division has been permitted on a motion to instruct under clause 7(c) of rule XXII (which permits multiple motions to instruct after the conferees have failed to report for 20 calendar days and 10 legislative days), provided separate substantive propositions are presented. *Manual* § 921.

§ 14. Motions to Table

Because a motion to lay on the table is a summary motion, its only purpose being to defeat the pending proposition, it has been held that the motion to table is not subject to a demand for a division of the question. 5 Hinds § 6140. A division of the question is not in order even if the motion is applicable to two or more separate and distinct propositions, such as a series of resolutions. 5 Hinds § 6138. A motion to table a resolution and pending amendments is likewise indivisible. 5 Hinds §§ 6139, 6140.

§ 15. Senate Amendments

Generally; Motions to Concur

On the question of agreeing or disagreeing to a Senate amendment, it is not in order to demand a division so as to vote separately on different portions of the amendment. 5 Hinds §§ 6151, 6156. The amendment must be voted on as a whole. 8 Cannon § 3175. However, when two or more Senate amendments are considered en bloc in the House, a separate vote may be had on each amendment. 8 Cannon §§ 2383, 2400, 3191. A special order of business may create a division of the question on concurring in a Senate amendment. See SPECIAL ORDERS OF BUSINESS. After the stage of disagreement, clause 10 of rule XXII permits separate votes on rejecting nongermane portions of Senate amendments. See GERMANENESS OF AMENDMENTS.

Motions to Concur with an Amendment

A House amendment proposed in a motion to concur in a Senate amendment with an amendment is divisible if the proposed House amendment is in divisible form. *Manual* § 921. However, such a motion may not be divided between concurring and amending. 8 Cannon § 3176.

A proposed House amendment to a Senate amendment is not divisible if the House amendment is in the form of a motion to strike and insert, as such motions are specifically indivisible under House rule. Deschler-Brown Ch 30 § 48; § 11, supra.

Motions to Recede and Concur

A division may be demanded on a motion to recede from disagreement and concur in a Senate amendment. 5 Hinds § 6209; 8 Cannon §§ 3197-

3199. The question having been divided and the House having receded, a motion to amend takes precedence over the motion to concur (5 Hinds §§6209-6211; 8 Cannon §3198), even after the previous question has been ordered on both motions (*Manual* §525).

C. Consideration of Divided Propositions

§16. In General

Amendment and Debate; Putting the Question

Where a division of the question has been demanded on separable portions of a proposition subject to amendment, amendments to the separable portions remain in order. However, once the Chair has put the question on the first portion, no further amendments to that portion are in order. 94-2, Sept. 9, 1976, p 29538-40. After a vote has been taken on the first portion, the second is open to debate and amendment unless the previous question is ordered. *Manual* §921.

Where a division of the question is demanded on a separable portion of an amendment, the Chair puts the question first on the remaining portion of the amendment, and that portion on which a division is demanded may remain open for further debate and amendment. *Manual* §482. If a division of the question is demanded on more than one portion of an amendment, the Chair may put the question first on the unaffected portions of the amendment (if any), then (after further debate) on the first part on which a division is requested, and then (after further debate) on the subsequent divisible portions. *Manual* §921. Where neither portion of a divided question remains open to further debate or amendment, the question may be put first on the portion identified by the demand for division and then on the remainder. *Manual* §921.

Where the question on adopting an amendment is divided by special order of business (rather than on demand from the floor), the Chair may put the question on each divided portion of the amendment in the order in which it appears. *Manual* §921.

Voting

A question having been divided for a vote, the vote may be taken by one of the voting methods authorized by the House rules, such as voice vote, division vote, or record vote. See VOTING. The motion to reconsider applies separately to each portion of the divided question and continues to be available even after disposition of a motion to reconsider only one portion of the divided question. However, frequently the motion to reconsider each portion is laid on the table en bloc by unanimous consent. 5 Hinds § 5609; 105-2, Dec. 19, 1998, pp 28110-12.

Chapter 22
Election Contests and Disputes

Research References

U.S. Const. art. I, § 5
1 Hinds §§ 634-755
6 Cannon §§ 90-189
Deschler Ch 9
Manual §§ 701, 724, 853

§ 1. In General

Contests for seats in the House are governed by the Federal Contested Elections Act. 2 USC § 381. This statute, enacted in 1969, sets forth the procedure by which a defeated candidate may have a claim to a seat adjudicated by the House. The Act provides for the filing of notice of contest and other proceedings, for the taking of testimony of witnesses, and for a hearing by the Committee on House Administration on such depositions and other papers as have been filed with the Clerk. 2 USC §§ 381-396. Acting on committee reports, the House then disposes of the case by resolution. See § 4, infra.

The grounds for an election contest and the defenses available to the contestee, as well as the process of taking testimony and other procedures followed in determining the contest in committee, are treated elsewhere. See Deschler Ch 9 and Ch 9 Appendix for complete treatment of contested election cases from the 65th Congress (1917) through the 92d Congress (1972).

Notwithstanding the availability of the statutory election-contest procedures discussed herein, some election disputes have been presented directly to the House for consideration and committee investigation. See, *e.g.*, H.

Rept. 99-58. An investigation of a challenged election has been initiated pursuant to:

- An action by the House in directly referring to the Committee on House Administration the question of a Member-elect's right to a seat. Deschler Ch 2 § 6.
- A protest filed by an elector of the district concerned. Deschler Ch 9 § 17.1.
- A petition filed by another person challenging the qualifications of a Member-elect. Deschler Ch 9 § 17.3.

The latter two procedures have rarely been invoked and they preceded the adoption of the modern contested election statute.

The right to a seat in the House also may be affected by House action on a motion to expel, where a sitting Member's conduct is at issue. See ETHICS; COMMITTEE ON ETHICS.

§ 2. Jurisdiction and Powers

Generally

The Constitution authorizes each House to be the judge of the elections, returns, and qualifications of its Members. U.S. Const. art. I, § 5. Thus, the House is entitled to judge contested elections involving its seats, and is not bound by agreement of the parties or decisions of State tribunals. 6 Cannon §§ 90-92. The determination by the House as to the right to a seat is final, being considered a nonjusticiable political question. *Roudebush* v. *Hartke*, 405 U.S. 15 (1972).

Pursuant to the contested election statute, the House acquires jurisdiction of an election contest upon the filing of a notice of contest by a candidate. Deschler Ch 9 § 4.1. Ordinarily, the papers relating to the contest are transmitted by the Clerk to the Committee on House Administration (the committee with jurisdiction over elections contests under clause 1(k) of rule X. Such transmission is pursuant to the statute and needs no formal referral or other action by the House. 2 USC § 393(b); Deschler Ch 9 § 4. However, the House itself may initiate an election investigation if a Member-elect's right to take the oath is challenged by another Member, by referring the question to the committee. Deschler Ch 2 § 6. The House also may summarily dismiss a contest by resolution. Deschler Ch 9 §§ 4.4, 4.5.

Where two persons claim the same seat from the same district, the House may refuse to permit either candidate to take the oath pending a determination of their rights by the House. Deschler Ch 9 § 4.3.

Election contests may be investigated by a special committee, by a subcommittee of the Committee on House Administration, or by *ad hoc* panels. Deschler Ch 9 §§5.2-5.4.

Recounts of Votes

To obtain an order from the House for a recount of votes in an election contest, the contestant should show that remedies to secure a recount under State law have been exhausted and that evidence and testimony have been taken in the matter. Deschler Ch 9 §§41.1, 41.3. Although the committee with jurisdiction has authority to require a recount of votes for a contested seat in the House, the committee may decline to order such a recount where the highest court of the State has conducted a recount and where the contestant has not demonstrated that a recount would change the result of the election. 96-2, Mar. 4, 1980, pp 4490, 4491.

§3. Parties

Under the controlling statute, ''a candidate for election'' to the House ''in the last preceding election'' is given the right to initiate a contest by filing the notice required by law. 2 USC §382(a). The statute defines ''candidate'' to mean one whose name was on the official ballot or who received write-in votes under certain conditions. 2 USC §381(2). Thus, a candidate in the primary whose name was not on the ballot in the general election lacks the requisite standing to initiate a contest, and this was true even under the predecessor contested election statute. Deschler Ch 9 §19.01. Similarly, the House has dismissed a contest filed by one who was a candidate in a special election to fill a vacancy but was not a candidate in a succeeding run-off election. 95-1, Oct. 27, 1977, p 35408.

A lack of standing of a contestant to initiate the contest is a defense that may be raised at the option of the contestee by motion. 2 USC §383(b).

§4. Consideration and Disposition

Precedence and Privilege

Under article I, section 5 of the Constitution and rule IX, the consideration of a contested election case constitutes a question of privilege. 3 Hinds §§2579, 2580, 2626. It takes precedence over the consideration of veto messages from the President (5 Hinds §§6641, 6642), special orders of business (3 Hinds §2554), and business in order on Calendar Wednesday (8 Cannon §2276).

Reports and Resolutions

The House generally disposes of election contests by acting on a resolution, which under the modern practice is reported from the Committee on House Administration. *Manual* § 724. A resolution is used to dispose of the case even where dismissal has been stipulated by the parties. Deschler Ch 9 § 52.5.

Under clause 5 of rule XIII, committee reports relating to the right of Members to their seats are privileged and are so reported from the floor. *Manual* § 853. Resolutions disposing of an election contest also are questions of privilege and may be called up at any time. 105-2, Feb. 12, 1998, pp 1323, 1324. However, unreported resolutions are subject to the notice requirement of rule IX. *Manual* § 701; Deschler Ch 9 §§ 42.3, 42.4.

The resolution may:

- Declare one of the parties entitled to the seat. Deschler Ch 9 §§ 42.2, 62.2.
- Declare one of the parties not competent to bring the contest. Deschler Ch 8 § 13.1.
- Declare that neither party should be seated pending a committee investigation. Deschler Ch 9 § 42.15.
- Declare the seat vacant. Deschler Ch 9 §§ 42.11, 42.12.
- Dispose of the contest upon expiration of a specified day. *Manual* § 701.
- Dismiss the contest. See § 5, infra.
- Provide for payment or reimbursement from the applicable accounts of the House for costs incurred in the contest or its investigation. Deschler Ch 8 § 13.4; Deschler Ch 9 §§ 45.1-45.6; see also 2 USC § 396 (permitting the committee to allow any party reimbursement for reasonable expenses in the case).

§ 5. — Dismissal

A motion to dismiss will lie under the Federal Contested Elections Act to permit the contestee to interpose certain defenses to the contestant's claim or notice of contest. 2 USC § 383(b). Such a motion may be acted on by the House pursuant to a privileged resolution reported from the Committee on House Administration. *Manual* §§ 850, 853.

Under this statute, the burden of proof is on the contestant to present sufficient evidence, even before the formal submission of testimony, to overcome the motion to dismiss. Deschler Ch 9 § 35.7. A motion to dismiss will lie where the contestant has not adduced evidence or forwarded testimony in the manner prescribed by law or has failed to demonstrate that there is some documentable basis for the allegations. Deschler Ch 9 §§ 25.1-25.5. Under the statute, the contestant has the burden of proving sufficient evidence to show that the result of the election would be changed or that the

House should conduct a complete recount. 95-1, May 9, 1977, p 13954; 99-1, Oct. 2, 1985, p 25665. Evidence that the contestant received more votes than the contestee in a *prior* election is insufficient. 95-1, Oct. 27, 1977, p 35408. Merely suggesting the probability of error in the tabulation of votes, without offering evidence of a change in the election result, is likewise insufficient. 95-1, May 9, 1977, p 13954. Where the number of illegal votes shown by clear and convincing evidence to have been cast in an election is less than the total margin of victory of the contestee, the House may adopt the recommendation of the Committee on House Administration dismissing the election contest. The clear and convincing standard was used rather than a proportionate reduction methodology that would have allocated the illegal votes scientifically between the parties. 105-2, Feb. 12, 1998, pp 1323, 1324.

§ 6. —Debate and Voting; Amendment

Generally

Resolutions disposing of election contests have been determined by voice vote and without debate. Deschler Ch 9 § 42.5. Normally, however, debate on the resolution is under the hour rule, with extensions of time permitted by unanimous consent. The debate may be divided among certain Members, with the previous question considered as ordered at the conclusion thereof. Deschler Ch 9 §§ 42.9, 59.1. The Member supporting the recommendation of the committee in the contest is entitled to close debate. Deschler Ch 9 § 42.8.

The resolution may be subject to a demand for a division of the question if its form permits (Deschler Ch 9 § 42.14) and to a motion to recommit with instructions (Deschler Ch 9 § 42.16). The resolution is not subject to amendment unless the Member controlling the time for debate yields for that purpose or the previous question is voted down. Deschler Ch 9 § 42.17. If the manager of the resolution yields for an amendment, the floor is lost to the proponent of the amendment. Deschler-Brown Ch 29 § 30.8. Where the previous question is ordered on both the resolution of dismissal and on the preamble, the preamble is not separately voted on or amended except as part of a motion to recommit. 105-2, Feb. 12, 1998, pp 1333, 1334.

Participation by the Parties

If not a sitting Member, the contestant in an election contest may be permitted on the floor under clause 2 of rule IV during the consideration of the case in the House but must abide by the rules of proper decorum. *Manual* § 622; Deschler Ch 4 § 4.5; Deschler Ch 9 § 42.6. Furthermore, such contestant is not allowed to participate in the debate absent an order of the House. 1 Hinds §§ 662, 666.

If a sitting Member, a contestee may participate in debate on the resolution disposing of the contest and insert remarks in the *Congressional Record*. Deschler Ch 9 §§ 42.6, 42.7; 105-2, Feb. 12, 1998, p 1327. Such contestee also may vote on the resolution. 99-1, Oct. 2, 1985, p 25670.

Chapter 23
Election of Members

Research References

U.S. Const. art. I, § 5, cl. 1
1 Hinds §§ 277-633
6 Cannon §§ 38-89
Deschler Ch 8

§ 1. In General

Generally

Although Congress has enacted extensive legislation to protect the right to vote and to secure the process against fraud, bribery, and illegal conduct, the actual mechanism for conducting and holding congressional elections has been left largely to the States. Deschler Ch 8 §§ 5, 7. However, under article I, section 5, clause 1 of the Constitution, the ultimate validity of elections rests on determinations by the House and Senate as final judges of the elections and returns of their respective Members. Deschler Ch 8 § 5. Therefore, where the conduct of election officials or of candidates and their agents constitutes fraud or illegal control of election machinery, the House or Senate may void an election and refuse to administer the oath to a Member-elect. Deschler Ch 8 § 7; see Deschler Ch 8 for complete treatment of elections and election campaigns.

Apportionment and Reapportionment

Since the admission of Alaska and Hawaii to statehood, the total membership of the House has remained fixed by statute at 435 seats. *Manual* § 227. By law, these 435 seats are automatically apportioned among the States according to each decennial census. 2 USC § 2a.

Under this law, a statistical model known as the ''method of equal proportions'' is used to determine the number of Representatives to which each State is entitled. Although other methods for apportioning House seats may be permitted, the equal proportions method chosen by Congress has been upheld under the Constitution and was plainly intended to reach as close as practicable the goal of ''one person, one vote.'' *Massachusetts* v. *Mosbacher*, 785 F. Supp. 230 (D. Mass. 1992), *rev'd* on other grounds *Franklin* v. *Massachusetts*, 505 U.S. 788 (1992). The courts also have recently upheld under Federal law and the Constitution a counting methodology used by the Census Bureau in a decennial census. This method, known as ''imputation,'' was held to be different than ''sampling,'' a method prohibited under section 195 of title 13, United States Code. *Utah* v. *Evans*, 536 U.S. 452 (2002). The method of apportioning the seats in the House is vested exclusively in Congress, and neither States nor courts may direct greater or lesser representation than that allocated by statute. Deschler Ch 8 § 1. The States create their own congressional districts, which must be redrawn after reapportionment so that each district is as equally populated as practicable. *Manual* § 229.

Section 2a of title 2, United States Code, mandates the manner in which a State must conduct an election after any apportionment but before the State is redistricted. Section 2a addresses an election where the number of Representatives has not changed, has increased, or has decreased. The authority under section 2a(c) of title 2 for a State to retain an at-large seat pending its redistricting should be read in light of section 2c of title 2, which requires all States entitled to more than one seat to elect representatives only from single-Member districts. *Manual* § 227.

Reapportionment proposals have been considered in the House, but have no privileged status under the Constitution and cannot interrupt the regular proceedings of the House. Deschler Ch 8 § 2. Reapportionment legislation also has been considered in the Committee of the Whole. Deschler Ch 8 § 2.5. Under clause 1(l) of rule X, proposals relating to apportionment are within the jurisdiction of the Committee on the Judiciary.

§ 2. Campaign Practices

The power of Congress to regulate the election process extends to the regulation of campaign practices. Deschler Ch 8 § 10. The Federal Election Campaign Act established a new and comprehensive code for campaign practices and expenditures, and contains provisions for investigations and enforcement. 2 USC § 431.

The Federal Election Commission is the agency empowered with primary jurisdiction over the administration, interpretation, and civil enforcement of the Federal Election Campaign Act. *Federal Election Comm'n* v. *American Intern. Demographic Services, Inc.*, 629 F. Supp. 317 (E.D. Va. 1986). However, the House itself has the power to judge elections and to determine whether a candidate was improperly elected to a seat. If violations of the election campaign statutes are so extensive as to render an election void, the House may deny the right to a seat. Deschler Ch 8 § 12.

Under clause 1(k) of rule X, the Committee on House Administration has jurisdiction over measures relating to the election of the President, Vice President, or Members of Congress and over measures relating to the raising, reporting, or use of campaign contributions for House candidates. Investigations of specific elections or election practices usually are undertaken by that committee. See, *e.g.*, 105-2, H. Res. 355, Feb. 12, 1998, p 453. Investigations of Members' elections may be conducted under the statutory election-contest procedures or offered on the floor of the House as questions of privilege. *Manual* § 701; see ELECTION CONTESTS AND DISPUTES. Formerly, investigations were undertaken by select committees created to review election campaigns and proceedings, which were created by privileged resolution reported from the Committee on Rules. Deschler Ch 15 § 1.3. Under the modern practice, investigations are undertaken by the Committee on House Administration.

A Member's resignation during an investigation effectively terminates the investigation, because the Committee on House Administration has no further jurisdiction in the matter thereafter. 95-1, May 4, 1977, p 13391.

Under clause 5 of rule XIII, a resolution reported from the Committee on House Administration relative to the right of a Member to a seat is considered as privileged. Deschler Ch 8 § 13.5.

§ 3. Certificates of Election

Certificates of election are issued by each State after congressional elections have been conducted and the results tabulated. The certificates, also termed "credentials," are sent to the Clerk of the House for use in composing the Clerk's roll. Although the certificate is not essential to the administration of the oath, any Member or Member-elect has the right to object thereto, by delivering a challenge either to the validity of the election or to the validity of the certificate itself. Deschler Ch 8 § 15. For a discussion of challenging the administration of the oath, see OATHS.

The House (and not the Speaker or other official) determines whether a Member may be sworn in after an election certificate has been challenged. If a challenge has been directed to a mere irregularity in the form of the certificate, the House will ordinarily seat the Member-elect and declare such individual finally entitled to the seat. Deschler Ch 8 § 17.1. However, if a certificate is challenged through an election contest or by an allegation of election irregularities, the House may authorize the Member-elect to be sworn but provide that the question of the final right to the seat be referred to committee. That procedure often is followed where a certificate is on file in order not to deprive a State of representation in the House because of protracted proceedings. Deschler Ch 8 § 16.4. Another procedural option that may be pursued by the House is to declare that neither candidate be sworn and that the question of *prima facie* and final right to the seat be referred to committee. *Manual* § 204.

A circumstance which may require the nullification of a certificate is the intervening death or disappearance of the Member-elect named therein. Deschler Ch 2 §§ 4.8, 4.9.

The House does not always require a certificate in seating a Member-elect. If such individual appears without a certificate but the election is uncontested and unquestioned, the House may authorize such Member-elect to be sworn by unanimous consent. *Manual* § 204. A photographic copy of the original certificate has been accepted without invoking the unanimous-consent procedure. 106-1, June 8, 1999, p 3773. In some cases where a certificate is delayed, the State represented will deliver informal communications to the House attesting to the validity of the election of the Member-elect. The House may accept such communications by unanimous consent in the absence of a certificate. Deschler Ch 2 § 3.3. Even where a Member-elect arrives without a certificate and the election of such individual is disputed, the House may by resolution authorize the swearing of such Member-elect. Deschler Ch 8 § 17.2.

§ 4. Resignations; Deaths; Filling Vacancies

A Member properly submits a resignation to an official designated by State law and simply informs the House of such action, the latter communication being satisfactory evidence of the resignation. *Manual* § 19; 1 Hinds § 567; Deschler-Brown-Johnson Ch 37 § 3.

Where a vacancy arises in the House by death, resignation, declination, or action of the House, the vacancy must be officially declared in order that a special election may be held. Deschler-Brown-Johnson Ch 38 § 2. Usually, the State executive declares the vacancy to exist, particularly in cases of death, declination, or resignation. Deschler Ch 8 § 9. The State executive then issues a writ of election to fill the vacancy. U.S. Const. art. I, § 2, cl. 4. If a Governor does not recognize the existence of a vacancy, such as in the case of a presumed death not susceptible of proof, the House itself may initiate the action to have the seat declared vacant. Deschler Ch 8 § 9.5. Such a declaration is proper where independent House action has created a vacancy by expulsion or exclusion of a Member. Deschler Ch 8 § 9. In such cases, the House, by privileged resolution, directs the Speaker to notify the State executive. *Manual* § 22. The State executive also is notified where the Member purports to resign directly to the Speaker, rather than to the relevant State official of such Member's State as is customary. Deschler-Brown-Johnson Ch 37 § 3.2.

Under clause 5 of rule XX, in the case of the death of a Member, the Speaker may lay before the House such documentation from Federal, State, or local officials deemed pertinent. Deschler-Brown-Johnson Ch 38 § 5.

A resolution declaring a seat vacant is used where a Member-elect is unable to take the oath or declines the office due to an incapacitating illness. *Manual* § 22; Deschler-Brown-Johnson Ch 38 § 2.17. In one instance, a letter to the Speaker from the attending physician was inserted in the *Congressional Record* to document the physical condition of the Member-elect. The letter stated that she was in a coma and would be unable to take the oath. *Manual* § 205. The House, by declaring the seat vacant by majority vote, was in effect judging a constitutional qualification of the Member; that is, the requirement that she take the oath. The resolution was not tantamount to an expulsion, which requires a two-thirds vote to adopt.

The House has adopted a resolution expressing the sense of the House that each State should examine its existing statutes, practices, and procedures governing special elections so that, in the event of a catastrophe, vacancies in the House may be filled in a timely fashion. 107-2, H. Res. 559, Oct. 2, 2002, p 18919. See also Deschler-Brown-Johnson Ch 38 § 5.

Chapter 24

Electoral Counts; Selection of President and Vice President

Research References

U.S. Const. amend. XII
3 Hinds §§ 1911-1980
6 Cannon §§ 438-441
Deschler Ch 10
Manual §§ 219-223

§ 1. In General; Election of President and Vice President

Both the House and Senate formally participate in the process by which the President and Vice President are elected. Congress is directed by the Constitution to receive, and in joint session to count, the electoral votes certified by the States. If no candidate receives a majority of the electoral vote, the House is directed to elect the President, and the Senate is directed to elect the Vice President. U.S. Const. amend. XII; *Manual* § 219.

The House has on two occasions, in 1801 and 1825, proceeded to elect a President where no candidate had a majority of electoral votes. 3 Hinds §§ 1983, 1985. Both Thomas Jefferson and John Quincy Adams were chosen after prolonged debate and repeated ballots in the House. Under both the original constitutional provision and the 12th amendment, balloting was by States, with each State having one vote.

There have been instances in which the result of the electoral vote has differed from the result of the popular vote. 3 Hinds §§ 1953-1956; 107-1, Jan. 6, 2001, pp 115, 136. Generally, however, the electoral vote has followed the popular vote because of the manner in which electors are chosen under State law. Deschler Ch 10 § 1.

Under the procedures governing the electoral count (as enacted in 1887 and codified in chapter 1 of title 3 of the United States Code), certificates identifying the electors are prepared and transmitted to the Archivist. 3 USC § 6. The electors of each State meet and vote on the first Monday after the second Wednesday in December at a place designated by the State legislature. 3 USC § 7. The electors prepare certified lists of all persons receiving votes for President or Vice President. The certificates are transmitted to the seat of government and directed to the President of the Senate. U.S. Const. amend. XII; 3 USC §§ 8-11.

Under earlier procedure (before the Act of 1887), bills relating to the electoral vote count were considered of high constitutional and parliamentary privilege. 3 Hinds § 2578. Resolutions relating to the method of examining the electoral votes, or to procedural irregularities or fraud in connection therewith, also were considered as privileged. 3 Hinds §§ 2573, 2576, 2577. The procedures established in the Act of 1887 rendered these precedents largely obsolete. 3 USC §§ 1-19.

When addressing a dispute over the election of President and Vice President in the state of Florida, the Supreme Court indicated its view of a section of the statute addressing a State's ability to determine ''controversy or contest'' as to the appointment of electors. 3 USC § 5; *Bush* v. *Palm Beach County Canvassing Bd.*, 531 U.S. 70 (2000). Ultimately, the Supreme Court found that the Florida Supreme Court violated the Equal Protection Clause of the 14th amendment by ordering certain counties to conduct manual recounts of the votes for President and Vice President without establishing standards for those recounts. *Bush* v. *Gore*, 531 U.S. 98 (2000).

§ 2. Joint Session to Count the Electoral Vote

The electoral count occurs in a joint session of the two Houses in the Hall of the House at 1 p.m. on the sixth day of January succeeding every meeting of electors (or an alternate day set by law). 3 USC § 15; *Manual* § 220; 3 Hinds § 1819; Deschler Ch 10 § 2. Sections 15-18 of title 3 of the United States Code prescribe in detail the procedure for the count. Nevertheless, the two Houses traditionally adopt a concurrent resolution providing for the meeting in joint session to count the vote, for the appointment of tellers, and for the declaration of the state of the vote. 3 Hinds § 1961; Deschler Ch 10 § 2.1. This concurrent resolution is privileged. 3 Hinds §§ 2573-2577. Sections 15-18 of title 3 of the United States Code are in effect joint rules of the two Houses for the occasion and govern the procedures both in the joint session and in each House in the event the two Houses divide to consider an objection. Deschler Ch 10 § 2.6.

Under clause 12 of rule I, the Speaker may declare a recess in connection with the joint session. The Speaker may decline to recognize for one-minute speeches or extensions of remarks before recessing for the joint session. Deschler Ch 10 § 2.3.

§ 3. Consideration of Certificates of Electors

Generally

A joint session to count the electoral votes is presided over by the President of the Senate. 3 USC § 15. In the absence of the President of the Senate, the President pro tempore of the Senate presides and calls the session to order. Deschler Ch 10 § 2.5.

No debate is allowed in the joint session. 3 USC § 18; *Manual* § 220.

Counting of Certificates

The electoral votes are counted by tellers who have been appointed on the part of the House by the Speaker and on the part of the Senate by the Vice President. Deschler Ch 10 §§ 3.1-3.4.

The certificates and other papers relating to the electoral count are presented and acted on in alphabetical order by States. 3 USC § 15. Where more than one set of certificates have been received from a State, and each set purports to be the duly appointed electors from that State, the Vice President presents the certificates, with all attached papers, in the order in which they have been received. Deschler Ch 10 § 3.5.

The certificates of votes given by the electors are opened by the President of the Senate and handed to the tellers, who read them in the presence and hearing of the two Houses. Deschler Ch 10 § 1. Traditionally, the reading of each certificate is dispensed with by unanimous consent after the first State has been read. However, on one occasion, no attempt was made to dispense with the reading of the certificates. On that occasion, the tellers read only a sufficient part of each certificate to reveal that it was signed by the pertinent electors, duly attested, regular in form, and authentic. *Manual* § 220; 107-1, Jan. 6, 2001, pp 101-15.

Where there are conflicting electoral certificates from the same State, the two Houses during the joint session may by unanimous consent determine which certificate is to be accepted as valid. The tellers may then be directed to count the votes in the certificate deemed valid. Deschler Ch 10 § 3.5.

Objections

An objection to the counting of any electoral vote must be in writing and signed by a Member and a Senator. 3 USC § 15; 109-1, Jan. 6, 2005, p 198. An objection not signed by a Senator is invalid. 107-1, Jan. 6, 2001, p 104. In the event that a timely objection in proper form is raised in connection with the count, the joint session divides, and the objection is considered by each House in separate session. Deschler Ch 10 § 3.6; 109-1, Jan. 6, 2005, p 199. The Act of 1887 prescribes the procedure to be followed in debate after the two Houses have separated. 3 USC § 17. On only two occasions (in 1969 and 2005) has an objection been perfected, requiring the two Houses to separate and consider the objection pursuant to the Act of 1877. 91-1, Jan. 6, 1969, p 146; 109-1, Jan. 6, 2005, p 199. In the House a motion to lay the objection on the table is not in order. Deschler Ch 10 § 3.7. In one instance the Senate agreed by unanimous consent to modify the terms set by the statute with respect to the division of time for debate. Deschler Ch 10 § 3.8.

If either the House or the Senate rejects the objection, the presiding officer of the joint session directs the tellers to record the votes as submitted. Deschler Ch 10 § 3.6; 109-1, Jan. 6, 2005, p 242.

Other Questions Arising in the Matter

In addition to the joint sessions dividing to consider an objection to the counting of any electoral vote, it divides to consider an ''other question arising in the matter.'' 3 USC §§ 15-18; *Manual* § 220. Such a question also must be in writing and signed by both a Member and a Senator. *Manual* § 220; 107-1, Jan. 6, 2001, p 104. Examples of an ''other question arising in the matter'' include: (1) an objection for lack of a quorum; (2) a motion that either House withdraw from the joint session; and (3) an appeal from a ruling by the presiding officer. *Manual* § 220. Such questions are not debatable in the joint session. 3 USC § 18.

§ 4. Presidential Disability; Filling Vice Presidential Vacancies

In addition to its responsibilities in ascertaining and counting the electoral votes cast for President and Vice President, Congress has the duty under the Constitution to resolve disputes as to Presidential disability. U.S. Const. amend. XXV §§ 3, 4. Messages relating to Presidential incapacity are laid before the House. In 1985, 2002, and 2007, the Speaker laid before the House two communications from the President of the United States (1) advising of the President's temporary incapacity to discharge the constitutional powers and duties of the Office of President and directing that the Vice President discharge those duties in his stead and (2) subsequently advising of the President's determination that he was able to resume those powers and duties. *Manual* § 256.

The House and Senate also act on the nomination of a Vice President to fill a vacancy. The Constitution provides that in such cases the President shall nominate a Vice President who shall take office upon confirmation by a majority vote of both Houses. U.S. Const. amend. XXV § 2. Messages from the President transmitting the nomination of a Vice President under this provision are laid before the House by the Speaker. The nomination is referred to the Committee on the Judiciary, which has jurisdiction over matters relating to Presidential succession. Deschler Ch 10 §§ 4.1, 4.2. The House and Senate consider the nomination by acting separately on simple resolutions. Deschler Ch 10 § 4.3.

Chapter 25
Ethics; Committee on Ethics

§ 27. Letter of Reproval

Research References

U.S. Const. art. I, § 5, cl. 2; § 6, cl. 1
2 Hinds §§ 1236-1289
6 Cannon §§ 236-238
Deschler Ch 12 §§ 2-18
Manual §§ 62, 721b, 759, 806, 853, 1095-1103
House Ethics Manual, 111th Cong.

A. Introductory

§ 1. In General

Authority; Definitions and Distinctions

The authority of the House to discipline its Members flows from the Constitution. It provides that each House may ''punish its Members for disorderly Behaviour, and, with the concurrence of two thirds, expel a Member.'' U.S. Const. art. I, § 5, cl. 2.

Among the sanctions that the House may impose under this provision, the rules of the Committee on Ethics outline the following:

- Expulsion from the House of Representatives.
- Censure.
- Reprimand.
- Fine.
- Denial or limitation of any right, power, privilege, or immunity of the Member if under the Constitution the House of Representatives may impose such denial or limitation.
- Any other sanction determined by the Committee to be appropriate.

Rule 24, Committee on Ethics, 112th Cong; see §§ 19-27, infra.

These sanctions are not mutually exclusive. In a given case, a Member may be censured, fined, and deprived of seniority. Deschler Ch 12 § 12.1. A Member also may be reprimanded and ordered to reimburse the costs of the committee's investigation. *Manual* § 64.

Imprisonment of a Member is a form of punishment that is theoretically within the power of the House to impose, but such action has never been taken by the House. Deschler Ch 12 § 12. The disciplinary measures referred to herein are separate and distinct from the sanctions of fine or imprisonment that may be available under a criminal statute at the State or Federal level. See § 9, infra.

Exclusion Distinguished

The power of exclusion is derived from the right of each House to determine the qualifications of its Members, whereas the power of expulsion stems from its authority to discipline Members for misconduct. This distinction has not always been recognized. In 1870 a Member was excluded from the 41st Congress on the ground that he had sold appointments to the Military Academy. 1 Hinds §464. In 1967, after an investigating committee recommended that a Member be fined and censured for improperly maintaining his wife on the clerk-hire payroll and for improper use of public funds for private purposes, the House voted to impose a stronger penalty—to exclude him by denying him his seat. Deschler Ch 12 §§14.1, 16.1. However, the Supreme Court determined such exclusion was not a sanction to be invoked in cases involving the misconduct of a Member. It is available only for failure to meet the constitutional qualifications of Members as to age, citizenship, and inhabitancy. *Powell* v. *McCormack*, 395 U.S. 486 (1969).

§2. Committee on Ethics

Generally

Before the 90th Congress, select temporary committees were created to consider allegations of improper conduct against a Member and to recommend such disciplinary measures as might be appropriate. Deschler Ch 12 §2. In the 90th Congress, the Committee on Standards of Official Conduct was established as a standing committee of the House. 90-1, H. Res. 418, Apr. 13, 1967, p 9425. The committee was renamed the Committee on Ethics in the 112th Congress. 112-1, Jan. 5, 2011, p ____. Under clause 5(a)(5) of rule XIII, the committee may report as privileged resolutions recommending action by the House with respect to the official conduct of any Member, officer, or employee of the House. *Manual* §853.

Legislative Jurisdiction

The jurisdiction of the Committee on Ethics, as set forth in clause 1(g) of rule X, consists of measures relating to the Code of Official Conduct. *Manual* §737. Measures proposing to amend the Code are not privileged for immediate consideration when reported by that committee but may be considered in the House pursuant to a special order of business from the Committee on Rules. See *Manual* §853.

Investigative Jurisdiction; Recommendations and Reports

Pursuant to clause 3 of rule XI, the Committee on Ethics is authorized to conduct investigations, hold hearings, and report any findings and recommendations to the House. *Manual* § 806. This committee has been given similar responsibilities under House resolutions authorizing specific investigations. Where the House has directed the committee to conduct such a specific investigation, it has, on occasion, authorized the committee to take staff depositions, to serve subpoenas within or without the United States, and to participate by special counsel in relevant judicial proceedings. See, *e.g.,* 95-1, H. Res. 252, Feb. 9, 1977, pp 3966, 3975; 96-2, H. Res. 608, Mar. 27, 1980, p 6995. The committee also has been authorized to investigate, with expanded subpoena authority, persons other than Members, officers, and employees. 94-2, H. Res. 1054, Mar. 3, 1976, p 5165-68.

By resolutions considered as questions of the privileges of the House, the committee has been directed:

- To investigate illegal solicitation of political contributions in the House Office Buildings by unnamed sitting Members.
- To review GAO audits of the operations of the ''bank'' in the Office of the Sergeant-at-Arms.
- To disclose the names and pertinent account information of Members found to have abused the privileges of the ''House bank.''
- To investigate violations of confidentiality by staff engaged in the investigation of the operation and management of the Office of the Postmaster.

Manual § 703.

Recent Major Revisions to the Ethics Process

In the 105th Congress the House adopted a resolution sponsored by the chair and ranking minority member of a bipartisan leadership task force on reform of the ethics process. The resolution included provisions amending the rules of the House as follows:

- Establishment of a ''pool'' of non-committee Members who may be assigned to serve on investigative subcommittees, and exclusion of service on such subcommittee from the limitation on subcommittee service. Clause 5 of rule X.
- Authority for the chair and ranking minority member jointly to appoint members from the ''pool'' to serve on an investigative subcommittee. Clause 5 of rule X.
- Requirement that a complaint placed on the committee agenda before expiration of the time limit set forth in the rules of the committee be referred to an investigative subcommittee only by an affirmative vote of the members of the committee. Clause 3 of rule XI.
- Change in the duration of service on the committee. Clause 5 of rule X.

- Requirement that each meeting be held in executive session unless opened by an affirmative vote of a majority of the members, and requirement that each adjudicatory subcommittee hearing or full-committee sanction hearing be open unless closed by an affirmative vote of a majority of its members. Clause 3(c) of rule XI.
- Requirement of a confidentiality oath by a Member, officer, or employee having access to committee information. Clause 3(d) of rule XI.
- Exception for committee votes taken in executive session from requirement that committees disclose record votes. Clause 3(b) of rule XIII.
- Permission for a non-Member to file information offered as a complaint only if a Member certifies the information is submitted in good faith and warrants committee consideration. Clause 3(b)(2)(B) of rule XI.
- Authority for the chair and ranking minority member of the committee jointly to gather preliminary additional information with regard to a complaint or information offered as a complaint. Clause 3(b)(1) of rule XI.
- Authority for a subcommittee to authorize and issue a subpoena only by affirmative vote of a majority of its members. Clause 2(m)(3) of rule XI.
- Authority for the committee to refer substantial evidence of a violation of law to Federal or State authorities either with approval of the House or by an affirmative vote of two-thirds of the members of the committee. Clause 3(a)(3) of rule XI.
- Authority for the committee to take appropriate action in the case of a frivolous complaint. Clause 3(e) of rule XI.

The resolution also included provisions requiring the committee to adopt the following committee rules (which were codified in clause 3 of rule XI in the 108th Congress):

- Guaranteeing the ranking minority member the right to place an item on the agenda.
- Setting specified standards for staff, providing for appointment of staff, permitting the retention of outside counsel or temporary staff, and permitting both the chair and the ranking minority member one additional staff member.
- Permitting only the chair or ranking minority member to make public statements regarding matters before the committee, unless otherwise determined by a vote of the committee.
- Providing the chair and ranking minority member 14 calendar days or five legislative days (whichever occurs first) to determine whether information offered as a complaint constitutes a complaint.
- Granting the chair and ranking minority member, unless otherwise determined by an affirmative vote of the majority of committee members, 45 calendar days or five legislative days (whichever occurs later) after the date they determine the information filed constitutes a complaint to: (1) recommend disposition of the complaint; (2) establish an investigative subcommittee; or (3) request an extension.

- Requiring the chair and ranking minority member to establish an investigative subcommittee to consider a complaint not disposed of by the expiration of the time limit.
- Providing for disposal of information not constituting a proper complaint.
- Setting parameters for the composition of investigative and adjudicatory subcommittees.
- Establishing a standard of proof for the adoption of a statement of alleged violation.
- Authorizing expansion of the scope of an investigation by an investigative subcommittee upon an affirmative vote of a majority of the members of the full committee.
- Authorizing an investigative subcommittee to amend its statement of alleged violation any time before it is transmitted to the committee and granting 30 calendar days for a respondent to file an answer to the amended statement of alleged violation.
- Establishing procedures to protect the due process rights of respondents.
- Requiring the committee to transmit to the House upon an affirmative vote of a majority of its members an investigative subcommittee report stating that it did not adopt a statement of alleged violation.
- Detailing a mode of proceeding upon an approved waiver of an adjudicatory hearing, including committee reporting requirements and opportunity for respondent views.
- Clarifying that, when the committee authorizes an investigation on its own initiative, the chair and ranking minority member shall establish an investigative subcommittee.

105-1, H. Res. 168, Sept. 18, 1997, pp 19317-20; *Manual* § 806.

Office of Congressional Ethics

In the 110th Congress, the House adopted a resolution establishing an Office of Congressional Ethics (OCE). This independent, nonpartisan office consists of 6 members: three appointed by the Speaker (with the concurrence of the Minority Leader) and three appointed by the Minority Leader (with the concurrence of the Speaker). The OCE functions as a clearinghouse where alleged violations of the applicable ethics rules are subject to preliminary investigation. Unlike the Committee on Ethics, the OCE receives allegations from any source (not just Members), and a request by any two members of the board triggers an automatic preliminary review by the OCE. A further vote is required to commence a second-phase review.

The OCE informs the Committee on Ethics of its progress throughout the investigatory process, and also provides notice to the Member being investigated. Upon the completion of an investigation, the OCE reports to the Committee one of three conclusions: (1) the OCE recommends that the complaint be dismissed; (2) the OCE recommends that the complaint be investigated by the Committee; or (3) the OCE has come to no conclusion due to a tie vote of the board. Conforming changes made to clause 3 of rule XI require the Committee on Ethics either to make public the OCE recommendation or to begin an investigation of its own. 110-1, H. Res. 895, Mar. 11, 2008, p 3741.

§ 3. —Membership; Eligibility for Committee Service; Disqualification

The Committee on Ethics, unlike other standing committees of the House (where the majority party has a preponderance of the elected membership), is composed of 10 members in equal numbers from the majority and minority parties. Clause 5(a)(3) of rule X. Service on the committee also is limited to no more than three Congresses in any 10-year period. However, a member of the committee may serve during a fourth Congress as either the chair or the ranking minority member of the committee. *Manual* § 759. At the beginning of each Congress, the Speaker and the Minority Leader each name 10 Members from their respective parties who are not members of the Committee on Ethics to be available to serve on investigative subcommittees thereof. Clause 5(a)(4) of rule X.

Clause 3(b)(4) of rule XI provides that a member of the committee shall be ineligible to participate in a committee proceeding relating to such Member's own conduct. Under this rule, where it was contended that four members of the committee were ineligible to adjudicate a complaint because of their personal involvement in the relevant conduct, the Speaker named four other Members to act as members of the committee in all proceedings on the complaint in the same political-party ratio represented by the party affiliation of the four ineligible members. *Manual* § 806a.

Clause 3(b)(5) of rule XI permits members of the committee to disqualify themselves from participation in any committee investigation in which such members certify that they could not render an impartial decision and authorizes the Speaker to appoint such replacements as necessary for that investigation. Under this rule, where a member of the committee submits an affidavit of disqualification in a disciplinary investigation of another Member, or where a member of the committee is the subject of an ethics inquiry and has notified the Speaker of such Member's ineligibility, the Speaker may appoint another Member to serve on the committee during the investigation. *Manual* § 806.

§ 4. —Publications; Advisory Opinions

Under clause 3(a)(4) of rule XI, the Committee on Ethics is authorized to issue and publish advisory opinions (also known as ''pink sheets'') with respect to the general propriety of any current or proposed conduct. The committee's advisory opinions are incorporated in the *House Ethics Manual.* The *House Ethics Manual* also includes advisory opinions issued by the former Select Committee on Ethics, which was established during the 95th Congress and was the precursor of the present standing committee. Recent advisory opinions may be found on the committee's website.

Two prior publications, *Gifts and Travel* and *Campaign Activity*, published as booklets in the 106th and 107th Congresses, respectively, were incorporated into the 2008 *House Ethics Manual.* Advisory opinions issued by the committee also may be found in the appendix to Chapter 12 of Deschler's Precedents. Additional information also is available from the committee's website.

In accordance with section 803(i) of the Ethics Reform Act of 1989, the committee has established an Office of Advice and Education. The primary responsibility of the office is to provide information and guidance to Members, officers, and employees regarding all applicable standards of conduct. This includes the ethics training for House employees mandated by House rules. Clause 3(a)(6) of rule XI.

§ 5. Initiating an Investigation; Complaints

Generally

In addition to an investigation directed by House resolution, called up as a question of the privileges of the House, an investigation of particular conduct may be initiated pursuant to adoption of a resolution reported from the Committee on Rules. See, *e.g.*, 96-2, H. Res. 608, Mar. 27, 1980, p 6995-98. A resolution directing the committee to investigate a possible unauthorized disclosure of classified information by the Speaker in violation of House rules was introduced through the hopper and referred to the Committee on Rules. 100-2, Sept. 30, 1988, p 27329. A resolution requiring the Committee on Standards of Official Conduct (now Ethics) to empanel an investigative subcommittee any time a Member has been indicted or otherwise formally charged with criminal conduct was adopted in the 110th Congress and carried forward in subsequent Congresses.

Under clause 3(b)(1)(A) of rule XI, an investigation of particular conduct also may be initiated by the Committee on Ethics, if approved by a majority vote of the members of that committee. An investigation also may be initiated pursuant to information offered as a complaint filed with the committee by a Member. A complaint may be filed by a non-Member if the complaint is accompanied by a certification from a Member that the information is submitted in good faith and warrants committee consideration.

Clause 3(b)(2) of rule XI; *Manual* § 806. As noted earlier, an investigation may also be initiated by a transmittal from the Office of Congressional Ethics. See § 2, supra.

Under clause 3(b)(1) of rule XI, the chair and ranking minority member of the committee jointly may gather additional information concerning alleged conduct that is the basis of a complaint until they have established an investigative subcommittee or either of them has placed on the agenda of the committee the issue of whether to establish such subcommittee. *Manual* § 806.

Complaint Requirements; Unfounded Charges

Information offered as a complaint filed with the committee must comply with the requirements of clause 3(b)(2) of rule XI, including the requirement that it be in writing and under oath. *Manual* § 806. Each complaint received by the committee is examined to determine whether it complies with that rule. Complaints that are not in compliance are returned. Those that comply with the rule are considered by the committee for appropriate disposition.

Under clause 3(e)(1) of rule XI, a complaint determined by the Committee on Ethics to be frivolous may give rise to action by that committee. A Member who presented false charges against another Member has himself become the subject of a select committee investigation and report. In 1908 the House adopted a resolution approving a select committee report finding a Member in contempt and in violation of his obligations as a Member where he had presented false charges of corruption against another Member. 6 Cannon § 400.

Disclosure

Clause 3(b)(6) of rule XI requires a vote of the Committee on Ethics to authorize the public disclosure of the content of a complaint or the fact of its filing.

Debate

References in floor debate to the content of a complaint or the fact of its filing are governed by the rules of decorum in debate under clause 1 of rule XVII. Under this stricture a Member should refrain from references in debate to the official conduct of a Member where such conduct is not the subject then pending before the House by way of either a report of the Committee on Ethics or another question of the privileges of the House. This stricture also precludes a Member from reciting news articles discussing a Member's conduct, reciting the content of a previously tabled resolution raising a question of the privileges of the House, or even referring to a Member's conduct by mere insinuation.

The fact that a complaint has been filed does not open up its allegations to debate on the floor. Notice of an intention to offer a resolution as a question of the privileges of the House under rule IX does not render a resolution ''pending'' and thereby permit references to the conduct of a Member proposed to be addressed therein. *Manual* § 361.

§ 6. Persons Subject to Disciplinary Procedures

The investigative authority that is given under clause 3(a)(1) of rule XI to the Committee on Ethics over alleged violations extends to ''Members, Delegates, the Resident Commissioner, officers, and employees of the House.'' *Manual* § 806. The Speaker has been subject to the investigative authority of this committee. 101-1, Statement of the Committee on Standards of Official Conduct (now Ethics) *In re* Wright, Apr. 17, 1989; H. Res. 31, H. Rept. 105-1, *In re* Gingrich, Jan. 21, 1997, p 459. A Delegate has been subject to censure for misconduct. 2 Hinds § 1305. With respect to violations by House officers or employees, the rules of the committee authorize it to recommend to the House dismissal from employment, reprimand, fine, or any other sanction determined by the committee to be appropriate. Rule 24, Rules of the Committee on Ethics, 112th Cong.

On one occasion, the House, by adopting a resolution presented as a question of privilege (dealing with the unauthorized disclosure of a House report), authorized the Committee on Standards of Official Conduct (now Ethics) to investigate persons not associated with the House. 94-2, H. Res. 1042, Feb. 19, 1976, p 3914. The House considered it necessary to enlarge the subpoena authority of the committee to carry out this investigation. 94-2, H. Res. 1054, Mar. 3, 1976, p 5165. Private citizens have been censured or reprimanded by the Speaker at the bar of the House for attempting to bribe a Member or for assaulting a Member. 2 Hinds §§ 1606, 1616-1619, 1625; 6 Cannon § 333.

Under clause 3(a)(3) of rule XI, the committee may report to the appropriate Federal or State authorities, either with the approval of the House or by an affirmative vote of two-thirds of the members of the committee, any substantial evidence of a violation of a law by a Member, officer, or employee of the House that is applicable to the performance of such individual's duties or the discharge of such individual's responsibilities that may have been disclosed in a committee investigation.

B. Basis for Imposing Sanctions

§7. In General; The Code of Official Conduct

Generally

Before the 90th Congress, there was no formal code of conduct for Representatives. However, in 1968 the rules were amended to establish a Code of Official Conduct for Members and employees of the House. 90-1, H. Res. 1049, Apr. 3, 1968, p 8803; rule XXIII. The Code, along with rules XXIV and XXV, contain provisions governing the receipt of compensation, gifts, and honoraria. It also addresses the use of campaign funds, proscribes discrimination in employment, and bars certain ''non-House'' uses of House stationery. *Manual* §§1095-1104. Rule XXVII, added in the 110th Congress, contains rules governing disclosure of negotiations for future employment and recusal in cases of conflicts of interest. This rule applies to Members, officers, and employees of the House.

Conduct Reflecting Discredit on the House

Under the Code of Official Conduct, disciplinary measures may be invoked against a Member, officer, or employee on the ground that such person has violated the requirement in clause 1 of the Code of Official Conduct to behave ''at all times'' in a manner that reflects ''creditably'' on the House. *Manual* §1095. Examples of disciplinary measures recommended by the Committee on Ethics against certain Members for conduct that violated clause 1 of the Code include:

- Failure to report campaign contributions and perjury. Certain Members were officially reprimanded by the House. H. Res. 1415, H. Rept. 95-1742, *In re* McFall, Oct. 13, 1978, p 37005; H. Res. 1416, H. Rept. 95-1743, *In re* Roybal, Oct. 13, 1978, p 37009.
- Conviction by a jury on bribery or other corruption charges. Member was expelled by the House. H. Res. 794, H. Rept. 96-1387, *In re* Myers, Oct. 2, 1980, p 28953; H. Res. 495, H. Rept. 107-594, *In re* Traficant, July 24, 2002, p 14319.
- Misuse of the congressional clerk-hire allowance for personal gain. Member was censured by the House by a unanimous vote and was required to make restitution of monies in the amount that he had personally benefited. H. Res. 378, H. Rept. 96-351, *In re* Diggs, July 31, 1979, p 21584.
- Engagement in sexual relationships or other inappropriate conduct with pages employed by the House. H. Res. 265, H. Rept. 98-295, *In re* Studds, July 20, 1983, p 20030; H. Res. 266, H. Rept. 98-296, *In re* Crane, July 20, 1983, p 20020; 109-2, H. Res. 1065, Sept. 29, 2006, p 21334.

The committee may find that a Member has brought discredit to the House, but recommend no formal sanction. H. Rept. 104-876, *In re* Collins; H. Rept. 105-797, *In re* Kim. The committee also may send the offending Member a letter of reproval. H. Rept. 106-979, *In re* Shuster.

The House voted to reprimand the Speaker for bringing discredit on the House. H. Res. 31, H. Rept. 105-1, *In re* Gingrich, Jan. 21, 1997, p 393.

Adhering to the ''Spirit and Letter'' of the Rules

Clause 2 of the Code of Official Conduct provides that a Member, officer, or employee of the House must ''adhere to the spirit and the letter'' of the rules of the House and to the rules of its committees. *Manual* § 1095. This rule has been interpreted to mean that a Member or employee may not do indirectly what the Member or employee would be barred from doing directly. Advisory Opinion No. 4, Select Committee on Ethics, 95th Cong.

In 1988 the Committee on Standards of Official Conduct (now Ethics) concluded that a Member's acceptance of an illegal gratuity on three occasions constituted action that discredited the House as an institution in violation of clause 1 of rule XXIII; and, having violated the ''spirit'' of clause 1, he also violated clause 2 of rule XXIII. H. Rept. 100-506, *In re* Biaggi. Although purposeful violation of any rule of the House could potentially be considered an infraction under clause 2 of rule XXIII, the committee has issued advisory opinions touching on some of the rules that specifically pertain to Members' conduct. In addition to the restrictions contained in the Code of Conduct, rules XXIV (Limitations on Use of Official Funds), XXV (Limitations on Outside Earned Income and Acceptance of Gifts), XXVI (Financial Disclosure), and XXVII (Disclosure by Members and Staff of Employment Negotiations) have been addressed by the committee in its *House Ethics Manual.*

§ 8. Code of Ethics for Government Service

A Code of Ethics to be adhered to by all government employees, including office holders, was adopted by concurrent resolution in 1958. 85-2, H. Con. Res. 175, July 11, 1958; *House Ethics Manual*, 111th Cong. The Committee on Standards of Official Conduct (now Ethics) has indicated that the Code of Ethics is an expression of traditional standards of conduct that continues to be applicable, even though the Code was enacted merely in the form of a concurrent resolution that expired with the adjournment of the Congress in which it was adopted. H. Rept. 94-1364, *In re* Sikes.

The Code of Ethics requires that any person in government service should, among other things, give a full day's labor for a full day's pay; never accept favors or benefits under circumstances that ''might be construed as influencing the performance of governmental duties;'' engage in no business with the government, either directly or indirectly, that is inconsistent with the conscientious performance of governmental duties; and never use any confidential information in the performance of governmental duties as a means of making a private profit.

The ethical standards of this Code have provided the basis for disciplinary proceedings against Members. See, *e.g.*, H. Rept. 100-506, *In re* Biaggi. In one instance, charges concerning the use of a Member's official position for pecuniary gain were heard by the committee. The committee found that the Member had failed to report his ownership of certain stock and that he bought stock in a bank following active efforts in his official capacity to obtain a charter for the bank. These charges resulted in a reprimand of the Member. H. Res. 1421, H. Rept. 94-1364, *In re* Sikes, July 29, 1976, p 24379.

§ 9. Violations of Statutes

Generally

Members of Congress, unless immunized by the Speech or Debate Clause of the Constitution, are subject to the same penalties under the criminal laws as are all citizens. *Manual* § 93; Deschler Ch 12 § 3. In addition to rules XXIII through XXVII, the Federal criminal code addresses the conduct of Members, officers, and employees with respect to bribery of public officials (18 USC § 201), claims against the Government (18 USC §§ 203-205, 207(e), 216), and public officials acting as agents of foreign principals (18 USC § 219). The violation of such statutes may be considered by the Committee on Ethics in recommending disciplinary actions to the House.

Thus, a Member's conviction under section 201 of title 18, United States Code, of accepting an illegal gratuity was cited as one of the grounds for the committee's recommendation that the Member be expelled. H. Rept. 100-506, *In re* Biaggi. The committee may find that a Member has violated certain statutes but recommend no formal sanction. H. Rept. 104-876, *In re* Collins; H. Rept. 105-797, *In re* Kim. The committee also may send the offending Member a letter of reproval. H. Rept. 106-979, *In re* Shuster. The House voted to reprimand a Speaker for violating certain provisions of the Internal Revenue Code. 105-1, H. Res. 31, H. Rept. 105-1, *In re* Gingrich, Jan. 21, 1997, p 393.

Any disciplinary measure that the House invokes against a Member for an alleged or proven violation of such a statute is separate and distinct from sanctions that may be sought by law enforcement authorities at the State or Federal level. Criminal prosecution may precede or follow committee investigation or House censure for the same offense. See *United States* v. *Diggs*, 613 F.2d 988 (D.C. Cir. 1979), cert. denied, 446 U.S. 982 (1980); H. Res. 378, H. Rept. 96-351, *In re* Diggs, July 31, 1979, p 21584.

Clause 3 of rule XI authorizes the Committee on Ethics to report to the appropriate Federal or State authorities, by majority vote with the approval of the House or by two-thirds vote of the committee alone, any substantial evidence of a violation of an applicable law by a Member, officer, or employee of the House, that may have been disclosed in a committee investigation. *Manual* § 806. During the committee's investigation of Speaker Gingrich, the committee received documents that may have proved useful to the Internal Revenue Service. The House adopted the recommendation of the committee to make those documents available to the Internal Revenue Service and to establish a liaison to aid the transfer of documents. H. Res. 31, H. Rept. 105-1, *In re* Gingrich, Jan. 21, 1997, p 393.

Conviction as Basis for Committee Action

Rule 18(e) of the rules of the Committee on Ethics requires the committee to undertake an investigation with regard to any felony conviction of a Member, officer, or employee of the House in a Federal, State, or local court. The rule further provides that the investigation may proceed at any time before sentencing. See, *e.g.*, H. Rept. 107-594, *In re* Traficant. The committee may review evidence presented at the Member's trial, including the trial transcript, transcripts of recorded phone conversations, and oral intercepts. H. Rept. 100-506, *In re* Biaggi. Examples of disciplinary measures recommended by the Committee on Ethics based on criminal convictions include bribery convictions or findings as to the receipt of money by a Member for exercising his influence in the House. H. Rept. 96-1387, *In re* Myers; H. Rept. 96-856, *In re* Flood; H. Rept. 96-1537, *In re* Jenrette; H. Rept. 97-110, *In re* Lederer; H. Rept. 100-506, *In re* Biaggi; H. Rept. 107-594, *In re* Traficant.

In 1980, charges involving alleged bribes of Members of Congress led to investigations by both the Committee on Standards of Official Conduct (now Ethics) and the Department of Justice. The committee was authorized to conduct an inquiry into such alleged improper conduct, to coordinate its investigation with the Justice Department, to enter into agreements with the Justice Department, and to participate, by special counsel, in any judicial proceeding concerning or relating to the inquiry. 96-2, H. Res. 608, Mar. 27, 1980, p 6995; 97-1, H. Res. 67, Mar. 4, 1981, p 3529.

The House may choose to initiate disciplinary proceedings against a Member upon a Member's conviction even when that Member has not exhausted all of the appeals in the criminal process. See § 19, infra.

§10. Misuse of Hiring Allowance; False Claims

Clause 8 of rule XXIII prohibits a Member from retaining anyone on payroll who does not perform duties commensurate with the compensation received. Closely related to this rule is the False Claims Act, which imposes liability on persons making claims against the government knowing such claims to be false or fraudulent. 31 USC §3729; 18 USC §287. Because Members must formally authorize salary payments to their aides, they may be in violation of Federal law if they know that such payments are being made to an aide who is not doing official work commensurate with such pay, or if such person is drawing on clerk-hire funds to meet personal or congressional expenses. See *United States* v. *Diggs*, 613 F.2d 988 (D.C. Cir. 1979), cert. denied, 446 U.S. 982 (1980). The False Claims Act is applicable where a Member submits false travel vouchers to the Clerk of the House. See *U.S. ex rel. Hollander* v. *Clay*, 420 F. Supp. 853 (D.D.C. 1976). Liability under the Act likewise arises where a Member has falsely certified certain long-distance phone calls as being official calls in order to obtain reimbursement for them. *United States* v. *Eilberg*, 507 F. Supp. 267 (E.D. Pa. 1980).

§11. Discrimination in Employment

Clause 9 of rule XXIII includes provisions barring discrimination against any individual with respect to compensation or other conditions of employment because of such individual's race, color, religion, or sex, including marital or parental status, disability, age, or national origin. The Committee on Standards of Official Conduct (now Ethics) has concluded that sexual harassment is a form of discrimination in employment that is prohibited by clause 9. In one case the committee issued a letter of reproval to a Member for his conduct in interacting with two female employees on his staff. H. Rept. 101-293, *In re* Bates.

The earliest form of the rule on "employment practices" grew out of the Fair Employment Practices Resolution first adopted in the 100th Congress. 100-2, H. Res. 558, Oct. 3, 1988, p 27840; 101-1, H. Res. 15, Jan. 3, 1989, p 85. The terms of that resolution were incorporated by reference in a standing rule in the 102d Congress. 102-1, H. Res. 5, Jan. 3, 1991, p 39. It was codified in full text, with certain amendments, in the 103d Congress. 103-1, H. Res. 5, Jan. 5, 1993, p 49. The Employment Practices rule was overtaken by the earliest form of a rule addressing the "application of certain laws" in the 103d Congress. 103-2, H. Res. 578, Oct. 7, 1994, p 29326. The Application of Laws rule, in turn, was overtaken by the Congressional Accountability Act of 1995. 2 USC § 1301. Certain savings provisions appear in section 506 of that Act. 2 USC § 1435.

§ 12. Campaign Fund Irregularities

Members of the House are governed by many restrictions and regulations concerning the use of campaign funds and must comply with various campaign finance procedures. These requirements are found primarily in the Federal Election Campaign Act of 1971. 2 USC § 431. Under this statute, the Federal Election Commission was established as an independent regulatory agency with jurisdiction over Federal campaign finance practices. 2 USC §§ 437c-438.

Clause 6 of rule XXIII requires that Members use campaign funds solely for campaign purposes and specifically prohibits the personal use of such funds. This includes the requirements that Members keep campaign funds separate from personal funds; may not convert campaign funds to personal use except for reimbursement for legitimate, verifiable prior campaign expenses and official expenses (subject to the limitations in clause 1(b)(2) of rule XXIV); and may not expend campaign funds for other than *bona fide* campaign or political purposes. The committee has taken the position that any use of campaign funds that personally benefits the Member rather than exclusively and solely benefiting the campaign is not a ''bona fide campaign purpose.'' H. Rept. 99-933, *In re* Weaver; H. Rept. 100-526, *In re* Rose. Although campaign funds may be invested, a candidate who borrows money from such candidate's own campaign is presumed to be receiving a personal benefit; that is, the use of the money.

The Committee on Standards of Official Conduct (now Ethics) has found that Members have violated clause 6 of rule XXIII by transferring campaign funds to personal accounts or borrowing from their campaign funds. See, *e.g.*, H. Rept. 96-930, *In re* Wilson; H. Rept. 99-933, *In re* Weaver.

The House has adopted reports of the committee recommending reprimand of Members who have failed to report a campaign contribution or have converted a campaign contribution to personal use. See, *e.g.*, H. Res. 1415, H. Rept. 95-1742, *In re* McFall, Oct. 13, 1978, p 37005; H. Res. 1416, H. Rept. 95-1743, *In re* Roybal, Oct. 13, 1978, p 37009. In two cases, Members were found to have violated Federal election campaign laws, but no formal sanctions were issued. H. Rept. 104-876, *In re* Collins; H. Rept. 105-797, *In re* Kim.

Clause 7 of rule XXIII requires any proceeds from testimonials or other fundraising events to be treated by Members as campaign contributions.

§13. Solicitation of Contributions From Government Employees

A Federal statute prohibits Members of Congress (and candidates for Congress) from soliciting political contributions from employees of the House and from other Federal government employees. 18 USC §602. Under this statute it must actually be known that the person who is being solicited is a Federal employee. Inadvertent solicitations to persons on a mailing list during a general fundraising campaign are not prohibited. H. Rept. 96-930, *In re* Wilson. Because the statute by its terms is directed at protecting "employees," it does not prevent one Member from soliciting another Member. See 6 Cannon §401 (in which the House adopted a resolution construing the predecessor statute).

In 1985, the Committee on Standards of Official Conduct (now Ethics) initiated a preliminary investigation into charges that a "Dear Colleague" letter had been used to solicit Members' staffs in House office buildings. However, the committee took the view that the statute was directed against coercive activities; that is, political "shakedowns." The committee concluded that, in the absence of any evidence of "victimization" (*i.e.*, coercion of congressional staff) the solicitations were not precluded by that law. H. Rept. 99-277. The committee concluded, however, that neither staff (paid or volunteer) while on official time, nor Federal office space at any time, should be used to prepare or distribute material involving solicitations of political contributions. H. Rept. 99-227; see also H. Rept. 99-1019.

§14. Limitations on Earned Income; Honoraria

Clause 1 of rule XXV places restrictions upon the amount of outside-earned income a Member, officer, or employee may receive. This provision limits the amount of aggregate outside-earned income in a calendar year to 15 percent of an annual congressional salary. The limitation applies to earned income for personal services, rather than monies that are essentially a return on equity. In this regard, the facts of a particular case will be regarded as controlling, rather than the characterization of such monies as outside-earned income. Advisory Opinion No. 13, Select Committee on Ethics, 95th Cong. (reprinted in H. Rept. 95-1837).

Under clause 3 of rule XXV, a Member, officer, or employee may receive neither an advance payment on copyright royalties nor copyright royalties under a contract unless it is first approved by the Committee on Ethics as complying with the requirement that the royalties are received from an established publisher under usual and customary contractual terms.

A restriction against honoraria is imposed by clause 1 of rule XXV. In 1989 special outside counsel concluded that Speaker Wright had retained excessive honoraria and other outside income, styled as "royalties," which he accepted from special interest groups from the sale of his book. 101-1, Statement of the Committee on Standards of Official Conduct (now Ethics) *In re* Wright, Apr. 17, 1989.

§ 15. Acceptance of Gifts

Clause 5 of rule XXV permits acceptance of a gift only if it has an individual value of less than $50 and a cumulative value from any one source in the calendar year of less than $100 (the value of perishable food sent to an office is allocated among the individual recipients and not to the Member). Clause 5 defines the term "gift" and outlines various exceptions to the rule. The Committee on Standards of Official Conduct (now Ethics) in the 96th Congress recommended the censure of a Member for misconduct that included the acceptance of gifts of money from a person with a "direct interest in legislation" before Congress. The committee determined that certain checks that had been marked "loans" were not true loans. On the basis of this and other violations, the House, after rejecting a motion to recommit that would have permitted a reprimand, voted to censure. H. Res. 660, H. Rept. 96-930, *In re* Wilson, June 10, 1980, p 13801. In 1988 the committee concluded that a Member's acceptance of illegal gratuities in trips to St. Maarten and Florida established *per se* violations of the gift rule since those events, both individually and in the aggregate, far exceeded the $100 limit then imposed by the gift rule. H. Rept. 100-506, *In re* Biaggi.

In the 110th Congress, rule XXV was amended to prohibit the acceptance of any gifts from registered lobbyists, and to clarify the valuation of tickets to sporting and entertainment events for purposes of the gift rule.

In 1977 the committee was empowered to investigate the alleged receipt by Members of "things of value" from the Korean government. 95-1, H. Res. 252, Feb. 9, 1977, p 3966. Subsequently, the House adopted a committee report recommending the reprimand of a Member on the basis of the committee's finding that he had failed to disclose, in a questionnaire sent to all Members by the committee, his receipt of currency and valuables worth more than $100 from representatives of Korea. H. Res. 1414, H. Rept. 95-1741, *In re* Wilson, Oct. 13, 1978, p 36976.

In the 110th Congress, rule XXV was amended to provide restrictions on privately funded travel for Members. Such restrictions include prohibitions on funding by registered lobbyists, certification requirements by Members, and a prohibition on using any funds for travel aboard private aircraft. Reimbursement for official travel was also made subject to new disclosure requirements.

The current *House Ethics Manual* incorporates the prior publication *Gifts and Travel* from the 106th Congress.

§ 16. Financial Disclosure

Title I of the Ethics in Government Act of 1978 requires Members, officers, and certain employees of the House to file an annual Financial Disclosure Statement. 5 USC App §§ 101-111. This law, which is incorporated into House rule XXVI, was intended to regulate and monitor possible conflicts of interest due to outside financial holdings. *Manual* § 1103.

In the 94th Congress the House reprimanded a Member for certain conduct occurring during prior Congresses, which included failure to make proper financial disclosures. H. Res. 1421, H. Rept. 94-1364, *In re* Sikes, July 29, 1976, p 24379. The Committee on Standards of Official Conduct (now Ethics) has concluded that a Member accepted certain gifts that were subject to mandatory disclosure under the Ethics in Government Act. H. Rept. 100-506, *In re* Biaggi; H. Rept. 105-797, *In re* Kim.

§ 17. Professional Practice Restrictions

Members are subject to various restrictions relating to their professional affiliations while serving in the House. Thus, Members are prohibited from receiving compensation for legal services before agencies of the Federal government. Clause 2 of rule XXV; 18 USC § 205. Under this rule, Members, officers, and certain senior employees may not:

- Receive compensation from affiliation with a firm providing professional services for compensation that involve a fiduciary relationship except for the practice of medicine.
- Permit their names to be used by any such firm or other entity.
- Practice a profession for compensation that involves a fiduciary relationship except for the practice of medicine.
- Serve for compensation on the board of directors of any association, corporation, or other entity.
- Receive compensation for teaching without prior notification and approval.

Manual § 1099.

§ 18. Acts Committed in a Prior Congress or Before Becoming a Member

Under clause 3(b)(3) of rule XI, the Committee on Ethics may not investigate an alleged violation of a law, rule, regulation, or standard of conduct that was not in effect at the time of the alleged violation. Also excepted from investigation are alleged violations that occurred before the third previous Congress unless the committee determines that such matters were directly related to an alleged violation that occurred in a more recent Congress. *Manual* § 806.

Historically, it has been within the prerogative of the House to censure a Member for misconduct occurring in a prior Congress, notwithstanding the reelection of such Member. Deschler Ch 12 § 16. However, the question whether the offense was known to such Member's constituency at the time of the election is a factor to be considered. 2 Hinds § 1286. Thus, in 1976 the House adopted the recommendation of the committee that a Member be reprimanded for certain conduct occurring during prior Congresses that involved financial irregularities but declined to recommend punishment for prior conflict-of-interest conduct that had occurred in 1961, where such conduct had apparently been known to a constituency that had continually reelected him. H. Res. 1421, H. Rept. 94-1364, *In re* Sikes, July 29, 1976, p 24379.

The House has asserted jurisdiction under article I, section 5 of the Constitution to inquire into the misconduct of a Member occurring before his last election and to impose at least those sanctions short of expulsion. H. Res. 378, H. Rept. 96-351, *In re* Diggs, July 31, 1979, p 21584; 2 Hinds § 1283. In one case, the committee investigated violations of Federal election laws that allegedly occurred before the respondent became a Member. H. Rept. 105-797, *In re* Kim.

Expulsion thus far has been applied to Members only with respect to offenses occurring during their terms of office and not to action taken by them before their election. Deschler Ch 12 § 13. A resolution calling for the expulsion of a Member was reported adversely by the committee and tabled by the House, where the Member had been convicted of bribery under California law for acts occurring while he served as a county tax assessor and before his election to the House. The committee found that although the conviction related to moral turpitude, it did not relate to official conduct while a Member of Congress. H. Res. 1392, H. Rept. 94-1478, *In re* Hinshaw, Sept. 8, 1976, p 29274, Oct. 1, 1976, p 35111.

If a Member's term of office expires before a pending resolution of expulsion against such Member is adopted, the proceedings are discontinued. 2 Hinds § 1276.

C. Nature and Forms of Disciplinary Measures

§19. In General

Kinds of Disciplinary Measures

The primary disciplinary measures that may be invoked by the House against a Member include expulsion, censure or reprimand, fines or other economic sanctions (such as reimbursement of the investigative costs of the committee), and deprivation of seniority or committee status.

Reprimand is appropriate for serious violations, censure is appropriate for more-serious violations, and expulsion of a Member is appropriate for the most serious violations. Rule 24(g), Rules of the Committee on Ethics, 112th Cong.

Generally, the type of disciplinary measure invoked will depend on the nature of the offense charged. Where there are mitigating circumstances, the committee sometimes issues a public letter of reproval. See, *e.g.*, H. Rept. 100-526, *In re* Rose; H. Rept. 106-979, *In re* Shuster. This letter may include a direction to the Member to apologize. H. Rept. 101-293, *In re* Bates. The House itself may extract an apology from the offending Member. 2 Hinds §§1650, 1657.

Effect of Court Conviction or Pendency of Judicial Proceedings

Under a former practice, where a Member had been convicted of a crime, the House would defer taking disciplinary action until the judicial processes had been exhausted. 6 Cannon §238. Under the more recent practice, the House may choose—as it did in the 96th and 107th Congresses—to initiate disciplinary proceedings against a Member for conduct even when that Member has not exhausted all of the appeals in the criminal process. H. Res. 378, H. Rept. 96-351, *In re* Diggs, July 31, 1979, p 21584; H. Res. 495, H. Rept. 107-594, *In re* Traficant, July 24, 2002. p 14299. Although a criminal conviction may be appealed, such a course of action and its outcome have no bearing on either the timing or the nature of the decision reached by the House. H. Rept. 100-506, *In re* Biaggi.

Clause 10 of rule XXIII provides that a Member who is convicted of a crime for which a prison sentence of two or more years could be imposed should refrain from committee business and from voting in the House until judicial or executive proceedings reinstate the Member's presumption of innocence or until reelection to the House after conviction. *Manual* §1095.

Resolutions and Reports

A resolution proposing disciplinary action against a Member may be called up in the House as a question of privilege. *Manual* § 703; 2 Hinds § 1254; 3 Hinds §§ 2648-2651. Where the Committee on Ethics after investigation recommends that disciplinary action be taken against a Member by the House, it normally files a privileged report with a form of resolution proposing the action. However, where the committee finds an allegation without merit or issues a lesser sanction, such as a letter of reproval, the committee files its report for the information of the House without an accompanying resolution. Where a Member is defeated (including in a primary), the committee may choose to report violations to the House at the end of the Congress without recommending sanctions. H. Rept. 105-797, *In re* Kim.

Under clause 3(a) of rule XI, the committee may recommend to the House from time to time such administrative actions as it may consider appropriate to establish or enforce standards of official conduct. However, a letter of reproval or other administrative action of the committee that resulted from an investigation under clause 3(a)(2) may be implemented only as a part of its report to the House. The rule also requires that the committee report to the House on the final disposition of any case it has voted to investigate. *Manual* § 806.

A resolution adopting a committee report may be offered as follows:

> *Resolved*, That the House of Representatives adopt the report by the Committee on Ethics dated __________ in the matter of Representative __________.

Consideration and Debate

A disciplinary resolution presents a question of privilege. *Manual* § 63. If reported by the Committee on Ethics (or a derivation thereof), a disciplinary resolution may be called up at any time after the committee has filed its report. *Manual* § 63. An unreported resolution may be called up by any Member as privileged under rule IX *with* proper notice (or by the Majority or Minority Leader *without* notice). *Manual* § 703; 3 Hinds § 2649; 108-2, Oct. 8, 2004, p 22734; 109-2, Sept. 29, 2006, p 21334; 110-1, June 5, 2007, p 14600; 111-2, Apr. 14, 2010, p ____.

Clause 2(a)(16) of rule IV permits an accused Member to be accompanied by counsel on the floor of the House when the committee's recommendation on such Member's case is under consideration by the House. *Manual* § 678.

Debate on a disciplinary resolution reported by the committee is under the hour rule, the chair of the committee being recognized for the entire hour. 8 Cannon §2448; Deschler Ch 12 §16. Debate on a resolution raising a question of the privileges of the House (which may include a disciplinary resolution) offered from the floor under rule IX also is debatable for one hour but the hour is equally divided between the proponent and the Majority Leader, Minority Leader, or a designee. *Manual* §699.

The manager of a disciplinary resolution may yield time to the Member charged to speak or to yield to other Members. 107-2, July 24, 2002, p 14309. In one instance the Member charged, after declining to speak, yielded all of his time to another Member. 96-1, July 31, 1979, p 21584.

A Member whose expulsion is proposed may be permitted to present a written defense. 2 Hinds §1273. However, if the previous question is moved on a proposition to censure, the effect may be to prevent the Member charged from making an explanation or presenting a defense. After the House has voted to censure, it is too late for the Member to be heard on the resolution itself. 2 Hinds §1259; 5 Hinds §5459.

Debate on a pending privileged resolution recommending disciplinary action against a Member necessarily may involve personalities. However, clause 1 of rule XVII still prohibits the use of language that is personally abusive or profane. During the actual pendency of such a resolution, a Member may discuss a prior case reported to the House by the Committee on Ethics for the purpose of comparing the severity of the sanction recommended in that case with the severity of the sanction recommended in the pending case, provided that the Member does not identify, or discuss the details of the past conduct of, a sitting Member. *Manual* §361.

The Speaker also has advised that Members should refrain from references in debate to the motivations of a Member who filed a complaint before the Committee on Standards of Official Conduct (now Ethics), to personal criticism of a member of the committee, and to an investigation undertaken by the committee, including the suggestion of a course of action or the advocacy of an interim status report by the committee. *Manual* §361.

Because an accurate record of disciplinary proceedings is important, the House may agree by unanimous consent to ban revisions or extensions of remarks delivered during the floor debate. Compare 96-2, May 29, 1980, p 12661, with 107-2, July 24, 2002, p 14319 (general leave granted).

It is for the House and not the Speaker to judge the conduct of Members. It is, accordingly, not a proper parliamentary inquiry to ask the Chair to interpret the application of a criminal statute to a Member's conduct. *Manual* §1095.

Effect of Resignation

The resignation of a Member at a time when expulsion proceedings against such Member are pending generally results in the suspension or discontinuance of the proceedings. 2 Hinds § 1275; 6 Cannon § 238. Similarly, where a Member resigns after having been found guilty of improper conduct (and deserving of censure) by a committee of investigation, the House may discontinue the proceeding. 6 Cannon § 398. However, the House may adopt a resolution censuring such conduct even after the resignation has been submitted. 2 Hinds §§ 1239, 1273, 1275.

§ 20. Expulsion

The House has the power under the Constitution to expel a Member by a two-thirds vote. U.S. Const. art. I, § 5, cl. 2. The discretionary power of the House to expel one of its Members has been said to be unlimited. 6 Cannon § 78. However, the House has consistently refused to expel a Member for acts unrelated to status as a Member or to public trust and duty. H. Rept. 56-85; 1 Hinds § 476. In 1976 an expulsion resolution was reported adversely and tabled by the House where a Member had been convicted of bribery under State law for acts occurring before his election to the House, because the conviction did not relate to his official conduct while a Member of Congress. Deschler Ch 12 § 13.1.

The power to expel extends to all cases where the offense is such as to be inconsistent with the trust and duty of the Member. *In re* Chapman, 166 U.S. 661, 669 (1897). The purpose of expulsion is not merely to provide punishment but also to remove a Member whose character and conduct demonstrate an unfitness to participate in the deliberations and decisions of the House and whose presence in it tends to bring that body into contempt and disgrace. 2 Hinds § 1286. The fundamental governing consideration underlying expulsion proceedings is whether the individual charged has displayed conduct inconsistent with the trust and duty of a Member. *In re* Chapman, 166 U.S. 661, 669 (1897).

The House has considered proposals to expel on several occasions. Expulsion was used during the Civil War against three Members charged with being in rebellion against the United States or with having taken up arms against it. 2 Hinds §§ 1261, 1262. More recently, the House expelled a Member who had been convicted in a Federal court of bribery and conspiracy in accepting funds to perform official duties. H. Res. 794, H. Rept. 96-1387, *In re* Myers, Oct. 2, 1980, p 28953. The Committee on Standards of Official Conduct (now Ethics) recommended the expulsion of two Members who had, among other acts of misconduct, accepted illegal gratuities.

H. Rept. 97-110, *In re* Lederer; H. Rept. 100-506, *In re* Biaggi. Both cases terminated with the Members' resignations.

In 2002 the House expelled a Member for illegal activities that resulted in Federal criminal convictions including (1) trading official acts and influence for things of value; (2) demanding and accepting salary kickbacks from his congressional employees; (3) influencing a congressional employee to destroy evidence and to provide false testimony to a Federal grand jury; (4) receiving personal labor and the services of his congressional employees while they were being paid by the taxpayers to perform public service; and (5) filing false income tax returns. H. Res. 495, H. Rept. 107-594, *In re* Traficant, July 24, 2002, p 14299.

Following the expulsion of a Member, the Clerk notifies the Governor of the relevant State of the action of the House. 107-2, July 24, 2002, p 14319.

There have been many instances in which an expulsion proposal considered in the House has failed, either because it was not supported by a two-thirds vote or because the House preferred some lesser penalty. This has occurred where a Member was charged with:

- Publishing an article alleged to be in violation of the privileges of the House. 2 Hinds § 1245.
- Abuse of the leave to print. 6 Cannon § 236.
- Involvement in an affray on the floor of the House. 2 Hinds § 1643.
- Assaulting a Senator. 2 Hinds § 1621.
- Uttering words alleged to be treasonable. 2 Hinds §§ 1253, 1254.
- Accepting money for nominating a person to the military academy. 2 Hinds § 1274.
- Attempting to bribe Members of Congress by offering them shares of stock at sums below their actual value. 2 Hinds § 1286.
- Assaulting another Member for words spoken in debate. 2 Hinds § 1656.
- Using offensive language toward another Member on the floor and deceiving the Speaker when the Speaker attempted to control the debate. 2 Hinds § 1251.
- Seeking improper dismissal of parking tickets and making misstatements of fact in a memorandum relating to an associate's criminal probation record. H. Res. 440, H. Res. 442, H. Rept. 101-610, *In re* Frank, July 26, 1990, pp 19705, 19717.

§ 21. —Procedure; Resolutions of Expulsion

Generally; Form

Expulsion proceedings may be initiated by the introduction of a resolution containing explicit charges, as follows:

Whereas, the Hon.______________, a Member of the House of Representatives from the State of______________, has, upon this day______________: Therefore, be it

Resolved, That the said______________, be, and is hereby, expelled from the House of Representatives.

2 Hinds §§ 1254, 1261, 1262.

Under the more recent practice, allegations of misconduct have not been included in the resolution as reported from the Committee on Ethics but rather in the accompanying report:

Resolved, That pursuant to article I, section 5, clause 2 of the United States Constitution, Representative______________, be, and is hereby, expelled from the House of Representatives.

H. Res. 495, H. Rept. 107-594, *In re* Traficant, July 24, 2002, p 14300.

The resolution should be limited in its application to one Member only, although several may be involved. Separate resolutions should be prepared on each Member. Deschler Ch 12 § 13.

A resolution proposing expulsion may provide for a committee to investigate and report on the matter. Referral of such a resolution normally is made to the Committee on Ethics. Deschler Ch 12 § 13. The resolution is subject to the motion to lay on the table. *Manual* § 63.

Under the Constitution, a resolution of expulsion requires the support of two-thirds of those Members present and voting. An amendment proposing expulsion may be agreed to by a majority vote; but, on the proposition as amended, a two-thirds vote is required. 2 Hinds § 1274. An amendment providing for censure is not germane to a resolution of expulsion. 6 Cannon § 236 (distinguishing 5 Hinds § 5923).

§ 22. Censure; Reprimand

Generally

Censure and reprimand are two other forms of discipline that may be administered pursuant to article I, section 5, clause 2 of the Constitution, which authorizes the House to punish a Member for disorderly behavior. *Manual* § 62. These punitive measures are ordered in the House by a majority of those voting, a quorum being present. The House itself must order the sanction. The Speaker does not have the unilateral authority to censure a Member. Deschler Ch 12 § 16.

During its history, the House has censured or reprimanded numerous Members and Delegates. The House on occasion has made a distinction between censure and reprimand, the latter being somewhat less punitive. Censure is administered by the Speaker to the Member at the bar of the House, perhaps in a manner specified in the resolution, including the reading of the censure resolution. See, *e.g.*, 96-1, July 31, 1979, p 21592; 96-2, June 10, 1980, p 13820; 111-2, Dec. 2, 2010, p ____. On the other hand, reprimand is administered to the Member merely by the adoption of a committee report. Deschler Ch 12 § 16; 105-1, Jan. 21, 1997, p 459. In one recent case, the House chose to adopt a resolution offered from the floor as a question of the privileges of the House ''disapproving'' of the indecorous behavior of a Member. 111-1, H. Res. 744, Sept. 15, 2009, p ____.

If necessary, the Member to be censured may be arrested and brought to the bar for the Speaker's pronouncement. 2 Hinds §§ 1251, 1305. The censure appears in full in the Journal. 2 Hinds § 1656; 6 Cannon § 236. In rare instances, the House has reconsidered a vote of censure or expunged a censure from the Journal of a preceding Congress. 2 Hinds § 1653; 4 Hinds §§ 2792, 2793.

§ 23. —Grounds; Particular Conduct

The conduct for which censure may be imposed is not limited to acts relating to the Member's official duties. The power to censure extends to any reprehensible conduct that brings the House into disrepute. Deschler Ch 12 § 16.

Many early cases of censure involved the use of unparliamentary language (2 Hinds §§ 1247-1249, 1251, 1305), assaults on a Member or Senator (2 Hinds §§ 1621, 1656), or insults to the House by the introduction of offensive resolutions (2 Hinds §§ 1246, 1256). During the Civil War, some Members whose sympathies lay with the Confederacy were censured for uttering treasonable words. 2 Hinds §§ 1252-1254. Censure was also invoked on the basis of evidence of corrupt acts by a Member. 2 Hinds §§ 1239, 1273, 1274, 1286.

More recent cases have seen censure or reprimand invoked against a Member for:

- Ignoring the processes and authority of the New York State courts, and improperly using government funds. Deschler Ch 12 § 16.1. Censure recommendation was rejected in favor of other penalties. § 1, supra.
- Failing to report certain financial holdings, in violation of the Code of Official Conduct, and investing in stock in a bank, the establishment of which he was promoting, in violation of the Code of Ethics for Government Service. H. Res. 1421, H. Rept. 94-1364, *In re* Sikes, July 29, 1976, p 24377.
- Failing to report a campaign contribution as required by law. H. Res. 1415, H. Rept. 95-1742, *In re* McFall, Oct. 13, 1978, p 37005.

- Failing to report a campaign contribution, converting a campaign contribution to personal use, and testifying falsely to the committee under oath. H. Res. 1416, H. Rept. 95-1743, *In re* Roybal, Oct. 13, 1978, p 37009.
- Unjust enrichment through increasing an office employee's salary. H. Res. 378, H. Rept. 96-351, *In re* Diggs, July 31, 1979, p 21584.
- Receiving money from a person with direct interest in legislation, in violation of clause 4 of rule XXIII and transferring campaign funds into office and personal accounts. H. Res. 660, H. Rept. 96-930, *In re* Wilson, June 10, 1980, p 13801.
- Sexual misconduct with a page. H. Res. 265, H. Rept. 98-295, *In re* Studds, July 20, 1983, p 20030; H. Res. 266, H. Rept. 98-296, *In re* Crane, July 20, 1983, p 20020.
- Filing false financial disclosure statements in violation of the Ethics in Government Act. H. Res. 558, H. Rept. 98-891, *In re* Hansen, July 31, 1984, p 21650.
- "Ghost voting," improperly diverting government resources, and maintaining a "ghost employee" on his staff. H. Res. 335, H. Rept. 100-485, *In re* Murphy, Dec. 18, 1987, p 36266.
- Seeking improper dismissal of parking tickets and for misstating facts in a memorandum relating to an associate's criminal probation record. H. Res. 440, H. Rept. 101-610, *In re* Frank, July 26, 1990, p 19717.
- Using official resources to solicit funds for an educational center, failing to file complete financial disclosure forms, and failing to pay taxes on certain property. H. Res. 1737, H. Rept. 111-661, *In re* Rangel, Dec. 2, 2010, p ____.

§ 24. — Censure Resolutions

Generally

The censure of a Member is imposed pursuant to a resolution adopted by the House. Deschler Ch 12 § 16. The resolution may take the following form:

> *Resolved*, That the Member from ____________, ____________, in ____________________ has been guilty of a violation of the rules and privileges of the House and merits the censure of the House for the same.
>
> *Resolved*, That said ______ be now brought to the bar of the House by the Sergeant-at-Arms, and the censure of the House be administered there by the Speaker.

2 Hinds § 1259.

The resolution may call for direct and immediate action by the House. Deschler Ch 12 § 16. Such a resolution should be drafted to apply to only one Member, although two or more Members may be involved. 2 Hinds §§ 1240, 1621.

A resolution of censure presents a question of privilege. 3 Hinds §§2649-2651; 6 Cannon §239. The Speaker may recognize a Member to offer a resolution of censure after the question on agreeing to a resolution calling for expulsion has been decided adversely. 6 Cannon §236. A resolution reported from committee may be adopted with an amendment converting the resolution from one of censure to one of a lesser sanction, such as reprimand. Deschler Ch 12 §16.1; 95-2, Oct. 13, 1978, p 37009.

Effect of Apologies or Explanations

In situations involving censure for unparliamentary language or behavior, the House may accept an apology or explanation from the Member and terminate the proceedings. 2 Hinds §§1250, 1257, 1258, 1652. The resolution of censure may be withdrawn. 2 Hinds §1250. If the House already has voted to censure, it may reconsider its vote and decide against censure. 2 Hinds §1653.

§25. Fines; Restitution of Funds

Pursuant to its constitutional authority to punish its Members, the House may levy a fine as a disciplinary measure against a Member for certain misconduct. U.S. Const. art. I, §5, cl. 2; Deschler Ch 12 §17. The fine may be coupled with certain other disciplinary measures deemed appropriate by the House. Examples of such fines include the following:

- For improper expenditure of House funds for private purposes, a fine of $25,000, to be deducted in monthly installments from the Member's salary. 91-1, H. Res. 2, Jan. 3, 1969, p 29.
- For misuse of congressional clerk-hire, restitution of monies in the amount in which the Member personally benefited by such misuse. H. Res. 378, H. Rept. 96-351, *In re* Diggs, July 31, 1979, p 21584.
- For a serious violation that, in the opinion of the Committee on Standards of Official Conduct (now Ethics), was more serious than one deserving reprimand but less serious than one deserving censure, reimbursement to the committee for the cost of conducting the investigation, which was $300,000. H. Res. 31, H. Rept. 105-1, *In re* Gingrich, Jan. 21, 1997, p 393.
- For failure to pay certain taxes, an order to pay restitution to the appropriate taxing authority and provide proof to the Committee of such payment. H. Res. 1737, H. Rept. 111-661, *In re* Rangel, Dec. 2, 2010, p ____.

Fines imposed by the House are separate and distinct from those for which a Member might be liable under Federal law.

§ 26. Deprivation of Status; Caucus Rules

Seniority Status

Deprivation of seniority status is a form of disciplinary action that may be invoked by the House against a Member under article I, section 5, clause 2 of the Constitution. Thus, the House may reduce a Member's seniority to that of a first-term Representative. Deschler Ch 12 § 18.2. The House may also reduce a Member's committee seniority as a result of party discipline enforced through the Member's party caucus. Deschler Ch 12 § 18.1. Members have also been removed from standing committees amid allegations of ethical misconduct. 109-2, June 16, 2006, p 11618.

Committee Participation; Committee Chair

The chair of a committee of the House may be subjected to a variety of disciplinary measures for misconduct in that capacity as chair. In one instance, a party caucus removed a Member from his position as chair of a committee based on a report disclosing certain improprieties concerning his travel expenses and clerk-hiring practices. Deschler Ch 12 § 9.2. The members of a committee may, consistent with the House rules, restrict a chair's authority to appoint special subcommittees or transfer authority from the chair to the membership and the subcommittee chairs. Deschler Ch 12 §§ 12.3, 12.4. The House, through the adoption of a resolution, may restrict the power of the chair to provide for funds for investigations by subcommittees. Deschler Ch 12 § 12.2. A resolution alleging that a Member willfully abused his power as chair of a committee investigating campaign finance improprieties by unilaterally releasing records of the committee in contravention of its rules, and expressing disapproval of such conduct, constitutes a question of the privileges of the House. 105-2, H. Res. 431, May 14, 1998, p 9276. For examples of similar resolutions alleging abuse of the powers of a committee chair offered as questions of the privileges of the House, see 108-1, July 18, 2003, p 18698 and 110-1, Jan. 24, 2007, p 2139.

Rule 25 of the rules of the Republican Conference requires the chair of any committee or subcommittee to step aside temporarily when indicted for a felony for which a prison sentence of two or more years could be imposed. Rule 26 imposes a similar requirement on a member of the leadership. Rule 27 imposes a more stringent requirement that the chair of any committee or subcommittee be replaced when censured by the House or convicted of a felony for which a prison sentence of two or more years could be imposed. Rules of the Republican Conference, 112th Cong. Rules 48 through 51 of the rules of the Democratic Caucus impose similar stepaside requirements on its chairs or ranking minority members. Rules of the Democratic Caucus, 112th Cong.

Under clause 10 of rule XXIII, a Member, Delegate, or Resident Commissioner who has been convicted by a court of record for the commission of a crime for which a prison sentence of two or more years could be imposed should refrain from participation in the business of each committee of which such individual is a member.

Voting by a Member Convicted of Certain Crimes

Under clause 10 of rule XXIII, a Member who has been convicted by a court of record for the commission of a crime for which a prison sentence of two or more years could be imposed should refrain from voting on any question in the House or the Committee of the Whole, unless or until judicial or executive proceedings result in reinstatement of the presumption of innocence or until reelection to the House after the date of such conviction.

§ 27. Letter of Reproval

A letter of reproval is a sanction the Committee on Ethics may impose by majority vote. Rule 24(c), Rules of the Committee on Ethics, 112th Cong. The committee may issue a letter of reproval as indicated in the following examples:

- For bringing discredit to the House with respect to a Member's ongoing professional relationship with a former member of his staff, with respect to his campaign committee, and for violating House gift restrictions. H. Rept. 106-979, *In re* Shuster.
- For bringing discredit to the House by conduct in interacting with two female employees. H. Rept. 101-293, *In re* Bates.
- Where the committee cited mitigating circumstances. H. Rept. 100-526, *In re* Rose.

A letter of reproval may direct the Member to apologize. Deschler Ch 12 § 13; H. Rept. 101-293, *In re* Bates.

Chapter 26
Germaneness of Amendments

Research References

5 Hinds §§ 5801-5924
8 Cannon §§ 2908-3064
Deschler-Brown Ch 28
Manual §§ 467, 928-940, 1089

A. Generally

§ 1. Introduction

Evolution of Rule

The House adopted its first germaneness rule in 1789, amended it in 1822, and has retained the rule in every subsequent Congress. Clause 7 of rule XVI states that no motion or proposition on a "subject different from that under consideration shall be admitted under color of amendment." *Manual* § 928.

It is a fundamental rule of the House that a germane relationship must exist between an amendment and the matter sought to be amended. No such rule existed under the practice of the early common law or under the rules of Parliament. It was not until 1883 that the British Parliament adopted a rule requiring "relevancy" of amendments. Erskine-May, 9th ed., p 325. Most State legislatures now also have germaneness requirements.

Before the advent of a germaneness requirement, a legislative assembly could by an amendment change the entire character of any bill or other pending proposition. It might entirely displace the original subject under consideration, and in its stead adopt one wholly foreign to it, both in form and in substance. 5 Hinds § 5825; Deschler-Brown Ch 28 §§ 1, 17.2; 105-2, Dec. 19, 1998, p 28102. Thus, the purpose of the rule is to maintain an orderly legislative process, and to prevent hasty and ill-considered legislation. It prevents the presentation to the House of propositions that might not reasonably be anticipated, and for which it might not be properly prepared. 8 Cannon § 2993.

Application of Rule Limited to Amendments

The germaneness rule applies to amendments and not to the relationship between the various propositions set forth within the bill itself. 5 Hinds § 6929; Deschler-Brown Ch 28 § 1. A bill may be composed in the first instance to embrace different subjects. The germaneness rule may preclude the introduction of a new subject by way of amendment during consideration of the bill. 5 Hinds § 5825. For example, a point of order will not lie against an appropriation in a general appropriation bill because it is not germane to the rest of the bill. Deschler-Brown Ch 28 § 17.1.

A point of order will not lie against a special order of business reported from the Committee on Rules "self-executing" the adoption in the House or in the Committee of the Whole of a nongermane amendment to a measure because the amendment is not separately before the House during consideration of the special order of business. *Manual* § 928. For a discussion of the germaneness of amendments to special orders of business reported from the Committee on Rules, see § 3, infra.

Application Before Adoption of Rules

The germaneness requirement has been held applicable in the House even before the adoption of the rules, under a theory of general parliamentary law based upon precedent. *Manual* § 60.

§ 2. Germaneness Defined; Factors To Be Considered

In General

For an amendment to be germane, it must be one that would appropriately be considered in connection with the bill. 8 Cannon § 2993. The concept implies more than the mere "relevance" of one subject to another. The fact that two subjects are related does not necessarily render each of them germane to the other. 8 Cannon §§ 2970, 2971, 2995; Deschler-Brown Ch 28 § 3.57. The germaneness of an amendment may depend on the relative scope of the amendment compared with that of the proposition sought to be amended. A proposition of narrow or limited scope may not be amended by a proposition of a more general nature, even though both propositions may be related to each other. § 10, infra. For example, to a bill authorizing emergency loans to livestock producers, an amendment changing the word ''livestock'' to ''agricultural'' was held to broaden the class of producers covered by the bill and, therefore, to be not germane. Deschler-Brown Ch 28 § 9.27.

Factors Considered in Determining Germaneness

In evaluating an amendment to determine its germaneness, the Chair considers the relationship of the amendment to the pending text, as perfected. The Chair considers the relationship between the amendment and an existing statute that the pending bill seeks to amend only if the existing statute is so comprehensively amended by the pending bill as to render amendable all its provisions. *Manual* § 939; 8 Cannon § 2942; Deschler-Brown Ch 28 § 12.10. The Chair considers the relationship of the amendment to the text to which it is offered and does not generally rely on language in accompanying reports not contained in the pending text. Deschler-Brown Ch 28 § 2.3.

The stage of the reading in the House or Committee of the Whole also must be considered when evaluating the germaneness of a particular amendment. An amendment that might be considered germane if offered at the end of the reading of the bill for amendment may not be germane if offered during the reading, before all the provisions of the bill are open to consideration. Deschler-Brown Ch 28 § 18.1; § 3, infra.

The germaneness of an amendment is not to be judged by the apparent motives of the Member offering it. Deschler-Brown Ch 28 § 46.1. In ruling on germaneness, the Chair does not determine the legal effect of the bill, law, or amendment in question. The Chair rules only on whether the amendment addresses a ''subject different'' from that under consideration. Deschler-Brown Ch 28 §§ 35.64-35.66.

The title or heading of a bill is not controlling (although it may be informative) in evaluating the germaneness of amendments offered to propositions in the bill. The scope of a measure is determined by its provisions and not by the phraseology of its formal title. Deschler-Brown Ch 28 § 2.4. Thus, the heading of a portion of a bill as ''Miscellaneous'' will not alone permit amendments to that portion that are not germane to its actual content; but the provisions under such a heading may be sufficiently diverse to permit an amendment to be tested, in effect, by its germaneness to the bill as a whole rather than merely that portion. *Manual* § 929; Deschler-Brown Ch 28 § 2.5.

§ 3. Proposition to Which Amendment Must Be Germane

Generally

The germaneness of an amendment is based on its relationship to the particular portion of the bill then open for amendment. The amendment should be germane to the particular paragraph, section, or title to which it is offered and not anticipate the subject matter of other portions not yet read or portions that have been passed in the reading. *Manual* § 929; 5 Hinds §§ 5811-5820; 8 Cannon § 2922; Deschler-Brown Ch 28 § 2. For example, the test of germaneness of an amendment offered to a title of a bill being read for amendment by titles is its relationship to the pending title as perfected and not to the particular section within that title addressed by the amendment. *Manual* § 929.

The germaneness of an amendment inserting a new portion is based on the relationship of the amendment to the portions of the bill that have been read. For example, the germaneness of an amendment adding a new title to the end of the bill is based on the relationship of the amendment to the entire bill. *Manual* § 929. Similarly, an amendment inserting a new section need not necessarily be germane to the preceding section of the bill, it being sufficient that the amendment be germane to the sections of the bill read to that point. By the same reasoning, an amendment in the form of a new paragraph need not be germane to the paragraph immediately preceding or following it. *Manual* § 929; 8 Cannon §§ 2932-2935.

Amendments to Pending Amendments

The test of germaneness of an amendment to a pending amendment is its relationship to the pending amendment and not to the bill to which that pending amendment has been offered. Deschler-Brown Ch 28 § 2.24. It follows that the test of germaneness of a substitute for a pending amendment is the relationship between the substitute and the amendment and not between the substitute and the pending bill. Deschler-Brown Ch 28 § 2.17. Similarly, the test of germaneness of an amendment to an amendment in the nature of a substitute is the relationship between those two propositions, and not between the amendment and the pending bill. Deschler-Brown Ch 28 § 21.23.

Consideration of Entire Bill

An amendment might be germane at the end of the reading of the bill for amendment, even though it would not have been germane if offered during the reading. Where a bill is, by unanimous consent, considered as read and open to amendment at any point, the test of germaneness of an amendment thereto is its relationship to the entire bill and not just its relationship to the particular section to which offered. *Manual* § 929; Deschler-Brown Ch 28 §§ 2.6, 2.31, 19.21. An amendment that adds a new portion at the end of the bill is evaluated by the relationship of the amendment to the entire bill. *Manual* § 929.

The test of germaneness in the case of a motion to recommit with instructions is the relationship of the instructions to the perfected bill taken as a whole and not merely their relationship to the separate portion of the bill specifically proposed to be amended in the instructions. *Manual* § 929.

Effect of Prior Amendments

In evaluating the germaneness of an amendment, the Chair considers the relationship of the amendment to the bill as modified by the adoption of any prior amendment and is not bound solely by the provisions of the original text. Thus, a perfecting amendment may be ruled out as not germane where it pertains to text that has been stricken from the bill. *Manual* § 929; Deschler-Brown Ch 28 §§ 2.9, 2.13, 35.32.

Effect of Pendency of Motion to Strike

A perfecting amendment to a title in a bill may be offered while there is pending a motion to strike the title. Such an amendment is to the pending text and not to the motion to strike; and thus the amendment is required to be germane to the text to which offered rather than the motion to strike. *Manual* § 929.

Amendments to Special Orders of Business Reported from the Committee on Rules

An amendment offered to a special order of business reported from the Committee on Rules (for example, waiving germaneness points of order against a specified amendment to be offered) must be germane to that resolution. A special order of business reported from the Committee on Rules providing for the consideration of a bill relating to a certain subject may be amended neither by an amendment that would substitute the consideration of a different proposition nor an amendment that would permit the additional consideration of a nongermane amendment to the bill. *Manual* § 928.

§4. Tests of Germaneness

Generally; Nonexclusiveness of Tests

Various tests may be invoked to determine the germaneness of an amendment. These tests are not mutually exclusive. *Manual* §935. The Chair, in evaluating germaneness, first must understand the nature and scope of the pending portion of the proposition being amended and then the relationship of the offered amendment to that pending text. The Chair follows the most appropriate line of precedent in rendering a ruling.

An amendment may satisfy one of the tests and yet be ruled out because of its failure to satisfy another. An amendment may thus be subject to a germaneness point of order, even though it is in some sense related to the pending proposition.

This principle is illustrated in the following precedents:

Held Not Germane

Text	Amendment
Excluding a Member-elect. . . .	Expelling the Member-elect (5 Hinds §5924)
Expelling a Member. . . .	Censuring the Member (6 Cannon §236)
Relating to interstate commerce. . . .	Relating to foreign commerce (8 Cannon §2918)
Proposing a committee investigation. . . .	Requesting a committee report (5 Hinds §5887)
Assigning clerks to committees. . . .	Assigning clerks to Members (5 Hinds §5901)
Erecting a building for a mint. . . .	Changing coinage laws (5 Hinds §5884)
Raising price of agricultural products by creation of corporation. . . .	Raising price by cooperative marketing (8 Cannon §2912)
Repealing a specific mortgage refinancing program. . . .	Regulating financial sector employee compensation. (112-1, Mar. 10, 2011, p ___)
Increasing food supplies by educational and demonstrational methods. . . .	Increasing food supplies by sale of fertilizer (8 Cannon §2980)

Held Not Germane—Continued

Text	Amendment
Enforcing State liquor laws. . . .	Enforcing State firearm laws (*Manual* § 932)

§ 5. —Subject Matter

Clause 7 of rule XVI precludes amendments ‘‘on a subject different from that under consideration.’’ This test of germaneness implies more than mere ‘‘relevance.’’ The test is whether or not a new subject is introduced by the amendment. An amendment relating to a subject to which there is no reference in the pending text may be subject to a point of order that it is not germane to the bill. *Manual* § 932; Deschler-Brown Ch 28 § 3; see also § 2, supra.

This principle is illustrated in the following precedents:

Held Germane

Text	Amendment
Creating a canal by one route. . . .	Changing route (5 Hinds § 5909)
Creating a board of inquiry. . . .	Specifying time of report (5 Hinds § 5915)
Creating two boards with separate duties. . . .	Creating one board with authorization to discharge the duties of both boards (8 Cannon § 3064)
Rescinding an order for adjournment. . . .	Fixing new date for adjournment (5 Hinds § 5920)
Regulating immigration. . . .	Providing an educational test for immigrants (5 Hinds § 5873)
Controlling public places in the District of Columbia. . . .	Removing fence of Botanic Garden (5 Hinds § 5914)
Appropriating funds for acquisition of information pertaining to agricultural products. . . .	Appropriating funds for an investigation incident thereto (8 Cannon § 3060)
Authorizing the construction of naval vessels. . . .	Providing that the vessels be constructed in government plants (8 Cannon § 3063)

Held Germane—Continued

Text	Amendment
Revising food safety laws and providing new regulatory authorities. . . .	Providing for the preemptive purchase of food related to such authorities (111-1, July 30, 2009, p ____)
Addressing the interrelation of House committees and imposing requirements for filing and content of committee reports. . . .	Addressing the content of reports from the Committee on Appropriations and the jurisdictional responsibilities of that committee and legislative committees (Deschler-Brown Ch 28 § 35.89)
Ameliorating procedures relating to mortgage foreclosure under the National Housing Act. . . .	Placing a moratorium on foreclosures of mortgages in economically depressed areas (Deschler-Brown Ch 28 § 3.36)
Addressing certain sections of the Clean Air Act with respect to the impact of shortages of energy resources on standards imposed under that Act. . . .	Addressing another section of that Act suspending for a temporary period the authority of the EPA Administrator to control automobile emissions (*Manual* § 932)
Prescribing the functions of a new Federal Energy Administration and conferring wide discretionary powers on its Administrator. . . .	Directing the Administrator to issue preliminary summer guidelines for citizen fuel use (Deschler-Brown Ch 28 § 33.15)
Requiring a general study of factors affecting domestic production of automobiles	Requiring a study of a particular factor—currency exchange rates—affecting that production (Deschler-Brown Ch 28 § 10.6)

Held Not Germane

Text	Amendment
Admitting religious refugees. . . .	Admitting political refugees (8 Cannon § 3047)
Limiting immigration. . . .	Disseminating information to attract a better class of immigrants (8 Cannon § 3048)

Held Not Germane—Continued

Text	Amendment
Prohibiting mailing of revolvers. . . .	Prohibiting mailing of publications advertising revolvers (8 Cannon § 3052)
Authorizing arbitration of claims against the government. . . .	Appropriating funds to pay claims so arbitrated (8 Cannon § 3057)
Eliminating wage discrimination based on the sex of the employee. . . .	Eliminating discrimination based on race (Deschler-Brown Ch 28 § 3.18)
Providing for comprehensive reform of immigration laws. . . .	Increasing the number of law enforcement officials, including U.S. Marshalls (whose responsibilities go beyond enforcement of immigration laws) (109-2, Sept. 21, 2006, p 18861)
Authorizing the use of American civilians to operate an early-warning system in the Sinai. . . .	Requiring that the U.S. contribution to the U.N. peace-keeping forces in the Middle East be proportionately reduced (Deschler-Brown Ch 28 § 3.47)
Establishing a cotton research program and promoting the marketing of cotton. . . .	Providing for research with respect to training and utilization of displaced farm labor in the cotton industry (Deschler-Brown Ch 28 § 3.5)
Extending the phased subsidization of certain categories of nonprofit mail. . . .	Establishing a new class of mail and postal rate therefor (Deschler-Brown Ch 28 § 9.54)
Reducing tax liabilities of individuals and businesses by providing diverse tax credits within the Internal Revenue Code. . . .	Providing rebates to recipients under retirement and survivor benefit programs (Deschler-Brown Ch 28 § 35.52)
Governing the political activities of Federal employees and containing certain restrictions on Federal employment relative to such activities. . . .	Prohibiting any employment or compensation, from whatever source, for candidates for office (Deschler-Brown Ch 28 § 9.50)
Addressing access to committee hearings and meetings. . . .	Addressing committee staffing (Deschler-Brown Ch 28 § 35.91)

Held Not Germane—Continued

Text	Amendment
Addressing the administrative structure of a new department. . . .	Prohibiting the department from withholding funds to carry out certain objectives (Deschler-Brown Ch 28 § 34.25)
Providing for the settlement of tribal claims. . . .	Setting new fuel procurement objectives for Federal agencies (110-2, June 25, 2008, p 13755)
During consideration of one of two reconciliation bills reported by the Committee on the Budget. . . .	Changing prospectively and indirectly the other reconciliation bill not then pending before the House (*Manual* § 932)
Reauthorizing the National Sea Grant College Program. . . .	Amending existing law to provide for automatic continuation of appropriations in the absence of timely enactment of a regular appropriation bill (*Manual* § 932)
Opposing concessional loans to a country and outlining principles governing the conduct of industrial cooperation projects of U.S. nationals in that country. . . .	Waiving other provisions of law by requiring changes in tariff schedules to achieve overall trade reciprocity between that country and the United States (*Manual* § 932)
Authorizing the deployment of troops to implement a peace agreement. . . .	Expressing support for the armed forces in carrying out such mission (*Manual* § 932)
Addressing enforcement of State liquor laws. . . .	Addressing enforcement of State firearm laws (*Manual* § 932)

Proposals Relating to Studies

To a proposal authorizing a program to be undertaken, an amendment providing for a study to determine the feasibility of undertaking such a program may be germane. Deschler-Brown Ch 28 § 30.37 (in effect overturning 8 Cannon § 2989). Conversely, an amendment requiring certain action is not germane to a proposal that would merely require a study. Accordingly, to a proposition establishing a commission to study a matter, an amendment directing an official to undertake and accomplish that matter is not germane. Deschler-Brown Ch 28 § 3.69. However, if an amendment to a proposal to study a matter merely requires the submission of proposed legislation to implement the study, the amendment may be germane. Deschler-Brown Ch 28 § 3.14.

§ 6. — Committee Jurisdiction

Generally

Committee jurisdiction over the subject of an amendment is a relevant test to be applied in determining the germaneness of that amendment. *Manual* § 934; Deschler-Brown Ch 28 § 4. Thus, to a bill providing agricultural price supports to stimulate domestic production, an amendment repealing price control for all commodities (within the jurisdiction of the Committee on Banking and Currency) would not be germane. *Manual* § 934. Similarly, an amendment changing the statement of policy contained in a bill is not germane if its effect is to fundamentally change the purpose of the bill and to emphasize a subject within the jurisdiction of another committee. Deschler-Brown Ch 28 § 4.11. Likewise, an amendment conferring authority on an executive official not mentioned in the pending proposition is not germane where the subject of that authority is not within the jurisdiction represented in the pending proposition. *Manual* § 934.

The chair of the Committee of the Whole may determine the germaneness of an amendment based upon the discernible committee jurisdictions as to subject matter without infringing upon the Speaker's prerogatives under rule XII to determine committee jurisdiction over introduced legislation. Deschler-Brown Ch 28 § 4.71. The fact that the amendment is contained in a motion to recommit the bill with instructions does not dispense with the requirement that the subject matter of the amendment be within the jurisdiction represented in the pending text. *Manual* § 930.

However, the fact that the subject matter of an amendment lies within the jurisdiction of a committee other than that having jurisdiction over the introduced bill does not necessarily dictate the conclusion that the amendment is not germane. Committee jurisdiction is but one of the tests of germaneness. In ruling on the question, the Chair must take into consideration other factors, including the fact that the introduced bill may have been broadened or narrowed by amendment. *Manual* § 929. Where the bill is amended in Committee of the Whole to include matters within the jurisdiction of other committees, further similar amendments may be germane. Deschler-Brown Ch 28 § 4.54. The Chair also may take into account the fact that the portion of the bill being amended itself contains language related to the amendment that is not within the jurisdiction of the committee reporting the bill. *Manual* § 934. An amendment in the nature of a substitute may be in order even though an incidental portion of the amendment, if considered separately, might be within the jurisdiction of another committee. Deschler-Brown Ch 28 § 30.36.

Committee jurisdiction over the subject of an amendment is most relevant where the pending text is entirely within one committee's jurisdiction and where the amendment falls within another committee's purview. Deschler-Brown Ch 28 § 4.99. Thus, committee jurisdiction is a relevant test where an authorization bill that is solely within one committee's jurisdiction is proposed to be amended by permanent changes of laws within another committee's jurisdiction. Deschler-Brown Ch 28 § 24.1. Committee jurisdiction over the subject of an amendment may not be the most apt test of germaneness where the proposition being amended contains provisions so comprehensive as to overlap several committees' jurisdictions. *Manual* § 934.

This principle is illustrated in the following precedents:

Held Not Germane

Text	Amendment
A bill reported from the Committee on International Relations (now Foreign Affairs) dealing with humanitarian and evacuation assistance in South Vietnam. . . .	Providing for payment of costs of settlement of evacuees in the U.S., a matter within the jurisdiction of the Committee on the Judiciary (Deschler-Brown Ch 28 § 4.52)
A bill reported from the Committee on Armed Services containing diverse provisions relating to national defense policy, military procurement, and personnel. . . .	Requiring reports on the Soviet Union's compliance with its arms control commitments, a matter within the jurisdiction of the Committee on Foreign Affairs (Deschler-Brown Ch 28 § 4.26)
A bill within the jurisdiction of the Committee on Armed Services and the Committee on Foreign Affairs regarding the redeployment of U.S. troops and related diplomatic issues. . . .	Proposing revisions to the Foreign Intelligence Surveillance Act, an act within the jurisdiction of the Committee on the Judiciary and the Permanent Select Committee on Intelligence (110-1, July 12, 2007, p 18844)
A bill reported from the Committee on Merchant Marine and Fisheries authorizing various activities of the Coast Guard. . . .	Urging cooperation of other nations as to certain Coast Guard and military operations, a matter within the jurisdiction of the Committee on Foreign Affairs (Deschler-Brown Ch 28 § 4.46)

Held Not Germane—Continued

Text	Amendment
A bill reported from the Committee on Natural Resources providing for a study of two rivers for inclusion in the National Wild and Scenic Rivers System. . . .	Providing for comprehensive energy legislation within the jurisdiction of seven different committees (110-2, Sept. 10, 2008, p 18417)
A bill reported from the Committee on Public Works and Transportation amending the Federal Water Pollution Control Act. . . .	Amending the Clean Air Act (a statute within the jurisdiction of the Committee on Energy and Commerce) to regulate ''acid rain'' (Deschler-Brown Ch 28 § 4.3)
A bill authorizing environmental research and development activities of an agency for two years. . . .	Adding permanent regulatory authority by amending a law not within the jurisdiction of the committee reporting the bill (Deschler-Brown Ch 28 § 4.1)
A bill relating to intelligence activities of the executive branch. . . .	Effecting a change in the rules of the House by directing a committee to impose an oath of secrecy on its members and staff (*Manual* § 934)
A bill reported from the Committee on Science and Technology (now Science, Space, and Technology) authorizing environmental *research and development activities* of an agency for two years. . . .	Expressing the sense of Congress as to the agency's *regulatory and enforcement activity*—a matter within the jurisdiction of another committee (Deschler-Brown Ch 28 § 4.2)
A bill reported from the Committee on Interior and Insular Affairs designating certain wilderness areas in Oregon. . . .	Providing unemployment and retraining entitlement payments to persons affected by such wilderness designations, a matter falling within the jurisdiction of other committees (Deschler-Brown Ch 28 § 4.8)
A bill reported from the Committee on Agriculture providing a one-year price support for milk. . . .	Relating to tariff duties on imported dairy products, a matter within the jurisdiction of the Committee on Ways and Means (Deschler-Brown Ch 28 § 4.74)

Held Not Germane—Continued

Text	Amendment
A bill reported from the Committee on Public Works and Transportation relating to grants to State and local governments for local public works construction projects. . . .	Providing grants to such governments to assist them in providing public services, a program within the jurisdiction of the Committee on Government Operations (Deschler-Brown Ch 28 § 4.99)
A bill reported from the Committee on Ways and Means providing taxes and tax incentives to conserve energy. . . .	Precluding the purchase of fuel-inefficient automobiles by the government, a subject within the jurisdiction of the Committee on Government Operations (Deschler-Brown Ch 28 § 4.21)
A bill reported from the Committee on Interstate and Foreign Commerce to conserve energy resources by regulating the production, allocation and use of those resources. . . .	Reducing energy consumption by the Federal government by a reduced work-week for Federal civilian employees, a matter within the jurisdiction of the Committee on Post Office and Civil Service (Deschler-Brown Ch 28 § 4.13)
A bill reported by the Committee on Ways and Means dealing only with import duties and quotas on sugar. . . .	Eliminating all price support payments for sugar, a matter within the jurisdiction of the Committee on Agriculture (Deschler-Brown Ch 28 § 4.73)
A bill reported from the Committee on International Relations (now Foreign Affairs) providing foreign economic assistance. . . .	Providing foreign *and domestic* economic assistance, a matter within the jurisdiction of the Committee on Banking (Deschler-Brown Ch 28 § 3.46)
A bill reported from the Committee on Energy and Commerce relating to mentally ill individuals. . . .	Prohibiting certain uses of general revenue-sharing funds (a matter within the jurisdiction of another committee) in certain areas (Deschler-Brown Ch 28 § 4.104)

Held Not Germane—Continued

Text	Amendment
A bill reported from the Committee on Education and Labor (now Education and the Workforce) authorizing a variety of civilian national service programs. . . .	Establishing a contingent military service obligation (a matter within the jurisdiction of the Committee on Armed Services) (*Manual* § 934)
A bill reauthorizing programs administered by two agencies within one committee's jurisdiction. . . .	Providing for authority that is more general in scope, affecting agencies within the jurisdiction of other committees (*Manual* § 934)
A bill reported by the Committee on Transportation and Infrastructure reforming and privatizing Amtrak. . . .	Rescinding previously appropriated funds for certain administrative expenses, a matter within the jurisdiction of the Committee on Appropriations (*Manual* § 934)
A concurrent resolution expressing a sense of Congress with respect to the availability of public funds for expenses incurred in the evaluation of a problem. . . .	Addressing legislative responses to that problem, within the jurisdiction of other committees (*Manual* § 934)
A bill reported from the Committee on Government Reform and Oversight proposing to alter responsibilities of executive branch agencies under an existing law. . . .	Proposing to extend the application of that law to entities of the legislative branch, a matter within the jurisdiction of the Committee on House Administration (*Manual* § 934)
A resolution authorizing the deployment of troops to implement a peace agreement, within the jurisdiction of the Committee on International Relations. . . .	Expressing support for the armed forces carrying out such mission, within the jurisdiction of both the Committees on Armed Services and International Relations (*Manual* § 934)
A bill comprehensively amending agricultural law and addressing some laws outside the jurisdiction of the Committee on Agriculture. . . .	Proposing to extend an existing dairy compact and create three new dairy compacts, within the jurisdiction of the Committee on the Judiciary (*Manual* § 934)

§ 7. —Fundamental Purpose

Another test used by the Chair in determining germaneness is one in which the fundamental purpose of the bill is compared with the fundamental purpose of the amendment. *Manual* § 933. If the purpose or objective of an amendment is unrelated to that of the bill to which it is offered, the amendment may be held not germane. 8 Cannon § 2911; Deschler-Brown Ch 28 § 4.10. This test is particularly applicable to an amendment in the nature of a substitute. Deschler-Brown Ch 28 § 5. If the purpose of a highway bill is to connect points A and B, an amendment specifying a different *route* between A and B would reflect the same fundamental purpose. However, an amendment connecting A and D would have a different purpose and would not be germane. 5 Hinds § 5909.

An amendment changing the statement of policy contained in a bill is not germane if its effect is to fundamentally change the purpose of the bill. Deschler-Brown Ch 28 § 4.11. An amendment changing the law with respect to the operations of one agency is not germane to a bill relating to the operations of a different agency. Deschler-Brown Ch 28 § 5.24.

In determining the fundamental purpose of a bill or an amendment offered thereto, the Chair may examine the broad scope of the bill and the stated purpose of the amendment and need not be bound by ancillary purposes that are merely suggested by the amendment. *Manual* § 933; Deschler-Brown Ch 28 § 5.12. An amendment in the form of a new title may be germane to a bill as a whole where that bill contains additional provisions not necessarily confined to the primary purpose, so long as the amendment falls within the overall parameters of the bill. Deschler-Brown Ch 28 § 5.20.

This principle is illustrated in the following precedents:

Held Germane

Text	Amendment
Authorizing funds to provide humanitarian and evacuation assistance and authorizing the use of United States troops to provide that assistance. . . .	Authorizing funds for military aid to a foreign country to be used by that country to further the fundamental purpose of the bill (Deschler-Brown Ch 28 § 5.23)
Enforcing the right to vote as guaranteed by the 15th amendment to the Constitution. . . .	Protecting freedom of speech and other first amendment rights whose abridgment might affect the exercise of voting rights (Deschler-Brown Ch 28 § 5.3)

Held Germane—Continued

Text	Amendment
Enforcing constitutional voting rights by requiring preservation of Federal election returns. . . .	Providing for court appointment of voting referees to insure protection of voters' rights (Deschler-Brown Ch 28 § 5.2)
Criminalizing use of a firearm during the commission of a felony that may be prosecuted in a Federal court. . . .	Criminalizing carrying of a firearm during the commission of a felony that may be prosecuted in either a State or Federal court (Deschler-Brown Ch 28 § 12.10)
Providing an omnibus surface transportation authorization for highway-related projects as well as roadways. . . .	Authorizing funds for certain highway projects that would incidentally permit completion of a related flood control project (Deschler-Brown Ch 28 § 5.12)
Authorizing the construction of a trans-Alaska oil-gas pipeline pursuant to procedural safeguards promulgated by the Secretary of the Interior. . . .	Containing similar procedures and including the condition that all participants be assured rights against discrimination as set forth in the Civil Rights Act (Deschler-Brown Ch 28 § 5.1)
Freezing the obligation of funds for fiscal year 1996 for missile defense until the Secretary of Defense rendered a specified readiness certification. . . .	Permitting an increase in the obligation of such funds on the basis of legislative findings concerning readiness, as each proposition addressed the relationship between 1996 funding levels for missile defense and readiness (*Manual* § 933)

Held Not Germane

Text	Amendment
Proposing a constitutional amendment relating to the election of the President and Vice President by popular vote rather than through the electoral college process. . . .	Proposing an apportionment of Representatives and concerning the size of congressional districts (Deschler-Brown Ch 28 § 8.12)

Held Not Germane—Continued

Text	Amendment
Authorizing military assistance programs to foreign nations. . . .	Authorizing a contribution to the U.N. International Atomic Energy Agency (Deschler-Brown Ch 28 § 42.52)
Authorizing law enforcement agency grants to purchase photographic and fingerprint equipment for law enforcement purposes. . . .	Providing for the purchase of bulletproof vests (Deschler-Brown Ch 28 § 3.78)
Extending the advisory and informational authority of the Council on Wage and Price Stability to encourage *voluntary programs* to resist inflation. . . .	Authorizing the President to issue *orders and regulations* stabilizing economic transfers, including wages and prices (Deschler-Brown Ch 28 § 6.20)
Establishing a new office within a government department. . . .	Abolishing the department (Deschler-Brown Ch 28 § 4.109)
Enabling agencies of the government to formulate policies relating to energy conservation. . . .	Prohibiting certain uses of fuel (for school busing) and imposing criminal penalties for such use (Deschler-Brown Ch 28 § 5.15)
Extending various laws relating to higher education. . . .	Imposing restrictions on preschool, elementary, and secondary education policy (Deschler-Brown Ch 28 § 35.58)
Providing funding for urban highway transportation systems. . . .	Broadening the bill to include rail transportation (Deschler-Brown Ch 28 § 4.62)
Requiring registration and public disclosure by lobbyists but not regulating or prohibiting their activities. . . .	Regulating their activities by placing a ceiling on their monetary contributions to Federal officials and prohibiting lobbying within certain areas (Deschler-Brown Ch 28 § 5.31)
Relating to the minting and issuance of public currency. . . .	Providing for a commemorative coin intended for private circulation (Deschler-Brown Ch 28 § 5.27)
Impeaching the President. . . .	Censuring the President (*Manual* § 933)

Held Not Germane—Continued

Text	Amendment
Authorizing a State attorney general to bring a civil action in Federal court against a person who has violated a State law regulating intoxicating liquor. . . .	Singling out certain violations of liquor laws on the basis of their regard for any and all firearms issues (*Manual* § 933)
Authorizing a State attorney general to bring a civil action in Federal court against a person who has violated a State law regulating intoxicating liquor. . . .	Creating new Federal laws to regulate intoxicating liquor (*Manual* § 933)

§ 8. —Accomplishing Result of Bill by Different Method

In order to be germane, an amendment must not only have the same end as the matter sought to be amended, but also must contemplate a method of achieving that end that is closely allied to the method encompassed in the bill or other matter sought to be amended. *Manual* § 933; Deschler-Brown Ch 28 § 6.4. Under this principle, when a proposition to accomplish a certain purpose by one method is pending, an amendment seeking to achieve the same purpose by another closely related method is germane. Deschler-Brown Ch 28 § 5.14. For example, if the purpose of a bill is to support the health of school children by mandating oranges in a school lunch program, an amendment providing free vitamin C supplements may be germane. Likewise, a proposition to accomplish a certain result by two alternative methods may be amended by language proposing to accomplish that result by a third, closely related method. Deschler-Brown Ch 28 § 6.8. However, an amendment to accomplish a similar purpose by an unrelated method, not contemplated by the bill, is not germane. Deschler-Brown Ch 28 § 6.4.

This principle is illustrated in the following precedents:

Held Germane

Text	Amendment
Accomplishing a result through regulation by an executive branch agency. . . .	Achieving the same result through the use of another governmental entity (Deschler-Brown Ch 28 § 6.8)

Held Germane—Continued

Text	Amendment
Conducting a broad range of programs involving energy sources, including environmental research related to the development of energy sources. . . .	Authorizing the Council on Environmental Quality to evaluate environmental effects of energy technology (Deschler-Brown Ch 28 § 6.9)
Providing loan guarantee programs for all States and subdivisions. . . .	Providing direct loans (and limiting them to New York) (Deschler-Brown Ch 28 § 6.4)
Subjecting employers who fail to apprise their workers of health risks to penalties under certain laws and regulations. . . .	Subjecting employers to penalties prescribed in the amendment (*Manual* § 933)
Freezing the obligation of funds for fiscal year 1996 for missile defense until the Secretary of Defense rendered a specified readiness certification. . . .	Permitting an increase in the obligation of such funds on the basis of legislative findings concerning readiness, as each proposition addressed the relationship between 1996 funding levels for missile defense and readiness (*Manual* § 933)

Held Not Germane

Text	Amendment
Conserving energy through the imposition of civil penalties on manufacturers of low-miles-per-gallon automobiles. . . .	Conserving energy through tax rebates to purchasers of high-miles-per-gallon automobiles (Deschler-Brown Ch 28 § 6.12)
Establishing an independent agency within the executive branch to accomplish a particular purpose. . . .	Emphasizing committee oversight and authorizing committees to order the agency to take certain actions (Deschler-Brown Ch 28 § 6.36)
Authorizing the Attorney General to participate in litigation based on discrimination in public facilities. . . .	Establishing a Community Relations Service to assist in resolving disputes arising from discriminatory practices (Deschler-Brown Ch 28 § 9.11)

Held Not Germane—Continued

Text	Amendment
Authorizing the promulgation of national drinking water standards to protect public health from contaminants. . . .	Requiring the negotiation and enforcement of international agreements to accomplish that purpose (Deschler-Brown Ch 28 § 6.25)
Controlling crime through research and training. . . .	Controlling crime through regulation of the sale of firearms (Deschler-Brown Ch 28 § 6.6)
Extending unemployment compensation benefits during a period of economic recession. . . .	Stimulating economic growth by tax incentives and regulatory reform (*Manual* § 933)
Promoting technological advancement by fostering Federal research and development. . . .	Promoting same by changes in tax and antitrust laws (*Manual* § 933)
Providing financial assistance to domestic agriculture through a system of price support payments. . . .	Protecting domestic agriculture by restricting imports in competition therewith (Deschler-Brown Ch 28 § 6.18)
Addressing substance abuse through prevention and treatment. . . .	Imposing civil penalties on drug dealers (*Manual* § 933)
Impeaching the President. . . .	Censuring the President (*Manual* § 933)
Authorizing a State attorney general to bring a civil action in Federal court against a person who has violated a State law regulating intoxicating liquor. . . .	Singling out certain violations of liquor laws on the basis of their regard for any and all firearms issues (*Manual* § 933)
Authorizing a State attorney general to bring a civil action in Federal court against a person who has violated a State law regulating intoxicating liquor. . . .	Creating new Federal laws to regulate intoxicating liquor (*Manual* § 933)

§ 9. —Individual Proposition or Class Not Germane to Another

One individual proposition is not germane to another individual proposition. *Manual* § 936; 8 Cannon §§ 2951-2953, 2963-2966; Deschler-Brown Ch 28 §§ 8.23, 8.33. Thus, in theory, a bill regulating the transportation of apples could not be amended by language regulating the transportation of oranges. However, if an individual proposition is rendered general in its scope by amendment, it is then subject to further amendment by propositions of the same class. 8 Cannon § 3003.

An individual proposition is not germane to another individual proposition merely because they are related. Thus, to a bill amending one subsection of law dealing with one prohibited type of activity, an amendment to another subsection dealing with a related but separate prohibited type of activity is not germane. Deschler-Brown Ch 28 § 8.7.

Where a bill covers two or more subjects within a readily definable class, it is not germane to add subjects outside of that class by way of amendment. Deschler-Brown Ch 28 § 3.80. Likewise, to a bill pertaining to several functions within an identifiable class of activity, an amendment adding a function outside that class would not be germane. *Manual* § 936.

To a bill dealing with relief for one class, an amendment seeking to include another class is not germane. Deschler-Brown Ch 28 § 13.19. Thus, to a bill providing financial relief for one class—agricultural producers—an amendment was held not germane where it extended such relief to another class, commercial fishermen, particularly where relief to the latter class was within the jurisdiction of another committee. Deschler-Brown Ch 28 § 4.70.

To a bill extending certain provisions to specified categories within a certain class of employees, an amendment extending those provisions to an additional category of employees within that same class is germane. Deschler-Brown Ch 28 § 12.1. However, such an amendment is not germane if it brings other classes of employees within the scope of the bill. Deschler-Brown Ch 28 § 13.1.

This principle is illustrated in the following precedents:

Held Not Germane

Text	Amendment
Providing for the relief of one individual. . . .	Providing for similar relief of another (5 Hinds §§ 5826-5929)
Exterminating the boll weevil. . . .	Including the gypsy moth (5 Hinds § 5832)
Providing a clerk for a committee. . . .	Providing a clerk for another committee (5 Hinds § 5833)
Providing for an additional judge in one territory. . . .	Providing additional judges in other territories (5 Hinds § 5830)

Held Not Germane—Continued

Text	Amendment
Providing relief for dependents of persons in the Army. . . .	Extending benefits to dependents in the National Guard (8 Cannon § 2953)
Pensioning veterans of Indian wars. . . .	Pensioning veterans of Mexican wars (8 Cannon § 2960)
Appropriating funds for only one year (and containing no provisions extending beyond that year). . . .	Extending the appropriation to another year (*Manual* § 936; 8 Cannon § 2913)
Relating to congressional actions on the budget. . . .	Repealing the Impoundment Control Act, thereby addressing Presidential authority to rescind or defer (Deschler-Brown Ch 28 § 4.89)
Siting a certain type of repository for a specified kind of nuclear waste. . . .	Prohibiting the construction at another site of another type of repository for another kind of nuclear waste (*Manual* § 936)
Disposing of tin from the national stockpile. . . .	Disposing of silver from the national stockpile (Deschler-Brown Ch 28 § 8.33)
Providing financial assistance to the States for construction of public school facilities. . . .	Providing loans to assist in the construction of private schools (Deschler-Brown Ch 28 § 8.39)
Settling a particular railway labor dispute. . . .	Settling another dispute between a different railroad company and its employees (Deschler-Brown Ch 28 § 8.34)
Prohibiting a certain type of activity. . . .	Including another class of prohibited activities (Deschler-Brown Ch 28 § 8.7)
Designing certain coins. . . .	Specifying the metal content of other coins (Deschler-Brown Ch 28 § 8.35)
Regulating poll-closing time in Presidential *general* elections. . . .	Extending the provisions to Presidential *primary* elections (Deschler-Brown Ch 28 § 8.13)

Held Not Germane—Continued

Text	Amendment
Relating to the civil service system for Federal civilian employees. . . .	Including other classes of employees (postal and District of Columbia employees) (Deschler-Brown Ch 28 § 8.4)
Providing a cost-of-living adjustment for foreign service retirees. . . .	Providing a comparable adjustment in annuities for Federal civil service employees (Deschler-Brown Ch 28 § 8.6)
Determining the equitability of Federal pay practices under statutory systems applicable to agencies of the executive branch. . . .	Extending the determination of fairness to pay practices in the legislative branch (Deschler-Brown Ch 28 § 13.8)
Providing for payment from the Senate contingent fund of certain travel expenses incurred by Senate employees. . . .	Providing additional travel allowances, payable from the House contingent fund, to Members of the House (Deschler-Brown Ch 28 § 13.7)
Authorizing grants to States for purchase of one class of equipment (photographic and fingerprinting equipment) for law enforcement purposes. . . .	Including assistance for the purchase of a different class of equipment (bulletproof vests) (Deschler-Brown Ch 28 § 8.37)
Addressing violent crimes. . . .	Addressing nonviolent crimes, such as crimes of fraud and deception or crimes against the environment (*Manual* § 936)
Naming a facility after a specific person. . . .	Substituting the name of a different person (8 Cannon § 2955) where it could not be shown that the amendment merely intended a return to the facility's existing designation (105-2, Feb. 4, 1998, pp 784, 790)
Addressing whether public funds should be available for specified endeavors of one group. . . .	Addressing the same question for unrelated endeavors of another group (*Manual* § 936)

Held Not Germane—Continued

Text	Amendment
Altering responsibilities of executive branch agencies under an existing law. . . .	Extending the application of that law to entities of the legislative branch (*Manual* § 936)
Appropriating or authorizing appropriations for a single year and containing no provisions beyond that year. . . .	Extending the authorization or appropriation for another year (*Manual* § 936)
Constitutional amendment on flag desecration. . . .	Constitutional amendment on a Balanced Federal Budget or on the Social Security Trust Fund (109-1, June 22, 2005, p 13539)

§ 10. —General Amendments to Specific or Limited Propositions

A specific proposition may not be amended by a proposition more general in scope. *Manual* § 937; 5 Hinds § 5843; 8 Cannon §§ 2997, 2998; Deschler-Brown Ch 28 § 9. Thus, an amendment applicable to fruits of all kinds would not be germane to a bill dealing only with apples. An amendment applicable to all departments and agencies is not germane to a bill limited in its application to certain departments and agencies. Deschler-Brown Ch 28 § 9.22. Even an amendment that merely strikes words from a bill may be ruled out if the amendment has the effect of broadening the scope of the bill. § 17, infra.

A substitute for an amendment must be confined in scope to the subject of the amendment. Deschler-Brown Ch 28 § 9.42. Thus, an amendment rewriting an entire concurrent resolution on the budget was held not germane to a perfecting amendment that proposed certain changes in figures for one of the years covered by the resolution. Deschler-Brown Ch 28 § 9.38.

This principle is illustrated in the following precedents:

Held Not Germane

Text	Amendment
Admitting a Territory. . . .	Admitting several Territories (5 Hinds § 5837)
Relating to all corporations in interstate commerce. . . .	Relating to all corporations (5 Hinds § 5842)

Held Not Germane—Continued

Text	Amendment
Applying proposition to one bureau of the Navy Department. . . .	Applying proposition to the Navy Department as a whole (8 Cannon § 2997)
Prohibiting speculation in cotton. . . .	Prohibiting speculation in cotton, wheat, and corn (8 Cannon § 3001)
Designating a single National Historic Trail. . . .	Altering regulations for all Historic Trails (110-2, July 10, 2008, p 14584)
Amending a law in one particular. . . .	Repealing the law (5 Hinds § 5924; 8 Cannon § 2949)
Authorizing loans to farmers in certain areas. . . .	Authorizing loans without geographical restriction (8 Cannon § 3235)
Terminating a specific mortgage refinancing program. . . .	Authorizing a study of mortgages generally (112-1, Mar. 10, 2011, p ____)
Authorizing foreign economic assistance to *certain qualifying nations*. . . .	Requiring reports on human rights violations by *all foreign countries* (Deschler-Brown Ch 28 § 35.58)
Restricting the use of funds for military operations in South Vietnam. . . .	Extending that restriction to other countries in Indochina (Deschler-Brown Ch 28 § 9.48)
Amending the Constitution to prohibit the U.S. or any State from denying persons 18 years of age or older the right to vote. . . .	Requiring the U.S. and all States to treat persons 18 years and older as having reached the age of legal majority for all purposes under the law (*Manual* § 937)
Criminalizing obstruction of court orders relating to desegregation of public schools. . . .	Extending criminalization to all court orders (Deschler-Brown Ch 28 § 9.12)
Relating to *official conduct* of Federal employees. . . .	Relating to *any criminal conduct* of those officials (Deschler-Brown Ch 28 § 9.49)

Held Not Germane—Continued

Text	Amendment
Extending the benefits of a Federal program to one class (public schools). . . .	Extending the benefits to a broader category—all nonprofit institutions in depressed areas (Deschler-Brown Ch 28 § 39.18)
Amending existing law to promote economic development through financial assistance to local communities. . . .	Requiring a study of the impact of *all* Federal, State, and local laws and regulations on employment opportunities (Deschler-Brown Ch 28 § 9.35)
Addressing mental health. . . .	Addressing a variety of public health programs (Deschler-Brown Ch 28 § 4.104)
Suspending temporarily certain requirements of the Clean Air Act. . . .	Suspending temporarily other requirements of all other environmental protection laws (Deschler-Brown Ch 28 § 4.5)
Authorizing activities of certain government agencies for a temporary period. . . .	Permanently changing existing law to cover a broader range of government activities (*Manual* § 937)
Appropriating or authorizing funds for only one year. . . .	Extending the appropriation or authorization to another year (Deschler-Brown Ch 28 § 9.2)
Amending an existing law to authorize a program. . . .	Restricting authorizations under that or any other act (*Manual* § 937)
Striking from a bill one activity from those covered by the law being amended. . . .	Striking an entire subsection of the bill, thereby eliminating the applicability of existing law to a number of activities (*Manual* § 937)
Continuing funding within one executive department. . . .	Addressing funding for other departments or addressing the compensation of all Federal employees (*Manual* § 937)
Relating to one aspect of Federal spending (U.S. contributions to an international financial institution). . . .	Relating to the entire Federal budget, mandating that total outlays not exceed receipts (Deschler-Brown Ch 28 § 35.48)

Held Not Germane—Continued

Text	Amendment
Appropriating funds for a program for one fiscal year. . . .	Relating to eligibility for funding in any fiscal year (Deschler-Brown Ch 28 § 15.24)
Prohibiting the use of funds appropriated for a fiscal year for a specified purpose. . . .	Prohibiting the use of funds appropriated for that or any prior fiscal year for an unrelated purpose (Deschler-Brown Ch 28 § 9.20)
Proposing a temporary change in law. . . .	Proposing permanent changes in that law (*Manual* § 937)
Amending an authority of an agency under an existing law. . . .	Expressing the sense of Congress on regulatory agencies generally (*Manual* § 937)
Establishing an office in the Department of the Interior to manage biological information. . . .	Addressing requirements of compensation for constitutional takings by other regulatory agencies (*Manual* § 937)
Waiving a requirement in existing law that an authorization be enacted before the obligation of certain funds. . . .	Enacting by reference bills containing not only that authorization but also other policy matters (*Manual* § 937)
Relating only to a certain appropriation account in a bill. . . .	Relating not only to that account but also to funds in other acts (*Manual* § 937)
Raising an employment ceiling for one year. . . .	Addressing in permanent law a hiring preference system for such employees (*Manual* § 937)
Authorizing Federal funds for qualifying State national service programs. . . .	Conditioning a portion of such funding on the enactment of State laws immunizing volunteers in nonprofit or public programs, generally, from certain legal liabilities (*Manual* § 937)
Addressing particular educational requirements imposed on educational agencies. . . .	Addressing any requirements imposed on educational agencies by the underlying bill (*Manual* § 937)

Held Not Germane—Continued

Text	Amendment
Reauthorizing programs administered by the Economic Development Administration and the Appalachian Regional Commission. . . .	Waiving any Federal regulation that would interfere with economic development (*Manual* § 937)
Prohibiting a certain class of abortion procedures. . . .	Prohibiting any or all abortion procedures (*Manual* § 937)
Addressing a class of imported goods (those produced by forced labor). . . .	Addressing all imported goods from one specified country (*Manual* § 937)

§ 11. —Specific Amendments to General Propositions

A general proposition may be amended by a specific proposition or one more limited in nature if within the same class. *Manual* § 938; 8 Cannon §§ 3002, 3009, 3012; Deschler-Brown Ch 28 § 10. Thus, a bill regulating the transportation of fruits of all kinds could be amended by language applicable specifically to oranges. Where a bill seeks to accomplish a general purpose by diverse methods, an amendment that adds a specific method to accomplish that result may be germane. Deschler-Brown Ch 28 § 6.47. Thus, to a bill authorizing a broad program of research and development, an amendment directing specific emphasis during the administration of that program was held germane. Deschler-Brown Ch 28 § 10.9.

To a proposition conferring a broad range of authority to accomplish a particular result, an amendment granting specific authority to achieve that result is germane. Deschler-Brown Ch 28 § 10.10.

An amendment defining a term in a bill may be germane so long as it relates to the bill (but may not rely on a relationship to a law being amended by the bill in aspects not the subject of the bill). Thus, to a bill clarifying the definition of persons or institutions under certain civil rights statutes, an amendment providing that the term ''person'' for the purpose of the bill shall include unborn children was held germane. Deschler-Brown Ch 28 § 10.1.

This principle is illustrated in the following precedents:

Held Germane

Text	Amendment
Appropriating a lump sum for rivers and harbors. . . .	Designating specific projects on which a lump sum should be expended (8 Cannon §§3004, 3008)
Providing for a decennial census of the entire population of the United States. . . .	Relating to the alien population of the United States (8 Cannon §3005)
Authorizing a commission to report on the public domain. . . .	Specifying a report on a designated area of the public domain (8 Cannon §3007)
Establishing an executive agency and conferring broad authority thereon. . . .	Directing that agency to conduct a study of a subject within the scope of that authority (Deschler-Brown Ch 28 §42.27)
Conferring wide discretionary powers upon an energy administrator. . . .	Directing the administrator to issue preliminary summer guidelines for citizen fuel use (Deschler-Brown Ch 28 §33.15)
Authorizing the Federal Energy Administrator to restrict exports of certain energy resources. . . .	Directing that official to prohibit the exportation of petroleum products for use in military operations in Indochina (Deschler-Brown Ch 28 §33.12)
Directing the President to require all government agencies to use economy-model motor vehicles. . . .	Limiting the number of ''fuel-inefficient'' passenger motor vehicles that the government could purchase (Deschler-Brown Ch 28 §10.11)
Seeking to accomplish a general purpose (support of the arts and humanities) by diverse methods. . . .	Authorizing the employment of unemployed artists through the National Endowment for the Arts (Deschler-Brown Ch 28 §6.47)
Addressing a range of criminal prohibitions. . . .	Addressing another criminal prohibition within that range (*Manual* §938)
Addressing violent crimes. . . .	Addressing violent crimes involving the environment (*Manual* §938)

§ 12. —Adding to Two or More Propositions

A measure containing two or more diverse propositions within the same class may be amended by an amendment adding a third proposition on the same subject. *Manual* § 938; 8 Cannon § 3016; Deschler-Brown Ch 28 § 11. For example, a bill regulating the transportation of apples and oranges could be amended by language extending the bill to bananas. To a bill bringing two new categories within the coverage of existing law, an amendment to include a third category of the same class may be germane. Deschler-Brown Ch 28 § 11.16. Likewise, where a bill contains several unrelated titles on a general subject, an amendment adding a further title within that general subject is germane. *Manual* § 929. Where a bill defines several unlawful acts, an amendment proposing to include another unlawful act of the same class is germane. Deschler-Brown Ch 28 § 11.21.

On the other hand, where a bill covers two or more subjects within a readily definable class, it is not germane to add subjects outside of that class by way of amendment. *Manual* § 938. Thus, to a bill authorizing the Secretary of the Treasury to strike two types of national medals honoring the bicentennial, an amendment permitting private mints to strike State medals was held not germane. 92-2, Feb. 2, 1972, pp 2180-82.

To a bill containing definitions of several of the terms used therein, an amendment may be germane that modifies one of the definitions and adds another (Deschler-Brown Ch 28 § 30.34) or that further defines other terms used in the bill (Deschler-Brown Ch 28 § 11.2).

This principle is illustrated in the following precedents:

Held Germane

Text	Amendment
Admitting several Territories into the Union. . . .	Admitting another Territory (5 Hinds § 5838)
Constructing buildings in two cities. . . .	Constructing similar buildings in several other cities (5 Hinds § 5840)
Providing a number of restrictions on an expenditure. . . .	Adding another restriction (8 Cannon § 3010)
Providing for a number of Army camps. . . .	Providing for an additional camp (8 Cannon § 3012)
Authorizing payment to several employees for injuries. . . .	Authorizing payment to another employee for such injuries (8 Cannon § 3015)

Held Germane—Continued

Text	Amendment
Collecting statistics on agriculture, manufacture, and mining. . . .	Collecting statistics on insurance (8 Cannon § 3016)
Relating to motor trucks and passenger-carrying automobiles. . . .	Relating also to motorcycles and trailers (7 Cannon § 1415)
Setting forth diverse findings and purposes related to a general subject. . . .	Setting forth a further finding or purpose related to that subject (Deschler-Brown Ch 28 § 11.23)
Prohibiting indirect assistance to several foreign countries. . . .	Including additional countries within that prohibition (Deschler-Brown Ch 28 § 12.9)
Relating to diverse political rights of the people of the District of Columbia. . . .	Conferring upon that electorate the additional right of electing a nonvoting Delegate to the Senate (Deschler-Brown Ch 28 § 11.25)
Funding several departments and agencies. . . .	Funding subway construction in the District of Columbia (*Manual* § 938)
Extending coverage of gun control laws to rifles, shotguns, and ammunition. . . .	Relating to registration of firearms by the purchasers thereof (Deschler-Brown Ch 28 § 11.36)
Criminalizing a number of activities in the field of interstate consumer credit transactions. . . .	Criminalizing a further activity, ''loansharking'' (Deschler-Brown Ch 28 § 11.15)
Extending the coverage of the Flammable Fabrics Act to include wearing apparel and household furnishings. . . .	Extending such coverage further to include children's toys (Deschler-Brown Ch 28 § 11.16)
Reducing tax liabilities in several diverse ways—including tax credits. . . .	Adding an additional tax credit (Deschler-Brown Ch 28 § 11.34)
Providing farm programs for dairy products, wool, feed grains, cotton and wheat. . . .	Adding a new program for poultry and eggs (Deschler-Brown Ch 28 § 11.28)
Addressing violent crimes. . . .	Addressing violent crimes involving the environment (*Manual* § 938)

§ 13. Appropriation Bills

An amendment offered to a general appropriation bill must be germane to the part of the bill that is under consideration. Deschler-Brown Ch 28 § 15. An amendment offered to an appropriation bill is judged by the general tests of germaneness that are set forth elsewhere in this chapter. § 4, supra; § 25, infra. Although general appropriation bills are normally read by paragraph, an amendment that increases an appropriation by transferring amounts from an account in another paragraph is normally offered under the protection of clause 2(f) of rule XXI. Therefore, in modern practice, the germaneness rule does not preclude such a transfer amendment. *Manual* § 929.

Subject to clause 2(c) of rule XXI (requiring that limitation amendments to general appropriation bills be offered at the end of the reading of the bill for amendment), an amendment limiting the use of funds by a particular agency funded in a general appropriation bill may be germane to the paragraph carrying the funds or to any general provisions portion of the bill affecting that agency or all agencies funded by the bill. However, an amendment limiting funds in a general appropriation bill for activities prescribed by laws unrelated to the functions of departments and agencies addressed by the bill was held not germane. *Manual* § 929.

Germaneness is an express requirement of any amendment sought to be introduced pursuant to the Holman rule, which permits legislative matter in general appropriation bills under certain circumstances. *Manual* § 1062; see APPROPRIATIONS.

This principle is illustrated in the following precedents:

Held Germane

Text	Amendment
Appropriating certain funds and permitting them to remain available beyond the fiscal year covered by the bill. . . .	Placing certain restrictions on their use, to become effective after the expiration of the fiscal year (Deschler-Brown Ch 28 § 15.27)
Appropriating funds for foreign assistance programs. . . .	Denying funds therein to pay arrearages or dues of members of the United Nations (Deschler-Brown Ch 28 § 15.8)
Appropriating funds for the Department of Agriculture and including a specific allocation of funds for animal disease and pest control. . . .	Limiting funds in the Act for chemical pesticides where their use would be prohibited by State or local law (Deschler-Brown Ch 28 § 15.7)

Held Germane—Continued

Text	Amendment
Appropriating funds for the Department of Defense. . . .	Limiting funds in the Act for financing of certain military operations (Deschler-Brown Ch 28 § 15.27)

Held Not Germane

Text	Amendment
Prohibiting aid to one nation unless a certain condition is met. . . .	Prohibiting aid to another nation pending certain actions, and referring to funds in other Acts (Deschler-Brown Ch 28 § 15.15)
Continuing appropriations pending enactment of regular appropriation bills and curtailing certain government expenditures. . . .	Requiring an agency to report to each Member the total Federal expenditures in the congressional district represented by each Member and directing the Members to take certain steps to effect a reduction in expenditures (Deschler-Brown Ch 28 § 15.48)
Continuing appropriations for certain departments and agencies for one month. . . .	Restricting the total administrative budget expenditures for the fiscal year and thus affecting funds not continued by the bill (Deschler-Brown Ch 28 § 15.17)
Providing supplemental appropriations for certain specified departments of government. . . .	Affecting appropriations for virtually all departments and agencies of government (Deschler-Brown Ch 28 § 15.14)
Continuing the availability of appropriated funds and also imposing diverse legislative conditions on the availability of appropriations. . . .	Changing permanent law as to the eligibility of certain recipients (Deschler-Brown Ch 28 § 15.26)
Appropriating funds for an agency for one year. . . .	Changing the appropriation figure but also adding language having the effect of permanent law (Deschler-Brown Ch 28 § 27.24)

Held Not Germane—Continued

Text	Amendment
Appropriating funds for a certain purpose for one government agency. . . .	Appropriating funds for another government agency for the same general purpose (Deschler-Brown Ch 28 § 15.37)
Providing appropriations for certain departments and agencies. . . .	Limiting funds therein to activities prescribed by laws unrelated to the functions of departments and agencies addressed by the bill (*Manual* § 929)

B. Application of Rule to Particular Forms of Amendment

§ 14. In General

The rule requiring germaneness of amendments has been applied to many forms of propositions having amendatory effect, including an amendment to a particular part of a bill (§ 15, infra), amendments to amendments (8 Cannon § 2924), and motions to recommit with instructions (§ 20, infra). The rule applies to amendments recommended by committee as well as to amendments offered from the floor. § 19, infra.

The form in which an amendment is offered may affect the determination of whether the amendment is germane. Thus, whether an amendment adds a new title to a bill or adds language to an existing title may affect the determination of whether the amendment is germane. § 16, infra.

§ 15. Amendments to Particular Portion of Bill

An amendment must be germane to the particular portion of the bill that is open to amendment; that is, an amendment must be germane to the pending paragraph, section, or title. *Manual* § 929; Deschler-Brown Ch 28 § 18. The Chair will evaluate the germaneness of an amendment by comparing the amendment to the pending portion of the bill without considering the bill as a whole. Deschler-Brown Ch 28 § 18.3.

The test of germaneness of an amendment is its relationship to the pending portion of the bill, as amended to that point. *Manual* § 929. For this reason, an amendment inserting a new section may be ruled out because it is not germane to the bill as read to that point. However, a similar amendment may be allowed subsequently when the scope of the bill has been broadened by additional sections passed in the reading or adoption of additional amendments. Deschler-Brown Ch 28 §18.1. An amendment that would be germane if offered when the bill is first taken up may not be germane to the bill, as modified, after portions of the bill have been stricken by amendment. 8 Cannon §2910.

§16. Adding New Section or Title

An amendment in the form of a new title, section, or paragraph need not necessarily be germane to the title, section, or paragraph immediately preceding it. The Chair will evaluate the relationship of the amendment to as much of the bill as has been read. 8 Cannon §§2932, 2935; Deschler-Brown Ch 28 §19. If an amendment is offered at the conclusion of the reading, the Chair will evaluate the relationship of the amendment to the bill as a whole, as perfected. *Manual* §929; Deschler-Brown Ch 28 §19.3. For this reason, an amendment that might not be germane when offered to a particular title of a bill may be considered germane if offered as a new title. Deschler-Brown Ch 28 §18.7. This test is applied even though the amendment in effect modifies (albeit indirectly) a provision previously read and passed. Deschler-Brown Ch 28 §19.11.

In determining the application of this test, the Chair must take into account whether the text is being read by titles, sections, or paragraphs. Thus, the test of the germaneness of an amendment in the form of a new section to a title of a bill being read by *titles* is the relationship between the amendment and the pending title. Deschler-Brown Ch 28 §3.11.

§17. Striking Text

An amendment striking language from a bill may not be germane if the result of the amendment extends the scope of the provisions of the bill to subjects other than those originally presented. 8 Cannon §2920. Deschler-Brown Ch 28 §20. A pro forma amendment merely to ''strike the last word'' to secure time for debate in the Committee of the Whole is germane. *Manual* §928.

§18. Substitute Amendments

The test of the germaneness of a substitute amendment is its relationship to the amendment to which it is offered and not its relationship to the underlying bill. *Manual* §929; Deschler-Brown Ch 28 §21. A substitute must be confined in scope to the subject of the amendment and must relate to the same portion of the bill being addressed by the amendment. Deschler-Brown Ch 28 §§9.42, 21. Thus, for an amendment establishing a termination date for the Federal Energy Administration, a substitute not dealing with the date of termination, but providing instead a reorganization plan for that agency, was ruled out as not germane. Deschler-Brown Ch 28 § 21.1.

However, for an amendment changing certain language in a pending section, a substitute changing that text and also adding language in the section may be germane if it has the effect of dealing with the same subject in a related and more limited way. Deschler-Brown Ch 28 § 32.16.

§ 19. Committee Amendments

The rule of germaneness applies to committee amendments as well as to those offered by individual Members. 5 Hinds § 5806; Deschler-Brown Ch 28 § 22. A committee amendment that is not germane to the bill as introduced may require a waiver in the rule providing for the consideration of the underlying bill. Deschler-Brown Ch 28 § 45.2.

§ 20. Recommittals; Instructions to Committees

The germaneness rule applies to instructions in a motion to recommit a bill to a committee. It is not in order to propose as part of a motion to recommit any proposition that would not have been germane if proposed as an amendment to the bill on the floor. *Manual* §§ 929, 930; 5 Hinds §§ 5529-5541; 8 Cannon §§ 2708-2712. In one instance, for example, during consideration of a bill authorizing military expenditures, a motion to recommit with instructions was ruled not germane because it contained provisions seeking to prescribe foreign policy objectives. Deschler-Brown Ch 28 § 23.3.

The test of germaneness in the case of a motion to recommit with instructions is the relationship of the instructions to the bill taken as a whole as perfected (and not merely to the separate portion of the bill specifically proposed to be amended in the instructions). *Manual* § 930. This is so even where the instructions do not propose a direct amendment to the bill but merely contain general instructions to the committee to pursue an unrelated approach or to instruct the committee not to report the bill back to the House until an unrelated contingency occurs. 8 Cannon § 2704; Deschler-Brown Ch 28 § 23.9.

A point of order against a motion to recommit with instructions has been entertained before completion of the reading of such motion where the matter contained in the instructions has been ruled not germane when offered as an amendment in the Committee of the Whole (Deschler-Brown Ch 28 § 23.3) or after a non-germane portion of the instructions has been read (*Manual* § 628).

C. Amendments Imposing Qualifications or Limitations

§21. In General; Exceptions or Exemptions

As pointed out earlier in this chapter, a general subject may be amended by a specific proposition of the same class. §11, supra. Under an extension of this principle, an amendment that makes a specific exception to or exemption from a general proposition is germane. 8 Cannon §3028; Deschler-Brown Ch 28 §29. Thus, to a section dealing with a designated class, an amendment exempting from the provisions of the section a certain portion of that class may be germane. 8 Cannon §3026. Provisions restricting authority may be modified by amendments providing exceptions to those restrictions. 8 Cannon §3024.

This principle is illustrated in the following precedents:

Held Germane

Text	Amendment
Deporting aliens. . . .	Exempting a portion of such aliens from deportation (8 Cannon §3029)
Prohibiting courts from issuing injunctions in labor disputes. . . .	Excepting all labor disputes affecting public utilities (8 Cannon §3024)
Prohibiting an administrator from setting ceiling prices above a certain level for domestic crude oil. . . .	Exempting new crude petroleum sold by producers of less than 30,000 barrels per day (Deschler-Brown Ch 28 §29.13)
Limiting discretionary powers conferred in a bill. . . .	Providing an exception from that limitation (Deschler-Brown Ch 28 §35.13)
Requiring NLRB certification of employee elections of unions as bargaining agents only where there has been a secret ballot. . . .	Excepting an employer that has undermined the election or is otherwise estopped from challenging it (Deschler-Brown Ch 28 §35.24)
Denying benefits to recipients failing to meet a certain qualification. . . .	Denying the same benefits to some recipients but excepting others (Deschler-Brown Ch 28 §29.11)

§22. Conditions or Qualifications

A condition or qualification sought to be added by way of amendment must be germane to the provisions of the bill. *Manual* §940; Deschler-

Brown Ch 28 § 30. An amendment is not germane if it makes the effectiveness of a bill contingent upon an unrelated event or determination. Deschler-Brown Ch 28 § 31.22. Thus, an amendment making the implementation of a funding program contingent upon compliance with unrelated legislation is not germane. Deschler-Brown Ch 28 § 30.23. For discussion of postponements pending contingencies, see § 26, infra.

On the other hand, an amendment imposing a condition may be in order if it imposes a prerequisite that comes within the general subject covered by the bill. For example, where a bill provided a comprehensive grant program that included within its scope the welfare of law enforcement officers, an amendment requiring States to enact a law enforcement officers' grievance system as a prerequisite to receiving grants under the bill was held to come within the general subject of law enforcement improvement covered by the bill and was held germane. Deschler-Brown Ch 28 § 30.30.

Assistance to a particular class of recipient covered by a bill may not by amendment be conditioned on actions or inaction by another class of recipient or agent not covered by the bill. Deschler-Brown Ch 28 § 30.29. For example, an amendment conditioning the availability to certain recipients of funds in an authorization bill upon their compliance with Federal law *not otherwise applicable to those recipients* and within the jurisdiction of other House committees may be ruled out as not germane. Deschler-Brown Ch 28 § 34.37.

This principle is illustrated in the following precedents:

Held Germane

Text	Amendment
Authorizing funds for a variety of programs that satisfy several stated requirements, in order to accomplish a general purpose. . . .	Conditioning the availability of those funds upon implementation of another program related to that general purpose (Deschler-Brown Ch 28 § 30.30)
Providing for scholarships. . . .	Providing requirements for eligibility for such scholarships (Deschler-Brown Ch 28 § 30.11)
Authorizing funds for military procurement and construction. . . .	Barring use of the funds in military operations in North Vietnam (Deschler-Brown Ch 28 § 30.6)

Held Germane—Continued

Text	Amendment
Authorizing the insurance of vessels. . . .	Denying such insurance to vessels charging exorbitant rates (8 Cannon § 3023)
Authorizing an agency to undertake certain activities. . . .	Allowing Congress to disapprove regulations issued pursuant thereto (Deschler-Brown Ch 28 § 33.11)
Requiring certain intelligence information to be given to the House. . . .	Imposing relevant conditions of security on the handling of such information in committee (*Manual* § 940)

§ 23. Restrictions or Limitations

Restrictions and limitations sought to be added to a bill by way of amendment must be germane to the provisions of the bill. *Manual* § 940; Deschler-Brown Ch 28 § 32. Thus, to a bill amending a statute, an amendment prohibiting assistance under that Act or under any other Act for a particular purpose, and affecting laws not being amended by the bill, may be ruled out as not germane. Deschler-Brown Ch 28 § 35.62.

This principle is illustrated in the following precedents:

Held Germane

Text	Amendment
Authorizing change in railroad rates. . . .	Excluding rate increases (8 Cannon § 3022)
Authorizing aid to shipping. . . .	Limiting such aid to ships equipped with life-saving devices (8 Cannon § 3027)
Authorizing use of oil-burning engines on ships. . . .	Prohibiting use of such engines if constructed outside of the United States (8 Cannon § 3032)
Furnishing medical services and facilities. . . .	Prohibiting the use of such services to perform certain abortions (Deschler-Brown Ch 28 § 32.7)
Providing unlimited terms of service for judges. . . .	Restricting terms to four years (8 Cannon § 3031)

Held Germane—Continued

Text	Amendment
Transferring specified property solely for the purpose of providing shelter to the homeless and protecting the public health. . . .	Requiring reversion of the property if not used for that charitable purpose as defined under a provision of the Internal Revenue Code (Deschler-Brown Ch 28 § 32.12)
Providing Federal funds to States for certain purposes. . . .	Restricting payment of those funds to States that enact certain laws relating to the activities being funded (*Manual* § 940)

Held Not Germane

Text	Amendment
Repairing naval vessels. . . .	Prohibiting such repairs in navy yards (in order to make them at less expense elsewhere) by restricting funds in portions of the bill not open to amendment (8 Cannon § 3034)

§ 24. — Discretionary Powers

To a proposition conferring discretionary authority, an amendment limiting or restricting the exercise of that authority is germane. 8 Cannon § 3022; Deschler-Brown Ch 28 § 33. Such an amendment may be germane, even though it incorporates as a term of measurement a qualification or condition applicable to entities beyond the scope of the bill. Deschler-Brown Ch 28 § 33.23. For example, to a proposition that the Administrator of Veterans' Affairs be authorized to establish a maximum interest rate for loans, an amendment stating that "the rate fixed shall not be higher than the FHA rate" was held germane. Deschler-Brown Ch 28 § 33.28.

Although a proposition reorganizing existing discretionary agency authority may be amended by imposing limitations on the exercise of those functions, an amendment directly changing policies in the substantive law to be administered by that agency is not germane. Deschler-Brown Ch 28 § 33.13.

This principle is illustrated in the following precedents:

Held Germane

Text	Amendment
Authorizing funds for the National Aeronautics and Space Administration. . . .	Prohibiting contracts for "support" services except where certain cost comparisons were made (Deschler-Brown Ch 28 § 33.27)
Conferring authority on the President to establish rules for ordering priorities among petroleum users and requiring that vital services in the areas of education and transportation shall receive priority. . . .	Restricting that regulatory authority by requiring that petroleum products allocated for public school transportation be used only between the student's home and the school closest thereto (Deschler-Brown Ch 28 § 33.9)
Prescribing the functions of a new Federal Energy Administration by conferring wide discretionary powers on the administrator. . . .	Limiting the authority of the administrator in setting prices for propane gas by requiring an equitable allocation of production costs (Deschler-Brown Ch 28 § 33.17)
Prescribing the functions of a new Federal Energy Administration. . . .	Prohibiting the promulgation of petroleum rationing rules without prior approval by Congress (Deschler-Brown Ch 28 § 33.16)
Authorizing an agency to undertake certain activities. . . .	Providing that regulations issued pursuant to that authority may be disapproved by Congress (Deschler-Brown Ch 28 § 33.11)
Continuing U.S. participation under the International Development Association Act. . . .	Directing opposition in that forum to loans to nations not party to a nuclear nonproliferation treaty (Deschler-Brown Ch 28 § 33.29)
Containing diverse provisions relating to authorities of the Department of Defense. . . .	Precluding the use of certain land for deployment of a weapons system pending a study (Deschler-Brown Ch 28 § 11.17)

§ 25. — Use of Funds

Amendments that merely place restrictions on the use of funds that are authorized or referred to in the bill are generally upheld as germane. Deschler-Brown Ch 28 § 34. An amendment seeking to restrict the use of funds must be limited to the subject matter and scope of the provisions sought to be amended. *Manual* § 940. The amendment must be confined to the agencies, authorities, and funds addressed by the bill and may not be more comprehensive in scope. Deschler-Brown Ch 28 § 32.6. A limiting amendment may be held not germane if it places restrictions on funds authorized or appropriated in other bills. Deschler-Brown Ch 28 § 31.30. To be germane, the amendment restricting the use of funds must relate solely to those funds and may not apply to another related category of funds. Deschler-Brown Ch 28 § 34.23.

An amendment limiting the use of funds by a particular agency funded in a general appropriation bill may be germane at more than one place in the bill. Subject to clauses 2(c) and (d) of rule XXI, the amendment may be offered when the paragraph carrying such funds is pending, or to an appropriate ''general provision'' portion of the bill affecting that agency or all agencies funded by the bill. Deschler-Brown Ch 28 § 15.1.

This principle is illustrated in the following precedents:

Held Germane

Text	Amendment
Authorizing supplemental appropriations for military procurement, development, and construction. . . .	Prohibiting use of those funds to carry out military operations in North Vietnam (Deschler-Brown Ch 28 § 34.10)
Appropriating funds for an additional Washington airport. . . .	Limiting the amount to be used for the construction of an access road (Deschler-Brown Ch 28 § 34.32)
Authorizing an investigation and incidental travel to be undertaken by a committee of the House. . . .	Restricting use of the funds permitted in such travel (Deschler-Brown Ch 28 § 34.5)
Authorizing appropriations to enter into contracts for the development of synthetic fuels. . . .	Prohibiting use of the funds to enter into contracts with any major oil company (Deschler-Brown Ch 28 § 34.28)
Authorizing appropriations for contributions to the United Nations Environmental Fund. . . .	Prohibiting use of those funds to assist in the reconstruction of North Vietnam (93-1, May 15, 1973, pp 15747, 15752)

Held Germane—Continued

Text	Amendment
Authorizing appropriations for the National Science Foundation. . . .	Prohibiting use of those funds for research on a live human fetus outside the womb (93-1, June 22, 1973, p 20946)
Establishing a rural electrification and telephone revolving fund for insured and guaranteed loans. . . .	Providing that no such funds be used outside the United States or its possessions (93-1, Apr. 4, 1973 p 10395)
Continuing U.S. participation under the International Development Association Act. . . .	Prohibiting use of U.S. contributions as loans for the purchase of nuclear weapons or materials (Deschler-Brown Ch 28 § 32.5)
Restricting the availability of funds to a certain category of recipients. . . .	Restricting further the availability of those funds to a subcategory of the same recipients (Deschler-Brown Ch 28 § 34.4)
Providing assistance for mass transportation programs and permitting certain school systems to be eligible applicants for school bus subsidies. . . .	Prohibiting use of funds to implement programs intended to overcome racial imbalance in school systems (Deschler-Brown Ch 28 § 34.20)
Authorizing funds and limited use of troops for a specific purpose. . . .	Denying funds for deployment of troops beyond a certain period of time (Deschler-Brown Ch 28 § 34.13)
Providing Federal funds to States for certain purposes. . . .	Restricting payment of those funds to States that enact certain laws relating to the activities being funded (*Manual* § 940)

Held Not Germane

Text	Amendment
Changing a dollar amount in operating expenses for an agency. . . .	Prohibiting a certain activity and the use of any funds therefor (*Manual* § 940)

Held Not Germane—Continued

Text	Amendment
Establishing a new Department of Education and addressing only the administrative structure of the department. . . .	Prohibiting the use of funds to compel the transportation of students or teachers with the goal of establishing racial or ethnic balance (Deschler-Brown Ch 28 § 34.38)
Approving an increase in the U.S. quota to the International Monetary Fund and authorizing dealing in gold in connection therewith. . . .	Prohibiting the alienation of gold to *any* international organization or its agents, or to *any* person or organization acting for certain purchasers (Deschler-Brown Ch 28 § 32.6)
Striking a provision prohibiting the use of funds in the bill for a designated oil land lease in California. . . .	Prohibiting use of funds in the bill *or in any other act* for that lease *and other* California leases (Deschler-Brown Ch 28 § 15.21)
Providing general appropriations. . . .	Limiting funds therein to activities prescribed by laws unrelated to the functions of departments and agencies addressed by the bill (*Manual* § 940)

§ 26. Postponing Effectiveness Pending Contingency

Amendments that merely postpone the effective date of the legislation to a date certain without stating a condition have been held germane. Thus, to a title of a bill establishing procedures permitting either House of Congress to disapprove an impoundment of appropriated funds by the President, an amendment delaying the effective date of that title to a day certain was held germane. *Manual* § 940. Similarly, to an amendment abolishing the Federal Energy Administration on a date certain and transferring some of its functions to other agencies at that time, an amendment delaying the termination date of that agency for one year was held germane. Deschler-Brown Ch 28 § 32.10.

An amendment may make the effectiveness of a bill subject to a condition if that condition is related to the provisions of the bill. Deschler-Brown Ch 28 § 31.33. An amendment delaying operation of a proposed amendment pending a determination of a fact is germane when the fact to be determined relates solely to the subject matter of the bill. 8 Cannon § 3029; Deschler-Brown Ch 28 § 31.18. However, an amendment is not germane if it delays the effectiveness of a bill contingent upon actions not involved in the administration of the affected program and that extend in scope beyond the authorities contained in the bill. Deschler-Brown Ch 28 § 31.1.

An amendment delaying the operation of proposed legislation pending an unrelated contingency is not germane. *Manual* § 940; 8 Cannon § 3037; Deschler-Brown Ch 28 § 31. Thus, an amendment making the implementation of Federal legislation contingent upon the enactment of unrelated State legislation is not germane. Deschler-Brown Ch 28 § 31.5. It is not germane for an amendment to render a measure contingent upon an unrelated congressional action. For example, to a bill authorizing appropriations for radio broadcasting to Cuba, an amendment prohibiting use of those funds until Congress considered a constitutional amendment mandating a balanced budget was ruled out as nongermane, imposing an unrelated contingency requiring separate congressional action on another subject. Deschler-Brown Ch 28 § 31.39. Likewise, an amendment to an appropriation bill delaying the availability of the appropriation pending an unrelated contingency—the enactment of certain revenue legislation—was held not germane. Deschler-Brown Ch 28 § 31.8.

An amendment may subject the operation of the bill to an external benchmark, so long as it does not constitute an unrelated condition. For example, an abstract fiscal standard may be used as the measure of availability of funding provided by the bill, or as the measure of applicability of a fiscal or budgetary feature of the bill. Deschler-Brown Ch 28 § 34.1.

This principle is illustrated in the following precedents:

Held Germane

Text	Amendment
Authorizing funds for elementary and secondary education. . . .	Prohibiting use of those funds ''so long as the present . . . . Commissioner of Education occupies that office'' (Deschler-Brown Ch 28 § 31.42)
Funding cost-of-living salary increase for Members. . . .	Restricting availability of those funds during months in which there is an increase in the public debt (Deschler-Brown Ch 28 § 34.1)

Held Germane—Continued

Text	Amendment
Authorizing appropriations for humanitarian and evacuation assistance to war refugees in South Vietnam. . . .	Making that authorization contingent on a report to Congress on the costs of a portion of the evacuation program (Deschler-Brown Ch 28 § 34.12)
Authorizing defense assistance to a foreign nation. . . .	Delaying that assistance until that nation's former ambassador testified before a House committee (Deschler-Brown Ch 28 § 31.33)

Held Not Germane

Text	Amendment
Extending funding for housing and urban renewal. . . .	Making such funding contingent on enactment of legislation raising additional revenue (Deschler-Brown Ch 28 § 31.11)
Appropriating funds for emergency fuel assistance. . . .	Making such funding contingent on enactment of an oil windfall profit tax (Deschler-Brown Ch 28 § 31.8)
Authorizing funds for one Federal agency. . . .	Making such funding contingent on appropriations for another Federal agency (110-1, May 2, 2007, p 11094)
Authorizing funds for construction of atomic energy facilities. . . .	Making such project contingent upon the enactment of Federal or State fair-housing measures (Deschler-Brown Ch 28 § 31.5)
Authorizing appropriations for the Arms Control and Disarmament Agency. . . .	Making such authorization contingent on the Soviet Union ceasing "to supply military articles to our enemy in Vietnam" (Deschler-Brown Ch 28 § 31.32)
Authorizing funds for foreign assistance. . . .	Making aid to a nation contingent upon the enactment of tax reform measures by that nation (Deschler-Brown Ch 28 § 31.37)

Held Not Germane—Continued

Text	Amendment
Authorizing military assistance to Israel and funds for the United Nations Emergency Force in the Middle East. . . .	Making such funds to Israel contingent on Presidential certification of the existence of a designated level of energy supplies for the U.S. (Deschler-Brown Ch 28 § 31.22)
Authorizing the development of certain military missile systems. . . .	Making expenditures contingent on the impact of U.S. grain sales on Soviet military preparedness (Deschler-Brown Ch 28 § 31.24)
Rescinding an agency's funds for motor vehicle seat belt and passive restraint *research and education*. . . .	Conditioning the availability of *all* funds pending State compliance with Federal standards for *mandatory seat belt use* (Deschler-Brown Ch 28 § 15.19)

D. Relation to Existing Law

§ 27. Amendments to Bills Amending Existing Law

The germaneness rule may provide the basis for a point of order against an amendment that is offered to a bill amending existing law. A germaneness point of order may be sustained where the proposed amendment relates to the existing law rather than to the pending bill. *Manual* § 939; 8 Cannon §§ 2916, 3045; Deschler-Brown Ch 28 § 35. Unless a bill so extensively amends existing law as to open up the entire law to amendment, the germaneness of an amendment to the bill depends upon its relationship to the subject of the bill and not to the entire law being amended. Deschler-Brown Ch 28 § 35.95. A bill amending several sections of one title of the U.S. Code does not necessarily bring the entire title under consideration so as to permit an amendment to any portion thereof. Deschler-Brown Ch 28 § 35.

Where a bill amends existing law in one narrow particular, an amendment proposing to modify such existing law in other particulars will generally be ruled out as not germane. Deschler-Brown Ch 28 § 35.65. Likewise, if a bill amending existing law relates to a single subject or has a single purpose, an amendment is not germane that proposes to modify the law further in a manner not related to the purpose of the bill. Deschler-Brown Ch 28 §§ 35.51, 41.4. Where a proposition narrowly amends one section of existing law by changing a specific program therein, that section of law is not open to a further amendment that would enlarge the scope of the pending proposition. 92-1, Dec. 8, 1971, p 45536.

To a proposition modifying a limited portion of existing law, an amendment further modifying that portion may be germane. Deschler-Brown Ch 28 § 35.19. Such an amendment may add exceptions or definitions modifying the proposition if related to the same subject. Deschler-Brown Ch 28 § 35.24. However, an amendment repealing the law is not germane. Deschler-Brown Ch 28 § 36.1.

This principle is illustrated in the following precedents:

Held Not Germane

Text	Amendment
Amending a section of title 5 of the U.S. Code granting certain rights to employees of executive agencies. . . .	Extending those rights to legislative branch employees as defined in a different section of that title (Deschler-Brown Ch 28 § 35.95)
Amending a portion of an existing law to extend the authorization for U.S. contributions to the International Monetary Fund. . . .	Amending another section of that law mandating that the total budget outlays of the Federal government shall not exceed its receipts (Deschler-Brown Ch 28 § 35.48)

§ 28. Amendments to Bills Repealing Existing Law

Where a bill repealing several sections of an existing law is pending, an amendment proposing to repeal the entire law may be germane. Where the bill seeks to repeal only one provision of an existing law, an amendment modifying that provision (rather than repealing it) also may be germane. Deschler-Brown Ch 28 § 37. On the other hand, to a bill repealing one narrow subsection of existing law, an amendment proposing a comprehensive revision of the whole law is not germane. Deschler-Brown Ch 28 § 37.7.

This principle is illustrated in the following precedents:

Held Not Germane

Text	Amendment
Repealing Chinese Exclusion Acts. . . .	Relating to immigration generally (Deschler-Brown Ch 28 § 37.6)

Held Not Germane—Continued

Text	Amendment
Repealing a narrow provision of an existing Act. . . .	Expressing congressional policy as to the pending bill *and* to the administration of the whole Act (Deschler-Brown Ch 28 § 37.9)
Repealing a narrow subsection of law relating to the order of induction of selective service registrants. . . .	Placing restrictions on the assignment of personnel to Vietnam without their consent (Deschler-Brown Ch 28 § 37.8)

§ 29. Amendments to Bills Incorporating Other Laws by Reference

A general rule of germaneness is that an amendment to a law in the jurisdiction of one committee is not germane to a bill in the jurisdiction of another committee. See § 6, supra. However, where the pending bill incorporates by reference provisions of a law from another committee and conditions the effectiveness of the bill upon actions taken pursuant to a section of that law, an amendment to alter that section of the law may be germane. Deschler-Brown Ch 28 § 4.100. Furthermore, a bill incorporating by reference procedural requirements contained in other Acts may be broad enough to permit an amendment similarly referring to, *but not directly amending*, other statutes and intending to accomplish the result sought to be effected by the portion of the bill to which offered. For example, to a bill including requirements for certification of Federal land use activities as compatible with approved State management programs and incorporating by reference certain statutory provisions, an amendment applying the procedures contained in those statutes to approval of such Federal land use programs in lieu of the certification procedures in the bill was held germane. Deschler-Brown Ch 28 § 4.100. On the other hand, to a bill citing but not amending a law on one subject, an amendment incorporating that law by reference to broaden its application to the subject of the bill is not germane. Deschler-Brown Ch 28 § 41.21.

Effect of Disclaimers

Ordinarily, the inclusion of language in a bill ''disclaiming'' any substantive effect of the bill on other provisions of law would not render germane amendments that do in fact affect that law. However, where disclaimer language in a bill is accompanied by other provisions changing a category of law cited in the disclaimer, an amendment further addressing the relationship between the bill and laws cited in the disclaimer may be germane. Deschler-Brown Ch 28 § 42.54.

§ 30. Amendments to Bills Continuing or Extending Existing Laws

A bill extending an existing law may open up the law being extended to germane amendments. Deschler-Brown Ch 28 § 39. A bill continuing and reenacting an existing law may be amended by a proposition modifying in a germane manner the provisions of the law being extended. Deschler-Brown Ch 28 § 39.28. To a bill extending an existing law in modified form, an amendment proposing further modification of the law is germane. Deschler-Brown Ch 28 § 39.19. However, while a bill ''extending existing law'' may open up the law being extended to germane amendments, a proposition that merely extends an official's authority under that law does not necessarily open up the entire law to amendment. Deschler-Brown Ch 28 § 39.27.

This principle is illustrated in the following precedents:

Held Germane

Text	Amendment
Continuing for one year the Mexican farm labor program.	Requiring a determination that reasonable efforts have been made to hire domestic workers (Deschler-Brown Ch 28 § 39.14)
Amending and extending the Elementary and Secondary Education Act. . . .	Providing that no funds in the Act be used for the transportation of students or teachers ''in order to meet provisions of'' the Civil Rights Act of 1964 (Deschler-Brown Ch 28 § 39.19)
Reenacting a law to extend the existence of the Federal Energy Administration, including the authority to conduct energy programs. . . .	Restricting the method of submitting energy action proposals to Congress (Deschler-Brown Ch 28 § 39.30)
Extending the existence of the Federal Energy Administration and authorizing appropriations for that agency. . . .	Requiring that agency to promulgate regulations to assure that the agency hearings be conducted in certain areas (Deschler-Brown Ch 28 § 39.31)

Held Not Germane

Text	Amendment
Extending the authority of the Administrator of Veterans' Affairs to establish a maximum interest rate for insured loans to veterans. . . .	Altering provisions of existing law and modifying the authority of the administrator to manage the loan program (Deschler-Brown Ch 28 §39.27)
Providing for a temporary extension of certain intelligence laws. . . .	Altering provisions of those laws on a permanent basis (110-2, Feb. 13, 2008, p 2116)
Extending the school milk program and making ''preschool programs operated as part of the school system'' eligible for benefits. . . .	Extending further such benefits to programs operated by nonprofit institutions in depressed areas (Deschler-Brown Ch 28 §39.18)

§31. Amendments Changing Law to Bills Not Changing That Law

Generally

An amendment that amends a law not contemplated in the bill under consideration and not related to the text before the House is subject to a germaneness point of order. Thus, to a bill amending one law, an amendment changing the provisions of another law is not germane. Deschler-Brown Ch 28 §42. Likewise, to a bill making appropriations for the current fiscal year, an amendment permanently changing existing law is not germane and thus is not in order, even though it tends to reduce expenditures for that year. Deschler-Brown Ch 28 §42.57. The number and variety of laws being amended by the underlying text may also affect the germaneness of an amendment changing an additional law. *Manual* §939.

The germaneness of an amendment may be affected by the adoption of other amendments that broaden the scope of the pending bill. For example, where a bill authorizing foreign military assistance was broadened by amendment to address permanent law relating to economic relations with foreign nations, an amendment to remove military and economic trade sanctions against Rhodesia was held germane to the bill as a whole in its perfected form. 95-2, Aug. 2, 1978, p 23938.

This principle is illustrated in the following precedents:

Held Not Germane

Text	Amendment
Reorganizing existing discretionary governmental authority and vesting it in a new agency. . . .	Directly changing policies in the substantive law to be administered by that agency (Deschler-Brown Ch 28 § 42.23)
Consolidating certain functions under a new agency and limiting its policy-making authority to that contained in existing law. . . .	Prescribing new policy by amending a law not amended by the bill (Deschler-Brown Ch 28 § 42.24)
Providing in part for increased salaries for Members of Congress and legislative employees. . . .	Relating to audits of financial transactions of the House and the Architect of the Capitol under another law (Deschler-Brown Ch 28 § 42.45)
Amending the Fair Labor Standards Act with respect to the effect of imports on the domestic labor market. . . .	Amending the Tariff Act of 1930 with respect to the importation of merchandise from Communist nations (Deschler-Brown Ch 28 § 42.2)
Establishing a Federal Energy Administration but not amending existing laws relating to energy conservation policy. . . .	Repealing the Emergency Daylight Saving Time Energy Conservation Act (Deschler-Brown Ch 28 § 42.21)
Regulating the importation of liquefied natural gas, but not directly amending the Natural Gas Act. . . .	Amending the Natural Gas Act to prohibit the FPC from regulating the price of natural gas at the well-head (Deschler-Brown Ch 28 § 42.20)
Amending certain Acts to provide for market adjustment and price support programs for wheat and feed grains. . . .	Amending another Act to direct the President to conduct an investigation into imports of specified agricultural products (Deschler-Brown Ch 28 § 42.11)
Changing for one year an existing law establishing price supports for several agricultural commodities. . . .	Waiving the provisions of another law relating to price supports for another agricultural commodity (Deschler-Brown Ch 28 § 42.17)
Amending several provisions of an existing law. . . .	Repealing a section of another law (*Manual* § 939)

Waivers or Repeals

An amendment repealing existing law has been held not germane to a bill not amending that law. Deschler-Brown Ch 28 § 42.21. An amendment may be subject to a point of order on the basis that it contains the language ''notwithstanding any other provision of law'' if it has the effect of waiving a statute not amended by the bill. Deschler-Brown Ch 28 § 42.17. In one such instance, the Chair noted that the waivers in the bill were waivers of a narrow class of existing laws, whereas the amendment waived various unspecified laws not within the scope of the pending measure. Deschler-Brown Ch 28 § 42.18.

E. House-Senate Relations

§ 32. Senate Germaneness Rules

In contrast to House practice, there is no general Senate rule prohibiting nongermane amendments. However, questions of germaneness of amendments to general appropriation bills are submitted to the Senate without debate under Senate rule XVI. The Chair does not rule on the question. Another rule prohibits nongermane amendments to bills after cloture has been invoked. See clause 2 of Senate rule XXII. In addition, pursuant to unanimous-consent agreements, the Senate sometimes prohibits nongermane amendments to particular bills, or may prohibit a certain class of nongermane amendments to a bill. Deschler-Brown Ch 28 § 25; see also S. Doc. 101-28. Under section 305 of the Budget Act, amendments offered in the Senate to a concurrent resolution on the budget must be germane; and under section 310, a similar restriction applies to amendments to budget reconciliation bills. *Manual* § 1127.

§ 33. Motions to Instruct Conferees

The rule that amendments must be germane applies to amendments to a motion to instruct conferees. 8 Cannon §§ 3230, 3235; Deschler-Brown Ch 28 § 28. The test of an amendment to a motion to instruct conferees is the relationship of the amendment to the subject matter of the House and Senate versions of the bill (*Manual* § 930) and not to the original motion to instruct.

Where an amendment in the nature of a substitute has been proposed by one House for the entire bill passed by the other House, provisions in either the bill or the substitute may be addressed in motions to instruct conferees. 8 Cannon § 3230.

§ 34. Senate Provisions in Conference Reports and in Amendments in Disagreement

Formerly, a Senate amendment was not subject to the point of order that it was not germane to the House bill. 8 Cannon § 3425. Today, under changes in the rules enacted in 1972, points of order may be made against nongermane Senate matter in a conference report or in a proposal to concur in a Senate amendment (with or without amendment). If sustained, separate votes may be demanded on portions of Senate amendments and conference reports containing language that would not have been germane if offered in the House. Clause 10 of rule XXII; *Manual* § 1089.

Clause 10 of rule XXII permits points of order against language in a conference report that was originally in the Senate bill or amendment and that would not have been germane if offered to the House-passed version, and permits a separate motion to reject such portion of the conference report if found nongermane. For purposes of that rule, the House-passed version, against which the Senate provisions are compared, is that version finally committed to conference, taking into consideration all amendments adopted by the House, including House amendments to Senate amendments. Deschler-Brown Ch 28 § 27.

Pursuant to clause 10 of rule XXII, where the Speaker sustains a point of order that a portion of a conference report containing a Senate amendment is not germane to the House bill, a motion to reject that portion of the conference report is in order and is subject to 40 minutes of debate. Deschler-Brown Ch 28 § 26.29.

The Member representing the conference committee recognized in opposition to a motion to reject a nongermane Senate provision pursuant to clause 10 of rule XXII, and not the proponent of the motion, has the right to close debate thereon. *Manual* § 1090. After the 40 minutes of debate permitted by that rule, it is then in order, following the disposition of the motion to reject, to make further points of order and motions to reject. If any such motion is adopted, the conference report shall be considered as rejected and the pending question shall be, in the case of a House bill with a Senate amendment, whether the House will recede from disagreement to the Senate amendment and concur therein with an amendment consisting of the portion of the conference report not rejected. Deschler-Brown Ch 28 § 26.31.

Clause 10 of rule XXII also permits points of order against nongermane Senate matter in motions to concur or concur with amendment in Senate amendments, the stage of disagreement having been reached. If such a point of order is sustained, a separate motion to reject such nongermane matter is permitted. *Manual* §§ 931, 1089. Clause 10 is not applicable to a provision contained in a motion to recede and concur with an amendment that is not contained in any form in the Senate version, the only requirement in such circumstances being that the motion as a whole be germane to the Senate amendment as a whole under the House germaneness rule. Deschler-Brown Ch 28 § 27.12.

This principle is illustrated in the following precedents:

Held Not Germane

House Bill	Senate Amendment
Continuing the operations of an executive department for one year. . . .	Prohibiting the availability of any funds appropriated for foreign military base agreements absent congressional approval (93-1, Sept. 11, 1973, pp 29243-46)
Exempting from tariff duty certain equipment and repairs for vessels operated by the United States. . . .	Extending benefits under the unemployment compensation program (Deschler-Brown Ch 28 § 26.30)
Requiring that a percentage of U.S. oil imports be carried on U.S. flag vessels. . . .	Relating to the construction of vessels with certain anti-pollution requirements (Deschler-Brown Ch 28 § 26.29)
Containing several diverse amendments to the Internal Revenue Code to provide individual and business tax credits. . . .	Authorizing appropriations for special payments to social security recipients (Deschler-Brown Ch 28 § 26.27)
Improving automotive fuel efficiency by imposing fuel economy standards upon manufacturers. . . .	Providing loan guarantees for automotive research and development (Deschler-Brown Ch 28 § 26.15)

§ 35. Amendments to Senate Amendments

An amendment offered in the House to a Senate amendment must ordinarily be germane to the particular Senate amendment to which it is offered, it not being sufficient that the amendment be germane to the provisions of the bill if the Senate amendment merely inserts new matter and does not strike House provisions. 5 Hinds § 6188; 8 Cannon § 2936; *Manual* § 931. Thus, during consideration of a Senate amendment reported in disagreement by conferees, a proposal to amend must be germane to the Senate amendment. Deschler-Brown Ch 28 § 27.35. Although a Senate amendment proposing legislation on a general appropriation bill is subject to an amendment of a similar character in the House, the requirement remains that the House amendment be germane to the Senate amendment. Deschler-Brown Ch 28 § 27.

The test of the germaneness of an amendment to an amendment contained in a motion to concur in a Senate amendment is the relationship between the offered amendment and the motion, and not the relationship between that amendment and the Senate amendment to which the motion has been offered. Deschler-Brown Ch 28 § 27.6.

The test of germaneness of an amendment in the nature of a substitute to a Senate amendment—proposed in a motion to concur therein with an amendment—is the relationship between the proposed amendment in its entirety and the Senate amendment in its entirety (and not the relationship between any one provision of the amendment and any one provision of the Senate amendment). Deschler-Brown Ch 28 §§ 27.11, 27.12.

The rule of germaneness applies to motions to recede and concur in a Senate amendment with an amendment. Such a motion must be germane to the Senate amendment. Deschler-Brown Ch 28 § 27. However, where a Senate amendment proposes only to strike language in a House bill, the test of the germaneness of a motion to recede and concur with an amendment is the relationship between the language in the motion and the provisions in the House bill proposed to be stricken by the Senate amendment. *Manual* § 931.

These principles are illustrated in the following precedents:

Held Germane

Senate Amendment	House Amendment
Appropriating funds for a Senate office building extension, providing a funding ceiling on such extension, and providing for the transfer of personnel and equipment to such extension. . . .	Reducing the appropriation and the funding ceiling, and providing that such extension upon completion meet certain personnel needs (96-1, Aug. 2, 1979, p 22007)
Containing diverse provisions relating to the organization and administration of the Federal courts, including appointment of additional district and circuit judges. . . .	Containing comparable provisions and in addition permitting courts of appeals of a certain size to establish administrative units (Deschler-Brown Ch 28 § 27.12)

Held Germane—Continued

Senate Amendment	House Amendment
Appropriating funds for termination of the civil supersonic aircraft. . . .	Appropriating funds for termination of payment of the airlines' contribution to development costs (92-1, July 29, 1971, p 28053)

Held Not Germane

Senate Amendment	House Amendment
Prohibiting use of specified funds as compensation for certain former employees. . . .	Enlarging the class of persons ineligible for such compensation (Deschler-Brown Ch 28 § 27.34)
Prohibiting use of funds in a general appropriation bill for only one basing mode for the MX missile. . . .	Authorizing appropriations for research and development of another weapons system (Deschler-Brown Ch 28 § 27.19)
Providing for payment, from the Senate contingent fund, of certain additional travel expenses incurred by Senate employees. . . .	Providing additional travel allowances to Members of the House from the House contingent fund (Deschler-Brown Ch 28 § 27.35)
Striking a provision in a general appropriation bill that precluded the use of funds therein by the Environmental Protection Agency to control air pollution by regulating parking facilities. . . .	Prohibiting use of those EPA funds temporarily to implement any plan requiring the review of *any* indirect sources of air pollution (Deschler-Brown Ch 28 § 27.14)
Appropriating funds for asbestos hazards abatement in schools. . . .	Earmarking funds for the refinancing of a recycling program of a specified city (Deschler-Brown Ch 28 § 27.1)

F. Procedural Matters; Points of Order

§ 36. In General

A point of order against an amendment to a proposition on germaneness grounds is generally treated the same way as other points of order. As noted earlier, the rule is not self-enforcing, and requires a Member to raise the point of order at the appropriate time. Deschler-Brown Ch 28 § 44. The proponent of the amendment bears the burden of proof that the amendment is germane to the underlying matter. 8 Cannon § 2995.

For more on points of order, including timeliness and debate thereon, see POINTS OF ORDER; PARLIAMENTARY INQUIRIES. For a discussion of special order of business resolutions, which may waive the germaneness rule or otherwise alter the normal tests of germaneness, see SPECIAL ORDERS OF BUSINESS.

Chapter 27
Impeachment

Research References

U.S. Const. art. I, §§ 2, 3; art. II, § 4
3 Hinds §§ 2001-2515
6 Cannon §§ 454-552
Deschler Ch 14
Manual §§ 173-176; 601-620

A. Generally

§ 1. In General; House and Senate Functions

Impeachment is a constitutional remedy to address serious offenses against the system of government. It is the first step in a remedial process—that of removal from public office and possible disqualification from holding further office. The purpose of impeachment is not punishment; rather, its function is primarily to maintain constitutional government. Deschler Ch 14 App. pp 726-728; 105-2, Dec. 19, 1998, pp 28107-9.

Impeachment proceedings have been initiated more than 60 times since the adoption of the Constitution. 3 Hinds § 2294; 6 Cannon § 498; Deschler

Ch 14 § 1. Nineteen of these cases resulted in impeachment by the House: President Andrew Johnson in 1868, Secretary of War William W. Belknap in 1876, Senator William Blount in 1797, President William J. Clinton in 1998, and 15 Federal judges. Only eight impeachments have led to Senate convictions—all of them Federal judges.

An impeachment is instituted by a written accusation, called an ''Article of Impeachment,'' which states the offense charged. The articles serve a purpose similar to that of an indictment in an ordinary criminal proceeding. *Manual* § 609.

The power of impeachment is bifurcated by the Constitution. The House is given the ''sole Power of Impeachment,'' and the Senate is given ''the sole Power to try all Impeachments.'' U.S. Const. art. I, § 2, cl. 5; § 3, cl. 6. Impeachments may be brought against the ''President, Vice President, and all civil Officers of the United States.'' Conviction of ''Treason, Bribery, or other high Crimes and Misdemeanors'' is followed by ''removal from Office'' and may include ''disqualification to hold'' further public office. U.S. Const. art. I, § 3, cl. 7; art. II, § 4.

The term ''impeach'' is used in different ways at various stages of the proceedings. A Member rises on the floor to ''impeach'' an officer in presenting a resolution or memorial. 3 Hinds § 2469. The House votes to ''impeach'' in the constitutional sense when it adopts an impeachment resolution and accompanying articles. § 8, infra. The Senate then conducts a trial on these articles and either convicts by two-thirds vote or acquits the ''impeached'' Federal official. § 9, infra.

§ 2. Who May Be Impeached

The ''President, Vice President, and all civil Officers of the United States'' are subject to removal under the impeachment clause of the Constitution. U.S. Const. art. II, § 4. A private citizen who has held no public office may not be impeached. 3 Hinds §§ 2007, 2315.

The term ''civil Officers'' in article II, section 4 of the Constitution refers to those appointed by the President under article II, section 3, clause 2. The term is broad enough to include all officers of the United States who hold their appointment from the Federal government, whether their duties be executive, administrative, or judicial, or whether their position be high or low. Impeachment—Selected Materials, Committee on the Judiciary, H. Doc. No. 93-7, Oct. 1973, p 691. On the other hand, military officers are not subject to impeachment, since they are subject to disciplinary measures according to military codes. 3 Willoughby, The Constitution (1929) § 929; 9 Hughes, Federal Practice (1931) § 7228.

A Member of Congress is not a ''civil Officer'' within the meaning of the impeachment provisions of the Constitution. 3 Hinds §§2310, 2316. The contention that a Senator was not a civil officer within the meaning of the impeachment provisions of the Constitution was sustained by the Senate in 1799. The Senate dismissed impeachment charges brought to its bar by the House, finding that an impeachment of a Senator was beyond its jurisdiction. 3 Hinds §2318; §4, infra.

Federal judges are subject to removal under the impeachment provisions of the Constitution. Of the 19 impeachments reaching the Senate, 15 have been directed at Federal judges, and in eight of these cases the Senate voted to convict: Pickering in 1803 (3 Hinds §§2319-2341); Humphreys in 1863 (3 Hinds §§2385-2397); Archbald in 1912 (6 Cannon §§498-512); Ritter in 1936 (S. Doc. No. 74-200, 1936); and Claiborne, Nixon, Hastings, and Porteous in 1986, 1988, 1989, and 2010, respectively (*Manual* §176).

Impeachment proceedings were initiated against a Member of the President's Cabinet in 1876, when impeachment charges were filed against William W. Belknap, who had been Secretary of War. The House and Senate debated the power of impeachment at length and determined that the Secretary remained amenable to impeachment and trial even after his resignation. 3 Hinds §§2007, 2467. In 1978, the House voted to table a privileged resolution impeaching Andrew Young, the United States Ambassador to the United Nations. 95-2, July 13, 1978, p 20606.

A Commissioner of the District of Columbia has been held not to be a civil officer subject to impeachment under the Constitution. 6 Cannon §548. Under section 596(a) of title 28, United States Code, an independent counsel appointed to investigate the President may be impeached. A resolution impeaching such independent counsel constitutes a question of the privileges of the House under Rule IX. *Manual* §604.

Effect of Resignation

The House and Senate have the power to impeach and try an accused official who has resigned. Deschler Ch 14 §2. It was conceded (in the Belknap impeachment proceeding described above) that a Cabinet Secretary remains amenable to impeachment and trial even after his resignation. 3 Hinds §§2317, 2318. As a practical matter, however, the resignation of an official about to be impeached generally puts an end to impeachment proceedings because the primary objective—removal from office—has been accomplished. This was the case in the impeachment proceedings begun against President Richard M. Nixon in 1974 and Judge George English in 1926. Deschler Ch 14 §§2.1, 2.2. President Nixon resigned following the decision of the Committee on the Judiciary to report to the House recommending his impeachment, and further proceedings were discontinued. 93-2, H. Rept. 93-1305, p 29361. Judge English resigned before commencement of trial by the Senate and the proceedings were discontinued at that point. 6 Cannon § 547. Judge Delahay (1873) and Judge Kent (2009) likewise resigned prior to Senate proceedings.

§ 3. Grounds for Impeachment

Generally

The Constitution defines the grounds for impeachment and conviction as "Treason, Bribery, or other high Crimes and Misdemeanors." U.S. Const. art. II, § 4. When the House determines that grounds for impeachment exist, the articles of impeachment are presented to the Senate. Any one of the articles may provide a sufficient basis or ground for conviction. Deschler Ch 14 § 3.

The phrase "high Crimes and Misdemeanors" has been interpreted broadly. The framers of the Constitution adopted the phrase from the English practice. At the time of the Constitutional Convention, the phrase "high crimes and misdemeanors" had been in use for more than 400 years in impeachment proceedings in the British Parliament. Some of these impeachments charged high treason; others charged high crimes and misdemeanors. The latter included both statutory offenses and nonstatutory offenses. Many of the charges involved abuse of official power or trust. Deschler Ch 14 App. pp 706-708.

An offense must be serious or substantial in nature to provide grounds for impeachment. This requirement flows from the language of the clause itself—"*high* Crimes and Misdemeanors." Although there is some authority to the contrary, it is generally accepted that the adjective "high" modifies "Misdemeanors" as well as "Crimes." Impeachment—Selected Materials, Committee on the Judiciary, H. Doc. No. 93-7, Oct. 1973, p 682. As to what constitutes a serious, impeachable offense, one commentator has said:

> To determine whether or not an act or a course of conduct is sufficient in law to support an impeachment, resort must be had to the eternal principles of right, applied to public propriety and civil morality. The offense must be prejudicial to the public interest and it must flow from a willful intent, or a reckless disregard of duty. . . . It may constitute an intentional violation of positive law, or it may be an official dereliction of commission or omission, a serious breach of moral obligation, or other gross impropriety of personal conduct that, in its natural consequences, tends to bring an office into contempt and disrepute.

Brown, The Impeachment of the Federal Judiciary, 26 Harv. L. Rev. 684, 703, 704 (1912).

The time when the offenses were committed is a factor to be taken into consideration. In 1973 the House declined to take any action on a request by Vice President Agnew for an investigation into allegations of impeachable offenses where the offenses were not committed during his term of office as Vice President and where the offenses were pending before the courts. 93-1, Sept. 25, 1973, p 31368.

Exactly 100 years earlier, in a case that also involved the Vice President, the Committee on the Judiciary found that Schuyler Colfax could not be impeached for an alleged offense committed before his term of office as Vice President (the alleged conduct occurring while he was Speaker). 3 Hinds §2510.

Presidential Impeachments

In 1998 the Committee on the Judiciary recommended to the House four articles of impeachment against President Clinton, two of which the House adopted. 105-2, H. Res. 611, Dec. 19, 1998, pp 28110-12. The first and third articles, which the House adopted, charged the President with providing perjurious testimony to a Federal grand jury and with obstructing justice in a Federal civil action. The second and fourth articles, which the House rejected, charged him with providing perjurious testimony in a Federal civil deposition and with abuse of power for failing to adequately respond to questions asked by the Committee on the Judiciary during the impeachment inquiry. 105-2, H. Rept. 105-830, pp 108, 118, 119, 121. President Clinton was acquitted in the Senate on both articles adopted by the House. 106-1, Feb. 12, 1999, pp 2375-79.

In 1974 the grounds for invoking the impeachment power against the President were illustrated when the House initiated an inquiry into President Nixon's conduct as a result of charges arising out of a 1972 break-in at the Democratic National Headquarters in the Watergate Office Building in Washington, DC. The Committee on the Judiciary recommended to the House three articles of impeachment against President Nixon in July 1974. The articles charged him with abuse of his Presidential powers, obstruction of justice, and contempt of Congress. Deschler Ch 14 §3.7. Before the full House voted on these articles, President Nixon resigned. His resignation terminated further action on the issue, although the articles were submitted to and accepted by the House by adoption of a resolution of "acceptance" considered under suspension of the rules rather than a resolution of impeachment. 93-2, Aug. 20, 1974, pp 29219-362.

In 1868 the House impeached President Andrew Johnson on the ground that he had violated the Tenure of Office Act by dismissing a Cabinet chief. Johnson was acquitted in the Senate. 3 Hinds §§2440, 2443.

Judicial Impeachments

Since Federal judges hold office ''during good Behaviour,'' it has been suggested that misbehavior properly defines the bounds of ''high Crimes and Misdemeanors'' or even that lack of good behavior constitutes an independent standard for impeachment. U.S. Const. art. III, § 1; 6 Cannon § 464. The more modern view, however, is that the ''good Behaviour'' clause more aptly describes judicial tenure; that is, the clause does not constitute a standard for impeachability but merely means that Federal judges hold office for life unless they are removed under some other provision of the Constitution. Under this view, the power of removal together with the appropriate standard are contained solely in the impeachment clause. Impeachment—Selected Materials, Committee on the Judiciary, H. Doc. No. 93-7, Oct. 1973, p 666.

The grounds for impeachment of Federal judges were scrutinized in 1970 during an inquiry of a special subcommittee of the Committee on the Judiciary into the conduct of Associate Justice Douglas of the Supreme Court. The report of that special subcommittee concluded that a Federal judge could be impeached for judicial conduct that is either criminal or a serious abuse of public duty, or for nonjudicial conduct that is criminal. Deschler Ch 14 § 3.13 (proceedings discontinued for lack of evidence). The committee report recommending impeachment of President Clinton also discussed judicial impeachments. 105-2, H. Rept. 105-830, pp 110-18.

§ 4. — Impeachable Misconduct

Impeachments have commonly involved charges of misconduct incompatible with the official position of the office holder. This conduct falls into three broad categories: (1) abusing or exceeding the lawful powers of the office; (2) behaving officially or personally in a manner grossly incompatible with the office; and (3) using the power of the office for an improper purpose or for personal gain. See Deschler Ch 14 App. p 719.

Abusing or Exceeding the Powers of the Office

The impeachment by the House of Senator William Blount in 1797 was based on allegations that he attempted to incite an Indian attack in order to capture certain territory for the British. He was charged with engaging in a conspiracy to compromise United States neutrality and with attempting to oust the President's lawful appointee as principal agent for Indian affairs. 3 Hinds §§ 2294-2318. Although the Senate found that it had no jurisdiction over the trial of an impeached Senator, it expelled him for having been guilty of a ''high misdemeanor, entirely inconsistent with his public trust and duty as a Senator.'' Deschler Ch 14 App. p 720.

The impeachment of President Andrew Johnson in 1868 was likewise based on allegations that he had exceeded the power of his office. Johnson was charged with violation of the Tenure of Office Act, which purported to limit the President's authority to remove members of his own Cabinet. Johnson, believing the Act unconstitutional, removed Secretary of War Stanton and was impeached by the House three days later. Johnson was acquitted in the Senate. 3 Hinds §§ 2440, 2443.

A serious abuse of the powers of the office was a charge included among the recommended articles impeaching President Nixon in 1974. The Committee on the Judiciary found that his conduct ''constituted a repeated and continuing abuse of the powers of the Presidency in disregard of the fundamental principle of the rule of law in our system of government.'' Deschler Ch 14 § 3.7.

The House adopted an article of impeachment against President Clinton alleging that he obstructed justice in the course of a Federal civil action. However, the House rejected an article of impeachment against President Clinton alleging that he engaged in conduct that resulted in abuse of his office by inadequately responding to 81 written questions posed by the Committee on the Judiciary. 105-2, H. Res. 611, Dec. 19, 1998, pp 28110-12; 105-2, H. Rept. 105-830, p 121. President Clinton was acquitted by the Senate on that article adopted by the House. 106-1, Feb. 12, 1999, p 2375-79.

Behavior Grossly Incompatible with the Office

Judge John Pickering was impeached by the House in 1803 for errors in a trial in violation of his trust and duty as a judge, and for appearing on the bench during the trial in a state of intoxication and using profane language. Pickering was convicted in the Senate and removed from office. 3 Hinds §§ 2319-2341.

Associate Supreme Court Justice Samuel Chase was impeached by the House in 1804. The House charged Chase with permitting his partisan views to influence his conduct in certain trials. His conduct was alleged to be a serious breach of his duty to judge impartially and to reflect on his competence to continue to exercise the power of the office. Chase was acquitted in the Senate. 3 Hinds §§ 2342-2363.

Judge West Humphreys was impeached by the House and convicted in the Senate in 1862 on charges that he joined the Confederacy without resigning his Federal judgeship. Judicial prejudice against Union supporters also was alleged. 3 Hinds §§ 2385-2397.

Judge Mark W. Delahay was impeached by the House in 1873 for ''personal habits,'' including intoxication and certain alleged corrupt transactions. He resigned prior to the commencement of proceedings in the Senate. 3 Hinds §§ 2504, 2505.

Judge George English was impeached by the House in 1926 for showing judicial favoritism and for failure to give impartial consideration to cases before him. It was alleged that his favoritism had created distrust of his official actions and destroyed public confidence in his court. 6 Cannon §§ 544-547. Judge English resigned before commencement of trial by the Senate, and the proceedings were discontinued.

Judge Samuel B. Kent was impeached in the House in 2009 for sexual misconduct with court employees, and for making false statements relating to such conduct to federal officials. Judge Kent resigned just after commencement of trial in the Senate, and the proceedings were discontinued. 111-1, July 22, 2009, p ____.

The House adopted an article of impeachment against President Clinton alleging that he prevented, obstructed, and impeded the administration of justice in a Federal civil action. 105-2, Dec. 19, 1998, pp 28110-12. President Clinton was acquitted by the Senate of that article of impeachment. 106-1, Feb. 12, 1999, pp 2375-79.

Using the Office for an Improper Purpose or Personal Gain

In 1826 Judge James Peck was impeached by the House for taking action against a lawyer who had publicly criticized one of his decisions, imprisoning him, and ordering his disbarment. The House charged that such conduct was unjust, arbitrary, and beyond the scope of his judicial duties. Peck was acquitted in the Senate. 3 Hinds §§ 2364-2366. Vindictive use of power also constituted an element of the charges in the articles of impeachment voted against Judge Charles Swayne in 1903. It was alleged that he maliciously and unlawfully imprisoned two lawyers and a litigant for contempt. 3 Hinds §§ 2469-2485.

Several impeachments have alleged the use of office for personal gain or the appearance of financial impropriety while in office. Secretary of War William Belknap was impeached by the House in 1876 for receiving substantial payments in return for his making of an appointment. He was acquitted in the Senate. 3 Hinds §§ 2444-2468.

The use of office for direct or indirect personal monetary gain was also involved in the impeachments of Judges Charles Swayne (1903), Robert Archbald (1912), George English (1926), Harold Louderback (1932), Halsted Ritter (1936), Samuel Kent (2009), and Thomas Porteous (2010). Judge Swayne was charged with falsifying expense accounts. Judge Archbald was charged with using his office to secure business favors from litigants and potential litigants before his court. Judges English, Louderback, and Ritter were charged with misusing their power to appoint and set the fees of bankruptcy receivers for personal profit. 3 Hinds §§2469-2485 (Swayne); 6 Cannon §§498-512 (Archbald); §§544-547 (English); §§513-524 (Louderback); 74-2, Jan. 14, 1936, p 5602 (Ritter).

In 1986 the House agreed to a resolution impeaching Federal District Judge Harry Claiborne, who had been convicted of falsifying Federal income tax returns. His final appeal was denied by the Supreme Court and he began serving his prison sentence. Because he declined to resign, however, Judge Claiborne was still receiving his judicial salary and, absent impeachment, would resume the bench on his release from prison. Consequently, a resolution of impeachment was introduced and the Committee on the Judiciary reported to the House four articles of impeachment against Judge Claiborne. The resolution was called up as a question of privilege and adopted. After trial in the Senate, Judge Claiborne was convicted on three of the four articles of impeachment and removed from office on October 9, 1986. *Manual* §176.

In the 100th Congress, the House agreed to a resolution reported from the Committee on the Judiciary impeaching Federal District Judge Alcee Hastings. The resolution specified 17 articles of impeachment, some of them addressing allegations of which the judge had been acquitted in a Federal criminal trial. 100-2, H. Res. 499, Aug. 3, 1988, p 20206. The judge was convicted in a trial before the Senate in the 101st Congress. 101-1, Oct. 20, 1989, pp 25329-35.

In 1989 the House voted to impeach Federal District Judge Walter L. Nixon, Jr., after he had been convicted on two counts of perjury before a grand jury about his relationship to a man whose son was being prosecuted for drug smuggling. The impeachment resolution charged that Judge Nixon had given false information about whether he had discussed the case with the local district attorney and attempted to influence its outcome. 101-1, May 10, 1989, p 8814. The Senate convicted Judge Nixon on two of the three articles of impeachment and removed him from office. 101-1, Nov. 3, 1989, pp 27102-4.

In 2010 the House voted to impeach Federal District Judge Thomas Porteous for engaging in corrupt financial relationships with attorneys and other court officials, knowingly making false statements in bankruptcy proceedings, and knowingly making false statements to the United States Senate and the Federal Bureau of Investigation regarding his nomination to the office of District Judge. The Senate convicted him on all four articles of impeachment and removed him from office. 111-2, Dec. 8, 2010, p ____.

Noncriminal Misconduct

In the history of impeachments under the Constitution, the most closely debated issue has been whether impeachment is limited to offenses indictable under the criminal law—or at least to offenses that constitute crimes—or whether the word ''Misdemeanors'' in the impeachment clause extends to noncriminal misconduct as well. Although the precedents are not entirely uniform, the majority clearly favor the broader definition. As stated in the Ritter impeachment, the modern view is that the provision for impeachment in the Constitution applies not only to high crimes and misdemeanors as those words were understood at common law, but also to acts that, though not defined as criminal, adversely affect the public interest. 69-1, H. Rept. 69-653, pp 9, 10.

The historical evidence establishes that the phrase ''high crimes and misdemeanors''—which over a period of centuries evolved into the English standard of impeachable conduct—had a special and distinctive meaning, and referred to a category of offenses that subverted the system of government. Deschler Ch 14 App. p 724. The American experience with impeachment likewise reflects the view that impeachable conduct need not be criminal. Of the 19 impeachments voted on by the House since 1789, at least 11 involved one or more allegations that did not charge a violation of criminal law. Deschler Ch 14 App. p 725. The impeachment of Judge Pickering in 1803 was the first such proceeding to result in conviction and was based, at least in part, on noncriminal misconduct. The first three articles involved a series of flagrant errors on the part of the judge in his conduct of a case. 3 Hinds § 2319. Similarly, in 1974, in recommending articles impeaching President Nixon, the House Committee on the Judiciary concluded that the President could be impeached not only for violations of Federal criminal statutes but also for abuse of the power of his office and for refusal to comply with proper subpoenas of the committee. Deschler Ch 14 § 3.7.

Less than one-third of all the articles the House has adopted have explicitly charged the violation of a criminal statute or used the word ''criminal'' or ''crime'' to describe the conduct alleged. Much more common in the articles are allegations that the officer has violated specific duties or an oath or seriously undermined public confidence in such officer's ability to perform his official functions. Deschler Ch 14 App. p 723.

The theory of the proponents of impeachment of President Johnson was succinctly put by one of the managers in the Senate trial:

> An impeachable high crime or misdemeanor is one in its nature or consequences subversive of some fundamental or essential principle of government or highly prejudicial to the public interest, and this may consist of a violation of the Constitution, of law, of an official oath, or of duty,

> by an act committed or omitted, or, without violating a positive law, by the abuse of discretionary powers from improper motives or for an improper purpose.

The Constitution of the United States of America—Analysis and Interpretation, p 615, Government Printing Office, 2002.

The House adopted an article of impeachment against President Clinton alleging that he gave perjurious, false, and misleading testimony to a Federal grand jury. However, the House rejected an article of impeachment against President Clinton alleging that he gave perjurious, false, and misleading written and deposed testimony in a Federal civil action. 105-2, H. Res. 611, Dec. 19, 1998, pp 28110-12. Some argued that neither allegation could be the subject of a successful criminal prosecution and thus would not be sufficient to establish an impeachable offense. 105-2, H. Rept. 105-830, p 211.

§ 5. Effect of Adjournment

An impeachment may proceed only when Congress is in session. 3 Hinds §§ 2006, 2462. However, an impeachment proceeding does not expire with adjournment. An impeachment proceeding begun in the House in one Congress may be resumed in the next Congress. 3 Hinds § 2321; 111-1, Jan. 13, 2009, p ____. An official impeached by the House in one Congress may be tried by the Senate in the next Congress. *Manual* § 620; 3 Hinds §§ 2319, 2320.

Although impeachment proceedings may continue from one Congress to the next, the authority of the managers appointed by the House expires at the end of a Congress; and managers must be reappointed when a new Congress convenes. *Manual* § 620. Managers on the part of the House are reappointed by resolution. *Manual* § 604; Deschler Ch 14 § 4.2. Thus, the articles of impeachment against Judge Alcee Hastings were presented in the Senate during the second session of the 100th Congress (100-2, Aug. 3, 1988, p 20223) but were still pending trial by the Senate in the 101st Congress, when the House reappointed managers (101-1, Jan. 3, 1989, p 84). The articles of impeachment against President Clinton were presented to the Senate after the Senate had adjourned *sine die* for the 105th Congress, and the Senate conducted the trial in the 106th Congress. *Manual* § 620.

B. Procedure in the House

§ 6. In General; Initiation and Referral of Charges

Generally

Under the modern practice, an impeachment is normally instituted by the House by the adoption of a resolution calling for a committee investigation of charges against the officer in question. This committee may, after investigation, recommend the dismissal of charges or it may recommend impeachment. Impeachment—Selected Materials, Committee on the Judiciary, H. Doc. No. 93-7, Oct. 1973, p 699. A resolution recommending impeachment is reported to the House simultaneously with the articles of impeachment setting forth the grounds for the proposed action. § 8, infra. Following the adoption of a resolution to impeach, the House appoints managers to conduct the impeachment trial in the Senate. The Senate is then informed of these facts by resolution. *Manual* § 607; Deschler Ch 14 § 9. When this resolution reaches the Senate, the Senate advises the House as to when the Senate will receive the managers appointed by the House. The managers then present themselves and the impeachment articles to the Senate, the House reserving the right to file additional articles later. *Manual* § 608a; Deschler Ch 14 §§ 10, 11.

Initiation of Charges

In most cases, impeachment proceedings in the House have been initiated either by introducing a resolution of impeachment through the hopper or by offering a resolution of impeachment on the floor as a question of the privileges of the House. *Manual* § 603; Deschler Ch 14 § 5.

In the House, various events have been credited with setting an impeachment in motion, including:

- Charges initiated by a petition from one or more citizens and referred to committee. 3 Hinds §§ 2364, 2491, 2494.
- Charges transmitted in a message from the President. 3 Hinds §§ 2294, 2319; 6 Cannon § 498.
- Charges transmitted from the legislature of a State. 3 Hinds § 2469.
- Charges arising from a grand jury investigation. 3 Hinds § 2488.
- Charges arising from an independent counsel investigation under section 595(c) of title 28, United States Code. *Manual* § 603.

In the 93d Congress, Vice President Agnew used a letter to the Speaker to attempt to initiate an investigation by the House of charges against him of possible impeachable offenses, but the House took no action on the request. *Manual* § 603.

In the 105th Congress, an independent counsel transmitted to the House under section 593 of title 28, United States Code, a communication containing evidence of alleged impeachable offenses by the President. The House adopted a privileged resolution reported by the Committee on Rules referring the communication to the Committee on the Judiciary, immediately releasing portions to the public, restricting Members' access to the communication, and restricting access to committee meetings and hearings on the communication. Later, the House adopted a privileged resolution reported by the Committee on the Judiciary authorizing an impeachment inquiry by that committee. *Manual* § 603.

Referral to Committee

Resolutions introduced through the hopper that directly call for an impeachment are referred to the Committee on the Judiciary, whereas resolutions merely calling for a committee investigation with a view toward impeachment are referred to the Committee on Rules. Deschler Ch 14 §§ 5.10, 5.11. In the 105th Congress the House adopted a privileged resolution reported by the Committee on Rules referring a communication from an independent counsel alleging certain impeachable offenses to the Committee on the Judiciary. Later, the House adopted a privileged resolution reported by the Committee on the Judiciary authorizing an impeachment inquiry by that committee. *Manual* § 603.

All impeachments to reach the Senate since 1900 have been based on resolutions reported by the Committee on the Judiciary. Before that committee's creation in 1813, impeachments were referred to a special committee for investigation. *Manual* § 603; 6 Cannon § 657.

§ 7. Committee Investigations

Committee impeachment investigations are governed by those portions of Rule XI relating to committee investigative and hearing procedures, and by any rules and special procedures adopted by the House and by the committee for the inquiry. *Manual* § 605; Deschler Ch 14 § 6.3. The House may by resolution waive or supplement a requirement of these rules in a particular case. In several recent instances, the House agreed to a resolution authorizing the counsel to the Committee on the Judiciary to take depositions of witnesses in an impeachment investigation and waiving the provision of Rule XI that requires at least two committee members to be present during the taking of such testimony. Deschler Ch 14 § 6.3; 105-2, H. Res. 581, Oct. 8, 1998, p 24679; 110-2, H. Res. 1448, Sept. 17, 2008, p 19502; 111-1, H. Res. 424, May 12, 2009, p ____. Authorities to conduct an investigation in one Congress have been "re-invigorated" in a subsequent Congress. 111-1, H. Res. 15, Jan. 13, 2009, p ____.

Under the earlier practice the committee sometimes made its inquiry *ex parte*. 3 Hinds §§ 2319, 2343, 2385. However, the modern trend is to permit the accused to testify, present witnesses, cross-examine witnesses, and be represented by counsel. 3 Hinds §§ 2445, 2470, 2471, 2501, 2518; Deschler Ch 14 § 6; 105-2, H. Rept. 105-830. Constitutionality, see § 9, infra.

Confidentiality of Material; Access

The House and the Committee on the Judiciary may adopt procedures to ensure the confidentiality of impeachment inquiry materials and to limit access to such materials. Deschler Ch 14 §§ 6.9, 15.3; 105-2, H. Res. 525, Sept. 11, 1998, pp 20020, 20021. Where a Federal court subpoenas certain evidence gathered by the committee in an impeachment inquiry, the House may adopt a resolution granting such limited access to the evidence as will not violate the privileges of the House or its sole power of impeachment under the Constitution. Deschler Ch 14 § 6.13.

Subcommittee Investigations

An investigative subcommittee charged with an impeachment inquiry is limited to the powers expressly authorized by the House or by the full committee. Deschler Ch 14 § 6.11; 105-2, H. Res. 581, Oct. 8, 1998, p 24679. After completing its investigation, the subcommittee ordinarily submits recommendations to the full committee as to whether impeachment is warranted. See, *e.g.*, Final Report of the Special Subcommittee on H. Res. 920 of the Committee on the Judiciary, 91-2, committee print, Sept. 17, 1970.

Form

For forms of resolutions authorizing an investigation of the sufficiency of grounds for impeachment and conferring subpoena power and authority to take testimony, see Deschler Ch 14 § 6.

§ 8. Consideration in the House; Voting

Generally

The respondent in an impeachment proceeding is impeached by the adoption of the House of articles of impeachment. Only a majority vote is necessary, whereas a two-thirds vote of Members present is required in the Senate for conviction and removal. U.S. Const. art. I, § 3; Impeachment—Selected Materials, Committee on the Judiciary, H. Doc. No. 93-7, Oct. 1973, p 700. In this regard, as is the usual practice, the committee's recommendations as reported in the resolution are not binding on the House until they are adopted. In 1933 the House voted to impeach Judge Harold Louderback, even though the Committee on the Judiciary found insufficient grounds to warrant impeachment. 6 Cannon § 514.

Impeachment Propositions as Privileged

A resolution impeaching an officer is highly privileged under the Constitution and therefore supersedes other pending business, including an election contest. *Manual* § 604; 3 Hinds §§ 2045-2048, 2581; 6 Cannon § 468. Such a resolution, if reported, may be considered immediately in the House as a question of privilege. It is, therefore, not subject to the three-day layover requirement of rule XIII. *Manual* § 604. It does not lose its privilege from the fact that a similar proposition has been considered previously during the same session. 3 Hinds § 2408. However, a resolution offered from the floor simply proposing an investigation is not privileged, even though impeachment may be a possible consequence. 3 Hinds §§ 2050, 2546; 6 Cannon § 463.

Although charges or resolutions of impeachment are privileged, they cannot be presented while another Member has the floor unless yielded to for that purpose. Deschler Ch 14 § 5.2. A resolution of impeachment offered from the floor by a Member (other than the Majority or Minority Leader) is not privileged for immediate consideration because it is subject to the notice requirement of rule IX. *Manual* § 699.

A committee to which resolutions of impeachment have been referred may report and call up as privileged resolutions incidental to the consideration of the impeachment question. *Manual* § 604; Deschler Ch 14 § 5.8. If, however, such a resolution is offered on the floor by a Member on such Member's own initiative and not reported from the committee to which the impeachment has been referred, it is not privileged for immediate consideration because it is subject to the notice requirement of rule IX. See *Manual* § 699.

Propositions incidental to an ongoing impeachment proceeding taken up as privileged (3 Hinds § 2400) have included:

- Reports relating to the investigation (3 Hinds § 2402; Deschler Ch 14 § 8.2).
- Resolutions providing for the selection of managers (6 Cannon § 517).
- Propositions to abate an impeachment proceeding (6 Cannon § 514).
- Proposals to confer subpoena authority or to provide funding for the investigation (*Manual* § 604; 6 Cannon § 549).
- Resolutions authorizing depositions by committee counsel (*Manual* § 604).

Following adoption of the articles of impeachment, the House adopts resolutions appointing managers to present the articles before the Senate, notifying the Senate of the adoption of articles and appointment of managers, and authorizing the managers to prepare for and to conduct the trial in the Senate. *Manual* § 607; 6 Cannon §§ 499, 500, 514, 517. These privileged incidental resolutions may be merged into a single indivisible privileged resolution. *Manual* § 607.

On several occasions the Committee on the Judiciary, having been referred a question of impeachment, reported a recommendation that impeachment was not warranted and, thereafter, called up the report as a question of privilege. Deschler Ch 14 § 1.3. Under section 596(a) of title 28, United States Code, an independent counsel appointed to investigate the President may be impeached; and a resolution impeaching such independent counsel constitutes a question of the privileges of the House under rule IX. *Manual* § 604.

Debate; Motions

Propositions of impeachment are considered under the general rules of the House applicable to other simple House resolutions, unless the House otherwise provides by special order of business. Deschler Ch 14 § 8; 105-2, Dec. 18, 1998, pp 27846, 27847. Since 1912, the House has considered the resolution together with the articles of impeachment. Deschler Ch 14 § 8.2. The House may consider the resolution and articles under a unanimous-consent agreement fixing and controlling the time for debate. Deschler Ch 14 §§ 8.1, 8.4; 105-2, Dec. 18, 1998, pp 27846, 27847. The motion for the previous question and the motion to recommit are applicable, and a separate vote may be demanded on each article of impeachment contained in the resolution. *Manual* § 606a; Deschler Ch 14 §§ 8.8-8.10. The resolution also is subject to a motion to lay on the table before debate thereon. Deschler-Brown Ch 29 § 1.15.

A wide range of debate is permitted on impeachment proposals, and a Member may refer to the political, social, and even the familial background of the accused. Deschler Ch 14 § 8.5. However, Members must abstain from language personally offensive. *Manual* § 370. Furthermore, Members must abstain from references to the personal conduct of sitting Members of the House or Senate. *Manual* § 370.

To a privileged resolution of impeachment, an amendment in the motion to recommit proposing instead to censure (which is not privileged) was held not germane. *Manual* § 604.

C. Procedure in the Senate

§ 9. In General

The sole power to try impeachments is vested in the Senate under the Constitution. U.S. Const. art. I, § 3, cl. 6. On the day of the trial, the Senate resolves itself into a court for the trial of the impeachment. Deschler Ch 14 § 11.5. The President of the Senate presides over the trial, except in the case of the impeachment of the President of the United States or the Vice President, in which case the Chief Justice presides. Deschler Ch 14 § 11. Upon organization of the court, the managers appear and the trial of the case proceeds. In the later practice, the resolution and articles of impeachment have been considered together and exhibited simultaneously in the Senate by the House managers. 6 Cannon §§ 501, 515; Deschler Ch 14 § 11. Objections to the articles of impeachment on the ground that they duplicate and accumulate separate offenses have been overruled. Deschler Ch 14 §§ 3.4, 13.6.

For precedents relating to the conduct of Senate impeachments, see S. Doc. 93-102, ''Procedure and Guidelines for Impeachment Trials in the United States Senate.'' For a detailed description of the impeachment trial against President Clinton, see *Manual* § 608a.

The presentation of the evidence follows a traditional sequence. The evidence against the accused is first presented by the managers. Evidence in defense is then presented by the accused, and the concluding evidence is presented by the managers. The accused is permitted to testify in answer to the charges contained in the articles. 6 Cannon §§ 511, 524; Deschler Ch 14 § 12.11. Counsel are permitted to appear, to be heard, to argue on preliminary and interlocutory questions, to deliver opening and final arguments, to submit motions, and to present evidence and examine and cross-examine witnesses. Deschler Ch 14 § 12. House counsel did not participate in the trial of President Clinton.

The use of a Senate committee in judicial impeachment proceedings does not violate any constitutional rights or offend fundamental notions of justice. *Hastings* v. *United States Senate, Impeachment Trial Committee*, 716 F. Supp. 38 (D.D.C. 1989). In one recent case, the court denied the claim of a former Federal judge that conviction voted by the Senate on two articles of impeachment adopted by the House was void because the judge was not afforded trial before the ''full'' Senate, rather than before a Senate committee. The court ruled that the Senate's denial of the former judge's motion for hearing before the full Senate, while according him the opportunity to present and cross-examine witnesses before the 12-member committee, and an opportunity to argue both personally and by counsel before the full Senate, did not make the controversy justiciable or the claim meritorious. *Nixon* v. *United States*, 744 F. Supp. 9 (D.D.C. 1990), *aff'd* 938 F.2d 239 (D.C. Cir. 1991), *aff'd* 506 U.S. 224 (1993).

At the conclusion of the evidence, there is argument, followed by deliberation by the Senate in executive session and a vote in open session. Deschler Ch 14 § 13. Before the vote, the proceedings may be dismissed in the Senate on the advice of the House managers. Deschler Ch 14 § 2.2.

§ 10. Voting and Judgment

Under the Constitution, a two-thirds vote of Senators present is required to convict an accused on an article of impeachment. The articles are voted on separately under the Senate rules. U.S. Const. art. I, § 3, cl. 6; Deschler Ch 14 § 13. The yeas and nays are taken on each article. 3 Hinds §§ 2098, 2339. In some instances, the Senate has adopted an order to provide a method of voting and putting the question separately and successively on each article. 6 Cannon § 524; Deschler Ch 14 § 13.2.

The Constitution provides for removal from office on conviction and also allows the further judgment of disqualification from holding further office. U.S. Const. art. I, § 3, cl. 7. No vote is required on removal following conviction, since removal follows automatically from conviction under this constitutional provision. Deschler Ch 14 § 13.9. However, the further judgment of disqualification from holding future office requires a majority vote. Deschler Ch 14 § 13.10. The Senate has held that a question on removal and disqualification is divisible. 3 Hinds § 2397; 6 Cannon § 512.

The impeachment and removal from office of a Federal District Judge did not necessarily disqualify him from holding office as a Member of the House, absent any specific action taken by the Senate to disqualify him from future Federal office. *Waggoner* v. *Hastings,* 816 F. Supp. 716 (S.D. Fla. 1993).

Chapter 28
Journal

Research References
U.S. Const. art. I, § 5
4 Hinds §§ 2726-2883
6 Cannon §§ 623-637
Deschler Ch 5 §§ 8-14
Manual §§ 68-74a, 582, 583, 621, 902

§ 1. Generally; Publication

The Journal is a record of the proceedings of each legislative day in the House. The Journal—and not the *Congressional Record*—is the official record of the proceedings of the House. *Manual* § 582; 4 Hinds § 2727. Certified copies thereof are admissible in judicial proceedings. 28 USC § 1736.

The Constitution requires the House to keep a Journal and publish it excepting such matters as may require secrecy. U.S. Const. art. I, § 5. The purpose of this constitutional requirement is to ensure that the proceedings of the House be a matter of public record. Deschler Ch 5 § 8.

§ 2. Matters Entered in the Journal

The content of the Journal is governed by the Constitution, by statute, and by the rules and practices of the House. Deschler Ch 5 § 10. The Constitution sets forth the general requirement that the ''proceedings'' of the House be kept in the Journal. U.S. Const. art. I, § 5; *Manual* § 68. It further specifies that the Journal reflect votes taken by the yeas and nays, as well as veto messages from the President. U.S. Const. art. I, § 7. Since such matters are always entered in the Journal, no motion or request to that effect is necessary. § 3, infra; Deschler Ch 5 § 10.4. Except as limited by these constitutional requirements, the House has the discretion to determine the content and format of its Journal, and it controls the extent to which House business is particularized therein. Deschler Ch 5 § 10.

Exclusions

The Journal records House actions and proceedings. It is not a verbatim transcript. Deschler Ch 5 §§ 10.2, 10.3. It does not include:

- The rationale for, or all the circumstances attending, House action. 4 Hinds §§ 2811, 2812.
- Verbatim accounts of debate and special-order speeches. Deschler Ch 5 § 10.3.
- The deliberations of the Committee of the Whole, except for recorded votes.
- Unanimous-consent requests that meet with objection. Deschler Ch 5 § 10.2.
- Motions that are not entertained. 4 Hinds §§ 2813, 2844.
- Parliamentary inquiries. 4 Hinds § 2842.

Inclusions

Proceedings that are reflected in the Journal include:

- Public bills, resolutions, and documents introduced and referred under the rules, by number, title, and committee of reference. *Manual* § 816.
- Private bills, petitions, and memorials introduced and referred, with the exception of those measures of obscene or insulting character. *Manual* § 818.
- The name of the Member introducing the measure, together with the words ''by request,'' if appropriate. Deschler Ch 5 § 10.7.
- Special orders of business providing for the consideration of a measure.
- The disposition of measures called up for consideration in the House or Committee of the Whole.
- Questions of order arising during the proceedings of the House. *Manual* § 647.
- Reports of committees delivered to the Clerk for printing and reference, by title or subject. *Manual* § 831.
- Motions entertained by the Speaker—including motions to amend—unless withdrawn on the same day. *Manual* §§ 580, 902.
- Motions to discharge when signed by the requisite number. *Manual* § 892.
- The discharge of the Committee of the Whole from the further consideration of a bill. Deschler Ch 5 § 10.9.

- Presentation of conference reports and the disposition thereof. *Manual* § 542.
- Messages from the Senate or from the President, including veto messages. U.S. Const. art. I, § 7; *Manual* § 815.
- Unanimous-consent requests agreed to by the House, and action taken pursuant thereto.
- The names of Members managing debate in the House under a special order of business and the time allocated therefor.
- Expungements from the *Congressional Record* ordered by the House. Deschler Ch 5 § 10.10.
- Disciplinary censure of a Member pursuant to order of the House. 2 Hinds § 1251.
- The time of adjournment. *Manual* § 647.
- Announcements by the Speaker of the whole number of the House.

§ 3. —Votes and Quorum Calls

The Constitution requires that votes taken by the yeas and nays be entered in the Journal. U.S. Const. art. I, § 5. The Journal also records the result of other votes and states in general terms the subject of those votes. 4 Hinds § 2804. The Journal also discloses:

- The names of those Members voting on each side of the question, as well as those not voting, when a recorded vote is taken pursuant to rule XX. *Manual* § 1014.
- The names of those Members recorded on a quorum call taken pursuant to clause 2 of rule XX. *Manual* § 1014.
- The names of those Members recorded by tellers when the Speaker directs a vote be taken by this procedure in lieu of the electronic system. *Manual* § 1019.
- The names of those Members voluntarily appearing to be recorded as present when a call of the House is conducted under clause 5 of rule XX. *Manual* § 1021.
- The names of those Members recorded as absent after a quorum call. *Manual* § 1019.
- The names of those present sufficient to establish a quorum. *Manual* § 1020.

§ 4. Reading and Approval

Pursuant to clause 1 of rule I, the Speaker is authorized to announce the approval of the Journal. The Speaker's approval of the Journal is deemed agreed to subject to a vote on demand of any Member. *Manual* § 621.

SPEAKER: The Chair has examined the Journal of the last day's proceedings and announces to the House [his] [her] approval thereof. Pursuant to clause 1 of rule I, the Journal stands approved.

MEMBER: M__. Speaker, pursuant to clause 1 of rule I, I demand a vote on agreeing to the Speaker's approval of the Journal.

SPEAKER: The question is on agreeing to the Speaker's approval of the Journal. Those in favor will say "Aye," those opposed "No." The "____ " have it.

MEMBER: M__. Speaker, I ask for the Yeas and Nays . . . [or] . . . I object to the vote on the ground that a quorum is not present and make a point of order that a quorum is not present.

Since the approval of the Journal is legislative business and is in order only in legislative sessions, it is not in order when the House has precluded *any* legislative business during a pro forma session. 96-2, Jan. 7, 1980, p 25. By unanimous consent, the House has also precluded the approval of the Journal during morning-hour debates.

At one time, the reading of the Journal of each legislative day was mandatory and could be dispensed with only by unanimous consent or under suspension of the rules. 4 Hinds § 2747; 6 Cannon § 625. Today, however, the Journal is considered as read after the Speaker's approval thereof. *Manual* § 621. However, if the Speaker's approval is disagreed to, clause 1 of rule I authorizes one motion that the Journal be read. § 6, infra. When the reading is ordered, a motion to amend the Journal is in order after the reading is completed. § 9, infra.

The Speaker's announcement of the approval of the Journal no longer requires the presence of a quorum. *Manual* § 621. However, if a Member objects to a vote on the question of approval, reading, or amendment of the Journal on the grounds that a quorum is not present, and a quorum is not present, a record vote is automatic. Clause 6(a) of rule XX. That vote may be postponed to a designated place within the same legislative day under clause 8(a) of rule XX. The vote may not be reconsidered under clause 1 of rule I.

Since the Journal is the official record of the proceedings of the House, its approval is not subject to the requirement that it correspond with the *Congressional Record.* Deschler Ch 5 § 14.2. The Journal is controlling in the event of a discrepancy between the Journal and the *Record.* Deschler Ch 5 § 8.1. There should be no delay in the approval of the Journal merely because its description of an action taken is inconsistent with the description of the same matter in the *Record.* Deschler Ch 5 § 14.2. The reading of the Journal may not be interrupted by a request to correct the *Record.* Deschler Ch 5 § 12.23.

§ 5. —Precedence; Interruptions

When the House convenes for a new legislative day, the approval of the Journal is the first order of business after the daily prayer, even if it is the second legislative day on the same calendar day. *Manual* § 869. It follows that the transaction of House business, however highly privileged, is not in order before such approval. Deschler Ch 21 § 2.12. Thus, the approval of the Journal takes precedence over reports from the Committee on Rules, as well as the presentation of conference reports. *Manual* § 1077; 6 Cannon § 630; Deschler Ch 5 § 12.2. Similarly, motions incident to the approval of the Journal, such as a motion to amend it, take precedence over motions relating to the consideration of bills. Deschler Ch 5 § 18.8. However, certain procedural matters are permitted to intervene even though the approval of the Journal is pending. They include:

- Simple motions to adjourn. Deschler Ch 5 § 12.3.
- Administration of the oath to a Member-elect. Deschler Ch 5 § 12.5.
- Parliamentary inquiries. Deschler Ch 5 § 12.15.
- The reception of messages from the Senate (Deschler Ch 5 § 12.12) or the President (Deschler Ch 5 § 12.20).
- Questions of privilege affecting the House collectively. 2 Hinds § 1630.
- Arraignments of impeachment. 6 Cannon § 469.

The House may by unanimous consent specifically authorize that certain proceedings be taken up prior to the Journal, or the Speaker may declare a short recess under clause 12 of rule I. Deschler Ch 5 § 12.8. The Speaker has the discretion to entertain unanimous-consent requests made before the taking up of the Journal, but may decline to do so if a reading thereof is pending. Deschler Ch 5 §§ 12.9, 12.11.

Where the House adjourns on consecutive days without having approved the Journal of the previous day's proceedings, the Speaker puts each question *de novo* in chronological order as the first order of business after the daily prayer on the subsequent day. *Manual* § 621.

§ 6. Motion That the Journal Be Read

If the Speaker's approval of the Journal is disagreed to under clause 1 of rule I, one motion that the Journal be read is in order:

MEMBER: M__. Speaker, I move that the Journal be read.

SPEAKER: The question is, shall the Journal be read?

The motion is privileged but not debatable and may not be reconsidered. *Manual* § 621; Deschler-Brown Ch 29 § 6.38.

§ 7. Reading Practices and Customs

Journal readings are conducted in accordance with the customs of the House. Deschler Ch 5 § 11.1. When the Clerk reads the Journal for the previous day, the Clerk omits such matters as the names of Members responding to record votes and the texts of messages received. The reading of the Journal by the Clerk may be terminated by unanimous consent. Deschler Ch 5 § 11; 101-2, Mar. 19, 1990, p 4488. It also may be suspended temporarily or waived in the event of disorder on the floor or pending a discussion of the validity of the previous day's adjournment. 2 Hinds § 1630; 4 Hinds § 2759. Members may, however, demand that the Journal be read in full. Deschler Ch 5 § 11.3.

§ 8. Motion to Approve

A motion to approve the Journal is ordinarily unnecessary under the modern practice of the House, because the Speaker is authorized under clause 1 of rule I to examine it and announce approval thereof. However, the Speaker's approval may be put to a vote on demand of a Member. *Manual* § 621. If the Speaker's approval is disagreed to, and a reading of the Journal is completed, a motion that the Journal be approved as read may be entertained:

> MEMBER [*after the Clerk has concluded the reading of the Journal*]: M__. Speaker, I move that the Journal as read stand approved.
>
> SPEAKER: The question is, shall the Journal of the last day's proceedings stand approved?

If the motion to approve is adopted by the House, further motions incident to the reading or correction of the Journal are out of order. If the motion to approve is rejected by the House, the Journal is subject to amendment unless the previous question is ordered. § 9, infra.

The motion to approve the Journal as read should be made when the Clerk completes the reading, but the Speaker may entertain such a motion, even though it interrupts the reading, in the absence of a timely objection thereto. Deschler Ch 5 §§ 14.3-14.6.

The motion to approve is debatable until the previous question is ordered on that motion.

The motion to approve may be disposed of by the adoption of a motion to lay on the table, even though the previous question has been demanded on the motion to approve. Deschler Ch 5 § 14.8. In such cases the motion to table the motion to approve is entertained first. Deschler Ch 5 § 14.8.

§9. Amendments and Corrections

Errors or omissions in the previous day's Journal may be corrected by motion or by unanimous consent:

> MEMBER [*after obtaining recognition*]: M__. Speaker, I move to amend the Journal by inserting [*or by striking or by striking and inserting*].

The Member offering the motion is recognized under the hour rule. *Manual* §621. The motion to amend the Journal is in order after the Journal has been read. The motion to amend is not in order after the approval of the Journal by the House. The motion to amend takes precedence over the motion to approve but will not be admitted after the previous question on the motion to approve has been demanded. *Manual* §621; Deschler Ch 5 §§13.2, 13.3.

Matters extraneous to the Journal, such as an expression of an opinion by a Member as to a ruling made by the Chair on the previous legislative day, may not be offered by way of the motion to amend. 4 Hinds §2848.

The motion to amend is applicable only to the Journal of the previous day. Corrections relating to a Journal of a *prior* legislative day are made by unanimous consent. Deschler Ch 5 §13.

An amendment to the Journal, such as a motion to expunge a portion thereof, should not be used as a substitute for a motion to reconsider. 4 Hinds §2790. However, the House may decide what constitutes its proceedings, even to the extent of omitting things actually done or of recording things not done. *Manual* §71; 4 Hinds §2784. None of the rulings on permissible amendments to correct the Journal had the effect of collaterally changing the tabling of a motion to reconsider. *Manual* §71.

Chapter 29
Lay on the Table

Research References
5 Hinds §§ 5389-5442
8 Cannon §§ 2649-2660
Deschler Ch 23 §§ 9-13
Manual §§ 445, 911, 914

§ 1. In General; Effect

The motion to table (or, under the more formal terminology of clause 4 of rule XVI, to "lay on the table") is used to summarily and adversely dispose of a proposition pending in the House. *Manual* § 914; Deschler Ch 23 § 9.1. The table referred to in rule XVI is the Clerk's table, not the Speaker's table. 5 Hinds § 5389 (note).

The language "to lay on the table"—to the extent that it implies that the tabled matter is only temporarily in abeyance—is misleading. The motion is not used simply to put aside a pending matter. The action of the House in adopting the motion to table a proposition is equivalent to a final adverse disposition thereof, and does not merely represent a refusal to consider it. Deschler Ch 23 § 9.1; 95-2, Aug. 15, 1978, p 26204. In this respect the House practice differs from general parliamentary usage, which permits the use of the motion to temporarily suspend consideration of a matter. Under the modern practice in the House, a tabling action is ordinarily as much a final adverse decision as a negative vote on the passage of a bill. 5 Hinds § 6540 (note). With few exceptions, matters laid on the table may be taken therefrom only by unanimous consent or by a motion to suspend the rules. § 8, infra. The pending proposition being disposed of finally and adversely, the adoption of the motion may have the effect of depriving a Member of the right to debate a proposition previously offered. Deschler Ch 23 § 9.2.

If the House rejects the motion to table a proposition, the proposition is before the House for disposition. Deschler Ch 23 §§ 9.19, 12.3. The rejection of a motion to lay on the table does not constitute a "decision" on the underlying proposition; thus, withdrawal of the proposition after such rejection is permissible. 103-2, Mar. 17, 1994, pp 5402, 5403.

§ 2. When in Order

The motion to table is in order only in the House and not in the Committee of the Whole. 4 Hinds §§ 4719, 4720; 8 Cannon §§ 2330, 2556a; Deschler Ch 23 §§ 9.29, 9.30. It does not apply to motions to go into the Committee of the Whole. 6 Cannon § 726. It is not applicable to propositions that are not debatable or amendable, except a motion to discharge a resolution of inquiry. *Manual* § 914; 5 Hinds § 5407.

A motion to table a proposition is in order after the proposition is called up for consideration but before debate thereon. 95-2, July 13, 1978, p 20606; 98-2, Oct. 4, 1984, p 30042. The motion is in order before the Member entitled to prior recognition for debate on the pending proposition has begun debate. 5 Hinds §§ 5393-5395; 6 Cannon § 412; 8 Cannon § 2649. The motion comes too late after the Chair has put the question on the pending proposition and asked for a vote. 96-1, Sept. 20, 1979, p 25512; *cf.* 109-2, June 22, 2006, pp 12298, 12299. The motion is in order after the previous question has been moved on the pending proposition but may not be made after the previous question has been ordered or after the yeas and nays have been ordered thereon. 5 Hinds §§ 5408, 5415-5422; 8 Cannon § 2655; Deschler Ch 23 § 9.

§ 3. Precedence

Generally

Under the rule, the motion to table is preferential. Deschler Ch 23 §§ 9, 11.2. It yields to the motion to adjourn and to the question of consideration. *Manual* § 911; 5 Hinds § 4943; Deschler Ch 23 § 9. However, it enjoys precedence over the motions for the previous question, to postpone, to refer, and to amend. Clause 4 of rule XVI; *Manual* § 911. A motion to table a measure is thus of higher privilege than a motion to refer the measure to a committee. 5 Hinds § 5303; Deschler Ch 23 § 12.5.

As Related to the Motion for the Previous Question

Pending the ordering of the previous question on a proposition that is under debate, the motion to table the proposition is preferential and is voted on first. *Manual* §914; Deschler Ch 23 §§9.11, 12.1. Although a motion to table is not in order after the previous question has been ordered on a pending proposition, if the previous question is voted down, the motion to table again becomes in order and is preferential. 5 Hinds §§5415-5422; Deschler Ch 23 §§9.21, 12.2.

§4. Application to Particular Propositions

Generally; Bills and Resolutions

The motion to table has been held specifically applicable to:

- A House bill. 5 Hinds §5426.
- A House bill with Senate amendments. 5 Hinds §6140.
- A vetoed bill. 4 Hinds §3549.
- A House resolution and an amendment thereto. 5 Hinds §6139.
- A series of resolutions on a particular subject. 5 Hinds §6138.
- A privileged resolution. 95-2, July 13, 1978, p 20606.
- A resolution proposing an impeachment or authorizing an impeachment investigation. 6 Cannon §541; Deschler Ch 23 §9.14.
- A resolution raising a question of the privileges of the House. 6 Cannon §560; Deschler Ch 23 §9.25.
- A resolution to expel a Member. 94-2, Oct. 1, 1976, p 35111.
- A resolution establishing a select committee. Deschler Ch 23 §9.22.
- A resolution of inquiry adversely reported from committee. Deschler Ch 23 §9.17.
- A concurrent resolution providing for adjournment *sine die*. Deschler Ch 23 §9.10.
- An appeal from a decision of the Speaker. 8 Cannon §3453; Deschler Ch 23 §9.3.
- A privileged resolution from a party caucus or conference electing Members to committees. *Manual* §914.

Special Orders of Business

Special orders of business reported from the Committee on Rules and called up under clause 5 of rule XIII are not subject to the motion to table, as clause 6 of rule XIII prohibits dilatory motions. *Manual* §§857, 914. However, after rejection of the previous question, the motion to table has been applied to a resolution providing a special order of business. Deschler Ch 23 §9.23.

The motion to table may not be applied to a resolution providing a special order of business if the resolution is before the House under the operation of the discharge rule, because such rule prohibits such intervening motion. Deschler Ch 23 § 9.28.

Conference Reports

In the later practice, the motion to table has not been applied to conference reports because this would carry the entire bill and amendments of the other House to the table and would leave no opportunity for the House and Senate to have a second conference. *Manual* § 914; 5 Hinds §§ 6539, 6540.

§ 5. Application to Particular Motions

The motion to table is applicable to debatable motions for the disposal of another matter, such as a motion to refer or a motion to recede and concur in a Senate amendment in disagreement. *Manual* § 914; 5 Hinds § 5433. The motion has been held specifically applicable to:

- A motion to postpone to a day certain. 8 Cannon §§ 2654, 2657.
- A motion to rerefer a bill to a committee. Deschler Ch 23 § 9.12.
- A motion to instruct conferees. Deschler Ch 23 §§ 9.7, 9.8.
- A motion to reconsider a vote. 8 Cannon §§ 2652, 2659; 95-2, Apr. 20, 1978, p 10990.
- A motion to discharge a resolution of inquiry (even though not debatable). 5 Hinds § 5407.
- A motion for a secret session pursuant to clause 9 of rule XVII (even though not debatable). 110-1, May 10, 2007, p 12177.

The motion to table may not be applied to a motion relating to the order of business or to any motion that is neither debatable nor amendable. Deschler Ch 23 §§ 9.26, 9.27. The motion is inapplicable to:

- A motion for the previous question. 5 Hinds §§ 5410, 5411.
- A motion to dispose of measures on which the previous question has been ordered. 8 Cannon §§ 2653, 2655.
- A motion to recommit made after the ordering of the previous question, including a debatable motion to recommit with instructions. *Manual* § 1002a; 5 Hinds §§ 5412-5414; 8 Cannon §§ 2653, 2655.
- A motion to dispense with further proceedings under a call of the House. Deschler Ch 23 §§ 9.26, 12.4.
- A motion to go into the Committee of the Whole. 5 Hinds § 5404; 6 Cannon § 726.
- A motion limiting the time for debate. 5 Hinds § 5403.
- A motion to suspend the rules. *Manual* § 886; 5 Hinds §§ 5405, 5406; Deschler Ch 23 § 9.
- A motion that when the House adjourn it stand adjourned until a day and time certain. *Manual* § 914.
- A motion to adjourn. *Manual* § 912.

The motion to table may not be applied to a motion to discharge a committee under clause 2 of rule XV unless the proposition before the committee is a vetoed bill or a resolution of inquiry. *Manual* § 914; 5 Hinds § 5407; 6 Cannon § 415; Deschler Ch 23 §§ 9.15, 9.16.

§ 6. Offering the Motion; Debate and Disposition

Generally; Debate

The motion to table, although customarily made orally from the floor, is subject to a timely demand that it be in writing. Deschler Ch 23 § 10.1.

MEMBER: M__. Speaker, I move that the House lay the ________ [*proposition*] on the table.

The motion to table is not debatable. Clause 4 of rule XVI; *Manual* § 914; 5 Hinds § 5301; 6 Cannon § 412; 8 Cannon § 2465; Deschler Ch 23 § 9.6. However, debate may be permitted by unanimous consent. 98-2, Oct. 4, 1984, p 30042.

Disposition of Motion

It has been established that the motion to table:

- May not be amended. *Manual* § 914; 5 Hinds § 5754.
- May not be divided for a vote. 5 Hinds §§ 6138-6140.
- May be reconsidered pursuant to motion. 5 Hinds §§ 5628, 5629, 6288; 8 Cannon § 2785.
- May be repeated after intervening business, but a call of the House alone is not considered sufficient intervening business. 5 Hinds §§ 5398-5401.

§ 7. Collateral Matters Carried to the Table

A bill or other proposition may be carried to the table when the House votes to table a proposal that is closely related thereto. Thus, when a proposed amendment to a pending measure is tabled, the pending measure also goes to the table. 5 Hinds §§ 5423, 5424; 8 Cannon § 2656. This rule is applied even where a Senate amendment to a House bill is tabled. 5 Hinds § 5424. The tabling of a bill has been held to result in the tabling of a pending motion to print the bill. 5 Hinds § 5426. The tabling of a proposal, however, will not result in the tabling of a connected matter unless it is directly and intimately related thereto. 8 Cannon § 2658. It has been held, for example, that:

- The tabling of an amendment to the Journal does not carry the Journal to the table. 5 Hinds §§ 5435, 5436.
- The tabling of a proposition for adverse disposition of a pending matter does not carry to the table the matter proposed to be disposed of. 8 Cannon § 2660.
- The tabling of a motion to reconsider a vote does not carry with it the proposition voted on. 8 Cannon §§ 2652, 2659.
- The tabling of a motion to instruct conferees does not carry with it the bill in disagreement. 8 Cannon § 2658.
- The tabling of a resolution providing for the termination of impeachment proceedings does not carry with it such proceedings. 6 Cannon § 538.
- The tabling of a preamble does not carry with it accompanying resolutions already agreed to. 5 Hinds § 5430.
- The tabling of a resolution does not take with it a connected resolution already agreed to. 5 Hinds § 5428.
- The tabling of a motion to receive a petition does not carry the petition with it. 5 Hinds §§ 5431-5433.
- The tabling of an appeal from a decision of the Speaker on a question of order does not carry with it the matter that was pending when the question of order arose. 5 Hinds § 5434.
- The tabling of a motion to postpone consideration of a Senate amendment does not carry with it pending motions for disposition of the amendment. 8 Cannon § 2657.

A motion to refer or a motion to recede and concur in a Senate amendment in disagreement may be laid on the table without carrying the pending matter to the table because other motions remain available for disposition of the pending amendment. *Manual* § 914.

§ 8. Taking From the Table; Reconsideration

A matter once laid on the table may be taken therefrom only by suspension of the rules (or similar process) or by unanimous consent unless it is a matter of privilege. *Manual* § 445; 5 Hinds § 6288; Deschler Ch 23 §§ 13.1, 13.2. Such matters of privilege include questions of privilege (5 Hinds §§ 5438, 5439), propositions to impeach (3 Hinds § 2049), and bills vetoed by the President (5 Hinds § 5439). An affirmative vote on a motion to table may be reconsidered pursuant to a timely motion therefor. 5 Hinds § 5628; 8 Cannon § 2785.

Moreover, a measure that has been tabled by the House may be presented again in similar but not identical form. 4 Hinds § 3385. However, under modern practice, a tabled resolution raising a question of the privileges of the House (even where the motion to reconsider that vote was laid on the table), may be offered again in identical form on a subsequent day if still constituting a question of privilege. *Manual* § 713; 104-1, Nov. 17, 1995, p 33846.

Chapter 30
Messages Between the Houses

Research References
5 Hinds §§ 6590-6662
8 Cannon §§ 3333-3353
Deschler-Brown Ch 32 §§ 1, 2
Manual §§ 330, 560-569, 873, 874

§ 1. In General; Uses

The House of Representatives and the Senate communicate and coordinate their activities by sending formal messages to each other. These messages between the two Houses constitute the sole source of official information regarding actions taken by the other House. 8 Cannon §§ 3342, 3343. The Chair does not take public notice of the proceedings of the Senate unless they are formally brought to the attention of the House by message from the Senate. Deschler-Brown Ch 32 § 2.14.

Messages between the House and Senate are used for a variety of legislative purposes:

- To indicate the final disposition by one House of a bill originating in the other.
- To convey the official papers accompanying a bill from one House to the other.
- To transmit the action of one House on an amendment of the other.
- To request the return of a bill.
- To convey information relating to a committee of conference and a report relating thereto.
- To transmit information relating to the election of an officer and other organizational matters.
- To indicate House or Senate action on a vetoed bill.
- To convey information or documents relating to an impeachment proceeding or electoral count.

- To dispose of questions regarding a breach of privilege by one House against the other.

Such messages also have been used on rare occasions to transmit or exchange confidential information between the two Houses. 5 Hinds § 5250.

The Clerk or a subordinate delivers the messages of the House to the Senate. Senate messages are delivered to the House by the Secretary of the Senate or a subordinate. 5 Hinds § 6592.

§ 2. Reception of Messages

The refusal of one House to receive a message from the other is a breach of the practice of comity between the two Houses. Deschler-Brown Ch 32 § 1.3. The reception of a message from the Senate is a highly privileged matter and may interrupt the consideration of a bill, even though the previous question has been ordered thereon. Deschler-Brown Ch 32 § 1.4; 5 Hinds § 6602. Messages are received during debate, the Member having the floor yielding at the request of the Speaker. *Manual* § 561. Such a message may be received in the absence of a quorum and pending a motion for a call of the House. *Manual* § 562; 8 Cannon § 3339. The Speaker may receive the message even before the approval of the Journal. *Manual* § 562.

A message from the Senate may not be received when the House is in the Committee of the Whole, but the Committee may rise (formally or informally) to permit the reception of such messages. *Manual* § 564.

Whereas it was formerly the custom to transmit messages only when both Houses were sitting (5 Hinds §§ 6601, 6602), the present practice permits the reception of messages regardless of whether the other House is in session (8 Cannon § 3338). Clause 2(h) of rule II permits the reception by the Clerk of messages from the President or Senate notwithstanding the recess or adjournment of the House.

§ 3. Messages Relating to Bills

Generally

The House ordinarily does not take formal notice of Senate action on bills until such action has been communicated in the normal parliamentary manner. 3 Hinds § 2656; *Manual* § 528a; but see 100-1, Dec. 11, 1987, p 35049.

Messages from the Senate concerning House bills with Senate amendments or Senate bills that require action by the Committee of the Whole go to the Speaker's table and may be referred to the appropriate standing committees in the same manner as public bills introduced in the House.

Manual § 873. Those which do not require consideration in the Committee of the Whole may be laid before the House for consideration pursuant to clause 2 of rule XIV. *Manual* § 874; see SENATE BILLS; AMENDMENTS BETWEEN THE HOUSES.

Senate messages giving notice of measures passed or approved are entered in the Journal and published in the *Congressional Record. Manual* § 815.

Requests for the Return of a Bill

A message from the Senate requesting that the House return a bill must be presented to the House for consideration. Deschler-Brown Ch 32 § 2.9. A request of the Senate for the return of a bill to correct an error is treated as privileged in the House and may be disposed of by unanimous consent or by motion. *Manual* § 565. When a request of the Senate for the return of a bill is treated as privileged, the Chair may immediately put the question on the request without debate. Deschler-Brown Ch 32 § 2.8. The House may by unanimous consent agree to a request of the Senate for the return of a Senate bill even where the bill has been referred to a House committee. Deschler-Brown Ch 32 § 2.2. A request of the House for return of a bill messaged to the Senate is not privileged where no error is involved, as it cannot be a substitute for reconsideration. The House by unanimous consent agreed to a request from the Senate for the return of a Senate bill, to the end that the Senate effect a specified (substantive) change in its text. *Manual* § 565. For a discussion of reconsideration of a vote, see RECONSIDERATION.

§ 4. Errors; Lost Documents

A proposition to correct an error in a message by one House to the other presents a question of privilege. 3 Hinds § 2613. One House may correct an error in its message to the other, the receiving House concurring in the correction. 5 Hinds § 6607. If the Clerk of the House or Secretary of the Senate commits an error in delivering a messaged document, such officer may be directed to correct it. In one instance, where the Secretary had delivered only one of two Senate amendments to a House bill, the mistake was not discovered until after the House had disagreed to the Senate amendment. The Senate then directed the Secretary to correct the mistake, the correction was received, and the House acted on the two amendments *de novo*. 5 Hinds § 6590. In another instance, where a figure was changed in the enrolling process in the Senate after the House had concurred in a Senate amendment and cleared the measure for the President, a concurrent resolution ratifying such enrollment was agreed to by the Senate (but not taken up in the House). 109-2, S. Con. Res. 80, Feb. 8, 2006, pp 1208, 1209.

Where an official document intended for delivery to the Senate is lost and cannot be retrieved, the preparation of official duplicates thereof may be provided for pursuant to concurrent resolution. Such resolutions are privileged for consideration. In such cases the Clerk attests to the authenticity of an existing printed copy or duplicate original. *Manual* § 704.

Chapter 31
Morning Hour; Call of Committees

Research References
4 Hinds §§ 3118-3141
6 Cannon §§ 751-755; 7 Cannon § 944
Deschler Ch 21 § 4
Manual §§ 869, 880, 881, 951

§ 1. In General; Place in Order of Business

Generally

The morning hour call of committees under clause 4 of rule XIV is a rarely-used procedure for calling up for consideration in the House bills that have been reported by committees and that are on the House Calendar. *Manual* § 880. Other avenues that are more frequently used for this purpose are special orders of business from the Committee on Rules; suspension of the rules; unanimous-consent agreements; and, historically, Calendar Wednesday (all of which are discussed under separate titles in this work). Because of the availability of these more effective procedures, and because most reported bills are referred to the Union Calendar, the morning hour call has become largely obsolete. Deschler Ch 21 § 4. However, since the demise of the Consent Calendar in the 104th Congress and the Corrections Calendar in the 109th Congress, the morning hour call of committees remains an alternative to motions to suspend the rules as a way of disposing of relatively noncontroversial bills on the House Calendar.

Morning-hour Debate Distinguished

In the 103d Congress the House established a procedure for ''morning-hour debates.'' *Manual* § 951. Under this practice, which is permitted by a standing order adopted by unanimous consent each Congress, the House meets before the regular convening hour on certain legislative days to entertain up to five-minute speeches from lists submitted by the Majority and Minority Leaders. Generally, no business is permitted during such periods. See CONSIDERATION AND DEBATE for further discussion of this practice.

Calendar Wednesday Distinguished

Unprivileged measures on the House or Union Calendar may be considered when committees are called alphabetically under the Calendar Wednesday rule. Clause 6 of rule XV. Before the 111th Congress, Calendar Wednesday was routinely dispensed with by unanimous consent. The rule now contains a notice requirement, and without such notice, the call of Committees does not occur. *Manual* § 900; see also CALENDAR WEDNESDAY.

Order of Morning Hour Business; Precedence

The morning hour is listed seventh in the rule governing the order of business in the House, coming just after ''unfinished business.'' Clause 1 of rule XIV. A bill once brought up on the morning hour call continues before the House in that order of business until disposed of, unless withdrawn by authority of the committee with jurisdiction over the bill. 4 Hinds § 3120. Such withdrawal must occur before amendment or other House action on the bill. 4 Hinds § 3129. Once consideration of the bill has begun under the morning hour rule, the House may not on motion postpone its further consideration to a day certain. 4 Hinds § 3164. However, other more highly privileged matters, such as a privileged report from the Committee on Rules, may intervene. 4 Hinds § 3131.

§ 2. Procedure; Business Considered

Generally

The morning hour rule provides that, after the disposition of unfinished business, the Speaker shall call each standing committee, ''in regular order,'' followed by select committees. Clause 4 of rule XIV. This rule is interpreted to mean that committees are to be called seriatim in the order in which they are listed in rule X. 6 Cannon § 751. Each committee, when named, may then call from the House Calendar a bill it has previously reported. Clause 4 of rule XIV. Bills called up under this procedure are debated under the hour rule, with debate being confined to the bill under consideration. Deschler Ch 21 § 4.2.

Business Considered During the Morning Hour

In the early practice the morning hour was used for the reception of reports from committees. 4 Hinds § 3118. In 1890 the rule was amended so as to devote the morning hour to ''any bill'' on the House Calendar reported by a committee ''on a previous day.'' *Manual* § 880. Thus, the bill must actually be on the House Calendar, and properly there, in order to be considered; a bill on the Union Calendar may not be brought up during the morning hour call of committees. 4 Hinds §§3122-3126; 6 Cannon §753.

Committee Authorization

A Member calling up a bill under the morning hour rule must be authorized to do so by the committee reporting the bill. Deschler Ch 21 §4.2. In the event of a dispute as to whether committee authorization was in fact granted, the Speaker may decline to resolve the matter on the ground that such an issue gives rise to a question of fact to be resolved by the committee. 4 Hinds §3127. The Speaker may, however, rule on the question of authorization based on statements by the chair and other members of the reporting committee. 4 Hinds §3128.

§3. Duration; Interruption or Termination

Generally

The term ''morning hour'' is to some extent misleading, since, under the modern rule, the call of committees does not necessarily terminate in one hour. 4 Hinds §3119. Morning hour does not terminate until the call is exhausted, until the House adjourns or votes to go into Committee of the Whole, or until other privileged matter intervenes. *Manual* §§881-883; 4 Hinds §3131. Under the modern practice, privileged business is always available to obviate morning hour business. After the intervening business is concluded, the morning hour call of committees is resumed unless the House adjourns. 4 Hinds §3133.

Motions to go into Committee of the Whole

House rules permit the interruption of the morning hour call of committees by a motion to go into Committee of the Whole. Clause 5 of rule XIV; see COMMITTEES OF THE WHOLE. Under this rule, the motion lies ''after one hour'' of the call of committees, and may be made for the purpose of taking up a particular bill. *Manual* §882. The motion may interrupt the call of committees after the expiration of one hour and may be made even sooner if the call of committees is exhausted before the hour expires. 4 Hinds §§3131, 3141.

Before expiration of the hour, the Speaker has declined to permit the call to be interrupted by a committee report or by a unanimous-consent request to consider a bill that is not on the House Calendar. 4 Hinds §§3130, 3132.

Chapter 32
Motions

Research References
5 Hinds §§ 5300-5358
8 Cannon §§ 2609-2640
Deschler Ch 23
Manual §§ 460, 902-905

§ 1. In General

Most motions that are used in the House are specifically provided for by House rule. They are governed by separate procedural requirements, serve different purposes, and are treated under separate titles elsewhere in this work, such as ADJOURNMENT; LAY ON THE TABLE; POSTPONEMENT; PREVIOUS QUESTION; RECONSIDERATION; REFER AND RECOMMIT; and SUSPENSION OF RULES.

Motions must also conform to certain common procedural requirements; for example, a Member offering a motion must seek recognition and address the Chair. § 3, infra. Although recognition for a motion is always at the Speaker's discretion, the Speaker will ordinarily be bound to entertain any motion that is in order under the rules of the House and in accordance with its parliamentary practices. 4 Hinds § 3550; see also RECOGNITION. Where a motion not in order under the rules of the House is, by unanimous consent, considered and agreed to, it controls the procedure of the House until carried out, unless the House takes affirmative action to the contrary. Deschler Ch 23 § 1.1.

§ 2. Form; Reading of Motion

Under clause 1 of rule XVI, a motion entertained in the House or in the Committee of the Whole must be reduced to writing if demanded by a Member. If offered in the House, the motion is entered on the Journal unless withdrawn on the same day. *Manual* § 902. Not every motion is in writing when proposed. When a point of order is raised, the Chair may give the proponent an opportunity to reduce the motion to writing before putting the question thereon. *Manual* § 902.

Clause 2 of rule XVI requires that a motion be stated by the Speaker or read by the Clerk before it can be debated. *Manual* § 904; 5 Hinds § 4937. The Clerk's reading may be dispensed with only by unanimous consent or special order of business. *Manual* § 904.

Where there is a misunderstanding about the wording of a pending motion, the Chair may restate the motion. However, it is not in order to ask that the motion be rereported by the Clerk except by unanimous consent. Deschler Ch 23 §§ 2.4, 2.5. If there is doubt, the motion voted on is the motion as stated by the Chair in putting the question and not as stated by the Member in offering the motion. Deschler Ch 23 § 2.3.

§ 3. Recognition to Offer

A Member may not offer a motion without seeking recognition and addressing the Chair. *Manual* §§ 394, 945. A Member desiring to offer a motion must actively seek recognition from the Chair before another motion to dispose of the pending question has been adopted. Clause 2 of rule XVII states: ''When two or more Members, Delegates, or the Resident Commissioner rise at once, the Speaker shall name the Member, Delegate, or Resident Commissioner who is first to speak. . . .'' *Manual* § 949.

A motion is not pending until the Chair has recognized its proponent thereon. For this reason, the Chair often asks ''For what purpose does the gentle______ rise?'' when a Member seeks recognition. By this question the Chair determines whether the Member proposes a motion that is entitled to precedence. *Manual* § 953; 2 Hinds § 1464; 6 Cannon §§ 289-291, 293. As a proper exercise of the Speaker's discretion, there is no appeal from such denial. *Manual* § 953; 6 Cannon § 292; 8 Cannon §§ 2429, 2646, 2762.

In certain rules the Chair's discretion in recognition is explicitly stated. In clause 7(b) of rule XX, the Speaker may recognize a Member to move a call of the House at any time; and further proceedings under a call are considered as dispensed with ''unless the Speaker recognizes for a motion'' to compel attendance of absentees. In clause 4 of rule XVI, the motion that the Speaker be authorized to declare a recess or the motion to set the day's adjournment to a day and time certain is entertained ''in the discretion of the Speaker.'' Other motions in rule XVI are given a precedence under the rules that the Chair must acknowledge.

The Member in charge of the pending bill is entitled at all stages to prior recognition for allowable motions intended to expedite the bill. 2

Hinds § 1457; 6 Cannon §§ 300, 301. However, the fact that a Member has the floor on one matter does not necessarily entitle such Member to prior recognition on a motion relating to another matter. 2 Hinds § 1464. Except when a Member in charge of a measure occupies the floor in debate, such Member must yield to Members proposing preferential motions. 5 Hinds §§ 5391-5395. Ordinarily, when an essential motion made by the Member in charge is decided adversely, the right to prior recognition passes to the Member leading the opposition to the motion. Deschler Ch 23 § 1.2; see also RECOGNITION. As to precedence among particular motions, see motions listed in § 1, supra.

§ 4. Dilatory Motions

Clause 1 of rule XVI, which was adopted in 1890, states that "a dilatory motion may not be entertained by the Speaker." *Manual* § 902. The Speaker may decline to entertain such motions on his or her own initiative or on a point of order from the floor. 5 Hinds §§ 5715-5722.

Hinds has said that a motion must be made manifestly for delay in order to justify its rejection as dilatory. 5 Hinds § 5714. Yet the determination of whether a motion is dilatory is entirely within the discretion of the Chair. Deschler Ch 23 § 4.1. Indeed, the Speaker determines a question of dilatoriness not necessarily by the length of time at issue or the character of the underlying business. Rather, the Speaker determines whether under the circumstances the motion is made with intent to delay the business of the House. 8 Cannon § 2804.

The Speaker may decline to entertain debate or an appeal on a question as to the dilatoriness of a motion if to do so would defeat the object of the rule. 5 Hinds § 5731. For discussion of dilatory motions pending consideration of a report from the Committee on Rules, see *Manual* § 857. For the rule prohibiting offering of dilatory motions during consideration of certain measures, see *Manual* §§ 857, 858.

§ 5. Withdrawal; Reoffering

Generally

A motion having been made, clause 2 of rule XVI places it in the possession of the House but permits its withdrawal at "any time before a decision or amendment thereon." *Manual* § 904. This rule is interpreted to mean that a motion may be withdrawn in the House as a matter of right unless the House has taken some action thereon, such as a motion for the previous question or the ordering of the previous question. *Manual* § 905; 5 Hinds §§ 5355, 5489; Deschler Ch 23 § 1. The House does not vote on the withdrawal of the motion, if timely. *Manual* § 460. Unanimous consent is not required if withdrawal occurs before a decision is made on the motion as offered or there is an amendment thereof. Deschler Ch 23 § 2.7.

A motion may be withdrawn although an amendment may have been offered to the motion and be pending. 5 Hinds § 5347; 8 Cannon § 2639. A motion may be withdrawn before action thereon even though it is under consideration as unfinished business postponed from the preceding day. 95-1, June 17, 1977, p 19693.

Action by the House that will preclude withdrawal of a motion includes the ordering of the yeas and nays on the motion. 5 Hinds § 5353. Unanimous consent to withdraw the motion is required where the yeas and nays have been ordered. Deschler Ch 23 § 2.9. However, a motion may be withdrawn after a voice and a division vote thereon where the Chair has not announced the result and where another type of vote might be had on the motion. The Chair may decline to permit a withdrawal while counting a vote. *Manual* § 905; 96-1, Nov. 13, 1979, p 32185.

Modification of Motion; Reoffering

A Member having the right to withdraw a motion before a decision thereon has the resulting power to modify the motion (as by withdrawing and offering a modified form). 5 Hinds § 5358. However, the proponent does not necessarily have the right to reoffer the motion, especially where it is a secondary motion under clause 4 of rule XVI; such motions may properly be offered only at the times designated by the rule. Deschler Ch 23 § 1.

For withdrawal of particular motions and withdrawal of amendments, see AMENDMENTS and WITHDRAWAL.

Chapter 33
Oaths

Research References

U.S. Const. art. I, § 5; art. VI, cl. 3
1 Hinds §§ 6-22
Deschler Ch 2 §§ 5, 6
Manual §§ 197-206

§ 1. In General; Administering the Oath of Office

Generally

The Constitution requires that every Senator and every Representative swear or affirm to support the Constitution of the United States. U.S. Const. art. VI, cl. 3. Clause 1 of rule II carries the same requirement for elected officers. For administration of the oath to officers, see OFFICERS AND OFFICES. The form of the oath and the procedure for its administration are regulated by statute. 2 USC § 25. Form of oath, see 5 USC § 3331 and *Manual* § 197.

Until a Member-elect has subscribed to the oath, such individual does not enjoy all the rights and prerogatives of a Member of Congress. Deschler Ch 2 § 2.1. Members who have not taken the oath are not entitled to vote or to introduce bills. *Manual* § 300; 8 Cannon § 3122. However, unsworn Members have participated at the beginning of a session in organizational business, such as the election of the Speaker. 1 Hinds § 224. Where two unsworn Members participated in more than mere organizational business, the House later ratified (by simple resolution) certain actions after the administration of the oath to Members-elect *en masse*. 112-1, Jan. 7, 2011, p ____. Although a Member has been named to a committee before taking the oath, under the modern practice the election of such a Member to a standing committee may be made effective only upon being sworn. 4 Hinds § 4483; 106-1, H. Res. 6, Jan. 6, 1999, pp 235-37.

In the early practice of the House, it was the custom to administer the oath by State delegations. Beginning with the 71st Congress, however,

Members-elect have been sworn in *en masse*. 6 Cannon § 8. Under this practice the Speaker administers the oath of office to all Members-elect at one time on opening day, although a Member-elect whose right to take the oath has been challenged may be asked to stand aside. *Manual* § 203. A Member-elect who does not take the oath of office on opening day may appear later in the well, in response to the Speaker's invitation, and take the oath. Deschler Ch 2 § 5.14. The Speaker also administers the oath to Delegates-elect, the Resident Commissioner from Puerto Rico, and Members-elect elected to fill vacancies. Deschler Ch 2 §§ 3.6, 5.

Credentials as Basis for Taking the Oath

Although the Clerk will not as a general rule enroll Members-elect who appear without certificates of election, the House itself may authorize, by unanimous consent, the administration of the oath to Members-elect who appear without appropriate formal credentials. 1 Hinds §§ 162-168, 553-564; Deschler Ch 2 § 3.5. For example, a Member-elect may be sworn on the basis of letters or telegrams from the executive department of the State of representation, attesting to the results of the election. Deschler Ch 2 §§ 3.1-3.4. The House may authorize the administration of the oath where credentials have not yet arrived, pursuant to a statement by another Member-elect or a State official that the election in issue is neither contested nor questioned. Deschler Ch 2 § 3. Unofficial State communications, including faxes and electronic scans, declaring the results of the election may be laid before the House before the unanimous-consent request for the administration of the oath. Deschler Ch 2 § 3.4.

Authorization by Resolution

The administration of the oath may be authorized by resolution after a challenge to the right to be sworn has been made. Such resolutions have included provisions collateral to the actual administration of the oath, such as a condition that the final right to the seat be referred to the Committee on House Administration. Deschler Ch 2 § 5.

Failure or Refusal to Take the Oath

Members-elect entitled to take the oath may decline it by resigning before taking a seat, because membership cannot be imposed on one without one's consent. 2 Hinds §§ 1230-1234. A Member-elect may be permitted to defer taking the oath, without declining the seat, until such time as questions regarding the requisite qualifications are resolved. Deschler Ch 2 § 5. However, where a Member-elect fails to appear to take the oath, the House may provide by resolution that, if such Member-elect fails to appear to take the oath by a certain date, the seat will be declared vacant. Deschler Ch 2 § 5.7.

In the 97th Congress, the House, by majority vote, declared vacant a seat where the Member-elect was unable to take the oath because of an incapacitating illness. In that case, the medical prognosis showed no likelihood of improvement. The constitutional basis for the declaration of the vacancy by majority vote was not expressly stated in the resolution. Nevertheless, the power of the House under article I, section 5 of the Constitution to judge the qualifications of its Members by majority vote has been justified by the Supreme Court. In *Powell* v. *McCormack*, 395 U.S. 486, 520 (1969), the Court stated in a footnote that in addition to age, citizenship, and inhabitancy, the article VI requirement for taking the oath could be argued to be a qualification.

Precedence

The administration of the oath is a matter of high privilege. *Manual* § 201. The oath may be administered before the reading of the Journal and takes precedence of a motion to amend the Journal. 1 Hinds § 171. It has been held in order to administer the oath in the absence of a quorum, during a roll call, and on Calendar Wednesday. *Manual* §§ 200, 201; 1 Hinds § 174; 6 Cannon § 22. The administration of the oath is in order even after the previous question has been ordered on a pending matter. Deschler Ch 2 § 5.17. Debate on a resolution reported from the Committee on Rules may be interrupted to allow a new Member to take the oath of office. Deschler Ch 2 § 5.18.

The Act of June 1, 1789, provides that on the organization of the House, and previous to entering on any other business, the oath shall be administered by any Member (generally the Member with longest continuous service) to the Speaker and by the Speaker to the other Members and Clerk (when elected). *Manual* § 198; 2 USC § 25; 1 Hinds §§ 130, 131; 6 Cannon § 6. The Act was cited by the Clerk in recognizing for nominations for Speaker as being of higher constitutional privilege than a resolution to postpone the election of a Speaker and instead provide for the election of a Speaker pro tempore pending the disposition of certain ethics charges against the nominee of the majority party. *Manual* § 198.

§ 2. Absent Members and the Oath; Use of Deputies

The Speaker, or a deputy named by the Speaker, may be authorized by resolution to administer the oath of office to a Member-elect absent because of illness or because of some illness in the family. Deschler Ch 2 §§ 5.8-5.12. The resolution may authorize the administration of the oath at some location other than the House. 1 Hinds § 170; 6 Cannon § 14. Persons who may be designated by the Speaker to administer the oath to an absent Member-elect include another Member (Deschler Ch 2 § 5.10), a State or county judge (Deschler Ch 2 § 5.11), or a Federal district court judge (105-1, Feb. 4, 1997, p 1381). The deputy so designated reports thereon to the House, which report may take the form of a letter. Deschler Ch 2 §§ 5.8, 5.10, 5.12.

§ 3. Challenging the Right To Be Sworn

Generally

Any Member-elect may challenge the right of any other Member-elect to be sworn when the Speaker directs the Members-elect to rise to take the oath of office. *Manual* § 202; Deschler Ch 2 § 6. The fact that the challenging party has not been sworn is no bar to such individual's right to invoke this procedure. 1 Hinds § 141. Challenging parties must base the challenge either on their own responsibility as a Member-elect or on specified facts or documents. Deschler Ch 2 § 6.2. Such challenges are generally directed at a single Member-elect, but in several instances the challenge has been directed against an entire State delegation. 1 Hinds §§ 457, 460-462; Deschler Ch 2 § 6.4. The authority to challenge the right of a Member-elect to be sworn is based on the Constitution, which designates the House as the sole judge of the elections, returns, and qualifications of Members. U.S. Const. art. I, § 5, cl. 1. See generally ELECTION OF MEMBERS. See also *Manual* §§ 202-203.

Procedure

When a challenge is proposed, the Speaker asks the challenged Member not to rise to take the oath with the rest of the membership *en masse*. The House, and not the Speaker, determines the action to be taken in such cases. *Manual* § 199; Deschler Ch 2 § 6.1. Debate on the right of the Member-elect to be sworn is not in order until after the remaining Members have been sworn. Deschler Ch 2 § 6.3. The pendency of a challenge does not preclude the entertainment of other business before the House, and all other organizational business may be completed before a challenge is resolved. 1 Hinds § 474; Deschler Ch 2 § 6.

Several courses of action are open to the House in disposing of a challenge. First, the House may simply seat a Member by authorizing the administration of the oath pursuant to a resolution determining the right to the seat. Deschler Ch 2 § 6.5. Second, the House may by resolution authorize the administration of the oath based on the Member-elect's *prima facie* right to the seat, but at the same time refer the determination of the final right to committee. 1 Hinds §§528-534. Finally, the House may by resolution refer the *prima facie* as well as the final right to the seat to committee, without authorizing the administration of the oath. Deschler Ch 2 §§6.6, 6.7.

Resolutions relating to the right of a challenged Member-elect to be sworn are privileged. *Manual* §201. The resolution is open to amendment where the House has not ordered the previous question thereon. Deschler Ch 23 §22.4. The challenged Member-elect may, by unanimous consent, be permitted to participate in debate on the resolution. Deschler Ch 2 §2.5. The time for debate on the resolution may be extended by unanimous consent. Deschler-Brown Ch 29 §26.33.

The seating of a Member-elect does not prejudice a contest pending under the Federal Contested Elections Act over final right to the seat. 2 USC §§381-396; *Manual* §203. In response to parliamentary inquiries, the Chair informed the House that a notice of contest had been filed with the Clerk. 105-1, Jan. 7, 1997, p 120; 110-1, Jan. 4, 2007, p 5.

As to the procedure to be followed in contested elections, see ELECTION CONTESTS AND DISPUTES.

§4. Oath Relating to Classified Information

Clause 13 of rule XXIII, the Code of Official Conduct, prescribes an oath to be executed by all Members, officers, and employees of the House before they obtain access to classified information:

> I do solemnly swear (or affirm) that I will not disclose any classified information received in the course of my service with the House of Representatives, except as authorized by the House of Representatives or in accordance with its rules. *Manual* §1095.

The Committee on Ethics has interpreted this clause as applying to classified information provided by "any person," not merely to data furnished by the House or by the executive branch. *Memorandum for All Members, Officers and Employees,* July 12, 1995.

Chapter 34
Office of the Speaker

Research References

1 Hinds §§ 186-234; 2 Hinds §§ 1307-1412
6 Cannon §§ 23, 24, 247-282
Deschler Ch 6 §§ 1-14
Manual §§ 621-639, 970

§ 1. Role of Speaker

The Speaker is the presiding officer of the House and is charged with numerous duties and responsibilities by law and by House rules. As the presiding officer of the House, the Speaker maintains order, manages its proceedings, and governs the administration of its business. *Manual* § 622; Deschler Ch 6 §§ 2-8. The major functions of the Speaker with respect to the consideration of measures on the floor include recognizing Members who seek to address the House (*Manual* § 949), construing and applying the House rules (*Manual* § 627), and putting the question on matters arising on the floor to a vote (*Manual* § 630).

The Speaker's role as presiding officer is an impartial one, and the Speaker's rulings serve to protect the rights of the minority. 88-1, June 4, 1963, pp 10151-65. In seeking to protect the interests of the minority, the Speaker has even asked unanimous consent that an order of the House be vacated where the circumstances so required. 89-1, May 18, 1965, p 10871.

§ 2. Term of Office; Vacancy

Term Limit

The Speaker's term of office begins when the oath of office is taken, which immediately follows the election of the Speaker and opening remarks. The term ends on the expiration of the Congress in which such individual was elected, unless sooner terminated by resignation, death, or removal from office. Deschler Ch 6 § 2. During the 104th through 107th Congresses, the Speaker's term of office was limited to four consecutive Congresses. That rule was repealed in the 108th Congress. *Manual* § 635a.

Vacancy

The Office of Speaker may be declared vacant by resolution, which may be offered as a matter of privilege. *Manual* § 315; 6 Cannon § 35. Under clause 8(b)(3) of rule I, adopted in the 108th Congress, the Speaker is required to deliver to the Clerk a list of Members in the order in which each shall act as Speaker pro tempore in the case of a vacancy in the Office of Speaker. Deschler-Brown-Johnson Ch 38 § 5. The Member acting as Speaker pro tempore under this provision may exercise such authorities of the Office of Speaker as may be necessary and appropriate pending the election of a Speaker or Speaker pro tempore. A vacancy in the Office may exist by reason of the physical inability of the Speaker to discharge the duties of the Office.

The House does not formally accept the resignation of a Speaker. 1 Hinds §§ 225, 232; Deschler-Brown-Johnson Ch 37 § 9.

§ 3. Election

Speaker Chosen from Members

Article I, section 2 of the Constitution directs that the House choose its Speaker and other officers. The Speaker is the only House officer who traditionally has been chosen from the sitting membership of the House. *Manual* § 26. The Constitution does not limit eligibility to that class, but the practice has been followed invariably. The Speaker's term of office thus expires at the end of such individual's term of office as a Member, whereas the other House officers continue in office "until their successors are chosen and qualified." Clause 1 of rule II; 1 Hinds § 187.

Nomination and Vote

The general practice for election of Speaker begins with nominations from each party caucus followed by a *viva voce* vote of the Members-elect. Relying on the Act of June 1, 1789, the Clerk recognized for nominations for Speaker as being of higher constitutional privilege than a resolution to postpone the election of a Speaker and instead provide for the election of a Speaker pro tempore pending the disposition of certain ethics charges against the nominee of the majority party. 2 USC § 25; *Manual* § 27.

Under the modern practice, the Speaker is elected by a majority of Members-elect voting by surname, a quorum being present. *Manual* § 27; 1 Hinds § 216; 6 Cannon § 24. The Clerk appoints tellers for this election. However, the House, and not the Clerk, decides by what method it shall elect. 1 Hinds § 210. For former practices relating to the election of the Speaker, see *Manual* § 27; 1 Hinds §§ 212, 214, 218; 8 Cannon § 3883.

In two instances the House agreed to choose and subsequently did choose a Speaker by a plurality of votes but confirmed the choice by majority vote. In 1849 the House had been in session 19 days without being able to elect a Speaker, no candidate having received a majority of the votes cast. The voting was *viva voce*, each Member responding to the call of the roll by naming the candidate for whom he voted. Finally, after the fifty-ninth ballot, the House adopted a resolution declaring that a Speaker could be elected by a plurality. 1 Hinds § 221. In 1856 the House again struggled over the election of a Speaker. Ballots numbering 129 had been taken without any candidate receiving a majority of the votes cast. The House then adopted a resolution permitting the election to be decided by a plurality. 1 Hinds § 222. On both of these occasions, the House ratified the plurality election by a majority vote.

§ 4. Jurisdiction and Duties; Rulings

The Speaker presides over the business of the House. In executing the duties of the Office, the Speaker:

- Calls the House to order and announces approval of the Journal. *Manual* §§ 621, 622.
- Refers bills and other matters to committee. *Manual* § 816.
- Disposes of business on the Speaker's table. *Manual* §§ 873-875.
- Designates Speakers pro tempore, and appoints chairs of the Committee of the Whole. *Manual* §§ 632, 970.
- Recognizes Members. Deschler Ch 6 §§ 3.16-3.23.
- States a question in prescribed form. *Manual* § 630.
- Supervises the timing of debate and other proceedings in the House. Deschler Ch 6 § 3.25.
- Rules on points of order and responds to parliamentary inquiries. Deschler Ch 6 § 3.
- Makes appointments pursuant to statute, House rules, and House resolutions. Deschler Ch 6 § 6. For appointments to committees, see COMMITTEES.

- Certifies to a U.S. Attorney persons found to be in contempt of a House committee. Deschler Ch 6 § 3.40.
- Declares the House in recess in the event of an emergency pursuant to the inherent power of the Office, pursuant to clause 12 of rule I, or pursuant to a House resolution authorizing such action. Deschler-Brown-Johnson Ch 39 § 2; see RECESS.
- Changes convening time (within constitutional limit) during an adjournment of not more than three days, in the case of imminent impairment of the place of reconvening. Clause 12(c) of rule I; Deschler-Brown-Johnson Ch 40 § 1.
- Convenes the House in a place at the seat of government other than the Hall of the House whenever it is in the public interest. Clause 12(d) of rule I; Deschler-Brown-Johnson Ch 40 § 2.
- Signs various documents, including warrants and subpoenas. Clause 4 of rule I.
- Makes preliminary decisions as to questions of privilege. 3 Hinds §§ 2649, 2650, 2654.
- Determines the presence of a quorum, conducts quorum counts, and counts certain votes. *Manual* §§ 55, 630, 810, 1012; 4 Hinds § 2932.
- Announces the absence of a quorum without unnecessary delay. 6 Cannon § 652.
- Maintains order in debate. *Manual* § 960.
- Administers censure by direction of the House. 6 Cannon §§ 236, 237.
- Designates Members to travel on official business of the House. *Manual* § 636.
- Appoints Members to conference committees. *Manual* §§ 536, 637.
- Rules on the validity of conference reports. *Manual* § 628; 5 Hinds §§ 6409, 6410, 6414, 6416, 6409-6413; 8 Cannon §§ 3256, 3264.
- Declares the House adjourned when the hour previously fixed for adjournment arrives. 5 Hinds § 6735.
- Approves assignment of leadership staff to the floor. Clause 2(a) of rule IV.

Many matters have been held to be beyond the scope of the Speaker's responsibility under the rules. The Speaker does not:

- Construe the legislative or legal effect of a pending measure or comment on the merits thereof. *Manual* § 628; Deschler Ch 6 §§ 4.20, 4.21.
- Determine whether Members have abused leave to print. *Manual* § 628.
- Respond to hypothetical questions, render anticipatory rulings, or decide a question not directly presented by the proceedings. *Manual* § 628; Deschler Ch 6 §§ 4.13, 4.14.
- Determine questions that are within the province of the chair of the Committee of the Whole. *Manual* § 971; 5 Hinds § 6987.
- Pass on the constitutional powers of the House, the constitutionality of House rules, or the constitutionality of amendments offered to pending bills. *Manual* § 628.

- Resolve questions on the consistency of an amendment with the measure to which it is offered, or with an amendment that already has been adopted, or on the consistency of proposed action with other acts of the House. *Manual* §§466, 628; 5 Hinds §5781.
- Answer inquiries as to the availability of amendments not yet offered. Deschler Ch 27 §3.37.
- Decide whether a Member should be allowed to display an exhibit in debate, except under the Speaker's duty to preserve decorum. *Manual* §622; Deschler Ch 6 §4.10.
- Rule on the sufficiency or effect of committee reports or whether the committee has followed instructions. *Manual* §628; 2 Hinds §1338; 4 Hinds §§4404, 4689; Deschler Ch 6 §§4.22, 4.23.
- Rule on the propriety or expediency of a proposed course of action. *Manual* §628.
- Construe the consequences of a pending vote. Deschler Ch 6 §§4.27, 4.28.
- Determine whether a Member should be censured or whether an office held is incompatible with membership in the House, these being matters for the House to decide. 2 Hinds §1275; 6 Cannon §253.
- Look behind the unambiguous language of a special order of business adopted by the House when interpreting its language. *Manual* §628.

For jurisdiction and duties of the chair of the Committee of the Whole, see COMMITTEES OF THE WHOLE.

§5. Participation in Debate and Voting

Debate

Although the Speaker's usual role is that of the presiding officer, there have been many instances in which the Speaker has made a statement from the Chair or in which the Speaker has relinquished the Chair and participated in the debate on the floor. *Manual* §358. The Speaker may take the floor for purposes of debate both in the House and in the Committee of the Whole. If the Speaker is to participate in debate on the floor of the House, another Member is called to the Chair to serve as Speaker pro tempore. *Manual* §358; 2 Hinds §1360.

Voting

Under the early rules of the House, the Speaker was barred from voting except under certain circumstances. 5 Hinds §5964. Today, the Speaker has the same right as other Members to vote but only occasionally exercises it. *Manual* §631. The Speaker may vote on any matter that comes before the House, and is required to vote where such vote would be decisive or where the House is engaged in voting by ballot. Clause 7 of rule I; *Manual* §631. The duty of giving a decisive vote may be exercised after the intervention of other business, if a correction of the roll shows a condition wherein such vote would be decisive. 5 Hinds §§ 6061-6063. On an electronic vote, the Chair may direct the Clerk to record the Speaker's vote and verify that instruction by submitting a vote card. *Manual* § 631.

§ 6. The Speaker Pro Tempore

Appointment or Election

The Speaker may appoint a Speaker pro tempore. Such an appointment may not exceed three legislative days, except that in the case of illness the Speaker's appointment may extend to 10 days with the approval of the House. Clause 8 of rule I. For longer periods, a Speaker pro tempore is elected by the House. *Manual* § 632. A Member sometimes is designated Speaker pro tempore by the Speaker and subsequently elected by the House. Deschler Ch 6 § 12.76. If the Speaker appoints a Speaker pro tempore only for purposes of signing enrolled bills and joint resolutions, such an appointment may extend for a ''specified period of time'' with the approval of the House. Clause 8 of rule I. The Speaker may appoint alternate Members to sign enrolled bills. *Manual* § 634. Under clause 8(b)(3) of rule I, adopted in the 108th Congress, the Speaker is required to deliver to the Clerk a list of Members in the order in which each shall act as Speaker pro tempore in the case of a vacancy in the Office of Speaker.

A Speaker pro tempore is elected pursuant to resolution. Deschler Ch 6 § 14.1. The resolution may be offered by the chair of the majority party caucus or by the Majority Leader. Deschler Ch 6 § 14. A Speaker pro tempore by designation leaves the Chair pending the offering of a resolution electing such individual as Speaker pro tempore. Deschler Ch 6 §§ 11.7, 14.1.

Oath of Office

The oath of office is administered to an elected Speaker pro tempore, but not to a designated Speaker pro tempore. Deschler Ch 6 § 11. The oath is administered to an elected Speaker pro tempore by the Speaker, by the Dean of the House, or by another Member. Deschler Ch 6 §§ 11.4-11.6.

Who May Serve

Under clause 8 of rule I, the Speaker pro tempore must be a Member of the House. *Manual* § 632. Such Member usually is a member of the majority party (Deschler Ch 6 § 10), such as the Majority Leader (Deschler Ch 3 § 17.5) or the Majority Whip (Deschler Ch 3 § 23.5). However, the Dean of the House also has served in that capacity. 89-1, Jan. 19, 1965, p 946. On rare ceremonial occasions the Minority Leader has been designated Speaker pro tempore. Deschler Ch 6 § 12.7.

Powers and Functions

The Speaker pro tempore, as the occupant of the Chair, exercises many functions that normally fall within the purview of the Speaker. Routine functions that are within the scope of authority of a Speaker pro tempore include calling the House to order, making various announcements, answering parliamentary inquiries, putting the question, counting for a quorum, ruling on points of order, and designating another Speaker pro tempore. Deschler Ch 6 §§ 9, 10. When the Office of Speaker is vacant, the Member acting as Speaker pro tempore under clause 8(b) of rule I may exercise such authorities of the Office as may be necessary and appropriate pending the election of a Speaker or Speaker pro tempore.

The authority of a Speaker pro tempore to exercise certain powers depends on whether such individual is designated, designated and approved, or elected. The powers of a designated Speaker pro tempore, compared with those of an elected Speaker pro tempore, are relatively limited. Deschler Ch 6 §§ 10, 14.

Absent unanimous consent or specific House approval, a designated Speaker pro tempore may not:

- Administer the oath of office to a Member-elect. Deschler Ch 6 § 12.8.
- Appoint conferees or make appointments of additional conferees. Deschler Ch 6 §§ 12.9, 12.10.
- Appoint Members to attend a funeral. Deschler Ch 6 § 12.14.

By contrast, an elected Speaker pro tempore may, for example, appoint conferees, administer the oath of office to a Member-elect, and preside at a joint session of Congress. Deschler Ch 6 §§ 12.8, 14, 14.8. Until 1983, unanimous consent was required for a Speaker pro tempore to spread upon the Journal a veto message from the President. Deschler Ch 6 § 12.11. Current practice allows even a designated Speaker pro tempore this authority without unanimous consent.

Chapter 35
Officers and Offices

Research References
U.S. Const. art. I, § 2
1 Hinds §§ 235-283
6 Cannon §§ 25-34
Deschler Ch 6 §§ 15-22
Manual §§ 640-670

§ 1. House Officers

In General

The Constitution directs that the House choose its Speaker and other officers. U.S. Const. art. I, § 2. The "other officers" not specified by title in the Constitution have carried various titles. Currently they are the Clerk, Sergeant-at-Arms, Chief Administrative Officer, and Chaplain. *Manual* § 640. Traditionally only the Speaker, and not these other officers, has been chosen from the sitting membership of the House. *Manual* § 26; see OFFICE OF THE SPEAKER. The Speaker's term of office thus expires at the end of such individual's term of office as a Member, whereas the other House officers continue in office until their successors are chosen and qualified. Clause 1 of rule II; 1 Hinds § 187.

In the 102d Congress the position of the Postmaster, for many years an elected officer of the House, was eliminated. *Manual* § 668. The Doorkeeper of the House, formerly an elected officer of the House, was not reestablished beginning in the 104th Congress. The responsibilities of that position were transferred to the Sergeant-at-Arms. *Manual* § 663.

Other offices established in the rules of the House or by statute are occupied by appointed officials. Rule II contains authority for an Office of General Counsel (clause 8), Historian (clause 7), and Inspector General (clause 6). The duties and appointing authority for the positions of Legislative Counsel, Law Revision Counsel, and Parliamentarian are carried in law. See *Manual* §§ 1118, 1120, 1122.

The Clerk

The Clerk has specific responsibilities spelled out in House rules, in statute, or as delegated by the House. The Clerk presides when a new Congress convenes. Clause 2 of rule II; *Manual* §§ 641-645. The Clerk has duties related to the conduct of House business. For example, the Clerk is responsible for processing bills, preparing the Journal, taking and tallying votes, and receiving messages from the President and the Senate when the House is not in session. *Manual* §§ 642, 647, 648, 652. To assist the House in its consideration of measures, the Clerk reads bills and motions (*Manual* §§ 428, 904), reads names alphabetically during the taking of certain votes and elections (*Manual* § 1015), notes all questions of order and decisions thereon and places them in the Journal (*Manual* § 647), reports disorderly words of a Member who has been called to order (*Manual* § 960), certifies to the passage of all bills and resolutions (*Manual* § 648), makes corrections during engrossment (*Manual* § 479), presents enrolled bills to the Speaker for signature and transmittal to the Senate (*Manual* § 575), and presents enrolled bills to the President (*Manual* § 648).

The Clerk also calls various calendars at the direction of the Speaker (*Manual* § 895), receives petitions and private bills (*Manual* § 818), disseminates copies of amendments offered in the Committee of the Whole (*Manual* § 978), and provides a place where Members may sign discharge petitions (*Manual* § 892). The Clerk also supervises the official reporters of the House, subject to the direction and control of the Speaker. *Manual* § 685.

In one instance, the Clerk carried out the duties of his own office as well as those of the Sergeant-at-Arms, having been elected to serve concurrently as Sergeant-at-Arms following the death of the incumbent. Deschler Ch 6 § 16.3.

The Clerk may designate and authorize one or more employees to perform the duties of the Office during an absence, except for such duties as are imposed on the Clerk by statute. *Manual* § 651. The designation may provide that such authorization is to remain in effect until revoked. 91-1, Oct. 29, 1969, p 32076. The designation is laid before the House by the Speaker. Deschler Ch 6 § 18.18.

Sergeant-at-Arms

The duties of the Sergeant-at-Arms on the floor are prescribed by House rules and by statute. Clause 3 of rule II; 2 USC § 78; *Manual* §§ 656-660. Under these provisions the Sergeant-at-Arms maintains order and executes arrest warrants for persons cited for contempt of the House or of a committee. In addition the Sergeant-at-Arms enforces the prohibition against Members walking across or out of the Hall of the House while the Speaker is addressing the House (*Manual* § 962), appoints officers to send for and arrest absent Members when so ordered by the Speaker or the House under clause 5 or 6 of rule XX (*Manual* §§ 1021-1025), and brings absent Members before the House (*Manual* § 1026). Pursuant to clause 12(c) of rule I, the Sergeant-at-Arms notifies the Speaker of an imminent impairment of the place of reconvening in order to allow alternate arrangements for convening the House. *Manual* § 639. The Sergeant-at-Arms is also responsible for the production of a ''catastrophic quorum failure report'' under clause 5(c) of rule XX. See QUORUMS.

Chief Administrative Officer

The Chief Administrative Officer (CAO) of the House has the operational and financial responsibility for functions assigned by the Committee on House Administration. The CAO is subject to the oversight of that committee and reports to it semiannually on the financial and operational status of each function under the jurisdiction of the CAO. Clause 4 of rule II.

The Chaplain

The Chaplain offers a prayer at commencement of each day's sitting of the House. Clause 5 of rule II. The prayer, which does not require a quorum, is offered daily after the House is called to order by the Speaker or a Speaker pro tempore is appointed. Deschler Ch 6 §§ 21.1, 21.2.

The daily prayer has been offered by visiting clergy of various denominations and nationalities. Deschler Ch 6 § 21.9. In the unexpected absence of the Chaplain, the prayer has been offered by a Member who was an ordained minister. 93-1, May 31, 1973, p 17441.

§ 2. Election and Oath

Election

The Clerk, Sergeant-at-Arms, Chief Administrative Officer, and Chaplain are elected for each Congress by resolution. Deschler Ch 6 § 16 (with forms). Before the House recodified its rules in the 106th Congress, the House was required under former rule II to elect its Speaker and other officers by a *viva voce* vote following nominations. 1 Hinds §§ 204, 208. However, even then, the officers mentioned in the rule, other than Speaker, were usually chosen by resolution, which is not a *viva voce* election. 1 Hinds §§ 193, 194. Officers have been elected prospectively. 110-1, Feb. 6, 2007, p 3156.

At the commencement of a Congress, each party's caucus selects one nominee for each such office. The majority submits its slate of nominees, and the minority usually submits a substitute amendment containing its slate. The House then votes on these slates (often disposing of them by voice vote), which may be offered by the caucus chairs. Deschler Ch 6 § 16. Such a resolution is offered from the floor as privileged and may be divided for a separate vote for the Chaplain, customarily an uncontested office. *Manual* § 640; Deschler Ch 6 § 16.2.

Oath

Each elected officer of the House takes the oath prescribed by law, which is administered by the Speaker. 5 USC § 3331 (with form); Deschler Ch 6 § 17. An officer elected to hold an additional office concurrently takes a separate oath for the additional office. Deschler Ch 6 § 17.1. The oath has been administered to an officer-elect before the effective date of such individual's election. 92-2, June 26, 1972, p 22387; see generally OATHS.

§ 3. Removal From Office

Both the Speaker and the House have the authority to remove the Clerk, Sergeant-at-Arms, or Chief Administrative Officer. Clause 1 of rule II; *Manual* § 640. An officer of the House may be removed from office pursuant to the adoption of a simple resolution, which may be offered as a matter of privilege. 1 Hinds §§ 284, 288-290; 6 Cannon § 35. For removal of the Speaker, see OFFICE OF THE SPEAKER. As a basis for removal of an officer, the House has considered allegations as follows:

- That the Clerk altered and falsified a House document. 1 Hinds § 284.
- That the Clerk was negligent in the administration of the contingent fund or misappropriated House funds. 1 Hinds §§ 283, 287.
- That the Doorkeeper was guilty of misconduct or corruption in office. 1 Hinds §§ 288, 289.

§ 4. Vacancies

The Speaker may make temporary appointments to fill vacancies in the Offices of the Clerk, the Sergeant-at-Arms, the Chief Administrative Officer, and the Chaplain. 2 USC § 75a-1. Pursuant to this authority, the Speaker has temporarily filled vacancies caused by the death or resignation of an officer. See, *e.g.*, Deschler Ch 6 § 6.25. Such appointments are effective until such time as the House acts by the adoption of a resolution to fill the vacancy on a permanent basis. Such a resolution is presented as a question of privilege. *Manual* § 701. The resignation of an elected officer of the House is subject to acceptance by the House. *Manual* § 640; Deschler-Brown-Johnson Ch 37 § 9.

§ 5. Other Offices Established by Rule II

Office of Inspector General

Under clause 6 of rule II, the Inspector General conducts audits of the financial and administrative functions of the House. The Inspector General is appointed by the Speaker, the Majority Leader, and the Minority Leader, acting jointly, and is subject to the policy direction and oversight of the Committee on House Administration. *Manual* § 667.

Office of General Counsel

Under clause 8 of rule II the General Counsel provides legal assistance and representation to the House. The General Counsel is appointed by the Speaker and functions under the direction of the Speaker. *Manual* § 670.

The General Counsel is authorized by law to appear in any proceeding before a State or Federal court (except the United States Supreme Court) without compliance with admission requirements of such court. 2 USC § 130f(a). Furthermore, the law requires the Attorney General to notify the General Counsel of a determination not to appeal a court decision affecting the constitutionality of an Act. 2 USC § 130f(b).

Office of the Historian

Under clause 7 of rule II the Historian of the House of Representatives is appointed by the Speaker. *Manual* § 669.

§ 6. Offices Established by Law

Government Accountability Office

The preparation, utilization, and distribution (to committees and Members) of reports by the Government Accountability Office, and its authority to assign its employees to duty with congressional committees, are regulated by sections 231-236 of the Legislative Reorganization Act of 1970. 31 USC § 711-720. This office was formerly known as the General Accounting Office. 31 USC § 702 note.

Office of Compliance

The Office of Compliance was established by the Congressional Accountability Act of 1995. 2 USC § 1381. The office is composed of five individuals appointed jointly by the Speaker, the Majority Leader of the Senate, and the Minority Leaders of the House and the Senate. The office has regulatory, enforcement, and educational responsibilities under the Act. Section 1382 provides for a General Counsel to be appointed by the Chair of the Compliance Board to exercise the authorities of the Office of Compliance.

Office of the Legislative Counsel

The Office of the Legislative Counsel of the House of Representatives evolved from a single Legislative Drafting Service established for the Congress by the Act of February 24, 1919. 40 Stat. 1057, 1141. The currently applicable provisions of law setting forth the purpose and functions of the office and providing for its administration are contained in title V of the Legislative Reorganization Act of 1970. 2 USC §§ 281, 282. The purpose of the office is to advise and assist the House, its committees, and its Members in the achievement of a clear, faithful, and coherent expression of legislative policies.

Congressional Budget Office

The Congressional Budget Office was established by the Congressional Budget Act of 1974. 2 USC § 601. The office is headed by a director appointed by the Speaker and the President pro tempore. 2 USC § 601. The functions of the office include providing assistance to the House and Senate Committees on the Budget and Appropriations and the Senate Committee on Finance in the discharge of matters within their jurisdictions and to other committees to assist them in complying with the provisions of the Act. 2 USC § 602.

The Office of the Law Revision Counsel

The Office of the Law Revision Counsel was established by the Committee Reform Amendments of 1974 to develop a codification of the laws of the United States. 2 USC § 285.

Office of the Parliamentarian

A Parliamentarian has been appointed by the Speaker in every Congress since 1927. Before 1927 the "Clerk at the Speaker's Table" performed the function of the Parliamentarian. In the 95th Congress the House formally and permanently established an Office of the Parliamentarian to be managed, supervised, and administered by a nonpartisan Parliamentarian appointed by the Speaker. 2 USC § 287. The compilation and preparation of the precedents of the House of Representatives was authorized in the 93d Congress by the Committee Reform Amendments of 1974. 2 USC § 28a. The printing and distribution of the precedents was also authorized by law. 2 USC §§ 28, 28b-e, 29.

For a list of other House offices, commissions, and joint entities, see *Manual* §§ 1113-1125h.

§ 7. Service of Process

Rule VIII governs the procedure for House response to a judicial or administrative subpoena served on a Member, Delegate, Resident Commissioner, officer, or employee of the House. *Manual* § 697. Examples of service of process on officers include those on the Speaker, the Clerk, and the Sergeant-at-Arms. Deschler Ch 11 §§ 16.2-16.4, 16.7-16.9, 16.11. Examples of service of process on employees include those on current and former employees of a committee, an employee of the House Republican Conference, and a former employee of a former House select committee who was subpoenaed to give a deposition about his recollection of certain executive session transactions. 93-2, Sept. 30, 1974, p 33020; 94-1, Sept. 23, 1975, p 29824; 97-1, Jan. 22, 1981, pp 694, 695. For a discussion of how an officer must comply with service of process under rule VIII, see QUESTIONS OF PRIVILEGE.

Legal counsel, through the Department of Justice, is available to an officer of the House (but not its Members) to defend the officer against actions brought against such officer while discharging official duties or executing an order of the House. 2 USC § 118. For a discussion of this statutory procedure, as well as House authorization by resolution for the appointment of legal counsel to represent an officer, Member, or employee who has been served with process, see QUESTIONS OF PRIVILEGE. Legal counsel is also available through the Office of General Counsel under clause 8 of rule II, which provides legal assistance and representation to Members, committees, officers, and employees in complying with legal process under rule VIII. § 5, supra.

Chapter 36
Order of Business; Privileged Business

Research References
4 Hinds §§ 3056-3152
6 Cannon §§ 708-757
Deschler Ch 21 §§ 1-8, 28-31
Manual §§ 869-901

A. The Daily Order of Business

§ 1. In General; Varying the Order of Business

Generally

The order or sequence in which business is taken up for floor consideration is governed by various House rules. A general rule for the "daily order of business" is set forth in clause 1 of rule XIV. *Manual* § 869. The order of business may be affected by rule XV, Business in Order on Special Days, which includes: Suspensions (clause 1), the Discharge Calendar (clause 2), the Private Calendar (clause 5), and Calendar Wednesday (clause 6). *Manual* §§ 885-901. The order of business specified by rule XV may be varied by a special order of the House as described in CONSIDERATION AND DEBATE and SPECIAL ORDERS OF BUSINESS.

Although rule XIV states the daily order of business, it does not bind the House to a fixed daily routine. Other House rules make certain important subjects privileged so as to permit the daily order of business to be interrupted or even supplanted entirely for days at a time. See §§ 4-7, infra. Indeed, clause 1 of rule XIV qualifies the daily order of business with the following parenthetical: "(unless varied by the application of other rules and except for the disposition of matters of higher precedence)." Although privileged matters may interrupt the order of business, procedural questions—such as a vote on adopting a special order of business, a motion to resolve into the Committee of the Whole, or the question of consideration—may precede their consideration. This system enables the House to give precedence to its most important business without losing the power by majority vote to go to any other measures on its calendars. For a list of privileged matters that may interrupt the order of business, see *Manual* §§ 870, 871.

The order of business also may be affected by the Speaker's discretionary authority to recognize Members on particular questions. See RECOGNITION. Pursuant to clause 6 of rule XIV, all questions relating to the priority of business shall be decided without debate.

Scheduling Business

The business of the House is scheduled by the Speaker and the Members who constitute the leadership of the majority party, acting in concert with the leadership of each standing committee and the Committee on Rules. Deschler Ch 21 § 1. The daily or weekly agenda of the House is ordinarily formulated by the Leadership and implemented by special orders of business reported from the Committee on Rules and adopted by the House. The legislative schedule for the House is announced to the Members by the Majority Leader or Whip or a designee or, rarely, by the Speaker. Deschler Ch 21 § 1.1. Such announcement is usually a response to a question asked by the Minority Whip or a designee during a "customarily long one-minute speech" or "colloquy" at the end of the legislative week. 105-2, Mar. 27, 1998, pp 5037-40.

§ 2. Sequence of Particular Business

The general rule specifying the daily order of business is set forth in clause 1 of rule XIV as follows:

- First: Prayer by the Chaplain.
- Second: Reading and approval of the Journal, unless postponed under clause 8 of rule XX.
- Third: The Pledge of Allegiance to the Flag.
- Fourth: Correction of reference of public bills.
- Fifth: Disposal of business on the Speaker's table as provided in clause 2.
- Sixth: Unfinished business as provided in clause 3.
- Seventh: The morning hour for the consideration of bills called up by committees as provided in clause 4.

- Eighth: Motions that the House resolve into the Committee of the Whole House on the state of the Union subject to clause 5.
- Ninth: Orders of the day.

Ranked first in the daily order of business is the prayer. No business is in order before the prayer, which is offered daily when the House meets. Deschler Ch 21 § 2.

The next order of business is the approval of the Journal. Only messages from the President or the Senate may be received and questions of the privileges of the House raised before the approval of the Journal. No other business, including privileged business, may intervene. See JOURNAL.

Following the approval of the Journal is the Pledge of Allegiance to the Flag, which is led by a Member at the invitation of the Speaker. One-minute speeches, although not provided for by rule XIV, are sometimes entertained by unanimous consent following the Pledge of Allegiance. § 3, infra. It is then in order to offer motions or unanimous-consent requests to correct the reference of public bills. See INTRODUCTION AND REFERENCE OF BILLS.

Rule XIV next provides for the disposal of business on the Speaker's table. Under clause 2 of rule XIV, such business consists of the referral of executive communications, messages from the President, and messages from the Senate; motions to dispose of certain Senate bills and resolutions; and motions to dispose of Senate amendments. *Manual* § 873. Messages from the President and messages from the Senate are matters of privilege and may be received, laid before the House, and disposed of whenever business permits. Deschler Ch 21 § 2. Disposition of Senate bills, see SENATE BILLS; AMENDMENTS BETWEEN THE HOUSES.

Under the prescribed order of business in rule XIV, the motion to resolve into Committee of the Whole is in order after the morning hour for consideration of bills reported by committees and before "orders of the day." The morning hour and "orders of the day" have not been used in many years, the House relying instead on special orders of business, which often supersede the regular order of business for lengthy periods. 4 Hinds § 3056; see SPECIAL ORDERS OF BUSINESS.

An order of business resolution reported from the Committee on Rules, permitting the Speaker to declare that the House resolve into the Committee of the Whole to consider a particular bill, gives precedence to such declaration when no other business is pending. Clause 2(b) of rule XVIII. Under clause 4 of rule XVIII, the motion to resolve into the Committee of the Whole is privileged for consideration of general appropriation bills. The motion to resolve into the Committee of the Whole may also be made privileged by the provisions of a statute. Deschler Ch 21 § 30.8.

As to when particular matters are in order, see APPROPRIATIONS; CALENDARS; CONFERENCES BETWEEN THE HOUSES; DISTRICT OF COLUMBIA BUSINESS; PRIVATE CALENDAR; QUESTIONS OF PRIVILEGE; QUORUMS; RESOLUTIONS OF INQUIRY; and VETO OF BILLS.

§ 3. The Daily Practice

The sequence of events on the House floor on any given day may, and usually does, vary from the order prescribed by clause 1 of rule XIV. Certain customs and norms have developed over recent years that allow Members to express their concerns on matters not pending before the House or scheduled for consideration in the daily or weekly agenda. One-minute speeches, special-order speeches, and ''morning-hour'' debate are all vehicles for this type of free expression. See CONSIDERATION AND DEBATE.

On each legislative day, certain events do occur in a predictable order. The prayer, the approval of the Journal, and the Pledge of Allegiance all occur in sequence, although the actual vote on the approval of the Journal (if demanded) may be postponed.

Before reaching the scheduled business of the day, the Speaker usually agrees to recognize Members for one-minute speeches. The Speaker may limit the number if the anticipated legislative schedule is full. See CONSIDERATION AND DEBATE for practices and norms relating to such speeches. Because of the precise language in the rules governing the Private Calendar and the discharge rule, one-minute speeches may await the disposition of those types or classes of business.

Following the disposition of one-minute speeches, and throughout the legislative day, the Chair lays down messages received from the President or the Senate. The Chair also makes announcements concerning appointments or informing the House of communications received in an official capacity.

Following one-minute speeches, the House normally proceeds to business holding a privileged status for that day. That special status may be set by a standing rule, by a special order of business reported by the Committee on Rules, or by an order previously adopted by the House either by unanimous consent or motion to suspend the rules.

Once this business is reached, the prescribed order is still subject to some flexibility. Certain record votes may be postponed or ''clustered'' to occur in sequence, pursuant to the Speaker's authority under clause 8 of rule XX.

When scheduled business has been completed, it is again customary for Members to be given an opportunity to address the House on other subjects.

Special-order speeches may be granted by designation of party leaders for up to one hour or 30 minutes per Member. Limits on the number and duration of such speeches are enforced by the exercise of the Speaker's power of recognition, which follows a policy established on opening day.

B. Privileged Business

§4. In General; Under the Constitution

Privileged business is business of such importance as to enjoy precedence over the regular order of business. It is business that can supersede or interrupt other matters that might otherwise be called up or be pending before the House. *Manual* §§853-857, 870, 871.

Privileged questions are to be distinguished from what are termed "questions of privilege." Privileged questions relate to the order or priority of business under the rules of the House, whereas "questions of privilege" pertain to the safety and dignity of the House, to the integrity of its proceedings, or to the rights or reputation of its members under rule IX. 3 Hinds §§2654, 2718; see QUESTIONS OF PRIVILEGE.

Privilege may derive from the Constitution, from the rules and practices of the House, and from statutes enacted pursuant to legislative rulemaking power. For example, a veto message from the President is privileged for consideration when received by the House. This privilege arises from article I, section 7, clause 2 of the Constitution. See VETO OF BILLS. Likewise, because the exclusive power of the House in the impeachment of civil officers arises from article I, section 2, clause 5 of the Constitution, the House has determined that propositions to impeach, and reports from a committee investigating charges of impeachment, are highly privileged. See IMPEACHMENT. Similarly, because article VI, clause 3 of the Constitution provides that Representatives shall take an oath, the administration of the oath to Members is privileged. A Member-elect appearing during a session may be administered the oath as a matter of the highest privilege that may interrupt other business. See OATHS.

Certain propositions are privileged for consideration because of indirect constitutional mandate. Examples include concurrent resolutions for adjournment *sine die* or to a day certain and motions incident to establishing a quorum, which are discussed in ADJOURNMENT and QUORUMS. However, privilege is not conferred merely because the question is one committed to the House under the Constitution. *Manual* §702. For example, a resolution to confirm the nomination of the Vice President, a duty committed to the

House under the 25th amendment to the Constitution, is not privileged for consideration. Deschler Ch 21 § 28.

§ 5. Business Privileged by House Rule

A variety of bills, reports, resolutions, and motions are privileged under the House rules. Some committees are given the power to report to the House at any time on certain subjects. See COMMITTEES. Certain kinds of committee reports are privileged, including reports on the contempt of witnesses, resolutions of inquiry, and election contests. These subjects are discussed in CONTEMPT, RESOLUTIONS OF INQUIRY, and ELECTION CONTESTS AND DISPUTES.

§ 6. —Privilege of Particular Business

The House rules make certain important subjects privileged, which permit the daily order of business to be interrupted or even supplanted entirely for days at a time. Among the privileged matters that may interrupt the order of business are:

- General appropriation bills. Clause 5 of rule XIII.
- Conference reports. Clause 7 of rule XXII.
- Motions to request or agree to a conference. Clause 1 of rule XXII.
- Special orders of business reported by the Committee on Rules. Clause 5 of rule XIII.
- Consideration of amendments between the Houses after disagreement. Clause 4 of rule XXII.
- Questions of privilege. Rule IX; see QUESTIONS OF PRIVILEGE.
- Bills coming over from a previous day with the previous question ordered. 5 Hinds §§ 5510-5517.
- Bills returned with the objections of the President. 4 Hinds §§ 3534-3536.

Some propositions are privileged for consideration on certain days of the week or month. On any Monday, Tuesday, or Wednesday, for example, the Speaker may recognize Members to move to suspend the rules and pass measures. Clause 1 of rule XV. The second and fourth Mondays of the month are set apart for District of Columbia business. Clause 4 of rule XV. Bills on the Private Calendar are called on the first Tuesday of the month and also on the third Tuesday if directed by the Speaker. Clause 5 of rule XV. The Speaker has the discretion to dispense with the call of the Private Calendar on the third Tuesday. *Manual* § 897.

Other classes of business not only are given a prescribed day but also are keyed to a specific reference in the order of business prescribed in clause 1 of rule XIV. For example, motions to discharge, when perfected and otherwise eligible, can be called up after the approval of the Journal. Clause 2 of rule XV. District of Columbia business is given a position following "disposal of such business on the Speaker's table as requires reference only." Clause 4 of rule XV. Both the provisions that designate a day for the class of business, and those that give the class a specified place in the order of business, can be changed by the House by adoption of a special order of business from the Committee on Rules, a unanimous-consent agreement, or a motion to suspend the rules.

The privileged status that is conferred on certain classes of business does not necessarily carry with it an exemption from applicable layover requirements of the House rules. Thus, a conference report may be called up for consideration as privileged business only after the report has been filed and is in compliance with the three-day and two-hour availability requirements of clause 8 of rule XXII. See CONFERENCES BETWEEN THE HOUSES.

When the Speaker is faced with competing Members seeking recognition for consideration of different items of business, it must first be determined whether one class or type of business is of a higher precedence than the other. In making these determinations, the Speaker relies on the rules of the House that give the matter precedence and on prior rulings of the Chair that may predetermine the choice. For a compilation of such rulings, see Deschler Ch 21 § 31. They are of lesser relevance in the modern practice because the House usually determines the order of consideration by adoption of a special order of business reported from the Committee on Rules. Also, the priority of propositions of equal privilege may be determined by the Chair as within the Chair's power of recognition.

§ 7. —Privileged Motions

Certain motions relating to the order of business are given precedence under the rules of the House. One example is the motion to suspend the rules, which may be used to change the order of business as well as to adopt a measure. See SUSPENSION OF RULES. The motion that the House resolve itself into the Committee of the Whole to consider a general appropriation bill is likewise privileged under the rules. See APPROPRIATIONS. For legislative procedures enacted in law (which may accord privileged status to certain motions), see CONGRESSIONAL PROCEDURES ENACTED IN LAW.

When called up pursuant to the provisions of the discharge rule under clause 2(d) of rule XV, a motion to discharge a committee is privileged; and the Speaker may decline to recognize for a matter not related to the proceedings. 7 Cannon § 1010. Such motions take precedence over business merely privileged under the general rules of the House. 7 Cannon § 1011; see DISCHARGING MEASURES FROM COMMITTEES.

If authorized, by vote or committee rule, by the committee (or committees) with jurisdiction over the bill, a motion to send a matter to conference is privileged under clause 1 of rule XXII. *Manual* § 1069. The motion is privileged at any time the House is in possession of the papers if the appropriate committee has authorized the motion and the Speaker recognizes for that purpose. *Manual* § 1070. A motion to discharge or instruct conferees is privileged under clause 7(c) of rule XXII. See CONFERENCES BETWEEN THE HOUSES.

For a discussion of precedence of secondary motions, see AMENDMENTS; LAY ON THE TABLE; POSTPONEMENT; PREVIOUS QUESTION; RECONSIDERATION; and REFER AND RECOMMIT.

Chapter 37
Points of Order; Parliamentary Inquiries

Research References

5 Hinds §§ 6863-6957
8 Cannon §§ 3427-3458
Deschler-Brown Ch 31 §§ 14, 15
Manual §§ 627-629, 641, 971

A. Points of Order

§ 1. In General; Form

Generally

A point of order is an objection that the pending matter or proceeding is in violation of a rule of the House. For a discussion of grounds for points of order, see § 7, infra. Any Member, Delegate, or the Resident Commissioner may make a point of order. 6 Cannon § 240. There have been rare instances in which the Speaker has insisted that a point of order be reduced to writing. 5 Hinds § 6865. However, the customary practice is for the Member to rise and address the Chair as follows:

> MEMBER: M__. Speaker (or M__. Chair), I make a point of order against the [amendment, section, paragraph]. The [amendment, section, paragraph] violates __________.

It is appropriate for the Chair to determine whether the point of order is being raised under a particular rule of the House. A Member should state a point of order explicitly, identifying the objectionable language. Deschler-Brown Ch 31 §§ 2.2, 2.3. On occasion, a Member has incorrectly demanded the "regular order," rather than make a point of order to assert, for example, that remarks are not confined to the question under debate. In such a case, the Chair may treat the demand as a point of order and rule thereon. *Manual* § 628.

The proper method for opposing a point of order is to speak on the point of order prior to the Chair's ruling and not by making a point of order against the point of order. Deschler-Brown Ch 31 § 7.3.

Effect

Where a point of order against the *consideration* of a bill is sustained, the bill is recommitted to the reporting committee or to its place on the appropriate calendar. See, *e.g., Manual* § 841. However, if the defect were a technical error in the report, the measure could be returned to the calendar by the filing of a supplemental report pursuant to clause 3(a)(2) of rule XIII. *Manual* § 838; 7 Cannon § 869. If a bill is on the wrong calendar and the Chair sustains a point of order against it for that reason, the bill is placed on the appropriate calendar. 4 Hinds § 4382.

If, during the consideration of a bill, a Member raises a point of order against certain language in a pending measure and the Chair sustains the point of order, the language is automatically stricken from the measure. 7 Cannon § 2148.

Under the former practice it was necessary for a Member on the floor to reserve points of order against appropriation bills before resolving into the Committee of the Whole, but this practice was eliminated in 1995 when the House adopted clause 1 of rule XXI. Under clause 1, points of order on general appropriation bills are "considered as reserved," which permits the Committee of the Whole to remove language in a bill referred to it by the House that violates House rules. *Manual* § 1035.

A point of order sustained against any part of an amendment is sufficient to invalidate the entire amendment. 5 Hinds § 5784. A point of order may be directed against an entire section or paragraph of a bill (depending on whether the bill is read by paragraph or by section). It also may be precisely aimed at a subpart thereof. However, the entire section or paragraph is vulnerable; and if a point of order is sustained against a portion of a pending provision, the entire provision may be ruled out of order unless prevented by a special order of business. 5 Hinds § 6883; Deschler-Brown Ch 31 §§ 1.24, 1.25. The stricken provision's headings and subheadings are likewise eliminated. 8 Cannon § 2353. Provisions ruled out on points of order in the Committee of the Whole are not reported to the House. 4 Hinds § 4906; 8 Cannon § 2428.

Multiple Points of Order

The Chair may entertain simultaneously more than one point of order against a paragraph. Deschler-Brown Ch 31 § 1.8. Typically, the Chair will decline to decide a point of order raised against a proposition until all other points of order on the same proposition have been submitted. 8 Cannon § 2310. Indeed, the Chair has the discretion to require all points of order against a pending proposition for alleged violation of a particular House rule to be stated at the same time. This procedure allows the Chair to rule separately on each point of order in such order as the Chair determines, or to permit the Chair to sustain one valid point of order without reaching the others. Deschler-Brown Ch 31 § 4.18. Thus, where several points of order are made against an amendment and the Chair sustains one of them, the remaining points of order need not be ruled on, as the amendment is no longer pending. Deschler-Brown Ch 31 § 1.12. Where the Chair entertains two points of order against a provision, the Chair may choose to sustain only one of them, even though both points of order are conceded by the manager of the bill. *Manual* § 628.

Cross References

Points of order based on particular rules or against particular propositions are addressed elsewhere in many other chapters in this work, such as AMENDMENTS; APPROPRIATIONS; CONSIDERATION AND DEBATE; and GERMANENESS OF AMENDMENTS.

§ 2. Role of the Chair

Generally

Under clause 5 of rule I, the Speaker decides "all questions of order, subject to appeal by a Member, Delegate, or Resident Commissioner." *Manual* § 627. When a Speaker pro tempore occupies the Chair, such Member decides questions of order. When the House is in Committee of the Whole, its Chair decides most questions of order independently of the Speaker. 5 Hinds §§ 6927, 6928. At the organization of a new Congress, before the election of a Speaker, questions of order are decided by the Clerk. Clause 2(a) of rule II; 1 Hinds § 64.

The Chair may examine the form of an offered amendment to determine its propriety and may rule it out of order even where no point of order is raised from the floor. Deschler-Brown Ch 31 § 6.11. Ordinarily, however, the Chair will rule out a proposition only when a point of order is raised and only when required under the circumstances to respond to the point of order. Deschler-Brown Ch 31 § 1.6. It is not the duty of the Speaker to decide any question that is not directly presented in the course of the proceedings of the House. 2 Hinds § 1314; see CONSIDERATION AND DEBATE. However, it is the duty of the Chair to initiate the call to order of a Member who engages in improper references to the actions of the Senate, its Members, or its committees, or to the President. *Manual* §§ 374, 961.

The Speaker may decline to rule on a point of order until the issue has been examined and studied. 3 Hinds § 2725; 8 Cannon §§ 2174, 2396. In reaching a decision on a point of order, the Chair may hear argument. *Manual* § 628; see § 9, infra.

Only on rare occasions has the Speaker submitted a question to the House itself for a decision, preferring to rule subject to appeal by any Member under clause 5 of rule I. *Manual* § 628; 4 Hinds §§ 3282, 4930; 5 Hinds § 5323.

Where the House has adopted an order permitting only certain amendments to be offered to a bill during its consideration in Committee of the Whole, the Chair is guided by the explicit unambiguous language of the rule, rather than by the intention of the Committee on Rules, in ruling whether a specific amendment is in the permitted class. *Manual* § 628. The Member offering an amendment in the Committee of the Whole pursuant to a special order of the House has the burden of proving that it meets the description of the amendment made in order. The Chair has advised the Committee that an amendment made in order was described by subject matter rather than by prescribed text and that the pending amendment fit such description. *Manual* § 993.

The Chair may consider argument on the meaning of an amendment in resolving any ambiguity in the language of the amendment when ruling on a point of order against it. Deschler-Brown Ch 31 § 8.9.

Consideration of Prior Rulings; Reversals

A decision by the Speaker or Chair is a precedent in resolving subsequent disputes where the same point of order is again in controversy. In looking to precedents to resolve a point of order, the House is applying a doctrine known in the courts as *stare decisis*, under which a judge looks to earlier cases involving the same question of law. In the same way, the House adheres to settled rulings and will not lightly disturb rationales that have been established by prior decision of the Chair. 2 Hinds § 1317; 6 Cannon § 248. However, although the Chair will normally not disregard a decision previously made on the same facts, such precedents may be examined, distinguished, and even overruled where shown to be erroneous. 4 Hinds § 4637; 8 Cannon §§ 2794, 3435. Indeed, the Chair may after further argument reverse the previous ruling on a point of order, for example, where existing law not previously called to the Chair's attention would justify the opposite ruling. 8 Cannon § 3435; Deschler-Brown Ch 31 § 1.5. The authoritative sources for proper interpretations of the rules are statements made directly from the Chair and not comments made by the Speaker in other contexts. *Manual* § 628.

§ 3. Reserving Points of Order

Generally

With certain exceptions, a point of order against a proposition may be held untimely if it is not made until after debate on the proposition has begun. § 4, infra. It is therefore not an uncommon practice for a Member to reserve a point of order against an amendment and then, after debate on the amendment, either press or withdraw the point of order. 8 Cannon § 3430. Reserving points of order against amendments, see AMENDMENTS.

The reservation of a point of order against an amendment is permitted at the discretion of the Chair and does not require unanimous consent. Deschler-Brown Ch 31 § 3.16. A Member wishing to reserve a point of order must rise and address the Chair. The Member may not reserve a point of order merely through private agreement with the Member in charge of the bill. 5 Hinds § 6867. The reserving Member need not specify the basis of the reservation. Deschler-Brown Ch 31 § 3.8. However, merely reserving the "right to object" to engage in a colloquy before making a point of order does not constitute the reservation of a point of order. 92-2, Apr. 18, 1972, p 13114.

Effect of Withdrawal

The reservation of a point of order being withdrawn, another Member may immediately renew the reservation or press a point of order. Deschler-Brown Ch 31 §§ 3.21-3.23. For a discussion of withdrawal of points of order generally, see § 11, infra.

§ 4. Time to Raise Points of Order

Generally

Unless otherwise provided by the rules of the House, a point of order against a proposition should be made when the proposition is presented for consideration, not after such consideration has begun. 5 Hinds § 6888. This principle is applied to points of order against bills and resolutions as well as to points of order against various motions, such as the motion to recommit. A point of order against a motion to recommit a bill must be made after the motion is read and comes too late after there has been debate thereon. Deschler-Brown Ch 31 § 4.25. A point of order against a motion to recommit may interrupt the reading of said motion where enough of the reading has been completed for the Chair to determine that the motion is not in order. 111-1, July 9, 2009, p ____. A point of order against a report involving the privileges of the House is properly raised after the report is read. Deschler-Brown Ch 31 § 4.5.

Under the rules of the House, certain points of order may be raised "at any time." For example, a point of order may be raised "at any time" under clause 4 of rule XXI, which prohibits the inclusion of appropriations in a bill or joint resolution reported by a legislative committee. *Manual* § 1065. A point of order may likewise be raised "at any time" under clause 5(a) of rule XXI, which prohibits inclusion of a tax or tariff measure in a bill or joint resolution reported by a committee that does not have jurisdiction over such measure. *Manual* § 1066. Such a point of order may be directed against language in a measure or against an amendment containing such language. In the former case, the point of order should be raised during the reading for amendment under the five-minute rule. Deschler Ch 25 § 12.14. In the latter case, the point of order should be raised before disposition of the amendment. Deschler-Brown Ch 31 § 5.29.

Effect of Intervening Debate

A point of order against a proposition ordinarily will be ruled out as untimely if debate on the merits of the proposition already has begun. 5

Hinds §§6891-6901; 8 Cannon §3440. However, the Chair will not permit brief debate to preclude a point of order by a Member who had diligently sought recognition for that purpose. 5 Hinds §6906. The Chair may recognize for a point of order against language in a bill notwithstanding intervening debate where the Member raising the point of order was standing, seeking recognition, before debate began. Deschler-Brown Ch 31 §6.39. Indeed, a Member who is standing and seeking recognition at the proper time to make a point of order may be recognized by the Chair, even though the Clerk has read past the language to which the point of order applies. Deschler-Brown Ch 29 §20.33. However, the mere fact that a Member was standing does not entitle such Member to make a point of order where such Member has not affirmatively sought recognition at the time the relevant nguage was read for amendment. Deschler-Brown Ch 31 §5.25.

Effect of Intervening Amendments

A point of order against a proposition ordinarily is untimely if raised after an amendment to the proposition has been offered. 5 Hinds §§6907-6911; 8 Cannon §3443. The point of order may be precluded even by a pro forma amendment. 8 Cannon §3445; 108-2, June 16, 2004, p 12565.

Points of order against a bill or portion thereof are considered by the Chair before the Chair recognizes Members to offer amendments. Deschler-Brown Ch 31 §5.1. If a bill is considered read and open to amendment at any point by unanimous consent, points of order should be stated before *any* amendments are offered. Deschler-Brown Ch 31 §5.5.

Although the reservation of a point of order by one Member inures to all Members who may then make the point of order when recognized by the Chair, withdrawal of a reservation by one Member requires other Members to either make or continue to reserve the point of order at that point, and a further reservation comes too late after there has been subsequent debate. Deschler-Brown Ch 31 §3.24.

§5. —Against Bills and Resolutions

Where the sustaining of a point of order against a measure would prevent its consideration, the appropriate time to make the point of order is when the measure is called up in the House or pending the motion or declaration to resolve into the Committee of the Whole, whichever procedure represents initial consideration of the measure. 8 Cannon §2252. A Member may not insist on a point of order against the consideration of a bill where the manager of the bill withdraws the motion that the House resolve itself into the Committee of the Whole for consideration of the bill. The point of order must be made anew if and when the motion is again made to resolve into Committee for consideration of that bill. Deschler-Brown Ch 31 § 4.6.

Although uncommon, a point of order challenging, for example, the privileged status of a resolution may be raised when the resolution is called up and before it is read. Deschler-Brown Ch 31 § 4.1. A point of order relating to the manner in which a resolution should be considered should be made before such consideration begins. 5 Hinds § 6890. A point of order that the text of a privileged resolution does not reflect the action of the reporting committee comes too late after there has been debate on the resolution. Deschler-Brown Ch 31 § 4.4.

§ 6. —Against Amendments

A point of order is properly made or reserved immediately after the reading of an amendment or following agreement to a unanimous-consent request that an amendment be considered as read. Deschler-Brown Ch 31 § 6.5. It should be disposed of before amendments to that amendment are offered. Deschler-Brown Ch 31 § 6.14. Once the amendment is agreed to in the Committee of the Whole and reported to the House, it is too late to raise a point of order against it, the proper time having been at the point the amendment was offered in Committee. 92-2, June 1, 1972, pp 19479, 19481, 19483. See generally AMENDMENTS.

§ 7. Application to Particular Questions; Grounds

A point of order ordinarily must be based on an objection that the pending matter or proceeding is in violation of some rule of the House. The Chair will ascertain and identify the particular rule being invoked when ruling on a point of order. 98-2, Oct. 2, 1984, p 28522.

Although questions of order arising under the rules are determined by the Chair, the Chair does not:

- Recognize for requests to suspend the rule governing admission to the floor. Clause 2(b) of rule IV; 5 Hinds § 7285.
- Rule on the sufficiency of committee reports or legal effect of language therein. Deschler Ch 19 § 7.17.
- Rule on questions of constitutionality, including the constitutional powers of the House. *Manual* § 628; 2 Hinds §§ 1255, 1318-1320; 8 Cannon §§ 2225, 3031, 3071, 3427; Deschler Ch 19 §§ 7.1-7.3, 8.10.
- Pass on the merits of a legislative proposition. Deschler Ch 19 § 7.4.
- Rule on the consistency of amendments or other proposed actions of the House. 2 Hinds §§ 1327-1336; 8 Cannon §§ 3237, 3458; Deschler Ch 19 §§ 7.5, 8.6-8.9.

- Construe the legislative or legal effect of a proposition. *Manual* § 628; 8 Cannon §§ 2280, 2841; Deschler Ch 19 § 7.16.
- Construe the general meaning or effect of an amendment or rule on whether it is ambiguous. Deschler Ch 19 §§ 8.1-8.5.
- Rule on hypothetical questions. 6 Cannon §§ 249, 253; Deschler Ch 19 §§ 7.6-7.8.
- Rule on the propriety or expediency of a proposed course of action. 2 Hinds §§ 1275, 1337.
- Consider contingencies that may arise in the future. 7 Cannon § 1409.
- Interpret a special order of business before it is adopted by the House. *Manual* § 628.
- Decide issues not presented in a point of order. Deschler Ch 19 § 6.1.
- Construe the result of a vote. Deschler Ch 6 § 4.28.
- Interpret the rules or procedures of the Senate. Deschler Ch 19 § 7.19.

The Speaker, and not the chair of the Committee of the Whole, rules on the propriety of amendments included in a motion to recommit with instructions. Deschler-Brown Ch 31 § 1.46

§ 8. Relation to Other Business

When a point of order is raised against a proposition, consideration of that proposition is precluded until the point of order is disposed of. The Chair should rule on the point of order before proceeding to other questions, such as the method of voting on the pending matter. 8 Cannon § 3432.

A timely point of order takes precedence over a parliamentary inquiry, and the deferral of a parliamentary inquiry gives no priority for that purpose because recognition is in the discretion of the Chair. Deschler-Brown Ch 31 § 11.4.

An amendment may not be offered to a proposition against which a point of order is pending. 8 Cannon § 2824. The previous question may not be demanded on a proposition until the point of order is resolved. 8 Cannon §§ 2681, 3433. Debate on the merits of the proposition is likewise precluded. 5 Hinds § 5055; 8 Cannon § 2556.

§ 9. Debate on Points of Order; Burden of Proof

In General; Recognition

Recognition for debate on a point of order is extended at the discretion of the Chair. 8 Cannon §§ 3446-3448. Members seeking to be heard must address the Chair separately and may not engage in "colloquies" on the point of order. Deschler-Brown Ch 31 § 7.17. The time allowed for debate on a point of order is likewise within the discretion of the Chair, who may decline to hear more when prepared to rule. *Manual* § 628. A Member speaking on a point of order does not control a fixed amount of time that can be reserved or yielded. 5 Hinds § 6919. Where a point of order is conceded by the manager of the bill, the Chair may sustain the point of order without debate. Deschler-Brown Ch 31 § 7.20.

Some points of order are not decided by a ruling from the Chair (beyond a threshold determination that the rule applies to the pending proposition), but instead trigger an automatic question of consideration. See QUESTION OF CONSIDERATION for examples of such points of order. With regard to unfunded mandates and earmark points of order, the statute or rule provides for 20 minutes of debate, equally divided between the Member raising the point of order and a Member opposed. *Manual* §§ 1068d, 1127.

Scope of Debate

The rule that debate on questions of order must be relevant is strictly construed. 8 Cannon § 3449. Debate is limited to the question of order and may not go to the merits of the proposition being considered. *Manual* § 628.

The Chair will not entertain unanimous-consent requests to permit Members to revise and extend their remarks on points of order. Deschler-Brown Ch 31 § 7.21. However, by unanimous consent, a Member may be allowed to revise and extend remarks *to follow* the ruling on the point of order. *Manual* § 628.

Burden of Proof

The proponents of an amendment have the burden of proof where a point of order is raised against the amendment on the grounds that it is not germane or that it proposes an unauthorized appropriation. 7 Cannon § 1179; 8 Cannon § 2995. Under House practice, those defending an item in an appropriation bill have the burden of showing the law authorizing it. 4 Hinds § 3597; 7 Cannon §§ 1179, 1276; 8 Cannon § 2387. Thus, a point of order having been raised, the burden of proving the authorization for language carried in an appropriation bill falls on the managers of the bill as proponents of the language. Deschler Ch 26 § 9.4. Similarly, the proponent of an amendment carries the burden of proving that the amendment does not increase levels of budget authority or outlays within the meaning of clause 2(f) of rule XXI. 107-1, Oct. 11, 2001, p 19368.

Where a point of order is raised against consideration of a bill on the ground that the report thereon does not adequately reflect all changes in existing law as required by clause 3(e) of rule XIII—the Ramseyer rule—the maker of the point of order has the burden of proof and must cite the specific statute that will be affected by the pending bill; in the absence of such citation the point of order will not be entertained. 8 Cannon § 2246.

§ 10. Waiver of Points of Order

Generally

Points of order may be waived by unanimous consent, by special order of business, or by consideration of a measure under suspension of the rules. Deschler-Brown Ch 31 § 9. In addition, a point of order is effectively waived when it is not timely raised. Where a motion that might have been subject to objection is, in the absence of a point of order, agreed to, it represents the will of the House and governs its procedure until the House orders otherwise. Deschler Ch 11 § 3.2.

By Special Order of Business

Special ''rules'' or resolutions from the Committee on Rules providing for the consideration of a bill often contain provisions expressly waiving points of order against the bill or certain language therein or amendments to be offered thereto. 7 Cannon § 769. A resolution waiving points of order against a certain provision in a bill has been agreed to by the House even after general debate on the bill has concluded and reading for amendment has begun. Deschler Ch 21 § 23.29. Such waivers are not implied merely by the fact that the special order of business provides for consideration of the bill. 98-1, Mar. 22, 1983, p 6502.

A special order of business may limit its waiver to a single point of order against consideration of a measure or against its provisions, or it may be so drafted as to constitute a blanket waiver of all points of order. Where a resolution providing for the consideration of a bill specifies that ''all points of order against said bill are hereby waived,'' the waiver is applicable only to the provisions of the bill and not to amendments. Deschler-Brown Ch 31 § 9.10. A special order of business providing for consideration of a measure may waive all points of order against provisions of the bill except specified text. Such a special order may include language to prevent a point of order against the vulnerable text from being applied to the remainder of a paragraph or section. See, *e.g.*, 107-1, July 17, 2001, p 13511.

A special order of business containing a waiver of section 425 of the Congressional Budget Act (unfunded intergovernmental mandates) is subject to a point of order under section 426 of that Act. Similarly, a special order of business containing a waiver of clauses 9(a) or 9(b) of rule XXI (earmarks) is subject to a point of order under clause 9(c) of rule XXI.

For further discussion, see SPECIAL ORDERS OF BUSINESS. See also CONSIDERATION AND DEBATE.

§ 11. Withdrawal of Points of Order

A point of order may be withdrawn at any time before the Chair rules. 8 Cannon § 3430. Once withdrawn, the point of order may immediately be renewed by another Member. 5 Hinds §§ 6875, 6906; 8 Cannon §§ 3429, 3430. As a rule, a point of order must be pressed, or further reserved, when the Chair inquires whether the objecting Member wishes to insist upon it, and comes too late after that Member has stated that such Member does not insist on, or continue to reserve, the point of order, and further debate has intervened. Deschler-Brown Ch 31 § 3.14.

§ 12. Appeals

Under clause 5 of rule I, a ruling of the Chair on a point of order may be subject to challenge through an appeal by a Member. *Manual* §§ 627, 629; 5 Hinds §§ 6938, 6939. An appeal also may be taken from the ruling of the chair of the Committee of the Whole on a point of order. Deschler-Brown Ch 31 § 13.3. However, a decision on a question of order is not subject to an appeal if the decision falls within the discretionary authority of the Chair. For a complete discussion of appeals, see APPEALS.

B. Parliamentary Inquiries

§ 13. In General

Recognition of Members for the purpose of propounding parliamentary inquiries is within the discretion of the Chair. 6 Cannon § 541. Inquiries concerning the parliamentary situation on the floor are properly directed to the Chair, and it is not in order for a Member to address them to the official reporters. Deschler-Brown Ch 31 § 14.14. The Chair may delay the response to a parliamentary inquiry pending examination of relevant House precedents. 8 Cannon § 2174. Responses to parliamentary inquiries are not subject to appeal. 5 Hinds § 6955; 8 Cannon § 3457. The Chair may take a parliamentary inquiry under advisement, especially when the inquiry does not relate to the pending proceedings of the House. *Manual* § 628a; 8 Cannon § 2174; 102-2, Apr. 7, 1992, p 8273; 103-1, May 26, 1993, p 11251.

The Chair may clarify a prior response to a parliamentary inquiry. *Manual* § 628a.

§ 14. Subjects of Inquiry

Proper Subjects of Inquiry

The Chair responds to parliamentary inquiries relating in a practical sense to the pending proceedings, such as inquiries relating to the application of the rules and precedents to a pending or otherwise pertinent situation. The Chair has entertained parliamentary inquiries concerning the following:

- The anticipated order of business. Deschler-Brown Ch 31 § 14.7.
- The status of the Clerk's progress in reading a document. Deschler-Brown Ch 31 § 14.12.
- The Speaker's authority as presiding officer. Deschler-Brown Ch 29 § 2.1.

Improper Subjects of Inquiry

The Chair may decline to entertain an inquiry on a subject not relevant to the pending question. Under this principle, the Chair has declined to respond to hypothetical questions, to questions not yet presented, and to requests to place pending proceedings in a historical context. *Manual* § 628a. The Chair has declined, for example, to anticipate whether language in a measure would trigger certain executive actions or to allocate debate time on a conference report not yet filed. Similarly, the Chair has declined to anticipate the precedential effect of a ruling or to respond to rhetorical or political characterizations of pending business.

A proper parliamentary inquiry relates to an interpretation of a House rule, not to an interpretation of a statute or of the Constitution. *Manual* § 628a. A Member may not, under the guise of a parliamentary inquiry, offer a motion or other proposition. Members must have the floor in their own right for that purpose. 8 Cannon § 2625.

In response to a parliamentary inquiry, the Chair has declined to:

- Judge the propriety of words spoken in debate pending a demand that those words be ''taken down'' as unparliamentary or judge the veracity of remarks in debate, or the propriety of words uttered earlier in debate.
- Reexamine and explain the validity of a prior ruling.
- Judge the accuracy of the content of an exhibit.
- Indicate which side of the aisle has failed under the Speaker's guidelines to clear a unanimous-consent request.
- Judge the construction or meaning of an amendment, which is a matter for the House, and not the Chair, to determine.
- Characterize an amendment on which a separate vote has been demanded.

Manual § 628a.

As to Orders of the House

The Chair ordinarily will not interpret a pending special order of business prior to its adoption or render other advisory opinions. For example, the Chair refused to respond to a parliamentary inquiry as to whether a resolution, reported from the Committee on Rules but not yet called up for consideration, would have the effect of violating the rights of Members. Questions concerning informal guidelines of the Committee on Rules for advance submission of amendments for possible inclusion under a special order of business may not be raised under the guise of a parliamentary inquiry. *Manual* § 628a.

§ 15. Timeliness of Inquiry

Generally

The Chair may decline to respond to a parliamentary inquiry that is untimely. The Chair does not respond to a parliamentary inquiry concerning the propriety of a proposition until the proposition is offered. Deschler-Brown Ch 31 § 15.11.

Inquiries Raised During Votes

During a vote, the Chair may refuse to entertain a parliamentary inquiry that is not related to the vote, although an inquiry relating to the conduct of the call may be entertained. *Manual* § 628a; Deschler-Brown Ch 31 §§ 15.14, 15.15. A parliamentary inquiry may not interrupt a division. However, such inquiries are entertained until the Chair asks those in favor of the proposition to rise. Deschler-Brown Ch 31 §§ 15.19, 15.20. Similarly, the Speaker may entertain a parliamentary inquiry after the yeas and nays are ordered, but before the vote. Deschler-Brown Ch 31 § 15.18.

The Chair may decline to entertain a parliamentary inquiry as to the cost of conducting the pending vote on the ground that the inquiry is not relevant to the pending question. 103-1, June 10, 1993, p 12482.

§ 16. As Related to Other Business

A parliamentary inquiry may interrupt matters of high privilege, such as an impeachment proceeding. 6 Cannon § 541. However, during the reading of a bill for amendment, a Member is not entitled to a parliamentary inquiry that would interrupt the reading of a paragraph or section of the bill. 8 Cannon § 2873.

The reading of the Journal may be interrupted by a parliamentary inquiry. 6 Cannon § 624. Furthermore, the Speaker may entertain a parliamentary inquiry relating to the order of business before the approval of the Journal. Deschler-Brown Ch 31 § 15.9.

During Debate

A Member may not be taken from the floor by a parliamentary inquiry but may yield for that purpose. The Chair exercises discretion in recognition for a parliamentary inquiry only when no other Member is occupying the floor for debate. *Manual* § 628a; Deschler-Brown Ch 31 §§ 15.1, 15.2.

Time consumed by a parliamentary inquiry is charged to the Member controlling time who yields for that purpose. When the Chair recognizes a Member for a parliamentary inquiry when no other Member has the floor, the Member controlling debate is not charged for the time so consumed. Deschler-Brown Ch 31 § 15.4.

Chapter 38
Postponement

Research References
5 Hinds §§ 5306-5318
8 Cannon §§ 2613-2617
Deschler Ch 23
Manual §§ 443-453, 911, 915, 998, 1030

§ 1. Postponement Generally

Authority for Motion or Declaration

Under clause 4 of rule XVI, a matter under debate may be postponed to a future day (or indefinitely) pursuant to a motion by any Member. *Manual* §§ 911, 915. A matter also may be postponed pursuant to the provisions of a special order of business. Deschler Ch 23 § 8.1. As adopted in the 111th Congress, clause 1(c) of rule XIX permits the Speaker to postpone further consideration of certain measures on which the previous question has been ordered. *Manual* § 1000a. In some instances the postponement of the consideration of a particular class of legislation has been recognized in statutes that reserve to the Congress the right to review certain executive branch actions. See *Manual* § 1130; *e.g.*, the Trade Act of 1974 (19 USC § 2192). For postponement relating to voting, see VOTING.

Postponement Motions

In the House there are two motions to postpone: (1) the motion to postpone to a day certain; and (2) the motion to postpone a matter indefinitely.

Both types of motions are provided for by clause 4 of rule XVI. Under that rule the motion to postpone to a day certain takes precedence over the motion to postpone indefinitely. The rule further provides that, once decided, neither motion may be made again on the same day at the same stage of the question. *Manual* § 911.

The two motions are distinguishable in several respects:

- The motion to postpone to a day certain takes precedence over various secondary motions in clause 4 of rule XVI, including the motions to refer or to amend (§ 3, infra), whereas the motion to postpone indefinitely yields to all those secondary motions (§ 7, infra).
- The motion to postpone to a day certain is debatable only within narrow limits (§ 5, infra), whereas debate on the motion to postpone indefinitely may be extended even to the merits of the pending proposition (§ 8, infra).
- The motion to postpone to a day certain merely suspends consideration of the pending measure until the date specified (§ 2, infra), whereas the motion to postpone indefinitely has the effect of finally disposing of the pending matter adversely (§ 6, infra).

Postponement of Measures in Committee of the Whole

The motion to postpone, either to a day certain or indefinitely, is not in order in the Committee of the Whole. *Manual* § 915; Deschler Ch 23 § 5. It is not in order in the House to move to postpone a bill where the bill is still being considered in the Committee. 4 Hinds § 4915; 8 Cannon § 2436.

Disposition of unfinished matters, see UNFINISHED BUSINESS.

§ 2. Motion to Postpone to a Day Certain

When in Order

When a question is under debate, the motion to postpone to a particular day is provided for by clause 4 of rule XVI. *Manual* §§ 911, 915. The motion is in order in the House and when the House is sitting as in the Committee of the Whole. 95-1, Nov. 1, 1977, p 36351. The motion is in order following the reading of the pending proposition and may be offered before the manager of the proposition has been recognized for debate. Deschler Ch 23 § 6.2; Deschler-Brown Ch 29 § 68.53. It is not in order after the previous question has been ordered on the pending matter. 5 Hinds §§ 5319-5321; 8 Cannon §§ 2616, 2617; Deschler Ch 23 § 6.1.

A motion to postpone to "the next legislative day" is construed as a motion to postpone to a day certain. 8 Cannon § 2657. The motion to postpone to a day certain may not specify a particular hour. 5 Hinds § 5307; Deschler Ch 23 § 5. It is not in order to move to postpone consideration of business to a day certain if that day is Calendar Wednesday, except by unanimous consent. 7 Cannon § 970; 8 Cannon § 2614. However, these precedents should be read in light of the current form of clause 6 of rule XV, which provides for Calendar Wednesday only when specifically noticed. See CALENDAR WEDNESDAY.

Form

MEMBER: M__. Speaker, I move that the [further] consideration of __________ [*the proposition*] be postponed until Friday next.

Effect of Motion

When the House adopts a motion to postpone a measure to a day certain, the effect is to suspend consideration of the measure until the day specified in the motion. 8 Cannon § 2614. A subsequent motion providing for an earlier consideration of the matter is not in order. 5 Hinds § 5308.

Application of Motion to Table

The motion to postpone to a day certain is subject to the motion to lay on the table. *Manual* § 914. The adoption of the motion to table carries only the motion to postpone—not the underlying measure—to the table. 8 Cannon § 2657.

Voting

A motion to postpone a proposition to a day certain may be determined by a simple majority vote, even though the proposition itself may require a two-thirds vote for passage. 7 Cannon § 1112. A bill that comes before the House on the day scheduled for it by a special order of business likewise may be postponed by a majority vote. 4 Hinds § 3177.

The vote on a motion to postpone a measure to a day certain is subject to a motion to reconsider. 5 Hinds § 5643.

§ 3. —Precedence

Clause 4 of rule XVI lists the motion to postpone to a day certain fourth among those motions available when a question is under debate. It follows the motions to adjourn and to lay on the table and the motion for the previous question, and thus the motion to postpone must yield to these more preferential motions. 5 Hinds § 5301; 8 Cannon § 2609. However, the motion to postpone to a day certain enjoys precedence over the motions to refer, to amend, and to postpone indefinitely. *Manual* § 911; 5 Hinds § 5301. The motion also takes precedence over the question of passing a bill vetoed by the President. Deschler Ch 23 § 7.1.

§ 4. —Application to Particular Propositions

The motion to postpone to a day certain has been applied to a wide variety of measures and questions, it being reasoned that otherwise the majority of the House could not exercise its will over the consideration of its business. 8 Cannon § 2613. However, the motion must be applied to the entire pending proposition, and not merely to a part thereof. 5 Hinds § 5306.

The motion to postpone consideration of a matter to a day certain is applicable to such propositions as:

- A bill coming before the House pursuant to a special order of business assigning the day for its consideration. 4 Hinds § 3177.
- A veto message, notwithstanding the constitutional mandate that the House "shall proceed to reconsider" a vetoed bill. 4 Hinds §§ 3542-3547; 7 Cannon §§ 1101, 1105, 1112; Deschler Ch 23 § 7.1.
- A resolution of disapproval under certain statutes. Deschler Ch 23 § 6.3.
- A resolution of censure reported from the Committee on Ethics. Deschler-Brown Ch 29 § 68.53.
- An appeal from the decision of the Chair. 8 Cannon § 2613.

The motion to postpone to a day certain is not applicable to:

- A motion to discharge a committee under clause 2 of rule XV. Deschler Ch 23 § 6.4.
- A special order of business from the Committee on Rules unless the previous question is rejected. *Manual* § 858; 5 Hinds § 4958.

§ 5. —Debate and Amendment

The motion to postpone to a day certain is subject to amendment. 5 Hinds § 5754; 8 Cannon § 2824. It is debatable within narrow limits. 5 Hinds § 5309. Debate is limited to the advisability of postponement only and may not go to the merits of the proposition to be postponed. 5 Hinds §§ 5310-5315; 8 Cannon § 2372; Deschler Ch 23 § 5.

In the House a motion to postpone to a day certain is debatable for one hour controlled by the Member offering the motion. Deschler-Brown Ch 29 § 68.56. Such Member may move the previous question on the motion and, if adopted, thereby terminate debate and preclude amendment. Deschler Ch 23 § 7.2. If a motion to table the motion is agreed to, debate on and amendments to the motion to postpone are precluded. 8 Cannon § 2654.

§ 6. Motion to Postpone Indefinitely

Authorization and Effect

The motion to postpone indefinitely is provided for by clause 4 of rule XVI. *Manual* §§ 911, 915. Adoption by the House of a motion to postpone a measure indefinitely constitutes final adverse disposition of that measure. Deschler Ch 23 § 5.

Application

The motion to postpone indefinitely has been held not to apply to a veto message from the President, a ruling that would appear to be reinforced by the constitutional mandate that the House must "proceed to reconsider" the measure. U.S. Const. art. I, § 7; 4 Hinds § 3548. However, the motion has been applied to various other legislative propositions, including:

- A House bill with Senate amendment. 5 Hinds § 6200.
- A Senate bill with House amendment. 5 Hinds § 6199.
- A resolution of disapproval of executive actions under certain statutes. Deschler Ch 23 § 6.3.
- A resolution relating to the election of House officers. 5 Hinds § 5318.

The motion to postpone indefinitely must be applied to the entire pending proposition and not merely to a part thereof. 5 Hinds § 5306.

Form

MEMBER: M__. Speaker, I move that the [further] consideration of ________ be postponed indefinitely.

§ 7. —Precedence; Application to Other Motions

In 1822 the House amended clause 4 of rule XVI to change the precedence of the motion to postpone indefinitely from its former place—immediately after the motion for the previous question—to the end of the list, where it remains to this day. *Manual* § 911. Accordingly, the motion to postpone indefinitely enjoys no precedence over the other secondary motions. 5 Hinds § 5301; Deschler Ch 23 § 8.1 (note). Because of its less preferential status, the motion is seldom used in the modern practice. It has been held specifically inapplicable to:

- A motion to refer. 5 Hinds § 5317.
- A motion to suspend the rules. 5 Hinds § 5322.
- A motion to resolve into Committee of the Whole, except under a statute providing for consideration of a resolution of disapproval that specifically allows the motion to postpone. *Manual* § 915; 6 Cannon § 726.

- A motion to discharge a committee under clause 2 of rule XV. Deschler Ch 23 § 6.4.

§ 8. —Debate and Amendment

The motion to postpone indefinitely is not amendable. Deschler Ch 23 § 8.1 (note). However, the motion is debatable, including debate on the merits of the pending proposition. 5 Hinds § 5316.

Debate on the motion may be precluded by statute with respect to a particular class of legislation. See, *e.g.*, the Trade Act of 1974, § 152(d)(3) (19 USC § 2192(d)(3)). Notwithstanding such a statute, the House may permit debate on the motion by unanimous consent. 98-1, Aug. 1, 1983, pp 21899, 21900.

Chapter 39
Previous Question

Research References

5 Hinds §§ 5443-5520, 5569-5604
8 Cannon §§ 2661-2694
Deschler Ch 23 §§ 14-24
Manual §§ 461-463, 994-1002

§ 1. In General

Function and Purpose

Clause 1 of rule XIX provides for the motion for the previous question. It is an essential motion in the House that is used during the consideration of a matter to terminate debate, foreclose the offering of amendments, and bring the House to an immediate vote on the main question. *Manual* § 994. It is the only motion used for this purpose in the House. 5 Hinds § 5456; 8 Cannon § 2662.

The import of the previous question, in Jefferson's language, is "shall the main question be now put?" *Manual* § 452. If the House disagrees to the motion, the main question is open to further consideration and the right of recognition transfers to a Member who opposed the motion. §§ 15, 16, infra.

The House practice in this regard is to be distinguished from that of the Senate, which does not admit the previous question. 8 Cannon § 2663.

Historical Background

In early Congresses, the previous question was used in the House for an entirely different purpose than it is today, having been modeled on the English parliamentary practice. As early as 1604, the previous question had been used in the Parliament to suppress a question that the majority deemed undesirable for further discussion or action. *Manual* §§ 442, 463. The Continental Congress adopted this device in 1778, but there was no intention of using it as a means of closing debate in order to bring the pending question to a vote. 5 Hinds § 5445.

Early interpretations of the rule in the House were consistent with its usage in the Continental Congress. However, in 1807, the House overruled a holding by Speaker Varnum that the ordering of the previous question precluded all debate on the main question. As a result, debates became very lengthy. In 1811, the House reversed its position by once again overruling Speaker Varnum to provide that there could be no debate after the previous question was ordered, and this decision was adhered to in subsequent rulings by the Speaker. 5 Hinds § 5445.

To moderate the harsh effects of the rule, seen by some as a way of suppressing a minority, the number required to order the previous question was changed from one-fifth to a majority, and a Member was given the right to call for 40 minutes of debate on a proposition if it had not been previously debated. 5 Hinds §§ 5445, 6821. In 1880, the rule was amended to permit the Speaker to entertain one motion to recommit, notwithstanding the ordering of the previous question. § 13, infra.

§ 2. Offering the Motion

Form

The motion for the previous question may be offered by any Member holding the floor. It must be made in writing if demanded, but is usually made orally:

> MEMBER: M__. Speaker, I move the previous question on the __________ [*proposition*].

SPEAKER: The question is on ordering the previous question.

The motion should precisely specify the scope that is intended. See §7, infra. The motion for the previous question may not include a provision that it is to take effect at a time certain. Such a motion may not include a provision, for example, "that the previous question be considered as ordered at 5 o'clock." 5 Hinds §5457.

Effect of a Special Order of Business

The ordering of the previous question on a bill may be required by language in a special order of business governing consideration of the bill. The rule may provide, for example:

> The previous question shall be considered as ordered on the bill and on any amendment thereto to final passage without intervening motion except: (1) one hour of debate on the bill equally divided and controlled by the chair and ranking minority member of the Committee on House Administration; and (2) one motion to recommit with or without instructions.

When the House is operating under such a rule, the Chair states that "under the rule, the previous question is ordered," and a motion for the previous question from the floor is unnecessary. 7 Cannon §776. Such a rule prohibits intervening motions, such as a motion to adjourn. *Manual* §912; Deschler-Brown-Johnson Ch 40 §3.4.

§3. —When in Order; Quorum Requirements

The previous question is one of those motions that is in order under clause 4 of rule XVI "when a question is under debate." As it is considered a fundamental rule of parliamentary procedure, it also is in order even before the rules of the House have been adopted. Deschler Ch 23 §14.1.

The motion for the previous question is in order in the House and in the House as in the Committee of the Whole. *Manual* §994; 5 Hinds §5456; 6 Cannon §639; 8 Cannon §2662; Deschler Ch 23 §14.10. The motion is not in order in the Committee of the Whole but may be moved in the House on an amendment reported from the Committee of the Whole. 4 Hinds §4716; Deschler Ch 23 §§14.8, 14.9.

The previous question is ordered by a majority of those voting, a quorum being present. However, less than a quorum may order the previous question on a motion incident to a call of the House. 5 Hinds §5458.

§ 4. — Who May Offer

During Debate in the House

The Member in charge of a pending measure has the prior right to recognition and may move the previous question at any time during the hour allotted to such Member and thereby cut off debate. 8 Cannon § 3231. The Member in charge may move the previous question upon regaining the floor after having yielded to another Member "for debate only." 8 Cannon § 2682. Other Members may not interpose the previous question during such time as the Member in charge is holding the floor, even though the Member in charge may not yet have begun to speak. *Manual* § 997; 2 Hinds § 1458. However, if the Member in charge of the pending measure does not move the previous question and loses the floor, any Member having the floor may so move. 5 Hinds § 5475. This is so even though the effect of moving the previous question may be to deprive the Member in charge of control of the measure. *Manual* § 997; 5 Hinds § 5476; 8 Cannon § 2685. If no Member moves the previous question after the expiration of the hour allotted to such Member, another Member may be recognized for a successive hour under the hour rule. Deschler-Brown Ch 29 § 67.13; 105-2, Dec. 18, 1998, p 27838.

Where time for debate in the House is equally divided and controlled by the majority and the minority, or between those in favor and those opposed, the previous question may not be moved until the other side has used or yielded back its time. The Chair may vacate the ordering of the previous question where it was improperly moved while the other side was still controlling time. *Manual* § 997.

Proponent of Amendment

A Member managing consideration of a measure may offer an amendment to the pending measure and move the previous question on the amendment and on the pending measure. *Manual* § 996. Although the previous question takes precedence over a motion to amend, the proponent of an amendment, having been recognized for debate after offering the amendment, may not be taken from the floor by another Member who seeks to move the previous question. Deschler Ch 23 § 20.7; § 6, infra. This rule is followed even though the amendment offered is merely a pro forma amendment. 92-2, May 8, 1972, pp 16154, 16157. However, a Member offering a preferential motion to dispose of a Senate amendment may not move the previous question on that motion as against the right of the Member in charge to the floor. 2 Hinds § 1459.

Effect of Yielding

A Member in charge of a pending measure may yield time to others for debate only and still retain the right to resume debate or move the previous question. 8 Cannon § 3383. However, where the Member in charge yields to another Member to offer an amendment to the measure, the first Member loses the floor and the Member offering the amendment is recognized for one hour and may move the previous question on the amendment and on the measure itself. Deschler-Brown Ch 29 § 33.9. In other words, the Member controlling the time may not yield to another Member to offer an amendment without losing the right to move the previous question. Deschler Ch 23 § 16.2. However, the Member so yielding may move the previous question on the pending measure following disposition of the amendment where the proponent of the amendment has not done so and where no other Member seeks recognition. Deschler Ch 23 §§ 16.3-16.5.

Under clause 4 of rule XVI, the motion for the previous question takes precedence, and may be offered by any Member, over an amendment offered by either the Member in charge of a pending measure or a second Member who was yielded time by the Member in charge. *Manual* § 997; Deschler Ch 23 §§ 14, 18.3.

§ 5. Precedence; Interruption of Other Matters

Generally

The motion for the previous question has the precedence given it by clause 4 of rule XVI. The Chair, having recognized a Member in charge of a bill for the motion for the previous question, may not recognize another Member to rise to a question of personal privilege. Deschler Ch 23 § 17.2. However, a message from the Senate, the administration of the oath, or the presentation of a conference report is in order, notwithstanding that the previous question has been moved or ordered on a pending proposition. 5 Hinds § 6449; Deschler Ch 23 §§ 19.3, 19.4.

A measure on which the previous question has been ordered takes precedence over a special order of business from the Committee on Rules, even if the special order provides for the immediate consideration of certain business. 5 Hinds § 5520.

Suspension of the Rules

The motion to suspend the rules may be entertained after the previous question has been moved and is admitted at the Speaker's discretion, notwithstanding the ordering of the previous question on a pending measure. *Manual* § 887; 5 Hinds §§ 6827, 6831-6833; 8 Cannon § 3418.

§ 6. —Precedence Over Other Motions

Generally

Under clause 4 of rule XVI, the motion for the previous question is listed third in the order of precedence after the motions to adjourn and to lay on the table. As such, the previous question has precedence over the motions to postpone, to refer, or to amend. *Manual* § 911; 5 Hinds § 5301; Deschler Ch 23 § 20.7. A Member making the motion also has priority over another Member seeking recognition for debate. Deschler Ch 23 § 19.1.

The Member in charge of a proposition and having the floor may demand the previous question, notwithstanding that another Member proposes a motion of higher privilege. However, the motion of higher privilege must be put before the question is put on the previous question. *Manual* § 997; 5 Hinds § 5480; 8 Cannon § 2684; Deschler Ch 23 § 16.6. A Member having the floor may not exclude a privileged motion simply by offering a motion of lower privilege and demanding the previous question thereon. 8 Cannon § 2609.

Adjournment

Under clause 4 of rule XVI, the motion to adjourn takes precedence over the motion for the previous question. *Manual* § 911; Deschler-Brown-Johnson Ch 40 § 3. However, a motion to adjourn is not in order after the previous question has been ordered on a bill to final passage under a special order of business prohibiting any intervening motion. *Manual* § 1002; 4 Hinds §§ 3211-3213; Deschler-Brown-Johnson Ch 40 § 3.4.

Lay on the Table

Under clause 4 of rule XVI, the motion to lay the pending proposition on the table takes precedence over the motion for the previous question. *Manual* § 911; 8 Cannon §§ 2658, 2660. However, the motion to table may not be applied to the motion for the previous question itself. 5 Hinds §§ 5410, 5411. The motion to table is not in order *after* the previous question is ordered, or even after the yeas and nays are ordered on the demand for the previous question. 5 Hinds §§ 5408, 5409, 5415-5422. A motion to table a motion to recommit is not in order after the previous question has been ordered on a bill to final passage under a special order of business prohibiting any intervening motion. *Manual* § 1002a.

Although the motion for the previous question yields to the motion to table, if the motion to table is rejected, the question recurs on the motion for the previous question that was pending when the motion to table was offered. Deschler Ch 23 § 20.1.

Referral or Recommittal

The previous question may be moved on a proposition while a motion to refer it is pending. 8 Cannon § 2678. However, the rule authorizing the motion to recommit (or commit) specifically permits the use of that motion after the previous question has been moved or ordered. *Manual* § 1001; see also § 13, infra.

Motions to Amend

The motion for the previous question takes precedence over the motion to amend. Deschler Ch 23 § 20.2. Thus, the motion for the previous question takes precedence over an amendment to, for example, a motion to recommit or a motion to instruct conferees. Deschler Ch 23 §§ 20.4, 20.5. If the motion for the previous question is voted down, the pending measure is subject to amendment. However, if the amendment is ruled out on a point of order, the previous question may again be moved and takes precedence over the offering of another amendment. Deschler Ch 23 § 20.3.

A Member, having obtained the floor to offer a preferential motion to dispose of a Senate amendment in disagreement, may not move the previous question on that preferential motion to the end that the Member in charge of the pending proposition is denied recognition for debate. *Manual* § 997; 2 Hinds § 1459.

§ 7. Scope of Motion; Application to Particular Propositions

Generally

Under clause 1 of rule XIX, the previous question may be moved and ordered on a single question, on a series of questions allowable under the rules, or on an amendment or amendments, or may embrace all authorized motions or amendments and include the bill or resolution to its passage, adoption, or rejection. *Manual* § 994. The motion should precisely specify the scope that is intended. However, where, during the consideration of a bill, a Member states merely "I move the previous question," without specifying the question to be voted on, the Speaker construes it as a motion for the previous question on the bill to final passage and as applicable to all intervening questions. 8 Cannon §§ 2673, 2674. When a series of questions are pending, and the previous question is moved without specifying the precise object of the motion, the Chair will apply the motion to all questions then pending in a related set. Deschler Ch 23 § 14.2. However, the Chair may apply an unqualified motion for the previous question on a divided question to only one portion thereof. 8 Cannon § 2676.

The motion for the previous question is generally applicable to any pending measure or motion that is subject to debate or amendment (*Manual* § 996) and has been held specifically applicable to:

- A proposition and a pending motion to refer the proposition to a committee. 5 Hinds § 5466; 8 Cannon § 2678.
- A pending resolution and an amendment thereto. *Manual* § 996.
- A question of approval of the Journal. Deschler Ch 23 § 14.6.
- A private bill under consideration during the call of the Private Calendar. Deschler Ch 23 § 14.5.
- A question of agreeing to a report of the Committee of the Whole that the enacting clause be stricken. 5 Hinds § 5342.
- A resolution to elect Members to committees. 8 Cannon § 2174.
- Certain amendments to a bill (leaving the remaining amendments open to debate and further amendment). 8 Cannon § 2679.
- All amendments to a bill other than a particular amendment. Deschler Ch 23 § 15.17.
- A substitute amendment. 5 Hinds § 5472.
- A question of privilege, including one involving censure of a Member or impeachment. 2 Hinds § 1256; 5 Hinds § 5460; 8 Cannon § 2672.
- A motion to limit debate pending a motion to go into the Committee of the Whole. 5 Hinds §§ 5203, 5473.
- A motion to postpone a matter to a day certain. Deschler Ch 23 § 18.2.

The previous question is not applicable to:

- A proposition that is not subject to debate or amendment or that is being considered under a procedure that precludes debate or intervening motions. 4 Hinds § 3077; Deschler Ch 23 § 14.12.
- A proposition against which a point of order is pending. 8 Cannon §§ 2681, 3433.
- A portion of a bill, including a single section. *Manual* § 996; 4 Hinds § 4930.
- More than one bill at a time (except by unanimous consent). 5 Hinds §§ 5461-5464.
- A measure being considered under a motion to suspend the rules. Deschler Ch 23 § 14.11.

Titles and Preambles

The rules of the House permit an amendment to the title of a bill after its passage. *Manual* § 922. The ordering of the previous question on a pending resolution does not cover the title or the preamble thereto unless the proponent of the motion so specifies. A motion to order the previous question on the preamble is in order following the vote on the resolution. 5 Hinds § 5469 (note 2); Deschler Ch 23 §§ 14.7, 18.4. However, the motion for the previous question may be applied at once to both a resolution and its preamble. *Manual* § 1002c.

Senate Amendments; Conference Reports

The previous question may be applied to a motion to dispose of a Senate amendment in disagreement, such as a motion to recede. Deschler Ch 23 § 15.6. However, a simple motion for the previous question applies to the immediate pending proposition only and not to other pending questions. 8 Cannon § 2676; but see Deschler Ch 23 § 14.2. Similarly, a motion for the previous question may not be applied to a question on agreeing both to a conference report and to a motion to ask for a further conference on amendments not included in the report. 5 Hinds § 5465. Likewise, when the previous question is ordered on a motion to send a matter to conference, it applies to that motion alone and does not extend to a subsequent motion to instruct conferees. 8 Cannon § 2675.

Incidental Questions

The previous question covers the main proposition but does not apply to questions that arise after the previous question has been ordered and that are merely incidental thereto. 8 Cannon § 2687. Thus, in one instance, it was held that the previous question applied to certain resolutions but not to the question of whether certain Members should be excused from voting thereon. 5 Hinds § 5467.

§ 8. Debate on Motion; Consideration and Disposition

Generally

The motion for the previous question is not debatable. *Manual* § 911; 5 Hinds § 5301; Deschler Ch 23 § 21.1. The motion cannot be amended. *Manual* § 452; 5 Hinds § 5754. It is not subject to a motion to table, and it cannot be postponed. *Manual* §§ 451, 998; 5 Hinds §§ 5322, 5410, 5411. Jefferson wrote, "to change it to tomorrow, or any other moment is without example and without utility." *Manual* § 452. Indeed, he felt that it would be "absurd" to postpone the previous question, it being his view that the same result could be had simply by voting against the previous question. *Manual* § 451.

Voting

The motion for the previous question is determined by a simple majority vote, and may be ordered by less than a quorum on a motion incident to a call of the House. 5 Hinds § 5458. A motion for the previous question on an amendment to a measure and on the measure is not divisible so as to obtain separate votes on ordering the previous question on the two propositions. *Manual* § 996; Deschler Ch 23 § 14.3. When the previous question is ordered on an amendment as well as the main proposition to which it is offered, the vote is taken first on the amendment and then immediately on the proposition. Deschler Ch 23 § 15.12. An order for the previous question does not preclude a demand for a division of the question and for a separate vote on distinct substantive propositions, such as a series of resolutions. 5 Hinds § 6149; 8 Cannon § 3173.

Withdrawal of Motion; Renewal

A Member may withdraw a motion for the previous question if the House has not acted thereon, and any Member entitled to the floor thereafter may renew that motion. 8 Cannon § 2683. If the House acts on the motion and rejects it, the motion nevertheless may be renewed after debate or other intervening business. Deschler Ch 23 §§ 14.4, 22.17.

Vacating the Ordering of the Previous Question

The action of the House in ordering the previous question is subject to the motion to reconsider. *Manual* § 1006; 5 Hinds § 5655; see § 14, infra. The ordering of the previous question also may be vacated by unanimous consent. 95-1, Oct. 6, 1977, p 32600. Thus, in one instance, unanimous consent was granted to permit the consideration of an amendment to a measure, even though the previous question was operating on the measure. Deschler Ch 23 § 14.13. The Chair has also vacated the ordering of the previous question when it was improperly moved while the other side was still controlling time. *Manual* § 997.

§ 9. Effect

Generally; As Precluding Further Consideration

Except as discussed in sections 13 and 14, infra, the adoption of the motion for the previous question stops all debate, precludes the offering of amendments, and brings the House to an immediate vote on the pending matter. 5 Hinds § 5321; Deschler Ch 23 §§ 15, 15.17. It cannot be modified, corrected, or changed, except by unanimous consent. 5 Hinds §§ 5482, 5485. A point of order against the pending matter on which the previous question has been ordered may be overruled as untimely. Deschler Ch 23 § 15.21. A motion ordinarily cannot be withdrawn once the previous question has been also moved on it. *Manual* § 905; 5 Hinds §§ 5355, 5489.

As Precluding Other Motions

With the exception of the motions to reconsider or to recommit (§§ 13, 14, infra), the ordering of the previous question precludes the application of various motions to dispose of the pending matter, including the motion to table (5 Hinds §§ 5412-5422; 8 Cannon § 2655), the motion to postpone (5 Hinds §§ 5319-5321; 8 Cannon §§ 2609, 2616, 2617), and a motion in the House to strike the enacting clause (Deschler Ch 23 § 15.13).

§ 10. —On Debate Generally

Effect of Demand

After the previous question has been moved on a proposition, no further debate on it is in order unless the previous question is rejected. Deschler Ch 23 § 15.1. All incidental questions, including ordinary questions of order, are likewise decided without debate. *Manual* § 1000; 5 Hinds §§ 5448, 5449. However, under the present practice, the Chair may recognize and respond to a parliamentary inquiry although the previous question may have been demanded. *Manual* § 1000. The demand precludes further debate on the question of overriding a Presidential veto. Deschler Ch 23 § 15.2.

Effect of Adoption

The ordering of the previous question on a proposition under debate has the effect of terminating that debate. 5 Hinds §§ 5443, 5444; 8 Cannon § 2662. The reading of a report or other paper, being in the nature of debate, is not in order thereafter. 5 Hinds §§ 5294, 5296. The proponent's right to close debate is likewise precluded. 5 Hinds §§ 4997-5000. Propositions on which pending debate has been terminated by the motion include: an amendment offered to a resolution reported by the Committee on Rules (Deschler Ch 23 § 15.10), an amendment in the nature of a substitute (Deschler Ch 23 § 15.11), and a motion to dispose of an amendment in disagreement between the Houses (Deschler Ch 23 § 15.8). However, a question involving the privileges of the House, subject to proper notice under rule IX, may have precedence over a pending proposition notwithstanding the ordering of the previous question, unless the previous question has been ordered without intervening motion (3 Hinds § 2532) or an explicit prohibition against dilatory motions is applicable.

Effect of a Special Order of Business Ordering the Previous Question

A special order of business governing consideration of a matter may order the previous question to adoption or passage without intervening motion (often excepting one motion to recommit). Such a resolution nevertheless would permit debate for 10 minutes on the motion to recommit a bill or joint resolution with instructions (*Manual* § 1001; Deschler Ch 23 § 15.15) but would preclude a motion to postpone or a motion to adjourn during pendency of the matter (*Manual* § 1002; 4 Hinds §§ 3211-3213). Alternatively, a special order of business that orders the previous question after debate may permit an intervening motion during debate, such as the motion to postpone. 96-2, Mar. 12, 1980, p 5388. In addition, such a rule enables the Speaker to postpone further proceedings at any time during consideration of the underlying measure pursuant to clause 1(c) of rule XIX.

§ 11. — On Divided Debate

Generally

When debate is divided by rule, or by the manager yielding control of time, the previous question may not be moved until the other side has used or yielded back its time. *Manual* § 997.

Forty-minute Debate

An exception to the rule that the previous question cuts off debate is found in clause 1 of rule XIX. It allows 40 minutes of debate where the previous question is ordered on a debatable proposition that in fact has not been debated. *Manual* § 999. This rule was adopted in 1880 to prevent passing measures without a word of debate, a frequent practice before that time. 5 Hinds § 6821. The right to 40 minutes of debate accrues only if the previous question is ordered, not merely moved. Deschler Ch 23 § 21.4. However, the 40 minutes of debate must be demanded before the House begins to vote on the main question. 5 Hinds § 5496.

Debate under the 40-minute rule is divided between the proponent of the pending proposition and an opponent. Deschler Ch 23 § 21.2.

If there has been any debate at all on the merits of the pending proposition before the ordering of the previous question, the 40 minutes of debate permitted by the rule cannot be claimed. 5 Hinds §§ 5499-5502. That time may not be demanded on a proposition that has been debated in the Committee of the Whole. 5 Hinds § 5505. The 40-minute rule does not apply to propositions that are themselves not debatable, such as a motion to close debate. 8 Cannon §§ 2555, 2690; Deschler Ch 23 § 21.7. The ordering of the previous question without debate by a special order of business resolution (not by motion) also would trigger the 40-minute rule. 103-2, July 29, 1994, pp 18611, 18615.

The word ''question'' in the 40-minute rule refers to the main question and does not refer to incidental motions, such as a motion to recommit a bill. 5 Hinds § 5497. ''Debate'' means debate on the main question and not on something incidentally connected therewith, such as a concurrent resolution correcting an error in the section numbers of the bill. 5 Hinds § 5508. Debate on a failed suspension constitutes ''debate'' such that moving the previous question on the bill without debate at a later time would not trigger the 40-minute rule. 5 Hinds §§ 5506, 5508.

The 40 minutes of debate may be claimed where the previous question has been ordered on an amendment that has not been debated either in the House or in the Committee of the Whole. 5 Hinds § 5503. However, the 40 minutes of debate may not be claimed with respect to an undebated amendment if the previous question was ordered both on the undebated amendment and the main proposition and the main proposition was debated. 5 Hinds § 5504.

The 40-minute rule does not apply at the inception of a Congress before the adoption of rules. 5 Hinds § 5509; Deschler Ch 23 § 21.6.

§ 12. — On Amendments

The previous question is an essential tool of the proponent of a proposition. After the previous question has been moved on a proposition, it is not subject to further amendment unless the motion is rejected by the House. Deschler Ch 23 § 15.5. If the previous question is ordered, no further amendments to the proposition are in order except for an amendment proposed in a motion to recommit with instructions. 8 Cannon § 3231; Deschler Ch 23 § 15.7; § 13, infra. Ordering the previous question precludes amendment to a special order of business reported by the Committee on Rules or to a motion to recommit with instructions. 8 Cannon §§ 2698, 2712, 3241; Deschler Ch 23 § 15.14.

Ordering the previous question on a proposition precludes amendments even if the question is not subject to debate. 5 Hinds §§ 5473, 5490. For example, the previous question may be applied in the House to the nondebatable motion to recommit in order to prevent amendment. *Manual* § 996.

Although unanimous consent may be granted for the consideration of an amendment even though the previous question has been ordered, the Speaker may decline to entertain unanimous-consent requests for that purpose. Deschler Ch 23 §§ 14.13, 15.18.

The motion for the previous question is not used in the Committee of the Whole. However, it is applicable to the work product that the Committee reports to the House. Where the previous question is ordered on some amendments reported from the Committee of the Whole, they must be disposed of before further consideration of the remaining amendments. Deschler Ch 23 § 15.19.

Amendments also are precluded where the House is operating pursuant to a special order of business providing that the previous question is "considered as ordered." Deschler Ch 23 §§ 15.15, 15.16.

§ 13. Recommittal

Generally

Clause 2 of rule XIX permits a motion to recommit (or commit) the pending measure to a committee either pending the motion for or after the ordering of the previous question. *Manual* § 1001. This provision was adopted in 1880 to afford "the amplest opportunity to test the sense of the House as to whether or not the bill is in the exact form it desires." 5 Hinds § 5443; see REFER AND RECOMMIT.

Amendment and Debate

Contrary to the early practice, the opponents of the bill are given priority in recognition to move to recommit it to a committee. *Manual* §§ 1001, 1002; 2 Hinds § 1456. The motion to recommit under this rule may be amended, as by adding instructions, unless such amendment is precluded by moving the previous question on the motion. 5 Hinds §§ 5582-5584; 8 Cannon § 2695.

A motion to recommit with instructions commonly provides that the committee report "forthwith." If the motion is adopted, the committee chair immediately reports to the House in conformity with the instructions; and the bill, as modified, is automatically before the House again. The House then votes separately on the amendments, which are not subject to further amendment if the previous question has been ordered on the bill to passage. The previous question, when ordered on the bill, continues in force until disposition of the bill and is not vitiated by its recommitment. Thus, where the previous question is moved on a resolution and an amendment thereto, and the House orders it recommitted with instructions to report with an amendment forthwith, the previous question remains operative to bar a subsequent amendment. 8 Cannon § 2677.

§ 14. Reconsideration

The vote on ordering the previous question on a measure is subject to the motion to reconsider. 5 Hinds § 5655. However, a motion to reconsider that vote may not be entertained if the House has partially executed that order, as by voting on an amendment. 5 Hinds §§ 5653, 5654. The vote ordering the previous question on a special order of business reported from the Committee on Rules may be reconsidered and such reconsideration is not dilatory under clause 6(b) of rule XIII. *Manual* §§858, 1006; see also RECONSIDERATION.

A motion to reconsider a vote on a proposition may be made after the previous question has been demanded on the proposition or even after it has been ordered and while it is operating. *Manual* §1005; 5 Hinds §§5656-5662. Under the modern practice, where the House votes to reconsider a proposition on which the previous question was operating when first voted on, no debate is in order except by unanimous consent. Deschler-Brown Ch 29 §6.51.

§15. Rejection of Motion—As Permitting Further Consideration

Generally

The defeat of the motion for the previous question on a pending proposition ordinarily opens up that proposition to further consideration, amendment, and debate. Deschler Ch 23 §§22.1-22.5. However, the rejection of the motion for the previous question on a measure that is not subject to amendment, such as a conference report, does not open the measure to amendment but only extends the time for debate thereon. Deschler Ch 23 §22.15. Similarly, if a pending proposition is not debatable, but is vulnerable to an amendment, the defeat of the previous question does not provide time for debate but only the opportunity for amendment. Deschler Ch 23 §22.8.

Motions

The rejection of the previous question can open a motion to further amendment. Examples include motions to instruct conferees, to recede and concur in a Senate amendment, to recommit a bill with instructions, and to recommit a conference report. Deschler Ch 23 §§22.12, 22.13, 22.16.

§16. —As Affecting Recognition

If the previous question is voted down on a proposition, recognition passes to an opponent of the motion for the previous question. Deschler Ch 23 §§23.1, 23.5. Thus, the previous question on a resolution being voted down, the Speaker may recognize a Member who led that effort, who may offer an amendment and be recognized for one hour. Deschler Ch 23 §§23.2, 23.5. However, recognition of such Member could be preempted by another Member with a preferential motion, such as the motion to lay on the table. *Manual* §954. The recognition of the Member is not precluded by the fact that such Member has been previously recognized to offer an amendment. Deschler Ch 23 § 23.4.

The practice of bestowing recognition on a Member leading the opposition upon rejection of the previous question is applied to a resolution from the Committee on Rules, to a motion to instruct conferees, and to a motion to recommit. Deschler Ch 23 §§ 23.6, 23.7; 107-2, Feb. 27, 2002, pp 2080-2085.

In recognizing one of the leaders of the opposition when the previous question is rejected, the Chair may give preference to a Member of the minority who was actively opposed to ordering the previous question. Deschler Ch 23 § 23.1. However, where no minority Member so qualified seeks recognition, a majority Member who opposed the previous question on the pending proposition may be recognized. Deschler Ch 23 § 23.8.

§ 17. Effect of Adjournment When Previous Question Operating

If the House adjourns without voting on a proposition on which the previous question has been ordered, the question becomes unfinished business on the next legislative day. 8 Cannon §§ 2693, 2694; Deschler Ch 23 §§ 15.22, 24.2. The proposition is taken up as unfinished business immediately after disposal of business on the Speaker's table. 5 Hinds §§ 5510-5517; 8 Cannon § 2674; Deschler Ch 23 § 24.2. Multiple bills coming over from a previous day with the previous question ordered thereon have precedence in the order in which the several motions for the previous question were made. 5 Hinds § 5518. A proposition coming over from the preceding day with the previous question ordered thereon has been held to take precedence over a motion for the disposition of a veto message from the President and to take precedence over a motion to go into the Committee of the Whole for the consideration of a bill privileged by special order of business. 8 Cannon §§ 2674, 2693; see generally UNFINISHED BUSINESS.

Chapter 40
Private Calendar

Research References
4 Hinds §§ 3266-3303
7 Cannon §§ 846-871
Deschler Ch 22 §§ 10-14
Manual §§ 895-897

§ 1. In General

Usage and Purpose; Referrals to the Calendar

The Private Calendar is used to facilitate the consideration of bills that are limited in their applicability to particular individuals or entities. Deschler Ch 22 § 10.

A formal calendar for private bills was established by rule during the 62d Congress. Before that time, private bills had been considered pursuant to special orders of business from the Committee on Rules. *Manual* § 896. Today, private bills when favorably reported are delivered to the Clerk for reference to the Private Calendar under the direction of the Speaker. *Manual* §§ 828, 831. The Speaker may correct the erroneous referral of a private bill to the Union Calendar or that of a public bill to the Private Calendar. *Manual* § 828; 7 Cannon § 859.

Generally, the Private Calendar and unanimous-consent requests are the exclusive procedures for consideration of private bills. The Speaker does not schedule them under suspension of the rules.

Measures Eligible

Resolutions and bills may be considered pursuant to the Private Calendar rule. Clause 5 of rule XV. The use of omnibus private bills—that is, the consolidation into one bill of numerous private bills that have been objected to by two or more Members when first called on the calendar—has been permitted under the rules since 1935. *Manual* § 895. The validity of this consolidation procedure has been sustained. Deschler Ch 22 § 13.1. See also § 6, infra.

Clause 4 of rule XII prohibits the introduction of certain private bills. See BILLS AND RESOLUTIONS.

§ 2. Calling the Calendar; When in Order

The Private Calendar is called up on the first and third Tuesdays of the month after the disposal of ''such business on the Speaker's table as requires reference only. . . .'' *Manual* § 895. The calling of the calendar is mandatory on the first Tuesday unless specifically dispensed with by the House and, within the Speaker's discretion, on the third Tuesday. Deschler Ch 22 § 11.

On the first Tuesday of the month, after disposition of matters requiring referral but before beginning the call, the Speaker has recognized a Member to call up a conference report (Deschler Ch 22 § 11.12), for a motion for a call of the House (100-1, July 8, 1987, p 18972), and for a unanimous-consent request (Deschler Ch 22 § 11).

The call has been entertained before the Speaker recognized for a privileged motion to discharge a committee from a resolution of inquiry (Deschler Ch 24 § 8.7) and before the consideration of a veto message carried over as unfinished business (94-1, Oct. 7, 1975, pp 32036-41).

On the third Tuesday, because the call is discretionary, the Speaker may entertain a unanimous-consent request for business not otherwise privileged, and the call does not displace other privileged business. Deschler Ch 22 § 11.3.

§ 3. Waivers; Dispensing with the Call

Deviations from the Private Calendar rule have been permitted by special order of business or by unanimous consent. By such means the House may:

- Permit a private bill to be considered at a time other than that specified by the rule. Deschler Ch 22 §§ 11.5-11.7.
- Transfer the entire calendar to days other than those specified. Deschler Ch 22 § 11.8.
- Dispense with the calendar altogether during a particular week. Deschler Ch 22 § 4.2.
- Take up other specified business during the time for the call of the calendar. Deschler Ch 22 § 11.11.

- Recommit a private bill on the calendar to committee. Deschler Ch 22 § 12.7.
- Restore to the calendar measures stricken therefrom. Deschler Ch 22 §§ 12.13-12.15.
- Rescind actions previously taken in connection with the calendar. Deschler Ch 22 §§ 12.16, 12.17.

Clause 5 of rule XV specifically provides for a privileged motion to dispense with all or part of the call of the Private Calendar by a two-thirds vote. *Manual* § 895; Deschler Ch 22 § 11.1. The motion is debatable for 10 minutes, divided between the proponent and an opponent of the motion. *Manual* § 895.

§ 4. Objections; Screening Procedures

Under clause 5 of rule XV, a bill called on the Private Calendar on the first Tuesday of the month that is objected to by two or more Members is automatically recommitted to the committee reporting it. On the third Tuesday of each month the same procedure is followed, with the exception that omnibus private bills are in order regardless of any objection. See § 6, infra.

By tradition, the Majority Leader and the Minority Leader each appoint three Members to serve as Private Calendar ''objectors'' during a Congress. Deschler Ch 22 § 15.3. These official objectors screen all bills that are placed on the calendar. When the calendar is called, the objectors may oppose or delay the consideration of any private bill that they feel is objectionable for any reason. The objectors may adopt and announce specific criteria that must be satisfied if a private bill is to be called up for consideration on the calendar. *Manual* § 896. For example, the objectors may require that a measure be on the calendar for at least seven days before being considered. Deschler Ch 22 § 12.1; 112-1, Mar. 31, 2011, p ____.

Form

SPEAKER: This is the day for the call of the Private Calendar. The Clerk will call the first bill on the Private Calendar.

[*The Clerk calls the first bill by calendar number and title.*]

SPEAKER: Is there objection to the consideration of the bill?. . .The Chair hears none. The Clerk will report the committee amendments. [*The Clerk reads the amendments.*]

SPEAKER: Without objection, the amendments are agreed to, the House bill is engrossed, read a third time and passed, and a motion to reconsider is laid on the table.

[*Or*]

(*If at least two Members object*) SPEAKER: Two objections are heard, and the bill is recommitted.

§ 5. Consideration and Debate

Bills

The Speaker may not entertain a reservation of the right to object to the consideration of a bill or resolution on the Private Calendar. *Manual* § 895. Bills called up from the Private Calendar are considered in the House as in the Committee of the Whole. Debate on bills in that forum is under the five-minute rule. However, where a private bill is considered independently of the calendar, pursuant to a special order of business from the Committee on Rules, the House may provide for consideration in the House or in the Committee of the Whole. Deschler Ch 22 § 11.5. If a private bill is being considered in the House by unanimous consent, debate follows the hour rule. Deschler Ch 22 § 13.6.

Amendments

Debate on amendments to bills called on the Private Calendar is limited to five minutes in favor of and five minutes in opposition to an amendment. Recognition in opposition to such an amendment goes first to a member of the committee reporting the bill. Deschler Ch 22 § 13.2. Recognition of Members seeking to extend the debate time ordinarily will be declined. Deschler Ch 22 §§ 13.4, 13.5. Pro forma amendments are not in order. Deschler Ch 22 §§ 13.13-13.17.

Motions to Strike the Enacting Clause

A motion to strike the enacting clause is in order during the consideration of a private bill, including an omnibus private bill. 8 Cannon § 2786; Deschler Ch 22 § 13.10. Such motion takes precedence over an amendment to strike a title of the bill and is debatable under the five-minute rule. Deschler Ch 22 §§ 13.11, 13.12.

Passing Over Calendared Measures

The House by unanimous consent may provide that a bill on the Private Calendar be passed over without prejudice. Deschler Ch 22 §§ 12.4-12.6. Such a bill retains its place on the calendar. A request that the bill be passed over comes too late after committee amendments to the bill have been adopted. 96-1, Dec. 18, 1979, pp 36758, 36759.

Form

SPEAKER: Today is the day for the call of the Private Calendar. The Clerk will call the first bill on the Private Calendar.

[*The Clerk calls the first bill by calendar number and title.*]

MEMBER: M__. Speaker, I ask unanimous consent that this bill be passed over without prejudice.

§ 6. Omnibus Private Bills

Generally

Omnibus private bills consist of individual private bills previously recommitted after two objections and grouped together under a single bill number for rereporting, consideration, and passage. Such omnibus private bills may not be objected to. 74-1, Mar. 26, 1935, p 4484. They are in order on the third Tuesday only, but they may be considered on the first Tuesday by unanimous consent. Deschler Ch 22 § 11.2. If an omnibus bill is passed by the House, it is resolved into individual bills for transmittal to the Senate and subsequently to the President. *Manual* §§ 895, 897.

Consideration and Debate

Omnibus private bills have preference over individual private bills on the calendar on the third Tuesday. Deschler Ch 22 § 11.4. Such bills are read by paragraph, and no amendments are entertained except to strike or reduce monetary amounts or provide limitations. Matters so stricken may not again be included in an omnibus bill during the session. *Manual* § 895. Where an omnibus private bill improperly includes an individual private bill previously laid on the table, the Chair upon sustaining such point of order may order the individual bill stricken from the omnibus bill. Deschler Ch 22 § 13.18.

Under clause 5 of rule XV, the Speaker may not entertain a reservation of the right to object to the consideration of an omnibus private bill. Amendments to measures on the Private Calendar are debatable under the five-minute rule. Debate is limited to ten minutes, divided between the proponent and an opponent. The rule does not admit a pro forma amendment or an extension of time under the five-minute rule. Deschler Ch 22 §§ 13.2-13.5.

§ 7. Disposition of Unfinished Business

Private Calendar bills unfinished on one Tuesday go over to the next Tuesday on which such bills are in order and are considered before the call of the other bills on the calendar. 7 Cannon § 854. Unfinished omnibus bills follow the same procedure and go over until the next Tuesday on which that class of business is again in order. Deschler Ch 22 § 11.13. However, when the previous question is ordered on a private bill, and the bill remains unfinished at adjournment, the bill comes up for disposition on the next legislative day. 8 Cannon §§ 2334, 2694.

§ 8. House-Senate Action on Private Bills

As in the case of public bills, Private Calendar bills are messaged to the Senate after passage by the House. Omnibus bills on their passage are resolved into several separate bills of which they are composed and are messaged to the Senate as individual bills and not as an omnibus bill. *Manual* § 895; Deschler Ch 22 § 14.1.

If amended by the Senate, further consideration and disposition by the House is effected by unanimous consent or by a special order of business. The House has, by suspension of the rules, adopted a resolution agreeing to an unrelated Senate amendment of a public character to a private bill. Deschler Ch 22 § 14.7. This is an exception from the general practice that the Speaker will not schedule private bills under suspension of the rules.

After passage in the House of an omnibus private bill, Senate bills pending on the Speaker's table that are identical or similar to those contained therein may be disposed of in the House by unanimous consent. Similarly, after disposition in the House of a private Senate bill, a similar House bill may be laid on the table by unanimous consent. This procedure is followed so that two measures involving the same private relief will not be messaged to the Senate. Deschler Ch 22 § 14.3.

Chapter 41
Question of Consideration

Research References
5 Hinds §§ 4936-4977
8 Cannon §§ 2436-2447
Deschler-Brown Ch 29
Manual §§ 906-910

§ 1. In General

Generally; Purpose and Effect

Clause 3 of rule XVI provides that when any motion or proposition is entertained, a Member may demand the question "[w]ill the House now consider it?" *Manual* § 906. This rule, which was adopted in its present form in 1880, permits the House by simple majority vote to refuse to consider business it may not want to consider on that day. 5 Hinds § 4936; 8 Cannon § 2447. The rule provides that the question is not to be put unless demanded. *Manual* § 906.

Any Member, Delegate, or the Resident Commissioner may demand the question of consideration, even against matters of the highest privilege and even though the Member in charge claims the floor for debate or to move the previous question. 5 Hinds §§ 4936, 4941, 4944, 4945, 5478; 6 Cannon § 404. The question of consideration is not debatable because such debate would defeat the purpose of the rule. 8 Cannon § 2447. If the House votes against consideration, it has the effect of preventing all debate on the pending measure at that time. The form for raising the question of consideration is as follows:

MEMBER: M__. Speaker, I raise the question of consideration.

SPEAKER: The gentle______ raises the question of consideration. The question is: Will the House now consider it [the motion or proposition]?

Where a report from the Committee on Rules is called up on the same legislative day on which reported, the Chair puts the question without demand pursuant to clause 6(a)(1) of rule XIII. *Manual* § 857; see SPECIAL ORDERS OF BUSINESS.

When in Order

The question of consideration is not in order after debate has begun and does not lie until the initial reading has been concluded. 5 Hinds §§ 4937-4939; 6 Cannon § 541; 8 Cannon § 2436. It may not be raised after the previous question has been ordered. 5 Hinds §§ 4965, 4966.

Voting on the Question

A negative vote on the question of consideration does not amount to a rejection of the proposition and does not prevent the measure from being brought before the House again. 5 Hinds § 4940. By the same token, an affirmative vote does not prevent the question of consideration from being raised on a subsequent day when the bill is again called up as unfinished business. 8 Cannon §§ 2438, 2447. If the question of consideration is raised but not voted on at adjournment it does not recur as unfinished business on the succeeding day. 5 Hinds §§ 4947, 4948.

It is in order to reconsider an affirmative vote on the question of consideration. Deschler-Brown Ch 29 § 5. However, it is not in order to reconsider a negative vote on the question of consideration. 5 Hinds §§ 5626, 5627.

As Related to Points of Order

A point of order against the eligibility for consideration of a bill, which if sustained might prevent consideration, should be made and decided before the question of consideration is put. *Manual* § 909. However, if the point of order relates merely to the manner of considering the bill, the point of order should be passed on after the House has decided the question of consideration. 5 Hinds § 4950. Points of order against a conference report are raised after the question of consideration has been decided in the affirmative. *Manual* § 909.

A point of order against consideration of a bill for failure of a proper quorum in committee to report was permitted despite unanimous consent of the House to immediately consider the bill because the unanimous-consent request was not accompanied by a waiver of points of order. Deschler Ch 20 § 17.13.

Other Methods of Preventing Consideration

Immediate consideration of a measure can be avoided by use of the motions to postpone or to refer. *Manual* §§ 915, 916. Successful application of the motion to lay the proposition on the table constitutes a final adverse disposition of the matter before the House. See LAY ON THE TABLE.

§ 2. Propositions Subject to the Question

The question of consideration has been applied to bills, resolutions, motions, and reports. It may be demanded against matters of highest privilege. *Manual* § 908; 5 Hinds § 4941. The question may be demanded:

- Against a committee report relating to the seating of a Member. 5 Hinds § 4941.
- Against a resolution raising a question of the privileges of the House. 6 Cannon § 560.
- Against a bill that has been made in order on a particular day by a special order of business. 4 Hinds § 3175; 5 Hinds §§ 4953-4957.
- Against a bill on the Union Calendar on Calendar Wednesday before resolving into the Committee of the Whole. 8 Cannon § 2445.
- Against the motion to reconsider. 8 Cannon § 2437.
- Against a conference report. 8 Cannon § 2439; Deschler-Brown Ch 29 § 5.12.
- Against a resolution to elect a Member to a standing committee. 104-1, July 10, 1995, p 18253.

§ 3. Propositions Not Subject to the Question

The question of consideration lies only against an individual proposition and may not be raised against a class of business, such as District of Columbia business generally. 4 Hinds §§ 3308, 3309; 5 Hinds § 4598.

Some legislative propositions are considered under special orders of business that provide for the "immediate consideration" of the proposition. Under that procedure the House decides the question of consideration by voting on the special order of business itself, and the question of consideration cannot be raised against the ultimate proposition. 5 Hinds §§ 4960-4963; 8 Cannon §§ 2440, 2441. The question of consideration is likewise inapplicable to a motion to resolve into the Committee of the Whole because the House expresses its will concerning consideration by voting on the motion. *Manual* § 908; Deschler-Brown Ch 29 § 5.6. Under modern practice, special orders of business authorize the Speaker to declare the House resolved into Committee of the Whole without motion, thereby precluding the question of consideration or any vote of the House. Clause 2(b) of rule XVIII; *Manual* § 972.

Other propositions held not subject to the question of consideration include:

- A bill returned with the President's veto. 5 Hinds §§ 4969, 4970.
- A motion relating to the order of business. 5 Hinds §§ 4971-4976; 8 Cannon § 2442.
- A motion to discharge committees. 5 Hinds § 4977.
- Propositions before the House merely for reference. 5 Hinds § 4964.
- A motion under clause 2(d) of rule XIV to take from the Speaker's table a Senate bill substantially the same as a House bill already favorably reported and on the House Calendar. 8 Cannon § 2443.
- Reports from the Committee on Rules relating to the rules or order of business. Clause 6 of rule XIII; *Manual* § 858; 5 Hinds §§ 4961-4963.

§ 4. Application to Points of Order Against Unfunded Mandates

Sections 423-426 of the Congressional Budget Act establish committee report requirements and points of order against consideration. *Manual* § 1127; see also UNFUNDED MANDATES.

Section 425(a)(2) establishes a point of order against consideration of any bill, joint resolution, amendment, motion, or conference report that would increase the direct costs of Federal intergovernmental mandates by an amount that exceeds the threshold in section 424(a)(1) unless it also provides spending authority or authorizes sufficient appropriations to cover the costs. Section 426(a) of the Act establishes a point of order against consideration of any rule or order that waives the application of section 425. Points of order under sections 425 and 426(a) of the Budget Act are disposed of not by a ruling of the Chair but by the question of consideration. Section 426(b)(2) establishes as a threshold premise for cognizability of a point of order under section 425 or 426(a) the specification of precise legislative language that is alleged to constitute a Federal mandate.

Form

THE SPEAKER: The gentle______ from __________ makes a point of order that the resolution violates section 426(a) of the Congressional Budget Act of 1974. The gentle______ has met the threshold burden to identify the specific language in the resolution on which the point of order is predicated. Such a point of order shall be disposed of by the question of consideration. The gentle______ from __________ and a Member opposed will each control 10 minutes. After debate, the Chair will put the question of consideration, to wit: "Will the House now consider the resolution?"

§ 5. Application to Points of Order Against Earmarks

Clauses 9(a) and 9(b) of rule XXI provide that it shall not be in order to consider certain measures that do not comply with disclosure requirements regarding earmarks, limited tax benefits and limited tariff benefits. See BUDGET PROCESS. Any Member may raise a point of order against consideration of such measures if the Chair is made aware of a lack of compliance with a disclosure requirement. Clause 9(c) of rule XXI provides that it is not in order to consider a special order of business or other order that waives the application of clause 9(a) or 9(b). The method of disposing of a point of order against such special order of business or other order or a conference report to accompany a general appropriation bill is the question of consideration. Clause 9(c) of rule XXI provides for 20 minutes of debate on the question of consideration, equally divided between the Member making the point of order and an opponent.

Form

THE SPEAKER: The gentle______ from __________ makes a point of order that the [resolution/conference report] violates clause 9(a) [or 9(b)] of rule XXI. Under clause 9(c) of rule XXI, the gentle______ from __________ and the gentle______ from __________ each will control 10 minutes on the question of consideration. Following debate, the Chair will put the question of consideration as follows: ''Will the House now consider the [resolution/conference report]?''

§ 6. Application to Points of Order Under the Statutory Pay-As-You-Go Act

The Statutory Pay-As-You-Go Act of 2010 established a new budget enforcement mechanism to require that new direct spending and revenue legislation enacted into law not increase the deficit. Pub. L. 111-139. Section 4(g) of the Act requires that the Chair put the question of consideration with respect to certain measures that contain an emergency designation under the Act. In such cases, the Chair puts the question of consideration without debate. The Chair does so before resolving into the Committee of the Whole for consideration of the measure. 111-1, Jan. 26, 2009, p ____. The failure of the Chair to put the question may be rendered moot by subsequent action of the House. 111-2, July 1, 2010, p ____.

The requirement that the Chair put the question of consideration on certain measures that carried an emergency designation under the House Pay-As-You-Go rule was eliminated when that rule was repealed in the 112th Congress. 112-1, H. Res. 5, Jan. 4, 2011, p ____.

Form

THE SPEAKER: The [measure] contains an emergency designation for the purposes of pay-as-you-go principles under section 4(g)(1) of the Statutory Pay-As-You-Go Act of 2010. Accordingly, the Chair must put the question of consideration under section 4(g)(2) of the Statutory Pay-As-You-Go Act of 2010. The Chair will put the question of consideration as follows: "Will the House now consider the [measure]?"

Chapter 42
Questions of Privilege

I. Introductory

II. Privilege of the House

A. BASIS OF PRIVILEGE

B. CONSIDERATION

III. Personal Privilege

A. BASIS OF PRIVILEGE

B. CONSIDERATION

Research References
3 Hinds §§ 2521-2725
6 Cannon §§ 553-622
Deschler Ch 11
Manual §§ 287-309, 698-713

I. Introductory

§ 1. In General

Definitions and Distinctions

The term ''privilege'' arises frequently in the rules governing the procedures of the House. It may refer to questions of the privileges of the House, to questions of personal privilege, to the privilege of Members from arrest, or to the privilege of certain motions. This chapter focuses on questions of the privileges of the House and on questions of personal privilege.

Questions of privilege are to be distinguished from privileged questions. The latter relate merely to the order or priority of business under the rules of the House, and the former pertain to the safety and dignity of the House or the integrity of its proceedings or to the rights or reputation of its Members (3 Hinds §§ 2654, 2718). Privileged questions, see ORDER OF BUSINESS; PRIVILEGED BUSINESS; *Manual* §§ 853-857.

Questions of privilege are classified by rule IX as (1) those affecting the rights of the House collectively, its safety, dignity, and the integrity of its proceedings, and (2) the rights, reputation, and conduct of Members, individually, in their representative capacity only. This rule, adopted in 1880, was based on procedures that had been followed in the House as a matter of longstanding custom. 3 Hinds § 2521. The rule was amended in the 103d Congress to permit the Speaker to postpone consideration of certain questions of privilege for up to two legislative days and to designate a time for consideration within that period. See § 14, infra.

Questions of the privileges of the House are brought before it in the form of a resolution. § 14, infra. Questions of personal privilege are raised by a Member from the floor when recognized for debate for that purpose. § 19, infra.

Privilege of Members From Arrest

Under the Constitution, Senators and Representatives are privileged from arrest, except for ''treason, felony, and breach of the peace,'' during attendance at a session and in going to and returning therefrom. U.S. Const. art. I, § 6. This privilege may be invoked in cases not covered by the exceptions, as where there has been an arrest for fraud and delinquency in connection with a civil proceeding. 3 Hinds § 2676. The exception has been construed to mean all indictable crimes. 3 Hinds § 2673. The privilege does not protect a Member from arrest in any criminal case. *Manual* § 91. Thus, a Member may be arrested and prosecuted for a felony specified in a timber protection statute; and the fact that Congress was in recess at the time of his arrest is no defense. *Williamson* v. *United States*, 207 U.S. 425 (1908). An investigation by committee of a Member's arrest to determine whether it was in violation of the privilege may be initiated by resolution. 3 Hinds § 2673. For more detailed analysis of this privilege, see Deschler Ch 7 § 18.

Privilege of Speech or Debate

Article I, section 6, clause 1 of the Constitution provides that Members or Senators "shall not be questioned in any other place" for "any speech or debate in either House." This clause precludes judicial inquiry into the motivation, preparation, and content of a Member's speech. *Manual* § 93. All speech, debate, and remarks on the floor are privileged, as is material inserted in the *Congressional Record* by a Member with the consent of the House. Deschler Ch 7 § 16. However, the Supreme Court has upheld a grand jury inquiry into the possession and nonlegislative use of classified documents by a Member. *Gravel* v. *United States*, 408 U.S. 606 (1972). The Court has also sustained the validity of an indictment of a Member for accepting an illegal bribe to perform legislative acts. *United States* v. *Brewster*, 408 U.S. 501 (1972). This clause does not prevent the House from applying rules relating to "proper debate" and from adopting procedures to deal with transgressions of those rules. *Manual* § 303.

§ 2. Precedence of Questions of Privilege

Under rule IX, a question of privilege has been held to take precedence over all questions except the motion to adjourn. This precedence is given to both questions of the privileges of the House and to questions of personal privilege. "The rights and privileges of the Members of the House, in the discharge of their functions, are sacred," said Speaker Reed in 1890, "and the House can undertake no higher duty than the conservation of all those rights and privileges intact. Even if the case arises under dubious circumstances, it is proper for the House to pause and give suitable heed to any question which any Member raises with regard to his rights and privileges as a Member." 3 Hinds § 2524. Under clause 2 of rule IX, the right to bring a question of privilege before the House without notice is restricted.

Manual §§ 699, 713. Only the Majority and Minority Leaders can now raise such a question "at any time." See § 14, infra.

Under rule IX questions of privilege have been held to take precedence over other business. *Manual* § 709; 3 Hinds § 2523. For example:

- Reading of messages from the President (which are received but do not displace the question of privilege). 5 Hinds §§ 6640-6642.
- District of Columbia business under clause 4 of rule XV. Deschler Ch 11 § 5.8.
- Calendar Wednesday business under clause 7 of rule XV. 7 Cannon §§ 908-910; Deschler Ch 11 § 5.7.
- Special orders for the consideration of business. 3 Hinds §§ 2524, 2525, 2554.
- Reports from the Committee on Rules. 8 Cannon § 3491.
- Motions to resolve into Committee of the Whole. 8 Cannon § 3461.
- Motions to reconsider. 5 Hinds §§ 5673-5676.
- Motions to suspend the rules. 3 Hinds § 2553; 6 Cannon §§ 553, 565.
- Scheduled special-order speeches. Deschler-Brown Ch 29 § 10.75.
- Senate amendments undisposed of after rejection of a conference report. 3 Hinds § 2531.

In general, one question of privilege may not take precedence over another. 3 Hinds §§ 2534, 2552, 2581. The Chair's power of recognition (and scheduling prerogative under rule IX) determines which of two matters of equal privilege is considered first. *Manual* § 709.

Because only one question of privilege may be pending at a time, another Member will not be recognized during such time to present another question of privilege. This stricture includes questions of personal privilege. *Manual* § 711; 3 Hinds § 2533; Deschler Ch 11 § 5.4.

A question of privilege loses its privilege when connected with or amended by a proposition not privileged. 3 Hinds § 2551; 5 Hinds § 5890.

Precedence Over the Previous Question

The question of privilege takes precedence over the consideration of a motion for the previous question. Deschler Ch 11 § 5.9. It supersedes the consideration of a proposition and must be disposed of first, even where the previous question has been ordered on such proposition, unless the previous question has been ordered to final passage under a special order of business prohibiting any intervening motions. 3 Hinds §§ 2522, 2532; 6 Cannon § 561; Deschler Ch 11 § 5.3.

Interruptions

By rising to a question of privilege, a Member may not deprive another Member of the floor. 5 Hinds § 5002; 8 Cannon §§ 2458, 2528; Deschler

Ch 11 § 23.2. However, the latter may yield time for preliminary debate on the question. Deschler Ch 11 § 23.3. Such a question may not interrupt a roll call or yea-and-nay vote. 5 Hinds §§ 6051, 6052, 6058; 6 Cannon §§ 554, 564.

A question of privilege may interrupt the consideration of a bill under a special order of business. 3 Hinds §§ 2524, 2525. It has precedence at a time set apart by special order for other business. 6 Cannon § 560. A question of the privileges of the House may interrupt the reading of the Journal (Deschler Ch 11 § 5.6), whereas a question of personal privilege may not (Deschler Ch 11 § 23.1).

A Member's announcement of intent to offer a resolution as a question of privilege may take precedence over a special order of business reported from the Committee on Rules. However, where a special order of business is pending, such announcements are counted against debate on the resolution absent unanimous consent to the contrary. *Manual* § 709.

As Unfinished Business

A question of privilege pending at the time of adjournment becomes unfinished business on the next day. Deschler Ch 11 § 5.5. It takes precedence over unfinished business that is privileged under rule XIV (order of business). *Manual* § 709.

II. Privilege of the House

A. Basis of Privilege

§ 3. Introductory; What Constitutes a Question of Privilege

Elements Generally

Under rule IX questions of the privileges of the House are those that affect its rights collectively, "its safety, dignity, and the integrity of its proceedings. . . ." *Manual* § 698. A question asserted to involve the privileges of the House must include one or more of the elements specified by rule IX. Deschler-Brown Ch 31 § 1.53. A Member may not by raising a question of the privileges of the House attach privilege to a question not otherwise in order under the rules of the House. Deschler-Brown Ch 29 § 9.58.

Organization of the House and Seating of Members

Questions relating to the organization of the House (1 Hinds §§ 22-24) and the right of Members to their seats (3 Hinds §§ 2579-2587), as well as various questions incidental thereto (1 Hinds § 322; 2 Hinds § 1207; 3 Hinds

§ 2588), have been held to give rise to questions of the privileges of the House (*Manual* § 701). The same is true of a proposition declaring the Office of the Speaker vacant (6 Cannon § 35) and the resignation of a Member from a select or standing committee (*Manual* § 704). A resolution electing a House officer is presented as a question of privilege. *Manual* § 701.

Safety and Dignity; Comfort and Convenience

A resolution directing an investigation into the safety of Members in light of alleged structural deficiencies in the Capitol gives rise to a question of the privileges of the House, as does a resolution directing the appointment of a select committee to inquire into fire safety of the environs of the House. A resolution directing the Sergeant-at-Arms to alert House personnel of the dangers of electronic security breaches gives rise to a question of the privileges of the House. *Manual* § 705.

Questions relating to the comfort and convenience of Members and employees have been held to give rise to a question of the privileges of the House. 3 Hinds §§ 2629-2633. For example, a resolution expressing the sense of the House as to the proper attire for Members during sessions of the House and a resolution relating to a sanitary environment for House employees were held to raise a question of privilege. *Manual* § 705; 3 Hinds §§ 2632, 2633. However, certain subjects relating purely to the convenience of Members are not necessarily entertained as privileged. For example, a resolution authorizing an additional attendant for the Members' bathroom and a resolution authorizing a new lunchroom for Members were held not to raise a question of privilege. 3 Hinds §§ 2635, 2636.

Integrity of the Legislative Process

Among the subjects giving rise to a question of the privileges of the House are questions relating to the integrity of its proceedings. *Manual* § 704; 3 Hinds §§ 2597-2601, 2614. For example:

- The presence on the floor of unauthorized persons. 3 Hinds §§ 2624-2626.
- The conduct of those in the press gallery. 3 Hinds § 2627.
- The integrity of the Journal. 2 Hinds § 1363; 3 Hinds § 2620.
- The protection of House records and files. 3 Hinds § 2659.
- The accuracy of House documents and messages. 3 Hinds § 2613.
- The integrity of the *Congressional Record*. *Manual* § 704.
- The integrity and regularity of an electronic vote. 110-1, Aug. 3, 2007, p 22769.
- The integrity of uninterrupted audio broadcast coverage of certain House proceedings. Deschler-Brown Ch 29 § 40.10.
- An unreasonable delay in transmitting an enrolled bill to the President. *Manual* § 704.

- The fraudulent introduction of a bill. 4 Hinds § 3388.
- The attempted bribery or corruption of Members. 2 Hinds § 1599; 6 Cannon § 580.
- An assault on a committee clerk. 2 Hinds § 1629.
- Investigation and report on the impact of a test involving television coverage of House proceedings. *Manual* § 684.
- Indecorous behavior of a former Member on the floor of the House and rooms leading thereto. *Manual* § 680.

The integrity of House proceedings also extends to the activities of its committees. The following have been the subject of resolutions raising a question of the privileges of the House:

- Use of an allegedly forged document at a committee hearing. *Manual* § 704.
- The public release of transcripts and other relevant documents relating to an investigation by a committee's task force of the operation and management of the Office of the Postmaster. *Manual* § 704.
- Unilateral release by a committee chair of committee records in contravention of its rules (adopted ''protocol''). *Manual* § 704.
- Intentional disregard of House rules and improper use of the Capitol Police. 108-1, July 23, 2003, p 19155.

A resolution directing a committee to investigate the circumstances surrounding the publication in a newspaper of a select committee report, which the House had ordered not to be released, gave rise to a question of the privileges of the House, because it related to the integrity of House proceedings and the sanctity of its records. Deschler-Brown Ch 29 § 18.12.

Effecting Changes in House Rules or Orders

A question of the privileges of the House may not be raised to effect a change in the rules of the House or their interpretation or to collaterally attack a rule or order properly adopted by the House at a previous time, the proper method of reopening the matter being a motion to reconsider. *Manual* § 706; Deschler Ch 11 § 3.2. Thus, a resolution collaterally challenging an adopted rule of the House by delaying its implementation was held not to give rise to a question of the privileges of the House. *Manual* § 706.

Similarly, it has been held that a question of the privileges of the House may not be raised to:

- Collaterally challenge a standing order establishing a joint meeting for a foreign head of state by withdrawing a pending invitation and prohibiting future invitations. *Manual* § 706.
- Direct the Speaker to follow certain customs in allowing one-minute speeches at the beginning of a session. Deschler-Brown Ch 29 § 10.58.

- Permit petitioners seeking redress of grievances to have access to the House floor. Deschler Ch 24 § 10.2.
- Broaden the rule relating to access by Members to committee records. 95-1, Dec. 6, 1977, p 38470.
- Direct that the party ratios of all standing committees, subcommittees, and staffs thereof be changed within a time certain to reflect overall party ratios in the House. Deschler-Brown Ch 31 § 1.51.
- Direct a committee to consider certain business, a motion to that effect not being in order under the rules. *Manual* § 706.
- Declare a recess to receive a petition. Deschler Ch 11 § 3.1.
- Effect a change in conference procedures. Deschler Ch 11 § 3.3.
- Direct a standing committee to release executive session material referred to it. *Manual* § 706.

A question of the privileges of the House may not be invoked to prescribe a special order of business for the House, because otherwise any Member would be able to attach privilege to a legislative measure merely by alleging impact on the dignity of the House based upon House action or inaction. For example, the following resolutions were held not to give rise to a question of the privileges of the House, but rather were held to be legislative matters to be considered under ordinary rules relating to priority of business:

- Alleging that the inability of the House to enact certain legislation constituted an impairment of the dignity of the House, the integrity of its proceedings, and its place in public esteem, and resolving that the House be considered to have passed such legislation.
- Precluding an adjournment of the House until a specified legislative measure is considered.
- Expressing congressional sentiment that the President take specified action to achieve a desired public policy even though involving executive action under a treaty (which it was the prerogative of the Senate to ratify).
- Directing that the reprogramming process established in law for legislative branch appropriations be subjected to third-party review for conformity with external standards of accounting but alleging no deviation from duly constituted procedure.
- Directing the Committee on Rules to report only ''open'' rules for the consideration of general appropriation bills.

Manual § 706; see also *Manual* § 702 for a discussion of legislative propositions purporting to present questions of the privileges of the House.

The constitutional validity of an existing rule of the House may not be challenged under the guise of a question of privilege, whether that existing rule was adopted by separate vote of the House or, instead, by its vote on the adoption of all of its rules. *Manual* § 706.

§ 4. Charges of Illegality or Impropriety

Specific Charges and General Criticism Distinguished

General criticism of the Congress, or the Members of the House, does not give rise to a question of the privileges of the House. Deschler Ch 11 §§ 8.1, 8.2. A resolution purporting to establish a committee to investigate vague allegations of "corruption in the House" was held not to give rise to a question of the privileges of the House. 3 Hinds § 2711. Allegations that are merely critical of the legislative process, such as charges of inactivity in regard to a subject reported from committee, are also insufficient. 93-2, June 24, 1974, pp 21596-98. Similarly, an allegation of unconstitutional abrogation of a treaty by the President was held insufficient. *Manual* § 706. However, an allegation of criminal conduct by the Congress has been presented as a question of the privileges of the House, as have charges that the House was being influenced by mobs or that a committee of the House was engaged in subversive activities. Deschler Ch 11 §§ 8.3, 8.4; 80-2, Mar. 10, 1948, p 2476.

Charges Involving Members

Charges against Members often have been made the basis of a question of personal privilege. §§ 17, 18, infra. Such charges may also give rise to a question of the privileges of the House where they involve elements of illegality or criminality so as to impugn the honor and dignity of the House itself. Thus, charges against Members of graft (7 Cannon § 911), of abusing the franking privilege (3 Hinds § 2705), of using "ghost" employees (*Manual* § 703), of improperly attempting to influence a vote (Deschler Ch 11 § 9.1), of giving away atomic secrets (Deschler Ch 11 § 9.2), and of illegally soliciting political contributions in a House office building (99-1, July 10, 1985, p 18397) have given rise to the privileges of the House. However, a mere allegation that a Member distributed an unauthorized questionnaire was held insufficient to give rise to a question of the privileges of the House. Deschler Ch 11 § 9.3.

A question of the privileges of the House may be based on charges against Members, even though they are not identified by name. 3 Hinds § 2705.

In 1992, resolutions relating to the operation of the "bank" in the Office of the Sergeant-at-Arms were presented as questions of the privileges of the House, including a resolution instructing the Committee on Standards of Official Conduct (now Ethics) to disclose the names and pertinent account information of Members and former Members found to have abused the privileges of the "bank." *Manual* § 703.

Charges Involving House Officers or Employees

Charges that an officer or employee of the House acted illegally or improperly may give rise to a question of the privileges of the House. 3 Hinds §§ 2628, 2645-2647; 6 Cannon § 35; Deschler Ch 11 § 10.3. Thus, a charge that an officer of the House conspired to influence legislation gives rise to a question of the privileges of the House. 3 Hinds § 2628. The same is true of an allegation that an officer of the House made secret motions in certain litigation without the knowledge of the House (Deschler-Brown Ch 29 § 30.4) or that an employee appeared in court without authorization as special counsel for a committee (Deschler Ch 11 § 10.3). Allegations of improper representation by counsel of the legal position of Members in a brief and allegations of unauthorized intervention by a committee employee in judicial proceedings also have given rise to questions of the privileges of the House. *Manual* § 703. On the other hand, merely alleging favoritism by the Speaker in making appointments or rudeness by the Doorkeeper in removing an occupant of the gallery has been held not to give rise to a question of the privileges of the House. Deschler Ch 11 §§ 10.1, 10.2.

In the 102d Congress, numerous resolutions relating to the financial operation of the Office of the Sergeant-at-Arms and the management of the Office of the Postmaster were presented as questions of the privileges of the House. Among them were resolutions terminating all bank and check-cashing operations in the Office of the Sergeant-at-Arms, directing the Committee on House Administration to conduct an investigation of the operation and management of the Office of the Postmaster, and directing the Committee on Standards of Official Conduct (now Ethics) to investigate alleged violations of confidentiality by certain staff members. *Manual* § 703.

§ 5. House Jurisdiction, Powers, and Prerogatives

Issues relating to the jurisdiction of the House or its prerogatives under the Constitution may give rise to a question of the privileges of the House. 2 Hinds §§ 1480-1537; 6 Cannon § 315; Deschler Ch 11 § 13. Matters that may be raised under this rule include jurisdictional questions relating to the prerogative of the House to originate revenue-raising legislation. 2 Hinds §§ 1480-1501; 6 Cannon § 315; Deschler Ch 11 § 13.1; see generally *Manual* § 102. Other similar matters that have given rise to a question of the privileges of the House include:

- The issuance of a court order restraining the publication of a committee report. Deschler Ch 11 § 13.3.
- The disclosure of House records in response to process issued by a Federal court. *Manual* § 291a.

- Intervention in judicial proceedings concerning the constitutionality of the one-House veto or other legislative review provision. 95-1, Nov. 2, 1977, p 366.
- The prerogative of the House when a bill has been "pocket vetoed." *Manual* § 702.
- The affirmative vote necessary to extend the time period for State ratification of a constitutional amendment. Deschler-Brown Ch 30 § 1.5.
- The constitutional authority of the House with respect to impeachment propositions. 3 Hinds §§ 2045-2048.

However, rule IX is concerned not with the privileges of the Congress as a legislative branch but only with the privileges of the House itself. Thus, neither the enumeration of legislative powers in article I, section 8 of the Constitution nor the prohibition in article I, section 9 against any withdrawal from the Treasury except by enactment of an appropriation renders a measure purporting to exercise or limit those powers a question of the privileges of the House. *Manual* § 702.

The revenue-raising prerogative of the House may be raised only when the House is in possession of the original papers. It may be raised with respect to a revenue provision that originated in conference. *Manual* § 702. The issue may not be raised after the House has adopted a conference report containing an additional revenue matter not in either the House or the Senate version. *Manual* § 702; Deschler Ch 13 § 14.2.

A resolution alleging that the President unconstitutionally abrogated a treaty (which is the prerogative of the Senate to ratify), and calling on the President to seek the approval of Congress prior to such abrogation, was held not to give rise to a question of the privileges of the House. *Manual* § 702.

Contempt Proceedings; Enforcement of Orders and Subpoenas

The power of the House to punish for contempt may be invoked as a basis for raising a question of the privileges of the House. That question has been held to arise where contemptuous conduct has been charged against a Member (2 Hinds § 1641), where a witness has refused to respond to an order to give testimony (*Manual* § 299; 3 Hinds § 1666; Deschler Ch 11 § 12), and where a person has been charged with an offense against the House, such as attempted bribery (2 Hinds §§ 1597, 1599). Committee reports relating to the refusal of a witness to be sworn or respond to a subpoena duces tecum in violation of section 192 of title 2, United States Code, likewise give rise to a question of the privileges of the House when called up by the reporting committee. Deschler Ch 11 §§ 12.2, 12.3.

§ 6. Intervention in Judicial Proceedings

The House sometimes authorizes special appearances on its own behalf in judicial proceedings relating to the powers and prerogatives of the House, and resolutions granting the authority to intervene in such cases may be called up as a question of privilege. The authority to intervene in judicial proceedings has been granted in cases involving the constitutionality of the one-House veto (or other legislative review provision) and the validity and effect of subpoenas issued by House committees or subcommittees. *Manual* § 291b; 94-2, July 1, 1976, p 21852.

As discussed in section 4, supra, charges of improper intervention in a judicial proceeding by an officer or employee of the House may give rise to a question of the privileges of the House. As such, the following resolutions have been held to constitute questions of the privileges of the House: (1) a resolution alleging unauthorized actions by a committee employee in intervening in judicial proceedings; (2) a resolution directing the Clerk to notify interested parties that the House regretted the use of official resources to present to the Supreme Court of Florida a legal brief arguing the unconstitutionality of congressional term limits, and that the House had no position on that question; and (3) a resolution alleging a chronology of litigation relating to the immunity of a Member from civil liability for bona fide official acts and expressing the views of the House thereon. *Manual* § 703.

The General Counsel of the House has the duty under clause 8 of rule II to provide legal assistance and representation to the House. *Manual* § 670. The General Counsel is authorized by law to appear in any proceeding before a State or Federal court (except the United States Supreme Court) without compliance with admission requirements of such court. 2 USC § 130f(a). Furthermore, the law requires the Attorney General to notify the General Counsel of a determination not to appeal a court decision affecting the constitutionality of an Act. 2 USC § 130f(b).

The House may authorize the Speaker to take any steps the Speaker considers necessary, including intervention as a party or submission of briefs *amicus curiae*, in order to protect the interests of the House. The House has adopted resolutions authorizing standing or select committees to make applications to courts in connection with their investigations. *Manual* § 291b. The House has directed the Speaker to certify to the United States Attorney the refusal of While House officials to produce documents and testify before a House committee. 110-2, Feb. 14, 2008, p 2190. The House also has authorized the chair of a subcommittee to intervene in a pending action on behalf of the subcommittee to obtain information in the possession of a Federal agency (the FTC). 94-1, Dec. 18, 1975, p 41707.

§ 7. Correcting the Congressional Record; Expungement

The accuracy and propriety of reports in the *Congressional Record* may give rise to a question of the privileges of the House. *Manual* § 704; 5 Hinds §§ 7005-7023; 8 Cannon §§ 3461, 3463, 3464; Deschler Ch 11 § 11. Accordingly, a resolution to request the Senate to expunge from the *Congressional Record* certain debate reflecting on the integrity of the House or that is offensive or otherwise improper may give rise to a question of the privileges of the House, as may resolutions to expunge from the *Record* matter improperly inserted under leave to print. Deschler Ch 11 § 11. However, neither a question of personal privilege nor a question of the privileges of the House arises during debate in which offensive language is used, the remedy being to demand that the objectionable words be taken down when spoken, pursuant to clause 4 of rule XVII. Deschler Ch 11 § 27.1. For further discussion of the procedure for taking down words, see CONSIDERATION AND DEBATE.

A resolution to correct inaccuracies in the *Congressional Record* is presented as a question of the privileges of the House. 5 Hinds § 7019; 8 Cannon § 3461; Deschler Ch 11 § 11.9. However, a resolution to restore to the *Record* remarks previously deleted by House order does not present a question of the privileges of the House, the proper method of reopening the matter being by motion to reconsider. Deschler Ch 11 § 11.10. A resolution directing the placement of an asterisk in the *Record* to indicate alleged factual inaccuracies in the President's state of the Union address (but not alleging inaccuracies in transcription) was held not to constitute a question of privilege. 108-1, Oct. 20, 2003, pp 25255, 25256.

§ 8. Service of Process

Generally

The service of judicial process on a Member, Delegate, Resident Commissioner, officer, or employee of the House has long been perceived as a matter relating to the integrity of House proceedings and as constituting a basis for raising a question of the privileges of the House. 7 Cannon § 2164; Deschler Ch 11 §§ 14.1-14.10. Rule VIII governs the procedure for House response to a judicial or administrative subpoena served on such persons. *Manual* § 697; § 9, infra.

The privileges of the House are invoked whether the recipient was served with a summons as a defendant or a subpoena as a witness and whether service of process was issued by a State or Federal court. Deschler

Ch 11 § 14. For example, the privileges of the House have been held to apply to service of process as follows:

- Civil actions, criminal proceedings, or courts martial. Deschler Ch 11 §§ 16.7, 16.9, 16.12, 16.17.
- Grand jury proceedings. Deschler Ch 11 § 15.
- Orders to appear and show cause for the failure to comply with a prior subpoena. Deschler Ch 11 § 14.9.
- Orders to appear for depositions or to answer interrogatories. Deschler Ch 11 §§ 14.10, 16.18.
- Preliminary proceedings in criminal cases. Deschler Ch 11 § 14.5.
- Administrative proceedings before Federal agencies. *Manual* § 697.

Under clause 6(b) of rule VIII, minutes or transcripts of executive sessions, or evidence received during such sessions, may not be disclosed or copied in response to a subpoena. A subpoena duces tecum requesting production of executive session records of a committee from a prior Congress may be laid before the House pending a determination as to its propriety. 97-1, Apr. 28, 1981, p 7603.

Service of Process on Officers or Employees

Examples of service of process on officers include those on the Speaker, the Clerk, and the Sergeant-at-Arms. Deschler Ch 11 §§ 16.2-16.4, 16.7-16.9, 16.11. Examples of service of process on employees include those on current and former employees of a committee, an employee of the House Republican Conference, and a former employee of a former House select committee who was subpoenaed to give a deposition about his recollection of certain executive session transactions. 93-2, Sept. 30, 1974, p 33020; 94-1, Sept. 23, 1975, p 29824; 97-1, Jan. 22, 1981, pp 694, 695.

§ 9. Procedure in Complying with Process under Rule VIII

Rule VIII provides general authority to a Member, Delegate, Resident Commissioner, officer, or employee of the House to comply with a judicial or administrative subpoena or judicial order directing appearance as a witness, or the disclosure of documents, relating to the official functions of the House. Such compliance must be consistent with the rights and privileges of the House. Accordingly, the Speaker is promptly notified upon service of a subpoena or judicial order, and the Speaker lays the notification before the House. Rule VIII does not require the text of the subpoena to be printed in the *Congressional Record*. *Manual* § 697.

Until the 95th Congress, the House would authorize a response to a subpoena by adopting a resolution raised as a question of the privileges of the House. This case-by-case approach was changed in the 95th and 96th

Congresses, when general authority was granted to respond to subpoenas and a procedure was established for automatic compliance without the necessity of a House vote. This standing authority formed the basis for the present rule, adopted in the 97th Congress. *Manual* § 697.

§ 10. —Resolutions Authorizing or Precluding Response

Although rule VIII establishes a procedure for automatic compliance with subpoenas without the necessity of a House vote, a question of the privileges of the House still may be raised to address the response of the House to a subpoena in any particular case. *Manual* § 697. For example, in the 102d Congress, the House considered as questions of the privileges of the House resolutions responding to a subpoena for certain records of the House, and to a contemporaneous request for such records from a special counsel. The resolutions authorized an officer of the House to release certain documents in response to the requests from the special counsel. *Manual* § 703.

Duration of Authorization

Resolutions authorizing a response to a subpoena or other judicial order are effective only during the Congress in which they are adopted. If the judicial proceedings in question extend into the next Congress, it may be necessary to seek another authorizing resolution, which may be offered as a question of privilege. Deschler Ch 11 §§ 18.1, 18.2. An authorization to ensure continuation of judicial proceedings commenced in a prior Congress has been included in the opening-day rules package of the next Congress. 111-1, Jan. 6, 2009, p ____.

§ 11. —Conditions or Limitations on Response

Prior to the adoption of rule VIII, when the House authorized a response to a subpoena by resolution on an ad hoc basis, the House occasionally imposed various conditions or limitations, such as:

- Permitting copies, but not original documents, to be produced. *Manual* § 291a; Deschler Ch 11 § 18.
- Limiting disclosure to certified copies of relevant documents. *Manual* § 291a.
- Prohibiting disclosure of information acquired in one's official capacity. Deschler Ch 11 § 17.6.
- Prohibiting disclosure of information not previously made public. Deschler Ch 11 § 17.10.
- Limiting disclosure to certain files and specified documents and only for inspection and copying. Deschler Ch 11 § 17.9.

- Permitting disclosure only on a determination of relevancy. 94-2, Mar. 31, 1976, p 8885.
- Permitting disclosure of certain documents but barring personal appearances. Deschler Ch 14 § 15.14.
- Permitting personal appearances but barring production of certain records. Deschler Ch 11 § 18.
- Permitting production of original documents for laboratory examination but providing for their return. *Manual* § 291a.
- Permitting a Member to respond only when the House is not in session. 94-1, Dec. 1, 1975, p 37888.

§ 12. Disclosure of Executive-Session Materials

The House traditionally has required that executive-session materials be released only when specifically permitted by authorizing resolution. Deschler Ch 11 § 18.4. This practice is continued under clause 6(b) of rule VIII, which states that under no circumstances shall any minutes or transcripts of executive sessions, or any evidence of witnesses in respect thereto, be disclosed or copied. *Manual* § 697. Before the adoption of rule VIII, the House by resolution asserted the privileges of the House against the release of executive-session materials or permitted the disclosure only after a judicial finding of relevancy. *Manual* § 291a.

§ 13. Providing for Legal Counsel

Statutory Authorization

Legal counsel, through the Department of Justice, is available to an officer of the House (but not its Members) to defend the officer against actions brought against such officer while discharging official duties or executing an order of the House. The district attorney for the district where the action is brought is directed on request to enter an appearance on behalf of the officer. 2 USC § 118. This procedure has been followed in actions involving the House, the Speaker, the chair of the Committee on Rules, the Clerk, and the Sergeant-at-Arms. *Manual* § 291b; Deschler Ch 11 § 16.

Authorization by Resolution

Occasionally, the House has authorized by resolution the appointment of special counsel to represent an officer or Member or employee who has been served with process. Such a resolution ordinarily is presented as a question of the privileges of the House. Deschler Ch 11 §§19.1, 19.3. Pursuant to such a resolution, the House has authorized:

- The Speaker to appoint or retain counsel to represent the House and its employees. Deschler Ch 11 §19.1.
- The chair of a committee, with the approval of the Speaker, to retain special counsel. *Manual* §291b.
- The Sergeant-at-Arms, with the approval of the Speaker and the chair of the Committee on House Administration, to retain special counsel. *Manual* §291b.
- The retention of special counsel to represent the interests of a subcommittee. *Manual* §291b.
- The retention of special counsel to represent members of a committee and its employees. Deschler Ch 11 §19.2.

Representation by General Counsel

Clause 8 of rule II provides for an Office of General Counsel to provide legal assistance and representation to the House. The office assists and provides representation to Members, committees, officers, and employees in complying with legal process under rule VIII.

B. Consideration

§14. Raising and Presenting the Question

In the House; Use of Resolutions

Questions of the privileges of the House are brought before the House in the form of a resolution. 3 Hinds §2546; 8 Cannon §3464; Deschler Ch 11 §4.2. Under rule IX such a resolution is privileged when called up by any Member. 3 Hinds §2536; §2, supra. However, its privilege is subject to a two-day notice requirement for Members other than the Majority Leader or the Minority Leader, which must include an announcement of the form of the resolution. Such announcement may be dispensed with by unanimous consent. *Manual* §699. The Speaker designates the time for consideration within two legislative days after the announcement, which may include immediate consideration. Under rule IX the Majority and Minority Leaders may offer the resolution at any time, yielding only to the motion to adjourn. *Manual* §699. The form of the announcement follows:

Form

MEMBER (OTHER THAN MAJORITY OR MINORITY LEADER): M__. Speaker, pursuant to clause 2(a)(1) of rule IX, I rise to give notice of my intent to raise a question of the privileges of the House. The form of the resolution is as follows: [*Note:* The Member may read the resolution in full or may ask unanimous consent to dispense with the reading.]

SPEAKER: Under rule IX, a resolution offered from the floor by a Member other than the Majority Leader or the Minority Leader as a question of the privileges of the House has immediate precedence only at a time designated by the Chair within two legislative days after the resolution is properly noticed. Pending that designation, the form of the resolution noticed by the gentle____ from ______ will appear in the *Record* at this point. The Chair will not at this point determine whether the resolution constitutes a question of privilege. That determination will be made at the time designated for consideration of the resolution.

The form of calling up the resolution follows:

Form

MEMBER: M__. Speaker, I rise to a question of the privileges of the House, and offer the resolution previously noticed.

SPEAKER: The Clerk will report the resolution. [Clerk reports the resolution in full. *Manual* § 713.]

SPEAKER: The resolution qualifies.

[*Or*]

SPEAKER: Does the gentle______ wish to present argument on why the resolution is privileged under rule IX to take precedence over other questions?

[*Or*]

OPPONENT: M__. Speaker, I make a point of order that the gentle______ does not present a question of privilege.

SPEAKER: The Chair will entertain argument as to whether the resolution constitutes a question of privilege.

Under rule IX, a question of the privileges of the House having been raised, the Speaker initially decides whether the question presented constitutes a question of the privileges of the House, and rules as to the validity of the question raised. *Manual* § 713; Deschler Ch 11 §§ 6.1, 6.2. The Speaker makes this decision at the time the question of privilege is called up, not at the time notice is given. *Manual* § 713. Appeal may be taken from the Chair's ruling, however, because the final determination as to the validity of the question rests with the House. Deschler Ch 11 § 6.3.

The question having been properly raised on the floor by a Member, the Speaker must entertain the question and rule on its admissibility. 2 Hinds § 1501; 3 Hinds §§ 2648-2650; Deschler Ch 11 § 1; 6 Cannon § 35. If the matter is not admissible as a question of the privileges of the House, the Speaker may refuse recognition. Deschler Ch 11 § 6.1.

The resolution must show a *prima facie* breach of the privileges of the House. The mere statement that the privileges of the House have been violated does not present a question of privilege. Deschler Ch 11 § 4.1.

A question of privilege may not be presented during a call of the House in the absence of a quorum unless it relates to the immediate proceedings. 3 Hinds § 2545. A Member's announcement of intent to offer a resolution as a question of privilege may take precedence over a special order of business reported from the Committee on Rules. However, where a special order of business is pending, such announcements are counted against debate on the resolution absent unanimous consent to the contrary. *Manual* § 709.

In Committee of the Whole

A question of the privileges of the House may not be raised in the Committee of the Whole. Deschler Ch 11 § 4.3. A breach of the privilege in the Committee of the Whole relates to the dignity of the House and, if such breach is raised, the Committee rises and reports to the House. 2 Hinds § 1657. Without the Committee's report to the House, the question of privilege cannot be raised in the House. 4 Hinds § 4912.

§ 15. Debate; Disposition

A resolution offered under rule IX is read in full. *Manual* § 700. A Member offering the resolution is recognized under the hour rule. Deschler Ch 11 § 7.1. Under clause 2(a) of rule IX, the hour allotted for debate on a resolution offered *from the floor* as a question of the privileges of the House must be equally divided between the proponent of the resolution and the Majority Leader or the Minority Leader or a designee, as determined by the Speaker. *Manual* § 699. Members must confine remarks in debate to the question raised. Deschler Ch 11 § 7.2.

A question of the privileges of the House is subject to disposition by the ordinary motions permitted under clause 4 of rule XVI (*Manual* § 709), including:

- The motion to lay on the table. 5 Hinds § 5438; 6 Cannon § 560.
- The motion for the previous question. 5 Hinds § 5460; 8 Cannon § 2672; Deschler Ch 11 § 7.3.
- The motion to postpone. 3 Hinds § 2536.
- The motion to refer (or to commit) to committee. *Manual* § 713; 8 Cannon § 3461; Deschler Ch 11 § 7.4.

Tabling a resolution raising a question of the privileges of the House is considered a final adverse disposition of that resolution, although the question may be rephrased and presented anew or reoffered on a subsequent day. 5 Hinds § 5438. Any appeal from a decision by the Speaker disposing of the question is likewise subject to the motion to lay on the table. Deschler Ch 11 § 6.3.

A committee report that is submitted as a matter involving the privileges of the House may be considered on the same day reported, notwithstanding the three-day availability rule under clause 4(a) of rule XIII. Deschler Ch 11 § 5.10. A proposition to discharge a committee from a question of privilege is itself privileged. 3 Hinds § 2709.

A resolution that presents a proper question of the privileges of the House (alteration of subcommittee hearing transcripts) may propose the creation of a select investigatory committee with subpoena authority to report back to the House by a certain date. *Manual* § 704.

III. Personal Privilege

A. Basis of Privilege

§ 16. In General

Under clause 1 of rule IX, questions of personal privilege are defined as those that affect the ''rights, reputation, and conduct'' of individual Members in their representative capacity. Under this rule, a Member may rise to a question of personal privilege from the floor to respond to criticism of integrity in such Member's representative capacity. *Manual* §§ 708, 711. A statement challenging the integrity of an official transcript of a committee hearing, thus impugning the integrity of those Members responsible for its preparation, has given rise to a question of personal privilege. Deschler Ch 11 § 25.2. However, charges that do not involve the Member in a representative capacity, such as charges relating to conduct before becoming a Member, do not give rise to a question of personal privilege. 3 Hinds §§ 2691, 2723, 2725.

To give rise to a question of personal privilege, the criticism must reflect directly on the Member's integrity or reputation. Deschler Ch 11 § 24.1. Mere statements of opinion about or general criticism of a Member's actions, voting record, or views, do not constitute grounds for a question of personal privilege. 3 Hinds §§ 2712-2714; Deschler Ch 11 §§ 24.2, 24.3. Thus, a charge that a Member's actions amount to a ''public scandal,'' even when made by the President (6 Cannon § 525), or that a Member distributed certain improper questionnaires (Deschler Ch 11 § 24.1), or that a Member filed a minority report that had been written by employees of a political party (Deschler Ch 11 § 24.4), does not give rise to a question of personal privilege.

Published charges relating to the House or the Members generally or to ''persons advocating'' a certain measure, with no Member being named or otherwise identified, do not give rise to a question of personal privilege. Deschler Ch 11 §§33.1-33.3.

A question of privilege may not be used to collaterally attack the rules or orders of the House. A refusal by those in charge of the time for general debate on a bill to allot time to a Member does not give that Member grounds for a question of personal privilege. Deschler Ch 11 §24.

§17. Charges by a Fellow Member; Words Used in Debate

Generally

Statements off the floor by a Member accusing another Member of lying or intentionally making a false statement may give rise to a question of personal privilege. Similarly, statements by a Member impugning another Member's motives or veracity, accusing another Member of traitorous acts, of gross political interference with a government contract, of an abuse of personal power, or of sponsoring a smear campaign may give rise to a question of personal privilege. 3 Hinds §2717; Deschler Ch 11 §§26.2-26.8. It is not necessary that the Member be identified by name if it is clear from other sources that the reference was to a particular Member. 3 Hinds §2709; 6 Cannon §§616, 617; Deschler Ch 11 §26.1.

Words Uttered in Debate or Inserted in the Congressional Record

A question of personal privilege may not be based on language uttered on the floor of the House in debate or conveyed by an exhibit used in debate, the remedy being a timely demand that the objectionable words be taken down when spoken. *Manual* §708; 8 Cannon §2537; Deschler Ch 11 §27.1; see generally CONSIDERATION AND DEBATE. However, a Member may base such a question on objectionable remarks inserted under leave to revise and extend remarks. 8 Cannon §2537; Deschler Ch 11 §§27.2-27.5. A Member may also base such a question on press accounts of remarks uttered on or off the floor impugning such individual's character or personal motives. *Manual* §708. Charges reflecting on a Member's integrity or reputation, inserted in the *Congressional Record* by a Senator, also may give rise to a question of personal privilege. Deschler Ch 11 §§27.6-27.9.

§18. Charges in the Press

Generally

Criticism of a Member in the press may give rise to a question of personal privilege where the criticism reflects on integrity or conduct in a representative capacity. Deschler-Brown Ch 29 §10.75. However, vague charges in newspaper articles (6 Cannon §570), criticisms (3 Hinds §§2712-

2714), or even misrepresentations of the Member's speeches or acts or responses in an interview have been held insufficient grounds (*Manual* § 708; 3 Hinds §§ 2707, 2708). The mere allegation that there has been a violation of the rules of the House, such as that votes have been improperly paired or that a bill has been placed on the incorrect calendar, does not give rise to a question of personal privilege. 3 Hinds § 2616; 8 Cannon § 3094. However, where the allegation impugns a Member's character or motives or reflects on reputation or integrity, a question of personal privilege may arise. Deschler-Brown Ch 29 § 60.27. For example, language in a newspaper asserting that a Member would divide the Nation and that he was a spokesman for the forces of betrayal was held to involve a question of personal privilege. Deschler Ch 11 § 31.3. Charges that a Member is a fascist sympathizer or that he has engaged in conduct inimical to the national security also have given rise to questions of personal privilege. Deschler Ch 11 §§ 31.4-31.18. Other charges in the press that have given rise to a question of personal privilege include allegations of:

- Misuse of public funds. Deschler Ch 11 § 30.1.
- Conflict of interest. Deschler Ch 11 §§ 30.6, 30.7.
- Deceptive or disgraceful conduct reflecting on the House. Deschler Ch 11 §§ 30.2, 30.15, 30.16.
- Dereliction of duties. Deschler Ch 11 § 30.3.
- Confiscation of evidence. Deschler Ch 11 § 30.4.
- Unworthy motives in taking certain legislative action. 6 Cannon § 576; 8 Cannon § 2216.
- Improper conduct in agency dealings. Deschler Ch 11 § 30.17.
- Abuse of the franking privilege. Deschler Ch 11 § 30.18.
- Engagement in improper lobbying activities. Deschler Ch 11 § 30.6.
- Introduction of legislation in which the Member had a personal interest. Deschler Ch 11 § 30.7.
- Wrongful claim of "out of pocket" expenses in a fundraising activity. 94-2, Feb. 23, 1976, p 4062.

Criticism of Committee Activities

Criticism impugning the motives or actions of a chair or member of a committee may give rise to a question of personal privilege. Deschler Ch 11 § 30.11. Thus, a Member has been recognized to rise to a question of personal privilege to respond to the following press charges:

- Allegation of improper disposition of classified documents from committee files. 94-2, Mar. 9, 1976, p 5825.
- Allegations of abuse of power or improper action in carrying out committee responsibilities. Deschler Ch 11 §§ 30.8-30.14.
- Allegation of improper hire of staff who did no work for the committee. 94-2, May 25, 1976, p 15344.

- Denigration of Member in televised committee proceedings. *Manual* § 708.
- Allegation that a committee chair had been buying votes. *Manual* § 708.

Normally, however, a question concerning charges as to the propriety of committee procedure, as distinct from charges against the Member's conduct in a representative capacity, should be raised as a question of the privileges of the House, assuming that the dignity and integrity of the House proceedings are at issue.

Charges of Illegality

Charges in the press that a Member did something illegal in such Member's representative capacity give rise to a question of personal privilege. 3 Hinds § 1829; Deschler Ch 11 §§ 29.1, 29.3. Such a question has arisen on publication of charges that a Member committed the following acts:

- Treason or sedition. Deschler Ch 11 § 29.6.
- Forgery. Deschler Ch 11 § 29.2.
- Corruption and bribery. 3 Hinds § 1830.
- Criminal conspiracy or perjury. Deschler Ch 11 § 29.5.
- Tax evasion and irregularities. Deschler Ch 11 §§ 29.4, 29.5.
- Violation of the securities laws. 95-2, June 2, 1978, p 16056.

Speaker Wright rose to a question of personal privilege to respond to a ''statement of alleged violations'' pending in the Committee on Standards of Official Conduct (now Ethics); and, pending the committee's disposition of his motion to dismiss, announced his intention to resign as Speaker and as a Member. Speaker Gingrich rose to a question of personal privilege to discuss his own official conduct previously resolved by the House. A committee chair rose to a question of personal privilege to discuss his own official conduct, which question was based on a letter of reproval reported by the Committee on Standards of Official Conduct (now Ethics). *Manual* § 708. A committee chair rose to a question of personal privilege to discuss alleged violations of Federal tax law. 110-2, Sept. 10, 2008, p 18419.

Charges of Impropriety

A charge of vote-selling in a conflict-of-interest case or involvement with an organization being investigated by a Senate committee or of conduct characterized as reprehensible has given rise to a question of personal privilege. Deschler Ch 11 §§ 28.1-28.3. Speaker Hastert rose to a question of personal privilege to respond to charges of impropriety in his selection of a Chaplain. *Manual* § 708.

The publication of vague charges accusing Members of impropriety, however, does not give rise to a question of personal privilege or of the privileges of the House. 3 Hinds § 2711. No question of personal privilege was held to arise from the publication of remarks attributed to a Member who denied making them. 3 Hinds § 2708.

Charges Impugning Veracity

Published charges that a Member made a false statement may give rise to a question of personal privilege. 3 Hinds § 2718; Deschler Ch 11 §§ 32.1, 32.2. For such a charge to give rise to this question of privilege, however, it must be alleged that the Member made a false statement knowingly, with intent to deceive. 3 Hinds § 2721. A mere difference of opinion over a factual matter, where there is no intent to deceive, does not give rise to a question of personal privilege. 3 Hinds §§ 2720, 2721.

B. Consideration

§ 19. Raising the Question; Procedure

Unlike questions of the privileges of the House, which must be raised by resolution, questions of personal privilege are ordinarily raised orally. Deschler Ch 11 § 20.

The Member, before proceeding with debate on a question of personal privilege, must state to the Speaker the grounds on which the question is based. Deschler Ch 11 § 21.1. In ruling on the question, the Speaker may insist that the offending material, if published, be submitted for examination. Compare Deschler Ch 11 § 21.2 with § 21.3.

MEMBER: M__. Speaker, I rise to a question of personal privilege.

SPEAKER: The gentle______ will state the question of personal privilege. . . .

[*Or*]

SPEAKER: The Chair is aware of valid bases for the gentle______'s question of personal privilege. The gentle______ is recognized for one hour.

In Committee of the Whole

Questions of personal privilege are raised in the House, not in the Committee of the Whole. Deschler Ch 11 § 21.4. Early precedents suggest, however, that a question of personal privilege may be raised in the Committee of the Whole if the matter in issue arose during the Committee proceedings. 3 Hinds §§ 2540-2544. A question of personal privilege alleged to have arisen in the Committee of the Whole cannot be raised in the House unless the matter was reported to it by the Committee. *Manual* § 711; 4 Hinds § 4912; see also § 17, supra, for a discussion that words spoken in debate do not give rise to a question of personal privilege.

§ 20. Debate on the Question

Debate on a question of personal privilege is ordinarily under the hour rule. 5 Hinds § 4990; 8 Cannon § 2443; Deschler Ch 11 § 22.1. The Member recognized on the question controls the hour. *Manual* § 713. A Member wishing to respond to another Member's debate on a question of personal privilege may do so in a special-order speech. Deschler Ch 11 § 22.2.

In rising to a question of personal privilege, the Member should confine all remarks to the statements or issues giving rise to the question. *Manual* § 713; 5 Hinds §§ 5075, 5076. However, the Member is entitled to discuss related matters necessary to challenge the charge that has been made against such Member. Deschler Ch 11 § 22.5. Members should limit their remarks to the matter concerning themselves personally, and should not use debate time to level charges against other Members. 5 Hinds § 5078; 8 Cannon §§ 2481-2483. Remarks should be kept within limits consistent with the spirit of the rule, and Members may not use the privilege as a vehicle for discussions not otherwise in order. 8 Cannon § 2448.

In lieu of raising a question of personal privilege, a Member may use a one-minute or special-order speech to respond to the charge or allegation. Deschler Ch 11 § 22.4. Another option available to the Member is merely to insert remarks in the *Congressional Record*, without using debate time. 94-2, Feb. 23, 1976, p 4062.

Chapter 43
Quorums

Research References

U.S. Const. art. I, § 5
4 Hinds §§ 2884-3055
6 Cannon §§ 638-707
Deschler Ch 20
Manual §§ 982, 1014-1029

A. Generally; Quorum Requirements

§ 1. In General

Constitutional Requirements and the House Rules

Under the Constitution, a majority of each House constitutes a quorum to do business, although a smaller number may adjourn from day to day or compel the attendance of absent Members. U.S. Const. art. I, § 5, cl. 1. Because the presence of a quorum is a constitutional requirement, and because a point of order of no quorum is the only method available to a Member to enforce that requirement, the Speaker has been reluctant to withhold recognition for a point of order of no quorum when raised in accordance with the rules of the House. Deschler Ch 20 §§ 14.2, 14.3. Quorum requirements for committees, see COMMITTEES.

The Constitution does not further define those legislative proceedings that are to constitute "business" for purposes of the quorum requirement. "Business" in this context has become a term of art that, under the House rules and precedents, does not encompass all parliamentary proceedings. For example, the prayer, administration of the oath, and certain motions incidental to a call of the House do not constitute business requiring a quorum. Deschler Ch 20 § 18 (note 10). Indeed, clause 7(a) of rule XX specifically prohibits the entertainment of a point of order of no quorum unless a question has been put to a vote. See § 3, infra. The House has determined by adopting such a rule that the mere conduct of debate, where the Chair has not put the pending proposition to a vote, is not conducting "business" under article I, section 5, clause 1 of the Constitution. Because the adoption of such a rule is viewed by the House as a proper exercise of its rule-making authority under article I, section 5, clause 2 of the Constitution, there is no constitutional basis for a point of order of no quorum during debate in the House. *Manual* § 1029.

Presumptions as to the Presence of a Quorum

A quorum is presumed to be present unless a point of no quorum is entertained and the Chair announces that a quorum is in fact not present or unless the absence of a quorum is disclosed by a vote or by a call of the House. Deschler Ch 20 § 1. Although it is not the duty of the Chair to take cognizance of the absence of a quorum unless otherwise disclosed, failure of a quorum to participate in a record vote cannot be ignored. The Chair must announce that fact although it was not objected to from the floor. 4 Hinds §§ 2953, 2963; 6 Cannon §§ 565, 624; Deschler Ch 20 § 1.

§ 2. What Constitutes a Quorum

A quorum of the House is defined as a majority of those Members sworn and living, whose membership has not been terminated by resignation or by House action. *Manual* § 53; 4 Hinds §§ 2889, 2890; 6 Cannon § 638; Deschler Ch 20 § 1; § 5, infra. Thus, when there are no vacancies, a quorum to do business is 218 Members. When the membership has been reduced by reason of death, resignation, expulsion, disqualification, or removal to 432, a quorum to do business is 217 Members. 94-2, June 18, 1976, p 19312. This long-standing practice was codified in the 108th Congress by adoption of clause 5(c) (now 5(d)) of rule XX. Clause 5(d) also requires the Speaker to announce the reduced whole number of the House, which is not subject to appeal. In the case of a death, the Speaker may lay before the House such documentation from Federal, State, or local officials deemed pertinent.

Clause 5(c) of rule XX provides for the calculation of a ''provisional'' quorum should catastrophic circumstances prevent Members from responding to a quorum call. Such catastrophic circumstances include ''natural disaster, attack, contagion or similar calamity rendering Representatives incapable of attending the proceedings of the House.'' Clause 5(c)(4)(A). In such circumstances, Members who are able to respond to a call of the House constitute the ''provisional number of the House'' and a quorum is determined on the basis of this number. *Manual* § 1024a.

Under clause 6(a) of rule XVIII, a quorum in the Committee of the Whole is 100 Members. *Manual* § 982. The quorum required in the House as in the Committee of the Whole is a quorum of the House and not a quorum of the Committee of the Whole. 6 Cannon § 639.

§ 3. Business Requiring a Quorum; Effect of Quorum Failure

In General

In Jefferson's time, the Speaker did not take the Chair until a quorum for business was present. *Manual* § 310. Under the early practice, a quorum was required during debate (4 Hinds §§ 2935-2939) and for other routine activities of the House, such as the reading of the Journal (4 Hinds § 2733), the consideration of committee reports (4 Hinds § 2947), and the calling up of measures (4 Hinds § 2943).

Under the modern practice, the Speaker takes the Chair at the hour to which the House has adjourned, and there is no requirement that the House proceed immediately to establish a quorum. *Manual* §§ 310, 621. Although the Speaker has the authority to recognize for a motion for a call of the

House at any time, a point of order of no quorum does not lie in the House unless the Speaker has put the pending question to a vote. Clause 7(a) of rule XX; *Manual* § 1027; § 12, infra. Accordingly, for example, the Chair may not entertain a point of order of no quorum during debate in the House or during the offering of the prayer or the administration of the oath.

The pendency of a unanimous-consent request in the House is not equivalent to the Chair's putting a pending question to a vote and does not permit a point of order of no quorum under clause 7(a) of rule XX. Deschler-Brown Ch 29 § 23.13.

Business Precluded in Absence of Quorum

The House cannot conduct business after the absence of a quorum has been announced. *Manual* § 55; Deschler Ch 20 §§ 1.5, 10.4. This includes business by unanimous consent. *Manual* § 1025. Even the Member who made the point of order of no quorum cannot then withdraw it by unanimous consent, as such a request would constitute business. 4 Hinds §§ 2928-2931; 6 Cannon § 657; Deschler Ch 20 § 10.4 (note). For example, where the announced absence of a quorum has resulted in a vote by the yeas and nays under clause 6 of rule XX, the House may not, even by unanimous consent, vacate the vote in order to conduct another voice vote in lieu of the record vote.

When the House authorizes the Speaker under clause 5 of rule XX to compel the attendance of absent Members, the Speaker requests the Sergeant-at-Arms to proceed with necessary and efficacious steps to secure a quorum. The Speaker then announces that, pending the establishment of a quorum, no further business, including unanimous-consent requests for recess authority, may be entertained. *Manual* § 1025.

If a quorum does not respond on a call of the House or on a record vote, even the most highly privileged business must terminate. 4 Hinds § 2934; 6 Cannon § 662. The House then has only two alternatives: to adjourn or to continue the proceedings under a pending call of the House until a quorum of record is obtained. Deschler Ch 20 §§ 10.10-10.12. If a call of the House is ordered, the House must first secure a quorum before disposing of the pending matter *de novo*. Deschler Ch 20 §§ 10.5-10.7.

For a discussion of quorum failures due to catastrophic circumstances, see § 2, supra.

§4. Motions Requiring a Quorum

In General

Under clause 7(a) of rule XX, the putting of a question to a vote triggers the admissibility of a point of order of no quorum, thereby permitting the Speaker to entertain a point of order of no quorum if the motion is one that requires a quorum for adoption. *Manual* §1027. Thus, a Member may make a point of order of no quorum when the Speaker has put the question on a motion to suspend the rules. However, where the Speaker postpones further proceedings on a motion to suspend the rules, the question is no longer being put to a vote for purposes of permitting a point of order of no quorum until the question recurs as unfinished business. *Manual* §1026.

Motions Incident to a Call of the House

The motion for a call of the House, or a motion incidental to a call of the House, does not require a quorum for adoption. *Manual* §1025; Deschler Ch 20 §2.8. Under clause 7(b) of rule XX, further proceedings are considered dispensed with when a quorum is established pursuant to the call unless the Speaker recognizes for a motion to compel attendance of Members. *Manual* §1028. For a discussion of motions in order during a call of the House, see *Manual* §1024.

The Motion to Adjourn

A quorum is not required on an affirmative vote on a simple motion to adjourn. Deschler Ch 20 §§8.7, 8.8. However, a point of no quorum on a negative vote on adjournment is in order and, if sustained, precipitates a call of the House. *Manual* §1025; 6 Cannon §700; Deschler Ch 20 §8.13.

A quorum is required for the adoption of a motion that when the House adjourns that day it adjourn to a day and time certain. *Manual* §913. A quorum also is required on a concurrent resolution providing for adjournment *sine die* but not on a motion to adjourn that implements such a concurrent resolution. Deschler Ch 20 §§8.9, 8.10.

The Motion to Rise

A quorum is not required on an affirmative vote on a simple motion that the Committee of the Whole rise (see §6, infra), but a negative voice vote or division vote permits a point of no quorum pending the demand for a recorded vote. See Deschler Ch 20 §16.7. A quorum is required on an affirmative vote on a motion to rise and report. 4 Hinds §2973.

§ 5. The Count to Determine a Quorum

Counting Those Present Together With Those Voting

Until 1890 the view prevailed in the House that it was necessary for a majority of the Members to vote on a matter submitted to the House in order to satisfy the constitutional requirement for a quorum. Under that practice the opposition might break a quorum simply by refusing to vote. 4 Hinds § 2977. That practice was changed in 1890 with the historic ruling by Speaker Reed, later embodied in clause 4(b) of rule XX, that Members present in the Chamber but not voting would be counted in determining the presence of a quorum. *Manual* § 1020; 4 Hinds § 2895; Deschler Ch 20 § 3. This ruling was upheld by the Supreme Court in *United States v. Ballin*, 144 U.S. 1 (1892), the Court declaring that the authority of the House to transact business is ''created by the mere presence of a majority.'' Since 1890, the point of order as to the absence of a quorum is that no quorum is present, not that no quorum has voted. 4 Hinds § 2917.

A quorum may be expressed as a fraction in which the numerator is the number of Members who are present and the denominator is the number of Members who are extant. As the issue in *Ballin* was Speaker Reed's method of counting the number of Members present, the decision of the Supreme Court addressed the numerator of this fraction. In dictum the Court examined the question ''how shall the presence of a majority be determined?'' and observed that, because the Constitution does not prescribe any method for determining the presence of such majority, it is within the competency of the House ''to prescribe any method which shall be reasonably certain to ascertain the fact.'' In 1906, consistent with the dictum in *Ballin*, Speaker Cannon employed the still-current method of counting the number of Members extant. After reviewing the perspectives of his predecessors across the 19th century and with special regard for the considered judgment of the Senate on the same question (Senate rule VI), Speaker Cannon held that once the House is organized for a Congress ''a quorum consists of a majority of those Members chosen, sworn, and living, whose membership has not been terminated by resignation or by the action of the House.'' 4 Hinds § 2890; 6 Cannon § 638.

Under clause 5(d) of rule XX (adopted in the 108th Congress), upon the death, resignation, expulsion, disqualification, or removal of a Member, the Speaker announces any adjustment to the whole number of the House. Such an announcement is not subject to appeal. In the case of a death, the Speaker may lay before the House such documentation from Federal, State, or local officials deemed pertinent. See § 2, supra.

Method of Counting

Speaker Reed also ruled in 1890 that it was the function of the Speaker to determine the presence of a quorum in such manner determined to be accurate and suitable by the Chair's own count or by various other methods. 4 Hinds § 2932. Under rule XX, the Speaker may direct the use of the electronic system in the Chamber to record the names of the Members voting or present. *Manual* § 1014. In lieu of using the electronic system (if, for example, there is a malfunction in the electronic system), the Speaker has the discretion to direct that the presence of Members be recorded by clerks or direct that a quorum call be taken by an alphabetical call of the roll. *Manual* §§ 1015, 1019.

Under clause 4(b) of rule XX, the Chair may count Members who are present and do not vote as follows:

- Members who are visible, including those behind the railing. Deschler Ch 20 § 3.6.
- Members in the process of leaving the Chamber. Deschler Ch 20 § 3.5.
- The Member then occupying the Chair. Deschler Ch 20 § 3.7.

However, the Chair may not count the following Members:

- Members in the cloakrooms out of sight. Deschler Ch 20 § 3.10.
- Members entering the Chamber after the Chair announces the result of the quorum call. Deschler Ch 20 §§ 3.11-3.13.

In any case, the Chair's count of a quorum is conclusive and may not be challenged on appeal. *Manual* § 629.

The number of Members present for the purpose of determining the absence of a quorum may be established by a count of the number of Members voting on a pending proposition. Deschler Ch 20 § 2.13. However, the Chair's count of those Members standing on a division vote in the House does not demonstrate the absence of a quorum because the Chair, in taking such a vote, does not count all Members present in the Chamber but only those standing. Deschler Ch 20 § 2.18.

Recounts

When the Chair is counting to determine if a quorum is present, the Chair may recount the House before announcing the result of the count. Such recount may be in response to a statement of a Member that more Members had entered the Chamber since the first count, thereby establishing a quorum. Deschler Ch 20 § 3.18.

B. Points of Order of No Quorum

§ 6. When in Order; Former and Modern Practice Distinguished

In the House

Under the former practice, a point of no quorum was in order in the House at any time, even when a Member had the floor in debate. Deschler Ch 20 § 13.8. The right of the Member to the floor was suspended until a quorum was secured. Deschler Ch 20 § 13.9. A point of no quorum could interrupt the reading of the Journal or the reading of a resolution, even though the resolution was privileged for consideration. Deschler Ch 20 §§ 13.11, 13.12, 13.14.

Under the modern practice, the use of points of order of no quorum in the House has been sharply curtailed. Under clause 7(a) of rule XX, a point of no quorum is not in order unless a question has been put to a vote, notwithstanding the failure of a quorum to have voted on a prior item of business no longer pending. 95-1, Sept. 16, 1977, p 29563. Therefore, a point of order of no quorum may not be made during the offering of the prayer, the administration of the oath, the reception of messages from the President or the Senate, the reading of the Journal, or special orders. The refusal of the Chair to entertain a point of order of no quorum where prohibited by clause 7(a) is not subject to appeal. *Manual* § 629. Furthermore, the Chair will not entertain a unanimous-consent request to waive the provisions of clause 7(a) of rule XX. 93-2, Dec. 9, 1974, p 38664.

In Committee of the Whole

A similarly restrictive rule applies to points of order of no quorum in the Committee of the Whole. Clause 6(b) of rule XVIII states that, ''after a quorum has once been established on a day,'' the Chair may not entertain a point of order that a quorum is not present unless the Committee is operating under the five-minute rule and the Chair has put the pending question to a vote. *Manual* § 982. A Member may make a point of order of no quorum while the Chair is counting those standing in the Committee to support a demand for a recorded vote and before the Chair's final announcement of the count. At that point the Chair must immediately begin counting for a quorum, and the request for a recorded vote remains pending following the establishment of a quorum. *Manual* § 1012. The Chair will resume the count for a recorded vote when the requesting Member withdraws the point of order of no quorum (which is the usual practice).

The restriction of clause 6 of rule XVIII against making a point of order of no quorum ''after a quorum has once been established on a day'' means on that day during consideration of the pending bill, because the House resolves itself into a new Committee of the Whole on each bill, with a new chair. *Manual* § 982. The rule restricting points of order of no quorum in the Committee after a quorum has once been established is applicable whether the quorum was established by a regular quorum call or a "short" quorum call. 95-2, June 8, 1978, p 16778. For a discussion of a regular quorum call and a short quorum call, see § 17, infra.

Although a point of order of no quorum may be raised during general debate in the Committee of the Whole, the Chair is given the discretion to entertain it under clause 6(b) of rule XVIII. *Manual* § 982.

A point of order of no quorum does not lie in the Committee against the adoption of a motion that the Committee rise, because that motion (as distinguished from the motion to rise and report) does not require a quorum for adoption. Clause 6(d) of rule XVIII; 4 Hinds §§ 2972, 2975.

§ 7. Objections to Vote Taken in Absence of Quorum

In the House

The rules of the House permit a Member to object to a vote taken in the absence of a quorum. An objection to such a vote under clause 6 of rule XX, if timely made, necessarily precipitates a call of the House (unless the House adjourns or the Chair postpones proceedings under clause 8 of rule XX) and, simultaneously, a vote by the yeas and nays on the pending question. *Manual* § 1025.

The objection to a vote permitted by clause 6 of rule XX applies only to votes on questions requiring a quorum. Thus, an objection may not be raised under the rule to an affirmative vote on a motion to adjourn or to a vote on a motion incidental to a call of the House, neither of which requires a quorum for adoption. 4 Hinds § 2994; 6 Cannon § 681; Deschler Ch 20 § 2.

For further discussion of the "automatic" vote by the yeas and nays that ensues under clause 6 of rule XX, see § 14, infra.

Effect of Postponement

When a Member objects to a vote on the ground that a quorum is not present, and further proceedings are postponed under clause 8 of rule XX or by unanimous consent, the Speaker puts the question *de novo* when the measure is again before the House as unfinished business. Members then have the same right to object on that ground as when the question was originally put. Deschler Ch 21 § 3.18. *Manual* § 1026. In the Committee of the Whole, when proceedings resume on a request for a recorded vote on an amendment postponed under clause 6(g) of rule XVIII, the voice vote is acknowledged and the request is announced as pending. At this time, a point of order of no quorum may be made.

§ 8. Timeliness and Diligence in Raising Objections

In General

An objection to a vote because of the absence of a quorum must be timely raised. Such an objection comes too late when the Speaker has announced the result of the vote and a motion to reconsider has been laid on the table. Deschler Ch 20 §§ 13.23, 13.24. However, such objections have been held to be timely and in order when they were made:

- After the Chair announced that the noes on a voice vote prevailed but before the House proceeded to other business. Deschler Ch 20 § 13.16.
- After a parliamentary inquiry that immediately followed the announcement of the result of a voice or division vote. 6 Cannon § 698; Deschler Ch 20 § 13.18.
- After a refusal of a demand for the yeas and nays following a division vote. Deschler Ch 20 § 13.19.
- After a sufficient number have risen to order the yeas and nays but before the start of the vote. Deschler Ch 20 § 13.1.

Timeliness in Seeking Recognition

An objection to a voice vote on the ground that a quorum is not present is timely even after the Chair announces the vote if the Member was standing and seeking recognition at the time the question was put. Deschler Ch 20 § 13.1. However, the Speaker may decline to recognize a Member to object to a vote because of the absence of a quorum where the Member has not shown the proper diligence in seeking recognition. Deschler Ch 20 § 13.26. In order to raise such an objection, a Member must be standing and actively seeking recognition when the Chair announces the result of the vote. Deschler Ch 20 § 13.25. The mere fact that a Member is standing does not constitute notice to the Chair that such Member is seeking recognition to make such an objection. Deschler Ch 20 § 13.2.

§ 9. When Dilatory; Effect of Prior Count

In General

Although the presence of a quorum is a constitutional requirement, and the Speaker has on occasion expressed reluctance to hold a point of order of no quorum dilatory for that reason, it has long been recognized as within the prerogative of the Chair to refuse to entertain a point of no quorum if the Chair determines that it was made for the sole purpose of delay where the presence of a quorum, as evidenced by an immediately preceding vote or quorum call, is apparent. 5 Hinds §§5724, 5725; 8 Cannon §2808; Deschler Ch 20 §14. Since rule XVIII and rule XX were amended to restrict recognition for points of no quorum to instances where the Chair has put a question to a vote, the use of repeated points of order as a dilatory tactic has lost its efficacy.

§10. Withdrawal of Point of Order

A point of order that a quorum is not present may be withdrawn, provided the absence of a quorum has not been announced by the Chair; and such withdrawal does not require unanimous consent. Deschler Ch 20 §18.5. A point of order of no quorum is considered withdrawn where the Chair exercises any postponement authority under clause 6(g) of rule XVIII or clause 8 of rule XX. *Manual* §§984, 1026.

A point of no quorum may not be withdrawn after the absence of a quorum has been announced by the Chair (4 Hinds §2928-2930; 6 Cannon §657; Deschler Ch 20 §18), even where the Member making the point of order attempted to withdraw it but was not observed by the Chair (103-1, June 10, 1993, p 12481). The point may not then be withdrawn even by unanimous consent, because the House may not conduct business, including the disposition of unanimous-consent requests, in the announced absence of a quorum. Deschler Ch 20 §18.7. The same rule is followed in the Committee of the Whole. Deschler Ch 20 §18.6.

A point of no quorum may not be reserved or withheld after the Chair has announced that a quorum is not present, no business being in order until a quorum is established. Deschler Ch 20 §§18.10, 18.11.

C. Quorum Calls

§11. In General

In the House

A motion for a call of the House is recognized under general parliamentary law and under the Constitution. 4 Hinds §2981. The Constitution authorizes a number smaller than a quorum to compel the attendance of absent Members. U.S. Const. art. I, §5.

Rule XX authorizes three separate procedures for a call of the House. They are as follows:

- The call of the House under clause 6 whenever objection is raised to a vote taken in the absence of a quorum. *Manual* § 1025. This call is sometimes referred to as an "automatic" call because it proceeds by operation of the rule and does not require a motion. See § 14, infra.
- The call of the House under clause 7(b), which permits the Speaker the discretion to recognize for a motion for a call of the House at any time. See § 12, infra.
- The call of the House under clause 5 that is used in the absence of a quorum to compel the attendance of absent Members. The Speaker may recognize for that motion, which must be adopted by a majority comprising at least 15 Members. See § 13, infra. The call under this clause is sometimes referred to as the "old" form of the call, clause 5 having been first adopted in 1789.

In Committee of the Whole

The provisions of clauses 5, 6, and 7 of rule XX, relating to quorum calls in the House, do not apply in Committee of the Whole. Accordingly, although a point of order that a quorum is not present will lie in the Committee of the Whole when a question is put, a Member may not object to a vote in the Committee on the ground that a quorum is not present. Deschler Ch 20 § 16.1; § 6, supra. In the Committee of the Whole, the quorum call and the vote occur seriatim and not simultaneously as they do in the House under clause 6 of rule XX. The requirement of, and the procedures for, obtaining a quorum in Committee of the Whole are found in clause 6 of rule XVIII. See § 17, infra.

§ 12. The Motion for a Call

Under clause 7(b) of rule XX, a nondebatable motion for a call of the House is permitted at any time subject to clause 7(c). Clause 7(c) precludes such motion after the previous question has been ordered unless the Speaker determines by actual count that a quorum is not present. A motion for a call of the House is in order notwithstanding language in clause 7(a) of rule XX that a point of order of no quorum may not be entertained unless the Speaker has put a pending question to a vote. *Manual* §§ 1027-1029. Under this rule, the Speaker has the discretion at any time to recognize a Member to offer the motion. Thus, the Speaker may refuse recognition. *Manual* § 1029. The motion is privileged if entertained by the Chair. It may be entertained after another Member has been recognized but before such Member has begun debate. Deschler-Brown Ch 29 § 23.15. When a Member is under recognition for debate, another Member may be recognized to move a call of the House only if yielded to for that purpose. 105-2, July 23, 1998, p 16989. The motion is not debatable. 6 Cannon §§ 683, 688.

If the motion is rejected, the House proceeds with business. Deschler-Brown Ch 29 § 20.20. However, if the motion is adopted by a record vote, and a quorum is established thereby, a call of the House must proceed unless rescinded by unanimous consent. 94-1, Oct. 22, 1975, p 33688.

§ 13. The Call to Compel Attendance of Absent Members

In General

Clause 5 of rule XX, enabling 15 Members to order a call of the House, dates from the earliest Congresses, and for many years was the only rule for procuring the attendance of Members. 4 Hinds § 2982. The automatic call of the House under clause 6, having been provided for by rule in 1896, is described as the call of the House in the new form. It supersedes the old form of the call except in cases in which the absence of a quorum is established by some means other than a vote. 4 Hinds § 3041. The call of the House on motion under clause 5 or clause 7(b) is in order at the Chair's discretion. On the other hand, the automatic call under clause 6 ensues while the House is voting. *Manual* §§ 1021-1025; 4 Hinds § 2990.

Recognition for the motion is within the Speaker's discretion, and the motion may not be adopted by fewer than 15 affirmative votes (which may include the Chair). Unless that number is present, the motion for the call is not entertained. 4 Hinds § 2983. The motion requires a majority vote for adoption, and a minority of 15 (or more) favoring the call is not sufficient. 4 Hinds § 2984.

If a majority votes to compel attendance under this rule, absentees are notified. *Manual* § 1021. Warrants may be issued by order of a majority of those present, and those for whom no sufficient excuse is made may be arrested by the Sergeant-at-Arms. § 19, infra. Members who appear voluntarily are admitted to the Hall and report their names to the Clerk to be entered on the Journal as present. *Manual* § 1021.

When a call of the House is ordered under this rule, the Speaker may direct the taking of the call by electronic device or by a call of the roll. *Manual* §§ 1014, 1015. A motion to adjourn takes precedence over a call of the House. 8 Cannon § 2642.

Under the modern practice, clause 5 is seldom used. It should be read in light of rule XX clause 7(a), which precludes a point of order of no quorum except when the Chair has put a question to a vote, and clause 7(b), which gives the Speaker discretion to recognize for a call of the House at any time. *Manual* §§ 1027, 1028.

§ 14. The Automatic Call

In General

Under clause 6 of rule XX, a call of the House ensues whenever a quorum fails to vote on any question that requires a quorum (assuming that the House does not adjourn), if in fact a quorum is not present and objection to the vote is made for that reason. The rule provides for a call of the House and states that the yeas and nays on the pending question ''shall at the same time be considered as ordered.'' *Manual* § 1025. The call of the House under this clause is sometimes referred to as the ''automatic call'' because it is mandated under the conditions specified by the rule. Deschler Ch 20 § 2; 6 Cannon § 695.

Under this rule the Speaker has the discretion to conduct the call by electronic device or to order a call of the roll by the Clerk. *Manual* § 1025; Deschler Ch 20 § 4.2. When the roll is called by the Clerk, the roll is called twice; and those appearing after their names are called may vote. 4 Hinds § 3052. The Speaker may count the House to determine whether a quorum is present. If the count discloses a quorum, the Speaker declares, pursuant to clause 6 of rule XX, that a quorum is constituted; the Speaker is not required to announce the actual count. *Manual* § 1025.

Although arrest of Members is rare in modern practice, Members who do not respond to the call are subject to arrest by the Sergeant-at-Arms. See § 19, infra.

The Speaker is authorized to declare that a quorum is constituted if those voting on the question, together with those who are present, make up a majority of the House. *Manual* § 1025. Such a declaration dispenses with further proceedings. See § 20, infra. The pending question is then decided by a majority of those voting, a quorum being present. *Manual* § 1025.

Invoking the Call

The automatic call of the House under clause 6 of rule XX may be invoked by a Member who rises following the announcement of the result of a vote to state:

> M__. Speaker, I object to the vote on the ground that a quorum is not present and make a point of order that a quorum is not present.

If no Member rises to object that a record vote discloses that a quorum is not present, the Speaker takes the initiative to declare the absence of a quorum, thereby invoking the automatic call. Deschler Ch 20 § 2.

The automatic call does not apply when the House is voting on a question that does not require a quorum, such as a motion incidental to a call of the House or a motion to adjourn decided in the affirmative. *Manual* § 1025; 4 Hinds § 2994; 6 Cannon § 681.

§ 15. Use of Electronic Equipment

In General

The Speaker is authorized under clause 2(a) of rule XX to use the electronic equipment in the Chamber to record those present for any quorum call. *Manual* § 1014. The use of this equipment is not mandatory. The Speaker has discretion, for example, to direct the Clerk to call the roll where a quorum fails to vote on any question and objection is made for that reason. Deschler Ch 20 § 4.2. The Speaker also has the discretion under rule XX to direct that the quorum call be taken by clerk tellers under clause 4 or by an alphabetical call of the roll under clause 3, rather than by electronic device. Deschler Ch 20 § 4.1. These alternatives are normally used when the electronic system is inoperable. Clause 2(b) of rule XX.

Response Time

On a call of the House conducted by electronic device, the Members have not less than 15 minutes to respond. Clause 2 of rule XX; *Manual* § 1014. After the 15 minutes have expired, the Chair may allow additional time for Members to respond before announcing the result. Deschler Ch 20 § 4.3.

At the beginning of a new Congress, the Speaker has inserted in the *Congressional Record* an announcement that, in order to expedite the conduct of quorum calls (as well as votes) by electronic device, the cloakrooms were directed not to forward to the Chair individual requests to hold a quorum call open. The Speaker has also announced that each occupant of the Chair would have the Speaker's full support in striving to close each electronic quorum call at the earliest opportunity and that Members should not rely on signals relayed from outside the Chamber to assume that quorum calls will be held open until they arrive. At the same time, the Chair will not close a quorum call while Members are in the well attempting to record their presence. *Manual* § 1014.

§ 16. Names Published and Recorded on a Call

Under clause 2(a) of rule XX, the names of those Members who respond to a quorum call are entered in the Journal and published in the *Congressional Record*. *Manual* § 1014. When the call is taken by clerks, the clerks record the names of those present and note the names of absentees. *Manual* § 1019. Members responding to a quorum call ordered on motion under clause 5 of rule XX must report their names to the Clerk to be entered in the Journal. *Manual* § 1021. When an automatic call of the House ensues under clause 6 of rule XX, Members brought in by the Sergeant-at-Arms are noted as present. *Manual* § 1025.

Under clause 4(b) of rule XX, any Member may demand, or the Speaker may require, that the names of those Members not voting be noted by the Clerk, recorded in the Journal, and reported to the Speaker, along with the names of those Members voting, in determining the presence of a quorum. *Manual* § 1020. The Speaker may direct the Clerk to note the names of Members under this rule even on a vote for which no quorum is necessary. 8 Cannon § 3152.

§ 17. Quorum Calls in Committee of the Whole

Regular and "Notice" Quorum Calls Distinguished

Quorum calls in the Committee of the Whole—to secure the presence of at least 100 Members—are governed by the provisions of clause 6 of rule XVIII. That rule permits two kinds of quorum calls in the Committee: a "regular" quorum call and a "notice" or "short" quorum call. *Manual* § 982.

A "regular" quorum call is initiated under clause 6(a) of rule XVIII. That rule sets forth the circumstances under which the Chair is to invoke the procedures normally available to the Speaker for quorum calls in the House under the applicable provisions of rule XX. Specifically, clause 2(a) of rule XX allows at least 15 minutes for Members to respond and requires the publication of the names of those Members answering present. *Manual* § 1014; see generally §§ 15, 16, supra.

A "notice" or "short" quorum call is permitted under clause 6(c) of rule XVIII. That provision permits the Chair, at any time during a call, subject to the prior announcement, to determine and declare that a quorum is present. Proceedings under the call are then considered vacated, and the Committee resumes its business. This provision permits the Chair to announce in advance, at the time the absence of a quorum is ascertained, that proceedings will be vacated when a quorum appears. It also enables the Chair to convert to a regular quorum call in the event that a quorum does not appear. The Chair need not convert to a regular quorum call precisely at the expiration of 15 minutes if a quorum (100 Members) has not responded on a "notice" quorum call but may continue to exercise discretion to vacate proceedings at any time during the entire period permitted for the conduct of the call by clause 2(a) of rule XX. *Manual* § 982.

When in Order

Under clause 6(a) of rule XVIII, the first time that a Committee of the Whole finds itself without a quorum on a day, the Chair must invoke one of the quorum call procedures that are available under rule XX. Thereafter, quorum calls are permitted only during proceedings under the five-minute rule when the Chair has put a pending question to a vote. A point of order of no quorum during general debate is permitted only at the discretion of the Chair. *Manual* § 982.

Method of Taking

Before installation of the electronic system in the Chamber, quorum calls in the Committee of the Whole were effected by a call of the roll. 4 Hinds § 2966. Under the modern practice, quorum calls are taken by electronic device, but the Chair has the discretion to effect the call by an alphabetical call of the roll or by clerk tellers. Clause 6(a) of rule XVIII, which incorporates by reference clauses 2, 3, and 4(a) of rule XX. Thus, the Chair may direct that a ''notice'' quorum call be conducted pursuant to the provisions of clause 4(a) of rule XX—by depositing quorum tally cards with clerk tellers—in lieu of conducting the call by electronic device or a call of the roll. Deschler-Brown Ch 30 § 31.9.

The so-called automatic call authorized by clause 6 of rule XX in the House is not permitted in the Committee of the Whole. See Deschler Ch 20 § 7.

Reports as to Absentees

The Committee of the Whole rises and the Chair reports the names of absentees to the House only in the event that a quorum fails to respond to the quorum call under clause 6 of rule XVIII.

§ 18. Motions in Order During the Call

Generally

With the exception of the motion to adjourn, the only motions in order during a call of the House are those in furtherance of the effort to secure a quorum. 6 Cannon § 682. Motions held not in order include:

- Motion to recess. 4 Hinds §§ 2995, 2996.
- Motion to dispense with further proceedings under the call. 4 Hinds § 2992.
- Motion to excuse Members from voting. 4 Hinds § 3007.
- Motion relating to deductions from the pay of Members. 4 Hinds § 3011.

Motions that are intended to secure a quorum and therefore in order during the call of the House include:

- Motion that the Speaker issue warrants for the arrest of absent Members. 6 Cannon § 681.
- Motion that the Sergeant-at-Arms take absent Members into custody. 4 Hinds § 3029; 6 Cannon § 685.
- Motion that the Sergeant-at-Arms report progress in securing a quorum. 6 Cannon § 687.
- Motion for the previous question on a proposition incident to a call of the House. 5 Hinds § 5458.
- Motion to reconsider a vote incident to a call of the House. 5 Hinds §§ 5607, 5608.

Motions to Adjourn

The motion to adjourn takes precedence over a call of the House. Deschler Ch 20 §§ 8.14, 8.15. The vote on the motion is taken before the call of the House, even when the motion for the call was offered but not finally agreed to before the motion to adjourn. Deschler Ch 20 § 8. Although the motion to adjourn is not entertained after the call of the House has been ordered, it again becomes available after Members have been given an opportunity to record their presence. Deschler Ch 20 §§ 8.22, 8.23. If the call is taken by roll call, the motion to adjourn again becomes in order after the conclusion of the second call of the roll if a quorum has not been established. Deschler Ch 20 § 8.19. If the call is taken by electronic device, the motion to adjourn again becomes in order after the expiration of 15 minutes and need not await the announcement of the result of the call. Deschler Ch 20 §§ 4.4.

Clause 6 of rule XX, which authorizes automatic votes by the yeas and nays, permits the House to adjourn in the absence of a quorum and before a call of the House. Clause 6(c) gives the Speaker discretion to recognize a motion to adjourn after the vote has been completed but before the result has been announced if the motion has been seconded by a majority of those present, to be ascertained by actual count of the Speaker. *Manual* § 1025.

§ 19. Securing Attendance; Arrests

Under Clause 6 of Rule XX

The attendance of absent Members may be secured under clause 6 of rule XX, which provides for the automatic vote by the yeas and nays. Under this rule, the Sergeant-at-Arms ‘‘shall proceed forthwith’’ to bring in absent Members whenever a quorum fails to vote, a quorum is not present, and objection is made for that reason. A Member who is arrested is brought by the Sergeant-at-Arms before the House and permitted to vote. *Manual* § 1025. Compulsory attendance or arrest has been rare in the modern practice.

Under the conditions specified by this rule, the Sergeant-at-Arms is required to detain those who are present and to bring in absentees. 4 Hinds §§ 3045-3048. It is not necessary that specific authorization be given by a motion (Deschler Ch 20 § 5.14) or by a resolution adopted by those present (4 Hinds § 3049). However, to make an arrest under this rule, the Sergeant-at-Arms must have possession of a warrant signed by the Speaker. Deschler Ch 20 § 5.10 (note). Although the Speaker possesses full authority to issue a warrant of arrest for absent Members under this rule (6 Cannon §§ 680, 702), the Speaker usually does not do so without House authorization (Deschler Ch 20 § 5.10). The warrant takes the following form (4 Hinds § 3041):

> To __________, Sergeant-at-Arms of the House of Representatives, or such officer's deputies:
>
> Whereas clause 6 of rule XX of the House of Representatives provides as follows: ________________
>
> Whereas the conditions specified in said rule have arisen, and the following-named Members of the House are absent, to wit: ____________________
>
> Now, therefore, by virtue of the power vested in me by the House, I hereby command you to execute the said order of the House, by taking into custody and bringing to the bar of the House said above-named Members; and make due return in what manner you execute the same.
>
> [Sealed, signed by the Speaker, and attested by the Clerk]

When arrested, Members are (1) arraigned at the bar, (2) discharged from arrest, (3) questioned by the Speaker as to whether or not they wish to vote, and (4) permitted to vote. 4 Hinds § 3044.

Under Clause 5 of Rule XX

The use of the Office of the Sergeant-at-Arms to procure the presence of Members in the Chamber also is permitted by clause 5 of rule XX, which authorizes the Speaker to recognize a motion, which requires 15 Members to adopt, to compel the attendance of absent Members. § 13, supra. Under the rule, a majority of those present, numbering at least 15 Members, may order officers appointed by the Sergeant-at-Arms to send for and arrest absentees for whom no excuse is made. Members whose attendance has been secured in this manner are detained until discharged under conditions determined by the House. *Manual* §§ 1021, 1023. Those present may prescribe a fine as the condition on which an arrested Member may be discharged. 4 Hinds § 3013.

Under this rule, in the absence of a quorum in the House, a motion (or other proposition) to arrest absentees and bring them into the Chamber is in order. 4 Hinds § 3018; Deschler Ch 20 § 5.6. To compel the attendance of absentees by arrest under this rule, the motion:

- Must be supported by 15 affirmative votes, and those voting to compel attendance must be in the majority. Deschler Ch 20 § 5.9 (note).
- Is in order after a single call of the roll. 4 Hinds § 3015.
- Is in order during proceedings to secure a quorum. 6 Cannon § 685.
- Is not debatable. 6 Cannon § 686.
- May not order the arraignment of absent Members at a future meeting of the House. 4 Hinds §§ 3032-3034.

The motion for the arrest of absentees is in the form of an order to the Sergeant-at-Arms, as follows (Deschler Ch 20 § 5.11):

> *Ordered*, That the Sergeant-at-Arms take into custody and bring to the bar of the House such Members as are absent without leave.

Unless directed by an appropriate motion, the Sergeant-at-Arms, under clause 5 of rule XX, has no authority to compel the attendance of absent Members. Deschler Ch 20 § 5.9. A motion that merely states that those who are not present are to be "sent for" and "returned," and not allowed to leave until the completion of certain business, has been interpreted as requiring the Sergeant-at-Arms to notify absentees but not as bestowing the authority to arrest them and bring them into the Chamber under custody. In that case, no timely point of order was raised against the motion due to lack of a quorum. Therefore, the motion was held to be binding on the Speaker and other Members. Deschler Ch 20 § 5.3.

After agreement to the appropriate motion, warrants for the arrest of absent Members are signed by the Speaker or Speaker pro tempore. Deschler Ch 20 § 5. Leave for a committee to sit during sessions does not release its members from liability to arrest. 4 Hinds § 3020.

Closing or Locking the Chamber Doors

Although it was Jefferson's view that as a matter "[o]f right, the door of the House ought not to be shut," the House rules have from time to time given the Speaker the authority to order the closing of the Chamber doors in connection with securing a quorum. *Manual* § 380; Deschler Ch 20 § 6. Clause 4 of rule XX, adopted in 1972, states that "the doors may not be closed except when ordered by the Speaker" pursuant to a quorum call. *Manual* § 1019. The precursor of this rule gave the Speaker the discretion, in securing a quorum, to order the doors closed or even locked. Deschler Ch 20 § 6.2 (note).

In 1919, Speaker Gillett, after putting the question on ordering a call of the House, directed the Doorkeeper to lock the Chamber doors but then sustained a point of order that the doors should be closed only on a call of the House. 6 Cannon §703. However, in one instance the doors were locked ''until disposition of the pending business'' (the reading of the Journal). This action was taken by order of the House rather than by order of the Speaker. Deschler Ch 20 §6.5. In 1968, Speaker McCormack ordered the doors to the Chamber closed and locked during a call of the House pursuant to the rule and instructed the Doorkeeper to let no Members leave the Hall. Deschler Ch 20 §6.3.

§20. Dispensing With Further Proceedings

Under the former practice, after a quorum had responded on a call of the House, it was necessary to move to dispense with further proceedings under the call before the House could proceed with pending business. See 4 Hinds §3039. Under the modern practice, clause 7(b) of rule XX eliminates the motion to dispense with further proceedings under a call of the House following establishment of a quorum. *Manual* §1028. Under this rule, when a quorum has been established pursuant to a call of the House, the Speaker ordinarily simply announces that further proceedings under the call are dispensed with unless the Speaker exercises the discretion to recognize for a motion to compel the attendance of Members under clause 5(b) of rule XX.

Chapter 44
Reading, Passage, and Enactment

Research References

U.S. Const. art. I, § 7
4 Hinds §§ 3364-3481
7 Cannon §§ 1027-1083
Deschler Ch 24 §§ 11-16
Manual §§ 104, 105, 396, 397, 497, 498, 573-577, 941-944

§ 1. In General; Stages in Passage

The various steps in the usual legislative process begin with the introduction of a measure and include its referral to committee, committee consideration, reporting of the measure to the House, and consideration and debate in the House or the Committee of the Whole (where the first and second readings occur). These matters are covered elsewhere in this work. See INTRODUCTION AND REFERRAL; COMMITTEES; COMMITTEES OF THE WHOLE; and CONSIDERATION AND DEBATE.

The following checklist describes the possible steps beginning with the ordering of the previous question on passage of a bill through its enactment into law:

- Previous question ordered on bill and all amendments to final passage.
  Note: When the previous question is ordered, debate is terminated and the House then votes first on any pending

amendment or amendments, including any reported from the Committee of the Whole. If the previous question is not ordered, the bill and any amendments thereto are open to further debate and possible further amendment. See PREVIOUS QUESTION.

- Demand for separate vote on amendments adopted in the Committee of the Whole.

  Note: A demand for a separate vote in the House on an amendment adopted in the Committee of the Whole is in order following the Speaker's announcement that the previous question has been ordered, but such separate votes are not actually taken until after the House votes on any remaining amendments en bloc. *Manual* § 337; Deschler Ch 27 § 36.20. A Member cannot demand a separate vote on an amendment *rejected* in the Committee of the Whole. Deschler Ch 27 § 36.12.

- Question put *en gros* on those amendments on which a separate vote was not demanded.

- Question put on each amendment on which a separate vote was demanded.

  Note: Votes are normally taken in the order in which the amendment appears in the bill. However, if amendments have been considered under a special order of business prescribing the order for their consideration, the amendments are voted on in the order in which they were considered in Committee of the Whole. *Manual* § 337; see also AMENDMENTS.

- Question put on engrossment and third reading (third reading by title only).

  Note: This is normally a pro forma question. Engrossment is the printing of the measure on special paper, and the ''third reading'' requires merely a reading of the title. *Manual* § 941. The question is ordinarily approved by voice vote. However, a record vote may be ordered, and a negative vote rejects the bill. On Senate bills the question is put on the third reading but not engrossment because such bills are engrossed by the Senate. For engrossment generally, see § 6, infra. Any amendment to a preamble of a joint resolution should be made after engrossment and pending the third reading. *Manual* § 414.

- Motion to recommit offered.

  Note: A Member opposed to the bill may offer a motion to recommit the measure to committee. A Member may offer a simple motion to recommit (which, if adopted, ends further consideration of the bill) or a motion to recommit with instructions. *Manual* §§ 1001, 1002. The motion may instruct the committee to report the bill back to the House ''forthwith'' with an amendment. Only one proper motion may be considered. See REFER AND RECOMMIT.

- Question put on ordering the previous question on motion to recommit.

  Note: Amendments to the motion cannot be offered if the previous question on the motion has been ordered. *Manual* §§916, 917, 1001, 1002. This comports with the House rule giving precedence to the motion for the previous question over the motion to amend. *Manual* §911. If the previous question is rejected, and an amendment is offered, the previous question is again moved on the amendment and the motion (as amended).

- Question put on motion to recommit (as amended or not).

  Note: If recommitted with instructions, the bill is reported back ''forthwith'' with amendment(s), the amendment(s) are again put to a vote, and the vote recurs on engrossment and third reading.

- Question put on passage of bill.

  Note: As a general rule, after a bill is passed there can be no further alteration of it. The Clerk may be authorized by unanimous consent to make technical and conforming (or even substantive) changes in the engrossment. *Manual* §500.

- Amendment to title of bill.

  Note: An amendment to the title is not in order until after the bill itself is passed and is not debatable. If the committee reported the bill to the House with an amendment to the title, the amendment to the title is adopted by unanimous consent initiated by the Chair. *Manual* §922.

- Motion to reconsider.

  Note: The motion to reconsider may be used to revisit passage or a step leading thereto. See RECONSIDERATION. While a motion to reconsider is pending, the bill cannot be sent to the Senate.

- Motion or unanimous-consent request to lay the motion to reconsider on the table.

  Note: The pro forma motion or unanimous-consent request to table the motion to reconsider is used to preclude a subsequent motion to reconsider, and it is the accepted parliamentary mode of making the vote in question final. In practice, the two motions often are made simultaneously. 8 Cannon §2784. The Speaker often performs this perfunctory role, as when declaring, after the announcement of a vote, ''without objection, a motion to reconsider is laid on the table.'' Deschler Ch 23 § 34. See generally RECONSIDERATION.

- Transmittal of bill to Senate.

  Note: After passage of a bill in the House, the engrossment is attested by the Clerk of the House and transmitted to the Senate.

- Consideration of bill by Senate.

- Return of bill to House.

  Note: If a House bill is passed by the Senate without amendment, the Senate messages the bill back to the House, where it is enrolled under the supervision of the Clerk. *Manual* § 648; see § 10, infra. If a House bill is returned with amendment, such amendment is disposed of by unanimous consent, by motion to suspend the rules, or by a special order of business. However, a Senate amendment not requiring consideration in the Committee of the Whole is privileged, as is a motion to disagree to the Senate amendment and request or agree to a conference with the Senate (if offered by direction of relevant committees). On very rare occasions, the Speaker has referred a bill with Senate amendments to the House committee having jurisdiction. *Manual* § 816. For an explanation of House procedure for consideration of Senate amendments, see SENATE BILLS; AMENDMENTS BETWEEN THE HOUSES and *Manual* §§ 528-528d. For a discussion of conferences, see CONFERENCES BETWEEN THE HOUSES and *Manual* §§ 530-559.

- Submission of conference report.

  Note: The committee of conference having met, a report embodying their recommendation is submitted together with a joint explanatory statement of the managers from each House.

- Adoption of conference report.

  Note: Approval by the House and Senate of the conference report and mutual agreement to any amendments in disagreement constitute final congressional approval of the bill. The two Houses act seriatim on the report, the one agreeing to the conference normally acting first. However, a conference report ordinarily must be acted on as a whole; that is, either adopted or rejected in its entirety. If the conferees disagree on certain numbered amendments, the amendments are submitted to each Chamber individually and acted upon separately. Every amendment must be agreed to in identical form by both

Houses before congressional action on the bill is complete. See CONFERENCES BETWEEN THE HOUSES.

- Enrollment of bill.
  Note: A bill that is finally passed by both Houses is enrolled by the House in which it originated; that is, it is printed on special paper (*i.e.*, parchment; 1 USC § 107) under the supervision of an enrolling clerk. After its accuracy has been approved by the Clerk, an enrolled bill is presented to the House and Senate, where it is signed by the Speaker and the President of the Senate, respectively. *Manual* § 648; see § 10, infra.
- Delivery of bill to the President for approval or veto.
  Note: An enrolled bill, having been signed by the Speaker and the President of the Senate, is delivered to the White House for Presidential approval. The President has 10 days (excluding Sundays) in which to sign the bill or veto it by returning it to the originating House with any objections. The bill may also be subject to a "pocket veto" if Congress, by final *sine die* adjournment, has prevented its return. See VETO OF BILLS.
- Passage of bill over Presidential veto.
  Note: A veto override requires a vote of two-thirds by the yeas and nays, a quorum being present, in each Chamber. If a vote to override a veto succeeds in the originating House, the measure is sent to the second House. If the veto is overridden there, the bill becomes law without the President's signature. *Manual* § 109.
- Deposit of measure in National Archives.
  Note: When an enrolled bill is signed by the President or enacted over a veto, it becomes a public law and is sent to the National Archives and published in *Statutes at Large*, an annual volume that compiles all bills that become law. An Act passed over the President's veto is transmitted to the Archivist by the House last acting on it.

§ 2. Readings

The reading of a bill is an essential step toward its passage. Deschler Ch 24 § 11. The First Congress adopted a rule requiring three separate and distinct readings of each bill brought before the House. 4 Hinds § 3391.

Clause 8 of rule XVI provides that a bill or joint resolution must be read three times. The first reading is by title; the second reading for amendment in the Committee of the Whole is by paragraph or section; and the third reading is by title. *Manual* § 941. The second, or full reading, is pursuant to clause 5 of rule XVIII. The three readings referred to in rule XVI are to be distinguished from the procedures involved in reading a bill for amendment. See AMENDMENTS. In practical terms a ''first reading'' in the Committee of the Whole contemplated in rule XVIII is in full, but this reading ordinarily is dispensed with by special order of business. The reading for amendment by paragraphs or sections is the second actual reading in the Committee of the Whole.

For a discussion of reading papers in debate, see CONSIDERATION AND DEBATE.

§ 3. —First Reading

Under clause 8 of rule XVI, the first reading of a bill in the House is in full. *Manual* § 941. The first reading of a bill in the Committee of the Whole is in full under clause 5 of rule XVIII. *Manual* § 978. Formerly, a bill was read the first time by title at the time of its introduction before the House. However, since 1890 all bills have been introduced by filing them with the Clerk (placing them in the bill ''hopper'' at the rostrum). 4 Hinds § 3391. Today, the titles of all bills introduced are printed in the Journal and the *Congressional Record*, thus fulfilling the purpose of the former first-reading rule. *Manual* § 942.

§ 4. —Second Reading

Generally

The second reading in the Committee of the Whole is required by clause 5 of rule XVIII. That reading is normally by paragraph or section. *Manual* § 980. Clause 8 of rule XVI has no provision for a second reading in the House. Therefore, in the House, bills are considered read a second time when they are taken up for action.

The Clerk, and not the chair of the Committee of the Whole, reads bills the second time. *Manual* § 428. If consideration of the bill is not completed on the day it is called up, the bill is read by title when it is called up on subsequent days.

Demanding a Reading in Full; Dispensing with Readings

Although clause 5(a) of rule XVIII requires a full reading of a bill (which may be demanded by any Member) before general debate, in practice verbatim readings are usually dispensed with by unanimous consent, by suspension of the rules, or by special order of business. Deschler Ch 24 § 11; Deschler Ch 27 § 7.1; *Manual* § 942.

It has been held that a motion to dispense with the reading in full is not in order. 8 Cannon §§2335, 2436. The Committee of the Whole may dispense with the reading by motion if the motion is made privileged, as by a special order of business. Deschler Ch 24 § 11.1 (note).

Measures Subject to Reading in Full

Clause 8 of rule XVI requires a reading ''in full'' only of ''bills and joint resolutions.'' However, the rule traditionally has been extended to privileged concurrent and simple resolutions as well. Such resolutions include adjournment resolutions, questions of privilege, and special orders of business reported by the Committee on Rules. See, *e.g.*, *Manual* §713. A concurrent or simple resolution called up by unanimous consent is not read in full; rather, only the title is read. When a measure is read in full, it is the text as originally introduced that is read. Proposed committee amendments, including those in the nature of a substitute, are not included in this reading. Deschler Ch 24 §11. Even when a substitute amendment has been reported to the House, it is the introduced bill that is read. 7 Cannon §1054.

Interruption of Reading

The reading of a bill may be interrupted by the presentation of a matter of higher privilege, such as the reception of a message, a question of privilege, or the arrival of the time designated for adjournment. See 5 Hinds §6448 (reading interrupted by presentation of conference report).

§5. —Third Reading

The third reading of a bill under clause 8 of rule XVI is by title only and comes after the order for engrossment and before the question on passage of the bill is put. *Manual* §941. The Speaker states: ''The question is on the engrossment and third reading of the bill.'' This is a pro forma question that is routinely approved by voice vote just before the measure itself is put to a vote. However, a record vote may be ordered on the question of engrossment and third reading. If the question is decided in the negative, the bill is considered rejected. 4 Hinds §3420. If the third reading is omitted and the bill passes, the defect can be rectified by reconsideration. 4 Hinds §3406.

At one time a Member could demand a reading *in full* of the engrossment, but this procedure was stricken from the rules in 1965. Deschler Ch 24 §11.

§ 6. Engrossment of House-passed Bills

After a bill has passed the House, the Clerk prepares a certified copy for transmission to the Senate. This copy is the official copy of the measure as passed by the House, and is referred to as the engrossment. That term also refers to the process by which a bill is engrossed; that is, printed on special paper under the supervision of the Clerk. House-passed measures or House amendments to Senate measures are engrossed on distinctive blue paper. The Clerk attests to the engrossment, and the Clerk's signature gives rise to the presumption that the bill was correctly engrossed. 4 Hinds § 3428. Senate bills and amendments are engrossed by that body on white paper and bear the signature of the Secretary of the Senate. A limited number of the blue and white engrossments are printed for official use of the House and the Senate and are the prints used by conferees in working out their agreements.

The engrossment of a House-passed bill is under the control of the House, not of the Committee of the Whole. Thus, a unanimous-consent request relating to the engrossment of a bill is properly made in the House following the passage of the bill and is not in order in the Committee of the Whole. Deschler Ch 24 § 12.2.

§ 7. — Correcting Errors in Engrossment

Before Transmittal of Bill to the Senate

Before the House has messaged its legislative action to the Senate, the House may, by unanimous consent, authorize the Clerk to make changes in the engrossment of a House-passed bill. This procedure may be used, for example, to direct the Clerk to correct or change the table of contents, to amend or strike cross references, or to change section numbers and make other technical changes. Deschler Ch 24 §§ 12.10, 12.12. By unanimous consent the Clerk also may be authorized to make designated substantive changes in the engrossment of a bill passed by the House. However, the Chair may require that the changes be read by the Clerk. 99-1, Feb. 27, 1985, p 3888; 99-1, June 27, 1985, p 17875. In one instance, the House by unanimous consent authorized the Clerk to engross in its introduced form a bill recently passed in an amended form under suspension of the rules. 106-2, July 27, 2000, p 16607.

The engrossment of House amendments to Senate bills that have not been messaged to the Senate may likewise be corrected by unanimous consent, the Clerk being directed to make the necessary change. Deschler Ch 24 §§ 12.8, 12.9, 12.11. Thus, in one instance, by unanimous consent, the

Clerk was authorized to correct the engrossment of a House amendment to a Senate bill passed on the preceding day to reflect the adoption in Committee of the Whole of an amendment that was inadvertently not reported to the House. 94-1, May 7, 1975, p 13363. The same procedure has been used to correct the engrossment of a House amendment to a Senate bill by deleting a provision inadvertently included in the measure. 99-2, Oct. 9, 1986, p 30102.

After Transmittal of Bill to Senate

After a bill has been messaged to the Senate, the House must request that the Senate return the bill for correction. The House makes its request by resolution, which may also authorize the Clerk to reengross the bill with specified changes. Deschler Ch 24 § 12.5. A resolution in the House requesting the return of a bill of the Senate to correct an error made by the Clerk in preparing the engrossment of a House amendment was treated as a question of privilege under rule IX. *Manual* § 565; 3 Hinds § 2613.

Where both Houses have acted on the measure a concurrent resolution may effect changes in the final enrollment. See § 12, infra.

§ 8. —Correcting Printing Errors; "Star Prints"

An engrossment may be "star printed" (that is, reprinted with a star to indicate the reprinting) to rectify a typographical error made by the Government Printing Office (GPO). This procedure is designed to substitute a reprinted bill and to show the exact form in which the bill was actually passed. Deschler Ch 24 § 12.1.

The star print procedure is appropriate to correct GPO printing errors in a bill until both Houses have acted on the measure. Thereafter, a concurrent resolution to correct an enrollment is used to correct printing errors in a bill. Deschler Ch 24 § 14.7.

§ 9. Transmittal of Bills Between the Houses

A bill, having passed one House and having been engrossed and attested, is transmitted to the other House by message. Deschler Ch 24 § 12.1. One House may message to the other a request to return a bill for the correction of errors or otherwise. *Manual* § 565; 3 Hinds § 2613; 4 Hinds §§ 3460-3465. A request by the Senate for the return of a bill, if alleging an error in preparation, is treated as privileged in the House. However, if not alleging error but rather seeking a substantive change, such a request would require unanimous consent. *Manual* § 565. The question is put to the House without debate. 95-1, Aug. 3, 1977, p 26538. The House may by unanimous consent agree to a request of the Senate for the return of a Senate bill, even where the bill has been referred to a House committee. 91-1, July 10, 1969, p 19095.

§ 10. Enrollment of Bills Passed by Both Houses

When a bill or joint resolution has passed both Houses, the papers are delivered to the House that originated the measure, and a final version—called the enrolled bill—is prepared. If the bill originated in the House, it is enrolled under the supervision of the Clerk. *Manual* § 648. The enrollment is printed on distinctive paper under special supervision of the enrolling clerks of the House or the Senate. 1 USC § 107; Deschler Ch 24 § 14. This printing requirement may be waived by the enactment of a joint resolution, or, during the last six days of the session, by the adoption of a concurrent resolution. 1 USC § 106; *Manual* § 574. The enrolled bill is signed by the presiding officers of the House and the Senate and is delivered to the President for approval. See §§ 11-13, infra. If approved by the President, the measure is sent to the National Archives. 1 USC § 106a.

It has been held that the validity of an enrolled bill signed by the President cannot be questioned on account of the pendency of a motion to reconsider, the signing of the enrolled bill by the Speaker and Vice President being complete and unimpeachable evidence of its passage. See *Field* v. *Clark*, 143 U.S. 649 (1892).

§ 11. — Certification and Signing

Approval and Certification

A House-enrolled bill or joint resolution must be approved as to form and accuracy by the Clerk, although this requirement on rare occasions has been waived by unanimous consent. *Manual* § 648; 4 Hinds § 3452. In addition, House-enrolled bills are certified by the Clerk as having originated in the House. Senate enrollments are delivered to the House after similar examination and certification by the Secretary of the Senate. Deschler Ch 24 § 15.

Signing

Ordinarily, enrollments are signed first by the Speaker and then by the President of the Senate. 4 Hinds § 3429. In early Congresses the Speaker could not sign an enrolled bill in the absence of a quorum. 4 Hinds § 3458. Today, under clause 4 of rule I, the Speaker has standing authority to sign enrolled bills even if the House is not in session; and bills passed at one session may be signed by the Speaker at the next session. *Manual* § 624; 7 Cannon § 1075. The Committee of the Whole may rise informally without motion to enable the Speaker to assume the Chair to lay an enrolled bill before the House. *Manual* § 625.

Signing by the Speaker Pro Tempore

A Speaker pro tempore elected by the House may sign enrolled bills. 2 Hinds § 1401. Under clause 8(b)(2) of rule I, the Speaker may appoint a Member to act as Speaker pro tempore only to sign enrolled bills for a specified period of time, subject to the approval of the House. However, a Member merely called to the Chair during the day or designated by the Speaker for a purpose other than to sign enrolled bills, may not exercise this function. 2 Hinds §§ 1399, 1401; 6 Cannon § 276.

§ 12. —Corrections in Enrollment

Generally; Authorizing Corrections Before Enrollment

The Clerk of the House may be authorized by concurrent resolution to make certain corrections in the enrollment of a House bill. 7 Cannon § 1068. The authorizing resolution may be agreed to by one House even before the bill to be corrected has passed the other House. In one instance the House agreed to a concurrent resolution correcting the enrollment of a joint resolution before the consideration of a conference report on that measure. 99-1, Dec. 11, 1985, pp 35957, 35958.

Corrections made in this manner often involve nothing more than spelling errors or an error in the title of a bill. However, a concurrent resolution may authorize the Clerk to make extensive substantive changes. Deschler Ch 24 §§ 14.5-14.7.

Corrections in enrolled bills are normally made by the House that originated the bill, but the concurrent resolution authorizing the changes may originate in either House. Thus, the House may originate a concurrent resolution directing the Secretary of the Senate to make corrections in the enrollment of a Senate bill. Deschler Ch 24 § 14.18.

Authorizing Corrections After Enrollment

The correction of a bill, even after its enrollment, may be ordered by concurrent resolution of the two Houses. 4 Hinds § 3451; 7 Cannon § 1041. If the enrolled bill has not been signed by the respective presiding officers, the resolution may simply direct the Clerk to reenroll the bill with a correction. Deschler Ch 24 § 14.14. If the enrolled bill has been so signed, the two Houses by concurrent action may authorize the rescission or cancellation of the signatures and a reenrollment. 4 Hinds §§ 3453-3459; Deschler Ch 24 § 14.13. In the same way, signatures may be canceled on a bill prematurely enrolled. 4 Hinds § 3454; Deschler Ch 24 §§ 15.12, 15.13. The resolution may not only rescind the action of the Speaker and President of the Senate in signing the bill but also may direct the Clerk to reenroll the bill with certain changes or to provide for its return to the Senate. Deschler Ch 24 §§ 14.9-14.11.

Correction or Recall of Bills Delivered to the President

Corrections or changes in enrolled bills that have been delivered to the White House but not signed into law traditionally have been effected by a concurrent resolution, considered by unanimous consent, that requests the return of the bill and vacates the signatures of the Speaker and the President of the Senate. The resolution may direct a reenrollment with corrections by the Clerk of the House or the Secretary of the Senate, as appropriate. 4 Hinds §§ 3507, 3508; Deschler Ch 24 §§ 16.1-16.4. Bills retrieved and corrected under this procedure are resubmitted to the President for approval. However, in one instance, a concurrent resolution was used to request the recall of a bill from the White House, to rescind the signatures of the two presiding officers and to postpone the bill indefinitely. Deschler Ch 24 § 16.5.

The use of concurrent resolutions to recall a bill to correct an error is appropriate only with respect to bills that have not been signed, or are presumed not to have been signed, by the President. 4 Hinds § 3507 (note). Once a bill has been signed, it becomes law; and changes in it can be effected only by amending the measure pursuant to the passage of a bill or joint resolution. Thus, where the President signed a bill from which a section was inadvertently omitted during enrollment, the Congress immediately passed a joint resolution amending the law to insert the omitted section. Deschler Ch 24 § 14.19.

Consideration of Resolution

Concurrent resolutions making corrections in an enrolled bill are not privileged for consideration and are normally considered by unanimous consent. See, *e.g.*, Deschler Ch 24 § 14.5. However, they also may be considered under suspension of the rules (93-2, Aug. 5, 1974, p 26796), or under a special order of business reported from the Committee on Rules (93-2, Dec. 13, 1974, p 39596). Such a resolution may also be taken up pursuant to a special order of business from the Committee on Rules ''hereby'' adopting that resolution. *Manual* § 855.

§ 13. Delivery of Measures to the President

Bills

The Constitution requires that every bill that passes the House and the Senate be presented to the President of the United States for approval. U.S. Const. art. I, § 7. In early Congresses a joint committee took enrolled bills to the President. 4 Hinds § 3432. However, in the later practice, the Clerk of the House or the Secretary of the Senate has responsibility for the enrollment of bills and for presenting the bills from that House to the President. Such presentation is recorded in the Journal. *Manual* § 577.

Enrolled bills pending at the close of a session have at the next session of the same Congress been ordered to be presented as if no adjournment had taken place. 4 Hinds §§ 3487, 3488. Enrolled bills signed by the presiding officers at one session have been sent to the President and approved at the next session of the same Congress. 4 Hinds § 3486. Bills enrolled in one Congress have been presented to the President and been signed by the President after the convening of the next Congress. *Manual* § 577.

Joint Resolutions

A joint resolution is a bill so far as the processes of Congress are concerned, with the exception of joint resolutions proposing amendments to the Constitution. 4 Hinds § 3375. Joint resolutions proposing amendments to the Constitution require a two-thirds vote to pass and are not sent to the President for approval. *Manual* § 397; 4 Hinds § 3483; 5 Hinds § 7040. Such joint resolutions, after passage by both Houses, are delivered to the Archivist. 1 USC § 106b.

Concurrent Resolutions

It has been the uniform practice of the Congress, since the organization of the government, not to present concurrent resolutions to the President for approval and to avoid incorporating in such resolutions any matter of strict legislation requiring such presentation. Concurrent resolutions have been used merely to express the sense of Congress on a given subject, to adjourn for longer than three days, or to accomplish some purpose in which both Houses have a common interest but with which the President has no concern. Such resolutions have "never embraced legislative provisions proper and hence have never been deemed to require executive approval." *Manual* § 396; 4 Hinds § 3483.

Chapter 45

Recess

Research References

5 Hinds §§ 6663-6671

8 Cannon §§ 3354-3362

Deschler-Brown-Johnson Ch 39

Manual §§ 586, 911, 913

§ 1. In General

Under clause 12(a) of rule I, the Speaker may declare a recess ''for a short time'' when no question is pending before the House. Under clause 12(b) of rule I, the Speaker or chair of the Committee of the Whole may declare an emergency recess when notified of an imminent threat to the safety of the House. Recesses also may be declared by the Speaker pursuant to authority granted by the House by privileged motion. § 2, infra. Except in case of emergency under clause 12(b) of rule I, recesses are not permitted in the Committee of the Whole except with the permission of the House. 5 Hinds §§ 6669-6671; 8 Cannon § 3357.

Recess is to be distinguished from adjournment. Recesses are taken during a legislative day, whereas adjournments terminate a legislative day. Another distinguishing feature is that, during a recess, the Mace remains in place on the rostrum, indicating that the House continues in session. Bills may be introduced and reports may be filed through the hopper.

Except for an emergency recess under clause 12(b) of rule I, a recess may not interrupt a call of the roll or a recorded vote, even though the House has previously given authority to declare a recess at any time. 5 Hinds §§ 6054, 6055. However, when the hour previously fixed for a recess arrived, the Chair declared the House in recess during a division vote. 5 Hinds § 6665.

§ 2. House Authorization; Motions

The House may specifically authorize the Speaker to declare a recess, but in modern practice, the standing authority in clause 12(a) of rule I (to declare a recess when no question is pending) has made such specific authorizations infrequent. The House may, by motion, by unanimous consent, by suspension of the rules, or by special order of business, authorize the Speaker to declare a recess. Clause 4 of rule XVI; *Manual* §§ 83, 586, 911, 913; Deschler Ch 21 § 11.8. The authority may be for a single recess on a given day, for several recesses subject to the call of the Chair, or for more than one day. 104-1, Dec. 15, 1995, p 37107 (motion); 104-1, Dec. 21, 1995, p 38475 (special order of business). However, no recess declared by the Speaker or authorized by the House alone can exceed three days (not including Sundays) because that would violate the constitutional requirement for Senate consent. U.S. Const. art. I, § 5; see also § 3, infra.

The Speaker also may be authorized to declare a recess:

- At any time during the remainder of the day. 87-2, Sept. 12, 1962, p 19258.
- On the following day. 86-1, May 26, 1959, p 9155.
- During the remainder of the week. 90-1, Dec. 15, 1967, p 37126.
- At any time on certain days of the week. 88-2, Apr. 7, 1964, p 7119.
- At any time on the legislative days of Friday and Saturday and if necessary on Sunday. 97-1, Nov. 19, 1981, p 28211.
- At any time during the remainder of the session. Deschler Ch 21 § 11.8.
- On a specific day to accommodate a joint meeting. 110-1, Nov. 1, 2007, p 29042.

Motions to Authorize a Recess

Clause 4(c) of rule XVI permits the Speaker to entertain ''at any time'' a motion authorizing the Chair to declare a recess. The motion may be adopted by simple majority vote.

Rule XVI gives the motion for a recess a privileged status equal to that of the motion to adjourn, which is a motion of the highest precedence and privilege. *Manual* §§ 911, 912; see ADJOURNMENT. Before the adoption of this rule in 1991, the motion to authorize a recess was not privileged in the House and could be entertained only by unanimous consent (8 Cannon § 3354), although a privileged motion to recess was permitted by rule from 1880 to 1890 (8 Cannon § 3356).

A motion to authorize the Speaker to declare a recess is not debatable or amendable. *Manual* §§ 911, 913.

Quorum Requirements

A vote by the House to authorize the Speaker to declare a recess requires a quorum. 4 Hinds §§2955-2960. A motion for a recess cannot be entertained if the absence of a quorum has been declared. 4 Hinds §2958-2960. However, when the hour previously fixed for a recess arrives, the Chair declares the House in recess, even if a quorum is not present. 5 Hinds §§6665, 6666.

§3. Duration of Recess

Generally

The Speaker may be authorized by the House to declare a recess to a time certain on that day (92-2, Oct. 14, 1972, p 36474), or to declare a recess until a time certain on the following calendar day (97-1, Nov. 20, 1981, p 28628). Overnight recess may be authorized, in which event the same legislative day is retained. 98-1, Nov. 10, 1983, p 32200. A recess does not terminate a legislative day, and a legislative day may not be terminated during recess. 8 Cannon §3356. In rare circumstances, upon the expiration of an overnight recess, the House is called to order and the Chaplain offers the prayer. 104-1, Dec. 18, 1995, p 37310; 107-1, Sept. 12, 2001, pp 16752, 16753.

When a recess is declared, the bell and light system will so indicate with six bells and six lights. Termination of a recess is indicated by three bells and three lights.

The Speaker has been authorized to declare recesses at any time during a Thursday-evening-to-Monday-noon period subject to the call of the Chair. 98-1, Nov. 10, 1983, p 32197. However, a recess cannot extend longer than three days by House order alone, because of the constitutional requirement that neither House may adjourn for more than three days without the consent of the other. See ADJOURNMENT. Authority for such adjournments is provided by concurrent resolution, whereas adjournments of three days or less may be ordered by the House alone. 94-1, Feb. 6, 1975, pp 2641, 2642.

Recess for a Short Time; Emergency Recess

The Speaker is permitted by clause 12(a) of rule I to declare a recess for "a short time . . . subject to the call of the Chair," when no question is pending before the House. The Speaker has used this authority to recess the House overnight. See, *e.g.*, 106-2, Dec. 14, 2000, p 26657; 107-1, May 3, 2001, pp 7134-37; 110-1, July 25, 2007, p 20762.

The House stood in recess on the legislative day of September 11, 2001, from 9:52 a.m. on September 11 until 10:03 a.m. on September 12.

107-1, Sept. 11, 2001, pp 16750-52; Deschler-Brown-Johnson Ch 39 § 2.17. As a result of the events of September 11, the House adopted clause 12(b) of rule I in the 108th Congress. Clause 12(b) authorizes the Speaker, even when business is pending, to declare an emergency recess when notified of an imminent threat to the safety of the House. This clause was amended in the 110th Congress to provide the same authority to the chair of the Committee of the Whole.

The Speaker's declaration of a recess for a ''short time'' under clause 12 of rule I may follow the postponement of a question under clause 8 of rule XX because, after postponement, a question is no longer pending before the House. The Speaker also has the authority to postpone consideration of a measure under clause 1(c) of rule XIX. These authorities have become familiar scheduling techniques of the majority leadership in the modern practice of the House.

The customary inquiry by the Chair, ''For what purpose does the gentle______ rise?'' does not immediately confer recognition, such that a Member's mere revelation that such Member seeks to offer a motion to adjourn does not suffice to make that motion ''pending'' so as to prevent a declaration of a short recess. Deschler-Brown-Johnson Ch 39 §§ 2.22, 2.24.

Emergency Convening Authority

During any recess or adjournment of not more than three days, if the Speaker is notified by the Sergeant-at-Arms of an imminent impairment of the place of reconvening, then the Speaker may, in consultation with the Minority Leader, postpone the time for reconvening within the three-day limit prescribed by the Constitution. In the alternative, the Speaker, under the same conditions, may reconvene the House before the time previously appointed solely to declare the House in recess within that three-day limit. Clause 12(c) of rule I.

The House has entered an order authorizing the Speaker or a designee, during any recess or adjournment of not more than three days, to reconvene the House at a time other than that previously appointed, within the three-day limit prescribed by the Constitution, based on a determination that the public interest so warrants and after consultation with the Minority Leader. 112-1, H. Res. 479, Dec. 6, 2011, p ____.

§ 4. Purpose of Recess

Where the Speaker is given authority to declare a recess by unanimous consent or a special order of business, the specific purpose of the recess may be stipulated. The Speaker may be authorized to declare the House in recess in order to:

- Attend to a Member who has suddenly taken ill on the floor of the House. 91-1, July 8, 1969, p 18614.
- Await the receipt of a message from the President. 91-1, Jan. 17, 1969, pp 1188-92.
- Await a message from the Senate. 91-1, Feb. 7, 1969, p 3268.
- Await a report from a committee on certain emergency legislation. 91-2, Mar. 4, 1970, p 5867.
- Await a conference report. 92-1, Dec. 14, 1971, pp 46884-88.
- Await a report from the Committee on Rules. 91-2, Mar. 4, 1970, p 5867.
- Await Senate action on a House joint resolution continuing appropriations for several departments of the government that are without funds. 95-1, Nov. 4, 1977, p 37066.
- Await or attend a joint meeting to receive certain dignitaries. 92-1, Sept. 8, 1971, p 30845.
- Receive former Members of the House in the Chamber. 95-2, May 19, 1978, p 14660.
- Permit Members to attend certain ceremonies. 93-2, Dec. 19, 1974, p 41604.
- Make preparations for a secret session of the House. 96-1, June 20, 1979, p 15711.

Recesses for many of the purposes outlined above, as well as for unannounced purposes, are now accomplished under the Speaker's authority to declare a short recess under clause 12(a) of rule I.

Chapter 46

Recognition

Research References

2 Hinds §§ 1419-1479; 5 Hinds §§ 4978-5079
6 Cannon §§ 283-313; 8 Cannon §§ 2448-2478
Deschler-Brown Ch 29 §§ 8-23
Manual §§ 354-357, 949-956, 958, 959, 966, 997

A. Introduction; Power of Recognition

§ 1. In General; Seeking Recognition

In order to address the House or to offer a motion or make an objection, a Member first must secure recognition from the Speaker or from the chair of the Committee of the Whole. Clause 1 of rule XVII; *Manual* § 945. Under the rule, the Chair has the power and discretion to determine who will be recognized and for what purpose. 2 Hinds §§ 1422-1424; see generally § 2, infra. To determine a Member's claim to the floor, the Chair may ask for what purpose a Member seeks recognition and may grant recognition for the specific purpose indicated. *Manual* § 953.

Duty to Rise and Remain Standing

Members must seek recognition at the proper time in order to protect their rights to make points of order or to offer amendments. Deschler-Brown Ch 29 § 20.25. A Member must be standing and must address the Chair in order to be recognized and may not remain seated at the committee table while engaging in debate. Deschler-Brown Ch 29 §§ 8.4, 8.5. Although a Member controlling the floor in debate must remain standing, a Member who inadvertently sits down and then immediately stands again before the Chair recognizes another Member may be permitted to retain control of the floor. Deschler-Brown Ch 29 § 33.22.

The mere placing of an amendment on the Clerk's desk does not bestow recognition. Deschler-Brown Ch 29 § 19.6. Where numerous amendments that might be offered to a bill have been left with the Clerk, the Chair may remind all Members seeking to offer amendments not only to stand but to seek recognition at the appropriate time. Deschler-Brown Ch 29 § 8.17. A Member recognized in support of an amendment may yield to another for a question or a brief statement, but the Member must remain standing in order to protect such individual's right to the floor. Deschler-Brown Ch 29 § 29.8.

Form

The language used to obtain the floor and to grant recognition to Members follows a traditional format of long standing:

MEMBER: M__. Speaker (or M__. Chair). . . .

> *Note:* This form of address is used whether the Member is seeking recognition to offer a proposition or interrupt a Member having the floor. 5 Hinds § 4979; 6 Cannon § 193. Such salutations as "Gentlemen of the House" or

> ''Ladies and gentlemen'' are not in order. 6 Cannon §285.

SPEAKER (or CHAIR): For what purpose does the gentle______ seek recognition?

> *Note:* This question enables the Chair to determine whether the Member proposes a matter that may be entitled to precedence or is otherwise in order under the rules of the House. 6 Cannon §§289-291.

MEMBER: I rise to offer a motion to __________ *(or raise other stated business)*.

SPEAKER (or CHAIR): The Chair recognizes the gentle______ from __________ *(Member's State)*.

Recognition to Interrupt a Member

A Member who wishes to interrupt another who has the floor must obtain recognition from the Chair. Deschler-Brown Ch 29 §8.2. However, in most cases, it is within the discretion of the Member occupying the floor to determine when and by whom such Member shall be interrupted. *Manual* §§364, 946.

Cross References

Recognition is governed in specific instances and in specific parliamentary situations by practices covered fully elsewhere in this work; for example, AMENDMENTS; PREVIOUS QUESTION; REFER AND RECOMMIT; and RECONSIDERATION. For the Speaker's announced policy of conferring recognition for unanimous-consent requests for the consideration of certain measures, see UNANIMOUS-CONSENT AGREEMENTS.

§2. Power and Discretion of Chair

In Jefferson's time, the Speaker was required by House rule to recognize the Member who was ''first up.'' 2 Hinds §1420. In case of doubt, there was an appeal from the Speaker's recognition of a particular Member. 2 Hinds §§1429-1434. This practice was changed, beginning in 1879, when the House adopted a report asserting that ''discretion must be lodged with the presiding officer.'' The report alluded to the practice of listing those Members desiring to speak on a given proposition but indicated that the Chair should not be obligated to follow the order stipulated. Rather, the report recommended that the Chair be free to exercise ''a wise and just discretion in the interest of full and fair debate.'' 2 Hinds §1424. Today clause 2 of rule XVII gives the Chair the power and discretion to decide who shall be recognized, and that decision is no longer subject to appeal. *Manual* §§949, 953; 8 Cannon §§2429, 2646; 109-2, June 22, 2006, p 12299. There has been no appeal from a decision of the Speaker on a question of recognition since 1881. *Manual* § 356.

Of course, the recognition of particular Members often is governed by the rules and precedents pertaining to the order of business or by special orders of business from the Committee on Rules. See §§ 3, 4, infra. However, where matters of equal privilege are pending, the order of their consideration is subject to the Speaker's discretionary power of recognition. Deschler-Brown Ch 29 § 9.55. It follows that, when more than one Member seeks recognition to call up privileged business, it is within the discretion of the Speaker whom to recognize. Clause 2 of rule XVII; Deschler-Brown Ch 29 § 9.56.

Clause 6 of rule XIV, which provides that questions relating to the priority of business are to be decided by a majority without debate, may not be invoked to inhibit the Speaker's power of recognition. *Manual* § 884.

§ 3. Limitations; Bases for Denial

The Speaker's power of recognition is subject to limitations imposed by the rules, such as clause 7 of rule XVII (prohibiting the Chair from recognizing a Member to draw attention to gallery occupants) and clause 2 of rule IV (restricting use of and admission to the Hall of the House). *Manual* §§ 677, 678, 966; Deschler-Brown Ch 29 § 11.10. The Chair's power of recognition also is governed by established practice and precedent, such as the long-standing tradition that a member of the committee reporting a bill is first recognized for motions to dispose of the bill (see § 11, infra) and the Speaker's announced policy of conferring recognition for unanimous-consent requests for the consideration of certain measures (see UNANIMOUS-CONSENT AGREEMENTS).

§ 4. Alternation in Recognition

In the House

Under the standing rules of the House, the Member reporting or calling up a measure is entitled to recognition for one hour, during which time such Member may yield to others. At the close of that hour, unless the previous question is moved, the ranking Member in opposition *may* be recognized for an hour with the same privilege of yielding. Thereafter, until the previous question is invoked, other Members favoring and opposing the measure are recognized alternately, preference again being given to members of the committee reporting the measure. *Manual* § 955; 8 Cannon § 2460.

Absent a special order of business making party affiliation pertinent, the Chair alternates according to differences on the pending question rather than according to political affiliation. 2 Hinds § 1444. Where the special order of business allots control of time to "the chair and the ranking minority member of the committee" (which is ordinarily the case in the modern practice) the term "minority" is construed to refer to the minority party in the House and not to those in the minority on the pending question. 7 Cannon § 767. However, a special order of business that allots control of time to those for and against a proposition does not necessarily require a division between the majority and minority parties of the House but, rather, a division between those actually favoring and opposing the measure. 7 Cannon § 766. Rules found in provisions of law establishing procedures for overturning executive decisions normally provide for equal division of time for debate between those favoring and those opposing a proposition, without designating who should control the time. Therefore, it is within the discretion of the Chair to recognize a Member supporting and a Member opposing the measure. *Manual* § 1130; 7 Cannon § 785.

In Committee of the Whole

A similar alternation procedure is followed during general debate in the Committee of the Whole. The usual practice is for the Chair to alternate between those given control of debate time under a special order of business, usually the chair and ranking minority member. 7 Cannon § 875; Deschler-Brown Ch 29 § 28.15.

It is the usual practice in the Committee of the Whole, during consideration of a measure under the five-minute rule, to alternate between majority and minority members, giving priority to members of the reporting committee in the order of seniority on the full committee. Deschler-Brown Ch 29 § 21.1. The Chair follows this principle whether recognizing Members to debate a pending amendment or to offer an amendment. Deschler-Brown Ch 29 § 13.9. Because the Chair normally has no knowledge whether specific Members oppose or support the pending proposition, the Chair cannot strictly alternate between both sides of the question. Deschler-Brown Ch 29 § 25.14. However, when an amendment is offered initially, clause 5 of rule XVIII (the five-minute rule) contemplates that the five minutes allotted the proponent is followed by recognition of a Member in opposition to the amendment.

B. Right to Recognition; Priorities

§ 5. In General

Clause 2 of rule XVII directs the Speaker to ''name the Member, Delegate, or Resident Commissioner who is first to speak'' when two or more Members rise at once. The Speaker or Chair has the discretion to determine the order or sequence in which Members will be recognized in debate. *Manual* § 949; Deschler-Brown Ch 29 §§ 9.2, 12.1, 19.20. However, the Chair's determination of priorities is governed by many factors, such as whether the pending proposition has been reported by a committee, whether it is given priority or is privileged under the rules, and whether the rules and practices of the House dictate a priority in recognition. For example, in recognizing a Member for a motion to recommit (who must qualify as being opposed to the bill), the Speaker gives preference to the Minority Leader and then to minority members of the committee reporting the bill in order of their rank on the committee. Deschler Ch 23 § 27.18; see generally REFER AND RECOMMIT.

§ 6. Priorities of Committee Members

Priority of Committee Members Over Nonmembers

Absent a special order of business providing to the contrary, the members of the committee reporting a bill are entitled to priority in recognition over nonmembers for debate on the bill. *Manual* §§ 953, 955; 2 Hinds §§ 1438, 1448; 6 Cannon §§ 306, 307; § 14, infra. Members of the committee reporting a bill also have priority in recognition to make points of order against proposed amendments to the bill. Deschler-Brown Ch 29 § 13.3.

The practice of according priority to committee members is an ancient one, having been adapted from that of the English Parliament. It is reasoned that the members of the reporting committee—having worked for months, if not years, on the legislation—are naturally more familiar with its strengths and weaknesses. Deschler-Brown Ch 29 § 13.12. They are entitled to priority in recognition, even over the Member who introduced the bill. Deschler-Brown Ch 29 § 13.13. However, if the proposition has been brought directly before the House independently of a committee, the proponent may be entitled to priority in recognition for motions and debate. § 10, infra.

Recognition of Committee Chairs

The chair of the reporting committee usually has charge of the bill and is entitled at all stages to priority in recognition for allowable motions intended to expedite it. Deschler-Brown Ch 29 §§ 12.2, 24. If the chair is opposed to the bill, however, the chair ordinarily yields priority in recognition to a member of the committee who favors the bill. 2 Hinds § 1449.

Priorities as Between Committee Members

Recognition is extended to committee members on the basis of their committee seniority, with the Chair alternating between members of the majority and the minority. Deschler-Brown Ch 29 § 13.25; § 4, supra. Where opposition is relevant to recognition and no committee member rises in opposition to the measure, any Member may be recognized in opposition. 7 Cannon § 958.

Effect of Failure to Seek Recognition

Although members of the committee reporting a bill under consideration have preference in recognition, a member may lose such preference if recognition is not sought in a timely manner. Deschler-Brown Ch 29 § 13.13. The Chair may recognize another on the basis that the committee member, though standing, is not actively seeking recognition. Deschler-Brown Ch 29 § 13.14.

§ 7. Right of Member in Control

Where a Member has been placed in charge of a bill by the reporting committee, or has been so designated by a special order of business from the Committee on Rules, the Member named as manager is recognized to call up the measure. Clause 3(a) of rule XVII; Deschler-Brown Ch 29 § 27.1; 110-1, Jan. 18, 2007, p 1624. Preference in recognition is accorded to the manager over other Members. Clause 3(a) of rule XVII; Deschler-Brown Ch 29 § 24.1. This priority in recognition of the Member in charge prevails in both the House and in the Committee of the Whole. Clause 3(a) of rule XVII; Deschler-Brown Ch 29 §§ 12.10, 14.3.

The Member in charge of the bill also is entitled at all stages to priority in recognition for allowable motions intended to expedite the bill, from the time of its first consideration to the time of consideration of Senate amendments and conference reports. 2 Hinds §§ 1451, 1452, 1457; 6 Cannon §§ 300, 301. For example, the Member who has been recognized to call up a measure in the House has priority in recognition to move the previous question thereon, even over the chair of the committee reporting that measure. *Manual* § 953.

The fact that a Member has the floor on one matter does not necessarily entitle such Member to priority in recognition on a motion relating to another matter. 2 Hinds § 1464. Before the Member in charge has begun debate, a Member proposing a preferential motion is entitled to recognition. 5 Hinds §§ 5391-5395. However, once debate has begun, a Member may not deprive the Member in charge of the floor by offering a debatable motion of higher privilege than the pending motion. *Manual* § 953; 2 Hinds §§ 1460-1463; 6 Cannon §§ 297-299; 8 Cannon §§ 2454, 3183, 3193, 3197, 3259.

§ 8. Right to Open and Close General Debate

Generally

Clause 3(a) of rule XVII provides that the Member reporting a measure from a committee is entitled to open and close general debate on that measure. *Manual* § 958. Otherwise, clause 3(b) of rule XVII precludes a Member from speaking twice on the same question without leave of the House. *Manual* § 959. Under the modern practice, however, where a special order of business places the control of debate in a "manager," or divides the time between the chair and ranking minority member of the committee reporting the measure, those controlling the time may yield to other Members as often as they desire, and are not restricted by this rule. *Manual* § 959. The minority member controlling one-half of the time must consume it or yield it back before the closing of debate. Deschler-Brown Ch 29 § 24.19. A majority manager of the bill who represents the primary committee of jurisdiction is entitled to close general debate (in this case, as against another manager representing an additional committee of jurisdiction). *Manual* § 958.

The manager of a bill for purposes of closing general debate may be the chair of the reporting committee or a designated majority member of that committee. Deschler-Brown Ch 29 §§ 7.3, 7.4.

The right of the manager to open and close general debate under clause 3 of rule XVII is recognized in both the House and the Committee of the Whole. Deschler-Brown Ch 29 § 7.4.

Rights of Proponents

The manager of a bill in control of the time, and not its proponent, is ordinarily entitled to close general debate. Deschler-Brown Ch 29 § 7.4. Where existing law provides that general debate in the Committee of the Whole on a joint resolution shall be equally divided and controlled by proponents and opponents, a proponent has the right to open and close general debate. 99-1, Apr. 23, 1985, p 8964. Where a joint resolution having no "sponsor" and having not been referred to a committee was made in order by a special order of business, its proponent was recognized to open and close general debate, there being no other ''manager'' of the pending resolution. 99-2, Apr. 16, 1986, pp 7611, 7629.

§ 9. —To Close Debate on Amendments

Recognition of Manager of Bill for Motion to Close Debate

In the Committee of the Whole, the Member managing the bill is entitled to priority in recognition to move to close debate on a pending amendment over other Members who desire to debate the amendment or to offer amendments thereto. Deschler-Brown Ch 29 § 78.9.

Recognition of Manager of Bill for Closing Controlled Debate on an Amendment

Under clause 3(c) of rule XVII, a manager of a bill or other representative of the committee in opposition to, and not the proponent of, an amendment has the right to close debate on an amendment on which debate has been limited and allocated under the five-minute rule in Committee of the Whole, including a minority manager. This principle prevails even where the manager of the bill is the proponent of a pending amendment to the amendment. *Manual* § 959.

The Chair will assume that the manager of a measure controlling time in opposition to an amendment is representing a committee of jurisdiction, even where the measure called up is unreported, where an unreported compromise text is made in order as original text in lieu of committee amendments or where the committee reported the measure without recommendation. Where the pending text includes a provision recommended by a committee of sequential referral, a member of that committee is entitled to close debate against an amendment thereto. Where the rule providing for the consideration of an unreported measure designates managers who do not serve on a committee of jurisdiction, those managers are entitled to close controlled debate against an amendment thereto. The majority manager of the bill may be recognized to control time in opposition to an amendment thereto, without regard to the party affiliation of the proponent, where the special order of business allocates control to ''a Member opposed.'' The right to close debate in opposition to an amendment devolves to a member of the committee of jurisdiction who derived debate time by unanimous consent from a manager who originally had the right to close debate. The proponent of a first-degree amendment who controls time in opposition to a second-degree amendment that favors the original bill over the first-degree amendment does not qualify as a ''manager'' within the meaning of clause 3(c) of rule XVII in opposing. *Manual* § 959.

Recognition of Proponent of Amendment

Under certain circumstances, the proponent of an amendment may close debate where the amendment is not opposed by a manager. For example, the proponent may close debate where neither a committee representative nor a Member assigned a managerial role by the governing special order of business opposes the amendment. Where a committee representative is allocated control of time in opposition to an amendment, not by recognition from the Chair but by a unanimous-consent request of a third Member who was allocated the time by the Chair, then the committee representative is not entitled to close debate as against the proponent. Similarly, the proponent of the amendment may close debate where no representative from the reporting committee opposes an amendment to a multijurisdictional bill; where the measure is unreported and has no ''manager'' under the terms of a special order of business; or where a measure is being managed by a single reporting committee and the Member controlling time in opposition, though a member of a committee having jurisdiction over the amendment, does not represent the reporting committee. *Manual* § 959.

C. Recognition on Particular Questions

§ 10. In General; As to Bills

Under long-standing practice, special orders of business give control of general debate in the House or in the Committee of the Whole to the chair and ranking minority member of the reporting committee(s), and recognition is extended accordingly. In the absence of the chair and ranking minority member designated by the rule, the Chair recognizes the next ranking majority and minority members for control of such debate, who may either be informally designated during a temporary absence upon informing the Chair or who may be formally designated by unanimous consent for the remainder of the debate. Deschler-Brown Ch 29 § 9.4. If, on the other hand, the proposition has been brought directly before the House independently of a committee, the proponent who calls up the measure is entitled to priority in recognition for motions and debate. 2 Hinds §§ 1446, 1454; 8 Cannon § 2454.

For a discussion of recognition to offer amendments, see AMENDMENTS. For a discussion of recognition for parliamentary inquiries and points of order, see POINTS OF ORDER; PARLIAMENTARY INQUIRIES.

Discharged Bills

If a bill has not been reported from committee, but is before the House pursuant to a motion to discharge, the proponents of that motion are entitled to priority in recognition for the purpose of managing the bill. Deschler-Brown Ch 29 § 27.5. For a discussion of recognition of Members for debate on the motion, see clause 2 of rule XV; *Manual* § 892; DISCHARGING MEASURES FROM COMMITTEES. In recognizing a Member to control time for debate in opposition to a discharged bill, the Chair recognizes the chair of the committee having jurisdiction of the subject matter if opposed. Deschler-Brown Ch 29 § 25.16.

Measures Called Up by Unanimous Consent

Where a measure is called up in the House pursuant to a unanimous-consent agreement that does not specify the debate time, the Member calling up the bill is recognized for one hour, and amendments may not be offered by other Members unless yielded to for that purpose or unless a motion for the previous question is rejected. Deschler-Brown Ch 29 § 24.24. By contrast, a measure called up in the House as in the Committee of the Whole is considered under the five-minute rule.

For the Speaker's policy of conferring recognition for unanimous-consent requests for the consideration of certain measures, see UNANIMOUS-CONSENT AGREEMENTS.

§ 11. For Motions

As noted in section 7, supra, the Member in charge of a bill is entitled at all stages to priority in recognition for allowable motions intended to expedite the bill, subject to a determination by the Chair that another Member has a motion of higher precedence. Thus, where one Member moves a call of the House, and another Member immediately moves to adjourn, the Chair will recognize the latter because the motion to adjourn is of higher privilege. 8 Cannon § 2642. If a preferential motion is debatable, a Member must offer it before the other Member has begun debate. This is so because a Member may not, by attempting to offer a preferential motion, deprive another Member, who has begun to speak, of the floor. 8 Cannon § 3197.

A Member may lose the right to the floor if neglecting to claim it before another Member with a preferential motion has been recognized. 2 Hinds § 1435. A Member desiring to offer a motion must actively seek recognition from the Chair before another motion to dispose of the pending question has been adopted. The fact that the Member may have been standing at that time is not sufficient to secure recognition. Deschler-Brown Ch 29 § 8.19. Moreover, the mere offering of a motion does not confer recognition. Where another Member has shown due diligence, such Member may be recognized. Deschler-Brown Ch 29 § 23.2. The first half of a voice vote having been taken, a Member may still be recognized for a proper motion before the second half of the voice vote occurs. 109-2, June 22, 2006, p 12299; see also *Manual* § 490.

For treatment of recognition to offer particular kinds of motions, see PREVIOUS QUESTION, SUSPENSION OF RULES, UNANIMOUS-CONSENT AGREEMENTS, and other chapters dealing with specific motions.

§ 12. Of Opposition After Rejection of Motion

Generally

Where an essential motion by the Member in charge of a measure is defeated, the right to priority in recognition passes to a Member opposed, as determined by the Speaker. *Manual* § 954; 2 Hinds §§ 1465-1468; Deschler-Brown Ch 29 § 15.6. Thus, where a motion for the previous question is rejected on a pending resolution, the Chair recognizes the Member perceived by the Chair to have led the opposition to that motion. 6 Cannon § 308; Deschler-Brown Ch 29 § 15.11. Recognition of that Member is not precluded by the fact that such Member was previously recognized and offered an amendment that was ruled out on a point of order. 91-1, Jan. 3, 1969, p 27.

The principle that the defeat of an essential motion offered by the Member in charge causes recognition to pass to the opposition is applicable in the following instances:

- House rejects a motion to lay an adversely reported resolution of inquiry on the table. Deschler-Brown Ch 29 § 15.3.
- House rejects a motion for the previous question on a resolution reported from the Committee on Rules. Deschler-Brown Ch 29 § 15.14.
- House rejects a motion for the previous question on a resolution relating to the seating of a Member-elect. Deschler-Brown Ch 29 § 15.15.
- House rejects a motion for the previous question on a resolution to discipline a Member of the House. 6 Cannon § 236.
- House rejects a motion for the previous question on a resolution providing for adoption of rules. 6 Cannon § 308.
- House rejects a motion for the previous question on a motion to recommit. 107-2, Feb. 27, 2002, p 2083.
- House rejects a motion to dispose of a Senate amendment reported from conference in disagreement. *Manual* § 954. (Recognition passes to opposition for disposition of that Senate amendment only.)
- Committee of the Whole reports a bill adversely. 4 Hinds § 4897; 8 Cannon § 2430.
- Committee of the Whole reports a bill with the recommendation that the enacting clause be stricken. 8 Cannon § 2629.

This principle applies only to an *essential* motion by the Member in charge of the bill. A motion to postpone consideration to a day certain is not an essential motion, the defeat of which would require recognition to pass to a Member opposed. Deschler-Brown Ch 29 § 15.2. The mere defeat of an amendment proposed by the Member in charge does not always cause the right to priority in recognition to pass to the opponents. 2 Hinds § 1478. In any case, the recognition for a motion by a Member in opposition may be preempted by a motion of higher precedence. *Manual* § 954.

Effect of Rejection of Motion for Previous Question on Conference Report or Rejection of Conference Report

The right to priority in recognition ordinarily passes to a Member of the opposition when the House refuses to order the previous question on a conference report, because control passes to the opposition upon rejection of the motion for the previous question. 2 Hinds §§ 1473, 1474; 5 Hinds § 6396. However, the invalidation of a conference report on a point of order, although equivalent to its rejection by the House, does not give the Member raising the question of order the right to the floor and does not affect the right to recognition. 6 Cannon § 313; 8 Cannon § 3284. Rejection of a conference report after the previous question has been ordered thereon does not cause recognition to pass to a Member opposed to the report, and the manager retains control to offer the initial motion to dispose of amendments in disagreement. *Manual* § 954; 2 Hinds 1477.

§ 13. As to Special Orders of Business

Calling Up Special Orders of Business

Recognition to call up special order of business resolutions reported from the Committee on Rules may be sought pursuant to the provisions of clause 6(d) of rule XIII. *Manual* § 861. Ordinarily, only a member of the Committee on Rules designated to call up a special order of business from the committee may be recognized for that purpose. Deschler-Brown Ch 29 § 18.13. Where a special order of business has been reported by the committee and has not been called up within the seven legislative days specified by clause 6(d), recognition to call it up may be extended to any member of that committee, including a minority member. Deschler-Brown Ch 29 § 18.13. The Member calling up the resolution must have announced the intention one calendar day before seeking recognition. See *Manual* § 861. Because calling up such a resolution is privileged, the Speaker would be obliged to recognize for this purpose unless another matter of equal privilege was proposed, in which case the order of consideration would be determined pursuant to the Speaker's discretionary power to grant recognition. Deschler-Brown Ch 29 § 9.55.

Recognition for Debate

A Member recognized to call up a special order of business or resolution by direction of the Committee on Rules controls one hour of debate thereon and may offer one or more amendments thereto. Deschler-Brown Ch 29 § 24.26. Such Member need not have the specific authorization of the committee to offer an amendment. *Manual* § 858. A resolution previously offered and debated but subsequently withdrawn may be called up again and the Member calling it up is recognized for a full hour. Deschler-Brown Ch 29 § 18.17. Other Members may be recognized only if yielded time. Deschler-Brown Ch 29 § 29.23. The resolution is not subject to amendment from the floor by another Member unless the Member in charge yields for that purpose or the House rejects a motion for the previous question. 6 Cannon § 309; Deschler-Brown Ch 29 § 30.5.

Ordinarily the manager's amendments are voted on after debate and after the previous question is ordered on the amendments and on the resolution. 101-2, Sept. 25, 1990, p 25575.

§ 14. Under the Five-Minute Rule

Generally; Effect of a Special Order of Business

Recognition of Members to offer amendments in the Committee of the Whole under the five-minute rule is within the discretion of the Chair and cannot be challenged on a point of order. Deschler-Brown Ch 29 § 9.6. The Chair does not anticipate the order in which amendments may be offered nor does the Chair declare in advance the order in which Members proposing amendments will be recognized. Deschler-Brown Ch 29 § 21.3. The Chair endeavors to alternate recognition to offer amendments between majority and minority Members (giving priority to committee members). *Manual* § 980. Of course, if a special order of business reported from the Committee on Rules specifies those Members who are to control debate, the Chair will extend recognition accordingly. However, where the special order of business merely *makes in order* the consideration of a particular amendment, it does not confer a privileged status on the amendment and does not, absent legislative history establishing a contrary intent by the Committee on Rules, alter the principle that recognition to offer an amendment under the five-minute rule is within the discretion of the chair of the Committee of the Whole. 95-2, May 23, 1978, p 15095. Under the modern practice, special orders of business often provide discretionary priority in recognition to Members who have preprinted their amendments in the *Congressional Record*. See, *e.g.*, 107-2, H. Res. 428, May 22, 2002, pp 8675, 8676. As to the effect of special orders of business on the control and distribution of debate time, see CONSIDERATION AND DEBATE.

Priority of Committee Members over Noncommittee Members

Committee amendments to a pending section are considered before the Chair entertains amendments from the floor. Deschler Ch 27 §§ 26.1-26.3. When entertaining amendments from the floor during the five-minute rule, the Chair follows certain guidelines as a matter of long-standing custom. Among them is that recognition is first accorded to members of the committee reporting the bill over Members of the House who are not on that committee. Deschler-Brown Ch 29 § 21.1. Thus, the Chair normally will recognize a member of a committee reporting a bill to offer a substitute for an amendment before recognizing a noncommittee member, although that committee member may have been recognized separately to debate the original amendment. Deschler-Brown Ch 29 § 13.20. Members of the committee reporting a pending bill are entitled to priority in recognition over noncommittee members, without regard to their party affiliation. Thus the Chair may accord priority in recognition to minority members of the reporting committee over majority noncommittee members to offer amendments. Deschler-Brown Ch 29 § 13.11.

Priorities as Between Committee Members

In bestowing recognition under the five-minute rule, the Chair gives preference to the chair and ranking minority member of the committee reporting the bill under consideration. Deschler-Brown Ch 29 § 12.12. Thereafter, the Chair endeavors to alternate between majority party and minority party members of the reporting committee. *Manual* § 981. Priority in recognition to offer amendments is extended to members of the full committee reporting the bill (typically in order of seniority), and the Chair does not accord priority in recognition to members of the subcommittee that considered the bill over other members of the full committee. Deschler-Brown Ch 29 § 13.6. However, in five-minute debate on appropriation bills the Chair has the discretion to recognize members of the subcommittee handling the bill first, and then recognize members of the full committee. Deschler-Brown Ch 29 § 12.8.

§ 15. —Under Limited Five-Minute Debate

The House may, by unanimous consent, agree to limit or extend debate under the five-minute rule in the Committee of the Whole, whether or not that debate has commenced. In the Committee of the Whole, debate under the five-minute rule may be limited by the Committee by unanimous consent or, after preliminary debate, by motion. See CONSIDERATION AND DEBATE. When such a limitation has been agreed to, the general rules of recognition applied under the five-minute rule are considered abrogated. Deschler-Brown Ch 29 § 22.14. Decisions regarding recognition during the remaining time, a division of time not having been ordered as part of the limitation, are largely within the discretion of the Chair. Deschler-Brown Ch 29 § 22.15. The Chair has the discretion to either (1) permit continued debate under the five-minute rule, (2) allocate the remaining time among those desiring to speak, or (3) divide the time between a proponent and an opponent to be yielded by them (which has become the prevailing practice). *Manual* § 987. The order in which Members desiring to speak are recognized is also within the discretion of the Chair. The Chair may take into account such factors as their committee status, whether they have amendments at the desk, and their seniority. Deschler-Brown Ch 29 § 22.12.

§ 16. As to House-Senate Conferences

Recognition to Seek a Conference

A motion to send a measure to conference is authorized by clause 1 of rule XXII. *Manual* § 1069; see CONFERENCES BETWEEN THE HOUSES. The motion is in order if the appropriate committee has authorized the motion and the Speaker chooses to recognize for that purpose. Deschler-Brown Ch 29 § 17.1. The Speaker will not recognize for the motion where the Senate amendment in question has been referred to the House committee or committees with jurisdiction and they have not yet had the opportunity to consider the amendment. *Manual* § 1070.

Recognition for debate and control of debate time on the motion, see CONFERENCES BETWEEN THE HOUSES.

Motions to Instruct Conferees

Recognition to offer a motion to instruct House conferees on a measure initially being sent to conference is the prerogative of the minority. The Speaker recognizes the ranking minority member of the committee reporting the bill if that member seeks recognition to offer the motion after the request or motion to go to conference is agreed to and before the Speaker's appointment of conferees. Deschler-Brown Ch 33 § 11.1. Where two minority members of the committee that has reported a bill seek recognition to offer a motion to instruct conferees pending their appointment by the Speaker, the Chair will recognize the highest ranking minority member of that committee. *Manual* § 541.

If a motion for the previous question is voted down on a motion to instruct the managers on the part of the House, the motion is open to amendment and the Speaker may recognize a Member opposed to ordering the previous question to control the time and offer an amendment. Deschler Ch 23 § 23.7.

For recognition for debate and control of debate time on a motion to instruct, see CONFERENCES BETWEEN THE HOUSES.

Calling Up Conference Reports

A conference report is normally called up for consideration in the House by the senior majority manager on the part of the House, and such Member may be recognized to do so, even though such Member did not sign the report and in fact was opposed to it. Deschler-Brown Ch 29 § 17.7. If the senior House conferee cannot be present on the floor to call up the report, the Speaker may recognize a junior majority member of the conference committee. Deschler-Brown Ch 29 § 27.6. The Speaker also may extend recognition to call up the report to the conferee who serves as chair or ranking majority member of a committee with jurisdiction. 6 Cannon § 301; Deschler-Brown Ch 29 § 27.7. Where a conference consists of conferees appointed from more than one committee, the conference report may be called up by the chair of a committee that was not the primary committee in the House. 97-2, Dec. 21, 1982, pp 33299, 33300.

For recognition to dispose of amendments between the Houses or for debate thereon, see SENATE BILLS; AMENDMENTS BETWEEN THE HOUSES.

Chapter 47
Reconsideration

Research References
5 Hinds §§ 5605-5705
8 Cannon §§ 2774-2795
Deschler Ch 23 §§ 33-41
Manual §§ 1003-1011

§ 1. Generally; Use of Motion

In General

By long tradition, the vote of the House on a proposition usually is not final and conclusive until there has been an opportunity to reconsider it. A proposition is not regarded as passed until a motion to reconsider it is disposed of or precluded. The motion to reconsider under clause 3 of rule XIX is the procedural device that permits the House to review its action on a given proposal. Its purpose is to allow the House to reflect on the wisdom of its action on the proposition. Deschler Ch 23 § 33.

Historical Background

Although not mentioned in the first rules of the House, adopted in 1789, the motion to reconsider was at that time well known in parliamentary practice. 5 Hinds § 5605. The motion was used in the Continental Congress and in the House from its first organization. It was made the subject of a rule of the House in 1802. *Manual* § 1003. In 1811, the rule was modified by limiting the time during which the motion might be offered to "the same or succeeding day" as the vote to be reconsidered. The rule was further revised in 1880, but has existed in the rules since then with only minor changes. 5 Hinds § 5605.

Use in Committee of the Whole

The motion to reconsider is in order in the House and in the House as in the Committee of the Whole but not in the Committee of the Whole. 4 Hinds §§ 4716-4718; 8 Cannon §§ 2324, 2325, 2793; Deschler Ch 23 §§ 33, 39.10; 104-1, May 11, 1995, p 12713. Indeed, a request to reconsider a vote is not in order in the Committee even by unanimous consent. Deschler Ch 23 § 39.12. However, on occasion, in lieu of a motion to reconsider, the Chair has allowed a unanimous-consent request to vacate the proceedings whereby an amendment had been adopted. Deschler Ch 23 § 39.13.

Entering and Calling Up Distinguished

A distinction should be made between *entering* the motion and offering or calling up the motion. Entering the motion and offering the motion can be separate events. 8 Cannon § 2785. One Member may enter the motion, and another Member may call up the motion. § 4, infra. In the modern practice, the motion is rarely entered but rather is considered as pending when offered. The motion must be offered within the two-day period allowed by the rule, but a motion merely entered during that time may remain pending indefinitely. §§ 5, 8, infra.

§ 2. Pro Forma Motions Distinguished

Normally, the Speaker declares, after the announcement of a vote, "without objection, a motion to reconsider is laid on the table." Deschler Ch 23 § 34. The effect of this declaration is to preclude a subsequent motion to reconsider, and it is the accepted parliamentary mode of making the vote in question final. Deschler Ch 23 § 34.5. Thereafter, the proposition may be taken up again only by special order of business, unanimous consent, or suspension of the rules. 5 Hinds § 5640; see also Deschler Ch 23 § 38.5. A Member who is opposed to the tabling of the motion to reconsider must object to the Speaker's declaration in a timely manner and is well advised to notify the Speaker in advance of an intention to seek genuine reconsideration. Deschler Ch 23 § 34. If such objection is made, one Member may move to reconsider and another Member may immediately move to table that motion. 5 Hinds § 5637. Disposition of the motion to reconsider is permitted while the previous question is operating. 8 Cannon § 2784.

§ 3. Effect of Motion

Effect When Motion Is Entered

After the House has voted on a proposition and a motion to reconsider it is entered, the effect is to suspend the proposition. *Manual* § 1007; 5 Hinds § 5704; Deschler Ch 23 § 33. The motion is thereafter considered as pending and, if not acted on, will remain pending, even in succeeding sessions of the same Congress. 5 Hinds § 5684. However, when a Congress expires without the House having acted on the motion, the motion fails, and the original proposition stands or falls according to the original vote. 5 Hinds § 5704 (footnote).

A motion to reconsider a bill having been entered, the Speaker will normally decline to sign its enrollment until the motion is disposed of. 5 Hinds § 5705. However, where a bill has been signed by the President, it cannot be impeached on the ground that a motion to reconsider it is still pending. 5 Hinds § 5705 (note).

Effect of Agreement to Motion

When a motion to reconsider is adopted, the question immediately recurs on the proposition to be reconsidered. 5 Hinds § 5703; Deschler Ch 23 § 33. Thus, when the House agrees to a motion to reconsider a vote on an amendment, the amendment is again pending and the Chair may put it to a vote *de novo*. 5 Hinds § 5704. Likewise, when the House agrees to reconsider a vote ordering the yeas and nays (by majority vote), the question immediately recurs on ordering the yeas and nays (by one-fifth of those present). *Manual* § 1007; 5 Hinds §§ 5689-5691. However, if the proposition originally voted on was a motion for the previous question, that motion may be withdrawn after the House has voted to reconsider it, on the theory that the action of the House has effectively ''nullified'' the vote on the previous question. 5 Hinds § 5357. For further discussion of the effect of the motion to reconsider, see *Manual* § 1007.

As Precluding Repetition of Motion

When a motion to reconsider has been offered and acted upon, a second motion to reconsider is not ordinarily in order. Deschler Ch 23 § 39.16. Otherwise, it is reasoned, motions to reconsider could be offered interminably. Thus, a vote ordering the previous question may be reconsidered only once. *Manual* § 1006; 5 Hinds § 5655. One motion to reconsider the yeas and nays having been acted on, another motion to reconsider is not in order. 5 Hinds

§ 6037. Similarly, the motion to reconsider a vote on a proposition having been adopted, and that vote having again been taken, a second motion to reconsider may not be offered unless the nature of the proposition has been changed by amendment. *Manual* § 1006; 5 Hinds §§ 5685-5688; 8 Cannon § 2788; Deschler Ch 23 § 33. The general rule that precludes the repetition of the motion is applied even where the House rejects the first motion by laying it on the table. 5 Hinds § 5632; Deschler Ch 23 § 39.15. However, the tabling of a motion to reconsider the vote whereby the House has amended a Senate amendment does not preclude the House from acting on a subsequent Senate amendment to the same proposition or considering any other proper motion to dispose of an amendment that might remain in disagreement after further Senate action. *Manual* § 1006.

§ 4. Who May Offer Motion

Clause 3 of rule XIX requires the Member entering the motion to be "on the prevailing side" but permits the motion to be called up by "any Member." *Manual* §§ 1003, 1004. Under this rule, the *entering* of the motion and the *offering* of the motion are regarded as separate events. 8 Cannon § 2785. However, under the modern practice the motion rarely is "entered" but is considered pending when offered. Thus, the Member offering a motion not previously entered must qualify as being on the prevailing side of the issue to be reconsidered. *Manual* § 1004; 2 Hinds § 1454.

With respect to pro forma motions to reconsider (see § 2, supra), any Member may object to the Chair's statement that "without objection" a motion to reconsider a vote just taken be laid on the table and need not have voted on the prevailing side to make such an objection. However, if objection is made, only a Member who voted on the prevailing side may offer the motion to reconsider the vote. *Manual* § 1004.

Likewise ineligible to move the reconsideration of a record vote are Members who were absent at the time of the vote (5 Hinds § 5619), or who failed to vote (8 Cannon § 2774).

In the case of a tie vote (a tie vote resulting in the defeat of the proposition), a Member voting in the negative qualifies as voting on the prevailing side. 5 Hinds § 5616. In the case of a proposition that did not receive a requisite two-thirds vote for approval, a Member voting in the negative qualifies. 5 Hinds §§ 5617, 5618. However, the motion to reconsider may not be applied to a negative vote on the motion to suspend. *Manual* § 886a; 5 Hinds § 5645; 8 Cannon § 2781.

When a vote is not recorded, any Member, regardless of how such Member voted, may enter the motion. *Manual* § 1004; 8 Cannon § 2775;

Deschler Ch 23 § 33. Any point of order relating to the eligibility of the Member to offer the motion should be raised before the ordering of the vote on the motion. Deschler Ch 23 § 35.4. The Chair, having voted on the prevailing side, may offer the motion to reconsider by stating the pendency of the motion. A Delegate or the Resident Commissioner may not offer the motion to reconsider. *Manual* § 1004.

§ 5. When Motion Is In Order

During the Continental Congress, there was no time limit on when the motion to reconsider could be offered, and the Congress often reconsidered matters passed on a preceding day or even several days or months before. 5 Hinds § 5605. Today clause 3 of rule XIX provides that the motion is in order "on the same or succeeding day" as that vote; and, once entered, may be called up by any Member. This means that the motion to reconsider may be offered or entered at any time during the day on which the vote sought to be reconsidered is taken (5 Hinds § 5674) or on the next legislative day after the question to be reconsidered was voted on (Deschler Ch 23 § 35.5). The entry of the motion during the two days prescribed by the rule is in order even after the previous question is ordered or when a question of the highest privilege is pending. 5 Hinds § 5673; 8 Cannon § 2785.

Once the motion has been entered within the two-day period, it remains pending indefinitely, even into a succeeding session of the same Congress. 5 Hinds § 5684; 8 Cannon § 2787. When a motion to reconsider relates to a bill belonging to a particular class of business, the consideration of the motion is in order only when that class of business is again in order. 5 Hinds § 5677; 8 Cannon §§ 2785, 2786. For example, a motion to reconsider the vote on a bill on the Private Calendar properly entered may be taken up for consideration only on a Private Calendar day. 8 Cannon § 2786.

In accordance with the general rule that the motion to reconsider is in order at any time during the two days prescribed by the rule, the motion has been held in order:

- After a demand for the previous question on a related matter (5 Hinds § 5656) or while the previous question is operating (5 Hinds §§ 5657-5672).
- Pending a motion to go into the Committee of the Whole. 8 Cannon § 2785.
- At a time set apart for other business if the matter sought to be reconsidered is entertained during such time by unanimous consent. 5 Hinds § 5683.
- After a bill to be reconsidered has gone to the Senate. 5 Hinds §§ 5666, 5667.

- After the Senate has been informed of agreement by the House to a Senate amendment. 5 Hinds § 5672.
- After a bill has gone to the President. 5 Hinds § 5668.

However, an entered motion is not in order:

- While another Member has the floor or while another question is pending before the House. 5 Hinds § 5673; 8 Cannon § 2785.
- While the House is dividing on a motion. 8 Cannon § 2791.
- In Committee of the Whole. § 1, supra.

See also §§ 8, 12, infra.

§ 6. Use in Standing Committees

The motion to reconsider is in order in the procedure of standing committees. 8 Cannon § 2213. Thus, the motion to reconsider may be entered in a committee on the same day as the vote to be reconsidered, or on the next day the committee convenes with a quorum present at which business of that class is in order. *Manual* §§ 416, 1005; Deschler Ch 23 § 33. Sometimes the motion must be applied to a series of propositions seriatim to achieve a desired result. In a committee, reconsideration of an amendment may require that the motion to report first be reconsidered, and then the ordering of the previous question on the measure, before a motion can be offered to reconsider the amendment. *Cf.* 8 Cannon § 2789.

A motion to reconsider is sometimes used in a committee, when it has obtained a quorum, to order reports on bills approved earlier in the day in the absence of a quorum. Deschler Ch 23 § 39.1.

§ 7. Forms

Following are the forms for entering the motion to reconsider, for subsequently calling it up and bringing it to a vote, and for offering the so-called pro forma motion.

Entering the Motion

MEMBER: I enter a motion to reconsider the vote by which the bill H.R. ____ was passed [*or rejected*].

Offering the Motion

MEMBER: I move to reconsider the vote by which the bill H.R. ____ was passed [*or rejected*].

SPEAKER: The gentle______ moves to reconsider the vote on H.R. ____. As many as are in favor of the motion say ''aye.''

Pro Forma Motion—By the Speaker

SPEAKER: Without objection, a motion to reconsider is laid on the table.
Note: Any Member may object to the Chair's statement that "without objection" a motion to reconsider a vote just taken be laid on the table (the Member need not be on the prevailing side). However, if objection is heard, only a qualified Member may call for reconsideration of the vote, and another Member may move to lay that motion to reconsider on the table. *Manual* § 1004.

§ 8. Precedence and Privilege of Motion

Under clause 3 of rule XIX, when no other question is pending, the motion to reconsider takes precedence over all other questions except the consideration of a conference report or a motion to adjourn. *Manual* §§ 1003, 1005; 8 Cannon § 2787. For example, the motion to reconsider takes precedence of a motion to go into the Committee of the Whole. 8 Cannon § 2785. However, the motion is subject to the question of consideration (8 Cannon § 2437) and the motion to lay on the table (8 Cannon § 2652), unless the Chair has put the question on the motion to reconsider (*Manual* § 1009). The precedence given the motion by the rule permits it to be offered even after the previous question has been moved or while it is operating. 5 Hinds §§ 5656-5662; 8 Cannon § 2784. A motion to reconsider a secondary motion (such as a motion to postpone) that was rejected is highly privileged and may be entertained by the Chair even after the manager of the main proposition has yielded time to another Member and before that Member has begun debate. 96-2, May 29, 1980, p 12663.

§ 9. Quorum Requirements

In general, the motion to reconsider cannot be agreed to in the House in the absence of a quorum when the vote to be reconsidered requires a quorum. 5 Hinds § 5606; Deschler Ch 23 § 33. A quorum is not necessary on a motion to reconsider the vote whereby the yeas and nays were ordered because the yeas and nays may be ordered by one-fifth of the Members present. 5 Hinds § 5693.

§ 10. Debate and Voting; Withdrawal

Debate

If debatable, the motion to reconsider is debated under the hour rule. Deschler Ch 23 § 41.1. Debate is under the control of the Member offering the motion if the proposition proposed to be reconsidered was debatable. 5

Hinds § 5696; 8 Cannon § 2792. If the proposition proposed to be reconsidered was not debatable, then the motion calling for reconsideration is itself not debatable. 5 Hinds §§ 5694, 5695, 5698; Deschler Ch 23 § 33. Thus, the motion to reconsider a vote ordering the previous question is not debatable. *Manual* § 1010.

An earlier view was that a motion to reconsider a vote may be debatable even if the previous question was operating at the time of such vote, on the theory that the vote of the House ''exhausted the previous question so as to open up the motion to debate.'' 5 Hinds § 5494. However, the current view is that, if the proposition to be reconsidered was voted on under the operation of the previous question, the motion to reconsider is not debatable because a primary function of the previous question is to terminate debate. *Manual* § 1010; 5 Hinds §§ 5656, 5701; Deschler Ch 23 § 38.7; Deschler-Brown Ch 29 § 6.49 (note). If the motion is agreed to, and if that proposition is again taken up, it is voted on without debate unless the ordering of the previous question itself is reconsidered. Deschler-Brown Ch 29 § 6.49.

Voting

A simple majority vote is sufficient to adopt a motion to reconsider, even when the vote reconsidered requires two-thirds for affirmative action. *Manual* § 1008; 5 Hinds §§ 5617, 5618; 8 Cannon § 2795. A majority vote also is required to reconsider a vote ordering the yeas and nays, although one-fifth is sufficient to order the yeas and nays. 5 Hinds §§ 5689-5692; 8 Cannon § 2790. If the House votes to reconsider, the yeas and nays may be ordered again by one-fifth. 5 Hinds § 5689. The motion to reconsider, and a motion to table such motion, are subject to postponement. Clause 8 of rule XX.

Withdrawal of Motion

The motion to reconsider having been entered within the time specified by the rules—that is, on the same or succeeding day as the vote on the proposition to be reconsidered—it may not be withdrawn without the consent of the House. *Manual* § 1003.

§ 11. Application to Particular Propositions

Generally

Clause 3 of rule XIX applies whenever ''a motion has been carried or lost. . . .'' *Manual* § 1003. The term ''motion'' in this rule has been construed so as to permit reconsideration of a wide variety of propositions. See §§ 12-14, infra. The motion is applicable whether the passage of the proposition required a simple majority or a two-thirds vote. 8 Cannon §2778. However, the motion is not in order when dilatory and manifestly for the purpose of delay. 5 Hinds §§5731-5733, 5735, 5739; 8 Cannon §§2797, 2815, 2822.

House Orders

The motion to reconsider applies to the vote on a House order, although the execution of that order has begun. 3 Hinds §2028; 5 Hinds §5665. The motion may be applied to a vote ordering the yeas and nays (5 Hinds §§5689-5691; 6029; 8 Cannon §2790) or to a vote refusing the yeas and nays (5 Hinds §5692) or to the vote by which the House refuses to order a third reading of a bill (8 Cannon §2777). The motion to reconsider also may be used to reopen the proceedings whereby the House has voted to expunge certain matter from the *Congressional Record.* Deschler Ch 23 §39.7.

The motion may not be applied to the vote by which the House has decided a question of parliamentary procedure submitted by the Speaker for the decision of the House. *Manual* §1006; 8 Cannon §2776; Deschler Ch 23 §33. However, the motion may be applied to a vote laying an appeal on the table. Compare 5 Hinds §5630 with 5 Hinds §5631.

Referrals

Under clause 4 of rule XIX, measures referred to a committee may not be brought back into the House on a motion to reconsider. *Manual* §1011. This rule, which was adopted in its present form in 1880, was intended to prevent a Member from bringing back into the House, on a motion to reconsider, any matter that such Member had obtained unanimous consent to introduce or submit for reference. 5 Hinds §5647. The rule was intended to apply to the initial formal reference to a committee and not to a motion to recommit. Deschler Ch 23 §39.6. However, it is too late to reconsider a vote by which a measure was recommitted to committee after the committee report has been made. 5 Hinds §5651.

In Relation to Previous Question

The motion to reconsider may be applied only once to a vote ordering the previous question. 5 Hinds §5655; 8 Cannon §2790. It may not be applied to a vote ordering the previous question that has been partially executed. For example, if the previous question has been ordered on a bill and an amendment thereto, and the amendment has been disposed of, the vote upon which the previous question was ordered is not subject to reconsideration. 5 Hinds §§5653, 5654. However, if the special order of business governing consideration of a measure orders the previous question on the measure, and on any amendment thereto, to final adoption or passage without intervening motion except one motion to recommit (which is the modern practice), the vote upon which an amendment was disposed of is subject to reconsideration. 111-1, June 17, 2009, p ____.

§ 12. — Other Motions and Requests

Generally

The motion to reconsider is applied to permit the House to review its vote on certain motions, including:

- An affirmative vote on a motion for the previous question, unless the previous question has been partially executed, as by a vote on certain amendments. 5 Hinds §§ 5653-5655; Deschler Ch 23 § 33.
- A vote on the motion to lay on the table, whether decided in the affirmative or in the negative. 5 Hinds §§ 5628, 5629, 5695, 6288; 8 Cannon § 2785; Deschler Ch 23 § 38.1. However, a motion to lay a motion to reconsider on the table is not subject to reconsideration. 5 Hinds §§ 5632-5640.
- An affirmative vote on a motion to go into the Committee of the Whole. 5 Hinds § 5641; Deschler Ch 23 § 33.
- An affirmative vote on the question of consideration. *Manual* § 907.
- An agreement by the House to a unanimous-consent request. 8 Cannon § 2794; Deschler Ch 23 § 33.
- An affirmative vote on a motion to suspend the rules. *Manual* § 886a.

When Not Applicable

The motion to reconsider may not be applied to votes rejecting certain motions, such as:

- A vote rejecting a motion to go into the Committee of the Whole. 5 Hinds § 5641.
- A vote rejecting the question of consideration. 5 Hinds §§ 5626, 5627; Deschler Ch 23 § 39.14.
- A vote rejecting the motion to suspend the rules. *Manual* § 886a; 5 Hinds § 5645; 8 Cannon § 2781; Deschler Ch 23 § 33.
- A vote rejecting a motion to recess. 5 Hinds § 5625.
- A vote rejecting a motion to adjourn. 5 Hinds §§ 5620-5622.
- A vote rejecting a motion to fix the day to which the House would adjourn. 5 Hinds § 5624. But see 5 Hinds § 5623.

Certain motions or questions are not subject to the motion to reconsider because of the adoption of ''expedited procedures'' prescribed by statute and intended to bring a legislative matter to a final conclusion without all the procedural protections normally accorded. See *Manual* § 1130 for examples of such laws. Another example is found in section 305(a) of the Congressional Budget Act of 1974, which precludes the motion to reconsider the vote by which a concurrent resolution on the budget is agreed to or disagreed to and the vote on adoption of a conference report on the same.

§ 13. —Bills and Resolutions; Amendments

The motion to reconsider may be applied to the vote by which a bill or joint resolution was passed (5 Hinds § 5666), including a private bill (4 Hinds §§ 3468, 3469); to a vote on the engrossment of the bill (5 Hinds § 5663); to a vote refusing to order a third reading of the bill (8 Cannon § 2777); and to a vote by which a measure was recommitted to committee (Deschler Ch 23 § 39.6). The motion also is applied to permit reconsideration of a vote on a resolution. 5 Hinds § 5609.

The motion to reconsider may be applied to permit reconsideration of a vote on an amendment; however, if the motion is not offered until after the passage of the amended bill, such reconsideration can be secured only after a successful motion to reconsider the vote on the passage of the bill. *Cf.* 8 Cannon § 2789. Similarly, to entertain a motion to reconsider a vote on an amendment to an amendment, it is first necessary to vote to reconsider the vote by which the original amendment, as amended, was disposed of. Deschler Ch 23 § 33.

§ 14. —Amendments Between the Houses; Conference Reports

A motion to reconsider may be applied to a vote on a Senate amendment to a House bill. The fact that the House has informed the Senate that it has voted to agree to such an amendment does not prevent a motion to reconsider that vote. 5 Hinds § 5672. However, such a motion must be timely offered. See § 15, infra. After a conference has been agreed to and the managers for the House appointed, it is too late to move to reconsider the vote whereby the House acted on an amendment in disagreement. 5 Hinds § 5664.

The motion to reconsider may be applied to a vote on a conference report or to a vote recommitting a conference report. Deschler Ch 23 §§ 39.4, 39.5. After disposition of a conference report and amendments reported therefrom in disagreement, it is in order to move to reconsider the vote on a motion disposing of one of the amendments. *Manual* § 1006.

Tabling a motion to reconsider ordinarily prevents the House from reconsideration of the vote in question. However, the laying on the table of a motion to reconsider the vote whereby the House has amended a Senate amendment does not preclude the House from acting on a subsequent Senate amendment to the same proposition or considering any other proper motion to dispose of an amendment that might remain in disagreement after further Senate action. *Manual* § 1006.

§ 15. —Measures Sent to the Senate or the President

The motion to reconsider may be applied to a measure that has been sent to the Senate. If that motion is agreed to, a motion to recall the measure is privileged. 5 Hinds §§ 5666, 5667, 5669. Older precedents suggest that reconsideration of the vote on the measure may be permitted even if the measure has passed both Houses and even if the measure has been sent to the President. 4 Hinds §§ 3466-3469; 5 Hinds § 5668. It would appear, however, that once the bill has been signed by the President, it cannot be called into question pursuant to a pending motion to reconsider the measure. 5 Hinds § 5704 (note). If the President returns the bill to the House with objections, and the House votes on the passage of the bill notwithstanding the objections of the President, that vote is not subject to the motion to reconsider because the Constitution expressly provides for that vote as one in the nature of reconsideration. U.S. Const. art. I, § 7, cl. 2; *Manual* § 109; 5 Hinds § 5644; 8 Cannon § 2778.

Chapter 48
Refer and Recommit

Research References

5 Hinds §§ 5521-5604
8 Cannon §§ 2695-2773
Deschler Ch 23 § 25
Manual §§ 420, 427, 448-451, 494, 916, 917, 1001-1002c

A. Generally; Motions

§ 1. In General

When a bill is introduced, it is referred to one or more committees by direction of the Speaker. See BILLS AND RESOLUTIONS. When a bill is reported by a committee, it is referred to the appropriate calendar by direction of the Speaker. See CALENDARS.

Motions for the referral, committal, or recommittal of a matter to a committee are permitted at certain narrowly circumscribed stages of the legislative process. These motions are:

- The ordinary motion to refer "when a question is under debate" under clause 4 of rule XVI. *Manual* §§ 911, 916.
- The motion to recommit (or commit, as the case may be) a matter to a committee pending or after the ordering of the previous question thereon under clause 2 of rule XIX. *Manual* § 1001.
- The motion to refer a bill to a committee pending a vote in the House on a motion to strike the enacting words as provided in clause 9 of rule XVIII. *Manual* §§ 988, 989.

When the House recodified its rules in the 106th Congress, it consolidated the last sentence of former clause 1 of rule XVII and certain provisions of former rule XVI clause 4, addressing the motion to recommit, under clause 2 of rule XIX. *Manual* § 1001.

§ 2. Form and Effect of Motion

MEMBER: M__. Speaker, I move to refer (or commit or recommit) the bill (or resolution) to the Committee on ______.

Such motion may or may not be subject to debate, depending on the applicable rule. The motion itself may not include a preamble, argument, or explanation. 5 Hinds § 5589; 8 Cannon § 2749. The motion may include instructions. See §§ 17-20, infra. The "straight" motion (without instructions) sends a measure to a specified committee and leaves the disposition thereof to the discretion of the committee. Deschler Ch 23 § 25.

A "straight" motion to recommit and a motion to recommit with instructions have equal precedence. 8 Cannon §§ 2714, 2758.

§ 3. Referral to Particular Committees

The motion to refer, commit, or recommit may propose a referral to a named standing committee, or to two or more standing committees, without regard to the usual rules governing committee jurisdiction. 4 Hinds §§ 4375, 4401; 5 Hinds § 5527; Deschler Ch 23 § 25. The motion may provide for referral to a committee other than that reporting the underlying measure. 8 Cannon § 2696.

A matter may be referred on motion to the Committee of the Whole (5 Hinds §§ 5552, 5553, 6631) or to a select committee, including one that is established pursuant to the motion (4 Hinds § 4401). However, motions for the referral of a matter to a subcommittee are not in order. 8 Cannon § 2739.

§ 4. Motions in Committee of the Whole

The motions permitted by House rules for the referral of a matter do not apply in Committee of the Whole. 4 Hinds § 4721; 8 Cannon §§ 2326, 2327. It is in order under certain circumstances in the Committee to move that the Committee rise and report back to the House with the *recommendation* that the measure under consideration be recommitted. Such a motion is usually precluded by the language of a special order of business from the Committee on Rules ordering the previous question. If such a motion is permitted, it is entertained only at the completion of the reading of the bill for amendment. *Manual* § 916; 4 Hinds §§ 4761, 4762; Deschler Ch 23 § 26.5.

The House, while acting in the House as in the Committee of the Whole, may refer a matter to a committee. 4 Hinds §§ 4931, 4932.

B. The Simple Motion to Refer

§ 5. In General

Generally; When to Offer

A simple motion to refer is permitted by clause 4(a) of rule XVI "when a question is under debate." *Manual* §§ 911, 916. This motion is in order pending the consideration of the underlying matter. The motion may be offered by any Member, who need not qualify as being in opposition to the pending question. Deschler Ch 23 § 25.

The motion to refer under clause 4 of rule XVI may be offered before the proponent of the proposition is recognized to control debate on the underlying measure. Deschler-Brown Ch 29 § 68.51. The motion may not be offered while another Member holds the floor in debate. 6 Cannon § 468;

8 Cannon § 2742. Once disposed of, it cannot be offered again at the same stage of the question on the same day. *Manual* § 918.

Application of Motion

A measure before the House under the general rules of the House is subject to the motion. The motion is applicable to: a measure called up from the House Calendar (including a resolution from the Committee on House Administration); a resolution adopting the rules of the House; an article of impeachment; and a resolution raising a question of the privileges of the House. 6 Cannon § 549; Deschler Ch 1 § 9; Deschler-Brown Ch 29 § 68.51. The motion has been applied to a vetoed bill, with or without the veto message. 4 Hinds §§ 3550, 3551; for referral of Presidential messages, see *Manual* § 875.

Referral With Instructions

The motion to refer may include instructions or be amended to include instructions. 5 Hinds § 5521. If the previous question is rejected on the motion, amendments including proper instructions in the motion are in order. *Manual* § 917. For a discussion of instructions generally, see §§ 17-20, infra.

§ 6. Precedence; Relation to Other Motions

The motion to refer under clause 4 of rule XVI takes precedence over the motions to amend or to postpone indefinitely, but yields to the motions to adjourn, to table, for the previous question, or to postpone to a day certain. *Manual* § 911. Thus, the Chair may recognize the Member seeking to offer the preferential motion before the less preferential motion is read. *Manual* § 916. The motion to refer is subject to the motion to table. *Manual* §§ 911, 914.

The motion for the previous question takes precedence over the motion to refer under clause 4 of rule XVI. *Manual* §§ 911, 916. However, where the motion to refer under that rule is preempted by the motion for the previous question on a resolution on which there has been no debate, rejection of the motion for the previous question leaves the motion to refer pending. 101-2, Mar. 22, 1990, pp 4996-98.

§ 7. Debate on Motion

A motion to refer under clause 4 of rule XVI (before the previous question is ordered) is separately debatable pending the consideration of the underlying matter. *Manual* § 713. The motion is debatable under the hour rule. Deschler-Brown Ch 29 § 68.51. The scope of the debate is narrowly confined and may not extend to the merits of the underlying matter. 5 Hinds §§5564-5568; 6 Cannon §549. Such debate is terminated by the adoption of the previous question on the motion. Deschler Ch 23 §25.

C. Referral Pending Motion to Strike Enacting Clause

§8. In General

Clause 9 of rule XVIII permits the offering of a motion to refer a measure to a committee, which may include instructions, pending concurrence by the House in a recommendation from the Committee of the Whole that the enacting clause of a measure be stricken. *Manual* §988. As noted elsewhere, the recommendation that the enacting clause be stricken may interrupt and supersede the offering of amendments in Committee of the Whole and, if agreed to by the House, defeats the bill. See COMMITTEES OF THE WHOLE.

The motion to refer permitted by this rule is to be distinguished from the motion to recommit that may be made pending final passage of the bill under clause 2 of rule XIX. The motion to recommit pending passage ensures the right of the minority to have a final opportunity to perfect the bill or to return it to committee. §14, infra. In contrast, the motion to refer under rule XVIII comes before action on the recommendation that the enacting clause be stricken and allows the friends of the original bill to avert its demise by referring it to committee where it may be considered in the light of the action of the House. 8 Cannon §2629.

The motion to refer permitted by rule XVIII may include instructions to report back forthwith with an amendment to the underlying bill. *Manual* §989.

The recommendation that the enacting clause be stricken may not be combined with a recommendation that the bill be recommitted to a committee. Deschler Ch 19 §10.10.

Automatic Recommittal

When the House disagrees with the recommendation of the Committee of the Whole to strike the enacting words and does not refer the bill under the provisions of the rule, the bill is recommitted to the Committee of the Whole, where it becomes unfinished business. This process is automatic and does not require a motion. 5 Hinds §§5326, 5345, 5346; 8 Cannon §2633.

D. Referral Pending or After Ordering the Previous Question

§ 9. In General; When in Order

The motion to recommit (or commit, as the case may be) is authorized under clause 2 of rule XIX. Under this rule, the motion is in order pending the motion for the previous question or after the previous question has been ordered on passage or adoption. The motion may be made with instructions and may provide for referral to a standing or select committee. *Manual* § 1001. It is not necessary that the underlying proposition be reported from a committee. 95-2, July 12, 1978, p 20504. Only one proper motion to commit is in order under the rule. *Manual* § 1002b; 5 Hinds § 5577.

If the previous question has been ordered on a proposition on which there has been no debate, and a Member insists on the 40 minutes of debate permitted by rule, the motion to commit should be made only after such debate. *Manual* § 999; 99-1, May 8, 1985, p 11072.

When the previous question is ordered on all stages of a bill to final passage, the motion to commit is not in order before engrossment or third reading. *Manual* § 1002; 5 Hinds §§ 5578-5581. The motion to commit may be made pending the demand for the previous question on passage or adoption but, at that stage, is subject to the motion to table. 5 Hinds § 5576.

Instructions With Motion

A motion to commit under clause 2 of rule XIX may be offered with instructions, such as an instruction to report back with an amendment. *Manual* § 1002b. Thus, a motion to commit a resolution electing minority Members to standing committees may be offered with instructions to a select committee to report back ''forthwith'' with an amendment adding the names of additional Members. Deschler-Brown Ch 29 § 23.55. For a discussion of instructions generally, see §§ 17-20, infra.

Amendments to Motion

A motion to commit may be amended, as by adding instructions, unless the previous question is ordered on the motion. 5 Hinds §§ 5582-5584; 8 Cannon § 2695.

§ 10. Application of Motion

The rule authorizing the motion to commit, pending or after the previous question, is construed as applying across a broad range of legislative business, including:

- Bills and joint resolutions. 5 Hinds § 5576.
- Simple resolutions and concurrent resolutions. 5 Hinds § 5573; Deschler-Brown Ch 29 § 23.54.
- Conference reports if the other House has not discharged its managers. See CONFERENCES BETWEEN THE HOUSES.
- Senate amendments being considered in the House before the stage of disagreement. 5 Hinds § 5575.
- A resolution stating a question of privilege, such as a disciplinary resolution, or a resolution certifying the contempt of a committee witness. Deschler Ch 23 § 26.13; Deschler-Brown Ch 29 § 68.51.
- A resolution electing Members to standing committees. Deschler-Brown Ch 29 § 23.55.

The motion to commit may not be separately applied to amendments to the underlying proposition. Deschler Ch 23 § 25. When the previous question has been ordered on a simple resolution and a pending amendment thereto, the motion to commit should be offered after the vote on the amendment. 5 Hinds §§ 5585-5588.

The motion does not apply to special orders of business reported by the Committee on Rules because clause 6(b) of rule XIII prevents the Speaker from entertaining dilatory motions until reports from such committee are disposed of. 5 Hinds §§ 5598-5601; Deschler Ch 23 § 25.11. However, if the motion for the previous question is rejected, this restriction no longer strictly applies. *Manual* § 858.

§ 11. Who May Offer Motion; Recognition

As noted elsewhere in this chapter, priority in recognition on a motion to recommit a bill pending final passage under clause 2 of rule XIX is given to an opponent of the bill. § 14, infra. Thus, an opponent, with preference given first to the Minority Leader or a designee and then to a minority member of the reporting committee (in order of seniority on the committee), has priority in recognition to offer the motion under rule XIX. *Manual* § 1001. However, if the underlying matter is a resolution offered from the floor as a question of the privileges of the House, the Member offering the motion to commit need not qualify as opposed to the resolution. Deschler-Brown Ch 29 § 23.60.

It is the prerogative of the minority, when the House is operating under general parliamentary procedure, to offer a motion to commit the resolution adopting the rules, but the minority Member offering the motion need not qualify as opposed to the resolution (because rule XIX has yet to be adopted). *Manual* § 60.

§ 12. Debate on Motion

Under clause 2 of rule XIX, a motion to commit with instructions is not separately debatable after the previous question is ordered on the underlying simple or concurrent resolution. 5 Hinds § 5582. Thus, the previous question having been ordered on a resolution before adoption of the rules, the motion to commit—even one including instructions—is not debatable. *Manual* § 60. As to the debate permitted on a motion to recommit pending final passage of a bill or joint resolution, see § 15, infra.

E. Recommittal Pending Final Passage

§ 13. In General

The motion to recommit a bill or joint resolution after the previous question has been ordered on the question of final passage is authorized by clause 2 of rule XIX. Clause 2(b), which permits debate on the motion, does not apply to simple resolutions, concurrent resolutions, or conference reports. *Manual* § 1001; § 15, infra. A Member wishing to raise or reserve a point of order against the motion to recommit may do so after the motion is offered but before debate has begun thereon. 104-1, June 22, 1995, p 16842.

When in Order

The motion to recommit a bill is typically made after the engrossment and third reading of the bill. Deschler Ch 23 § 29.1; *cf.* 107-2, June 13, 2002, p 10240. A Member seeking to offer the motion must be standing and addressing the Chair after the engrossment and third reading of the bill and before the Chair puts the question on passage of the bill. The motion comes too late when the Chair has put the question on passage and has announced the apparent result of the vote. Deschler Ch 23 §§ 29.5, 29.6.

Repetition of Motion

Clause 2 permits only one motion to recommit after the previous question has been ordered. However, if the motion is ruled out on a point of order, its proponent or another qualifying Member is entitled to offer a proper motion to recommit. *Manual* § 1002b; 8 Cannon § 2713.

Amendments to Motion

A motion to recommit is subject to amendment until the previous question is ordered on the motion. Deschler Ch 23 § 25.1. If the previous question on the motion is not ordered, the motion is open to amendment. Deschler Ch 23 § 25.2. The amendment must be germane to the pending measure and not necessarily to the original motion. *Manual* § 1002a; see § 17, infra. In order to be recognized for an amendment to such motion, a Member must either be yielded to for that purpose by the proponent or the previous question must be defeated. 107-2, Feb. 27, 2002, pp 2080-85. Any point of order against an amendment to the motion should be raised immediately following the reading of the amendment. *Manual* § 924.

§ 14. Who May Offer Motion; Recognition

SPEAKER: Is the gentle______ opposed to the measure?

This is the threshold question to be put by the Chair in determining a Member's qualification to offer a motion to recommit. Deschler Ch 23 § 25. At one time the applicable rule was construed to give the friends of the bill an opportunity to correct any errors in the bill before the House voted on passage. 8 Cannon § 2762. Under clause 2 of rule XIX, the Speaker is required to give preference in recognition to a Member who is opposed to the bill, whether the motion is made with or without instructions. *Manual* § 1002c. This rules change was intended to allow the minority a final opportunity to return the bill to committee or (through instructions) to have its version of the bill brought to a vote. Deschler Ch 23 § 25.

In recognizing a Member to move to recommit, the Chair does not attempt to assess the degree of that Member's opposition and takes the Member's word. The Chair makes no distinction between Members who are unqualifiedly opposed and those who phrase their opposition "to the bill in its present form." It is not the province of the Chair to direct a Member, having qualified as opposed, to vote against the measure after rejection of the motion to recommit. *Manual* § 1002c.

Among Members opposed to the bill, the Speaker will first look to the Minority Leader or a designee, then to minority members of the committee reporting the bill (in order of seniority on the committee), then to other minority Members, and finally to majority Members. *Manual* § 1002c. These principles of recognition are followed even where a bill under consideration is not reported from committee. See 89-1, Sept. 29, 1965, p 25439; 96-1,

Nov. 28, 1979, pp 33904, 33906, 33914. Priority in recognition to the Minority Leader or a designee is imputed from the form of clause 6 of rule XIII. § 16, infra.

It is not too late for a senior member of the committee to seek recognition where another minority Member has qualified as opposed to the bill but where such individual's motion has not yet been read by the Clerk. Deschler Ch 29 § 8.21.

Recognition for Amendments to Motion

If the previous question is not ordered on a motion to recommit, the person offering an amendment to the motion does not have to qualify as being opposed to the bill. Deschler Ch 23 § 27.14. A Member who, in the Speaker's determination, led the opposition to ordering the previous question on the motion to recommit—such as the chair of the committee reporting the bill—is entitled to offer an amendment to the motion regardless of party affiliation. *Manual* § 1002c.

§ 15. Debate on Motion

Generally

Under a prior form of the rule, the straight motion to recommit was not debatable whether offered pending the previous question on the measure or after the previous question had been ordered. 5 Hinds § 5582; Deschler Ch 23 § 25. However, in the 111th Congress, clause 2 of rule XIX was amended and the motion to recommit a bill or joint resolution is now debated under the terms of clause 2(b)(1) whether or not such motion contains instructions. *Manual* § 1002a. Under that rule, a motion to recommit a bill or joint resolution on which the previous question is ordered to passage is debatable for 10 minutes, five minutes in favor of the motion and five opposed. Under clause 2(c) debate may be extended to one hour, equally divided, upon demand of the majority floor manager of the bill. *Manual* § 1001. The debate permitted by the rule is inapplicable to a simple or concurrent resolution or a conference report. *Manual* § 1002a.

Control of Debate Time

The Member in support of a motion to recommit with instructions is recognized for five minutes and must use or yield back all of that time. Such Member may not reserve a portion thereof. However, the Member offering the motion may, at the conclusion of the 10 minutes of debate, yield to another Member to offer an amendment to the motion if the previous question has not been ordered on the motion. *Manual* § 1002a.

A Member recognized for five minutes in opposition to a motion to recommit with instructions controls the floor for debate only and may not yield to another Member to offer an amendment to the motion to recommit. Deschler Ch 23 § 30.4. Where debate time on a motion to recommit with instructions has been lengthened by a special order of business, the Chair has allowed time to be allocated and controlled and has permitted the Member controlling time in opposition to close debate. 95-2, Aug. 10, 1978, p 25500.

§ 16. Effect of Special Orders of Business

Clause 6(c) of rule XIII precludes the Committee on Rules from reporting a special order of business which would prevent the motion to recommit a bill or joint resolution from being made as provided in clause 2(b) of rule XIX. That prohibition includes a motion to recommit with instructions if offered by the Minority Leader or a designee, except on a Senate bill or joint resolution for which the text of a House-passed measure has been substituted. *Manual* § 857.

The prohibition is applicable only to the recommittal of a bill or joint resolution pending initial final passage and does not apply to a special order of business restricting the recommittal of a simple or concurrent resolution. *Manual* § 859. The Committee on Rules has reported special orders of business precluding a motion to recommit at subsequent stages; that is, during consideration of amendments between the Houses. See SENATE BILLS; AMENDMENTS BETWEEN THE HOUSES. For an exchange of correspondence between the chair and ranking minority member of the Committee on Rules regarding this practice, see 104-2, Jan. 24, 1996, pp 1228, 1229.

F. Motions With Instructions

§ 17. In General

The motion to refer, commit, or recommit may include instructions. Such instructions may direct a designated committee to take a specified action, such as to study a subject germane to the underlying measure. *Manual* § 1002b; Deschler Ch 23 § 25. A committee may be instructed as follows:

- To report ''forthwith'' with an amendment. § 18, infra.
- To consider the bill in relation to the President's energy message and to promptly hold hearings thereon. 95-1, Apr. 29, 1977, p 12886.
- To hold hearings and promptly report recommendations on how to amortize the cost of the bill. 101-2, Mar. 29, 1990, p 6042.

- To examine possible measures to reduce oil prices and report amendments containing such measures. 106-2, Mar. 22, 2000, p 3295.
- To hold hearings on a proposal and to solicit the views of administration officials. Deschler Ch 23 § 26.2; 100-2, July 27, 1988, p 19146.
- To examine the sufficiency of a contempt citation and report back to the House. Deschler Ch 23 § 32.11.

Under a previous form of the rule, a motion to recommit a bill or joint resolution with instructions could specify that the committee report back "promptly." Unlike a motion to recommit "forthwith," where amendatory instructions are carried out immediately (see below), a "promptly" motion sent the bill back to committee whose eventual report (if any) was not immediately before the House. The instructions contained in such a motion were advisory only. Such "promptly" instructions, while no longer applicable to bills and joint resolutions, remain available for simple or concurrent resolutions. *Manual* § 1002b.

Amendments to Instructions

A motion to recommit with instructions may be amended if the previous question has not been ordered thereon. A substitute amendment which strikes all of the proposed instructions and inserts others in their place is in order if germane to the pending measure, and does not violate the right of the minority to move to recommit. 8 Cannon § 2759. An amendment offered to an instruction must be germane to the bill, not necessarily to the original instruction. *Manual* § 930.

§ 18. Instructions to Report "Forthwith"

The House may recommit a bill to committee with instructions to report an amendment "forthwith." Such instructions must be complied with immediately. *Manual* § 1002b. The House has used this procedure even with respect to an amendment in the nature of a substitute for the entire bill. Deschler Ch 23 § 32.16.

Having been instructed to report "forthwith," the committee is not required to convene and consider the measure. The chair or other designated committee member immediately rises and announces that, pursuant to the instructions of the House, the measure is reported back to the House with the instructed amendment. Deschler Ch 23 § 25. The House then votes on the amendment and, if it is adopted, again on engrossment and third reading of the bill before final passage, as shown in the following example:

> SPEAKER: The question is on the engrossment and third reading of the bill.

Note: The question is then put. If it carries, the bill is ordered to be engrossed and read a third time, and is read the third time.

MEMBER: I have a motion to recommit at the desk.

SPEAKER: Is the gentle______ opposed to the bill?

MEMBER: I am, M__. Speaker [in its present form].

SPEAKER: The gentle______ qualifies. The Clerk will report the motion to recommit.

CLERK: The gentle______ from ______ moves to recommit the bill, H.R. ____, to the Committee on __________ with instructions to report the bill forthwith with the following amendment: ____________

Note: The motion is subject to 10 minutes of debate or up to one hour if demanded by the floor manager of the bill, equally divided between the proponent and a Member opposed to the motion. § 15, supra.

SPEAKER: Without objection, the previous question is ordered on the motion to recommit. The question is on the motion to recommit.

Note: A vote having been taken and announced in the affirmative, the chair of the designated committee rises:

CHAIR: M__. Speaker, pursuant to the instructions of the House on the motion to recommit, I report back the bill, H.R. __________, with an amendment.

SPEAKER: The Clerk will report the amendment. [*After Clerk reports the amendment.*] The question is on the amendment.

Note: The amendment is voted on; if it is adopted, the Speaker again puts the question on engrossment and third reading of the bill; if agreed to, the question is on passage of the bill.

§ 19. Dividing the Question on Instructions

On a motion to recommit with instructions, it is not in order to demand a separate vote on the instructions or various branches thereof. 5 Hinds §§ 6134-6137; 8 Cannon §§ 2737, 3170. However, when a bill is reported back to the House with an amendment pursuant to such instructions, a division of the question may be demanded on the amendment if the question is otherwise in a divisible form. *Manual* § 921. A motion to recommit a bill to conference with various instructions may not be divided. *Manual* § 921; see generally DIVISION OF THE QUESTION FOR VOTING.

§ 20. Instructions Subject to a Point of Order

A motion to recommit may not propose to do that which may not be done by amendment under the rules of the House. *Manual* § 1002b; 5 Hinds §§ 5529-5541.

For instance, a motion to recommit may not:

- Propose an amendment that is not germane. 5 Hinds §§ 5529-5541, 5834, 5889; 8 Cannon §§ 2705, 2707, 2708.
- Amend or eliminate an amendment adopted by the House (unless permitted by special order of business). 5 Hinds § 5531; 8 Cannon §§ 2712, 2714, 2715, 2720-2724; Deschler Ch 23 § 32.20.
- Propose an amendment in violation of clauses 2, 4, 5, or 10 of rule XXI. 5 Hinds §§ 5533-5540; 112-1, Mar. 3, 2011, p ____.
- Propose an amendment in violation of the Congressional Budget Act. *Manual* § 1127.
- Change the rules of the House by authorizing a committee to report at any time (5 Hinds § 5543) or by directing a committee to report by a date certain (5 Hinds § 5549). However, it has been held in order to reoffer an amendment rejected by the House. 5 Hinds §§ 5543, 5549; 8 Cannon § 2728.
- Contain an amendment in the form of a limitation to a general appropriations bill that has not been offered in the Committee of the Whole. See APPROPRIATIONS.
- Contain argument. *Manual* § 1002b.

Where a special order of business providing for the consideration of a bill prohibited the offering of amendments to a certain title of the bill (at any point during consideration), it was held not in order to offer a motion to recommit with instructions to amend the restricted title. However, that precedent should be read in light of clause 6(c)(2) of rule XIII, which precludes the Committee on Rules from reporting a rule that would prevent a motion to recommit from including amendatory instructions. *Manual* § 1002b.

Under clause 6(c) of rule XIII, the Committee on Rules may not report a special order of business denying to the Minority Leader or a designee the right to offer a motion with instructions. *Manual* § 857. If the special order of business reported from the Committee on Rules permits a motion to recommit "with or without instructions," amendatory instructions are protected; and a motion to recommit may include instructions (otherwise in order) that modify an amendment previously agreed to by the House. This is true even if the House has adopted an amendment in the nature of a substitute. The insertion of the phrase "one motion to recommit *with or without instructions*" has become routine in special orders reported by the Committee on Rules (but is unnecessary in a special order of business that precludes amendments prior to the stage of recommittal).

The Chair does not anticipate the content of a motion to recommit and will not rule in advance as to whether particular instructions which might be offered as part of such a motion would be in order. Deschler-Brown Ch 28 § 23.

Chapter 49
Resolutions of Inquiry

Research References

3 Hinds §§ 1856-1910
6 Cannon §§ 404-437
Deschler Ch 15 § 2
Manual §§ 864-868

§ 1. In General

The resolution of inquiry is one of the methods used by the House to obtain information from the executive branch. Deschler Ch 15 § 2. Resolutions of inquiry are accorded privileged status under clause 7 of rule XIII. *Manual* §§ 864, 866.

A resolution of inquiry is simple rather than concurrent or joint in form. *Manual* § 865. The resolution normally provides that the information be furnished directly to the House.

A resolution of inquiry need not contain a statement as to the purpose for which the information is sought. 96-1, June 15, 1979, p 15027. In fact, the inclusion of a preamble will effectively destroy the privilege that the resolution might otherwise enjoy. See § 6, infra.

The wording of the resolution will vary depending on the person to whom the resolution is directed. The House traditionally ''requests'' the President and ''directs'' the heads of executive departments to furnish information. *Manual* § 865. The resolution may include the qualifying phrase, ''if not incompatible with the public interest,'' or words to that effect. 3 Hinds § 1896; 6 Cannon § 436; Deschler Ch 15 § 2.8.

§ 2. To Whom Resolutions May Be Directed

Resolutions of inquiry are directed to the President or to a cabinet officer. Deschler Ch 15 § 2. Clause 7 of rule XIII refers to ''the head of an executive department.'' That term does not extend beyond Cabinet officers to subordinate officials. Thus, a resolution of inquiry directed to the Federal Reserve Board (6 Cannon § 406) or to the Director of the CIA (Deschler Ch 15 § 2.1) would not be privileged for consideration.

Normally, resolutions of inquiry direct the respondent to furnish information directly to the House, and it has been questioned whether directing the respondent to furnish information to a committee of the House would impair the privilege. Deschler Ch 15 § 2.26; but see 3 Hinds § 1860.

§ 3. Subjects of Inquiry

A wide variety of information—relating to both foreign and domestic affairs—may be sought pursuant to a resolution of inquiry. The House has agreed to such resolutions to obtain information on:

- Agreements between the President and the British Prime Minister. Deschler Ch 15 § 2.13.
- The relationship between the President's brother (Billy Carter) and the Libyan Government. 96-2, Sept. 10, 1980, p 24948.
- The dismantlement and removal of industrial plants from postwar Germany. Deschler Ch 15 § 2.15.
- Sales to foreign countries of goods in short supply. Deschler Ch 15 § 2.22.
- Domestic availability of petroleum and coal. Deschler Ch 15 § 2.23.
- The construction of certain river improvements and the costs thereof. 3 Hinds § 1875.
- Information in possession of the Department of Justice relative to a certain kidnapping case, including the names of those questioned in the investigation. Deschler Ch 15 § 2.19.
- Documents containing a list of public school systems receiving Federal aid that bus school children to achieve racial balance or indicating the use of Federal funds for such busing. Deschler Ch 15 § 2.24.
- Department of Defense documents regarding U.S. military assistance to certain nations. Deschler Ch 15 § 2.12.
- Information from the Secretary of State regarding a U.S. military alert ordered in October, 1973. 93-2, Apr. 9, 1974, p 10177.
- Information from the Secretary of Defense relative to congressional support for the C-5B aircraft. 97-2, Aug. 3, 1982, p 18947.
- Information from the President relative to U.S. activities in Honduras and Nicaragua. 98-1, May 4, 1983, p 11097.
- Information from the President relating to U.S. supplies of crude oil and refined petroleum products. 96-1, June 14, 1979, p 14951.

- Evidence compiled by the Department of Justice and the FBI in connection with the ABSCAM investigation (relating to bribery of certain Members and other public officials), and information on the amount of Federal spending thereon. 96-2, Feb. 27, 1980, pp 4071, 4078.

Documents that have been sought pursuant to a resolution of inquiry include reports on foreign affairs, such as the so-called Pentagon Papers (Deschler Ch 15 §2.2), certain text of communications between the Department of State and a U.S. Embassy (Deschler Ch 15 §2.3), maps showing certain military operations (Deschler Ch 15 §2.8), military statistical data (Deschler Ch 15 §2.11), papers in the custody of the Special Prosecutor (Deschler Ch 15 §2.17), and a letter from the Director of the FBI to the Secretary of Commerce (Deschler Ch 15 §2.20). A resolution of inquiry, reported adversely in 1993, requested the President to furnish certain documents concerning the White House travel office and the FBI. 103-1, July 20, 1993, p 16207.

§4. Privilege of Resolution

For a resolution of inquiry to have privileged status, or for the motion to discharge to have that status, the resolution must be addressed to the President or to a member of the President's Cabinet. 3 Hinds §1861; 6 Cannon §406. To be privileged, the resolution should not contain a preamble. 3 Hinds §§1877, 1878; 6 Cannon §§422, 427. It must seek facts rather than opinions and may not require an investigation. 3 Hinds §§1872-1874; 6 Cannon §§427, 429, 432; §7, infra. A resolution may be held to require an investigation where it calls for information that is not within the purview of the executive to whom the resolution is addressed. 3 Hinds §1874; 6 Cannon §410. The point of order that a resolution of inquiry is not privileged should be raised after the resolution has been read but before debate thereon. See POINTS OF ORDER; PARLIAMENTARY INQUIRIES.

§5. —Resolutions Calling for Opinions

To enjoy privileged status, a resolution of inquiry should seek factual information only. It may not be considered as privileged if it calls for an opinion or for such facts as would inevitably require the statement of an opinion to answer the inquiry. *Manual* §866; 3 Hinds §§1872, 1873; 6 Cannon §413; Deschler Ch 15 §2. A request for documents only is normally construed not to require an expression of opinion.

Resolutions of inquiry have lost their privileged status because they sought opinions rather than facts, for example:

- The names of those certifying to an appointment unless the disclosure would be ''distressing'' to anyone named. 72-1, Feb. 5, 1932, p 3453.
- An ''analysis'' of a country's past and present military capability. 92-1, July 7, 1971, p 23816.
- The rationale for American involvement in South Vietnam. Deschler Ch 15 § 2.1.
- The extent of damage to facilities struck by bombs. Deschler Ch 15 § 2.7.

§ 6. Committee Functions

Referrals and Reports; Joint Referrals

Resolutions of inquiry are introduced through the hopper and referred to the appropriate committees for consideration and report. Under clause 7 of rule XIII, committees are required to report resolutions of inquiry back to the House within 14 legislative days, exclusive of the day of introduction and the day of discharge. 3 Hinds §§ 1858, 1859. The 14-day reporting period may be extended by unanimous consent. *Manual* § 864; 97-2, July 12, 1982, p 15773. In the case of a multiple referral, all committees must either report or be discharged before consideration, but the modern practice is to refer such resolutions to a single committee only.

Discharge

If a committee fails to file its report on the resolution to the House within the 14-day period, the House may consider the resolution by adopting a motion to discharge as follows:

> MEMBER: M__. Speaker, I move to discharge the Committee on __________ from the further consideration of the resolution, H. Res. ____, a privileged resolution of inquiry.

This motion is privileged for consideration after the 14-day period even though there may have been some delay in the transmittal of the resolution to the committee. *Manual* § 867; 3 Hinds § 1871. The motion to discharge is not debatable. *Manual* § 867. A motion to table the motion to discharge is in order but is likewise not debatable. 6 Cannon § 415. However, if the motion to discharge is agreed to, the question recurs on agreeing to the resolution of inquiry; and that question is debatable. 6 Cannon § 417.

A committee also may be discharged from consideration of a resolution of inquiry by unanimous consent, even where a motion to discharge is not yet eligible for consideration under clause 7 of rule XIII. Deschler Ch 15 §§ 2.17, 2.18.

§7. Consideration in the House

Generally; Calling Up

A resolution of inquiry, if in proper form, is privileged, and a report thereon is presented from the floor rather than through the hopper. 103-1, July 20, 1993, p 16207. Subject to three-day report availability under clause 4 of rule XIII, the resolution may be called up in the House and considered anytime after it has been reported by (or discharged from) a committee to which it was referred. 6 Cannon §414; Deschler Ch 24 §8.13. It may not be called up as privileged before being referred to committee. *Manual* §866. The privilege of the resolution is not affected by an adverse report. Indeed, an adverse report on the resolution is itself submitted as privileged. 6 Cannon §§404, 410.

The reported resolution retains its privilege after being referred to the calendar. 6 Cannon §407. If it is ruled out because it was submitted through the hopper, it may be immediately resubmitted from the floor without loss of privilege. 6 Cannon §419.

Who May Call Up

When a resolution of inquiry has been reported by committee within the 14-day time frame, only an authorized member of that committee may call up the resolution for consideration. 6 Cannon §413; §4, supra. By reporting a resolution of inquiry, even adversely, within 14 legislative days, the committee of jurisdiction retains control of the resolution, and a Member not authorized by the committee cannot call up the resolution. *Manual* §867; 8 Cannon §2310.

Three-Day Availability Requirement

The consideration of a resolution of inquiry in the House is ordinarily subject to the three-day availability requirement of clause 4 of rule XIII. *Manual* §850. However, the House has considered it on the day reported where no point of order was raised, or pursuant to a unanimous-consent request. Deschler Ch 24 §§8.13, 8.14.

Debate; Motions

The Member calling up a privileged resolution of inquiry is recognized to control one hour of debate, whether the resolution is reported from committee or is before the House pursuant to a motion to discharge. *Manual* §867.

A motion to table will lie against a pending resolution of inquiry, whether reported favorably or adversely. Deschler Ch 15 §2. The motion to table is preferential. *Manual* § 914. The motion may be offered before or after debate on the resolution. *Manual* § 867.

Effect of Adjournment

A resolution of inquiry undisposed of by the House at adjournment at the end of the day retains its privilege and is the unfinished business when that class of business is again in order under the rules. 6 Cannon § 412. On that day, the resolution may be called up and debated *de novo*. 96-1, June 14, 1979, p 14951; 96-1, June 15, 1979, p 15027.

§ 8. Executive Branch Responses

Resolutions of inquiry ordinarily have been complied with pursuant to principles of comity between the branches of government. Deschler Ch 15 §§ 2, 3. Responses submitted to the House by the officer named in the resolution are laid before the House and referred to the committee or committees reporting the resolution. 96-2, Sept. 17, 1980, p 25887.

The House rules contain no specific provision for enforcing resolutions of inquiry, and there have been a number of instances in which the officer named has refused or declined to provide some or all of the information sought. For examples of conflicts with the executive branch over resolutions of inquiry, see *Manual* § 868; 6 Cannon §§ 434, 435. In such cases the House may renew its inquiry or demand a further or more complete answer. 3 Hinds §§ 1890, 1891; 6 Cannon § 435. For the power of the House to issue subpoenas and to enforce them pursuant to contempt procedures, see CONTEMPT.

Chapter 50

Rules and Precedents of the House

Research References

U.S. Const. art. I, § 5
8 Cannon §§ 3376-3396
Deschler Ch 5 §§ 1-7
Manual §§ 58-61a, 283-286, 387, 388, 1130

§ 1. In General

Adoption of Rules

The Constitution empowers each House to determine the rules of its proceedings. U.S. Const. art. I § 5; *Manual* § 58. The House may not by its rules ignore constitutional restraints or violate fundamental rights, and there should be a reasonable relation between the mode or method of proceeding established by the rule and the result that is sought. However, within these limitations, the House is free to adopt such rules as it sees fit. *Yellin* v. *United States*, 374 U.S. 109 (1963).

It is customary for the House at the beginning of each Congress to adopt the rules by which it is to be governed during its meetings. In so doing, the House ordinarily will adopt the rules applicable in the previous Congress with such amendments as it considers necessary. Deschler Ch 1 § 10.5. Such rules are adopted or amended pursuant to a simple resolution that is called up as privileged and debated under principles of ''general parliamentary law.'' See ASSEMBLY OF CONGRESS. Changes in the rules from the prior Congress normally emanate from the conference or caucus of the party that commands a majority and thus has the responsibility for organizing the House.

Even before adoption of rules, it is in order to consider as privileged a resolution in the nature of a special order of business that makes in order the subsequent consideration of a resolution adopting the rules for the newly organized House. *Manual* § 60; 5 Hinds 5450.

When a member of the majority party offers a resolution providing rules for the new Congress:

- The resolution is debatable for one hour.
- The resolution is not subject to amendment unless the previous question is rejected or the manager of the resolution yields for an amendment. Deschler Ch 1 § 10.9.
- A motion to refer (with instructions) is in order before debate begins, but this motion is subject to being laid on the table. *Manual* § 60.
- A motion to commit is in order pending or following the ordering of the previous question, which is the prerogative of the minority, but the proponent need not qualify as opposed to the resolution; and it is not debatable. *Manual* § 60; 5 Hinds § 5604.
- A majority vote is required to adopt a resolution establishing rules for a new Congress.

The right of the House to determine the rules of its proceedings may not be impaired by repetition of dilatory motions. 5 Hinds § 5707.

Publication

The standing rules of the House are published each Congress in the *House Rules and Manual* pursuant to resolution. *Manual,* p iii. This comprehensive volume also includes, among other pertinent material, portions of *Jefferson's Manual,* which was prepared by Thomas Jefferson for his own guidance while he was President of the Senate from 1797 to 1801. Under clause 1 of rule XXIX, the principles recorded in *Jefferson's Manual* govern the proceedings of the House where the principles are applicable and not inconsistent with the standing rules and orders of the House. *Manual* § 1105.

Statutory Rules and Joint Rules

In some cases, Congress has enacted statutes setting forth rules and procedures to be followed when the House considers certain kinds of legislation, for example, the Congressional Budget and Impoundment Control Act of 1974. Such statutes are enacted as an exercise of the rule-making power of Congress, are reincorporated by reference in the preface of the resolution adopting the rules of each House and in clause 1 of rule XXIX, and are carried in the *House Rules and Manual. Manual* §§ 1127-1130; Deschler Ch 5 § 3.

Joint rules, although in common use until 1876, are rarely used today except to govern a joint session to count electoral votes. *Manual* § 220; Deschler Ch 10 § 2.6.

Rules Based on Precedent or Custom

As Asher Hinds noted in his work on the precedents of the House, much of what is known as parliamentary law is not part of the formal written rules of the House but springs from precedent or long-standing custom. 1 Hinds, Introduction, p iii. Such precedent may be invoked to resolve a procedural question in the absence of an express written rule on the subject. Deschler Ch 5 § 3; see also 6 Cannon, Preface, p v; Deschler, Preface, pp iii-xiv. More frequently, the precedents of the House are used to show the scope and application of one of its formal rules. A noteworthy example is the House germaneness rule, which is set forth very concisely in clause 7 of rule XVI, yet has been interpreted through thousands of precedents since its adoption in 1789. *Manual* §§ 928-940; Deschler-Brown Ch 28.

The precedents of the House, which are based primarily on the rulings of the Speaker or chair of the Committee of the Whole, are compiled in *Hinds' Precedents* (1907), *Cannon's Precedents* (1936), *Deschler's Precedents* (1977) and *Deschler-Brown Precedents*. *Deschler-Brown-Johnson Precedents*, which is currently being compiled, is authorized by 2 USC § 28b.

§ 2. Binding Effect

Parliamentary law—a term that encompasses both formal rules and usages—has come to be recognized as binding on the assembly and its members, except as it may be varied by the adoption by the membership of special rules or through some other authorized procedural device. *Landes* v. *State ex rel Matson*, 67 NE 189 (Ind. 1903).

On the theory that a government of laws is preferable to a government of men, the House has repeatedly recognized the importance of following its precedents and obeying its well-established procedural rules. See, *e.g.*, 2 Hinds § 1317. The House adheres to settled rulings, and will not lightly disturb procedures that have been established by prior decision of the Chair. Deschler, Preface, p vi. However, the Speaker or Chair may refuse to follow a precedent even though it is relevant to a pending question, where it is the only precedent on the point and was not carefully reasoned. 6 Cannon § 48.

§ 3. Construction

When a timely point of order is raised, it is the duty of the Chair to determine whether language in a pending measure conforms to the rules of the House, although the Chair may properly decline to do so where points of order against the provisions have been waived by a special order of business. Deschler Ch 21 § 23.3. In construing a rule, the Speaker may look beyond its terms and consider all the facts and circumstances in order to determine the intention of the House in adopting the rule. Deschler Ch 5 § 6.3. In construing the rules, the Chair may be guided by the general principle that the object of a parliamentary body is action, and not stoppage of action. *Manual* § 902.

The absence of a formal rule governing a particular procedure does not necessarily mean that the procedure is permitted. Indeed, acts or proceedings not expressly authorized by the rules may be deemed inconsistent with, or in violation of, the rules. Deschler Ch 5 § 6.4.

Where two rules of the House are in irreconcilable conflict, the one adopted later controls. Deschler Ch 5 § 6.1. Similarly, where the rules of the House and a subsequent legislative enactment are not consistent, the enactment must prevail. Deschler Ch 5 § 6.2. Similarly, a rule adopted after an enactment may supersede those provisions of the statute that would otherwise govern House procedure. Deschler Ch 5 § 6.

§ 4. Changing or Waiving Rules

Generally

Pursuant to its authority under article I, section 5 of the Constitution, the House may change or waive the rules governing its proceedings. 94-1, Mar. 20, 1975, p 7677; 95-1, Nov. 1, 1977, p 36310. This is so even with respect to rules enacted by statute. *Manual* § 857. Once the rules have been adopted at the convening of the House in a new Congress, further amendments to the rules are generally implemented by resolution reported from the Committee on Rules. A rule may in effect be suspended or modified through the use of certain procedural devices, such as a unanimous-consent request. Deschler Ch 5 § 5.

A motion to amend the rules of the House does not present a question of ''constitutional'' privilege. 8 Cannon § 3377. A question of the privileges of the House may not be invoked to effect a change in the rules of the House or their interpretation. *Manual* § 706; see generally QUESTIONS OF PRIVILEGE.

The effect of a proposed change in the rules or a proposed special order of business is a matter for debate and not within the jurisdiction of the Chair to decide on a parliamentary inquiry during its pendency. *Manual* § 628; Deschler Ch 5 § 5.12.

For the motion to suspend the rules, see SUSPENSION OF RULES.

By Resolution

Amendments to the rules are generally offered in the form of a privileged resolution reported and called up by the Committee on Rules. Such a resolution may not be amended unless the Member in charge yields for that purpose or the previous question is voted down. Deschler Ch 5 § 5.8. The resolution may be considered in the Committee of the Whole pursuant to the terms of a special order of business reported from the Committee on Rules. Deschler Ch 5 § 5.6.

Although a resolution from the Committee on Rules to amend a House rule is privileged, a resolution offered from the floor to amend a House rule is not privileged for consideration as against a demand that business proceed in the regular order. 8 Cannon § 3377; Deschler Ch 5 § 5.1.

Clause 2 of rule XV, the discharge rule, has also been used to bring a proposed rules change before the House. *Manual* § 892.

By Unanimous Consent

Minor changes in the standing rules may be considered by unanimous consent. Deschler Ch 5 § 5.2. The House may by unanimous consent waive the requirements of a particular rule unless the rule itself provides that it is not subject to waiver even by unanimous consent. See, *e.g.*, clause 7 of rule XVII.

By Special Order of Business

The House may adopt a special order of business from the Committee on Rules that has the effect of setting aside the standing rules of the House insofar as they impede the consideration of a particular bill. Deschler Ch 21 § 19.7. The special order of business may waive one or more—or indeed all—points of order against consideration of a particular bill or against provisions therein. For example, the special order of business may waive points of order that could otherwise be raised against legislative provisions in an appropriation bill, points of order based on the germaneness requirement, or points of order based on the Ramseyer rule. Deschler Ch 5 § 7. A rule that waives a point of order under section 425 of the Congressional Budget Act of 1974 (unfunded intergovernmental mandates) is itself subject to a point of order under section 426 of that Act. A rule that waives a point of order against earmarks (as provided for by clauses 9(a) and 9(b) of rule XXI) is not in order, and a point of order raised against such a rule is disposed of by the question of consideration, as provided by clause 9(c) of rule XXI. See BUDGET PROCESS; QUESTION OF CONSIDERATION.

A special order of business that ''self-executes'' the adoption of an amendment is not subject to a point of order that the amendment would otherwise be subject to because the amendment is not separately before the House during consideration of the special order of business. For example, a special order of business has been held not subject to points of order for ''self-executing'' an amendment that violated clause 7 of rule XVI (germaneness) (*Manual* § 928), clause 2 of rule XXI (legislation on an appropriation bill) (*Manual* § 1044), and clause 4 of rule XXI (appropriation on a legislative bill) (*Manual* § 1065).

For a full discussion of special orders of business, see SPECIAL ORDERS OF BUSINESS.

Chapter 51

Senate Bills; Amendments Between the Houses

I. Disposition of Senate Bills on the Speaker's Table

II. Senate Amendments

A. Before the Stage of Disagreement

B. Reaching the Stage of Disagreement

C. After the Stage of Disagreement; Motions

Research References

4 Hinds §§ 3090, 3108-3111, 4796-4808
5 Hinds §§ 6163-6253, 6308, 6310, 6324
6 Cannon § 730;
7 Cannon §§ 799, 819, 825;
8 Cannon §§ 3177-3208, 3211
Deschler-Brown Ch 32
Manual §§ 485-488, 519, 521-529, 873, 874, 1069-1076

I. Disposition of Senate Bills on the Speaker's Table

§ 1. In General

The House and Senate must agree on every detail of a bill before it can be enrolled and presented to the President. U.S. Const. art. 1, § 7. The inability of the two Houses to agree on even the slightest amendment to a bill causes the loss of the bill. 5 Hinds § 6233.

Senate bills and joint resolutions messaged from the Senate to the House go to the Speaker's table for disposition pursuant to clause 2 of rule XIV. Under this rule, Senate bills may be referred by the Speaker to the appropriate standing committees in the same manner as public bills introduced by the Members. *Manual* §§ 873, 874; see §§ 5, 6, infra. However, Senate bills and resolutions that are ''substantially the same'' as House measures favorably reported, and not required to be considered in the Committee of the Whole, may be disposed of in the House by motion authorized by the reporting committee. Clause 2 of rule XIV; see § 2, infra. Senate bills that do not satisfy the conditions specified by that rule may be called up under unanimous consent, suspension of the rules, or special order of business, but not by motion. 95-2, Feb. 23, 1978, p 4480; §§ 3, 4, infra. Simple resolutions of the Senate that do not require House action are not referred. 7 Cannon § 1048.

For a discussion of the House's prerogative to originate revenue-raising legislation with regard to Senate amendments, see QUESTIONS OF PRIVILEGE, § 5.

§ 2. By Motion

Generally

Under clause 2 of rule XIV, a Senate bill or resolution received in the House after a House measure "substantially the same" has been reported favorably and placed on the House Calendar or Private Calendar is privileged. It may be called up from the Speaker's table for consideration on motion directed by all reporting committees having initial jurisdiction of the House bill. *Manual* § 873; 4 Hinds §§ 3097, 3101, 3102; 6 Cannon §§ 727, 734. The fact that a House bill substantially the same as the Senate bill has already passed the House and gone to the Senate does not detract from the privilege of the Senate bill under the rule. 6 Cannon § 734. Under the modern practice, this rule is rarely used because few measures qualify (most bills and joint resolutions reported in the House are referred to the Union Calendar).

The motion to call up the Senate bill is not subject to the question of consideration but is subject to a point of order if the conditions specified by the rule are not satisfied. 8 Cannon § 2443. The prerequisites of the rule are:

- The Senate bill must be substantially the same as the House bill. 4 Hinds §§ 3098, 3099, 3107-3111; 6 Cannon § 737.
- The Senate bill must not require consideration in the Committee of the Whole, and, if private, must not involve an appropriation. 4 Hinds §§ 3101; 3102.
- The Senate bill must come to the House after the House bill is placed on the calendar. 4 Hinds § 3096; 6 Cannon § 738.
- The House bill must be on the House Calendar or Private Calendar (not the Union Calendar). 4 Hinds §§ 3089, 3097.
- Under clause 2 of rule XIV, all reporting committees having initial jurisdiction of the House measure must authorize the motion. *Manual* § 873.

In determining whether the House bill is substantially the same as the Senate bill, amendments recommended by the House committee must be considered. 6 Cannon §§ 734, 736. Although a committee must authorize the calling up of the Senate bill, the actual motion need not be offered by a member of the committee. 4 Hinds § 3100; 6 Hinds § 739. The authority of a committee to call up a bill must be given at a formal meeting of the committee. 8 Cannon §§ 2211, 2212.

Although the rule has been interpreted to apply to private Senate bills that do not involve an appropriation (4 Hinds § 3102), in modern practice Senate private bills on the Speaker's table are considered by unanimous consent during the call of the Private Calendar, whether they are substantially the same as a House-passed private bill or not.

Form

The Member authorized by the committee to call up the Senate bill rises and addresses the Chair:

> MEMBER: M__. Speaker, by direction of the Committee on __________, I call from the Speaker's table Senate bill S.____, H.R. ____, having been reported and placed on the House Calendar.
>
> SPEAKER: The gentle______ calls from the Speaker's table the bill S.____, which the Clerk will report.

Floor Consideration

Senate bills called up under this procedure are considered under the general rules of the House, the Member in charge being recognized for one hour. 6 Cannon § 738. The procedure is as follows:

- The bill is read in full.
- The Member in charge uses or allots the hour to which such Member is entitled.
- If the previous question is not moved at the expiration of the first hour, another Member may be recognized for an hour.

§ 3. By Unanimous Consent

A Senate measure may be taken from the Speaker's table and called up for consideration in the House by unanimous consent. Deschler-Brown Ch 32 §§ 3.4, 4.4, 4.5. Consideration in the House by unanimous consent is permitted even where the Senate measure ordinarily would require consideration in the Committee of the Whole. Deschler-Brown Ch 32 § 3.7.

A unanimous-consent request to consider a Senate bill on the Speaker's table may provide for its consideration in the House under the hour rule. It also may include a provision that a specified amendment be considered as pending. 97-2, Oct. 1, 1982, pp 27362, 27365-68.

The House also may agree to a unanimous-consent request to take a Senate bill from the Speaker's table and to strike all after the enacting clause and insert in lieu thereof certain text. Deschler-Brown Ch 32 § 3.4. For the Speaker's guidelines for recognition of a unanimous-consent request to consider a Senate measure on the Speaker's table, see *Manual* § 956 and RECOGNITION.

§ 4. By Special Order of Business

The House may adopt a resolution reported from the Committee on Rules that provides for consideration in the House of a Senate bill on the Speaker's table, even if the measure would otherwise require consideration in the Committee of the Whole. Deschler-Brown Ch 32 § 3.5.

The Committee on Rules may report a special order of business permitting consideration in the House of a Senate measure from the Speaker's table and preclude all intervening motions except, in the case of a bill or joint resolution, the motion to recommit as protected by clause 6(c) of rule XIII. Deschler Ch 21 § 27; see SPECIAL ORDERS OF BUSINESS.

§ 5. Referral to Committee

Under clause 2(b) of rule XIV, the Speaker has the discretion to refer Senate bills to committees in the same manner as public bills originating in the House (as described in clause 2 of rule XII) unless the Senate bills qualify for consideration under clause 2(d) of rule XIV. *Manual* §§ 873, 874; 6 Cannon § 727; § 2, supra. Simple resolutions from the Senate that do not require any action by the House are not referred. 7 Cannon § 1048.

§ 6. —Speaker's Discretion

It is the practice to refer promptly bills messaged from the Senate. Nevertheless, clause 2(b) of rule XIV is merely discretionary and not mandatory. *Manual* § 873; 4 Hinds § 3111. Furthermore, the length of time such bills may remain on the Speaker's table before being referred is within the Speaker's discretion. 6 Cannon § 727. Under the modern practice, the Speaker may hold a Senate bill at the table when a comparable House bill has been reported or ordered reported by a House committee or when the Senate measure violates a House rule (such as the rule against commemorations, clause 5 of rule XII) or the Constitution (such as the origination clause, article 1, section 7). For a discussion of referral of House bills with Senate amendments, see § 7, infra.

II. Senate Amendments
A. Before the Stage of Disagreement

§ 7. In General; Referral to Committee

Referrals by the Speaker

Senate amendments to House bills messaged from the Senate normally remain at the Speaker's table to be disposed of by unanimous consent, by special order of business, or by motion. However, before consideration of any motions to dispose of Senate amendments, the Speaker has the authority under clause 2 of rule XIV to refer such amendments to the appropriate committees and to impose any conditions permitted by clause 2 of rule XII, such as a time limitation for committee consideration. *Manual* §§ 528a, 873. For example, the Speaker may refer only a portion of the Senate amendment to the standing committee with subject matter jurisdiction, without referring the remainder of the Senate amendment to the committee with jurisdiction over the original House bill. Deschler-Brown Ch 32 § 5.29.

The Speaker may hold at the desk or refer Senate amendments that remain undisposed of after House action. For example, the Chair indicated that should a resolution providing for concurring in Senate amendments to a House bill be rejected, the bill and amendments would remain on the Speaker's table for further action by the House. Deschler-Brown Ch 32 § 5.45. Likewise, if objection is made to a unanimous-consent request to disagree to the amendments and agree to a conference, the Speaker is not required to send the bill and amendments directly to the committee having jurisdiction thereof. The Speaker may hold the bill on the table until the Committee on Rules has an opportunity to act or until the House takes other action. Deschler-Brown Ch 32 § 5.5.

Referrals By Motion

A motion to refer a Senate amendment that is under debate may be offered pursuant to clause 4 of rule XVI. *Manual* § 916. That motion takes precedence over the motions to agree, disagree, or amend. *Manual* § 528b; 5 Hinds §§ 6172-6174. Pursuant to clause 2 of rule XIX, the motion to refer is in order even after the previous question has been ordered on a motion to concur in the Senate amendment. However, a motion to commit under clause 2 does not apply to a motion to dispose of a Senate amendment after the stage of disagreement where the motion to commit is used to displace a pending preferential motion. *Manual* § 1002.

Referrals By Special Order of Business

A Senate amendment may be referred to a standing committee pursuant to the terms of a special order of business from the Committee on Rules. Deschler-Brown Ch 32 § 5.33.

§ 8. Consideration in the House

Under clause 2 of rule XXII, House bills with Senate amendments that do not require consideration in the Committee of the Whole may be disposed of by privileged motion. *Manual* § 1071. This rule is applied to Senate amendments to House amendments as well as to Senate amendments to House bills. Deschler-Brown Ch 32 § 6.1. This rule is rarely used because few measures qualify (most Senate amendments require consideration in the Committee of the Whole because they raise revenue or they directly or indirectly make appropriations of money or property). *Manual* § 528a.

§ 9. Consideration in Committee of the Whole

House bills with Senate amendments that require consideration in the Committee of the Whole may not be called up in the House as privileged for immediate consideration before the stage of disagreement. *Manual* § 528a; 6 Cannon § 731. The only exception is a motion to ask or agree to a conference under clause 1 of rule XXII. 4 Hinds §§ 3149, 3150; 8 Cannon §§ 3185, 3194. Reaching the stage of disagreement, see § 16, infra.

Under clause 3 of rule XXII, an amendment of the Senate to a House bill is subject to the point of order that it first must be considered in the Committee of the Whole if, originating in the House, it would be subject to that point of order. *Manual* §§ 1072-1074. The point of order permitted by this rule applies only before the stage of disagreement has been reached on the Senate amendment. It is too late to raise a point of order that Senate amendments should have been considered in Committee of the Whole after the House has disagreed thereto and the amendments have been reported from conference. *Manual* § 1073.

Because of these restrictions against immediate consideration of Senate amendments in the House, it was at one time common practice to refer such amendments to the appropriate standing committee. 6 Cannon § 731. After committee consideration, they were taken up in the Committee of the Whole. 4 Hinds §§ 3108, 3109. Under the modern practice, most Senate amendments are disposed of by a special order of business reported from the Committee on Rules, by unanimous consent, or under suspension of the rules. §§ 11-13, infra.

§ 10. Consideration by Order of the House

If the House agrees to a request to take up a Senate amendment before the stage of disagreement, and if the request specifies the disposition sought (to concur, to amend, or to disagree), only that action is in order. Such a special request does not place the Senate amendment before the House for any alternative disposition. If, on the other hand, a Senate amendment is placed before the House by unanimous consent or a special order of business merely "for consideration," various motions are in order in the following order of priority: to concur with an amendment, to concur, or to disagree. A motion to concur with an amendment can itself be amended, if the motion for the previous question is rejected, to propose another amendment. Similarly, where the House has adopted a special order of business providing for the consideration in the House of a motion to concur in Senate amendments that otherwise require consideration in the Committee of the Whole, only the motion to concur, made in order by the special order of business, is in order. Other motions to dispose of the Senate amendments may not be offered as privileged pending, or even after rejection, of that motion. The rejection of such a motion does not result in disagreement to that amendment or permit disposition of that amendment by other motions (the stage of disagreement not having been reached). Deschler-Brown Ch 32 § 5.34.

§ 11. —By Special Order of Business

Generally

Resolutions from the Committee on Rules may be used to authorize the consideration in the House of a motion to dispose of Senate amendments before the stage of disagreement that would otherwise require consideration in the Committee of the Whole. Such rules often authorize the chair of a designated committee to offer a specified motion to dispose of the Senate amendments. At this stage, the special order of business need not protect the motion to recommit because the bill is not at the stage of initial passage and thus clause 6(c) of rule XIII does not apply. *Manual* § 859.

If a motion for the previous question is voted down on a resolution providing for consideration of the Senate amendments, the resolution is open to germane amendment. Deschler Ch 21 § 27.18. If a resolution providing for concurring in Senate amendments to a House bill before the stage of disagreement is rejected, the bill and amendments remain on the Speaker's table for further action by the House. Deschler Ch 21 § 27.20.

‘‘Hereby’’ Special Orders of Business

On occasion the Committee on Rules has recommended a so-called ‘‘hereby’’ special order of business. Such a resolution, if adopted by the House, orders a disposition of a Senate amendment, often before the stage of disagreement. Such a resolution eliminates the need for a motion to dispose of the amendment. Such rule is sometimes referred to as a ‘‘hereby’’ special order because the House, in adopting the resolution as drafted, ‘‘hereby’’ agrees to the disposition of the amendment as proposed by that resolution. If the House adopts a resolution, no further action by the House is required. The amendment is never itself before the House for separate consideration. Deschler Ch 21 §§ 27.16, 27.19.

Special orders of this nature may include provisions for a motion to dispose of Senate amendments as well as ''hereby'' provisions applicable to a related proposition.

The adoption of a ''hereby'' resolution disposing of a Senate amendment obviates the requirement of consideration in Committee of the Whole under clause 3 of rule XXII that would otherwise apply. *Manual* § 1073.

Special Orders of Business and the Motion to Recommit

Clause 6 of rule XIII precludes the Committee on Rules from preventing a motion to recommit with instructions a bill or joint resolution on which the previous question has been ordered to passage. *Manual* § 857. Under that stricture, the Committee on Rules may not propose that the House ''hereby'' pass a bill or joint resolution or provide for initial passage thereof without intervening motion (unless it is the text of a previously House-passed measure).

§ 12. —By Unanimous Consent

Generally

Senate amendments may be considered in the House by unanimous consent, even though such amendments normally would require consideration in Committee of the Whole. Typically, the House will agree by unanimous consent to take from the Speaker's table a House bill with Senate amendments and concur in or otherwise dispose of the amendments or permit the consideration of those amendments in the House. Deschler-Brown Ch 32 § 5.7.

This procedure may be invoked to permit the House to consider a Senate amendment and concur therein with an amendment consisting of the text of a House-passed bill. 95-1, May 11, 1977, p 14390. In one instance, pursuant to a single unanimous-consent request, the House amended a Senate amendment with the text of another bill introduced in the House, insisted on the House amendment, and requested a conference. 97-2, Mar. 16, 1982, p 4227. In another instance, the House by unanimous consent made in order the consideration of a motion to disagree to *any* Senate amendment that might be added to a House-passed bill then pending in the Senate. Subsequently, pursuant to this authority, the House considered and adopted a motion disagreeing to a Senate amendment. 99-2, Aug. 15, 1986, p 22132.

Guidelines for Recognition

Recognition for unanimous consent to consider a Senate amendment on the Speaker's table may be subject to announced guidelines imposed by the Speaker as a precondition to such recognition. For example, the Speaker may indicate an intention to recognize only the chair or other authorized member of the committee with jurisdiction for such unanimous-consent requests. *Manual* § 956.

Form of Request as Affecting Votes

The pendency of a unanimous-consent request to take from the Speaker's table a measure with a Senate amendment and concur in the amendment precludes the necessity for a vote on the amendment because the amendment would be disposed of if the request is granted. Deschler-Brown Ch 32 §§ 5.11, 9.14. The failure of a Member to object to the unanimous-consent request constitutes final House action on the measure, thereby precluding a vote on the amendment. However, a unanimous-consent request invoked merely to consider a Senate amendment in the House permits a vote on a subsequent motion to concur in the Senate amendment. Deschler-Brown Ch 32 § 5.14.

§ 13. —By Suspension of the Rules

The House may consider a proposition, offered under suspension of the rules, taking a House bill with one or more Senate amendments from the Speaker's table and concurring in, disagreeing to, or making some other disposition of, the amendment(s). Deschler-Brown Ch 32 § 5.25.

A motion to suspend the rules and take a House bill with Senate amendments from the Speaker's table and concur in the amendments with a designated amendment may set forth the designated amendment in the text of a resolution. Under prior practice, the language of the designated amendment was included in the motion itself. 95-1, July 12, 1977, p 22483; Deschler-Brown Ch 32 § 5.22. The House also has agreed to a motion to suspend the rules and agree to a resolution whereby the House agreed to the Senate amendment with a further amendment, insisted on the House amendment, and requested a conference with the Senate. 98-2, Aug. 8, 1984, p 22963.

The suspension procedure in such cases does not require a resolution when the language to be voted on directly is in the Senate message and the House is not originating new language. For example, the House has agreed to a motion to suspend the rules and take from the Speaker's table a Senate bill with a Senate amendment to House amendments thereto, and to concur in the Senate amendment. 95-1, Oct. 18, 1977, pp 34086, 34087, 34091.

§ 14. —By Sending to Conference

House bills returned with Senate amendments requiring consideration in the Committee of the Whole may be taken from the Speaker's table and sent to conference by unanimous consent. 6 Cannon § 732. Such amendments also may be sent to conference by motion under the provisions of clause 1 of rule XXII if the House is in possession of the official papers. Deschler-Brown Ch 29 § 17.1. That rule provides that a motion to disagree with an amendment of the Senate to a House proposition and to request or agree to a conference with the Senate is always in order if the Speaker has chosen to recognize for that purpose and if the motion is made by direction of the committee having jurisdiction of the subject matter of the proposition. *Manual* §§ 1069, 1070. On a bill that has been referred to more than one committee, the motion must be authorized by the primary committee and all committees of initial referral reporting thereon. Under clause 2(a)(3) of rule XI, a committee may adopt a rule directing the chair to offer such a motion whenever the chair considers it appropriate. A committee of sequential referral need not authorize a motion made by direction of the committee that reported the bill. *Manual* § 1070; see generally CONFERENCES BETWEEN THE HOUSES.

While a privileged motion to go to conference under clause 1 of rule XXII is pending, preferential motions to concur or to concur with amendment are not in order (the stage of disagreement not having been reached). Deschler-Brown Ch 32 § 5.

§ 15. Motions; Precedence Before Stage of Disagreement

The stage of disagreement not having been reached on a Senate amendment, motions in the House to dispose of the amendment are not privileged and require unanimous consent or a special order of business from the Committee on Rules, the only exception being a motion to ask or agree to a conference under clause 1 of rule XXII. Deschler-Brown Ch 32 § 5.34. However, if a Senate amendment is considered pursuant to an order of the House that does not specify the motion to be considered, the amendment may then be disposed of by invoking one of the motions shown in Chart No. 1 (§ 16, infra). Such motions are available in the specified sequence and are arranged in order of precedence. *Manual* § 528b.

The relative preference of motions at this stage favors allowing the House to perfect the amendment; that is, to first consider any amendments to the Senate amendment before considering whether to agree or disagree to it. Thus, at this stage, the motion to concur with an amendment takes precedence over the motion to concur. *Manual* § 528b. These motions yield to the motion under clause 1 of rule XXII to disagree and send to conference, which must be made by direction of the pertinent committees.

A motion in the House to dispose of a Senate amendment to a House bill is itself subject to the secondary motions ordinarily applicable to any question that is under debate—to table, to postpone to a day certain, to refer, and to amend—all of which remain privileged under clause 4 of rule XVI, the last three yielding to the motion for the previous question. *Manual* § 528b. Thus, an amendment to a motion to concur in a Senate amendment with an amendment may not be offered unless the Member having the floor yields for that purpose, or unless a motion for the previous question on the motion is defeated. Deschler-Brown Ch 32 § 11.20.

Where a motion to recede and concur in an amendment reported from conference in disagreement is divided on demand, and the House votes to recede, the motion to concur with an amendment may be offered as preferential to the motion to concur (the House having retreated from the stage of disagreement). 95-2, Oct. 5, 1978, p 33698. If the motion to concur with an amendment is rejected, the question recurs on the original proposal to concur in the Senate amendment. Deschler-Brown Ch 32 § 9.16. On rejection of a motion to concur in a pending Senate amendment, a motion to concur with an amendment or a motion to disagree is in order. Deschler-Brown Ch 32 § 9.17.

A motion to concur in a Senate amendment with an amendment (before the stage of disagreement) is not subject to a demand for a division of the question. 8 Cannon § 3176. Divisibility after the stage of disagreement, see §§ 20, 21, infra.

B. Reaching the Stage of Disagreement

§ 16. In General

Reaching the stage of disagreement is a critical threshold in the disposition of amendments between the Houses. Before the stage of disagreement is reached on Senate amendments, motions in the House to dispose of amendments that require consideration in Committee of the Whole are not privileged and require unanimous consent unless other action is made in order by a special order of business or by the prescription in clause 1 of rule XXII, relating to motions to ask or agree to a conference. §§ 8, 11, 15, supra. After the stage of disagreement has been reached, motions in the

House to resolve the matter in disagreement are privileged and do not require unanimous consent for their consideration. § 17, infra. The stage of disagreement having been reached, a bill with Senate amendments may be called up as privileged when the House is in possession of the papers. 8 Cannon § 3194.

Whether the House has reached the stage of disagreement also is important in determining the kinds of motions that may be sought and the precedence thereof. These motions (*Manual* § 528) are shown in Chart No. 1 and are listed in preferential order.

MOTIONS TO DISPOSE OF SENATE AMENDMENTS

SENATE AMENDMENT

Motions before the stage of disagreement	Motions after the stage of disagreement
1. Concur with amendment(s)	1. Recede and concur
2. Concur	2. Recede and concur with amendment(s)
3. Disagree and request or agree to conference	3. Insist on disagreement and request or agree to a (further) conference
4. Disagree	4. Insist on disagreement
	5. Adhere

Chart No. 1.

The stage of disagreement between the two Houses is reached when the House has either disagreed to the Senate amendments or has insisted on its own amendments to a Senate measure and has messaged that action to the Senate. *Manual* §§ 528a, 1074. For example, where the House concurred in a Senate amendment to a House bill with an amendment, insisted on the amendment, and requested a conference, and the Senate then concurred in the House amendment with a further amendment, the matter was privileged in the House for further disposition because the House had communicated its insistence and request for a conference to the Senate. *Manual* § 1074.

The House has reached the stage of disagreement on a bill when it has disagreed to a Senate amendment or insisted on a House amendment (with or without requesting or agreeing to a conference) and has informed the Senate of its action by message. Only previous insistence or disagreement by the House itself (and not merely disagreement, insistence, or amendment by the Senate) places the House in disagreement. *Manual* §§ 528a, 528c; Deschler-Brown Ch 32 § 7.5.

Once the stage of disagreement has been reached on a bill with amendments, the House remains in the stage of disagreement until the matter is finally disposed of, and motions for its disposition are privileged whenever the House is in possession of the papers. This principle applies both where the stage of disagreement is reached without a conference, and where matters remain in disagreement after conferees have reported. *Manual* § 528c. Where a Senate amendment reported from conference in disagreement remains in disagreement following subsequent action by the House and the Senate, a further motion to dispose of that Senate amendment in the House is privileged under clause 4 of rule XXII and subject to one hour of debate. *Manual* § 1075.

C. After the Stage of Disagreement; Motions

§ 17. In General; Privilege of Motions

Under clause 4 of rule XXII, once the stage of disagreement has been reached and the House is in possession of the papers, motions in the House to resolve the matter in disagreement are privileged and no longer require unanimous consent for their consideration. Deschler-Brown Ch 32 § 7.3. For example, the House having disagreed to a Senate amendment and the Senate having insisted thereon, motions to dispose of the matter in disagreement are privileged for consideration in the House.

Once the stage of disagreement has been reached between the two Houses on an amendment, motions in the House to dispose of the matter at subsequent permissible stages of amendment remain privileged. For example, where the House concurred in a Senate amendment to a House bill with an amendment, insisted on the House amendment and requested a conference, and the Senate then concurred in the House amendment with a further amendment, the matter was privileged for further disposition in the

House because the stage of disagreement had been reached. Deschler-Brown Ch 32 § 7.5.

§ 18. Motions in Order; Precedence of Motions

Generally

The stage of disagreement having been reached on a Senate amendment, the amendment is subject to disposition in the House by various motions. The primary motions to dispose of the amendment, arranged in preferential order, are shown in Chart No. 1 (§ 16, supra). *Manual* § 528d. These motions have precedence in the order shown without regard to the order in which they might be offered. 5 Hinds § 6324. A demand for the previous question by the Member in charge of a bill does not preclude consideration of a preferential motion to dispose of the amendment in disagreement. 8 Cannon § 3204.

In theory, once at the stage of disagreement, preferential status is accorded to a motion that tends most directly to bring the Houses into agreement. 8 Cannon § 3204; Deschler-Brown Ch 32 § 7.8. Thus, the stage of disagreement having been reached, a motion to recede and concur takes precedence over a motion to recede and concur with an amendment and a motion to insist on disagreement, because the motion to recede and concur most promptly tends to bring the two Houses together. *Manual* § 528d.

For a discussion of the preferential status of a motion to insist on disagreement to a Senate amendment reported from conference in disagreement, where the original motion to dispose of the matter portends legislation on an appropriation bill within the jurisdiction of another committee, see clause 8(b)(3) of rule XXII; *Manual* § 1084; CONFERENCES BETWEEN THE HOUSES. Where the matter in disagreement is a House amendment, see § 29, infra.

Secondary Motions

Secondary motions applicable when any question is under debate, such as the motion to table, to refer, or to postpone, are available to dispose of a Senate amendment and are in order when preferential. *Manual* § 911. The motion to table a Senate amendment in disagreement is preferential over other motions to dispose of the amendment. § 19, infra. The motion to refer a Senate amendment is preferential only to the motion to adhere to disagreement. *Manual* § 528d. A motion to recommit with instructions to report back forthwith with an amendment may not be offered after the previous question has been ordered on a motion to recede and concur, a motion of higher privilege. *Manual* § 1002; Deschler-Brown Ch 32 § 7.5. Motions to postpone, either to a day certain or indefinitely, may be presumed to have the lowest privilege with respect to a Senate amendment after the stage of disagreement has been reached. *Manual* § 528d.

§ 19. — To Lay on the Table

The stage of disagreement having been reached, a motion to table a Senate amendment to a House bill is in order and takes precedence over other motions to dispose of the amendment, including the motion to insist on disagreement. Adoption of a motion to table the amendment carries the bill to the table. *Manual* § 528d; 5 Hinds §§ 5424, 6201-6203; Deschler-Brown Ch 32 § 7.22.

Laying on the table a motion to dispose of a Senate amendment should be distinguished from the tabling of the Senate amendment itself. *Manual* §§ 528d, 914. A privileged motion to dispose of a Senate amendment in disagreement is itself subject to the motion to table. *Manual* § 519. Thus, a motion to recede and concur is subject to the motion to table (Deschler-Brown Ch 32 § 7.27), as is the motion to recede and concur with an amendment (Deschler-Brown Ch 32 § 7.26). A motion to table a privileged motion to dispose of an amendment between the Houses is in order before debate thereon or at the end of debate (and before the previous question is ordered). *Manual* § 914; 5 Hinds §§ 5393-5395.

Adoption of a motion to table a motion to dispose of an amendment represents final adverse disposition of that motion at that stage of the question, but would not necessarily dispose of the amendment or the bill, because other motions could still be available to dispose of the amendment. See Deschler-Brown Ch 32 § 7.10.

§ 20. — To Recede and Concur

In General

After the stage of disagreement has been reached, a motion to recede and concur is highly preferential, yields only to a motion to table (§ 19, supra), and takes precedence over:

- A motion to recede and concur with an amendment. 8 Cannon §§ 3198, 3202.
- A motion to insist on disagreement. 5 Hinds § 6208; 8 Cannon § 3194.
- A motion to disagree (or insist) and request a conference. *Manual* § 528d.
- A motion to adhere. 5 Hinds § 6271.

A motion to recede and concur is in order even after a motion for the previous question has been demanded on a motion of lesser privilege, such as a motion to insist. 5 Hinds § 6208.

If the House agrees to the motion to recede and concur, other less preferential motions to dispose of the amendment fall and are not voted upon. Deschler-Brown Ch 32 § 10.25. However, if the House rejects the motion to recede and concur, further action must be taken to dispose of the amendment. *Manual* § 488. If the motion to recede and concur in the Senate amendment is defeated, a further motion relating to the amendment in disagreement is in order. Deschler-Brown Ch 32 § 10.27. If a motion to insist on disagreement to the Senate amendment was pending, the question would recur on that motion. Deschler-Brown Ch 32 § 10.28.

Dividing the Question

The question on a motion to recede and concur in a Senate amendment may be divided on demand of any Member. 8 Cannon § 3203. The division may be demanded as a matter of right under clause 5 of rule XVI. *Manual* § 921. The House does not vote on whether to permit a division of the question. Deschler-Brown Ch 32 § 10.11.

If the question on receding and concurring is divided before the ordering of the previous question, the hour rule for debate applies to each motion separately. See Deschler-Brown Ch 32 §§ 8.1, 10.13.

If the question has been divided and the motion to recede is agreed to, then the question of concurring is before the House. Deschler-Brown Ch 32 § 10.20. However, the House having receded, it is no longer in the stage of disagreement with the Senate on that amendment, and in that event a motion to amend takes precedence over the motion to concur. 5 Hinds §§ 6209, 6210; 8 Cannon § 3198. Thus, where a motion to recede and concur has been divided, and the House recedes, a motion to concur with an amendment then takes precedence over the motion to concur, is considered as pending if part of the original motion, and is voted on first. *Manual* § 528d; 95-2, Oct. 5, 1978, p 33698-701.

§ 21. —To Recede and Concur With Amendment

A Senate amendment in disagreement is subject to disposition in the House pursuant to a motion to recede from disagreement and concur in the amendment with an amendment. See, *e.g.*, 97-1, May 20, 1981, p 10319. This motion ordinarily yields to the motion to recede and concur but takes precedence over the motion to insist and over the motion to adhere. *Manual* § 528d; 5 Hinds §§ 6219-6223; 8 Cannon §§ 3200, 3202.

A motion to recede and concur with an amendment is subject to amendment if the motion for the previous question is voted down or if the Member in control of the floor yields for that purpose. Deschler-Brown Ch 32 §§ 11.19, 11.21. Where one motion to recede and concur with an amendment is rejected, another motion to recede and concur with a different amendment may be offered. Deschler-Brown Ch 32 § 11.12.

A motion to recede from disagreement to a Senate amendment and concur therein with an amendment may, on demand of any Member, be divided to permit separate votes; the House votes first on the motion to recede, and (if the House does recede) then on the motion to concur with an amendment. 94-1, Oct. 7, 1975, p 32064; 99-1, Nov. 1, 1985, pp 30147, 30163. If the House refuses to recede, the motion to further insist is in order. § 22, infra.

§ 22. — To Insist

A Senate amendment in disagreement may be disposed of pursuant to a motion to insist on disagreement or a compound motion to insist on disagreement and request a (further) conference. Because the motion to insist on disagreement and request a conference is more likely to bring the two Houses together, that motion takes precedence over the simple motion to insist. *Manual* § 528d. Where both Houses insist and neither House asks for a conference or recedes, the bill fails. 5 Hinds § 6228.

A motion to insist on disagreement to a Senate amendment yields to preferential motions, such as a motion to recede and concur in the amendment but takes precedence over the motion to refer. 5 Hinds § 6225; 8 Cannon § 3183. A motion to insist on disagreement and request a further conference is not in order so long as preferential motions to dispose of amendments in disagreement are pending. Deschler-Brown Ch 33 § 29.50.

The motion to insist on disagreement is in order and most commonly used after the House has refused to recede from disagreement to a Senate amendment. See, *e.g.*, Deschler-Brown Ch 32 §§ 12.2, 12.9. Thus where the House refuses to recede from its disagreement to a Senate amendment—the motion to recede and concur having been divided on demand of a Member—the motion to insist on disagreement is in order. Deschler-Brown Ch 32 § 12.10. Underlying these precedents is the reasoning that because the refusal of the House to recede is not equivalent to insisting upon disagreement, the House may vote separately on that question pursuant to the motion to insist on disagreement. Deschler-Brown Ch 32 § 12.8.

A motion to insist on disagreement and request a further conference may be in order after the rejection of a conference report or after the conference managers have reported a Senate amendment in disagreement. Deschler-Brown Ch 32 §§ 11.13, 12.13. For example, on rejection of a motion to recede and concur in a Senate amendment with an amendment, the manager may be recognized to offer a motion that the House insist on its disagreement to the amendment. 96-1, May 23, 1979, p 12489. Where a motion to recede and concur with an amendment to an amendment reported in disagreement from conference has been divided, and the motion to recede is rejected, the manager is entitled to recognition to offer a motion to insist on disagreement. 94-1, Sept. 24, 1975, pp 30081, 30082.

Rejection of a motion to insist on disagreement to a Senate amendment is not tantamount to concurrence. Further action is required to dispose of the Senate amendment. Indeed, a motion to insist having been rejected, the same Member who had offered the motion may be recognized, absent recognition of another Member, to offer a motion to recede and concur. Deschler-Brown Ch 32 § 12.8. Similarly, the rejection of a motion to recede and concur is not equivalent to the adoption of a motion that the House insist on disagreement. Deschler-Brown Ch 32 § 12.5.

Under clause 8(b)(3) of rule XXII, a motion to insist on disagreement to a Senate amendment to a general appropriation bill reported in disagreement by a conference committee is preferential and separately debatable if the original motion to dispose of the Senate amendment proposes to change existing law and the motion to insist is timely offered by the chair of a committee of jurisdiction or a designee. Under clause 8(b)(3), the previous question is considered as ordered on such motion to its adoption without intervening motion. *Manual* § 1084.

§ 23. —To Refer to Committee

A Senate amendment in disagreement may be disposed of pursuant to a motion to refer (or recommit) to committee when and if such motion is preferential. The simple motion to refer is preferential only to the motion to adhere. *Manual* § 528d. The motion to refer must yield to motions of higher preferential status, such as the motion to recede and concur and the motion to insist. 5 Hinds § 6225; 8 Cannon § 3259. A motion to recommit with instructions may be offered, but it too must yield to preferential motions to dispose of the amendment. Thus, a motion to recommit with instructions to report back forthwith with an amendment may not be offered after the previous question has been ordered on a motion to recede and concur, a motion of higher privilege. *Manual* § 1002; Deschler-Brown Ch 32 § 7.5. However, after the House has receded from disagreement to a Senate amendment, a motion to amend is preferential, so that, after the previous question is ordered on a motion to concur, a motion to recommit with instructions to amend would be in order. 8 Cannon § 2744.

§ 24. —To Adhere

Where the House has expressed its disagreement to a Senate amendment and the amendment remains in disagreement after a Senate response thereto, a motion that the House adhere to its disagreement is in order. See, *e.g.*, 5 Hinds § 6239. The motion to adhere is rarely used in modern practice, but when both Houses have insisted, neither inclining to recede, it is in order. This motion yields to motions of higher precedence, such as the motion to recede and concur and the motion to insist. *Manual* § 528d; 5 Hinds § 6324. When both Houses adhere, the bill fails, even though the disagreement may be over a very minor amendment. 5 Hinds §§ 6163, 6233-6240, 6313, 6324, 6325.

The adoption of a motion of higher preferential status—to recede from disagreement to the amendment—precludes a motion to adhere to the same amendment. However, the House may recede from its disagreement to certain amendments and adhere to it as to other amendments to the same bill. 5 Hinds § 6229; for adherence to House amendments, see § 29, infra.

Adherence is to be distinguished from insistence in that adherence represents an uncompromising position and may not be accompanied by a request for a conference. The House that votes to adhere does not ask for a conference, although it may agree to one, whereas the other House may vote to insist and, at the same time, seek a conference. 5 Hinds §§ 6241, 6308. One House, having adhered, may recede from its adherence and agree to a conference asked by the other, or it may vote to further adhere. 5 Hinds § 6251.

§ 25. Debate; Recognition

Debate in the House on a privileged motion to dispose of a Senate amendment in disagreement is under the hour rule. Deschler-Brown Ch 32 § 8.1. Under clause 8(d) of rule XXII, when an amendment is reported from conference in disagreement, the Speaker recognizes the manager of the report for a motion to dispose of the amendment. The motion is debatable for one hour, equally divided between the majority and minority parties. Pursuant to clause 8(d)(2) of rule XXII, if the floor managers for both parties support the conference report, a Member opposed may claim one-third of the time for debate. See CONFERENCES BETWEEN THE HOUSES. The equal division of debate between the majority and minority parties under clause 8(d) technically applies only to conference reports and to motions to dispose of amendments reported from conference in disagreement and does not apply to the Member offering the initial motion to dispose of an amendment in disagreement that has not been reported from conference but that is subsequently before the House. Deschler-Brown Ch 32 § 7.4. However, the current practice in the House is to divide the time in this fashion on all motions to dispose of amendments still in disagreement following a conference. *Manual* § 1086.

Although a motion to dispose of the amendment in disagreement may be displaced by a preferential motion, the Member offering the preferential motion does not thereby gain control of time for debate. Deschler-Brown Ch 33 § 29.12. For example, although the motion to concur in a Senate amendment takes precedence over the motion to disagree where the stage of disagreement has been reached, the Member offering the preferential motion does not thereby gain control of the time for debate, which remains in the control of the proponent of the original motion under the hour rule. Deschler-Brown Ch 32 § 7.14. Similar rules are applied to amendments reported from conference in disagreement; that is, the proponent of the preferential motion does not thereby gain control of the time for debate. Deschler-Brown Ch 32 § 8.1.

Although the manager of a conference report is entitled to prior recognition to offer motions to dispose of amendments in disagreement, such individual is not entitled to offer two motions, one preferential to the other, to be pending at the same time. However, where the first motion to insist on disagreement has been superseded by a preferential motion to recede and concur, then the initial motion is no longer pending. When the House votes to recede on the first portion of that divided question, the manager may be recognized to offer another motion to concur with an amendment, which would be preferential to the remaining proposal to concur. Deschler-Brown Ch 32 § 8.2. This is to be contrasted with the situation where the bill manager offers a motion to dispose of a Senate amendment that is rejected by the House. In that case, recognition to offer a subsequent motion to dispose of the pending Senate amendment shifts to a Member who led the opposition to the rejected motion. See *Manual* § 954.

§ 26. Disposition of Nongermane Senate Provisions

Under clause 10 of rule XXII, points of order may be made and separate votes demanded on motions to reject portions of conference reports and Senate amendments in disagreement containing language that would not have been germane if offered in the House. Clause 10 permits points of order against language in a conference report that was originally in a Senate bill and that would not have been germane if offered to the House-passed version, and permits a separate motion to reject such portion of the conference report if found nongermane. *Manual* §§ 931, 1089, 1090. Clause 10 permits a similar procedure if a Senate amendment or portion thereof would have been nongermane if offered in the House. Motions to reject under these clauses are subject to 40 minutes of debate, equally divided between a proponent and an opponent of the motion. *Manual* §§ 1089, 1090; see GERMANENESS. Under the modern practice, conference reports are considered pursuant to a special order of business that waives all points of order against the conference report and its consideration, including clause 10 of rule XXII.

III. House Amendments to Senate Measures

§ 27. In General; Degree of Amendment

A Senate bill may be subject to amendment by the House when the bill is called up in the House pursuant to a unanimous-consent request or a motion authorized by a special order of business from the Committee on Rules. §§ 2-4, supra. A Senate amendment to a House measure also is subject to amendment by the House. The motion to concur with an amendment is in order before the stage of disagreement, and the motion to recede and concur with an amendment is in order after the stage of disagreement. §§ 15, 21, supra. As pointed out elsewhere, however, an amendment to an amendment to an amendment is in the third degree and not in order absent unanimous consent, suspension of the rules, or a special order of business providing such procedure. See AMENDMENTS. This rule governs the two Houses, according to *Jefferson's Manual*, and is applicable to amendments between the Houses, as shown in Chart No. 2. *Manual* § 529.

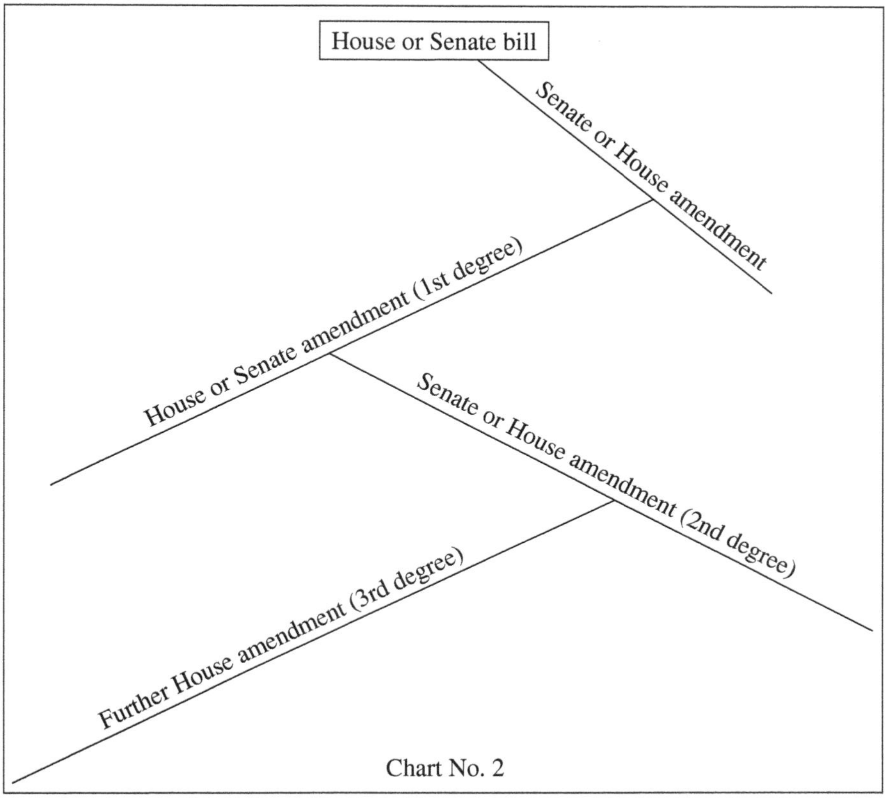

Chart No. 2

Where a bill of one House is amended by the other, the originating House may respond with an amendment, and the second House may offer an amendment to that amendment, but there the process stops; any further amendment is in the third degree and not in order. 5 Hinds § 6163. An amendment of one House being amended by the other, the first amending House may amend the last amendment, but further amendment is not permissible. 5 Hinds §§ 6176-6178. Thus, where a Senate amendment to a House bill has been reported in disagreement, and a House amendment thereto is amended by a further Senate amendment, motions in the House to agree or disagree to the Senate amendment to the House amendment are in order, but a motion to concur with a further amendment would be in the third degree and not in order. Deschler-Brown Ch 32 § 6.4. Likewise, where there is pending in the House a motion to amend a Senate amendment to a House amendment to a Senate bill, and the House adopts the motion, the Senate may then either concur in or disagree to the House amendment, but a further Senate amendment would be in the third degree. 94-1, Dec. 15,

1975, pp 40711, 40712. However, a conference report recommending amendments at this stage is not subject to a point of order that the amendments are in the third degree.

The House may consider a third-degree amendment by unanimous consent, under suspension of the rules, or pursuant to a special order of business from the Committee on Rules. Unanimous-consent requests have been used to seek consideration of amendments in the fourth or fifth degree. 99-2, Mar. 20, 1986, p 5796. If the House adopts an amendment pursuant to such a procedure, the Senate may consider itself no longer bound by Jefferson's proscription against third-degree amendments and amend further.

§ 28. Germaneness Requirements

An amendment offered in the House to a Senate amendment (that merely inserts new matter and does not strike House provisions) must ordinarily be germane to the particular Senate amendment to which it is offered, its germaneness to the provisions of the bill being insufficient. *Manual* § 931; 5 Hinds § 6188. The test of germaneness of an amendment in the nature of a substitute to a Senate amendment—proposed in a motion to concur therein with an amendment—is the relationship between the proposed amendment in its entirety and the Senate amendment (and not the relationship between any one provision of the amendment and any one provision of the Senate amendment). *Manual* § 931. A special order of business may waive the germaneness requirement. See, *e.g.*, 106-2, Sept. 27, 2000, p 19708.

A motion to recede and concur in a Senate amendment with an amendment must be germane to the Senate amendment. Deschler-Brown Ch 28 § 27.1. However, where a Senate amendment proposes to strike language in a House bill, the test of the germaneness of a motion to recede and concur with an amendment is the relationship between the language in the motion and the provisions in the House bill proposed to be stricken by the Senate amendment, as well as to the matter to be inserted by the Senate amendment. Deschler-Brown Ch 28 § 27.9.

Clause 10 of rule XXII permits points of order against portions of motions to concur or concur with amendment in nongermane Senate amendments, the stage of disagreement having been reached. If such points of order are sustained, the rule permits separate motions to reject such nongermane matter. *Manual* §§ 1089-1091; for more comprehensive discussion, see GERMANENESS OF AMENDMENTS.

§ 29. Amending House-passed Amendments; Receding, Insisting, Adhering

Generally

Jefferson reasoned that, although the House may modify an amendment from the Senate, the House cannot amend its own amendment ''because they have, on the question, passed it in that form.'' *Manual* § 526. Thus, although the House may recede from or insist on its own amendment, it may not couple an amendment with such an action. 5 Hinds § 6163. Indeed, few motions are available to enable the House to act on its own amendment to a Senate measure. These motions (*Manual* § 528b), which are used primarily when the Senate has disagreed to the House amendment, are as follows:

- To recede.
- To insist and request or agree to a conference.
- To insist.
- To adhere.

These motions have precedence in the House in the order named without regard to the order in which they might be offered. 5 Hinds § 6324. Accordingly, the Senate having disagreed to a House amendment, the House may recede from or insist on its own amendment. When both Houses have insisted, neither inclining to recede, it is in order to adhere. 5 Hinds § 6163.

Receding

The House may recede from its own amendment to a Senate bill by motion or by unanimous consent. *Manual* § 524; Deschler-Brown Ch 32 §§ 10.3, 10.5. If the House recedes from its own amendment, the bill is passed unamended, unless the Senate has concurred in the House amendment with a Senate amendment. Deschler-Brown Ch 32 § 10. If the House recedes from its amendment to a Senate amendment, further House action is in order: the House may either concur in the Senate amendment or amend it. *Manual* § 528d.

The stage of disagreement having been reached on a House amendment to a Senate amendment to a House proposition, the House may recede from its amendment and, having receded, may then concur in the Senate amendment with a different amendment (and such separate actions are not tantamount to the House's receding from its own amendment with an amendment as proscribed by *Jefferson's Manual*). *Manual* § 526. Of course, where the House has previously concurred in a Senate amendment with an amendment, the House does not, merely by receding from its amendment, concur in the Senate amendment. *Manual* § 524.

Insisting

The motion to insist on a House amendment yields to the motion to recede therefrom. 5 Hinds § 6270. However, where both Houses insist and neither asks for a conference or recedes, the bill fails. 5 Hinds § 6228.

The compound motion to insist on a House amendment and request or agree to a conference takes precedence over simple motions to insist or to adhere. Preferential status is accorded to the compound motion because of the greater likelihood that it will resolve the differences between the two Houses. *Manual* § 528b.

Adhering

Although it has been permitted, adherence before the stage of disagreement has been extremely rare and is used infrequently under the modern practice, even after the stage of disagreement. 5 Hinds § 6303. The motion to adhere to an amendment is the least-privileged motion, yielding to the motion to recede and the motion to insist. In addition, the ordinary motions applicable to any question that is under debate—to table, to postpone to a day certain, and to refer—remain privileged under clause 4 of rule XVI. *Manual* § 528b.

It has been held that after the previous question has been moved on a motion to adhere, a motion to recede may not be offered. 5 Hinds § 6310.

Effect of Adherence; Adherence as Related to Conferences

When both Houses adhere—one House adhering to its amendment and the other to its disagreement therewith—the bill fails. 5 Hinds §§ 6163, 6313, 6325. Adherence is to be distinguished from insistence in that adherence represents an uncompromising position and may not even be accompanied by a request for a conference. 5 Hinds § 6308. However, one House, having adhered, may recede from its adherence and agree to a conference asked by the other, or it may vote to further adhere. 5 Hinds § 6251. Conferences often have been asked and granted where only one House has adhered. 5 Hinds §§ 6241-6244.

Chapter 52
Special Orders of Business

Research References
4 Hinds §§ 3152-3265
7 Cannon §§ 758-845
Deschler Ch 21 §§ 16-19
Manual §§ 734, 855, 857-859

§ 1. In General

Jurisdiction and Authority

A resolution that specifies the manner in which a measure is to be taken up and the procedures to be followed during its consideration is called a ''special order of business'' or ''special rule.'' Such a resolution, once adopted by the House, gives privilege to the measure to be considered. Deschler Ch 21 § 16. The Committee on Rules has jurisdiction to report such resolutions under clause 1(o) of rule X. *Manual* § 733. By adoption of a special order of business by majority vote, the House establishes the parameters of its agenda on an ad hoc basis. Special orders of business are distinct from ''special-order speeches,'' which are discussed in CONSIDERATION AND DEBATE.

Because of the wide diversity of their use in the legislative process, special orders of business are discussed in many other chapters in this work. Measures not taken up under a special order of business may be taken up by unanimous consent or considered under suspension of the rules or are privileged in their own right under other standing rules or statutes.

Restrictions on Authority of the Committee on Rules

The broad power of the Committee on Rules to report resolutions varying the order of business or providing a special order is expressly restricted by clause 6(c) of rule XIII, which protects the motion to recommit. *Manual*

§ 857. The restriction relating to the motion to recommit, which is considered a fundamental prerogative of the minority, preserves the opportunity to include proper instructions in the motion to recommit a bill or joint resolution as described in clause 2(b) of rule XIX. *Manual* § 857.

In the 104th Congress, the restriction relating to the motion to recommit was extended to prohibit the Committee on Rules from recommending a rule or order that would prevent a motion by the Minority Leader or a designee to recommit a bill or joint resolution with instructions to report back an amendment otherwise in order, except in the case of a Senate bill or joint resolution for which the text of a House-passed measure is being substituted. *Manual* § 857. For a discussion of the restriction before it was extended to include amendatory instructions, see *Manual* § 859. In the 111th Congress, clause 2 of rule XIX was amended to provide that the instructions contained in the motion to recommit a bill or joint resolution must direct the committee to report amendment(s) back to the House "forthwith" (resulting in the amendment(s) being immediately before the House for consideration). For more on the motion to recommit, see REFER AND RECOMMIT; see also *Manual* § 1002b.

A special order of business providing for consideration of a bill under suspension of the rules does not violate clause 6 of rule XIII because no motion to recommit is available under suspension. *Manual* § 859; 8 Cannon § 2267.

Section 425 of the Congressional Budget Act of 1974 precludes consideration of a measure imposing Federal intergovernmental mandates above a specified threshold amount. *Manual* § 1127; 2 USC § 658e(a). Section 426 precludes the consideration of a special order of business that waives points of order under section 425 of the Congressional Budget Act. However, this restriction is "enforced" by a Member raising a point of order against the rule and then the House disposing of the question of consideration on the rule. The attention of the House is thus focused on the waiver. After limited debate, the House may decide to proceed with consideration of the rule. See UNFUNDED MANDATES.

In similar fashion, clause 9 of rule XXI establishes a point of order against consideration of certain measures for failure to disclose (or disclaim the presence of) certain earmarks, tax benefits, and tariff benefits, and permits a vote on the question of consideration of a rule waiving such a point of order. See BUDGET PROCESS.

Application to Various Measures

The privilege of the Committee on Rules to report special orders of business extends to special orders for the consideration of individual bills or classes of bills or the consideration of a specified amendment to a bill and the prescription of a mode of considering such amendment. 5 Hinds § 6774; 8 Cannon § 2258; see § 6, infra.

Customarily, a committee that has reported, or has jurisdiction over, a measure requests the Committee on Rules to provide a special order of business for its consideration. However, the Committee on Rules also may provide for consideration of an unreported bill (the adoption of the resolution discharges the committees to which the bill was referred). 8 Cannon § 2259; Deschler Ch 21 §§ 16.15-16.17; 93-2, Oct. 17, 1974, p 36020. It may even provide for the consideration of a bill that has not yet been introduced or permit consideration of a measure that comes into existence by virtue of adoption by the House of the special order of business. *Manual* § 855; 8 Cannon § 3388. For example, it may provide for consideration of a joint resolution originated upon adoption of the special order of business consisting of the text of a Senate-passed joint resolution identical to a measure previously rejected by the House under a separate statutory approval procedure. 99-2, Apr. 15, 1986, p 7531.

The Committee on Rules also may recommend a ''hereby'' resolution that provides for a concurrent resolution correcting the enrollment of a bill to be considered as adopted by the House upon the adoption of the special order of business. Similarly, it may provide that a Senate amendment pending at the Speaker's table and otherwise requiring consideration in Committee of the Whole be ''hereby'' considered as adopted upon adoption of the special order of business or considered as adopted with a further specified amendment. *Manual* § 855; Deschler Ch 21 § 16.11. In both cases, there is no bill or joint resolution pending initial final passage. Therefore, the stricture under clause 6(c) of rule XIII against denying a motion to recommit with instructions is not operative.

A special order of business may make in order two or more propositions. It also may link more than one passed measure separately considered into one engrossment. *Manual* § 476.

Special orders of business that prescribe procedures for the consideration of conference reports and amendments between the Houses may:

- Waive points of order against a conference report and against its consideration. 107-1, Dec. 12, 2001, p 25089.
- Provide for the immediate consideration of a conference report when it is eventually reported from the committee of conference. Deschler Ch 21 § 16.
- Permit a motion to ''hook-up'' a House-passed measure with a similar Senate-passed measure and a motion to go to conference. 107-1, July 12, 2001, p 13097.

- Provide for a motion to dispose of Senate amendments to a House bill. 104-1, Dec. 13, 1995, p 36290.
- Permit a third-degree amendment to be offered to a Senate amendment. 103-1, Sept. 30, 1993, p 23148.
- Allow conferees to refile a conference report in a corrected form without a new meeting or new signatures. 104-1, Nov. 17, 1995, p 33741.
- With respect to a measure in conference, discharge managers on the part of the House and lay the bill on the table or dispose of an amendment in disagreement (the House being in possession of the official papers). 5 Hinds § 6526; 110-1, Dec. 12, 2007, p 34003.

The Committee on Rules has reported as privileged a special order of business nearly identical to one previously rejected by the House, but it was held not to constitute "another of the same substance" within the meaning of *Jefferson's Manual* because it provided a different scheme for general debate. *Manual* § 515.

At the convening of a new Congress, a special order of business has been offered as privileged to provide for consideration in the House of a resolution to adopt the rules of a new Congress. *Manual* § 60.

Waivers

The Committee on Rules may report and call up as privileged resolutions temporarily waiving or altering any rule of the House, including statutory provisions enacted as an exercise of the rulemaking authority of the House, that would prohibit the consideration of a bill or otherwise establish an exclusive procedure for consideration of a particular type of measure. *Manual* § 857. For example, the Committee on Rules has reported as privileged a joint resolution repealing the statutory requirement—a joint rule—that each House adjourn *sine die* not later than July 31. *Manual* § 1106.

Points of order do not lie against the consideration of a special order of business for waiving points of order against a measure, as it is for the House to determine, by a majority vote on the adoption of the resolution, whether certain rules should be waived. Deschler Ch 21 § 16.9. However, a House or statutory rule may contain language restricting the authority of the Committee on Rules to recommend a waiver. See UNFUNDED MANDATES; QUESTION OF CONSIDERATION.

Under clause 6(g) of rule XIII, a special order of business shall, "to the maximum extent possible," be specific with respect to any waiver of a point of order against the underlying measure or against its consideration. *Manual* § 863.

§ 2. Reporting Special Orders of Business

Generally; Typography

Under clause 3(g) of rule XIII, a report from the Committee on Rules repealing or amending a standing rule must include a Ramseyer-type comparative print; that is, appropriate typography showing the proposed omissions or insertions. This clause does not apply to resolutions that merely provide temporary waivers of rules during the consideration of particular legislative business. *Manual* § 848.

Privilege and Precedence of Reports

A report from the Committee on Rules enjoys high privilege. 8 Cannon § 2260. A report from the Committee on Rules takes precedence over a motion to consider a measure that is ''highly privileged'' pursuant to a statute enacted as an exercise of the rulemaking authority of the House, acknowledging the constitutional authority of the House to change its rules at any time. *Manual* § 857. It also takes precedence over a privileged motion to discharge a committee and has been called up before District of Columbia business that is privileged on District Day. Deschler Ch 21 §§ 17.7, 17.8.

Although highly privileged, a report from the Committee on Rules yields to the presentation of conference reports (5 Hinds § 6449) and to a question of the privileges of the House (8 Cannon § 3491). A report is not in order after the House has voted to go into Committee of the Whole. 5 Hinds § 6781.

Once a special order of business is under debate, the House can postpone further consideration and proceed to other business only by unanimous consent. Deschler Ch 21 § 17.11. However, under clause 2 of rule XVI, the manager of the resolution can withdraw it from consideration before a decision has been made thereon. Deschler Ch 21 § 18.41. If the resolution is later reoffered, debate under the hour rule begins anew. Deschler Ch 21 § 17.11 (note).

Reporting to the House; Calling Up

Under clause 6(d) of rule XIII, the Committee on Rules must present a special order of business resolution to the House within three legislative days of the time when it orders a report with respect to the underlying measure. *Manual* § 861.

Ordinarily, a report from the Committee on Rules is called up for consideration by a member of that committee who has been so authorized. However, under clause 6(d) of rule XIII, if the report has been on the House Calendar for seven legislative days without being called up, any member of the committee may call it up provided the member gives notice of one calendar day of an intention to do so. This rule may be invoked by a minority member of the committee. *Manual* § 861.

Under clause 6(e) of rule XIII, in the event an adverse report is made by the Committee on Rules on a special order of business, any Member of the House may call up the report and move the adoption of the resolution on a day when motions to discharge committees are in order. *Manual* § 861; see DISCHARGING MEASURES FROM COMMITTEES.

Same-day Consideration

Although it is always in order to call up for consideration a resolution reported from the Committee on Rules relating to the order of business, it may not be considered on the same legislative day as reported under clause 6(a) of rule XIII unless so determined by a vote of not less than two-thirds of the Members voting, a quorum being present. This requirement does not apply to resolutions called up during the last three days of a session. *Manual* § 857. The Committee on Rules may report a resolution waiving this requirement. 93-2, Dec. 19, 1974, p 41572.

The two-thirds vote needed for same-day consideration does not alter the requirement that a simple majority must actually adopt the resolution. Deschler Ch 21 § 18.7. If consideration is ordered by a two-thirds vote, a point of order that the resolution has not been printed does not lie. *Manual* § 857.

Under clause 6(a)(2) of rule XIII, the two-thirds vote requirement for same-day consideration does not apply if the only effect of a rule is to waive the three-day layover requirement for a particular reported bill or the three-day layover and two-hour availability requirement for a conference report and amendments in disagreement. *Manual* § 857.

A report filed by the Committee on Rules at any time before the convening of the House on the next legislative day may be called up for immediate consideration without the two-thirds requirement. If the House continues in session into a second calendar day and then meets again that day, or convenes for two legislative days on the same calendar day, any report filed on the first legislative day may be called up on the second without the question of consideration being raised. *Manual* § 857.

§ 3. Forms

Filing a Rule

MEMBER: M__. Speaker, by direction of the Committee on Rules, I present a privileged report for filing under the rule.

SPEAKER: The Clerk will report the title of the resolution. [*After Clerk reports title.*] Referred to the House Calendar and ordered printed.

Calling Up a Rule

MEMBER: M__. Speaker, by direction of the Committee on Rules, I call up House Resolution ____ and ask for its immediate consideration.

SPEAKER: The Clerk will report the resolution. [*Unanimous consent to waive the reading in full is normally not entertained.*] The gentle______ from ____ is recognized for one hour.

Calling Up Rule on Same Day It Is Filed

MEMBER: M__. Speaker, by direction of the Committee on Rules, I present a privileged report.

SPEAKER: The Clerk will report the title of the resolution. [*After Clerk reports title.*] Referred to the House Calendar and ordered printed.

MEMBER: M__. Speaker, by direction of the Committee on Rules, I call up House Resolution ——— and ask for its immediate consideration.

SPEAKER: The Clerk will report the resolution. [*Unanimous consent to waive the reading in full is normally not entertained.*] The question is, will the House consider the resolution. [*If two-thirds of those voting, a quorum being present, vote in the affirmative.*] Two-thirds of those present having voted in the affirmative, the resolution shall be considered.

§ 4. Consideration of Special Orders of Business

Debate

Special orders of business reported from the Committee on Rules are considered in the House under the hour rule. Therefore, a Member recognized to call up a special order of business by direction of the Committee on Rules manages one hour of debate. Deschler Ch 21 § 18. Other Members may be recognized only if yielded time. Deschler Ch 21 § 18.15. It is customary for the Member calling up the resolution to yield 30 minutes of the hour to a minority member of the Committee on Rules for purposes of debate only. Deschler Ch 21 § 18.15 (note). The minority member is permitted to yield time in segments to other Members.

Debate on a special order of business may range to the merits of the measure to be made in order because the question of consideration of the bill is involved. However, it should not range to the merits of a measure not to be considered under that special order of business. *Manual* § 948.

Amendments and Divisibility

Under clause 5(b) of rule XVI, a special order of business resolution is not divisible. *Manual* § 919. The manager of the special order of business may offer one or more amendments thereto, and authorization of the committee is not required. Deschler Ch 21 § 18.23. The resolution is not otherwise subject to amendment from the floor unless the manager yields for that purpose or unless the House fails to order the previous question. Deschler Ch 21 § 18.19.

Dilatory Motions Not Permitted

The question of consideration may not be raised against a report from the Committee on Rules. 5 Hinds §§ 4961, 4962; 8 Cannon §§ 2440, 2441. The clause forbidding dilatory motions has been construed strictly. 5 Hinds §§ 5740-5742. As such, the following have been excluded:

- A motion to commit or recommit after the ordering of the previous question. 5 Hinds §§ 5593-5601; 8 Cannon §§ 2270, 2750, 2753.
- An appeal from the Chair's decision not to entertain the question of consideration or a motion to lay the pending resolution on the table. 5 Hinds § 5739.
- A motion to postpone to a day certain. *Manual* § 858.
- A motion to table an amendment offered by the manager of the rule. *Manual* § 858.

A motion to reconsider the vote on the motion for the previous question on the rule (and on any pending amendment thereto) is not dilatory and may be laid on the table without carrying with it the resolution itself. *Manual* § 858; 5 Hinds § 5739.

In the event that the motion for the previous question is rejected on a privileged resolution from the Committee on Rules, the provisions of clause 6(b) prohibiting "dilatory" motions no longer strictly apply. As such, the resolution is subject to proper amendment, further debate, or a motion to table or refer, subject to being preempted by a preferential motion offered by another Member. *Manual* § 858.

Only one motion to adjourn is admissible during the consideration of a report from the Committee on Rules, and the motion may not be offered when another Member has the floor. *Manual* § 858. Where the House adjourns during the consideration of a report from the Committee on Rules, further consideration of the report becomes unfinished business on the following day, and debate resumes from the point where interrupted. *Manual* § 858.

Rejection of Motion for Previous Question

In the event that the motion for the previous question is rejected, the Member who has led the opposition will be recognized for one hour unless preempted by a preferential motion, such as the motion to table, which may be offered by any Member. The Member recognized may yield time, may offer an amendment to the resolution, and may move the previous question on the amendment and the resolution. Deschler Ch 21 § 18.

Voting

A special order of business requires a majority vote for adoption. 4 Hinds § 3169. Under clause 8 of rule XX, the Speaker has the authority to postpone for up to two legislative days a record vote on the motion for the previous question or on the adoption of a rule. *Manual* § 1030; see VOTING.

§ 5. Modification of Special Orders of Business

By Resolution

The Committee on Rules may report a privileged resolution modifying the operation or effect of a previous special order of business adopted by the House. Such a resolution may provide additional procedures to govern the further consideration of a measure already pending in Committee of the Whole and may include limitations on further debate or amendments. 8 Cannon § 2258; Deschler Ch 21 §§ 16.26, 16.27.

By Unanimous Consent in the House

A unanimous-consent request to modify the terms established by a special order of business providing for the consideration of a measure in the Committee of the Whole may be made after its adoption by the House and before completion of consideration of the underlying measure in the Committee. 99-2, Sept. 24, 1986, p 25890.

A unanimous-consent request may not be entertained in the Committee of the Whole if the request would materially modify procedures required by a special order of business adopted by the House. Such requests must be made in the House. For examples of requests that may not be entertained in the Committee of the Whole, see COMMITTEES OF THE WHOLE; *Manual* § 993.

Although the House may alter the terms of an adopted special order of business to make an additional amendment in order in the Committee of the Whole, the Chair may decline to entertain a unanimous-consent request to admit an additional nongermane amendment unless assured the request has been cleared. This practice is consistent with the Speaker's announced policy of conferring recognition for unanimous-consent requests for the consideration of unreported bills and resolutions only when assured that the majority and minority floor and committee leaderships have no objection. *Manual* §§ 857, 956.

The Member offering an amendment in the Committee of the Whole pursuant to a special order of the House has the burden of proving that it meets the description of the amendment made in order. *Manual* § 993.

By Unanimous Consent in the Committee of the Whole

The chair of the Committee of the Whole may entertain a unanimous-consent request to modify a special order of business if the request proposes merely an incidental or minor change to the special order. For examples of unanimous-consent requests have been entertained in Committee of the Whole, see COMMITTEES OF THE WHOLE; *Manual* § 993.

By unanimous consent the House may delegate to the Committee of the Whole authority to entertain unanimous-consent requests to change procedures contained in an adopted special order of business. *Manual* § 993.

§ 6. Procedures Prescribed by Special Orders of Business

In recent Congresses, special orders of business have provided for the consideration of amendments in a variety of ways, from ''open'' rules (which are silent on the amendment structure) to ''closed'' (which preclude all amendments). In between these two extremes, special orders of business have:

- Specified consideration that is open in part and restricted in part. 106-1, Aug. 4, 1999, p 19460.
- Permitted only specified amendments. 107-1, Aug. 1, 2001, p 15414.
- Required first-degree amendments to be printed in the *Congressional Record*. 107-1, July 19, 2001, p 13870.
- Specified that certain amendments be ''considered as adopted,'' often referred to as ''self-executed.'' 107-1, Aug. 1, 2001, p 15414.
- Authorized the floor manager to offer en bloc amendments consisting of the text of other amendments made in order. 107-1, Sept. 19, 2001, p 17221.
- Left the amendment process open only for a specified period of time. 106-2, May 10, 2000, p 7481.

Although the Committee on Rules may announce a policy that it intends to make in order only preprinted amendments, the committee may in fact, without violating a rule of the House, report a special order of business making in order an unprinted amendment. *Manual* § 857.

An amendment may be ''self-executed'' by adoption of a special order of business even if, considered separately, it would violate a rule of the

House. For example, a special order may ''self-execute'' an amendment that contains:

- An appropriation in violation of clause 4 of rule XXI. *Manual* § 855.
- An appropriation in violation of clause 2 of rule XXI. *Manual* § 855.
- Nongermane provisions in violation of clause 7 of rule XVI. *Manual* § 855.

Normally, a rule that precludes any amendment, or permits only one amendment, provides for the consideration of the measure in the House. A rule that permits more than one amendment normally provides for consideration in the Committee of the Whole.

One procedure involving the consideration of amendments is called ''king of the hill.'' Although regular order does not permit further amendments to a text once it has been amended in its entirety, a ''king of the hill'' rule permits several substitute amendments to be voted on in the Committee of the Whole, with only the last one adopted to be considered as finally adopted and reported to the House. The Committee on Rules also has reported a special order of business providing for a variation of that procedure. This procedure permits consideration of conflicting amendments in a series, with only the one winning the most votes being finally voted on in the House.

Special orders of business often make in order as original text something other than the text of the introduced measure. For example, the base text may be specified to be:

- A substitute reported by the committee of jurisdiction (the most common text made in order). 107-1, May 10, 2001, p 7772.
- A substitute reported by the committee of primary jurisdiction modified by amendments reported by a committee of secondary jurisdiction. 107-2, Apr. 10, 2002, p 4140.
- The text of another introduced bill or a specified preprinted amendment (such as in the report accompanying the special order of business). 107-1, Oct. 3, 2001, p 18585.
- An amendment first adopted in the Committee of the Whole. 104-1, Aug. 2, 1995, p 21678.
- Introduced text as modified by amendments printed in the report accompanying the special order of business. 107-1, Dec. 6, 2001, p 24143.
- A ''committee print'' representing reported text not yet available as a Union Calendar print. 109-1, Sept. 29, 2005, p 21777.

The Committee on Rules may report resolutions that provide special procedures to expedite consideration or accomplish specific results. For example, a resolution may authorize priority in recognition for the offering of amendments to Members who had their amendments preprinted in the *Congressional Record.*

Chapter 53
Suspension of Rules

Research References

5 Hinds §§ 6790-6862
8 Cannon §§ 3397-3426
Deschler Ch 21 §§ 9-15
Manual §§ 885-891

§ 1. Generally; Motions to Suspend

In General

A motion to suspend the rules is authorized by clause 1 of rule XV, adopted in its original form in 1822. *Manual* § 885. The privileged motion is in order only on the days specified by the rule or by special order of the House. §§ 4, 5, infra. Recognition for the motion is at the discretion of the Speaker. § 6, infra. It is debatable for 40 minutes, is not amendable, and requires a two-thirds vote for adoption. §§ 7, 8, 10, infra.

Effect of Rejection of the Motion

Rejection of a motion that the House suspend the rules and pass a bill does not constitute a rejection of the bill. The Speaker may schedule it again under suspension of rules. 107-2, July 15, 2002, July 23, 2002, pp 12832, 13949. The Committee on Rules may report a resolution authorizing the consideration of such bill. 8 Cannon § 3392; Deschler Ch 21 § 15.8.

§ 2. Uses of the Motion

In General

In the early practice, the motion to suspend the rules was used only to enable a matter to be taken up. *Manual* § 886; 5 Hinds §§ 6852, 6853. Under the modern practice, it is possible by one motion both to bring a matter before the House and to pass it. The proponent moves "that the House suspend the rules and pass the bill." *Manual* § 886a; 5 Hinds §§ 6846, 6847. In this form, all rules that ordinarily would impede an immediate vote on passage of a measure are set aside. The underlying bill is passed without the intervention of questions such as ordering the previous question, third reading, recommittal, or division of the question. § 5, infra.

A motion to suspend the rules may provide for passage of an unreported bill. 5 Hinds § 6850. Indeed, the motion to suspend may provide for a series of procedural steps, such as the reconsideration of the vote passing a bill, the amendment of the bill, and its passage again. 5 Hinds § 6849. Forms for offering motion, see § 6, infra.

To Pass Legislative Measures

Under the modern practice, the motion to suspend the rules is used frequently to pass legislative measures that are perceived to have a broad degree of support and little need for prolonged debate. It also is available to bring before the House bills that would otherwise be subject to a point of order. 8 Cannon § 3424; Deschler Ch 21 § 9. The motion may provide for the passage of a bill, even if the bill has not been reported or referred to any calendar or previously introduced. *Manual* § 886; 8 Cannon § 3421. Following are some examples of measures considered under suspension of the rules:

- An amendment to the Constitution (both the motion and the amendment requiring a two-thirds vote). Deschler Ch 21 § 9.21.
- A bill or resolution submitted from the floor and not considered by a committee. Deschler Ch 21 § 9.19.
- A bill that is pending before a committee but that has not been reported. Deschler Ch 21 § 9.
- A Senate bill. Deschler Ch 21 § 9.3.
- An amendment to a Senate bill and a motion to insist on the House amendment and request a conference. 103-2, Mar. 24, 1994, p 6515.
- A resolution to disagree to a Senate amendment to a House joint resolution and agree to a request for a conference. Deschler Ch 21 § 9.13.
- A conference report. 8 Cannon §§ 3406, 3423.
- A motion to recommit a conference report. Deschler Ch 21 § 9.5.
- A motion to agree to Senate amendments. 8 Cannon § 3425.

- A resolution to concur in a Senate amendment to a House bill with a further House amendment. *Manual* § 886.
- A motion to reconsider the vote by which a bill passed, amend the bill, and pass the bill again. 5 Hinds § 6849.
- A motion to take a measure from the table. 5 Hinds §§ 5640, 6288.
- A bill consisting of the text of two bills previously passed by the House. *Manual* § 886.

To Provide Special Orders of Business

In the early practice of the House, the motion to suspend the rules was used frequently to adopt special orders of business. 5 Hinds § 6820 (note). Today, special orders of business usually are adopted by a simple majority vote of the House on a report from the Committee on Rules. 4 Hinds § 3169; 5 Hinds § 6790. Special orders of business also are often adopted by unanimous consent. See UNANIMOUS-CONSENT AGREEMENTS. However, motions to suspend the rules still may be used to consider, for example, the following:

- A request to repeal or change a rule of the House. 5 Hinds § 6862.
- A request to permit several bills to be reported. 5 Hinds § 6857.
- A resolution extending the time for debate on a motion. Deschler Ch 21 § 9.18.

§ 3. Rules Suspended by Adoption of Motion

In General

If not otherwise qualified or if not specifically prohibited by House rule, a motion to suspend the rules suspends all rules, including the standing rules of the House, the unwritten law and practice of the House, and the parliamentary rules stated in *Jefferson's Manual.* 5 Hinds § 6796; 8 Cannon § 3406. No points of order against the consideration of the bill may be raised, such as points of order based on defects in reporting the bill (such as the lack of quorum when reporting), Ramseyer rule violations, or the like. Deschler Ch 21 §§ 9.7-9.12; *Manual* § 886.

Rules Not Subject to Suspension

Certain rules are not subject to suspension. 5 Hinds §§ 7270, 7283, 7285. Among these rules are:

- The rule relating to the use of the Hall of the House. *Manual* § 677.
- The rule relating to the privileges of the floor. *Manual* § 678.
- The rule prohibiting the introduction of occupants of the gallery. *Manual* § 966.

§ 4. When Motion Is In Order; Notice

Under clause 1 of rule XV, the motion to suspend the rules is in order only on the calendar days of Monday, Tuesday, and Wednesday and during the last six days of a session. *Manual* § 885. However, the Speaker may be authorized to recognize for motions to suspend the rules on other days by unanimous consent or by special order of business. *Manual* § 887; Deschler Ch 21 §§ 10.2, 10.3. The "last six days" are not applicable until both Houses have agreed to a concurrent resolution establishing a date for *sine die* adjournment (or until the final six days of a session under the Constitution). Deschler Ch 21 § 10.9.

Notice Requirements

The rules of the House require no advance notice to Members of bills called up under suspension. *Manual* § 886. Copies of reports on bills considered under suspension are not required to be available in advance. *Manual* § 886. However, most bills considered in the House pursuant to a motion to suspend the rules are on a list maintained by the leadership that identifies those bills on which motions to suspend will be entertained by the Speaker on a given day. This informal list is maintained to give notice to the Members, and ordinarily only such bills as have been cleared with the leadership through this procedure are brought up under suspension. Deschler Ch 21 § 9. A special order of business providing an additional day for the consideration of motions to suspend the rules may require advance notice of one hour on the floor. If so, unanimous consent is required to permit the Chair to entertain the motion prior to that time. *Manual* § 886.

§ 5. Precedence of Motion; Application of Other Motions

When the Motion Takes Precedence

The motion to suspend the rules and pass a measure is privileged in the House if made on a day on which the Speaker is authorized to recognize for such motions. *Manual* § 887. Thus the Speaker may recognize for such a motion notwithstanding the pendency on Monday of a request for recognition to consider District of Columbia business, the matters being of equal privilege. Deschler Ch 21 § 10.7.

A motion to suspend the rules may be entertained even where the yeas and nays have been demanded on another highly privileged motion or the previous question has been ordered on another matter. 5 Hinds §§ 6827, 6831-6833, 6835; 8 Cannon § 3418.

When Motion Yields

When a question of the privileges of the House (such as an election contest) is pending, that question takes precedence over a motion to suspend the rules. 5 Hinds § 6825. Similarly, if a question concerning the administration of the oath of office of a Member is pending, a motion to suspend the rules is not in order. 5 Hinds § 6826. The motion also yields to the consideration of a bill under a special order of business (5 Hinds § 6838), motions from the Discharge Calendar (7 Cannon § 1018), and the motion to adjourn (5 Hinds §§ 5743-5746). However, pending a motion to suspend the rules, only one motion to adjourn is in order, unless the failure of a quorum is demonstrated. 5 Hinds §§ 5744, 5746; 8 Cannon § 2823; Deschler Ch 21 § 13.16. Because a resolution raising a question of the privileges of the House takes precedence over a motion to suspend the rules, such resolution may be offered between motions to suspend the rules on which the Speaker has postponed record votes. *Manual* § 709.

Because two motions to suspend the rules cannot be pending at the same time, a pending motion must be disposed of before another one may be entertained by the Chair. 5 Hinds § 6814, 6837.

Application of Other Motions

Many motions that commonly are offered during the consideration of a measure are inapplicable to the motion to suspend. The motion to suspend may not be tabled (5 Hinds § 5406), postponed by motion (5 Hinds § 5322), recommitted (5 Hinds § 6860), or divided for a vote (5 Hinds §§ 6141-6143, 6860). The motion to amend may not be applied to a motion to suspend the rules. 5 Hinds § 5405. The motion for the previous question is not applicable to a proposition being considered under suspension. Deschler Ch 21 § 13.17.

The motion to reconsider may not be applied to a negative vote on the motion to suspend. *Manual* § 886a; 5 Hinds § 5645; 8 Cannon § 2781.

§ 6. Offering of Motion; Recognition

The Speaker's Discretion

On suspension days, recognition for a motion to suspend the rules lies entirely within the discretion of the Speaker. 5 Hinds §§ 6791-6794; 8 Cannon §§ 3402-3404; Deschler Ch 21 §§ 11.4-11.6. The Speaker has the discretion to recognize for a motion to suspend the rules on a bill even though the House previously has rejected a similar motion on the same bill. 103-2, Oct. 4, 1994, pp 27663, 27754.

Measures called up under suspension normally are cleared with the leadership, and the Speaker may decline recognition for a motion that does not comply with this practice. Deschler Ch 21 § 11.6. However, the Speaker has the discretion to recognize for a motion to suspend the rules and pass legislation that has not been scheduled in advance. Deschler Ch 21 § 9.22; § 4, supra.

Before 1991 the motion to suspend the rules required a second, so that the House, without debate, could decline to entertain the motion. A second usually was considered ordered by unanimous consent. However, if challenged, the question was resolved by a vote with tellers. *Manual* § 889.

The Speaker ordinarily extends recognition to the chair or other member of the committee having jurisdiction over the subject matter of the proposition and not to the original sponsor of the measure. Deschler Ch 21 §§ 11.10-11.13. The Chair does not require that the motion be authorized by the committee. Deschler Ch 21 § 11.11.

Forms

M__. Speaker, I move that the House suspend the rules and pass the bill, H.R. __________ [as amended].

> *Note:* The title of the bill is read by the Clerk; the Member's motion need not recite the title.

M__. Speaker, I move that the House suspend the rules and agree to House Resolution __________ [as amended].

M__. Speaker, I move that the House suspend the rules and concur in the Senate amendment to the bill H.R. __________.

M__. Speaker, I move that the House suspend the rules and adopt [or recommit] the conference report on H.R. __________.

M__. Speaker, I move that the House suspend the rules and agree to the resolution I send to the desk.

§ 7. Consideration and Debate

Reading Requirements

Under the early practice, it was held that the motion to suspend the rules did not dispense with the reading of the bill thereby called up for consideration. 5 Hinds § 5277; 8 Cannon § 3400. However, under the modern practice, the motion itself is offered by the proponent and the title is read by the clerk. Other reading requirements are deemed waived. *Manual* § 886; Deschler Ch 21 § 14.4.

Debate

Under clause 1(c) of rule XV, motions to suspend the rules are debatable for 40 minutes, equally divided between the proponent of the motion and an opponent. *Manual* § 891. This is so, even though the proposition presented is itself not otherwise debatable. 5 Hinds § 6822. In the case that the mover is opposed to the bill, a Member in favor may be recognized for debate. 8 Cannon § 3416. A Member rising to claim the time in opposition may be challenged by another Member:

> MEMBER: Is the gentle______ seeking recognition opposed to the motion? If not, I demand the time in opposition.

Following are the priorities in recognition for control of time in opposition to a motion to suspend the rules:

- Opponents have priority.
- Among opponents, members of the committee of jurisdiction have priority.
- Among committee members opposed, minority members have priority in order of full-committee seniority.

5 Hinds § 6802; 8 Cannon § 3415. The Chair will not examine the degree of a Member's opposition to the motion. *Manual* § 891.

The allocation of the time is within the discretion of the Members controlling it. Deschler Ch 21 § 13.10. Alternation of recognition between Members on both sides of the aisle is not required. 2 Hinds § 1442; Deschler Ch 21 § 13.9. No Member may speak in debate on the motion unless yielded time by a Member in control of the time. Deschler Ch 21 § 13.7. Time yielded to a Member may not be reserved or yielded to a third Member. Deschler Ch 21 § 13.5.

The proponent of the motion is entitled to open and close debate in favor of the motion. Deschler Ch 21 §§ 13.13, 13.14.

Debate should be confined to the object of the motion and may not range to the merits of a bill not scheduled for suspension on that day. *Manual* § 948.

The House may by unanimous consent or resolution alter the normal procedure for debate on the motion. In so doing, the House may extend the time for debate or designate the Members to control the time. 8 Cannon § 3414; Deschler Ch 21 §§ 13.3, 13.18. If time is extended by unanimous consent, the Chair may divide that time equally between the proponent and the opponent. 8 Cannon § 3415.

§ 8. Amendments

Amendments from the floor are not in order to propositions being considered under suspension of the rules. 5 Hinds §§ 5405, 6858, 6859; Deschler Ch 21 § 14.8. Only those amendments included in the motion to suspend are in order, and the Member offering the motion may not yield to other Members for further amendment. Deschler Ch 21 § 14.6. This prohibition against offering amendments applies to pro forma amendments and to motions to strike the enacting clause. Deschler Ch 21 §§ 14.11, 14.12. After a motion to suspend the rules and pass a bill has been offered, it may be amended either by withdrawing the motion and reoffering it in new form; or the manager of the motion may modify it by unanimous consent. Deschler Ch 21 § 14.3; 107-1, Dec. 5, 2001, p 24039.

The bill and any proposed amendments in the motion are reported (usually by title only) and considered as one entity and are printed in the *Congressional Record* in full. Amendments are not voted on separately. Deschler Ch 21 §§ 14.4, 15.5. Committee approval of such amendments is not required. *Manual* § 886; Deschler Ch 21 § 14.2.

§ 9. Withdrawal of Motion

A motion to suspend the rules may be withdrawn at any time before the Chair puts the question and a voice vote is taken thereon. 5 Hinds §§ 6840, 6844; 8 Cannon §§ 3405, 3419. The motion may be withdrawn by unanimous consent, even after the Speaker has put the question on its adoption and postponed further proceedings. Deschler Ch 21 § 13.23.

§ 10. Voting on Motion

In General

Clause 1(a) of rule XV requires a two-thirds vote for the adoption of a motion to suspend the rules. *Manual* § 885. That requirement is construed as two-thirds of the Members present and voting for or against the motion (votes of those "present" are not counted except to establish the required quorum). Deschler Ch 21 § 15.2 (note).

The motion to reconsider may not be applied to a negative vote on the motion because such disposition is not final; that is, an identical motion may be entertained. § 1, supra. The motion to reconsider may be applied to an affirmative vote on the motion. *Manual* § 886.

Postponing Votes

A record vote on a motion to suspend the rules may be postponed by the Speaker under the conditions specified by clause 8 of rule XX. Under this rule, the Speaker may postpone such a vote to a designated time or place in the legislative schedule within two legislative days. The Chair's customary announcement of an intent to postpone, which is made before consideration of a series of motions, is not a necessary prerequisite to the postponement authority. *Manual* § 1030. At the designated time, the Speaker puts the question on each motion on which further proceedings have been postponed. For a discussion of postponing votes generally, see VOTING.

Once the Speaker has postponed record votes to occur at a designated place in the legislative schedule, the time for such votes may be redesignated within the appropriate period. *Manual* § 1030.

Where proceedings are postponed for a *de novo* vote by voice in response to a point of no quorum, the point of order of no quorum is not ripe until the question recurs as unfinished business. 95-1, Sept. 26, 1977, p 30948. It is too late to demand a record vote on the motion after the Speaker has announced that further proceedings on that motion have been postponed. The demand is not in order until the motion is again before the House as unfinished business. 93-2, June 17, 1974, p 19334.

Chapter 54
Unanimous-Consent Agreements

Research References

4 Hinds §§ 3058-3060, 3155-3159
7 Cannon §§ 758-763
Deschler Ch 23 §§ 42-48
Manual §§ 872, 950, 956, 993

§ 1. In General; Effect of Agreement

Generally

A request for unanimous consent is in effect a motion to suspend the order of business temporarily. Granting the request permits some action that is not in dispute and to which no Member has any objection. *Manual* § 872; 4 Hinds §§ 3058, 3059; 8 Cannon § 2794. An objection by any Member terminates the request. Deschler Ch 23 § 45.6.

The practice in the House of allowing some actions to be taken by unanimous consent began in the 1830's, when the House, responding to the increased pressure of legislative activity, unanimously agreed to a special order of business permitting it to consider a bill which was not in the regular order of business. 4 Hinds § 3155. This use has now become commonplace. In the modern practice of the House, many items of business are considered as a result of unanimous-consent requests. The device also is used to facilitate consideration of measures by waiving the reading or limiting or extending the time for debate. §§ 7, 8, infra; see also CONSIDERATION AND DEBATE.

Availability in the Committee of the Whole

Unanimous-consent requests are in order both in the House and, to a lesser extent, in the Committee of the Whole. For example, the Committee may by unanimous consent permit the withdrawal of an amendment under clause 5 of rule XVIII, limit debate other than general debate set by the House, or provide that a bill be considered as read and open to amendment unless in conflict with a House order or special order of business. *Manual* § 993; 8 Cannon § 2553. However, unanimous consent may not be requested in the Committee of the Whole on matters properly addressed only in the House. *Manual* § 993; Deschler Ch 23 §§ 48.15, 48.16; § 8, infra.

§ 2. Recognition of Members for Requests

Generally; Speaker's Guidelines

The recognition of Members to offer unanimous-consent requests is in the discretion of the Chair. Deschler Ch 23 § 45.4. A Member seeking unanimous consent must be recognized by the Chair for a stated purpose, and a Member so recognized may not seek the further consent of the House for some other purpose. Thus, a Member may not be recognized to consider a particular bill where such Member has been recognized only to speak for one minute. Deschler Ch 23 § 48.3.

The Speaker has announced and enforced a policy of conferring recognition for unanimous-consent requests for the consideration of unreported bills and resolutions only when assured that the majority and minority floor and committee leaderships have no objection. This policy minimizes attempts to force Members to go on record as objecting to a variety of unanimous-consent requests. The policy has been extended to the following:

- Requests relating to reported bills.
- Requests for immediate consideration of matters (separately unreported) comprising a portion of a measure already passed by the House.
- Requests to consider a motion to suspend the rules and pass an unreported bill (on a nonsuspension day).
- Requests to permit consideration of (nongermane) amendments to bills.
- Requests to permit expedited consideration of measures on subsequent days, as by waiving the requirement that a bill be referred to committee for 30 legislative days before a motion to discharge may be presented under clause 2 of rule XV.

- Requests relating to Senate-passed bills on the Speaker's table, including one identical to a House-passed bill and a Senate concurrent resolution to correct an enrollment.
- Constituent parts of a single request combining final disposition of several separate measures.

For further examples, see *Manual* § 956.

In addition, with respect to unanimous-consent requests to dispose of Senate amendments to House bills on the Speaker's table, the Chair will entertain such a request only if made by the chair of the committee with jurisdiction, or by another committee member authorized to make the request. *Manual* § 956; Deschler Ch 21 § 1.23.

The Speaker's enforcement of this policy of recognition is not subject to appeal. ''Floor leadership'' in this context has been construed to apply only to the Minority Leader and not to the entire hierarchy of minority leadership, where the Chair had been assured that the Minority Leader had given consent.

It is not a proper parliamentary inquiry to ask the Chair to indicate which side of the aisle has failed under the Speaker's guidelines to clear a unanimous-consent request, but the Chair may indicate the absence of such clearance for the *Congressional Record.*

For a discussion of recognition for unanimous-consent requests to vary procedures in the Committee of the Whole governed by a special order of business adopted by the House, see *Manual* § 993; § 8, infra.

§ 3. Timeliness

Unanimous-consent requests must be timely. Deschler Ch 23 § 45.4. They cannot be entertained:

- In the House after the House has voted to go into the Committee of the Whole. 4 Hinds § 4727.
- When the absence of a quorum has been announced in the House. 6 Cannon §§ 660, 686, 689.
- During proceedings incident to securing a quorum of the Committee of the Whole. 8 Cannon § 2379.
- During the pendency of a unanimous-consent request by another Member. Deschler Ch 23 § 48.1.

An objection to a unanimous-consent request must be timely. It is ordinarily too late to object to a unanimous-consent request after the Chair has asked if there is objection and has announced that the Chair hears none. Deschler Ch 23 § 45.3. Thus, when unanimous consent has been given for the consideration of a bill, amendments may be offered and may not be prevented by a subsequent objection of a Member. 5 Hinds § 5782.

§ 4. Stating the Request; Withdrawal

A Member seeking the unanimous consent of the House on some matter should rise and address the Chair. The Chair may decline to entertain a request that includes alternatives (6 Cannon § 709; Deschler Ch 23 § 43.2) or includes a request made contingent upon another (6 Cannon § 709).

It is the Speaker's statement of the request as put to the House that is controlling, and the Speaker may refuse to recognize an objection to the request made before such statement of the request. Deschler Ch 23 §§ 43.1, 45.2.

A Member may withdraw a unanimous-consent request at any time before House action thereon, and unanimous consent to do so is not required. Deschler Ch 23 § 43.4.

§ 5. Objecting to the Request

Generally

An objection to a unanimous-consent request terminates the request, even if the objecting Member attempts to subsequently withdraw the objection. Deschler Ch 23 § 45.6. Because a request for unanimous consent is in effect a request to suspend the order of business temporarily, a demand for the "regular order" may be made at any time while the request is being stated and requires the request to be disposed of immediately. *Manual* § 381; 4 Hinds § 3058.

An objection to a unanimous-consent request may be made by any Member, including the Speaker or the chair of the Committee of the Whole. 8 Cannon § 3383; Deschler Ch 23 §§ 42, 45.5. A Delegate may also object. *Manual* § 675; 6 Cannon § 241.

When objecting to a unanimous-consent request, a Member must rise and be identified for the *Congressional Record. Manual* § 872; 2 Hinds § 1137. If the Chair repeats the request, the objection is properly made to the request as put by the Chair, not as put by the Member making the request. Deschler Ch 23 § 45.2.

§ 6. Reserving Objections

A Member may reserve the right to object to a unanimous-consent request and by so doing obtain the floor. Deschler Ch 23 § 42. A Member reserving the right to object to a unanimous-consent request holds the floor under that reservation subject to a demand for the regular order by any Member or by the Chair. Deschler Ch 23 § 46.6. A Member controlling the floor under a reservation of the right to object loses the floor if the request is withdrawn or if the regular order is demanded. 6 Cannon §§287, 288; Deschler Ch 23 §§46.3, 46.4. If the regular order is demanded by a Member standing, the reserving Member must either object or withdraw the reservation. Deschler Ch 23 §46.6.

§7. Particular Uses Relative to Business of the House

The unanimous-consent procedure is commonly used to change the regular order or waive the application of a particular rule. Under this practice, the House may waive the requirement of a rule unless the rule in question specifies that it is not subject to waiver, even by unanimous consent. Deschler Ch 23 §42. The unanimous-consent procedure is applied across a wide range of House business.

Unanimous-Consent Requests Involving Consideration or Adoption or Passage of a Measure

Unanimous consent may be used to provide for the consideration of a measure in the House, to vary the consideration of a measure in the House that is being considered under the general rules of the House or under an existing special order of business, or to adopt or pass a measure. For example, unanimous-consent requests may be used as follows:

- To consider a nonprivileged measure. Deschler Ch 23 §47.4.
- To consider a bill under the general rules of the House. Deschler-Brown Ch 29 §3.4.

  Note: If on the Union Calendar, the bill will then normally be considered in the Committee of the Whole. However, the bill may be called up pursuant to the agreement and then by unanimous consent considered in the House as in the Committee of the Whole. 4 Hinds §4923.
- To provide a special order for the consideration of certain business (such as motions to suspend the rules on a day not set aside for suspensions). 4 Hinds §§3165, 3166; 7 Cannon §§758-760.
- To alter the terms of a special order of business. 7 Cannon §763.
- To transact other business on a day set apart for a special purpose. 5 Hinds §7246.
- To agree to transact no business during a stated period. 7 Cannon §§760, 761.
- To take from the Speaker's table a House bill with a Senate amendment and to consider such an amendment in the House. *Manual* §528a.
- To permit the House to recede from its own amendment to a Senate amendment before the stage of disagreement. 89-2, Apr. 18, 1966, p 8207.
- To permit consideration in the House on any subsequent day of a bill to be introduced by the chair of the Committee on Appropriations. 97-2, June 23, 1982, p 14989.

- To waive all points of order against consideration in the House of an unreported joint resolution providing further continuing appropriations for the current fiscal year, consider it as read for amendment, close it to amendment by ordering the previous question to passage without intervening motion except debate and one motion to recommit. 107-2, Sept. 26, 2002, p 18146.
- To discharge the Committee of the Whole from further consideration of a bill being read for amendment under a special order of business, and provide that certain amendments be considered as agreed to. 98-1, Nov. 18, 1983, p 34160.
- To consider a measure on the Union Calendar in the House by waiving all points of order against consideration, self-execute a compromise substitute in lieu of the committee amendments, and close the measure to amendment by ordering the previous question on the bill, as amended, to passage without intervening motion except debate and one motion to recommit with or without instructions. 106-2, Apr. 13, 2000, p 5566.
- To adopt or pass, in a single request, several measures, including any amendments thereto. See, *e.g.*, 107-2, Nov. 14, 2002, p 22513.
- To enlarge the time for debate on a motion to suspend the rules. 8 Cannon § 3414.
- To specify the time at which a measure is to be called up—either immediately or on a subsequent day. 106-1, July 22, 1999, p 17309.

Unanimous-Consent Requests to Effect a Variety of Business of the House

In addition to facilitating consideration of legislative matters, unanimous-consent requests may used be as follows:

- To swear in a Member-elect pending arrival of the requisite credentials. 6 Cannon § 12.
- To refer a bill for the payment of a private claim against the government to a committee other than the Judiciary or Foreign Affairs. Clause 2(d) of rule XII.
- To correct a reference to committee. *Manual* § 714.
- To permit a committee additional time to file a report. 8 Cannon § 2783.
- To insert extraneous material in the *Congressional Record* or to permit Members to revise and extend their remarks or to vacate such permission. 5 Hinds § 6990; Deschler Ch 23 § 47.11.
- To postpone consideration of a measure, such as a resolution from the Committee on Rules, or to postpone certain votes thereon. Deschler Ch 23 § 47.8.
- To entertain a proposition for a recess. 8 Cannon § 3357.

  Note: Clause 12 of rule I permits the Speaker, without unanimous consent, to declare a ''short'' recess when no business is pending or an ''emergency'' recess when notified of an imminent threat.

- To suspend the order of business to permit the House to vacate an action taken on a bill. 6 Cannon § 711.
- To withdraw papers accompanying bills after they have been submitted to the House. 5 Hinds § 7259.
- To file a report while the House is not in session. 8 Cannon § 2252.
- To withdraw a report from a standing committee. 8 Cannon § 2312.
- To allow a Member to proceed in order after the Chair has ruled words out of order. *Manual* § 961.
- To change unparliamentary words spoken in debate or to withdraw or delete such words from the *Congressional Record.* 8 Cannon §§ 2538, 2540; Deschler Ch 23 §§ 47.9, 47.10.
- To address the House for one minute before offering a motion. Deschler Ch 23 § 47.7.

§ 8. Particular Uses Relative to Business of the Committee of the Whole

Unanimous-consent requests are frequently used in the House and in the Committee of the Whole to vary the rules governing consideration of a measure. However, the Committee of the Whole may by unanimous consent permit only minor variances from a special order of business adopted by the House. The variances must be congruent with the special order of business governing consideration of the measure in the Committee of the Whole. *Manual* § 993.

The following unanimous-consent requests may be considered in the Committee of the Whole:

- To dispense with the first reading of a bill. 8 Cannon § 2436.
- To dispense with the reading of an amendment. Deschler Ch 23 § 47.2.
- To withdraw a pending amendment. Clause 5 of rule XVIII; *Manual* § 978.
- To return to a portion of a bill passed in the reading for amendment. 8 Cannon § 2929.
- To permit a supporter of an amendment to claim debate time allocated by special order of business to an opponent, where no opponent seeks recognition. *Manual* § 993.
- To shorten the time set by a special order of business for debate on a particular amendment. *Manual* § 993.
- To lengthen the time set by a special order of business for debate on a particular amendment under terms of control congruent with those set by the order of the House. *Manual* § 993.
- To permit one of two committees controlling time for general debate pursuant to a special order of business to yield control of its time to the other. *Manual* § 993.

- To permit the offering of pro forma amendments for the purpose of debate under a ''modified-closed'' special order of business limiting both amendments and debate thereon but not specifically preempting pro forma amendments. *Manual* § 993.
- To close debate on titles of a bill that have not been read. Deschler Ch 23 § 47.1.
- To close or limit debate under the five-minute rule and to modify that time limit. *Manual* § 987.
- To permit the reading of an amendment considered as read by special order of business. *Manual* § 993.

The following unanimous-consent requests are not in order in the Committee of the Whole:

- To change the scheme for control or duration of general debate specified by the House (except to allow transfers of time among committees allotted time by the House). *Manual* § 993.
- To entertain a motion to reconsider. Deschler Ch 23 § 39.12.
- To excuse a Member from voting in the Committee of the Whole. Deschler-Brown Ch 30 § 3.3.
- To permit an amendment to be offered to the underlying bill where a special order of business permitted its consideration only as a perfecting amendment to a committee amendment. *Manual* § 993.
- To permit a substitute to be read for amendment by section where the special order of business did not so provide. *Manual* § 993.
- To restrict ''en blocking'' authority granted in a special order of business. *Manual* § 993.
- To preempt the Chair's discretion under clause 6 of rule XVIII to postpone and cluster votes or to schedule further consideration of a pending measure to a subsequent day. *Manual* § 993.
- To postpone a vote on an appeal of a ruling of the Chair. *Manual* § 993.
- To permit an amendment to an amendment rendered unamendable by a special order of business or to permit an amendment to an amendment already adopted. *Manual* § 993.
- To permit consideration of an amendment out of the order specified in a special order of business. *Manual* § 993.
- To permit consideration of an additional amendment or to authorize a supplemental report from the Committee on Rules in lieu of the original report referred to in the special order of business. *Manual* § 993.
- To permit another to offer an amendment where the special order of business vested the authority to offer such amendment in a specified Member. *Manual* § 993.
- To permit a division of the question on an amendment rendered indivisible by a special order of business. *Manual* § 993.

- To extend the time limitation for consideration of amendments beyond that set by a special order of business requiring the Chair to put the question on the pending amendments at the expiration of certain hours of consideration. *Manual* § 993.
- To prohibit the offering of an amendment otherwise in order. *Manual* § 980.

§ 9. Limitations on Requests; Grounds for Denial of Recognition

It cannot be assumed that the House has authority to waive any rule by unanimous consent. Sometimes the rule itself contains a specific provision that cannot be suspended by unanimous consent. The rules specifically prohibit the use of the unanimous-consent procedure as follows:

- To permit unauthorized persons to be admitted to the House floor. Clause 2 of rule IV.
- To bring to the attention of the House an occupant of the galleries. Clause 7 of rule XVII.
- To delete the name of the first sponsor of a bill or resolution. Clause 7(b)(2) of rule XII.

In addition, there are many rules that are not subject to waiver by unanimous consent under the practice of the House. Deschler-Brown Ch 29 § 11.1. For example, the following unanimous-consent requests are not in order in the House:

- To permit Members to record their votes after the announcement of the result. Deschler-Brown Ch 30 § 36.1.
- To extend a special-order speech beyond the cut-off time specified in the Speaker's announced policies. *Manual* § 950.
- To permit a Member to give a second one-minute speech. *Manual* § 950.
- To revise and extend arguments in the *Congressional Record* on points of order (it being essential that the Chair's ruling be responsive to arguments actually made). *Manual* § 628.
- To insert in the *Congressional Record* a colloquy between Members that did not actually occur. *Manual* § 692.

Requests Denied Recognition at the Speaker's Discretion

The Speaker may decline to recognize for a unanimous-consent request that is improper or inappropriate under the particular circumstances, as where proper notice cannot be given to interested Members. Deschler Ch 23 § 48.2. The Speaker may do so by exercising the discretionary power of recognition. Deschler Ch 23 § 42. Thus the Speaker may decline to recognize for a unanimous-consent request:

- To permit a Member to address the House on a private bill being considered on the Private Calendar (proceedings which normally preclude debate). Deschler Ch 23 § 48.8.
- To permit the House to rerefer a bill to a committee whose chair has not been consulted on the matter. Deschler Ch 23 § 48.5.
- To consider a measure after the Members have been informed that there will be no further legislative business for the day. Deschler Ch 23 §§ 48.6, 48.7.
- To reduce to five minutes the time for the first vote in a series of postponed votes, because the bell and light system would not give adequate notice of the initial five-minute vote. *Manual* § 1030.
- To direct the clerk of a committee, without its approval, to remove from committee offices certain documents and bring such documents to the well of the House Deschler Ch 23 § 48.4.

For a discussion of the Speaker's guidelines for conferring recognition for unanimous-consent requests for the consideration of certain measures, see § 2, supra.

§ 10. Modification or Revocation of Agreement

An agreement entered into by unanimous consent may be modified or vacated by unanimous consent at the pleasure of the House. 7 Cannon § 946. Thus, by unanimous consent, the House may vacate a previous unanimous-consent agreement permitting all Members to revise and extend their remarks on a particular measure. 98-1, Nov. 15, 1983, p 32746. A unanimous-consent agreement also may be revoked pursuant to a majority vote on a resolution reported from the Committee on Rules as to the order of business. 8 Cannon § 3390.

The Speaker will not entertain a unanimous-consent request to preclude recognition for consideration of a certain matter. Agreement to such a request would render the restriction an order of the House. The Speaker prefers to retain the scheduling of legislation as the prerogative of the majority leadership, subject to the Speaker's guidelines for unanimous-consent requests as discussed in section 2, supra.

Chapter 55
Unfinished Business

Research References
4 Hinds §§ 3112-3114, 4735, 4736
6 Cannon §§ 740, 741
Deschler Ch 21 § 3
Manual §§ 869, 876-879

§ 1. In General

Unfinished business is business that was carried over from a previous day and is in order immediately after disposition of business on the Speaker's table under clauses 1 and 2 of rule XIV, which set forth the daily order of business in the House. *Manual* §§ 869, 873. The resumption of unfinished business under clause 3 may be preempted by business of higher privilege, such as a motion to discharge on a discharge day. Deschler Ch 21 § 3. Unfinished business may not be called up under clause 1 of rule XIV if the order of business under that rule has been supplanted, as it always is. See ORDER OF BUSINESS; PRIVILEGED BUSINESS.

The Speaker has the discretionary authority under clause 8 of rule XX to postpone certain questions and to "cluster" them for voting at a designated time or place in the legislative schedule. The postponement authorized by the rule must be to a time within two subsequent legislative days, with the exception of questions relating to the approval of the Journal, which may be postponed only to a time on the same legislative day. *Manual* §§ 877, 1030. Once announced, the time for taking postponed votes may be redesignated within the permissible period by the Chair. *Manual* § 1030. When the House adjourns on the second legislative day after postponement of a question under clause 8 of rule XX, without resuming proceedings thereon, the question remains unfinished business on the next legislative day. *Manual* §§ 877, 1030; see VOTING.

Certain categories of business that are postponed until a designated time are resumed at the discretion of the Chair. In addition to votes under clause 8 of rule XX discussed supra, consideration of a veto message postponed to a day certain provides an example. Deschler Ch 21 § 28.4. Additionally, beginning in the 111th Congress, the Speaker has the authority to postpone further consideration of certain measures on which the previous question has been ordered, and resume such consideration at the Speaker's discretion. *Manual* § 1000a. Generally, however, unfinished business coming over from a previous day does not automatically come before the House for consideration but must be called up by a Member in charge. Deschler Ch 21 § 3.

If the matter called up as unfinished business was under debate at the time of postponement, debate does not begin anew but recommences from the point where it was interrupted. *Manual* § 915.

§ 2. Business Unfinished at Adjournment

Clause 3 of rule XIV provides that, with certain exceptions, business pending and unfinished at adjournment is to be resumed after business on the Speaker's table is finished and at the same time each day thereafter until disposed of. *Manual* § 876; see also clause 8 of rule XX. For example, where the House adjourns during consideration of a report from the Committee on Rules, further consideration of the report becomes the unfinished business on the following day, and debate resumes from the point where interrupted. *Manual* § 877.

Ordinarily, under clause 3 of rule XIV, any general legislative business that is unfinished at adjournment goes over to the succeeding day, whereas motions that relate merely to the sequence or order of business do not. *Manual* §§ 876, 877. Thus, a motion relating to the order of business does not recur as unfinished business on a succeeding day, even though a vote had been ordered on it. 4 Hinds § 3114. Likewise, the question of consideration, when not disposed of at adjournment, does not recur as unfinished business on a succeeding day but may be raised anew on a subsequent day when the matter is again before the House. 5 Hinds §§ 4947, 4948; 8 Cannon § 2438. Those special classes of business that are in order only on days of the week designated by House rule are not covered by clause 3 of rule XIV. See § 4, infra.

When the House adjourns on the second legislative day after postponement of a question under clause 8 of rule XX without resuming proceedings thereon, the question remains unfinished business on the next legislative day. When the House adjourns while a motion to instruct conferees under clause 7(c) of rule XXII is pending, the motion to instruct becomes unfinished business on the next day and does not need to be renoticed. *Manual* § 877.

§ 3. —Where Previous Question Ordered

If the House adjourns without voting on a proposition on which the previous question has been ordered, the question comes up as unfinished business on the next legislative day. *Manual* § 878; 5 Hinds §§ 5510-5517; 8 Cannon § 2691. The previous question having been ordered on a matter, its consideration on the succeeding day becomes preferential and may supersede action on other business, even though privileged. Thus, a resolution coming over from the preceding day with the previous question ordered was held to take precedence over a motion to dispose of a veto message from the President. 8 Cannon § 2693. Similarly, a bill coming over from the preceding day with the previous question ordered was held to take precedence over business made in order by a special order of business. 5 Hinds § 5520.

§ 4. —On Days Designated for Special Classes of Business

Consistent with clause 3 of rule XIV, business unfinished at adjournment and belonging to a class of business that is in order only on certain days is not taken up again until the next day eligible for the call of the appropriate calendar or for that class of business. 8 Cannon § 2334; Deschler Ch 21 § 3. This practice is followed with respect to:

- Private bills considered on certain Tuesdays. See PRIVATE CALENDAR.
- Matters considered at the Calendar Wednesday call of committees. See CALENDAR WEDNESDAY.
- District of Columbia bills on certain Mondays. See DISTRICT OF COLUMBIA BUSINESS.
- Bills brought up under the rule setting apart days for motions to suspend the rules (but not those postponed under clause 8 of rule XX). 8 Cannon § 3412; Deschler Ch 21 §§ 3.30, 3.31.
- Bills brought up under the rule setting apart days for motions to discharge committees. See DISCHARGING MEASURES FROM COMMITTEES.

§ 5. Voting as Unfinished Business

When a vote is postponed or when a quorum fails to vote on a question and the House adjourns, the vote may recur as unfinished business on the following day. Deschler Ch 21 § 3. For votes postponed by the Speaker under clause 8 of rule XX, see § 1, supra. Votes on unfinished business in the House are put *de novo*, if previously postponed, and Members have the same rights as when the question was first put, unless the yeas and nays or a recorded vote was ordered before postponement. Deschler Ch 21 § 3.18. Thus, when a vote is postponed pursuant to clause 8 of rule XX, having been objected to for lack of a quorum when initially before the House, the yeas and nays or a recorded vote may be demanded when the vote recurs as unfinished business. *Manual* § 76; Deschler-Brown Ch 30 §§ 56.5, 56.6; see VOTING. The Speaker also may postpone proceedings again when the vote recurs on such vote previously objected to for lack of a quorum. For a discussion of postponed votes in Committee of the Whole, see § 7, infra.

§ 6. Business Postponed to a Day Certain

Where a measure before the House is postponed to a day certain, either by motion or by unanimous consent, the measure becomes the unfinished business on the day to which postponed. Deschler Ch 21 § 3. This practice is followed with respect to postponed conference reports and to veto messages that are postponed to a day certain. Deschler Ch 21 §§ 8.17, 8.18; see also POSTPONEMENT.

§ 7. In Committee of the Whole

Unfinished Business

Business unfinished when the Committee of the Whole rises remains unfinished and is to be considered first in order when the House next goes into Committee of the Whole to consider that business. 4 Hinds § 4735. The House or the Speaker, pursuant to declaration authority under clause 2 of rule XVIII, and not the Committee of the Whole, controls resumption of consideration. The chair of the Committee of the Whole will not entertain unanimous-consent requests to fix the time of resumption of consideration of a bill. *Manual* § 993.

When the House resolves into Committee of the Whole for the consideration of a bill on which reading for amendment was begun on the previous day, the Committee proceeds with the reading of the bill. 8 Cannon § 2336.

Postponed Requests for Recorded Votes

Under clause 6(g) of rule XVIII, the chair of the Committee of the Whole may postpone and cluster requests for recorded votes on amendments to a subsequent place and time during the amendment process as determined by the Chair. When proceedings resume on a request for a recorded vote on an amendment so postponed, the voice vote is acknowledged and the request is announced as pending. An electronic vote ordered on the postponed request may be reduced to not less than two minutes, provided the first vote in a series is 15 minutes. *Manual* § 984; see also AMENDMENTS.

Chapter 56
Unfunded Mandates

Research References

Deschler-Brown Ch 31 § 1.57
Manual §§ 790, 843, 910, 991, 1081, 1127
Congressional Budget Act of 1974, §§ 421-428 (2 USC §§ 658-658g, 1502, 1515)

§ 1. In General

Part B was added to title IV of the Congressional Budget and Impoundment Control Act of 1974 by the Unfunded Mandates Reform Act of 1995. These provisions were enacted to require an assessment and full consideration of the impact of legislative and regulatory proposals on public and private sectors. H. Rept. 104-1. The Act explicitly declared that Part B was enacted as an exercise of congressional rulemaking powers. *Manual* § 1127; 2 USC § 1515.

§ 2. Definition of Mandate

The Unfunded Mandates Reform Act defines a ''Federal intergovernmental mandate'' as (1) an enforceable duty on State, local, or tribal government, or a reduction in the authorization of appropriations for Federal financial assistance provided to those governments for compliance with such duty, or (2) a provision which compels State and local spending for participation in an entitlement program under which at least $500 million is provided to States and localities annually. *Manual* § 1127; 2 USC § 1502.

A ''Federal private sector mandate'' is defined as an enforceable duty on the private sector or a reduction in the authorization of appropriations for Federal financial assistance provided to the private sector for compliance with such a duty. *Manual* § 1127; 2 USC § 1502.

§ 3. Committee Responsibilities

Under the Act, the Congressional Budget Office (CBO) must provide an authorizing committee with a detailed cost estimate for each bill reported by such committee containing mandates that have the requisite annual aggregate impact (adjusted for inflation) on the public sector (*i.e.*, State and local government) or on the private sector. A committee must publish this CBO estimate in the committee report or in the *Congressional Record* before consideration of the legislation on the House floor. 2 USC § 658b.

A committee report also must include:

- An assessment of the costs and benefits of the mandate.
- A statement of the degree to which the Federal funding of an intergovernmental mandate would disadvantage the private sector.
- A statement of the amount of assistance authorized to pay for the mandate.
- A statement whether the committee intends that the mandate be unfunded.
- A statement whether the legislation intends to preempt State and local law.

2 USC § 658b.

§ 4. Points of Order

It is not in order to consider a bill or joint resolution reported by a committee containing an intergovernmental mandate unless the committee has published a CBO estimate. 2 USC § 658b. There is no point of order against consideration of a measure containing a private sector mandate, even though CBO must provide, and committees must publish, similar cost estimates for private sector mandates as they do for intergovernmental mandates. See § 3, supra.

A point of order also would lie on the floor against consideration of a bill, joint resolution, amendment, motion, or conference report that imposes intergovernmental mandates exceeding the requisite level on State and local governments unless the legislation:

- Funds the mandates through new budget authority or new entitlement authority;
- Includes an authorization for appropriations for the direct costs of the mandate; and
- Provides for an evaluation of and reaction to the direct costs of the mandate by the relevant Federal agency and expedited procedures in the Congress to address such evaluation.

Manual § 1127; 2 USC § 658d.

A point of order under the Act may not be raised against an appropriation bill or an amendment thereto, with certain exceptions. *Manual* § 1127; 2 USC § 658c. The Act not only establishes a point of order against consideration of a measure containing an unfunded intergovernmental mandate (2 USC §658d), but it also establishes a point of order against a resolution providing a special order of business that waives a point of order against a measure, or self-executes the adoption of an amendment, containing an unfunded intergovernmental mandate (2 USC §658e). A special order of business "hereby" concurring in a Senate amendment that precludes the opportunity to raise a point of order constitutes a waiver of the application of the point of order. 109-2, Feb. 1, 2006, pp 549, 550.

§5. Disposition of Points of Order

A point of order against consideration of a bill is properly raised pending the Speaker's declaration that the House resolve into the Committee of the Whole for such consideration. A point of order against consideration of a resolution providing a special order of business must be made when the special order is called up and comes too late after the resolution has been adopted. *Manual* §1127; 2 USC §658e.

In order to be cognizable by the Chair, each point of order must specify the precise language on which it is premised. A point of order may be raised against more than one provision. *Manual* §1127; 2 USC §658e. In the case of a special order of business, the precise language subject to the point of order is normally the waiver of points of order against consideration of the underlying measure, including amendments thereto.

Each point of order raised is separately debatable for 20 minutes, equally divided between the Member initiating the point of order and an opponent. Debate on the point of order against a special order of business is on the question whether the House should consider the measure. The Members controlling debate on the point of order may reserve time, and a manager of a measure who controls time for debate against the point of order has the right to close debate. *Manual* §1127; 2 USC §658e.

After debate the Chair puts one question of consideration with respect to the proposition that is the subject of the points of order. The Chair puts the question of consideration without intervening motion except one motion that the House adjourn. Disposition of the question of consideration of a bill or resolution shall be considered also to determine a like point of order against an amendment made in order as original text. *Manual* §1127; 2 USC §658e.

Chapter 57
Veto of Bills

Research References

U.S. Const. art. I § 7
4 Hinds §§ 3520-3552
7 Cannon §§ 1094-1115
Deschler Ch 24 §§ 17-23
Manual §§ 104, 107-109, 112-114, 1130(6B)

§ 1. In General; Veto Messages

Generally

The authority for the President to disapprove, or veto, a bill is spelled out in article I, section 7 of the Constitution. The same clause addresses the process by which Congress can override a veto and enact a measure into law.

The President has a 10-day period in which to approve or disapprove a bill. The President can sign the bill into law or return it to the House of its origination with a veto message detailing why the President chooses not to sign. If the President fails to give approval by signing the bill during that period, the bill will become law automatically, without a signature. However, in very limited circumstances the President may, by withholding a signature, effect a ''pocket veto.'' If before the end of a 10-day signing period the Congress adjourns *sine die* and thereby prevents the return of the bill, the bill does not become law if the President has taken no action regarding it. At this stage, the bill can become a law only if the President signs it. Deschler Ch 24 § 17. For a discussion of pocket vetoes, see § 7, infra.

The 10-day period given the President under the Constitution in which to approve or reject a bill begins on the day after the bill is presented to the President. The day on which the bill is presented to the President is not counted in the computation, and Sundays also are excluded. Deschler Ch 24 § 17.1.

Under the usual practice, bills are considered to have been ''presented to the President'' when they are delivered to the White House. However, bills delivered to the White House while the President was abroad have been held by the White House, under arrangements agreed to with the presenting House, for presentation to the President upon return to the United States. *Manual* § 105.

When the President exercises the veto authority, the enrollment is returned with a sealed message setting forth the objections. An enrolled House bill returned to the Clerk during a recess with a ''memorandum of disapproval'' setting forth the objections of the President has been treated by the House as a return veto. *Manual* §§ 107, 113.

§ 2. House Action on Vetoed Bills

The Speaker lays a veto message before the House on the day it is received. Deschler Ch 24 § 20.1. It is then read and entered in the Journal. *Manual* § 108. The Speaker announces:

> The objections of the President will be spread at large upon the Journal and the message and bill will be printed as a House document.

When the message is laid before the House, the question on passage is considered as pending. No motion from the floor to reconsider the bill is necessary. 7 Cannon §§ 1097-1099. If the House does not wish to proceed immediately to reconsider the bill, the motions to lay on the table, to postpone consideration to a day certain, or to refer to committee are available. See § 4, infra. The House also may agree, by unanimous consent, to postpone consideration of a veto message to another day. 101-2, Jan. 23, 1990, p 5; 105-1, Nov. 13, 1997, p 26564; 111-2, Jan. 12, 2010, p ____. Under clause 4 of rule XVI, and under the precedents, the motion for the previous question takes precedence over a motion to postpone or to refer when a question is under debate. However, where the Speaker has laid before the House a veto message from the President but has not yet stated the question to be on overriding the veto, that question is not ''under debate'' and the motion for the previous question does not take precedence. *Manual* § 108. If the House wishes to proceed to the consideration of the message and address the question of passing the bill over the President's veto, it can defeat any preferential motion that is offered and proceed to the main question.

If no preferential motion is offered, the Chair then states the question as follows:

> The pending question is whether the House will, on reconsideration, pass the bill, the objections of the President to the contrary notwithstanding.

§ 3. — Consideration as Privileged

The consideration of a veto message from the President is a matter of high privilege and may interrupt consideration of a pending matter (such as a conference report) if the previous question has not been ordered on that matter. 95-2, Oct. 5, 1978, p 33704. Although its consideration may be postponed to a day certain, it remains highly privileged and becomes the unfinished business on that day. Deschler Ch 24 §§ 22.1, 22.2. A vetoed bill may be laid on the table. However, because it is still highly privileged, a motion to take it from the table is in order at any time. *Manual* § 108; 4 Hinds § 3550; 5 Hinds § 5439; 7 Cannon § 1105. If a veto message is referred to committee, a motion to discharge the committee from further consideration of the message also is highly privileged. 4 Hinds § 3532.

A vetoed bill received in the House from the Senate is considered as if received directly from the President and supersedes the regular order of business. *Manual* § 107; 4 Hinds § 3537; 7 Cannon § 1109. The privilege accorded vetoed bills does not extend to a bill reported in lieu of a vetoed bill. 4 Hinds § 3531; 7 Cannon § 1103.

Although highly privileged, the consideration of a vetoed bill yields to:

- Unfinished business from the preceding day with the previous question ordered. 8 Cannon § 2693.
- Certain matters being considered as questions privileged under the Constitution, such as contested elections or impeachment. 5 Hinds § 6642; 3 Hinds § 2053.
- A motion to adjourn. 4 Hinds § 3523.

§ 4. — Motions in Order

Generally

The mandate under article I, section 7 of the Constitution, that the House ''shall . . . proceed to reconsider'' a vetoed bill, means that the House considers it under the rules of the House, with the ordinary motions under the House rules available. *Manual* § 108. The motions to lay the bill on the table, to postpone to a day certain, and to refer take precedence in the order named over the question of reconsideration of passage, the objections of the President to the contrary notwithstanding, until the previous question is ordered. A Member may not move the previous question on the question of reconsideration where the Chair has not yet stated the question to be pending on overriding the veto. *Manual* § 108; see also 7 Cannon § 1105; § 2, supra.

Postponement

Although the House often takes immediate action on a veto message from the President, the consideration of the message may be postponed to a day certain by unanimous consent or by motion. 4 Hinds §§ 3542-3547; Deschler Ch 24 § 21.9. Such a postponement is not in violation of the constitutional requirement that the House "shall . . . proceed to reconsider" a vetoed bill. *Manual* § 108. The postponement has been for as long as eight months and into the next session of the same Congress. 99-1, Dec. 17, 1985, p 37477. The motion to postpone further consideration of a veto message is debatable for one hour. *Manual* § 108.

When consideration of a veto message is postponed to a day certain, it becomes unfinished business on that day, and its consideration does not require a motion from the floor. Deschler Ch 24 § 22.1. At that time, the veto message may be voted on, tabled, referred to committee, or again postponed as the House determines. *Manual* § 108.

Referral to Committee

A veto message from the President may be referred to a committee by unanimous consent or by motion. 4 Hinds § 3550; Deschler Ch 24 § 21.5. Such a referral is in order in the House even on a bill that the Senate has already passed over the President's veto. 94-2, Jan. 26, 1976, p 874.

A motion to refer a veto message to committee takes precedence over the question of reconsideration. 7 Cannon § 1100. However, although the ordinary motion to refer may be applied to a vetoed bill, the motion is not in order pending the demand for the previous question or after it is ordered on the constitutional question of reconsideration. 7 Cannon § 1102.

Discharge of Committee

A motion to discharge a committee from the consideration of a vetoed bill is privileged. 4 Hinds § 3532. Under the modern practice, such motion is debatable under the hour rule. *Manual* § 108. The motion is renewable every legislative day, notwithstanding the tabling of a prior motion. 100-2, Aug. 10, 1988, p 21589. If a motion to discharge is agreed to, the veto message is pending as unfinished business. *Manual* § 108.

Amendability

A vetoed bill is not amendable in the House, nor in a committee following referral. 4 Hinds § 3551; *cf.* 4 Hinds § 5644.

§ 5. —Debate

Debate on the question of overriding the President's veto of a bill is under the hour rule. Deschler Ch 24 § 22.7. The previous question may be moved by the manager at any time during the debate. Deschler Ch 24 § 22.9. The Chair normally recognizes the chair of the committee or subcommittee that managed the bill to control the debate on the veto message.

§ 6. —Voting; Disposition of Bill

Under article I, section 7 of the Constitution, a vetoed bill becomes law when it is reconsidered and passed by the requisite two-thirds vote in each House. The two-thirds vote required to pass the bill is two-thirds of the Members voting, a quorum being present, and not two-thirds of the total membership of the House. 4 Hinds §§ 3537, 3538; 7 Cannon § 1111. Article I, section 7, further requires that the vote on passage of a bill over the President's veto must be by the yeas and nays. Deschler Ch 24 § 22.10.

The motion to reconsider is not in order on the vote on the question of overriding a veto. 5 Hinds § 5644; 8 Cannon § 2778.

When a vetoed House bill is reconsidered and passed in the House, the House sends the bill and veto message to the Senate and informs that body that it passed by the constitutional two-thirds vote. When the House fails to pass a bill over the President's veto, the bill and veto message are referred to committee, and the Senate is informed of the action of the House. Deschler Ch 24 § 23.

§ 7. Pocket Vetoes

Generally; Use After Final Adjournment

Under the Constitution, if the President neither signs nor returns a bill within 10 days (Sundays excepted), it becomes law as if it had been signed, unless Congress by its adjournment ''prevents its return.'' U.S. Const. art. I, § 7. The President is said to ''pocket veto'' a bill where no action is taken on the bill during the 10-day period and where the Congress adjourns *sine die* before the expiration of that time in such a manner as to prevent the return of the bill to the originating House. *Manual* § 112; Deschler Ch 24 § 18; *The Pocket Veto Case*, 279 U.S. 655, 680 (1929) (dicta).

A constitutional debate still lingers with respect to the conditions under which the President may exercise the pocket veto authority during other types of adjournment of a Congress. The executive and legislative branches have sometimes held different perspectives with respect to the conditions surrounding an adjournment and their impact on the return of a bill disapproved by the President.

During Intersession Adjournments

The Supreme Court has held that the President's return of a bill to the originating House was prevented when the Congress adjourned its first session *sine die* fewer than 10 days after presenting the bill to the President for approval. Because neither House was in session to receive the bill, the President was prevented from returning it, and a pocket veto was upheld. *The Pocket Veto Case*, 279 U.S. 655 (1929). A more recent appellate court decision held that the return of a bill during an adjournment between sessions was not prevented within the meaning of the Constitution where the originating House had appointed an agent for the receipt of Presidential veto messages. The decision further stated that the validity of a pocket veto is governed not by the type or length of adjournment but by whether the conditions of the adjournment impede the actual return of the bill. *Barnes* v. *Kline*, 759 F.2d 21 (D.C. Cir. 1985), *vacated as moot*, *Burke* v. *Barnes*, 479 U.S. 361 (1987). As part of the concurrent resolution providing for the *sine die* adjournment of the first session, the Congress has affirmed its position that an intersession adjournment does not prevent the return of a bill where the Clerk and the Secretary of the Senate are authorized to receive messages during the adjournment. *Manual* § 113. Under clause 2(h) of rule II, the Clerk is authorized to receive messages from the President at any time that the House is not in session. *Manual* § 652. On certain occasions, when the second session of a Congress convenes, the House has asserted its right to reconsider a bill returned with a Presidential ''memorandum of disapproval'' received during the *sine die* adjournment that follows the first session. *Manual* § 113; 101-2, Jan. 23, 1990, p 3.

During Intrasession Adjournments

An adjournment of Congress during a session does not prevent the President from returning a bill disapproved of, as long as appropriate arrangements are made by the originating House for the receipt of Presidential messages during the adjournment. Thus, it has been held that a Senate bill cannot be pocket vetoed by the President during an ''intrasession'' adjournment of Congress for more than three days to a day certain, where the Secretary of the Senate has been authorized to receive Presidential messages during such adjournment. *Kennedy* v. *Sampson*, 511 F.2d 430 (D.C. Cir. 1974); see also *Kennedy* v. *Jones*, 412 F. Supp. 353 (D.D.C. 1976). The Supreme Court has held that the adjournment of the House of origin for a period not exceeding three days while the other House of the Congress remained in session, does not prevent the return of a vetoed bill to the House of origin. *Wright* v. *United States*, 302 U.S. 583 (1938).

In one instance the House and Senate reconsidered and passed a bill that was ostensibly pocket vetoed during an intrasession adjournment. The Administrator of General Services at the Archives (now Archivist), upon receiving instructions from the Department of Justice, declined to promulgate the bill as public law on the day it was received. The question as to the efficacy of the congressional action in passing the bill over the President's veto was mooted when the House and Senate passed an identical bill that was signed into law. *Manual* § 113.

''Protective Return''

Presidents have, on occasion, asserted the ability to employ what is known as a ''protective return'' veto, whereby a bill is not signed, but returned to Congress with a ''memorandum of disapproval,'' asserting pocket veto authority. In such instances, the House has regarded the President's actual return of the bill without a signature as a return veto and proceeded to reconsider the bill over the President's objections. *Manual* § 113.

For a joint letter from Speaker Foley and Minority Leader Michel to the President, and a response thereto by Attorney General Thornburg, on the use of pocket veto authority during an intrasession adjournment, see 101-2, Jan. 23, 1990, p 3. For joint letters from Speakers and Minority Leaders reiterating their predecessors' concerns in this area, see 106-2, Sept. 19, 2000, p 18594; 106-2, Nov. 13, 2000, pp 26022, 26023; 110-2, Oct. 2, 2008, p ____; 111-2, May 26, 2010, p ____. For discussions of the constitutionality of intersession or intrasession pocket vetoes, see Kennedy, ''Congress, The President, and The Pocket Veto,'' 63 Va. L. Rev. 355 (1977), Spitzer, ''The ''Protective Return'' Pocket Veto: President Aggrandizement of Constitutional Power'' 31 Presidential Studies Quarterly 720 (2001), and Hearing, Subcommittee on Legislative Process, Committee on Rules, on H.R. 849, 101st Congress.

§ 8. Line Item Veto Authority

The Line Item Veto Act took effect on January 1, 1997. 2 USC §§ 691-691f. The Act gave the President the authority to cancel discrete dollar amounts of discretionary budget authority, new direct spending, and limited tax benefits contained in Acts sent for approval. Cancellations were effective unless disapproved by law. Such disapprovals could be enacted under the congressional review procedures set forth in the Act. The President has exercised this cancellation authority on a couple of occasions. See H. Doc. 105-147, H. Doc. 105-115, and H. Doc. 105-116. In *Clinton* v. *City of New York*, 524 U.S. 417 (1998), the Supreme Court held that the cancellation authority of the Line Item Veto Act violated the presentment clause of article I, section 7 of the Constitution. Although the congressional review procedures remain in the law, the Court decision makes it unlikely that they will be invoked. See *Manual* § 1130(6B).

Chapter 58
Voting

Research References

U.S. Const. art. I §§ 5, 7
5 Hinds §§ 5925-6105
8 Cannon §§ 3065-3162
Deschler-Brown Ch 30
Manual §§ 75-80, 630, 631, 1012-1034

A. Generally

§ 1. In General; Kinds of Votes

Generally

The rules of the House identify four methods of voting that are in regular use in the full House:

- Voice votes under clause 6 of rule I in which Members express their voting preference simply by calling out "aye" or "no" in unison.
- Division votes under clause 1(a) of rule XX in which Members stand to be counted as either for or against a proposition.
- Yea-and-nay votes, which require the support of one-fifth of the Members present under article I, section 5 of the Constitution or which are ordered automatically when a Member objects to a pending vote on the ground that a quorum is not present under clause 6 of rule XX. Yea-and-nay votes usually are taken by electronic device.
- Recorded votes under clause 1(b) of rule XX, which require the support of one-fifth of a quorum (44 when a quorum is 218). A recorded vote is considered to be a vote by the yeas and nays when taken in the House.

When the House is operating in the Committee of the Whole, all of these commonly used methods of voting are available except for the yeas and nays, which is a vote used only in the House. Under clause 6(e) of rule XVIII, a recorded vote may be ordered in the Committee of the Whole when the demand is supported by at least 25 Members. The automatic vote by the yeas and nays, when a vote is objected to on the grounds that a quorum is not present, is not available in the Committee of the Whole.

Sometimes these voting methods are used in various combinations, one after the other, depending on the circumstances. In the usual case, the Chair first puts a question to a vote by voice under clause 6 of rule I. A record vote may then be demanded.

Less frequently used, but still available under rule XX, are the following: (1) roll call votes, in which each Member's response is given orally as the Clerk calls the roll in alphabetical order (clause 3 of rule XX); and (2) votes by tellers with clerks, in which each Member fills out and signs a vote tally card and submits it to a designated teller (clause 4 of rule XX).

Clause 10 of rule XX requires that the question on final passage of general appropriation bills, budget resolutions, or bills increasing certain Federal income tax rates, or conference reports thereon, be taken by the yeas and nays. Article I, section 7 of the Constitution requires that the question of passing a bill over the veto of the President also must be by the yeas and nays. Under clause 12 of rule XXII, the vote to authorize a closed conference committee meeting also is required to be taken by the yeas and nays.

All votes are in order only when the Chair puts the question. Unauthorized votes, as where a Member asks for a "straw" vote or a "show of hands" are not in order. Deschler-Brown Ch 30 § 2.3.

For a discussion of voting in committees, see COMMITTEES.

Voting by Ballot in Elections

Voting on an election in the House by ballot, although authorized by clause 11 of rule XX, is largely obsolete. *Manual* § 1034. There has been no instance of voting by ballot under this rule since 1868, when the managers of an impeachment proceeding were elected by ballot. 3 Hinds § 2417.

§ 2. The Electronic Voting System

In General

The electronic voting system was installed in the House Chamber in 1972 pursuant to the Legislative Reorganization Act of 1970 and adopted as a voting method by amendments to rule XX. *Manual* § 1012. The new system replaced the lengthy call of the roll and votes by cards with the clerks. Instead, votes are conducted by a computerized device that simultaneously receives and records votes cast by Members during the voting period. A master computer processes voting information for immediate and subsequent retrieval. Members may still vote by card with the clerks in the well, who enter the information into the computer system.

Verification of Vote; Changing Votes

Forty-six electronic voting stations are available in the Chamber. After using one of them, a Member may verify that the vote has been properly recorded by reinserting the voting card in an alternate voting station. Illumination of the button corresponding to the last vote preference will indicate that the vote has been recorded by the system. If the voting system fails, the Chair may allow Members additional time to check the electronic display panel to verify whether their votes were properly recorded. 103-1, Sept. 29, 1993, p 23030.

A Member may change a vote by depressing one of the other buttons. Changes may be made at any time during a five-minute vote, or during the first 10 minutes of a 15-minute vote. With less than five minutes remaining during a 15-minute vote, changes must be made in the well. Changes may also be made in the well after the voting stations have been closed but before the Chair's announcement of the result. *Manual* § 1014. For a discussion of vote changes generally, see § 25, infra.

Effect of Malfunction

Clause 2(b) of rule XX authorizes the Chair to conduct record votes and quorum calls under the alternate procedures prescribed in rule XX when the electronic voting system malfunctions. For example, the Chair may vacate the results of an electronic vote in progress when the system malfunctions and direct that the record vote be conducted by call of the roll under clause 3 of rule XX. *Manual* § 1014a. The Chair may also announce that Members who have been recorded before the malfunction of the electronic device will be included in the new tally of those voting. Deschler-Brown Ch 30 § 31.15. When the system again becomes operative, its use resumes at the Chair's discretion. Deschler-Brown Ch 30 § 31.11.

The question whether the electronic voting system is functioning reliably is in the discretion of the Chair, who may base a judgment on certification by the Clerk. For example, the Speaker continued to use the electronic system, even though the electronic display panel was temporarily inoperative, where the voting stations continued in operation and Members were able to verify their votes. On the other hand, the Chair vacated the results of an electronic vote and directed that the record vote be taken by call of the roll where the electronic display panel malfunctioned, and the Chair could not obtain verification from the Clerk that the vote would be recorded with 100 percent accuracy. *Manual* § 1014a. A malfunction of the monitor at the majority or minority table will not prevent use of the electronic system where an alternate monitor may be used. 93-2, Aug. 7, 1974, p 27219.

§ 3. Prohibitions Against Voting by Proxy or for Absent Members

Whether in the House or the Committee of the Whole, Members must vote in person. *Manual* § 674; 7 Cannon § 1014. No one other than a Member may cast a vote or record a Member's presence. A Member may not cast a vote on behalf of another Member, and an authorization to that end is forbidden by clause 2 of rule III.

The use of an electronic voting card belonging to a Member who is *in absentia*—sometimes referred to as ''ghost voting''—is considered a serious breach of ethics. A Member's participation in such activity, either by direction or by subsequent acquiescence or ratification, is a matter warranting sanction by the House. The House has reprimanded a Member for failing to prevent unauthorized use of a voting card. Deschler-Brown Ch 30 § 3.16.

B. Role of the Chair; Duties

§ 4. In General; Putting the Question

An essential step in bringing a pending proposition to a vote occurs when the Speaker or Chair states and then puts the question as prescribed by clause 6 of rule I. *Manual* § 630. It is a breach of order for the Speaker to refuse to put a question that is in order. *Manual* § 304.

A question may be put to a vote only by the Chair. It is not in order for a Member having the floor to usurp the role of the Chair in this regard, as by asking for a demonstration of support, such as a ''straw vote'' before the question is put. *Manual* § 630; Deschler-Brown Ch 30 § 2.3. The proposition as stated by the Chair in putting the question, and not as stated by the sponsoring Member, is the proposition voted upon. 6 Cannon § 247.

Putting the question on engrossment and third reading before passage of a bill or joint resolution is required by clause 8 of rule XVI. However, where a statute requires the vote to occur on final passage immediately following the conclusion of general debate, the Speaker puts the question on final passage without putting the question on ordering the previous question or on engrossment and third reading. 99-1, Apr. 23, 1985, p 9085.

§ 5. Voting by the Chair

Right to Vote

The Speaker has the same right to vote as other Members, and the Speaker has exercised this right even in contravention of early House rules attempting to limit the Speaker's voting authority. *Manual* § 631; 5 Hinds §§ 5964, 5966. The Speaker may vote "aye" or "no" at any time before the final announcement of the vote. Deschler-Brown Ch 30 § 21.2. On an electronic vote, the Speaker may direct the Clerk to record the Speaker's vote and verifies that instruction by submitting a vote card. *Manual* § 631. On roll call votes, the Speaker's name is not called except at the Speaker's request, and then at the end of the roll. *Manual* § 631. Members, other than the Speaker, who are occupying the Chair vote by submitting a voting card to the Clerk, who then enters the vote.

In the early history of the House, Speakers exercised the right to vote sparingly. 5 Hinds § 5964 (note). In more recent Congresses, it has become more common for Speakers to vote, especially on important legislation.

Duty to Vote

Under clause 7 of rule I, the Speaker is not required to vote "except when such vote would be decisive . . . ." *Manual* § 631. The Speaker may vote to cause a tie and thus defeat a measure or to break a tie and thus pass or adopt a measure. 8 Cannon § 3100; Deschler Ch 6 § 5.

§ 6. Chair's Responsibility as to the Count

One of the responsibilities of the Speaker is to count the number of Members rising in support of, or against, a pending proposition, as where a vote is taken by division. One of the suppositions on which parliamentary law is founded is that the Speaker will not betray the duty to make an honest count of the vote. 5 Hinds § 6002. The integrity of the Chair in counting a vote is not subject to a direct challenge. *Manual* § 629; 8 Cannon § 3115. Appeals may not be taken from the Chair's count of the number rising to demand a vote. 8 Cannon § 3105; Deschler-Brown Ch 30 § 33.5. An appeal also will not lie from a count of those supporting the demand for the yeas and nays (Deschler-Brown Ch 30 § 26.8) or from a decision refusing recapitulation of a vote (8 Cannon § 3128). The remedy of a Member dissatisfied with the Speaker's count of Members rising, as on a division vote, is to demand a record vote. 8 Cannon §§ 3115-3118.

C. Rights and Duties of Members

§7. In General; Duty to Vote

The casting of a vote (or the refusal to cast a vote) is the responsibility of the individual Member. Although clause 1 of rule III states that Members "shall vote on each question put . . . ", in practice the House does not enforce this provision. *Manual* §671. The Speaker has no power to compel a Member to vote. 5 Hinds §5942. House actions to compel a Member to cast a vote have been uniformly unsuccessful. 5 Hinds §§5943-5948. By the same token, the House does not excuse a Member from voting other than by granting "leaves of absence" under clause 1 of rule III. A unanimous-consent request in the Committee of the Whole to excuse a Member from voting will not be entertained. Deschler-Brown Ch 30 §3.3.

§8. Disqualification to Vote

Generally; Conviction of Crime

The precedents suggest that the House has no authority to deprive a Member of the inherent right to vote. *Manual* §672; 5 Hinds §§5952, 5966, 5967; 8 Cannon §3072.

Clause 10 of rule XXIII, part of the Code of Official Conduct, provides that a Member who is convicted of a crime for which a prison sentence of two or more years could be imposed "should" refrain from voting in the House or the Committee of the Whole until reinstatement of the presumption of innocence or until such Member is reelected to the House. *Manual* §1095. The term "conviction" in clause 10 is construed to include a plea of guilty or a certified finding of guilt even though sentencing may occur later. H. Rept. 94-76.

Personal or Pecuniary Interest

Clause 1 of rule III provides that a Member is not required to vote where such Member has a "direct personal or pecuniary" interest in the question. *Manual* §671. In rare instances the Speaker has ruled that a Member, because of such Member's personal interest in the outcome, should not vote. 5 Hinds §§5955, 5958. However, ordinarily the Member—and not the Chair—determines this question. 5 Hinds §§5950, 5951; 8 Cannon §3071; Deschler-Brown Ch 30 §3.1. The Speaker will not sustain a point of order challenging the personal or pecuniary interest of Members in a pending question, and will defer to the judgment of each Member as to the directness of the interest. *Manual* §672.

Members may abstain from voting on a measure because of a personal or pecuniary interest in the measure being considered and thus announce an intention to be recorded as ''present'' on the issue. Deschler-Brown Ch 30 §§ 3.5, 3.7.

Where the subject of a vote before the House affects an entire class, the personal interest of Members who belong to the class is not such as to disqualify them from voting. 5 Hinds § 5952. In one instance, for example, during consideration of a bill providing financial assistance to States and political subdivisions, the Speaker indicated that the bill was sufficiently general in scope that Members holding municipal bonds or who had other financial interests dependent on the fiscal affairs of a particular city would merely be within a class of similarly situated individuals whose pecuniary interest would not be so direct as to preclude them from voting on the bill. Deschler-Brown Ch 30 § 3.10.

D. Nonrecord Votes

§ 9. In General; Voice Votes

Votes not of record are those for which no official public record is required of the names or votes of the participating Members. There are two types of nonrecord votes. The first is a voice vote under clause 6 of rule I. The second is a vote by division under clause 1(a) of rule XX. § 10, infra. Authority for demanding a vote by tellers was eliminated from the rules in the 103d Congress. § 11, infra.

Voice votes are the simplest and most commonly used of all voting procedures. Such votes are based on the volume of sound produced by Members as they respond either ''aye'' or ''no'' to the question put by the Chair. *Manual* § 630; 5 Hinds § 5926. If the Chair is in doubt about the result, or if any Member requests it, a division vote is in order. *Manual* § 1012. In a division vote, those in favor and then those opposed are asked to stand and be counted. § 10, infra.

In most situations, the Speaker must put the pending question to a voice vote under clause 6 of rule I before entertaining a demand for a recorded vote or the yeas and nays. Deschler-Brown Ch 30 § 7.1.

§ 10. Voting by Division

Generally; Form

A demand for a division (standing) vote is in order following the taking of a voice vote, although this method of voting is rarely used in modern practice. Deschler-Brown Ch 30 § 17.1. Under clause 1 of rule XX, after a voice vote, if the Speaker is in doubt or a division is demanded, "[t]he House shall divide . . . . Those in favor of the question shall first rise from their seats to be counted, and then those opposed." *Manual* § 1012. Only one demand for a vote by division on a pending question is in order. Deschler-Brown Ch 30 § 11.9.

MEMBER: M__. Speaker, I demand a division.
CHAIR: A division is demanded. As many as are in favor will rise and stand until counted. . . .
The ayes will be seated and the noes will stand.

Timeliness

A demand for a division comes too late when the Member making it was not seeking recognition at the time the Chair announced the result of the voice vote. Deschler-Brown Ch 30 § 9.9. However, the mere announcement of a voice vote does not preclude a demand for a division provided that no intervening business has transpired and the proponent of a division was seeking recognition at the time of the announcement. Deschler-Brown Ch 30 § 9.5.

Precedence of Demand for Recorded Vote or Yea-and-Nay Vote

A demand for the yeas and nays in the House under article I, section 5 of the Constitution takes precedence over a demand for a division. Deschler-Brown Ch 30 § 14.1.

A demand for the yeas and nays may be made before or after a division vote, or even while a division vote is being announced. 5 Hinds § 6039. However, the demand may not interrupt a division while the Chair is counting. *Manual* § 1012; Deschler-Brown Ch 30 § 10.3. A demand for a division vote is not precluded by the fact that the yeas and nays have been refused. 8 Cannon § 3103.

When the Chair has put the question and is in doubt as to the result, the Chair has the discretion under clause 1(a) of rule XX to conduct a vote by division before entertaining a demand for a record vote. Deschler-Brown Ch 30 § 9.2. The Chair may also entertain a demand for a record vote without first conducting a division. Deschler-Brown Ch 30 § 9.3. However, the Chair's count cannot be interrupted by a demand for a record vote. Deschler-Brown Ch 30 § 10.4.

Interruptions During the Count

The Chair generally declines to recognize Members while counting those standing on a division vote. Parliamentary inquiries are entertained before (not after) the Chair asks those in favor of the proposition to rise.

Deschler-Brown Ch 30 § 10.2. Under clause 7 of rule XXII, a conference report may not be presented while the House is dividing. *Manual* § 1077. Messages are not received during a division. *Manual* § 562.

Because a vote by division takes no cognizance of Members present but not voting, the number of votes counted by division does not necessarily establish a lack of a quorum. *Manual* § 1012. Accordingly, the Chair may interrupt the count of Members standing in favor of a proposition in order to count for a quorum pursuant to a point of order that a quorum is not present. *Manual* § 1012.

§ 11. Teller Votes

Under the earlier practice of the House, a Member could demand a teller vote if supported by a sufficient number of Members. 5 Hinds § 5986. However, teller votes are almost never used in modern practice, as the rule authorizing a demanded teller vote was abolished in 1993. *Manual* § 1013. While used infrequently, under clause 4 of rule XX, the Speaker may direct a vote by tellers. For an explanation of the method of taking teller votes, see Deschler-Brown Ch 30 § 16. For a discussion of teller votes and the Speaker's discretion, see § 18, infra.

E. Votes of Record

§ 12. Yea-and-Nay Votes; Recorded Votes

Yea-and-Nay Votes Distinguished

There are two primary methods of taking a vote of record in the House of Representatives. Voting by the yeas and nays under article I, section 5 of the Constitution is the preeminent method of voting and its initiation is to be distinguished from the recorded vote available under separate House rules. Clause 6 of rule XX also orders the yeas and nays in the absence of a quorum whenever a vote is objected to for lack of a quorum. *Manual* § 1025. Yea-and-nay votes are not in order in the Committee of the Whole. 4 Hinds § 4722. Recorded votes, on the other hand, are available in both the House (clause 1(b) of rule XX) and the Committee of the Whole (clause 6(e) of rule XVIII).

Yea-and-nay votes require the support of one-fifth *of those present.* § 14, infra. On the other hand, a recorded vote in the House requires the support of one-fifth *of a quorum* (44 when a quorum is 218). Deschler-Brown Ch 30 § 34.1. A request for a recorded vote in the Committee of the Whole must be supported by 25 Members under clause 6(e) of rule

XVIII. It is the Chair's statement of the demand, and not the Member's request, that controls whether one-fifth of those present or one-fifth of a quorum is required to support the demand. Deschler-Brown Ch 30 § 2.2.

Demanding a Recorded Vote

Under the rules, a recorded vote is in order in the House or in the Committee of the Whole after the question has been put to a voice vote:

> CHAIR: The question is on the amendment offered by the gentle______ from __________. [voice vote]
> MEMBER: M__. Speaker [or M__. Chair], I demand a recorded vote.
> CHAIR: The gentle______ asks for a recorded vote. As many as are in favor of taking this vote by a recorded vote will stand and remain standing until counted.

A demand for a recorded vote in the House under clause 1 of rule XX must be supported by one-fifth of a quorum (usually 44 Members). Deschler-Brown Ch 30 § 34.1. The demand must be supported by 25 Members in the Committee of the Whole under clause 6(e) of rule XVIII. The count of Members standing to support a demand for a recorded vote is not subject to challenge by appeal. Deschler-Brown Ch 30 § 33.5.

In the House, a request for a recorded vote must yield to the constitutional prerogative of a Member to demand the yeas and nays. § 14, infra. However, a request for a recorded vote may be made following a demand for the yeas and nays, if that demand is withdrawn or does not receive the required support. Deschler-Brown Ch 30 §§ 33.2, 33.3. Even the Member who has withdrawn a demand for the yeas and nays may request a recorded vote under clause 1(b) of rule XX. Deschler-Brown Ch 30 § 33.4. Where one-fifth of the Members present have refused to order the yeas and nays on a motion, and that motion later becomes the unfinished business of the House, a Member may still demand a recorded vote on the motion but may not renew a demand for the yeas and nays. Deschler-Brown Ch 30 § 55.5.

Timeliness of Demand for Recorded Vote; Interruptions

A request for a recorded vote is in order only after the Chair has put the question to a voice vote. Deschler-Brown Ch 30 § 7.1. It cannot interrupt a voice vote or a vote by division that is in progress. *Manual* § 1012; Deschler-Brown Ch 30 § 7.1. The demand is not timely if the Member making it is not seeking recognition at the time that the result of the vote is announced by the Chair. Deschler-Brown Ch 30 § 33.18. However, a Member's demand for a recorded vote may be made after the Chair announces the result of a division vote if no other business has intervened. Deschler-Brown Ch 30 § 9.5.

A demand for a recorded vote on an amendment comes too late after the amendment has been voted on and disposed of and the Chair has inquired as to the purpose of another Member seeking recognition. Deschler-Brown Ch 30 §§ 24.6, 33.17. However, a mere inquiry relating to a pending motion, raised after the Chair has announced the result of a voice vote, does not constitute such intervening business as to preclude the right of a Member to demand a recorded vote on the pending motion. *Manual* § 1012. If the demand comes too late, it is within the province of the Chair to recognize for a unanimous-consent request to vacate proceedings and thereby set the stage for putting the question a second time so a recorded vote can be demanded. Deschler-Brown Ch 30 § 33.18.

Repetition or Renewal of Demand

Only one request for a recorded vote on a pending question is in order. *Manual* § 1012. Thus, a request for a recorded vote on a pending question having been refused, a second request is not in order following a division vote on that question. Deschler-Brown Ch 30 § 33.7.

A similar rule is followed in the Committee of the Whole. Where the Committee has refused a request for a recorded vote, the request may be renewed only by unanimous consent. Deschler-Brown Ch 30 § 33.9. This is true even where the absence of a quorum is disclosed immediately following the Chair's announcement of the refusal or where a quorum call has intervened. Deschler-Brown Ch 30 §§ 33.10, 33.11. However, the request remains pending where the Chair had interrupted the count of Members standing in support of the demand in order to count for a quorum. 97-2, Aug. 5, 1982, p 19658. For a request to be once denied, the Chair must have finalized the count. In one instance, the chair of the Committee of the Whole, having announced that an insufficient number of Members had arisen in support of a request for a recorded vote on an amendment (but having hedged that announcement with the word ''apparently'' and having refrained from stating the conclusion that the recorded vote was refused), nevertheless entertained a point of no quorum, tacitly treating the request for a recorded vote as not yet finalized. 107-1, Oct. 11, 2001, p 19385.

Withdrawal of Demand

A demand for a recorded vote may be withdrawn without unanimous consent before the Chair finalizes the count. Deschler-Brown Ch 30 §§ 33.20, 33.21.

Postponement of Vote

For a discussion of the Chair's authority to postpone votes in the House and in the Committee of the Whole, see §§ 22, 23, infra.

§ 13. Ordering the Yeas and Nays

In General; When Required

The yeas and nays usually are in order only after they are demanded by a Member and the demand is supported by a sufficient number of Members. § 14, infra. However, in some cases the yeas and nays are required by law or by House rule. Under article I, section 7 of the Constitution, a vote by the yeas and nays is required to pass a bill over the President's veto. 4 Hinds § 3520; 7 Cannon § 1110; see also VETO OF BILLS.

The yeas and nays are to be "considered as ordered" when the question is put on certain measures such as a bill providing general appropriations or certain income tax rate increases or a concurrent resolution on the budget. Clause 10 of rule XX. The yeas and nays are automatically ordered under the House rules when a vote has been objected to for lack of a quorum, thereby precipitating a simultaneous quorum call. § 16, infra. A vote by the yeas and nays is required to authorize a closed conference committee meeting under clause 12 of rule XXII. *Manual* § 1093. Such a vote also may be required by statute. See, *e.g.*, 50 USC § 1545 (War Powers Resolution); 50 USC § 1622 (termination of national emergency).

Effect of Ordering

The ordering of the yeas and nays ordinarily brings the pending proposition to a vote but does not necessarily preclude all other business. A motion to adjourn may be admitted after the yeas and nays are ordered and before the vote has begun. 5 Hinds § 5366. Consideration of a conference report or a motion to reconsider the vote by which the yeas and nays have been ordered also has been permitted to intervene. *Manual* § 80; 5 Hinds § 6029; 8 Cannon § 2790.

Effect of Adjournment

An order for the yeas and nays remains in effect during an adjournment and is taken up whenever the bill again comes before the House. 8 Cannon § 3108. However, should a quorum fail to vote and the House adjourn, the question recurs *de novo* when the bill again comes before the House. Deschler Ch 20 §§ 8.2, 10.17.

§ 14. Demanding the Yeas and Nays

In General

A demand for the yeas and nays is in order after the question has been put. Deschler-Brown Ch 30 § 7.1. However, a vote by the yeas and nays is taken only if a sufficient number of Members rise in support of the demand. Under article I, section 5 of the Constitution, the demand must be supported by one-fifth of the Members present. *Manual* §§ 75, 77.

> MEMBER: M__. Speaker, I demand the yeas and nays.
>
> SPEAKER: The yeas and nays are requested. As many as are in favor of taking this vote by yeas and nays will rise and remain standing until counted.
>
> A sufficient number having arisen, the yeas and nays are ordered. [*Or*] An insufficient number having arisen, the yeas and nays are refused.

It is well established that a quorum is not necessary to the ordering of the yeas and nays. *Manual* § 76; 5 Hinds §§ 6016-6028. In ascertaining whether one-fifth of those present support a demand for the yeas and nays, the Speaker counts the entire number present as well as those who rise in favor of the demand. 8 Cannon §§ 3111, 3120. A request for a rising of those opposed to the demand is not in order. 8 Cannon §§ 3112-3114. The Chair ordinarily first counts those supporting the demand and then counts the House. Latecomers in support of the demand are included in the count until it is closed by the Chair. *Manual* § 78. The Speaker's count of the House on this question is not subject to appeal. *Manual* § 78.

When in Order

The Speaker must put the question before a demand for the yeas and nays is in order. *Manual* § 76. The demand is in order after the Speaker has put the question to a voice vote, is announcing the result of a division, and even after the announcement of such a vote if the House has not passed on to other business. 5 Hinds §§ 6039-6041. However, a demand for the yeas and nays comes too late after the Speaker has put the question on a motion and announced the result and the House has proceeded to other business. Deschler-Brown Ch 30 § 24.6. It is likewise untimely where the Chair has put a question to a voice vote, announced the result, and by unanimous consent laid the motion to reconsider on the table, where the Member was not seeking recognition when the question was put. Deschler-Brown Ch 29 § 8.25.

Precedence of Demand

Being of constitutional origin, a demand for the yeas and nays in the House takes precedence over a demand for a recorded vote. Deschler-Brown Ch 30 § 33.2. A demand for the yeas and nays likewise takes precedence over a demand for a division vote. Deschler-Brown Ch 30 § 14.1.

Demands as Dilatory; Repetition of Demand

The constitutional provision authorizing a demand for the yeas and nays is liberally construed. 8 Cannon § 3110. The demand may be made by any Member and cannot be denied merely on the ground that it is dilatory. 5 Hinds § 5737; 8 Cannon § 3107. However, the yeas and nays having been refused once may not be demanded again on the same question. 5 Hinds § 6029. It is not in order during the various processes of a division vote to repeat a demand for the yeas and nays that has been rejected. 5 Hinds § 6030.

Withdrawal

When the demand for the yeas and nays has been supported by one-fifth of the Members present, it is too late for the Member making the demand to withdraw it except by unanimous consent. Deschler-Brown Ch 30 § 24.8.

§ 15. Voting by the Yeas and Nays

In General

Under the earlier practice, yea-and-nay votes were cast in response to the Clerk's call of the roll of Members in alphabetical order. Today, yea-and-nay votes almost invariably are cast by use of the electronic voting system. However, the Speaker has the discretion under clause 3 of rule XX to have the Clerk call the roll for the yeas and nays. *Manual* § 1015. The Speaker may also direct the Clerk to call the roll, in lieu of taking the vote by electronic device, when the voting system is temporarily inoperative. Deschler-Brown Ch 30 §§ 31.8-31.10.

Reconsideration

A motion to reconsider a vote ordering the yeas and nays or refusing the yeas and nays is in order. *Manual* § 79; 5 Hinds §§ 5692, 6029; 8 Cannon § 2790. A yea-and-nay vote itself is likewise subject to reconsideration. If the House (by a majority vote) agrees to reconsider, the yeas and nays again may be ordered by one-fifth of those present. 5 Hinds §§ 5689-5691. However, if the House, having reconsidered, again orders the yeas and nays, a second motion to reconsider is not in order. 5 Hinds § 6037.

Disclosure of Member's Vote

A Member's vote, whether ''yea,'' ''nay,'' or ''present,'' appears in the *Congressional Record* and, as required by article I, section 5 of the Constitution, in the House Journal. *Manual* § 75. However, there is no requirement that a Member's vote be announced publicly during the vote. *Manual* § 76.

§ 16. Automatic Yea-and-Nay Votes

Any nonrecord vote in the House may be objected to for lack of a quorum under clause 6 of rule XX, thereby precipitating, in the absence of a quorum, a quorum call and a simultaneous automatic ordering of the yeas and nays. 6 Cannon § 697; Deschler-Brown Ch 30 § 23. Clause 6 provides that ''[w]hen a quorum fails to vote on a question, a quorum is not present, and objection is made for that cause . . . . there shall be a call of the House . . . . and the yeas and nays . . . . shall at the same time be considered as ordered.'' *Manual* § 1025. An automatic call under this rule is not in order in Committee of the Whole. *Manual* § 1026.

The Speaker may direct that an automatic vote in the House be taken by electronic device. The Speaker also has the discretion to direct the Clerk to call the roll. Deschler-Brown Ch 30 § 31.9.

Procedures under clause 6 of rule XX when a quorum fails to vote are applicable regardless of the method of voting, but do not apply when the House is voting on a question that does not require a quorum, such as a motion incidental to a call of the House. 4 Hinds §§ 2994, 3053; 6 Cannon §§ 681, 691, 697, 703. Although a quorum is not required to adjourn, a point of no quorum on a negative vote on adjournment, if sustained, precipitates a call of the House under the rule. 6 Cannon § 700; Deschler-Brown Ch 30 § 11.4.

For a further discussion of quorums and voting, see QUORUMS.

§ 17. Roll Call Votes

In General

Because of the availability of the electronic voting system, roll call votes are rarely taken under the modern practice. Today roll call votes ordinarily are taken only during the process of electing a Speaker—where the Members respond by surname—or in the event of a malfunction of the electronic voting system. *Manual* § 27; Deschler-Brown Ch 30 § 31.15. Nevertheless, the Speaker has broad discretionary power to invoke a roll call vote, in lieu of taking the vote by electronic device, even where a quorum fails to vote on any question and objection is made for that reason. *Manual* § 1014; Deschler Ch 20 § 4.2.

The Clerk calls the roll of Members in alphabetical order by surname. 5 Hinds § 6046. The Speaker's name may be called at the close of the roll at the direction of the Speaker. 5 Hinds § 5965. The roll is called twice—the second roll call being limited to those Members who failed to respond to the first call. 4 Hinds § 3052. A Member may cast a vote even after such Member's name has been called, provided the result of the vote has not been announced. *Manual* § 1015.

Interruptions

A motion to adjourn may be offered before the roll call begins. 4 Hinds § 3050. Under clause 6(c) of rule XX, after Members have had the requisite opportunity to respond by the yeas and nays but before a result has been announced, a motion that the House adjourn is in order if seconded by a majority of those present (to be ascertained by actual count by the Speaker). If the House adjourns pursuant to such a motion, the yeas and nays are vacated.

A roll call may be interrupted for the reception of messages and by the arrival of the hour fixed for adjournment *sine die*. *Manual* § 1018; 5 Hinds §§ 6715-6718. However, a roll call, once under way, may not be interrupted by:

- A motion to adjourn (except as provided in clause 6(c) of rule XX). 5 Hinds § 6053.
- A parliamentary inquiry, unless related to the vote. 5 Hinds §§ 6054, 6058; 8 Cannon § 3132.
- A question of personal privilege. 5 Hinds § 6058; 6 Cannon §§ 554, 564.
- The arrival of the hour fixed for another order of business. 5 Hinds § 6056.
- The arrival of the hour fixed for a recess. 5 Hinds §§ 6054, 6055; 8 Cannon § 3133.
- The presentation of a conference report. 5 Hinds § 6443.

§ 18. Teller Votes With Clerks

"Tellers with clerks" refers to a voting method adopted in 1971 to make it possible to record the votes of individual Members in the Committee of the Whole. Clause 4 of rule XX; *Manual* § 1019. Under this rarely used voting practice, the Chair has the discretion to order the Clerk to "record the names of those Members voting on each side of the question . . . . " Each Member is given a tally card on which to enter a voting preference and a signature. The Members then deposit these cards in ballot boxes located in the Chamber, with the "aye" boxes located up the aisle at the rear of the Chamber at the Chair's left and the "no" boxes located up the aisle at the Chair's right.

Tellers with clerks as a voting method fell into disuse in 1972 with the adoption of the more efficient electronic voting system. See § 2, supra. Tellers with clerks remains as a backup procedure to be used in the event of malfunction of the electronic system or in the event the Clerk is unable to call the roll. *Manual* § 1019.

§ 19. Pairing

General Pairs; Specific Pairs

The practice of announcing general pairs was deleted from the rules in the 106th Congress. For a history of the former rule, see *Manual* § 1031.

"Live" Pairs

Although rarely used, the announcement of live pairs, which involve an agreement between one Member who is present and voting and another on the opposite side of the question, who is absent, is still permitted under clause 3 of rule XX. *Manual* § 1015. By agreement, the voting Member withdraws the previous vote and instead votes "present" by submitting an amber "present" card. Deschler-Brown Ch 30 § 4.

> MEMBER: M__. Speaker, on the vote just recorded I voted "aye" (or "no"). I have a pair with the gentle______ from __________ and desire to change my vote and be recorded as "Present."
>
> CHAIR: The Clerk will call the gentle______'s name.

Such announcements must be made before the vote is finally declared. Deschler-Brown Ch 30 § 4.11.

F. Voting Periods; Time Limitations

§ 20. In General; 15-minute Votes

15-minute Votes

Under clause 2(a) of rule XX and clause 6(g) of rule XVIII, Members have a minimum of 15 minutes from the time of the ordering of a record vote in the House or in the Committee of the Whole. The Chair has the discretion to close the vote and to announce the result at any time after 15 minutes have elapsed or to allow additional time for Members to record their votes before announcing the result. *Manual* § 1014. Thus, no point of order lies against the decision of the Chair to close a vote taken by electronic device after 15 minutes have elapsed, such decision being within the Chair's sole discretion. *Manual* § 1014.

At the beginning of a new Congress, the Speaker has inserted in the *Congressional Record* an announcement that, in order to expedite the conduct of votes by electronic device, the cloakrooms were directed not to forward to the Chair individual requests to hold a vote open. The Speaker has also announced that each occupant of the Chair would have the Speaker's full support in striving to close each electronic vote at the earliest opportunity and that Members should not rely on signals relayed from outside the Chamber to assume that votes will be held open until they arrive. At the same time, the Chair will not close a vote while a Member is in the well attempting to vote. *Manual* § 1014. Where the Chair has prematurely attempted to close a vote while voting cards submitted in the well were still being tabulated, the Chair has allowed such tabulation to continue before announcing the final outcome of the vote. 110-1, Aug. 2, 2007, p 22545.

It is not in order, even by unanimous consent, to permit a Member to have a vote recorded after the announcement of the result, even though the Member claims to have been in the Chamber before the announcement. Deschler-Brown Ch 30 §§ 36.2, 36.4. However, Members may, by unanimous consent, announce how they would have voted if permitted. See §§ 25-27, infra.

Voting Alerts; Bell and Light System

A legislative call system alerts Members to the taking of a vote as well as to the kind of vote and to the duration of the voting period. This system uses bells and lights that are activated through clocks located throughout the House and its adjacent office buildings. *Manual* § 1016. A mechanical malfunction of this call system does not result in the retaking of a vote except by unanimous consent. 8 Cannon §§ 3153, 3154. Such failure does not permit a Member to be recorded following the conclusion of the call. *Manual* § 1016. In one instance, the Committee of the Whole agreed by unanimous consent to vacate a recorded vote on an amendment, permitting a new recorded vote to be taken, where it was alleged that erroneous clocks outside the Chamber and on the televised proceedings had misled Members as to the amount of time available. 98-1, May 3, 1983, p 10773.

The system, comprising bells and lights, is used as follows:

- Recorded vote, yeas and nays, or automatic record vote taken either by electronic system or by use of tellers with ballot cards—two bells and two lights on left indicate a vote by which Members are recorded by name. Bells are repeated five minutes after the first ring.
- Recorded vote, yeas and nays, or automatic record electronic vote to be followed immediately by possible five-minute vote under clause 8(c) or 9 of rule XX or clause 6(f) or 6(g) of rule XVIII—two bells rung at beginning of first vote, followed by five bells, indicate that the Chair will order five-minute votes if record vote is ordered immediately thereafter. Two bells repeated five minutes after first ring. Five bells on each subsequent electronic vote.
- Recorded vote in the Committee of the Whole to be followed immediately by possible vote of less than five minutes under clauses 6(f) or 6(g) of rule XVIII—two bells rung at beginning of first vote, followed by two bells indicate that Chair will order less-then-five-minute votes if recorded vote is ordered immediately thereafter. Two bells repeated five minutes after first ring. Two bells on each subsequent electronic vote.
- Record vote—two bells, followed by a brief pause, then two bells, indicate such a vote taken by a call of the roll in the House. The bells are repeated when the Clerk reaches the ''R's'' in the first call of the roll.
- Regular quorum call—three bells and three lights on left indicate a quorum call either in the House or in Committee of the Whole by electronic system or by clerks. The bells are repeated five minutes after the first ring. Where quorum call is by call of the roll, three bells followed by a brief pause, then three more bells, with the process repeated when the Clerk reaches the ''R's'' in the first call of the roll, are used.
- Regular quorum call in Committee of the Whole, which may be followed immediately by five-minute electronic recorded vote—three bells rung at beginning of quorum call, followed by five bells, indicate that the Chair will order five-minute vote if record vote is ordered on pending question. Three bells repeated five minutes after first ring. Five bells for record vote on pending question if ordered.
- Notice or short quorum call in Committee of the Whole—one long bell followed by three regular bells, and three lights on left, indicate that the Chair has chosen, using the authority under clause 6 of rule XVIII, to vacate proceedings when a quorum of the Committee appears. Bells are repeated every five minutes unless the call is vacated by the ringing of one long bell and the extinguishing of three lights or the call is converted into a regular quorum call and three regular bells are rung.
- Adjournment—four bells and four lights on left.
- A five-minute vote—five bells and five lights on left.
- Recess of the House—six bells and six lights on left.
- Civil Defense Warning—twelve bells, sounded at two-second intervals, with six lights illuminated.
- The light on the far right—seven—indicates that the House is in session.

§21. Five-Minute Votes in the House; "15-and-5" Votes

Generally

Under clause 9 of rule XX, the Speaker may reduce to five minutes the time for electronic voting on any question arising without intervening business after an electronic vote on another question if notice of possible five-minute voting was issued before the first electronic vote.

These votes, often referred to as "15-and-5" votes, are in order before other business intervenes. For example, clause 9 of rule XX does not give the Chair the authority to reduce to five minutes the vote on a motion to recommit occurring immediately after a recorded vote on an amendment reported from the Committee of the Whole, and the Chair will not entertain a unanimous-consent request to reduce that vote to five minutes after Members have already left the Chamber with the expectation that the next vote will be a 15-minute vote. *Manual* §1032.

By Unanimous Consent

The House may by unanimous consent authorize the Speaker to reduce the time to respond to a recorded vote. By unanimous consent, the House reduced to five minutes the minimum time for a required record vote on a motion to authorize a closed conference meeting, to be taken immediately following another record vote previously postponed. 98-1, Aug. 1, 1983, p 22029. The Chair has declined to recognize for a unanimous-consent request to reduce to five minutes the first vote in a series because the bell and light system would not give adequate notice of an initial five-minute vote. Under extraordinary circumstances, when many consecutive votes are taken, the House may set the response time at two minutes by unanimous consent. *Manual* §1032.

§22. Postponed and Clustered Votes in Committee of the Whole

Two-Minute Votes

Although 15 minutes is the usual minimum time for Members to respond on a recorded vote in the Committee of the Whole, the Chair has the discretion, under some circumstances, to reduce such time to not less than two minutes. Prior to the 112th Congress, such period was five minutes, with two-minute voting authorized on an ad hoc basis by unanimous consent. *Manual* §984. The Chair has the discretion under clause 6 of rule XVIII to reduce to two minutes the period for a recorded vote following a regular 15-minute quorum call. *Manual* §982. An announcement of a possible two-minute vote is normally made by the Chair in advance. 98-1, May 4, 1983, p 11063.

Postponed Votes on Amendments

Under clause 6(g) of rule XVIII, the chair of the Committee of the Whole may postpone a request for a recorded vote on any amendment. Proceedings on that amendment may be resumed at the Chair's discretion. Clause 6(g) further permits the Chair to reduce to two minutes the time for electronic voting on any postponed question that follows another electronic vote without intervening business, provided the first vote in any series is a 15-minute vote. *Manual* § 984.

Before the adoption of clause 6(g) of rule XVIII, the chair of the Committee of the Whole could not entertain a unanimous-consent request to reduce below 15 minutes the minimum time for recorded votes or to postpone and cluster votes on amendments. *Manual* § 984. Special orders of business before adoption of clause 6(g) routinely provided the chair of the Committee of the Whole authority to postpone and cluster requests for recorded votes. When a special order of business provided such authority, the Chair held the following (also applicable to the Chair's authority under the standing rule):

- The use of postponement authority, and the order of resuming proceedings on postponed questions, is entirely within the discretion of the Chair.
- An amendment pending as unfinished business, where proceedings on a request for a recorded vote have been postponed, may be modified by unanimous consent on the initiative of its proponent.
- A request for a recorded vote on an amendment on which proceedings have been postponed may be withdrawn by unanimous consent before proceedings resume on the request as unfinished business, in which case the amendment stands disposed of by the voice vote thereon.
- Authority to postpone a request for a recorded vote does not permit the Chair to postpone a vote on an appeal of a ruling of the Chair, even by unanimous consent.
- The Committee of the Whole by unanimous consent may vacate postponed proceedings, thereby permitting the Chair to put the question *de novo*.
- The Chair may resume proceedings on unfinished business consisting of a "stack" of amendments even while another amendment is pending.
- The offering of a pro forma amendment to discuss the legislative program, or an extended one-minute speech by a Member to express gratitude to the Members on a personal matter, may be considered intervening business such as to preclude a two-minute vote under this authority.

Manual § 984.

§23. Postponed and Clustered Votes in the House

The Speaker has discretionary authority under clause 8 of rule XX to postpone certain questions and to "cluster" them for voting at a designated time or place in the legislative schedule, and, after the vote on the first such question, to reduce to five minutes the vote on all of the additional questions so postponed. *Manual* §1030. The rule specifically permits the Speaker to postpone the following questions:

- Approval of the Journal.
- Passing a bill or joint resolution or adopting a concurrent resolution or a resolution (or ordering the previous question thereon).
- Agreeing to a motion to suspend the rules.
- Agreeing to an amendment reported from the Committee of the Whole.
- Agreeing to a motion to reconsider or agreeing to a motion to lay on the table a motion to reconsider.
- Agreeing to a conference report or to a motion to instruct conferees (or ordering the previous question thereon).

These categories are not mutually exclusive. For example, the Speaker may "cluster" a vote on the approval of the Journal with motions to suspend the rules. 107-2, Oct. 16, 2002, p 20749. Where the proposition does not fall within one of the categories listed in clause 8 of rule XX, the Chair does not have discretionary authority to postpone a vote but may do so by unanimous consent. *Manual* §1030.

For all such categories, the postponement authority under clause 8 of rule XX must be to a place designated within two legislative days, with the exception of the question of agreeing to the Speaker's approval of the Journal. That question may be postponed only to a time on the same legislative day. *Manual* §1030. The Speaker may simultaneously designate separate times for the resumption of proceedings on separate postponed questions. Once the Speaker has postponed votes to a designated place in the legislative schedule, the Speaker may redesignate the time when the votes will be taken within the appropriate period. *Manual* §1030.

The discretionary authority of the Speaker to postpone votes under clause 8 of rule XX arises after a vote of record is ordered or when a vote is objected to for lack of a quorum. *Manual* §1030. The authority of the Speaker to postpone such a vote does not continue once a record vote has commenced or once the Speaker has announced the absence of a quorum. Deschler-Brown Ch 30 §56.1.

In exercising the authority under this rule, the Speaker may announce that the consideration of certain postponed questions may be interrupted by other privileged business. 97-1, Dec. 15, 1981, p 31506. The "clustering" of record votes on postponed matters does not prevent the Chair from entertaining a unanimous-consent request between postponed votes. However, if constituting intervening business, the first vote after the request would have to be a 15-minute vote unless reduced to five minutes by unanimous consent. *Manual* § 1030.

G. Vote Changes, Corrections, and Announcements

§ 24. In General; Vote Changes

A Member who has voted may change such vote at any time before the final announcement of the result. *Manual* § 1014; 5 Hinds §§ 5931, 5934, 6093, 6094. During that time a ''present'' vote may be changed as well as an ''aye'' or ''no'' vote. 5 Hinds § 6060. However, a Member may not withdraw a vote entirely without leave of the House. 5 Hinds § 5930.

Changes in votes cast are barred following the announcement of the result of the vote, even by unanimous consent. Deschler-Brown Ch 30 § 6.1. However, the Speaker may announce a change in the result of a vote taken by electronic device when required to correct an error in identifying a voting card submitted in the well. *Manual* § 1014.

When a vote is being taken by electronic device, a Member is permitted to change such vote by reinserting the voting card in a voting station during the first 10 minutes of a 15-minute vote or by the Clerk's announcement in the well after the Chair has asked for changes. During five-minute votes or two-minute votes, a Member is permitted to change a vote at the voting stations at any time. Following the expiration of the minimum time for voting by electronic device and the closing of electronic voting stations, but before the Speaker's announcement of the result, any Member may either change a vote or cast an initial vote in the well by use of a ballot card. *Manual* § 1014; see also § 2, supra.

A Member who wishes to change a vote on a recorded vote conducted by tellers with clerks may announce such vote change in the well before the announcement of the result. Deschler-Brown Ch 30 § 40.6. If the correction is made before the announcement of the result by the Chair, unanimous consent is not required. Deschler-Brown Ch 30 § 40.1.

When a Member changes a vote following a record vote and before the announcement of the result by the Chair, the change appears in the *Congressional Record.* This occurs even where the Member changes a vote twice, thereby reverting to the original voting stance. Deschler-Brown Ch 30 § 39.6.

§ 25. Correcting the Congressional Record and the Journal

Electronic Votes

The Chair presumes the technical accuracy of the electronic system if properly used and relies on the responsibility of Members to correctly cast and verify their votes. Deschler-Brown Ch 30 § 31.3. The Speaker declines to entertain requests to correct the Journal or the *Congressional Record* on votes taken by electronic device. *Manual* § 1014. Recognition for such a request may be denied despite assurances by the Member that the vote had been verified by reinserting the voting card. Deschler-Brown Ch 30 § 6.2. However, the incorrect transcription by the official reporters of a change announced by the Clerk may be corrected in the *Record* by unanimous consent. Deschler-Brown Ch 30 § 31.16. Also, by unanimous consent the House may permit the correction of the *Record* and the Journal to delete a vote that was not actually cast. *Manual* § 1014.

The Speaker has declined to entertain a unanimous-consent request to correct a vote taken by electronic device although the Member was recorded as voting on a day when such Member was on leave from the House, no explanation having been offered for the discrepancy. Deschler-Brown Ch 30 § 32.4 However, the Speaker may announce a change in the result of a vote taken by electronic device when required to correct an error in identifying a voting card submitted in the well. Deschler-Brown Ch 30 § 32.5. For a report of the Committee on Standards of Official Conduct (now Ethics) on voting anomalies, see H. Rept. 96-991.

After the announcement of the result of such a vote, although it is not permissible to change a vote, a Member may seek unanimous consent to explain in the *Congressional Record* where such Member's vote was incorrectly recorded or, though cast, was not recorded. § 27, infra. In entertaining such requests, the Chair does not pass judgment on the Member's explanation as to how the vote was improperly recorded or how, though present and having voted, such Member was not recorded, nor does the Chair challenge the Member's word on how such Member voted. Deschler-Brown Ch 30 § 38.1.

Nonelectronic Votes

When the electronic voting system is not in use, and a Member is incorrectly recorded on a roll call, such Member may correct the vote before the announcement of the result, with the corrected vote being properly recorded and the change duly noted in the *Congressional Record. Manual* § 1015. When a vote actually given fails to be recorded during a call of the roll, the Member may, before the approval of the Journal, demand as a matter of right that correction be made. 5 Hinds §§ 5969, 6061, 6062; 8 Cannon § 3143.

Members who have been incorrectly recorded on a vote taken by clerks pursuant to clause 4 of rule XX have, by unanimous consent, had their votes corrected following the announcement of the result. The Chair will not entertain such requests after further business has been transacted. Deschler-Brown Ch 30 § 40.3.

A Member ascertaining that an absent colleague has been inadvertently recorded on a nonelectronic roll call vote may have the vote deleted by unanimous consent, before the announcement of the result. Deschler-Brown Ch 30 § 37.1.

§ 26. Recapitulations

A Member may not demand a recapitulation of a vote taken by electronic device. Deschler-Brown Ch 30 § 31.6. The recapitulation of such votes is refused because all Members may determine whether they were correctly recorded by examining the electronic display panel over the Speaker's rostrum and because, even if the display panel is inoperative, individual votes and vote totals may be verified through the voting and monitoring stations. Deschler-Brown Ch 30 § 31.7.

Record votes that do not involve the use of the electronic voting system are subject to recapitulation at the discretion of the Speaker, either before or after the announcement of the result. *Manual* § 1015; 5 Hinds §§ 6049, 6050; 8 Cannon §§ 3125, 3128; Deschler-Brown Ch 30 §§ 28.2, 28.4.

§ 27. Personal Explanations

Members who are absent for a record vote may announce how they would have voted had they been present. Deschler-Brown Ch 30 § 41.1.

> MEMBER: M__. Speaker, on roll call ______, I was unavoidably detained as a result of ______________________. Had I been present I would have voted "[aye] [nay]" I ask unanimous consent that this statement appear in the *Congressional Record* following the announcement of the vote.

Alternatively, a Member may submit a signed statement for printing in the *Congressional Record* without personally announcing an intent. The explanation will appear in the *Record* immediately following the missed vote if the explanation is received the day of the vote. If the explanation is submitted in writing rather than announced on the floor, the explanation will appear in distinctive type. If the explanation is submitted any time after the day of the vote, it appears in the ''Extensions of Remarks'' portion of the *Record.*

Neither the rules nor the practice of the House permit a Member to announce after a record vote how absent colleagues would have voted if present. 6 Cannon § 200.

If the Member's explanation alleges that such Member was present but not recorded, the Chair does not, by entertaining the request, pass judgment on the Member's explanation. Deschler-Brown Ch 30 § 38.1.

H. Majority Votes; Super-majority Votes

§ 28. In General; Tie Votes

''The voice of the majority decides . . . where not otherwise expressly provided,'' wrote Jefferson, expressing a fundamental precept of parliamentary law. *Manual* § 508. Most business that comes before the House is decided by a majority vote, and, under clause 6 of rule XIV, all questions relating to the priority of business are decided by a majority. *Manual* § 884. Under clause 1(c) of rule XX, a rule in effect since the First Congress, if the vote on a proposition is a tie, the proposition is defeated. *Manual* § 1013; 5 Hinds §§ 5926, 5964.

Two-thirds Votes

Under the Constitution or by House rule, a two-thirds vote is expressly required in the House on:

- Amendment to the Constitution. U.S. Const. art. V; *Manual* § 190.
- Passage of a bill over a veto. U.S. Const. art. I § 7; *Manual* § 104.
- Dispensing with the call of the Private Calendar. Clause 5 of rule XV; *Manual* § 895.
- Same-day consideration of reports from the Committee on Rules. Clause 6 of rule XIII; *Manual* § 857.
- Suspension of the rules. Clause 1 of rule XV; *Manual* § 885.
- Expulsion of a Member. U.S. Const. art. I § 5; *Manual* § 62.
- Removal of political disabilities. U.S. Const. amend. XIV § 3; *Manual* § 230.

A two-thirds vote means two-thirds of those voting, a quorum being present, and not two-thirds of the entire membership. Deschler-Brown Ch 30 § 5. Such a vote requires an affirmative vote by two-thirds of those Members actually voting; Members who indicate only that they are ''present'' are not counted in determining the two-thirds figure. Deschler-Brown Ch 30 § 5.2; 5 Hinds § 7027; 8 Cannon § 3503; 7 Cannon § 1111.

Three-fifths Votes

Under clause 5(b) of rule XXI, certain income tax rate increases can be passed or adopted only by a vote of not less than three-fifths of the Members voting.

Chapter 59
Withdrawal

Research References
5 Hinds §§ 5347-5358
Deschler Ch 23 §§ 2, 36, 43; Deschler Ch 27 § 20
Manual §§ 902, 904, 905, 922, 925, 978

§ 1. In General

Withdrawal of a Motion

Clause 2 of rule XVI states that a motion, once entertained, may be "withdrawn at any time before a decision or amendment thereon." *Manual* § 904. A motion may be withdrawn although an amendment has been offered to it and is pending. 5 Hinds § 5347; 6 Cannon § 373; 8 Cannon § 2639.

Examples of motions that may be withdrawn under the rule include:

- A motion to suspend the rules. *Manual* § 905.
- A motion that the House resolve into the Committee of the Whole for the consideration of a bill. *Manual* § 905.
- A motion to instruct conferees. *Manual* § 905.
- A motion to dispose of an amendment reported from conference in disagreement. See, *e.g.*, Deschler-Brown Ch 32 § 10.30.

A motion that the House resolve into the Committee of the Whole for the consideration of a bill may be withdrawn pending a point of order against consideration of the bill. If the motion is withdrawn, the Chair is not obligated to rule on the point of order. *Manual* § 905; 8 Cannon § 3405.

The proponent of a motion to dispose of an amendment reported in disagreement, having withdrawn the motion, may change the amendment included in the motion and offer it again in its modified form. Deschler-Brown Ch 32 § 8.3.

A motion may be withdrawn in the Committee of the Whole only by unanimous consent. Deschler Ch 23 § 2.10.

Unanimous consent is not required to withdraw a pending unanimous-consent request. *Manual* § 905.

Withdrawal of a Measure

Under clause 2 of rule XVI, a resolution, including a privileged resolution, may be withdrawn at any time before a decision is made thereon or before an amendment thereto is adopted. For example, where the Speaker has put the question on adoption of a resolution to a voice vote without the ordering of the previous question, and the yeas and nays have not been ordered, the resolution may be withdrawn. *Manual* § 905. If the resolution is called up in the House again, the Member calling up the resolution is recognized for one hour, notwithstanding the fact that the resolution previously has been considered, debated, and then withdrawn before action is taken thereon. *Manual* § 905. Withdrawal of a pending resolution is not in order when the absence of a quorum has been announced by the Chair. *Manual* § 905.

A conference report called up for consideration in the House may be withdrawn from consideration at any time before action is taken thereon. Deschler-Brown Ch 33 § 20.9.

Withdrawal of an Amendment

An amendment may be withdrawn in the House at any time before an amendment is adopted thereto or a decision is had thereon. 5 Hinds § 5753; 6 Cannon § 587; 8 Cannon § 2332. The same right to withdraw an amendment exists in the forum known as "the House as in the Committee of the Whole." 4 Hinds § 4935. Therefore, that right exists in standing committees where general procedures of that forum apply. *Manual* § 427.

Under clause 5 of rule XVIII, unanimous consent is required to withdraw an amendment in Committee of the Whole, unless withdrawal authority was conferred by the House. *Manual* § 905; 5 Hinds § 5221; 6 Cannon § 570; 8 Cannon §§ 2465, 2859, 3405. However, unanimous consent is not required to withdraw an amendment that is at the Clerk's desk but that has not been offered by the Member. Deschler Ch 27 § 20.5.

Where a substitute amendment is withdrawn by unanimous consent, an amendment to the substitute also is withdrawn. Deschler Ch 27 § 20.9. The withdrawal of an amendment by unanimous consent does not preclude its being reoffered at the same stage of the proceedings, and unanimous consent is not required to reoffer the amendment if otherwise in order. Deschler Ch 27 § 20.10.

The chair of the Committee of the Whole will entertain a unanimous-consent request to withdraw an amendment even when a point of order is pending against the amendment or against a substitute therefor. Deschler Ch 27 §§20.6, 20.7.

§2. Decisions That Prevent Withdrawal

A decision that prevents withdrawal may consist of the following:

- The ordering of the yeas and nays, either directly on the motion or on a motion to lay it on the table. 5 Hinds §§5353, 5354.
- The ordering of the previous question, or the demand therefor. *Manual* §905; 5 Hinds §5489.
- The refusal to lay on the table. 5 Hinds §§5351, 5352; 8 Cannon §2640.

Where the Chair postpones a voice vote under clause 8 of rule XX when an objection has been made for lack of a quorum, and that question comes up later as postponed unfinished business, the proponent unilaterally may withdraw it, because it becomes a question *de novo*. *Manual* §905; see, *e.g.*, 101-1, July 24, 1989, pp 15794, 15818.

§3. Right to Modify Derived from Right to Withdraw

As a general principle, modifications to a pending motion, if in order at all, must be approved by the House. There is one narrow exception to this principle. A Member having the right to withdraw a motion before a decision is made thereon, and immediately thereafter reoffer it, has the resulting right to modify the motion without approval of the House. *Manual* §905; 5 Hinds §5358.

For example, a Member having the right to withdraw a motion to instruct conferees before a decision is made thereon, and the right to offer a different motion at the same stage of proceedings (one not subject to notice requirements), has the resulting power to modify the motion. *Manual* §905. Similarly, a Member having the right to withdraw a resolution offered as a question of privilege, and the right to offer a different resolution as a question of privilege immediately thereafter (one not subject to notice requirements), has the resulting power to modify the resolution without the concurrence of the House. Deschler Ch 23 §1.

In most cases, however, the right of withdrawal and resubmission in a modified form does not exist. For example, a resolution such as a special order of business resolution reported by the Committee on Rules, may not be modified except by direction of the reporting committee or with concurrence of the House. In the case of a nonprivileged motion, the proponent may not be guaranteed the right to immediately reoffer the motion, especially where it is a secondary motion under clause 4 of rule XVI. Thus, although an amendment to a motion pending in the House may be withdrawn by the Member offering the amendment before it is acted upon, such Member is not guaranteed the right to reoffer that amendment, and therefore does not have the right to modify the amendment without the consent of the House. Deschler Ch 23 § 1.

Other secondary motions specified under clause 4 of rule XVI, such as the motions to lay on the table, for the previous question, to postpone to a day certain, to refer, and to postpone indefinitely, may be withdrawn before action is taken thereon but may not be modified without the consent of the House. The motion that when the House adjourns it adjourn to a day and time certain is in order only at the Speaker's discretion and is therefore subject to modification by the offeror only with the consent of the House. Deschler Ch 23 § 1.

In the Committee of the Whole, amendments may be withdrawn only by unanimous consent, so the doctrine of unilateral modification is never applicable in that forum.

Pursuant to a unanimous-consent request offered by the manager of the pending motion, the House may modify a suspension motion during its consideration or after the vote has been postponed *de novo* under clause 8 of rule XX. See, *e.g.*, 102-2, July 2, 1992, p 17220; 103-2, Oct. 3, 1994, p 27364. However, the more common practice is for the manager to withdraw the motion and for the Speaker to recognize such Member to reoffer the motion in a modified form, in which case the debate on the motion begins anew. Deschler Ch 21 § 14.3.

§ 4. Points of Order

Generally

A motion may be withdrawn pending a point of order against its consideration. If the motion is withdrawn, the Chair is not obligated to rule on any point of order raised against it. *Manual* § 905; 8 Cannon § 3405. Similarly, a motion that the House resolve into the Committee of the Whole for the consideration of a bill may be withdrawn pending a point of order against consideration of the bill. *Manual* § 905.

A motion may be withdrawn even after the previous question has been ordered on an appeal from a decision of the Chair on a point of order against the motion. Furthermore, the motion being withdrawn, all proceedings on the appeal fall thereby. 5 Hinds § 5356.

The chair of the Committee of the Whole may recognize for a unanimous-consent request to withdraw an amendment before ruling on a point of order. Deschler Ch 27 § 20.6.

Point of Order for Lack of Quorum

When a point of order of no quorum is made, the point of order may be withdrawn until announcement of the absence of a quorum, after which the point of order may not be withdrawn even by unanimous consent. Deschler Ch 20 § 18. Objection to a voice vote for lack of a quorum having been withdrawn, and demand for a division having been made, an objection to the division vote for lack of a quorum is in order. If a quorum is not present, the yeas and nays are automatic. Deschler Ch 20 § 18.4.

Withdrawal of a pending resolution is not in order when the absence of a quorum has been announced by the Chair. *Manual* § 905.

Withdrawal of Reservation of Point of Order

The reservation of a point of order by one Member inures to all. However, withdrawal of a reservation by one Member requires other Members to either make or continue to reserve the point of order at that point, and a further reservation comes too late after there has been debate. Deschler-Brown Ch 31 § 3.14.

Words Taken Down

When a demand is made that certain words used in debate be taken down, such words may be withdrawn by unanimous consent in the House or in the Committee of the Whole. Deschler-Brown Ch 29 §§ 51.1, 51.2. The Speaker may suggest that a Member who had uttered unparliamentary words request unanimous consent to withdraw them. Deschler-Brown Ch 29 § 51.11. No debate is in order pending a request to withdraw unparliamentary words. Deschler-Brown Ch 29 § 51.8. Like any other point of order, withdrawal of the demand that words be taken down does not require unanimous consent. *Manual* § 628.

§ 5. Requests for Record Votes

A demand for a recorded vote may be withdrawn before the Chair begins to count Members supporting the demand, and unanimous consent is not required. Deschler-Brown Ch 30 § 33.20. Where a demand for a recorded vote is pending, it may be withdrawn by the maker, but it is not in order to condition its withdrawal on the House's acceptance of a modification to the motion on which the vote is being taken. Deschler-Brown Ch 30 § 33.23. Although a demand for the yeas and nays, once supported by one-fifth of those present, cannot be withdrawn, the House may, by unanimous consent, vacate the proceedings and take the vote *de novo*. Deschler-Brown Ch 30 § 33.24. In one instance a Member who demanded a recorded vote asked unanimous consent to withdraw his demand when, the recorded vote being under way, the electronic system failed. Deschler-Brown Ch 30 § 33.22.

INDEX

(The main headings in this index, shown in boldface type, refer to corresponding chapter titles. Section references are to sections specified within the identified chapter. Cross references are to headings in this index.)

AMENDMENTS—Continued

AMENDMENTS—Continued

COMMITTEE OF THE WHOLE—
Continued

COMMITTEE OF THE WHOLE—
Continued

GERMANENESS OF AMENDMENTS

GERMANENESS OF AMENDMENTS—Continued

LEGISLATION ON APPROPRIATION BILLS— Continued

LEGISLATION ON APPROPRIATION BILLS— Continued

PRIVILEGED BUSINESS—Continued

PRIVILEGES OF THE HOUSE

PRIVILEGES OF THE HOUSE—Continued

PRIVILEGE, PERSONAL, QUESTION OF

REFERRAL OF BILLS, RESOLUTIONS, AND OTHER MATTER—Continued

REFERRAL OF BILLS, RESOLUTIONS, AND OTHER MATTER—Continued

RESIDENT COMMISSIONER, see DELEGATES AND RESIDENT COMMISSIONER

RESIGNATION

RESOLUTIONS OF INQUIRY, see INQUIRY, RESOLUTIONS OF

REVENUE LEGISLATION, PREROGATIVE OF HOUSE TO ORIGINATE

RISE OR RISE AND REPORT, MOTION TO, see COMMITTEE OF THE WHOLE

RULES OF THE HOUSE

www.ingramcontent.com/pod-product-compliance
Ingram Content Group UK Ltd.
Pitfield, Milton Keynes, MK11 3LW, UK
UKHW051118290926
15471UKWH00010B/1739

9 781780 39